BEHAVIORAL ASSESSMENT OF CHILDHOOD DISORDERS

Second Edition

SELECTED CORE PROBLEMS

Edited by
ERIC J. MASH
University of Calgary

and

LEIF G. TERDAL
Oregon Health Sciences University

THE GUILFORD PRESS
New York   London

To Heather and Marge

© 1988 The Guilford Press
A Division of Guilford Publications, Inc.
72 Spring Street, New York, NY 10012

Printed in the United States of America

Last digit is print number: 9 8 7 6 5 4 3 2 1

Library of Congress Cataloging in Publication Data

Behavioral assessment of childhood disorders.

    1. Mental illness—Diagnosis. 2. Behavioral
assessment of children. 3. Psychodiagnostics.
I. Mash, Eric J. II. Terdal, Leif G., 1937–
RJ503.5.B44 1988   618.92'89075   88-24684
ISBN 0-89862-143-7

CONTRIBUTORS

RUSSELL A. BARKLEY, PhD, Department of Psychiatry, University of Massachusetts Medical Center, Worcester, Massachusetts

BILLY A. BARRIOS, PhD, Department of Psychology, University of Mississippi, University, Mississippi

KEITH A. CRNIC, PhD, Department of Psychology, Pennsylvania State University, University Park, Pennsylvania

REX FOREHAND, PhD, Department of Psychology, University of Georgia, Athens, Georgia

DONALD P. HARTMANN, PhD, Department of Psychology, University of Utah, Salt Lake City, Utah

CHRISTINE HOVANITZ, PhD, Department of Psychology, University of Cincinnati, Cincinnati, Ohio

ALAN E. KAZDIN, PhD, Department of Psychiatry, Western Psychiatric Institute and Clinic, University of Pittsburgh School of Medicine, Pittsburgh, Pennsylvania

ERIC J. MASH, PhD, Department of Psychology, University of Calgary, Calgary, Alberta, Canada

ROBERT J. McMAHON, PhD, Department of Psychology, University of Washington, Seattle, Washington

CRIGHTON NEWSOM, PhD, Department of Psychology, Muscatatuck Developmental Center, Butlerville, Indiana

ARNOLD RINCOVER, PhD, Surrey Place Centre, Toronto, Ontario, Canada

H. GERRY TAYLOR, PhD, McGill–Montreal Children's Hospital Learning Centre, Montreal, Quebec, Canada

LEIF G. TERDAL, PhD, Department of Medical Psychology and Crippled Children's Division, Oregon Health Sciences University, Portland, Oregon

DAVID A. WOLFE, PhD, Department of Psychology, University of Western Ontario, London, Ontario, Canada

PREFACE

This book is about assessment and diagnosis, child psychopathology, child development, clinical psychology, psychometrics, social values, ethics, and behavior therapy. When we first made this statement in the Preface to the first edition of this volume,[1] we did so only to sensitize readers to our view that all assessments of children with problems are embedded in a complex network of overlapping disciplines and bodies of knowledge. The complexities of developing children and their social systems are a fact that renders any narrow approach to child and family assessment inadequate. Since the appearance of the first edition of this book, new empirical findings and new conceptualizations in the areas of child psychopathology and child development have served to further establish the complexity and richness surrounding the assessment of childhood disorders.

This *Selected Core Problems* edition represents a shortened version of the second edition of *Behavioral Assessment of Childhood Disorders*.[2] It includes only those chapters from the complete edition that deal with core childhood disorders.[3] It is hoped that the narrower em-

phasis and abbreviated length of this edition will facilitate its use in educational settings and by professionals who wish to focus their assessment efforts on behavior and learning problems during childhood.

This text considers the assessment of disturbed children and families from a behavioral perspective. In its simplest formulation, such a perspective emphasizes that assessment should proceed as an empirically based enterprise. The approach taken in this volume is one that considers behavioral assessment as a general problem-solving strategy for understanding disturbed children and their families. It is believed that the effectiveness of these strategies can be enhanced through knowledge pertaining to specific childhood disorders, such that the methods to be used in assessment are directed at understanding those parameters which have been identified as important for particular classes of problems.

Although there is currently no singular definition of behavioral assessment, commonly occurring concepts have included a focus on individualized assessments, recognition of the

---

[1] Mash, E. J., & Terdal, L. G. (Eds.). (1981). *Behavioral assessment of childhood disorders*. New York: Guilford Press.

[2] Mash, E. J., & Terdal, L. G. (Eds.). (1988). *Behavioral assessment of childhood disorders* (2nd ed., unabridged). New York: Guilford Press.

[3] By core childhood disorders we are referring to the more common behavior and learning problems of childhood. For the most part, these are the childhood difficulties that often result in referrals to mental health, educational, and pediatric professionals for treatment. They include attention-deficit hyperactivity disorders, conduct disorders,

childhood depression, childhood fears and anxieties, mental retardation, autism, learning disabilities, and abusive and neglectful family situations. Additional chapters that are included in the unabridged version of this volume cover the assessment of problems in social relationships (H. Hops and C. R. Greenwood); chronic illness and pain (S. B. Johnson); tics and Gilles de la Tourette's syndrome (R. A. Barkley); brain-injured children (J. M. Fletcher); enuresis and encopresis (D. M. Fielding and D. M. Doleys); sexual abuse (V. V. Wolfe and D. A. Wolfe); childhood obesity (J. P. Foreyt and G. K. Goodrick); anorexia and bulimia nervosa (J. P. Foreyt and J. K. McGavin); and parent–adolescent conflict (S. L. Foster and A. L. Robin).

importance of situational influences on behavior, and the use of multimethod assessment strategies. A continuing theme has been the need to formulate assessment information in a way that is meaningful for clinical decision making about individual children and their families.

The face of child behavior assessment has changed dramatically over the past decade and these changes are reflected throughout this new edition. From its early roots which emphasized the direct observation of molecular responses, behavioral assessment has become increasingly systems oriented and sensitive to the interactions between behaviors, cognitions, and affects as they unfold within the child's larger social network.

Recent work in behavioral assessment has shown an increasing emphasis on developmental factors, a heightened interest in diagnosis and classification, a concern for the decision-making processes surrounding assessment, attention to prevention-oriented assessments, and recognition of the need for theoretical models to guide assessment research and practice.

In this second edition we have again attempted to include chapters covering a wide range of core childhood disorders. All chapters have been completely updated and revised to reflect the qualitative changes that have taken place in the field since the time of the first edition. The problem-oriented focus of this volume makes it not only a book about assessment but also a book about child psychopathology. Each chapter first provides a detailed analysis of the disorder under consideration prior to examining specific assessment methods. We hope that this book will be appropriate for use in assessment, child psychopathology, and behavior therapy courses at the advanced undergraduate and graduate levels in areas such as psychology, education, counseling, social work, and medicine, and that it will satisfy a need in applied settings and training programs for practitioners who wish to introduce new child assessment procedures into their work.

We would like to extend our thanks to the contributors to this volume for the consistently high quality of their chapters and for their receptiveness to editorial feedback. We are also grateful to Seymour Weingarten at The Guilford Press for his unqualified support of this project. During the preparation of this book, Eric Mash was supported by a University of Calgary Sabbatical Fellowship and by research grants from Health and Welfare Canada and the Alberta Mental Health Advisory Council. This support greatly facilitated work on this volume.

Eric J. Mash
Leif G. Terdal

CONTENTS

PART I

INTRODUCTION

1 BEHAVIORAL ASSESSMENT OF CHILD AND FAMILY DISTURBANCE

ERIC J. MASH
University of Calgary

LEIF G. TERDAL
Oregon Health Sciences University

From the time of their conception, children in our society are assessed, evaluated, and labeled. These processes, which are guided by the implicit assumptions about development held by significant others and the society (Kagan, 1983), are applied to the children's physical growth, cognitive status, social and emotional development, educational achievement, and psychological functioning. Parents, teachers, physicians, siblings, peers, and the social community all participate in this ongoing evaluative process, as do the children themselves. For most children, these evaluations occur primarily in the course of everyday social transactions and, to a lesser extent, during periodic formal evaluations best characterized as "routine" (e.g., regular medical checkups). As a result of these assessments, some children are identified as *deviating* from a normal course of development with regard to their behavior, their physical condition, or their violation of social norms and expectations. When a negative valence is assigned to this deviation, a child is especially likely to be labeled as belonging to a category of children who show similar char-

acteristics. It is these children and their families who may then come to the attention of society's professional assessors, who will utilize special strategies to build upon the assessments that have already taken place (Messick, 1983). This book is concerned with those special strategies for the assessment of child and family disorders encompassed under the label "behavioral assessment."

Recent discussions of behavioral assessment (Bornstein, Bornstein, & Dawson, 1984; Ciminero, Calhoun, & Adams, 1986; Cone, 1987; Cone & Hoier, 1986; Mash & Terdal, 1981a; R. O. Nelson, 1983; Ollendick & Hersen, 1984) and of childhood disorders (Achenbach, 1978, 1985; Achenbach & Edelbrock, 1984; Quay & Werry, 1986; A. O. Ross & Pelham, 1981) have pointed out the continuing lack of conceptual and methodological clarity in both of these areas. Although there is much agreement regarding the need for systematic assessments of children (particularly those exhibiting or at risk for problems), there has been and continues to be a good deal of disagreement regarding how childhood disorders should be conceptualized;

what child characteristics, adaptations, and contexts should be assessed; by whom and in what situations they should be assessed; what methods should be employed; and how the outcomes of such assessments should be integrated, interpreted, and utilized. In spite of these disagreements, however, there exists a general consensus regarding the importance of developing effective assessment strategies not as an endpoint but rather as a prerequisite for improving and evaluating services for children (Achenbach & Edelbrock, 1981; Blau, 1979). Such a "functional–utilitarian" approach to the behavioral assessment of children and families is perhaps the major theme underlying this volume—a theme transcending many of the conceptual and methodological problems, differences, and preferences that emerge in the current discussion.

Despite numerous attempts to define the field (e.g., Evans & Nelson, 1977, 1986; Hayes & Nelson, 1986; Hersen & Bellack, 1981; Mash & Terdal, 1981b; R. O. Nelson & Hayes 1979; 1981; Ollendick & Hersen, 1984), there is presently no single agreed-upon definition of child behavior assessment. Nor do we believe that there is likely to be one. However, there *are* characteristically occurring concepts (e.g., the importance of contextual influences), methods (e.g., the use of multimethod strategies that often include direct observations), and purposes (e.g., treatment design and evaluation) that serve to define the field (Mash, 1979; O'Leary, 1979). The purpose of this introductory chapter is to outline some of the current concepts and practices associated with the behavioral assessment of disturbed children and families, and to discuss several of the broader issues and concerns surrounding their development and utilization.

RECENT DEVELOPMENTS

In the introductory chapter to the first edition of this volume, we stated (Mash & Terdal, 1981b): "Recognizing the likelihood of ongoing and future changes in assessment strategies related to new empirical findings, emergent ideas, practical concerns, and shifts in the broader sociocultural milieu in which assessments are carried out, this chapter—indeed, this book—should be viewed as a working framework for understanding current behavioral approaches to the assessment of children" (p. 4).

As reflected throughout the present volume,

the face of child behavior assessment has changed dramatically during the 1980s. Some of the more noteworthy developments to be discussed include the following:

1. A greater emphasis on incorporating developmental considerations into the design, conduct, and interpretation of assessments (Edelbrock, 1984), the implementation of treatments (Kendall, Lerner, & Craighead, 1984; McMahon & Peters, 1985), and the study of child and family psychopathology (e.g., Digdon & Gotlib, 1985; Fincham & Cain, in press; Sroufe & Rutter, 1984).

2. A heightened interest in issues related to diagnosis and classification, with concomitant efforts to integrate extant diagnostic practices with behavioral assessment strategies (Barlow, 1986; S. L. Harris & Powers, 1984; Kazdin, 1983).

3. An elaborated view of behavioral assessment as an ongoing decision-making process. This view has generated discussions concerning the judgmental factors influencing this complex information-processing task (Evans, 1985; Kanfer, 1985; Kanfer & Busemeyer, 1982; Tabachnik & Alloy, in press), and efforts to develop both clinically (Herbert, 1981) and empirically (Loeber, Dishion, & Patterson, 1984) derived decision-making models for specific problems and populations.

4. A growing concern for prevention-oriented assessments (Roberts & Peterson, 1984), emanating from current social issues and concerns surrounding divorce (Emery, 1982; Forehand, Middleton, & Long, 1986; Kurdek, in press), single-parent families (Stevenson, Colbert, & Roach, 1986) and stepfamilies (Santrock & Sitterle, 1987; Santrock, Sitterle, & Warshak, in press), working mothers (Cotterell, 1986), unemployment (Kates, 1986), children in day care (Molnar, 1985), home accidents (Christopherson, 1986; Mori & Peterson, 1986; L. Peterson & Mori, 1985), child abductions (Flanagan, 1986), sexual abuse (Finkelhor & Associates, 1986; Mrazek, 1983; Wolfe & Wolfe, 1988), family violence (Azar, 1986; A. P. Goldstein, Keller, & Erne, 1985; Kelly, 1983; Neidig & Friedman, 1984), and adolescent suicide (Select Panel for the Promotion of Child Health, 1981; Zigler, 1984).

5. A growing emphasis on understanding the interrelated influences of child and family cognitions (Bandura, 1986; Coie & Dodge, 1986; Karoly, 1981) and affects (Gottman & Levenson, 1986) on behavior, as assessed within the context of ongoing social interactions (e.g.,

Bradbury & Fincham, in press-a, in press-b; Gottman & Levenson, 1985; Hops *et al.*, 1987).

6. The extension of behavioral assessment concepts and practices into health care settings (Karoly, 1985; Mindell *et al.*, 1986) within the general frameworks of behavioral–developmental pediatrics (Gross & Drabman, in press; Lutzker & Lamazor, 1985) and pediatric behavioral medicine (S. A. Hobbs, Beck, & Wansley, 1984).

7. An increasing recognition of the need for empirically driven theoretical models as the basis for organizing and implementing assessment strategies with children and families (McFall, 1986; Patterson, 1986; Patterson & Bank, 1986).

8. The introduction of technological advances, particularly the use of computers during both the data-collecting and decision-making phases of assessment (Ancill, Carr, & Rogers, 1985; Carr & Ghosh, 1983; Gardner & Breuer, 1985; Holden, 1985a; Romanczyk, 1986). This has stimulated further interest in the utility and feasibility of using actuarial models for clinical decision making (Achenbach, 1985; Mash, 1985; Rachman, 1983; Wiggins, 1981).

9. A conceptual and methodological convergence on ecologically oriented systems models (Belsky, Lerner, & Spanier, 1984; Bronfenbrenner, 1979, 1986; Hartup, 1986a, 1986b) as the appropriate framework for organizing and understanding assessment information derived from children and families (Evans, 1985; Wasik, 1984). This has led to a heightened interest in the assessment of whole-family variables (Forman & Hagan, 1984; Holman, 1983; Rodick, Henggeler, & Hanson, 1986) and the relationships between family systems and the broader sociocultural milieu (Barling, 1986; Dunst & Trivette, 1985, 1986; Parke, MacDonald, Beital, & Bhavnagri, 1987).

It should be apparent from this brief and selective overview of recent developments that current approaches to child and family behavioral assessment are complex and varied. They extend well beyond earlier views of child behavior assessment as being synonymous with the direct observation of easily defined target behaviors.

SOME GENERAL OBSERVATIONS ON BEHAVIORAL ASSESSMENT

Several writers (Mash & Terdal, 1981b: R. O. Nelson, 1983) have described the seemingly meteoric rise of behavioral assessment during the 1960s and 1970s. This rapid growth of the field was reflected in numerous books, conference papers, symposia, book chapters and journal articles. This growth has continued into the 1980s, as reflected in several recent publications (Ciminero *et al.*, 1986; Hayes & Nelson, 1986; Mash & Terdal, 1981a; Ollendick & Hersen, 1984). In considering current developments in behavioral assessment, several general observations are germane to the discussion that follows:

1. Although the growth of the field has been rapid, it has not been without some "disillusionments" (R. O. Nelson, 1983), "second looks" (Achenbach & Edelbrock, 1984), and "growing pains" (Hartmann, 1983). Expressions of dissatisfaction have been directed both at the techniques of behavioral assessment and at its conceptual adequacy. For example, R. O. Nelson (1983) has called attention to the lack of convergence across both differing and similar measures of the same behavior; the impracticality of many recommended behavioral assessment techniques, especially direct observation; and the inability of the field to generate a set of well-standardized and psychometrically sound behavioral assessment procedures. Dissatisfactions with the conceptual foundations of behavioral assessment have focused on such issues as how information concerning a specific child can be related to knowledge concerning similar children obtained in other situations at other times; difficulties surrounding the assessment of covert and/or infrequently occurring events; and the potential limitations of molecular analysis for the detection of larger patterns of behaviors (Achenbach, 1985).

2. While there was formerly a disproportionate emphasis in the literature on the behavioral assessment of adults relative to children, this imbalance has been righted to a degree with the appearance of several books whose primary focus is on child behavior analysis and assessment (e.g., Gelfand & Hartmann, 1984; Mash & Terdal, 1981a; Ollendick & Hersen, 1984). In addition, recent texts on child behavior therapy have provided increased coverage of assessment issues and procedures (e.g. Herbert, 1981; Hersen & Van Hasselt, 1987; Ollendick & Cerny, 1981). Attention to the behavioral assessment of children and families has also been stimulated by recent conceptual and methodological advances in developmental psychology and behavioral pediatrics, and by the growing popularity of systems-oriented, family-focused approaches to treatment. Conceptuali-

zations that view adults and children as partners in an interacting network of systems and subsystems create a context in which child and adult assessments are viewed as equally important in any attempts to understand system perturbations.

3. The structure and content of child behavioral assessment strategies and methods, while maintaining an idiographic focus, have shown an increasingly greater sensitivity to the unique characteristics and needs of the population being assessed. In this regard, coding schemes for observing families of conduct-disordered or hyperactive children (Carlson, 1984) may be quite different from those designed for observing families in which a child is developmentally delayed (Dunst, 1984) or a family member is clinically depressed (Hops *et al.*, 1986). The movement toward population-specific assessments is also evident in the increasing recognition of the need to design assessments that are sensitive to the developmental characteristics of the child and family being evaluated. Future elaborations of a problem-specific approach to child and family assessment will probably require the development of conceptual models for specific disorders that indicate what variables are important to assess, and the empirical specification of the parameters most relevant to the description and modification of particular disorders (Mash, 1985).

4. Along with the need for population-specific assessments, recent research would also suggest the presence of a number of nonspecific assessment parameters that cut across differing types of child and family problems. For example, McKinny and Peterson (1987) found that within a population of developmentally delayed children the children's diagnosis did not contribute significantly to the parents' reported stress, relative to such factors as spouse support, perceived control, and other child characteristics. Also, the types of disturbance exhibited by children in families characterized by marital discord, divorce, and parental psychopathology (e.g., alcoholism, depression, or schizophrenia) are often quite similar. Lee and Gottlib (1986) suggest that common to these types of family disruptions are parental distress, an increased self-focus, and the consequent unavailability of parents to meet the emotional needs of their children. To the extent that differing problems present common sources of stress (e.g., reduction in time for self, marital strain), the use of standardized measures of common effects across different populations will probably serve to complement both the idiographic and population-specific information needed in behavioral assessments.

5. It has become commonplace for writers on behavioral assessment to cite surveys that call attention to (a) the discrepancy between idealized recommendations as to how behavioral assessments are to be carried out, and how such assessments are actually conducted in clinical practice; and (b) the fact that many behaviorally oriented clinicians still use personality tests and projective techniques (Ford & Kendall, 1979; Piotrowski & Keller, 1984; Swan & MacDonald, 1978; Wade, Baker, & Hartmann, 1979). However, it should be noted that many of these "we don't do that in real life" surveys have not focused specifically on assessment practices with children and families, and there is some evidence to indicate that child behavioral assessment is viewed as an integral component in the training of clinical child psychologists (Elbert, 1985a, 1985b), and in the assessment of specific child problems such as hyperactivity (Rosenberg & Beck, 1986).

Implicit in criticisms concerning the failure to translate behavioral assessment principles into practice has been the tendency to equate behavioral assessment with direct observation, and then to note the impracticality of carrying out such observations in the clinical context. While such a narrow perspective on behavioral assessment may exist in the abstract, it does not reflect current clinical practices or research. Behavioral assessments have evolved into problem-solving strategies that utilize a wide range of methods. The exclusion of direct observation from an assessment is not synonymous with the exclusion of a behavioral assessment approach. Nevertheless, the richness of observational assessments and their potentially large clinical yield compel us to continue to seek ways in which observational assessments can be made more viable in clinical practice (Mash & Barkley, 1986). We have recommended that one way in which high-quality observational data can be collected in an economically viable fashion is through the development of specialized assessment centers that have the resources and expertise to carry out observations on a contractual basis (Mash, 1984; Mash & Barkley, 1986).

6. Advances in child behavioral assessment have been seriously hampered by the failure to develop well-standardized and widely used

measures of child and family characteristics. Agreement on how certain child and family behaviors should best be described and measured for particular purposes is a prerequisite for the advancement of knowledge in the field, and yet the proliferation of idiosyncratic assessment devices has continued. It would seem that an agreed-upon set of procedures for measuring activity in an overactive child, or patterns of family interaction in an abusive family situation, would not be that difficult; however, this goal has eluded behavioral assessors. Some have argued against standardization, espousing the view that the use of preferred, well-standardized, reliable, and well-validated assessment devices may conflict with the idiographic, problem-oriented focus in behavioral assessment (e.g., R. O. Nelson, 1983). However, we believe that psychometrically sound and well-standardized assessment procedures can be effectively used in a flexible problem-solving framework that is sensitive to the individual needs of specific families and situations.

DEFINING BEHAVIORAL ASSESSMENT

The development and continuing evolution of behavioral assessment strategies for the assessment of disturbed children and families has been inextricably related to concomitant and parallel changes in the theoretical models and clinical practices of child and family behavior therapy (Hersen & Van Hasselt, 1987; A. O. Ross, 1981), behavior modification (G. Martin & Pear, 1983), applied behavior analysis (Sulzer-Azaroff & Mayer, 1977), and more recently behavioral pediatrics (Gross & Drabman, in press; Krasnegor, Arasteh, & Cataldo, 1986). Part of the difficulty in precisely defining child behavior assessment relates to the fact that concepts and practices in the aforementioned fields have been continually evolving, and the constructs and procedures that may be admissible by some are not accepted by others. In addition to the heterogeneity within these fields, which are presumed to have certain shared assumptions, there have also been recent efforts to integrate the behaviorally oriented therapies with other approaches (Kendall, 1982). Such attempts at rapprochement, which in the child and family areas are typified by recent efforts to integrate behavioral and family systems ap-

proaches (e.g., Alexander & Parsons, 1982; S. L. Harris, 1984; Foster & Robin, 1988; Weiss, 1980), further obscure the boundaries between what constitutes "behavioral" intervention and what does not. These therapeutic integrations have also prompted integration at the level of assessment from the standpoints both of what is to be assessed and of how these assessments are to be carried out.

While the practice of behavioral assessment is by no means restricted to situations in which behavioral treatments are to be introduced, it is believed that current views of behavioral assessment can best be understood within the context of behavioral intervention. Early behavioral approaches to the treatment of child and family disorders involved the specification of target behaviors and their alteration through the arrangement or rearrangement of antecedent and consequent stimulus events in a manner loosely conforming to the learning principles encompassed under the operant, classical, and observational learning paradigms (Ullmann & Krasner, 1965). Although these applications were varied, they did nevertheless have a number of cardinal features, including a focus on easily defined and observable events, current behaviors and situational determinants, and the child as the primary target for assessment and treatment (Bijou & Peterson, 1971). At that time behavioral assessment consisted primarily of obtaining frequency, rate, and duration measures describing the behaviors of interest, and the "pinpointing, recording, and consequating" of these target behaviors provided a direct and often effective method for producing behavioral change.

The significance of systematic assessments of target behaviors during the early development of child and family behavior therapy cannot be overstated. The early work stimulated a broadly empirical approach to problems in clinical child psychology, established continuity between assessment and intervention by emphasizing the need to evaluate treatment outcomes using objective behavioral measures, reinforced the need for individualized assessments, sensitized assessors to the evaluation of behavior in context, and led to the development of assessment methods having high face validity (Kanfer, 1979; R. O. Nelson, 1983; O'Leary, 1979).

As behavior therapy with children and families evolved, a much greater emphasis was placed on evaluating the child as part of a larger network of interacting social systems and subsystems (Patterson, 1976, 1982; Wahler, 1976); this was consistent with parallel developments in the field of developmental psychology (Belsky, 1981; Bronfenbrenner, 1986). While assessments continued to be viewed as individualized in relation to the system under consideration (e.g. the family), they did not necessarily occur at the level of the individual. In other words, a much wider range of variables—encompassing such things as the marital relationship, family stress, and social isolation and support, as well as the relationships between these variables and the parent–child interaction (e.g., Brody, Pillegrini, & Sigel, 1986; Pannaccione & Wahler, 1986)—were often targeted for assessment and treatment. Within the various subsystems that were designated, increasing recognition was given to the important role of cognition and affect in mediating child and family change, as well as to the role of more distal stimulus events (Wahler & Graves, 1983). These developments have changed the nature of behavioral assessment from target behavior measurement to a more general set of problem-solving strategies encompassing a wider range of system variables and a greater variety of methods than were characteristic of earlier work (Evans, 1985; Evans & Nelson, 1977, 1986; Kanfer, 1985; Kanfer & Busemeyer, 1982; Kanfer & Nay, 1982; Wasik, 1984).

In this volume, the term "child behavior assessment" is used to describe a range of deliberate problem-solving strategies for understanding both disturbed and nondisturbed children and their social systems, including their families and peer groups. These strategies employ a flexible and ongoing process of hypothesis testing regarding the nature of the problem, its causes, likely outcomes in the absence of intervention, and the anticipated effects of various treatments. Such hypothesis testing proceeds from a particular assumptive base and is carried out in relation to existing data, for certain purposes, and through the use of specific methodologies. The nature of this assumptive base, the relevant data sets, the relevant methodologies, and the particular purposes are elaborated upon in this and subsequent chapters. We also believe that the deployment of any child behavioral assessment strategy should not preclude the complementary use of alternative conceptual frameworks and methods, where such methods can be shown to assist in our understanding of the problem and our efforts to bring

about change. It is our feeling that the generation of better hypotheses to test at the idiographic level can best proceed from an understanding of the general theories and principles of psychological assessment (e.g., Anastasi, 1982; Cronbach, 1984; Nunnally, 1978), information concerning normal child and family development (e.g., Field, Huston, Quay, Troll, & Finley, 1982; Mussen, 1983), and knowledge regarding populations of children and families showing similar types of problems including information about incidence, prevalence, developmental characteristics, biological factors and system parameters (e.g., Achenbach, 1982; Quay & Werry, 1986). This general viewpoint is reflected throughout the chapters in this volume.

A COMMENT ON BEHAVIORAL VERSUS TRADITIONAL ASSESSMENT

A number of writers (Mash & Terdal, 1981b; R. O. Nelson, 1983) have noted that much of the early impetus for the development of behavioral assessment strategies during the 1960s was derived from a dissatisfaction with the conceptual foundations and techniques of the prevalent assessment models of that time. The "offending" paradigms, which included the medical, psychodynamic, and psychometric traditions (Achenbach, 1985), were lumped together under the general rubric of "traditional" assessment approaches. Early definitions of behavioral assessment were frequently based upon contrasts with a potpourri of assumptions and techniques characteristic of these traditional approaches (e.g., Bornstein *et al.*, 1984; Cone & Hawkins, 1977; Goldfried & Kent, 1972; Hartmann, Roper, & Bradford, 1979; Mash & Terdal, 1976, 1981b; Mischel, 1968). These contrasts often reflected statements regarding what behavioral assessment was not, rather than what it was. As behavioral assessment has become less and less insular and provincial, the contrasts between behavioral and traditional approaches to assessment are becoming less and less clear (Hartmann, 1983).

We feel that the continuing depiction of behavioral assessment primarily in terms of contrasts with traditional approaches has a number of potentially negative consequences. First, the categories "behavioral" and "traditional" have each been shown to encompass a heterogeneous range of conceptual and methodological approaches to assessment, and global comparisons between the two categories inevitably obscure a host of important and subtle distinctions that exist within each approach (Mash & Terdal, 1981b). Second, we feel that the "behavioral versus traditional" contrast tends to perpetuate a view of the field as predominantly reactionary, when in fact there are many strengths of the behavioral assessment approach that have been shown to stand on their own merit. Third, definitions of behavioral assessment that are based on contrasts with traditional views tend to foster the blanket acceptance or rejection of certain ideas (e.g., stable traits) or procedures (e.g., personality tests) when such categorical decisions are often unnecessary or undesirable within the problem-solving model being advocated here. Finally, it would appear that the practices of clinicians and researchers concerned with child and family assessment do not easily conform to these global designations, and the boundaries between behavioral and traditional approaches are, as noted, becoming less and less clear (Haynes, 1983). The actual use of concepts and procedures characterized as traditional *or* behavioral is often based on a variety of pragmatic considerations reflecting administrative requirements (e.g., billing practices, journal criteria for defining abnormal populations), normative assessment practices in a particular clinical or research context, resources for assessment, and individual preferences and priorities. We believe that efforts to maintain a radical definition of behavioral assessment—one that requires the presence of certain essential characteristics, such as a focus on observable behavior, a natural-science perspective, idiographic analysis, and criterion-referenced performance (see Cone & Hoier, 1986, for a lucid description of this position)—could result in the abandonment of a "behavioral identity" by many individuals who feel that their practices do not strictly adhere to such a narrow and constraining definition and who do not wish to exclude concepts and techniques that they believe to be both clinically and empirically useful.

BEHAVIORAL ASSESSMENT OF CHILD AND FAMILY DISTURBANCE: A PROTOTYPE-BASED VIEW

Rather than attempting to define behavioral assessment in terms of its necessary or defining features, we believe that a prototype-based view (e.g., Cantor, Smith, French, & Mezzich, 1980) may best depict the current state of the field. Within such a framework, the general category "behavioral assessment" is based on sets of imperfectly correlated features, referred to as "prototypes" (Rosch, 1978). Assessment cases having the largest number of general category features would be considered to be the most typical examples of behavioral assessment. The prototypical view also recognizes that within the more general category of behavioral assessment there can exist a hierarchically but imperfectly nested set of subcategories (e.g., Cantor *et al.,* 1980), such as "behavioral assessment with young children" or "behavioral assessment of adolescents." Behavioral assessment strategies may be quite different, depending on the specific parameters associated with differing types of child and family problems; for example, the prototype for behavioral assessment with a 3-year-old noncompliant child may be quite different from that for a depressed and suicidal adolescent. This view is consistent with the relativistic, contextually based, and idiographic nature of most behavioral assessment strategies, and with the organization of the present volume around categories of commonly occurring childhood disorders.

Since judgments concerning whether or not any particular assessment protocol fits the category of behavioral assessment appear to be of little consequence in and of themselves, we have not attempted to rigorously derive either a conceptually or an empirically based prototype of behavioral assessment. Rather, we simply wish to use the prototype-based view to represent some of the more commonly occurring conceptual, strategic, and procedural features of behavioral assessment (Mash, 1979). These include the following:

1. Behavioral assessment approaches are often based on conceptualizations of personality and abnormal behavior that focus on the child's thoughts, feelings, and behaviors as they occur in specific situations, rather than as manifestations of some global underlying traits or dispositions.

2. Behavioral assessment approaches are predominantly idiographic and individualized (Wolpe, 1986). They focus on understanding the individual child and family, rather than on nomothetic comparisons that attempt to describe individuals primarily in relation to dimensions derived from group norms.

3. Behavioral assessments emphasize the role of situational influences on behavior. It is recognized that the patterning and organization of an individual's behavior across situations may be highly idiographic (Mischel, 1968, 1973), and it is therefore important to describe both behaviors *and* situations. The theoretical debates surrounding the issue of situational specificity have been extensive (Bem & Funder, 1978; Endler & Magnusson, 1976) and are not discussed here. However, the pragmatic outcomes of the emphasis on situational specificity in behavioral assessment have been a greater sensitivity to the need to measure situational dimensions, and a corresponding increase in the range of environments sampled; for example, home, school, playground, and supermarket observations (e.g., Holden, 1985b) have been added to those samples of the child's and parent's behavior previously obtained under highly controlled and noninteractive testing conditions in the clinic.

4. Behavioral approaches have emphasized the instability of child and family behavior over time. This is in contrast to other approaches that emphasize the consistency of behavior over time, concomitant with the stable and enduring nature of underlying causes. Conceptually, at least, behavioral views would predict either consistency or variability in behavior over time as a function of the degree of stability or variation in context. However, because externally and internally induced situational variation appears to be the norm rather than the exception throughout childhood, the predominant behavioral view has been one that predicts the relative absence of consistency in behavior over time.

This view, however, fails to capture the complexity of the question in a number of ways. First, consistency can be assessed in relation to many levels of behavior, and, depending on the specificity of the behavior under consideration, different results may obtain. If a child's behavior is described in terms of a highly idiographic response topography (e.g., whining), then we may find little consistency over time; by contrast, behavioral definitions based on broader response classes (e.g., aggression) that encompass a wide range of behaviors, both within and across age levels, may have more enduring qualities. Furthermore, if we look at response functions rather than specific topographies, we may find that phenotypically different responses may still be reflective of a dynamic stability in which certain patterns of adjustment are repeated over time. As stated by Garber

(1984), "although there is little evidence of homotypic continuity—symptomatic isomorphism from early childhood—there is some evidence that children may show consistency in their general adaptive or maladaptive pattern of organizing their experiences and interacting with their environment" (p. 34). This organizational–developmental viewpoint has been supported by findings from longitudinal studies of development, which have suggested that patterns that are expressed in early relationships may repeat themselves over time (Cicchetti & Braunwald, in press; Kaye, 1984; Sroufe & Fleeson, 1986). The type of child and family characteristic being assessed also has implications for the question of temporal stability. For example, some characteristics (e.g., achievement motivation, dependency and passivity in females, serious aggressive behavior, and intellectual mastery) may show stability over time, whereas others may not (Garber, 1984; Loeber, 1982).

5. Behavioral assessments are by their nature systems-oriented. They are directed at describing and understanding (a) characteristics of the child and family, (b) the contexts in which such characteristics are expressed, and (c) the structural organizations and functional relationships that exist between situations and behaviors, thoughts, and emotions.

6. Behavioral approaches generally emphasize contemporaneous controlling variables rather than historical causes. However, where information concerning factors that are temporally remote (e.g., age of onset) can facilitate an understanding of current influences, it is not uncommon that such information will be sought. For example, knowing that a mother was physically abused as a child may help to understand her current attitudes and behavior toward her own child (Cicchetti & Rizley, 1981). Similarly, knowledge of early attachment patterns may assist in understanding a child's current patterns of social disturbance (Laney & Lewis, 1985).

7. Behavioral approaches are more often concerned with behaviors, cognitions, and affects as direct samples of the domains of interest rather than as signs of some underlying or remote causes. For example, assessments focusing on a child's irrational cognitions (e.g., Leitenberg, Yost, & Carroll-Wilson, 1986) or misattributions (Dodge & Somberg, 1987) consider these events as functional components of the problem to be modified, rather than as symptoms of some other problem. Neverthe-

less, an increasing emphasis in behavioral assessment on response–system covariations (Kazdin, 1982b; Voeltz & Evans, 1982) suggests that the assessment of some factors may be of interest primarily because of their relationship to some other more central aspect of the problem.

8. Behavioral approaches focus on obtaining assessment information that is directly relevant to treatment. "Relevance for treatment" usually refers to the usefulness of information in pinpointing treatment goals, selecting targets for intervention, designing and implementing interventions, and evaluating the outcomes of therapy.

9. Behavioral approaches rely on a multimethod assessment strategy, which emphasizes the importance of using different informants and a variety of procedures, including observations, interviews, and questionnaires. The inherent superiority of one method over another is not assumed, but should be based on the purposes and needs associated with specific assessments (McFall, 1986). Nevertheless, direct observations of behavior in naturalistic contexts (Foster & Cone, 1986; Reid, Baldwin, Patterson, & Dishion, 1987) are more commonly used in child and family behavioral assessment than in other approaches.

10. Behavioral approaches have attempted to maintain a low level of inference in interpreting assessment findings (Goldfried & Kent, 1972).

11. Behavioral assessments are ongoing and self-evaluating. Instead of assessments' being made on one or two occasions prior to treatment, the need for further assessment is dictated by the efficacy of the methods in facilitating desired treatment outcomes.

12. Behavioral assessments should be empirically anchored. The assessment strategy—in particular, the decision as to which variables to assess—should be derived from (a) an accumulation of knowledge concerning the characteristics of the child and family being assessed, and (b) the literature on specific disorders. Where assessments are theoretically driven, the theories should be closely tied to the data.

COMMON ASSESSMENT PURPOSES

Inherent in the view of behavioral assessment as an ongoing problem-solving strategy is the recognition that assessment of children and families are always carried out in relation to one or more purposes. Along with the assessor's working assumptions and conceptualizations about child and family behavior, these purposes will determine which individuals, behaviors, and settings are evaluated; the choice of assessment methods; the way in which findings are interpreted; the specification of assessment and treatment goals; and the manner in which these goals are evaluated. Most questions surrounding the assessment of child and family disturbance can be considered only within the context of the intended assessment purpose; therefore, decisions regarding the appropriateness or usefulness of particular methods and procedures are always relative to the needs of the situation. Discussions concerning the relative merits of information obtained via self-report versus direct observation have little meaning outside of the assessment context. A multicategory observational code system may be appropriate for assessments designed to identify potential controlling variables to be altered with treatment, but inappropriate for evaluating the outcome of a highly focused intervention.

Many writers (e.g., Bornstein et al., 1984; Cone & Hawkins, 1977; Hawkins, 1979; Kanfer & Nay, 1982; Mash & Terdal, 1976, 1980) have outlined the more common purposes for which child and family assessments are conducted. Broadly conceived, these include the following: (1) diagnosis, or assessment activities focusing on determining the nature or cause of the child's and family's problem: (2) prognosis, or generating predictions concerning future behavior under specified conditions; (3) treatment design, or the gathering of information that will assist in the development and implementation of effective interventions; and (4) evaluation, or assessments intended to evaluate treatment effectiveness and/ or acceptability. Although these purposes characterize behavioral assessment of children and families, they are not specific to any one theoretical, methodological, or therapeutic orientation. Because these purposes have been discussed previously and are addressed in relation to specific disorders in the chapters following, we comment on them only briefly here.

Diagnosis

The four purposes of assessment mentioned above often occur in phases for individual cases

(Bornstein *et al.*, 1984). Early diagnostic assessments are concerned with questions relating to general screening and administrative decision making (e.g., can the child be appropriately served by a particular agency or educational program?), whether or not there is a problem (e.g., does the child's behavior deviate from an appropriate behavioral or social norm?), and the nature and extent of the problem (e.g., what is it that the child is doing or not doing that results in a distressed school or family situation?).

As noted by Achenbach (1985), the term "diagnosis" has acquired two meanings. The first views diagnosis and classification as equivalent, and focuses on the formal assignment of cases to specific categories drawn from either a system of disease classification (Prugh, Engel, & Morse, 1975), such as the Diagnostic and Statistical Manual of Mental Disorders, third edition (DSM-III; American Psychiatric Association, 1980, 1987), or from empirically derived taxometric categories, prototypes, or typologies (Achenbach, 1985). The second and much broader meaning given to the term "diagnosis" considers it to be an analytic information-gathering process in which efforts are directed at understanding the nature of a problem, its possible causes, treatment options, and outcomes. While behavioral assessment strategies are more consistent with the broader view of diagnosis, behavioral assessors have also continued to use formal diagnoses as an organizational framework for their work (S. L. Harris, 1979; S. L. Harris & Powers, 1984; Kazdin, 1983; Nathan, 1981; Powers, 1984).

The diagnostic phase within behavioral assessment is conducted with the expectation that assessment will lead directly to recommendations for treatment. The questions often asked during the diagnostic phase of behavioral assessment are (1) What is the child doing, either overtly or covertly, that brings him or her into conflict with the environment? and (2) What are the potential controlling variables for these problems? Behavioral diagnoses are often highly individualized and based on direct empirical support. The methods employed during the early diagnostic phases of behavioral assessment tend to be global and extensive—they have been described as showing "broad bandwidth but low fidelity"—and the use of unstructured interviews, global self-report instruments, observational narratives, and multicategory code systems is common.

Prognosis

Every child and family assessment carries with it some projection regarding short- and long-term outcomes under varying conditions. Knowledge concerning the likely outcomes for certain behaviors during later periods of development is required for making judgments concerning deviancy. Since many childhood problems are not intrinsically pathological and are exhibited to some extent by most children, decisions regarding whether or not to treat often depend on prognostic implications (Achenbach, 1985). Implicit in any decision to initiate intervention is a projection that things will remain the same, improve, or deteriorate in the absence of treatment, or that outcomes will differ as a function of differing treatments. Often, treatments are directed at enhancing developmental processes rather than at removing symptoms or restoring a previous level of functioning (Achenbach & Edelbrock, 1984). Information concerning developmental processes may also provide the basis for anticipatory interventions in high-risk situations where prognoses are known to be poor (Kendall *et al.*, 1984). There are also a host of decisions related to children's mental health and the legal system (Reppucci, Weithorn, Mulvey, & Monahan, 1984) in which behavioral assessors may be requested or required to provide prognostic information (e.g., the parent's ability to provide an adequate environment for the child).

Very often questions conerning prognosis are considered in relation to longitudinal information, as derived, for example, from studies of "resiliency and invulnerability" in high-risk children (Garmezy & Rutter, 1983, 1985; Garmezy & Tellegen, 1984). For example, findings reported by Masten (1986) indicate that children with more resources (e.g., intellectual ability, stable and supportive families) are generally more competent and show more adaptive patterns of dealing with stress, particularly when they are girls. While data such as these can provide a basis for prediction in general, their applicability to decision making in regard to individual children and their families is not always clear. Studies of individual children at risk who do well may provide suggestions as to the types of interventions that could be appropriate in high-risk situations. For example, Masten (1986) describes one high-risk boy who coped extremely well with stress by creating a more positive environment for himself through drawing on adults outside the home, maintaining a positive outlook and disposition, and consciously using humor in his interactions.

Longitudinal studies of long-term outcomes for differing childhood disorders also provide information concerning prognosis (Loeber & Dishion, 1983). For example, Kelso and Stewart (1986) followed up 53 conduct-disordered boys 2 years later and found that 45% no longer had the disorder. Outcomes for 85% of the boys could be predicted via a discriminant function, which revealed the best predictors of persisting conduct disorders to be a variety of antisocial or aggressive symptoms, fire setting, early age of onset, and child deviance.

Questions concerning prognosis are frequently raised early in the assessment process. However, such questions are also important following treatment in assessing the likelihood that treatment gains will be maintained (Karoly & Steffen, 1980). In the adult area, studies that have shown the prognosis for maintenance with certain types of problems to be poor (e.g., abuse of alcohol) have led to the development of creative programs for relapse prevention. With a few exceptions, the systematic assessment of treatment maintenance has received less attention in the child and family areas.

Design

The design phase of behavioral assessment focuses on obtaining information that is directly relevant to the formulation of effective treatment strategies. This gathering of information includes further specification and measurement of potential controlling variables (e.g., patterns of social rewards and punishments, irrational cognitions or misattributions), determination of the child's own resources for change (e.g., behavioral assets and or/self-controlling behaviors), assessment of potential social and physical resources that can be utilized in carrying out treatment, assessment of the motivation for treatment of both the child and significant others, indication of potential reinforcers, specification of realistic and specific treatment objectives, and recommendations as to the types of treatments that are most likely to be effective.

Hypothesis testing during this phase is the norm, and determining the effectiveness of or the need for further assessment is an iterative process based on whether specified goals are achieved. The assessment procedures characterizing this phase are more problem-focused

than during the diagnostic phase, and specific types of problem checklists (e.g., fear survey schedules, measures of activity level, depression inventories), observational situations (e.g., command–compliance analogues), and behavior codes (e.g., on-task behavior, self-stimulation, aggression) are often used.

Evaluation

The evaluation phase of behavioral assessment is ongoing, and commonly involves the use of procedures designed to determine whether treatment objectives are being met, whether changes that have occurred are attributable to specific interventions, whether the changes are long-lasting and generalizable to other situations, whether the treatment, is economically viable, and whether treatments and treatment outcomes are subjectively acceptable to the participants. Assessments for determining whether treatment goals are being met require the measurement of targeted objectives over time. Such measurement will indicate the presence or absence of change, which in many cases may be adequate. However, to determine whether changes are a function of the treatments introduced, it is necessary to collect observations within the constraints of a single-subject experimental design (Barlow & Hersen, 1984). While such designs have been, and continue to be, an integral component of behavior therapy and assessment, a key question at the present time concerns the adequacy of single-case designs for representing the often complex system relationships that characterize many of the treatment goals in child and family interventions.

Evaluations relative to the acceptablility of treatments and treatment changes have been discussed under the headings of social validity (Kazdin, 1977; Wolf, 1978), treatment acceptability (Kazdin, 1981, 1984), and consumer satisfaction (Kiesler, 1983; LeBow, 1982; McMahon & Forehand, 1983). Behavioral assessors have also become increasingly sensitive to some of the measurement issues surrounding long-term follow-up (Mash & Terdal, 1980); such issues are especially pertinent to interventions for children, which must be gauged against ongoing or projected developmental changes. The methods used for evaluation tend to be highly focused and specific in comparison to earlier assessment phases.

The purposes described thus far relate to clinical decision making for individual children, since this is characteristically the focus for most behavioral assessments. There is also a need to recognize that broader societal and institutional purposes often underlie assessment practices with children. These include classification for administrative record keeping, program development and evaluation, policy planning, and the advancement of scientific knowledge (Hawkins, 1979). The types of assessment methods needed to meet these purposes may differ substantially from those required for the assessment of individual children and families.

CHILDREN'S FUNCTIONING AND ITS DETERMINANTS

Childhood Disorders versus Target Behaviors

While early behavioral approaches to child and family disorders were explicit in their rejection of classification systems characteristic of the medical and psychodynamic models of psychopathology (Ullmann & Krasner, 1965), it has been noted that many books written from the behavioral perspective have organized their subject matter according to chapters roughly corresponding to traditional diagnostic units (e.g., Barlow, 1981; Hersen & Van Hasselt, 1987; Mash & Barkley, in press; Mash & Terdal, 1981a; Morris & Kratochwill, 1983; Ullmann & Krasner, 1969; A. J. Yates, 1970). Such an organization is also characteristic of this volume, and reflects the view that children and families often present themselves for assessment showing characteristic patterns, clusters, or constellations of problems rather than single or isolated target symptoms. We believe that assessment can best proceed from an empirically based understanding of such characteristic patterns or "packages of behavior." As noted by Barlow (1986), "the identification of behaviors and cognitions that seem to cluster together is not an insidious influence but rather something that all behavior therapists engage in formally or informally as a first step preceding a thorough behavioral analysis" (p. 100).

There is both clinical and empirical evidence to suggest that broad patterns of child disturbance labeled "undercontrolled" (e.g., aggression, delinquency, hyperactivity) and "overcontrolled" (e.g., fears, anxiety, depression, somatic complaints, withdrawal) are relatively stable over time and across raters (Achenbach & Edelbrock, 1978). We concur with Kanfer's (1979) position that "different problem areas require development of separate methods and conceptualizations that take into account the particular parameters of that area," and that "it may turn out that in some domains progress in behavioral assessment will be blocked until conceptual models or data are available to permit a functional analysis on which target selection for assessment and rules for generalization of observations can be based" (p. 39).

There continues to be a pressing need for conceptual models of child and family disorder to guide our behavioral assessments in both clinical and research contexts (McFall, 1986). One of the best-articulated theory-driven empirically based models for behavioral assessment that has emerged thus far is represented by Gerald Patterson's (1982) work with children and families exhibiting antisocial problems. Through the use of multiple methodologies, and complex statistical methods such as structural equation modeling (Connel & Tanaka, 1987; Joreskog & Sorbom, 1983), a number of empirically derived constructs and their relationships have been implicated in the development of antisocial behavior (Patterson, 1986; Patterson & Bank, 1986). While this work has occurred primarily in a research context, it suggests several molar and micro variables (e.g., whether the child is rejected or perceived as antisocial by others; the likelihood of the child's unprovoked negative behavior toward parents and siblings, and its duration; the extent to which parents monitor their children and spend time with them; and the parents' inept discipline, as reflected in their use of explosive forms of punishment, negative actions and reactions, and inconsistent/erratic behavior) that are probably important to assess in any clinical context with antisocial children and families. Each chapter in this volume provides one or more conceptual models and an empirical base for the disorder being considered, and the assessment strategies presented are intended to follow from this framework.

The specification of particular categories of childhood disorders as a basis for discussing assessment strategies is suggestive of the syndrome and trait views that behavioral assessors have previously avoided. However, as described by Achenbach and Edelbrock (1978, p. 1294), there are different ways of viewing the role of syndromes in the classification of children:

1. The syndrome may be viewed as representing a personality or character type that endures beyond the immediate precipitating events requiring professional attention.
2. The syndrome may be viewed as a reaction type, whose form is as much a function of specific precipitating stresses as of individual characteristics.
3. The syndrome may be viewed as a collection of behaviors that happen to be statistically associated because the environmental contingencies supporting them are statistically associated.
4. The syndrome may be viewed as reflecting dimensions or traits, so that children are best described individually in terms of their scores on all syndromes rather than by categorization according to their resemblance to a particular syndrome.

The view of syndromes as reflecting either reaction types or classes of correlated behaviors would appear consistent with many of the assumptions underlying behavioral assessment. Nevertheless, the views listed above are not necessarily independent of one another. It may be that reaction types that become well established early in develoment eventually emerge as enduring, but not necessarily irreversible, character types. For example, recent work has suggested that preferential orientations toward others, self, and the object world when confronted with interactive stress may be exhibited by infants as young as 6 months of age (Tronick & Gianino, 1986).

The concept of syndromes in behavioral work with children and families is represented in work that has examined the notions of ''response class'' and ''response covariation'' (e.g., Kazdin, 1982b, 1983; Voeltz & Evans, 1982; Wahler, 1975). These notions imply that (1) certain behaviors tend to *co-occur,* or to be correlated with one another; and (2) that certain behaviors tend to *covary,* such that changes in one are associated with changes in the other. In both cases, the behaviors that co-occur or covary may be topographically similar *or* dissimilar. Research into response covariation has suggested indirect paths of clinical intervention—for example, when decreases in a child's noncompliant behavior lead to a reduction in bedwetting (Nordquist, 1971) or stuttering (Wahler, Sperling, Thomas, Teeter, & Luper, 1970). The existence of such response clusters has important implications for assessment, in

that mapping out these relationships and co-variations is likely to suggest courses of intervention that are maximally effective (i.e., where the least intrusive and most cost-efficient procedures may be used to bring about the most widespread change).

While an extensive discussion of research issues surrounding the concepts of response class and response covariation is beyond the scope of the current chapter, it would appear that a number of important questions need to be addressed before these concepts can have widespread applicability in child and family behavioral assessment.

1. First, there is currently little information as to how one goes about identifying response classes. Potential response classes have been derived via serendipitous discovery, from clinically described syndromes, from conceptual models or theories about child and family disorders, from statistical methods for grouping data (Achenbach, 1985; Skinner, 1981), and through systematic functional analysis (D. R. Peterson, 1968). In light of the potentially infinite number of topographically dissimilar responses that could be related, guidelines are needed for limiting the number and range of responses to be assessed.

2. Response-class representations are miniature systems (e.g., Minuchin, 1985), and guidelines are needed for mapping out the structural organizations and functional relationships that describe a particular response class, as well as describing its relationships to other systems (e.g., relationships between response classes).

3. While the focus in child and family behavioral assessment has been on *response* classes, we are more often talking about constellations of responses, cognitions, emotions, and physiological reactions. The more varied and complex our response classes become, the more they seem to approximate some of the more classical descriptions of clinical syndromes.

4. Are response classes to be defined idiographically, or can we expect them to have some generality across individuals?

5. The relationship between response classes and situations has received little attention (Wahler & Graves, 1983). Can we expect that response classes will be situation-specific, as some research has suggested (Patterson & Bechtel, 1977), or will some response clusters show generality across situations?

6. Most discussions of response classes have focused on the individual. However, it would

be equally feasible to identify response clusters for more complex social units—for example, sibling dyads or the family.

While these issues are in need of further investigation, research on response covariation has sensitized behavioral assessors to the fact that consideration of only a narrow range of target behaviors fails to adequately represent the more general network of behaviors of which this behavior may be a part, or the fact that the behavior may be functionally embedded in a larger social system (Kazdin, 1985).

The view of child and family disorders underlying this volume is based on commonalities in patterns of behavior and behavior-context disturbances, rather than on target symptoms. Many discussions of behavioral assessment have focused on assessment techniques, such as the interview, self-report, and direct observation (e.g., Ollendick & Hersen, 1984). However, this volume considers these techniques only in relation to the specific problem contexts in which they are to be used. A. O. Ross (1978) notes that "the emphasis in behavior therapy should be on the conceptualization of problems and not on specific techniques" (p. 592). This statement is equally applicable to behavioral assessment. Although some general principles are undoubtedly associated with the development and use of particular behavioral assessment techniques, the nature of an interview with the parent of a depressed child should be different from that conducted with the parent of a socially aggressive child. It is believed that an understanding of the parameters associated with childhood depression (see Kazdin, Chapter 4, this volume) or conduct disorders (see McMahon & Forehand, Chapter 3, this volume), in coordination with the general principles of behavioral interviewing (e.g., Turkat, 1986), will serve to generate more specialized and ultimately more useful assessments in each of these areas.

Classification and Diagnosis

Probably the most controversial area in the assessment and treatment of disturbed children and families has been the use of diagnostic labels based upon global classification systems. In commenting on the high proportion (estimates of 40%) of clinic-referred children who were (and sometimes still are) labeled in global and nondescript terms such as "adjustment reaction" (Cerreto & Tuma, 1977), Dreger et al.

(1964) stated, "[L]ooked at realistically, what this means is that after the elaborate procedures used in most clinics are completed, the child is placed in a category, which says exactly what we knew about him in the first place, that he has a problem" (p. 1). In some studies, as many as 30% of parents surveyed who had been in contact with professionals indicated that their children had been described with three or more labels (Gorham, DesJardins, Page, Pettis, & Scheiber, 1975), and over time the same labels may be used to describe different sets of clinical phenomena (Zachary, Levin, Hargreaves, & Greene, 1981). The differing systems for the classification of childhood disorders have received extensive discussion (e.g., Achenbach & Edelbrock, 1978; Hobbs, 1975; Kessler, 1971; Phillips, Draguns, & Bartlett, 1975; Quay, 1979), and such discussions (e.g., Achenbach, 1985; Cantwell, 1980; Morey, Skinner, & Blashfield, 1986; Nathan, 1981; Rutter & Shaffer, 1980; Spitzer & Cantwell, 1980) have increased in number since the development of DSM-III (American Psychiatric Association, 1980) and its recent revision, DSM-IIIR (American Psychiatric Association, 1987).

There is in the literature some consensus regarding the general neglect of meaningful taxonomic frameworks for describing children and families, and the need for classification systems for guiding theory, research, and practice. For example, Achenbach and Edelbrock (1978) state that "the study of psychopathology in children has long lacked a coherent taxonomic framework within which training, treatment, epidemiology, and research could be integrated" (p. 1275). However, all classification systems to emerge thus far have met with varying degrees of criticism, although their use has increased over the past 10 years. For example, Nathan (1986) states, "For the most part, when more effective treatments have been developed or more light has been shed on etiology, it has not been by virtue of one or another classification scheme that this has come about" (p. 201).

While behavioral assessors have become increasingly accepting of the need for a classification system of child and family disorders, and of existing systems such as DSM-III (S. L. Harris & Powers, 1984; C. Peterson & Rahrer, 1986; Powers, 1984; Taylor, 1983), there continue to be expressions of dissatisfaction with the currently available approaches (Evans & Nelson, 1986), especially those based on the

Kraepelinian tradition. These dissatisfactions center around such things as empirical inadequacy (McLemore & Benjamin, 1979; McReynolds, 1975; Schacht & Nathan, 1977); implicit etiological assumptions that underlie the categories (e.g., Group for the Advancement of Psychiatry, 1974); the subjective-impressionistic criteria used to derive individual categories; the failure to provide empirically based operational criteria for assignment to categories; the static nature of the categories when applied to the developing child; the lack of demonstrated relevance for treatment; the potentially undesirable consequences of labeling; and a general lack of sensitivity to contextual influences.

Nevertheless, behavioral assessors have failed to provide an alternative classification scheme, in spite of a long-standing recognition of the need to do so (Adams, Doster, & Calhoun, 1977; Arkowitz, 1979; Ferster, 1965). The lack of behavioral assessment development in this area probably reflects the priority for idiographic, treatment-oriented goals. It is not clear that the development of global classification systems for childhood disorders will do much to facilitate these goals, although they have the potential to improve communication, the combining of data from diverse sources, epidemiological study, comparison of treatments, and understanding of causes (Kessler, 1971).

Classification efforts for childhood disorders have followed several traditions. The first has involved the development of clinically derived categories for classification based upon subjective consensus, as characterized by those syndromal systems developed by the Group for the Advancement of Psychiatry (1974), the World Health Organization (the multiaxial classification of Rutter, Shaffer, & Shepherd, 1975), and the American Psychiatric Association (1980, 1987). Although it is beyond the scope of this chapter to review these systems in any detail (see Achenbach, 1985, for an excellent review of classification paradigms), commonly occurring categories are exemplified by those provided in DSM-III. These include groupings for attention deficit disorders, conduct disorders, and anxiety–withdrawal disorders. Other categories include those for mental retardation; developmental disorders of a pervasive and specific nature; and problems related to eating, speech, and stereotyped movements. DSM-III criteria for assignment to these categories are presented throughout the chapters of this vol-

ume. Generally, they include such things as the presence of a specified number of "behaviors," a minimum time period during which the specified behavior(s) must be present, age criteria, and exclusionary criteria if the problem is a function of other disorders. In recognizing that a simple enumeration of symptoms may not be sufficient in planning treatment and predicting individual outcomes, DSM-III also provides a multiaxial classification scheme in which the first two axes include all categories of mental disorder, and the remaining three deal with physical disorders and conditions (Axis III), severity of psychosocial stressors (Axis IV), and highest level of adaptive functioning in the past year (Axis V). However, only the first three axes constitute an "official" diagnostic evaluation, and the amount of differentiation for Axes I and II is disproportionately large when compared with that for the others.

Efforts to increase the accuracy and reliability of psychiatric diagnoses have resulted in the development of a number of structured and semistructured interview procedures for obtaining information to assist in making a diagnosis. The use of such standardized procedures for the identification of groups of patients in behaviorally oriented assessment and treatment outcome studies has increased over the past 5 years, and DSM-III terminology is increasingly finding its way into behavioral assessment research with children and families. Some have suggested that the DSM-III criteria could provide direction regarding the range of behaviors that might then be assessed in a more intensive idiographic fashion (Powers, 1984). It is likely that until behavioral assessors are willing and able to invest the time and resources to develop and to promote an empirically based classification alternative to DSM-III, administrative requirements, the need to communicate with other professionals, and the need for a taxonomy to direct and organize research and clinical activities will all contribute to increased acceptance and use of the DSM-III typologies by behavioral assessors.

A second major approach to the classification of childhood disorders is an empirical one, involving the utilization of multivariate statistical methods such as factor analysis and cluster analysis (Achenbach, 1985). Such approaches assume that there are a number of independent dimensions for behavior and that all children possess these sets of behavior to varying degrees. In contrast to the previously described approaches characterized by the use of clinically derived categories emphasizing qualitatively different types of childhood disorder, the dimensional approach, which focuses on empirically derived categories of behavioral covariation, seems more consistent with the assumptions of behavioral assessment if not with the practice. Although empirically derived classifications are more objective and potentially more reliable, they also possess associated problems. No classification system can be better than the items that comprise it, and, as noted by Achenbach (1985), "subjective judgement is involved in selecting the samples and attributes to be analyzed, the analytic methods, and the mathematical criteria" (p. 90). Other concerns include possible interactions between the methods of data collection (e.g., ratings, direct observations, questionnaires) or the informants (e.g., parents vs. teachers) and the dimensions that emerge, and the lack of sensitivity of the global trait dimensions to situational influences (e.g., age of child, duration of the disorder, setting in which behavior is rated, time at which the ratings are made).

The multivariate studies (see Achenbach & Edelbrock, 1978) are consistent in identifying the two broad dimensions of child behavior labeled "undercontrolled" and "overcontrolled." More specific syndromes that have been verified via confirmatory factor analysis include aggressive, attentional problems with hyperactivity, anxious depressed, cruel (girls only), delinquent, obsessive–compulsive, schizoid thought disorder, sex problems, socially inept, somatic complaints, and uncommunicative–withdrawn (Achenbach, 1985, p. 107).

Much of the recent impetus for the development of multivariate classification approaches in child and family assessment has come from the extensive work of Thomas Achenbach and Craig Edelbrock with the Child Behavior Checklist and Revised Child Behavior Profile (Achenbach & Edelbrock, 1983; Edelbrock & Achenbach, 1985). It would not be possible to do justice to the scope and magnitude of this work in this brief discussion, and the interested reader is referred to an eloquent exposition on the "merits of multivariates" by Achenbach (1985). Briefly, however, Achenbach (1985) describes a number of advantages associated with utilizing a taxometric integration of prototypical syndromes, in which an individual child may be classified on the basis of the similarity of his or her profile of syndrome scores with the centroid of each previously derived profile type. Beginning with the rationale that child syndromes consist of imperfectly correlated features, the argument is made that a prototype-based view of classification (Cantor et al., 1980) is preferable to one that employs the assignment of individuals to categories based on the presence of a small number of essential or cardinal features. While it has been recognized that the conceptual derivation of prototypes for syndromes is possible (e.g., Horowitz, Post, French, Wallis, & Siegelman, 1981; Horowitz, Wright, Lowenstein, & Parad, 1981), operational definitions of prototypical syndromes can be generated via multivariate analyses. It is argued that the use of quantitative indices, standardized assessment data, and computerized data processing will permit the integration of large and complex data sets; will reduce the likelihood that information-processing biases will influence clinical judgments; and will enable the clinician to focus on other aspects of assessment and treatment that are not easily standardized.

In light of current views of behavioral assessment as a problem-solving strategy that seeks to assess multiple child and family characteristics utilizing a variety of methods, the use of actuarial approaches in behavioral assessment seems most appropriate (Mash, 1985; Rachman, 1983). The multivariate emphasis on empirical decision making is quite consistent with many of the behavioral assessment assumptions. In addition, multivariate approaches are becoming increasingly multidimensional. For example, Achenbach (1985) has proposed a provisional multiaxial approach to assessment that describes children of different ages on five axes: (I) Parent Perceptions, (II) Teacher's Perceptions, (III) Cognitive Assessment, (IV) Physical Conditions, and (V) Clinician's Assessment. These axes are intended to reflect different settings, different informants, and different assessment methods. While this approach is promising, and clearly offers more than the current multi-axial elaborations of DSM-III, the approach as presented, is decidedly deficient in terms of its contextual or its developmental emphasis. For example, during the first 2 years of life the primary emphasis is on information concerning developmental milestones and clinical impressions; a rich data base describing interactive developmental processes, such as attachment quality, emotional regulation, purposeful communication, and cognitive development, receives little attention. The specific axes that are proposed also tend to confound settings, informants, methods, and the dimension being assessed. Nevertheless this approach is consistent with the multitrait–multimethod emphasis in behavioral assessment (Nay, 1979), and reflects the emergence of multivariate assessment strategies that rely on a wider range of methods and informants than was previously the case.

As reflected throughout this volume, the use of existing multivariate assessment procedures in child and family behavioral assessment has increased considerably. This reflects a greater interest in child and parent perceptions as mediators of behavior and behavior change (e.g., Forehand, Wells, McMahon, Griest, & Rogers, 1982; Mash & Johnston, 1983b), the relationships that have been found between these measures and direct observations of behavior (e.g., Mash & Johnston, 1983a; Patterson & Bank, 1986), and the availability and ease of use of these procedures. Many of the criticisms of the multivariate approach by behavioral assessors have been based on a dissatisfaction with the often global and ambiguous content being assessed, the fact that information has been based heavily on subjective reports, and the general lack of sensitivity to situational influences. However, these criticisms are not inherent to the approach per se, since it would be quite possible to derive "syndromes" that were based on other theories, had different contents, employed other methods (e.g., direct observation), and sampled a broader range of settings than those currently available. Conceivably, syndromes of "reaction types" could also be derived that were specific to particular situations (e.g., profiles for reaction types to stressful family events, medical procedures, academic tasks, etc.).

More serious criticism of the multivariate strategy within a behavioral assessment framework pertains to the nomothetic emphasis on comparisons between an individual child and some group norm, and the apparent lack of relevance of dimensional systems for treatment (D. R. Peterson, 1968). However, it would appear that behavioral assessors have integrated the standardized multivariate assessments into clinical practice in formulating treatment goals— for example, where the parent's perceptions may be that the child is "deviant," but observations of the child's behavior would suggest otherwise (e.g., Mash, Johnston, & Kovitz, 1983)—and as one outcome measure for assessing the impact of treatment.

A third approach to classification follows from a developmental perspective on child psychopathology. While this perspective is often taken, albeit unsystematically, in clinical practice, it does not seem to have had a significant impact on institutionalized diagnostic practices with children thus far. For example, many of the DSM-III categories for children are simple extensions of those used to categorize adults, and the focus of the multivariate approaches has been on the categorization of isolated behaviors and traits rather than on the patterns of adaptation that are more characteristic of developmental change. Garber (1984) has presented an insightful developmental perspective on classification, and has outlined many of the complexities and challenges that underlie this approach. Central to this view is the need to assess children's levels of functioning within different developmental domains (e.g., emotional, cognitive, social, physiological) and their patterns of coping in relation to major developmental tasks (e.g., regulation of biological functions, attachment, dependency, self-control, conformity to rules). Children are diagnosed in relation to their success or failure in negotiating normative developmental expectations and demands, and it is believed that diagnostic models should emphasize adaptations and organizations of behavior at various developmental levels, rather than static traits, signs, or symptoms.

The developmental perspective is quite consistent with the emphasis in behavioral assessment on describing children's reactions in relation to situational demands, but it presents some formidable challenges in practice; not the least of these are mapping out and defining "normative" developmental sequences and creating a relevant taxonomy of developmental tasks. Nevertheless, current longitudinal studies in child development and developmental psychopathology (Sroufe & Rutter, 1984) are beginning to provide a rich data base from which developmental adaptations may be assessed and classified, especially in the first few years of life (e.g., Greenspan & Lourie, 1981) and more recently during middle childhood (e.g., Masten, 1986). The developmental perspective on classification, and developmental models in general, have much to contribute to the behavioral assessment of children and families.

The classification systems that we have discussed thus far, especially DSM-III and the
multivariate approach, have tended to focus on
the individual child. They are derived from
models that view childhood disorders as residing in the child, rather than in the reciprocal
relationships between the child and the larger
social system in which he or she functions.
Classification models for describing larger social systems, such as the parent–child dyad
(Egeland & Sroufe, 1981; Oldershaw, 1986),
the marital relationship (Weiss & Margolin,
1986), or the family (Mink, Meyers, & Nihara,
1984; Mink, Nihara, & Meyers, 1983; Moos
& Moos, 1978), are only beginning to emerge.
It is believed that these types of classification
approaches have the potential for incorporating
the behavioral emphasis on situational influence
into our diagnostic practices. Similarly, there
continues to be an enormous need in assessments with children and families for the development of taxonomies that describe situations
(Mischel, 1977; Schlundt & McFall; 1987),
although this has been recognized for some time
(e.g., Bossard & Boll, 1943). Most of our
assessment procedures still focus on individuals, and the degree of measurement sophistication that has been achieved in describing the
situations in which children and families function is still quite primitive, often reflecting
obvious topographical features of the setting
(e.g., home vs. school). More elaborated classification schemes reflecting the differentiation
that occurs within settings are needed, and
previous work on the ecological assessment of
environments should provide some direction in
this regard (e.g., Vincent & Trickett, 1983).
For example, the Classroom Environment Scale
(Moos & Trickett, 1974) looks at classroom
environments in terms of relationship (e.g.,
involvement, affiliation, teacher support), personal (e.g., task orientation, competition), system maintenance (e.g., order and organizations, rule clarity, teacher control), and system
change (e.g., innovation) dimensions.

Outcomes of Labeling Children

A great deal has been written about the positive
and negative aspects of assigning diagnostic
labels to children. On the positive side, it is
argued that labels help to summarize and order
observations; to facilitate communication among
professionals with different backgrounds; to guide
treatment strategies in a global fashion; to put
therapists in touch with a pre-existing relevant
body of more detailed research and clinical
data; and, consistent with scientific goals, to
facilitate etiological, epidemiological, and
treatment outcome studies (Rains, Kitsuse,
Duster, & Friedson, 1975). On the negative
side are criticisms regarding how effectively
currently available diagnostic labels achieve any
of the aforementioned purposes, as well as a
concern about possible negative outcomes associated with assigning labels to children, including how others tend to perceive and react
to the children (Bromfeld, Weisz, & Messer,
1986) and how the labels influence children's
perceptions of themselves and their behavior
(Guskin, Bartel, & MacMillan, 1975).

The use of existing labels can bias professionals toward seeing psychopathology in children, although there is some evidence to suggest that behavior therapists may be less easily
biased by labels (Langer & Abelson, 1974).
Several studies have shown that a particular
behavior, if believed to be exhibited by a "disturbed" or "handicapped" child, may produce
different reactions than when it is believed to
be exhibited by a "nondisturbed" child (Ste-
ven-Long, 1973). Labeling children as "behaviorally disturbed" or as "normal" has also
been shown to result in distortions in recall on
the part of trained observers, for negative behaviors (B. T. Yates, Klein, & Haven, 1978)
and, under some circumstances, for positive
behaviors (B. T. Yates & Hoage, 1979). B. T.
Yates *et al.* (1978) found a tendency for observers to overestimate the occurrence of negative behavior in a group labeled "behaviorally
disturbed," and to underestimate the occurrence of negative behavior in a group labeled
"normal." Other studies have shown the role
that labels play in producing negatively stereotypical expectations on the part of teachers
(G. G. Foster, Ysseldyke, & Reese, 1975).
These illustrative studies, as well as many others, provide indirect support for some of the
potentially negative effects of diagnostic labeling by professionals. Furthermore, recent work
on the "cognitive economics" (Achenbach,
1985; Mischel, 1979) of clinical information
processing suggests that many sources of bias
may surround human judgments, including those
involved in the assignment of labels.

On the positive side, some investigators have
suggested that the use of labels may serve as a

convenient reference point for tolerance toward and acceptability of particular sets of child behaviors (Algozzine, Mercer, & Countermine, 1977); may provide parents with closure and understanding regarding what might be wrong with their children (Fernald & Gettys, 1978); and is consistent with the natural tendencies of humans to think in terms of categories. If parents believe that a label explains why their child is the way he or she is, then attention may be directed at coping with the problem rather than at searching for the "real" cause through successive contacts with agencies and professionals. Whether such suggested "benefits" outweigh the negative effects of labeling has yet to be demonstrated.

It is believed that the most important outcomes associated with the labeling of disturbed children may not be those involving the assignment of static labels or diagnoses by professionals. Rather, the informal labeling processes surrounding child and family behavior and the interpretations of formal labels by parents, teachers, and children themselves are likely to have the greatest impact (e.g., Coie & Pennington, 1976; Compas, Friedland-Bandes, Bastien, & Adelman, 1981; Dollinger, Thelan, & Walsh, 1980). Further study and assessment of the beliefs (Sigel, 1985) and "everyday cognitions" (Sternberg & Wagner, in press) that describe how parents and teachers use labels to organize their experiences with both normal and disturbed children, and how such labeling influences their responses to and feelings about children, are likely to increase our understanding of disordered behavior. Several lines of research that appear promising in this regard include studies that have examined labeling and attribution processes in parents of disturbed (Larrance & Twentyman, 1983) and nondisturbed (Dix, Ruble, Grusec, & Nixon, 1986) children, and those that have looked at "parents as problem solvers" in common but often difficult, child-rearing situations (e.g, crying, noncompliance, refusal, trips to the supermarket) (Holden, 1985a, 1985b, 1985c). Labeling is a prepotent human response, and there is a need to find ways of assessing some of the natural and common ways in which child behaviors are ordered by those interacting with children. In identifying the types of labels that are used, the conditions under which they are used, and the effects associated with their use, it is likely that we will need to consider the unique characteristics of the interactants, as well as those universal processes that characterize humans as information processors (Kanfer, 1985).

Etiological Assumptions Regarding Childhood Disorders

The most prevalent misconception associated with behavioral views of child and family disorders has been that deviant behaviors are acquired exclusively as a function of interactions with the external physical and social environments. Implicit in this view is that child and family deviancy represent faulty learning, and therefore that in assessing the problem one should look for causes in the external environment, giving minimal attention to organismic events or internal cognitions and affects.

To be sure, early behavioral views of child and family disorder emphasized the significant role of environmental events as relevant controlling conditions, but even then did not do so to the exclusion of other important variables. If anything, the behavioral and social learning viewpoints that emerged in the 1960s (e.g., Bandura, 1969; Kanfer & Phillips, 1970; Ullmann & Krasner, 1965) provided a more balanced approach to the study of child and family psychopathology, which had previously emphasized physical causes such as brain dysfunction, or internal events such as unconscious impulses and drives. It was unfortunate that the attempt to give greater weight to important and observable environmental influences was inaccurately perceived by many as the complete rejection of all intraorganismic controlling variables. Current work on the behavioral assessment of children and families examines a broad range of internal and external controlling factors.

A number of general points related to a behavioral assessment perspective on childhood disorders can be made:

1. The first concerns multiple causality. Given that the child is embedded in a complex and changing system, it is likely that many potentially relevant controlling variables contribute to the problem, including physical and social environmental events, as well as orgnasimic variables of both a physiological and a cognitive nature.

2. No *a priori* assumptions are made regarding the primacy of controlling variables in con-

tributing to child and family disorders. This view rejects particular sets of controlling variables as necessarily more important than others (e.g., physical vs. social causes) either contemporaneously or historically, and is intended to counteract the popular belief in many child assessment and treatment settings that the identification of malfunctioning physical systems through medical examination, neuropsychological testing, or historical information somehow provides a more fundamental explanation of why the child is exhibiting problems. Such an analysis is both incomplete and inaccurate, because it gives greater weight to physical causes in explaining child behavior and ignores potential environmental factors of equal importance.

3. Although there are no assumptions in behavioral assessment regarding the primacy of controlling conditions with respect to etiology, primacy may be given to certain variables when such variables are suggested by data, or for the sake of methodological and practical expediency. Variables that are observable, easily measured, and readily modified may become the focus for assessment when such an approach facilitates remediation of the problem.

4. It is assumed that there is an ongoing and reciprocal interaction between relevant controlling variables, so that attempts to identify original causes in assessment are not likely to be fruitful. "Causes" that occur earlier in development (e.g., birth injury or social deprivation) cannot be assumed to be more significant contributors to the child and family's difficulties than current physical conditions and social processes.

5. The processes by which relevant controlling variables for most deviant child and family behaviors exert their influence are assumed to be similar and often continuous with those underlying nondeviant behavior, and general principles related to both physiology and learning apply equally for both types of behavior.

6. Although controlling variables that are contemporaneous and situationally present are frequently emphasized as "causes" in behavioral views of child and family disorders, there is also the need to consider both extrasituational and temporally more remote causes. For example, external stressors such as marital discord (O'Leary, 1984) may have direct effects on a mother's immediate reaction to her child's behavior. Passman and Mulhern (1977) have shown that a mother's punitiveness toward her child may increase with the amount of external stress to which she is exposed, and Wahler (1980) has reported an inverse relationship between extrafamily contracts and child behavior problems. There is increasing evidence to suggest that children's *in situ* behaviors represent only one contributor to parental reaction (e.g., Mash & Johnston, 1983a), which may be influenced by external factors of the types just mentioned (Dunst & Trivette, 1986), as well as by the general rules and strategies that parents follow in interacting with their children (Lytton, 1979; Sigel, 1985). It is not surprising, therefore, that treatment-induced behavioral alterations in the child do not always lead to subsequent changes in parental behavior and perceptions.

DIMENSIONS OF CHILD AND FAMILY BEHAVIOR ASSESSMENT

One of the most important characteristics of developing children is the active dialogue that transpires between each child and his or her biological makeup, physical and social environments, and the cultural milieu into which he or she is born (D'Antonio & Aldous, 1983; Lamb, 1982). Guided by genetic endowment and neuromuscular maturation, relentlessly working at understanding the surrounding physical realities and social expectations, the child is nurtured, shaped, and socialized. No passive partner in this dialogue, the child in return shapes the world around him or her, setting his or her own expectations and demands (Bell & Harper, 1977; Emery, Binkoff, Houts, & Carr, 1983). This developmental engagement is characterized by conflict and equilibrium in the cognitive, emotional, and social domains, and almost always by quantitative and qualitative movement and change. It begins at the time of conception and continues thereafter. Any consideration of the assessment of children and families must begin with recognition of the ebb and flow of this developmental dialogue, because it has critical implications for the manner in which child behaviors are conceptualized, measured, classified, diagnosed, changed, and evaluated. The recognition that child and family behaviors are embedded within normative developmental sequences guided by organizational principles, and that they occur within a leveled context of micro- and macrosocial influences (Bronfenbrenner, 1979, 1986), necessitates a view of child behavior assessment that reflects both the uniqueness and the multidimensionality of children. This leads to a number of important generalizations regarding assessment:

1. Developing children represent a unique population for which there are special assessment considerations of a conceptual, methodological, and practical nature.

2. The assessment of childhood disorders necessarily involves normative judgments as to what constitutes (a) developmental deviation, (b) performance variation in relation to an appropriate reference group, (c) developmentally appropriate adaptation to a range of situational demands, and (d) unexpected deviation from some projected course of individual development. Of necessity, judgments will usually include comparisons of a child to both individual and group norms.

3. Assessment of children and their families invariably involves multiple targets, including somatic and physiological states, behaviors, cognitions, and affects.

4. Given the large number and range of factors at the individual and systems levels that are implicated for most types of child and family disorders, decision rules are needed for the selection of meaningful targets for assessment and intervention (Evans, 1985; Kanfer, 1985; Mash, 1985).

5. Similarly, when one considers the potentially infinite number of variables and their interactions that *could* be assessed in disturbed family systems, empirically validated decision rules are needed for the individual case, in order to determine what factors *should* be assessed using what methods.

6. The range of situations in which children function is necessarily various and includes the family, the day care setting, school, and formal and informal peer groups. Embedded within each of these more global settings are numerous subsettings. In light of this, multisituational analysis is the rule, and one of the tasks of assessment is often to determine which aspects of performance are unique to specific contexts and which aspects transcend situational variations.

7. The pervasiveness of developmental change and situational variation in children suggests the need to assess patterns of behavior over time, as well as more global situational consistencies.

Special Considerations

Although the assessment of adults has much in common with the assessment of children, there are several characteristic conditions and constraints associated with the assessment of children that are not ordinarily encountered when assessing adults (Achenbach, 1985). The uniqueness of child assessment follows from generalizations about children as a group, characteristics of children at different ages that may interact with the types of assessments being carried out, and commonalities within the types of situations in which children ordinarily function and in which they are assessed.

Rapid and Uneven Developmental Change

With respect to generalizations about children as a group, the most noteworthy characteristic is rapid and uneven developmental change (Ciminero & Drabman, 1977; Evans & Nelson, 1977). Such change has implications both for judgments concerning childhood deviancy and for the selection of appropriate methods for assessment. Some studies have described both the age trends characterizing many child behaviors (e.g., Achenbach & Edelbrock, 1981; Mac Farlane, Allen, & Honzik, 1954) and ways in which the social significance and meaning of a problem may vary with the age of the child (Prugh *et al.*, 1975). Behaviors that are common at an earlier age (e.g., tantrums) may be considered inappropriate in an older child, and some authors have noted that certain types of childhood disorders (e.g., conduct disorders) seem to reflect instances of "arrested socialization" (Patterson, 1982).

Developmental deviation has been defined empirically in relation to a variation from some observed behavioral norm (Achenbach & Edelbrock, 1981), and theoretically either in terms of a deviation from some expected behavioral pattern characteristic of particular stages of cognitive or psychosexual development (Santostefano, 1978), or in terms of the child's failure to reorganize his or her behavior over time in relation to age-appropriate developmental adaptations (Greenspan & Porges, 1984). A behavioral assessment approach would place greater emphasis on developmental norms based upon observed behavior or observed patterns of behavior in context than on norms derived from inferred theoretical constructs.

Cross-sectional and longitudinal data describing age trends for a range of normal and problem child behaviors are just now beginning to accumulate (e.g., Larzelere, Amberson, Martin, Handler, & Alibrando, 1985), and much of this information comes from the developmental literature. Prior data based on global parent reports (e.g., Achenbach & Edelbrock, 1981; MacFarlane *et al.,* 1954) are being buttressed by direct observations of ongoing social interactions. Information concerning proportions of children at different ages exhibiting various problems is also being reinforced with more specific information concerning children's success or failure in making age-related adaptations, such as the formation of a secure attachment, the development of purposeful communication systems, and the regulation of emotions. Much of this research has been described under the heading of developmental psychopathology and is just beginning to find its way into clinical assessments with children and families. Making normative judgments in the context of adaptations over time is quite compatible with child behavioral assessment, since the organizational approach requires a careful specification of situational demands (e.g., developmental tasks).

Normative information describing "qualitative" shifts across ages is still needed. Although such shifts across time are difficult to assess, it would appear that many child behaviors, such as fears (Barrios & Hartmann, Chapter 5, this volume) and hyperactivity (D. M. Ross & Ross, 1982), change both quantitatively and qualitatively with age. Judgments regarding deviancy must be made in relation to both types of change.

Rapid and uneven developmental change also carries implications for the stability of assessment information over time. Assessment of behavior at one age may not be predictive of behavior at a later time, especially when assessments are obtained with very young children. For example, in examining aggressive behavior in males, Olweus (1979) reported that the degree of stability tended to decrease linearly as the interval between the two times of measurement increased, and that stability in aggressive behavior could be broadly described as a positive linear function of the interval covered and the subject's age at the time of first measurement.

Plasticity and Modifiability

A second characteristic of children as a group that has implications for assessment and treatment relates to the plasticity and modifiability of the young in relation to environmental influences. That child behavior is under the strong and immediate social control of parents and other children suggests that the need for assessment of these environmental influences is greater than might be the case for assessments with adults. While it may be true that children are generally under greater environmental influence than adults, it is also the case that reciprocal influence is the norm from early development onward.

Age and Sex Characteristics

A third characteristic of developing children as a group is that they are various, both within and across ages. Several writers have emphasized the need for an integration of behavioral and developmental approaches to assessment and treatment (Edelbrock, 1984; Evans & Nelson, 1986; S. L. Harris & Ferrari, 1983; McMahon & Peters, 1985). Developmental characteristics such as a child's age and sex have implications not only for judgments regarding deviancy, but also for the assessment methods that are most appropriate. One obvious difference relates to the constraints placed on the use of child self-report measures as a function of age-related verbal and cognitive abilities. The nature of children's reaction to being observed and their understanding of assessment purposes may also vary with age. Assessments of young children may be affected by the children's wariness of strangers, whereas adolescents may be wary of assessment by adults, but for quite different reasons.

A child's sex also plays an important role in judgments of deviancy, with concomitant implications for the interpretations of assessment information. Numerous studies have shown that both the norms that are used in making judgments about child behavior and the overt behavioral reactions of parents and teachers will vary as a function of whether the child is male or female. Other studies have shown sex differences for different types of childhood disorders (see Eme, 1979, for review). The factors emerging from multivariate studies of child behavior problems differ for boys versus girls

(Achenbach & Edelbrock, 1983), and recent work suggests that the same disorder (e.g., depression) may manifest itself in different ways, depending on the sex of the child (Sroufe & Rutter, 1984). Longitudinal research has also suggested that the stability of certain personality dimensions over time may be greater for boys than for girls (Block & Gjerde, 1986).

Commonalities in Assessment Situations

There are several commonalities in the types of assessment situations in which children are evaluated that also have implications for assessment (Achenbach, 1985; Evans & Nelson, 1977). Childhood distress is typically framed in terms of its impact on others. That children are typically referred by adults means that some children may not be experiencing subjective distress and may not understand the reasons for assessment (Reid *et al.*, 1987). It also suggests the need to consider those factors that have been shown to influence referral, including social class (S. L. Harris, 1974) and type of problem (Lorion, Cowen, & Caldwell, 1974).

There is also a strong relationship between learning and behavior problems during childhood (Taylor, Chapter 8, this volume), and behavioral assessments are often carried out in the context of cognitive or intellectual evaluations (Kaufman & Reynolds, 1984). This interrelationship between learning and behavior problems reflects the more general observation that problematic child behavior rarely occurs in isolation. This typically means that child assessment is multidisciplinary, involving a range of professionals—educators, psychologists, and a variety of medical personnel.

It is also the norm that children who are referred for assessment will undergo repeated evaluations. This is especially the case for children with chronic conditions, for which repeated evaluation and planning may be dictated by legislative requirements. Repeated evaluation also applies to children with less severe problems, reflecting both the fragmentation that is characteristic of mental health delivery systems for children and, more positively, the re-evaluation of children following remedial behavioral or educational programming. Repeated evaluations require the development of assessment methods that are robust across ages and relatively insensitive to the effects of practice.

Normative Comparisons

Child behavioral assessors, with their emphasis on the functioning of individual children and families, have given little attention to the development of normative information that attempts to establish an individual child's position on some dimension relative to the performance of other members of a suitable reference group (Furman & Drabman, 1981). In emphasizing the role of assessment for monitoring changes associated with treatment, the focus has been on the establishment of intra-individual as opposed to group norms. For example, such intraindividual normative comparisons are implicit in any assessment that examines the performance of a child relative to the same child's behavior under baseline conditions. Although intraindividual comparisons of this type will identify the child as improving, not improving, or getting worse, they provide little guidance as to whether the child's performance is meaningful with respect to some generally accepted performance criterion as derived from significant others or cultural informants (Kazdin, 1977).

Assessment approaches emphasizing the child's performance not in relation to some reference group's average, but rather in relation to specific performance criteria, would appear to be consistent with the treatment emphasis of behavioral approaches (Hartmann *et al.*, 1979; Kendall *et al.*, 1984). Such edumetric or criterion-referenced testing approaches (Carver, 1974) seem especially applicable in areas such as academic performance, athletic skill, or job completion, or where easily identifiable and sometimes absolute performance goals are specifiable. On the other hand, in areas related to social behavior and adjustment, the current lack of availability of accepted standards of performance makes a criterion-referenced approach more difficult to apply. However, recent efforts to identify the types of child social behaviors that may lead to popularity with peers or that are reinforced by peers (Cone & Hoier, 1986; Hops & Greenwood, 1981), or the types of child responses that are likely to be either approved of or viewed as disturbing by adults (Mooney & Algozzine, 1978), may one day provide a basis for generally acceptable criterion standards in some of the more subjective areas of social behavior. Conceptual frameworks such as McFall's (1982) model of social performance, which distinguishes between social skills (e.g., behavioral components) and social competence (e.g., components based on social judgments) have the potential for delineating the specific behavioral components that may lead to judgments of skilled performance under certain conditions.

In considering the applicability of group norms in behavioral assessment, it is important to examine issues related to the utility of normative comparisons generally and to the kinds of normative information that are likely to be most useful (Edelbrock, 1984). Hartmann *et al.* (1979) have outlined a number of potential uses for normative comparisons in behavioral assessment. These include the following:

1. Normative comparisons are frequently useful in the identification of deficient or excessive performance, as would be the case if a child engaged in excessively high rates of aggressive behavior. Normative information about rates of aggression shown in comparable situations by comparable children would serve as a basis for identifying the child as potentially problematic, depending on social judgments and environmental reactions to the behavior.

2. Where presenting complaints about children reflect parental expectations that differ markedly from existing norms, as might be the case in some abusive family situations (Mash *et al.*, 1983; Wolfe, Chapter 9, this volume), the focus and type of intervention may be quite different than would be the case in the absence of such normative information.

3. Where norms exist that suggest certain types of childhood problems to be both common and transient (e.g., early reactions to separation, certain fears, bedwetting) at particular ages, such information may lead to decisions concerning the need for intervention. This is not to argue that such normative difficulties may not be of concern for the child and family and that some educative–coping strategies would not be helpful (Furman, 1980). Normative behavior should not be considered to be "normal" without careful consideration of the context in which it occurs and its relationships to other responses and other individuals. Most normative behaviors, especially those derived from multivariate studies, are typically presented in terms of their frequency of occurrence for the general population. For example, Edelbrock (1984) notes that "arguing" was reported as a problem by more than half of the parents of nonreferred children, and "the fact that it is such a common complaint about normal chil-

dren suggests that it should not receive high priority as a target for clinical treatment" (p. 29). However, it may well be that the "functions" of arguing in a referred population may be qualitatively different than in a nonreferred population, so that in one group arguing functions as a cue for further escalation of coercive behavior, whereas in the other group it may not (Patterson, 1982). Under these circumstances, frequent reports of arguing in nonclinic groups would not provide a sound basis for giving this response a low priority in treatment. Nevertheless, under some circumstances, knowledge that a problem is common and transient could diminish the need for extensive clinical intervention.

4. Where norms exist for skilled versus inept performances, such information may be used for establishing both intermediate treatment targets and ultimate treatment goals.

5. Norms may be useful for grouping children into relatively homogeneous treatment groups, which subsequently could produce greater precision with respect to the types of treatment most appropriate for children with particular types of difficulties.

6. Normative information permits the direct comparison of studies using differing samples of children.

7. Normative information for specific assessment measures may enhance the comparability of findings obtained through different data sources. For example, measures of parent report and direct observation may yield equivalent information should the scores on each reflect a similar degree of deviation, as in the case of a child rated one standard deviation above the mean on the two different measures.

8. Normative information may be useful in evaluating the clinical significance or social validity of treatment outcomes.

While the above-described uses of norms refer primarily to norms for behavior, normative information regarding situational determinants may also help to identify some situations as being at high risk for the development of particular problems. For example, normative information regarding the quality of the child's school environment (e.g., high expectations, good group management, effective feedback and praise, setting of good models of behavior by teachers, pleasant working conditions, and giving students positions of trust and responsibility) may serve as a basis for the detection of early problems where such conditions are deficient, with a subsequent focus on prevention (Rutter, 1979). Similarly, norms regarding the presence or absence of certain family background variables for particular childhood disorders—for example, those related to a parental history of alcoholism (Lee & Gotlib, 1986) or child abuse (Wolfe, 1985)—may also serve to identify some children as being at risk. In general, norms concerning contextual factors have not received as much attention as norms concerning individual behavior.

Multiple Targets

Behavioral assessments of children have typically been directed at behavior and at potential controlling variables. While early approaches tended to focus on behavior as reflected in the overt motor reactions of the child, more recent views have adopted a broader view of child behavior that encompasses intraorganism activity, including physiological reaction, cognitions, and affects. Controlling variables for behavior are those antecedent and consequent events in the social and physical environments that serve to influence the occurrence of the behavior. The heuristic "S-O-R-K-C" serves as a convenient way of organizing relevant classes of assessment information into broad categories of antecedent and consequent events, any one of which may be designated as targets for treatment (Kanfer & Phillips, 1970).

"S" refers to prior stimulation, or the external and internal environments that have some functional relationship to the behavior. Given that the functional properties of environments for many child behaviors have not been empirically established, assessment often involves the designation of S variables that are hypothesized to be important.

"O" refers to the biological status of the organism (i.e., the child), including the range of genetic, physiological, neurological, biochemical, and mechanical variables that influence the form and function of behavior. The numerous studies supporting the interaction between biological and social variables in child behavior and development require that information regarding the child's biological condition be brought to bear in any assessment, if only at times to be eliminated as a possible relevant determinant for specific types of child behavior. Such information is especially important with children, given the frequent and rapid physical changes that occur throughout

childhood and adolescence. The blending of assessment information related to biological and social variables has increased dramatically, concomitant with the increased use of behavioral procedures in child health settings (e.g., Johnson, 1988; Krasnegor et al., 1986) and the growing recognition of the potential importance of biological factors in understanding both normal variations in child temperament (Garcia-Coll, Kagan, & Reznick, 1984) and more dysfunctional childhood disorders (Kazdin, Chapter 4, this volume).

"R" refers to the response, which has been taken in behavioral assessment as encompassing motor behavior, cognitive–verbal behavior, and physiological emotional behavior (Cone, 1979). Following from both theory and practical concerns, early developments in behavioral assessment occurred largely with respect to the measurement of motor behavior, and to a lesser extent in relation to physiological responses. However, there has been an increasing emphasis on the definition and measurement of more covert cognitive events, including construction competencies, encoding strategies, expectancies, values, plans, self-statements, and metacognitive processes (e.g., Karoly, 1981; Kendall & Hollon, 1981; Mischel, 1973). In addition, the assessment of cognitive events has evolved away from a focus on single individuals to one of examining the cognitions that are operative in a variety of social systems and subsystems (e.g, marital relationships, mother–child relationships, etc.) (Bradbury & Fincham, in press-a).

While responses as treatment targets have focused largely on content, there is also much useful information to suggest that the structural and qualitative elements of the response may be as important as the content of the response per se, if not more so. For example, Wahler and Dumas (1986) and others have identified patterns of responses in which mothers adopt an indiscriminate response style; that is, their responses are independent of the immediately preceding child behavior. Mischel (1977) has discussed how such indiscriminate responding involving nonconformance to changes in the situation may be maladaptive. Yet, to date, there has been little systematic effort to target and modify structural response properties.

"K" refers to the contingency relationships between behavior and its consequences, including such things as the frequency and timing of response outcomes. Schedules of reinforcement

(Ferster & Skinner, 1953) clearly influence the form and topography of behavior and consititute an important category of assessment information. It has been suggested, for example, that under continuous reward conditions the performance of hyperactive and normal children may not differ, whereas hyperactive children may exhibit response decrements under conditions of partial reward (Firestone & Douglas, 1975).

"C" refers to the consequences of behavior and may include a wide variety of social and nonsocial events that vary in their valence. Consequences are typically embedded within naturalistic social exchanges (Snyder & Patterson, 1986) and have accompanying affective components that have not, until recently, received much attention (Furman & Masters, 1980). As is the case with prior stimulation, it is important to distinguish between events following behavior that are functionally related in altering future probabilities and consequent events that are contiguous but that have not been demonstrated to have response-controlling properties (Mash & Terdal, 1976).

It should be evident from this brief overview that the S-O-R-K-C designations, although useful in organizing assessment information, are arbitrary and reflect a somewhat static view of the relationship between child behavior and context. The categories are foci of convenience, and responses may serve as antecedents or consequences depending on one's perspective and purpose. With the view that child–behavior–environment relationships are continuous, ongoing, interactive, and embedded in many different systems, it becomes apparent that behavior may be a controlling variable for environmental events and for itself, as emphasized in much of the work on behavioral self-regulation (Karoly, 1981). Many studies have shown that a child's behavior may alter the contingency systems to which he or she is exposed. For example, children's reactions immediately prior to adult-administered consequences such as punishment have been shown to influence the amount of punishment they receive (Parke & Sawin, 1977). Children who seek to make reparations for their misdeeds receive less punishment from adults than those who act defiantly. These points highlight some of the complexities of S-O-R-K-C definitions and their interactions. As child behavior assessments are increasingly guided by systems models, the need to elaborate the structural and functional

S-O-R-K-C relationships both between individuals and between systems of individuals has increased.

Selection of Treatment Goals

The identification of problem behaviors that are targeted for change within a behavioral intervention program, has been a hallmark of behavioral assessments with children and families. However, several writers (Hawkins, 1975; Mash, 1985) have called attention to the fact that many reports begin with a designation of the problem to be treated, with little information as to the decisional processes utilized in this selection. Several recent papers (Evans, 1985; Kanfer, 1985; Kazdin, 1985; Kratochwill, 1985; Mash, 1985) have addressed a number of important points associated with the selection of target behaviors. These include the following:

1. Models of behavior therapy and assessment that focus on a single target behavior as being synonymous with the goals of treatment may often provide incomplete representations of both the assessment and change process.

2. A more appropriate representation of the problem space for child and family behavioral assessment is provided by a systems model that encompasses a wide range of potentially important individuals, responses, and contexts that might be contributing to the problematic situation.

3. Such system representations of the child and family's problems require the development of decision rules for determining how best to conceptualize the system of interest and what aspects of the system should be modified in order to bring about the most widespread and meaningful changes.

4. In practice, the decision rules that are often employed reflect the theoretical preferences and subjective judgments of practicing clinicians (Kanfer, 1985). Such clinical decision making has been shown to be subject to a variety of information-processing errors (Achenbach, 1985; Tabachnik & Alloy, in press), many of which stem from the basic limitations (e.g., limited attention and memory) of human information processors in dealing with complex data sets under conditions that often involve time pressures and high levels of uncertainty (Cantor, 1982).

5. In light of the above-listed limitations, many writers have acknowledged that an actu-

arial approach to the selection of treatment goals and the ways these goals might be most effectively achieved offers promise as an adjunct to clinical decision making (Achenbach, 1985; Cattell, 1983; Meehl, 1954; Rachman, 1983). The increasing availability of high-speed microprocessors is likely to facilitate such an approach (Romanczyk, 1986).

6. If treatment goals are to be conceptualized in a systems framework, then the derivation of empirically based decision rules for intervention requires that the structural and functional interrelationships between different aspects of the system be documented and described. The identification of constellations of target behaviors and response covariations becomes important (Kazdin, 1982b, 1985; Voeltz & Evans, 1982).

7. Target behavior selection is conceptualized as a dynamic and ongoing process in which information derived from assessment and the impact of various interventions may be utilized in reformulating treatment goals.

8. Such an approach is consistent with the behavioral assessment emphasis on the important relationship between assessment and treatment. With this approach, not only is assessment information leading to treatment recommendations, but treatment outcomes are also being utilized in determining the need for additional assessment and reformulation of the problem.

The points made above call attention to the fact that the specification of target behaviors for the child is, *by itself*, not likely to provide a sufficient representation of the family's difficulties or the range of desired treatment goals. Nevertheless, information concerning the types of child behaviors that are often the focus of intervention can provide useful information within the context of a broader decision-making framework (Mash & Terdal, 1981b). Such information reflects both conceptual and empirical guidelines that commonly underlie target behavior selection.

Some of the more commonly mentioned conceptual guidelines include the following:

1. The behavior is considered to be physically dangerous to the child and/or to others in the child's environment.

2. The behavior should provide an entry point into the natural reinforcement community of the child.

3. The target behaviors selected should be positive, in order to avoid a problem focus in treatment.

4. Behaviors that are viewed as essentials for development are frequently given high priority. For example, language, cognitive development and school performance, motor skills, rule-governed behavior (Karoly, 1981), and, more recently, peer relationships (Hartup, 1979; Hops & Greenwood, Chapter 6, this volume) are frequently targeted behaviors. Implicit in this emphasis is the notion that many of these behaviors are embedded in normal developmental sequences, such that the failure to take corrective action early will result in cumulative deficits, with the child falling even further behind.

5. Behaviors that are viewed as essential early elements for more complex response chains have also been given priority. Classes of general imitative behavior and parrticular cognitive styles have been viewed as requisite behaviors that permit the occurrence of a range of other responses.

6. Behaviors that maximize the flexibility of the child in adapting to changing new environments are viewed as important treatment targets. The recent emphasis on teaching general coping skills and self-control strategies is consistent with this notion.

7. Behaviors that dramatically alter the existing contingency system for the child, such that maladaptive environmental reactions to the child are altered, are viewed as likely to contribute to long-term benefit (Stokes, Fowler, & Baer, 1978).

Some of the more commonly cited empirical criteria for selecting particular child behaviors for treatment are as follows: (1) The behaviors are consistent with some developmental or local norms for performance. (2) The behaviors have been shown, as a result of careful task analysis, to be critical components for successful performance; teaching classroom survival skills (e.g., attending, peer discussion about classwork) as described by Hops and Cobb (1973) is an example of this approach. (3) The behaviors are subjectively rated as positive by recognized community standards (Wolf, 1978). (4) The behaviors effectively discriminate between "skilled" and "nonskilled" performers. (5) The behaviors' natural history is known to have a poor long-term prognosis.

The preceding guidelines represent tentative decision-making rules in the selection of treatment targets, and should always be considered in relation to the broader context in which the child is being assessed.

Multisituational Analysis

Information regarding the context in which the child's behavior, cognitions, and affects occur is an essential ingredient for any child behavioral assessment concerned with the identification of relevant controlling variables to be utilized in the design of effective treatments. This is especially important, because the range of situations in which children function is diverse. The criterion as to what constitutes "competent" performance is likely to vary with the parameters of the situation, suggesting the need for situation-specific measures of behavior (e.g., Dodge, McClaskey, & Feldman, 1985). Identification of the functional properties of specific setting events permits behavioral alterations based on the utilization of stimulus control procedures (Wahler & Fox, 1981). Situational analysis, especially with respect to physical environments or structure, has been referred to as "ecological assessment" (Willems, 1973, 1974), and, in spite of its acknowledged importance in child behavior assessment, it continues to be an area of relative neglect. It is believed that greater within-situation differentiation, which recognizes both the differences and the potential similarities in dissimilar environments, is necessary if the potential of situational analysis in developing effective treatments is to be realized.

One type of molecular situational analysis has examined differential child responses to varying antecedent social stimuli, as has been the case with studies examining the effects of parents' utilizing different types of commands or language constructions in directing their children's behavior (Forehand, 1977). Other studies have attempted to identify differing types of home, classroom, or institutional situations or task structures that might be predictive of particular child responses. For example, certain home situations involving the mother's being occupied, or those possessing time constraints (e.g., dinnertime [Jewett & Clark, 1979], bedtime, getting dressed, going to school) or elements of social evaluation (e.g., shopping trips, visits to others' homes, visits to restaurants), seem to create a high risk for the occurrence of problematic behavior in both normal and disturbed children (Barkley, Chapter 2, this volume; Barkley & Edelbrock, 1987).

Other studies have examined classroom activity structures that are predictive of different types of child social and academic behavior; these structures have included instructional arrangements (Greenwood, Delquadri, Stanley, Terry, & Hall, 1985), group versus individual activities (Patterson & Bechtel, 1977), quiet versus noisy conditions (Whalen, Henker, Collins, Finck, & Dotemoto, 1979), self-paced versus other-paced activities (Whalen et al., 1979), room size, seating arrangements, groupings of children based on different levels of ability, and formal versus informal task requirements (Jacob, O'Leary, & Rosenblad, 1978). Similar variables have been examined in institutional and day care environments. In addition, general environmental conditions related to space, noise, and temperature are variables of potential importance. For example, Russell and Bernal (1977) reported systematic variations in the rates of desirable and undesirable child behavior in the home, associated with temporal and climatic variables such as time of day, day of the week, precipitation, and temperature. That children characteristically come into contact with multiple settings suggests the importance of further specification of situational variables and their functional relationship with behavior.

It is likely the case that situational variation will mediate not only behaviors, but cognitions and affects of family members as well. For example, in looking at cognitions relating to perceptions of equity within the marital relationship, Skitka (1986) found that such perceptions differed, depending on the family context that was being assessed (e.g., sex, finances, etc.). There is a need to develop a taxonomy of situations that can guide both research and applied work in child and family behavior assessment (e.g., Schlundt & McFall, 1987). Are there groups of situations that can be specified on the basis of classificatory principles paralleling those relating to the classification of behavior? In attempting to build such situational taxonomies, we should be cognizant of the following remarks by Mischel (1977):

> Depending on one's purpose many different classifications are possible and useful. To seek any single "basic" taxonomy of situations may be as futile as searching for a final or ultimate taxonomy of traits; we can label situations in as many different ways as we can label people. It is important to avoid emerging simply with a trait psychology of situations, in which events and settings, rather than people, are merely given

different labels. The task of naming situations cannot substitute for the job of analyzing how conditions and environments interact with people in them. (pp. 337–338).

Expanded Temporal and Contextual Base

A core assumption of early approaches to the behavioral assessment of children was the focus on contemporaneous behavior and controlling conditions. Current influences were viewed as being proximal in time not only to the behavior being assessed, but also to the situation. For example, an observational assessment of parent–child interaction looked for "causes" of child behavior as reflected in the responses (e.g., cues and reinforcers) provided to the child by the parent in that situation. Developmental–historical information was not given a particularly important role, so that the parent's response to the child was viewed as being a direct reaction to the child's ongoing behavior in the situation rather than as a function of the cumulative effect of many prior negative interactions with the child. The finding that parents of aggressive, in contrast to normal, children may punish the children more, even when they are behaving appropriately (Patterson, 1976), suggests that parents may be responding to more than the immediate behaviors of their children.

Similarly, early behavioral assessments of children tended to ignore some of the broader contextual variables that were related to ongoing child behaviors. However, such factors as parental personality, family climate, peer group relations, marital relationships, and community support systems have been shown to be potent sources of control for child behavior—indeed, as important as the reactions of significant others to the child's behavior at the time of its occurrence. Some studies have shown the warmth and permissiveness of the home to be a significant factor in the effectiveness of social reinforcement by parents (Patterson, Littman, & Hinsey, 1964). Others have demonstrated that maternal punitiveness to the child can be influenced by the degree of external stress placed on the mother in the situation (Passman & Mulhern, 1977). Friedrich (1979) reported that marital satisfaction was the best overall predictor of the coping behaviors of mothers of handicapped children, and Wahler (1980) has reported a positive relationship between problem child behavior and the degree of "insularity" of the family.

Given that so many of these situationally and temporally more remote distal events have been shown to represent important determinants of both the behavior of family members (e.g., Dumas, 1986; Patterson & Bank, 1986) and of treatment outcomes (Dumas & Wahler, 1983), the exclusive reliance on contemporaneous information in behavioral assessment is no longer tenable. Although still important for behavioral assessments, contemporaneous information should be buttressed and interpreted within a broader temporal and social context.

METHODS OF ASSESSMENT

The methods used by child and family behavioral assessors cannot in and of themselves be considered unique (Evans & Nelson, 1986), and for the most part are the same as those used more generally in assessments with clinical populations (e.g., G. Goldstein & Hersen, 1984; Rutter, Tuma, & Lann, 1987). The use of structured (Edelbrock & Costello, 1984) and nonstructured interviews (Bierman, 1983; Gross, 1984; Turkat, 1986), behavioral checklists and questionnaires (Barkley, 1987; Finch & Rogers, 1984; Jensen & Haynes, 1986; McMahon, 1984), self-monitoring procedures (Bornstein, Hamilton, & Bornstein, 1986), analogue methods (Hughes & Haynes, 1978; Nay, 1986), psychophysiological recordings (Kallman & Feuerstein, 1986), and direct observations of behavior (S. L. Foster & Cone, 1980, 1986) obviously predates the emergence of behavioral assessment as a distinct field of study. At the present time, the uniqueness of behavioral assessment methods is reflected in (1) the use of multimethod strategies; (2) the flexible use of such methods within a decision-making model based on the behavioral assessment prototype; (3) an emphasis on the use of assessment instruments whose content represents a sample of the behaviors, cognitions, and affects of interest rather than being an indirect sign of some underlying trait; (4) an emphasis on the use of assessment instruments designed to sample relevant situational content; and (5) the use of assessment instruments and measures that can be employed repeatedly over time, in an evaluation framework directed at assessing whether or not the goals of treatment are being met.

We do not intend to review in detail the voluminous number of behavioral assessment methods that have been utilized with children and families, or to discuss the many issues associated with their use. There are now many comprehensive reviews of the methods of behavioral assessment (e.g., Ciminero *et al.*, 1986; Ciminero & Drabman, 1977; Evans & Nelson, 1977, 1986; Filsinger & Lewis, 1981; Hersen & Bellack, 1981; Ollendick & Hersen, 1984). In the discussion that follows, we highlight some of the more prevalent concerns and issues associated with the use of particular methods, as well as some of the more recent methodological developments in child and family behavioral assessment. We emphasize again that the major underlying theme of this volume is that discussions of methods are best carried out in relation to specific types of child and family difficulties. Nevertheless, since part of the assessment task is to initially identify the problem category that best describes the individual child and his or her family, it is also the case that some methods (e.g., screening instruments, diagnostic interviews) are not specific to populations of children.

Selection of Methods

In studying and helping children and families who are experiencing problems, it would seem that we have identified much of the universe of content that we are interested in. If we combine the literatures dealing with the clinical assessment of children and families with writings in child development, child psychopathology, behavior therapy, and family therapy, there appears to be no shortage of assessment instruments, albeit there is certainly variability in their psychometric quality. Literally hundreds of different coding systems have been used to describe child compliance; even in newer areas of assessment, such as social support and family stress, the numbers of available measures are large (Dunst & Trivette, 1985). What is lacking at this time seems to be an agreed-upon set of decisional criteria and rules concerning which of the available measures are best suited for particular purposes, and when and how these measures are to be used (Hartmann, 1984).

In practice, the most frequently used decisional criteria often equate the quantity of assessment information with its quality. The rather crude heuristic here is that the "best" assessments are those that sample as many domains

as possible using the widest variety of methods. Traditional "test batteries," in which children presenting for treatment often receive a standardized evaluation that includes an interview with the parent and child, an IQ test, a projective personality test, and a test for organicity or perceptual dysfunction, illustrate this approach. Criticisms of these procedures as being insufficient for diagnosis and treatment have come from both behaviorally and nonbehaviorally oriented clinicians (e.g., Santostefano, 1978).

While there is a good deal of empirical support for the notion that different methods may and often do yield different information about a child, the hypothesis that using as many different methods as possible will result in a truer or more useful description of the child and family has not been tested. In some cases, the accumulation of greater amounts of information in the clinical context may actually serve to reduce accuracy while increasing judgmental confidence (Nisbett, Zukier, & Lemley, 1981). Given larger amounts of information, the effect of diagnostic data can be diluted by the presence of an increased number of nondiagnostic features. It is important that behavioral assessors give some attention to the incremental validity associated with using multiple methods, in order to avoid the perpetuation of potentially unnecessary and costly procedures. Presumably, such incremental validity can be assessed by examining the relationship between amount and types of assessment information obtained as it relates to the effectiveness of treatment (Mash, 1979; Nelson, 1983).

The multiple purposes for which assessments with children and families are carried out suggest that not all children should be assessed in all possible ways. What are some of the factors that will probably contribute to decision making regarding the selection of methods? Although it is not possible to discuss these factors in detail here, the choice of assessment methods in a particular case will probably be based on such things as the purpose of the assessment (e.g., screening vs. treatment evaluation), nature of the problem behavior (e.g., overt vs. covert, chronic vs. acute), characteristics of the child (e.g., age, cognitive and language skills) and of the family (e.g., social class, education, single parent vs. intact marriage), the assessment setting (e.g., classroom, home, or clinic), characteristics of the assessor (e.g., conceptual preferences, level of training, available time), and characteristics of the method (e.g., complexity and amount of technical resources or training required, sensitivity to particular interventions). Some of the more common considerations in the selection of particular methods for specific populations of children are discussed in each of the chapters of this volume. However, in light of the complexity of information underlying the choice of assessment methods, we believe that an actuarial approach may eventually lead to more precise statements concerning which measures might best be employed for an individual case.

Standardization, Reliability, and Validity

The need for standardized measures in child psychopathology, family assessment, and child development generally, and in child and family behavioral assessment in particular, has been pointed out by many writers (Kanfer, 1972; Mash, 1985). In spite of this recognition, there has been a proliferation of methods for assessing children and families that are idiosyncratic to the situation in which they are used, unstandardized, and of unknown reliability and validity (Strosahl & Linehan, 1986). The early rejection of many traditionally used psychological tests by behavioral assessors, concomitant with an emphasis on individually focused and prescriptive assessments, created a void that was filled by instruments having high face validity but unknown psychometric properties (e.g., Cautela, Cautela, & Esonis, 1983).

The fact that the same instruments have not been used repeatedly by different assessors has limited the accumulation of meaningful reliability and validity information. This state of affairs is especially prevalent with children and families. With the exception of a small number of self-report measures of children's fears, anxieties, and social skills, and a slightly larger number of observational coding schemes that were originally developed as research instruments for studying children in the home and classroom (e.g., Forehand & McMahon, 1981; Mash, Terdal, & Anderson, 1973; O'Leary, Romanczyk, Kass, Dietz, & Santogrossi, 1971; Reid, 1978; Wahler, House, & Stambaugh, 1976), there are few standardized behavioral assessment methods for children and families. In fact, the more standardized measures of child and family behavior that have been used with increasing frequency in behavioral research and

practice appear to be those that have been developed out of other traditions. These include, for example, parent report instruments of child behavior (e.g., Achenbach & Edelbrock, 1983), measures of children's depression or anxiety (e.g., Kovacs, 1978; Spielberger, 1973), and measures of marital satisfaction or distress (e.g., Spanier, 1976).

It is evident that if behavioral assessment with children and families is to have any scientific or clinical merit, the proliferation of idiosyncratic assessment methods must be replaced by the development and utilization of more standardized and population-specific behavioral assessments. There has been some movement in this direction with the availability of observational codes describing specific problems such as family aggression (Reid, 1978), depression (Hops et al., 1986), hyperactivity (Abikoff, Gittelman, & Klein, 1980), and autism (Freeman & Schroth, 1984), and analogue measures designed to assess specific problems such as attention deficit disorder (Milich, Loney, & Landau, 1982).

Some have argued against the development of a standardized set of behavioral assessment techniques (Cone & Hoier, 1986; R. O. Nelson, 1983). These arguments appear to be based on (1) the notion that the individuality and contextual specificity of child and family behavior would require an inordinately large number of techniques to sample all situations and behaviors of interest, therefore rendering a standardized approach impractical; and (2) the inappropriateness of using psychometric criteria as the basis for development and selection of particular standardized measures. In regard to the latter reason, it is presumed that behavioral conceptualizations based upon response instability over time and upon situational specificity of behavior are incompatible with the trait-oriented assumptions underlying psychometric concepts such as reliability and validity. For example, if one rejects the view that stable traits manifest themselves in similar ways over time, then viewing variability of scores over time as reflecting an unreliable measuring instrument rather than inherent behavioral inconsistency would be inappropriate. Similarly, concurrent validity has little meaning if one accepts cross-situational variability as the norm, because a lack of situational consistency reflects things as they are, rather than an invalid measurement procedure (Kazdin, 1979).

Several writers have discussed these con-

cerns and have noted ways in which psychometric considerations might be applied to behavioral assessment, even with its differing
assumptions (Cone, 1977; Hartmann, 1976).
Others have advocated the use of "other than
psychometric" criteria—for example, accuracy—for assessing the adequacy of behavioral
assessment procedures (Cone & Hoier, 1986).
The myriad of issues surrounding the relevance
of psychometric concepts for behavioral assessment has been discussed extensively by behavioral assessors (Cone, 1977, 1978, 1981; Cone
& Hoier, 1986; Hartmann et al., 1979; Johnson
& Bolstad, 1973; Strosahl & Linehan, 1986),
and the interested reader is referred to the sources
cited for further discussion. However, a few
brief comments are in order.

First, in spite of ongoing debate, there has
been little resolution of these issues—perhaps
because the arguments reflect fundamental differences in views regarding the utility of differing models of human functioning in the context of clinical assessment. The key issue centers
around the compatibility or lack of compatibility of the idiographic and nomothetic approaches to assessment. While recognizing the
arguments on both sides of this issue, we would
concur with the view that these approaches are
complementary and that both are necessary to
our understanding, assessment, and treatment
of child and family disorders. This view is
expressed in the following passage by Strosahl
and Linehan (1986):

> By using nomothetic principles, the behavioral
> assessor starts with a framework within which
> the idiographic elements of the individual case
> can be developed and refined. Nomothetic prin-
> ciples deliver hypotheses that can be tested idi-
> ographically. Conversely, idiographic data can
> sometimes point the way for nomothetic research,
> which in turn can be used to guide further idio-
> graphic testing. (p. 36).

We believe that current approaches to the
behavioral assessment of child and family disturbance, as illustrated throughout the chapters
of this volume, already reflect some integration
of the nomothetic and idiographic approaches.
This is suggested by an increasing concern for
diagnostic issues and normative information,
the use of multivariate procedures for the assessment of traits, and efforts to aggregate information about individuals into broader patterns of responding.

Interviews with Parents and Others

Regardless of assessors' therapeutic orientations, and in spite of numerous criticisms concerning reliability and validity, the interview
continues to be the most universally used clinical assessment procedure (Matarazzo, 1983).
However, the interviewer's behaviors and expectations, the information obtained in the interview, the meaning assigned to that information, and the extent of standardization will
vary among theoretical orientations. Consequently, the interviews used in the behavioral
assessment of children and families are often
quite different in purpose and style from those
conducted by clinicians with other orientations
(Turkat & Meyer, 1982). As an information-
gathering procedure, clinical interviews are
usually used flexibly over repeated occasions
and are frequently integrated with other types
of assessment information, such as the opportunity to observe families interacting and to
assess such things as problem-solving skills,
compliance to treatment, and nonverbal communications.

Given that a social learning conceptualization
of child and family disorders requires some
understanding of reciprocal social relationships,
and because children are typically referred by
adults, it is almost always necessary to obtain
descriptions from adults about the nature of the
children's difficulties, social circumstances,
physical status, and general development. Most
typically a child's parent(s), usually the mother,
will be the primary informant. However, other
adults (e.g., teachers, relatives, and neighbors)
and other children (e.g., siblings and peers)
although less frequently called upon, can provide potentially useful assessment information
as well.

An interview with a parent will provide information about the child, about the parent, and
about the parent–child relationship. The relative focus given to each of these areas will vary
with the nature of the presenting problem and
the purposes for which the interview is carried
out. Until recently, behavioral assessors have
given relatively less attention to obtaining information about parents themselves than about
children and parent–child relationships. However, recent work identifying relationships between parental characteristics and children's
functioning in both family and school (e.g.,
Forehand, Long, Brody, & Fauber, 1986), and

between parental affects such as depression and child behavior (e.g., Hammen *et al.,* 1986), suggests that the base for information gathering in the behavioral interview needs to include a focus on the child, the parent(s), sibling relationships, and the marriage, as well as on the relationships between these various systems.

Several writers have outlined the varying purposes for which behavioral interviews are conducted (Haynes, 1978; Turkat, 1986). These purposes have been summarized by Haynes and Jensen (1979); their points, adapted to interviews with parents, include the following:

1. Gathering information about parental concerns, expectations, and goals.
2. Assessing parental perceptions and feelings about the child's problems, concerns, and goals.
3. Identifying possible factors that may be maintaining or eliciting problem behaviors.
4. Obtaining historical information about problem and nonproblem behaviors and about prior treatment efforts.
5. Identifying potentially reinforcing events for both child and parent.
6. Educating the parent with respect to the nature of the childhood problem, its prevalence, its prognosis, and its possible etiologies.
7. Providing the parent with an adequate rationale for proposed interventions.
8. Assessing the parent's affective state, motivation for changing the situation, and resources for taking an active role in helping to mediate behavior change.
9. Obtaining informed consent.
10. Providing data for the assessment of treatment outcomes.
11. Communicating with parents about procedures and setting realistic goals for assessment and intervention.

The multiplicity of purposes described means that the degree of structure, the content, and the style of parental interviews will vary greatly, and a lack of uniformity is often the rule rather than the exception. There are several general points related to behavioral interviews with parents that require discussion.

Generality and Flexibility

The first point involves the level of generality and flexibility of the interview. Typically, in-

terviews with parents have been used either as diagnostic or screening instruments to determine treatment eligibility or as methods of gaining information that will facilitate the design of effective treatments. These purposes necessarily define the interview as being general, and also require the interviewer to adapt his or her behavior to the various concerns being raised by parents. The degree of structure and standardization within parental interviews is usually low, but can be increased for other interview purposes—for example, when interview information is to be used as an outcome measure, or when the interview is being used to obtain a formal diagnosis (e.g., Puig-Antich & Chambers, 1978). Alternatively, if pretreatment questionnaires include life history information and/or reinforcement surveys, then initial interviews can be more structured in focusing on the information obtained from these questionnaires. The advantages of such increased standardization are probably greater reliability and validity.

A number of guidelines and standardized formats have been suggested for behavioral interviews with parents (e.g., Bersoff & Grieger, 1971; Holland, 1970; Kanfer & Grimm, 1977; Kanfer & Saslow, 1960; Wahler & Cormier, 1970). Although these formats are useful, they are also quite general and make no *a priori* assumptions regarding the specific interview content that is likely to be most meaningful. In effect, these nonspecific interview formats ignore the information available from informal assessments that may have already taken place, as well as the existing empirical literature related to the general class of problems the child and parent are experiencing. Typically, existing information and empirical findings are brought to bear under the ambiguous label of ''clinical skills.'' Clinical experience and training are presumed to lead the interviewer into asking the ''right'' questions within some of the general areas suggested by the formats that have been presented (Kanfer, 1985). Consistent with the theme of this book, we believe that problem-specific interview formats are needed. For instance, interviews with parents of autistic children should systematically probe for information regarding commonly identified problems, situations, and controlling variables (e.g., self-stimulation, language, possible negative reinforcers). Rather than assuming that interviewers will have the necessary specific information to guide interview content and process, we believe that interview schedules including disorder- and context-specific information will lead to more systematic, standardized, efficient, and useful interviews possessing greater reliability and validity.

Reliability and Validity

It should be emphasized that questions concerning reliability and validity are meaningful *only* in relation to the interview purpose. So, for example, if the purpose is to gain information about the mother's *perception* of the child as a possible controlling variable for her behavior toward her child, a lack of correspondence between maternal report and that of other informants is of less concern than if a mother's report is being used to establish actual rates of child behavior in order to assess treatment outcome.

With respect to reliability, primary concerns relate to such things as (1) whether information obtained on one occasion is comparable to information obtained on other occasions from the same parent (e.g., stability); (2) whether information obtained from the parent is comparable to information obtained from another informant—for example, mother versus father (i.e., interobserver agreement; Edelbrock, Costello, Dulcan, Conover, & Kalas, 1986; Schwarz, Barton-Henry, & Pruzinsky, 1985); (3) whether the information given by the parent is consistent with other information given by the parent in the same interview (i.e., internal consistency); and (4) whether the information obtained by one interviewer is comparable to that obtained by another interviewer with the same parent (i.e., method error).

The first reliablility concern mentioned is especially relevant in relation to interviews that require parents to report retrospectively on their children's developmental/social history, one of the more common elements of most child assessments (Yarrow, Campbell, & Burton, 1970). In reviewing the reliability of such recall by parents, Evans and Nelson (1977) concluded that these retrospective reports are likely to be unreliable and frequently distorted in the direction of socially desirable responses and dominant cultural themes. Interestingly, the degree of reliability appears related to the nature of the events that parents are reporting (e.g., pleasantness vs. unpleasantness) and the level of specificity of behavior being described (Lapouse & Monk, 1958).

It should be recognized, however, that although parental reports may conform to the demand characteristics of the interview situation, such characteristics may not always predict socially desirable responses. For example, there may be a parental bias toward reporting more negative behaviors and greater distress if eligibility for treatment is an issue, whereas posttreatment interviews may be discriminative for reports of positive child behavior and the absence of distress. This latter point is especially important when interview information is to be used as a measure of treatment outcome. Mothers of problem children may also be realistic about their children's behavior, in contrast to mothers of nonproblem children, who may describe their children in an overly positive fashion. Interobserver agreement in relation to mother–father and teacher report is difficult to evaluate, because disagreement may reflect differences in the situation in which each of these informants observes the child. In general, mothers may be more reliable informants than fathers and may provide descriptions of their children's behavior that are much more differentiated and situation-specific (McGillicuddy-DeLisi, 1985).

Interviews with other significant adults or with the child's friends, peers, or siblings may be potentially useful but have received little attention in assessment, in part because of ethical concerns associated with obtaining such information. For example, interviews with peers may further stigmatize the child as having a problem, with subsequent alterations in the manner in which others interact with the child. At the same time, data suggest that peer evaluations may be particularly sensitive in identifying children with problems (Cowen, Pederson, Babigian, Izzo, & Trost, 1973), although it is not known whether peer judgments regarding the specific nature of these problems are likely to be accurate. The general problems associated with securing verbal reports from children, particularly younger children, suggest that structured tasks or game-like assessment procedures involving child and peer interaction may be more sensitive measures than unstructured interviews with peers. Information obtained from siblings may also be important, in that many problem families are characterized by high rates of sibling conflict (Dunn & Munn, 1986). Some studies with nonproblem familes have suggested that children's views of their siblings are represented by patterns of positive and negative behaviors mixed with positive and negative feelings (Pepler, Corter, & Abramovitch, 1982). However, it may be that both perceptions and behaviors for siblings in problem families are more negatively toned (Patterson, 1982).

Structured Parental Reports about Child Behavior

In addition to unstructured interviews with parents, reports concerning child behavior and adjustment have also been obtained via other, more structured methods (Barkley, 1987; Humphreys & Ciminero, 1979; McMahon, 1984). The most widely used methods have been global behavior checklists requiring either binary judgments concerning the presence or absence of particular child behaviors (e.g., Louisville Behavior Check List—L. C. Miller, Hampe, Barrett, & Noble, 1971; Missouri Children's Behavior Checklist—Sines, 1986) or Likert-type scale ratings concerning the degree to which the behavior is present or perceived as a problem (e.g., Child Behavior Checklist and Revised Child Behavior Profile—Achenbach & Edelbrock, 1983; Conners Parent's Rating Scale—Conners, 1970; Parent Attitudes Test—Cowen, Huser, Beach, & Rappaport, 1970; Behavior Problem Checklist—Quay & Peterson, 1975; Yale Children's Inventory—Shaywitz, Schnell, Shaywitz, & Towle, 1986; Washington Symptom Checklist—Wimberger & Gregory, 1968). These checklists cover a wide range of presenting complaints and, to a lesser extent, child competencies; offer a degree of standardization that is uncharacteristic of clinical interviews; permit normative comparisons between children; are economical to administer and score; may be readily used as treatment outcome measures; and provide a rich measure of parents' perceptions of their children's behavior, including possible discrepancies in the perceptions of parents in the same family, and the discrepancies between parental perceptions and data derived through other sources.

In the clinical context, these checklists can serve as comprehensive but rough screening instruments, most typically during the diagnostic phase of assessment. They provide a rea-sonable estimate of parental perceptions of a child's overall behavior and adjustment as aggregated across a wide variety of situations. They fail to provide situation-specific information about behavior, or information that can be easily incorporated into a program of intervention. Most of the checklists noted above have been used with children of at least school age, but, consistent with an emphasis on prevention-oriented assessments, several measures have recently been developed for use with younger children and toddlers (e.g., Child Behavior Checklist for Ages 2–3—Achenbach, 1984; Behavior Checklist for Infants and Toddlers—Bullock, MacPhee, & Benson, 1984; Toddler Behavior Checklist—Larzelere, Martin, & Amberson, 1985). For children younger than 2, the most commonly used parent report measures have been subsumed under the general heading of temperament (e.g., Goldsmith & Campos, 1986; Rothbart, 1981).

As noted previously, extensive multivariate analyses of parent-completed checklists (see Achenbach, 1985) have yielded consistent factors; not surprisingly, these factors vary with the age and sex of the child and with the setting and informant (e.g., Gdowski, Lachar, & Kline, 1985). Within a behavioral assessment framework, such variations are consistent with the view that behaviors will vary in degree and type across situations, and that different informants will structure their views of the child in a different fashion. While there is a need for more measures with situational norms, the likelihood that the most frquently used checklists will be modified in this direction seems quite low, in light of the large-scale empirical efforts that often go into establishing a psychometrically sound normative data base for checklists. More typically, new measures tend to involve bigger and better efforts at restructuring old contents (e.g., Achenbach, Conners, & Quay, 1985).

One concern surrounding the use of parent checklists has been the degree of correspondence between reports by mothers versus fathers (e.g., Achenbach, McConaughy, & Howell, 1987). Some researchers have reported high agreement between parents on global checklists (e.g., z-transformed Pearson correlation of .69) for both narrow- and broad-band syndromes (Achenbach, 1985, p. 104). However, the degree of agreement or disagreement between parents will probably depend on the type of measure being compared (e.g., narrow-band syndromes vs. profiles) and the type of agreement index that is used. Reports by mothers versus fathers can lead to different profile interpretations and judgments of clinical significance (Hulbert, Gdowski, & Lachar, 1986). Furthermore, when different raters seeing children in different contexts have been compared, interrater agreement drops substantialy (r's $= .19$ and .37 for narrow- and broad-band syndromes, respectively; Achenbach, 1985). Such findings may have implications for the assessment of parental perceptions in divorced versus intact families.

In addition to global checklists and structured interviews, several parent-completed measures concerned with more focused content areas or problems have also been developed. These include, for example, parental ratings of a child's hyperactivity (e.g., Werry & Sprague, 1970), general development (e.g., Minnesota Child Development Inventory—Ireton & Thwing, 1974), personality (e.g., Personality Inventory for Children—Gdowski et al., 1985; Lachar, 1982; Wirt, Lachar, Klinedinst, & Seat, 1984), self-control (Kendall & Wilcox, 1979; W. M. Reynolds & Stark, 1986), and preferred reinforcers (Clement & Richard, 1976).

Another type of parent report, often used to monitor changes during treatment, has been parent recording of targeted child behavior. Typically, parents will collect baseline data on one or two general (e.g., compliance) or specific (e.g., swearing) behaviors that may subsequently be designated for modification. Less frequently, parents may also collect systematic data about antecedent and consequent events in order to identify potentially important controlling variables to be utilized in treatment. Many different forms have been presented to assist parents in recording their children's behavior (e.g., Madsen & Madsen, 1972). Such forms are common fare in almost all manuals that have been used in behaviorally oriented parent training programs (see Bernal & North, 1978, for a review of 26 commonly used parent training manuals). Records kept by parents have the advantage of providing ongoing *in situ* information about behaviors of interest that might not otherwise be accessible to observation, and may also provide secondary benefits that are not directly related to assessment. These include teaching parents better observation, tracking, and monitoring skills; assessing parental motivation; and providing parents with more realistic estimates of their children's rate of responding and with feedback regarding the effects of treatment. On the negative side, there are practical problems in getting parents to keep accurate records, and parental recordings of behavior may be reactive in the home situation, producing unrepresentative data. In addition, although parent recordings have been used extensively, there is little reliability or validity information available concerning their use.

Parents are of necessity the primary informants in child behavior assessment, because it is parental perception that determines what, if anything, will be done about their children. Furthermore, professionals' judgments regarding childhood disorder may be influenced more by what parents say about their children than by observed child behavior. Because parent-completed checklists can provide more information more quickly than could otherwise be obtained through interviews, and are also more economical with respect to cost, effort, and therapists' time, they are likely to receive continued use in child and family behavior assessment. We believe that the utility of such checklists for assessment and treatment of individual children can be enhanced through the inclusion of more situational content.

Parent Self-Ratings

Earlier discussions of behavioral assessment were not explicit concerning the importance of information reported by parents about themselves. However, recent writings have increasingly emphasized the importance of assessing parents' self-reported perceptions and feelings (Patterson, 1982). The earlier work in behavioral assessment tended to utilize parents' reports about themselves primarily in areas directly related to the children's problems (e.g., ''How does it make you feel when he does not listen to you?''). Parents' feelings, attitudes, and cognitions were considered as moderator variables, but usually in relation to their influences on how parents reacted to their children or as predictors of the likelihood that parents would involve themselves in treatment. While these considerations continue, parents' reports about themselves have increasingly been viewed as important to assess in understanding the nature of the families' problems and as potential targets for intervention. As in work in other areas (e.g., Bristol & Gallagher, 1986), the greater emphasis in behavioral assessment thus far has been on obtaining self-reports from mothers as opposed to fathers.

Parent self-ratings have included a variety of procedures designed to assess parental behavior and disciplinary practices, parental cognitions, and parental affects. One type of self-rating has been concerned with reported parenting practices. Such practices have been assessed via questionnaires that ask directly about the parents' reported use of rewards and punishments (e.g., Gordon, Jones, & Nowicki, 1979), or that provide the parents with brief written scenarios of child behavior or situations, to which the parents specify what they would do in those situations (e.g., Patterson & Colleagues, 1984). Similar assessments have presented either audiotaped (e.g., Grusec & Kuczynski, 1980; Martin, Johnson, Johansson, & Wahl, 1976) or videotaped (e.g., Disbrow & Doerr, 1983; H. Miller & Clarke, 1978; Wolfe & LaRose, 1986) samples of children's behavior, and the parents' verbal and/or physiological responses are recorded. Such analogue measures are a reflection of how parents think they would respond, and the degree of correspondence between expressed intent and actual parent behavior in these situations has received little empirical investigation.

The increasing focus on cognitive variables in behavioral assessment and treatment, and in the study of parent–child relationships more generally (e.g., Sigel, 1985), has led to the development of a host of self-report measures for describing different types of parental cognitions. Such measures have been used to assess the following:

1. General attitudes about children and child rearing (e.g., Parent Attitude Research Instrument—Schaefer & Bell, 1958; Belief Scale—Bristol, 1983a).
2. Satisfaction in areas concerned with spouse support, the child–parent relationship, parent performance, family discipline, and control (e.g., Parent Satisfaction Scale—Guidubaldi & Cleminshaw, 1985; Satisfaction with Parenting Scale—Crnic & Greenberg, 1983).
3. Parenting self-esteem, as reflected in degree of comfort in the parenting role and perceived effectiveness as a parent (e.g., Parenting Sense of Competence Scale—Gi-

baud-Wallston & Wandersman, 1978, and Mash & Johnston, 1986; Self Perceptions of the Parental Role—MacPhee, Benson, & Bullock, 1984).
4. Expectations for development and developmentally appropriate behavior (e.g., Parent Opinion Survey—Azar, Robinson, Hekemian, & Twentyman, 1984; Child Development Questionnaire—Mash & Johnston, 1980).
5. Attributional processes related to the causes of child behavior (e.g., Dix & Grusec, 1985; Larrance & Twentyman, 1983) or of specific problems such as enuresis (Butler, Brewin, & Forsythe, 1986).
6. Problem-solving skills in regard to commonly occurring child behaviors and child rearing situations (e.g., Holden 1985a, 1985b, 1985c; Parent Problem Solving Instrument—Wasik, Bryant, & Fishbein, 1980).
7. Empathy in general (e.g., Chlopan, McBain, Carbonell, & Hagen, 1985) and in the parenting domain (e.g., Feshbach, 1987; Newberger, 1978).
8. Emotional recognition (e.g., Camras, Ribordy, Spaccarelli, & Stefani, 1986; Kropp & Haynes, 1987).

Studies into the cognitive processes of parents have provided information concerning relationships between parental cognitions and behavior; possible differences in the cognitions of parents in disturbed versus nondisturbed families; and the ways in which parents process information about demanding child-rearing situations, including their use of anticipatory or proactive strategies (Holden, 1985d). Information concerning the decisional processes of parents seems especially relevant to formulating treatment goals, since the parents' problem-solving style may be directly targeted for treatment (e.g., Blechman, 1985). Many of the measures described have been used in a research context, and their potential utility in clinical assessment needs to be demonstrated. Furthermore, there are a number of different cognitive dimensions that are being assessed, and more work is needed to determine whether or not these dimensions are in fact distinct (Sigel, 1985).

An interest in how parents of problem (Mash, 1984; Mash & Johnston, 1983b), handicapped (Zeitlin, Williamson, & Rosenblatt, 1985), and nonproblem children cope with the stresses sur-

rounding child rearing has led to the development of several measures designed to assess
the "stresses" associated with being a parent
(e.g., Parenting Stress Index—Abidin, 1983),
the degree to which specific types of child
behavior may be perceived as "disturbing"
(e.g., Mooney & Algozzine, 1978), and the
impact on parents of specific handicapping child
conditions, such as hearing loss (Meadow-Orlans, 1986). Similarly, an interest in the social
networks surrounding disturbed families has led
to the development of a variety of measures
concerned with reports of perceived social support and/or social isolation (e.g., Bristol, 1983b;
Dunst, Jenkins, & Trivette, 1984; Salzinger,
Kaplan, & Artemyeff, 1983; Wahler, Leske, &
Rogers, 1979). For a comprehensive review of
measures concerned with family stress and social support, the reader is referred to Dunst and
Trivette (1985).

Much recent work has also been directed at
parents' reports of their own mood states, particularly depression (e.g., Billings & Moos,
1986; Forehand, Fauber, Long, Brody, & Slotkin, 1986). Thus far, little attention has been
directed at the assessment of other mood states
(e.g., anxiety) in the context of behavioral
family assessment. The most frequently utilized
measure of mood has been the Beck Depression
Inventory (BDI; Beck, Ward, Mendelson, Mock,
& Erbaugh, 1961). While the prevalence of
self-reported depression in mothers of problem
children is high, the causal sequences surrounding such mood states as determinants or outcomes of disturbed family interactions have not
yet been established (Patterson, 1982). There
is a rapidly growing literature documenting the
profound impact that maternal depression can
have on child functioning and family relationships, beginning in early infancy (Hammen *et
al.*, 1986).

It is also the case that mothers' feelings of
depression may negatively color their views of
their children. Friedlander, Weiss, and Traylor
(1986) reported a .71 correlation between maternal BDI scores and the Depression subscale
of the Child Behavior Checklist. Edelbrock
(1984) notes that parental endorsement of the
Child Behavior Checklist item "unhappy, sad,
or depressed" discriminated between clinically
referred and nonreferred children more strongly
than any other item. However, in light of the
high correlation between mothers' self-reports
of depression and ratings of their children, it is
not clear whether the sensitivity of this item

related to the mothers' or to the children's
depression. The fact that the same item best
discriminated between referred and nonreferred
children even when teacher ratings were used
(Edelbrock & Achenbach, 1985) suggests that
the item's sensitivity may not be due to a
negative response bias per se. Additional support for this view comes from a study (Billings
& Moos, 1986) showing that independent ratings of child functioning made by depressed
parents and their nondepressed spouses were
highly correlated (median $r = .59$). Nevertheless, even with nondepressed teachers or spouses,
ratings of a child as unhappy could reflect an
attribution that follows from a negative view of
the child and his or her behavior, rather than
being indicative of the child's actual distress.

In summary, parent self-ratings reflect a variety of important characteristics that may contribute to how parents react to, and are affected
by, their disturbed children. In addition, many
of the cognitions and affects being assessed are
likely to suggest fruitful areas for needed interventions. In considerations of the future use
and development of such self-ratings, a number
of evaluative criteria for selecting a self-report
inventory have been suggested, including
whether it can be administered repeatedly as an
outcome measure; whether it provides sufficient
specificity; whether it is sensitive to treatment
changes; whether it guards against common
self-report biases such as social desirability,
acquiescence, demand characteristics, faking,
or lying; and whether it possesses adequate
reliability, validity, and norms (Hartmann, 1984).
Many of the parent self-ratings that have been
used thus far in child and family behavior
assessment would not meet this criteria.

Child Self-Report

Concerns regarding the reliability, validity, and
practical difficulties associated with obtaining
self-report information from children, especially younger children, resulted in a minimal
reliance on such measures in early work in
child and family behavior assessment. More
recently, there has been an increase in the use
of interviews and child-completed checklists
and questionnaires (Bierman, 1983; Bierman &
Schwartz, 1986; Finch & Rogers, 1984)
throughout the various phases of assessment
and treatment. This increase is related to a
number of factors:

1. The growing recognition of children's unique position as observers of themselves and of their social environment.
2. An accumulation of data in support of the notion that cognitions and emotions directly influence children's behavior and often mediate the effects of intervention.
3. An increased emphasis on children's thoughts and feelings as potential targets for treatment, with a concomitant increase in the use of cognitively based therapy procedures.
4. A growing concern for childhood disorders such as depression (Cicchetti & Schneider-Rosen, 1984; Odom & DeKlyem, 1986) and anxiety (Gittelman, 1985), disorders that require the direct assessment of children's self-reported feelings.
5. A greater sensitivity to developmental issues in behavioral assessment, which has reinforced the notion that methods need to be adapted to the qualitatively different information-processing and interpersonal styles characteristic of children at different ages. While interviews and checklists of the types administered to adults may not be very informative with children in preschool or grade school, flexible interview formats that are consistent with a child's developmental level can provide important information concerning the child's behavior, thought processes, views of himself, or herself, and views of the environment.
6. The development and widespread availability of a number of well-standardized and psychometrically sound structured and semi-structured interview and questionnaire procedures.

Unstructured Interviews

The format and content of early assessment interviews with children should vary in relation to each child's developmental status, the nature of the child's problem, and the interview purpose. Purposes will vary, but typically include attempts to elicit information regarding children's perceptions of themselves and their problems, and efforts to obtain samples of how children handle themselves in a social situation with an adult (Greenspan, 1981; Gross, 1984). Children's views of the circumstances that have brought them to the clinic, expectations for improvement, and comprehension of the assessment situation are all important to assess, as is the manner in which the children interpret

significant events in their lives, such as divorce (Kurdek, 1986, in press). In addition, children's perceptions of their parents, siblings, teachers, and peers (Bierman & MacCauley, in press; Furman & Buhrmester, 1985a, 1985b; Hymel, 1986; Skeen & Gelfand, 1981) will probably influence their reactions to them, and are therefore especially important for understanding the problem, designing interventions, and assessing the suitability of employing such individuals as mediators in behavioral intervention programs. Interviews may also focus on obtaining more specific types of information that children are in a unique position to report, such as their preferred reinforcers or preferences for immediate versus delayed rewards.

Semistructured and Structured Interviews

Unstructured clinical interviews would appear to be extremely unreliable for purposes of diagnosis, where such diagnosis is concerned with assignment to diagnostic categories. Sources of unreliability stem from a variety of factors, including a lack of clarity concerning decision rules, and the operation of confirmatory biases and other types of judgmental errors (Achenbach, 1985; Costello, 1986). While the use of more structured interviews in clinical practice with children has not been widespread, such procedures have received increased use in research studies where the primary focus has been on identifying homogeneous populations of children conforming to particular diagnostic criteria. It appears likely that such interviews will receive increased use in clinical practice, in light of their easy adaptability to computerized administration and scoring (Stein, 1986) and the continuing administrative demands for assigning children to institutionalized diagnostic categories.

A number of structured and semistructured diagnostic interviews for children and adolescents have been developed over the past decade, each having different degrees of structure. These include the Diagnostic Interview for Children and Adolescents (Herjanic & Reich, 1982); the Schedule for Affective Disorders and Schizophrenia for School-Age Children (Chambers *et al.*, 1985; Puig-Antich & Chambers, 1978); Diagnostic Interview Schedule for Children and Adolescents (Costello, Edelbrock, & Costello, 1985; Costello, Edelbrock, Kalas, Kessler, & Klaric, 1982); the Interview Sched-

ule for Children (Kovacs, 1982, 1985); the
Child Assessment Schedule (Hodges, 1985);
the Mental Health Assessment Form (Kestenbaum & Bird, 1978); and the Psychological
Screening Inventory (Langner et al., 1976).

Numerous empirical investigations with these
interviews have produced interesting results that
have implications for the assessment of children
more generally. For example, the reliability of
the interview may interact with the particular
dimension (e.g., affective, cognitive, behavioral) being evaluated. Edelbrock, Costello,
Dulcan, Kalas, and Conover (1985) found that
in descriptions of internal states the reliability
of the interview was related to the child's age;
children under age 10 showed little consistency
in their interview reports, even over periods as
brief as 1 or 2 weeks. Young children showed
a particular tendency to change their responses
from affirmative during an initial interview to
negative in a second interview several days
later.

The potential utility of structured psychiatric
interviews for behavioral assessments is not
clear at this time. Certainly, the increased
standardization and gains in reliability associated with using these procedures provide some
advantage in both applied and basic research
with children and families. However, most of
the structured interview formats tend to produce
global indices concerning the presence or absence of a disorder, rather than the more specific information needed to formulate a picture
of a particular child, family, and peer group
for the purposes of intervention.

Few structured child interviews have been
developed specifically for use in behavioral
assessment. Bierman (1983) has presented some
extremely useful guidelines in this regard,
showing how empirical information about developmental processes (e.g., person perception
as related to age) may be used to guide the
types of questions that are asked in an interview. The few structured formats that have
been presented have been developed primarily
as research instruments (Patterson & Colleagues, 1984). It would seem that as behavioral assessors increase their interest in children's perceptions and feelings, some degree
of standardization in their interview procedures
is warranted. Presumably, such standardized
instruments should look at children's reports in
relation to a variety of commonly occurring
situations in the home and classroom.

Child-Completed Checklists
and Questionnaires

The use of child-completed checklists and questionnaires in child behavioral assessment has
also increased (Finch & Rogers, 1984). While
the content and response format for child-completed measures have varied with children's
developmental status, for the most part these
measures have been used with older children
and often as one measure of treatment outcome.
A wide variety of self-report instruments has
been developed for describing the cognitive,
affective, and behavioral domains. While many
of the early self-report measures tended to be
direct downward extensions of instruments initially developed for adults, currently used measures have followed more closely from work
with children. Some of the more frequently
used instruments and the areas they assess are
as follows:

1. General personality dimensions such as introversion–extraversion (e.g., Eysenck &
   Rachman, 1965).
2. Perceived locus of control (e.g., Bugental,
   Whalen, & Henker, 1977; Nowicki & Duke,
   1974; Nowicki & Strickland, 1972).
3. Social relationships and assertion (e.g.,
   Deluty, 1979; Hops & Lewin, 1984; Michelson & Wood, 1982; Ollendick, 1984;
   Scanlon & Ollendick, 1985).
4. Self-esteem and self-concept in general and
   in specific domains such as academic or
   social functioning (e.g., Coopersmith, 1967;
   Harter, 1982, 1983; Harter & Pike, 1984;
   Piers & Harris, 1963; Williams & Workman, 1978).
5. Reinforcer preferences (e.g., Clement &
   Richard, 1976; Tharp & Wetzel, 1969).
6. Anger (e.g., W. M. Nelson & Finch, 1978).
7. Depression (e.g., Kazdin, Chapter 4, this
   volume; Kovacs, 1978; Smucker, Craighead, Craighead, & Green, 1986).
8. Anxiety (e.g., see Barrios & Hartmann,
   Chapter 5, this volume; Castenada, Mc-
   Candless, & Palermo, 1956; C. R. Reynolds & Richmond, 1978; Silverman &
   Nelles, 1986; Spielberger, 1973).
9. Irrational cognitions such as catastrophiz-
   ing, overgeneralizing, personalizing, and
   selective abstraction, as expressed in the
   social, academic, and athletic domains (e.g.,
   Leitenberg et al., 1986).

10. Perceptions of family members (e.g., Furman & Buhrmester, 1985b; Hazzard, Christensen, & Margolin, 1983.
11. Perceptions of peers and peer relationships (e.g., Asher, Hymel, & Renshaw, 1984; Bierman & McCauley, in press).
12. Perceived behavior problems and competencies (e.g., Achenbach & McConaughy, 1985).

Specific examples of the items comprising many of these checklists are provided in the chapters that follow.

Self-Monitoring Procedures

A number of discussions of the types of self-monitoring procedures that have been used in assessment, as well as related methodological issues, are available (e.g., Bornstein et al., 1986; Shapiro, 1984). Children have used self-monitoring for such behaviors as classroom attending (Broden, Hall, & Mitts, 1971), academic responses (Lovitt, 1973), class attendance (McKenzie & Rushall, 1974), talking out in class (Broden et al., 1971), aggression (Lovitt, 1973), room cleaning (Layne, Rickard, Jones, & Lyman, 1976), and appropriate verbalizations (R. O. Nelson, Lipinski, & Boykin, 1978). In most instances, the use of self-monitoring procedures with children has been undertaken as part of a larger set of procedures of self-assessment, including recording and evaluation, that are intended to modify the behavior being monitored. There are few descriptions of children self-monitoring their own behavior and life situations in order to provide diagnostic information for developing treatments or measuring treatment outcome. Consequently, the assessment functions of self-monitoring procedures with children have not received much elaboration.

Direct Observations of Behavior: Some Comments and Cautions

We have previously described a direct observational procedure as a method for obtaining samples of behaviors and settings determined to be clinically important (in relation to diagnosis, design, prognosis, and evaluation), in a naturalistic situation or in an analogue situation that is structured in such a way as to provide information about behaviors and settings comparable to what would have been obtained in situ (Mash & Terdal, 1976). Direct observational methods usually involve the recording of behavior when it occurs; the use of trained and impartial observers following clearly specified rules and procedures regarding the timing of observations and their context; the use of previously designated categories that require a minimal degree of inference; and some procedure to check reliability (Cone & Foster, 1982; Hartmann, 1982; Reid et al., 1987).

The role ascribed to direct observations of ongoing child behavior as the sine qua non of early work in behavioral assessment (Johnson & Bolstad, 1973) was so great that the use of observational procedures has in some instances been viewed as synonymous with the practice of behavioral assessment. Many reports, for example, have presented only direct observations of target behavior as a measure of change. The strong and sometimes overzealous emphasis on direct observations as the primary data source in behavioral assessment was probably related to an increased recognition of the need for greater objectivity in clinical child assessment, and to the compatibility of direct and less inferential data sources with the nonmediational focus characterizing earlier behavior therapy approaches. There has, however, been a lessening emphasis on the exclusive use of direct observational procedures, concomitant with the increasing systems orientation in child and family assessment and the admissibility of cognitive and affective variables in both behavior therapy and assessment (Jacobson, 1985; Wasik, 1984).

The early behavioral assessment emphasis on direct observational procedures was part of the general reaction against the indirect and often highly inferential assessments characterizing traditional child assessments (Goldfried & Kent, 1972). Parent ratings, personality inventories, children's self-reports, and responses to projective test stimuli or doll-play situations, as they were traditionally used to generate inferences regarding emotional conflict and intrapsychic processes, often seemed far removed from the major presenting problems of the child and his or her family.

It has been argued that direct observation is less subject to bias and distortion than are verbal reports from either children or parents and teachers. However, this question cannot really be addressed without considering who the informant is, what child or family behavior is being described, and what the context and purposes for assessment are. Furthermore, support for this argument comes more from studies demonstrating poor reliability and validity associated with verbal report than from studies directly demonstrating observational data to be accurate and unbiased. In fact, many studies have shown that observed behavior can be readily distorted by biases on the part of both observers and those being observed. For example, Johnson and Lobitz (1974) demonstrated that normal parents could make their children look either "good" or "bad" when instructed to do so. However, it is possible that some types of problem families may find it difficult to make themselves "look good" to outside observers. For example, it has been reported that abusive mothers continue to behave in ways considered to be socially undesirable, even when they are being observed (Mash et al., 1983; Reid, Taplin, & Lorber, 1981). Nevertheless, in light of the demand characteristics of most observation situations (e.g., relating to diagnosis of the problem, eligibility for treatment, educational placement, legal adjudication, and evaluation of treatment change), it seems likely that most families will attempt to systematically influence what is being observed.

Although there have been a host of methodological investigations concerned with the issues surrounding the use of observational procedures (Kazdin, 1982a), these studies, taken together, have not been as informative as one would hope. One reason for this is that many of the studies have explored questions concerning bias and reactivity "in general," and questions of this nature do not really address the issues of bias and reactivity under highly specific conditions. Bias and reactivity are likely to vary as a function of the answers to the question "What is being assessed, who is being assessed, by whom, using what methods, for what purposes, and in what situations?"

The preceding general comments are not intended to diminish the importance of direct observational procedures for behavioral assessments of children and families. Rather, they are intended to caution against the steadfast adherence to observational methods as the best type of assessment under all circumstances, in the face of an increasing conceptual emphasis on cognitive and affective variables, contradictory empirical findings related to possible biases

and reactivity, the potential unrepresentativeness of observational data, the relativity of assessment purposes, and the many practical concerns associated with the use of observational procedures.

Observational Procedures with Children and Families

A wide range of observational procedures have been utilized in assessing children and families, ranging from simple single-behavior or single-purpose recording schemes that can be conducted with a minimal amount of observer training to complex and exhaustive multibehavior–multicontext interaction code systems (e.g., Conger, 1982; Dishion et al., 1984; Hops et al., 1986; Mash et al., 1973; Reid, 1978; Toobert, Patterson, Moore, & Halper, 1982; Wahler et al., 1976) requiring substantial initial and ongoing observer training (Fagot & Hagan, 1987; Reid, 1982). The factors involved in selecting an appropriate observational procedure are numerous and include such things as the stage of the assessment process, the characteristics of the behaviors of interest, the situation in which observation is to occur, observer characteristics, and technical resources (Mash & Terdal, 1981b).

There are currently several detailed discussions of direct observational procedures and of the methodological and practical issues surrounding their use (e.g., Foster & Cone, 1986; Hartmann, 1982). These issues are concerned with factors influencing the objectivity and reliability of observations, such as code system characteristics (e.g., number, complexity, and molecularity of categories); characteristics of the behaviors being observed (rate and complexity); methods of assessing reliability (e.g., awareness of reliability checks); observer characteristics (e.g., age, sex); methods of calculating reliability; sources of observer and observee bias under a range of conditions; reactivity to being observed; and ways in which observational data should be summarized and interpreted. An extensive discussion of these issues is beyond the scope of this chapter, but a sensitivity to methodological concerns of this kind is a necessary part of any observational assessment of children, because they have a direct bearing on the validity of the findings. A minimally acceptable set of criteria for any observational code would be that it is objective (e.g., two observers will classify behavior in the same way), that it has mutually exclusive subcategories, and that it provides data that are amenable to objective analysis. Given these minimal requirements, further validation as to a wide range of goals and purposes is possible.

Selecting Code Categories

The use of observational codes requires decisions relating to both the content (e.g., what categories to include) and the structure (e.g., number of categories, temporal base, mechanics for observing and recording) of the code system (Hawkins, 1982). With regard to content, the selection of particular categories of child and family behavior to observe—either in the construction of one's own code system or in the selection of an already existing code system—presupposes an existing set of hypotheses. There are many such implicit hypotheses underlying the existing observational code systems that have been used most often in behavioral assessment. For example, the greater prevalence and range of codes for categorizing child compliance and parental directiveness, relative to codes for children's and parents' affectional responses (e.g., Twardosz & Nordquist, 1983) have followed from and contributed to the development of hypotheses of disturbed family behavior centering around command–compliance sequences (e.g., Patterson, 1982). This is not to say that such hypotheses lack validity and/or utility, but rather that the nature of the existing code systems may favor some assessment outcomes over others. Most of the earlier observational codes for children focused on family interactions to a greater extent than interactions with peers, and for some time this limited our understanding of the importance of peer interactions and the relationships between family and peer group behavior.

For the most part, code selection and observational system construction have been carried out on a rational basis. Consistent with the view of maintaining low levels of inference, the family behaviors observed are often those directly reported as problematic by parents and teachers, or those that fit with the theories or experiences of the assessor. Established code systems, because of their procedural development, availability, and ease of application, often may be utilized inappropriately with particular populations or in situations at the differ from those established in the initial rationale for construction. We believe that category and code system selection can be improved with greater attention to the parameters associated with the specific populations of families being observed and the settings in which they function. Specialized codes of this nature are provided in the chapters of this volume related to conduct disorders, fears and anxieties, autism, and childhood depression. The categories included reflect behaviors and setting variables that have been empirically shown to be relevant for the populations under study.

It may also be useful to examine existing code systems in order to identify base rates at which particular categories are used in assessment, and the reasons given for their inclusion or exclusion. Such data are available in the literature but have not, with few exceptions (McIntyre et al., 1983), been systematically examined. In addition, the ways in which similar categories have been defined need further specification. It is not uncommon for similarly labeled behavior categories to be defined in quite different ways (Mash & Dalby, 1979), reflecting the lack of standardization mentioned previously. Such idiosyncratic code construction seems unnecessary and can only contribute to poor communication between assessors. Perhaps a behavior and setting code dictionary that provides standarized categories and definitions relevant to specific child populations and settings will lead to greater consistency in the use of observational procedures (Mash & Barkley, 1986).

Recently, there has been greater attention to observations that focus not only on molecular responses, but also on larger, more global units for describing family interaction. Implicit in this trend are the notions (1) that larger response chains have qualitative features of their own, and although molecular codes may not reveal these dimensions, subjective impressions by trained or "culturally sensitive" human observers may; and (2) that global ratings can provide a more efficiently obtained and equivalent integrative summary of the molecular responses. Weiss and Chaffin (1986) compared two marital code systems that were based on either global ratings of communication or on many specific categories, and found that the degree of overlap was moderate but not great ($r = .48$). It was pointed out that the two systems might be useful for different purposes and that, in light of the high costs of using complex category systems, the use of more global ratings might be explored. Several researchers have supplemented molecular observations with more global judgments and have found that experienced raters whose global judgments are averaged and composited can often provide reliable and valid indices of psychologically complex behaviors (Moskowitz & Schwarz, 1982; Weinrott, Reid, Bauske, & Brummett, 1981). It would appear that there are assets and liabilities associated with the use of molar and molecular ratings and that some combination of the two may be useful (Cairns & Green, 1979). If future empirical work can establish the utility, reliability, and validity of more global ratings for specific purposes, there would clearly be some practical advantage in using these procedures in the clinical context.

Early behavioral assessments focused not only on molecular response units, but also emphasized frequency, rate, and duration measures. Consistent with the recent interest in more global ratings, there is currently an interest not only in how much and for how long a behavior is seen, but also in the "qualitative" manner in which the behavior is expressed. For example, adult disciplinary reactions seem to be based not only on the type of child misbehavior, but also on how it is expressed. When noncompliance is accompanied by expressions of overt opposition such as anger and verbal refusal, stronger parental reactions may occur (Trickett & Kuczynski, 1986). There is currently a need to better define the qualitative features of responding that may influence both judgments and subsequent reactions. Recent work has suggested that the coding of nonverbal cues such as facial expressions (Gottman & Levenson, 1986), proxemic features such as how slowly or quickly the response is performed, the prosodic features of language, or the intensity of the behavior (Henker, Astor-Dubin, & Varni, 1986) may all reveal features of the interaction that may not be evident from molecular response codes. Other structural aspects of performance, such as latency and duration, may also provide important information. For example, Kotsopoulos and Mellor (1986) examined speech breath and speech latency variables with anxiety-disordered and conduct-disordered children. Children with anxiety disorders showed increased breath rate and lower output of speech per breath, whereas conduct disorder was associated with short initial hesitation before speaking, which could reflect an absence of specific cognitive processes such as planning.

There has also been an increased interest in coding the affective qualities of interactions, in part as a result of the many studies that have found relationships between depression and behavior problems in families. Some code systems have superimposed a more subjectively based valence code over the behavioral dimension. It is possible, for example, to code compliant behavior that has either positive or negative accompanying affect (Dishion et al., 1984). Other observational systems code specific affects such as anger, contempt, whining, sadness, or fear directly (Gottmann & Levenson, 1986), or code categories of affect such as aversive, dysphoric, happy, or caring (Hops et al., 1986). The work on affective coding in child and family behavioral assessment is relatively recent, and the empirical findings are sparse. In addition, most of this work has been conducted in a research context, and its direct applicability to clinical assessment and intervention is just being explored. Nevertheless, it would appear that this is a promising trend in the observational assessment of children and families, and one that will probably continue.

Settings for Observation

Following from a situation-specific view of behavior, observational assessments with children have been carried out in a wide range of settings, the most common of which are the clinic, the home, and the classroom (A. M. Harris & Reid, 1981; Zangwill & Kniskern, 1982). Other examples of observational settings have included institutional environments, such as group homes for delinquent adolescents; living environments for retarded or autistic children; playgrounds; supermarkets; and children's groups. More specific situations within each of these global settings have also provided structure for observation—for example, free play versus command–compliance instructions in the clinic, or observation at mealtime versus bedtime in the home.

A major concern associated with the choice of observational settings has been the degree of control that is imposed on the situation by the assessor. Behavioral assessors have previously emphasized the importance of observing in the child and family's natural environment, imposing the least amount of structure as possible, in order to see things "as they typically occur." This emphasis has reflected a reaction against the nonrepresentative and exclusive clinic observation conditions charasteristic of many clinical child assessments. Although *in situ* assessment is still recognized as an important part of behavioral assessment with children, there has also been an increased recognition that non-structured observations—in the home or preschool, for example—may not always be the most efficient or practical method for obtaining samples of the behaviors of interest.

Observation in natural environments may be especially unrevealing with behaviors that occur at a low rate or that are especially reactive to observation. Many nonstructured family and peer interactions consist of no interaction or low-rate "chatty" exchanges (Mash & Barkley, 1986). For example, in one study of non-problem families, over one-third of the observations were characterized by mutual non-involvement of family members (Baskett, 1985). In another study in which dominance and dependent behaviors were observed in the preschool, almost 8 weeks of observation were required in order to obtain generalizable data (Moskowitz & Schwarz, 1982). Such findings would suggest that in some circumstances the use of "evocative" situations, in order to highlight infrequently occurring response systems, may prove to be a potentially more efficient and reliable assessment strategy than the use of unstructured naturalistic observations.

In further contrasting naturalistic versus structured observations, the assumption that home observations are "natural" and that observations in the clinic or laboratory are "artificial" is an oversimplification. Home observations may at times provide us with artificial reactions to natural conditions, whereas clinic observations may provide us with natural reactions to artificial conditions. Which information is more meaningful depends a great deal on the purpose of the assessment. When cross-setting comparisons of behavior (e.g., home vs. clinic) do not agree, this cannot be assumed to be a function of the unrepresentativeness of behavior in the clinic unless there is some independent verification of the representativeness of the home observation. In most instances there is no such verification, and it is therefore inaccurate to equate representativeness with the naturalness of the physical setting, as is often done.

When home or classroom observations have been neither feasible nor appropriate, behavioral assessors have utilized a variety of structured laboratory or clinic observation settings for sampling the behaviors of interest (Hughes

& Haynes, 1978). Such analogue situations have provided a wide range of structures for assessing parent–child behaviors, including free-play interactions between mother and child; a variety of command–compliance situations, such as the mother having the child clean up or put away play materials, or occupy himself or herself while the mother is busy reading or talking on the telephone; academic task situations; problem-solving situations, such as figuring out how to play a game together; and highly structured observations of the social reinforcement properties or punishment styles of parents. The range of potentially relevant analogue situations to be used in behavioral assessment is restricted only by the ingenuity and physical resources of the assessor. The challenge, however, is for systematic reliability and validity assessment that would permit the use of more standardized and psychometrically well-developed analogues than has been the case thus far.

Using and Interpreting Observational Data

Direct observational data are utilized for a number of purposes: They can serve as treatment outcome measures, provide a data base for the construction of theories about childhood disorders (Patterson, 1982), and serve as a basis for making recommendations for treatment. In practice, the last-mentioned use is perhaps the most frequent but the least understood, because the processes by which direct observations have been translated into clinical recommendations are often poorly defined, unspecified, or oversimplified. For example, the observation of a positive adult response to a negative child behavior (e.g., teacher attention for misbehavior) or of a negative adult response to a positive child behavior (e.g., parental scoldings following a child's use of age-appropriate grammatical constructions) may lead to treatment recommendations centering around better contingency management. Alternatively, adult presentation of ambiguous antecedent cues for behavior (e.g., overly complex parental commands) may result in treatments centering around the alteration of stimulus control functions. However, in practice, these types of observation-based treatment recommendations represent informal hypothesis testing rather than systematically or empirically derived outcomes. It is also not clear whether such recommendations represent the fitting of observations to preferred and/or common hypotheses regarding contingencies, or the derivation of hypotheses that are genuinely based upon what has been observed.

Interpretations of observational data have typically followed from summarizations of child-behavior–adult-response sequences over relatively brief time intervals. It is often the pattern of behavior based upon interactional responses in immediately adjacent time intervals about which interpretations are made, with the assumption that immediate cues and reactions serve as major controlling events. A mother's reaction to her child's behavior is assumed to follow from the child's response that preceded it. However, the causes for both child and adult behavior may emanate from more remote points in observational sequences than those immediately adjacent in time; there is a need for empirical and conceptual criteria that can be utilized to formulate interpretations of observational data based on stylistic patterns of responding and in relation to more distal controlling events.

One recurrent issue in the use of observational procedures has been that of the costs involved. This has been noted as one factor in the lack of use of observational procedures by behavioral clinicians. Reid *et al.* (1987) note that in their setting, the cost (including dry runs, observer time, travel costs, and data summarization) of a comprehensive observational assessment encompassing six 1-hour sessions is $210.00—an amount less than the cost of a personality assessment. This figure seems quite reasonable, but it does not include indirect costs related to development, hardware, software, trained personnel, recording devices, and the like. So it would appear that carrying out observational assessments may be quite feasible and economical, *provided that the assessor already possesses the resources to do them*. Most practicing clinicians do not, in the same manner that most medical practitioners would be ill-equipped and ill-advised to carry out their own blood tests or brain scans. We have recommended (Mash & Barkley, 1986) that the development of specialized clinical research laboratories, which would function in a manner similar to medical laboratories, is necessary if sophisticated observational methods and data summarization procedures are to be integrated into clinical practice. Such laboratories would have a staff of highly trained observers, access to multiple coding systems, the necessary physical resources and equipment, the data-analytic

programs and empirically derived interpretive skills neccesary to deal with complex information, and the capability to provide immediate feedback and/or ongoing assessments of intervention efforts. The potential advantages of this general approach to assessment are enormous, since the degree of standardization, reliability, validity, and complexity of analyses underlying clinical decision making and treatment outcome evaluation in individual cases could be increased immeasurably. Perhaps most importantly, the precision of interpretation in a network of such observational laboratories would increase in an exponential fashion as a rapidly expanding data base permitted better decision making.

Family Assessment Methods

Concomitant with a growing trend toward conceptualizing (Sroufe & Fleeson, 1986) and treating (Alexander & Parsons, 1982; Szykula, 1986) childhood disorders in the context of the family, measures designed to tap family functioning have proliferated. Many of these "family measures" are being incorporated into the behavioral assessment of children and families (Foster & Robin, 1988). There is currently no shortage of measures to assess one thing or another about families, as several reviews bear witness (e.g., Forman & Hagan, 1984; Straus & Brown, 1978). Straus and Brown (1978), in a 40-year review of procedures for family measurement, indicated that the first 30 years revealed 319 measures whereas the final 10 years yielded 494 additional measures. If we were to consider work in clinical and developmental psychology since this 1978 review, one would posit an even greater exponential increase in the number of measures that have been developed to assess families (e.g., Filsinger, 1983; Holman, 1983).

One important question is this: What aspect of an assessment method makes it a "family" measure? Family assessment really occurs at two levels. At one level, family assessment is a strategy in which information is derived in order to understand the manner in which different family members relate to themselves and to one another. Information derived from the assessment of an individual family member's behaviors or feelings may be conceptually or empirically aggregated into a statement regarding how the family functions as a whole. This approach reflects the type of orientation that has characterized most of the work in child and family behavioral assessment thus far.

At the second level, family assessment encompasses measures that describe the functional or structural organization of the family at a level that is usually higher than that of the individual or dyad (Gjerde, 1986). Such views conceptualize families as systems, and attempt to describe the interdependencies, rules, relationships, and interactional processes that serve to regulate the system in the face of ongoing internal and external stressors. While many assessment procedures have included the word "family" in their title, most have not systematically tapped the kinds of functions characteristic of this view.

Measures designed to assess family dimensions have evolved from several traditions. Without question, the family therapy approaches have provided the richest conceptual base for describing families (Gurman & Kniskern, 1981; Minuchin, 1985). A discussion of these approaches is beyond the scope of this chapter; however, many family therapy constructs (e.g., enmeshment, adaptability, cohesion, triangulation, alliances, executive behavior, power locus, etc.) all seem to capture larger units of family functioning than the molecular recordings that have characterized much of the previous work in child and family behavioral assessment. Nevertheless, these concepts have not been well operationalized, and the methods for assessing them that have been devised by family therapists (see Forman & Hagan, 1984, for a review; Szapocznik, 1984) have not been been widely used in behavioral assessment.

Behavioral approaches to family assessment initially focused on specific dyads or observation of interactions when all family members were present. However, few of these studies attempted to describe family interactions in terms that went "beyond the dyad." When family dimensions emerged, these were empirically derived through the use of statistical transformations that tended to support a higher-order process such as coercion. However, these constructs have tended to be more theoretical than practical, and while the coercive interchanges of aggressive families have been well described, there is, for example, no single measure that can be used to describe the level of coercive process characterizing an entire family.

A third approach to describing family dimensions has evolved out of the developmental literature, with its emphasis on developmental systems and the emergence of early relationships (Hartup, 1986a, 1986b; Kaye, 1984). Much of this work has been with infants and preschoolers and has focused on such things as communication patterns and the quality of early attachments. Illustrative of the systems approach are those studies that have identified "higher-order" effects—for example, the way in which the behavior of family members may vary with the interpersonal structure of the interaction setting (e.g., which family members are present). For example, Gjerde (1986) found that the presence of the father enhanced the quality of mother–son relations, whereas presence of the mother reduced the quality of father–son relations. Also, mothers tended to show more differentiation between boys and girls when their husbands were present, whereas fathers did so when their wives were absent. This study and others like it point up the need to examine family interactions under a wide range of interpersonal contexts, and offer a rich conceptual and empirical base for carrying out behavioral assessments with families of young children. To date, however, few of the family measures that have been used in developmental investigations have been used extensively for the behavioral assessment of children and families in a clinical context.

One of the positive outcomes resulting from the increased interest in family assessment has been a much wider sampling of family subsystems than was previously the case in child and family behavioral assessment. This is especially true of measures designed to describe the marital (e.g., Margolin, 1983; Weiss & Margolin, 1986) and sibling (e.g., Brody & Stoneman, 1983; Mash & Johnston, 1983c) subsystems.

There is a trend toward the integration of some of the more global concepts and measures of families that have evolved from family systems views, and the operational specificity characteristic of behavioral assessments (see Foster & Robin, 1988). For example, Rodick et al. (1986) found that in families with balanced degrees of cohesion and adaptability, the mothers' communication was more supportive and explicit and the mother–child dyads evidenced significantly greater warmth and affection than in families with extremes of cohesion and adaptability. This study provides a good example of current efforts to operationalize subjectively defined global dimensions of family functioning by relating them to more directly observed empirical referents.

As the assessment focus has shifted toward understanding the dynamic systems in which children and families function, there has also been an increased interest in statistical methods that can be used to adequately describe the complexity of these systems. For example, in describing reciprocal social interaction over time, much recent attention has been given to sequential analysis as a primary data-analytic strategy (e.g., Bakeman & Gottman, 1986; Gottman, 1982; Gottman & Ringland, 1981; Gottman & Roy, in press; Whitehurst, Fischel, DeBaryshe, Caulfield, & Falco, 1986). Wampold (1986) has described some of the recent developments in this area as well as some of the difficulties, one of the primary ones being the way in which observations of sequential events can be integrated with more distal occurrences.

Formal Testing with Children

Regardless of whether behavioral assessment represents a break from traditional psychometric test approaches or a logical extension of such approaches, as some have suggested (Evans & Nelson, 1977), the fact remains that the use of developmental scales, intelligence and achievement tests (Kaufman & Kaufman, 1983; R. O. Nelson, 1980), perceptual–motor tests, and comprehensive neuropsychological assessments (see Fletcher, 1988) with children is common practice among both behavioral and nonbehavioral clinicians. The reader is referred to individual chapters in this volume for discussions of the utility of specific tests in behavioral assessments with specific populations of children.

SUMMARY

In this introductory chapter, we have described some of the more general issues characterizing the behavioral assessment of disturbed children and families. In doing so, we have tried to set the stage for the detailed discussions of the assessment of specific types of childhood disturbances in the chapters that follow.We have presented the view that behavioral assessment with children and families is best depicted as a general problem-solving strategy for understanding children's behavior and its determinants. It is a highly empirical approach to clinical child assessment that is based on an understanding of child development, child

psychopathology, and psychological testing. This problem-solving strategy is carried out in relation to recurring purposes, follows from a particular set of assumptions about children's behavior and its causes, designates particular behaviors and controlling variables as important, and employs multiple methods and informants.

Recent work in the area has become increasingly systems-oriented and sensitive to developmental parameters. A general theme that has been emphasized is that behavioral assessments of children and families will be most meaningful when they are derived in relation to specific types of childhood disorders. It is this theme that underlies most of the chapters that follow.

REFERENCES

Abidin, R. R. (1983). *Parenting Stress Index*. Charlottesville, VA: Pediatric Psychology Press.

Abikoff, H., Gittelman, R., & Klein, D. F. (1980). Classroom observation code for hyperactive children: A replication of validity. *Journal of Consulting and Clinical Psychology, 48*, 555–565.

Achenbach, T. M. (1978). Psychopathology of childhood: Research problems and issues. *Journal of Consulting and Clinical Psychology, 46*, 759–776.

Achenbach, T. M. (1982). *Developmental psychopathology* (2nd ed.). New York: Wiley.

Achenbach, T. M. (1984). *Child Behavior Checklist for Ages 2–3 (CBCL)*. Burlington: University of Vermont, Department of Psychiatry.

Achenbach, T. M. (1985). *Assessment and taxonomy of child and adolescent psychopathology*. Beverly Hills, CA: Sage.

Achenbach, T. M., Conners, C. K., & Quay, H. C. (1985). *The ACQ Behavior Checklist*. Unpublished manuscript, University of Vermont, Department of Psychiatry.

Achenbach, T. M.,, & Edelbrock, C. S. (1978). The classification of child psychology: A review and analysis of empirical efforts. *Psychological Bulletin, 85*, 1275–1301.

Achenbach, T. M., & Edelbrock, C. S. (1981). Behavioral problems and competencies reported by parents of normal and disturbed children aged four through sixteen. *Monographs of the Society for Research in Child Development, 46*, (1, Serial No. 188).

Achenbach, T. M., & Edelbrock, C. S. (1983). *Manual for the Child Behavior Checklist and Revised Child Behavior Profile*. Burlington: University of Vermont, Department of Psychiatry.

Achenbach, T. M., & Edelbrock, C. S. (1984). Psychopathology of childhood. *Annual Review of Psychology, 35*, 227–256.

Achenbach, T. M., & McConaughy, S. H. (1985). *Child Interview Checklist—Self-Report Form; Child Interview Checklist—Observation Form*. Burlington: University of Vermont, Department of Psychiatry.

Achenbach, T. M., McConaughy, S. H., & Howell, C. T. (1987). Child/adolescent behavioral and emotional problems: Implications of cross-informant correlations for situational specificity. *Psychological Bulletin, 101,* 213–232.

Adams, H. E., Doster, J. A., & Calhoun, K. S. (1977). A psychologically based system of response classification. In A. R. Ciminero, K. S. Calhoun, & H. E. Adams (Eds.), *Handbook of behavioral assessment* (pp. 47–78). New York: Wiley.

Alexander, J. G., & Parsons, B. V. (1982). *Functional family therapy.* Monterey, CA: Brooks/Cole.

Algozzine, B., Mercer, C. D., & Countermine, T. (1977). The effects of labels and behavior on teacher expectations. *Exceptional Children, 44,* 131–132.

American Psychiatric Association, (1980). *Diagnostic and statistical manual of mental disorders* (3rd ed.). Washington, DC: Author.

American Psychiatric Association. (1987). *Diagnostic and statistical manual of mental disorders* (3rd ed., rev.). Washington, DC: Author.

Anastasi, A. (1982). *Psychological testing* (5th ed.). New York: Macmillan.

Ancill, R. J., Carr, A. C. & Rogers, D. (1985). Comparing computerized self-rating scales for depression with conventional observer ratings. *Acta Psychiatrica Scandinavica, 71,* 315–317.

Arkowitz, H. (1979). Behavioral assessment comes of age. *Contemporary Psychology, 24,* 296–297.

Asher, S. R., Hymel, S., & Renshaw, P. D. (1984). Loneliness in children. *Child Development, 55,* 1456–1464.

Azar, S. T. (1986). A framework for understanding child maltreatment: An integration of cognitive behavioural and developmental perspectives. *Canadian Journal of Behavioral Science, 18,* 340–355.

Azar, S. T., Robinson, D. R., Hekimian, E., & Twentyman, C. T. (1984). Unrealistic expectations and problem-solving ability in maltreating and comparison mothers. *Journal of Consulting and Clinical Psychology, 52,* 687–691.

Bakeman, R., & Gottman, J. M. (1986). *Observing interaction; An introduction to sequential analysis.* New York: Cambridge University Press.

Bandura, A. (1969). *Principles of behavior modification.* New York: Holt, Rinehart & Winston.

Bandura, A. (1986). *Social foundations of thought and action: A social cognitive theory.* Englewood Cliffs, NJ: Prentice-Hall.

Barkley, R. A. (1987). A review of child behavior rating scales and checklists for research in child psychopathology (pp. 113–155). In M. Rutter, H. Tuma, & I. Lann (Eds.), *Assessment and diagnosis in child psychopathology.* New York: Guilford Press.

Barkley, R. A., & Edelbrock, C. (1987). Assessing situational variation in children's behavior problems: The Home and School Situations Questionnaires. In R. Prinz (Ed.), *Advances in behavioral assessment of children and families.* Greenwich, CT: JAI Press.

Barling, J. (1986). Father's work experiences, the father–child relationship and children's behaviour. *Journal of Occupational Behaviour, 7,* 61–66.

Barlow, D. H. (Ed.). (1981) *Behavioral assessment of adult disorders.* New York: Guilford Press.

Barlow, D. H. (1986). In defense of Panic Disorder with Agoraphobia and the behavioral treatment of panic: A comment on Kleiner. *The Behavior Therapist, 9,* 99–100.

Barlow, D. H., & Hersen, M. (1984). *Single case experimental designs: Strategies for studying behavior change* (2nd ed.). New York: Pergamon Press

Baskett, L. M. (1985). Understanding family interactions: Most probable reactions by parents and siblings. *Child and Family Behavior Therapy, 7,* 41–50.

Beck, A. T., Ward, C. H., Mendelson, M., Mock, J., & Erbaugh, J. (1961). An inventory for measuring depression. *Archives of General Psychiatry, 4,* 53–63.

Bell, R. Q., & Harper, L. V. (1977). *Child effects on adults.* Hillsdale, NJ: Erlbaum.

Belsky, J. (1981). Early human experience: A family perspective. *Developmental Psychology, 17,* 3–23.

Belsky, J., Lerner, R. M., & Spanier, G. B. (1984). *The child in the family.* New York: Random House.

Bem, D. M., & Funder, D. C. (1978). Predicting more of the people more of the time: Assessing the personality of situations. *Psychological Review, 85,* 485–501.

Bernal, M. E., & North, J. (1978). A survey of parent training manuals. *Journal of Applied Behavior Analysis, 11,* 533–544.

Bersoff, D. N., & Grieger, R. M. (1971). An interview model for the psychosituational assessment of children's behavior. *American Journal of Orthopsychiatry, 41,* 483–493.

Bierman, K. L. (1983). Cognitive development and clinical interviews with children. In B. B. Lahey & A. E. Kazdin (Ed.), *Advances in clinical child psychology.* (Vol. 6, pp. 217–250). New York: Plenum.

Bierman, K. L., & McCauley, E. (in press). Children's descriptions of their peer interactions. *Journal of Clinical Child Psychology.*

Bierman, K. L., & Schwartz, L. A. (1986). Clinical child interviews: Approaches and developmental considerations. *Journal of Child and Adolescent Psychotherapy, 3,* 267–278.

Bijou, S. W., & Peterson, R. F. (1971). Functional analysis in the assessment of children. In P. McReynolds (Ed.), *Advances in psychological assessment* (Vol. 2). Palo Alto, CA: Science and Behavior Books.

Billings, A. G., & Moos, R. H. (1986). Children of parents with unipolar depression: A controlled 1-year follow-up. *Journal of Abnormal Child Psychology, 14,* 149–166.

Blau, T. H. (1979). Diagnosis of disturbed children. *American Psychologist, 34,* 969–972.

Blechman, E. A. (1985). *Solving child behavior problems at home and school.* Champaign, IL: Research Press.

Block, J., & Gjerde, P. F. (1986, August). *Early antecedents of ego resiliency in late adolescence.* Paper presented at the meeting of the American Psychological Association, Washington, DC.

Bornstein, P. H., Bornstein, M. T., & Dawson, B. (1984). Integrated assessment and treatment. In T. H. Ollendick & M.Hersen (Eds.), *Child behavioral assessment: Principles and procedures* (pp. 223–243). New York: Pergamon Press.

Bornstein, P. H., Hamilton, S. B., & Bornstein, M. (1986). Self-monitoring procedures. In A. R. Ciminero, K. S. Calhoun, & H. E. Adams (Eds.), *Handbook of behavioral assessment* (2nd ed., pp. 176–222). New York: Wiley.

Bossard, J. H. S., & Boll, E. S. (1943). *Family situations: An introduction to the study of child behavior.* Philadelphia: University of Pennsylvania Press.

Bradbury, T. N., & Fincham, F. D. (in press-a). Affect and cognition in close relationships: Towards an integrative model. *Cognition and Emotion.*

Bradbury, T. N., & Fincham, F. D. (in press-b). Assessment of affect. In K. D. O'Leary (Ed.), *Assessment of marital discord*. Hillsdale, NJ: Erlbaum.

Bristol, M. M. (1983a). The Belief Scale. In M. Bristol, A. Donovan, & A. Harding (Eds.), *The broader impact of intervention: A workshop on measuring stress and support*. Chapel Hill, NC: Frank Porter Graham Child Development Center.

Bristol, M. M. (1983b). Carolina Parent Support Scale. In M. Bristol, A. Donovan, & A. Harding (Eds.), *The broader impact of intervention: A workshop on measuring stress and support*. Chapel Hill, NC: Frank Porter Graham Child Development Center.

Bristol, M. M., & Gallagher, J. J. (1986). Research on fathers of young handicapped children: Evolution, review, and some future directions. In J. J. Gallagher & P. M. Vietze (Eds.), *Families of handicapped persons* (pp. 81–100). Baltimore: Paul H. Brookes.

Broden, M., Hall, R. V., & Mitts, B. (1971). The effect of self-recording on the classroom behavior of two eighth grade students. *Journal of Applied Behavior Analysis, 4,* 191–199.

Brody, G. H., Pillegrini, A. D., & Sigel, I. E. (1986). Marital quality and mother–child and father–child interactions with school aged children. *Developmental Psychology, 22,* 291–296.

Brody, G. H., & Stoneman, Z. (1983). Children with atypical siblings: Socialization outcomes and clinical participation. In B. B. Lahey & A. E. Kazdin (Eds.), *Advances in clinical child psychology* (Vol. 6, pp. 285–325). New York: Plenum.

Bromfield, R., Weisz, J. R., & Messer, I. (1986). Children's judgements and attributions in response to the mental retarded label. *Journal of Abnormal Psychology, 95,* 81–87.

Bronfenbrenner, U. (1979). *The ecology of human development: Experiments by nature and design*. Cambridge, MA: Harvard University Press.

Bronfenbrenner, U. (1986). Ecology of the family as a context for human development: Research perspectives. *Developmental Psychology, 22,* 723–742.

Bugental, D. B., Whalen, C. K., & Henker, B. (1977). Causal attributions of hyperactive children and motivational assumptions of two behavior-change approaches: Evidence for an interactionist position. *Child Development, 48,* 874–884.

Bullock, D., MacPhee, C., & Benson, J. B. (1984). *Behavior Checklist for Infants and Toddlers*. Unpublished manuscript, University of Denver.

Butler, R. J., Brewin, C. R., & Forsythe, W. I. (1986). Maternal attributions and tolerance for nocturnal enuresis. *Behaviour Research and Therapy, 24,* 307–312.

Cairns, R. B., & Green, J. A. (1979). How to assess personality and social patterns: Observations or ratings? In R.B. Cairns (Ed.), *The analysis of social interactions: Methods, issues and illustrations* (pp. 209–226). Hillsdale, NJ: Erlbaum.

Camras, L. A., Ribordy, S., Spaccarelli, S., & Stefani, R. (1986). *Emotional recognition and production by abused children and mothers*. Unpublished manuscript, DePaul University.

Cantor, N. (1982). "Everyday" versus normative models of clinical and social judgment. In G.Weary & H. L. Mirels (Eds.), *Integrations of clinical and social psychology* (pp. 27–47). New York: Oxford University Press.

Cantor, N., Smith, E. E., French, R. deS., & Mezzich, J.

(1980). Psychiatric diagnosis as prototype categorization. *Journal of Abnormal Psychology, 89,* 181–193.

Cantwell, D. P. (1980). The diagnostic process and diagnostic classification in child psychiatry—DMS-III. *Journal of the American Academy of Child Psychiatry, 19,* 305–412.

Carlson, W. J. (1984). A factor structure of child home observation data. *Journal of Abnormal Child Psychology, 12,* 245–260.

Carr, A. C., & Ghosh, A. (1983). Accuracy of behavioural assessment by computer. *British Journal of Psychiatry, 142,* 66–70.

Carver, R. P. (1974). Two dimensions of tests: Psychometric and edumetric. *American Psychologist, 29,* 512–518.

Castenada, A., McCandless, B., & Palermo, D. (1956). The children's form of the Manifest Anxiety Scale. *Child Development, 27,* 317–326.

Catell, R. B. (1983). Let's end the duel. *American Psychologist, 38,* 769–776.

Cautela, J. R., Cautela, J., & Esonis, S. (1983). *Forms for behavior analysis with children*. Champaign, IL: Research Press.

Cerreto, M. C., & Tuma, J. M. (1977). Distribution of DSM-II diagnoses in a child psychiatric setting. *Journal of Abnormal Child Psychology, 5,* 147–153.

Chambers, W. J., Puig-Antich, J., Hirsch, M., Paez, P., Ambrosini, P. J., Tabrizi, M. A., & Davies, M. (1985). The assessment of affective disorders in children and adolescents by semi-structured interview: Test–retest reliability for school age children, present episode version. *Archives of General Psychiatry, 42,* 696–702.

Chlopan, B. E., McBain, M. L., Carbonell, J. L., & Hagen, R. L. (1985). Empathy: Review of available measures. *Journal of Personality and Social Psychology, 48,* 635–653.

Christopherson, E. R. (1986). Accident prevention in primary care. *Pediatric Clinics of North America, 33,* 925–933.

Cicchetti, D., & Braunwald, K. G. (in press). An organizational approach to the study of emotional development in maltreated infants. *Journal of Infant Mental Health*.

Cicchetti, D., & Rizley, R. (1981). Developmental perspectives on the etiology, intergenerational transmission, and sequelae of child maltreatment. *New Directions in Child Development, 11,* 31–55.

Cicchetti, D., & Schneider-Rosen, K. (Eds.). (1984). *Childhood depression*. San Francisco: Jossey-Bass.

Ciminero, A. R., Calhoun, D. S., & Adams, H. E. (Eds.). (1986). *Handbook of behavioral assessment* (2nd ed.). New York: Wiley.

Ciminero, A. R., & Drabman, R. S. (1977). Current developments in the behavioral assessment of children. In B. B. Lahey & A. E. Kazdin (Eds.), *Advances in clinical child psychology* (Vol. 1, pp. 47–82). New York: Plenum.

Clement, P.W., & Richard, R. C. (1976). Identifying reinforces for children: A Children's Reinforcement Survey. In E. J. Mash & L. G. Terdal (Eds.), *Behavior therapy assessment; Diagnosis, design,and evaluation* (pp. 207–216). New York: Springer.

Coie, D. D., & Dodge, K. A. (1986, August). *Hostile and instrumentally aggressive children: A social information processing perspective*. Paper presented at the meeting of the American Psychological Association, Washington, DC.

Coie, J. D., & Pennington, B. F. (1976). Children's perceptions of deviance and disorder. *Child Development, 47,* 407–413.

Compas, B. E., Friedland-Bandes, R., Bastien, R., & Adelman, H. S. (1981). Parent and child causal attributions related to the child's clinical problem. *Journal of Abnormal Child Psychology, 9,* 389–397.

Cone, J. D. (1977). The relevance of reliability and validity for behavioral assessment. *Behavior Therapy, 8,* 411–426.

Cone, J. D. (1978). The behavioral assessment grid (BAG): A conceptual framework and a taxonomy. *Behavior Therapy, 9,* 882–888.

Cone, J. D. (1979). Confounded comparisons in triple response mode assessment research. *Behavioral Assessment, 1,* 85–95.

Cone, J. D. (1981). Psychometric considerations. In M. Hersen & A. S. Bellack (Eds.), *Behavioral assessment; A practical handbook* (2nd ed., pp. 38–68). New York: Pergamon Press.

Cone, J. D. (1987). Behavioral assessment with children and adolescents. In M. Hersen & V. B. Van Hasselt (Eds.), *Behavior therapy with children and adolescents: A clinical approach.* (pp. 29–49). New York: Wiley.

Cone, J. D., & Foster, S. L. (1982). Direct observation in clinical psychology. In P. C. Kendall & J. N. Butcher (Eds.), *Handbook of research methods in clinical psychology* (pp. 311–354). New York: Wiley.

Cone, J. D., & Hawkins, R. P. (Eds.), (1977). *Behavior assessment: New directions in clinical psychology.* New York: Brunner/ Mazel.

Cone, J. D., & Hoier, T. S. (1986). Assessing children: The radical behavioral perspective. In R. J. Prinz (Ed.), *Advances in behavioral assessment of children and families* (Vol. 2, pp. 1–27). Greewich, CT: JAI Press.

Conger, R. D. (1982). *Social interactional scoring system: Observer training manual.* Unpublished manuscript, University of Illinois, Department of Human Development and Family Ecology.

Connell, J. P., & Tanaka, J. S. (Eds.). (1987). Special section on structural equation modeling. *Child Development, 58,* 1–175.

Conners, C. K. (1970). Symptom patterns in hyperkinetic, neurotic, and normal children. *Child Development, 4,* 667–682.

Coopersmith, S. (1967). *The antecedents of self-esteem.* San Francisco: W. H. Freeman.

Costello, A. J. (1986). Assessment and diagnosis of affective disorders in children. *Journal of Child Psychology and Psychiatry, 27,* 565–574.

Costello, A. J., Edelbrock, C., Kalas, R., Kessler, M. D., & Klaric, S. (1982). *The NIMH Diagnostic Interview Schedule for Children (DISC).* Pittsburgh, PA: Authors.

Costello, E. J., Edelbrock, C., & Costello, A. J. (1985). Validity of the NIMH Diagnostic Interview Schedule for Children: A comparison between psychiatric and pediatric referrals. *Journal of Abnormal Child Psychology, 13,* 579–595.

Cotterell, J. L. (1986). Work and community influences on the quality of child rearing. *Child Development, 57,* 362–374.

Cowen, E. L., Huser, J., Beach, D. R., & Rappaport, J. (1970). Parental perceptions of young children and their relation to indexes of adjustment. *Journal of Consulting and Clinical Psychology, 34,* 97–103.

Cowen, E. L., Pederson, A., Babigian, H., Izzo, L. D., & Trost, M. A. (1973). Long-term follow-up of early

detected vulnerable children. *Journal of Consulting and Clinical Psychology, 41,* 438–445.

Crnic, K. A., & Greenberg, K. (1983). *Inventory of Parent Experiences: Manual.* Unpublished manuscript, University of Washington.

Cronbach, L. J. (1984). *Essentials of psychological testing* (4th ed.). New York: Harper & Row.

D'Antonio, W. V., & Aldous, J. (Eds.). (1983). *Families and religions: Conflict and change in modern society.* Beverly Hills, CA: Sage.

Deluty, R. H. (1979). Children's Action Tendency Scale: A self-report measure of agressiveness, assertiveness, and submissiveness in children. *Journal of Consulting and Clinical Psychology, 47,* 1061–1071.

Digdon, N., & Gotlib, I. H. (1985). Developmental considerations in the study of childhood depression. *Developmental Review, 5,* 162–199.

Disbrow, M., & Doerr, H. (1983). *Parent–child interaction videotapes.* Unpublished material, University of Washington.

Dishion, T., Gardner, K., Patterson, G. R., Reid, J., Spyrou, S., & Thibodeaux, S. (1984). *The Family Process Code: A multidimensional system for observing family interactions.* Unpublished manual, Oregon Social Learning Center, Eugene.

Dix, T., & Grusec, J. E. (1985). Parent attribution processes in the socialization of children. In I. Sigel (Ed.), *Parental belief systems: The psychological consequences for children* (pp. 201–233). Hillsdale, NJ: Erlbaum.

Dix, T., Ruble, D. N., Grusec, J. E., & Nixon, S. (1986). Social cognition in parents: Inferential and affective reactions to children of three age levels. *Child Development, 57,* 879–894.

Dodge, K. A., McClaskey, C. L., & Feldman, E. (1985). Situational approach to the assessment of social competence in children. *Journal of Consulting and Clinical Psychology, 53,* 344–353.

Dodge, K. A., & Somberg, D. R. (1987). Hostile attributional biases among aggressive boys are exacerbated under conditions of threat to self. *Child Development, 58,* 213–224.

Dollinger, S. J., Thelan, M. H., & Walsh, M. L. (1980). Children's conceptions of psychological problems. *Journal of Clinical Child Psychology, 9,* 191–194.

Dreger, R. M., Lewis, P. M., Rich, T. A., Miller, K. S., Reid, M. P., Overlade, D. C., Taffel, C., & Flemming, E. L. (1964). Behavioral classification project. *Journal of Consulting Psychology, 28,* 1–13.

Dumas, J. E (1986). Indirect influence of maternal social contacts on mother–child interactions. *Journal of Abnormal Child Psychology, 14,* 205–216.

Dumas, J. E., & Wahler, R. G. (1983). Predictors of treatment outcome in parent training: Mother insularity and socioeconomic disadvantage. *Behavioral Assessment, 5,* 301–313.

Dunn, J., & Munn, P. (1986). Sibling quarrels and maternal intervention: Individual differences in understanding and aggression. *Journal of Child Psychology and Psychiatry, 27,* 583–597.

Dunst, C. J. (1984). *Parent–Child Interaction Rating Scale.* Unpublished scale, Western Carolina Center, Morganton, NC.

Dunst, C. J., Jenkins, V., & Trivette, C. M. (1984). The Family Support Scale: Reliability and validity. *Journal of Individual, Family, and Community Wellness, 1,* 45–52.

Dunst, C. J., & Trivette, C. M. (1985). *A guide to measures of social support and family behavior* (Monograph of the Technical Assistance Development System, No. 1). Chapel Hill, NC: University of North Carolina, Technical Assistance Development System.

Dunst, C. J., & Trivette, C. M. (1986). Looking beyond the parent–child dyad for the determinants of maternal styles of interaction. *Infant Mental Health Journal, 7,* 69–80.

Edelbrock, C. (1984). Developmental considerations. In T. H. Ollendick & M. Hersen (Eds.), *Child behavioral assessment: Principles and procedures* (pp. 20–37). New York: Pergamon Press.

Edelbrock, C., & Achenbach, T. M. (1985). *Manual for the Teacher's Report Form and Teacher Version of the Child Behavior Profile.* Burlington: University of Vermont, Department of Psychiatry.

Edelbrock, C., & Costello, A. J. (1984). Structured psychiatric interviews for children and adolescents. In G. Goldstein & M. Hersen (Eds.), *Handbook of psychological assessment.* (pp. 276–304). New York: Pergamon Press.

Edelbrock, C., Costello, A. J., Dulcan, M. J., Conover, N. C., & Kalas, R. (1986). Parent–child agreement of child psychiatric symptoms assessed via structured interview. *Journal of Child Psychology and Psychiatry, 27,* 181–190.

Edelbrock, C., Costello, A. J., Dulcan, M. J., Kalas, R., & Conover, N. C. (1985). Age differences in the reliability of the psychiatric interview of the child. *Child Development, 56,* 265–275.

Egeland, B., & Sroufe, L. A. (1981). Attachment and early maltreatment. *Child Development, 52,* 44–52.

Elbert, J. C. (1985a). Current trends and future needs in the training of child diagnostic assessment. In J. M. Tuma (Ed.), *Proceedings: Conference on training clinical child psychologists* (pp. 82–87). Baton Rouge: Louisiana State University, Department of Psychology.

Elbert, J. C. (1985b). Training in child diagnostic assessment. A survey of clinical psychology graduate programs. *Journal of Clinical Child Psychology, 13,* 122–133.

Eme, R. F. (1979). Sex differences in child psychopathology: A review. *Psychological Bulletin, 86,* 574–595.

Emery, R. E. (1982). Interparental conflict and the children of discord and divorce. *Psychological Bulletin, 92,* 310–330.

Emery, R. E., Binkoff, J. A., Houts, A. C., & Carr, E. G. (1983). Children as independent variables: Some clinical implications of child effects. *Behavioral Therapy, 14,* 398–412.

Endler, N. S., & Magnusson, D. (Eds.). (1976). *Interactional psychology and personality.* Washington, DC: Hemisphere.

Evans, I. M. (1985). Building systems models as a strategy for target behavior selection in clinical assessment. *Behavioral Assessment, 7,* 21–32.

Evans, I. M., & Nelson, R. O. (1977). Assessment of child behavior problems. In A. R. Ciminero, K. S. Calhoun, & H. E. Adams (Eds.), *Handbook of behavioral assessment* (pp. 603–681). New York: Wiley.

Evans, I. M., & Nelson, R. O. (1986). Assessment of children. In A. R. Ciminero, K. S. Calhoun, & H. E. Adams (Eds.), *Handbook of behavioral assessment* (2nd ed., pp. 601–630). New York: Wiley.

Eysenck, H. J., & Rachman, S. (1965). *The causes and cures of neurosis.* London: Routledge & Kegan Paul.

Fagot, B. I., & Hagan, R. (1987). *Coding of interactions: Is reliability really a problem?* Manuscript submitted for publication.

Fernald, C. D., & Gettys, L. (1978, August). *Effects of diagnostic labels on perceptions of children's behavior disorders.* Paper presented at the annual meeting of the American Psychological Association, Toronto.

Ferster, C. B. (1965). Classification of Behavioral pathology. In L. Krasner & L. P. Ullmann (Eds.), *Research in behavior modification: New developments and implications* (pp. 6–26). New York: Holt, Rinehart & Winston.

Ferster, C. B., & Skinner, B. F. (1953). *Schedules of reinforcement.* New York: Appleton-Century-Crofts.

Feshbach, N. (1987). *The construct of empathy and the physical maltreatment of children.* Manuscript submitted for publication.

Field, T. M., Huston, A., Quay, H. C., Troll, L., & Finley, G. E. (1982). *Review of human development.* New York: Wiley.

Filsinger, E. E. (1983). *Marriage and family assessment: A sourcebook for family therapy.* Beverly Hills, CA: Sage.

Filsinger, E. E., & Lewis, R. A. (Eds.). (1981). *Assessing marriage: New behavioral approaches.* Beverly Hills, CA: Sage.

Finch, A. J., & Rogers, T. R. (1984). Self-report instruments. In T. H. Ollendick & M. Hersen (Eds.), *Child behavioral assessment: principles and procedures* (pp. 106–123). New York: Pergamon Press.

Fincham, F. D., & Cain, K. M. (in press). Learned helplessness in humans: A developmental analysis. *Developmental Review.*

Finkelhor, D., & Associates. (1986). *A sourcebook on child sexual abuse.* Beverly Hills, CA: Sage.

Firestone, P., & Douglas, V. I. (1975). The effects of verbal and material rewards and punishers on the performance of impulsive and reflective children. *Child Study Journal, 7,* 71–78.

Flanagan, R. (1986). Teaching young children responses to inappropriate approaches by strangers in public places. *Child and Family Behavior Therapy, 8,* 27–43.

Fletcher, J. M. (1988). Brain-injured children. In E. J. Mash & L. G. Terdal (Eds.), *Behavioral assessment of childhood disorders* (2nd ed., unabridged, pp. 451–489). New York: Guilford Press.

Ford, J. D., & Kendall, P. C. (1979). Behavior therapists' professional behaviors: Converging evidence for a gap between theory and practice. *The Behavior Therapist, 2,* 37–38.

Forehand, R. (1977). Child noncompliance to parental requests: Behavioral analysis and treatment. In M. Hersen, R. M. Eisler, & P. M. Miller (Eds.), *Progress in behavior modification* (Vol. 5, 111–147). New York: Academic Press.

Forehand, R., Fauber, R., Long, N., Brody, G. H., & Slotkin, J. (1986). *Maternal depressive mood following divorce: An examination of predictors and adolescent adjustment from a stress model perspective.* Unpublished manuscript, University of Georgia.

Forehand, R., Long, N., Brody, G. H., & Fauber, R. (1986). Home predictors of young adolescents' school behavior and academic performance. *Child Development, 57,* 1528–1533.

Forehand, R. L., & McMahon, R. J. (1981). *Helping the noncompliant child: A clinician's guide to parent training.* New York: Guilford Press.

Forehand, R., Middleton, K., & Long, N. (1986). *Adolescent functioning as a consequence of recent parental divorce and the parent–adolescent relationship.* Unpublished manuscript, University of Georgia.

Forehand, R., Wells, K. C., McMahon, R. J., Griest, D. L., & Rogers, T. (1982). Maternal perceptions of maladjustment in clinic-referred children: An extension of earlier research. *Journal of Behavioral Asssssment, 4,* 145–151.

Forman, B. D., & Hagan, B. J. (1984). Measures for evaluating total family functioning. *Family Therapy, 11,* 1–36.

Foster, G. G., Ysseldyke, J. E., & Reese, J. H. (1975). I wouldn't have seen it, if I hadn't believed it. *Exceptional Children, 41,* 469–473.

Foster, S. L., & Cone, J. D. (1980). Current issues in direct observation. *Behavioral Assessment, 2,* 313–338.

Foster, S. L., & Cone, J. D. (1986). Design and use of direct observation procedures. In A. R. Ciminero, K. S. Calhoun, & H. E. Adams (Eds.), *Handbook of behavioral assessment* (2nd ed, pp. 253–324). New York: Wiley.

Foster, S. L., & Robin, A. L. (1988). Family conflict and communication in adolescence. In E. J. Mash & L. G. Terdal (Eds.), *Behavioral assessment of childhood disorders* (2nd ed., unabridged, pp. 717–775). New York: Guilford Press.

Freeman, B. J., & Schroth, P. C. (1984). The development of the Behavioral Observation System (BOS) for autism. *Behavioral Assessment, 6,* 177–187.

Friedlander, S., Weiss, D. S., & Traylor, J. (1986). Assessing the influence of maternal depression on the validity of the Child Behavior Checklist. *Journal of Abnormal Child Psychology, 14,* 123–133

Friedrich, W. N. (1979). Predictors of the coping behavior of mothers of handicapped children. *Journal of Consulting and Clinical Psychology, 57,* 1140–1141.

Furman, W. (1980). Promoting social development: Developmental implications for treatment. In B. B. Lahey & A. E. Kazdin (Eds.), *Advances in clinical child psychology* (Vol. 3, pp. 1–40). New York: Plenum.

Furman, W., & Buhrmester, D. (1985a). Children's perceptions of the personal relationships in their social networks. *Developmental Psychology, 21,* 1016–1024.

Furman, W., & Buhrmester, D. (1985b). Children's perceptions of the qualities of sibling relationships. *Child Development, 56,* 448–461.

Furman, W., & Drabman, R. (1981). Methodological issues in child behavior therapy. In M. Hersen, R. M. Eisler, & P.M. Miller (Eds.), *Progress in behavior modification* (Vol. 11, pp. 31–64). New York: Academic Press.

Furman, W., & Masters, J. C. (1980). Affective consequences of social reinforcement, punishment and neutral behavior. *Developmental Psychology, 16,* 100–104.

Garber, J. (1984). Classification of child psychopathology: A developmental perspective. *Child Development, 55,* 30–48.

Garcia-Coll, C., Kagan, J., & Raznick, J. S. (1984). Behavioral inhibition in young children. *Child Development, 55,* 1005–1019.

Gardner, J. M., & Breuer, A. (1985). Reliability and validity of a microcomputer assessment system for developmentally disabled persons. *Education and Training of the Mentally Retarded, 5,* 209–212.

Garmezy, N., & Rutter, M. (Eds). (1983). *Stress, coping, and development in children.* New York: McGraw-Hill.

Garmezy, N., & Rutter, M. (1985). Acute reactions to stress. In M. Rutter & L. Hersov (Eds.), *Child and adolescent psychiatry: Modern approaches* (2nd ed., pp. 152–176). Oxford: Blackwell Scientific Publications.

Garmezy, N., & Tellegen, A. (1984). Studies of stress resistant children: Methods, variables and preliminary findings. In F. Morrison, C. Lord, & D. Keating (Eds.), *Advances in applied developmental psychology* (Vol. 1, pp. 231–287). New York: Academic Press.

Gdowski, C. L., Lachar, D., & Kline, R. B. (1985). A PIC profile typology of children and adolescents: 1. Empirically derived alternative to traditional diagnosis. *Journal of Abnormal Psychology, 94,* 346–361.

Gelfand, D. M., & Hartmann, D. P. (1984). *Child behavior analysis and therapy* (2nd ed.). New York: Pergamon Press.

Gibaud-Wallston, J., & Wandersman, L. P. (1978, August). *Development and utility of the Parenting Sense of Competence Scale.* Paper presented at the meeting of the American Psychological Association, Toronto.

Gittelman, R. (1985). Anxiety disorders in children. In B. B. Lahey & A. E. Kazdin (Eds.), *Advances in clinical child psychology* (Vol. 8, pp. 53–79). New York: Plenum.

Gjerde, P. F. (1986). The interpersonal structure of family interaction settings: Parent adolescent relations in dyads versus triads. *Developmental Psychology, 22,* 297–304.

Goldfried, M. R., & Kent, R. N. (1972). Traditional versus behavioral assessment: A comparison of methodological and theoretical assumptions. *Psychological Bulletin, 77,* 409–420.

Goldsmith, H. H., & Compos, J. J. (1986). Fundamental issues in the study of early temperament: The Denver Twin Temperament Study. In M. E. Lamb, A. L. Brown, & B. Rogoff (Eds.), *Advances in developmental psychology* (Vol. 4, pp. 231–283). Hillsdale, NJ: Erlbaum.

Goldstein, A. P., Keller, H., & Erne, D. (1985). *Changing the abusive parent.* Champaign, IL: Research Press.

Goldstein, G., & Hersen, M. (1984). *Handbook of psychological assessment.* New York: Pergamon Press.

Gordon, D. A., Jones, R. H., & Nowicki, S. (1979). A measure of intensity of parental punishment. *Journal of Personality Assessment, 43,* 485–496.

Gorham, K. A., DesJardins, C., Page, R., Pettis, E., & Scheiber, B. (1975). Effect on parents. In N. Hobbs (Ed.), *Issues in the classification of children* (Vol. 2, pp. 154–188). San Francisco: Jossey-Bass.

Gottman, J. M. (1982). *Time-series analysis: A comprehensive introduction for social scientists.* New York: Cambridge University Press.

Gottman, J. M., & Levenson, R. W. (1985). A valid procedure for obtaining self-report of affect in marital interaction. *Journal of Consulting and Clinical Psychology, 53,* 151–160.

Gottman, J. M., & Levenson, R. W. (1986). Assessing the role of emotion in marriage. *Behavioral Assessment, 8,* 31–48.

Gottman, J. M., & Ringland, J. T. (1981).The analysis of dominance and bidirectionality in social development. *Child Development, 52,* 393–412.

Gottman, J., & Roy, A. (in press.) *Sequential analysis.* New York: Cambridge University Press.

Greenspan, S.I. (1981). *The clinical interview of the child.* New York: McGraw-Hill.

Greenspan, S. I., & Lourie, R. S. (1981). Developmental structuralist approach to the classification of adaptive and pathologic personality organizations: Infancy and early childhood. *American Journal of Psychiatry, 138,* 725–735.

Greenspan, S. I., & Porges, S. W. (1984). Psychopathology in infancy and early childhood: Clinical perspectives on the organization of sensory and affective-thematic experience. *Child Development, 55,* 49–70.

Greenwood, C. R., Delquadri, J. C., Stanley, S. O., Terry, B., Hall, R. V. (1985). Assessment of ecobehavioral interaction in school settings. *Behavioral Assessment, 7,* 331–348.

Gross, A. M. (1984). Behavioral interviewing. In T. H. Ollendick & M. Hersen (Eds.), *Child behavioral assessment: Principles and procedures* (pp. 61–79). New York: Pergamon Press.

Gross, A. M., & Drabman, R. S. (in press). *Handbook of clinical behavioral prediatrics.* New York: Plenum.

Group for the Advancement of Psychiatry. (1974). *Psychopathological disorders in childhood: Theoretical considerations and a proposed classification.* New York: Jason Aronson.

Grusec, J. E., & Kuczynski, L. (1980). Direction of effect in socialization: A comparison of the parent's versus the child's behavior as determinants of disciplinary techniques. *Developmental Psychology, 16,* 1–9.

Guidubaldi, J., & Cleminshaw, H. K. (1985). The development of the Cleminshaw–Guidubaldi Parent Satisfaction Scale. *Journal of Clinical Child Psychology, 14,* 293–298.

Gurman, A. S., & Kniskern, D. P. (Eds.). (1981). *Handbook of family therapy.* New York: Brunner/Mazel.

Guskin, S. L., Bartel, N. R., & MacMillan, D. L. (1975). Perspective of the labeled child. In N. Hobbs (Ed.), *Issues in the classification of children* (Vol. 2, pp. 185–212). San Francisco: Jossey-Bass.

Hammen, C. L., Gordon, D. S., Adrian, C., Burge, D., Jaenicke, C., & Hiroto, D. (1986, May). *Children of depressed mothers: Predictors of risk.* Paper presented at the annual meeting of the American Psychiatric Association, Washington, DC.

Harris, A. M., & Reid, J. B. (1981). The consistency of a class of coercive child behavior across school settings for individual subjects. *Journal of Abnormal Child Psychology, 9,* 219–227.

Harris, S. L. (1974). The relationship between family income and number of parent-perceived problems. *International Journal of Social Psychiatry, 20,* 109–112.

Harris, S. L. (1979). DSM-III—its implications for children. *Child Behavior Therapy, 1,* 37–46.

Harris, S. L. (1984). The family of the autistic child: A behavioral systems view. *Clinical Psychology Review, 4,* 227–239.

Harris, S. L., & Ferrari, M. (1983). Developmental factors in child behavior therapy. *Behavior Therapy, 14,* 54–72.

Harris, S. L., & Powers, M. D. (1984). Diagnostic issues. In T. H. Ollendick & M. Hersen (Eds.), *Child behavioral assessment: Principles and procedures* (pp. 38–57). New York: Pergamon Press.

Harter, S. (1982). The Perceived Competence Scale for Children. *Child Development, 53,* 87–97.

Harter, S. (1983). Developmental perspectives on the self-system. In E. M. Hetherington (Ed.), *Handbook of child psychology,* (4th ed.): *Vol. 4. Socialization, personality, and social development* (pp. 275–386). New York: Wiley.

Harter, S., & Pike, R. (1984). The pictorial scale of perceived competence and social acceptance for young children. *Child Development, 55,* 1969–1982.

Hartmann, D. P. (1976, September). *Must the baby follow the bathwater? Psychometric principles—behavioral data.* Paper presented at the annual meeting of the American Psychological Association, Washington, DC.

Hartmann, D. P. (1982). *Using observers to study behavior.* San Francisco: Jossey-Bass.

Hartmann, D. P. (1983). Editorial. *Behavioral Assessment, 5,* 1–3

Hartmann, D. P. (1984). Assessment strategies. In D. H. Barlow & M. Hersen (Eds.), *Single case experimental designs: Strategies for studying behavior change* (2nd ed., pp. 107–139). New York: Pergamon Press.

Hartmann, D. P., Roper, B. L., & Bradford, D. C. (1979). Some relationships between behavioral and traditional assessment. *Journal of Behavioral Assessment, 1,* 3–21.

Hartup, W. W. (1979). Peer relations and the growth of social competence. In M. W. Kent & J. E. Rolf (Eds.), *Primary prevention of psychopathology* (Vol. 3, pp. 150–170). Hanover, NH: University Press of New England.

Hartup, W. W. (1986a). On relationships and development. In W. W. Hartup & Z. Rubin (Eds.), *Relationships and development* (pp. 1–26). Hillsdale, NJ: Erlbaum.

Hartup, W. W. (1986a, October). *Relationships and regulation: Trends and issues in childhood socialization.* Paper presented at Future Directions in Child Psychology Conference, Iowa City, IA.

Hawkins, R. P. (1975). Who decided that was the problem? Two stages of responsibility for applied behavior analysis. In W. S. Wood (Ed.), *Issues in evaluating behavior modification.* Champaign, IL: Research Press.

Hawkins, R. P. (1979). The functions of assessment: Implications for selection and development of devices for assessing repertoires in clinical, educational, and other settings. *Journal of Applied Behavior Analysis, 12,* 501–516.

Hawkins, R. P. (1982). Developing a behavior code. In D. P. Hartmann (Ed.), *Using observers to study behavior* (pp. 21–35). San Francisco: Jossey-Bass.

Haynes, S. C., & Nelson, R. O. (1986). *Conceptual foundations of behavioral assessment.* New York: Guilford Press.

Haynes, S. N. (1978). *Principles of behavioral assessment.* New York: Gardner Press.

Haynes, S. N. (1983). Behavioral assessment. In M. Hersen, A. E. Kazdin, & A. S. Bellack (Eds.), *Clinical psychology handbook.* New York: Pergamon Press.

Haynes, S. N., & Jensen, B. J. (1979). The interview as a behavioral assessment instrument. *Behavioral Assessment, 1,* 97–106.

Hazzard, A., Christensen, A., & Margolin, G. (1983). Children's perceptions of parental behaviors. *Journal of Abnormal Child Psychology, 11,* 49–60.

Henker, B., Astor-Dubin, L., & Varni, J.W. (1986). Psychostimulant medication and perceived intensity in hyperactive children. *Journal of Abnormal Child Psychology, 14,* 105–114.

Herbert, M. (1981). *Behavioural treatment of problem children: A practice manual.* London: Academic Press.

Herjanic, B., & Reich, W. (1982). Development of a structured psychiatric interview for children. *Journal of Abnormal Child Psychology, 10,* 307–324.

Hersen, M., & Bellack, A. S. (Eds.). (1981). *Behavioral assessment: A practical handbook* (2nd ed.). New York: Pergamon Press.

Hersen, M., & Van Hasselt, V. B. (Ed.). (1987). *Behavior therapy with children and adolescents: A clinical approach.* New York: Wiley.

Hobbs, N. (1975). *Issues in the classification of children* (Vols. 1 & 2). San Francisco: Jossey-Bass.

Hobbs, S. A., Beck, S. J., & Wansley, R. A. (1984). Pediatric behavioral medicine: Directions in treatment and intervention. In M. Hersen, R. M. Eisler, & P. M. Miller (Eds.), *Progress in behavior modification* (Vol. 16, pp. 1–29). New York: Academic Press.

Hodges, K. (1985). *Manual for the Child Assessment Schedule (CAS).* Durham, NC: Duke University Medical Center.

Holden, G. W. (1985a). Analyzing parental reasoning with microcomputer-presented problems. *Simulation and Games, 16,* 203–210.

Holden, G. W. (1985b, July). *Caregiving experience and adults' cognitive responses to a problematic parent–child setting.* Paper presented at the Biennial Meeting of the International Society for the Study of Behavioural Development, Tours, France.

Holden, G. W. (1985c, April). *Diagnosing why a baby is crying: The effect of caregiving experience.* Paper presented at the Biennial Meeting of the Society for Research in Child Development, Toronto.

Holden, G. W. (1985d). How parents create a social environment via proactive behavior. In T. Garling & J. Valsiner (Eds.), *Children within environments* (pp. 193–215). New York: Plenum.

Holland, C. J. (1970). An interview guide for behavioral counseling with parents. *Behavior Therapy, 1,* 70–79.

Holman, A. M. (1983). *Family assessment: Tools for understanding and intervention.* Beverly Hills, CA: Sage.

Hops, H., Biglan, A., Sherman, L., Arthur, J., Friedman, L., & Osteen, V. (1987). Home observations of family interactions of depressed women. *Journal of Consulting and Clinical Psychology, 55,* 341–346.

Hops, H., Biglan, A., Sherman, L., Arthur, J., Warner, P., Holcomb, C., Oosternink, N., & Osteen, V. (1986). *Revised LIFE (Living in Familial Environments) system.* Unpublished manuscript, Oregon Research Institute, Eugene.

Hops, H., & Cobb, J. A. (1973). Survival behaviors in the educational setting: Their implications for research and intervention. In L. A. Hamerlynck, L. C. Handy, & E. J. Mash (Eds.), *Behavior change: Methodology, concepts and practice* (pp. 193–208). Champaign, IL: Research Press.

Hops, H., & Greenwood, C. (1981). Social skills deficits. In E. J. Mash & L. G. Terdal (Eds.), *Behavioral assessment of childhood disorders* (pp. 347–396). New York: Guilford Press.

Hops, H., & Lewin (1984). Peer sociometric forms. In T. H. Ollendick & M. Hersen (Eds.), *Child behavioral assessment: Principles and procedures* (pp. 124–147). New York: Pergamon Press.

Horowitz, L. M., Post, D. L., French, R. deS., Wallis, K. D., & Siegelman, E. Y. (1981). The prototype as a construct in abnormal psychology: 2. Clarifying disagreement in psychiatric judgements. *Journal of Abnormal Psychology, 90,* 575–585.

Horowitz, L. M., Wright, J. C., Lowenstein, E., & Parad, H. W. (1981). The prototype as a construct in abnormal psychology: 1. A method for deriving prototypes. *Journal of Abnormal Psychology, 90,* 568–574.

Hughes, H. M., & Haynes, S. N. (1978). Structured laboratory observation in the behavioral assessment of parent–child interactions: A methodological critique. *Behavior Therapy, 9,* 428–447.

Hulbert, T. A., Gdowski, C. L., & Lachar, D. (1986). Interparent agreement on the Personality Inventory for Children: Are substantial correlations sufficient? *Journal of Abnormal Child Psychology, 14,* 115–122.

Hymphreys, L. E., & Ciminero, A. R. (1979). Parent report measures of child behavior: A review. *Journal of Clinical Child Psychology, 5,* 56–63.

Hymel, S. (1986). Interpretations of peer behavior: Affective bias in childhood and adolesence. *Child Development, 57,* 431–445.

Ireton, H., & Thwing, E. J. (1974). *Minnesota Child Development Inventory.* Minneapolis: Behavior Science Systems.

Jacob, R. G., O'Leary, K. D., & Rosenblad, C. (1978). Formal and informal classroom settings: Effects on hyperactivity. *Journal of Abnormal Child Psychology, 6,* 47–59.

Jacobson, N. S. (1985). The role of observational measures in behavior therapy outcome research. *Behavioral Assessment, 7,* 297–308.

Jensen, B. J., & Haynes, S. N. (1986). Self-report questionnaires and inventories. In A. R. Ciminero, K. S. Calhoun, & H. E. Adams (Eds.), *Handbook of behavioral assessment* (2nd ed, pp. 150–179). New York: Wiley.

Jewett, J. F., & Clark, H. B. (1979). Teaching preschoolers to use appropriate dinnertime conversation: An analysis of generalization from school to home. *Behavior Therapy, 10,* 589–605.

Johnson, S. B. (1988). Chronic illness and pain. In E. J. Mash & L. G. Terdal (Eds.), *Behavioral assessment of childhood disorders* (2nd ed., unabridged, pp. 491–527). New York: Guilford Press.

Johnson, S. M., & Bolstad, O. D. (1973). Methodological issues in naturalistic observation: Some problems and solutions for field research. In L. A. Hamerlynck, L. C. Handy, & E. J. Mash (Eds.), *Behavior change: Methodology, concepts, and practice* (pp. 7–67). Champaign, IL: Research Press.

Johnson, S. M., & Lobitz, G. K. (1974). Parental manipulation of child behavior in home observations. *Journal of Applied Behavior Analysis, 7,* 23–32.

Joreskog, K. G., & Sorbom, D. (1983). *LISREL VI: Analysis of linear structural of relationships by maximum likelihood and least squares methods* (2nd ed.). Chicago: Natural Education Resources.

Kagan, J. (1983). Classifications of the child. In W. Kessen (Ed.), *Handbook of child psychology* (4th ed.): *Vol. 1. History, theory, and methods* (pp. 527–560). New York: Wiley.

Kallman, W. M., & Feuerstein, M.J. (1986). Psychophysiological procedures. In A. R. Ciminero, K. S. Calhoun, & H. E. Adams (Eds.), *Handbook of behavioral assessment* (2nd ed, pp. 325–352). New York: Wiley.

Kanfer, F. H. (1972). Assessment for behavior modification. *Journal of Personality Assessment, 36,* 418–423.

Kanfer, F. H. (1979). A few comments on the current status of behavioral assessment. *Behavioral Assessment, 1*, 37–39.

Kanfer, F. H. (1985). Target selection for clinical change programs. *Behavioral Assessment, 7*, 7–20.

Kanfer, F. H., & Busemeyer, J. R. (1982). The use of problem-solving and decision-making in behavior therapy. *Clinical Psychology Review, 2*, 239–266.

Kanfer, F. H., & Grimm, L. G. (1977). Behavioral analysis: Selecting target behaviors in the interview. *Behavior Modification, 1*, 7–28.

Kanfer, F. H., & Nay, W. R. (1982). Behavioral assessment. In G. T. Wilson & C. M. Franks (Eds.), *Contemporary behavior therapy: Conceptual and empirical foundations* (pp. 367–402). New York: Guilford Press.

Kanfer, F. H., & Phillips, J. S. (1970). *Learning foundations of behavior therapy.* New York: Wiley.

Kanfer, F. H., & Saslow, G. (1969). Behavioral diagnosis. In C. M. Franks (Ed.), *Behavior therapy: Appraisal and status* (pp. 417–444). New York: McGraw-Hill.

Karoly, P. (1981). Self-management problems in children. In E. J. Mash & L. G. Terdal (Eds.), *Behavioral assessment of childhood disorders* (pp. 79–126). New York: Guilford Press.

Karoly, P. (1985). *Measurement strategies in health psychology.* New York: Wiley-Interscience.

Karoly, P., & Steffen, J. J. (1980). *Improving the long-term effects of psychotherapy.* New York: Garden Press.

Kates, N. (1986). *The psychological impact of unemployment.* Unpublished manuscript, East Region Mental Health Services, Hamilton, Ontario.

Kaufman, A. S., & Kaufman, N. L. (1983). *Kaufman assessment battery for children.* Circle Pines, MN: American Guidance Services.

Kaufman, A. S., & Reynolds, C. R. (1984). Intellectual and academic achievement tests. In T. H. Ollendick & M. Hersen (Eds.), *Child behavioral assessment: Principles and procedures* (pp. 195–222). New York: Pergamon Press.

Kaye, K. (1984). Toward a developmental psychology of the family. In L. L'Abate (Ed.), *Handbook of family psychology and psychotherapy.* Homewood, IL: Dow Jones/Irwin.

Kazdin, A. E. (1977). Assessing the clinical or applied importance of behavior change through social validation. *Behavior Modification, 1*, 427–452.

Kazdin, A. E. (1979). Situational specificity: The two-edged sword of behavioral assessment. *Behavioral Assessment, 1*, 57–75.

Kazdin, A. E. (1981). Acceptability of child treatment techniques: The influence of treatment efficacy and adverse side effects. *Behavior Therapy, 12*, 493–506.

Kazdin, A. E. (1982a). Observer effects: Reactivity of direct observation. In D. P. Hartmann (Ed.), *Using observers to study behavior* (pp. 5–19). San Francisco: Jossey-Bass.

Kazdin, A. E. (1982b). Symptom substitution, generalization, and response covariation: Implications for psychotherapy outcome. *Psychological Bulletin, 91*, 349–365.

Kazdin, A. E. (1983). Psychiatric diagnosis, dimensions of dysfunction and child behavior therapy. *Behavior Therapy, 14*, 73–99.

Kazdin, A. E. (1984). Acceptability of aversive procedures and medication as treatment alternatives for deviant child behavior. *Journal of Abnormal Child Psychology, 12*, 289–302.

Kazdin, A. E. (1985). Selection of target behaviors: The relationship of the treatment focus to clinical dysfunction. *Behavioral Assessment, 7*, 33–47.

Kelly, J. A. (1983). *Treating child-abusive families: Intervention based on skills training.* New York: Plenum.

Kelso, J., & Stewart, M. A. (1986). Factors which predict the persistence of aggressive conduct disorder. *Journal of Child Psychology and Psychiatry, 27*, 77–86.

Kendall, P.C. (1982). Integration: Behavior therapy and other schools of thought. *Behavior Therapy, 13*, 550–571.

Kendall, P. C., & Hollon, S. D. (Eds.). (1981). *Cognitive-behavioral interventions: Assessment methods.* New York: Academic Press.

Kendall, P.C., Lerner, R. M., & Craighead, W. E. (1984). Human development and intervention in child psychopathology. *Child Development, 55*, 71–82.

Kendall, P. C., & Wilcox, L. E. (1979). Self-control in children: Development of a rating scale. *Journal of Consulting and Clinical Psychology, 47*, 1020–1029.

Kessler, J. W. (1971). Nosology in child psychopathology. In H. E. Rie (Ed.), *Perspectives in child psychopathology.* Chicago: Aldine-Atherton.

Kestenbaum, C. J., & Bird, H. R. (1978). A reliability study of the Mental Health Assessment Form for School-Age Children. *Journal of the American Academy of Child Psychiatry, 7*, 338–347.

Kiesler, C. A. (1983). Social psychological issues in studying consumer satisfaction with behavior therapy. *Behavior Therapy, 14*, 226–236.

Kotsopoulos, S., & Mellor, C. (1986). Extralinguistic speech characteristics of children with conduct and anxiety disorders. *Journal of Child Psychology and Psychiatry, 27*, 99–108.

Kovacs, M. (1978). Rating scales to assess depression in school aged children. *Acta Paedopsychiatrica, 46*, 305–315.

Kovacs, M. (1982). *The longitudinal study of child and adolescent psychopathology: I. The semi-structured psychiatric Interview Schedule for Children (ISC).* Unpublished manuscript.

Kovacs, M. (1985). ISC (The Interview Schedule for Children). *Psychopharmacology Bulletin, 21*, 991–994.

Krasnegor, N. A., Arasteh, J. D., & Cataldo, M. F. (Eds.). (1986). *Child health behavior: A behavioral pediatrics perspective.* New York: Wiley.

Kratochwill, T. R. (1985). Selection of target behaviors in behavioral consultation. *Behavioral Assessment, 7*, 49–62.

Kropp, J. P., & Haynes, O. M. (1987). Abusive and nonabusive mothers' ability to identify general and specific emotion signals of infants. *Child Development, 58*, 187–190.

Kurdek, L. A. (1986). Children's reasoning about parental divorce. In R. D. Ashmore & D. M. Brodzinsky (Eds.), *Thinking about the family: Views of parents and children* (pp. 233–276). Hillsdale, NJ: Erlbaum.

Kurdek, L. A. (in press). Children's adjustment to parental divorce: An ecological perspective. In J. P. Vincent (Ed.), *Advances in family intervention, assessment and theory* (Vol. 4). Greewich, CT: JAI Press.

Lachar, D. (1982). *Personality Inventory for Children (PIC) revised format manual supplement.* Los Angeles: Western Psychological Services

Lamb, M. E. (Ed.). (1982). *Nontraditional families: Parenting and child development.* Hillsdale, NJ: Erlbaum.

Laney, M. D., & Lewis, M. (1985, April). *Assessing affective involvement and style in early mother child interactions: Implications for emergent child psychopathology.* Paper presented at the meeting of the Society for Research in Child Development, Toronto.

Langer, E. J., & Abelson, R. P. (1974). A patient by any other name . . . : Clinician group difference in labeling bias. *Journal of Consulting and Clinical Psychology, 42,* 4–9.

Langner, T. S., Gersten, J. C., McCarthy, E. D., Eisenberg, G., Greene, E. L., Hersen, J. H., & Jameson, J. D. (1976). A screening inventory for assessing psychiatric impairment in children six to eight. *Journal of Consulting and Clinical Psychology, 44,* 286–296.

Lapouse, R., & Monk, M. A. (1958). An epidemiologic study of behavior characteristic in children. *American Journal of Public Health, 48,* 1134–1144.

Larrance, D. T., & Twentyman, C. T. (1983). Maternal attributions and child abuse. *Journal of Abnormal Psychology, 92,* 449–457.

Larzelere, R. E., Amberson, T. G., Martin, J. A., Handler, J., & Alibrando, S. A. (1985, August). *Developmental changes in discipline problems during the toddler years.* Paper presented at the meeting of the American Psychological Association, Los Angeles.

Larzelere, R. E., Martin, J. A., & Amberson, T. G. (1985). *Toddler Behavior Checklist, Form B.* Unpublished scale, Biola University, La Mirada, CA.

Layne, C. C., Rickard, H. C., Jones, M. T., & Lyman, R. D. (1976). Accuracy of self-monitoring on a variable ratio schedule of observer verification. *Behavior Therapy, 7,* 481–488.

LeBow, J. (1982). Consumer satisfaction with mental health treatment. *Psychological Bulletin, 91,* 244–259.

Lee, C. M., & Gotlib, I. H. (1986). *Family disruption and child adjustment: An integrative review.* Manuscript submitted for publication.

Leitenberg, H., Yost, L. W., & Carroll-Wilson, M. (1986). Negative cognitive errors in children: Questionnaire development, normative data, and comparisons between children with and without self reported symptoms of depression, low self-esteem, and evaluation anxiety. *Journal of Consulting and Clinical Psychology, 54,* 528–536.

Loeber, R. (1982). The stability of antisocial and delinquent child behavior: A review. *Child Development, 53,* 1431–1446.

Loeber, R., & Dishion, T. J. (1983). Early predictors of male delinquency: A review. *Psychological Bulletin, 94,* 68–99.

Loeber, R., Dishion, T. J., & Patterson, G. R. (1984). Multiple gating: A miltistage assessment procedure for identifying youths at risk for delinquency. *Journal of Research in Crime and Delinquency, 21,* 7–32.

Lorion, R. P., Cowen, E. L., & Caldwell, R. A. (1974). Problem types of children referred to a school-based mental health program. *Journal of Consulting and Clinical Psychology, 42,* 491–496.

Lovitt, T.C. (1973). Self-management projects with children with learning disabilities. *Journal of Learning Disabilities, 6,* 15–28.

Lutzker, J. R., & Lamazor, E. A. (1985). Behavioral pediatrics: Research, treatment, recommendations. In M. Hersen, R. M. Eisler, & P. M. Miller (Eds.), *Progress in behavior modification* (Vol. 19, pp. 217–253). New York: Academic Press.

Lytton, H. (1979). Disciplinary encounters between young boys and their mothers and fathers: Is there a contingency system? *Developmental Psychology, 15,* 256–268.

MacFarlane, J. W., Allen L., & Honzik, M. P. (1954). *A developmental study of the behavior problems of normal children between twenty-one months and fourteen years.* Berkeley: University of California Press.

MacPhee, D., Benson, J. B., & Bullock, D. (1984) *Self-perceptions of the parental role.* Unpublished manuscript, University of Denver.

Madsen, C. K., & Madsen, C. H. (1972). *Parents, children, discipline: A positive approach.* Boston: Allyn & Bacon.

Margolin, G. (1983). An interactional model for the behavioral assessment of marital relationships. *Behavioral Assessment, 5,* 103–127.

Martin, G., & Pear, J. *Behavior modification: What it is and how to do it* (2nd. ed.). Englewood Cliffs, NJ: Prentice-Hall.

Martin, S., Johnson, S., Johansson, S., & Wahl, G. (1976). The comparability of behavioral data in laboratory and natural settings. In E. J. Mash, L. A. Hamerlynck, & L. C. Handy (Eds.), *Behavior modification and families* (pp. 189–203). New York: Brunner/Mazel.

Mash E. J. (1979). What is behavioral assessment? *Behavioral Assessment, 1,* 23–29.

Mash, E. J. (1984). Families with problem children. In A. Doyle, D. Gold, & D. Moskowitz (Eds.), *Children in families under stress* (pp. 65–84). San Francisco: Jossey-Bass.

Mash, E. J. (1985). Some comments on target selection in behavior therapy. *Behavioral Assessment, 7,* 63–78.

Mash, E. J., & Barkley, R. A. (1986). Assessment of family interaction with the Response-Class Matrix. In R. J. Prinz (Ed.), *Advances in the behavioral assessment of children and families* (pp. 29–67). Greenwich, CT: JAI Press Inc.

Mash, E. J., & Barkley, R. A. (Eds.). (in press). *Behavioral treatment of childhood disorders.* New York: Guilford Press.

Mash, E. J., & Dalby, J. T. (1979). Behavioral interventions for hyperactivity. In R. L. Trites (Ed.), *Hyperactivity in children: Etiology, measurement, and treatment implication* (pp. 161–216). Baltimore: University Park Press.

Mash, E. J., & Johnston, C. (1980). *Child Development Questionnaire.* Unpublished scale, University of Calgary, Department of Psychology.

Mash, E. J., & Johnston, C. (1983a). A note on the prediction of of mothers' behavior with their hyperactive children during play and task situations. *Child and Family Behavior Therapy, 5,* 1–14.

Mash, E. J., & Johnston, C. (1983b). Parental perceptions of child behavior problems, parenting self-esteem and mother's reported stress in younger and older hyperactive aNd normal children. *Journal of Consulting and Clinical Psychology, 51,* 86–99.

Mash, E. J., & Johnston, C. (1983c). Sibling interactions of hyperactive and normal children and their relationship to reports of maternal stress and self-esteem. *Journal of Clinical Child Psychology, 12,* 91–99.

Mash, E. J., & Johnston, C. (1986). *Norms for the Parenting Sense of Competence Scale.* Unpublished manuscript, University of Calgary, Department of Psychology.

Mash, E. J., Johnston, C., & Kovitz, K. (1983). A comparison of the mother–child interactions of physically abused and non-abused children during play and task situations. *Journal of Clinical Child Psychology, 12,* 337–346.

Mash, E. J., & Terdal, L. G. (Eds.). (1976). *Behavior therapy assessment: Diagnosis, design, and evaluation.* New York: Springer.

Mash, E. J., & Terdal, L. G. (1980). Follow-up assessments in behavior therapy. In P. Karoly & J. J. Steffen (Eds.), *The long-range effects of psychotherapy: Models of durable outcome* (pp. 99–147). New York: Gardner Press.

Mash, E. J., & Terdal, L. G. (Eds.). (1981a). *Behavioral assessment of childhood disorders.* New York: Guilford Press.

Mash, E. J., & Terdal, L. G. (1981b). Behavioral assessment of childhood disturbance. In E. J. Mash & L. G. Terdal (Eds.). *Behavioral assessment of childhood disorders* (pp. 3–76). New York: Guilford Press.

Mash, E. J., Terdal, L. G., & Anderson, K. (1973). The Response-Class Matrix: A procedure for recording parent–child interactions. *Journal of Consulting and Clinical Psychology, 40,* 163–164.

Masten, A. S. (1986, August). *Patterns of adaptation to stress in middle childhood.* Paper presented at the meeting of the American Psychological Association, Washington, DC.

Matarazzo, J. D. (1983). Computerized psychological testing. *Science, 221,* 323.

McFall, R. M. (1982). A review and reformulation of the concept of social skills. *Behavioral Assessment, 4,* 1–33.

McFall, R. M. (1986). Theory and method in assessment: The vital link. *Behavioral Assessment, 8,* 3–10.

McGillicuddy-DeLisi, A. V. (1985). The relationship between parental beliefs and children's cognitive level. In I. Sigel (Ed.), *Parental belief systems: The psychological consequences for children* (pp. 7–24). Hillsdale, NJ: Erlbaum.

McIntyre, T. J., Bornstein, P. H., Isaacs, C. D., Woody, D. J., Bornstein, M. T., Clucas, T. J., & Long, G. (1983). Naturalistic observation of conduct disordered children: An archival analysis. *Behavior Therapy, 14,* 375–385.

McKenzie, T. L., & Rushall, B. S. (1974). Effects of self-recording on attendance and performance in a competitive swimming training environment. *Journal of Applied Behavior Analysis, 7,* 199–206.

McKinney, B., & Peterson, R. A. (1987). Predictors of stress in parents of developmentally disabled children. *Journal of Pediatric Psychology, 12,* 133–150.

McLemore, C. W., & Benjamin, L. (1979). Whatever happened to interpersonal diagnosis?: A psychosocial alternative to DSM-III. *American Psychologist, 34,* 17–34.

McMahon, R. J. (1984). Self-report instruments. In T. H. Ollendick & M. Hersen (Eds.), *Child behavioral assessment: Principles and procedures* (pp. 80–105). New York: Pergamon Press.

McMahon, R. J. & Forehand, R. (1983). Consumer satisfaction in behavioral treatment of children: Types, issues, and recommendations. *Behavior Therapy, 14,* 209–225.

McMahon, R. J., & Peters, R. DeV. (Eds.). (1985). *Childhood disorders: Behavioral–developmental approaches.* New York: Brunner/Mazel.

McReynolds, P. (1975). Historical antecedents of personality assessment. In P. McReynolds (Ed.), *Advances in psychological assessment* (Vol. 3, pp. 477–532). San Francisco: Jossey-Bass.

Meadow-Orlans, K. P. (1986). *Impact of a child's hearing loss: A questionnaire for parents.* Unpublished manuscript, Gallaudet College Research Institute, Washington, DC.

Meehl, P. H. (1954). *Clinical versus statistical prediction: A theoretical analysis and review of the evidence.* Minneapolis: University of Minnesota Press.

Messick, S. (1983). Assessment of children. In W. Kessen (Ed.), *Handbook of child psychology* (4th ed.): Vol. 1, *History, theory, and methods* (pp. 477–526). New York: Wiley.

Michelson, L., & Wood, R. (1982). Development and psychometric properties of the Children's Assertive Behavior Inventory. *Journal of Behavioral Assessment, 4,* 3–13.

Milich, R., Loney, J., & Landau, S. (1982). The independent dimensions of hyperactivity and aggression: A validation with playroom observation data. *Journal of Abnormal Psychology, 91,* 183–198.

Miller, H., & Clarke, D. (1978). *Effective parental attention* [Videotape]. Los Angeles: University of California at Los Angeles.

Miller, L. C., Hampe, E., Barrett, C., & Nobel, H. (1971). Children's deviant behavior within the general population. *Journal of Consulting and Clinical Psychology, 37,* 16–22.

Mindell, J. A., Andrasik, F., Quinn, S. J., Blake, D. D., Kabela, E., & McCarran, M. S. (1986, November). *Antecedents and consequences of pediatric headache: Validation of clinical interviews.* Paper presented at the meeting of the Association for Advancement of Behavior Therapy, Chicago.

Mink, I. T., Meyers, C. E., & Nihara, K. (1984). Taxonomy of family life styles: II. Homes with slow-learning children. *American Journal of Mental Deficiency, 89,* 111–123.

Mink, I. T., Nihara, K., & Meyers, C. E. (1983). Taxonomy of family life styles: I. Homes with TMR children. *American Journal of Mental Deficiency, 87,* 484–497.

Minuchin, P. (1985). Families and individual development: Provocations from the field of family therapy. *Child Development, 56,* 289–302.

Mischel, W. (1968). *Personality and assessment.* New York: Wiley.

Mischel, W. (1973). Toward a cognitive social learning reconceptualization of personality. *Psychological Review, 80,* 252–283.

Mischel, W. (1977). The interaction of person and situation. In D. Magnusson & N. S. Endler (Eds.), *Personality at the crossroads: Current issues in interactional psychology* (pp. 333–352). Hillsdale, NJ: Erlbaum.

Mischel, W. (1979). On the interface of cognition and personality: Beyond the person–situation debate. *American Psychologist, 34,* 740–754.

Molnar, J. M. (1985, August). *Home and day care contexts: Interactive influences on children's behavior.* Paper presented at the meeting of the American Psychological Association, Los Angeles.

Mooney, C., & Algozzine, B. (1978). A comparison of the disturbingness of behaviors related to learning disability and emotional disturbance. *Journal of Abnormal Child Psychology, 6,* 401–406.

Moos, R. H., & Moos, B. S. (1978). A typology of family social environments. *Family Process, 17,* 357–371.

Moos, R. H., & Trickett, E. J. (1974). *Classroom Environment Scale manual.* Palo Alto, CA: Consulting Psychologists Press.

Morey, L. C., Skinner, H. A., & Blashfield, R. K. (1986). Trends in the classification of abnormal behavior. In A. R. Ciminero, K. S. Calhoun, & H. E. Adams (Eds.), *Handbook of behavioral assessment* (2nd ed., pp. 47–75). New York: Wiley.

Mori, L., & Peterson, L. (1986). Training preschoolers in home safety skills to prevent inadvertent injury. *Journal of Clinical Child Psychology, 15,* 106–114.

Morris, R. J., & Kratochwill, T. R. (1983). *Treating children's fears and phobias: A behavioral approach.* New York: Pergamon Press.

Moskowitz, D. S., & Schwarz, J. C. (1982). Validity comparisons of behavior counts and ratings by knowledgeable informants. *Journal of Personality and Social Psychology, 42,* 518–528.

Mrazek, P. (1983). Sexual abuse of children. In B. B. Lahey & A. E. Kazdin (Eds.), *Advances in clinical child psychology,* (Vol. 6, pp. 199–216). New York: Plenum.

Mussen, P. H. (General Ed.). (1983). *Handbook of child psychology* (4th ed., 4 vols.). New York: Wiley.

Nathan, P. E. (1981). Symptomatic diagnosis and behavioral assessment: A synthesis? In D. H. Barlow (Ed.), *Behavioral assessment of adult disorders* (pp. 1–11). New York: Guilford Press.

Nathan, P. E. (1986). [Review of R. K. Blashfield, *The classification of psychopathology*]. *Behavioral Assessment, 8,* 199–201.

Nay, W. R. (1979). *Multimethod clinical assessment.* New York: Gardner Press.

Nay, W. R. (1986). Analogue measures. In A. R. Ciminero, K. S. Calhoun, & H. E. Adams (Eds.), *Handbook of behavioral assessment* (2nd ed., pp. 223–252). New York: Wiley.

Neidig, P. H., & Friedman, D. H. (1984). *Spouse abuse: A treatment program for couples.* Champaign, IL: Research Press.

Nelson, R. O. (1980). The use of intelligence tests in behavioral assessment. *Behavioral Assessment, 2,* 417–423.

Nelson, R. O. (1983). Behavioral assessment: Past, present, future. *Behavioral Assessment, 5,* 195–206.

Nelson, R. O., & Hayes, S. C. (1979). Some current dimensions of behavioral assessment. *Behavioral Assessment, 1,* 1–16.

Nelson, R. O., & Hayes, S. C. (1981). Nature of behavioral assessment. In M. Hersen & A. Bellack (Eds.), *Behavioral assessment: A practical handbook* (2nd ed., pp. 3–37). New York: Pergamon Press.

Nelson, R. O., Lipinski, D. P., & Boykin, R. A. (1978). The effects of self-recorders' training and the obtrusiveness of the self-recording device on the accuracy and reactivity of self-monitoring. *Behavior Therapy, 9,* 200–208.

Nelson, W. M., & Finch, A. J. (1978). *The Children's Inventory of Anger.* Unpublished manuscript, Xavier University, Cincinnati, OH.

Newberger, C. M. (1978). *Parental conceptions of children and child rearing: A structural developmental analysis.* Unpublished doctoral dissertation, Harvard University.

Nisbett, R. E., Zukier, H., & Lemley, R. E. (1981). The dilution effect. Nondiagnostic information weakens the implications of diagnostic information. *Cognitive Psychology, 13,* 248–277.

Nordquist, V. M. (1971). The modification of a child's enuresis: Some response–response relationships. *Journal of Applied Behavior Analysis, 4,* 241–247.

Nowicki, S., & Duke, M. P. (1974). A preschool and preliminary internal–external control scale. *Developmental Psychology, 6,* 874–880.

Nowicki, S., & Strickland, B. R. (1973). A locus of control scale for children. *Journal of Consulting and Clinical Psychology, 40,* 148–154.

Nunnally, J. C. (1978). *Psychometric theory* (2nd ed.). New York: McGraw-Hill

Odom, S. L., & DeKlyem, M. (1986). *Social withdrawal and depression in childhood.* Unpublished manuscript, Western Psychiatric Institute and Clinic, University of Pittsburgh, Pittsburgh, PA.

Oldershaw, L. (1986). *A behavioral approach to the classification of different types of physically abusive mothers.* Unpublished manuscript. University of Toronto.

O'Leary, K. D. (1979). Behavioral assessment. *Behavioral Assessment, 1,* 31–36.

O'Leary, K. D. (1984). Marital discord and children: Problems, strategies, methodologies, and results. In A. Doyle, D. Gold, & D. S. Moskowitz (Eds.), *Children in families under stress* (pp. 35–46). San Francisco: Jossey-Bass.

O'Leary, K. D., Romanczyk, R. G., Kass, R. E., Dietz, A., & Santogrossi, D. (1971). *Procedures for classroom observations of teachers and children.* Unpublished manuscript, State University of New York at Stony Brook.

Ollendick, T. H. (1984). Development and validation of the Children's Assertiveness Inventory. *Child and Family Behavior Therapy, 5,* 1–15.

Ollendick, T. H., & Cerny, J. A. (1981). *Clinical behavior therapy with children.* New York: Plenum Press.

Ollendick, T. H., & Hersen, M. (Eds.). (1984). *Child behavioral assessment: Principles and procedures.* New York: Pergamon Press.

Olweus, D. (1979). Stability of aggressive reaction patterns in males. *Psychological Bulletin, 86,* 852–875.

Pannaccione, V. F., & Wahler, R. G. (1986). Child Behavior, maternal depression, and social coercion as factors in the quality of child care. *Journal of Abnormal Child Psychology, 14,* 263–278.

Parke, R. D., MacDonald, K. B., Beital, A., & Bhavnagri, N. (1987). The role of the family in the development of peer relationships. In R. DeV. Peters and R. J. McMahon (Eds.), *Marriages and families: Behavioral-systems approaches.* New York: Brunner/Mazel.

Parke, R. D., & Sawin, D. B. (1977). *The child's role in sparing the rod.* Unpublished manuscript, University of Illinois.

Passman, R. H., & Mulhern, R. K. (1977). Maternal punitiveness as affected by situational stress: An experimental analogue of child abuse. *Journal of Abnormal Psychology, 86,* 565–569.

Patterson, G. R. (1976). The aggressive child: Victim and architect of a coercive system. In E. J. Mash, L. A. Hamerlynck, & L. C. Handy (Eds.), *Behavior modification and families* (pp. 267–316). New York: Brunner/Mazel.

Patterson, G. R. (1982). *Coercive family process.* Eugene, OR: Castalia.

Patterson, G. R. (1986). Performance models for antisocial boys. *American Psychologist, 41,* 432–444.

Patterson, G. R., & Bank, L. (1986). Bootstrapping your way in the nomological thicket. *Behavioral Assessment, 8,* 49–73.

Patterson, G. R., & Bechtel, G. C. (1977). Formulating situational environment in relation to states and traits. In R. B. Cattell & R. M. Greger (Eds.), *Handbook of modern personality theory* (pp. 254–268). Washington, DC: Halstead.

Patterson, G. R., & Colleagues. (1984). *Assessment protocol from the Oregon Social Learning Center Logitudinal Study.* Unpublished materials, Oregon Social Learning Center, Eugene.

Patterson, G. R., Littman, R. A., & Hinsey, W. C. (1964). Parental effectiveness as reinforcer in the laboratory and its relation to child-rearing practices and child adjustment in the classroom. *Journal of Personality, 32,* 180–199.

Pepler, D. J., Corter, C., & Abramovitch, R. (1982). *Am I my brother's brother? Sibling perceptions.* Paper presented at the Waterloo Conference on Child Development, Waterloo, Ontario, Canada.

Peterson, C., & Rahrer, S. (1986). A DSM-III training tool for child clinicians. *The Behavior Therapist, 9*(5), 105.

Peterson, D. R. (1968). *The clinical study of social behavior.* New York: Appleton-Century-Crofts.

Peterson, L., & Mori, L. (1985). Prevention of child injury: An overview of targets, methods, and tactics for psychologists. *Journal of Consulting and Clinical Psychology, 53,* 586–595.

Phillips, L., Draguns, J. G., & Bartlett, D. P. (1975). Classification of behavior disorders. In N. Hobbs (Ed.), *Issues in the classification of children* (Vol. 1, pp. 26–55). San Francisco: Jossey-Bass.

Piers, E. V., & Harris, D. B. (1963). *The Piers–Harris Self-Concept Scale.* Unpublished manuscript, Pennsylvania State University.

Piotrowski, C., & Keller, J. W. (1984). Attitudes toward clinical assessment by members of the AABT. *Psychological Reports, 55,* 831–838.

Powers, M. D. (1984). Syndromal diagnosis and the behavioral assessment of childhood disorders. *Child and Family Behavior Therapy, 6*(3), 1–15.

Prugh, D. G. Engel, M., & Morse, W. C. (1975). Emotional disturbance in children. In N. Hobbs (Ed.), *Issues in the classification of children* (Vol. 1, pp. 261–299) San Francisco: Jossey-Bass.

Puig-Antich, J., & Chambers, W. (1978). *Schedule for Affective Disorders and Schizophrenia for School-Aged Children.* New York: New York State Psychiatric Institute.

Quay, H. C. (1979). Classification. In H. C. Quay & J. S. Werry (Eds.), *Psychopathological disorders of childhood* (2nd ed., pp. 1–42). New York: Wiley.

Quay, H. C., & Peterson, D. R. (1975). *Manual for the Behavior Problem Checklist.* Unpublished manuscript.

Quay, H. C., & Werry, J. S. (Eds.). (1986). *Psychopathological disorders of childhood* (3rd ed.). New York: Wiley.

Rachman, S. (1983). Behavioral medicine, clinical reasoning, and technical advances. *Canadian Journal of Behavioural Science, 15,* 318–333.

Rains, P M., Kitsuse, J. I., Duster, T., & Friedson, E. (1975). The labeling approach to deviance. In N. Hobbs (Ed.), *Issues in the classification of children* (Vol. 1, pp. 88–100). San Francisco: Jossey-Bas.

Reid, J. B. (Ed.). (1978). *A social learning approach to family intervention: Vol. 2. Observation in home settings.* Eugene, OR: Castalia.

Reid, J. B. (1982). Observer training in naturalistic research. In D. P. Hartmann (Ed.), *Using observers to study behavior* (pp. 37–50). San Francisco: Jossey-Bass.

Reid, J. B., Baldwin, D. V., Patterson, G. R., & Dishion, T. J. (1987). Some problems relating to the assessment of childhood disorders: A role for observational data. In M. Rutter, A. H. Tuma, & I. Lann (Eds.), *Assessment and diagnosis in child psychopathology.* New York: Guilford Press.

Reid, J. B., Taplin, P. S., & Lorber, R. (1981). A social interactional approach to the treatment of abusive families. In R. B. Stuart (Ed.), *Violent behavior: Social learning approaches to prediction, management, and treatment* (pp. 83–101). New York: Brunner/Mazel.

Reppucci, N. D., Weithorn, L. A. Mulvey, E. P., & Monahan, J. (Eds.). (1984). *Children, mental health, and the law.* Beverly Hills, CA: Sage.

Reynolds, C. R., & Richmond, B. O. (1978). "What I Think and Feel": A revised measure of children's manifest anxiety. *Journal of Abnormal Child Psychology, 6,* 271–280.

Reynolds, W. M., & Stark, K. D. (1986). Self-control in children: A multimethod examination of treatment outcome measures. *Journal of Abnormal Child Psychology, 14,* 13–23.

Roberts, M. C., & Peterson, L. (Eds.). (1984). *Prevention of problems in childhood: Psychological research and applications.* New York: Wiley.

Rodick, J. D., Henggeler, S. W., & Hanson, C. L. (1986). An evaluation of the Family Adaptability and Cohesion Evaluation Scales and the Circumplex Model. *Journal of Abnormal Child Psychology, 14,* 77–87.

Romanczyk, R. G. (1986). *Clinical utilization of microcomputer technology.* New York: Pergamon Press.

Rosch, E. (1978). Principles of categorization. In E. Rosch & B. B. Lloyd (Eds.), *Cognition and categorization* (pp. 27–48). Hillsdale, NJ: Erlbaum.

Rosenberg, R. P., & Beck, S. (1986). Preferred assessment methods and treatment modalities for hyperactive children among clinical child and school psychologists. *Journal of Clinical Child Psychology, 15,* 142–147.

Ross, A. O. (1978) Behavior therapy with children. In S. L. Garfield & A. E. Bergin (Eds.), *Handbook of psychotherapy and behavior change: An empirical analysis* (2nd ed., pp. 592–620). New York: Wiley.

Ross, A. O. (1981). *Child behavior therapy: Principles, procedures and empirical basis.* New York: Wiley.

Ross, A. O., & Pelham, W. E. (1981). Child psychopathology. *Annual Review of Psychology, 32,* 243–278.

Ross, D. M., & Ross, S. A. (1982). *Hyperactivity: Research, theory, and action* (2nd ed.). New York: Wiley.

Rothbart, M. K. (1981). Measurement of temperament in infancy. *Child Development, 52,* 569–578.

Russell, M. B., & Bernal, M. E. (1977). Temporal and climatic variables in naturalistic observation. *Journal of Applied Behavior Analysis, 10,* 399–405.

Rutter, M. (1979). Maternal deprivation, 1972–1978: New findings, new concepts, new approaches. *Child Development, 50,* 283–305.

Rutter, M., & Shaffer, D. (1980). DSM-III: A step forward

or back in terms of the classification of child psychiatric disorders? *Journal of the American Academy of Child Psychiatry, 19,* 371–394.

Rutter, M., Shaffer, D., & Shepherd, M. (1975). *A multi-axial classification of child psychiatric disorders: An evaluation of a proposal.* Geneva: World Health Organization.

Rutter, M., Tuma, A. H., & Lann, I. (Eds.). (1987). *Assessment and diagnosis in child psychopathology.* New York: Guilford Press.

Salzinger, S., Kaplan, S., & Artemyeff, C. (1983). Mothers' personal social networks and child maltreatment. *Journal of Abnormal Psychology, 92,* 68–76.

Santostefano, S. (1978). *A biodevelopmental approach to clinical child psychology: Cognitive controls and cognitive control therapy.* New York: Wiley.

Santrock, J. W., & Sitterle, K. A. (1987). Parent–child relationships in stepmother families. In K. Pasley & M. Ihinger-Tallman (Eds.), *Remarriage and stepfamilies today: Research and theory.* New York: Guilford Press.

Santrock, J. W., Sitterle, K. A., & Warshak, R. A. (in press). Parent–child relationships in stepfather families. In P. Bronstein & C. P. Cowan (Eds.), *Fatherhood today: Men's changing role in the family.* New York: Wiley.

Scanlon, E. M., & Ollendick, T. H. (1985). Children's assertive behavior: The reliability and validity of three self-report measures. *Child and Family Behavior Therapy, 7,* 9–21.

Schacht, T., & Nathan, P. E. (1977). But is it good for psychologists? Appraisal and status of DSM-III. *American Psychologist, 32,* 1017–1025.

Schaefer, E. S., & Bell, R. Q. (1958). Development of a parent attitude research instrument. *Child Development, 29,* 339–361.

Schlundt, D. G., & McFall, R. M. (1987). Classifying social situations: A comparison of five methods. *Behavioral Assessments, 9,* 21–42.

Schwartz, J. C., Barton-Henry, M. L., & Pruzinsky, T. (1985). Assessing child rearing behaviors: A comparison of ratings made by mother, father and sibling on the CRPBI. *Child Development, 56,* 462–479.

Select Panel for the Promotion of Child Health. (1981). *Better health for our children: A national strategy* (4 vols.). Washington, DC: U.S. Government Printing Office.

Shapiro, E. S. (1984). Self-monitoring procedures. In T. H. Ollendick & M. Hersen (Eds.), *Child behavioral assessment: Principles and procedures* (pp. 148–165). New York: Pergamon Press.

Shaywitz, S. E., Schnell, C., Shaywitz, B. A., & Towle, V. R. (1986). Yale Children's Inventory: An instrument to assess children with attentional deficits and learning disabilities. I. Scale development and psychometric properties. *Journal of Abnormal Child Psychology, 14,* 347–364.

Sigel, I. (Ed.). (1985). *Parental belief systems: The psychological consequences for children.* Hillsdale, NJ: Erlbaum.

Silverman, W. K., & Nelles, W. B. (1986, November). *Further considerations in the assessment of childhood anxiety: Mothers' and children's reports.* Paper presented at the meeting of the Association for Advancement of Behavior Therapy, Chicago.

Sines, J. O. (1986). Normative data for the Revised Missouri Children's Behavior Checklist—Parent Form (MCBC-P). *Journal of Abnormal Child Psychology, 14,* 89–94.

Skeen, J. A., & Gelfand, D. M. (1981, April). *Children's perceptions of their mothers and fathers.* Paper presented at the meeting of the Western Psychological Association, Los Angeles.

Skinner, H. A. (1981). Toward the integration of classification theory and methods. *Journal of Abnormal Psychology, 90,* 68–87.

Skitka, L. J. (1986, April). *The role of gender and resources in equity considerations of interpersonal relationships.* Paper presented at the annual meeting of the Western Psychological Association, Seattle.

Smucker, M. R., Craighead, W. E., Craighead, L. W., & Green, B. (1986). Normative and reliability data for the Children's Depression Inventory. *Journal of Abnormal Child Psychology, 14,* 25–39.

Snyder, J., & Patterson, G. R. (1986). The effects of consequences on patterns of social interaction: A quasi-experimental approach to reinforcement in natural interaction. *Child Development, 57,* 1257–1268.

Spanier, G. B. (1976). Measuring dyadic adjustment: New scales for assessing marriage and similar dyads. *Journal of Marriage and the Family, 38,* 15–28.

Spielberger, C. D. (1973). *State–Trait Anxiety Inventory for Children.* Palo Alto, CA: Consulting Psychologists Press.

Spitzer, R. L., & Cantwell, D. P. (1980). The DSM-III classification of the psychiatric disorders of infancy, childhood, and adolescence. *Journal of the American Academy of Child Psychiatry, 19,* 356–370.

Sroufe, L. A., & Fleeson, J. (1986). Attachment and the construction of relationships. In W. Hartup & Z. Rubin (Eds.), *Relationships and development.* Hillsdale, NJ: Erlbaum.

Sroufe, L. A., & Rutter, M. (1984). The domain of developmental psychopathology. *Child Development, 55,* 17–29.

Stein, S. J. (1986). *Computer assisted diagnosis for children and adolescents.* Unpublished manuscript, University of Toronto, Department of Psychiatry.

Sternberg, R. J., & Wagner, R. K. (in press). *Practical intelligence: Nature and origins of intelligence in the everyday world.* Cambridge, England: Cambridge University Press.

Stevens-Long, J. (1973). The effect of behavioral context on some aspects of adult disciplinary practice and affect. *Child Development, 44,* 476–484.

Stevenson, M. B., Colbert, K. K., & Roach, M. A. (1986, October). *Transition to parenthood in adolescent and adult single mothers.* Unpublished manuscript, University of Wisconsin–Madison.

Stokes, T. F., Fowler, S. A., & Baer, D. M. (1978). Training preschool children to recruit natural communities of reinforcement. *Journal of Applied Behavior Analysis, 11,* 285–303.

Straus, M. A., & Brown, B. W. (1978). *Family measurement techniques.* Minneapolis: University of Minnesota Press.

Strosahl, K. D., & Linehan, M. M. (1986). Basic issues in behavioral assessment. In A. R. Ciminero, K. S. Calhoun, & H. E. Adams (Eds.), *Handbook of behavioral assessment* (2nd ed., pp. 12–46). New York: Wiley.

Sulzer-Azaroff, B., & Mayer, G. R. (1977). *Applying behavior-analysis procedures with children and youth.* New York: Holt, Rinehart & Winston.

Swan, G. E., & MacDonald, M. L. (1978). Behavior therapy in practice: A national survey of behavior therapists. *Behavior Therapy, 9,* 799–807.

Szapocznik, J. (1984). *Manual for family task rating.* Unpublished manuscript, University of Miami, Miami, FL.

Szykula, S. (1986). *Child focused stratregies and behavioral family therapy processes: Hypothetical case study comparisons.* Unpublished manuscript, University of Utah School of Medicine.

Tabachnik, N., & Alloy, L. B. (in press). Clinician and patient as aberrant actuaries: Expectation-based distortions in assessment of covariation. In L. Y. Abramson (Ed.), *Social cognition and clinical psychology.* New York: Guilford Press.

Taylor, C. B. (1983). DSM-III and behavioral assessment. *Behavioral Assessment, 5,* 5–14.

Tharp, R. G., & Wetzel, R. J. (1969). *Behavior modification in the natural environment.* New York: Academic Press.

Toobert, D., Patterson, G. R., Moore, D., & Halper, V. (1982). *MOSAIC: A multidimensional description of family interaction.* Unpublished technical report, Oregon Social Learning Center, Eugene.

Trickett, P. K., & Kuczynski, L. (1986). Children's misbehaviors and parental disciplinary strategies in abusive and nonabusive families. *Developmental Psychology, 22,* 115–123.

Tronick, E. Q., & Gianino, A. (1986). Interactive mismatch and repair: Challenges to the coping infant. *Zero to Three, 6,* 1–6.

Turkat, I. D. (1986). The behavioral interview. In A. R. Ciminero, K. S. Calhoun, & H. E. Adams (Eds.), *Handbook of behavioral assessment* (2nd ed., pp. 109–149). New York: Wiley.

Turkat, I. D., & Meyer, V. (1982). The behavior-analytic approach. In P. Wachtel (Ed.), *Resistance: Psychodynamic and behavioral approaches* (pp. 157–184). New York: Plenum.

Twardosz, S., & Nordquist, V. N. (1983). The development and importance of affection. In B. B. Lahey & A. E. Kazdin (Eds.), *Advances in clinical child psychology* (Vol. 6, pp. 129–168). New York: Plenum.

Ullmann, L. P., & Krasner, L. (Eds.). (1965). *Case studies in behavior modification.* New York: Holt, Rinehart & Winston.

Ullmann, L. P., & Krasner, L. (1969). *A psychological approach to abnormal behavior.* Englewood Cliffs, NJ: Prentice-Hall.

Vincent, T. A., & Trickett, E. J. (1983). Preventive interventions and the human context: Ecological approaches to environmental assessment and change. In R. D. Felner, L. A. Jason, J. N. Moritsugu, & S. S. Farber (Eds.), *Preventive psychology: Theory, research and practice* (pp. 67–86). New York: Pergamon Press.

Voeltz, L. M., & Evans, I. M. (1982). The assessment of behavioral interrelationships in child behavior therapy. *Behavioral Assessment, 4,* 131–165.

Wade, T. C., Baker, T. B. & Hartmann, D. P. (1979). Behavior therapists' self-reported views and practices. *The Behavior Therapist, 2,* 3–6.

Wahler, R. G. (1975). Some structural aspects of deviant child behavior. *Journal of Applied Behavior Analysis, 8,* 27–42.

Wahler, R. G. (1976). Deviant child behavior within the family: Developmental speculations and behavior change

strategies. In H. Leitenberg (Ed.), *Handbook of behavior modification and behavior therapy* (pp. 516–543). Englewood Cliffs, NJ: Prentice-Hall.

Wahler, R. G. (1980). The insular mother: Her problems in parent–child treatment. *Journal of Applied Behavior Analysis, 13,* 207–219.

Wahler, R. G., & Cormier, W. H. (1970). The ecological interview: A first step in out-patient child behavior therapy. *Journal of Behavior Therapy and Experimental Psychiatry, 1,* 279–289.

Wahler, R. G., & Dumas, J. E. (1986). Maintenance factors in coercive mother–child interactions: The compliance and predictability hypotheses. *Journal of Applied Behavior Analysis, 19,* 13–22.

Wahler, R. G., & Fox, J. J. (1981). Setting events in applied behavior analysis: Toward a conceptual and methodological expansion. *Journal of Applied Behavior Analysis, 14,* 327–338.

Wahler, R. G., & Graves, M. G. (1983). Setting events in social networks: Ally or enemy in child behavior therapy? *Behavior Therapy, 14,* 19–36.

Wahler, R. G., House, A. E., & Stambaugh, E. E. (1976). *Ecological assessment of child problem behavior: A clinical package for home, school, and institutional settings.* New York: Pergamon Press.

Wahler, R. G., Leske, G., & Rogers, E. D. (1979). The insular family: A deviance support system for oppositional children. In L. A. Hamerlynck (Ed.), *Behavioral systems for the developmentally disabled: Vol. 1. School and family environments* (pp. 102–127). New York: Brunner/Mazel.

Wahler, R. G., Sperling, K. A., Thomas, M. R., Teeter, N. C., & Luper, H. L. (1970). The modification of childhood stuttering: Some response-response relationships. *Journal of Experimental Child Psychology, 9,* 411–428.

Wampold, B. E. (1986). State of the art in sequential analysis: Comment on Lichtenberg and Heck. *Journal of Counseling Psychology, 33,* 182–185.

Wasik, B. H. (1984). Clinical applications of direct behavioral observation: A look at the past and the future. In B. B. Lahey & A. E. Kazdin (Eds.), *Advances in clinical child psychology* (pp. 156–193). New York: Plenum.

Wasik, B. H., Bryant, D. M., & Fishbein, J. (1980, November). *Assessing parent problem solving skills.* Paper presented at the meeting of the Association for Advancement of Behavior Therapy, Toronto.

Weinrott, M. R., Reid, J. B., Bauske, B. W., & Brummett, B. (1981). Supplementing naturalistic observations with observer impressions. *Behavioral Assessment, 3,* 151–159.

Weiss, R. L. (1980). Strategic behavioral marital therapy: Toward a model for assessment and intervention. In J. P. Vincent (Ed.), *Advances in family intervention, assessment and theory* (Vol. 1, pp. 229–271). Greenwich, CT: JAI Press.

Weiss, R. L., & Chaffin, L. (1986, May). *Micro- and macro-coding of marital interactions.* Paper presented at the meeting of the Western Psychological Association, Seattle.

Weiss, R. L., & Margolin, G. (1986). Assessment of marital conflict and accord. In A. R. Ciminero, K. S. Calhoun, & H. E. Adams (Eds.), *Handbook of behavioral assessment* (2nd ed, pp. 561–600). New York: Wiley.

Werry, J. S., & Sprague, R. L. (1970). Hyperactivity. In

C. G. Costello (Ed.), *Symptoms of psychopathology: A handbook* (pp. 397–417). New York: Wiley.

Whalen, C. K., Henker, B., Collins, B. E., Finck, D., & Dotemoto, S. (1979). A social ecology of hyperactive boys: Medication effects in structured classroom environments. *Journal of Applied Behavior Analysis, 12,* 65–81.

Whitehurst, G. J., Fischel, J. E., DeBaryshe, B., Caulfield, M. B., & Falco, F. L. (1986). Analyzing sequential relations in observational data: A practical guide. *Journal of Psychopathology and Behavioral Assessment, 8,* 129–148.

Wiggins, J. S. (1981). Clinical and statistical prediction: Where are we and where do we go from here? *Clinical Psychology Review, 1,* 3–18.

Willems, E. P. (1973). Go ye into all the world and modify behavior: An ecologist's view. *Representative Research in Social Psychology, 4,* 93–105.

Willems, E. P. (1974). Behavioral technology and behavioral ecology. *Journal of Applied Behavior Analysis, 7,* 151–165.

Williams, R. L., & Workman, E. A. (1978). The development of a behavioral self-concept scale. *Behavior Therapy, 9,* 680–681.

Wimberger, H. C., & Gregory, R. J. (1968). A behavior checklist for use in child psychiatry clinics. *Journal of the American Academy of Child Psychiatry, 7,* 677–688.

Wirt, R. D., Lachar, D., Klinedinst, J. K., & Seat, P. D. (1984). *Multidimensional description of child personality: A manual for the Personality Inventory for Children* (1984 rev. by D. Lachar). Los Angeles: Western Psychological Services.

Wolf, M. M. (1978). Social validity: The case for subjective measurement or how applied behavior analysis is finding its heart. *Journal of Applied Behavior Analysis, 11,* 203–214.

Wolfe, D. A. (1985). Child abusive parents: An empirical review and analysis. *Psychological Bulletin, 97,* 462–482.

Wolfe, D. A., & LaRose, L. (1986). *Child videotape series* [Videotape]. London, Ontario: University of Western Ontario.

Wolfe, V. V., & Wolfe, D. A. (1988). The sexually abused child. In E. J. Mash & L. G. Terdal (Eds.), *Behavioral assessment of childhood disorders* (2nd ed., unabridged, pp. 670–714). New York: Guilford Press.

Wolpe, J. (1986). Individualization: The categorical imperative of behavior therapy practice. *Journal of Behavior Therapy and Experimental Psychiatry, 17,* 145–153.

Yarrow, M. R., Campbell, J. D., & Burton, R. V. (1970). Recollections of childhood: A study of the retrospective method. *Monographs of the Society for Research in Child Development* (Vol. 35, Serial No. 138).

Yates, A. J. (1970). *Behavior therapy.* New York: Wiley.

Yates, B. T., & Hoage, C. M. (1979, December). *Mnemonic stigma in behavior observation: An interaction of diagnostic label, relative frequency of positive versus negative behavior, and type of behavior recalled.* Paper presented at the meeting of the Association for Advancement of Behavior Therapy, San Francisco.

Yates, B. T., Kline, S. B., & Haven, W. G. (1978). Psychological nosology and mnemonic reconstruction: Effects of diagnostic labels on observers' recall of positive and negative behavior frequencies. *Cognitive Therapy and Research, 2,* 377–387.

Zachary, R. A., Levin, B., Hargreaves, W. A., & Greene, J. A. (1981). *Trends in the use of psychiatric diagnoses for children: 1960–1979.* Unpublished manuscript, University of California at San Francisco.

Zangwill, W. M. & Kniskern, J. R. (1982). Comparison of problem families in the clinic and at home. *Behavior Therapy, 13,* 145–152.

Zeitlin, S., Williamson, G. G., & Rosenblatt, W. (1985). *Coping with stress model as used with families in an early intervention program.* Unpublished manuscript, John F. Kennedy Medical Center, Edison, NJ.

Zigler, E. (1984, November). *The child and the family in the 80's: Problems and social/behavioral solutions.* Paper presented at the annual meeting of the Association for Advancement of Behavior Therapy, Philadelphia.

PART II
BEHAVIOR DISORDERS

2 ATTENTION DEFICIT DISORDER WITH HYPERACTIVITY

RUSSELL A. BARKLEY
University of Massachusetts Medical Center

S ince the first edition of this chapter appeared more than 6 years ago (Barkley, 1981b), much has occurred in research on hyperactivity in children, or what has now come to be known as Attention Deficit Disorder with Hyperactivity (ADD/H) in the third edition of the *Diagnostic and Statistical Manual of Mental Disorders* (DSM-III; American Psychiatric Association, 1980). It remains one of the most frequently studied childhood disorders, probably reflecting its status as one of the problems most commonly referred to child guidance centers in this country. Greater information now exists on the nature of the disorder, its prevalence, its developmental course, its prognosis, and its etiology (see Ross & Ross, 1982, for review), and advances continue to be made on its theoretical conceptualization. Happily for many faced with the clinical demands of assessing and treating these children, more useful assessment techniques and treatment programs are now available than was previously the case. This chapter highlights information culled from the vast body of literature on this disorder, and briefly summarizes its current status in the field of child psychopathology. From this, guidelines are suggested for the clinical assessment of ADD/H in children.

OVERVIEW OF ATTENTION DEFICIT DISORDERS

History

One of the earliest papers to appear on the subject of ADD/H in children was that by Still (1902), in which children described in terms closely resembling modern-day descriptions of ADD/H and conduct disorders were believed to have suffered from "defects in moral control" and "volitional inhibition." Little additional research was published on ADD/H until the late 1940s. Scientific writers at that time were struck by the similarity of behavioral problems between ADD/H children and those having documented brain injury. As a result, overactivity, distractibility, inattention, and poor impulse control were believed to signify brain injury, despite the absence of hard neurological evidence (Strauss & Lehtinen, 1947). Distractibility and excessive activity were believed to be the chief difficulties of such children. From these notions would later spring the terms "minimal brain damage" and eventually "minimal brain dysfunction" (MBD; Clements & Peters, 1962). These terms were used to imply an underlying brain impairment (Wender, 1971), despite the dearth of medical evidence supporting the brain injury hypothesis (Rutter, 1977; H. G. Taylor, 1983).

By the late 1970s, the concept of MBD was on the wane (Rie & Rie, 1980), mainly due to a lack of evidence for any interrelationships among its symptoms (Routh & Roberts, 1972; Ullman, Barkley, & Brown, 1978; Werry, Weiss, & Douglas, 1964). The emphasis on overactivity as the hallmark of this disorder increased into the 1960s (Chess, 1960; Clements, 1966). But as more measures of other constructs were included in research, it became apparent that overactivity was not the only problem experienced by such children, nor was it necessarily the primary one. In a series of studies by Douglas and her colleagues, a persuasive case was made for attentional deficits and impulse control problems as the primary symptoms of this disorder (Douglas, 1972). Subsequently, substantial evidence has accumulated in support of this notion (Douglas, 1980, 1983; Douglas & Peters, 1979). So convincing was this body of research that in the revision of the DSM-II (American Psychiatric Association, 1968), the diagnosis Hyperkinetic Reaction of Childhood was replaced with Attention Deficit Disorder with or without Hyperactivity, and *three* primary symptoms were now described: inattention, impulsivity, and overactivity.

Presently, a child can be diagnosed as having Attention Deficit Disorder without Hyperactivity—that is, as having *only* problems with inattention and impulsivity. Although research supporting this latter subclassification was almost nonexistent, the very creation of such a subtype prompted further study into its possible existence (Edelbrock, Costello, & Kessler, 1984; Maurer & Stewart, 1980). This subtyping distinction has been obliterated in the revision of the DSM-III just published (DSM-IIIR), and ADD/H will be regarded as a single disorder. Recognizing the heterogeneity of symptoms of children with this disorder, the DSM-IIIR will permit a child to have one or more of the three primary deficits while still qualifying for the diagnosis.

By the early 1980s, several investigators were proposing that deficits in the self-regulation of behavior may account for many of the difficulties in ADD/H. Routh (1978) proposed that the regulation of behavior in accordance with situational demands may be defective. Others have hypothesized deficits in self-directed instruction (Kendall & Braswell, 1984), self-regulation of arousal to meet environmental demands (Douglas, 1983), or rule-governed behavior (Barkley, 1981a, 1981b, in press). The field seems to be partially returning to the early notion of Still (1902) that defects in volitional inhibition and the moral control of behavior are part of this disorder.

Definition, Diagnosis, and Primary Symptoms

A number of commonalities can be distilled from prior efforts at describing and defining ADD/H. These appear to include the following: (1) an emphasis on *age-inappropriate* levels of inattention, impulsivity, and overactivity; (2) the inability of the children to restrict their behavior to situational demands (self-regulation), relative to same-age normal children; (3) the emergence of these problems by early childhood; (4) the pervasiveness of these problems across several settings and/or caregivers; (5) the chronicity of these symptoms throughout development; and (6) the inability to account for these behavioral deficits on the basis of obvious developmental disabilities (i.e., mental retardation, severe language delay, etc.), neurological diseases (i.e., gross brain damage, epilepsy, etc.), or severe psychopathology (i.e., autism, schizophrenia, etc.).

Definition and Diagnostic Criteria

Many different definitions for ADD/H have been proposed throughout the history of this disorder. Few, however, have been particularly operational (Barkley, 1982). A great improvement in this state of affairs occurred in DSM-III, where guidelines for the types and number of behavioral descriptors, the age of onset, and the duration of these symptoms were specified. These criteria have recently been revised (American Psychiatric Association, 1987). These revised criteria are set forth in Table 1. They differ from those in the earlier DSM-III edition in: (1) having a single item list of symptoms instead of three separate listings of items under each symptom; (2) the cutoff score of 8 of 14 items was established in a clinical field trial; and (3) the condition of Affective Disorder no longer excludes the use of the diagnosis. The disorder is now referred to as Attention Deficit–Hyperactivity Disorder (AD-HD) and no attempt at subtyping into groups with or without hyperactivity has been made.

TABLE 1. Criteria for Diagnosing Attention Deficit–Hyperactivity Disorder from the DSM-IIIR

A. A period of six months or more during which at least eight of the following behaviors are present:
    (1) has difficulty remaining seated when required to
    (2) often fidgets with hands or feet or squirms in seat
    (3) has difficulty playing quietly
    (4) often talks excessively
    (5) often shifts from one uncompleted activity to another
    (6) has difficulty sustaining attention to tasks and play activities
    (7) has difficulty following through on instructions from others (not due to oppositional behavior or failure of comprehension), e.g., fails to finish chores
    (8) is easily distracted by extraneous stimuli
    (9) often interrupts or intrudes on others, e.g., butts into other children's games
    (10) often blurts out answers to questions before they have been completed
    (11) has difficulty waiting turn in games or group situations
    (12) often engages in physically dangerous activities without considering possible consequences (not for the purpose of thrill-seeking), e.g., runs into street without looking
    (13) often loses things necessary for tasks or activities at school or at home (e.g., toys, pencils, books, assignments)
    (14) often doesn't seem to listen to what is being said to him or her
B. Onset before the age of seven years.
C. Does not meet criteria for Pervasive Developmental Disorder.

Note: From the *Diagnostic and Statistical Manual of Mental Disorders* (3rd ed. rev.) by the American Psychiatric Association, 1987, Washington, DC: Author.

Although these criteria are an improvement over those in previous DSM editions, they continue to suffer from several difficulties. First, the symptom cutoff score was not established relative to those scores that might have been obtained by normal children. Hence, it is not clear how many normal children would meet the 8 of 14 cutoff criterion. Second, the symptoms listed were not chosen to represent a common dimension or factor in which the items truly interrelate as a function of a construct which they have in common (e.g., attention deficits). Finally, the age of onset and duration criteria do not have any rationale for their inclusion.

I have elsewhere (Barkley, 1982) proposed a more stringent set of guidelines. These have been modified somewhat and are presently as follows:

1. Parent and/or teacher complaints of inattention, impulsivity, overactivity, and poor rule-governed behavior (e.g., sustained compliance, self-control, and problem solving).
2. A score or scores two standard deviations above the mean for same-age, same-sex normal children on factors labeled as "Inattention" or "Hyperactivity" in well-standardized child behavior rating scales completed by parents or teachers.
3. Onset of these problems by 6 years of age.
4. Duration of these problems for at least 12 months.
5. An IQ greater than 85 or, if between 70 and 85, comparison to children of the same mental age in using criterion 2 above.
6. The exclusion of significant language delay, sensory handicaps (e.g., deafness, blindness, etc.), or severe psychopathology (e.g., autism, childhood schizophrenia).

It is possible for children to exhibit symptoms of ADD/H after the age of 6 years as a result of central nervous system trauma or disease. In such cases, I suggest that all of these criteria other than 3 must be met and that the disorder should be referred to as "acquired ADD/H secondary to _____" with the known etiology specified so as to distinguish such children from the more common developmental, idiopathic form of the disorder described in the vast majority of research on the subject.

It should be noted that these criteria do not preclude the children receiving additional DSM-IIIR diagnoses of Oppositional–Defiant Disorder or Conduct Disorder. As mentioned later, these disorders overlap substantially with ADD/H and would be expected to occur in the majority of such children.

I am in agreement with other experienced

researchers in this field (Werry, 1985) in viewing ADD/H as being on a dimension or continuum with normal child behavior. Deficits in attention, impulsivity, and activity may be to ADD/H what delays in intelligence are to mental retardation: Both conditions lie on a continuum with normal development and are established by using a somewhat arbitrary cutoff point along this continuum. Yet one must recognize the existence of borderline conditions lying near to but not beyond this cutoff point. The condition is not necessarily static, in that once so diagnosed a child always remains within this category. While ADD/H is generally chronic, with a high degree of stability over development for most children (see Campbell, Schleifer, & Weiss, 1978), those lying nearest to the cutoff point may move into or out of the class over development as their individual scores fluctuate.

From this viewpoint, the disorder might best be defined as follows: *ADD/H is a developmental disorder of attention span, impulsivity, and/or overactivity as well as rule-governed behavior, in which these deficits are significantly inappropriate for the child's mental age; have an onset in early childhood; are significantly pervasive or cross-situational in nature; are generally chronic or persistent over time; and are not the direct result of severe language delay, deafness, blindness, autism, or childhood psychosis.*

Primary Symptoms

Numerous studies have shown that ADD/H children are significantly different from normal children on measures of attention span, activity level, and impulse control (for review, see Ross & Ross, 1976, 1982; Whalen & Henker, 1980). However, many of these studies have also shown substantial disparities in the types of measures on which such differences occur, the kinds of settings in which the measures are taken, and the definitions used to select the ADD/H children; these factors have led to many failures to replicate the findings of others on these constructs (Barkley, 1982). While space precludes a full elucidation of the issue here, it is clear that the constructs of inattention, overactivity, impulsivity, and rule-governed behavior are not unitary, but multidimensional (Barkley & Ullman, 1975; Douglas & Peters, 1979; Milich & Kramer, 1984; Ullman *et al.,* 1978; Zettle & Hayes, 1982). There are many different types

of attention, activity, impulsivity, and rule-governed behavior and numerous ways to measure them, not all of which have consistently revealed differences between ADD/H and normal children. Moreover, research has not always been successful in demonstrating the more important distinction between ADD/H and other psychiatric disorders on measures of these primary symptoms (Firestone & Martin, 1979; Sandberg, Rutter, & Taylor, 1978; Shaffer, McNamara, & Pincus, 1974). And so, while this chapter may frequently refer to such constructs as if they are unitary and as if they consistently differentiate ADD/H from other groups of children, the complexity inherent in these terms and the disparity among studies should not be ignored.

CONCEPTUALIZATION OF ADD/H. I have elsewhere proposed, and have noted above, that ADD/H children may have an additional primary deficit in rule-governed behavior (Barkley, 1981a, 1981b, in press). Space precludes a fuller description of this construct and justification for its inclusion as a primary symptom. Suffice it to say here that "rule-governed behavior" refers to the ability of language (commands, directions, instructions, descriptions, etc.) or other symbol systems to serve as discriminative stimuli for behavior (Zettle & Hayes, 1982). Rules are contingency-specifying stimuli (Skinner, 1969), constructed either by the verbal community or by the individual, which specify relations (the contingencies) among antecedents, behavior, and consequences.

ADD/H children have considerable difficulties adhering to rules constructed for them by the social community (e.g., parents and teachers). At times they may not initiate compliance to direct instructions, may initiate it but fail to sustain it, or may sustain the compliance but in a form unacceptable to the community (see Barkley, 1985). In fact, most studies on ADD/H children using laboratory tasks of attention and impulsivity are studies of rule-governed behavior, in that instructions (rules) for performing the task are always given by the examiner. As a result, this voluminous body of experiments on attention span and impulsivity is hopelessly confounded by the construct of rule-governed behavior. Such studies have shown that ADD/H children have difficulties in *sustaining* compliance to the task instructions, especially when the task is boring and there are few or no consequences for doing so.

Finally, ADD/H children exercise poor problem solving in academic or social situations (Douglas, 1983). Problem solving (Skinner, 1969) is a form of rule-governed behavior in which the individual generates a series of questions or instructions (second-order rules) that, when followed, lead to the construction of a solution (first-order rule). One debate in the literature on self-control in ADD/H children (Kendall & Braswell, 1984) concerns whether their deficit is in knowing how to construct such second-order rules, which implies a skills deficit, or whether it is the compliance with the strategy that is deficient, which implies a performance or motivational deficit. Certainly deficits in the latter (governance by rules), over time, could lead to deficits in the former (learning rule construction).

It therefore seems that ADD/H children are primarily "contingency-shaped" in their behavior, as opposed to "rule-governed." That is, their behavior is more often under the control of the immediately occurring natural consequences in a situation than of its rules. Douglas (1983) seems to refer to this as a heightened sensitivity to immediate reinforcement, but I prefer to think of it as a diminished sensitivity to control by rules. It is quite possible that deficits in rule-governed behavior could actually result in the other primary deficits of ADD/H children, such as short attention span to tasks, poor impulse control, poor regulation of activity level to setting demands, deficient problem-solving and social skills, and poor regulation of emotions. While more research on this issue is clearly required, I believe that the literature is sufficiently compelling for us to include poor rule-governed behavior as one of the primary deficits in ADD/H children.

SITUATIONAL VARIATION. Much evidence demonstrates that ADD/H children do not display their primary problems, or display them to a consistent degree, in all situations (Barkley, 1981a; Zentall, 1984), under all contingencies (Barkley, in press), and with all caregivers with whom they may have contact (Tallmadge & Barkley, 1983). This no doubt leads to disagreements among various caregivers (i.e., parents, teachers, babysitters, grandparents, physicians) as to whether or not a child truly has ADD/H. When such doubt exists, parents, particularly mothers, are usually most readily blamed for the children's behavioral problems, since they most often appear to have the greatest difficulties with such children (Tallmadge & Barkley, 1983).

Several factors seem to contribute to this variation in behavioral problems across settings: (1) the degree of "structure" in a situation, or the extent to which a setting makes demands on ADD/H children to restrain their behavior and comply with situational rules and commands (Barkley, Karlsson, & Pollard, 1985; Jacob, O'Leary, & Rosenblad, 1978; Luk, 1985; Mash & Johnston, 1982); (2) the sex of a parent dealing with a child (Tallmadge & Barkley, 1983), in that fathers have somewhat fewer problems than mothers; (3) the nature of the tasks that ADD/H children are asked to do, as well as the frequency with which the instructions for the task are repeated to the children throughout their performance (relatively dull tasks involving sustained attention with no repetition of directions result in the poorest performance by ADD/H children); (4) the novelty or unfamiliarity of a situation; and (5) the contingencies, or schedule of consequences, operating during a particular setting or task. More immediate and more frequent reinforcement appears to result in more normal levels of performance in ADD/H children, whereas normal children can sustain accurate levels of performance under far less immediate or frequent consequences (Barkley, in press; Barkley, Copeland, & Sivage, 1980; Douglas & Parry, 1983).

SUBTYPING ADD/H. As noted earlier, ADD/H is a heterogeneous disorder. Recently, efforts have been made to classify these children into more homogeneous subtypes. One promising approach has been to subdivide ADD/H children based upon the presence and degree of aggressiveness (Loney & Milich, 1982; Milich & Loney, 1979). "Aggression" in these studies is not defined as physical attacks against others so much as a constellation of negative temperament (e.g., temper outbursts) and oppositional and defiant behavior (e.g., quarreling, refusing to cooperate, acting "smart"). ADD/H children who are also significantly aggressive tend to have more severe primary symptoms, greater academic performance problems, greater peer relationship problems, poorer outcome in adolescence and young adulthood, and a greater incidence of psychopathology in their parents than do ADD/H children not considered aggressive. The latter subgroup tends to have problems primarily in academic performance.

A second approach to subtyping has been to define ADD/H as either "situational" or "pervasive." Situational ADD/H is that defined as

ADD/H by either parents *or* teachers, while pervasive ADD/H is that defined as ADD/H by both. Children with pervasive ADD/H have been found to have greater behavioral disturbance, greater persistence of their disturbance over time, and greater cognitive and learning impairments (Schacher, Rutter, & Smith, 1981). However, these findings have not been replicated by others (Cohen & Minde, 1983; McGee, Williams, & Silva, 1984a, 1984b). It appears that the aforementioned subtyping approach based on degree of aggression may account for these results. Children with pervasive ADD/H are more likely to fall into the "ADD/H with aggression" subtype, and as a result may have greater problems with deviance, chronicity, and cognitive impairments than children with situational ADD/H.

A third subtyping distinction is that set forth in DSM-III as Attention Deficit Disorder with or without Hyperactivity. The results of studies on this classification have been conflicting. Several have not found important differences between ADD/H children and those without hyperactivity (Maurer & Stewart, 1980; Rubinstein & Brown, 1984). However, others have found that ADD/H children have greater conduct problems and oppositional behavior, greater peer relationship difficulties, and more academic performance problems than those without hyperactivity (Edelbrock *et al.,* 1984; King & Young, 1982). The results are only suggestive, however, since many of these studies have serious methodological flaws.

Related Characteristics

ADD/H children have been found to experience a number of cognitive, academic, emotional, social, and physical problems in addition to their primary problems. Such children seem more likely to have deficits in general intelligence (Safer & Allen, 1976; Tarver-Behring, Barkley, & Karlsson, 1985), academic achievement (Cantwell & Satterfield, 1978; Safer & Allen, 1976); depression and low self-esteem (Weiss, Hechtman, & Perlman, 1978), and poor peer acceptance (Johnston, Pelham, & Murphy, 1985; Pelham & Bender, 1982). ADD/H children also appear to have more minor physical anomalies (Quinn & Rapoport, 1974), although the reliability, specificity for this disorder, and meaning of such differences remain obscure (Krouse & Kauffman, 1982). Accidental poisonings and injuries (Hartsough & Lam-

bert, 1985; Stewart, Thach, & Freidin, 1970); allergies (Trites, Tryphonas, & Ferguson, 1980); motor incoordination (Denckla & Rudel, 1978); enuresis and encopresis (Safer & Allen, 1976); and vision, language, and chronic general health problems (Hartsough & Lambert, 1985) have all been observed to be more common in ADD/H than normal or non-ADD/H children. Studies comparing ADD/H and normal children on various psychophysiological measures have produced conflicting results, but what little agreement there is suggests greater variability in responding and underreactivity of responding in ADD/H children (Ferguson & Pappas, 1979; Hastings & Barkley, 1978; Rosenthal & Allen, 1978). Nevertheless, it is unclear what relationship such findings have to the behavioral problems of these children, their differential response to treatment, and the specificity of these findings for ADD/H as compared to other psychiatric disorders in children.

Prevalence

The occurrence of ADD/H in the population has been somewhat difficult to estimate, as a result of the considerable variation in definitions. Prevalence estimates range from as low as 1% to as much as 20% of the school-age population. A generally cited figure is 3–5% (American Psychiatric Association, 1980). Cut-off scores on teacher rating scales yield prevalence rates of 9–20% for boys and 2–9% for girls if a score greater than 1.5 standard deviations above the mean is used (O'Leary, Vivian, & Nisi, 1985; Trites, Dugas, Lynch, & Ferguson, 1979). More stringent cut off scores, such as the criterion of two standard deviations above the mean recommended earlier, yield 5–7% for boys and 2–4% for girls. Where different social definers (parents, teachers, physicians) are used, the incidence varies from 1.15% where agreement among all three definers is required to 4.92% where at least one definer reports the child to be ADD/H (Lambert, Sandoval, & Sassone, 1978). Boys are reported as having the disorder more often than girls, with ratios ranging from 4:1 to 9:1 across studies (Ross & Ross, 1976). A generally accepted ratio is 6:1. However, epidemiological studies seem to suggest that a ratio of 3:1 is more typical in the general population (Trites *et al.,* 1979). The prevalence also appears to vary somewhat with socioeconomic status (Lambert *et al.,* 1978), although the differences across levels of status are not especially impressive. The rate of occurrence of ADD/H fluctuates to some extent across countries (O'Leary et al., 1985; Trites et al., 1979), and Ross and Ross (1982) even noted that among Chinese-Americans in New York City and children residing in Salt Lake City, Utah, the prevalence of ADD/H was low to nonexistent. The reasons for this are not clear.

Developmental Course and Predictors of Outcome

It is commonly accepted that ADD/H arises early in childhood and that precursors of the disorder may, in fact, be identified in infancy. Infants of difficult temperament who are excessively active, have poor sleeping and eating habits, and are negative in their moods are at greater risk for later ADD/H than children having more normal temperaments (see Ross & Ross, 1982, for a review). Also, as noted earlier, infants with a higher frequency of minor physical anomalies may also be at greater risk for later behavioral disorders, such as ADD/H (Quinn & Rapoport, 1974). However, not all children who are eventually diagnosed as ADD/H have a history of minor anomalies or difficult temperament in infancy, and even those children who do are not necessarily destined to become ADD/H (Chamberlin, 1977).

By 3 years of age, over 50% of ADD/H children have begun to manifest behavioral problems, particularly overactivity, short attention span, and noncompliant behavior. "Child-proofing" the home is often necessary, given the greater risk noted earlier of accidental injuries and poisonings. As a result of noncompliance, toilet training at this age may be difficult and occur later than normal (Hartsough & Lambert, 1985). For those children who begin attendance at nursery or preschool programs, complaints from teachers concerning restlessness, inattention, and oppositional behavior appear to be common.

Research suggests that once children are noted to be excessive in those areas of behavior characteristic of ADD/H, their problems remain relatively stable over time from their preschool years into their early formal schooling (Campbell et al., 1978). By 6 years of age, over 90% of ADD/H children will have been identified as problematic by their parents or teachers. Continuing problems with attention span, on-task behavior, compliance with classroom rules and directions, and restlessness are noted. Many ADD/H children will have problems in their relationships with peers, due to their selfishness, immaturity, heightened emotionality, conduct problems, and general lack of age-appropriate social skills (Pelham & Bender, 1982). With exposure to broader social situations (school, community, public places), ADD/H children pose even greater management difficulties for their parents, particularly in unsupervised situations. At an age when children can often be trusted to follow appropriate social rules when outside of parental supervision, ADD/H children are often described by their parents as being incapable of being trusted when alone. Parents may now have difficulty getting baby-sitters to sit with these children because of the history of chronic behavioral problems under such conditions. Parents often find themselves spending most of the children's waking day supervising their activities. They may even come to spend less time with the children in recreational pursuits because of frequent management problems posed under such conditions. Stress in the parental role as well as reports of maternal depression may arise or increase at this time (Breen, 1985; Mash & Johnston, 1983a).

During middle to late childhood (6–11 years of age), complaints about ADD/H children at school may focus not only upon underachievement and failure to complete assignments, but disruptive classroom conduct, continuing poor social skills, and difficulties with self-control when outside of teacher supervision (hallways, riding the bus, recess, lunchtime, etc.). Learning disabilities may now be observed in approximately 25% or more of ADD/H children; whether or not they are noted, learning disabilities may emerge in many such youngsters. Some children eventually are placed for part of their school day within programs described with the unfortunate label of "emotionally disturbed." Nevertheless, smaller classroom environments allowing for greater teacher attention, more individualized instruction, and more frequent use of contingency management methods may be needed for elementary-age ADD/H children.

In the home, parents may now complain that these children are unable to take responsibility for routine chores and activities, such as dressing for school on time, cleaning their rooms, doing homework, or assisting with other household jobs. Neighborhood children may already have labeled ADD/H children as undesirable, due to their prior reputations for aggressiveness and immature conduct, as well as for their often poor athletic ability stemming from delayed motor development. Parents of ADD/H children bemoan the children's lack of friends and may find their children gravitating toward associations with other problematic children. Within the community, lying, stealing, and destructiveness of others' property may appear in those children with prior histories of aggressive and oppositional behavior. By late childhood, many ADD/H children report low self-esteem.

Several factors appear to play a role in the outcome during the teenage years. Those children with "pure" ADD/H not associated with significant aggressiveness or peer problems are likely to have problems primarily in school performance (Paternite & Loney, 1980); they are typically described as "underachieving." Those having associated aggression and conduct problems apparently fare much worse. Not only are school performance problems significant, but difficulties with predelinquent or delinquent behavior in the community may emerge, and peer relationship problems remain significant or increase in severity. Although ADD/H children are less active, inattentive, and noncompliant at this age than in their childhood years, significant problems with rebelliousness, defiance of authority, violation of family rules, and immature or irresponsible conduct are often described by parents. Some evidence suggests that ADD/H children may be more likely to abuse alcohol (Blouin, Bornstein, & Trites, 1978), while other research suggests not (Weiss, Hechtman, Perlman, Hopkins, & Wener, 1979); yet, the research by Weiss et al. (1979) suggests a greater likelihood of use of hallucinogens by ADD/H as compared to control children. ADD/H children also appear more likely to have car accidents than other teenagers (Weiss et al., 1979). Many continue to have feelings of low self-esteem, poor social acceptance, and depression (Hechtman, Weiss, & Perlman, 1980). Approximately 30% will fail to complete high school, and of those who do, most will fail to pursue any university degree program (Weiss, Hechtman, Milroy, & Perlman, 1985).

As young adults, ADD/H individuals appear to make a more adequate adjustment to their employment setting than they did to school (Weiss et al., 1978). Still, as many as 66% are reported to have continuing problems with restlessness, inattention, impulsivity, low self-esteem, and feelings of sadness and depression, compared to same-age controls (Hechtman et al., 1980; Weiss et al., 1985). Over 75% complain of interpersonal problems or significant psychological difficulties, and more of them will make suicide attempts than will normal or control subjects (Weiss et al., 1985). Between 23% and 45% may eventually receive a DSM-III diagnosis of Adult Antisocial Personality (Loney, Whaley-Klahn, Kosier, & Conboy, 1981; Weiss et al., 1985). Approximately 27% may be diagnosed as alcoholic by adulthood; while this rate is greater than that expected for normal adults, it is not different from the rate of alcoholism among the ADD/H individuals' siblings. Common genetic disposition or family environment rather than ADD/H itself, then, may be related to alcoholism in these children (Hechtman, Weiss, Perlman, & Amsel, 1984; Loney et al., 1981). In general, follow-up studies find ADD/H individuals as young adults to be doing less well socially, psychologically, academically, and occupationally than controls or even their own siblings (Loney et al., 1981; Thorley, 1984; Weiss et al., 1985). Such findings clearly indicate that adult disorders exist that are equivalent to ADD/H or are residual conditions of childhood ADD/H (Wender, Reimherr, & Wood, 1981; Wood, Reimherr, Wender, & Johnson, 1976).

Studies examining predictors of outcome in ADD/H children have identified low intelligence in childhood, aggressiveness and oppositional behavior, poor peer acceptance, emotional instability, and extent of parental psychopathology as predictors of poorer outcomes (Hechtman, Weiss, Perlman, & Amsel, 1984; Loney et al., 1981; Paternite & Loney, 1980). While extensive, long-term treatment during adolescence may make some improvement in outcome (Satterfield, Satterfield, & Cantwell, 1981), lesser degrees of treatment, including stimulant drug therapy, provide only marginal benefit to the adult outcome of this group (Hechtman, Weiss, & Perlman, 1984; Paternite & Loney, 1980).

Etiology

Various causes of ADD/H have been proposed, and many theorists now see the disorder as arising from multiple etiologies, much as they view other developmental disabilities (e.g., mental retardation). Brain damage was initially believed to be a primary cause of this disorder (Strauss & Lehtinen, 1947), but more recent research suggests that fewer than 5% of ADD/H children have hard evidence of neurological damage (Rutter, 1977). And, while it is possible for brain injury to lead to the development of attention deficits and hyperactivity, most brain-injured children do not develop such difficulties (Rutter, Chadwick, & Shaffer, 1983). Some research suggests potential neurotransmitter abnormalities in ADD/H children (Shaywitz, Cohen, & Shaywitz, 1978; Shaywitz, Shaywitz, Cohen, & Young, 1983), but such studies have often produced conflicting results and have relied on models of central neurotransmitter functioning based upon samples from peripheral systems (blood serotonin, urinary metabolites of neurotransmitters, etc.) that may or may not reliably reflect central biochemical activities. Research using computerized tomography (CT) scan techniques to evaluate ADD/H children has not found any significant structural abnormalities (Shaywitz, Shaywitz, Byrne, Cohen, & Rothman, 1983); however, decreased levels of cerebral blood flow in the frontal white matter and frontal–midbrain tracts have been reported in ADD/H as compared to dysphasic children (Lou, Henriksen, & Bruhn, 1984), suggesting decreased activity or stimulation in these regions (Fox & Raichle, 1985). Such findings may explain the observations of decreased reactivity to stimulation in psychophysiological research with ADD/H children (Hastings & Barkley, 1978). Finally, some investigators (Kinsbourne, 1977) have proposed that neurological immaturity may be a cause of ADD/H. While there is suggestive evidence from the behavioral symptoms and psychophysiological research for such a hypothesis, the notion remains both vague and difficult to test directly with current neurological evaluative methods.

Various environmental toxins have been proposed as causes of ADD/H in children. Some (Feingold, 1975) have proposed that toxic or allergic reactions to food additives such as artificial colorings cause over 60% of ADD/H in children. Placement on a diet relatively free of the offending additives is proposed as the most effective treatment. A substantial body of research has accrued suggesting that this is hardly the case (for reviews, see Conners, 1980; Mattes & Gittelman, 1981). This can be summarized as indicating that the vast majority of ADD/H children show no changes in behavior when placed on such diets; among the 5% who do, the changes noted are quite small, are usually limited to changes in parent or teacher rating scales, and can hardly be considered clinically therapeutic effects. Others (J. F. Taylor, 1980) have proposed that much of ADD/H behavior is a reaction to allergens in the environment. While ADD/H children may have more allergies than other children (Trites et al., 1980), there is no evidence that the removal of the suspected allergens or other treatment of the allergic children results in clinically significant improvements in the children, although minor improvements in behavior may be noted (Trites et al., 1980).

More recently, sugar in children's diets has been proposed as a cause of ADD/H, among other childhood disorders (Smith, 1976). While one study did show a significant relationship between levels of sugar consumed in the diets of ADD/H children and their rates of aggressiveness and activity in a clinic playroom, such relationships were not found for normal children, nor did the ADD/H children consume more sugar than the normal children (Prinz, Roberts, & Hantman, 1980). Furthermore, studies that have challenged ADD/H children with sucrose, using aspartame as the placebo control condition, have found no increases in ADD/H symptoms following the sucrose challenges (M. D. Gross, 1984; Wolraich, Milich, Stumbo, & Schultz, 1985).

Elevated blood lead levels have been implicated as a cause of ADD/H symptoms in children (David, 1974), with some studies finding as many as 25–35% of the group of lead-exposed children to have such symptoms (Baloh, Sturm, Green, & Gleser, 1975; de la Burde & Choate, 1972, 1974). However, other studies are conflicting in their results (Milar, Schroeder, Mushak, & Boone, 1981; Needleman et al., 1979) or have found the association to be weak at best (Gittelman & Eskenazi, 1983).

Some research exists to show an association between maternal alcohol consumption (Shaywitz, Cohen, & Shaywitz, 1980), as well as maternal smoking (Denson, Nanson, & McWatters, 1975; Nichols, 1980), during pregnancy and symptoms of ADD/H in the exposed children. However, the causal link here is unclear. While it may well be that ingestion of such substances during pregnancy results in toxic effects on the fetus such that ADD/H symptoms are more likely, it may also be that women who are more likely to have ADD/H children are, by virtue of their own increased risk of psychiatric disturbance, more likely to smoke or consume alcohol during pregnancy. The indication of a greater frequency of psychiatric disturbance and alcohol abuse among parents and relatives of ADD/H children, and the fact that fathers and stepfathers of ADD/H children were also found to smoke more heavily than normal (Denson et al., 1975), at least call into question the causal direction proposed among these variables.

Recently, a hereditary cause for ADD/H has been the focus of increased research. Investigators have long recognized the increased incidence of various psychiatric disorders (Befera & Barkley, 1985)—particularly psychopathy, antisocial personality, depression, conduct disorders, alcoholism, and ADD/H—among biological relatives of ADD/H children (Cantwell, 1975; Morrison & Stewart, 1971, 1973). The relatively high concordance for activity level among monozygotic twins (Lopez, 1965; Willerman, 1973), and the increased incidence of ADD/H among the biological parents and siblings of ADD/H children (Deutsch, 1984), are suggestive of some as yet unspecified mode of inheritance of these characteristics. Further support comes from the acknowledgment that Tourette syndrome is probably an inherited disorder in which there is a greater than normal incidence of ADD/H symptoms in the affected children and their relatives (Comings & Comings, 1984).

There have been few efforts to articulate a purely environmental cause for ADD/H in children. Block (1977) has proposed that an increase in the incidence of hyperactivity over time, coupled with a corresponding increase in the "cultural tempo" of our times, may have resulted in greater stimulation of our children and hence a greater likelihood of hyperactivity in those children already predisposed to such characteristics. Ross and Ross (1982), in their excellent review of the literature, find the evidence not especially compelling. Willis and Lovaas (1977) have proposed that ADD/H is a deficit in the stimulus control of behavior by parental commands that derives from poor child management techniques employed by the parents. While mothers of ADD/H children provide more commands and supervision to their children, this appears to be partly a function of the type of task required of the children (Tallmadge & Barkley, 1983) and the age of the children (Barkley, Karlsson, & Pollard, 1985;

Mash & Johnston, 1982), and is substantially diminished when the children are treated with stimulant medication (Barkley & Cunningham, 1980; Barkley, Karlsson, Strzelecki, & Murphy, 1984; Humphries, Kinsbourne, & Swanson, 1978). Such results suggest that the behavior of the mothers is more likely a reaction to than a chief cause of the behavioral difficulties in ADD/H children.

In summary, ADD/H is a disorder with potentially numerous etiologies, among which the biological causes appear to have the greatest support. Most likely, the causes of the disorder should be viewed much as one views those of mental retardation—multiple causes having a final common pathway inevitably affecting the development of particular abilities.

Implications for Assessment

The material just reviewed has a number of important implications for the clinical assessment of children with ADD/H:

1. The primary problems of these children appear to be in the areas of sustained attention, impulsivity, overactivity, and poor rule-governed behavior; accordingly, these should be the major targets of assessment and, of course, intervention. Given the considerably greater incidence of other disorders coexisting with ADD/H, such as learning disabilities, oppositional and defiant behavior, conduct disorders, enuresis and encopresis, and social skills deficits, a comprehensive assessment must also include methods to address these areas. This chapter does not discuss the assessment of these latter problems, as their evaluation is the subject of the other chapters in this text to which the reader should refer. Assessment methods must be chosen for their ability to evaluate these major domains of difficulty.

2. Given that current diagnostic criteria require that a child's behavioral problems be developmentally inappropriate for his or her mental age, assessment techniques having adequate normative data will be necessary.

3. The cross-situational or pervasive nature of ADD/H dictates that the evaluation collect information on the child's functioning in different settings and with different caregivers.

4. The chronic nature of ADD/H throughout childhood and adolescence makes it useful to have assessment methods that are appropriate across wide age ranges, with adequate normative data at each age. The need for periodic

reassessments of these children over time, to evaluate maturational changes in behavior as well as whether that behavior remains problematic or statistically atypical, should encourage the clinician to use such developmentally referenced techniques.

5. Given the greater prevalence of psychiatric disorders among the parents of ADD/H children, and the likelihood that such disorders may interfere with response to treatment, it will prove important to expand the scope of the evaluation to include some measures of the psychiatric status of the parents and siblings and their own needs for treatment.

ASSESSMENT

The evaluation of ADD/H children incorporates multiple assessment methods, relying upon several informants concerning the nature of the children's difficulties across multiple situations. Parent, child, and teacher interviews; parent and teacher rating scales of child behavior, and self-report scales for older children; laboratory measures of ADD/H symptoms; direct observational techniques; and parent self-report measures of relevant psychiatric conditions must all be part of the clinical protocol.

Parental Interview

Although often criticized for its unreliability and subjectivity, the parental interview remains an indispensable part of the clinical assessment of children. Whether accurate or not, parental reports provide an ecologically valid and important source of information concerning the children's difficulties. It is the parents' complaints that have often led to the referral of the children, that will affect their perceptions of and reactions to the children, and that will influence their adherence to the treatment recommendations. Moreover, the reliability and accuracy of the parental interview have much to do with the manner in which it is conducted and the specificity of the questions offered by the examiner. Interviewing that focuses upon the specific complaints and functional parameters of the children's problems provides the cornerstone upon which the remainder of the evaluation is built.

After obtaining the routine demographic data concerning a child and family, the interview proceeds to the major referral concerns of the parents (and those of the professional referring

the child, where appropriate). General descriptions by parents must be followed with specific questions by the examiner to elucidate the details of the problems and their functional relationships. The format of the behavioral interview provides a useful framework for approaching this task (see A. M. Gross, 1984; Morganstern, 1976). A functional-analytic interview probes not only for the specific nature, frequency, age of onset, and chronicity of the problematic behaviors, but also for the situational and temporal variation in the behaviors and their consequences. If the problems are chronic, which they often are, determining what has prompted the referral at this time reveals much about parental perceptions of a child's problems, current family circumstances related to the problems' severity, and parental motivation for treatment.

Following this, the examiner should review with the parents potential problems that may exist in the developmental domains of motor, language, intellectual, academic, emotional, and social functioning. Such information greatly aids in the differential diagnosis of a child's problems. To accomplish this requires that the examiner have an adequate knowledge of the diagnostic features of other childhood disorders, some of which may present superficially as ADD/H. For instance, many children with Pervasive Developmental Disorders (Childhood Onset) as defined by DSM-III may be viewed by their parents as ADD/H children, as they are more likely to have heard about the latter disorder than the former and will recognize some of the ADD/H qualities in their children. Questioning about inappropriate thinking, affect, social relations, and motor peculiarities may reveal a more seriously and pervasively disturbed child. Inquiry must be made as to the presence or history of tics in the child or the immediate biological family members. Where this is noted, the examiner should either recommend against the use of stimulant drugs in the treatment of such a child, or, at the very least, urge cautious use of low doses of such medicine to preclude the exacerbation of the child's tic disorder (Comings & Comings, 1984; Golden, 1983).

Developmental, medical, school, and family histories are then obtained. The last of these should include a discussion of potential psychiatric difficulties in the parents and siblings; marital difficulties; and any family problems centered around chronic medical conditions, employment difficulties, or other potentially stressful events within the family. Of course, the examiner will want to obtain some information about prior treatments received by the child and family for these presenting problems. Where the history suggests potentially treatable medical or neurological conditions (allergies, seizures, Tourette syndrome, etc.), a referral to a physician is essential. Without evidence of such problems, however, referral to a physician for examination usually fails to reveal any further information of use in the treatment of ADD/H children. An exception to this is where the use of stimulant medications is contemplated, in which case a referral to a physician is clearly indicated.

Following this generic interview, the examiner must pursue more details about the nature of the parent–child interactions surrounding the child's following of rules. All ADD/H children have problems complying or sustaining compliance with certain types of commands, directions, and assigned tasks. Such problems usually consist of failures to finish assigned activities, particularly when they are boring, effortful, and have few or no immediate consequences. More than 60% of ADD/H children, however, have also acquired a repertoire of oppositional, defiant, and coercive behaviors, and these naturally exacerbate conflictual interactions with parents over rules. Therefore, parents should be questioned about a child's ability to accomplish commands and requests in a satisfactory manner in various settings, to adhere to rules of conduct governing behavior in various situations, and to demonstrate self-control (rule following) appropriate to the child's age in the absence of adult supervision. To accomplish this, I have found it useful to follow the format set forth in Table 2, in which parents are questioned about their interactions with their children in a variety of home and public situations. Where problems are said to occur, the examiner follows up with questions 2–9 in Table 2.

Such an approach yields a wealth of information on the nature of parent–child interactions across settings; the type of noncompliance shown by the child (e.g., stalling, starting the task but failing to finish it, outright opposition and defiance, etc.); the particular management style employed by parents to deal with noncompliance; and the particular types of coercive behaviors used by the child as part of the noncompliance. This may add an additional 30–40 minutes to the parental interview, but is well worth the time invested where it is possible to do so. Where time constraints are problematic, a rating scale can be used that has been developed to provide similar types of information (see the discussion of the Home Situations

TABLE 2. Parental Interview Format

Situations to be discussed with parents	Follow-up questions for each problematic situation
General—overall interactions Playing alone Playing with other children Mealtimes Getting dressed in morning During washing and bathing While parent is on telephone While watching television While visitors are at home While visiting others' homes In public places (supermarkets, shopping centers, etc.) While mother is occupied with chores or activities When father is at home When child is asked to do a chore At bedtime Other situations (in car, in church, etc.)	1. Is this a problem area? If so, then proceed with questions 2 through 9. 2. What does the child do in this situation that bothers you? 3. What is your response? 4. What will the child do next? 5. If the problem continues, what will you do next? 6. What is usually the outcome of this interaction? 7. How often do these problems occur in this situation? 8. How do you feel about these problems? 9. On a scale of 0 to 10 (0 = no problem; 10 = severe problem), how severe is the problem to you?

Note. Adapted from interview used by C. Hanf, 1976, University of Oregon Health Sciences Center. Reprinted from *Hyperactive Children: A Handbook for Diagnosis and Treatment* by R. A. Barkley, 1981, New York: Guilford Press. Copyright 1981 by the Guilford Press. Reprinted by permission.

Questionnaire in "Parent Rating Scales," below). After parents complete the scale, they can be questioned about one or two of the problem situations, using the same follow-up questions as in Table 2.

This interview may also reveal that one parent, usually the mother, has more difficulty managing the ADD/H child than the other. Care should be taken to discuss differences in the parents' approaches to management and any marital problems this may have spawned. Such difficulties in child management can often lead to reduced leisure and recreational time for the parents, increased conflict within the marriage, and often conflict within the extended family if relatives should live nearby. The examiner should briefly inquire about the nature of parental and family social activities to determine how isolated, or insular, the parents are from the usual social support networks in which many parents are involved. Research by Wahler (1980) has shown that the degree of maternal insularity is significantly associated with failure in subsequent parent training programs. Where insularity is present to a significant degree, such a finding might suggest addressing the isolation as an initial goal of treatment, rather than progressing directly to child behavior management training with that family.

The parental interview can then conclude with a discussion of the child's positive characteristics and attributes, as well as potential rewards and reinforcers desired by the child that will prove useful in later parent training on contingency management methods. Some parents of ADD/H children have had such chronic and pervasive management problems that upon initial questioning they may find it hard to report anything positive about their children. Getting them to begin thinking of such attributes is actually an initial step toward treatment, as the early phases of parent training will teach parents to focus on and attend to desirable child behaviors (Forehand & McMahon, 1981).

Child Interview

Some time should always be spent directly interacting with ADD/H children. The length of this interview depends upon the age, intellectual level, and language abilities of the children. With young children, it may serve merely as a time to become acquainted, noting their appearance, behavior, developmental characteristics, and general demeanor. With older children and adolescents, this time can be fruitfully spent inquiring about the children's views of the reasons for the referral and evaluation, how they see the family functioning, any additional problems they feel they may have, how well they are performing at school, their degree of acceptance by peers and classmates, and what changes in the family they believe might make life for them happier at home. Like the parents, the children can be queried as to potential rewards and reinforcers they find desirable, which will prove useful in later contingency management programs.

A word of caution is appropriate: Children below the age of 12 are not especially reliable in their reports of their own problems or those of other family members, and the problem is compounded by the frequently diminished self-awareness and impulse control of typical ADD/H children. ADD/H children often show little reflection about the examiner's questions and may lie or distort information in a more socially pleasing direction. Some will report that they have many friends, have no interaction problems at home with their parents, and are doing well at school, in direct contrast with the extensive parental and teacher complaints of inappropriate behavior by these children.

While notation of the children's behavior, compliance, attention span, activity level, and impulse control within the clinic is useful, clinicians must guard against drawing any diagnostic conclusions from cases where the children are not problematic in the clinic or office. Many ADD/H children do not misbehave in clinicians' offices, and so heavy reliance upon such observations will clearly lead to false negatives in the diagnosis (Sleator & Ullmann, 1981). In some instances, the behavior of the children with their parents in the waiting area prior to the appointment may be a better indication of the children's management problems at home than is the children's behavior toward clinicians, particularly when this involves a one-to-one interaction between a child and an examiner.

Teacher Interview

At some point during or soon after the initial evaluative session with the family, contact with a child's teacher(s) is essential to further clarifying the nature of the child's problems. The vast majority of ADD/H children have problems with academic performance and classroom behavior, and the details of these difficulties need to be obtained. While this may initially be done by telephone, a visit to the classroom and direct observation and recording of a child's behavior, where time and resources permit, can prove quite useful in further documenting the ADD/H behaviors of the child and in planning later contingency management programs for the classroom. Teachers should also be sent the rating scales discussed below. These can be sent as a packet prior to an actual evaluation, so that the results are available for discussion with a child's parents during the interview, as well as with the teacher during the subsequent telephone contact or school visit.

This interview should focus upon the specific nature of a child's problems in the school environment, again following a functional-analytic or behavioral format. The settings, nature, frequency, consequating events, and eliciting events for the major behavioral problems should all be explored. The follow-up questions used in the parental interview on parent–child interactions and shown in Table 2 may prove useful here as well. Teachers should be questioned about potential learning disabilities in ADD/H children, given their greater likelihood of occurrence in this population. Where evidence suggests their existence, the evaluations of such children should be expanded to explore their nature and degree along the lines suggested by H. G. Taylor in Chapter 8 of this text. Even where learning disabilities do not exist, ADD/H children are more likely to have problems with sloppy handwriting, careless approaches to tasks, poor organization of their work materials, and academic "underachievement" relative to their tested abilities. The examiner should take time with the teachers to explore the possibility of these problems.

Parent Rating Scales

Child behavior checklists and rating scales have become an essential element in the evaluation and diagnosis of ADD/H in children. The availability of several scales, with excellent normative data across a wide age range of children and with excellent reliability and validity, makes their incorporation into the assessment protocol quite convenient and extremely useful. Such information is invaluable in determining the statistical deviance of these children's problem behaviors, the extent to which the children meet

the aforementioned diagnostic criteria, and the degree to which other problems may be present. As a result, it is useful to mail a packet of these scales out to parents prior to the initial appointment, asking that they be returned on or before the day of the evaluation. This permits the examiner to review and score them before interviewing the parents and allows for vague or significant answers to be elucidated in the interview.

Numerous child behavior rating scales exist, and the reader is referred elsewhere (Barkley, 1987a) for greater details on the more commonly used scales. Three of these are routinely used in our clinical assessment of ADD/H children, and these are briefly discussed below.

Child Behavior Checklist

The Child Behavior Checklist (CBCL; Achenbach & Edelbrock, 1983) is one of the most rigorously developed and standardized child behavior rating scales currently available for assessing the most common dimensions of child psychopathology. The CBCL consists of 20 items comprising a Social Competence scale and 118 items comprising a Behavior Problem scale. The Social Competence items are distributed across seven categories of information: sports, hobbies and activities, clubs and organizations, chores, friendships, and schooling. From these answers, three Social Competence scores are generated: Activities, Social Involvement, and School Performance. Scores can then be plotted on the Social Competence Profile, which contains the normative data for determination of the child's relative standing in the normal population in these competence areas. Separate profiles are available for both sexes and for four age ranges (2–3, 4–5, 6–11, and 12–16 years of age). This is one of the few rating scales in which any items pertaining to social competence are included.

The Behavior Problem scale has 118 items dealing with various behavioral, social, emotional, and physical problems. Factor analyses of the items were used to generate Child Behavior Profiles of the most common factors for each sex within each of the four age levels described above. Hence, there are different factor scores and Child Behavior Profiles for each of these eight groupings. For instance, for 6- to 11-year-old boys, the Profile contains factor scores for scales of Schizoid or Anxious, De-

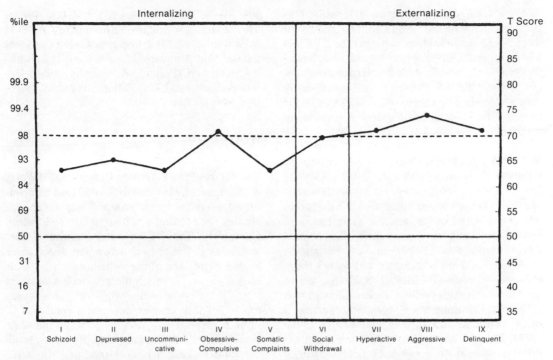

FIGURE 1. The Child Behavior Profile for 60 ADD/H boys on the CBCL. From *Hyperactive Children: A Handbook for Diagnosis and Treatment* by R. A. Barkley, 1981, New York: Guilford Press. Copyright 1981 by the Guilford Press. Reprinted by permission.

pressed, Uncommunicative, Obsessive–Compulsive, Somatic Complaints, Social Withdrawal, Hyperactive, Aggressive, and Delinquent. This attention to developmental changes in the dimensions of child psychopathology is a commendable advantage of this scale.

The normative data are based upon 1,300 children normally distributed across socioeconomic status and chosen by cluster sampling from census tracts in Washington, D.C., Maryland, and Virginia. Test–retest reliability, stability, and interparent agreement are quite satisfactory (see Achenbach & Edelbrock, 1983; Barkley, 1987a). Research has shown that the CBCL significantly discriminates ADD/H from normal and other psychiatric groups of children (Mash & Johnston, 1983a). The mean child Behavior Profile for 60 ADD/H boys (aged 6–11) is shown in Figure 1. It is clear that a large percentage of these ADD/H boys were also oppositional and aggressive, as noted from the significant clinical elevations (*t* score greater than 70) on the Aggressive and Delinquent scales, in addition to the elevation on the Hyperactive scale. The Obsessive–Compulsive scale

was also significantly elevated, primarily because some items loading on this scale pertain to sleep problems, excessive talking, and nervous movements.

Conners Parent Rating Scale—Revised

The most commonly used rating scales in research with ADD/H children have been the Conners Parent and Teacher Rating Scales. Several versions of both scales exist, but the most satisfactory normative data for the former scale are published for the Conners Parent Rating Scale—Revised (CPRS-R; Goyette, Conners, & Ulrich, 1978). This is a 48-item rating scale that can be scored to yield five factor scales: Conduct Problems, Learning Problems, Psychosomatic, Impulsive–Hyperactive, and Anxiety. Many of the items overlap with those on the CBCL. Nevertheless, the CPRS-R is useful in addition to the CBCL for a variety of reasons, chief among these being the substantial number of studies that have employed these scales for evaluating hyperactive children and their response to treatment. Another reason is that the CBCL does not have a separate Hyperactive scale on the Child Behavior Profile for 4- to 5-year-old children, whereas the CPRS-R yields separate factor scores for the Impulsive–Hyperactive and Conduct Problems scales. Finally, the CPRS-R is briefer and more easily repeated over short time intervals than is the longer CBCL, making it useful in evaluating response to treatment.

Normative data on the CPRS-R were collected on 750 children aged 3–17 years and are published elsewhere (Barkley, 1981a; Goyette et al., 1978). Information on test–retest reliability has not been published. Interparent agreement is adequate, and the scale has been shown not only to significantly discriminate ADD/H from non-ADD/H children, but also to be sensitive to stimulant drug and parent training interventions (Barkley, 1987a). Scores on the Conners scales decline somewhat from first to second administration, perhaps reflecting a practice effect, and so it is advised that if the CPRS-R is to be used to assess treatment effects, it should be given once before using it as a baseline or pretreatment measure.

Home Situations Questionnaire

The Home Situations Questionnaire (HSQ; Barkley, 1981a) was developed in order to evaluate *where* children were displaying their behavioral problems, as opposed to what type of problems they were having. The latter information is easily obtained by using the above-described rating scales, but few rating scales adequately assess the situational variation in children's behavioral disorders. The HSQ was developed from the interview format shown in Table 2. The scale itself is available elsewhere (Barkley, 1981a); it asks about 16 situations around the home and in public in which parents might have behavior problems with their children. Parents are asked to answer yes or no as to whether they have a problem in each setting, and, if so, to rate the severity of the problem using a scale from 1 (mild) to 9 (severe). Two scores are obtained: the number of problem situations, and the mean severity rating of these problems. In addition, inspection of the profile across the range of settings often provides useful information for planning contingency management interventions as part of parent training.

Adequate normative data and information on reliability (test–retest, interrater, etc.) are available for the HSQ (Barkley & Edelbrock, 1987). The scale significantly differentiates ADD/H from normal children and is sensitive to parent training and stimulant drug interventions (Barkley, Karlsson, Pollard, & Murphy, 1985; Befera & Barkley, 1985; Pollard, Ward, & Barkley, 1983).

Werry–Weiss–Peters Activity Rating Scale

The Werry–Peters Activity Rating Scale (Werry & Sprague, 1968) consists of 31 items concerning activity level, grouped into seven categories or settings: Mealtimes, Television, Homework, Play, Sleep, Away from Home, and School. Under each setting are listed three to five items describing behavior (e.g., "Gets up and down"), which the respondent answers "No," "Yes—a little bit," or "Yes—very much." These answers are given credits of 0, 1, or 2, respectively, and the score on the scale is the sum of these item credits. Routh, Schroeder, and O'Tuama (1974) modified the scale by dropping those items pertaining to school or homework, leaving 22 items for use. The only normative data available for the scale are those collected on a small sample of normal children of above-average socioeconomic status and intelligence (Routh et al., 1974). Interparent reliability agreements of .90 for the original scale (Werry, Weiss, Douglas, & Martin, 1966) and .82 for the modified version (Mash & Johnston, 1983a) have been reported. The scale significantly discriminates ADD/H from normal and non-ADD/H clinic-referred children (Barkley & Ullman, 1975; Ullman et al., 1978), but there is some controversy as to whether the scale actually assesses activity level, its situational inappropriateness, or child noncompliance (Barkley & Cunningham, 1980; Ross & Ross, 1982). The scale is sensitive to stimulant drug effects (Barkley, 1977a), as well as to treatment effects from parent training programs for ADD/H (Dubey, O'Leary, & Kaufman, 1983; Pollard et al., 1983).

Teacher Rating Scales

There are many rating scales for completion by teachers that measure various dimensions of psychopathology in children. The more commonly used scales are reviewed elsewhere (Barkley, 1987a). Of these, my colleagues and

I have found the following four scales to be the most useful in our clinical assessment protocol for ADD/H children.

Child Behavior Checklist— Teacher Report Form

The Child Behavior Checklist—Teacher Report Form (CBCL-TRF; Achenbach & Edelbrock, 1983) is quite similar to the parent version discussed above. The majority of items are the same as is the scoring procedure. The CBCL-TRF consists of two scales, Adaptive Functioning and Behavior Problem. The Adaptive Functioning scale is based upon eight categories of information obtained from the teacher, from which six scores are derived: School Performance, Working Hard, Behaving Appropriately, Learning, Happy, and a Summary score. These scores are then plotted on an Adaptive Functioning Profile, which contains the normative data. The Behavior Problem scale contains 118 items. These are scored to yield factor scale scores, which are then plotted on the Child Behavior Profile containing the normative data. Profiles are available for both sexes and for two age groups (6–11 and 12–16 years of age). The profiles for each age and sex are somewhat different, as factor analyses for each of these subject groups have revealed somewhat different dimensions of psychopathology. The factors for boys aged 6–11 are Anxious, Social Withdrawal, Unpopular, Self-Destructive, Obsessive–Compulsive, Inattentive, Nervous–Overactive, and Aggressive.

Normative data were collected on 1,100 normal children in a fashion similar to that used for the CBCL parent form. Test–retest reliability is satisfactory (Achenbach & Edelbrock, 1983), but no interteacher reliability information is available. The instrument discriminates ADD/H from other psychiatric disorders, as well as between ADD/H and attention deficit disorder without hyperactivity (Edelbrock et al., 1984). The sensitivity of the CBCL-TRF to treatment effects awaits investigation.

Conners Teacher Rating Scales

Two versions of the Conners Teacher Rating Scale (CTRS) exist, a 39-item version (Conners, 1969) and a 28-item revised version (CTRS-R; Goyette et al., 1978). The 39-item original scale is the most widely used rating scale for research with ADD/H children. The items are scored to yield six factor scales, using the normative data from Trites, Blouin, and La-Prade (1982): Hyperactivity, Conduct Problem, Emotional–Overindulgent, Anxious–Passive, Asocial, and Daydreams/Attendance. Norms were collected on 9,583 children aged 4–12 years. Test–retest and interteacher reliability estimates are quite satisfactory, and the scale is sensitive to stimulant drug and parent training interventions (Barkley, 1987a). While the items overlap with those of the CBCL-TRF, administration of both instruments can be useful, given the sizable body of literature available on the CTRS and its convenience in assessing treatment effects.

The 28-item CTRS-R is similar to the CPRS-R in its format and scoring. Items are scored to yield three factors: Conduct Problem, Hyperactive, and Inattentive–Passive. Normative data for the CTRS-R are available for 383 children aged 3–17 years (Goyette et al., 1978). The scale has adequate test–retest reliability (Edelbrock, Greenbaum, & Conover, 1985), has been shown to discriminate ADD/H from other children, and is sensitive to stimulant drug effects (Barkley, 1987a). In our clinic, the CTRS-R is used instead of the original CTRS, because (1) there is substantial overlap between the latter scale and the CBCL-TRF, which is also used in our clinic; (2) the CTRS-R is a shorter instrument; and (3) the three factor scales of the CTRS-R reflect the main areas of interest in our treatment programs. The CTRS-R is thus quite useful as a measure of treatment effectiveness when the greater information provided by the CTRS is not needed.

School Situations Questionnaire

Like the HSQ, the School Situations Questionnaire (SSQ; Barkley, 1981a) evaluates the common situations in which children pose behavior problems and is used as an adjunct with other classroom behavior rating scales. The SSQ asks about 12 situations (e.g., In the Hallways, In the Bathrooms, During Small-Group Work, etc.), and the teacher answers whether the child is a problem in any of them. If so, the teacher rates the severity of the problem on a scale from 1 (mild) to 9 (severe). Two measures are obtained: the number of problem settings, and their mean severity rating. Normative data are available (Barkley & Edelbrock, 1987) for the scale, as are estimates of its test–retest or interteacher reliability. The scale has been shown to discriminate ADD/H from normal children and to be sensitive to stimulant drug treatment (Barkley, Fischer, Newby, & Breen, 1987).

Self-Control Rating Scale

ADD/H children have substantial difficulties with self-control. To evaluate these deficits, Kendall and Wilcox (1979) developed the 33-item Self-Control Rating Scale (SCRS), containing specific questions about children's ability to inhibit behavior, follow rules, and control impulsive reactions. The scale yields a single summary score and has been shown to measure a relatively homogeneous construct that the developers call "self-control." The nature and specificity of the items make this scale quite useful with teachers (or parents) in evaluating self-control deficits in ADD/H children. However, normative data are available only for a small Minneapolis sample ($n = 110$) of children in third to sixth grades (Kendall & Wilcox, 1979). Test–retest coefficients are satisfactory, but no interteacher reliability estimates are available. The scale correlates significantly with direct classroom observations of off-task behavior and "bugging others," discriminates ADD/H children from normal children and those with other psychiatric disorders, and is sensitive to treatment effects from self-control training programs (Barkley, 1987a).

Self-Report Rating Scales for Children

Achenbach and Edelbrock (1983) have developed a child self-report rating scale quite similar to the CBCL, which is completed by children aged 11–18 years. Most items are similar to those on the parent and teacher forms of the CBCL, except that they are worded in the first person. No normative data or factor analyses exist for this scale, nor have studies utilized it with groups of ADD/H adolescents. Nevertheless, the scale may have some clinical utility for obtaining comparative information for parent and teacher responses.

Robin (1981) has developed a 44-item Issues Checklist, which is completed separately by an adolescent and each of his or her parents concerning issues in the home over which there may be conflict (homework, chores, dating, allowance, etc.). Each item can also be rated on a scale from 1 to 5 as to the degree of negative affect displayed during the discussions of the problematic issues. The scale can be used in conjunction with the direct observational measure described later for assessing parent–adolescent conflict in family interactions. Normative data are available for over 100 distressed and 68 nondistressed families. The scale is described by Foster and Robin (1988).

Laboratory Tests and Measures

In the first edition of the present chapter (Barkley, 1981b), I decried the unavailability of objective laboratory tests and instruments for evaluating attention span, activity level, and impulse control in ADD/H children. What measures were available had no normative data and therefore were of little clinical utility in establishing the deviance of these children from same-age normal peers on these constructs. Since 1981, there have been several promising developments in the standardization of a number of instruments, although much remains to be done before these devices can be recommended for widespread clinical use. These measures are grouped here under the constructs that they appear to assess.

Vigilance and Sustained Attention

Probably one of the most widely used measures of attention span or vigilance in the research literature on ADD/H children is the continuous-performance test (CPT). Variations of the method abound, but the most common one requires a child to observe a screen while individual letters or numbers are projected onto it at a rapid pace. The child is required to press a button when a certain stimulus or pair of stimuli in sequence appear. The measures derived from the method are usually the number correct, the number of stimuli the child misses (omissions), and the number of incorrect stimuli to which the child responds (commissions). The number correct and number of omissions are believed to assess vigilance or sustained attention, while the number of commissions may reflect both sustained attention and impulse control. This method has been shown to be one of the most reliable for discriminating ADD/H from normal children (Douglas, 1983) and is acutely sensitive to stimulant drugs effects (Barkley, 1977b). Klee and Garfinkel (1983) have found that the CPT measures also correlate significantly with the Daydreams/Attendance and Hyperactivity factors from the CTRS; the Coding and Arithmetic subtests of the Wechsler Intelligence Scale for Children—Revised (WISC-R), thought to assess attention, among other things; and the latency and error scores of the Matching Familiar Figures Test, believed to assess impulsivity (see "Impulse Control" below). The problems with the CPT in clinical use have always been the lack of a standardized procedure, a lack of normative data, and an often unwieldly apparatus.

Gordon (1983) has developed a small, solid-state, childproofed computerized device known as the Gordon Diagnostic System (GDS) for assessing vigilance and impulse control in ADD/H children. The impulse control measure is described in a later section. The measure of vigilance is a CPT in which numbers are randomly presented on a screen at a rate of one per second, and the child must watch for a 1 and then a 9 appearing in sequence. When this occurs, the child is to press a small button. The task lasts 12 minutes, and the three commonly derived measures are taken (number correct, omissions, commissions). Normative data are available, based on more than 700 children aged 3–16. Research has recently shown this version of the CPT to discriminate ADD/H and normal children (Gordon, 1985) and to be sensitive to stimulant drug treatment with ADD/H children (Barkley, Fischer, Newby, & Breen, 1987).

Several computer software programs for CPT-like tasks have been developed recently for use with personal computers. Klee and Garfinkel (1983) have developed one similar to the GDS but using sequences of letters. Normative data are not available as yet. Gregory Wright and Virginia Berman have written a program in which the child watches a computer monitor and depresses a button whenever an airplane-like shape appears on the screen. Various shapes are displayed in rapid succession on the screen, and if a child responds correctly, the pace of presentation increases; if he or she responds incorrectly, the pace slows. The method yields two measures, one of the child's variability of vigilance and the other of average level of correct responses. Norms are available for kindergarten through ninth grade. Research on the ability of the software program to discriminate ADD/H and normal children and on its sensitivity to stimulant drug effects is not presently available. Nevertheless, these software programs, along with the GDS, offer some promise of eventually yielding clinically useful, objective, convenient, and inexpensive measures of sustained attention for ADD/H children.

Impulse Control

Two methods of assessing impulsivity in ADD/H children have shown promise for clinical practice. The first, the Matching Familiar Figures Test (MFFT), has an extensive history of use in research assessing impulse control in normal and disturbed children. Originally developed by Kagan (1966), this easily administered matching-to-sample test involves the examiner presenting to the child a picture of a recognizable object. The child is allowed to study the picture for a few moments and then is shown an array of six very similar pictures. The child is to choose which picture most closely resembles the sample picture. The task involves 12 such sets, and the child's score is the mean time taken to the first response (latency) and the total number of errors (incorrectly identified pictures). Both measures have been found to discriminate ADD/H and normal children (Campbell, Douglas, & Morgenstern, 1971) and aggressive and nonaggressive ADD/H children (Milich, Landau, & Loney, 1981); to correlate with clinic playroom measures of activity level and attention (Milich et al., 1981); and to be sensitive to stimulant drug effects (Barkley, 1977b). The MFFT also shows a strong relationship to measures of academic achievement (Weithorn, Kagen, & Marcus, 1984). Normative data have been reported, based on a sample of 2,846 normal children aged 5–12 (Salkind & Nelson, 1980). A longer version of the MFFT using 20 stimulus sets (MFFT20) has been developed (Cairns & Cammock, 1978) and is believed to be more stable and reliable than the shorter version, particularly for children in the older age range (Messer & Brodzinsky, 1981). Norms for the longer version have been reported by Cairns and Cammock (1984).

The second test of impulsivity to offer some clinical utility is the delay task from the GDS, described above. In this task, the child sits before the device and is told to wait, then press a blue button on the device; if the child has waited long enough, he or she earns a point. The child is not told how long to wait before pushing the button—merely to wait, press the button, then wait again, then press the button. The task is comparable to a direct-reinforcement-of-latency procedure and may assess a different form of impulsivity from that measured by tasks such as the MFFT. The task produces three measures: the number of rewards (correct responses), the number of button presses (total responses), and the ratio of rewards to button presses (efficiency ratio). All three measures have been found to significantly discriminate ADD/H from non-ADD/H clinic-referred children, and to correlate significantly with ratings from the original CTRS and CPRS (Gordon, 1979). In a second study, McClure and Gordon (1984) found that only the total number of responses and the efficiency ratio significantly discriminated ADD/H from control children. The efficiency ratio was also found in this study to correlate significantly with both measures from the MFFT20 and the Hyperactivity factor of the CTRS. The investigators reported classifying 91% of the hyperactive sample correctly, using a cutoff score below .54 on the efficiency ratio of the delay task. The instrument, however, has not been shown to be sensitive to stimulant drug treatment (Barkley, Fischer, Newby, & Breen, 1987).

Milich and Kramer (1984) have provided an excellent review and critique of measures of impulsivity, which is worth reading prior to undertaking the clinical interpretation of these laboratory tests.

Activity Level

Like the constructs of attention span and impulsivity, activity level is a multidimensional construct having a multiplicity of definitions and measures. "Activity level" can refer to a wide range of phenomena, from cellular functions and electrophysiological measures to movement of a small muscle group or appendage to total body motion or locomotor movements. Which of these is meant when referring to the "hyperactivity" of the ADD/H child is not often made clear. In general, most prior research has focused on movement of the appendages, locomotor motion, or more vague and global concepts of "fidgetiness" and "out-of-seat" behaviors. The two latter concepts are discussed below under "Direct Observational Procedures," as that is how they are often assessed. Mechanical devices are often employed in evaluating the former types of activity

level, and so they are briefly discussed here as laboratory measures.

A wide array of devices measuring activity level has been used to study ADD/H children. Modified self-winding wrist watches, called "actometers," have been used to measure wrist and ankle activity (see Barkley, 1977b; Barkley et al., 1980; Tryon, 1984), as have pedometers attached to a waist belt, wrist, or ankle (Barkley, 1977a). Motion transducers using small mercury switches and attached to various locations on a child's trunk have also been used to measure hyperactivity (see Tryon, 1984). A new solid-state acceleration monitor was recently developed for 24-hour monitoring of activity (Porrino et al., 1983). Montagu and Swarbrick (1975) employed pneumatic pads on a playroom floor to record locomotor activity mechanically, while others have used grid-marked floors of playrooms to measure locomotion (Routh & Schroeder, 1976). Seat restlessness has been measured using stabilimetric cushions attached to a chair seat (Barkley, 1977a; Tryon, 1984).

Such instruments have not been widely used by clinicians, chiefly due to a lack of normative data, concerns about reliability, and issues of validity in obtaining representative samples of the type of "hyperactivity" that is the chief clinical complaint. Studies are conflicting as to whether such measures correlate significantly with direct observations of children's behavior and activity level in the home or classroom (Kendall & Brophy, 1981; Rapoport & Benoit, 1975). They have not been reliably found to relate significantly to parent, teacher, or clinician ratings of hyperactivity (Barkley & Ullman, 1975; Kendall & Brophy, 1981; Milich, Loney, & Landau, 1982; Routh & Schroeder, 1976; Shaffer et al., 1974; Ullman et al., 1978).

In summary, while adequate normative studies for these instruments may make them more appealing for establishing the statistical deviance of a child's attention span, impulse control, or activity level, such quantitative scores collected in isolation from the natural social environment have several limitations. Many of these measures are taken in laboratory playroom or analogue settings rather than in those natural settings most problematic to these children; this leaves their representativeness in question. The reliability of scores over time is also not well established. Moreover, the measures are highly influenced by situational factors (Porrino et al., 1983) and have only low-order correlations with other measures of these constructs, even when they are taken in the same settings at the same time (Barkley & Ullman, 1975; Ullman *et al.*, 1978). Such measures also correlate to a low degree, if at all, with measures of the same constructs taken in other settings, such as between clinic and home, clinic and classroom, testing room and classroom, and so on (Kendall & Brophy, 1981; Milich *et al.*, 1981; Rapoport & Benoit, 1975). More troublesome for treatment planning is the fact that laboratory measures often reveal little information about the possible controlling variables for activity level, attention, or impulse control. An understanding of such controlling variables is often essential to planning behavioral interventions. While these tests and measures have shown some use in monitoring drug treatment effects, they have, with a few exceptions (e.g., the MFFT), not yet shown that they are sensitive to other types of interventions for ADD/H children. Finally, there is little indication that these measures correlate significantly with those behaviors that parents and teachers find most objectionable in ADD/H children (Barkley & Cunningham, 1980).

Direct Observational Procedures

New developments have also taken place in the area of direct observational procedures for evaluating ADD/H children. Many of these remain in the research stages of their development, with normative data collection and treatment sensitivity studies still in process or waiting to be done. Nevertheless, several of them are sufficiently promising to warrant mention here. They vary in the focus of the target behaviors being assessed, the degree of training necessary for their reliable use, and the facilities and resources required for their implementation. As a result, not all clinicians or clinics will be able to adopt them, but to the extent that their use is feasible, their inclusion in an ADD/H assessment protocol is strongly endorsed.

ADD/H Behaviors

Various behavioral observation and recording methods have been developed specifically to capture the symptoms believed to be of primary concern in ADD/H children. Jacob *et al.* (1978) describe a procedure for recording ADD/H behaviors in the natural classroom setting, known as the Hyperactive Behavior Code, which uses an interval-sampling procedure to record the following categories: Solicitation (seeks inter-

action with teacher), Aggression, Refusal, Change of Position, Daydreaming, and Weird Sounds (nonspeech vocalizations or noises). These measures are collapsed into a single score representing hyperactive behavior. The developers have found the system to discriminate ADD/H from normal children, chiefly in formal or highly structured as opposed to informal classroom settings. The measure also correlates quite highly with teacher ratings on the Hyperactivity, Conduct Problem, and Daydreams/Attendance factors of the CTRS.

Another observational system developed for recording classroom ADD/H behavior is that by Abikoff, Gittelman-Klein, and Klein (1977). The system contains 14 behavioral categories scored on an interval-sampling basis. These categories pertain to off-task behavior, movement about the classroom, and other behaviors that occur more often in ADD/H than normal children. Of the 14 categories, 12 were found to significantly differentiate ADD/H and normal children. The system, however, may be cumbersome for clinical practice because of the large number of categories and the training time needed to score them reliably. Nonetheless, the system, like that of Jacob *et al.* (1978), would seem useful for clinicians wishing to make direct observations of ADD/H behaviors in the natural environment.

Milich and his colleagues have developed and validated an observation code for use in clinic playroom analogue settings. It has been found to discriminate ADD/H children from those who are purely aggressive, from those who are both ADD/H and aggressive, and from a group of psychiatric control children (Milich *et al.*, 1982). The measures derived from the coding procedure have also shown significant stability over a 2-year period in normal children (Milich, 1984). Two situations are employed in the clinic playroom: Free Play and a Restricted Academic Playroom Situation. The child is placed alone in the room and told to play freely with the toys during Free Play. Toys are available for play; four tables are in the room; and the floor of the playroom is divided into 16 squares by using black tape on the tile floors. During the Restricted Academic Playroom Situation, the child is requested to remain seated, to complete a series of worksheets using a task similar to the Coding subtest from the WISC-R, and not to play with any of the toys in the room.

Each situation lasts for 15 minutes. Throughout this time, observers are continuously recording six behavioral categories: Grid Crossings, Out of Seat, Fidgeting, Vocalization, On Task, and Attention Shifts. In the Restricted Academic Situation, two additional measures are taken: time spent touching forbidden toys, and the number of worksheet items completed by the child. The method seems to be promising for objective recording of ADD/H behaviors in a clinic analogue setting, particularly given its ability to discriminate between ADD/H with and without aggression and between these ADD/H subtypes and purely aggressive as well as clinical control groups. The stability of the measure over time, and its significant correlation with clinician ratings of hyperactivity as well as with the MFFT measure of impulsivity, are particularly impressive for such brief samples of clinic playroom behavior.

My colleagues and I have recently adapted the Milich Restricted Academic Playroom Situation for use in our clinical evaluations of ADD/H children and subsequent assessment of

their stimulant drug responding. Using a clinic playroom with a one-way observation mirror, the examiner places the ADD/H child and his or her mother in the playroom with instructions to play freely with toys for a short period of time (5 minutes). This merely serves as habituation period, and no behaviors are recorded. At the end of this time, the examiner instructs the mother to have her child sit at a small table at the opposite end of the room from where she is to sit on a sofa. The child is given a set of mathematics problems (five pages) selected from workbooks for his or her current grade level. The child is asked to remain seated and work on the math problems at a small table while the mother sits on a sofa and reads magazines. This situation lasts 15 minutes, during which the examiner is recording the initial occurrence of eight behavior categories during each 30-second interval. The recording form is shown in Figure 2, and the definitions of the categories are provided in Table 3. A tape recorder is

ACADEMIC SITUATION CODE SHEET

Interval #:	1	2	3	4	5	6	7	8	9	10	11	12	13	14	15	16	17	18
Off Task																		
Fidgeting																		
Vocalizing																		
Talks to M																		
Plays w/ Obj.																		
Out of Seat																		
Negative																		
M Commands																		

Interval =:	19	20	21	22	23	24	25	26	27	28	29	30	Total	Scoring		
Off Task														/30 =		%
Fidgeting														/30 =		%
Vocalizing														/30 =		%
Talks to M														/30 =		%
Plays w/ Obj.														/30 =		%
Out of Seat														/30 =		%
Negative														/30 =		%
M Commands														/30 =		%

Child's Name_____　Coder Initials_____　Date:_____

Session:　1　2　3　4　　　Is this a reliability check?　YES　NO
If so, with whom?_____

Comments:

FIGURE 2. The behavior coding sheet for the Restricted Academic Playroom Situation.

TABLE 3. Restricted Academic Playroom Situation: Instructions for Coding Playroom Behavior

Instructions for Conducting Observation:

Place the mother and child in a playroom having a one-way mirror and intercom facilities, a small table and chair at which the child will work, a larger chair or sofa and magazines for the mother, and a number of toys available for play. Instruct the mother and child to play together with the toys as they might do at home. Allow 5 minutes for play. This is a habituation period and is not used for recording behavior.

At the end of the 5 minutes, enter the room and instruct the mother to have her child accomplish a set of math problems (at least five pages in length). The child is to work at the small table and is not to bother his or her mother while she sits in the larger chair or sofa and reads magazines. The mother is then given the set of math problems and a pencil for her child to use. The math problems should be appropriate for the child's academic grade level. These problems can be taken from grade-level math books available at most educational stores.

After giving these instructions, the examiner returns to the observation room and begins the audiotape containing the interval-coding cues. This tape merely contains voice prompts indicating the beginning of each 30-second interval (i.e., "Begin 1, Begin 2, Begin 3, . . . Begin 30"). When the tape sounds the interval number, the coder proceeds to that column and places a check mark in that block corresponding to each behavior category observed to occur during that time interval. Each category is scored only once during a 30-second interval, regardless of how often it may occur. When the tape recorder sounds the next interval number, the coder moves to the next column and begins marking any behavior categories that occur in that interval.

The following behavior categories are recorded: Off Task, Fidgeting, Vocalization, Talks to Mother, Plays with Objects, Out of Seat, Negative Behavior for the Child, and Mother Commands. It is possible to score a child as showing any or all of these behavior categories within any 30-second coding interval.

There are 30 intervals to be coded (15 minutes × 2 intervals each minute). The following definitions are used for each behavior category.

Definitions of Behavior Categories:

1. *Off Task:* This category is checked if the child interrupts his or her attention to the tasks to engage in some other behavior. Off-task behaviors are looking around the room, playing with the pencil, looking at or playing with his or her clothing, talking to mother, or any other behavior where the child is not looking at the worksheets. A child can hum or whistle while working, kick his or her legs, or even stop using the pencil, and still remain "on task" as long as he or she maintains eye contact with the task. It is essentially the breaking of eye contact with the worksheets that constitutes "off-task" behavior.

2. *Fidgeting:* Any repetitive, purposeless motion of the legs, arms, buttocks, or trunk. Remember, it must occur at least twice in succession to be considered repetitive, and it should serve no purpose. Examples: swaying back and forth, kicking legs back and forth, swinging arms at sides, shuffling feet from side to side, or shifting buttocks about in the chair.

3. *Vocalization:* Any vocal noise or verbalization made by the child, excluding statements made toward the mother. Statements made out loud but to no one in particular (talking to self) are scored in this category. If the child initiates any verbal interaction with the mother, or responds to her interactions verbally, it is scored in the next category (Talks to Mother). Examples of vocalizing might be humming, whistling, clicking teeth together, making odd mouth noises, singing, talking to self, whispering to self, or throat clearing. Sniffing is not a vocalization.

4. *Talks to Mother:* Any verbal statement, question, comment, remark, or command directed toward the mother. Eye contact with the mother need not be made, so long as it is clear that the statement or question is directed at the mother.

5. *Plays with Objects:* If the child manually touches any other object in the room (except the mother) that is not related to the task (pencil, paper, and desk) or his or her body (including clothing), it is scored in this category. Playing with body parts or clothing or touching the mother is not scored here. Examples: touches other chairs, tables, curtains, or cabinets in the room; plays with the toys; touches the light switches; etc.

6. *Out of Seat:* Any time the child's buttocks break the flat surface of the seat in which he or she is sitting, it is coded in this category.

7. *Negative Behavior:* Any verbal or nonverbal display of anger, refusal, opposition, or discouragement toward the mother.

8. *Mother Commands:* Any imperative or interrogative directed toward the child that directs the child to perform some behavior or stop an ongoing behavior is scored here.

Scoring Dependent Measures:

The score for each behavior category is derived by counting the number of check marks for that category and dividing by 30 (or the actual number of intervals of observation) to yield a percentage of occurrence.

used to cue the observer to the beginning of each 30-second interval ("Begin 1, Begin 2, . . ."). Our procedure differs from the Milich procedure in several respects: The floor is not marked off into grids to record locomotion; the child's mother is in the room; a time-sampling procedure rather than a continuous recording procedure is used for scoring behavior; several additional behavior categories are coded as a result of having the mother in the room (Talks to Mother, Mother Commands, and Negative Behavior for the Child); and wrist and ankle actometers are not used for recording activity level. Separate scores (percentages of occurrence) can be derived and examined for each measure or collapsed to yield a Total ADD/H Behavior Score (total percentage of occurrence).

We have found that this measure significantly discriminates ADD/H from normal and non-ADD/H clinic children (Breen, 1985) and is quite sensitive to drug and dose effects of stimulant medication (Barkley, Fischer, Newby, & Breen, 1987). The coding procedure can be quickly learned and is easily used in facilities having rooms with one-way observation mirrors and intercoms. The recording form can also be used for recording classroom ADD/H behavior during periods of individual desk work simply by substituting Talks to Teacher/Peer for Talks to Mother, and Teacher Commands for Mother Commands.

Adult–Child Interactions

Because ADD/H children display significant problems with noncompliance, difficulties in completing assigned tasks, and in many cases defiant and oppositional behavior, it is useful to take some measures of the interactions of ADD/H children with adults. Most procedures developed for recording such interactions have concentrated on parent–child as compared to teacher–child dyads. Several parent–child interaction coding systems appear promising for inclusion in a clinical assessment protocol. These systems focus primarily upon recording noncomplaint and negative behaviors by the children, and commands and other controlling behaviors used by the parents.

A relatively easy-to-use coding system for recording noncompliance in parent–child interactions in a clinic playroom has been developed by Forehand and McMahon (see Chapter 3, this volume). For those interested in obtaining a more detailed assessment of parent–child interactions, more complicated observational systems have been developed. The Response-Class Matrix (Mash, Terdal, & Anderson, 1973) has been used extensively in research with ADD/H children, as well as in studies of other childhood disorders (see Mash & Barkley, 1986, for a review). The manual and coding forms are described elsewhere (Barkley, 1981a). The system requires two coders: One records parent behaviors and subsequent child behaviors, while the other codes the child behaviors as antecedents and the parent behaviors as consequences. Behaviors such as parental commands, questions, interactions, praise, negative reactions, and so on, are recorded, as are child behaviors such as compliance, play, questions, interactions, and negative reactions. Recording systems have also been developed by Patterson (1982), Wahler, House, and Stambaugh (1976), and Robinson and Eyberg (1981) for coding parent–child interactions, particularly in children with conduct problems. Like the Response-Class Matrix, these systems require extended time for training and may be cumbersome to use in the typical clinical setting, where time and resources are limited.

The aforementioned recording systems have been used chiefly for recording interactions between parents and preadolescent children. Such observation systems and their analogue settings may not be especially useful for evaluating the issues that bring families with adolescent ADD/H children to child guidance centers. In these cases, it would seem more useful to evaluate the areas of conflict existing between parents and adolescents, since an understanding of these is more likely to lead to useful treatment planning within a behavioral family therapy approach. Robin (1981) has developed a direct observational recording procedure for assessing conflicts in communication patterns between parents and adolescents. The system is discussed by Foster and Robin (1988), and would be an excellent substitute for those other coding systems where the subject of the evaluation is an ADD/H teenager.

Advantages and Limitations

Direct observational methods can overcome some of the limitations described earlier for laboratory measures, in that they are capable of recording behavior in its natural environment or in analogue settings structured to elicit behaviors representative of those problems occurring outside the clinic. In so doing, they offer more ecologically valid measures of the actual behaviors of ADD/H children about which parents and teachers are most concerned. The parent–child interaction coding systems, in particular, can record the antecedent and consequent events so essential to understanding the social context in which the ADD/H behaviors are occurring and to suggesting potential changes in the interactions as part of behavioral treatment. These procedures can also be used to monitor the changes in behavior brought about by both drug and behavioral interventions, particularly the latter, as they frequently focus upon the targets of such behavioral training programs (parental management of the children).

However, normative data are lacking on such observational systems, and this makes them less useful for determining the statistical deviance of child behaviors necessary in rendering a diagnosis. Such normative data, if collected, would be problematic because of the sensitivity of these observational systems to changes in environmental parameters, such as room size, lighting, furniture, toys, presence or absence of the examiner, and even examiner characteristics. These would apply to both clinic analogue and natural classroom observations. As a result, any norms might not prove useful in other clinics, where such conditions would certainly differ from those under which the norms were collected.

There are several ways of partially overcoming this dilemma. First, clinics can collect their own normative data, using their own standard observational systems and playroom procedures. Local university students, in return for stipends, course credit, or even completion of student research projects, can help to build up such a data base on normal children to be used for clinical purposes.

Second, where exact quantitative measures of deviation from the norm are not essential, using a method of yoked controls may help to provide an approximate indication of deviance. In a classroom observation, this is easily achieved by asking the teacher to point out a child representative of the typical children in the class and taking observations on this child during the same school visit used to record the ADD/H child's behavior. So long as the child's name is not disclosed to the observer, such observations should not violate ethical guidelines. For clinic analogue observations, having a normal

sibling of the ADD/H child come in for the observations provides useful contrasting information, particularly where parent–child interactions are being recorded. Such a procedure has been used by Tarver-Behring *et al.* (1985) to show that ADD/H children are less compliant with parental commands than their normal siblings.

Third, we may be reaching a state in the evolution of behavioral assessment paradigms where it is time to establish regional clinical/research centers that have the resources, facilities, and personnel necessary to conduct more comprehensive behavioral assessments, using standardized protocols for specialized disorders; surrounding community professionals can refer cases to these centers for those specific protocols (Mash & Barkley, 1986). Such a procedure can be likened to the establishment of regional magnetic resonance imaging (MRI) laboratories at large hospital/medical school complexes, to which patients with neurological diseases can be referred for complicated evaluations, the equipment for which is often far too expensive for typical clinicians to purchase themselves. These regional behavioral assessment centers would certainly have the resources necessary to develop normative data banks on the local population for addressing the question of statistical deviance of child behaviors. If this is done properly, such specialized assessment centers could be well received within the regions; could be cost-effective, given the large volume of service likely to result; and could be useful for large-scale research programs drawing upon the unique patient population.

Parent Self-Report Measures

It has become increasingly apparent that child behavioral disorders, their level of severity, and their response to intervention are in part a function of factors affecting parents and families at large. While this may sound trite or even gratuitous to the sophisticated clinician, it has taken quite some time for behavioral scientists to develop technologies adequate to the task of assessing this complex domain of interactions. Even now, this aspect of behavioral assessment remains in its infancy; yet some gains have occurred in our understanding of how distal events affect child behavior via their effects on parental behavior (Wahler & Graves, 1983). Related to this has been the burgeoning literature in ADD/H on the prevalence of psychiatric disorders among family members, as discussed earlier. That these problems might further influence the frequency and severity of behavioral problems in ADD/H children has been demonstrated in recent studies, particularly those by Mash (Mash & Johnston, 1983a, 1983b) on the role of parental stress, perceived competance, and self-esteem in parent–child interactions and ratings of child deviance in ADD/H families. Coupled with the research by Wahler (1980) on social isolation in mothers of behaviorally disturbed children and its influence on parent training outcome; the research by Forehand (see Chapter 3, this volume) on the separate and interactive contributions of maternal depression and marital discord to the decision to refer children for clinical assistance, to parent–child interactions, and to parental ratings of child deviance; and the research by Patterson (1982) on coercive family interaction processes, this literature indicates that some evaluation of parent variables is essential for the clinical assessment of ADD/H children. While space does not permit a thorough discussion of the clinical behavioral assessment of adults and their disorders (see Barlow, 1981), brief mention is made here of some assessment methods that may be of value in at least providing a preliminary screening for certain variables of importance to treatment in ADD/H children.

Marital Discord

Many instruments exist for evaluating marital discord in parents. A more thorough treatment of the behavioral assessment of marital discord can be found in the paper by Margolin (1983). However, the ones most often used in research on childhood disorders have been the Locke–Wallace Marital Adjustment Scale (Locke & Wallace, 1959) and its recent revision, the Locke–Thomes Marital Adjustment Scale (Locke & Thomes, 1980). The former is a 44-item scale, while the latter is a brief 19-item scale; both use a multiple-choice format designed to permit a quick assessment of marital discord. The score is the sum of the number of credits assigned to each answer across all items. However, individual items of the scale should be examined for significant marital issues that may affect later treatment recommendations. Research has found mothers of ADD/H children, particularly those of boys, to have higher ratings of discord than mothers of normal children (Befera & Barkley, 1985).

Maternal Depression

Mothers of ADD/H children are frequently more depressed than mothers of normal children (Befera & Barkley, 1985; Mash & Johnston, 1983a), and this may affect their responsiveness to behavioral parent training programs (Forehand & McMahon, 1981). A scale often used to provide a quick assessment of maternal depression is the Beck Depression Inventory (Beck, Rush, Shaw, & Emery, 1980). This is a 21-item multiple-choice questionnaire of self-reported levels of depression in the respondent. The score assigned to each answer is that listed beside the answer on the scale. The total score is the sum of the number of credits assigned to each endorsed answer across all items.

Parent Stress

Recent research suggests that parents of ADD/H children report more stress in their families and in their parental role than those of normal or clinic-referred non-ADD/H children (Breen, 1985; Mash & Johnston, 1983a). One measure used to evaluate this construct has been the Parenting Stress Index (PSI; Burke & Abidin, 1980). The original PSI is a 150-item multiple-choice questionnaire that can be scored to yield six scores pertaining to child behavioral characteristics (e.g. distractibility, mood, etc.), eight scores pertaining to maternal characteristics (e.g. depression, sense of competence as a parent, etc.), and two scores pertaining to situational and life stress events. These scores can be summed to yield three domain or summary scores: Child Domain, Mother Domain, and Total Stress. Test–retest reliability for the instrument has been reported to range from .70 to .90 for the domain scores over 3- to 4-week intervals (Abidin, 1983).

Summary

It should be clear from the foregoing that the assessment of ADD/H children is a complex and serious endeavor requiring adequate time (3–5 hours); knowledge of the relevant research and clinical literature (for starting places see Barkley, 1981a; Ross & Ross, 1976, 1982); skillful clinical judgment in sorting out the pertinent issues; and sufficient resources to obtain multiple types of information from multiple sources (parents, children, teachers), using a variety of assessment methods. A careful, comprehensive evaluation of an ADD/H child should include the following:

- Parent, child, and teacher interviews (all ages)
- The CBCL (ages 3–16)
- The CPRS-R (ages 3–17)
- The HSQ (all ages)
- The CBCL-TRF (ages 5–16)
- The CTRS (ages 3–17)
- The SSQ (all ages)
- The SCRS (ages 5–12)
- Child self-report ratings (ages 12–17)
- Lab measures of vigilance and impulse control (all ages)
- Clinic observations of ADD/H behaviors (ages 5–14)
- Clinic observations of parent–child interactions (ages 3–17)
- Ratings of marital discord, depression, and stress (all parents)

Where time and resources permit, direct observations of ADD/H behaviors in the classroom should also be made. At the very least, telephone contact with a child's teacher should be made to follow up on his or her responses to the teacher rating scales and to obtain more detail about the child's classroom behavior problems. To this list of assessment methods should be added those others necessary to address the specific problems often occurring in conjunction with ADD/H but discussed in other chapters of this text (e.g., learning disabilities, social skills deficits, enuresis and encopresis, etc.). Where resources do not permit direct observational measures to be taken in clinic analogue settings, then observations in the home or classroom should be attempted. Where this is not possible, then at the very least the interviews, rating scales, and lab measures noted above should be collected. These can be supplemented with parent or teacher diaries of selected target behaviors.

TREATMENT IMPLICATIONS

The multimethod assessment protocol suggested here for use with ADD/H children will certainly reveal a variety of areas of deviance or discomfort requiring clinical intervention, and perhaps even more detailed behavioral assessment than has been noted here. The subsequent treatments will, no doubt, be based upon those deficit areas found to be the most salient, the most significant to the concerns of

the referral agent (e.g., parent, physician, teacher, etc.), or of the most importance to present and later adjustment. Such treatment recommendations may range from minimal parent counseling concerning appropriate child behavior (for those children found to have no behavioral abnormalities) to residential treatment (for those ADD/H children having severe, chronic, or even dangerous forms of conduct problems). Between these extremes, treatment recommendations may focus on improving the primary ADD/H symptoms through stimulant medication or classroom behavioral interventions; the oppositional behavior of the young ADD/H child through parent training in effective child management procedures; the parent–adolescent conflicts of ADD/H teenagers via a behavioral problem-solving approach to family therapy; or the peer relationship problems through individual or group social skills training. The evaluation will, in most cases, reveal the need for multiple interventions for the ADD/H child, or even the other family members, in order to fully address the issues raised therein. Regardless of the treatments indicated from the initial evaluation, ongoing, periodic reassessment using many of the methods noted above will be necessary to document change (or the lack thereof) throughout treatment, maintenance of treatment gains over time after treatment termination, and generalization (or the lack of it) of treatment effects to other problematic behaviors and environments.

Treatments abound for ADD/H children (see Barkley, 1981a; Ross & Ross, 1982), but only some of these have demonstrated their efficacy. A brief review of those that have shown the greatest promise for dealing with the primary problems in ADD/H children follows, along with suggested methods for evaluating the outcomes of these particular therapies.

Stimulant Medication

There is overwhelming evidence for the efficacy of stimulant drugs in the treatment of ADD/H children (Barkley, 1977b; Cantwell & Carlson, 1978). Although they are not sufficient by themselves to ameliorate the myriad difficulties of such children, these drugs can be an indispensable part of a total treatment program (and sometime the most effective part) for children over 5 years of age with moderate to severe ADD/H. The primary effects of the stimulants (Ritalin, Dexedrine, Cylert) are improved attention span, decreased impulsivity, diminished task-irrelevant activity (especially in structured situations), and generally decreased disruptive behavior in social situations. Secondary effects from these changes appear to be increased compliance to commands and instructions (Barkley & Cunningham, 1980), productivity on academic assignments (Rapport, Stoner, DuPaul, Birmingham, & Tucker, 1985), and peer acceptance; decreased parent and teacher reprimands, supervision, and punishment (see Barkley, 1985); and occasionally improvements in handwriting. Approximately 75% of ADD/H children over 5 years of age respond positively to medication. The behavioral action of the medications is short-lived (3–8 hours), and thus the medications must be given several times each day for adequate behavioral control. The drugs can be used throughout childhood and adolescence if necessary. Most side effects are not serious, are dose-related, and dissipate within several days of treatment onset. In 1–2% of cases, tic reactions may develop. As noted earlier, children with a personal or family history of tics or Tourette syndrome seem most likely to develop these reactions. Some research suggests that children with higher pretreatment levels of anxiety are more likely to respond with adverse reactions.

A decision to refer an ADD/H child for a medication trial should be based upon the information obtained in the initial evaluation, particularly the following factors: (1) the age of the child and the duration and severity of the presenting problems; (2) the history and success of prior treatment efforts; (3) the absence of a personal or family history of tics or Tourette syndrome; (4) normal levels of anxiety in the child (rating scales may help here); (5) parental motivation for such treatment; (6) an absence of stimulant abuse in the parents; and (7) the likelihood that parents will employ the medication responsibly and in compliance with physician directions.

A protocol for evaluating stimulant drug and dose responding over a 3-week interval might use two doses of medication and a placebo (a 1-week trial per condition), with the child evaluated at the end of each week. A more complete description of these procedures has been given elsewhere (Barkley, Fischer, Newby, & Breen, 1987). Again, this protocol assumes that the more comprehensive initial evaluation discussed earlier has been conducted. The methods used to assess drug and dose responding might

include the CPRS-R and the CTRS-R; the HSQ and the SSQ; the Side Effects Questionnaire (see Barkley, 1981a); lab tests of vigilance and impulse control; clinic playroom observations of ADD/H behaviors during the Restricted Academic Playroom Situation (see the procedures by Milich's group and our group, described above); and a paired-associate learning task (see Douglas, Barr, O'Neill, & Britton, 1986).

Parent Training in Contingency Management

Many parent training programs exist for teaching parents to manage their behavior problem children (Dangel & Polster, 1984; Forehand & McMahon, 1981). Such parent training can be effective in improving parent–child interactions in ADD/H children (Dubey et al., 1983; Pollard et al., 1983). I have elsewhere described a program designed specifically for parents of ADD/H children (Barkley, 1981a, 1987b). The program is based upon the skills taught in the program by Forehand and McMahon (1981), but it includes additional sessions to provide information to families about ADD/H, to train them in establishing home token reinforcement systems, and to teach them to deal with misbehavior in public places. Briefly, the steps of the program cover these topics: (1) an overview of ADD/H; (2) the causes of child misbehavior; (3) developing and enhancing parental attending skills; (4) attending to child compliance; (5) implementing the home chip/point system; (6) time out from reinforcement; (7) managing children in public places; (8) coping with future behavior problems; and (9) a 1-month review and booster session.

A decision to employ parent training procedures should be based upon the information obtained in the initial evaluation with respect to the child's level of noncompliant, oppositional, or defiant behaviors at home, in addition to the primary ADD/H symptoms; the parents' educational and intellectual level, as well as degree of motivation for training; and the absence of a degree of maternal insularity, depression, stress, personal psychopathology, and marital discord sufficient to interfere with training. The age of the child will, of course, determine the appropriateness of this approach. In general, it seems useful for children 2 to 11 years of age; after that time, the problem-solving training for families of ADD/H children developed by Robin (see below) seems most appropriate. At least once throughout training and at posttreatment, the following assessment protocol might be used to evaluate treatment effects: the CPRS-R, the HSQ, and clinic analogue observations of parent–child interactions during task performance. The CBCL and several of the parent self-report measures might also be used where longer time spans are involved between pretreatment and posttreatment. These would be in addition to the weekly parent diaries kept as part of the parent training program.

Self-Control Training

Kendall and Braswell (1984) have developed a promising approach for training impulsive children in self-control strategies. The program appears useful with children and adolescents, but my personal experience suggests that older children with satisfactory or better verbal abilities are more likely to respond positively to individualized training in these procedures. The program utilizes a variety of problem tasks as vehicles to teach children to (1) inhibit responding, (2) repeat the problem or instruction, (3) describe the nature of the problem, (4) describe possible alternative approaches to the problem, (5) evaluate the possible consequences/outcomes of each, (6) undertake the problem solution while engaging in self-instructed guidance, and (7) evaluate their own performance. This encapsulation of the program does not do justice to its complexity, and the reader is referred to the text by Kendall and Braswell (1984) and to Douglas (1980) for more detailed descriptions of this approach. Contingency management methods are often incorporated into the training sessions to enhance motivation and sustain performance, while parents and/or teachers use similar contingency management methods and prompting of the skills to insure generalization of the skills to their settings. Research on the efficacy of self-control training with ADD/H children has been described by Abikoff (1985), Douglas, Parry, Marton, and Garson (1976), Kendall and Braswell (1984), and Whalen, Henker, and Hinshaw (1985).

The decision to make use of this program should be based upon information in the initial evaluation indicating adequate age, intelligence, and verbal abilities of the child; adequate parent and/or teacher motivation to implement generalization programs; and adequate child motivation to attend the individual training sessions. A possible assessment protocol for evaluating treatment effects might include the CPRS-R and the CTRS-R; parent and teacher ratings on the SCRS; clinic administration of vigilance tasks and the MFFT; and individualized testing of the child on several problems (e.g., mazes) by a second examiner (not the therapist) to evaluate generalization.

Parent–Adolescent Intervention

Robin (1981, 1985) has designed a useful approach to resolving conflicts in parent–adolescent interactions in families with ADD/H teenagers. The approach is often combined with advice to parents on contingency management methods appropriate to this age group (e.g., point systems, behavioral contracts, etc.). In my experience, by the time the typical ADD/H child reaches this age range (13–18 years), the most significant issues in the family center around the teenager's acceptance of responsibility (chores, homework, school performance, etc.), disagreements over the teenager's rights and privileges, and the social activities in which the teenager may be engaged. While problems with attention span, impulsivity, and proneness to emotionality are often better by this time than in earlier childhood, they remain somewhat problematic and appear to express themselves through these conflictual issues when combined with the normal striving for independence typical of this developmental stage. Where conduct problems and oppositional behavior persist into this stage, as they often do, the level of family conflict is greatly exacerbated. Robins's approach directs itself at resolving these conflicts, and it is strongly recommended where ADD/H children are too old for the child management program described elsewhere (Barkley, 1981a).

Briefly, this approach involves (1) training the parents and adolescent in a set of problem-solving steps to be used with each conflict area, (2) teaching the parents and adolescent a behavioral style for approaching the use of these steps, and (3) addressing irrational beliefs that may be held by the parents or adolescent and that may govern their evaluations of and subsequent demands upon each other. The approach is outlined more fully by Foster and Robin (1988), as are the assessment methods for evaluating initial conflicts and treatment effects. The decision to use this treatment program should be based upon various findings from the evaluation, not the least of which would be the age of the ADD/H adolescent, the severity of conduct disorders and oppositional behavior (the approach is not especially helpful with severe conduct disorders), the motivation of the adolescent and parents to enter into family therapy, and the level of verbal intelligence of the family members who are to participate.

Classroom Management

Given that the majority of ADD/H children exhibit behavioral problems in their classrooms, classroom interventions are likely to be employed with most such children. These may involve training of the teacher in contingency management methods (see Barkley, 1981a), transfer of the child to a special education class for behavioral disorders, or both. Token reinforcement programs, home-based evaluation/reinforcement programs, increased attending by teachers to child compliance, in-class time-out procedures, and behavioral contracts may all be employed in the reduction of ADD/H behaviors in the classroom. Certainly, whether the treatment is undertaken will be based upon a number of findings from the evaluation, including the level of school behavior and performance problems, the degree of parent and teacher commitment to complying with these methods, the extent of previous school interventions, the degree to which stimulant medication may address these difficulties, and the eligibility of the children for special educational programs under U.S. Public Law 94-142 and state statutes. An assessment protocol for evaluating treatment effects might include the CTRS, the SSQ, the SCRS, a daily/weekly school report card (see Barkley, 1981a), direct classroom observations of ADD/H behaviors, and teacher diaries of significant events. The CBCL-TRF could also be included where longer time spans between pretreatment and posttreatment assessments are involved.

Residential Treatment

A few ADD/H children and adolescents with severe oppositional behavior or conduct disorders will require placement in residential treatment centers in order to attempt intervention with them and their families. This will become clear from the evaluation if severe levels of aggression, delinquency, and conduct disorders

are noted on the rating scales and during the interview; if parents no longer exert control over the behavior of the children out of fear of physical retaliation, or the children have a history of running away from home; or if family functioning is so chaotic or disorganized as to make outpatient intervention unlikely to succeed.

Summary

In the majority of instances, multiple interventions are involved in treating the plethora of difficulties of ADD/H children and their families. These often include parent training in child management skills, classroom management programs, home-based reinforcement systems, self-control training of older children, and stimulant medication. For older children, problem-solving training of the adolescent and parents is usually substituted for the child management training program. While initial interventions are often short-term, periodic reintervention is often necessary as the children develop and display new problems commensurate with the parental and societal demands of later developmental stages and the children's inabilities to meet these demands adequately. Assessment and intervention are therefore closely intertwined in an ongoing process.

CONCLUSION

In this chapter, ADD/H is viewed as a developmental disorder of attention span, impulse control, activity level, and rule-governed behavior, in which the major behavioral difficulties have an onset in early childhood; are pervasive in nature; are frequently chronic throughout development; and are not the result of mental retardation, serious language delay, sensory deficits, or severe psychopathology. It occurs more frequently in males than in females. It has multiple etiologies, chief among which are biological contributions, yet it displays substantial situational variation and responsiveness to environmental influences. Numerous additional problems may coexist with ADD/H and make the assessment of the disorder a complex and challenging affair. The comprehensive assessment of ADD/H in children includes parent, teacher, and child interviews; parent and teacher rating scales; parent self-report measures; lab measures of attention span and impulse control; and direct observations of

ADD/H behaviors and parent–child interactions. The persistent nature of the disorder insures the need for periodic assessment and intervention throughout the development of these children.

REFERENCES

Abidin, R. R. (1983). *Parenting Stress Index*. Charlottesville, VA: Pediatric Psychology Press.

Abikoff, H. (1985). Efficacy of cognitive training interventions in hyperactive children: a critical review. *Clinical Psychology Review, 5,* 479–512.

Abikoff, H., Gittelman-Klein, R., & Klein, D. (1977). Validation of a classroom obeservation code for hyperactive children. *Journal of Consulting and Clinical Psychology, 45,* 772–783.

Achenbach, T. M., & Edelbrock, C. (1983). *Manual for the Child Behavior Checklist and Revised Child Behavior Profile*. Burlington: University of Vermont, Department of Psychiatry.

American Psychiatric Association. (1968). *Diagnostic and statistical manual of mental disorders* (2nd ed.). Washington, DC: Author.

American Psychiatric Association. (1980). *Diagnostic and statistical manual of mental disorders* (3rd ed.). Washington, DC: Author.

American Psychiatric Association. (1987). *Diagnostic and statistical manual of mental disorders* (3rd ed., rev.). Washington, DC: Author.

Baloh, R., Sturm, R., Green, B., & Gleser, G. (1975). Neuropsychological effects of chronic asymptomatic increased lead absorption. *Archives of Neurology, 32,* 326–330.

Barkley, R. A. (1977a). The effects of methylphenidate on various measures of activity level and attention in hyperkinetic children. *Journal of Abnormal Child Psychology, 5,* 351–369.

Barkley, R. A. (1977b). A review of stimulant drug research with hyperactive children. *Journal of Child Psychology and Psychiatry, 18,* 137–165.

Barkley, R. A. (1981a). *Hyperactive children: A handbook for diagnosis and treatment*. New York: Guilford Press.

Barkley, R. A. (1981b). Hyperactivity. In E. J. Mash & L. G. Terdal (Eds.), *Behavioral assessment of childhood disorders* (pp. 127–184). New York: Guilford Press.

Barkley, R. A. (1982). Specific guidelines for defining hyperactivity in children (attention deficit disorder with hyperactivity). In B. B. Lahey & A. E. Kazdin (Eds.), *Advances in clinical child psychology* (Vol. 5, pp. 137–180). New York: Plenum.

Barkley, R. A. (1985). The social interactions of hyperactive children: Developmental changes, drug effects, and situational variation. In R. McMahon & R. Peters (Eds.), *Childhood disorders: Behavioral–developmental approaches* (pp. 218–243). New York: Brunner/Mazel.

Barkley, R. A. (1987a). A review of child behavior rating scales and checklists for research in child psychopathology. In M. Rutter, A. H. Tuma, & I. Lann (Eds.), *Assessment and diagnosis in child psychopathology*. New York: Guilford Press.

Barkley, R. A. (1987b). *Defiant children: A clinician's manual for parent training*. New York: Guilford Press.

Barkley, R. A. (in press). The problem of stimulus control and rule-governed behavior in children with attention deficit disorder with hyperactivity. In J. Swanson & L. Bloomingdale (Eds.), *Emerging trends in research on attention deficit disorders*. New York: Plenum.

Barkley, R. A., Copeland, A. P., & Sivage, C. (1980). A self-control classroom for hyperactive children. *Journal of Autism and Developmental Disorders, 10,* 75–89.

Barkley, R. A., & Cunningham, C. E. (1980). The parent–child interactions of hyperactive children and their modification by stimulant drugs. In R. Knights & D. Bakker (Eds.), *Treatment of hyperactive and learning disordered children* (pp. 219–236). Baltimore: University Park Press.

Barkley, R. A. & Edelbrock, C. S. (1987). Assessing situational variation in children's behavior problems: The Home and School Situations Questionnaires. In R. Prinz (Ed.) *Advances in behavioral assessment of children and families* (Vol. 3, pp. 157–176). Greenwich, CT: JAI.

Barkley, R. A., Fischer, M., Newby, R., & Breen, M. (in press). Development of a multimethod clinical protocol for assessing stimulant drug responding in ADD children. *Journal of Clinical Child Psychology*.

Barkley, R. A., Karlsson, J., & Pollard, S. (1985). Effects of age on the mother–child interactions of ADD-H and normal boys. *Journal of Abnormal Child Psychology, 13,* 631–638.

Barkley, R. A., Karlsson, J., Pollard, S., & Murphy, J. (1985). Developmental changes in the mother child interactions of hyperactive boys: Effects of two dose levels of Ritalin. *Journal of Child Psychology and Psychiatry, 26,* 705–715.

Barkley, R. A., Karlsson, J., Strzelecki, E., & Murphy, J. (1984). Effects of age and Ritalin dosage on the mother–child interactions of hyperactive children. *Journal of Consulting and Clinical Psychology, 52,* 750–758.

Barkley, R. A., & Ullman, D. G. (1975). A comparison of objective measures of activity and distractibility in hyperactive and nonhyperactive children. *Journal of Abnormal Child Psychology, 3,* 231–244.

Barlow, D. H. (Ed.). (1981). *Behavioral assessment of adult disorders*. New York: Guilford Press.

Beck, A. T., Rush, A. J., Shaw, B. F., & Emery, G. (1980). *Cognitive therapy of depression*. New York: Guilford Press.

Befera, M., & Barkley, R. A. (1985). Hyperactive and normal girls and boys: Mother–child interactions, parent psychiatric status, and child psychopathology. *Journal of Child Psychology and Psychiatry, 26,* 439–452.

Block, G. H. (1977). Hyperactivity: A cultural perspective. *Journal of Learning Disabilities, 110,* 236–240.

Blouin, A. G., Bornstein, M. A., & Trites, R. L. (1978). Teenage alcohol abuse among hyperactive children: A five year follow-up study. *Journal of Pediatric Psychology, 3,* 188–194.

Breen, M. (1985). *ADD-H in girls: An analysis of attentional, emotional, cognitive, and academic behaviors and parental psychiatric status*. Manuscript submitted for publication.

Burke, W. T., & Abidin, R. R. (1980). Parenting Stress Index (PSI): A family system assessment approach. In R. R. Abidin (Ed.), *Parent education and intervention handbook*. Springfield, IL: Charles C Thomas.

Cairns, E., & Cammock, T. (1978). Development of a more reliable version of the Matching Familiar Figures Test. *Developmental Psychology, 11,* 244–248.

Cairns, E., & Cammock, T. (1984). The development of reflection–impulsivity: Further data. *Personality and Individual Differences, 5,* 113–115.

Campbell, S. B., Douglas, V. I., & Morganstern, G. (1971). Cognitive styles in hyperactive children and the effect of methylphenidate. *Journal of Child Psychology and Psychiatry, 12,* 55–67.

Campbell, S. B., Schleifer, M., & Weiss, G. (1978). Continuities in maternal reports and child behaviors over time in hyperactive and comparison groups. *Journal of Abnormal Child Psychology, 6.* 33–45.

Cantwell, D. (1975). *The hyperactive child.* New York: Spectrum.

Cantwell, D., & Carlson, G. (1978). Stimulants. In J. Werry (Ed.), *Pediatric psychopharmacology* (pp. 171–207). New York: Brunner/Mazel.

Cantwell, D., & Satterfield, J. H. (1978). The prevalence of academic underachievement in hyperactive children. *Journal of Pediatric Psychology, 3,* 168–171.

Chamberlin, R. W. (1977). Can we identify a group of children at age two who are at risk for the development of behavioral or emotional problems in kindergarten or first grade? *Pediatrics, 59* (Suppl.), 971–981.

Chess, S. (1960). Diagnosis and treatment of the hyperactive child. *New York State Journal of Medicine, 60,* 2379–2385.

Clements, S. D. (1966). *Task force one: Minimal brain dysfunction in children* (National Institute of Neurological Diseases and Blindness, Monograph No. 3). Washington, DC: U. S. Department of Health, Education and Welfare.

Clements, S. D., & Peters, J. E. (1962). Minimal brain dysfunction in the school-age child. *Archives of General Psychiatry, 6,* 185–197.

Cohen, N. J., & Minde, K. (1983). The "hyperactive syndrome" in kindergarten children: Comparison of children with pervasive and situational symptoms. *Journal of Child Psychology and Psychiatry, 24,* 443–455.

Comings, D. E., & Comings, D. G. (1984). Tourette's syndrome and attention deficit disorder with hyperactivity: Are they genetically related? *Journal of the American Academy of Child Psychiatry, 23,* 138–146.

Conners, C. K. (1969). A teacher rating scale for use in drug studies with children. *American Journal of Psychiatry, 126,* 884.

Conners, C. K. (1980). *Food additives and hyperactive children.* New York: Plenum.

Dangel, R. F., & Polster, R. A. (Eds.). (1984). *Parent training: Foundations of research and practice.* New York: Guilford Press.

David, O. J. (1974). Association between lower level lead concentrations and hyperactivity. *Environmental Health Perspective, 7,* 17–25.

de la Burde, B., & Choate, M. (1972). Does asymptomatic lead exposure in children have latent sequelae? *Journal of Pediatrics, 81,* 1088–1091.

de la Burde, B., & Choate, M. (1974). Early asymptomatic lead exposure and development at school age. *Journal of Pediatrics, 87,* 638–642.

Denckla, M. B., & Rudel, R. G. (1978). Anomalies of motor development in hyperactive boys. *Annals of Neurology, 3,* 231–233.

Denson, R., Nanson, J. L., & McWatters, M. A. (1975). Hyperkinesis and maternal smoking. *Canadian Psychiatric Association Journal, 20,* 183–187.

Deutsch, C. (1984, October). *Genetic studies of attention deficit disorder.* Paper presented at the High Point Hospital Conference on Attention and Conduct Disorder, Toronto.

Douglas, V. I. (1972). Stop, look, and listen: The problem of sustained attention and impulse control in hyperactive and normal children. *Canadian Journal of Behavioural Science, 4,* 259–282.

Douglas, V. I. (1980). Higher mental processes in hyperactive children: Implications for training. In R. Knights & D. Bakker (Eds.), *Treatment of hyperactive and learning disordered children* (pp. 65–92). Baltimore: University Park Press.

Douglas, V. I. (1983). Attention and cognitive problems. In M. Rutter (Ed.), *Developmental neuropsychiatry* (pp. 280–329). New York: Guilford Press.

Douglas, V. I., Barr, R. G., O'Neill, M. E., & Britton, B. G. (1986). Short term effects of methylphenidate on the cognitive, learning, and academic performance of children with attention deficit disorder. *Journal of Child Psychology and Psychiatry, 27,* 191–212.

Douglas, V. I., & Parry, P. A. (1983). Effects of reward on delayed reaction time task performance of hyperactive children. *Journal of Abnormal Child Psychology, 11,* 313–326.

Douglas, V., Parry, P., Marton, P., & Garson, C. (1976). Assessment of a cognitive training program for hyperactive children. *Journal of Abnormal Child Psychology, 4,* 389–410.

Douglas, V. I., & Peters, K. G. (1979). Toward a clearer definition of the attentional deficit of hyperactive children. In G. A. Hale & M. Lewis (Eds.), *Attention and the development of cognitive skills* (pp. 173–248). New York: Plenum.

Dubey, D. R., O'Leary, S. G., & Kaufman, K. F. (1983). Training parents of hyperactive children in child management: A comparative outcome study. *Journal of Abnormal Child Psychology, 11,* 229–246.

Edelbrock, C., Costello, A., & Kessler, M. D. (1984). Empirical corroboration of attention deficit disorder. *Journal of the American Academy of Child Psychiatry, 23,* 285–290.

Edelbrock, C., Greenbaum, R., & Conover, N. C. (1985). Reliability and concurrent relations between the teacher version of the Child Behavior Profile and the Conners Revised Teacher Rating Scale. *Journal of Abnormal Child Psychology, 13,* 295–304.

Feingold, B. (1975). *Why your child is hyperactive.* New York: Random House.

Ferguson, H. B., & Pappas, B. A. (1979). Evaluation of psychophysiological, neurochemical, and animal models of hyperactivity. In R. Trites (Ed.), *Hyperactivity in children* (pp. 61–92). Baltimore: University Park Press.

Firestone, P., & Martin, J. E. (1979). An analysis of the hyperactive syndrome: A comparison of hyperactive, behavior problem, asthmatic, and normal children. *Journal of Abnormal Child Psychology, 7,* 261–273.

Forehand, R., & McMahon, R. (1981). *Helping the noncompliant child: A clinician's guide to parent training.* New York: Guilford Press.

Foster, S. L., & Robin, A. L. (1988). Family conflict and communication in adolescence. In E. J. Mash & L. G. Terdal (Eds.), *Behavioral assessment of childhood disorders* (2nd ed., unabridged, pp. 717–775). New York: Guilford Press.

Fox, P. T., & Raichle, M. E. (1985). Stimulus rate determines regional brain blood flow in striate cortex. *Annals of Neurology, 17,* 303–305.

Gittleman, R., & Eskenazi, B. (1983). Lead and hyperactivity revisited. *Archives of General Psychiatry, 40,* 827–833.

Golden, G. S. (1983). Movement disorders in children: Tourette syndrome. *Developmental and Behavioral Pediatrics, 3,* 209–216.

Gordon, M. (1979). The assessment of impulsivity and mediating behaviors in hyperactive and non-hyperactive children. *Journal of Abnormal Child Psychology, 7,* 317–326.

Gordon, M. (1983). *The Gordon Diagnostic System.* Boulder, CO: Clinical Diagnostic Systems.

Gordon, M. (chair). (1985, August). *Assessment of ADD/ hyperactivity: Research on the Gordon Diagnostic System.* Symposium presented at the meeting of the American Psychological Association, Los Angeles.

Goyette, C. H., Conners, C. K., & Ulrich, R. F. (1978). Normative data for Revised Conners Parent and Teacher Rating Scales. *Journal of Abnormal Child Psychology, 6,* 221–236.

Gross, A. M. (1984). Behavioral interviewing. In T. H. Ollendick & M. Hersen (Eds.), *Child behavioral assessment* (pp. 61–79). New York: Pergamon Press.

Gross, M. D. (1984). Effects of sucrose on hyperkinetic children. *Pediatrics, 74,* 876–878.

Hartsough, C. S., & Lambert, N. M. (1985). Medical factors in hyperactive and normal children: Prenatal, developmental, and health history findings. *American Journal of Orthopsychiatry, 55,* 190–201.

Hastings, J. E., & Barkley, R. A. (1978). A review of psychophysiological research with hyperactive children. *Journal of Abnormal Child Psychology, 7,* 413–447.

Hechtman, L., Weiss, G., & Perlman, T. (1980). Hyperactives as young adults: Self-esteem and social-skills. *Canadian Journal of Psychiatry, 25,* 478–483.

Hechtman, L., Weiss, G., & Perlman, T. (1984). Young adult outcome of hyperactive children who received long-term stimulant treatment. *Journal of the American Academy of Child Psychiatry, 23,* 261–269.

Hechtman, L., Weiss, G., Perlman, R., & Amsel, R. (1984). Hyperactives as young adults: Initial predictors of outcome. *Journal of the American Academy of Child Psychiatry, 23,* 250–260.

Humphries, T., Kinsbourne, M., & Swanson, J. (1978). Stimulant effects on cooperation and social interaction between hyperactive children and their mothers. *Journal of Child Psychology and Psychiatry, 19,* 12–22.

Jacob, R. G., O'Leary, K. D., & Rosenblad, C. (1978). Formal and informal classroom settings: Effects on hyperactivity. *Journal of Abnormal Child Psychology, 6,* 47–59.

Johnston, C., Pelham, W. E., & Murphy, H. A. (1985). Peer relationships in ADDH and normal children: A developmental analysis of peer and teacher ratings. *Journal of Abnormal Child Psychology, 13,* 89–100.

Kagan, J. (1966). Reflection–impulsivity: The generality and dynamics of conceptual tempo. *Journal of Abnormal Psychology, 71,* 17–24.

Kendall, P. C., & Braswell, L. (1984). *Cognitive–behavioral therapy for impulsive children.* New York: Guilford Press.

Kendall, P. C., & Brophy, C. (1981). Activity and attentional correlates of teacher ratings of hyperactivity. *Journal of Pediatric Psychology, 6,* 451–458.

Kendall, P. C., & Wilcox, L. E. (1979). Self-control in children: Development of a rating scale. *Journal of Consulting and Clinical Psychology, 47,* 1020–1029.

King, C., & Young, D. (1982). Attentional deficits with and without hyperactivity: Teacher and peer perceptions. *Journal of Abnormal Child Psychology, 10,* 483–496.

Kinsbourne, M. (1977). The mechanism of hyperactivity. In M. Blaw, I. Rapin, & M. Kinsbourne (Eds.), *Topics in child neurology* (pp. 289–306). New York: Spectrum.

Klee, S. H., & Garfinkel, B. D. (1983). The computerized continuous performance task: A new measure of inattention. *Journal of Abnormal Child Psychology, 11,* 487–496.

Krouse, J. P., & Kauffman, J. M. (1982). Minor physical anomalies in exceptional children: A review and critique of research. *Journal of Abnormal Child Psychology, 10,* 247–262.

Lambert, N. M., Sandoval, J., & Sassone, D. (1978). Prevalence of hyperactivity in elementary school children as a function of social system definers. *American Journal of Orthopsychiatry, 48,* 446–463.

Locke, H. J., & Thomes, M. M. (1980). *The Locke Marital Adjustment Test: Its validity, reliability, weighting procedure, and modification.* Unpublished manuscript, University of Southern California.

Locke, H. J., & Wallace, K. M. (1959). Short marital adjustment and prediction tests: Their reliability and validity. *Marriage and Family Therapy, 21,* 251–255.

Loney, J., & Milich, R. (1982). Hyperactivity, inattention, and aggression in clinical practice. In M. Wolraich & D. Routh (Eds.), *Advances in behavioral pediatrics* (Vol. 2, pp. 113–147). Greenwich, CT: JAI Press.

Loney, J., Whaley-Klahn, M. A., Kosier, T., & Conboy, J. (1981, November). *Hyperactive boys and their brothers at 21: Predictors of aggressive and antisocial outcomes.* Paper presented at the meeting of the Society of Life History Research, Monterey, CA.

Lopez, R. C. (1965). Hyperactivity in twins. *Canadian Psychiatric Association Journal, 10,* 421–426.

Lou, H. C., Henriksen, L., & Bruhn, P. (1984). Focal cerebral hypoperfusion in children with dysphasia and/ or attention deficit disorder. *Archives of Neurology, 41,* 825–829.

Luk, S. (1985). Direct observations studies of hyperactive behaviors. *Journal of the American Academy of Child Psychiatry, 24,* 338–344.

Margolin, G. (1983). An interactional model for the behavioral assessment of martial relationships. *Behavioral Assessment, 5,* 103–128.

Mash, E. J., & Barkley, R. A. (1986). Assessment of family interaction with the Response-Class Matrix. In R. Prinz (Ed.), *Advances in behavioral assessment of children and families* (Vol. 2, pp. 29–67). Greenwich, CT: JAI Press.

Mash, E. J., & Johnston, C. (1982). A comparison of the mother–child interactions of younger and older hyperactive and normal children. *Child Development, 53,* 1371–1381.

Mash, E. J., & Johnston, C. (1983a). Parental perceptions of child behavior problems, parenting self-esteem, and mothers' reported stress in younger and older hyperactive and normal children. *Journal of Consulting and Clinical Psychology, 51,* 68–99.

Mash, E. J., & Johnston, C. (1983b). The prediction of mothers' behavior with their hyperactive children during play and task situations. *Child and Family Behavior Therapy, 5,* 1–14.

Mash, E. J., Terdal, L., & Anderson, K. (1973). The Response-Class Matrix: A procedure for recording parent–child interactions. *Journal of Consulting and Clinical Psychology, 40,* 163–164.

Mattes, J. A., & Gittelman, R. (1981). Effects of artificial food colorings in children with hyperactive symptoms. *Archives of General Psychiatry, 38,* 714–718.

Maurer, R. G., & Stewart, M. A. (1980). Attention deficit without hyperactivity in a child psychiatry clinic. *Journal of Clinical Psychiatry, 41,* 232–233.

McClure, F. D., & Gordon, M. (1984). Performance of disturbed hyperactive and nonhyperactive children on an objective measure of hyperactivity. *Journal of Abnormal Child Psychology, 12,* 561–572.

McGee, R., Williams, S., & Silva, P. A. (1984a). Background characteristics of aggressive, hyperactive, and aggressive–hyperactive boys. *Journal of the American Academy of Child Psychiatry, 23,* 280–284.

McGee, R., Williams, S., & Silva, P. A. (1984b). Behavioral and developmental characteristics of aggressive, hyperactive, and aggressive–hyperactive boys. *Journal of the American Academy of Child Psychiatry, 23,* 270–279.

Messer, S., & Brodzinsky, D. M. (1981). Three year stability of reflection–impulsivity in young adolescents. *Developmental Psychology, 17,* 848–850.

Milar, C. R., Schroeder, S. R., Mushak, P., & Boone, L. (1981). Failure to find hyperactivity in preschool children with moderately elevated lead burden. *Journal of Pediatric Psychology, 6,* 85–95.

Milich, R. (1984). Cross-sectional and longitudinal observations of activity level and sustained attention in a normative sample. *Journal of Abnormal Child Psychology, 12,* 261–276.

Milich, R., & Kramer, J. (1984). Reflections on impulsivity: An empirical investigation of impulsivity as a construct. In K. Gadow & I. Bialer (Eds.), *Advances in learning and behavioral disabilities* (Vol. 3). Greenwich, CT: JAI Press.

Milich, R., Landau, S., & Loney, J. (1981, August). *The inter-relationships among hyperactivity, aggression, and impulsivity.* Paper presented at the meeting of the American Psychological Association, Los Angeles.

Milich, R., & Loney, J. (1979). The role of hyperactive and aggressive symptomatology in predicting adolescent outcome among hyperactive children. *Journal of Pediatric Psychology, 4,* 93–112.

Milich, R., Loney, J., & Landau, S. (1982). The independent dimensions of hyperactivity and aggression: A validation with playroom observation data. *Journal of Abnormal Psychology, 91,* 183–198.

Montagu, J., & Swarbrick, L. (1975). Effect of amphetamine in hyperkinetic children: Stimulant or sedative? A pilot study. *Developmental Medicine and Child Neurology, 17,* 293–298.

Morganstern, K. P. (1976). Behavioral interviewing: The initial stages of assessment. In M. Hersen & A. S. Bellack (Eds.), *Behavioral assessment: A practical handbook* (pp. 51–76). New York: Pergamon Press.

Morrison, J. R., & Stewart, M. A. (1971). A family study of the hyperactive child syndrome. *Biological Psychiatry, 3,* 189–195.

Morrison, J. R., & Stewart, M. A. (1973). Evidence for a polygenetic inheritance in the hyperactive child syndrome. *American Journal of Psychiatry, 130,* 791–792.

Needleman, H. L., Gunnoe, C., Leviton, A., Reed, R., Peresie, H., Maher, C., & Barrett, P. (1979). Deficits in psychologic and classroom performance of children with elevated dentine lead levels. *New England Journal of Medicine, 300,* 689–695.

Nichols, P. (1980). Early antecedents of hyperactivity. *Neurology, 30,* 4–9.

O'Leary, K. D., Vivian, D., & Nisi, A. (1985). Hyperactivity in Italy. *Journal of Abnormal Child Psychology, 13,* 485–500.

Paternite, C., & Loney, J. (1980). Childhood hyperkinesis: Relationships between symptomatology and home environment. In C. K. Whalen & B. Henker (Eds.), *Hyperactive children: The social ecology of identification and treatment* (pp. 105–141). New York: Academic Press.

Patterson, G. R. (1982). *Coercive family process.* Eugene, OR: Castalia.

Pelham, W. E., & Bender, M. E. (1982). Peer relationships in hyperactive children: Description and treatment. In K. Gadow & E. Bialer (Eds.), *Advances in learning and behavioral disabilities* (Vol. 1, pp. 365–436). Greenwich, CT: JAI Press.

Pollard, S., Ward, E. M., & Barkley, R. A. (1983). The effects of parent training and Ritalin on the parent–child interactions of hyperactive boys. *Child and Family Behavior Therapy, 5,* 51–69.

Porrino, L. J., Rapoport, J. L., Behar, D., Sceery, W., Ismond, D. R., & Bunney, W. E. (1983). A naturalistic assessment of the motor activity of hyperactive boys. *Archives of General Psychiatry, 40,* 681–687.

Prinz, R. J., Roberts, W. A., & Hantman, E. (1980). Dietary correlates of hyperactive behavior in children. *Journal of Consulting and Clinical Psychology, 48,* 760–769.

Quinn, P. O., & Rapoport, J. L. (1974). Minor physical anomalies and neurological status in hyperactive boys. *Pediatrics, 53,* 742–747.

Rapoport, J. L., & Benoit, M. (1975). The relation of direct home observations to the clinic evaluation of hyperactive school age boys. *Journal of Child Psychology and Psychiatry, 16,* 141–147.

Rapport, M. D., Stoner, G., DuPaul, G. J., Birmingham, B. K., & Tucker, S. (1985). Methlyphenidate in hyperactive children: Differential effects of dose on academic, learning, and social behavior. *Journal of Abnormal Child Psychology, 13,* 227–244.

Rie, H. E., & Rie, E. D. (1980). *Handbook of minimal brain dysfunction.* New York: Wiley.

Robin, A. L. (1981). A controlled evaluation of problem-solving communication training with parent–adolescent conflict. *Behavior Therapy, 12,* 593–609.

Robin, A. L. (1985). Parent–adolescent conflict: A developmental problem of families. In R. McMahon & R. Peters (Eds.), *Childhood disorders: Developmental–behavioral approaches* (pp. 244–266). New York: Brunner/Mazel.

Robinson, E. A., & Eyberg, S. (1981). The dyadic parent–child interaction coding system: Standardization and validation. *Journal of Consulting and Clinical Psychology, 49,* 245–250.

Rosenthal, R. H., & Allen, T. W. (1978). An examination of attention, arousal, and learning dysfunctions of hyperkinetic children. *Psychological Bulletin, 85,* 689–715.

Ross, D. M., & Ross, S. A. (1976). *Hyperactivity: Research, theory, and action.* New York: Wiley.

Ross, D. M., & Ross, S. A. (1982). *Hyperactivity: Current*

issues, research, and theory (2nd ed.). New York: Wiley.

Routh, D. K. (1978). Hyperactivity. In P. Magrab (Ed.), *Psychological management of pediatric problems* (pp. 3–48). Baltimore: University Park Press.

Routh, D. K., & Roberts, R. D. (1972). Minimal brain dysfunction in children: Failure to find evidence for a behavioral syndrome. *Psychological Reports, 31,* 307–314.

Routh, D. K., & Schroeder, C. S. (1976). Standardized playroom measures as indices of hyperactivity. *Journal of Abnormal Child Psychology, 4,* 199–207.

Routh, D. K., Schroeder, C. S., & O'Tuama, L. (1974). Development of activity level in children. *Developmental Psychology, 10,* 163–168.

Rubinstein, R. A., & Brown, R. T. (1984). An evaluation of the validity of the diagnostic category of attention deficit disorder. *American Journal of Orthopsychiatry, 54,* 398–414.

Rutter, M. (1977). Brain damage syndromes in childhood: Concepts and findings. *Journal of Child Psychology and Psychiatry, 18,* 1–21.

Rutter, M., Chadwick, O., & Shaffer, D. (1983). Head injury. In M. Rutter (Ed.), *Developmental neuropsychiatry* (pp. 83–111). New York: Guilford Press.

Safer, R., & Allen, D. (1976). *Hyperactive children.* Baltimore: University Park Press.

Salkind, N. J., & Nelson, C. F. (1980). A note on the developmental nature of reflection–impulsivity. *Developmental Psychology, 6,* 237–238.

Sandberg, S. T., Rutter, M., & Taylor, E. (1978). Hyperkinetic disorder in psychiatric clinic attenders. *Developmental Medicine and Child Neurology, 20,* 279–299.

Satterfield, J. H., Satterfield, B. T., & Cantwell, D. P. (1981). Three-year multimodality treatment study of 100 hyperactive boys. *Journal of Pediatrics, 98,* 650–655.

Schacher, R., Rutter, M., & Smith, A. (1981). The characteristics of situationally and pervasively hyperactive children: Implications for syndrome definition. *Journal of Child Psychology and Psychiatry, 22,* 375–392.

Shaffer, D., McNamara, N., & Pincus, J. H. (1974). Controlled observations on patterns of activity, attention, and impulsivity in brain-damaged and psychiatrically disturbed boys. *Psychological Medicine, 4,* 4–18.

Shaywitz, S. E., Cohen, D. J., & Shaywitz, B. A. (1978). The biochemical basis of minimal brain dysfunction. *Journal of Pediatrics, 92,* 179–187.

Shaywitz, S. E., Cohen, D. J., & Shaywitz, B. A. (1980). Behavior and learning difficulties in children of normal intelligence born to alcoholic mothers. *Journal of Pediatrics, 96,* 978–982.

Shaywitz, B. A., Shaywitz, S. E., Byrne, T., Cohen, D. J., & Rothman, S. (1983). Attention deficit disorder: Quantitative analysis of CT. *Neurology, 33,* 1500–1503.

Shaywitz, S. E., Shaywitz, B. A., Cohen, D. J., & Young, J. G. (1983). Monoaminergic mechanisms in hyperactivity. In M. Rutter (Ed.), *Developmental neuropsychiatry* (pp. 330–347). New York: Guilford Press.

Skinner, B. F. (1969). *Contingencies of reinforcement: A theoretical analysis.* New York: Appleton-Century-Crofts.

Sleator, E. K., & Ullmann, R. K. (1981). Can the physician diagnose hyperactivity in the office? *Pediatrics, 67,* 13–17.

Smith, L. (1976). *Your child's behavior chemistry.* New York: Random House.

Stewart, M. A., Thach, B. T., & Freidin, M. R. (1970). Accidental poisoning and the hyperactive child syndrome. *Diseases of the Nervous System, 31,* 403–407.

Still, G. F. (1902). Some abnormal psychical conditions in children. *Lancet, 1,* 1008–1012, 1077–1082, 1163–1168.

Strauss, A. A., & Lehtinen, L. E. (1947). *Psychopathology and education of the brain-injured child.* New York: Grune & Stratton.

Tallmadge, J., & Barkley, R. A. (1983). The interactions of hyperactive and normal boys with their mothers and fathers. *Journal of Abnormal Child Psychology, 11,* 565–579.

Tarver-Behring, S., Barkley, R., & Karlsson, J. (1985). The mother–child interactions of hyperactive boys and their normal siblings. *American Journal of Orthopsychiatry, 55,* 202–209.

Taylor, H. G. (1983). MBD: Meanings and misconceptions. *Journal of Clinical Neuropsychology, 5,* 271–287.

Taylor, J. F. (1980). *The hyperactive child and the family.* New York: Random House.

Thorley, G. (1984). Review of follow-up and follow-back studies of childhood hyperactivity. *Psychological Bulletin, 96,* 116–132.

Trites, R. L., Blouin, A. G. A., & LaPrade, K. (1982). Factor analysis of the Conners Teaching Rating Scale based on a large normative sample. *Journal of Consulting and Clinical Psychology, 50,* 615–623.

Trites, R. L., Dugas, F., Lynch, G., & Ferguson, B. (1979). Incidence of hyperactivity. *Journal of Pediatric Psychology, 4,* 179–188.

Trites, R. L., Tryphonas, H., & Ferguson, H. B. (1980). Diet treatment for hyperactive children with food allergies. In R. Knights & D. Bakker (Eds.), *Treatment of hyperactive and learning disordered children* (pp. 151–166). Baltimore: University Park Press.

Tryon, W. W. (1984). Principles and methods of mechanically measuring motor activity. *Behavioral Assessment, 6,* 129–140.

Ullman, D. G., Barkley, R. A., & Brown, H. W. (1978). The behavioral symptoms of hyperkinetic children who successfully responded to stimulant drug treatment. *American Journal of Orthopsychiatry, 48,* 425–437.

Wahler, R. G. (1980). The insular mother: Her problems in parent–child treatment. *Journal of Applied Behavior Analysis, 13,* 207–219.

Wahler, R. G., & Graves, M. G. (1983). Setting events in social networks: Ally or enemy in child behavior therapy? *Behavior Therapy, 14,* 19–36.

Wahler, R. G., House, A. E., & Stambaugh, E. E. (1976). *Ecological assessment of child problem behavior.* New York: Pergamon Press.

Weiss, H., Hechtman, L., Milroy, T., & Perlman, T. (1985). Psychiatric status of hyperactives as adults: A controlled prospective 15-year follow-up of 63 hyperactive children. *Journal of the American Academy of Child Psychiatry, 24,* 211–220.

Weiss, G., Hechtman, L., & Perlman, T. (1978). Hyperactives as young adults: School, employer, and self-rating scales obtained during ten-year follow-up evaluation. *American Journal of Orthopsychiatry, 48,* 438–445.

Weiss, G., Hechtman, L., Perlman, T., Hopkins, J., & Wener, A. (1979). Hyperactives as young adults: A controlled prospective ten-year follow-up of 75 children. *Archives of General Psychiatry, 36,* 675–681.

Weithorn, C. J., Kagen, E., & Marcus, M. (1984). The relationship of activity level ratings and cognitive impulsivity to task performance and academic achievement. *Journal of Child Psychology and Psychiatry, 25,* 587–606.

Wender, P. H., Reimherr, F. W., & Wood, D. R. (1981). Attention deficit disorder ("minimal brain dysfunction") in adults. *Archives of General Psychiatry, 38,* 449–456.

Werry, J. S. (1985, June). *Differential diagnosis of ADD and conduct disorders.* Paper presented at the International Workshop on Attention Deficit Disorder, Gröningen, the Netherlands.

Werry, J. S., & Sprague, R. L. (1968). Hyperactivity. In C. G. Costello (Ed.), *Symptoms of psychopathology* (pp. 397–417). New York: Wiley.

Werry, J., Weiss, G., & Douglas, V. (1964). Studies of the hyperactive child: I. Some preliminary findings. *Canadian Psychiatric Association Journal, 9,* 120–130.

Werry, J., Weiss, G., Douglas, V., & Martin, J. (1966). Studies on the hyperactive child: III. The effect of chlorpromazine upon behavior and learning. *Journal of the American Academy of Child Psychiatry, 5,* 292–312.

Whalen, C. K., & Henker, B. (1980). *Hyperactive children: The social ecology of identification and treatment.* New York: Academic Press.

Whalen, C. K., Henker, B., & Hinshaw, S. P. (1985). Cognitive–behavioral therapies for hyperactive children: Premises, problems, and prospects. *Journal of Abnormal Child Psychology, 13,* 391–410.

Willerman, L. (1973). Activity level and hyperactivity in twins. *Child Development, 44,* 288–293.

Willis, T. J., & Lovaas, I. (1977). A behavioral approach to treating hyperactive children: The parent's role. In J. G. Millichap (Ed.), *Learning disabilities and related disorders* (pp. 119–140). Chicago: Year Book Medical Publications.

Wolraich, M., Milich, R., Stumbo, P., & Schultz, F. (1985). The effects of sucrose ingestion on the behavior of hyperactive boys. *Journal of Pediatrics, 106,* 675–682.

Wood, D. R., Reimherr, F. W., Wender, P. H., & Johnson, G. E. (1976). Diagnosis and treatment of minimal brain dysfunction in adults. *Archives of General Psychiatry, 33,* 1453–1460.

Zentall, S. (1984). Context effects in the behavioral ratings of hyperactivity. *Journal of Abnormal Child Psychology, 12,* 345–352.

Zettle, R. D., & Hayes, S. C. (1982). Rule-governed behavior: A potential theoretical framework for cognitive–behavioral therapy. In P. C. Kendall (Ed.), *Advances in cognitive–behavioral research* (Vol. 1, pp. 73–118). New York: Academic Press.

3 CONDUCT DISORDERS

ROBERT J. McMAHON
University of Washington

REX FOREHAND
University of Georgia

I n surveying the presenting problems of children described in the behavioral literature, it is clear that the vast majority of studies deal with children whose behavior can generally be described as "out of control" of the parents and/or other significant individuals in the community (e.g., teachers). Chief complaints of these children's parents include aggressiveness toward others (hitting, kicking, fighting); physical destructiveness; disobedience to adult authorities; temper tantrums; high-rate annoying behaviors (e.g., yelling, whining, high activity level, and threatening others); and, to a lesser extent, community rule violations such as stealing or fire setting (Loeber & Schmaling, 1985a). Typically, these behaviors do not occur in isolation but as a complex or "class," and children displaying such behaviors have been labeled "oppositional," "socially aggressive," and "conduct-disordered" by various authors (e.g., Patterson, 1974; Wahler, 1969).

The need for developing and evaluating effective assessment approaches for the conduct-disordered child is evidenced by the fact that these children comprise the largest group referred to mental health centers (Wells & Forehand, 1985). Depending upon the particular sample, these children can account for approximately 50% of the clinic population (Wolff,

1961). Boys are referred more often than girls for such problems (Kazdin, 1985), with ratios ranging from 4:1 to 12:1 (American Psychiatric Association, 1980, 1987). As we discuss later, conduct-disordered children also appear to manifest difficulties in a variety of other areas (Wells & Forehand, 1985).

Developmental studies of nonreferred children indicate that even these children may exhibit conduct disordered behaviors at some point in their childhood and adolescence (Edelbrock, 1985; MacFarlane, Allen, & Honzik, 1954). For both clinic-referred and nonreferred children, the number of problem behaviors declines with age (e.g., Moore & Mukai, 1983). However, children with severe conduct disorders are likely to exhibit similar patterns of behavior into adulthood if left untreated, and they have an increased likelihood of engaging in delinquent and criminal behavior (Loeber, 1982; Olweus, 1979; Robins, 1966). In his recent review, Loeber (1982) concluded that conduct-disordered children whose antisocial behavior has an earlier onset, is manifested in more than one setting, occurs at higher rates, and/or is manifested in several forms are at greatest risk for continued performance of these behaviors. As adults, not only are conduct-disordered children more likely to continue to engage in antisocial behavior; they are at increased risk for psychiatric impairment of various types, poor occupational adjustment, low educational attainment, marital distress/disruption, less social participation, and poor physical health (Kazdin, 1985). Given the frequency with which these families present themselves to mental health facilities for help, the effectiveness of behavioral treatment with these childhood disorders (Casey & Berman, 1985), and the likelihood of the continued occurrence of such behaviors if nothing is done, it is not surprising that much of the behavioral research with children has focused on this target population.

The primary purpose of this chapter is to present and evaluate critically the procedures currently used to assess conduct disorders in children. A secondary purpose is to familiarize the reader with the behavioral characteristics of conduct-disordered children and their families, and to present a conceptual framework for understanding the development and maintenance of conduct disorders in children.

CHARACTERISTICS OF CONDUCT-DISORDERED CHILDREN AND THEIR FAMILIES

Child Characteristics

Several different approaches have been used to describe and classify conduct-disordered children (Wells & Forehand, 1985). The most widely used system of classification is the *Diagnostic and Statistical Manual of Mental Disorders,* third edition (DSM-III; American Psychiatric Association, 1980). Within DMS-III, there are two major types of disorders that are pertinent to the present chapter: Conduct Disorder and Oppositional Disorder. The category of Conduct Disorder varies along two dimensions: Aggressive–Nonaggressive and Socialized–Undersocialized. The Nonaggressive dimension of Conduct Disorder involves behaviors such as truancy, lying, stealing, and substance abuse. These are behaviors that are nonviolent and do not involve confrontation with another person. Such behaviors have been labeled "covert antisocial behaviors" by Patterson (1982) and Loeber and Schmaling (1985a). In contrast, the Aggressive dimension involves behaviors in which the rights of others are directly violated (i.e., physical violence against persons or property). These have been labeled as "overt antisocial behaviors" (Loeber & Schmaling, 1985a; Patterson, 1982). The Socialized–Undersocial-

ized dimension pertains to whether the individual shows evidence of social attachment to others (Socialized) or fails to establish empathy or affection with others (Undersocialized). The second category within DSM-III that is relevant to this chapter is Oppositional Disorder. This category includes behaviors such as disobedience, stubbornness, violation of minor rules, tantrums, and backtalk.

Although DSM-III is widely used, several authors have emphasized that problems exist with this classification system for children. Achenbach (1985) has recently noted that the child categories have little basis in research, while Wells and Forehand (1985) have pointed out the questionable reliability and validity data for the child diagnostic categories. Agreement among clinicians' diagnoses has typically been poor (e.g., Mattison, Cantwell, Russell, & Will, 1979), and few validity studies have been conducted (Wells & Forehand, 1985).

At least partly in response to some of these criticisms, the DSM-III has been recently revised (DSM-IIIR; American Psychiatric Association, 1987). There have been several changes in the Conduct Disorder and Oppositional Disorder categories. With respect to the DSM-IIIR version of Conduct Disorder, the essential feature is a "persistent pattern of conduct in which the basic rights of others and major age-appropriate societal norms or rules are violated" (p. 53). The pattern must have continued for at least 6 months, and at least 3 of the following 13 behaviors must have been present: stolen without confrontation of a victim (more than once); run away from home overnight (at least twice, or once without returning); lied; set fires; truant from school; broken into someone else's house, building, or car; deliberate destruction of others' property; physical cruelty to animals; forced someone into sexual activity; used a weapon (in more than one fight); initiated physical fights; stolen with confrontation of a victim; physical cruelty to people. Rather than four subtypes based on aggressive–nonaggressive and socialized–undersocialized dimensions, the DSM-IIIR lists three subtypes of Conduct Disorder. The Solitary Aggressive Type, which corresponds roughly to the DSM-III subtype of Undersocialized Aggressive, is characterized by aggressive physical behavior initiated by the child and usually directed toward both adults and peers. The Group Type, which corresponds somewhat to the DSM-III subtype of Socialized Nonaggressive, is characterized by conduct problems that occur mainly as a group activity with peers. In contrast to its DSM-III counterpart, physical aggression may be manifested in the Group Type. Finally, the Undifferentiated Type is composed of children with a diagnosis of Conduct Disorder whose pattern of behavior does not fit neatly into either of the other subtypes. The DSM-IIIR notes that the Undifferentiated Type may be much more common than either of the other two subtypes.

Oppositional Disorder is now referred to as "Oppositional Defiant Disorder" in the DSM-IIIR. The essential feature is a "pattern of negativistic, hostile, and defiant behavior without the more serious violations of the basic rights of others that are seen in Conduct Disorder" (p. 56). Thus, the Conduct Disorder category subsumes the Oppositional Defiant Disorder category. The pattern of behavior must have a duration of at least 6 months, and at least five of the following nine behaviors must have been present and have occurred frequently: loses temper; argues with adults; actively defies or refuses adult requests or rules; deliberately does things that annoy other people; blames others for his or her own mistakes; touchy or easily annoyed by others; angry and resentful; spiteful or vindictive; swears. Age of onset has been eliminated as a diagnostic criteria, but is described as typically beginning by 8 years and usually not later than early adolescence. The severity (mild, moderate, severe) of both Conduct Disorder and Oppositional Defiant Disorder is now noted in the DSM-IIIR, based primarily on the number of different behaviors in which the child engages.

Because of the recent appearance of the DSM-IIIR, its psychometric properties are not known, and so it is not possible to ascertain at this time whether the changes noted above with respect to the diagnostic categories relevant to conduct disorders represent improvement over their DSM-III counterparts. A second approach for describing and classifying conduct-disordered children is through empirically derived syndromes (Achenbach, 1985). This approach assumes that there are a number of dimensions along which all children's behavior varies. These dimensions are relatively independent of one another, and, within each dimension, behaviors are highly related. In their reviews of the research on empirically derived syndromes of children's behavior, Quay (1979) and Achenbach and Edelbrock (1978) found that one factor that consistently emerged from studies could be labeled

"conduct disorder." Some of the most common behaviors identified by Quay (1979) as defining this syndrome are listed below:

- Fights
- Temper tantrums
- Disobedient
- Destructive
- Impertinent
- Uncooperative
- Disruptive
- Negative
- Restless
- Boisterous
- Irritable
- Attention-seeking
- Dominates others
- Lies
- Steals

As Wells and Forehand (1985) have noted, such empirically derived syndromes typically include behaviors from both the Conduct Disorder and the Oppositional Disorder categories of DSM-III, suggesting that there is not substantial evidence for a separate classification of Oppositional Disorder from Conduct Disorder. (A similar case might be made regarding the relevant DSM-IIIR disorders as well.) Indeed, interrater reliability has been shown to improve to near-acceptable levels ($\kappa = .67$) when the Conduct Disorder ($\kappa = .53$) and Oppositional Disorder ($\kappa = .39$) categories of DSM-III are combined (Werry, Methven, Fitzpatrick, & Dixon, 1983).

Close examination of the behaviors that are subsumed under the empirically derived conduct disorder dimension indicates that most are behaviors involving direct confrontation or disruption of the environment. They are the same type of behaviors that Patterson (1982) and Loeber and Schmaling (1985a) have labeled "overt antisocial behaviors." Exactly how these manifestations of conduct disorder relate to the more covert conduct-disordered behaviors (e.g., stealing, lying) is unclear; however, Loeber and Schmaling (1985a) recently have proposed that the two disorders represent endpoints of a single dimension. They have described a dimension of antisocial behavior that is anchored by covert behaviors (alcohol and drug use, truancy, stealing) on one pole and overt behaviors (temper tantrums, screaming, arguing, demanding, and impulsivity) on the other pole. Noncompliance is represented at the midpoint of the dimension.

TABLE 1. Developmental Progression of
Conduct-Disordered Behaviors

Oppositional	
Argues	Temper tantrums
Bragging	Stubborn
Demands attention	Teases
Disobeys at home	Loud
Impulsive	

Offensive	
Cruelty	Fights
Disobeys at school	Sulks
Screams	Swears
Poor peer relations	Lying/cheating

Aggressive	
Destroys	Bad friends
Threatens	Steals at home
Attacks	

Delinquent	
Sets fires	Truancy
Steals outside	Runs away
Alcohol/drug use	Vandalism

Note. From *Conduct Problems in Childhood and Adolescence: Developmental Patterns and Progressions* by C. Edelbrock, 1985, unpublished manuscript. Reprinted by permission of the author.

As we discuss in the next section, noncompliance is viewed by several investigators as a keystone behavior that links the two endpoints of the antisocial dimension.

Edelbrock (1985) has recently proposed a developmental model based on the empirically derived conduct disorder dimension, which describes a stepwise progression through four stages: "oppositional," "offensive," "aggressive," and "delinquent." This progression is presented in Table 1. In general, these four stages comprise progressions from overt to covert types of conduct-disordered behavior, from minor to more serious behaviors, and (to a lesser extent) from problems within the home setting to problems in the school and community. Behaviors represented in earlier stages tend to continue to be displayed even as the child engages in behaviors characteristic of higher stages of the model. At each successive stage, progressively smaller subsets of children appear to engage in the behaviors. Although this model must be considered as preliminary because of its primary reliance on parent ratings and cross-sectional data, it clearly suggests the utility of considering these developmental factors in the assessment, and ultimately the treatment, of conduct-disordered children.

If one generalizes across the two methods of classifying children's behavior, it would appear that conduct disorders include behaviors that are overt and directly disruptive to the environment, as well as behaviors that are covert and less immediately disruptive to the environment. While relatively little research has been conducted examining children with covert antisocial behaviors, substantial work has focused on children (and their families) who demonstrate overt conduct disorders. Much of this work has consisted of the comparison of children referred to clinics for conduct disorders (e.g., noncompliance, aggression) with nonreferred children. A number of researchers (Delfini, Bernal, & Rosen, 1976; Forehand, King, Peed, & Yoder, 1975; Green, Forehand, & McMahon, 1979; Griest, Forehand, Wells, & McMahon, 1980; Moore, 1975; Patterson, 1976, 1982) have conducted behavioral observation studies and found that behaviors representing overt conduct problems are more prevalent in clinic-referred children than in nonreferred children. An aggregate measure of overt conduct disorders typically has been used in these studies. However, in some studies (e.g., Griest *et al.*, 1980), discrete behaviors (e.g., noncompliance) have been examined and found to differ between the two groups.

With respect to covert conduct disorders, the relatively little research that has been conducted has focused on children who steal. Virtually all of this work has been conducted by Gerald R. Patterson and his colleagues at the Oregon Social Learning Center (see Patterson, 1982). In two investigations, the level of aversive behavior in family interactions demonstrated by children who stole was significantly higher than for nonreferred children, but significantly less than for socially aggressive children (Patterson, 1982; Reid & Hendricks, 1973). When children who demonstrate both stealing and social aggression are examined separately, they are found to be even more aversive than the children who are socially aggressive but who do not steal. The remaining children who steal exhibit levels of aversive behavior that are comparable to those of nonreferred children (Loeber & Schmaling, 1985b; Patterson, 1982). It also appears that children who steal are older at time of referral than children referred for overt types of conduct disorders (Reid & Hendricks, 1973) and are at greater risk for committing delinquent offenses as adolescents (Loeber & Schmaling, 1985b; Moore, Chamberlain, & Mukai, 1979).

Not only do conduct-disordered children exhibit higher levels of aversive behavior in the context of family interactions; they do so in interactions with peers as well. Parents of conduct-disordered children report that their children are less socially competent than other children and/or that they have poor peer relations (Achenbach & Edelbrock, 1983; Lorber & Patterson, 1981). Observational studies on school playgrounds indicate that aggressive children are more deviant in their peer interactions than their nonaggressive counterparts (e.g., Harris, Kreil, & Orpet, 1977). Furthermore, based on sociometric data, they are more likely to be rejected by their peers (e.g., Milich, Landau, Kilby, & Whitten, 1982).

In addition to behavioral differences between conduct-disordered and nonreferred children with respect to peer interactions, attention is also being paid to cognitive variables that may characterize the peer interactions of conduct-disordered children. In particular, much of this research has focused on possible tendencies to misattribute hostile intentions to others. Kenneth Dodge (e.g., Dodge, 1980; Dodge & Frame, 1982; Milich & Dodge, 1984) and others (e.g., Nasby, Hayden, & DePaulo, 1980) have presented data to suggest that aggressive children engage in the distortion of social cues in peer interactions in such a way that they are likely to attribute hostile intent to others in situations in which such intent is ambiguous or absent. This perception of hostile intent may then predispose such children to react aggressively. Patterson (1982) has suggested that this attributional bias also characterizes interactions within the families of conduct-disordered children. However, to date, there are no data that address this issue. In addition to the problems noted above, there are also data to suggest that aggressive children are deficient in social problem-solving types of skills (e.g., Asarnow & Callan, 1985; Deluty, 1981; Richard & Dodge, 1982), and that they evaluate aggressive interpersonal styles as more desirable than do nonaggressive children (Deluty, 1983). Aggressive delinquents have been found to be less empathic than their nonaggressive counterparts (Ellis, 1982).

Conduct-disordered children also frequently have other difficulties as well. There is a close association between conduct disorders and attention deficit disorder with hyperactivity (ADD/H), to the extent that Safer and Allen (1976) reported that 75% of children with ADD/H also have conduct-disordered types of problems. Interestingly, Loeber (1985) has recently proposed that hyperactivity may be the "driving force" in conduct-disordered children. That is, hyperactivity may be a necessary ingredient in order for children to display severe conduct disorder.

There is also an association between conduct disorders and depression, especially for boys. Chiles, Miller, and Cox (1980) reported that 23% of a group of adolescent delinquents admitted to a correctional facility met diagnostic criteria for a major affective disorder. In another investigation, preadolescent boys diagnosed as conduct-disordered were more likely to be depressed than were boys with other diagnoses (Steward, de Blois, Meardon, & Cummings, 1980). This relationship did not hold for girls. Conversely, a number of children diagnosed as having an affective disorder appear to be at risk for also receiving a diagnosis of conduct disorder (Kovacs, Feinberg, Crouse-Novac, Paulauskas, & Finkelstein, 1984; Puig-Antich, 1982). Puig-Antich (1982) reported that one-third of the sample of children who received a DSM-III diagnosis of Major Depressive Disorder also met the DSM-III criteria for Conduct Disorder. In the Kovacs et al. (1984) investigation, 7% of the children with Major Depressive Disorder and 11% of the children with Dysthymic Disorder were also given a diagnosis of Conduct Disorder.

Finally, conduct-disordered children often have a low level of academic achievement, which manifests itself in the early elementary grades and continues into high school. For example, low academic achievement in third grade and being held back during elementary school occurred three times more frequently in severely behavior-disordered junior high school students than in a matched control group (Safer, 1984). During the junior high school period, the behaviorally disordered children were more than 50 times more likely to be held back than were children in the control group. Deficits in various academic skills have also been correlated with adolescent delinquency (r's = .24–.37; Dishion, Loeber, Stouthamer-Loeber, & Patterson, 1984). Reading disabilities, in particular, are associated with conduct disorders (e.g., Sturge, 1982). In a large-scale epidemiological survey on the Isle of Wight (Rutter, Tizard, Yule, Graham, & Whitmore, 1976), one-third of the conduct-disordered children demonstrated specific reading retardation, which was defined as a 28-month or more lag in reading ability in normal-IQ children.

Family Characteristics

Many of the investigations described above concerning child behavior have also examined parental behavior. In general, it has been found that parents of clinic-referred conduct-disordered children demonstrate more commanding and critical behaviors toward their children; however, parents of clinic-referred and nonreferred children typically do not differ in the frequency of positive behaviors (e.g., verbal rewards) directed toward their children (see Rogers, Forehand, & Griest, 1981, for a review of these data).

Patterson and his colleagues have recently extended the parenting variables that have been examined to include the constructs of "inept discipline" and "monitoring" (Patterson, 1982; Patterson & Bank, 1986; Patterson & Dishion, 1985; Patterson & Stouthamer-Loeber, 1984). As assessed by multiple methods, inept discipline is characterized by failure to back up threats, persistent nagging in response to both trivial and significant deviant behaviors, and more extreme forms of physical punishment. Monitoring refers to the failure to be aware of or to believe reports of conduct-disordered behavior occurring outside the home. Poor parental disciplinary procedures and inadequate parental monitoring of school-age children's activities have been found to be positively associated with court records and self-reported delinquency behaviors on the part of the child (Patterson & Stouthamer-Loeber, 1984). In a group of younger children (fourth-grade boys), inadequate parental discipline was associated with coercive child behaviors in the home (Patterson & Bank, 1986). The monitoring construct was less salient for the younger children than for adolescents (e.g., Patterson & Stouthamer-Loeber, 1984), indicating a developmental change in the relative importance of this parenting behavior.

Patterson and his colleagues have also examined behavioral differences among the parents of children who are socially aggressive, children who steal, and children who are both socially aggressive and stealers. Patterson (1982) has reported that the parents of stealers are more distant and less involved in interactions with their children than parents of nonreferred children or parents of socially aggressive children. The mothers and siblings of socially aggressive children are more coercive than their counterparts in nonreferred families or families in which the child steals. Loeber and Schmaling (1985b) found that families with socially aggressive children and those with children who both fought and stole were more likely to demonstrate poorer monitoring skills and to have a rejecting mother.

In general, most of the research looking at parenting behavior has focused on mothers. However, Patterson and his associates have collected substantial amounts of data on fathers of conduct-disordered children (see Patterson, 1982, for a summary), and they have concluded that while fathers behave similarly to mothers in both conduct-disordered and nonreferred families, the frequencies of their behaviors are much lower. Patterson interprets these findings as indicative of the secondary role fathers seem to play with regard to child management in the family.

One point of considerable interest is the fact that, although clinic-referred and nonreferred children differ in conduct-disordered behaviors, there is considerable overlap in the distribution of scores of the children in the two groups. That is, a considerable number of children in the referred group cannot be differentiated on behavioral measures from children in the nonreferred group, and vice versa (e.g., Delfini et al., 1976; Lobitz & Johnson, 1975). In contrast to the overlap in behaviors of clinic-referred and nonreferred children, there is minimal overlap between groups when parent perception measures of child behaviors are utilized (Delfini et al., 1976; Griest et al., 1980; Lobitz & Johnson, 1975). This finding suggests that parent perception of the child, not child behavior per se, is the best discriminator between clinic-referred and nonreferred children. This is not surprising, given that parents typically initiate the referral process. Such a finding also would suggest that some children who are referred for the treatment of conduct disorders may not actually manifest clinically deviant levels of such behavior. Parents of clinic-referred and conduct-disordered children do seem to be more likely than the parents of nonreferred children to perceive neutral child behaviors as inappropriate, at least in the context of laboratory analogue studies employing written vignettes of parent–child interaction (Holleran, Littman, Freund, & Schmaling, 1982; Middlebrook & Forehand, 1985).

If some parents of clinic-referred children are mislabeling the behavior of their children, it is important to determine what characteristics of these parents or the families in general are responsible for this process. Recent research with the parents of conduct-disordered children has indicated that they experience more personal (e.g., depression, anxiety), interparental (marital conflict), and extrafamilial (e.g., isolation) distress than parents of nonreferred children (see Griest & Wells, 1983, for a review). In addition, they appear to experience higher frequencies of stressful events, both of a minor and of a more significant nature (Patterson, 1982, 1983). A number of investigations by Forehand and Patterson and their associates have supported the role of personal distress as one factor associated with parental misperceptions of their children (e.g., Forehand, Wells, McMahon, Griest, & Rogers, 1982; Griest, Wells, & Forehand, 1979; Patterson, 1982; Rickard, Forehand, Wells, Griest, & McMahon, 1981). For example, Richard et al. (1981) found two subgroups of clinic-referred children: (1) those who demonstrated higher levels of conduct disorders than nonreferred children and whose parents were not depressed, and (2) those who did not demonstrate higher levels of conduct disorders but whose parents were depressed. The authors concluded from this finding that maternal depression may well have been a significant factor in the parental perceptions of the children and the subsequent referral process. Brody and Forehand (1986) have presented data to support the hypothesis that it is the combination of maternal depression *and* child noncompliant behavior, rather than either factor alone, that is most closely associated with parental perceptions of child maladjustment. Interestingly, recent data suggest that the role of depression may not be limited to influencing parental perceptions. While Forehand, Lautenschlager, Faust, and Graziano (1986) recently confirmed the earlier findings that depression primarily is associated with parent perceptions, their data suggested that depression also influences parenting behavior, which then has an effect on child behavior. That is, some children may be perceived as deviant by their parents because of parental depression, but, at least to some extent, the depression also will change the parenting behavior directed toward those children (i.e., will increase the number of commands directed toward them) and, as a consequence, will increase the level of child deviant behavior (i.e., will increase noncompliant behavior).

Other investigators have focused on the role

of marital distress in these families (see K. D. O'Leary & Emery, 1984, for a review). It appears that for children who have been referred for the treatment of conduct-disordered types of behaviors, marital distress is positively related to parental perceptions of child maladjustment and to observed levels of child deviant behavior and parental negative behavior. These relationships seem to be stronger for boys than for girls (e.g., Rutter, 1970).

Forehand and Brody (1985) recently examined the relative and additive effects of depression and marital adjustment in a sample of mothers of clinic-referred conduct-disordered children. Marital satisfaction was related to child and parent behavior, whereas depression was related to parental perceptions of the child. There was no interaction between the two factors. Investigators utilizing different methodologies have also reported findings suggesting that marital adjustment may be less important than maternal depression in predicting parental perceptions of the child (Furey & Forehand, 1986; Schaughency & Lahey, 1985).

The perceptual biasing effect of high stress levels has been demonstrated by Middlebrook and Forehand (1985). Mothers of both clinic-referred conduct-disordered children and nonreferred children, who read vignettes describing mother–child interactions in which the mother was under high levels of stress, perceived neutral (but not clearly appropriate or inappropriate) child behaviors as more deviant than when the same neutral child behaviors occurred in situations in which the mother was experiencing a low level of stress. While mothers of clinic-referred conduct-disordered children perceived the neutral child behaviors as inappropriate, and mothers of nonreferred children perceived the neutral child behaviors as appropriate, there was no significant interaction between clinic status and stress level.

Some parents of conduct-disordered children may be quite isolated from friends, neighbors, and the community (e.g., Wahler, 1980). Research in this area has focused primarily on "insularity," a construct developed by Wahler at the University of Tennessee. Insularity is defined as a "specific pattern of social contacts within the community that is characterized by a high level of negatively perceived coercive interchanges with relatives and/or helping agency representatives and by a low level of positively perceived supportive interchanges with friends" (Wahler & Dumas, 1984, p. 387). Insularity has been shown to be positively related to negative parent behavior directed toward the child and oppositional child behavior directed toward the parent (Dumas & Wahler, 1985; Wahler, 1980), and to be associated with poor maintenance of treatment effects (Dumas & Wahler, 1983; Wahler, 1980; Wahler & Afton, 1980). Thus, when a mother has a large proportion of aversive interactions outside the home, the interactions between her and her child in the home are likely to be negative as well.

In summary, parents of conduct-disordered children not only experience elevated levels of problem behaviors from their children; they also exhibit higher levels of commanding and critical behaviors, as well as poor monitoring and disciplinary practices. Furthermore, they experience more personal, interparental, and extrafamiliar distress, which most investigators have postulated leads to the child behavior problems; however, sufficient data are not available to answer the directionality question at this time.

BEHAVIORAL FORMULATIONS OF CONDUCT DISORDERS IN CHILDREN

Although the focus of this section is on the various family factors that have been implicated in the development and maintenance of conduct disorders, it is important to briefly review some of the data relating to biological factors such as genetic influences and medical correlates. In addition, the role of the child's temperament is briefly described. For more extensive reviews of these factors, the reader is referred to Kazdin (1985) and Wells and Forehand (1985).

There is increasing evidence to suggest that there may be a genetic predisposition to the development of conduct disorders. Although the data base is rather limited, findings from twin and adoption studies alike have been consistent in their suggestion of genetic influences on the manifestation of conduct disorders and/or criminal behavior. For example, there is a greater concordance among identical twins than fraternal twins in terms of adult criminal behavior (Cloninger, Reich, & Guze, 1978) and higher rates of antisocial behavior as adults among adopted children whose biological parents engaged in antisocial behavior than when the parents did not engage in such behavior (Cadoret, 1978). In a sample of adopted children with aggressive conduct disorder, the

adoptive fathers were less likely to have been alcoholic or to have been diagnosed as having an antisocial personality than the fathers of nonadopted children with aggressive conduct disorder (Jary & Stewart, 1985). In a sample of 50 boys diagnosed as having an aggressive conduct disorder, the rate of the disorder in the full brothers of these children was twice that of the rate in half-brothers (Twito & Stewart, 1982). That we are most likely dealing with a genetic *predisposition* is demonstrated by the findings of Cadoret, Cain, and Crowe (1983), who found that the likelihood of adolescents' engaging in conduct-disordered behavior was greatly increased when both genetic and environmental influences were present.

There is some research to indicate that extremely aggressive forms of conduct-disordered behavior are associated with a history of head and face injuries, frequent hospital visits, and evidence of neurological abnormalities (Shanok & Lewis, 1981). Lewis, Pincus, Shanok, and Glaser (1982) reported that 18% of a sample of incarcerated delinquent boys met the criteria for psychomotor seizure disorder, which can include directed aggressive behavior as one of its manifestations. However, as noted elsewhere (Wells & Forehand, 1985), the evidence for neurological abnormalities and other medical indicators has come from investigations of delinquent, usually incarcerated, populations, with the most violent and aggressive children showing the greatest evidence of these medical indicators. There is little evidence that these variables are significant contributors in the development of milder forms of conduct disorders.

Temperament is currently viewed as involving dimensions of the individual's personality that are "largely genetic or constitutional in origin, exist in most ages and most societies, and are relatively stable, at least within major developmental areas" (Plomin, 1981, p. 269). Of particular interest is the "temperamentally difficult" child who is from the outset intense, irregular, negative, and nonadaptable (Thomas, Chess, & Birch, 1968).[1] Such a child is thought to be predisposed to the development of subsequent behavior problems, due to the increased likelihood of maladaptive parent–child interactions. Webster-Stratton and Eyberg (1982)

----

[1] See Goldsmith *et al.* (1987) for a discussion of current points of agreement and disagreement concerning the constructs of "temperament" and "temperamental difficulty."

have demonstrated moderate correlations between some dimensions of child temperament and parent reports of child conduct-disordered behavior (r's = .33–.48) and mother–child interactions (r's = .27–.47). Both clinic-referred and nonreferred groups of aggressive school-age boys have been found to have more adverse temperament scores than a control group (Kolvin, Nicol, Garside, Day, & Tweddle, 1982). The most compelling evidence for the role of child temperament in the development of conduct disorders comes from a causal analysis of familial and temperamental determinants of aggressive behavior in adolescent boys (Olweus, 1980). Using path-analytic techniques, Olweus found that the boys' temperament contributed substantially to the prediction of aggressive behavior. However, temperament variables did not contribute to the explanatory variance as much as did family variables (mother's negativism, mother's permissiveness of aggression). Wolkind and De Salis (1982) reported that maternal depression was associated with child behavior problems at 3½ years of age, but only when the child was ''temperamentally difficult'' at 4 months of age.

The most comprehensive behavioral formulation of the development of conduct disorders in children has been offered by Patterson (1982). Patterson emphasizes the coercive, or controlling, nature of conduct-disordered types of behavior and has developed a coercion hypothesis to account for their development and maintenance. According to this hypothesis, rudimentary aversive behaviors, such as crying, may be instinctual in the newborn infant. Such behaviors could be considered highly adaptive in the evolutionary sense, in that they quickly shape the mother in the skills necessary for the infant's survival (e.g., feeding and temperature control). Presumably, as most infants grow older, they substitute more appropriate verbal and social skills for the rudimentary coercive behaviors. However, according to Patterson, a number of conditions might increase the likelihood that some children will continue to employ aversive control strategies. For example, parents might fail to model or reinforce more appropriate prosocial skills and/or may continue to respond to the child's coercive behavior. As far as this latter point is concerned, Patterson (1982) has emphasized the role of negative reinforcement in the escalation and maintenance of coercive behaviors. In the negative-reinforcement model, coercive behavior on the part of one family member is reinforced when it results in the removal of an aversive event being applied to another family member. The following examples illustrate how parent and child are negatively reinforced for engaging in coercive behavior.

Application of aversive event

Mother gives command.
↓
Coercive child response

Child whines, screams, noncomplies.
↓
Removal of aversive event

Mother gives up (withdraws the command) rather than listen to whining and screaming child.

In this example, the child's coercive behaviors are negatively reinforced when the mother withdraws the aversive stimulus (command). In the following example, coercion escalates.

Application of aversive event 1

Mother gives command.
↓
Coercive child response

Child whines, noncomplies.
↓
Application of aversive event 2

Mother raises her voice, repeats command.
↓
Child response 2

Child yells louder, noncomplies.
↓
Aversive stimulus 3

Mother begins to yell, repeats command again.
↓
Removal of aversive child response

Child complies.

In this example, the mother's escalating coercive behavior is reinforced by the child's eventual compliance.

It is apparent in the preceding examples that negative reinforcement can function to increase the probability of the occurrence of aggressive control techniques by both child and parent. In addition, as this "training" continues over long periods, significant increases in the rate and intensity of these coercive behaviors occur as both family members are reinforced by engaging in aggressive behaviors. Furthermore, the child also observes his or her parents engaging in coercive responses, which provides the opportunity for modeling of aggression to occur (Patterson, 1976, 1982; Patterson & Reid, 1973).

Noncompliance (i.e., failure to follow parental requests), as demonstrated in the example above, is important, as Patterson (1982) and Loeber and Schmaling (1985a) have recently proposed that this behavior is the keystone in the development of *both* overt and covert forms of conduct-disordered behavior. Loeber and Schmaling (1985a) have found that noncompliance is positioned near the zero point of their unidimensional overt–covert scale of antisocial behaviors. Patterson reported that noncompliance is the primary behavior shared by children who manifest overt antisocial problems and those who manifest covert antisocial problems. Finally, several investigators (Patterson, 1982; Russo, Cataldo, & Cushing, 1981; Wells, Forehand, & Griest, 1980) have reported reductions in other antisocial behaviors when noncompliance is treated. These findings emphasize the importance of assessing and treating this behavior; as a result, noncompliance receives a major focus in this chapter.

From the coercion hypothesis, it is obvious that extended deviant interactions between a parent and a young child can result in the development and maintenance of coercive behaviors. Loeber (1982) has examined the role of the antisocial behavior itself in the maintenance process. After a thorough review, he concludes that the more extreme the antisocial or conduct-disordered behavior, the more stable it will be over time. The term "extreme" is defined by Loeber by the "density hypothesis" (children who manifest high rates of antisocial behavior early in life are more likely to continue), the "multiple-setting hypothesis" (children who demonstrate antisocial behavior in more than one setting are more at risk than those who show such behavior in only one setting), the "variety hypothesis" (children who demonstrate more varied antisocial behaviors are more at risk), and the "early-onset hypoth-esis" (children who show an earlier onset of delinquency are more at risk). Loeber presents data to support each of these hypotheses. It is clear that each of the hypotheses fits well into a coercive explanation for the development and maintenance of conduct disorders. For example, children who show high rates of difficult behavior early in life (e.g., "temperamentally difficult" children) would certainly be at higher risk to enter into and maintain a coercive cycle with their parents than children who do not demonstrate such behavior.

Patterson and his colleagues have recently elaborated on the coercion model and incorporated some of the more molar family influences described above (Patterson & Bank, 1986; Patterson & Dishion, 1985; Patterson & Stouthamer-Loeber, 1984). The prime elements in the development of child conduct disorders are hypothesized to be deficiencies in key parenting skills such as discipline, monitoring, positive reinforcement, problem solving, and involvement. Child variables are given somewhat less attention, although it is apparent from our earlier review that cognitive (e.g., attributional biases and interpersonal problem-solving skills) and temperamental variables are important to consider. Intrafamilial stressors (marital distress, personal adjustment problems, physical illness, etc.) and extrafamilial stressors (e.g., insularity) can lead to the disruption of the parenting skills. However, adequate levels of these parenting skills can potentially mediate the impact of some stressors, such as having a temperamentally difficult child.

Patterson's model is also now being conceptualized along developmental lines, in the sense that various stages or progressions have been hypothesized to precede and to be causally related to subsequent stages. The first stage consists of "basic training" in coercion in the home setting, much as described above. In a sample of 10-year-old boys and their families, Patterson and Bank (1986) found that inadequate parental discipline led to coercive child behaviors, which in turn produced conduct-disordered behavior in both the school and the home. In addition, the coercive behaviors led to further parental difficulties in disciplining. Poor parental discipline was also associated with less effective parental monitoring of the child; poor monitoring skills in turn led to conduct-disordered behavior, although to a lesser extent. As noted above, deficits in parental monitoring appear to account for increasing variance in older (adolescent) children (Patterson & Dishion, 1985).

Once the child's coercive behavior generalizes to the school, it is hypothesized to lead to peer rejection and a failure to develop adequate academic skills. Because of poor parental problem-solving and reinforcement skills (which have been implicated in the child's development of peer relationships) and the nature of the conduct-disordered child's behavior, he or she is also unlikely to be able to acquire the social skills necessary for successful adaptation to the home or school environment. As a result of these multiple difficulties in both home and school, the child's self-esteem is likely to suffer. (Although not specifically stated, it seems that these difficulties might also lead to depression in some of these children.) As the child grows older, association with deviant peers results from inadequate parental monitoring and the child's poor social skills. The association with deviant peers and the continued academic difficulties eventually lead to delinquent behavior (Patterson & Dishion, 1985).

While our formulations concerning the development and maintenance of conduct disorders in children are certainly not fully developed at this time, major advances have been made in recent years. As the scope of our lenses for viewing and conceptualizing the development and maintenance of conduct disorders becomes both more expansive (i.e., the ecological systems in which the behavior occurs are examined more thoroughly) and more microscopic (i.e., the nature of the individual behaviors included under the rubric of "conduct disorder" and their interrelationships are examined more thoroughly), our understanding will continue to grow. However, the current knowledge base concerning the development and maintenance of conduct disorders in children does provide us with a conceptual model to guide the behavioral assessment of the conduct-disordered child and his or her family. We now turn to a discussion of the assessment process itself.

ASSESSMENT OF CONDUCT DISORDERS IN CHILDREN

In this section of the chapter, we discuss the behavioral assessment of conduct-disordered children and their families. Three major areas of assessment are discussed separately: the assessment of child behavior per se and in an interactional context; the assessment of other child characteristics, such as temperament; and familial and extrafamilial factors, such as parent/teacher perceptions of the child, personal and marital adjustment of the parents, parental stress, maternal insularity, and parental satisfaction with treatment. In each section, the particular methods (e.g., interviews, questionnaires, observations) that are most appropriate for assessing the questions of interest are discussed. We focus our discussion of methods on assessment procedures that have been employed specifically with conduct-disordered populations. In some instances (e.g., where the choice of assessment procedures is limited), other assessment procedures are mentioned, but these are not described in detail. Although the emphasis is on preintervention assessment and a functional analysis of conduct disorders in children, many of these procedures can also be used to evaluate treatment as it progresses and treatment outcome at termination and follow-up.

Child Behavior Per Se and in an Interactional Context

The primary focus of a behavioral assessment of the conduct-disordered child is on the assessment of the referred child's behavior per se, and, because of the interactional nature of conduct disorders, on the behavior of relevant individuals in the child's environment. In virtually every case this means the parents, but the behavior of other relevant adults (e.g., teachers(s), babysitter, grandparents), siblings, and peers may also need to be assessed.

With respect to child behavior, the therapist should keep a number of points in mind when conducting the assessment. First and foremost, is the child in fact engaging in conduct-disordered types of behavior? If so, then the next step is to determine whether the behaviors are characteristic of overt, covert, or mixed patterns of conduct-disordered behavior (Loeber & Schmaling, 1985a, 1985b; Patterson, 1982). (Given the problems noted earlier concerning the reliability and validity of the DSM-III categories of Conduct Disorder and Oppositional Disorder and the lack of knowledge concerning the psychometric properties of their DSM-IIIR counterparts, it seems most appropriate at this time to focus on the empirically derived classification of conduct disorders.) In addition, given the importance of child noncompliance as a keystone behavior for both overt and covert types of conduct disorders (Loeber & Schmaling, 1985a; Patterson, 1982), the fact that it occurs very early in the progression of conduct disorders (Edelbrock, 1985), and the demonstrated utility of targeting this behavior in treatment (e.g., McMahon & Forehand, 1984; Russo et al., 1981), it is essential to assess child noncompliance in a thorough manner.

In the context of Patterson's coercion model (Patterson, 1982; Patterson & Bank, 1986; Patterson & Dishion, 1985; Patterson & Stouthamer-Loeber, 1984), and the developmental progression of conduct disorders proposed by Edelbrock (1985), information concerning the child's behavior can be used to provide some hypotheses as to how far the child has progressed in his or her development of these conduct-disordered behaviors and the extent to which these behaviors are being manifested in multiple settings. As noted earlier, more serious and covert behaviors (e.g., stealing) that also occur in settings outside the home (e.g., school) suggest a more advanced progression of conduct disorder, poorer prognosis, and a different treatment approach than for the child who engages in mild overt behaviors (e.g., arguing) only in the home setting.

Given the central theoretical role accorded to parenting skill deficits in the development and maintenance of child conduct disorders and the interactional nature of conduct disorders, it is essential to assess parent behavior in the context of interactions with the referred child. This is particularly true for mothers, but also for fathers as well. As noted above, while fathers usually have a secondary role in child management compared to mothers (Patterson, 1982), it is important to assess the extent to which the father is involved in child management, the quality of his interactions with the child, and the degree of consistency and support between parents. Finally, in situations in which the presenting problems of the child involve the school setting, siblings, and/or peers, then it will be necessary to obtain information concerning those areas as well.

In order to obtain a representative and meaningful account of the referred child's conduct-disordered behavior, particularly with regard to its interactional aspects, the behavior therapist must rely on multiple methods of assessment (Forehand, Griest, & Wells, 1979; Patterson & Bank, 1986). Interviews with the parents, child, and other relevant parties (e.g., teachers); be-

havioral rating scales; and behavioral observations in clinic, home and/or school settings can all be employed. Measures of these types that are particularly applicable to the assessment of conduct-disordered children are described below.

Behavioral Interviews

The interview is usually the first contact the therapist has with the identified client (i.e., the child) and with the significant adults in the child's life (i.e., parents, teachers). The primary function of the interview is to identify verbally the behaviors to be targeted for treatment and the stimulus conditions, both antecedent and consequent, currently maintaining the problem behaviors. Because the etiology of child conduct disorders is conceptualized primarily in terms of the child's interactions with others (parents in particular), the interview focuses on both adult and child behaviors and, more specifically, on the pattern of interaction between the child and the adult in question. As a consequence, the responses identified for treatment during the interview include parent and child behaviors and/or teacher and child behaviors.

INTERVIEW WITH PARENTS. There are two preliminary issues that must be considered prior to the parent interview (Forehand & McMahon, 1981). First, it is strongly recommended that both parents be involved in the initial interview if at all possible. This permits the therapist to obtain a more complete picture of interaction patterns between each parent and the child, the degree of consistency between parents in their child-rearing philosophy and behavior, and a behavioral sample of the marital interaction. It may also provide an opportunity for the therapist to prompt participation from a reluctant parent (usually the father) during the assessment process and perhaps in treatment as well. The second preliminary issue is whether the child will remain in the room during the parent interview. We prefer to interview the parents alone, since this allows the parents to discuss their relationship with their child more freely, and it avoids the situation in which excessive demands are placed on a young child. Behavioral samples of the parent–child interaction can be gathered more systematically through clinic or home observations.

The major purpose of the initial interview with the parents is to determine the nature of the typical parent–child interactions that are

Child: Interviewer(s):
Interviewee(s):   Date:

Setting	Description	Frequency	Duration	Parent Response	Child Response
Bedtime (A.M. and P.M.)					
Mealtime					
Bath time					
On phone					
Visitors—at home					
Visiting others					
Car					
Public places (stores, etc.)					
School					
Siblings					
Peers					
Other parent/relative					
Disciplinary procedures					
Other					

FIGURE 1. Problem guidesheet. From *Helping the Noncompliant Child: A Clinician's Guide to Parent Training* (p. 19) by R. L. Forehand and R. J. McMahon, 1981, New York: Guilford Press. Copyright 1981 by the Guilford Press. Reprinted by permission.

problematic, the antecedent stimulus conditions under which problem behaviors occur, and the consequences that accompany such behaviors. The interview typically begins with a general question, such as "Tell me what types of problems you have been having with your child," or "What brings you to the clinic?" In our experience, most parents, not surprisingly, respond globally to such a global question. To structure the way in which information is obtained from parents concerning current problematic parent–child interactions, we have found the interview format developed by Hanf (1970) and presented by us elsewhere (Forehand & McMahon, 1981) to be extremely useful. Although designed specifically for use with parents of 3- to 8-year-old children, many of the areas are relevant to children of all ages. The Problem Guidesheet that we employ in our interviews with these families is presented in Figure 1. Following the parents' statements of the primary concerns about their child, the therapist presents situations that may or may not be problem areas for the particular family.

Parents are asked whether their child is disruptive in situations such as the following: getting dressed in the morning, mealtimes, visiting in a friend's home, riding in the car, shopping, adult–adult conversations, parental telephone conversations, bath time, and bedtime. Information is also elicited as to whether the child experiences academic or behavioral difficulties in school, and about the child's relationship with other family members as well as peers. If the parents report that a particular behavior or setting is not problematic, the therapist moves to the next situation. If the parents report that a particular situation is a problem area for them, then the therapist examines the antecedent conditions of the situation ("What happens just before [the problem interaction]?"), the child's behavior ("What does the child do?"), the parents' response ("What do you do?"), and the child's reaction to the parents' intervention ("What does the child do then?").

The analysis of both the parents' and the child's behavior in the problem situation should be continued until the therapist has a clear understanding of the nature and extent of the parent–child interaction. Other relevant information, such as the frequency ("How often . . . ?") and duration ("How long . . . ?") of the problem behavior, should also be obtained. At this point, it is also appropriate to ask historical–developmental questions specific to the problem interaction. Following is a portion of an initial interview that exemplifies the analysis of a problem situation:

THERAPIST: Do you have any problems with Mark at bedtime?

PARENT: Oh my gosh, yes. It takes forever for him to go to sleep. He gets out of bed again and again.

T: Tell me about your family's routine during the half-hour before Marks' bedtime.

P: At 7:30 I help Mark with his bath. After he brushes his teeth and goes to the bathroom, I read him a story. Then Bob and I kiss him goodnight.

T: OK, then what happens?

P: Well, things are quiet for about 10–15 minutes. Then Mark is up. He gets out of bed and comes into the den where Bob and I are watching TV.

T: What does Mark do when he gets up?

P: He usually comes in and climbs in either Bob's or my lap and complains that he can't sleep.

T: What do you do then?

P: Sometimes we let him sit with us for a while, but usually I take him back to bed and tell him goodnight again.

T: What happens then?

P: Mark stays there for a while, but he's soon out again.

T: And then what do you do?

P: I may tell him he's being a bad boy. Then I take him back to bed. Usually I read him another story—hoping he'll get sleepy this time.

T: Does that work?

P: No, he's up again before I have time to get settled in my chair.

T: What happens then?

P: The whole thing repeats itself. I put him in bed, read him another story, and he gets up again.

T: How long does this go on?

P: For about 2 or 3 hours—until Bob and I go to bed.

T: What happens when you and your husband go to bed?

P: Mark still gets up, but we let him get in bed with us and he goes to sleep then.

T: How many nights a week does this happen?

P: Every night! I can't think of a night's peace in the last few months.

T: How long has Mark been doing this?

P: Oh, I would guess for about a year.

T: Have you or your husband tried any other ways of handling Mark at bedtime?

P: Sometimes I get angry and yell at him. Sometimes Bob tries spanking him, but then Mark just ends up crying all evening. At least my way, we have a little peace and quiet.

In this sample interview, the therapist obtained a description of the events preceding the problem situation fairly quickly. The therapist had to repeat "What happens then?" or some variation thereof several times until a clear description was obtained of the consequent events currently maintaining the problem behavior. Based on this assessment, the problem behavior—noncompliance at bedtime ("getting out of bed")—was occurring at a high rate and had been for some time.

The next sample interview centers around the same problem situation—bedtime—but in this clinical case the antecedent events emerged as the factors maintaining the problem interaction.

T: Do you have a problem with Timmy at bedtime?

P: Certainly! He's impossible. He starts to scream and cry the minute we put him to bed.

T: Tell me about your family's routine the half-hour before Timmy's bedtime.

P: Well, Timmy takes his bath and puts on his pajamas right after supper. Then we usually watch television together. He knows his bedtime is 8:30, so when the program ends his father says "bedtime." Then the problems begin. Timmy tries to stall, begging to see the next show. We ignore this. His father usually ends up carrying Timmy—screaming all the way— to bed.

T: What happens then?

P: He used to get up again and again. Each time we would spank him and put him back to bed. Now when we put him to bed the first time, we just lock his door. He cries for a while and then drops off to sleep.

T: How many nights a week does this happen?

P: Let me see. Nearly all the time.

T: Thinking back over the past week, how many nights out of the last seven have you had problems with Timmy at bedtime?

P: Mmmm. Four.

T: How long has Timmy been difficult at bedtime?

P: For the last 6 months.

Based on this interview assessment, the therapist concluded that the antecedent events (the abrupt announcement of bedtime and removal of the child to bed) were maintaining the child's whine–cry–scream behavior at bedtime. Instructing the parents to institute a prebedtime ritual, similar to that used by the parents in the first interview, quickly eliminated the problematic interactions at bedtime. The second interview sample is included here to emphasize the importance of assessing the antecedent conditions in any problematic parent–child interaction.

Wahler (Wahler & Cormier, 1970) has described a similar interview format, in that the parent completes preinterview checklists that list various home and community situations and inappropriate child behaviors. The behavior therapist then has the parents elaborate on the problem behaviors in each setting, including the parental consequences that occur following the child behaviors. Patterson (Patterson, Reid, Jones, & Conger, 1975) structures the initial interview with parents somewhat differently from our procedure (Forehand & McMahon, 1981) or from that of Wahler and Cormier (1970). Instead of focusing on situations, the therapist and parents together fill out a Symptom Checklist containing 31 child behavior problems. This checklist forms the basis of the Parent Daily Report observation measure discussed later in this chapter. The 31 problems are aggression, arguing, bedwetting, competitiveness, complaining, crying, defiance, destructiveness, fearfulness, fighting with siblings, fire setting, hitting others, hyperactiveness, irritability, lying, negativism, noisiness, noncomplying, not eating, pants wetting, pouting, running around, running away (wandering), sadness/unhappiness, soiling, stealing, talking back to mother, teasing, temper tantrums, whining, and yelling. As each behavior is read to the parents, a behavioral definition is also given, to insure that the parent understands the descriptive term used. The parents are asked to indicate whether they think that the behavior occurs often enough to be a real problem now and whether the behavior is something they wish to change. If the parents' answer is "yes," then they are asked about the setting in which the problem behavior occurs, how they have tried to handle the problem, and what they think causes the problem.

More recently, Patterson and his colleagues have developed a structured parent interview that focuses more on parent behavior than does the Symptom Checklist described above (see, e.g., Patterson & Bank, 1986). In the structured interview, each parent is asked a series of questions concerning the monitoring of the child, parental rejection, positive reinforcement directed to the child, parental discipline, problem solving, activities within the family, and the parent's future aspirations for the child. The parent is asked to note the frequency of a particular behavior or to rate his or her response on Likert-type scales. Following the interview, the interviewer completes a series of ratings based on his or her impressions of the parent. To date, this interview has been employed only in a large-scale longitudinal study on the development and maintenance of conduct-disordered/delinquent behavior (e.g., Patterson & Bank, 1986). Thus, its psychometric characteristics are relatively unknown, and it has yet to be employed in the context of treatment. It does provide a broad assessment of theoretically relevant parenting behaviors.

The interview as an assessment tool does not end with the first contact, but continues throughout treatment formulation and implementation. The interview is used to obtain information (e.g., potential rewards and punishers) necessary for the development of treatment programs, to assess the programs as they are implemented, and to alter these programs if necessary. Portions of Holland's (1970) interview guide provide questions appropriate for the specification of problem behaviors, the determination of reinforcers and punishers, and the development of treatment strategies (e.g., having the parents list reinforcers that they think will be effective in bringing about behavior changes; having the parents discuss situations in which desirable behaviors are to occur).

INTERVIEW WITH TEACHER. If the presenting problem concerns classroom behavior, an interview with the child's teacher(s) is also necessary. In addition, teachers are often in a better position than parents to report on children's academic achievement and social skills (Gross, 1983). Reading ability is of particular interest because of the high incidence of reading disability in conduct-disordered children (approximately one-third) (e.g., Rutter *et al.,* 1976). The interview with the teacher is structured similarly to Hanf's (1970) interview format used with parents, in that the therapist questions whether various classroom situations are problem areas. Situations to be covered are based on Barkley's (1981) School Situations Questionnaire and Wahler and Cormier's (1970) preinterview checklist; they include school arrival, individual desk work, small-group activities, recess, lunch, field trips, assemblies, free time in class, and particular academic topics (e.g., mathematics, social studies). If the teacher indicates that a particular situation is a problem, then the therapist obtains a description of the situation ("What is the class doing?"), the child's behavior in that situation ("What does the child do?"), the teacher's responses to the child ("What do you do?"), and the child's responses to the teacher's interventions ("What does the child do then?"). Other information relevant to the problem situation includes the frequency and duration of the problem and the role of other children in escalating or inhibiting the problem.

Information concerning the problematic teacher–child interactions is also obtained by questioning the teacher concerning what problem behaviors the child is exhibiting. To structure this part of the interview, it is helpful to focus first on common classroom rules. Typical questions to be asked are these: "Does the child leave his or her desk inappropriately?" "Does the child bother his or her classmates while they are working?" "Does the child talk out of turn?" "Does the child demand excessive teacher attention?" and so forth. Once a particular rule violation has been identified, then questions concerning antecedent events (e.g., "In what situations is the child more likely to hit another student?"), the exact behavior of the child, the teacher's responses to the child, and the child's responses to the teacher's interventions are asked, according to Hanf's (1970) interview format.

In talking with the teacher, the therapist is also interested in understanding exactly what the teacher considers appropriate student behavior in each of the problem situations (e.g., "What does the best-behaved child do in this situation?" "What do most children do in this situation?"). This information is necessary for the specification of treatment goals. The therapist also explores with the teacher potential rewards and punishments available in the classroom. The use of rewards and punishments acceptable to the teacher is essential if the teacher is to execute the treatment program developed by the therapist (cf. Witt & Elliott, 1985). Again, the interview guide developed by Holland (1970) provides questions appropriate for the development of treatment strategies. Throughout the interview, the therapist is evaluating both the willingness and the motivation of the teacher to work with the therapist and the skills of the teacher in carrying out the treatment program correctly. (For a more intensive coverage of interview procedures with the teacher, see the preceding section on interviewing parents).

INTERVIEW WITH CHILD. With very young children (5 years and younger), an individual interview is usually not beneficial, at least with respect to content. Recent findings suggest that children below the age of 10 are not reliable reporters of their own behavioral symptoms (Edelbrock, Costello, Dulcan, Kalas, & Conover, 1985; see below). However, even a few minutes spent privately with a younger child in a play situation or a walk to the soda machine provides the therapist with a subjective evaluation of the child's cognitive, affective, and behavioral characteristics (e.g., verbal skills, social skills) (Bierman, 1983). It also provides the therapist with an opportunity to assess the child's perception of why he or she has been brought to the clinic. With older children, an individual interview can provide the therapist with additional pertinent information.

The interview in the clinic setting typically begins with the statement, "Tell me why you are here today." After the child has responded, the therapist should explain his or her own view of why the child is at the clinic. The explanation might be this:

> Your parents are concerned because you and they don't seem to be getting along very well. They came to see us to get some help so things will be more pleasant for you and them at home.

If the problems are largely school-centered, this might be the explanation:

> Your parents are concerned because you and Mr./Ms. [teacher's name] aren't getting along very well. They came to the clinic with you to see if we could help so things would be more pleasant for you and your teacher at school.

The therapist then proceeds to ask the child about various situations at home and/or at school in an attempt to obtain the child's perception about what is happening in these problem situations. Sometimes such questioning is fruitless; at other times, the child's understanding of the situation and the role he or she plays is quite accurate. Other questions to ask a child include those in the following areas:

- Family—What kinds of things do you do with your father/mother/brothers/sisters? What can you do to make your father/mother happy/mad?
- School—Tell me about school. What do you like best at school? What do you dislike most at school?
- Social—Tell me about your friends. What kinds of things do you do with [friend's name]?
- Personal—What are your favorite things? What do you like to do most?

As part of the interview process, the child and therapist together can fill in a reinforcement survey (e.g., Cautela, Cautela, & Esonis, 1983) for use later in the development of treatment

programs. This type of structured activity can be helpful in building rapport.

In the context of the longitudinal study noted above, Patterson and his colleagues have developed a structured interview for children from the 4th through 10th grades (see Patterson & Bank, 1986). The interview includes questions concerning parental monitoring of the child, family relations, expectations concerning the use of alcohol, substance consumption, sources and amount of positive reinforcement for the child, peer behavior, chores, frequency of engaging in various overt and covert conduct-disordered behaviors, parental discipline, family problem solving, the child's perceptions of deviant behavior, and his or her future aspirations. As with the structured parent interview, the interviewer completes an impressions inventory following completion of the interview.

LIMITATIONS. For the behavior therapist, the interview is a necessary, but not a sufficient, assessment procedure. Despite its extensive use, the behavioral interview—its structure, reliability, and validity—has been researched very little. Several studies (e.g., Yarrow, Campbell, & Burton, 1970) have investigated maternal retrospective reports of child behavior and have found that developmental information is generally biased in the desired direction. There have been relatively few studies examining the validity or reliability of parents' descriptions of current child behavior, and even fewer data concerning the reliability and validity of children's self-reports. This situation has begun to change somewhat with the development of a variety of structured interview schedules for children and parents. While most of these instruments are still in relatively early stages of development (see Edelbrock & Costello, 1984, for a review), there have been some findings, especially with regard to the National Institute of Mental Health (NIMH) Diagnostic Interview Schedule for Children (DISC; Costello, Edelbrock, Dulcan, & Kalas, 1984), that are of clear relevance. The DISC is a highly structured interview for children aged 6–18 (the DISC-C) and their parents (the DISC-P) that can be administered in 40–60 minutes. Intended as a descriptive and screening instrument in epidemiological research, it provides scores in 27 symptom areas that parallel DSM-III categories. Four of those symptom areas refer specifically to conduct-disordered types of behavior: Conduct Disorder (and Aggressive and Nonaggressive subtypes) and Oppositionalism. In a recent investigation, age-related differences in test–retest (2–3 weeks) reliability were assessed on both the child and parent forms of the DISC (Edelbrock, Costello, *et al.*, 1985). On the DISC-C, the intraclass correlation coefficient (ICC) reliabilities for the Behavior/Conduct scales (including the four scales referring specifically to Conduct Disorder) averaged .69 compared to .57 for the Affective/Neurotic scales. For the four Conduct Disorder categories, the ICCs ranged from .65 to .76. In general, it was found that the reliabilities for all categories increased with the age of the child. In addition, while all the children were more likely to report fewer symptoms at the retest than at the initial interview, this was particularly true of the younger (6- to 9-year-old) children. On the basis of these data, Edelbrock and colleagues concluded that children below the age of 10 are not reliable in reporting their own behavioral symptoms. Reliabilities on the DISC-P were higher than on the DISC-C, with the average ICCs being .83 and .73 for the Behavior/Conduct and Affective/Neurotic scales, respectively. Reliabilities of the Conduct Disorder categories were higher as well, with ICCs ranging from .78 to .86. Interestingly, parents of younger children were slightly more reliable than were the parents of older children.

Data concerning the level of agreement between mothers and children on parallel forms of another structured interview, the Diagnostic Interview for Children and Adolescents, have been reported by Herjanic and Reich (1982). When chance levels of agreement between child and parent responses were controlled statistically, then mother–child agreement was unsatisfactory for 122 of 168 questions (73%) on this interview. Various asymmetries in maternal and child responses on this interview have been noted as well (Herjanic & Reich, 1982). Children reported symptoms related to anxiety, depression, somatic concerns, psychosis, and severe antisocial behavior (e.g., injured/killed an animal for fun) more frequently than did their mothers. Mothers were more likely to report symptoms related to school behavior problems and peer relationships.

These asymmetries have been reported by other investigators dealing specifically with conduct-disordered children. Loeber and Schmaling (1985b) have suggested that when one is dealing with overt types of conduct disorders (e.g., fighting), maternal and teacher reports may be preferable to child reports, since conduct-disordered children often underestimate their own aggressive behavior compared to maternal or teacher estimations (Kazdin, Esveldt-Dawson, Unis, & Rancurello, 1983; Ledingham, Younger, Schwartzman, & Bergeron, 1982). For example, Kazdin *et al.* (1983) found that children with a wide range of diagnoses on an inpatient psychiatric unit provided significantly less severe ratings of their aggressive and depressive symptoms than did their mothers and, to a lesser extent, their fathers. Correlations between children's and parents' responses on a semistructured interview for aggression were in the range of .23 to .37. By contrast, parents are *less* aware of the occurrence of covert types of conduct disorders. In an assessment of various forms of antisocial behavior in nearly 200 boys and their families, Loeber and Schmaling (1985b) reported that 40% of the mothers were not aware that their sons stole frequently. They suggest that more valid estimates of covert types of conduct-disordered behavior such as stealing are more likely to be obtained from children than from parents.

Research on the reliability and validity of teacher interviews is also lacking. Bolstad and Johnson (1977) compared the global labels (e.g., "Best-behaved," "average-behaved," and "least well-behaved") teachers used to describe children in their classrooms with teacher ratings on questionnaires, teacher estimates of child classroom behaviors, and behavioral observations in the classrooms. Their results suggest that teachers' verbal reports are valid, at least with respect to global labels. However, in a similar study, Green, Beck, Forehand, and Vosk (1980) found that while teachers were able to discriminate normal children from disturbed children (conduct-disordered or socially withdrawn) in their classrooms, they were less accurate in terms of differentiating between the conduct-disordered and socially withdrawn children. Additional studies on the reliability and validity of specific teacher verbal descriptions of child classroom behavior are not available.

In summary, the behavioral interview is, and will certainly continue to be, an indispensable part of behavioral assessment. The ongoing construction and development of structured parent and child interviews that include items assessing conduct-disordered behavior (e.g., Costello *et al.*, 1984), or that are designed specifically to assess conduct-disordered child behaviors and relevant parent behaviors (e.g., Patterson & Bank, 1986), are encouraging. However, because of the limited empirical basis of behavioral interviews at present, they must be used in conjunction with other assessment procedures in developing a valid functional analysis of the referral problem.

Behavioral Rating Scales

Behavioral rating scales "describe assessment instruments that are completed by adults in reference to a child's behavior or characteristics" (McMahon, 1984, p. 81). Advantages of these instruments are that they permit the assessment of a broad range of behaviors and behavioral dimensions, including low-frequency behaviors; require relatively little time to administer, score, and interpret; facilitate the gathering of normative data; are readily quantifiable; and incorporate the perceptions of significant individuals in the child's life such as parents or teachers (see Barkley, 1984, and McMahon, 1984, for more extensive discussions). Some of the rating scales can provide data relevant to diagnostic decisions. Behavioral rating scales have been extensively employed as treatment outcome measures with conduct-disordered children (Atkeson & Forehand, 1978), and they have also been a primary source of data concerning social validation (Kazdin, 1977) of treatment effects with conduct-disordered children and their families (e.g., Forehand, Wells, & Griest, 1980). Parents' and teachers' perceptions of the child are important treatment goals in their own right, and behavioral rating scales provide ready access to such data (see below).

There are literally hundreds of behavioral rating scales, and most of those include conduct-disordered types of behaviors along with other child behavior problems. We present brief reviews of three sets of behavioral rating scales that are well researched and that, based on current evidence, we feel to be most appropriate for clinical and research use with conduct-disordered children. Several other behavioral rating scales are also described here that have more limited applicability to conduct-disordered children. Our discussion of these rating scales focuses on aspects specific to the behavioral assessment of conduct disorders. For more extensive reviews of these scales, see Barkley (1984) and McMahon (1984).

CHILD BEHAVIOR CHECKLIST. The Child Behavior Checklist (CBCL; Achenbach & Edelbrock, 1983) is designed for use with children between the ages of 2 and 16. The goal of its developers is to provide a comprehensive behavioral assessment battery for behaviorally disordered children, with parallel forms of the CBCL for parents, teachers, youths, and observers. To date, only the parent and teacher forms have been completely standardized, although preliminary investigations have been completed with the youth self-report (Achenbach & Edelbrock, 1983) and observer (Reed & Edelbrock, 1983) versions.

The parent form of the CBCL currently consists of two different checklists: one completed by parents of children aged 4–16 (CBCL/4–16) and a newly developed checklist completed by parents of children aged 2–3 (CBCL/2–3). The CBCL/4–16 includes both Social Competence and Behavior Problem scales, while the CBCL/2–3 includes only Behavior Problem scales. The forms can be completed in approximately 10–20 minutes. The CBCL scores are summarized on either the Revised Child Behavior Profile (RCBP) (for the CBCL/4–16) or the Child Behavior Profile for Ages 2–3 (for the CBCL/2–3). Both profiles indicate the child's standing on various narrow-band and broad-band (Internalizing, Externalizing) syndromes. The RCBP has separate norms for boys and girls at three age levels (4–5, 6–11, 12–16). The Externalizing dimension includes conduct-disordered types of behavior problems on three of the scales (Aggressive, Delinquent, Cruel). The Aggressive scale is found for boys and girls at each age level, while the Delinquent scale is found at each age level except for 4- to 5-year-old girls. The Cruel scale is found only for girls at ages 6–11 and 12–16. On the Child Behavior Profile for Ages 2–3, the two Externalizing scales (Aggressive, Destructive) include conduct disorder types of behaviors. The relationship of these scales to corresponding DSM-III and DSM-IIIR categories is noted in Table 2. A Total Behavior Problem score can be derived as well. The Social Competence scales on the RCBP include items related to various activities, social relationships, and success in school.

The parent form of the CBCL/4–16 has been shown to possess quite adequate psychometric properties (Achenbach & Edelbrock, 1983). For example, the conduct-disorder-related scales of the RCBP correlate highly with their counterparts on the Conners Parent Rating Scale (Con-

TABLE 2. Correspondence of Child Behavior Profile Scales to DSM-III and DSM-IIIR Categories Pertaining to Conduct Disorders

DSM-III category	DSM-IIIR category	Child Behavior Profile scale
Conduct Disorder	Conduct Disorder	
Undersocialized, aggressive	Solitary aggressive	Aggressive[a]
		Cruel[b]
		Destructive[c]
Undersocialized, nonaggressive		—
Socialized, aggressive	Group	Delinquent[d]
Socialized, nonaggressive		Delinquent[e]
	Undifferentiated	Aggressive[a]
		Cruel[b]
		Delinquent[d,e]
		Destructive[c]
Oppositional Disorder	Oppositional Defiant Disorder	—

Note. Portions of this table were adapted from *Manual for the Child Behavior Checklist and Revised Child Behavior Profile* (p. 121) by T. M. Achenbach and C. S. Edelbrock, 1983, Burlington: University of Vermont, Department of Psychiatry. Copyright 1983 by the University of Vermont, Department of Psychiatry. Adapted by permission.
[a] All sex/age groups.
[b] Girls 6–11, 12–16.
[c] Boys and girls 2–3.
[d] Boys 4–5, 6–11, 12–16.
[e] Girls 6–11, 12–16.

ners, 1973) (r's = .76–.88) and the Revised Behavior Problem Checklist (Quay & Peterson, 1983) (r's = .52–.88). The parent form of the CBCL/4–16 is also sensitive to treatment changes resulting from parent training interventions for the treatment of conduct disorders (Webster-Stratton, 1984, 1985b).

Within inpatient groups, the CBCL/4–16 has been shown to differentiate boys with DSM-III diagnoses of Conduct Disorder or Major Depression from children with other diagnoses (Kazdin & Heidish, 1984). With respect to the conduct-disordered children (6- to 11-year-old boys), their parents reported significantly greater problems on the Aggressive and Delinquent narrow-band scales and on the Externalizing broad-band scale. They did not differ on the other scales of the CBP. Using each of these three scales, 94–99% of the boys diagnosed as conduct-disordered were correctly identified. However, there was a very low level of specificity (7–12%); that is, a large proportion of the boys who were identified as conduct-disordered on the CBP did not receive a diagnosis of Conduct Disorder using DSM-III criteria. (A similar pattern of high sensitivity and low specificity was found for the diagnosis of Major Depression as well.) It is worth noting that

Kazdin and Heidish adopted a relatively low cutoff score (one standard deviation above the mean) for classification as deviant, which, while maximizing sensitivity, may have decreased specificity. An additional factor contributing to the low specificity may be the relatively narrow DSM-III criteria for Conduct Disorder.

The CBCL/4–16 has also been shown to differentiate firesetters from nonfiresetters within a group of inpatient conduct-disordered children (Kolko, Kazdin, & Meyer, 1985). Mothers of firesetters endorsed significantly more items on the Hyperactive and Delinquent narrow-band scales and on the Externalizing broad-band scale of the RCBP. The children also received significantly lower scores on the Social scale. In general, these findings indicate that conduct-disordered children who set fires are more extreme in their behavior than conduct-disordered children who do not engage in firesetting.

The Behavior Problem items on the Teacher's Report Form of the CBCL (Edelbrock & Achenbach, 1984) have been adapted from the parent version of the CBCL, with several items being replaced by ones that are more appropriate to classroom situations. The teacher version of the Child Behavior Profile consists of eight or nine Behavior Problem scales derived from factor analysis; Internalizing, Externalizing, and Total Behavior Problem scores; and six scale scores related to school performance and adaptive functioning. There are separate profiles available for boys and girls at two age levels (6–11, 12–16).

Preliminary psychometric data on the Teacher's Report Form of the CBCL have been reported for the Profile for 6- to 11-year-old boys. The Teacher's Report Form has adequate test–retest reliability (e.g., the average r's for the Aggressive scale were .96, .75, and .68 for a 1-week, 2-month, and 4-month intervals, respectively; Edelbrock & Achenbach, 1984), and scores on the Externalizing scales (especially Aggressive) of the Teacher Profile correlate quite highly with the various scales of the revised Conners Teacher Rating Scale (e.g., the Aggressive scale of the Teacher Profile correlated .90 with the Conduct Problem scale of the revised Conners Teacher Rating Scale; Edelbrock, Greenbaum, & Conover, 1985). The Teacher's Report Form has also been shown to discriminate clinic-referred from nonreferred children (Edelbrock & Achenbach, 1984) and to differentiate children with Attention Deficit Disorder with and without Hyperactivity from children with other diagnoses (Edelbrock, Costello, & Kessler, 1984). Total Behavior Problem scores are correlated with classroom observational measures as obtained on the Direct Observation Form of the CBCL (Reed & Edelbrock, 1983).

The CBCL offers a number of compelling advantages. First, it represents the culmination of extensive empirical analyses of data gathered from a variety of informants concerning both child behavior problems and competencies. In fact, it is one of the few behavior rating scales to assess prosocial behaviors (McMahon, 1984). Second, its psychometric qualities appear to be more than adequate, and extensive normative data are provided for children of different ages and sexes (Achenbach & Edelbrock, 1981, 1983). Third, the development of equivalent forms for different informants should maximize the amount of information that can be gathered about the child and should permit comparisons across informants and situations. Fourth, the provision of both broad-band and narrow-band syndromes (including broad coverage of conduct-disordered types of behavior) in the RCBP means that the CBCL can be used for both general and more specific purposes, including classification, screening, diagnosis, and treatment evaluation. With conduct-disordered children, its comprehensive coverage may prove useful in screening for some of the associated features of conduct disorders discussed above, such as ADD/H and depression.

BEHAVIOR PROBLEM CHECKLIST. The Revised Behavior Problem Checklist (RBPC; Quay & Peterson, 1983), which consists of 89 items, is intended to widen the diagnostic scope and increase the psychometric robustness of the original Behavior Problem Checklist (BPC; Quay, 1977). It is usually completed by parents or teachers, and takes approximately 10–15 minutes to complete. Various factor analyses of the original BPC have yielded two very robust dimensions (Conduct Problem, Personality Problem), as well as two other broad-band dimensions (Inadequacy–Immaturity, Socialized Delinquency). Adequate reliability and validity coefficients have been obtained with either parents or teachers as informants (see Quay, 1977). Interparent agreement has been shown to be higher in nondistressed than in distressed samples, and higher for the Conduct Problem items than for the Personality Problem items (Jacob, Grounds, & Haley, 1982). High scores on the Conduct Problem scale have been associated with attribution of hostility to others (Nasby *et al.*, 1980). The BPC has been used occasionally to assess the outcome of treatment with children demonstrating conduct-disordered behavior (e.g., Oltmanns, Broderick, & O'Leary, 1977). In the Kazdin and Heidish (1984) investigation reported above, findings similar to those reported for the CBCL were found for the BPC. Boys with a DSM-III diagnosis of Conduct Disorder received higher scores on the Conduct Problem and Socialized Delinquency scales of the BPC than did children with other diagnoses. These two scales of the BPC were highly sensitive in identifying conduct-disordered children (75%–89%). (The Personality Problem scale was moderately sensitive [62%] in identifying children with a diagnosis of Major Depression.) Specificity was higher for both the Conduct Disorder and the Major Depression diagnoses on the BPC (44%–60%) than on the CBCL.

The RBPC is composed of six factors: Conduct Disorder, Socialized Aggression, Attention Problem, Anxiety Withdrawal, Psychotic Behavior, and Motor Excess (Quay & Peterson, 1983). Correlations between similar scales of the RBPC and the original BPC in various samples are quite high for the Conduct Disorder/ Conduct Problem (r's = .87–.95) and Socialized Aggression/Socialized Delinquency (r's = .92–.97) scales (Quay & Peterson, 1983). Norms are currently available for teacher ratings from kindergarten through 12th grade and for maternal ratings for children aged 5–16 years. Reliability estimates are comparable to those obtained with the original BPC, and support for various types of validity is promising. For example, teacher ratings on the Conduct Disorder scale have been shown to correlate highly with peer nominations of aggression ($r = .72$) and with observed levels of initiated aggression ($r = .60$) and cooperation ($r = -.45$) in peer interactions (Quay & Peterson, 1983). The RBPC has yet to be employed as a treatment outcome measure.

In a clinical setting, the RBPC can be considered for use as a general screening device, as an instrument for identifying dimensions of deviant behavior, and as a measure of treatment outcome. Although the RBPC has only recently appeared, the similarly of its factor structure to the widely researched BPC bodes well for its applicability to the behavioral assessment of conduct-disordered children. However, the limited number of dimensions of child behavior disorders and the omission of positive behaviors or competencies from the scale make it less useful than the CBCL.

EYBERG CHILD BEHAVIOR INVENTORY. The Eyberg Child Behavior Inventory (ECBI; Eyberg, 1980) is the only behavioral rating scale that has been explicitly developed to assess conduct disorders per se. The ECBI is completed by parents and is comprised of 36 items that describe specific conduct-disordered types of behaviors. All but a few of these items refer to overt, as opposed to covert, types of conduct disorder. Other items refer to attentional ("Has short attention span") or developmental ("Wets the bed") problems. Based on factor analyses, the ECBI does, in fact, appear to be a unidimensional scale measuring conduct disorders in children (Robinson, Eyberg, & Ross, 1980) and adolescents (Eyberg & Robinson, 1983a).

The ECBI is intended for use with children from ages 2 to 16, and takes less than 15 minutes to complete. Parents rate each item on both a 7-point frequency of occurrence (Intensity) scale and a yes–no problem identification (Problem) scale. The use of these two scales permits a much more fine-grained analysis of the presenting problems and may provide useful information concerning the role of parental perceptions of a child in the rating process (Robinson et al., 1980).

Normative data for children aged 2–12 (Robinson et al., 1980) and adolescents aged 13–16 (Eyberg & Robinson, 1983a), and tentative cutting points for treatment selection (Eyberg & Ross, 1978) have been presented. Despite sex differences on both dimensions of the ECBI (with boys scoring higher than girls), Robinson et al. (1980) chose to report normative data for children aged 2–12 by age only. This was not an issue for the normative sample of adolescents, for which no sex differences were found.

With respect to other psychometric considerations, adequate test–retest, split-half, and internal-consistency reliabilities have been reported (Eyberg & Robinson, 1983a; Robinson et al., 1980). Scores on both dimensions of the ECBI and on individual items have been shown to discriminate conduct-disordered children from other clinic-referred children and from normal children (Eyberg & Robinson, 1983a; Eyberg & Ross, 1978; Robinson et al., 1980). The ECBI has been found to correlate significantly with various clinic-based observational coding systems, but only modestly with a maternal report measure of child temperament (Robinson & Eyberg, 1981; Webster-Stratton, 1985a; Webster-Stratton & Eyberg, 1982). Responses on the ECBI have been shown to be independent of social desirability factors (Robinson & Anderson, 1983). The ECBI is also sensitive to behavioral treatment effects (e.g., Eyberg & Robinson, 1982; Eyberg & Ross, 1978; Webster-Stratton, 1984).

The ECBI shows a great deal of promise as a useful rating scale in clinical settings, where it can be employed as a screening instrument and as a treatment outcome measure. However, its unidimensional assessment of conduct disorders limits its utility as a screening instrument. In situations in which a broader screening is desired or when information pertinent to differential diagnosis is sought, then use of one of the broad-band behavioral rating scales described above is recommended.

OTHER BEHAVIORAL RATING SCALES. Conners (1969, 1970, 1973) developed a set of separate rating scales for parents (Conners Parent Rating Scale; CPRS) and teachers (Conners Teacher Rating Scale; CTRS), which were revised in 1978 by Goyette, Conners, and Ulrich. The Conners scales have been used primarily to discriminate hyperactive from non-hyperactive children (e.g., Werry, Sprague, & Cohen, 1975) and to assess the effects of various drug (Conners & Werry, 1979) or behavioral (S. G. O'Leary & Pelham, 1978) treatments with these children. However, there are two scales derived from subsets of items on the CPRS and CTRS that are relevant to the assessment of conduct-disordered children. The Abbreviated Symptom Questionnaire (ASQ; Conners, 1973) consists of 10 items common to both the parent and teacher forms. Although intended as a measure of hyperactivity per se, the ASQ is best regarded as a measure of both conduct disorders and hyperactivity (Barkley, 1984; Ullmann, Sleator, & Sprague, 1985), and would be an appropriate measure to employ when the identification of children with features of both conduct disorders and hyperactivity is required. Note that Ullmann et al. (1985) have presented data to indicate that the ASQ fails to select children whose primary difficulty is inattention (i.e., attention deficit disorder) as opposed to hyperactivity per se. In an attempt to discriminate conduct-disordered children from hyperactive children, Loney and Milich (1982) have developed the Iowa CTRS, which consists of 10 items from the CTRS. Half of the items load highly on the Conduct Problem factor and the remaining items load highly on the Hyperactivity factor of the CTRS. Separate norms and cutting scores for boys and girls at each of three grade levels (kindergarten to first grade, second to third grades, and fourth to fifth grades) have been presented (Murphy, Pelham, & Milich, 1985), and the differential validity of this version of the CTRS has been recently demonstrated (Milich & Fitzgerald, 1985).

Two additional rating scales deserve mention because of their extensive use as outcome measures of parental perceptions of conduct-disordered children and their ability to differentiate groups of clinic-referred conduct-disordered children from nonreferred children. These are the Parent Attitudes Test (PAT; Cowen, Huser, Beach, & Rappaport, 1970) and the revised version of the Becker Bipolar Adjective Checklist (Patterson & Fagot, 1967). However, the limited psychometric and normative data associated with these two rating scales and the presence of the more psychometrically sound alternatives presented above should preclude reliance on these measures. The PAT has been shown to discriminate between children rated as adjusted or maladjusted by their teachers (Cowen et al., 1970), and between nonreferred and clinic-referred conduct-disordered children (Forehand et al., 1975; Griest et al., 1980). It has been extensively employed as an outcome measure of parental perceptions of conduct-disordered children by Forehand and his colleagues (see McMahon & Forehand, 1984, for a review). Peed, Roberts, and Forehand (1977) found that a treatment group changed significantly more than a waiting-list control group on the Home Attitude and Behavior Rating scales of the PAT, but not on the Adjective Checklist scale of that instrument.

The revised version of the Becker Bipolar Adjective Checklist (Patterson & Fagot, 1967) consists of five factors: Hostile–Withdrawn, Relaxed Disposition, Aggression, Intellectual Efficiency, and Conduct Problems. Lobitz and Johnson (1975) found significant differences on all five factors between clinic-referred conduct-disordered children and matched control children, and the concurrent validity of three of the factors (Aggression, Conduct Problems, Relaxed Disposition) with the Parent Daily Report (a parental observation measure, described below) has been demonstrated (Chamberlain & Reid, 1987). The Becker Bipolar Adjective Checklist has been used frequently in research to evaluate treatment effectiveness with conduct-disordered children (e.g., Eyberg & Johnson, 1974; Patterson, 1974; Peed et al., 1977). Unfortunately, Peed et al. (1977) found that a waiting-list control group demonstrated changes similar to those displayed by a treatment group for all factors except Conduct Problems. These results bring into question the validity of the other factors for assessing the effectiveness of behavior therapy treatment programs.

In summary, there are several behavioral rating scales available for use in the assessment of conduct-disordered children. Depending upon the specific purposes of the assessment, the behavior therapist has a wide range of instruments from which to choose. These include a rating scale designed to focus solely on conduct disorders as rated by parents (the ECBI); a rating scale designed to assess broad-band dysfunctions as rated by parents and teachers (the RBPC); and a comprehensive set of instruments designed to assess both broad- and narrow-band dimensions of child disorders and that can be completed by parents, teachers, the children themselves, or independent observers (the CBCL). As well, two brief rating scales derived from the Conners scales can be used to identify children with features of both conduct disorders and hyperactivity (the ASQ) or to discriminate conduct-disordered from hyperactive children (the Iowa CTRS). On the basis of the available data, we feel that the CBCL and the ECBI are most likely to meet the needs of clinicians and researchers dealing with conduct disorders.

Behavioral Observation

Because of problems inherent in other assessment strategies (e.g., interviews, questionnaires), direct behavioral observation is the most widely accepted procedure for obtaining a reliable and valid description of current parent–child interactions and/or teacher–child interactions. Given the likelihood of perceptual biases from adults intimately involved with a child on a day-to-day basis (e.g., parents, teachers), sole reliance on their reports, whether by interview or questionnaire methods, is unwise (cf. Reid, Baldwin, Patterson, & Dishion, 1985). Through the appropriate use of behavioral observation, the therapist is able to obtain measures on the frequency and duration of child problem behaviors and on the relations between child and parent and/or teacher behaviors, and thus is able to quantify the problem interactions targeted for treatment. Comparisons of observational data with those gathered via other means can assist the clinician in determining whether the focus of treatment should be on the adult–child interaction or on adult perceptual and/or personal adjustment issues. In this section, we describe several observational systems developed for independent observers and currently in use for assessing interactions with conduct-disordered children in the clinic, home, and school settings. We also discuss observational measures for assessing conduct-disordered behaviors that can be employed by significant adults such as parents and teachers.

OBSERVATION IN THE CLINIC. Although extremely valuable to assessment and treatment, behavioral observations by independent observers in the natural environment are very expensive and time-consuming—that is, they lack efficiency. An assessment procedure that reduces the time and cost associated with observation in the natural setting is the observation of parent–child interactions in a structured setting in the clinic. Use of a structured clinic observation is advantageous for three reasons: It efficiently elicits the problem parent–child interactions; observation can occur unobtru-

sively through one–way windows; and the standard situation allows the therapist to make within- and between-client comparisons (Hughes & Haynes, 1978).

Typically, the structured setting is a playroom in a clinic, equipped with one-way windows and age-appropriate toys and games. Instructions to the parents may vary from "Play with your child" to highly specific guidelines for emitting a list of commands to the child. Similarly, behavioral observation systems vary in complexity. For a review and critique of behavioral observations in the clinic, the reader is referred to Hughes and Haynes (1978).

There are two widely used structured observation procedures available for assessing parent–child interactions in the clinic: the system developed by Forehand and his colleagues (Forehand & McMahon, 1981; Forehand, Peed, Roberts, McMahon, Griest, & Humphreys, 1978) and the Dyadic Parent–Child Interaction Coding System (DPICS; Eyberg & Robinson, 1983b). Both of these observation systems are modifications of the assessment procedure developed by Hanf (1970) for the observation of parent–child interactions in the clinic.

In the Forehand observation system, each parent–child pair is observed in a clinic playroom equipped with a one-way window and wired for sound. The playroom contains various age-appropriate toys, such as building blocks, toy trucks and cars, dolls, puzzles, crayons, and paper. An observer codes the parent–child interaction from an adjoining observation room. Prior to the clinic observation, each parent is instructed to interact with his or her child in two different contexts, referred to as the "Child's Game" and the "Parent's Game." In the Child's Game, the parent is instructed to engage in any activity that the child chooses and to allow the child to determine the nature and rules of the interaction. Thus, the Child's Game is essentially a free-play situation. In the Parent's Game, the parent is instructed to engage the child in activities whose rules and nature are determined by the parent. The Parent's Game is thus essentially a command situation.

The clinic observation consists of coding the parent–child interaction for 5 or 10 minutes in both the Child's and Parent's Games. Six parent behaviors and three child behaviors are recorded during the observation. The parent behaviors include rewards (praise or positive physical attention); attends (description of the child's behavior, activity, or appearance); questions (interrogatives); commands (including both alpha commands, which are directives to which a motoric response is appropriate and feasible, and beta commands, which are commands to which the child has no opportunity to demonstrate compliance); warnings (statements that describe aversive consequences to be delivered by the parent); and time out (removal of the child from positive reinforcement). The child behaviors are compliance, noncompliance, and inappropriate behavior (whine–cry–yell–tantrum, aggression, deviant talk).

Following the clinic observation, the data are summarized for both the Child's Game and the Parent's Game. Parent behaviors are expressed as rate per minute of attends, rewards, questions, alpha commands, beta commands, warnings, time outs, and total commands. Child behaviors are expressed in percentages: percentage of child compliance to alpha commands, percentage of child compliance to total commands, and percentage of child inappropriate behavior. In addition, the percentage of parental attention contingent upon child compliance (i.e., rewards plus attends emitted within 5 seconds following child compliance) is computed. Because the time spent in assessing the parent–child interactions is relatively short (10 minutes), this clinic observation procedure can be repeated at each clinic visit, thus providing the therapist with a continuous assessment of treatment effects. This same coding system has been used extensively for home observations of parent–child interactions (see McMahon & Forehand, 1984).

Figure 2 shows a sample score sheet for the observation of parent–child interactions during the Parent's Game in the clinic. Data are recorded in 30-second intervals. With one exception, the frequency of occurrence of each behavior is scored in each interval. Inappropriate behavior is recorded on an occurrence–nonoccurrence basis for each 30-second interval. The data from the sample observation are summarized at the bottom of the figure. As can be seen, the child who was being observed engaged in inappropriate behavior (e.g., whining, crying, hitting) in 40% of the ten 30-second observation intervals. His compliance to the total number of commands given by the parent was 19%. However, his compliance to clear, direct commands (alpha commands) was much higher (75%). The parent provided positive consequences to only 17% of the child's compliances. Differentiating child compliance to

alpha and to beta commands provides the therapist with information concerning the antecedent events maintaining child noncompliance. In this example, the large difference between the percentage of compliance to alpha commands and that to total commands indicated that modification of the parent's command behavior would be essential to treatment success. Based on this observation, the treatment goals would be (1) to teach the parent to give alpha commands, (2) to decrease the number of beta commands, (3) to increase the parent's positive consequation of child compliance, and (4) to decrease the child's inappropriate behavior by teaching the parent a time-out procedure.

Using this coding system, Forehand and Peed (1979) have reported an average interobserver agreement of 75%. The coding system possesses adequate test–retest reliability as well. Data from repeated observations of nonintervention parent–child interactions are stable and consistent with this coding system (Peed et al., 1977), yet the observation procedure is also sensitive enough to measure significant treatment effects in the clinic and home (see McMahon & Forehand, 1984, for a review).

Given that the coding system and structured situation produce a reliable and sensitive assessment instrument, the next question concerns the validity of the instrument. Forehand et al. (1975) found significant differences with respect to rate of parental commands and percentage of child compliance between clinic-referred and nonreferred parent–child interactions observed in a clinic. Griest et al. (1980) reported significant differences in compliance in the home setting between clinic-referred and nonreferred children. In other studies, parent–child interactions in the clinic have been shown to be similar to those observed in the home (Peed et al., 1977) and to predict child behavior in the home (Forehand, Wells, & Sturgis, 1978). More specifically, treatment effects observed in the clinic coincide with treatment effects observed in the home (Peed et al., 1977)

The second observational system for coding parent–child interaction in the clinic is the DPICS (Eyberg & Robinson, 1983b). Because of its common roots in the work of Hanf (1970), the DPICS is quite similar to the Forehand system. The parent–child dyad is observed for 5 minutes in three standard situations that vary in the degree to which parental control is required: Child-Directed Interaction (a free-play situation), Parent-Directed Interaction (the parent

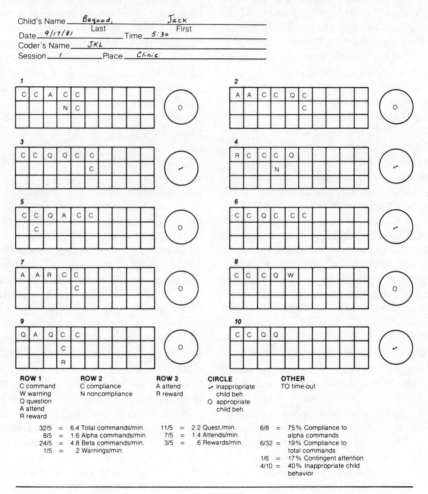

FIGURE 2. Sample score sheet for the observation of parent–child interactions during the Parent's Game in the clinic. From *Helping the Noncompliant Child: A Clinician's Guide to Parent Training* (p. 37) by R. L. Forehand and R. J. McMahon, 1981, New York: Guilford Press. Copyright 1981 by the Guilford Press. Reprinted by permission.

guides the child's activity), and Clean-Up (the parent attempts to get the child to pick up the toys in the clinic playroom).

There are 12 parent and 7 child behaviors that are scored. Many of the parent behaviors are based on those in Hanf (1970) and Patterson, Ray, Shaw, and Cobb (1969). Parent behaviors include direct and indirect commands, descriptive and reflective statements, descriptive/reflective questions, acknowledgment, irrelevant verbalization, unlabeled and labeled praise, physical positive and negative, and crit-

ical statement. Most of the child behaviors were selected from the list compiled by Adkins and Johnson (1972; see below). Child behaviors include cry, yell, whine, smart talk, destructive, physical negative, and change activity. There are also two sequences scored: parental response to deviant child behavior (respond, ignore) and child response to commands (compliance, noncompliance, no opportunity). The behaviors are scored continuously via frequency counts during each 5-minute observation. However, for some nondiscrete behaviors (e.g., yell), the observer is required to make use of a "5-second rule" in which the behavior is scored at the beginning of each 5-second period during which the behavior is occurring.

Several composite variables are formed from the individual behavioral categories and sequences (Robinson & Eyberg, 1981). These include total praise (labeled and unlabeled praise), total deviant (whine + cry + physical negative + smart talk + yell + destructive), total commands (direct + indirect commands), command ratio (direct commands/total commands), no opportunity ratio (no opportunity/total commands), compliance ratio (complies/total commands), and noncompliance ratio (noncomplies/total commands).

With respect to the psychometric properties of the DPICS, the data are encouraging. Interrater reliability has been assessed in several investigations, with correlation coefficients ranging from .65 to 1.00 (Aragona & Eyberg, 1981; Eyberg & Matarazzo, 1980; Robinson & Eyberg, 1981). In the primary standardization study, the mean reliability coefficients for parent and child behaviors were .91 and .92, respectively (Robinson & Eyberg, 1981). Kniskern, Robinson, and Mitchell (1983) reported coefficients for individual behaviors that ranged from .47 to .96. Only 2 of 19 behaviors (irrelevant verbalization, labeled praise) had reliability coefficients less than .72. Zangwill and Kniskern (1982) reported overall interobserver agreement figures of 69% and 68% for observations conducted in the clinic and home, respectively. There are no test–retest reliability figures, although families were observed twice over a 7-day period during the primary standardization study (Robinson & Eyberg, 1981).

Validation studies have indicated that the DPICS successfully discriminates families of conduct-disordered children and those of normal children, and conduct-disordered children and their siblings (Robinson & Eyberg, 1981). It is also sensitive to changes induced by treatment (Eyberg & Matarazzo, 1980; Eyberg & Robinson, 1982; Webster-Stratton, 1984). In the primary standardization study, the DPICS correctly classified 100% of normal nonreferred families, 85% of conduct-disordered clinic-referred families, and 94% of the combined group of families (Robinson & Eyberg, 1981). It also predicted 61% of the variance in parent-completed ECBI (Eyberg, 1980) scores pertaining to behavior problems in the home. However, in a recent study, Webster-Stratton (1985a) found

significant correlations between observed child behaviors and the ECBI only for the Parent-Directed Interaction observation format. Child behaviors in the Child-Directed Interaction format or in unstructured observation formats in the clinic and the home did not correlate with the ECBI.

Normative data on the DPICS are somewhat meager, since they are based on 22 mother–child pairs (Eyberg & Robinson, 1983b). Also, there are no data reported for the Clean-Up phase of the observation. Presumably because of the small sample size, the normative data are not grouped according to age and sex of the children.

Although the DPICS was developed as a clinic-based observation system, it has been employed in home observations on a number of occasions as well (Kniskern et al., 1983; Webster-Stratton, 1984, 1985a, 1985b; Zangwill & Kniskern, 1982). Most of these investigations have assessed the relationship between parent–child interaction as observed in the clinic and in the home. For example, Zangwill and Kniskern (1982) found that mother and child behaviors in a clinic-referred sample that were observed in the clinic correlated to a moderate degree with the same behaviors observed in the home. However, the rates of the behaviors tended to be higher in the clinic than in the home. Webster-Stratton (1985a) concluded that the similarity of the structure of the observations, rather than setting per se, was the key to clinic–home comparability. She found that the strongest correlations between clinic and home observations occurred when the clinic observations were relatively unstructured, thus making them similar in format to the home observations. However, she recommended that the Parent-Directed Interaction (analogous to the Parent's Game in Forehand's coding system) be employed as a "challenge test" in the clinic, since it elicited higher rates of deviant mother and child behaviors in her clinic-referred sample than either the Child-Directed Interaction or the unstructured clinic observation. On the basis of our own clinical experience with the Parent's Game and Child's Game observational formats, we feel that the Child-Directed Interaction format also provides useful data concerning the parent's reinforcement of appropriate child behavior and possible difficulties with parental directiveness (i.e., high rates of commands).

Patterson (1982, 1983) has hypothesized that

poor problem-solving skills are associated with increased maternal stress levels, higher levels of child coercive behavior, and deficits in the child's social skills. There have been limited attempts to assess familial problem solving with conduct-disordered families using observational methods in an analogue setting. To date, these efforts have focused primarily on adolescents and their parents. Robin and Weiss (1980) employed a modified version of the Marital Interaction Coding System (Weiss & Margolin, 1977) to assess problem-solving communication behavior (rather than problem solving per se). Mother and adolescent behaviors were coded as each dyad spent 10 minutes discussing each of two problematic issues. The coding system discriminated distressed from nondistressed mother–adolescent dyads on a number of different behaviors. A further revision of this coding system called the Parent–Adolescent Interaction Coding system (Robin, 1981; see Foster & Robin, Chapter 17, this volume), permits the assessment of specific problem-solving behaviors (e.g., consequential statements, specification of the problem). This coding system was found to be sensitive to changes in problem-solving behavior as a function of Robin's (1985) problem-solving communication training intervention.

Patterson (1983) has developed a similar analogue procedure for assessing parent–child problem-solving interactions. Three 10-minute discussion tasks are videotaped and coded: The parent and child each bring up something they would like changed in the family, and the family is asked to plan a weekend activity. In addition to coding specific behaviors, the observer completes a rating checklist concerned with the overall quality of the solutions reached by family members. Preliminary analyses have indicated that observed measures of mother irritability during problem solving and observer ratings of poor quality of solution are correlated with child coercive behavior in the home.

OBSERVATION IN THE HOME. Several behavioral coding systems have been developed to measure the behavior of conduct-disordered children in the home. Two of the systems that have been reported in the research literature as the most frequently used for home observation are presented in this section (Patterson et al., 1969; Wahler, House, & Stambaugh, 1976). A third system, designed for use in both the home and the clinic, has been presented in the preceding section on clinic observations (i.e.,

Forehand, Peed, et al., 1978). Its use in the context of the home setting is described. Finally a new coding system (Dishion, Gardner, Patterson, Reid, Spyrou, & Thibodeaux, 1984) that seems to represent significant improvements over other home observation coding systems is described briefly.

The Family Interaction Coding System (FICS) was developed by Patterson and his colleagues at the Oregon Research Institute and the Oregon Social Learning Center (Patterson et al., 1969; Reid, 1978). Although designed to record social interactions among family members in their natural setting (the home), the system is not completely unstructured. Prior to the observation, members of the family are given the following instructions: (1) Everyone in the family must be present; (2) no guests should be present during observations; (3) the family is limited to two rooms; (4) no telephone calls are to be made, and incoming calls must be answered briefly; (5) no television viewing is permitted; (6) no conversations may be held with observers while they are coding; and (7) therapy-related issues are not to be discussed with the observer (Reid, 1978).

Preintervention assessment usually consists of 6–10 hours of observation collected in approximately 1-hour segments. During an observation period, the subject's behavior and the responses by other family members to the subject's behavior are coded in order to provide a sequential account of the subject's interactions with other family members. Each member of the family is randomly designated the subject for 5-minute segments of the observation period. Interactions between the subject and other family members are recorded every 6 seconds. When each member has been observed for five minutes, the series is repeated once. A total of 29 behavioral categories are used to describe the subject–family interactions. These behavioral categories are divided into first- and second-order behaviors. First-order behaviors are those deemed most relevant for evaluating treatment outcome and/or contributing to coercion theory (Reid, 1978). The first-order behavioral categories are as follows: command, command negative, cry, humiliate, laugh, negativism, whine, yell, destructiveness, high rate, physical negative, physical positive, approval, compliance, disapproval, dependency, ignore, indulgence, noncompliance, play, tease, and work. The second-order behavioral categories are these: attention, no response, normative, receive, self-stimulation, talk, and touch. Reid (1978) provides complete definitions, with examples, for each of the 29 categories. A recent factor analysis of the FICS yielded a five-factor structure that accounted for nearly 40% of the variance in observed behaviors (Carlson, Williams, & Davol, 1984).

Following 6–10 hours of preintervention observation, the conduct-disordered child's behavior is summarized by computing the frequency of each aversive behavior and the frequency of total aversive behavior (TAB) (Reid, 1978). The TAB score is a composite of 14 code categories and is designed to measure general coerciveness. It has been shown to correspond closely with parent- and child-derived ratings of aversive behavior, thus lending support to its social validity (Hoffman, Fagot, Reid, & Patterson, 1987; Snyder, 1983). In addition, the relationship of particular antecedent and consequent behaviors can be examined (Patterson, 1982). As treatment progresses, observation data can also be used to determine changes in targeted and nontargeted deviant behavior (Patterson, Cobb, & Ray, 1973) and in parent consequation of conduct-disordered behaviors (Taplin & Reid, 1977).

The Standardized Observation Codes system (SOC; Wahler et al., 1976), developed at the University of Tennessee, is similar to Patterson et al.'s FICS in that it is designed to record a child's interactions with other persons in his or her environment. As with the FICS, certain rules are imposed on the family during the observation period. All family members must remain in the house, and all television sets, radios, and record players must be turned off. Observation periods are 30 minutes in length. The number of observation periods varies, depending on the length of time required to obtain a valid preintervention assessment. During each period, the observer watches the parent–child interaction for 10 seconds and records the behavioral categories over a 5-second period. Nineteen behavioral response categories are used to record the child's behavior, and six social event categories are used to record the behaviors of other persons in the child's environment; these 25 categories compose the SOC. The 19 categories of child behavior are as follows: compliance, opposition, aversive opposition, complaints, self-stimulation, object play, self-talk, sustained noninteraction, sustained schoolwork, sustained toy play, sustained work, sustained attending, mand adult, mand child,

social approach—adult, social approach—child, social interaction—adult, and social interaction—child. The six social event categories are these: instruction adult—nonaversive, instruction adult—aversive, social attention adult—nonaversive, social attention adult—aversive, social attention child—nonaversive, and social attention child—aversive. Data are typically expressed as the percentage of occurrence. The SOC includes a greater focus on positive behaviors than do most of the other observation systems. Wahler et al. (1976) provide definitions and behavioral examples for each of these categories.

When employed in the home setting, the coding system developed by Forehand, Peed, et al. (1978) is used to collect data in blocks of four 40-minute observations. The observations are conducted on different days and may be done at different times of the day. Family members are instructed to interact with each other in a normal fashion, although guidelines similar to those used by Patterson's and Wahler's groups are presented to the parent. The Forehand coding system only permits the behavior of a single adult and a single child to be recorded at a given time. If more than one parent is being observed, then separate observation sessions may occur with each parent and child, or the observer can code the behavior of each parent with the child in alternating 5-minute periods (Forehand & McMahon, 1981).

The reliability and validity of the FICS and the SOC are similar to those reported by Forehand (see "Observation in the Clinic," above). Patterson (1977, 1982) reports interobserver agreement ranging from 73% to 80% on the FICS, with the average agreement approximating 75%. Weinrott and Jones (1984) reported an ICC of .87 between observers on the FICS. When TAB scores in the first and second weeks of baseline are compared, the correlation is .78 (Patterson, 1982), supporting the short-term stability of this measure. Long-term stability (.74 at 1 year) of the TAB score has also been reported (Patterson, 1982). Reid (1978) has reported normative data based on 27 clinic-referred and 27 nonreferred families for each of the behavioral categories. Data are reported for the target children, mothers, fathers, and siblings. Wahler (1980; Wahler et al., 1976) has found that interobserver agreement with the SOC usually reaches 80% or better. Dumas and Wahler (1985) reported ICCs for a subsample of 10 of the 25 SOC categories. In all but one case, the ICCs were .83 or higher for session reliabilities. Interval-by-interval reliabilities as measured by kappa ranged from .51 to .81. In their study, Weinrott and Jones (1984) reported an average interobserver reliability of .97 for the SOC.

With respect to validity, the FICS has been shown to discriminate between clinic-referred and nonreferred children and their family members (see Patterson, 1982, for a review), and among various subtypes of conduct-disordered children (social–aggressive, hyperactive–aggressive, stealers), other clinic-referred children (e.g., abused), and normal children (Carlson et al., 1984; Hoffman et al., 1987). Correlations between TAB scores and other measures (e.g., parent reports, parent-collected data) support the concurrent validity of the FICS (e.g., Patterson, 1982). However, correlations between six specific categories shared between the FICS and the Parent Daily Report (see below) are much lower, suggesting only moderate convergence for these more specific categories. The FICS has been widely employed as a measure of treatment outcome and has been shown to be highly sensitive in this regard (see Patterson & Fleischman, 1979).

The validity data on Wahler's SOC are not as extensive. On Wahler's system, teacher-identified problem children displayed less appropriate behavior in both home and/or school than did teacher-identified nonproblem children (Moore, 1975; Snyder & Brown, 1983). Subsets of categories from the SOC have also been shown to discriminate insular from noninsular clinic-referred families at baseline (Dumas & Wahler, 1985) and in terms of the outcome of parent training interventions (Wahler & Afton, 1980).

Patterson and his colleagues (Dishion, Gardner, et al., 1984) have recently developed a new coding system for the large-scale longitudinal study they are conducting concerning the development and maintenance of conduct-disordered/delinquent behavior. The Family Process Code (FPC) is unique in that it includes reasonably broad coverage of prosocial as well as deviant behaviors; provides ratings of affect for each behavior that is coded; and records interactions in real time, which permits a more accurate assessment of the duration of behavior. The FPC includes three dimensions: Activity, Content, and Valence. The Activity dimension refers to the general setting in which the target person is being observed and includes work, play, read, eat, attend, and unspecified. The

Content dimension is comprised of 25 behaviors, which are approximately equally divided among positive, negative, and neutral behaviors. The behaviors are distributed into five major categories: verbal, vocal, nonverbal, physical, and compliance. The Valence dimension is a measure of affect (exuberant, positive, neutral, negative, unrestrained negative) that is recorded with every content code. The Activity, Content, and Valence dimensions are recorded on a hand-held automated data collection device that records data in real time, thus allowing a more sensitive assessment of duration.

Home observations using the FPC are structured in a manner similar to that described above for the FICS. Each observation is divided into 5- or 10-minute segments in which a particular member of the family is the focal subject. To date, the FPC has not been employed as a treatment outcome measure, and its psychometric characteristics have not been as thoroughly investigated as the FICS. Nonetheless, it represents some significant improvements over other observation systems for assessing conduct-disordered children and their families.

Patterson's research group has also developed an Observer Impressions Inventory (e.g., Weinrott, Reid, Bauske, & Brummett, 1981) to supplement the observational data from the FICS and the FPC. As described by Weinrott et al., this inventory consists of 25 items, most of which are rated on Likert-type scales, and is completed by the observer immediately following a home observation. A cluster analysis of the items revealed four dimensions—Hostility, Disorganization, Child Aggression, and Parental Reactivity to being Observed. The inventory possesses adequate internal consistency (alpha = .73–.88) and has been shown to discriminate between conduct-disordered and nonreferred families. Two of the four dimensions (Disorganization, Child Aggression) were significantly correlated with baseline TAB scores from the FICS (r's = .55 and .38, respectively), and predicted posttreatment TAB scores as well. Combining the Observer Impressions data with the baseline TAB scores resulted in the strongest predictor of deviant behavior at posttreatment. A revised version of the Observer Impressions Inventory consisting of 46 items has been shown to contribute significantly to the parental ''inept discipline'' construct described by Patterson and Bank (1986).

Each of the coding systems described above was developed for use in clinical research to provide a rigorous assessment of interactions between conduct-disordered children and their parents. The use of these systems in general clinical practice is desirable but rare. To obtain data on conduct-disordered behavior and antecedent and consequent events, the coding systems are, of necessity, complex. Partially as a result of their complexity, the time to train and maintain adequate levels of reliability by independent observers is lengthy. For example, most investigators (e.g., Forehand & McMahon, 1981; Reid, 1978) report a minimum of 20 hours of training prior to the start of observations and weekly 1-hour training sessions during the collection of observations. Weinrott and Jones (1984) report that the FICS requires approximately 60 hours of training.

In addition to training time, the observations themselves require a certain amount of time and flexibility. With the FICS there are six to ten 1-hour preintervention observations, two 1-hour observations during treatment, and eighteen 1-hour observations spread over the year following termination (Patterson et al., 1973). Home observations take place in the evening, just before dinner, so that the likelihood that the entire family will be present is maximized. Observations with the Forehand coding system occur in blocks of four 40-minute observations prior to treatment, immediately after treatment, and at various follow-up intervals. As noted above, observations are planned to coincide with the times when the problem child behaviors are more likely to occur, and thus requires more flexibility in the observers' schedules.

As is evident from the preceding discussion, few clinical settings have the resources to provide such extensive assessment. In general, we recommend the use of structured clinical observations to assess parent–child interactions. If there is a discrepancy between the clinic observations and the parent reports of interactions at home, home observations are necessary.

OBSERVATION IN THE SCHOOL. Direct observations in the school have the same practical problems as those previously mentioned for home observations. The necessity of training reliable observers and the lengthy observation time are similar. Unfortunately, unlike the case with home observation, the therapist does not have the option of observing teacher–child interactions in the clinic. Therefore, if the presenting problems concern behavior at school (whether in the classroom or on the play-

ground), observation in that setting is usually necessary.

As with teacher interviews, the therapist must first obtain the permission of the parents, the principal, and the teacher(s) before scheduling the observations. As with home observations, behavior observations in the classroom should be timed so as to occur when the problem interactions are most frequent. For example, if the teacher reports that the child is particularly disruptive during seat work in the morning, the observation should take place during that period, not during reading class in the afternoon.

In contrast to the clinic and home settings, behavioral observation systems designed specifically for assessing conduct-disordered types of behavior in the school setting have received relatively little attention. Both Patterson's group's and Forehand's systems, originally developed for use in the home and/or clinic, have been adapted for use in the school (Breiner & Forehand, 1981; Harris et al., 1977; Patterson et al., 1973). Harris has adapted the FICS to the school setting and has used it to assess cross-situational consistency in aggressive and prosocial boys in the classroom and on the playground (Harris, 1979, 1980; Harris et al., 1977; Harris & Reid, 1981). Her adaptation includes 22 categories of behavior, 9 of which comprise a Total Deviant composite score. Harris and Reid (1981) reported average interobserver agreements of 93% in the classroom and 86% on the playground. Breiner and Forehand (1981) modified the Forehand et al. (1978) coding system for use in the classroom setting. Interobserver agreement figures were 80% or higher for each teacher and child behavior. Wahler's group's coding system was originally developed for use in both the home and the school, although it does not appear to have been used extensively in the latter setting. Snyder and Brown (1983) did employ the SOC in a preschool setting to assess the environmental correlates of child noncompliance and oppositional behavior. Adoption of these coding systems has the advantage of facilitating cross-situational (home–school) comparisons during assessment of treatment outcome (Ciminero & Drabman, 1977).

A fourth coding system, developed by Cobb and Hops (1972), has been designed specifically for the acting-out child in the classroom. With this coding system, the behaviors of teachers and peers that precede and follow the conduct-disordered child's behavior are recorded, thus providing a sequential pattern identifying the antecedent and consequent events of the conduct-disordered child's behavior. There are 37 different behavioral categories, which can be grouped under eight headings: approvals and disapprovals, attention and looking at, management questions, talk academic, commands, disruption and inappropriate locale, physical negative and punishment, and miscellaneous. The coding manual by Cobb and Hops (1972) provides definitions and examples for each of the 37 categories. Using a modified form of the coding system that included 19 categories, Walker and Hops (1976) reported interobserver agreement reliabilities above 95%. Furthermore, the system discriminated between teacher-referred behavior problem children and their classroom peers in terms of appropriate behavior, and was sensitive to classroom intervention procedures.

Unfortunately, none of these observational systems have received extensive use, nor do they appear to have undergone rigorous evaluation of their psychometric properties. A possible exception is the recent appearance of the Direct Observation Form (DOF) of the CBCL (Reed & Edelbrock, 1983), which consists of 96 behavior problem items and a measure of on-task behavior. There is a high degree of overlap between the items on the DOF and the teacher (86 common items) and parent (73 common items) forms of the CBCL (see below). Six 10-minute observations of the child on different days and at different times of the day are collected. The child is observed for 10 minutes, during which the observer writes a narrative description of the child's behavior. At the end of each minute, the child is observed for 5 seconds, and the presence or absence of on-task behavior is recorded. At the end of the observation, the observer then completes the DOF. Each item is rated on a 4-point scale, with higher ratings indicative of greater intensity and/or duration. Thus, the DOF yields a total behavior problem score and a measure of on-task behavior. Reed and Edelbrock (1983) have reported acceptable levels of interobserver agreement for these two measures as well as for individual items on the DOF. The DOF scores are also correlated with corresponding teacher ratings on the Teacher Report Form of the CBCL, and they discriminate between referred and nonreferred children in the classroom. A newly available Profile for the DOF yields On-Task, Internalizing, Externalizing,

and Total Problem scores as well as scores for six narrow-band problem scales.

The DOF of the CBCL obviously requires additional investigation before it can be strongly recommended. To date, it has only been employed in a classroom setting, although it presumably could be used in the home as well. A limiting factor is that the DOF does not assess teacher behavior or aspects of the teacher–child interaction. However, considering the high level of methodological sophistication that has been involved in the development and evaluation of the parent and teacher versions of the CBCL and the results of the initial classroom investigation, it will probably become an important tool for the assessment of conduct-disordered children in the classroom and, perhaps, in home and clinic settings. That it is part of a behavioral assessment package including parent, teacher, and youth ratings adds to its attractiveness.

OBSERVATION BY SIGNIFICANT ADULTS. An alternative to observations by independent observers in the natural setting is to train significant adults in the child's environment to observe and record certain types of child behavior. Patterson (Patterson et al., 1975), Forehand (Forehand & McMahon, 1981; Furey & Forehand, 1983), and Wahler (Wahler et al., 1976) report the use of parents and/or teachers as observers in addition to the use of independent observers in the natural setting.

The Parent Daily Report (PDR; Chamberlain & Reid, 1987; Patterson et al., 1975) is a parent observation measure that is typically administered during brief (5 to 10-minute) telephone interviews. Developed in 1969, it exists in several forms. In the version reported by Patterson et al. (1975), the PDR consists of 31 deviant child behaviors. Parents are asked whether any of the behaviors have occurred in the past 24 hours, and if so, in which setting (home, school, community, other). In the version reported by Chamberlain and Reid (1987), the PDR consists of 33 deviant child behaviors and a single item referring to whether the parent has spanked the child in the past 24 hours. The setting in which the behavior occurs is not recorded in this version. Two scores are derived from the PDR: (1) Targeted Behaviors, which is the sum of all occurrences of behaviors targeted as problematic by parents at the initial interview; and (2) Total Behaviors, which is the sum of all occurrences of the total list of behaviors (Chamberlain & Reid, 1987).

The PDR is employed on a pretreatment basis

to assess the magnitude of behavior problems and as a check on information presented by the parents in the initial interview. It is also used during therapy to monitor the progress of the family. Finally, the PDR has been employed extensively as a measure of treatment outcome by Patterson and his colleagues (e.g., Patterson, 1974) and others (e.g., Webster-Stratton, 1984).

Reviews of the psychometric characteristics of the PDR are presented by Patterson (1982) and Chamberlain and Reid (1987); the latter have also reported normative data on the measure. The PDR possesses adequate intercaller and interparent reliability, as well as internal consistency and temporal stability. With respect to the latter, Chamberlain and Reid (1987) noted that, at least with nonreferred families, PDR scores tend to be inflated on the first day, but stable thereafter. This suggests that clinicians may wish to discard data from the first telephone interview with the PDR.

The PDR has been shown to correlate significantly with Patterson's FICS in populations of socially aggressive, stealing, and normal children (Patterson, 1982). However, as noted above, there is less correspondence between individual behaviors noted on the PDR and the FICS. Although the PDR has proven quite sensitive to treatment effects, Patterson (1982) has suggested that it is highly reactive in this regard, at least when compared to observational data gathered by independent observers. The PDR also converges with three of the five factors from the Becker Bipolar Adjective Checklist (Aggression, Conduct Problems, and Relaxed Disposition) (Chamberlain & Reid, 1987). These investigators also reported that social desirability factors seem to exert minimal influence on PDR scores, at least with nonreferred families.

Normative data on both PDR scores are presented in Chamberlain and Reid (1987) for parents of children aged 4–10. The mean daily number of problem behaviors reported for the PDR Targeted Behavior and PDR Total Behavior scores is 2.29 and 5.33, respectively. The PDR Targeted Behavior score is a more useful measure than the PDR Total Behavior score, since only the former score has adequate interparent reliability and concurrent validity with the FICS (Chamberlain & Reid, 1987).

A revised version of the PDR has been developed recently by Patterson and his colleagues for the longitudinal investigation of conduct-disordered children and their families mentioned above (see Patterson & Bank, 1986). Parents are asked whether they have disciplined the child in the past 24 hours for each of 15 overt and 8 covert conduct-disordered behaviors. If so, they are asked to describe the discipline procedures. This version of the PDR also includes sections on parental monitoring of the child, positive reinforcement directed to the child, and the occurrence of crises and social support.

A parallel form of the PDR for children has also been developed for use in this longitudinal study. The child is asked whether he or she has engaged in any of various overt and covert conduct-disordered behaviors, the state of his or her mood, and whether the parents have engaged in any of several monitoring behaviors (e.g., talk about the child's activities). Because both of these observational instruments are relatively new, data concerning their psychometric characteristics are limited. However, they do represent potential advances, in that areas other than child behavior per se are assessed (e.g., parental monitoring and discipline) and the child is being included as an informant.

With Forehand's parent observation procedure (Forehand & McMahon, 1981), parents select 3 problem behaviors from a list of 11 at the initial interview. These behaviors are as follows: whine, physical negative, humiliate, destructiveness, tease, smart talk, noncompliance, ignore, yell, demand attention, and temper tantrum. These behaviors were identified by Adkins and Johnson (1972) as aversive child behaviors, based on parental ratings and parental consequences applied to the behaviors. Parents are required to record the frequency of each of the three selected problem behaviors during the 24 hours preceding four home observations both before and after treatment. The independent observers collect the parent-recorded data at the end of each 24-hour period when they visit the home for observations. No reliability data have been reported. Furthermore, Forehand et al. (1979) reported that the parent-recorded data during the 24-hour period did not correlate significantly with observer measures of child compliance and child deviant behavior during a subsequent 40-minute observation, suggesting that the two methods of data collection may yield different conclusions.

A measure similar to the PDR, but which is not administered over the telephone and which includes prosocial as well as deviant behaviors, has been developed by Furey and Forehand (1983). Designed for parents of 2 to 8-year-old children, the Daily Child Behavior Checklist (DCBC) contains 28 displeasing (e.g., "nagged parent to play with them") and 37 pleasing (e.g., "slept through the night") behaviors. The items were derived from various behavior rating scales and from interviews with parents. Parents note the occurrence–nonoccurrence of each behavior on a daily basis for the preceding 24-hour period and whether its occurrence was pleasing or displeasing. Three scores are derived from the DCBC: the number of pleasing and displeasing behaviors, and a total score derived by subtracting the number of displeasing behaviors from the pleasing behaviors. Preliminary psychometric data presented by Furey and Forehand (1983, 1984) suggest that the DCBC warrants further investigation as a parent observation measure.

With the observation procedure described by Wahler et al. (1976), the adult (parent or teacher) records, at most, 2 of the 19 child behavior categories, and he or she also records the instructional and attention categories for the adult's own behavior. Wahler et al. report data to indicate that teachers can accurately record a child's conduct-disordered behavior in the classroom. No data are reported concerning the reliability of the teacher's recording of his or her own behavior.

Kubany and Sloggett (1973) developed a simple but reliable procedure for classroom teachers to estimate the amount of on-task, passive, and disruptive behaviors in which particular students are engaging. Recordings are made on either a 4-, 8-, or 16-minute variable interval schedule. A kitchen timer is used to signal recording times.

With certain low-rate behaviors, such as stealing, fire setting, and truancy, parent- and/or teacher-collected data may be the only sources of information on the occurrence of these behaviors. The coding procedure for teachers developed by Kubany and Sloggett (1973) described above can also be modified to record low-rate behaviors in the classroom. The teacher simply notes whether the behavior occurred at any time during the interval. Patterson and his colleagues (e.g., Patterson et al., 1975) have developed specific techniques for the assessment and treatment of children who steal. Because behaviors such as stealing are rarely observed, the target behavior is redefined as "the child's taking, or being in possession of, any-

thing that does not clearly belong to him" or the parent's "receiving a report or complaint by a reliable informant" (Patterson et al., 1975, p. 137). Jones (1974) reports the development of a brief daily interview similar to the PDR for collecting data on the occurrence–nonoccurrence of stealing by children between the ages of 5 and 15. The parent is queried as to whether stealing took place, and, if so, the item(s) stolen and their value, the location and social context of the theft, how the parent learned of the theft, and the parent's response to the theft. This Telephone Interview Report on Stealing and Social Aggression has adequate test–retest reliability and is sensitive to the effects of treatment procedures designed to reduce stealing (Reid, Hinojosa-Rivera, & Lorber, 1980).

SUMMARY. In summary, behavioral observation is, to date, the most reliable and valid assessment procedure for obtaining a functional analysis of conduct disorders in children. Unfortunately, it is also the most costly in terms of therapist time. As a result, efforts are being made to develop alternative observational procedures that are more efficient but that maintain or enhance the quality of the information obtained. For example, audiotape recording equipment has been employed in the home to collect observation data in several investigations (e.g., Christensen, Johnson, Phillips, & Glasgow, 1980; Johnson & Bolstad, 1975). An audiotape recording system developed by Christensen (1979) utilizes microphones placed unobtrusively in areas where interaction among family members is likely to occur on a frequent basis (e.g., the eating area). This approach to gathering observational data appears to generate minimal reactivity (Christensen & Hazzard, 1983), although savings in time are less clear, since the observational data must still be transcribed from the audiotapes.

Other investigators have focused their energies on the development of observational methods that are more feasible for practitioners in clinical settings. Budd and Fabry (1984) have designed an observation system, consisting of five brief structured activities, that assesses specific sets of child management techniques commonly employed with conduct-disordered children (e.g., giving instructions, differential attention). The activities can be used as general treatment outcome measures or used to monitor progress within a treatment session. Other researchers have focused on the assessment of parent and child behavior in different settings in the home and/or community. Sanders and Christensen (1983) have developed an observational methodology in which parent and child behaviors are observed in five home settings (mealtimes, getting ready for school, bathtime, bedtime, and structured play activity). Mc-Isaac, Hutchinson, and Roberts (1984) have recently attempted to develop clinic-based analogues for the assessment of two commonly reported problematic settings: when the parent is busy with his or her own activities and does not wish to be interrupted by the child, and during shopping trips.

Additional Child Characteristics

In earlier sections of this chapter, we have discussed various child attributes that, in at least some cases, are associated with conduct disorders such as medical difficulties, temperamental variables, specific behavior disorders such as ADD/H and depression, and academic and peer relationship problems. In this section, we briefly discuss the assessment of these factors.

Developmental/Medical History

Usually as part of the initial behavioral interview with the parents, a brief developmental and medical history of the child should be obtained. The purpose of this line of questioning with parents of conduct-disordered children is to determine whether there appear to be any medical factors that may be associated with either the development or maintenance of the conduct-disordered behavior (e.g., past or current evidence of neurological injury or disease, hearing difficulties, extended or frequent hospitalizations). The interview should cover difficulties during pregnancy, birth, and early childhood; ages at which developmental milestones such as sitting, standing, walking, and talking were reached; medical (especially neurological), speech, and hearing problems; and the presence–absence of various toileting problems. If the therapist suspects any of these problems, an appropriate referral (e.g., physician, audiologist) may need to be made prior to, or concomitant with, intervention.

Temperament

The most widely recognized classification of temperament comes from the New York Lon-gitudinal Survey (e.g., Thomas & Chess, 1977; Thomas et al., 1968), which identified nine dimensions of temperament: activity level, rhythmicity (regularity of sleeping, eating, etc.), approach to or withdrawal from new stimuli, adaptability to new situations, intensity of reaction, threshold of responsiveness, quality of mood, distractibility, and attention span. The therapist may choose to query the parents on these dimensions in the context of the developmental interview mentioned above, or temperament may be assessed in a more formal manner. A number of standardized parent interviews (e.g., Thomas & Chess, 1977) and questionnaires exist for assessing temperament; however, they present difficulties in terms of lengthy administration and scoring procedures and/or problems with respect to the adequacy of their psychometric properties (see Vaughn, Bradley, Joffe, Seifer, & Barglow, 1987). For example, the parent-completed questionnaires for children of different ages developed by Carey and his associates have been recommended as the instruments of choice for assessing temperament (Plomin, 1983). However, both the original and revised forms of the Infant Temperament Questionnaire (Carey, 1970; Carey & McDevitt, 1978) have recently been shown to lack discriminant validity (Vaughn et al., 1987). Although the questionnaires for 3-to 7-year old (Behavioral Style Questionnaire; McDevitt & Carey, 1978) and 8- to 12-year old children (Middle Childhood Temperament Questionnaire; Hegvik, McDevitt, & Carey, 1982) were not examined by Vaughn et al., if therapists do use these measures, they should be interpreted with caution. It is also worth noting that some of the subscales of the Child domain on the Parenting Stress Index (Abidin, 1983; see below) seem to tap into the dimensions of temperament listed above. Given that the Parenting Stress Index assesses other types of stressors as well, clinicians might find this instrument of greater utility. It should be noted that to our knowledge, none of these measures have been employed with conduct-disordered samples of children.

Other Behavior Disorders and Problems

As noted earlier, conduct disordered children may also present with problems related to ADD/H and/or depression. Behavioral rating scales that provide information about a wide range of narrow-band behavior disorders such as the CBCL (Achenbach & Edelbrock, 1983) can serve as a useful screening device. If there are significant elevations on the relevant scales of the CBCL, then a more thorough assessment of these disorders will need to be conducted. Information on the behavioral assessment of ADD/H and depression may be found in the chapters in this volume by Barkley and Kazdin, respectively.

As noted above, conduct-disordered children also have problems with peer interactions. If the information from behavioral interviews, questionnaires (e.g., the Social Competence scales of the CBCL; Achenbach & Edelbrock, 1983), and observations indicates that this is a problem area for a particular child, additional assessment of the child's social skills is necessary. The assessment should examine not only the behavioral aspects of the social skills difficulties, but cognitive and affective dimensions as well. Traditionally, assessment of social skills has involved behavioral observations, sociometric measures, and questionnaires. Hops and Greenwood (1988) provide strategies for the assessment of social skills.

If the presenting problem concerns classroom behavior, a functional analysis of the problem behaviors should also include an assessment of the child's academic behavior. Although interviews, observations, and rating scales can provide information concerning the child's academic behavior, additional evaluation in the form of intelligence and achievement tests is necessary to determine whether the child has learning difficulties in addition to his or her conduct disorder problems. Taylor (see Chapter 8, this volume) provides a complete review of assessment strategies with which to evaluate learning problems.

Familial and Extrafamilial Factors

In this section, we discuss the assessment of five familial and extrafamilial areas that are relevant to the assessment of conduct-disordered children: parent and teacher perceptions of child adjustment; parents' perceptions of their own personal and marital adjustment; parental stress; parental functioning in extrafamilial social contexts; and parental satisfaction with treatment.

Perceptions of Child Adjustment

As noted above, parents' perception of a child, rather than the child's behavior per se, is the best predictor of referral for conduct-disordered types of behavior. An analogous situation probably holds true in the classroom situation with teachers. Therefore, some measure of significant adults' perceptions of the child is an essential component of the assessment process. The behavioral rating scales described above are the most ready sources of such data. When examined in the context of behavioral observation data and the therapist's own impressions, these behavioral rating scales can be important indicators as to whether the informants (parents, teachers) appear to have a perceptual bias in their assessment of the referred child's behavior.

An alternative methodology for assessing potential perceptual biases in the parents of conduct-disordered children is the use of brief written scenarios or vignettes describing parent–child interactions in which a child displays a variety of inappropriate, neutral, and positive behaviors (Holleran et al., 1982; Middlebrook & Forehand, 1985). As noted above, findings from these investigations suggest that parents of conduct-disordered children are more likely to perceive neutral child behaviors as inappropriate. Audiotaped and videotaped analogues of parent–child interaction have been developed for assessing potential perceptual biases with physically abusive mothers (e.g., Bauer & Twentyman, 1985; Wolfe & LaRose, 1985). These methods have yet to be employed with the parents of conduct-disordered children.

Parental Personal and Marital Adjustment

Exposition and discussion of the various parental personal (e.g., depression, anxiety, substance abuse) and marital adjustment problems that may occur in parents of conduct-disordered children is beyond the scope of this chapter. Instead, a set of brief screening procedures is needed to ascertain whether a more complete and thorough assessment for a particular problem or group of problems is required. Questions related to these issues can best be incorporated into the initial interview with the parents. In some cases, the child can also be asked for his or her perceptions as well (e.g., "Does your dad ever seem to have too much to drink?" "How do your mom and dad get along with each other?"). In conjunction with the judicious use of the various self-report measures described below, the therapist should be able to make a decision as to the necessity of pursuing any of these areas in greater detail. Should that be the case, then excellent guidelines for conducting behavioral assessments for these types of problems are presented in Hersen and Bellack (1981).

With respect to the personal adjustment of the parents of children with conduct disorders, depression, particularly maternal depression, has received the most attention because of its theoretical (Patterson, 1982) and empirical (e.g., Forehand, Furey, & McMahon, 1984) relevance. The Beck Depression Inventory (BDI; Beck, Rush, Shaw, & Emery, 1980) has been the most frequently employed measure. The BDI consists of 21 items, each of which is scored on a 4-point scale, with higher scores indicating greater depression. The following cutoff points have been delineated: 0–9, no depression or minimal depression; 10–14, borderline depression; 15–20, mild depression; 21–30 moderate depression; 31–40, severe depression; 41–63, very severe depression.

Psychometric data on the BDI with various populations are quite extensive and are not reviewed here; suffice it to say that adequate reliability and validity have been established. For example, scores on the BDI correlate significantly with clinicians' ratings of depression (Metcalfe & Goldman, 1965) and with objective behavioral measures of depression (Williams, Barlow, & Agras, 1972). The BDI differentiates mothers of clinic-referred conduct disordered and nonreferred children (e.g., Griest et al., 1980), and, relative to other types of measures (e.g., behavioral observations of child behavior), has been found to be the best predictor of maternal perceptions of clinic-referred conduct-disordered children (Forehand et al., 1982; Griest et al., 1979). It has been shown to change in a positive direction following completion of a parent training program (Forehand et al., 1980), and to predict dropouts from treatment as well (McMahon, Forehand, Griest, & Wells, 1981).

A measure that has been employed to assess daily fluctuations in the mood state of mothers of conduct-disordered children is Lubin's (1967) Depression Adjective Check Lists (DACL).

Patterson (1982, 1983) has found mothers' depressed mood to be associated with maternal reports of higher frequencies of daily crises, and inversely associated with positive social contacts outside the family. However, these relationships occurred only for three of the five mothers in the sample.

It should be noted that neither the BDI nor the DACL is intended as an instrument for diagnosing depression; rather, the former is a measure of the severity of various depressive symptoms (particularly cognitive symptoms), and the latter is a measure of mood (Rehm, 1981). When employed with parents of conduct-disordered children, they are probably best regarded as indicators of parental personal *distress*, rather than depression per se. Patterson's (1976, 1980, 1982) data indicating that mothers of conduct-disordered children demonstrate elevations on most of the clinical scales of the Minnesota Multiphasic Personality Inventory compared to mothers of nonreferred children is consistent with this idea. Given the high intercorrelations of depression with measures of anxiety (e.g., the State–Trait Anxiety Inventory; Spielberger, Gorsuch, & Lushene, 1970), marital adjustment, and insularity, a similar conclusion might be drawn concerning these other measures as well (Forehand et al., 1984).

With respect to marital adjustment, two questionnaires have been used in much of the clinical research on marital discord: Locke's Marital Adjustment Test (MAT; Locke & Wallace, 1959) and the Dyadic Adjustment Scale (DAS; Spanier, 1976). The MAT is a reliable instrument that has been shown to discriminate between distressed and nondistressed couples (Locke & Wallace, 1959) and to predict rates of positive and negative interactional behaviors between spouses in the home (Wills, Weiss, & Patterson, 1974). A modified form of the MAT yields scores that are stable over an extended period of time (i.e., $2\frac{1}{4}$ years; Kimmel & van der Veen, 1974). The modified version of the questionnaire (presented in Kimmel & van der Veen, 1974) consists of 23 weighted items. Higher scores on the questionnaire indicate a greater degree of marital satisfaction. The following means and standard deviations were obtained for a sample of 149 wives and 157 husbands: wives, $M = 108.40$, $SD = 16.32$; husbands, $M = 110.22$, $SD = 16.28$.

In families in which a child has been referred for treatment of conduct-disordered behavior problems, marital distress as measured by the MAT has been found to be associated with deviant child behavior (Johnson & Lobitz, 1974), with self-reports of overt marital hostility (Porter & O'Leary, 1980), and with maternal depression as measured by the BDI (Rickard, Forehand, Atkeson, & Lopez, 1982). A composite measure of marital adjustment that included the MAT successfully discriminated the parents of aggressive boys from the parents of nonaggressive boys (Loeber & Dishion, 1984). The parents of boys who fought at home and at school experienced greater marital conflict than the parents of boys who fought in only one of the settings.

A factor analysis of the MAT by Kimmel and van der Veen (1974) yielded two factors, which they labeled Sexual Congeniality and Compatibility. The Compatibility factor was negatively correlated with a measure of the child's aggressive behavior in nonreferred families (Kimmel, 1970, cited in Kimmel & van der Veen, 1974). However, a recent investigation with clinic-referred families failed to find any relationship between two measures of child behavior (compliance, deviant behavior) and the Compatibility factor of the MAT (Schaughency, Middlebrook, Forehand, & Lahey, 1984). Schaughency et al. did find that child compliance was inversely related to the Sexual Congeniality factor of the MAT and that mothers of clinic-referred children whose behavior was not deviant had significantly lower scores on this factor than did mothers of clinic-referred children whose behavior was deviant. The authors concluded that low sexual congeniality may be an aspect of parental distress that contributes to inappropriate parent referrals for child treatment.

The DAS (Spanier, 1976) is a 32-item self-report inventory that contains four empirically validated subscales of marital adjustment: Dyadic Consensus (spouses' agreement regarding various marital issues), Dyadic Cohesion (extent to which partners involve themselves in joint activities), Dyadic Satisfaction (overall evaluation of the marital relationship and level of commitment to the relationship), and Affectional Expression (degree of affection and sexual involvement in the relationship). Spanier (1976) has reported adequate internal-consistency reliability figures for the total scale (.96) and for each of the subscales (.73–.94). The DAS is composed primarily of items from other marital adjustment scales, and thus has a high degree of content validity. The total score and each item have been shown to discriminate married from divorced individuals. The DAS correlates .93 with the Locke and Wallace (1959) version of the MAT (Spanier, 1976), and is positively correlated with positive interactions between spouses in the home (Robinson & Anderson, 1983). Robinson and Anderson did find the DAS to be moderately influenced by social desirability in a sample of nonreferred families.

In collecting normative data for this scale, Spanier (1976) reported a mean score of 114.8 and a standard deviation of 17.8 for a sample of 218 married couples. On the basis of these data, Jacobson and Anderson (1980) have suggested that a cutoff score of 97, which corresponds to one standard deviation below the mean of Spanier's (1976) normative sample, be used to classify individuals as maritally distressed. The mean of Spanier's normative sample (115) would seem to be a conservative cutoff score for maritally nondistressed couples. However, Bond and McMahon (1984) adopted a score of 107 as a cutoff for classifying mothers as maritally nondistressed, based on the mean score of 107.34 obtained by Houseknecht (1979) for a sample of 50 mothers.

Finally, the O'Leary–Porter Scale (Porter & O'Leary, 1980), which is a nine-item parent-completed questionnaire designed to assess the frequency of various forms of overt marital hostility (e.g., quarrels, sarcasm, and physical abuse) that are witnessed by the child, can also be administered. There is some evidence that this scale is more strongly associated with various scales of Quay's (1977) BPC (including Conduct Problem and Socialized Delinquency) than is the MAT, at least for clinic-referred boys (Porter & O'Leary, 1980).

Parental Stress

Patterson (1982, 1983) has hypothesized that minor day-to-day hassles (as well as major crises such as divorce, unemployment, etc.) can alter the parent–child interaction and can ultimately lead to conduct-disordered behavior in the child. Preliminary data on a small number of families have provided some support for this notion, in that daily fluctuations in the frequency of mother-reported crises are associated with maternal aversive behavior directed toward a child (Patterson, 1982, 1983). As noted above, high levels of maternal stress seem to be associated with maternal perceptual biases, such that mothers are more likely to perceive neutral child behavior as deviant in high-stress than in low-stress situations (Middlebrook & Forehand, 1985).

The Oregon Social Learning Center's (OSLC) Family Crisis List (Patterson, 1982) consists of 78 items related to a variety of stressful events in the areas of the family (e.g., argument with spouse), household and transportation (e.g., check bounced), economic (e.g., received unexpected bill), health (e.g., someone in the family is ill), school (e.g., child skipped school), social interchange (e.g., child had a serious disagreement with a neighbor or friend), and legal (e.g., policeman came to the door). The parent is asked to note which of the crises have occurred in the past 7 days. Patterson (1983) has recently revised and extended this measure. It now consists of 101 items that are rated for intensity and valence on a 7-point scale. Both the mother and father complete the checklist and note crises that have occurred over the past 24 hours. They complete the measure on 3 separate days. To date, neither form of the OSLC Family Crisis List has received adequate psychometric evaluation. Nonetheless, it might prove useful as a screening instrument to assist the therapist in noting parental perceptions of the frequency, intensity, and valence of various family-related stressors.

An alternative instrument that does have a reasonable psychometric foundation is the Parenting Stress Index (PSI; Abidin, 1983; Loyd & Abidin, 1985). The PSI is designed as a screening instrument for assessing relative levels of stress in the parent–child system. In its most recent revision, it consists of 101 items tapping into two major domains of stressors. Those in the Child domain concern the child's adaptability, reinforcing qualities, demandingness, activity level, mood, and acceptability to the parent. The Parent domain includes scales related to depression, attachment to the child, spousal and social system support, parental health, perceived restrictions of role, and the parent's sense of competence. Because the PSI defines stressors very broadly, and includes subscales of dimensions that are clearly related to conduct-disordered children and their families (e.g., child temperament, parental depression, extrafamilial social support), it may prove to be quite useful. However, to our knowledge, the PSI has not been employed specifically with

the families of conduct-disordered children. It has been used with mothers of hyperactive children (e.g., Mash & Johnston, 1983) and physically abused children (Mash, Johnston, & Kovitz, 1983).

Extrafamilial Functioning

As noted above, there is increasing recognition of the importance of assessing the extrafamilial functioning of parents of conduct-disordered children. The Community Interaction Checklist (CIC; Wahler, Leske, & Rogers, 1979), a brief interview designed to assess maternal insularity, is the only measure of its type to have been employed with conduct-disordered children and their families. Therefore, it is described here in some detail. The mother is asked to recall extrafamily contacts over the previous 24 hours. The number of contacts is recorded, as well as the identity of the contact person (e.g., friend, relative, helping agency representative), who initiated the contact, the duration of the contact and the distance from home, and the perceived valence of the contact (positive, negative, neutral). The CIC is usually administered by the observer after each home observation. Thus, multiple administrations of the CIC is the norm. Mothers are categorized as insular if they report at least twice as many daily contacts with relatives and/or helping agency representatives as with friends, and if at least one-third of the daily contacts are reported as neutral or aversive (Dumas & Wahler, 1983, 1985).

Because of the nature of the CIC, interobserver agreement figures are not available. However, internal consistency reliabilities of .79 or higher have been reported (e.g., Dumas & Wahler, 1983, 1985). Mothers characterized as insular on the CIC are more aversive and indiscriminate in the use of aversive consequences with their children than are noninsular mothers, and the children of insular mothers are more aversive (Dumas & Wahler, 1985). Coercive exchanges between insular mothers and their children are of longer duration than those involving noninsular mother–child dyads (Wahler, Hughey, & Gordon, 1981). Aversive maternal contacts with adults as measured on the CIC are associated with aversive maternal behavior directed toward the children on the same day (Wahler, 1980; Wahler & Graves, 1983). Finally, classification as insular on the CIC is a strong predictor of poor maintenance of the effects of parent training interventions for conduct-disordered children (Dumas & Wahler, 1983; Wahler, 1980; Wahler & Afton, 1980). Insular mothers had a success rate of approximately 50% in maintaining positive effects from parent training over a 1-year period (Dumas & Wahler, 1983). None of the mothers who were both insular and socioeconomically disadvantaged had a favorable outcome over the 1-year period.

Parental Satisfaction with Treatment

Within the past decade, behavior therapists have recognized the importance of social validity— that is, the necessity of demonstrating that therapeutic changes are "clinically or socially important to the client" (Kazdin, 1977, p. 429). One type of social validity is consumer satisfaction with the outcome of treatment (Wolf, 1978). Several authors (e.g., Margolis, Sorenson, & Galano, 1977; Yates, 1978) have suggested that consumer satisfaction with a particular treatment strategy or an entire treatment approach is likely to be a factor in the ultimate effectiveness of the intervention. In a recent review of consumer satisfaction with child behavior therapy, we (McMahon & Forehand, 1983) delineated four areas in which consumer satisfaction should be assessed: treatment outcome, therapists, treatment procedures, and teaching format. We found that the majority of studies have focused on adult participants in treatment (usually parents involved in parent training interventions for the treatment of conduct-disordered children, although teachers have occasionally been assessed). However, the children themselves have rarely been asked to evaluate their satisfaction with treatment, probably because of the difficulty in developing appropriate measures for children of various ages.

At present, there is no single consumer satisfaction measure that is appropriate for use with all types of interventions for conduct-disordered children and their families. However, a measure that we developed to assess parental satisfaction with a parent training program designed to modify child noncompliance and other conduct-disordered behaviors (Forehand & McMahon, 1981) is briefly described. The Parents' Consumer Satisfaction Questionnaire (PCSQ; McMahon, Tiedemann, Forehand, & Griest, 1984) assesses parental satisfaction with the overall program, the teaching format, the specific parenting techniques that

are taught, and the therapists. Items examining both the usefulness and difficulty of the teaching format and specific parenting techniques are included. In all of these areas, parents respond to items on a 7-point Likert-type scale. Parents also have the opportunity to reply to several open-ended questions concerning their reactions to the parenting program. The PCSQ is presented elsewhere (Forehand & McMahon, 1981).

Using the PCSQ, parents have generally reported high absolute levels of satisfaction with the various aspects of the parent training program at both treatment termination and at a 2-month follow-up (McMahon, Forehand, & Griest, 1981; McMahon et al., 1984). The PCSQ also differentiated mothers who participated in the basic parent training program from those who participated in the parent training program and who also received training in social learning principles. The latter group of mothers reported generally higher levels of satisfaction. Using a modified version of the PCSQ, Baum and Forehand (1981) found that parental satisfaction was maintained 1 to $4\frac{1}{2}$ years after treatment termination. Finally, Webster-Stratton (1984) reported similarly positive ratings of satisfaction from mothers of conduct-disordered children at posttreatment and at a 1-year follow-up, regardless of whether they participated in a videotape-based parent training program or in a more typical individual consultation form of parent training.

CONCLUSIONS

In this chapter, we have described characteristics of conduct-disordered children and their families, summarized current formulations of the development of conduct disorders, and detailed a variety of methods for assessing three important areas: child behavior per se and in an interactional context; other child characteristics; and familial and extrafamilial factors. The methods described include interviews with parents, teachers, and children; behavioral questionnaires of various types to assess adult perceptions of a child's adjustment, parental personal and marital adjustment, parental functioning outside the family, and satisfaction with treatment; and behavioral observations in the clinic, home, and school settings. As we have stressed throughout this chapter, a proper assessment of a conduct-disordered child must make use of multiple methods (e.g., behavioral rating scales, observation) completed by multiple informants (e.g., parents, teachers) concerning the child's behavior in multiple settings (e.g., home, school). Furthermore, it is essential that the familial and extrafamilial contexts in which the conduct-disordered child functions be assessed as well. Such comprehensive assessments are truly necessary, because current data indicate that the selection of treatment and the prognosis for these children are tied to the severity, duration, and pervasiveness of the conduct disorders (Loeber, 1982), as well as the extent to which familial and extrafamilial problems may be present.

With respect to this last point, behavior therapists have only recently acknowledged the importance of dealing with familial and extrafamilial factors (Griest & Wells, 1983; Wahler, 1980). At present, the methods being utilized to assess factors such as parental depression, marital adjustment, and insularity in the families of conduct-disordered children have, for the most part, been restricted to parental self-reports. Current investigations by Hops and his colleagues at the Oregon Research Institute (e.g., Biglan, Hops, & Sherman, in press), employing sophisticated observational methodology to assess familial interactions with depressed mothers, may prove quite useful in elaborating the role that this aspect of parental adjustment plays in the development and maintenance of conduct disorders in children. It is essential to establish whether other methods that have been developed to assess these areas of functioning provide equally useful or better data at a reasonable cost.

There is a growing awareness among behavior therapists of the need for conducting assessments that adequately incorporate multiple assessment procedures and deal with the interrelationships among these procedures (Achenbach & Edelbrock, 1984; Mash, 1985). This is especially important for behavior therapists working with conduct-disordered children. At present, however, most of the research has focused on the psychometric acceptability of single measures in assessing conduct-disordered children and their families. (In fact, much more work is needed in this area as well.) Reid *et al.* (1985) have suggested the use of a ''multiple-gating'' approach to the use of observational methods as a means of employing multiple assessment measures in a cost-effective

manner. In this approach, less costly assessment procedures (e.g., interviews, behavioral rating scales) would be employed as screening instruments with all children who are clinic-referred for the treatment of conduct disorders. More expensive assessment methods, such as observations in the home or school, would be used to assess only that subgroup of children for whom the less expensive methods have indicated the desirability of further assessment. An analogous procedure could be applied in the assessment of other child characteristics and familial and extrafamilial factors, in that low-cost methods such as interview questions (e.g., concerning the child's early temperament) and/or brief questionnaires (e.g., the BDI) would be employed as screening measures. Should additional assessment in these various areas be indicated, then a more through (and expensive) assessment (e.g., one employing observational procedures and/or structured interviews) could be conducted.

A few investigators have described preliminary formulations for matching clinic-referred families with specific interventions, including those applicable to conduct disorders (Blechman, 1981; Embry, 1984). However, the utility of these algorithms awaits empirical validation. It may even be premature at this point to develop such prescriptive instruments until we have a broader data base concerning the interrelationships among the various methods for assessing conduct-disordered children and their families.

In our view, the behavioral assessment of conduct-disordered children has come a long way since the first edition of this volume appeared in 1981. Not only have the nature of individual behaviors composing the conduct disorder dimension and their interrelationships been examined more thoroughly, there has also been an increased emphasis on the developmental, familial, and broader ecological contexts in which those behaviors are embedded. In essence, there is a greater awareness of the diversity of conduct-disordered children and of the fact that multiple causal and maintaining factors must be considered in behavioral assessment. This awareness has been translated into a greater appreciation for the importance of multimethod, multi-informant, and multi-setting assessment. While our knowledge of how best to assess conduct-disordered children is by no means complete, researchers and clinicians working with these children have reason to view the developments described in this chapter as clear-cut advances.

Acknowledgments

Preparation of this chapter was supported in part by Grant No. 410-84-1340 from the Social Sciences and Humanities Research Council of Canada. We would like to thank Elizabeth McCririck, Holly Austin, and Kimmy Chiu for their assistance in the preparation of the manuscript.

REFERENCES

Abidin, R. R. (1983). *Parenting Stress Index–Manual.* Charlottesville, VA: Pediatric Psychology Press.

Achenbach, T. M. (1985). Behavior disorders of childhood: Diagnosis and assessment, taxonomy and taxometry. In R. J. McMahon & R. DeV. Peters (Eds.), *Childhood disorders: Behavioral–developmental approaches* (pp. 55–89). New York: Brunner/Mazel.

Achenbach, T. M., & Edelbrock, C. S. (1978). The classification of child psychopathology: A review and analysis of empirical efforts. *Psychological Bulletin, 85,* 1275–1301.

Achenbach, T. M., & Edelbrock, C. S. (1981). Behavioral problems and competencies reported by parents of normal and disturbed children aged four through sixteen. *Monographs of the Society for Research in Child Development, 46*(1, Serial No. 188).

Achenbach, T. M., & Edelbrock, C. S. (1983). *Manual for the Child Behavior Checklist and Revised Child Behavior Profile.* Burlington: University of Vermont, Department of Psychiatry.

Achenbach, T. M., & Edelbrock, C. S. (1984). Psychopathology of childhood. *Annual Review of Psychology, 35,* 227–56.

Adkins, D. A., & Johnson, S. M. (1972, April). *What behaviors may be called deviant for children? A comparison of two approaches to behavior classification.* Paper presented at the meeting of the Western Psychological Association, Portland, OR.

American Psychiatric Association. (1980). *Diagnostic and statistical manual of mental disorders* (3rd ed.). Washington, DC: Author.

American Psychiatric Association. (1987). *Diagnostic and statistical manual of mental disorders* (3rd ed.–revised). Washington, DC: Author.

Aragona, J. A., & Eyberg, S. M. (1981). Neglected children: Mother's report of child behavior problems and observed verbal behavior. *Child Development, 52,* 596–602.

Asarnow, J. R., & Callan, J. W. (1985). Boys with peer adjustment problems: Social cognitive processes. *Journal of Consulting and Clinical Psychology, 53,* 80–87.

Atkeson, B. M., & Forehand, R. (1978). Parent behavioral training for problem children: An examination of studies using multiple outcome measures. *Journal of Abnormal Child Psychology, 6,* 449–460.

Barkley, R. A. (1981). *Hyperactive children: A handbook for diagnosis and treatment.* New York: Guilford Press.

Barkley, R. A. (1984). *A review of child behavior rating scales and checklists for research in child psychopathology.* Rockville, MD: Center for Studies of Child and Adolescent Psychopathology, Clinical Research Branch, National Institute of Mental Health.

Bauer, W. D., & Twentyman, C. T. (1985). Abusing, neglectful, and comparison mothers' responses to child-related and non-child-related stressors. *Journal of Consulting and Clinical Psychology, 53,* 335–343.

Baum, C. G., & Forehand, R. (1981). Long-term follow-up assessment of parent training by use of multiple-outcome measures. *Behavior Therapy, 12,* 643–652.

Beck, A. T., Rush, A. J., Shaw, B. F., & Emery, G. (1980). *Cognitive therapy of depression.* New York: Guilford Press.

Bierman, K. L. (1983). Cognitive development and clinical interviews with children. In B. B. Lahey & A. E. Kazdin (Eds.), *Advances in clinical child psychology* (Vol. 6, pp. 217–250). New York: Plenum.

Biglan, A., Hops, H., & Sherman, L. (in press). Coercive family processes and maternal depression. In R. DeV. Peters & R. J. McMahon (Eds.), *Social learning and systems approaches to marriage and the family.* New York: Brunner/Mazel.

Blechman, E. A. (1981). Toward comprehensive behavioral family intervention: An algorithm for matching families and interventions. *Behavior Modification, 5,* 221–236.

Bolstad, O. D., & Johnson, S. M. (1977). The relationship between teachers' assessment of students and the students' actual behavior in the classroom. *Child Development, 48,* 570–578.

Bond, C. R., & McMahon, R. J. (1984). Relationships between marital distress and child behavioral problems, maternal personal adjustment, maternal personality, and maternal parenting behavior. *Journal of Abnormal Psychology, 93,* 348–351.

Breiner, J. L., & Forehand, R. (1981). An assessment of the effects of parent training on clinic-referred children's school behavior. *Behavioral Assessment, 3,* 31–42.

Brody, G., & Forehand, R. (1986). Maternal perceptions of child maladjustment as a function of the combined influence of child behavior and maternal depression. *Journal of Consulting and Clinical Psychology, 54,* 237–240.

Budd, K. S., & Fabry, P. L. (1984). Behavioral assessment in applied parent training: Use of a structured observation system. In R. F. Dangel & R. A. Polster (Eds.), *Parent training: Foundations of research and practice* (pp. 417–442). New York: Guilford Press.

Cadoret, R. J. (1978). Psychopathology in adopted-away offspring of biologic parents with antisocial behavior. *Archives of General Psychiatry, 35,* 176–184.

Cadoret, R. J., Cain, C. A., & Crowe, R. R. (1983). Evidence for gene–environment interaction in the development of adolescent antisocial behavior. *Behavior Genetics, 13,* 301–310.

Carey, W. B. (1970). A simplified method for measuring infant temperament. *Journal of Pediatrics, 77,* 188–194.

Carey, W. B., & McDevitt, S. C. (1978). *Infant Temperament Questionnaire (Revised).* Unpublished instrument, copyright by the authors. (Available from W. B. Carey, 31 Front Street, Media, PA 19063).

Carlson, W. J., Williams, W. B., & Davol, H. (1984). A factor structure of child home observation data. *Journal of Abnormal Child Psychology, 12,* 245–260.

Casey, R. J., & Berman, J. S. (1985). The outcome of psychotherapy with children. *Psychological Bulletin, 98,* 388–400.

Cautela, J. R., Cautela, J., & Esonis, S. (1983). *Forms*

for behavior analysis with children. Champaign, IL: Research Press.

Chamberlain, P., & Reid, J. B. (1987). Parent observation and report of child symptoms. *Behavioral Assessment, 9*, 97–109.

Chiles, A., Miller, M. L., & Cox, G. B. (1980). Depression in an adolescent delinquent population. *Archives of General Psychiatry, 37*, 1179–1184.

Christensen, A. (1979). Naturalistic observation of families: A system for random audio recordings in the home. *Behavior Therapy, 10*, 418–422.

Christensen, A., & Hazzard, A. (1983). Reactive effects during naturalistic observation of families. *Behavioral Assessment, 5*, 349–362.

Christensen, A., Johnson, S. M., Phillips, S., & Glasgow, R. E. (1980). Cost effectiveness in behavioral family therapy. *Behavior Therapy, 11*, 208–226.

Ciminero, A. R., & Drabman, R. S. (1977). Current developments in the behavioral assessment of children. In B. B. Lahey & A. E. Kazdin (Eds.), *Advances in clinical child psychology* (Vol. 1, pp. 47–82). New York: Plenum.

Cloninger, C. R., Reich, T., & Guze, S. G. (1978). Genetic–environmental interactions and antisocial behavior. In R. D. Hare & D. Schalling (Eds.), *Psychopathic behavior: Approaches to research* (pp. 225–237). New York: Wiley.

Cobb, J. A., & Hops, H. (1972). *Coding manual for continuous observation of interactions by single subjects in an academic setting* (Report No. 9). Eugene: University of Oregon, Center at Oregon for Research in the Behavioral Education of the Handicapped.

Conners, C. K. (1969). A teacher rating scale for use in drug studies with children. *American Journal of Psychiatry, 126*, 884–888.

Conners, C. K. (1970). Symptom patterns in hyperkinetic, neurotic, and normal children. *Child Development, 41*, 667–682.

Conners, C. K. (1973). Rating scales for use in drug studies with children. *Psychopharmacology Bulletin, 9*, 24–84.

Conners, C. K., & Werry, J. S. (1979). Pharmacotherapy. In H. C. Quay & J. S. Werry (Eds.), *Psychopathological disorders of childhood* (2nd ed., pp. 336–386). New York: Wiley.

Costello, A. J., Edelbrock, C. S., Dulcan, M. K., & Kalas, R. (1984). *Testing of the NIMH Diagnostic Interview Schedule for Children (DISC) in a clinical population* (Contract No. DB-81-0027, final report to the Center for Epidemiological Studies, National Institute for Mental Health). Pittsburgh: University of Pittsburgh.

Cowen, E. L., Huser, J., Beach, D. R., & Rappaport, J. (1970). Parental perceptions of young children and their relation to indexes of adjustment. *Journal of Consulting and Clinical Psychology, 34*, 97–103.

Delfini, L. F., Bernal, M. E., & Rosen, P. M. (1976). Comparison of deviant and normal boys in home settings. In E. J. Mash, L. A. Hamerlynck, & L. C. Handy (Eds.), *Behavior modification and families* (pp. 228–248). New York: Brunner/Mazel.

Deluty, R. H. (1981). Alternative-thinking ability of aggressive, assertive, and submissive children. *Cognitive Therapy and Research, 5*, 309–312.

Deluty, R. H. (1983). Children's evaluations of aggressive, assertive, and submissive responses. *Journal of Clinical Child Psychology, 12*, 124–129.

Dishion, T., Gardner, K., Patterson, G., Reid, J., Spyrou, S., & Thibodeaux, S. (1984). *The Family Process Code: A multidimensional system for observing family interactions* (Oregon Social Learning Center Technical Report). (Available from Oregon Social Learning Center, 207 E. 5th Avenue, Suite 202, Eugene, OR 97401)

Dishion, T. J., Loeber, R., Stouthamer-Loeber, M., & Patterson, G. R. (1984). Skill deficits and male adolescent delinquency. *Journal of Abnormal Child Psychology, 12*, 37–54.

Dodge, K. A. (1980). Social cognition and children's aggressive behavior. *Child Development, 51*, 162–170.

Dodge, K. A., & Frame, C. L. (1982). Social cognitive biases and deficits in aggressive boys. *Child Development, 53*, 620–635.

Dumas, J. E., & Wahler, R. G. (1983). Predictors of treatment outcome in parent training: Mother insularity and socioeconomic disadvantage. *Behavioral Assessment, 5*, 301–313.

Dumas, J. E., & Wahler, R. G. (1985). Indiscriminate mothering as a contextual factor in aggressive–oppositional child behavior: "Damned if you do and damned if you don't." *Journal of Abnormal Child Psychology, 13*, 1–17.

Edelbrock, C. (1985). *Conduct problems in childhood and adolescence: Developmental patterns and progressions.* Unpublished manuscript.

Edelbrock, C. S., & Achenbach, T. M. (1984). The Teacher Version of the Child Behavior Profile: I. Boys aged 6–11. *Journal of Consulting and Clinical Psychology, 52*, 207–217.

Edelbrock, C., & Costello, A. J. (1984). *A review of structured psychiatric interviews for children.* Rockville, MD: Center for Studies of Child and Adolescent Psychopathology, Clinical Research Branch, National Institute of Mental Health.

Edelbrock, C., Costello, A. J., Dulcan, M. K., Kalas, D., & Conover, N. (1985). Age differences in the reliability of the psychiatric interview of the child. *Child Development, 56*, 265–275.

Edelbrock, C., Costello, A. J., & Kessler, M. D. (1984). Empirical corroboration of attention deficit disorder. *Journal of the American Academy of Child Psychiatry, 23*, 285–290.

Edelbrock, C., Greenbaum, R., & Conover, N. C. (1985). Reliability and concurrent relations between the Teacher Version of the Child Behavior Profile and the Conners Revised Teacher Rating Scale. *Journal of Abnormal Child Psychology, 13*, 295–303.

Ellis, P. L. (1982). Empathy: A factor in antisocial behavior. *Journal of Abnormal Child Psychology, 10*, 123–133.

Embry, L. H. (1984). What to do? Matching client characteristics and intervention techniques through a prescriptive taxonomic key. In R. F. Dangel & R. A. Polster (Eds.), *Parent training: Foundations of research and practice* (pp. 443–473). New York: Guilford Press.

Eyberg, S. M. (1980). Eyberg Child Behavior Inventory. *Journal of Clinical Child Psychology, 9*, 29.

Eyberg, S. M. & Johnson, S. M. (1974). Multiple assessment of behavior modification with families: Effects of contingency contracting and order of treated problems. *Journal of Consulting and Clinical Psychology, 42*, 594–606.

Eyberg, S. M., & Matarazzo, R. G. (1980). Training parents as therapists: A comparison between individual parent–child interaction training and parent group didactic training. *Journal of Clinical Psychology, 36,* 492–499.

Eyberg, S. M., & Robinson, E. A. (1982). Parent–child interaction training: Effects on family functioning. *Journal of Clinical Child Psychology, 11,* 130–137.

Eyberg, S. M., & Robinson, E. A. (1983a). Conduct problem behavior: Standardization of a behavioral rating scale with adolescents. *Journal of Clinical Child Psychology, 12,* 347–357.

Eyberg, S. M., & Robinson, E. A. (1983b). Dyadic Parent–Child Interaction Coding System: A manual. *Psychological Documents, 13.* (Ms. No. 2582)

Eyberg, S. M., & Ross, A. W. (1978). Assessment of child behavior problems: The validation of a new inventory. *Journal of Clinical Child Psychology, 7,* 113–116.

Forehand, R., & Brody, G. (1985). The association between parental personal/marital adjustment and parent–child interactions in a clinic sample. *Behaviour Research and Therapy, 23,* 211–212.

Forehand, R., Furey, W. M., & McMahon, R. J. (1984). The role of maternal distress in a parent training program to modify child non-compliance. *Behavioural Psychotherapy, 12,* 93–108.

Forehand, R., Griest, D., & Wells, K. C. (1979). Parent behavioral training: An analysis of the relationship among multiple outcome measures. *Journal of Abnormal Child Psychology, 7,* 229–242.

Forehand, R., King, H. E., Peed, S., & Yoder, P. (1975). Mother–child interactions: Comparison of a non-compliant clinic group and a nonclinic group. *Behaviour Research and Therapy, 13,* 79–84.

Forehand, R., Lautenschlager, G. J., Faust, J., & Graziano, W. G. (1986). Parent perceptions and parent–child interactions in clinic-referred children: A preliminary investigation of the effects of maternal depressive moods. *Behaviour Research and Therapy, 24,* 73–75.

Forehand, R., & McMahon, R. J. (1981). *Helping the noncompliant child: A clinician's guide to parent training.* New York: Guilford Press,

Forehand, R., & Peed, S. (1979). Training parents to modify noncompliant behavior of their children. In A. J. Finch, Jr., & P. C. Kendall (Eds.), *Treatment and research in child psychopathology* (pp. 159–184). New York: Spectrum.

Forehand, R., Peed, S., Roberts, M., McMahon, R., Griest, D., & Humphreys L. (1978). *Coding manual for scoring mother–child interaction* (3rd ed.). Unpublished manuscript, University of Georgia.

Forehand, R., Wells, K. C., & Griest, D. L. (1980). An examination of the social validity of a parent training program. *Behavior Therapy, 11,* 488–502.

Forehand, R., Wells, K. C., McMahon, R. J., Griest, D. L., & Rogers, T. (1982). Maternal perceptions of maladjustment in clinic-referred children: An extension of earlier research. *Journal of Behavioral Assessment, 4,* 145–151.

Forehand, R., Wells, K. C., & Sturgis, E. T. (1978). Predictors of child noncompliant behavior in the home. *Journal of Consulting and Clinical Psychology, 46,* 179.

Furey, W., & Forehand, R. (1983). The Daily Child Behavior Checklist. *Journal of Behavioral Assessment, 5,* 83–95.

Furey, W. M., & Forehand, R. (1984). An examination of predictors of mothers' perceptions of satisfaction with their children. *Journal of Social and Clinical Psychology, 2,* 230–243.

Furey, W. M., & Forehand, R. (1986). What factors are associated with mothers' evaluations of their clinic-referred children? *Child and Family Behavior Therapy, 8,* 21–42.

Goldsmith, H. H., Buss, A. H., Plomin, R., Rothbart, M. K., Thomas, A., Chess, S., Hinde, R. A., & McCall, R. B. (1987). Roundtable: What is temperament? Four approaches, *Child Development, 58,* 505–529.

Goyette, C. H., Conners, C. K., & Ulrich, R. F. (1978). Normative data on revised Conners Parent and Teacher Rating Scales. *Journal of Abnormal Child Psychology, 6,* 221–236.

Green, K. D., Beck, S. J., Forehand, R., & Vosk, B. (1980). Validity of teacher nominations of child behavior problems. *Journal of Abnormal Child Psychology,* 397–404.

Green, K. D., Forehand, R., & McMahon, R. J. (1979). Parental manipulation of compliance and noncompliance in normal and deviant children. *Behavior Modification, 3,* 245–266.

Griest, D. L., Forehand, R., Wells, K. C., & McMahon, R. J. (1980). An examination of differences between nonclinic and behavior-problem clinic-referred children and their mothers. *Journal of Abnormal Psychology, 89,* 497–500.

Griest, D. L., & Wells, K. C. (1983). Behavioral family therapy with conduct disorders in children. *Behavior Therapy, 14,* 37–53.

Griest, D. L., Wells, K. C., & Forehand, R. (1979). An examination of predictors of maternal perceptions of maladjustment in clinic-referred children. *Journal of Abnormal Psychology, 88,* 277–281.

Gross, A. M. (1983). Conduct disorders, In M. Hersen (Ed.), *Outpatient behavior therapy: A clinical guide* (pp. 307–332). New York: Grune & Stratton.

Hanf, C. (1970). *Shaping mothers to shape their children's behavior.* Unpublished manuscript, University of Oregon Medical School.

Harris, A. (1979). An empirical test of the situation specificity/consistency of aggressive behavior. *Child Behavior Therapy, 1,* 257–270.

Harris, A. (1980). Response class: A Guttman scale analysis. *Journal of Abnormal Child Psychology, 8,* 213–220.

Harris, A., Kreil, D., & Orpet, R. (1977). The modification and validation of the Behavior Coding System for school settings. *Educational and Psychological Measurement, 37,* 1121–1126.

Harris, A., & Reid, J. B. (1981). The consistency of a class of coercive child behaviors across school settings for individual subjects. *Journal of Abnormal Child Psychology, 9,* 219–227.

Hegvik, R. L., McDevitt, S. C., & Carey, W. B. (1982). Middle Childhood Temperament Questionnaire. *Developmental and Behavioral Pediatrics, 3,* 199–200.

Herjanic, B., & Reich, W. (1982). Development of a structured psychiatric interview for children: Agreement between child and parent on individual symptoms. *Journal of Abnormal Child Psychology, 10,* 307–324.

Hersen, M., & Bellack, A. S. (Eds.). (1981). *Behavioral assessment: A practical handbook* (2nd ed.). New York: Pergamon Press.

Hoffman, D. A., Fagot, B. I., Reid, J. B., & Patterson, G. R. (1987). Parents rate the Family Interaction Coding System: Comparisons of problem and nonproblem boys using parent-derived behavior composites. *Behavioral Assessment, 9,* 31–40.

Holland, C. J. (1970). An interview guide for behavioral counseling with parents. *Behavior Therapy, 1,* 70–79.

Holleran, P. A., Littman, D. C., Freund, R. D., & Schmaling, K. B. (1982). A signal detection approach to social perception: Identification of negative and positive behaviors by parents of normal and problem children. *Journal of Abnormal Child Psychology, 10,* 547–558.

Hops, H., & Greenwood, C. R. (1988). Social skills deficits. In E. J. Mash & L. G. Terdal (Eds.), *Behavioral assessment of childhood disorders* (2nd ed., unabridged, pp. 263–315). New York: Guilford Press.

Houseknecht, S. K. (1979). Childlessness and marital adjustment. *Journal of Marriage and the Family, 41,* 259–265.

Hughes, H. M., & Haynes, S. N. (1978). Structured laboratory observation in the behavioral assessment of parent–child interactions: A methodological critique. *Behavior Therapy, 9,* 428–447.

Jacob, T., Grounds, L., & Haley, R. (1982). Correspondence between parents' reports on the Behavior Problem Checklist. *Journal of Abnormal Child Psychology, 10,* 593–608.

Jacobson, N. S., & Anderson, E. A. (1980). The effects of behavior rehearsal and feedback on the acquisition of problem-solving skills in distressed and non-distressed couples. *Behaviour Research and Therapy, 18,* 25–36.

Jary, M. L., & Stewart, M. A. (1985). Psychiatric disorder in the parents of adopted children with aggressive conduct disorder. *Neuropsychobiology, 13,* 7–11.

Johnson, S. M., & Bolstad, O. D. (1975). Reactivity to home observations: A comparison of audio recorded behaviors with observers present or absent. *Journal of Applied Behavior Analysis, 8,* 181–185.

Johnson, S. M., & Lobitz, G. K. (1974). The personal and marital adjustment of parents as related to observed child deviance and parenting behaviors. *Journal of Abnormal Child Psychology, 2,* 193–207.

Jones, R. R. (1974). *"Observation" by telephone: An economical behavior sampling technique (Oregon Research Institute Technical Report No. 14*[1]). Eugene: Oregon Research Institute.

Kazdin, A. E. (1977). Assessing the clinical or applied importance of behavior change through social validation. *Behavior Modification, 1,* 427–452.

Kazdin, A. E. (1985). *Treatment of antisocial behavior in children and adolescents.* Homewood, IL: Dorsey Press.

Kazdin, A. E., Esveldt-Dawson, K., Unis, A. S., & Rancurello, M. D. (1983). Child and parent evaluations of depression and aggression in psychiatric inpatient children. *Journal of Abnormal Child Psychology, 11,* 401–413.

Kazdin, A. E., & Heidish, I. E. (1984). Convergence of clinically derived diagnoses and parent checklists among inpatient children. *Journal of Abnormal Child Psychology, 12,* 421–436.

Kimmel, D. C., & van der Veen, F. (1974). Factors of marital adjustment in Locke's Marital Adjustment Test. *Journal of Marriage and the Family, 36,* 57–63.

Kniskern, J. R., Robinson, E. A., & Mitchell, S. K. (1983). Mother–child interaction in the home and laboratory setting. *Child Study Journal, 13,* 23–29.

Kolko, D. J., Kazdin, A. E., & Meyer, E. C. (1985). Aggression and psychopathology in childhood fireset-ters: Parent and child reports. *Journal of Consulting and Clinical Psychology, 53,* 377–385.

Kolvin, I., Nicol, A. R., Garside, R. F., Day, K. A., & Tweddle, E. G. (1982). Temperamental patterns in aggressive boys. In R. Porter & G. M. Collins (Eds.), *Temperamental differences in infants and young children* (Ciba Foundation Symposium No. 89, pp. 252–255). London: Pitman.

Kovacs, M., Feinberg, T. L., Crouse-Novak, M. A., Paulauskas, S. L., & Finkelstein, R. (1984). Depressive disorders in childhood: I. A longitudinal prospective study of characteristics and recovery. *Archives of General Psychiatry, 41,* 229–237.

Kubany, E. S., & Sloggett, B. B. (1973). Coding procedure for teachers. *Journal of Applied Behavior Analysis, 6,* 339–344.

Ledingham, J. E., Younger, A., Schwartzman, A., & Bergeron, G. (1982). Agreement among teacher, peer, and self-ratings of children's aggression, withdrawal, and likeability. *Journal of Abnormal Child Psychology, 10,* 363–372.

Lewis, D. O., Pincus, J. H., Shanok, S. S., & Glaser, G. H. (1982). Psychomotor epilepsy and violence in a group of incarcerated adolescent boys. *American Journal of Psychiatry, 139,* 882–887.

Lobitz, G. K., & Johnson, S. M. (1975). Normal versus deviant children: A multimethod comparison. *Journal of Abnormal Child Psychology, 3,* 353–374.

Locke, H. J., & Wallace, K. M. (1959). Short marital-adjustment and prediction tests: Their reliability and validity. *Marriage and Family Living, 21,* 251–255.

Loeber, R. (1982). The stability of antisocial and delinquent child behavior: A review. *Child Development, 53,* 1431–1446.

Loeber, R. (1985, November). The selection of target behaviors for modification in the treatment of conduct disordered children: Caretaker's preferences, key-stone behaviors, and stepping stones. In B. B. Lahey (Chair), *Selection of targets for intervention for children with conduct disorder and ADD/hyperactivity.* Symposium conducted at the meeting of the Association for Advancement of Behavior Therapy, Houston.

Loeber, R., & Dishion, T. J. (1984). Boys who fight at home and school: Family conditions influencing cross-setting consistency. *Journal of Consulting and Clinical Psychology, 52,* 759–768.

Loeber, R., & Schmaling, K. B. (1985a). Empirical evidence for overt and covert patterns of antisocial conduct problems: A meta-analysis. *Journal of Abnormal Child Psychology, 13,* 337–352.

Loeber, R., & Schmaling, K. B. (1985b). The utility of differentiating between mixed and pure forms of antisocial child behavior. *Journal of Abnormal Child Psychology, 13,* 315–336.

Loney, J., & Milich, R. S. (1982). Hyperactivity, inattention, and aggression in clinical practice. In M. Wolraich & D. K. Routh (Eds.), *Advances in developmental and behavioral pediatrics* (Vol. 2, pp. 113–147). Greenwich, CT: JAI Press.

Lorber, R., & Patterson, G. R. (1981). The aggressive child: A concomitant of a coercive system. In J. P. Vincent (Ed.), *Advances in family intervention, assessment and theory* (Vol. 2, pp. 47–87). Greenwich, CT: JAI Press.

Loyd, B. H., & Abidin, R. R. (1985). Revision of the Parenting Stress Index. *Journal of Pediatric Psychology, 10,* 169–177.

Lubin, B. (1967). *Manual for the Depression Adjective Check Lists*. San Diego: Educational and Industrial Testing Service.

MacFarlane, J., Allen, L., & Honzik, M. (1954). *A developmental study of the behavior problems of normal children between 21 months and 14 years*. Berkeley: University of California Press.

Margolis, R. B., Sorenson, J. L., & Galano, J. (1977). Consumer satisfaction in mental health delivery services. *Professional Psychology, 8*, 11–16.

Mash, E. J. (1985). Some comments on target selection in behavior therapy. *Behavioral Assessment, 7*, 49–64.

Mash, E. J., & Johnston, C. (1983). Sibling interactions of hyperactive and normal children and their relationship to reports of maternal stress and self-esteem. *Journal of Clinical Child Psychology, 12*, 91–99.

Mash, E. J., Johnston, C., & Kovitz, K. (1983). A comparison of the mother–child interactions of physically abused and non-abused children during play and task situations. *Journal of Clinical Child Psychology, 12*, 337–346.

Mattison, R., Cantwell, D. P., Russell, A. T., & Will, L. (1979). A comparison of DSM-II and DSM-III in the diagnosis of childhood psychiatric disorders. *Archives of General Psychiatry, 36*, 1217–1222.

McDevitt, S. C., & Carey, W. B. (1978). The measurement of temperament in 3–7 year old children. *Journal of Child Psychology and Psychiatry, 19*, 245–253.

McIsaac, L., Hutchinson, B., & Roberts, M. (1984, November). *An empirical evaluation of two clinic analogs for preschool children: The "mother-busy" and "store" situations*. Paper presented at the meeting of the Association for Advancement of Behavior Therapy, Philadelphia.

McMahon, R. J., (1984). Behavioral checklists and rating scales. In T. H. Ollendick & M. Hersen (Eds.), *Child behavioral assessment: Principles and procedures* (pp. 80–105). New York: Pergamon Press.

McMahon, R. J., & Forehand, R. (1983). Consumer satisfaction in behavioral treatment of children: Types issues, and recommendations. *Behavior Therapy, 14*, 209–225.

McMahon, R. J., & Forehand, R. (1984). Parent training for the noncompliant child: Treatment outcome, generalization, and adjunctive therapy procedures. In R. F. Dangel & R. A. Polster (Eds.), *Parent training: Foundations of research and practice* (pp. 298–328). New York: Guilford Press.

McMahon, R. J., Forehand, R., & Griest, D. L. (1981). Effects of knowledge of social learning principles on enhancing treatment outcome and generalization in a parent training program. *Journal of Consulting and Clinical Psychology, 49*, 526–532.

McMahon, R. J., Forehand, R., Griest, D. L., & Wells, K. C. (1981). Who drops out of treatment during parent behavioral training? *Behavioral Counseling Quarterly, 1*, 79–85.

McMahon, R. J., Tiedemann, G. L., Forehand, R., & Griest, D. L. (1984). Parental satisfaction with parent training to modify child noncompliance. *Behavior Therapy, 15*, 295–303.

Metcalfe, M., & Goldman, E. (1965). Validation of an inventory for measuring depression. *British Journal of Psychiatry, 111*, 240–242.

Middlebrook, J. L., & Forehand, R. (1985). Maternal perceptions of deviance in child behavior as a function of stress and clinic versus nonclinic status of the child: An analogue study. *Behavior Therapy, 16*, 494–502.

Milich, R., & Dodge, K. A. (1984). Social information processing in child psychiatric populations. *Journal of Abnormal Child Psychology, 12*, 471–490.

Milich, R., & Fitzgerald, G. (1985). Validation of inattention/overactivity and aggression ratings with classroom observations. *Journal of Consulting and Clinical Psychology, 1985, 53*, 139–140.

Milich, R., Landau, S., Kilby, G., & Whitten, P. (1982). Preschool peer perceptions of the behavior of hyperactive and aggressive children. *Journal of Abnormal Child Psychology, 10*, 497–510.

Moore, D. R. (1975). *Determinants of deviancy: A behavioral comparison of normal and deviant children in multiple settings*. Unpublished manuscript, University of Tennessee.

Moore, D. R., Chamberlain, P., & Mukai, L. (1979). Children at risk for delinquency: A follow-up comparison of aggressive children and children who steal. *Journal of Abnormal Child Psychology, 7*, 345–355.

Moore, D. R., & Mukai, L. H. (1983). Aggressive behavior in the home as a function of the age and sex of control-problem and normal children. *Journal of Abnormal Child Psychology, 11*, 257–272.

Murphy, D. A., Pelham, W. E., & Milich, R. S. (1985, November). *Normative and validity data on the Iowa Conners Teacher Rating Scale*. Paper presented at the meeting of the Association for Advancement of Behavior Therapy, Houston.

Nasby, W., Hayden, B., & DePaulo, B. M. (1980). Attributional bias among aggressive boys to interpret unambiguous social stimuli as displays of hostility. *Journal of Abnormal Psychology, 89*, 454–468.

O'Leary, K. D., & Emery, R. E. (1984). Marital discord and child behavioral problems. In M. D. Levine & P. Satz (Eds.), *Middle childhood: Development and dysfunction* (pp. 345–364). Baltimore: University Park Press.

O'Leary, S. G., & Pelham, W. E. (1978). Behavior therapy and withdrawal of stimulant medication with hyperactive children. *Pediatrics, 61*, 211–217.

Oltmanns, T. F., Broderick, J. E., & O'Leary, K. D. (1977). Marital adjustment and the efficacy of behavior therapy with children. *Journal of Consulting and Clinical Psychology, 45*, 724–729.

Olweus, D. (1979). Stability of aggressive reaction patterns in males: A review. *Psychological Bulletin, 86*, 852–857.

Olweus, D. (1980). Familial and temperamental determinants of aggressive behavior in adolescent boys: A causal analysis. *Developmental Psychology, 16*, 644–660.

Patterson, G. R. (1974). Interventions for boys with conduct problems: Multiple settings, treatments, and criteria. *Journal of Consulting and Clinical Psychology, 42*, 471–781.

Patterson, G. R. (1976). The aggressive child: Victim and architect of a coercive system. In E. J. Mash, L. A. Hamerlynck, & L. C. Handy (Eds.), *Behavior modification and families* (pp. 267–316). New York: Brunner/Mazel.

Patterson, G. R. (1977). Naturalistic observation in clinical assessment. *Journal of Abnormal Child Psychology, 5*, 309–322.

Patterson, G. R. (1980). Mothers: The unacknowledged victims. *Monographs of the Society for Research in Child Development, 45* (5, Serial No. 186).

Patterson, G. R. (1982). *Coercive family process*. Eugene, OR: Castalia.

Patterson, G. R. (1983). Stress: A change agent for family process. In N. Garmezy & M. Rutter (Eds.), *Stress, coping and development in children* (pp. 235–262). New York: McGraw-Hill.

Patterson, G. R., & Bank, L. (1986). Bootstrapping your way in the nomological thicket. *Behavioral Assessment, 8,* 49–73.

Patterson, G. R., Cobb, J. A., & Ray, R. S. (1973). A social engineering technology for retraining the families of aggressive boys. In H. Adams & L. Unikel (Eds.), *Issues and trends in behavior therapy* (pp. 139–224). Springfield, IL: Charles C Thomas.

Patterson, G. R., & Dishion, T. J. (1985). Contributions of families and peers to delinquency. *Criminology, 23,* 63–79.

Patterson, G. R., & Fagot, B. I. (1967). Selective responses to social reinforcers and deviant behavior in children. *Psychological Record, 17,* 369–378.

Patterson, G. R., & Fleischman, M. J. (1979). Maintenance of treatment effects: Some considerations concerning family systems and follow-up data. *Behavior Therapy, 10,* 168–185.

Patterson, G. R., Ray, R. S., Shaw, D. A., & Cobb, J. A. (1969). *Manual for coding of family interactions* (rev. ed.). New York: Microfiche Publications.

Patterson, G. R., & Reid, J. B. (1973). Intervention for families of aggressive boys: A replication study. *Behaviour Research and Therapy, 11,* 383–394.

Patterson, G. R., Reid, J. B., Jones, R. R., & Conger, R. E. (1975). *A social learning approach to family intervention. Families with aggressive children* (Vol. 1). Eugene, OR: Castalia.

Patterson, G. R., & Stouthamer-Loeber, M. (1984). The correlation of family management practices and delinquency. *Child Development, 55,* 1299–1307.

Peed, S., Roberts, M., & Forehand, R. (1977). Evaluation of the effectiveness of a standardized parent training program in altering the interaction of mothers and their noncompliant children. *Behavior Modification, 1,* 323–350.

Plomin, R. (1981). Heredity and temperament: A comparison of twin data for self-report questionnaires, parental ratings, and objectively assessed behavior. In L. Gedda, P. Parisi, & W. E. Nance (Eds.), *Progress in clinical and biological research: Twin research 3, Part B. Intelligence, personality, and development* (Vol. 69B). New York: Alan R. Liss.

Plomin, R. (1983). Childhood temperament. In B. B. Lahey & A. E. Kazdin (Eds.), *Advances in clinical child psychology* (Vol. 6, pp. 45–92). New York: Plenum.

Porter, B., & O'Leary, K. D. (1980). Marital discord and childhood behavior problems. *Journal of Abnormal Child Psychology, 8,* 287–295.

Puig-Antich, J. (1982). Major depression and conduct disorder in prepuberty. *Journal of the American Academy of Child Psychiatry, 21,* 118–128.

Quay, H. C. (1977). Measuring dimensions of deviant behavior: The Behavior Problem Checklist. *Journal of Abnormal Child Psychology, 5,* 277–287.

Quay, H. C. (1979). Classification. In H. C. Quay & J. S. Werry (Eds.), *Psychopathological disorders of childhood* (2nd ed., pp. 1–42). New York: Wiley.

Quay, H. C., & Peterson, D. R. (1983). *Interim manual for the Revised Behavior Problem Checklist.* Unpublished manuscript, University of Miami.

Reed, M. L., & Edelbrock, C. (1983). Reliability and validity of the Direct Observation Form of the Child Behavior Checklist. *Journal of Abnormal Child Psychology, 11,* 521–530.

Rehm, L. P. (1981). Assessment of depression. In M. Hersen & A. S. Bellack (Eds.), *Behavioral assessment* (2nd ed., pp. 246–295). New York: Pergamon Press.

Reid, J. B. (Ed.). (1978). *A social learning approach to family intervention: Observation in home settings* (Vol. 2). Eugene, OR: Castalia.

Reid, J. B., Baldwin, D. V., Patterson, G. R., & Dishion, T. J. (1985). *Some problems relating to the assessment of childhood disorders: A role for observational data.* Unpublished manuscript, Oregon Social Learning Center, Eugene.

Reid, J. B., & Hendricks, A. F. C. J. (1973). A preliminary analysis of the effectiveness of direct home intervention for treatment of pre-delinquent boys who steal. In L. A. Hamerlynck, L. C. Handy, & E. J. Mash (Eds.), *Behavior change: Methodology, concepts, and practice* (pp. 209–219). Champaign, IL: Research Press.

Reid, J. B., Hinojosa-Rivera, G., & Lorber, R. (1980). *A social learning approach to the outpatient treatment of children who steal.* Unpublished manuscript, Oregon Social Learning Center, Eugene.

Richard, B. A., & Dodge, K. A. (1982). Social maladjustment and problem solving in school-aged children. *Journal of Consulting and Clinical Psychology, 50,* 226–233.

Rickard, K. M., Forehand, R., Atkeson, B. M., & Lopez, C. (1982). An examination of the relationship of marital satisfaction and divorce with parent–child interactions. *Journal of Clinical Child Psychology, 11,* 61–65.

Rickard, K. M., Forehand, R., Wells, K. C., Griest, D. L., & McMahon, R. J. (1981). Factors in the referral of children for behavioral treatment: A comparison of mothers of clinic-referred deviant, clinic-referred nondeviant, and nonclinic children. *Behaviour Research and Therapy, 19,* 201–205.

Robin, A. L. (1981). A controlled evaluation of problem-solving communication training with parent–adolescent conflict. *Behavior Therapy, 12,* 593–609.

Robin, A. L. (1985). Parent–adolescent conflict: A developmental problem of families. In R. J. McMahon & R. DeV. Peters (Eds.), *Childhood disorders: Behavioral–developmental approaches* (pp. 244–265). New York: Brunner/Mazel.

Robin, A. L., & Weiss, J. G. (1980). Criterion-related validity of behavioral and self-report measures of problem-solving communications skills in distressed and non-distressed parent–adolescent dyads. *Behavioral Assessment, 2,* 339–352.

Robins, L. N. (1966). *Deviant children grown up.* Baltimore: Williams & Wilkins.

Robinson, E. A., & Anderson, L. L. (1983). Family adjustment, parental attitudes, and social desirability. *Journal of Abnormal Child Psychology, 11,* 247–256.

Robinson, E. A., & Eyberg, S. M. (1981). The Dyadic Parent–Child Interaction Coding System: Standardization and validation. *Journal of Consulting and Clinical Psychology, 49,* 245–250.

Robinson, E. A., Eyberg, S. M., & Ross, A. W. (1980). The standardization of an inventory of child conduct problem behaviors. *Journal of Clinical Child Psychology, 9,* 22–29.

Rogers, T. R., Forehand, R., & Griest, D. L. (1981). The conduct disordered child: An analysis of family problems. *Clinical Psychology Review, 1,* 139–147.

Russo, D. C., Cataldo, M. F., & Cushing, P. J. (1981).

Compliance training and behavioral covariation in the treatment of multiple behavior problems. *Journal of Applied Behavior Analysis, 14,* 209–222.

Rutter, M. (1970). Sex differences in children's responses to family stress. In E. J. Anthony & C. Koupernik (Eds.), *International yearbook for child psychiatry and allied disciplines: Vol. 1., The child in his family* (pp. 165–196). New York: Wiley.

Rutter, M., Tizard, J., Yule, W., Graham, P., & Whitmore, K. (1976). Research report: Isle of Wight studies, 1964–1974. *Psychological Medicine, 6,* 313–332.

Safer, D. J. (1984). Subgrouping conduct disordered adolescents by early risk factors. *American Journal of Orthopsychiatry, 54,* 603–612.

Safer, D. J., & Allen, R. P. (1976). *Hyperactive children: Diagnosis and management.* Baltimore: University Park Press.

Sanders, M. R., & Christensen, A. P. (1983). *An analysis of children's oppositional behavior and parents' coercive behavior across five parenting environments.* Paper presented at the Sixth National Conference on Behavior Modification, Adelaide, South Australia.

Schaughency, E. A., & Lahey, B. B. (1985). Mothers' and fathers' perceptions of child deviance: Roles of child behavior, parental depression, and marital satisfaction. *Journal of Consulting and Clinical Psychology, 53,* 718–723.

Schaughency, E. A., Middlebrook, J. L., Forehand, R., & Lahey, B. B. (1984, November). *The relationship of separate facets of marital adjustment to child behavior problems.* Paper presented at the meeting of the Association for Advancement of Behavior Therapy, Philadelphia.

Shanok, S. S., & Lewis, D. O. (1981). Medical histories of female delinquents: Clinical and epidemiological findings. *Archives of General Psychiatry, 38,* 211–213.

Snyder, J. (1983). Aversive social stimuli in the Family Interaction Coding System: A validation study. *Behavioral Assessment, 5,* 315–331.

Snyder, J., & Brown, K. (1983). Oppositional behavior and noncompliance in preschool children: Environmental correlates and skills deficits. *Behavioral Assessment, 5,* 333–348.

Spanier, G. B. (1976). Measuring dyadic adjustment: New scales for assessing the quality of marriage and similar dyads. *Journal of Marriage and the Family, 38,* 15–28.

Spielberger, C. D., Gorsuch, R. L., & Lushene, R. E. (1970). *STAI: Manual for the State–Trait Anxiety Inventory.* Palo Alto, CA: Consulting Psychologists Press.

Stewart, M. A., de Blois, S., Meardon, J., & Cummings, C. (1980). Aggressive conduct disorder of children: The clinical picture. *Journal of Nervous and Mental Disease, 168,* 604–610.

Sturge, C. (1982). Reading retardation and antisocial behaviour. *Journal of Child Psychology and Psychiatry, 23,* 21–31.

Taplin, P. S., & Reid, J. B. (1977). Changes in parent consequation as a function of family intervention. *Journal of Consulting and Clinical Psychology, 45,* 973–981.

Thomas, A., & Chess, S. (1977). *Temperament and development.* New York: Brunner/Mazel.

Thomas, A., Chess, S., & Birch, H. G. (1968). *Temperament and behavior disorders in children.* New York: New York University Press.

Twito, T. J., & Stewart, M. A. (1982). A half-sibling study of aggressive conduct disorder: Prevalence of disorders in parents, brothers and sisters. *Neuropsychobiology, 8,* 144–150.

Ullmann, R. K., Sleator, E. K., & Sprague, R. L. (1985). A change of mind: The Conners abbreviated rating scales reconsidered. *Journal of Abnormal Child Psychology, 13,* 553–565.

Vaughn, B. E., Bradley, C. F., Joffe, L. S., Seifer, R., & Barglow, P. (1987). Maternal characteristics measured prenatally are predictive of ratings of temperamental "difficulty" on the Carey Infant Temperament Questionnaire. *Developmental Psychology, 23,* 152–161.

Wahler, R. G. (1969). Oppositional children: A quest for parental reinforcement control. *Journal of Applied Behavior Analysis, 2,* 159–170.

Wahler, R. G. (1980). The insular mother: Her problems in parent–child treatment. *Journal of Applied Behavior Analysis, 13,* 207–219.

Wahler, R. G., & Afton, A. D. (1980). Attentional processes in insular and noninsular mothers. *Child Behavior Therapy, 2*(2), 25–41.

Wahler, R. G., & Cormier, W. H. (1970). The ecological interview: A first step in out-patient child behavior therapy. *Journal of Behavior Therapy and Experimental Psychiatry, 1,* 279–289.

Wahler, R. G., & Dumas, J. E. (1984). Changing the observational coding styles of insular and noninsular mothers: A step toward maintenance of parent training effects. In R. F. Dangel & R. A. Polster (Eds.), *Parent training: Foundations of research and practice* (pp. 379–416). New York: Guilford Press.

Wahler, R. G., & Graves, M. G. (1983). Setting events in social networks: Ally or enemy in child behavior therapy? *Behavior Therapy, 14,* 19–36.

Wahler, R. G., House, A. E., & Stambaugh, E. E. (1976). *Ecological assessment of child problem behavior: A clinical package for home, school, and institutional settings.* New York: Pergamon Press.

Wahler, R. G., Hughey, J. B., & Gordon, J. S. (1981). Chronic patterns of mother–child coercion: Some differences between insular and noninsular families. *Analysis and Intervention in Developmental Disabilities, 1,* 145–156.

Wahler, R. G., Leske, G., & Rogers, E. S. (1979). The insular family: A deviance support system for oppositional children. In L. A. Hamerlynck (Ed.), *Behavioral systems for the developmentally disabled: Vol. 1. School and family environments* (pp. 102–127). New York: Brunner/Mazel.

Walker, H. M., & Hops, H. (1976). Use of normative peer data as a standard for evaluating classroom treatment effects. *Journal of Applied Behavior Analysis, 9,* 159–168.

Webster-Stratton, C. (1984). Randomized trial of two parent-training programs for families with conduct-disordered children. *Journal of Consulting and Clinical Psychology, 52,* 666–678.

Webster-Stratton, C. (1985a). Comparisons of behavior transactions between conduct-disordered children and their mothers in the clinic and at home. *Journal of Abnormal Child Psychology, 13,* 169–184.

Webster-Stratton, C. (1985b). Predictors of treatment outcome in parent training for conduct disordered children. *Behavior Therapy, 16,* 223–242.

Webster-Stratton, C., & Eyberg, S. M. (1982). Child temperament: Relationship with child behavior problems and parent–child interactions. *Journal of Clinical Child Psychology, 11*, 123–129.

Weinrott, M. R., & Jones, R. R. (1984). Overt versus covert assessment of observer reliability. *Child Development, 55*, 1125–1137.

Weinrott, M. R., Reid, J. B., Bauske, R. W., & Brummett, B. (1981). Supplementing naturalistic observations with observer impressions. *Behavioral Assessment, 3*, 151–159.

Weiss, R. L., & Margolin, G. (1977). Assessment of marital conflict and accord. In A. R. Ciminero, K. S. Calhoun, & H. E. Adams (Eds.), *Handbook of behavioral assessment* (pp. 555–602). New York: Wiley.

Wells, K. C., & Forehand, R. (1985). Conduct and oppositional disorders. In P. H. Bornstein & A. E. Kazdin (Eds.), *Handbook of clinical behavior therapy with children* (pp. 218–265). Homewood, IL: Dorsey.

Wells, K. C., Forehand, R., & Griest, D. L. (1980). Generality of treatment effects from treated to untreated behaviors resulting from a parent training program. *Journal of Clinical Child Psychology, 9*, 219–219.

Werry, J. S., Methven, R. J., Fitzpatrick, J., & Dixon, H. (1983). The interrater reliability of DSM-III in children. *Journal of Abnormal Child Psychology, 11*, 341–354.

Werry, J. S., Sprague, R. L., & Cohen, M. N. (1975). Conners Teacher Rating Scale for use in drug studies with children: An empirical study. *Journal of Abnormal Child Psychology, 3*, 217–229.

Williams, J. G., Barlow, D. H., & Agras, W. S. (1972). Behavioral measurement of severe depression. *Archives of General Psychiatry, 27*, 330–333.

Wills, T. A., Weiss, R. L., & Patterson, G. R. (1974). A behavioral analysis of the determinants of marital satisfaction. *Journal of Consulting and Clinical Psychology, 42*, 802–811.

Witt, J. C., & Elliott, S. N. (1985). Acceptability of classroom intervention strategies. In T. R. Kratochwill (Ed.), *Advances in school psychology* (Vol. 4, pp. 251–288). Hillsdale, NJ: Erlbaum.

Wolf, M. M. (1978). Social validity: The case for subjective measurement, or how applied behavior analysis is finding its heart. *Journal of Applied Behavior Analysis, 11*, 203–214.

Wolfe, D. A., & LaRose, L. (1985, November). A video-simulated stress procedure for abusive parents: Multimodal assessment of parental tolerance, arousal, and coping. In J. Lutzker (Chair), *Child abuse and neglect: Treatment, research, and theory.* Symposium conducted at the meeting of the Association for Advancement of Behavior Therapy, Houston.

Wolff, S. (1961). Symptomatology and outcome of preschool children with behaviour disorders attending a child guidance clinic. *Journal of Child Psychology and Psychiatry, 2*, 269–276.

Wolkind, S. N., & De Salis, W. (1982). Infant temperament, maternal mental state, and child behavioural problems. In R. Porter & G. M. Collins (Eds.), *Temperamental differences in infants and young children* (Ciba Foundation Symposium No. 89, pp. 221–233). London: Pitman.

Yarrow, M. R., Campbell, J. D., & Burton, R. V. (1970). Recollections of childhood: A study of the retrospective method. *Monographs of the Society for Research in Child Development, 35*(5).

Yates, B. T. (1978). Improving the cost-effectiveness of obesity programs: Three basic strategies for reducing the cost per pound. *International Journal of Obesity, 2*, 249–266.

Zangwill, W. M., & Kniskern, J. R. (1982). Comparison of problem families in the clinic and at home. *Behavior Therapy, 13*, 145–152.

PART III
EMOTIONAL DISORDERS

4 CHILDHOOD DEPRESSION

ALAN E. KAZDIN
Western Psychiatric Institute and Clinic
University of Pittsburgh School of Medicine

Childhood depression is a major area of research in clinical child psychology and child psychiatry. The current attention can be traced to many influences. First, major advances have been made in the diagnosis, assessment, etiology, and treatment of affective disorders in adults (see Clayton & Barrett, 1983; Depue, 1979; Paykel, 1982a). Findings with adults point to areas of research with children where similar evidence might be obtained on the nature of the dysfunction or where precursors of adult depression might be identified. Second, recent developments in psychiatric diagnosis have facilitated the application of diagnostic criteria to children and adolescents. Criteria for invoking diagnoses have become more explicit and have enhanced research on childhood disorders in general. Third, research and clinical work have advanced because of recent developments in the assessment of childhood depression. The emergence of a number of measures has permitted the scrutiny of depressive symptoms and their correlates in clinic and nonclinic populations.

The present chapter reviews and evaluates current techniques of assessing childhood depression. Alternative techniques are illustrated. Issues and limitations of current measurement strategies are also presented. Several central topics are covered as well, including the emergence of childhood depression as an area of research, characteristics of depression in childhood and adolescence, current diagnostic criteria, developmental considerations, and etiological models of depression.

ASSUMPTIONS ABOUT CHILDHOOD DEPRESSION

Although advances have been made in the investigation of childhood depression, research has lagged well behind the advances made in the study of depression in adults. The delay in studying depression in children is not entirely unique to this disorder. In general, assessment, diagnosis, and treatment for children have been less well studied than they have for adults. Assumptions about the nature of depression in children have also been responsible for the delay. Doubts have been expressed whether depression is manifested in children, and if so, the form(s) that it may take. Although no one has ever doubted that children can experience sad affect, views have varied regarding whether children can suffer from the full set of affective, somatic, cognitive, and behavioral symptoms characteristic of major depression in adults.

Elaboration of various assumptions requires distinguishing depression as a symptom from depression as a syndrome. As a *symptom,* "depression" refers merely to sad affect and obviously is quite common. As a *syndrome,* "depression" refers to a constellation or group of symptoms that go together. Sadness may only be a part of a larger set of problems that may include loss of interest in activities, feelings of worthlessness, sleep disturbances, changes in appetite, and others.[1]

Early Psychoanalytic Views

The dominant conceptual views in child clinical work have been based on variations of psychoanalytic theory that assert that depression as a disorder does not occur in children (e.g., Mahler, 1961; Rie, 1966). Certainly, some forms of depression have been widely acknowledged. For example, Spitz (1946) discussed the reaction in infancy precipitated by separation from the mother. This reaction, referred to as "anaclitic depression," may include several signs such as sadness, withdrawal, apprehension, weepiness, retarded reaction to external stimuli, slowed movement, dejection, loss of appetite and weight, and insomnia. Anaclitic depression is viewed as a result of the experience of object loss. Although many of these symptoms resemble the clinical picture of adult depression, anaclitic depression as originally formulated is not parallel to affective disorders in adults. Adult depression emerges in many forms, only some of which might be attributed to specific environmental events.

Depression as a clinical disorder in children, similar to major depression in adults, has not been considered to be possible in prominent psychoanalytic positions. According to orthodox psychoanalytic theory, depression as a disorder has been considered to be a phenomenon of the superego. Alternative explanations of the emergence of depression have been advanced, including the argument that depression results from aggression directed against oneself (Roch-

lin, 1965), from a conflict that arouses guilt (Beres, 1966), and from low self-esteem that results from a discrepancy between the real and ideal self (Rie, 1966). In each of these positions, depression depends on a well-developed superego. Since superego development is hypothesized not to mature until adolescence, the appearance of a full clinical syndrome of depression in childhood is precluded.

Ego-analytic models of depression acknowledge the possible appearance of the disorder in children (Anthony, 1975; Bemporad & Wilson, 1978). Depressive states and approximations of a depressive disorder can emerge at different ages and are considered to vary as a function of psychosexual development, experience, and perceptual and cognitive skills. Thus, contemporary psychoanalytic views are compatible with the appearance of childhood depression as a disorder. Yet the dominant view has been that depression as a disorder does not exist in children. Consequently, it has not been specifically studied in clinical work or included as a viable diagnostic category for children.

Masked Depression

A second major conceptual position has acknowledged that depression can exist in children, but contends that its manifestations differ significantly from those of adult depression. The essential features, such as dysphoric mood and pervasive loss of interest, may not be present. Rather, this view proposes that there is an underlying depression that is manifest in several other symptoms or forms of psychopathology. Depression is said to be "masked" or expressed in "depressive equivalents." Children may be depressed, but their affective disorder can only be inferred from the presence of other complaints evident in childhood (Cytryn & McKnew, 1972, 1974; Glaser, 1968; Malmquist, 1977; Toolan, 1962). The symptoms that putatively mask depression have included the full gamut of clinical problems evident in childhood. As a partial list, temper tantrums, hyperactivity, disobedience, running away, delinquency, phobias, somatic complaints, irritability, separation anxiety, and underachievement have been identified as depressive equivalents (see Kovacs & Beck, 1977).

There is a problem inherent in the notions of masked depression and depressive equivalents: It is not clear how to distinguish masked depression or depressive equivalents from entirely

---

[1] It is important to clarify further the terminology that is used in the present chapter. The term "symptom" is used to refer to a particular behavior, broadly conceived, and may include a characteristic of affect, cognition, or behavior. There is no implication that a "symptom" reflects a particular etiological model or underlying cause. This use is consistent with the current notion of symptoms in diagnostic practices. For present purposes, the notions of "syndrome" and "disorder" are used interchangeably in reference to depression. "Syndrome" refers to multiple symptoms or behaviors that go together. "Disorder" refers to a syndrome when more is known about the constellation of symptoms. A characteristic family history, biological correlates, predictable clinical course or outcome, and other factors suggest the utility of viewing a syndrome as more than merely a collection of correlated behaviors. Current diagnostic practices consider major depression as a disorder in the sense noted here.

different disorders in which depression is not implicated. Consequently, these concepts have, in current use, been regarded as unnecessary, empirically unverifiable, and in general not particularly meaningful (Anthony, 1975; Cytryn, McKnew, & Bunney, 1980; Kovacs & Beck, 1977).

Despite their limitations, the notions of masked depression and depressive equivalents have indirectly contributed to subsequent research on childhood depression. The idea that depression is masked at least acknowledges that depression can exist in children. Also, the position implies that depression may frequently be associated with other forms of childhood psychopathology, which may obscure or overshadow the presence of depression. Many of the symptoms that have been considered to mask depression may also be present, but they reflect other symptoms or disorders and can be distinguished from depression. Depression does not necessarily accompany other disorders, but when it does, depression may be overlooked if it is not explicitly sought through careful assessment (Carlson & Cantwell, 1979).

The notions of masked depression and depressive equivalents are also significant because they raise the possibility that depression in childhood will be manifested in ways that differ from depression in adulthood. The differences among children, adolescents, and adults may not be in whether depression is masked, but in essential and/or associated features that can be objectively assessed. Beyond the search for differences in symptoms as a function of age, a broader developmental perspective is raised by the notions of masked depression and depressive equivalents. The course of development of depressive symptoms, and the connections between biological and environmental processes at one age and depressive symptoms at later ages, are raised implicitly by this view as well (cf. Cicchetti & Schneider-Rosen, 1984; Sroufe & Rutter, 1984).

Depressive Symptoms as Part of Normal Development

Another conceptual position on the nature of childhood depression suggests that symptoms of depression may emerge in children over the course of normal development, but may dissipate over time (Lefkowitz, 1980; Lefkowitz & Burton, 1978). A premise of this view is that if the clinical symptoms of depression are typical of childhood or relatively prevalent, and if they remit with age, they should not be regarded as evidence of "psychopathology." The view that childhood depression may not represent a distinct dysfunction in children has been a partial reaction to the notion of masked depression, which permits virtually any sign of deviance to constitute evidence for depression. Epidemiological research has shown that many so-called "depressive equivalents," such as temper tantrums, fears, or enuresis, are relatively common over the course of childhood (e.g., Lapouse, 1966). These behaviors often are not diagnostically significant, because they are not necessarily related to adjustment in general, and they diminish over time (Lapouse, 1966; Werry & Quay, 1971).

Even behaviors that relate more specifically to the syndrome of depression, as defined in current taxonomy, may be relatively common. For example, as a measure of sadness, crying has been shown to vary significantly as a function of age. At 6 years of age, approximately 18% of children have been reported to cry two to three times per week; the percentage decreases markedly by puberty to 2% (Werry & Quay, 1971). Similarly, poor appetite, occasionally a symptom of depression, is relatively common in 5-year-old girls and boys (37% and 29%, respectively) but drops sharply by age 9 (9% and 6%, respectively) (MacFarlane, Allen, & Honzik, 1954). This indicates that characteristics of depression are often seen at different points in child development.

Despite these findings, there is a central problem with the notion that depression is a developmental phenomenon. Depression (dysphoria) as a symptom or other specific symptoms may emerge at different points of development. Whether the group of symptoms that defines the syndrome emerges at varying points in childhood is an entirely different matter. Even if the full syndrome were shown to have a relatively high prevalence at a particular age, this does not by itself mean that a disorder does not exist or that it should not be treated (Costello, 1980). Moreover, childhood depression may be a precursor of adolescent and adult depression, in which case its early identification might be important.

As already noted, the notion that depression is part of normal development emerged when the diagnostic criteria for depression were so diffuse that virtually any deviance in a child was taken as a possible sign for depression.

The current specification of diagnostic criteria for the syndrome of depression overcomes many of the concerns that gave rise to this view. Nevertheless, the view that depressive symptoms may emerge over the course of development has been important. The view directs attention to the fact that symptoms of depression may vary over the course of child development and helps to alert clinicians and researchers, so that the developmentally common symptoms are not confused with the full set of symptoms that define the syndrome.

Depression as a Syndrome or Disorder

A fourth view is that depression in childhood exists and that the essential features of the disorder are similar in children, adolescents, and adults (e.g., Cantwell, 1982; Puig-Antich & Gittelman, 1982). This position was adopted in the third edition of the *Diagnostic and Statistical Manual of Mental Disorders* (DSM-III; American Psychiatric Association, 1980), in which the criteria for diagnoses in the Affective Disorders group are delineated and applied independently of age. The statement that these essential features can be used to diagnose depression in children, adolescents, and adults alike was made *a priori* in DSM-III, but, this by implication, raises the issue as an empirical question: That is, can depression be diagnosed in children, adolescents, and adults using the same criteria? This question has now been answered affirmatively by several investigations in which psychiatric interviews have been administered to children or adolescents and their parents (e.g., Carlson & Cantwell, 1980; Chiles, Miller, & Cox, 1980; Kashani, Barbero, & Bolander, 1981; Kashani, Husain, Shekim, Hodges, Cytryn, & McKnew, 1981; Puig-Antich, Blau, Marx, Greenhill, & Chambers, 1978). The fact that depression as a clinical syndrome can be diagnosed in children, adolescents, and adults does not mean that the manifestations of the disorder are necessarily identical. DSM-III recognized that there may be different features for varying ages and developmental levels. For example, for young children, separation anxiety and school refusal may accompany depression. In adolescents, on the other hand, withdrawal from activities and school difficulties may be evident. To date, the specific differences in depressive disorders that might be associated with age, gender, and stages of psychological,

behavioral, and biological maturation have not been empirically elaborated.

The view of childhood depression as a syndrome or disorder has gained dominance in the last few years, largely because of the success in applying unmodified adult diagnostic criteria to children and adolescents. Also, empirical evidence is beginning to emerge that elaborates the affective, behavioral, cognitive, motivational, and biological components of childhood depression (see Cantwell & Carlson, 1983; Puig-Antich & Gittelman, 1982).

CHARACTERISTICS OF DEPRESSION

Prevalence

Questions of major interest obviously include the extent to which children experience depressive symptoms and the constellation of symptoms that defines the disorder. Depression has been studied in the population of normal children and adolescents, as well as various clinic samples. Most research has addressed the prevalence of severe depressive symptoms by identifying subsamples whose scores on self-report, parent, and peer inventories reflect relatively extreme levels of depression. For example, using a peer-based measure, Lefkowitz and Tesiny (1985) found severe depression (extreme scores exceeding two standard deviations above the mean) in 5.2% of a sample of over 3,000 normal third-, fourth-, and fifth-grade children. In another study, 7.3% and 1.3% of high school students showed moderate and severe levels of depression, respectively, using cutoff criteria developed with adults (Kaplan, Hong, & Weinhold, 1984). These and other studies have utilized different methods of assessing depression and different criteria for defining extreme scores. Hence, their results are difficult to compare.

Other studies have utilized diagnostic criteria to evaluate depression as a disorder. In the general population, approximately 2% have been given a diagnosis of Major Depression in randomly selected child populations aged 7–12, using DSM-III criteria (Kashani *et al.,* 1983; Kashani & Simonds, 1979). In clinical populations, estimates have ranged from approximately 2% to 60% (Kashani, Husain, *et al.,* 1981), although more typical estimates fall between 10% and 20% (Puig-Antich & Gittelman, 1982).

An issue of interest is the possibility of differences in prevalence of depressive disorders as a function of gender. The interest stems from the fact that in adulthood, depression generally is more prevalent among women than among men. To date, research has typically found no sex differences in prevalence of depressive disorders in clinic and nonclinic samples of children aged 6–12 (e.g., Kashani et al., 1983; Lefkowitz & Tesiny, 1985; Lobovits & Handal, 1985). On the other hand, research has suggested that among adolescents, the prevalence is greater in females than in males (e.g., Mezzich & Mezzich, 1979; Reynolds, 1985). Moreover, differences in severity of depression between males and females appear to begin in early adolescence and to increase over the next several years (Kandel & Davies, 1982). Differences in prevalence rates between adolescent males and females are not always found (Kaplan et al., 1984). Consequently, further work and large-scale epidemiological studies are still needed.

As for the overall prevalence rates for children and adolescents, there remain rather large discrepancies in the currently available studies. The large discrepancies may result in part from the different ages that are studied. For example, using DSM-III diagnostic criteria, evidence suggests that young children (aged 1–6 years) referred for treatment may have markedly lower rates (1%) of Major Depression than children aged 9–12 (13%) (Kashani, Cantwell, Shekim, & Reid, 1982; Kashani, Ray, & Carlson, 1984). Also, differences in prevalence rates may be due to the different measures that are used; the difficulty in administering similar measures to children of different ages; and, perhaps most importantly, the different diagnostic criteria that are invoked. The clarity of prevalence data for depressive disorders among children is likely to improve with the increased use of standardized descriptive criteria for diagnostic purposes, the development of standard diagnostic interviews, and evidence that diagnoses can be invoked with acceptable reliability (e.g., Chambers et al., 1985; Orvaschel, Puig-Antich, Chambers, Tabrizi, & Johnson, 1982).

Current Diagnostic Criteria

The development of diagnostic systems for children must be viewed in light of the contemporary evolution of diagnosis for adults. A historically significant development occurred in the early 1970s when a group of researchers at Washington University (St. Louis) published diagnostic criteria for use in research with adults (Feighner et al., 1972). These criteria were designed to specify a uniform set of symptoms or behavioral characteristics for diagnosing particular disorders. The criteria required specific core or essential symptoms and a select set of additional symptoms from a larger set that needed to be present for a particular disorder to be diagnosed. A disorder was defined by the specific symptoms that a patient showed, free from etiological inferences about the nature of the dysfunction. The Feighner criteria, as they came to be called, were expanded into the Research Diagnostic Criteria (RDC); Spitzer, Endicott, & Robins, 1978), based on the same descriptive model but encompassing a wider range of disorders.

For present purposes, it is important to note that the approach of the Feighner criteria and the RDC served as a model for developing criteria for DSM-III. The RDC were designed primarily for researchers and restricted to a limited set of disorders. Consequently, many patients who come for treatment would not fall into a particular RDC category. DSM-III was designed to handle the exigencies of clinical practice, which require a broader range of diagnostic categories. The same descriptive model used in the RDC was adopted for DSM-III, but the range of disorders was expanded.[2]

Prior to the development of the RDC and DSM-III, separate criteria had been proposed for childhood depression by Weinberg and his colleagues (e.g., Ling, Oftedol, & Weinberg, 1970; Weinberg, Rutman, Sullivan, Pencik, & Dietz, 1973). Although the criteria represented an advance in operationalizing the dysfunction for children, the actual criteria that were invoked were somewhat broad. As a result, children who met the Weinberg criteria tended to have other psychiatric diagnoses as well (cf. Carlson & Cantwell, 1980; Cytryn, McKnew, Bartko, Lamour, & Hamovitt, 1982). With DSM-III, diagnoses of particular disorders became more clearly associated with specific

---

[2] There were some differences between the RDC and DSM-III for invoking the diagnosis of Major Depression, including the number and duration of symptoms, and the criterion of whether the patient has been referred for help or shows impairment of functioning. The major differences pertained to the different subtypes of depression. The RDC permitted greater differentiation among alternative subtypes, and alternative subtypes were not mutually exclusive (see J. B. W. Williams & Spitzer, 1982).

TABLE 1. DSM-IIIR Criteria for Major Depression

A. *Inclusion Criteria:* At least five of the following symptoms have been present during the same 2-week period; at least one of the symptoms was either (1) depressed mood or (2) loss of interest or pleasure.

   (1) depressed mood most of the day, nearly every day (either by subjective account, e.g., feels "down" or "low," or is observed by others to look sad or depressed)

   (2) loss of interest or pleasure in all or almost all activities nearly every day (either by subjective account or is observed by others to be apathetic)

   (3) significant weight loss or weight gain (when not dieting or binge-eating, e.g., more than 5% of body weight in a month) or decrease or increase in appetite nearly every day (in children consider failure to make expected weight gains)

   (4) insomnia or hypersomnia nearly every day

   (5) psychomotor agitation or retardation nearly every day (observable by others not merely subjective feelings of restlessness or being slowed down; in children under 6, hypoactivity)

   (6) fatigue or loss of energy nearly every day

   (7) feelings of worthlessness or excessive or inappropriate guilt (either may be delusional) nearly every day (not merely self-reproach or guilt about being sick)

   (8) diminished ability to think or concentrate, or indecisiveness nearly every day (either by subjective account or observed by others)

   (9) thoughts that he or she would be better off dead or suicidal ideation nearly every day, or suicide attempt

B. *Exclusion Criteria*

   (1) an organic etiology has been ruled out (i.e., either there was no new organic factor or change in a pre-existing organic factor) as precipitating the disturbance or the disturbance has persisted for at least 1 month beyond the cessation of the precipitating organic factor

   (2) not a normal reaction to the loss of a loved one (Uncomplicated Bereavement)

   (3) at no time during the disturbance have there been delusions or hallucinations for as long as 2 weeks in the absence of prominent mood symptoms

   (4) not superimposed on Schizophrenia, Schizophreniform Disorder or Paranoid Disorder

---

Note. Adapted from *Diagnostic and Statistical Manual of Mental Disorders* (3rd ed. rev.) by the American Psychiatric Association, 1987, Washington, DC: Author.

symptom criteria, independent of a person's age. Although children may evince unique characteristics in their manifestations of depression, the current approach is to apply the diagnosis when the core criteria have been met.

Beginning in 1983, the diagnostic categories were re-evaluated to incorporate research findings on alternative disorders and experience in applying the specific diagnostic categories. A revision of the DSM-III criteria has emerged and is referred to as DSM-IIIR (American Psychiatric Association, 1987). In DSM-IIIR several changes were made in various disorders in terms of clarifying the criteria, changing subtypes, and deleting and adding alternative disorders. For affective disorders, the changes were relatively minor. Depression is part of a larger category referred to as Mood (rather than Affective) Disorders. The criteria for major depression in DSM-IIIR are illustrated in Table 1.

As in DSM-III, depressive symptoms may be included in other types of disorders as well. Table 2 enumerates several other categories of depressive disorders. As evident in the table, mild forms of depression may appear (Dys-

thymic Disorder) when the full set of symptoms and the severity of symptoms that meet criteria for Major Depression are not evident. The symptoms may not be clinically significant because they are interrupted by only brief periods of normal mood. Also, current evidence suggests that a mild form of depression places children at risk for major depressive episodes (Kovacs *et al.,* 1984). Other manifestations of depressive symptoms may emerge (Table 2). In each of the disorders, there may be sad affect, loss of interest in the usual activities, and other symptoms. The severity, duration, and precipitants of the symptoms are major determinants of the type of depressive disorder that is defined. A careful assessment is required in order to evaluate the severity and duration of the symptoms and to make judgments about specific events from which they may have emerged.[3]

---

[3] In addition to the problems listed in Table 2, disorders in which mania is present may also be associated with depression. "Mania" refers to elevated mood, euphoria, and excessive activity. Diagnoses may include mania or mania combined with periods of depression, as in bipolar

TABLE 2. DSM-IIIR Diagnostic Categories That Include Depressive Symptoms Other than Major Depressive Disorder

Disorder or Condition and Key Characteristics

Dysthymia

Essentially a mood disorder in which the symptoms of major depression are evident in less severe form. The symptoms may be chronic lasting for at least 2 years (1 year for children and adolescents) during which there has been depressed mood most of the day more days than not.

Separation Anxiety Disorder

Many of the symptoms of depression such as sadness, excessive worrying, sleep dysfunction, somatic complaints, apathy, and social withdrawal may emerge as part of fear of separation from those to whom the child is attached. In such cases, the symptoms may be clearly associated with the theme of separation. For example, worrying may have a specific focus on worry about being away from the parent. Similarly, somatic complaints may occur to remain at home or to foster increased attention to the child.

Adjustment Disorder with Depressed Mood

Depressive symptoms may emerge as a reaction to an identifiable psychosocial stressor such as divorce of the parents, leaving friends during a move away from home, or serious illness of a parent. In such cases, the symptoms are in temporal proximity (within 3 months) of the stressor. The reaction is viewed as a maladaptive reaction because the person's functioning in everyday life is disrupted or because the symptoms are in excess of a "normal" or usually expected reaction. The symptoms are likely to remit after a period of adjustment with the new circumstances.

Uncomplicated Bereavement

Within DSM-IIIR, bereavement resembles an Adjustment Disorder in terms of its association with a particular event. However, it is not listed as a disorder because it is considered as a normal reaction to the loss of a loved one. Bereavement is often associated with several depressive symptoms or a full depressive syndrome and temporary impairment in school and social functioning. Yet, the reaction is not regarded as clinically significant unless the symptoms remain well beyond a "reasonable" period of adjustment or begin to recur with repeated episodes long after the loss.

Note. Adapted from *Diagnostic and Statistical Manual of Mental Disorders* (3rd ed. rev.) by the American Psychiatric Association, 1987, Washington, DC: Author.

Developmental Considerations

The criteria for diagnosing depression in children have been developed from investigation of adults. There is always the risk that extensions to children will miss the mark because of the failure to take developmental considerations into account. Developmental changes in affective, cognitive, biochemical, motoric, and other systems are likely to be important in the manifestations of depression in children. For these reasons, the need to adopt a developmental perspective is invariably recommended in studying childhood depression (e.g., Anthony, 1975; Cicchetti & Schneider-Rosen, 1984; Sroufe & Rutter, 1984).

Within DSM-IIIR criteria, as noted earlier, the possibility of different symptoms emerging as a function of age is acknowledged. And researchers occasionally have suggested that specific symptoms (e.g., separation anxiety,

enuresis, conduct disorder) are likely to be associated with depression in children. However, there has been no firm empirical base to date that would serve as a basis for age-specific criteria.

An important issue for the field has been to elaborate the developmental differences in depression. Multivariate studies of child symptoms suggest that there may well be developmental differences. For example, Achenbach and Edelbrock (1983) studied parent checklist ratings of boys and girls in different age groups (4–5, 6–11, and 12–16). A Depression factor emerged in analyses of Child Behavior Checklist ratings of all groups except boys and girls aged 12–16. For boys in this age range, no Depression factor emerged. For girls, the Depression factor clustered with items specifically related to withdrawal; being secretive, shy, and timid; and liking to be alone. For the groups where a Depression factor did emerge, the specific symptoms that clustered on this factor varied as a function of sex and age. For example, for boys aged 6–11, suicidal talk was associated with other symptoms of depression,

_____
depressive disorder or cyclothymia (analogous to Dysthymic Disorder). These are not covered here because mania is relatively rare in children (Rapoport & Ismond, 1984).

although this was not the case at ages 4–5. For girls aged 6–11, feeling persecuted and anxiety were associated with other depressive symptoms; at ages 4–5, these symptoms were not part of the Depression factor. The results suggest that depressive symptoms may be organized quite differently as a function of age and gender.

To date, research has shown many similarities between the manifestations of depression in children and in adults. For example, studies have shown that many cognitive attributes (e.g., attributional style, locus of control, hopelessness, cognitive distortion), biological correlates (e.g., in response to drug challenges, measures of endocrine functioning), and overt behaviors are similar in depressed children and adults (e.g., Kaslow, Rehm, & Siegel, 1984; Kazdin, Esveldt-Dawson, Sherick, & Colbus, 1985; Kazdin, Rodgers, & Colbus, 1986; Moyal, 1977; Puig-Antich, 1983; Seligman et al., 1984). In these studies, the search for developmental differences has encompassed a relatively broad age range (e.g., 6–14 years of age). Similarities in cognitive processes, symptoms of depression, and the correlates of depression among different age groups at this point have been the rule rather than the exception.

There are differences that have been found between depression in children and adults. First, data for adults indicate that depression is more prevalent in women than in men, at least in Western cultures, with a female-to-male ratio of approximately 2:1 (Whybrow, Akiskal, & McKinney, 1984). Studies of children have not revealed consistent sex differences in prevalence of major depression (Carlson & Cantwell, 1979; Kashani et al., 1982). On the other hand, some differences have been found between depressed boys and girls that have not been evident with adults. For example, associations between depression and other characteristics (e.g., nonverbal behavior, unpopularity, somatic complaints) appear to be higher and more consistent among girls than among boys (Jacobsen, Lahey, & Strauss, 1983; Kazdin, Sherick, Esveldt-Dawson, & Rancurello, 1985).

Second, some of the serious concomitants of depression are clearly less evident in children. As a major case in point, suicide in children below the age of 12 is extremely rare (Hawton, 1986), and as a result of the low base rate, suicide is less likely to be manifested in childhood depression. On the other hand, suicidal ideation, threats, and attempts are not that rare and are often evident in patient samples, especially those with depressive disorder (Carlson & Cantwell, 1982; Pfeffer, Conte, Plutchik, & Jerrett, 1979). Third, biological correlates of depression are not all the same for children and adults. For example, electroencephalographic (EEG) sleep patterns characteristic of depressed adults have not been evident among depressed children (Goetz et al., 1983; Young, Knowles, MacLean, Boag, & McConville, 1982).

In general, the literature does not provide evidence that characteristics of depression and its associated features are identical throughout the developmental spectrum. However, the claims for the differences in depression as a function of development appear to be based primarily on clinical observations (e.g., Bemporad & Wilson, 1978; Herzog & Rathbun, 1982) rather than on firm data. A deficiency in the research is in referring to and studying developmental differences only in terms of chronological age of the child samples. Further work is needed that examines depression in relation to principles that guide developmental processes more broadly (e.g., holism, differentiation) or in terms of theoretically germane concepts (e.g., Piagetian stages) (cf. Cicchetti & Schneider-Rosen, 1984; Sroufe & Rutter, 1984). In advance of such research, developmental differences will remain elusive. For present purposes, however, it is important to note that major domains of affect, cognition, and behavior show many similarities between children and adults.

Identification of Depression in Everyday Life

The discussion above covers the major categories into which depression is classified in DSM-IIIR. However, it is important not to focus exclusively on these diagnostic categories or to view them as fixed or exhaustive. Depressive symptoms may be associated with a variety of conditions, such as a response to actual or threatened events (e.g., parental divorce or separation) or existential and identity crises, even though a child or adolescent may not meet the criteria for a specific disorder. A major issue for parents, teachers, and others in everyday life is to identify whether the child's behavior warrants clinical referral or special treatment.

The initial concern is what to look for in order to identify depression in children. Consider school performance as an example. Research has suggested a variety of signs and domains of child performance that may reflect depressive symptoms. Peer relations (e.g., unpopularity), poor schoolwork (e.g., lack of interest in studying), reduced achievement (e.g., test performance, grades), impairment on cognitive tasks, and acting out in the classroom have all been found to be associated with depression (see Jacobsen *et al.*, 1983; Lefkowitz & Tesiny, 1980; Tesiny, Lefkowitz, & Gordon, 1980). Yet these characteristics are likely to be associated with all sorts of dysfunctions (e.g., conduct disorder) beyond depressive disorders. This does not mean that the type of problems noted above are unimportant. However, as a guide to identification of depression in children, they may be nonspecific.

Identification of depression in everyday situations, such as at school or at home, needs to focus more specifically on characteristics of the dysfunction. There some general guidelines that may be helpful. The initial focus of attention, of course, is whether the core symptoms of depression (e.g., sad affect and loss of interest in activities) are evident. Yet it is not the presence of one or a few symptoms alone that should be accorded significance. For example, sad affect is very much a part of everyday experience, and is "normal" in response to a variety of not-well-specified environmental and physiological events. Indeed, studies suggest that as an isolated symptom, depression among elementary-school-age children is quite common. For example, one study found that 17% of school-age children were sad, although only about 2% of the children met criteria for major depression (Kashani & Simonds, 1979). Thus, the presence of sadness alone should not necessarily be regarded as significant.

For a symptom or set of symptoms to take on significance, one should look for several characteristics:

1. The symptom should reflect a change in behavior. Many children simply appear moody, apathetic, and slow in their activities in general, and these characteristics may not warrant special attention. Depression becomes significant as a change from ordinary behavior.

2. Consistency in duration or continuation of depressed affect is also significant. Mood may change rapidly, and by definition is short-lived. If there is a period of, say, a week or two where there is depressed affect or other symptoms that are sustained, their possible significance is increased.

3. The absence of a clear precipitant often is important. If the child or significant others cannot identify specific events that account for the change in mood, interest, or other symptoms, this is noteworthy. Similarly, the inability to alter the mood or to controvert the symptoms through the usual ministrations of parents, teachers, and peers is important information.

4. The impact of the symptoms on everyday functioning is a major criterion. If changes in school performance, attendance, and participation in activities are associated with the onset of the symptoms, then special attention may be warranted.

As depression receives increased professional attention, there is increased sensitivity to its presence in children and adolescents. It is important, of course, to better identify disorders so that they can be prevented and treated. A potential problem with increased professional attention is that there may be an increased propensity to label dysfunction that does not warrant identification. For these reasons, specific diagnostic criteria and the possible manifestations of depressive symptoms in everyday life that are of a magnitude to warrant possible attention need to be underscored. The difficult task for persons in everyday life is to judge whether the symptoms appear to impede a child's daily functioning, whether they appear to be stable or emerge repeatedly at different time intervals, or whether they seem to distinguish the child clearly from his or her peers.

ETIOLOGICAL MODELS: AN OVERVIEW

Identification of the causes of affective disorders is obviously of great interest. The literature on the etiology of these disorders is complex, because of the different subtypes of dysfunction, as well as the multiplicity of models proposed to account for them. Moreover, for many different models, research has advanced considerably on the mechanisms associated with depressive symptoms. For present purposes, an overview of models is provided to convey current approaches.[4] The models have been developed and researched in the context of adult dysfunction, and only recently have the models been extended to children. Although the alternative models can be divided into several different overall approaches or schools of thought, they are highlighted here under two major ru-

---

[4] The models of depression cannot begin to be detailed here; the reader is encouraged to seek other sources (e.g., Paykel, 1982a; Rehm & Kaslow, 1984).

brics—namely, psychosocial and biological models.

Psychosocial Models

Psychosocial models are approaches that emphasize intrapsychic, behavioral, and interpersonal underpinnings of depression. There are a number of different views, only some of which are sampled here.

Psychoanalytic Models

Psychoanalytic models of depression have included multiple positions (see Mendelson, 1982). The positions focus on intrapsychic influences, beginning with the view of Freud, which emphasized unsatisfied libidinal strivings (particularly object loss—e.g., as reflected in a parent who fails to fulfill the child's needs). The child's identification with the parents' values and ideals has also been accorded an important role. The self-criticism and self-rejection of depressed persons are attributed to the battle of the ego and superego within the individual that reflects these values. The self-directed criticism and internal conflict reflect anger and hostility toward the parent (Freud, 1917/1957).

Freud's views, not fully detailed here, served as a point of departure for several psychoanalytic positions among his followers (e.g., Abraham, Rado, and Bibring). Such factors were identified as repeated disappointment in relation to one's parents, fixation at the oral stage, aggression turned inward, excessive craving for narcissistic gratification, loss of self-esteem resulting from the unsatisfied need for affection, feelings of helplessness, and others.

These views attributed the causes of depression to experiences in childhood. Constitutional factors were recognized by Freud and his followers as accounting for selected forms of depression and increasing the need for excess gratification and sensitivity to frustrations from inadequate affection. Many specific features of psychoanalytic views, such as low self-esteem and helplessness, have played a role in other models and have been the subject of considerable research. However, psychoanalytic views themselves have not generated a great deal of research. Consequently, they cannot be viewed as empirically well grounded.

Behavioral Models

Several behavioral models of depression have emerged in the last decade (see Clarkin & Glazer, 1981). As a general statement, the models focus on learning, environmental consequences, and skill acquisition and deficits. Symptoms of depression are considered to result from problems in interacting with the environment.

Lewinsohn (1974) has advanced the view that depression results from the loss or reduction of reinforcement from the environment. The person's behavior does not produce sufficient positive reinforcement from others, and the individual becomes passive, withdraws from interactions, and shows the affective and cognitive symptoms of depression. Alternatively, punishing and aversive consequences (unpleasant outcomes) may also result from person–environment interactions and lead to the symptoms. Support for the view has derived from several studies that show the relationship between mood and other depressive symptoms and the number of reinforcing (pleasant) activities in which persons engage, and from treatment outcome studies that demonstrate a relationship between increases in pleasant activities and decreases in depressive symptoms (Lewinsohn, 1974; Lewinsohn & Arconad, 1981).

A related behavioral model suggests that social skills deficits underlie depression. The view overlaps with the position advanced by Lewinsohn, because social skills deficits may lead to reduced or limited reinforcement from the environment. Also, social interactions are central sources of positive reinforcement that have been reduced in depressed persons. Social skills deficits may also cause depressed persons to fail to meet interpersonal demands and to suffer anxiety and lack of reinforcement as a result. Evidence for this position has also come from research showing interpersonal deficits in the behaviors of depressed persons, as reflected in nonverbal behavior, affective expression, and reciprocity of interactions (e.g., Blumberg & Hokanson, 1983; Libet & Lewinsohn, 1973). In addition, social skills and assertion training programs have led to improvements in depression in several studies (see Rehm & Kaslow, 1984).

Rehm (1977) has proposed a self-control model of depression, which focuses on the individual's maladaptive or deficient self-regulatory processes in coping with stress. Aspects of how individuals self-monitor, self-evaluate, and self-reinforce behavior are central. Persons with deficits in these self-regulatory skills are likely to focus on negative events, to set overly stringent criteria for evaluating their performance, and to administer little reinforcement to themselves, among other characteristics. The model is integrative insofar as it combines and draws upon other psychosocial models. Thus, reduced activity and lack of reinforcement (*à la* Lewinsohn) are incorporated into the model along with attributions of helplessness and negativism (*à la* Seligman and Beck), highlighted below.

Cognitive Models

Cognitive and behavioral models of depression are not always easily distinguishable, because versions within each camp often rely upon similar constructs, such as attributions and lack of social reinforcement. Also, treatment procedures often overlap considerably, as in the use of practice exercises and activities in everyday life. Nevertheless, cognitive views emphasize the perceptual, attributional, and belief systems that underlie depressive symptoms. Beck's (1976) model emphasizes the importance of the cognitive triad of depression—namely, negative views of oneself, the world, and the future. The negative cognitions are considered to affect the person's judgment about the world and interpersonal interactions, and to account for affective, motivational, and behavioral symptoms of depression. Systematic errors in thinking, such as overgeneralizing specific events and misinterpreting experience in general, can be identified to reflect the pervasive focus on negative aspects of experience. Support for Beck's view has derived from studies showing features of the cognitive triad in depressed samples. In addition, several treatment studies have shown that cognitive therapy, which focuses specifically on maladaptive cognitions, leads to improvements in depression (see Beck, Rush, Shaw, & Emery, 1980; Rehm & Kaslow, 1984).

Seligman (1975) has proposed a learned helplessness model of depression. The model proposes that depression results from people's experiences and expectations that their responses do not influence events in their lives. Helplessness leads to passivity, social impairment, slowed activity, and other symptoms of depression. The model grew out of animal laboratory research showing that animals became helpless after exposure to unavoidable shock. When they could later escape from the shock, they failed to do so. The model was extended by focusing on the perceptions and attributions of depressed persons, who often feel they cannot influence their environment (Abramson, Seligman, & Teasdale, 1978). The specific attributions that people have about why they cannot control their environment (e.g., due to internal or external factors) and the pervasiveness of these influences (e.g., specific to a situation or general) affect the symptoms that may emerge (e.g., reduced self-esteem). Studies have supported the model by identifying alternative attributional patterns associated with or resulting from helplessness induction techniques (Abramson *et al.*, 1978).

Another cognitively based position proposes that depression is related to deficits in interpersonal problem-solving skills (D'Zurilla & Nezu, 1982). Persons who are depressed, when compared to nondepressed controls, evince deficits in generating alternative solutions to social problems, engaging in means–ends thinking, and making decisions (Nezu & Ronan, 1985). Problem-solving skills, when present, appear to act as a buffer against the impact of negative life events (Billings & Moos, 1982). In response to negative events or stress, depressive symptoms are more likely to emerge because of deficits in problem-solving skills. This model focuses on the specific cognitive deficits that may mediate management of stress and interpersonal interactions.

Socioenvironmental Views

Socioenvironmental models have focused on life events that may influence the onset or emergence of symptoms of depression. The view is included here as psychosocial because it is not only the stressful event itself, but also the person's perception or cognitive appraisal of that event, that is important. The significance of stressful events as precursors to depressive symptoms is recognized in everyday life. Bereavement, for example, frequently includes multiple symptoms of depressive disorder linked specifically to death of a loved one. Moreover, the risk of suicide is greatly increased following death of a relative or spouse, suggesting that extremes of hopelessness and depression may follow stressful events (Bunch, 1972; MacMahon & Pugh, 1965).

Research has supported the role of stressful life events in depressive disorders. Persons who are depressed or who later meet criteria for depression report significantly more stressful life events than do matched controls. Although higher levels of such events characterize other patient groups (schizophrenic or mental patients), depression still seems to be associated with greater levels of such events (Paykel, 1982b). In addition, stressful events appear to precede by a few weeks or months the onset of an episode or relapse (Brown, Harris, & Peto, 1973; Paykel & Tanner, 1976). Attempts to identify the type of events that are uniquely related to depression (e.g., loss of a relative) and severity of the events (e.g., life-threatening) have not revealed consistent patterns.

Biological Models

Psychosocial models of depression, particularly cognitive and behavioral models, have flourished and have generated a host of treatments. At the same time, remarkable progress has been made in biological views of the nature of depression. Assessment and treatment techniques have emerged from these models as well.

Biochemical Models

There are a number of biochemical agents that have been implicated in depression, only a few of which can be mentioned here (see Usdin, Asberg, Bertilsson, & Sjoqvist, 1984). Research has focused on the identification of neurotransmitters that may underlie depression (see Zis & Goodwin, 1982). Different transmitters have been studied. Monoamines, especially catecholamine and indoleamine, have received attention in a variety of types of studies. The general view has been that affective disorders are characterized by a deficit (e.g., depression) or excess (e.g., mania) in one or more neurotransmitters, or by an imbalance of these transmitters. Support for this view in relation to monoamines comes from several quarters. For example, drugs that increase catecholamine output can act as antidepressants, whereas drugs that decrease output can act as antimanics. Also, concentrations of amines and their metabolites in the urine, cerebrospinal fluid, and plasma indicate altered amine functioning among persons with affective disorders.

Neuroendocrine abnormalities have also been studied (e.g., Sachar, 1982). The focus has a broad-based rationale. Symptoms of depression include disturbances of mood, sex drive, sleep, appetite, and autonomic activity, which as a whole suggest dysfunction of the hypothalamus. Also, the neurotransmitters (especially noradrenaline, serotonin, and acetylcholine) that have been implicated in depressive disorders regulate the sorts of neuroendocrine agents that control pituitary function and hormonal responses. Different hormone systems have been studied. For example, depressed patients have been shown to hypersecrete cortisol and not to suppress cortisol secretion in response to drug challenge (administration of dexamethasone) (see Carroll, 1983). Also, hyposecretion of growth hormone has been found in response to insulin-induced hypoglycemia (Carroll, 1978). Growth hormone is believed to be mediated by neurotransmitters that may be deficient among depressed patients.

Genetic Models

The genetic influences in different depressive disorders have been established for some time. Close relatives of persons with major depression are more likely to have the disorder than are unrelated persons (see Depue & Monroe, 1979; Nurnberger & Gershon, 1982). The precise concordance varies with the criteria used to define depression, subtypes of depression, ages of the sample and relatives, and other factors. Different lines of evidence have supported the role of inheritance. The evidence from twin studies has been relatively consistent. Monozygotic twins show about 65% concordance for affective disorders, compared to approximately 14% for dizygotic twins (see Gershon, Targum, Kessler, Mazure, & Bunney, 1977). The strong familial ties of affective disorders have also been supported with studies of adoptees and studies of parents and children of index populations.

The genetic evidence has helped foster diverse types of research, including the identification of subtypes of affective disorders, with their specific genetic loadings, biological correlates, family histories, and patterns of treatment response. Research has also explored biological markers (i.e., genetic, biochemical, or related characteristics that permit identification of who is at risk for affective disorders). Ideally, these markers consist of stable characteristics that can be detected whether or not a person is currently showing the symptoms of depression. Several biological markers have been investigated.[5]

---

[5] Some of the biological markers that have been studied include urinary metabolites of monoamines (e.g., 3-meth-

Another line of work is to identify the mode of genetic transmission (e.g., monogenetic vs. polygenetic, recessive vs. dominant, X-linked models, and combinations of these views.)

These lines of research are obviously inter-related. The idea of biological markers has implications for different types of affective disorder. Also, if specific markers are identified, they may have implications regarding mode of genetic transmission. If the marker can be traced to a chromosomal location, insights regarding both transmission and the mechanism of action may result.

General Comments

The discussion above is intended only to high-light selected views of the causes of affective disorders. The list is by no means exhaustive (see Akiskal & McKinney, 1975). Different models might be presented (e.g., sociological, existential), as well as specific views within particular models (e.g., alternative neurotrans-mitters and endocrine systems, the modes of action through which stress is considered to promote depression).

The models are presented in a highlighted fashion to point to their areas of emphasis. Actually, the models overlap greatly. Many of the differences are not in the identification of specific factors, but in their relative weighting and in whether a given factor is accorded a central or causal role in generating depressive symptoms or is considered the consequence of some other source of influence. For example, life events and stressors are acknowledged as significant in cognitive, social skills, and bio-chemical models (e.g., Depue, 1979; Paykel, 1982a).

Few efforts have been provided to integrate alternative views that span different models (e.g., psychosocial, biological). As one exam-ple, Akiskal (1979; Akiskal & McKinney, 1975) has provided a biobehavioral model that inte-

grates (1) genetic vulnerability; (2) develop-mental events (e.g., early object loss); (3) psy-chosocial events (e.g., life events as stressors); (4) physiological stressors (e.g., medical con-ditions, disease, results of childbirth); and (5) personality traits (e.g., stable characteristics that influence reactivity to stress). These influ-ences are proposed to alter the central nervous system and to converge on a final common biological pathway that is implicated in the biological substrates of responses to environ-mental reinforcement. Specifically, the areas of the diencephalon are proposed, because they mediate arousal, mood, motivation, and psy-chomotor functions (see Akiskal, 1979; Why-brow et al., 1984). The idea of an integrated model is obviously attractive, if for no other reason than the acknowledgment of the legiti-macy of alternative perspectives and areas of research.

With regard to childhood depression, no at-tempts have been made to subject broad models to empirical test. The initial task has been to evaluate the extent to which models studied primarily with adult samples apply to children. For example, biological evidence on various markers of depression (e.g., cortisol, growth hormone abnormalities) has shown several con-sistencies between depressed adults and chil-dren (Puig-Antich, 1983). Similarly, studies of various cognitive features of depression show such consistencies (e.g., Haley, Fine, Mar-riage, Moretti, & Freeman, 1985; Seligman et al., 1984). Recent research has shown dimin-ished social interaction of depressed children with parents and peers, relative to normal and nondepressed patient control children (Kazdin, Esveldt-Dawson, et al., 1985; Puig-Antich et al., 1985a, 1985b). The findings are similar to those evident in studies of social behavior among adult samples. In general, these studies have indicated the heuristic value of applying models of depression developed with adult samples to childhood depression.

As with adults, the data suggest that depres-sion encompasses a broad range of affective, cognitive, motoric, and other features. There has been considerable discussion about the unique features of depression in children and the need to consider developmental differences (Cic-chetti & Schneider-Rosen, 1984). To date, em-pirical research has shown more similarities than differences in processes, correlates, and central features of depression across the devel-opmental spectrum.

---

oxy-4-hydroxyphenylethylene glycol [MHPG]), measures of blood and plasma (e.g., red blood catechol-o-methyl-transferase [COMT] and platelet monoamine oxidase [MAO]), cell membrane characteristics (e.g., lithium ion ratio), neuroendocrine function (e.g., level and diurnal variation of cortisol, resistance to cortisol suppression in response to dexamethasone), and sleep characteristics (e.g., latency to onset of rapid eye movement [REM] sleep and decreased deep sleep as reflected in delta wave).

CURRENT ASSESSMENT METHODS

Over the last several years, major advances have been made in the development of assessment techniques for children and adolescents. The range of measures has increased, and data have become available on the psychometric properties of individual measures. The advances are critical because they elaborate specific methods that can be used to identify children who show symptoms of depression, and also to provide normative information to help identify those departures that warrant special attention. Although measures have emerged that are specific to alternative models of depression, as noted above, most current measures assess the specific symptoms included in the diagnosis of depression and ask raters to evaluate the presence, absence, or severity of individual symptoms. Several different assessment modalities are identified and illustrated below. Given the proliferation of assessment devices, the reader is referred to alternative sources for more detailed discussions of individual measures (see Cantwell & Carlson, 1983; Kazdin, 1981; Kazdin & Petti, 1982; Strober & Werry, in press).

Self-Report

Self-report is clearly one of the most widely used assessment methods. Self-report is especially important in assessing depression, given that key symptoms (e.g., sadness, feelings of worthlessness, and loss of interest in activities) reflect subjective feelings or perceptions. In addition, self-report measures have been used extensively and successfully for the assessment of depressive symptoms in adults. Consequently, their extension to children is natural. Indeed, a number of measures reflect direct adaptations of instruments developed for adults.

An extraordinarily large number of self-report measures have become available. They are enumerated with key references in Table 3. The measures differ in the goals to which they are directed (e.g., diagnosis vs. assessment of severity of symptoms), in the type of symptoms they emphasize (e.g., cognitive vs. affective), and in their empirical status. Also, the measures have been developed in a variety of ways, such as direct adaptation of measures developed with adults, reliance upon diagnostic criteria, the ability to discriminate populations, or expert opinions of the item content (see Kazdin & Petti, 1982).

In clinical settings, one of the primary purposes of assessment of depression is to obtain a diagnosis. For such uses, diagnostic interviews are utilized, such as the Schedule for Affective Disorders and Schizophrenia for School-Age Children (K-SADS; Chambers, Puig-Antich, & Tabrizi, 1978). The measure is modeled after the format of the Schedule for Affective Disorders and Schizophrenia (Endicott & Spitzer, 1978), which has been used for diagnosis of disorders in adults. In the K-SADS, a wide range of possible diagnoses are covered by the material, although the primary focus is on affective disorders. The measure consists of an unstructured interview, followed by a structured portion where the respondent is asked about the presence, severity, and duration of a number of symptoms. An outline of major areas encompassed by the unstructured interview and guidelines for administration are given in Figure 1. After the unstructured interview is completed, the more structured portion of the interview begins. During this portion, a wide range of specific symptoms are evaluated. For each symptom, the interviewer asks questions to determine whether the symptom is present, and if so, to what degree. A sample item and the range of questions that might be asked to obtain the information are also presented in Figure 1.

The measure is administered separately to the parent and then the child, a process that may require anywhere from 45 to 90 minutes. Discrepancies are resolved to reach a consensus on the presence of specific symptoms covered in the DSM. The K-SADS has been utilized in a number of studies and has been shown to reflect treatment effects as well (using ratings of symptom severity) (e.g., Kashani et al., 1983; Puig-Antich et al., 1978). Other diagnostic instruments are available as well (see Table 3) and have also been used to evaluate individual symptoms or different types of affective disorder (Herjanic & Reich, 1982; Kovacs et al., 1984).

Although diagnosis of depression is of obvious interest, self-report inventories, questionnaires, and interviews designed to measure severity of symptoms are used more frequently. The most widely used measure is the Children's Depression Inventory (CDI; Kovacs, 1981). The measure, adapted originally from the Beck Depression Inventory (BDI), includes 27 items that assess the cognitive, affective, and behavioral signs of depression. Each item presents three alternative statements. Children select one of the three alternatives that characterizes them

TABLE 3. Selected Self-Report Measures, Interviews, and Clinical Rating Scales for Childhood and Adolescent Depression

Measure	Response format	Age range	Special features
1. Children's Depression Inventory (CDI; Kovacs & Beck, 1977)	27 items, each rated on scale of 0–2.	7–17	Derivative of Beck Depression Inventory (BDI). Items reflect affective, cognitive, and behavioral symptoms.
2. Short Children's Depression Inventory (Short CDI; Carlson & Cantwell, 1979)	13 items, rated on scale of 0–4.	7–17	Derivative of Short BDI. Departs slightly from CDI in duration required for symptoms to be endorsed and in response alternative format.
3. Children's Depression Scale (CDS; Lang & Tisher, 1978)	66 items, each item on a card; cards sorted into boxes reflecting scale of 1–5.	9–16	Depression subscales reflect affective symptoms, social problems, preoccupation with sickness and death, and guilt. Also, positive subscale measuring pleasure and enjoyment.
4. Self-Rating Scale (Birleson, 1981)	18 items, scored on a 3-point scale.	7–13	Items reflect range of affective, cognitive behavioral symptoms. Sample item: "I like to have fun."
5. Modified Zung (M-Zung; Lefkowitz & Tesiny, 1980)	16 items; yes–no format for presence or absence.	Fourth- and fifth-graders (approx. 10–11)	Derived from adult scale; modifications include reduced number of items, rewording, and different response format. Sample item: "Do you often feel like crying?"
6. Face Valid Depression Scale for Adolescents (DSA; Mezzich & Mezzich, 1979)	35 items, scored 0–1 (true–false) as characteristic of respondent.	12–18	Derived from Minnesota Multiphasic Personality Inventory items that clinicians selected. Includes items specific to adolescents, as well as items common to adolescents and adults. Sample item: "Do you want to leave home?"
7. Center for Epidemiological Studies Depression Scale (modified for children) (CES-D; Weissman, Orvaschel, & Padian, 1980)	20 items, each on scale of 0–4.	6–17	Derivative of adult scales of same name. Many items dealing with friends and parents. Sample item: "Have you wanted to do something opposite of what your parents wanted?"
8. Beck Depression Inventory (modified for adolescents) (BDI-A; Chiles, Miller, & Cox, 1980)	33 items, each on a scale varying from 0 to 2, 3, or 4 points.	13–15	Derivative of BDI. Change in language rather than content.
9. Reynolds Adolescent Depression Scale (RADS; Reynolds & Coats, 1985)	30 items, each on a 4-point scale.	High school students	Items derived from symptoms included in major, minor, and unipolar depression.
10. Bellevue Index of Depression (BID; Petti, 1978)	40 items, each rated on 4-point scale for severity and 3-point scale for duration.	6–12	Items devised on the basis of the Weinberg criteria; interview can be given separately to child, parents, and others; recommendation is to combine scores from different sources.
11. Bellevue Index of Depression—Revised (BID-R; Kazdin, French, Unis, & Esveldt-Dawson, 1983)	26 items, each rated on a 5-point scale for severity and 3-point scale for duration.	6–13	Similar to BID; fewer items, scores not combined from different sources.
12. Behavior Inventory for	27 items rated by cli-	<13	Approximately two-thirds of items de-

(continued)

TABLE 3. (*continued*)

Measure	Response format	Age range	Special features
Depressed Adolescents (Chiles *et al.*, 1980)	nicians on varying Likert-type formats based on multiple sources of information.		rived from Hamilton Rating Scale for Depression; others derived especially for this scale. Sample item: "The adolescent cries frequently while alone."
13. Children's Depression Rating Scale (CDRS; Poznanski, Cook, & Carroll, 1979)	16 items scored after interview; symptoms rated on 6-point scale for severity.	6–12	Devised from format of Hamilton Rating Scale for Depression. Administered also to parents and others to combine different sources.
14. Children's Affective Rating Scale (CARS; McKnew, Cytryn, Efron, Gershon, & Bunney, 1979)	Three items (mood, verbal behavior, and fantasy), each rated on 10-point scale for severity following interview.	5–15	Global clinical ratings rather than self-report of problems by child.
15. Interview Schedule for Children (ISC—Form C; Kovacs, 1978)	Multiple items and subitems covering symptoms of depression, conduct disorders, and other symptom constellations; rated on 10-point scale for severity for most items.	8–13	Current phenomenology of child; duration varies to reflect current conditions; specific symptoms queried with varying durations. Parent and child are administered interview.
16. Schedule for Affective Disorders and Schizophrenia for School-Age Children (K-SADS; Chambers, Puig-Antich, & Tabrizi, 1978)	Multiple items covering several disorders based on RDC; depression symptom areas rated for degree of severity for scales varying in point values.	6–16	Modeled after adult SADS; provides several diagnoses based on RDC. Parent and child are interviewed.

within the last 2 weeks. For example, children are asked to select one of each set of these alternatives: "a. I am sad once in a while"; "b. I am sad many times"; or "c. I am sad all of the time." For each item, the child's score (0, 1, or 2) is based on the more extreme statement that is endorsed (in the direction of depression).

The CDI has been shown to have high internal consistency (e.g., Cronbach's $\alpha > .80$) and moderate test–retest reliability (from 1 week up to 6 months); to distinguish clinic from nonclinic groups of children; and to correlate in the expected directions with measures of related constructs, such as self-esteem, negative cognitive attributions, hopelessness, and others (e.g., Kazdin, French, Unis, Esveldt-Dawson, & Sherick, 1983; Kovacs, 1981; Saylor, Finch, Baskin, Furey, & Kelly, 1984; Saylor, Finch, Spirito, & Bennett, 1984; Seligman *et al.*, 1984). Normative data have appeared in these and other studies to facilitate evaluation of the level of dysfunction of children relative to their same-age and same-gender peers (Finch, Saylor, & Edwards, 1985). In general, the CDI is one of the better-researched measures to date. The measure has been used for children 6 years and older (Kazdin, Rodgers, & Colbus, 1986; Kovacs, 1981).

The findings have also raised ambiguities regarding the CDI. For example, selected findings in the studies above have indicated that the CDI does not necessarily predict depression scores from other measures and does not invariably discriminate depression from other diagnoses or from maladjustment. Complexities

FIGURE 1. Illustration of unstructured and structured interview format of the K-SADS. From *The Ongoing Development of the Kiddie-SADS (Schedule for Affective Disorders and Schizophrenia for School-Age Children)* by W. J. Chambers, J. Puig-Antich, and M. A. Tabrizi, 1978, October, paper presented at the meeting of the American Academy of Child Psychiatry, San Diego. Reprinted by permission of Dr. Puig-Antich.

UNSTRUCTURED INTERVIEW

The interviewer should first introduce himself to the child or parent and explain the purpose of the interview. He should then obtain or confirm enough demographic information so as to orient himself (see scoring sheet).

The aim of this part of the assessment is to obtain an overall view of the presenting problems, onset of the episode and duration. The unstructured interview with the parent is likely to be more productive than the one with the child in assessing these clinical parameters.

> Hello, I am Dr. _____ (here you spend a few minutes in general conversation in order to make the child feel at ease). I would like to talk with you about the kinds of problems which made your parents bring you to see us, so I can think about how to help you best.
> Could you first tell me your . . . (demographic information)?
> What is your main trouble?
> Why did you come here?
> Why did your parents bring you here?
> What did they say?
> Can you guess why?
> What is the last thing that happened which made your parents bring you here?

If possible, try to get a history of the present illness in the unstructured interview. You are likely to get it, in many children, especially over 8 years old.

IF PATIENT BLAMES OTHERS OR FOCUSES ON PERIPHERAL ISSUES:
> Yes, I understand that (e.g., the other children at school pick on you).
> For how long have they done this?
> Do you know why they pick on you instead of the other children?
> Do you do anything to bother them?
> Do you do anything that makes them angry?
> Do you do anything that makes your teacher angry?
> Have you been having any worries lately?
> Have you been having any problems lately?
> Have you been having any difficulties lately?

IF A SYMPTOM IS IDENTIFIED:
> When did you first notice you were having this (symptom)?
> How different has this trouble been from the way you were before?
> How different has this trouble been from the way you usually are?
> When was it worse?

IF THE CHILD'S STATEMENT IS TOO BRIEF: Can you tell me more about that?
IF THE CHILD HAS MORE TO ADD: What else has been troubling you?
IF STATEMENTS ARE HARD TO UNDERSTAND: Can you explain what you mean by that?
IF THE CHILD IS VAGUE: Could you give me an example of (_____)?
IF NO OTHER RESPONSE IS FORTHCOMING: Why did you come to the hospital?

AFTER A SYMPTOM IS IDENTIFIED AND EXPLORED:
> Do you have any other troubles?
> Do you have any other problems?
> Do you have any other worries?
> Do you have any other things bothering you?

If any other problems are brought up, explore each one individually like the first one.

WHEN THE CHILD HAS NO OTHER DIFFICULTIES TO REPORT:
> Anything else troubling you?
> Anything else you would like more help with?

Many children will be unable to provide reliable time data. This is developmentally normal. If the child does not provide such data in the first questioning, he will probably not provide

(continued)

FIGURE 1. (*continued*)

it at all. Most children under 18 years of age will be unable to give chronological data. Do not assail the child with questions if questioning so far is unproductive. Just proceed to the structured interview. An easy, friendly manner is essential for the success of the interview.

During the unstructured interview with the parent the same technique should be followed, modifying the questions appropriately to refer to the child. After the unstructured interview is completed, the interviewer will frequently have a clear picture of onset and length of present episode, major symptomatology, and periodicity (mood disorders). Sometimes this information can only come from the parent(s). In this case the child should be told what parents have reported, and he should be allowed to confirm or refute such information. The interviewer should then make a clinical judgment on onset and length of present episode and then rate mode of onset and duration.

When interviewing children who are not psychiatric patients the same approach is to be followed, without any reference to referral or main complaint.

> I would like you to tell me about any worries, problems, fears, difficulties, or troubles you are having now.

STRUCTURED INTERVIEW (Sample Item)

NEGATIVE SELF-IMAGE

Includes feelings of inadequacy, inferiority, failure and worthlessness, self-deprecation, self-belittling. Rate with disregard of how "realistic" the negative self-evaluation is.

How do you feel about yourself? Are you down on yourself?	0 No information.
Do you like yourself as a person? Why? Describe yourself.	1 Not at all.
Do you ever think of yourself as ugly? When? How often?	2 Slight: Occasional feelings of inadequacy.
Do you think you are bright or stupid? Why? Do you often think like that?	3. Mild: Often feels somewhat inadequate, or would like to change his looks or his brains or his personality.
Do you think you are better or worse than your friends?	
Is any one of your friends worse than you are?	4. Moderate: Often feels like a failure, or would like to change two of the above.
What things are you good at? Any others?	
What things are you bad at?	5. Severe: Frequent feelings of worthlessness, or would like to change all three. Occasionally says he hates himself.
How often do you feel this way about yourself?	
What would you like to change about you?	

---

have also emerged in the test–retest data. For brief intervals such as 1 week, low and high–retest correlations have been found (r's = .38 vs. .87) for normal and emotionally disturbed children, respectively (Saylor, Finch, Spirito, & Bennett, 1984). More typically, moderate test–retest correlations have been found spanning periods of several weeks (Kazdin, French, Unis, & Esveldt-Dawson, 1983; Kovacs, 1981). There may be important differences in the stability of CDI severity scores as a function of age, sex, and clinic versus nonclinic samples

(Saylor, Finch, Spirito, & Bennett, 1984). In general, the CDI remains the most widely used and researched measure of childhood depression. Nevertheless, the need to evaluate its psychometric properties and normative base remains.

As shown in Table 3, there are many other self-report measures. One of these that may merit special attention is the Children's Depression Scale (Lang & Tisher, 1978). The measure is noteworthy because its 66 items encompass several subscales for specific areas of depressive symptoms (affective responses, social problems, self-esteem, preoccupation with sickness and death, and guilt) and positive affective experiences as well. The use of multiple subscales may permit more fine-grained analyses of developmental differences in depression than do other scales that sample relatively few symptom areas.

The measures in Table 3 typically have been developed for children and adolescents and often are recommended for use up to ages 17 or 18. However, occasionally, measures developed for adults (e.g., the BDI) are also used with adolescents (e.g., Strober, Green, & Carlson, 1981). Thus, for adolescents the range of available measures is broad.

Ratings by Adults

Significant others, primarily parents and teachers, are often asked to evaluate a child's depression. For present purposes, ratings by clinicians are included here as well. Their "significance" stems from their special expertise rather than their familiarity with the child. Several different types of measures are available. The most commonly used measures are general scales that assess a variety of different types of symptoms or constellations of behavior, only one of which is depression. For example, the Personality Inventory for Children is a parent-rated scale that includes multiple areas of child dysfunction (Wirt, Lachar, Klinedinst, & Seat, 1977). A subscale of the instrument includes 46 true–false items to measure depression separately from the larger scale (e.g., Lobovits & Handal, 1985).

A second type of rating by significant others involves the adaptation of self-report measures. Measures such as the CDI (or other measures listed in Table 3) are altered for the parent or adult to convey that the child's depression is evaluated. The alterations are minor, with changes in instructions or wording of the items. For example, parents and teachers occasionally are asked to complete the CDI for children under their care (e.g., Helsel & Matson, 1984). With alternate forms for children and adults, direct comparisons can be made to evaluate correspondence of responses.

A third type of measure in this category is one specifically designed to assess depression and related symptoms. One such measure worth highlighting is the Children's Depression Rating Scale (CDRS; Poznanski, Cook, & Carroll, 1979). The measure is an adaptation of the Hamilton Rating Scale for Depression (Hamilton, 1967), which has been widely used to measure depression in adults. The current version (CDRS-R) is a 17-item interview concerning symptoms of depression, each of which is rated on a Likert-type scale for severity of dysfunction. The symptoms may be inferred from the content of the child's verbal report as well as from nonverbal behavior in the inter-

TABLE 4. Illustrative Item (Anhedonia) from the CDRS

CAPACITY TO HAVE FUN (0–7)

0. Unable to rate.
1. Interest and activities realistically appropriate for age, personality, and social environment. Shows no appreciable change with present illness. Any feelings of boredom are transient.
2. Doubtful.
3. Mild. Describes some activities realistically available several times a week but not on a daily basis. Shows interest but not enthusiasm. May express some episodes of boredom more than once a week.
4. Mild to moderate.
5. Moderate. Is easily bored. Complains of "nothing to do." Participates in structured activities with a "going through the motions" attitude.
6. Moderate to severe. Shows no enthusiasm or real interest. Has difficulty naming activities. May express interest primarily in activities that are (realistically) *unavailable* on a daily or weekly basis.
7. Severe. Has no initiative to become involved in any activities. Primarily passive. Watches others play or watches TV but shows little interest in the program. Requires coaxing and/or pushing to get involved in the activity.

Note. From "Preliminary Studies of the Reliability and Validity of the Children's Depression Rating Scale" by E. O. Poznanski, J. A. Grossman, Y. Buchsbaum, M. Banegas, L. Freeman, & R. Gibbons, 1984, *Journal of the American Academy of Child Psychiatry, 23,* p. 193. Copyright 1984 by the American Academy of Child Psychiatry. Reprinted by permission.

TABLE 5. PNID Items

1. Often plays alone? (D)	12. Doesn't play? (D)
2. Thinks they are bad? (D)	13. Often smiles? (H)
3. Doesn't try again when they lose? (D)	14. Doesn't take part in things? (D)
4. Often sleeps in class? (D)	15. Doesn't have much fun? (D)
5. Often looks lonely? (D)	16. Is often cheerful? (H)
6. Often says they don't feel well? (D)	17. Thinks others don't like them? (D)
7. Says they can't do things? (D)	18. Often looks sad? (D)
8. Often cries? (D)	19. Who would you like to sit next to in
9. Often looks happy? (H)	class? (P)
10. Likes to do a lot of things? (H)	20. Who are the children you would like to
11. Worries a lot? (D)	have for your best friends? (P)

Note. "Assessment of Childhood Depression" by M. M. Lefkowitz and E. P. Tesiny, 1980, *Journal of Consulting and Clinical Psychology, 48,* p. 44. Copyright 1980 by the American Psychological Association. Reprinted by permission of the authors. Items 1–18 are prefaced by "who" for administration. The three subscales of the measure include Depression (14 D items), Happiness (4 H items), and Popularity (2 P items). Item analyses suggested that item 2 not be included in the scale, bringing to 13 the number of items used to score depression.

view (e.g., appearance of sad affect, hypoactivity). Evaluation of the symptoms ultimately depends upon the judgment of the clinician, who may rely upon multiple sources of information, including interviews of the child, parent, or others. The information is integrated into a single rating. An example of the rating format is provided in Table 4, which presents the item to measure anhedonia (impairment of the capacity to have fun).

Although evaluation of the CDRS in its original or revised form has been sparse, studies have appeared indicating high interjudge agreement (r's > .75) in rating children, high correlations (r's > .85) of the CDRS with global clinical ratings of depression, and high test–retest performance ($r = .81$ up to 6 weeks) (Poznanski *et al.*, 1979; Poznanski, Cook, Carroll, & Corzo, 1983; Poznanski *et al.*, 1984).

Ratings by Peers

Peer ratings have been used to evaluate diverse facets of psychopathology, including depression. The advantage of peers is that they observe each other in a wide range of settings and for extended periods, and consequently have a reasonably good basis for their evaluations. Peer measures occasionally have been constructed by altering items from self-report inventories so that they can be rated by peers (e.g., Malouff, 1984).

For children, the primary peer-based measure is the Peer Nomination Inventory for Depression (PNID; Lefkowitz & Tesiny, 1980). The measure depends upon the group context, because peers within the group (e.g., the same classroom at school) are asked about characteristics of different children. The measure, presented in Table 5, consists of 20 items in which children are asked several specific questions. The 20 items comprise three subscales: Depression, Happiness, and Popularity. In response to each question, the child identifies the peer(s) to whom the characteristic applies. A child's own score is the sum (or proportion) of nominations he or she receives on each of the subscales.

The measure has been carefully evaluated in studies that have provided evidence for internal consistency ($\alpha > .85$), test–retest stability (from 2 to over 6 months), and interrater agreement. Also, normative data have been gathered for over 3,000 third-, fourth-, and fifth-grade children. Validation studies have shown only weak relations between PNID scores and self-report or teacher ratings of depression. Yet PNID scores correlate with school performance, self-concept, teacher ratings of work skills and social behavior, and peer ratings of happiness and popularity (Lefkowitz, Tesiny, & Gordon, 1980; Lefkowitz & Tesiny, 1985; Tesiny & Lefkowitz, 1982).

Direct Observations of Overt Behavior

Many characteristics of depression are overt behaviors or observable characteristics, such as diminished social and motor activity, sad facial expression, slowed speech, and others (see Greden & Carroll, 1981; Jacobson, 1981). In the literature with adult populations, some attention has been given to direct observations of overt behavior. The primary focus has been on measures of nonverbal behavior. Research has shown that depressed adults, when compared to normal controls or other patient groups, often show reduced eye contact with others; slower speech; and fewer hand, head, and body movements during conversation (e.g., Jones & Pasna, 1979; Waxer, 1976). Studies have also shown that recovery from a depressive episode and response to antidepressant medication are reflected in changes in nonverbal behaviors (e.g., Fisch, Frey, & Hirsbrunner, 1983; R. E. Miller, Ranelli, & Levine, 1977).

Although nonverbal behavior has been rather extensively studied with depressed adults, few direct extensions have been reported with children. In one investigation with child psychiatric patients aged 7–12, nonverbal behaviors were assessed during interviews and evaluated in relation to self-report and parent report measures of child depression and psychiatric diagnosis (Kazdin, Sherick, et al., 1985). Nonverbal behaviors were assessed as each child answered questions about everyday life (e.g., "What have you been doing in school?") or told stories in response to Thematic Apperception Test cards. Nonverbal behaviors included eye contact, facial expressiveness, response latency, bodily movements, gestures, frowning, and others. The results revealed low negative correlations for child and parent reports of depression and nonverbal behaviors such as facial expressiveness, body movements and gestures, and a positive correlation with tearfulness. There were, however, important gender differences, with girls showing more consistent relationships between nonverbal behaviors and measures of depression.

Nonverbal behavior during interviews does

TABLE 6. Behavioral Codes for Direct Observation of Behavior

A. *Social Activity:* Behaviors in this category consisted of engaging in social interaction or activities in which such interaction was central. Four behaviors were included in this category.

   (1) *Talking*—verbally interacting with another child in which there was an exchange of comments or ongoing dialogue. Single verbal statements that were unreciprocated were not included.

   (2) *Playing a Game*—participating in a game such as a board game or other activity with one or more individuals.

   (3) *Participating in a Group Activity*—engaging in behavior with a group of individuals not necessarily involving a structured game; interacting with a group, taking turns, looking at materials together, working together on a special task.

   (4) *Interacting with Staff*—contacting staff members including conversing or playing with staff.

B. *Solitary Behavior:* Behaviors scored in this category consisted of engaging in activities that did not involve participation with other persons. The activities were performed alone, independently, or in a parallel fashion with others rather than in conjunction with them. Five behaviors were included in this category.

   (1) *Playing a Game Alone*—engaging in a game activity (board game, cards, or task with play materials) involving only oneself.

   (2) *Working on an Academic Task*—reading, studying, or writing by oneself.

   (3) *Listening and Watching*—looking, listening, and reacting to a TV program or radio or music by oneself.

   (4) *Straightening One's Room*—putting one's belongings in the proper place or cleaning one's room.

   (5) *Grooming*—engaging in behaviors related to self-care. Three areas were observed, including getting dressed or changing clothes, grooming (combing one's hair, brushing teeth), and cleaning or washing oneself (showering, bathing).

C. *Affect-Related Expression:* Codes in this category were selected to reflect the display of affective expression. Four codes were included that reflected both nonverbal and verbal behaviors.

   (1) *Smiling*—using facial muscles to upturn the corners of the mouth and/or facial expressions of joy or pleasure.

   (2) *Frowning*—lowering one's eyebrows or downward turning of the mouth and/or facial expressions of displeasure.

   (3) *Arguing*—tense, emotional, verbal interaction including loud voice, shouting, loss of temper, or verbal outburst of anger.

   (4) *Complaining*—verbal expression of unhappiness, dissatisfaction.

not exhaust the range of options for direct observation. Research with adults has suggested the utility of observing behavior during daily functioning. For example, J. G. Williams, Barlow, and Agras (1972) observed talking, smiling, and several motor behaviors of depressed patients. They found moderate to high negative correlations of a total sum of these behaviors with clinician and self-report ratings of depression. Overt behaviors observed on the ward have also reflected improvements in treatment and predict posthospital adjustment better than clinician and self-report ratings (Fossi, Faravelli, & Paoli, 1984; J. G. Williams *et al.,* 1972).

Direct observations have been made of inpatient children aged 8–13, who were observed during free-time periods over the course of a week (Kazdin, Esveldt-Dawson, *et al.,* 1985). Behaviors were observed to comprise three categories: social activity, solitary behavior, and affect-related expression. Within each category, several specific behaviors were identified. Table 6 shows the overall categories and the constituent behaviors that were observed. The primary interest was in evaluating the three overall categories, because pilot data indicated that the base rates for the individual behaviors were quite low. Children were observed for 35-minute periods over a week. Each behavior was recorded as present or absent during 5-minute intervals in each of the periods.

Children high in depression, as defined by a parent interview measure (the Bellevue Index of Depression—Revised), engaged in significantly less social behavior and evinced less affect-related expression than did children low in depression. These results are consistent with studies of depressed adults that have found deficiencies in social interaction and expressions of affect (e.g., Lewinsohn & Shaffer, 1971; Linden, Hautzinger, & Hoffmann, 1983).

The codes shown in Table 6 do not, of course, exhaust the range of options for direct observations. Other studies have reported the use of direct observation in examining on-task and disruptive classroom behavior, completion of activities of daily living (Michelson, DiLorenzo, & Petti, 1981), and role-play performance where specific features of depression are operationalized and evaluated (Frame, Matson, Sonis, Fialkov, & Kazdin, 1982). Apart from the need to expand upon currently available observational codes, research needs to consider more systematically the antecedents, settings

(e.g., home, school), and consequences associated with such behaviors.

Psychophysiological and Biological Assessments

Psychophysiological and biological assessments encompass a number of laboratory-based measures. These measures supplement the more commonly used rating scales and interviews. Moreover, the measures often have implications for testing etiological views and biological correlates of affective disorders.

Assessment of neuroendocrine functioning has been evaluated more extensively among children than other biological strategies have been. The research has followed rather extensive exemplars from the literature on adults. Adult depressed patients (endogenous depressives) have been shown to secrete excess cortisol during depressive episodes—a characteristic that returns to normal during recovery (see Depue & Kleiman, 1979). Cortisol hypersecretion is assessed by drawing blood repeatedly (e.g., over a 24-hour period). Plasma concentrations of cortisol show more frequent periods of secretion, higher peak values, and greater amounts of secretion. Research has also shown that endogenous depressed adults hyposecrete growth hormone in response to insulin-induced hypoglycemia. This research has been extended to children, showing similar findings with depressed patients (see Puig-Antich, 1983).

Electrophysiological recordings of adults have been used extensively to evaluate sleep of depressed patients. Decreased total sleep time, decreased delta wave sleep, shortened REM latency, and early-morning and intermittent awakenings are some of the many characteristics shown to distinguish depressed adults (see Kupfer *et al.,* 1983). Evaluations of sleep architecture among depressed children have not shown consistent differences parallel to those obtained with adults (e.g., Goetz *et al.,* 1983; Young *et al.,* 1982). The discrepancy of findings between adult and child populations may prove significant, given the continuity of many other biological correlates over the developmental spectrum.

The above-described measures do not exhaust the biological correlates that have been studied in children. The primary focus has been on the assessment of biological markers that have emerged in research on adult depressives, as noted earlier. Biological assessments make a major contribution in understanding depression and its possible biological substrates. The measures reflect a different level of assessment from assessment of symptoms experienced by the child or dysfunction evident to parents and teachers. The relationship between the presence of specific symptoms and results from biological assessments of the sort highlighted here remains to be explored in children.

Other Measures

The modalities described up to this point reflect the measures most commonly used to assess depression. However, other types of measures have occasionally been used as well. Projective techniques have received attention in a few investigations. These techniques, of course, are designed to present ambiguous stimuli and response opportunities to the child. Investigations have evaluated different facets of the Rorschach test (e.g., Decina *et al.*, 1983), the Thematic Apperception Test (e.g., Kazdin, Sherick, *et al.*, 1985; Riddle & Rapoport, 1976), the Children's Apperception Test (Cytryn & McKnew, 1974), and the Draw-a-Person Test (Gordon, Lefkowitz, & Tesiny, 1980). In general, measures derived from these instruments have not yielded reliable differences between depressed and nondepressed youths. When differences have emerged, molecular responses (e.g., number of color responses on the Rorschach) with unclear theoretical or applied significance have been identified.

MEASURES OF RELATED CONSTRUCTS

There are a number of constructs related to depression that are often included in an assessment battery because they focus on a particular facet of depressive symptoms or derive from a model about the important ingredients associated with depression. The constructs and sample measures are only briefly noted here.

Self-Esteem

"Self-esteem" consists of self-reported valuations of personal worth. Diminished self-esteem is a generic characteristic that may be associated with several types of dysfunction; of course, it may also occur in the absence of any dysfunction. Low self-esteem is part of the symptom picture of depression (e.g., feelings of worthlessness) and also plays a prominent role in alternative models of depression (Beck, 1976).

Assessment of self-esteem is usually conducted by presenting multiple statements in a self-report inventory. Children are asked to decide whether descriptive statements are true or untrue of them. For example, the Coopersmith Self-Esteem Inventory (Coopersmith, 1967) includes 58 items to which children respond as like or not like them. Sample items refer to such personal characteristics as how proud the child is of his or her school work, whether he or she often feels ashamed, or whether he or she ever feels like a failure. Evidence has shown that measures of childhood depression are negatively correlated in the moderate range with the Coopersmith measure or related measures of self-esteem (e.g., Kazdin, French, Unis, & Esveldt-Dawson, 1983).

Self-esteem scales such as the Coopersmith Inventory typically yield total scores that are obtained by summing items across several areas of functioning. The assumption has been that self-esteem is a global index of self-perception. An alternative view is that there are many areas of functioning, and that people may feel differently about themselves in relation to them. A recently devised self-report inventory that reflects this view is the Perceived Competence Scale for Children (Harter, 1982). This measure of self-esteem samples three specific spheres of functioning: (1) cognitive competence, (2) social competence, and (3) physical competence. A fourth area, overall self-worth, is also included. Sample items include self-ratings of how good the child is at schoolwork (cognitive competence), how popular he or she is (social competence), how well he or she performs in sports (physical competence), and the extent to which the child views himself or herself as a good person (global self-worth). Data suggest that children can readily distinguish separate areas of competence. The use of a self-esteem scale that differentiates areas of self-perceived competence may be quite useful for investigation of depression. Fine-grained evaluation of different areas of competence, and perhaps of competence in different situations, may be informative in evaluating developmental, gender, and diagnostic variations.

Hopelessness

"Hopelessness" refers to negative expectations toward the future. Hopelessness is related to depression in different ways. One symptom diagnostically relevant to depression is suicidal attempt or ideation. Hopelessness has been consistently shown to correlate with suicidal behavior in adults (Beck, Kovacs, & Weissman, 1975). Indeed, the relation between depression and suicidal behavior (when studied through partial correlation) is mediated by the level of hopelessness. Hopelessness, like self-esteem, is also posited as a central feature of depression in cognitive views of depression.

A measure has been available for some time to assess hopelessness among adults (Beck, Weissman, Lester, & Trexler, 1974). Recently, a parallel measure has been developed for children. The Hopelessness Scale for Children (Kazdin, Rodgers, & Colbus, 1986) includes 17 true–false items that ask children how they see the future and how the future is likely to

turn out for them (see Figure 2). As with adults, hopelessness in children has been shown to correlate with depression, to predict suicidal ideation and behavior, and to be related to diminished self-esteem (Kazdin, French, Unis, Esveldt-Dawson, & Sherick, 1983; Kazdin, Rodgers, & Colbus, 1986). To date, this hopelessness measure has been used only with patient samples (aged 6–13). Data on normal children, and variations in hopelessness and its correlates over the course of development, have yet to be reported.

Social Behavior

Social skills, social competence, and social interaction have been frequently studied in relation to adult depression. While deficits in social behavior and diminished social interac-

---

FIGURE 2. The Hopelessness Scale for Children. An item is scored as reflecting hopelessness if the answer is true (T) or false (F), as noted at the end of each item.

Instructions to the Child:
   These sentences are about how some kids feel about their lives. Your answers let us know about how kids feel about things. I am going to read each sentence to you. I'd like you to tell me if the sentence is *true* for you or *false* for you. If the sentence is how you feel, you would say it is *like you* or *true*. If the sentence is *not* how you think or feel, you would say it is *not like you* or *false*.
   Let's try some examples:

A. When I grow up, I want to be a teacher.	true	false
B. I don't think I will have a pet when I grow up.	true	false

(Stop to explain what the answer given by the child means.)
There are no right or wrong answers. Just tell me if the sentence is like you or not like you—true or false.

1. I want to grow up because I think things will be better (F).	true	false
2. I might as well give up because I can't make things better for myself (T).	true	false
3. When things are going badly, I know that they won't be bad all of the time (F).	true	false
4. I can imagine what my life will be like when I'm grown up (F).	true	false
5. I have enough time to finish the things I really want to do (F).	true	false
6. Someday, I will be good at doing the things that I really care about (F).	true	false
7. I will get more of the good things in life than most other kids (F).	true	false
8. I don't have good luck and there's no reason to think I will when I grow up (T).	true	false
9. All I can see ahead of me are bad things, not good things (T).	true	false
10. I don't think I will get what I really want (T).	true	false
11. When I grow up, I think I will be happier than I am now (F).	true	false
12. Things just won't work out the way I want them to (T).	true	false
13. I never get what I want, so it's dumb to want anything (T).	true	false
14. I don't think I will have any real fun when I grow up (T).	true	false
15. Tomorrow seems unclear and confusing to me (T).	true	false
16. I will have more good times than bad times (F).	true	false
17. There's no use in really trying to get something I want because I probably won't get it (T).	true	false

tion are not explicitly part of the diagnostic criteria, a loss of interest in usual activities is a core symptom, and many of these activities are social in nature. In addition, social behavior has occupied a prominent place in behavioral and cognitive models of depression.

In research with adults, deficits in the social behavior of depressed patients have been demonstrated with a wide array of measures focusing both on molar and on molecular behaviors (e.g., communication patterns, participation in activities, expressions of affect, eye contact, and hand gestures accompanying speech) (Hinchliffe, Lancashire, & Roberts, 1971; Lewinsohn & Shaffer, 1971; Linden et al., 1983). For children, several measures of social behavior are available, including interviews, informant reports, peer and sociometric ratings, behavioral role-play tests, naturalistic observations, and others (see Hops & Greenwood, 1988; Michelson, Sugai, Wood, & Kazdin, 1983). To date, these have not been systematically evaluated in the context of childhood depression.

One measure recently developed to sample a broad range of social behaviors is the Matson Evaluation of Social Skills with Youngsters (MESSY; Matson, Rotatori, & Helsel, 1983). The scale includes 92 items that address multiple areas of social functioning, such as social isolation, expression of hostility, conversational skills, making friends, and others. Each item (e.g., "I know how to make friends," "I gripe or complain often") is rated on a 5-point Likert scale. Separate forms are available so that the child or an adult can evaluate performance (Matson, Esveldt-Dawson, & Kazdin, 1983; Matson, Rotatori, & Helsel, 1983). Research with this scale has demonstrated relationships between deficiencies in social functioning and severity of depression (Helsel & Matson, 1984). These results are consistent with findings from studies in which children's social behavior has been assessed by parents' ratings of the children's participation in activities and social interaction and by direct observation of the children (Kazdin, Esveldt-Dawson, et al., 1985; Kazdin, Rodgers, & Colbus, 1986).

Life Events

"Life events" refer generally to external factors in the environment that can induce stress. The events may vary along several dimensions, including their perceived valence (e.g., positive, negative, or mixed); their magnitude or intensity (e.g., severity of negative events, such as losing a friend who moves away vs. death of a parent); and their concentration (e.g., one or a few vs. several within a specific time period). The assessment of stressors as part of the evaluation of depression has received considerable attention among adults. The impact of stressors in precipitating or facilitating the emergence of depression has been recognized in socioenvironmental, cognitive, and biological models. However, little attention has yet been accorded the assessment of stressors in childhood depression.

A number of measures are available (see Johnson, 1982). Their usual format is to list several different events to the child, who indicates whether or not they occurred. Additional information may be solicited to evaluate their perceived impact. For example, the Life Events Checklist enumerates 46 events (e.g., change of schools, divorce of parents) that are endorsed by the child as having occurred or not (Johnson & McCutcheon, 1980). The type of event (good, bad) and its impact on the child's life (1 = no effect, 4 = great effect) are also evaluated. The measure has been shown to correlate significantly with difficulty in coping with personal problems, depression, and several other measures of adjustment (see Johnson & McCutcheon, 1980).

Additional Constructs

An important characteristic of depression is that virtually all facets of the individual's functioning may be affected. Consequently, many other constructs and measurement strategies than those listed above may be of interest for the purposes of clinical research. Other constructs that are close to and partially overlap with those discussed above include measures of attributional style, as measured by the Kastan Children's Attributional Style Questionnaire (Kaslow et al., 1984); locus of control, as measured by the Internal–External Scale for Children (Nowicki & Strickland, 1973); child perception of rewarding events, as measured by the Children's Reinforcement Schedule (Cautela, Cautela & Esonis, 1983); and children's feelings of loneliness, as measured by the Loneliness Questionnaire (Asher & Wheeler, 1985). There are a number of constructs that might be of interest for which child measures are currently unavailable. For example, there are well-developed measures for adults of the inability to experience pleasure (anhedonia) and suicidal ideation; the absence of similar well-developed measures for children has impeded research on these constructs.

Because many different areas of performance are likely to be affected by depressive states, it may be useful to consider the inclusion of scales designed to measure adaptive functioning across multiple areas. For example, scales such as the School Behavior Checklist (L. C. Miller, 1972) or the Child Behavior Checklist (Achenbach & Edelbrock, 1983) assess several types of behavioral problems (internalizing, externalizing) as well as prosocial behavior (participation in activities, extraversion), and may be useful in demonstrating the breadth of dysfunction.

CURRENT ISSUES AND CONSIDERATIONS FOR MEASUREMENT SELECTION

The discussion above presents many types of measures of depression, as well as measures of related areas. The large number of measures currently available does not mean that assessment strategies are well developed. Actually, several fundamental questions can be raised about current measures, how they are to be used and interpreted, and their relevance for research and practice.

Child Report

The bulk of assessment devices include child self-report measures. A major issue in the use of such measures is the extent to which children are able or willing to report on their depressive symptoms. This concern does not merely derive from the fact that children might deny symptoms. Rather, measures often ask subtle questions about the presence of specific symptoms, whether a child can identify the basis for a symptom, the duration and intensity, and so on. Research has clearly established that both clinic and nonclinic samples can report on their depressive symptoms (Cantwell & Carlson, 1983). However, evidence suggests that children report fewer symptoms than do parents and clinicians in their evaluations of the children (Kazdin, French, Unis, & Esveldt-Dawson, 1983; Orvaschel *et al.*, 1982; Tisher & Lang, 1983).

The lower estimates of symptoms that children report do not necessarily indict self-report measures. The questions of interest are the extent to which the measures predict performance in other areas or over time, and the relationship of child reports to other sources of information designed to assess depressed affect. Evidence to date suggests that self-report among patient and nonpatient samples is related to a number of other areas of performance (e.g., suicidal attempt and ideation, hopelessness, self-esteem, and negative attributional style), as noted earlier.

Correspondence of Measures

An issue that has frequently emerged is the extent to which measures of depression correspond with each other. The primary issue is the relation of reports from different sources such as parents, teachers, and peers. Reports of children generally do not correlate very well with reports of their parents, teachers, and/or peers (Kazdin, Esveldt-Dawson, Unis, & Rancurello, 1983; Saylor, Finch, Baskin, Furey, & Kelly, 1984; Tesiny & Lefkowitz, 1982). The correlations are occasionally significant, but their magnitude typically ranges between .00 and .30. Obviously, the shared variance in ratings of depression from different sources is quite small.

The lack of correspondence, now evident in several studies, raises the question of whose reports are to be believed. For research, the issue is the extent to which child, parent, teacher, peer, or combined reports are better predictors of other criteria such as family history, long-term prognosis, and treatment course. In everyday experience, reports of depressive symptoms in a child, whether from the child or an adult, should be attended to. Both reports have shown to be related to other important criteria. For example, as noted above, child reports of depression correlate with other facets of experience and behavior. Parent reports tend to correlate with social behavior and affect-related expression (Kazdin, Esveldt-Dawson, Sherick, & Colbus, 1985). Peer and teacher reports correlate with popularity and academic performance, respectively (Tesiny & Lefkowitz, 1982; Tesiny *et al.*, 1980).

The major difficulty in validating reports from alternative raters has been the absence of independent criteria that are free from the bias or input of one of the raters. For example, psychiatric diagnosis or even clinical judgment may not be independent criteria because they invariably rely upon child or parent reports. Because ratings of children's depression from alternative sources correlate with important facets of dysfunction or child behavior, they all may reflect potentially useful information. Yet, for purposes of understanding the relative utility of alternative measures, it will be important to identify alternative sources and measures that predict severity of dysfunction, onset of affective disorders, and response to treatment. Such research remains to be completed.

Inventories to Diagnose Depressive Disorders

An important issue both for research and practice is the use of self-report inventories and questionnaires to diagnose depression or to identify children with relative severity of symptoms. In studies of nonclinic cases, performances on measures such as the CDI are used to define depressed samples, based upon cutoff scores. Although the degree of departure from normal can be clearly delineated with inventories of severity, only the diagnostic interviews specifically address criteria for reaching a psychiatric diagnosis. Children with severe scores on measures such as the CDI may not necessarily meet diagnostic criteria for major depression, and vice versa. In general, children with a diagnosis of depression score higher on self-report measures than do those without such diagnoses (e.g., Asarnow & Carlson, 1985; Moretti, Fine, Haley, & Marriage, 1985), although the differences are not always clinically or statistically significant (e.g., Kazdin, French, Unis, & Esveldt-Dawson, 1983; Saylor, Finch, Spirito, & Bennett, 1984). Thus, self-report inventories are not equivalent to diagnostic interviews in the information they provide.

Biological Assessment

The use of biological assessment raises a number of issues that warrant mention. Because many of the procedures are invasive, concerns emerge about subjecting youths to discomfort and risk. Some techniques currently in use (e.g., insulin-induced hypoglycemia) are risky and simply not feasible for clinical use. Other techniques evaluated with adults (e.g., lumbar puncture) are useful for obtaining information about neurochemistry but have understandably been avoided with children. Although some of the biological measures do corroborate diag-

noses, they do not invariably provide confirming evidence.

For example, in a recent study, a biological measure (growth hormone secretion during sleep) accurately identified half of a sample of depressed children (Puig-Antich et al., 1984). While this finding is highly significant on conceptual grounds, the measure will not be sufficient for screening or diagnostic purposes until higher levels of identification are obtained. Biological measures nevertheless are likely to be refined and to serve multiple functions apart from validation of other assessment techniques. Such measures will help to identify mechanisms underlying depressed symptoms and markers for diagnosis, treatment prescriptions, and prognosis.

General Comments

The assessment of childhood depression is an area of extraordinary research activity. Although many measures are currently available, relatively few have been well tested in studies evaluating some of the obvious forms of reliability and validity. Some measures, such as the CDI, have been frequently evaluated and in diverse contexts. A number of other measures, still with few published data to their credit, might have a rich yield. As a case in point, the Children's Depression Scale is designed to assess many facets of depression, such as social behavior, self-esteem, preoccupation with sickness and death, and others (see Table 3). This measure and several others have only begun to be explored (Tisher & Lang, 1983).

The bulk of the measures consist of lists of symptoms that children rate on Likert-type scales. Among the many such measures, it is likely that some will suffer from disuse and redundancy with more popular measures rather than from poor validity. Investigations are emerging at an accelerated rate on specific instruments; these typically provide normative data, information on psychometric characteristics of the measure, or correlates of severity of depression.

Assessment strategies include primarily self-report and parent report measures. Further research is likely to explore alternative modalities to assess depression. Psychophysiological assessment has not been well explored. For example, facial muscle contractions related to expressions of happiness and sadness have been studied with electromyography and have been shown to discriminate adult depressives from normals and other patient groups (e.g., Schwartz *et al.*, 1978). Such work has yet to be pursued with children or adolescents. Also, biological assessment procedures (e.g., neuroendocrine evaluations) are likely to increase, given the work with adults in this area. Psychophysiological and biological assessment can be very useful for several purposes, including early diagnosis and treatment evaluation. From the standpoint of assessment, such measures may be especially useful in providing criteria to help evaluate and validate more commonly used self-report and parent report measures. Although such measures are not bias-free, they do provide information that is independent of the reports of others.

CURRENT MEASURES IN PERSPECTIVE

Functional Analysis

Alternative conceptual views of depression point to different facets as causes or correlates of dysfunction. The positions argue for specific constructs and foci for both assessment and treatment. The wide range of views and the plethora of measures they encompass make it difficult to identify areas in need of further development in the area of assessment and to select alternative measures in clinical research. A metaconceptual framework relatively free from the specific substantive models of depression is useful, in order to examine current assessment strategies that are in use and to point to relevant areas of childhood depression that may warrant further attention.

A useful framework to integrate current measures is that of a behavioral-analytic or functional-analytic approach (Kanfer & Saslow, 1969). The approach is posed here to organize current assessment strategies for depression, rather than to argue for a substantive position with regard to the nature, characteristics, or conceptualization of depression as a disorder. A behavioral-analytic approach examines the stimuli (S), the organism (O) or individual client, the responses (R), the contingencies (K), and the consequences (C) of behavior. The "stimuli" are the possible antecedent events for depression (e.g., school failure, loss of a relative, divorce); the "organism" consists of those factors within the individual that may affect behavior (e.g., handicapping physical conditions, limited coping skills); the "re-

sponses" are those observed behaviors that serve as the focus of assessment and treatment (e.g., participation in activities, suicidal threats and gestures); the "contingencies" are the relationships (e.g., various reinforcement schedules) between behaviors and antecedent and consequent events in the environment (e.g., child–parent and child–peer interactions associated with, preceding, and resulting from the manifestation of depressive symptoms); and the "consequences" are the specific events (e.g., reinforcing, punishing, or absence of consequences) that follow behavior (e.g., social contacts with others). The S-O-R-K-C model points to different facets of depressive symptoms and the context in which they emerge that may be relevant to assess.[6]

From the standpoint of a functional-analytic model, current measurement strategies focus on relatively restricted areas of functioning. The vast majority of measures reviewed earlier focus on factors within the individual (or O portions of the S-O-R-K-C analysis). For example, self-report and parent report inventories and interviews of depression or related constructs typically refer to traits and states within the child. Dysphoria, feelings of worthlessness or hopelessness, and thoughts of suicide all illustrate the focus on internal states. Measures of biological states and processes also refer to internal characteristics of the organism. Although it is obviously useful not to consider cognitive and biological measures as equivalent, their common focus on the organism is significant to note.

The response (R) or behavioral domain is encompassed by fewer current measurement strategies. How the child behaves or responds (R) is encompassed by ratings completed by the child or by significant others. For example,

---

[6]The S-O-R-K-C model grew out of behavioral analysis, an approach that emphasizes the control that the environment exerts on behavior. Early formulations excluded the role of the organism (O) or the individual in the analysis (Lindsley, 1964). The O factor was added to emphasize the relevance of features within the individual that may influence performance (Kanfer & Saslow, 1969). Over the last decade, the O portion of the model has received increased emphasis in behavior therapy, with attention to cognitive processes that may influence behavior. Cognitions, only one type of internal factor that may influence performance, have received particularly great attention in the context of depression assessment and treatment research. Affective processes, another set of internal factors relevant to depressive symptoms, have received increased attention in developmental research (e.g., Masters, Felleman, & Barden, 1981).

parents or teachers may be asked to rate the extent to which the child complains of physical symptoms, cries, has difficulty falling asleep, or exhibits similar behaviors that characterize depression. Strictly speaking, of course, such evaluations are *ratings* of behavior rather than direct observations of behavior. Yet the referents are the child's actions. Direct observation of overt behavior reflects the R component of the S-O-R-K-C model. Relatively few studies in the child arena have examined overt behavior. As an assessment modality, overt behavior warrants much greater attention.

The mere fact that several measures are available to evaluate characteristics of the individual and behavior does not mean that these (O and R) domains are well developed. There are a number of areas within the O and R domains that may be relevant for which assessment techniques are currently unavailable. For example, anhedonia, or the inability to experience pleasure, has been studied in adult depressed patients; currently, measures to assess similar states in children remain to be developed. Similarly, measures of suicidal ideation and behavior have been developed for adults (Beck, Resnik, & Lettieri, 1974) but not for children. These and other gaps in assessment techniques point to O and R dimensions in need of further development.

Other dimensions of the S-O-R-K-C model have been relatively neglected in the measurement of childhood depression. For example, antecedent stimuli (S) have been infrequently assessed. A major candidate here would be the assessment of life events antedating the onset of depressive symptoms (e.g., parental separation, divorce, or death). In some cases, depressive symptoms can be readily traced to specific antecedent events (e.g., bereavement). Measurement of the antecedent stimuli may extend well beyond specific stressful events. Evaluation of parent variables and parent–child interaction may be relevant as well. For example, depressive disorders tend to run in families, so that children whose parents have suffered depressive episodes are at risk for depressive symptoms themselves. Also, mothers with affective disorder interact quite differently with their children than do parents without affective disorder. Depressed adults have been found to show multiple signs of impaired parenting, including diminished expressions of affection, lower levels of interaction in general, greater irritability and overprotectiveness, and

other characteristics (Orvaschel, 1983). In addition, emotional detachment and rejection by parents in early childhood appear to be related to subsequent depression in adulthood (Crook, Raskin, & Eliot, 1981; Lefkowitz & Tesiny, 1984).

To judge from these findings, antecedent stimuli that relate to depression may occur well before depression appears, and hence may be more appropriately evaluated in prospective longitudinal studies that assess early environmental stimuli and subsequent child depression. However, there may also be concurrent stimuli (e.g., parental child-rearing practices, maternal depressive episodes) in the settings in which children function that relate to the onset, severity, and cessation of depressive symptoms. For example, a recent study found that inpatient children who were current victims of physical abuse showed greater severity of depression than matched control patients who had not experienced physical abuse (Kazdin, Moser, Colbus, & Bell, 1985). Severity of depression was much greater when a child was a victim of both current and past physical abuse, as opposed to either current or past abuse alone. These results merely illustrate the need to look at depressive symptoms in relation to both past and present events in children's lives.

The contingencies of reinforcement (K) and consequences (C) of depressive symptoms in children have rarely been studied. In research on adult depression by contrast, these areas have received considerable attention. For example, Lewinsohn has conducted studies on several measures that pertain to reinforcing activities and the rewards that depressed individuals reap from them (see Lewinsohn & Hoberman, 1982). One measure that has received considerable attention is the Pleasant Events Schedule. The measure lists numerous events and activities in which people can engage. Adults rate the frequency with which they have engaged in particular events (within the last 30 days) and how enjoyable each event was. Thus, the measure permits evaluation of reported responses (frequency of engaging in the events) as well as the contingencies (response–consequence connections) and consequences. Because the frequency of engaging in pleasant activities and the extent to which they produce enjoyment have been shown to relate to depression in adults, programmatic extensions to children are sorely needed.

Several measures have been advanced for

use with children that can assess features of the contingencies and consequences. Cautela *et al.*, (1983) have provided a number of measures to be completed by the child or parent that examine the extent to which specific activities may be reinforcing for the child. For example, the Children's Reinforcement Schedule lists 25 events, such as going on trips, playing ball, and playing with a pet. The child rates each of these on a 3-point scale reflecting the extent to which they are liked. On another measure, the Parents' and Children's Reinforcement Survey Schedule (Child Form), the child rates the extent to which he or she likes engaging in activities with each of his or her parents (e.g., being kissed, hugged, having a story read to him or her). These scales address how the child sees various potentially reinforcing consequences in the environment, and the connections between interactions with parents and their rewarding value. The measures thus focus on neglected aspects of the S-O-R-K-C analysis and would seem to be especially useful in the study of childhood depression. Other aspects of the consequences of behavior also warrant investigation in the context of childhood depression. For example, research with adults suggests that depressed affect leads to withdrawal and reduced social interaction of others (Coyne, 1976). Thus, the interpersonal consequences of behavior in depressed children would seem to be a worthwhile focus.

Current measures of childhood depression reflect breadth in terms of the modalities and methods of assessment. Yet, in terms of a functional analysis, antecedents and consequences of depression and the connections between depression and environmental events remain to be elaborated. There is a greater need to describe the context in which childhood depression occurs. This represents a shift in focus from the individual and his or her depressive symptoms to a more functional and interactional model. Measures that consider characteristics of individual children as well as those with whom they interact may not only enhance our understanding of depressive symptoms, but also direct attention to possible points of intervention to ameliorate or prevent depression. For example, recent work has suggested that depressed children evince deficiencies in their interactions with their families and peers (Puig-Antich *et al.*, 1985a, 1985b). Although these areas show improvements with treatment of depressive symptoms, deficits remain. The

assessment of child behavior in different contexts suggests the need to incorporate social interaction and social skills training into alternative treatment regimens.

Selection of Measures

No single measure has been shown to assess the multiple facets of dysfunction that depression can reflect or to evaluate the diverse models that are currently posed. For the clinician and researcher, it is obvious that assessment of depression needs to include multiple measures, encompassing different methods of assessment (e.g., interviews, direct observations), perspectives (e.g., child, parent, teacher), and domains (e.g., affect, cognitions, behavior). Apart from the advisability of multichannel assessment strategies in general, specific findings within the area of childhood depression lobby for the general recommendation. Findings have shown that there may be significant method variance in the assessment of depression, that different methods of assessment may not intercorrelate highly, and that measures that do not correlate highly with each other may still reliably predict different external criteria (e.g., social behavior, suicidal risk) (see Kazdin, Esveldt-Dawson, *et al.*, 1985; Kazdin, Esveldt-Dawson, Unis, & Rancurello, 1983; Saylor, Finch, Baskin, Furey, & Kelly, 1984; Saylor, Finch, Spirito, & Bennett, 1984). Based on these considerations, an assessment battery minimally should sample (1) different sources of information (e.g., typically the child and a significant other); (2) performance in different settings (e.g., typically performance at home and at school); (3) multiple domains of depressive symptoms (e.g., affect, cognitions, and behavior); and (4) overall adjustment in everyday life (e.g., as in measures of adjustment or psychopathology).

Other considerations may dictate more specifically the domains of assessment, specific constructs, and concrete assessment strategies. The conceptual model adhered to in clinical work or research obviously can dictate the measures that are used. Specific behavioral and cognitive models have led clinical researchers to select measures that focus on social skills, activities and reinforcing consequences, and negative attributions. Similarly, biological models have dictated the search for neurohumors and metabolites of endocrine function. Adoption of a particular model may not invariably lead one to specific measures. For example, psychodynamic models of childhood depression have yet to establish assessment techniques shown to reliably identify facets of depression in children.

Interest in specific symptoms may also dictate the measures that are selected. Salient symptoms or correlates may point to the need for specific measurement strategies. For example, the presence of suicidal ideation or attempts or sleep disturbances may focus the selection of available assessment devices or the improvisation of new measures for clinical work. Identification of depression through standardized measures may also be followed up with a functional analysis of the specific symptom pattern of the individual case.

For example, Frame *et al.*, (1982) evaluated and treated a 10-year-old boy hospitalized on an inpatient unit who met DSM-III criteria for Major Depression. The diagnosis was based on a standardized psychiatric interview; the severity of depression was also corroborated by scores on parent ratings of the child's depression (on the CDI and the Bellevue Index of Depression—Revised). Direct observation of the child revealed several specific behaviors that were associated with depression. These included turning the body away from others during social interaction; lack of eye contact; deficient speech (soft, brief, or delayed responses to prompts from others); and bland affect as reflected in lack of emotional tone and voice inflection and failure to employ facial, hand, and arm gestures while speaking. To assess these behaviors systematically, the investigators had the child engage in 12 role-play social interactions each day. The role-play situations involved everyday situations from home and hospital life, such as

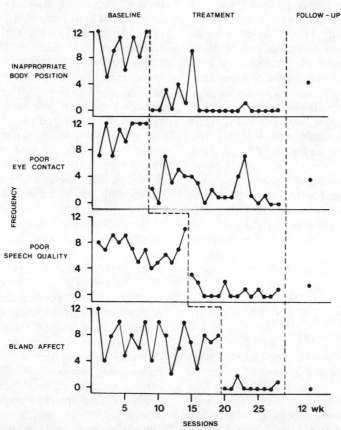

FIGURE 3. Frequency of social behaviors of a depressed boy as measured during assessment interviews. The treatment was applied to different behaviors at different points in time. From ''Behavioral Treatment of Depression in a Prepubertal Child'' by C. Frame, J. L. Matson, W. A. Sonis, M. J. Fialkov, and A. E. Kazdin, 1982, *Journal of Behavior Therapy and Experimental Psychiatry, 2,* p. 241. Copyright 1982 by Pergamon Press, Ltd. Reprinted by permission.

initiating conversation in the cafeteria with a new child patient admitted to the hospital. For each role-play situation, each of the behaviors (inappropriate body position, lack of eye contact while talking to the assessor, poor speech quality, and bland affect) was scored as present or absent.

A social skills training program was then provided for the child, in which he engaged in role play with a therapist to alter each of the specific behaviors noted above. The treatment consisted of modeling the appropriate behaviors in each area, providing opportunities for practice, and therapist praise and feedback. Treatment was conducted five times per week for approximately 5 weeks. The treatment was introduced in a multiple-baseline design across behaviors, in which the separate behaviors were focused on at different points in time.

As shown in Figure 3, when training in the first two behaviors (body positions and eye contact) was introduced, marked changes occurred. When training focused on other facets of interaction, these changed as well. Follow-up evaluation 12 weeks after treatment had been terminated indicated that the gains were maintained. In general, the case is useful in illustrating the individualization of assessment. Standardized diagnostic measures and inventories were useful in establishing that the child met the DSM-III criteria for Major Depression. However, measures were then individualized, based upon observation of specific responses that the child evinced in his interactions with others. These responses were then altered in treatment. A deficiency in the case was the absence of further assessment after treatment to determine whether depressive symptoms on standardized measures reflected change as well.

Treatment Research and the Assessment of Outcome

The selection of measures for evaluating treatment techniques raises a number of issues for which few data are available. Relatively little controlled outcome research is available on the treatment of childhood depression. Many different psychosocial techniques, such as interpersonal therapy, cognitive therapy, self-control therapy, social skills training, and others, have been tested in outcome research with adults. To date, few of these have been extended to childhood depression (e.g., Butler, Miezitis, Friedman, & Cole, 1980; Reynolds & Coats, 1985). The bulk of the treatment research with children and adolescents has utilized alternative medications. That research, beyond the scope of the present chapter, has shown therapeutic change and has identified variables (e.g., plasma levels of medication, subtype of depression) of which treatment response is a function (see Kazdin, Rancurello, & Unis, in press).

The outcome research with both child and adult populations has important implications for assessment. First, research with children has suggested that medications may not completely address the dysfunctions that depressed children show. For example, depressed children showed marked deficiencies in communications with their mothers and in peer relations, compared to nondepressed patients and normal controls (Puig-Antich et al., 1985a, 1985b). After treatment of depression with medication, mother–child interactions had improved, but they were not up to the level of those of normal children. In addition, peer relations had changed very little. These results suggest that medication may not address significant facets of performance relevant to depression. Because social skills deficits have been proposed as a major characteristic of depressed patients (Lewinsohn & Arconad, 1981), other types of treatment besides medications may be needed to address this area directly. From the standpoint of assessment, the results also suggest that social functioning should be included in any evaluations of treatment.

Research on adult patients has suggested that psychosocial treatments and medications may offer unique and complementary advantages in terms of the changes they produce (see Klerman & Schechter, 1982). Although there is some overlap in the impact of alternative treatments, medications tend to alter the symptoms of depression (e.g., affect, sleep dysfunction, vegetative signs), with relatively little impact on problems of living, social functioning, and interpersonal relationships. Psychosocial treatments appear to address these later problems, but with somewhat less impact on depressive symptoms. There are exceptions that fail to show the specific and complementary effects of these alternative forms of treatment (see Murphy, Simons, Wetzel, & Lustman, 1984; Simons, Garfield, & Murphy, 1984). From the standpoint of assessment, these findings also argue for assessment of interpersonal functioning in treatment outcome studies.[7]

General Comments

Current studies point to the need for assessment to encompass multiple measures, domains, methods, and areas of functioning. Although a particular type of measure or source of information is critical to assess (e.g., self-report), choices are difficult to justify favoring one measure over another within a given type of measure. Too few data are available to permit well-informed decisions about most measures. Within a given type of measure, there are many redundancies in the measures currently available. Also, the content of the items and the range of factors that are encompassed may be useful for directing assessment decisions. Across different sources of information, the information is less likely to be redundant. Separate raters provide different perspectives, and their evaluations are correlated with different criteria. It is still the case that for most measures, few or no reliability and validity data are available. Consequently, well-based recommendations can only be provided for a general measurement strategy of sampling broadly across assessment domains.

CONCLUSIONS

Research on affective disorders in children has begun relatively recently. Nevertheless, advances have been rapid. The primary reason for this is that research has drawn upon work on affective disorders with adults, where marked gains have been made in diagnosis, assessment, and treatment. Conceptual views, research paradigms, and laboratory methods that have been developed in research with adults have been extended to children.

Findings obtained for adults may not necessarily characterize children; however, such findings provide an excellent place to begin to identify what developmental differences there are. To date, studies have shown important consistencies between adults and children in

cognitive processes, behavioral repertoires, biological characteristics, and other facets of depression. In many obvious ways, due to the different activities and stages of physical and emotional development, it is likely that symptoms of depression and their correlates will differ in important ways across the developmental spectrum. To date, few differences have been found, although research in this area has only recently begun.

Advances in research can also be traced to the development of assessment techniques to measure depression and its correlates in children. A large number of inventories and interviews, to be completed by the child or by significant others, have emerged. Peer measures and direct observations of behaviors have also been developed. Assessment of childhood depression has raised a number of important issues, such as the tendency for children to underestimate their symptoms (at least when compared to estimates of others), the lack of correspondence or convergence in parent and child ratings of a child's depression, and the need to identify additional criteria to validate existing measures. A pervasive characteristic of current measures is the almost exclusive focus on symptom characteristics in the individual's repertoire. The antecedents and precipitants of depressive states and environmental events, and contingencies that contribute or sustain these states, warrant additional study.

Acknowledgments

Completion of this chapter was supported by a Research Scientist Development Award (MH00353) and by a grant (MH35408) from the National Institute of Mental Health.

---

[7]Medications raise a variety of other assessment issues if they are to be used in treatment outcome. The assessment of medication compliance, monitoring of diverse side effects, plasma levels of the medication, and other areas may need to be assessed, depending on the medication (see Kazdin, Rancurello, & Unis, in press).

REFERENCES

Abramson, L. Y., Seligman, M. E. P., & Teasdale, J. D. (1978). Learned helplessness in humans: Critique and reformulation. *Journal of Abnormal Psychology, 87,* 49–74.

Achenbach, T. M., & Edelbrock, C. S. (1983). *Manual for the Child Behavior Checklist and Revised Child Behavior Profile.* Burlington: University of Vermont, Department of Psychiatry.

Akiskal, H. S. (1979). A biobehavioral approach to depression. In R. A. Depue (Ed.), *The psychobiology of the depressive disorders* (pp. 409–437). New York: Academic Press.

Akiskal, H. S., & McKinney, W. T., Jr. (1975). Overview of recent research in depression: Integration of ten conceptual models into a comprehensive clinical frame. *Archives of General Psychiatry, 32,* 285–305.

American Psychiatric Association. (1980). *Diagnostic and statistical manual of mental disorders* (3rd ed.). Washington, DC: Author.

American Psychiatric Association. (1987). *Diagnostic and statistical manual of mental disorders* (3rd ed., rev.). Washington, DC: Author.

Anthony, E. J. (1975). Childhood depression. In E. J. Anthony & T. Benedek (Eds.), *Depression and human existence* (pp. 231–277). Boston: Little, Brown.

Asarnow, J. R., & Carlson, G. A. (Eds.) (1985). Depression Self-Rating Scale: Utility with child psychiatric inpatients. *Journal of Consulting and Clinical Psychology, 53,* 491–499.

Asher, S. R., & Wheeler, V. A. (1985). Children's loneliness: A comparison of rejected and neglected peer status. *Journal of Consulting and Clinical Psychology, 53,* 500–505.

Beck, A. T. (1976). *Cognitive therapy and the emotional disorders.* New York: International Universities Press.

Beck, A. T., Kovacs, M., & Weissman, A. (1975). Hopelessness and suicidal behavior: An overview. *Journal of the American Medical Association, 234,* 1146–1149.

Beck, A. T., Resnik, H. L. P., & Lettieri, D. J. (Eds.). (1974). *The prediction of suicide.* Bowie, MD: Charles Press.

Beck, A. T., Rush, A. J., Shaw, B. F., & Emery, G. (1980). *Cognitive therapy of depression.* New York: Guilford Press.

Beck, A. T., Weissman, A., Lester, D., & Trexler, L. (1974). The measurement of pessimism: The Hopelessness Scale. *Journal of Consulting and Clinical Psychology, 42,* 861–865.

Bemporad, J. R., & Wilson, A. (1978). A developmental approach to depression in childhood and adolescence. *Journal of the American Academy of Psychoanalysis, 6,* 325–352.

Beres, D. (1966). Superego and depression. In R. M. Lowenstein, L. M. Newman, M. Scherr, & A. J. Solnit (Eds.), *Psychoanalysis—a general psychology* (pp. 479–498). New York: International Universities Press.

Billings, A. G., & Moos, R. H. (1982). Psychosocial theory and research on depression: An integrative framework and review. *Clinical Psychology Review, 2,* 213–237.

Birleson, P. (1981). The validity of depressive disorder in childhood and the development of a self-rating scale: A research project. *Journal of Child Psychology and Psychiatry, 22,* 73–88.

Blumberg, S. R., & Hokanson, J. E. (1983). The effects of another person's response style on interpersonal behavior in depression. *Journal of Abnormal Psychology, 92,* 196–209.

Brown, G. W., Harris, T. O., & Peto, J. (1973). Life events and psychiatric disorders: Part II. Nature of causal link. *Psychological Medicine, 3,* 159–176.

Bunch, J. (1972). Recent bereavement in relation to suicide. *Journal of Psychosomatic Research, 16,* 361–366.

Butler, L., Miezitis, S., Friedman, R., & Cole, E. (1980). The effect of two school-based intervention programs on depressive symptoms in preadolescents. *American Educational Research Journal, 17,* 111–119.

Cantwell, D. P. (1982). Childhood depression. In B. B. Lahey & A. E. Kazdin (Eds.), *Advances in clinical child psychology* (Vol. 5, pp. 39–93). New York: Plenum.

Cantwell, D. P., & Carlson, G. A. (Eds.). (1983). *Affective disorders in childhood and adolescence: An update.* New York: Spectrum.

Carlson, G. A., & Cantwell, D. P. (1979). A survey of depressive symptoms in a child and adolescent psychiatric population. *Journal of the American Academy of Child Psychiatry, 18,* 587–599.

Carlson, G. A., & Cantwell, D. P. (1980). Unmasking masked depression in children and adolescents. *American Journal of Psychiatry, 137,* 445–449.

Carlson, G. A., & Cantwell, D. P. (1982). Suicidal behavior and depression in children and adolescents. *Journal of the American Academy of Child Psychiatry, 21,* 361–368.

Carroll, B. J. (1978). Neuroendocrine function in psychiatric disorders. In M. A. Lipton, A. DiMascio, & K. F. Killam (Eds.), *Psychopharmacology: A generation of progress* (pp. 487–497). New York: Raven Press.

Carroll, B. J. (1983). Neuroendocrine diagnosis of depression: The dexamethasone suppression test. In P. J. Clayton & J. E. Barrett (Eds.), *Treatment of depression* (pp. 1–30). New York: Raven Press.

Cautela, J. R., Cautela, J., & Esonis, S. (1983). *Forms for behavior analysis with children.* Champaign, IL: Research Press.

Chambers, W. J., Puig-Antich, J., Hirsch, M., Paez, P., Ambrosini, P. J., Tabrizi, M. A., & Davies, M. (1985). The assessment of affective disorders in children and adolescents by semistructured interview: Test–retest reliability. *Archives of General Psychiatry, 42,* 696–702.

Chambers, W. J., Puig-Antich, J., & Tabrizi, M. A. (1978, October). *The ongoing development of the Kiddie-SADS (Schedule for Affective Disorders and Schizophrenia for School-Age Children).* Paper presented at the meeting of the American Academy of Child Psychiatry, San Diego.

Chiles, J. A., Miller, M. L.., & Cox, G. B. (1980). Depression in an adolescent delinquent population. *Archives of General Psychiatry, 37,* 1179–1184.

Cicchetti, D., & Schneider-Rosen, K. (1984). Toward a transactional model of childhood depression. In D. Cicchetti & K. Schneider-Rosen (Eds.), *Childhood depression: New directions for child development* (pp. 5–27). San Francisco: Jossey-Bass.

Clarkin, J. F., & Glazer, H. I. (Eds.). (1981). *Depression: Behavioral and directive intervention strategies.* New York: Garland Press.

Clayton, P. J., & Barrett, J. E. (Eds.). (1983). *Treatment of depression.* New York: Raven Press.

Coopersmith, S. (1967). *The antecedents of self-esteem.* San Francisco: W. H. Freeman.

Costello, C. G. (1980). Childhood depression: Three basic but questionable assumptions in the Lefkowitz and Burton critique. *Psychological Bulletin, 87,* 185–190.

Coyne, J. C. (1976). Toward an interactional description of depression. *Psychiatry, 39,* 28–40.

Crook, T., Raskin, A., & Eliot, J. (1981). Parent–child relationships and adult depression. *Child Development, 52,* 950–957.

Cytryn, L., & McKnew, D. H. (1972). Proposed classification of childhood depression. *American Journal of Psychiatry, 129,* 149–155.

Cytryn, L., & McKnew, D. H. (1974). Factors influencing the changing clinical expression of the depressive process in children. *American Journal of Psychiatry, 131,* 879–881.

Cytryn, L., McKnew, D. H., Bartko, J. J., Lamour, M., & Hamovitt, J. (1982). Offspring of patients with affective disorders: II. *Journal of the American Academy of Child Psychiatry, 21*, 389–391.

Cytryn, L., McKnew, D. H., & Bunney, W. E. (1980). Diagnosis of depression in children: A reassessment. *American Journal of Psychiatry, 137*, 22–25.

Decina, P., Kestenbaum, C. J., Farber, S., Kron, L., Gargan, M., Sackeim, H. A., & Fieve, R. R. (1983). Clinical and psychological assessment of children of bipolar probands. *American Journal of Psychiatry, 140*, 548–553

Depue, R. A. (Ed.). (1979). *The psychobiology of the depressive disorders: Implications for the effects of stress.* New York: Academic Press.

Depue R. A., & Kleiman, R. M. (1979). Free cortisol as a peripheral index of central vulnerability to major forms of polar depressive disorders: Examining stress–biology interactions in subsyndromal high-risk persons. In R. A. Depue (Ed.), *The psychobiology of the depressive disorders.* (pp. 177–204). New York: Academic Press.

Depue, R. A., & Monroe, S. M. (1979). The unipolar–biopolar distinction in the depressive disorders: Implications for stress–onset interaction. In R. A. Depue (Ed.), *The psychobiology of the depressive disorders* (pp. 23–53). New York: Academic Press.

D'Zurilla, T. J., & Nezu, A. (1982). Social problem solving in adults. In P. C. Kendall (Ed.), *Advances in cognitive–behavioral research and therapy* (Vol. 1, pp. 202–274). New York: Academic Press.

Endicott, J., & Spitzer, R. L. (1978). A diagnostic interview: The Schedule for Affective Disorders and Schizophrenia. *Archives of General Psychiatry, 35*, 837–844.

Feighner, J. P., Robins, E., Guze, S. B., Woodruff, R. A., Winokur, G., & Munoz, R. (1972). Diagnostic criteria for use in psychiatric research. *Archives of General Psychiatry, 26*, 57–63.

Finch, A. J., Jr., Saylor, C. F., & Edwards, G. L. (1985). Children's Depression Inventory: Sex and grade norms for normal children. *Journal of Consulting and Clinical Psychology, 53* 424–425.

Fisch, H. U., Frey, S., & Hirsbrunner, H. P. (1983). Analyzing nonverbal behavior in depression. *Journal of Abnormal Psychology, 92*, 307–318.

Fossi, L., Faravelli, C., & Paoli, M. (1984). The ethological approach to the assessment of depressive disorders. *Journal of Nervous and Mental Disease, 172*, 332–341.

Frame, C., Matson, J. L., Sonis, W. A., Fialkov, M. J., & Kazdin, A. E. (1982). Behavioral treatment of depression in a prepubertal child. *Journal of Behavior Therapy and Experimental Psychiatry, 3*, 239–243.

Freud, S. (1957). Mourning and melancholia. In J. Strachey (Ed. and Trans.), *Standard edition of the complete psychological works of Sigmund Freud* (Vol. 14, pp. 243–258). London: Hogarth Press. (Original work published 1917)

Gershon, E. S., Targum, S. D., Kessler, L. R., Mazure, C. M., & Bunney, W. E., Jr. (1977). Genetic studies and biologic strategies in the affective disorders. *Progress in Medical Genetics, 2*, 101–164.

Glaser, K. (1968). Masked depression in children and adolescents. In S. Chess & A. Thomas (Eds.), *Annual progress in child psychiatry and child development* (Vol. 1, pp. 345–355). New York: Brunner/Mazel.

Goetz, R. R., Goetz, D. M., Hanlon, C., Davies, M., Weitzman, E. D., & Puig-Antich, J. (1983). Spindle characteristics in prepubertal major depressives during an episode and after sustained recovery: A controlled study. *Sleep, 6*, 369–375.

Gordon, N., Lefkowitz, M. M., & Tesiny, E. P. (1980). Childhood depression and the Draw-a-Person Test. *Psychological Reports, 47*, 251–257.

Greden, J. F., & Carroll, B. J. (1981). Psychomotor function in affective disorders: An overview of new monitoring techniques. *American Journal of Psychiatry, 138*, 1441–1448.

Haley, G., Fine, S., Marriage, K., Moretti, M., & Freeman, R. (1985). Cognitive bias and depression in psychiatrically disturbed children and adolescents. *Journal of Consulting and Clinical Psychology, 53*, 535–537.

Hamilton, M. A. (1967). Development of a rating scale for primary depressive illness. *British Journal of Social and Clinical Psychology, 6*, 278–296.

Harter, S. (1982). The Perceived Competence Scale for Children. *Child Development, 53*, 87–97.

Hawton, K. (1986). *Suicide and attempted suicide among children and adolescents.* Beverly Hills, CA: Sage.

Helsel, W. J., & Matson, J. L. (1984). Assessment of depression in children: The internal structure of the Child Depression Inventory (CDI). *Behaviour Research and Therapy, 22*, 289–298.

Herjanic, B., & Reich, W. (1982). Development of a structured psychiatric interview for children: Agreement between child and parent on individual symptoms. *Journal of Abnormal Child Psychology, 10*, 307–324.

Herzog, D. B., & Rathbun, J. M. (1982). Childhood depression: Developmental considerations. *American Journal of Diseases of Children, 136*, 115–120.

Hinchliffe, M. K., Lancashire, M., & Roberts, F. J. (1971). A study of eye-contact change in depressed and recovered psychiatric patients. *British Journal of Psychiatry, 119*, 213–215.

Hops, H., & Greenwood, C. R. (1988). Social skills deficits. In E. J. Mash & L. G. Terdal (Eds.), *Behavioral assessment of childhood disorders* (2nd ed., unabridged, pp. 263–315). New York: Guilford Press.

Jacobsen, R. H., Lahey, B. B., & Strauss, C. C. (1983). Correlates of depressed mood in normal children. *Journal of Abnormal Child Psychology, 11*, 29–40.

Jacobson, N. S. (1981). The assessment of overt behavior in depression. In L. P. Rehm (Ed.), *Behavior therapy for depression: Present status and future directions* (pp. 279–300). New York: Academic Press.

Johnson, J. H. (1982). Life events as stressors in childhood and adolescence. In B. B. Lahey & A. E. Kazdin (Eds.). *Advances in clinical child psychology* (Vol. 5, pp. 220–253). New York: Plenum.

Johnson, J. H., & McCutcheon, S. M. (1980). Assessing life stress in older children and adolescents: Preliminary findings with the Life Events Checklist. In I. G. Sarason & C. D. Spielberger (Eds.), *Stress and anxiety* (Vol. 7, pp. 111–125). Washington, DC: Hemisphere.

Jones, I. M., & Pasna, M. (1979). Some nonverbal aspects of depression and schizophrenia occurring during the interview. *Journal of Nervous and Mental Disease, 167*, 402–409.

Kandel, D. B., & Davies, M. (1982). Epidemiology of depressive mood in adolescents: An empirical study. *Archives of General Psychiatry, 39*, 1205–1212.

Kanfer, F. H., & Saslow, G. (1969). Behavioral diagnosis.

In C. M. Franks (Ed.), *Behavior therapy: Appraisal and status* (pp. 417–444). New York: McGraw-Hill.

Kaplan, S. L., Hong, G. K., & Weinhold, C. (1984). Epidemiology of depressive symptomatology in adolescents. *Journal of the American Academy of Child Psychiatry, 23,* 91–98.

Kashani, J. H., Barbero, G. J., & Bolander, F. D. (1981). Depression in hospitalized pediatric patients. *Journal of the American Academy of Child Psychiatry, 20,* 123–134.

Kashani, J. H., Cantwell, D. P., Shekim, W. O., & Reid, J. C. (1982). Major depressive disorder in children admitted to an inpatient community mental health center. *American Journal of Psychiatry, 139,* 671–672.

Kashani, J. H., Husain, A., Shekim, W. O., Hodges, K. K., Cytryn, L., & McKnew, D. H. (1981). Current perspectives on childhood depression: An overview. *American Journal of Psychiatry, 138,* 143–153.

Kashani, J. H., McGee, R. O., Clarkson, S. E., Anderson, J. C., Walton, L. A., Williams, S., Silva, P. A., Robins, A. J., Cytryn, L., & McKnew, D. H. (1983). Depression in a sample of 9-year old children. *Archives of General Psychiatry, 40,* 1217–1223.

Kashani, J. H., Ray, J. S., & Carlson, G. A. (1984). Depression and depression-like states in preschool-age children in a child development unit. *American Journal of Psychiatry, 141,* 1397–1402.

Kashani, J., & Simonds, J. F. (1979). The incidence of depression in children. *American Journal of Psychiatry, 136,* 1203–1205.

Kaslow, N. J., Rehm, L. P., & Siegel, A. W. (1984). Social-cognitive and cognitive correlates of depression in children. *Journal of Abnormal Child Psychology, 12,* 605–620.

Kazdin, A. E. (1981). Assessment techniques for childhood depression: A critical appraisal. *Journal of the American Academy of Child Psychiatry, 20,* 358–375.

Kazdin, A. E., Esveldt-Dawson, K., Sherick, R. B., & Colbus, D. (1985). Assessment of overt behavior and childhood depression among psychiatrically disturbed children. *Journal of Consulting and Clinical Psychology, 53,* 201–210.

Kazdin, A. E., Esveldt-Dawson, K., Unis, A. S., & Rancurello, M. D. (1983). Child and parent evaluations of depression and aggression in psychiatric inpatient children. *Journal of Abnormal Child Psychology, 11,* 401–413.

Kazdin, A. E., French, N. H., Unis, A. S., & Esveldt-Dawson, K. (1983). Assessment of childhood depression: Correspondence of child and parent ratings. *Journal of the American Academy of Child Psychiatry, 22,* 157–164.

Kazdin, A. E., French, N. H., Unis, A. S., Esveldt-Dawson, K., & Sherick, R. B. (1983). Hopelessness, depression and suicidal intent among psychiatrically disturbed inpatient children. *Journal of Consulting and Clinical Psychology, 51,* 504–510.

Kazdin, A. E., Moser, J., Colbus, D., & Bell, R. (1985). Depressive symptoms among physically abused and psychiatrically disturbed children. *Journal of Abnormal Psychology, 94,* 298–307.

Kazdin, A. E., & Petti, T. A. (1982). Self-report and interview measures of childhood and adolescent depression. *Journal of Child Psychology and Psychiatry, 23,* 437–457.

Kazdin, A. E., Rancurello, M., & Unis, A. S. (in press).

Childhood depression. In G. D. Burrows & J. S. Werry (Eds.), *Advances in human psychopharmacology* (Vol. 4). Greenwich, CT: JAI Press.

Kazdin, A. E., Rodgers, A., & Colbus, D. (1986). The Hopelessness Scale for Children: Psychometric characteristics and concurrent validity. *Journal of Consulting and Clinical Psychology, 54,* 241–245.

Kazdin, A. E., Sherick, R. B., Esveldt-Dawson, K., & Rancurello, M. D. (1985). Nonverbal behavior and childhood depression. *Journal of the American Academy of Child Psychiatry, 24,* 303–309.

Klerman, G. L., & Schechter, G. (1982). Drugs and psychotherapy. In E. S. Paykel (Ed.), *Handbook of affective disorders* (pp. 329–337). New York: Guilford Press.

Kovacs, M. (1978). *Interview Schedule for Children (ISC)* (10th revision). Unpublished manuscript, University of Pittsburgh School of Medicine.

Kovacs, M. (1981). Rating scales to assess depression in school-aged children. *Acta Paedopsychiatrica, 46,* 305–315.

Kovacs, M., & Beck, A. T. (1977). An empirical clinical approach towards a definition of childhood depression. In J. G. Schulterbrandt & A. Raskin (Eds.), *Depression in children: Diagnosis, treatment, and conceptual models* (pp. 1–25). New York: Raven Press.

Kovacs, M., Feinberg, T. L., Crouse-Novak, M., Paulauskas, S. L., Pollock, M., & Finkelstein, R. (1984). Depressive disorders in childhood: II. A longitudinal study of the risk for a subsequent major depression. *Archives of General Psychiatry, 41,* 643–649.

Kupfer, D. J., Spiker, D. G., Rossi, A., Coble, P. A., Ulrich, R., & Shaw, D. (1983). Recent diagnostic and treatment advances in REM sleep and depression. In P. J. Clayton & J. E. Barrett (Eds.) *Treatment of depression* (pp. 31–52). New York: Raven Press.

Lang, M., & Tisher, M. (1978). *Children's Depression Scale.* Victoria, Australia: Australian Council for Educational Research.

Lapouse, R. (1966). The epidemiology of behavior disorders in children. *American Journal of Diseases of Children, 111,* 594–599.

Lefkowitz, M. M. (1980). Childhood depression: A reply to Costello. *Psychological Bulletin, 87,* 191–194.

Lefkowitz, M. M., & Burton, N. (1978). Childhood depression: A critique of the concept. *Psychological Bulletin, 85,* 716–726.

Lefkowitz, M. M., & Tesiny, E. P. (1980). Assessment of childhood depression. *Journal of Consulting and Clinical Psychology, 48,* 43–50.

Lefkowitz, M. M., & Tesiny, E. P. (1984). Rejection and depression: Prospective and contemporaneous analyses. *Developmental Psychology, 20,* 776–785.

Lefkowitz, M. M., & Tesiny, E. P. (1985). Depression in children: Prevalence and correlates. *Journal of Consulting and Clinical Psychology; 53,* 647–656.

Lefkowitz, M. M., Tesiny, E. P., & Gordon, N. H. (1980). Childhood depression, family income, and locus of control. *Journal of Nervous and Mental Disease, 168,* 732–735.

Lewinsohn, P. M. (1974). Clinical and theoretical aspects of depression. In K. S. Calhoun, H. E. Adams, & K. M. Mitchell (Eds.), *Innovative treatment methods of psychopathology* (pp. 63–120). New York: Wiley.

Lewinsohn, P. M., & Arconad, M. (1981). Behavioral treatment of depression: A social learning approach. In

J. F. Clarkin & H. I. Glazer (Eds.), *Depression: Behavioral and directive intervention strategies* (pp. 33–67). New York: Garland/STPM.

Lewinsohn, P. M. & Hoberman, H. M. (1982). Depression. In A. S. Bellack, M. Hersen, & A. E. Kazdin (Eds.), *International handbook of behavior modification and therapy* (pp. 397–431). New York: Guilford Press.

Lewinsohn, P. M., & Shaffer, M. (1971). The use of home observations as an integral part of the treatment of depression: Preliminary report and case studies. *Journal of Consulting and Clinical Psychology, 37,* 87–94.

Libet, J., & Lewinsohn, P. M. (1973). The concept of social skill with special references to the behavior of depressed persons. *Journal of Consulting and Clinical Psychology, 40,* 304–312.

Linden, M., Hautzinger, M., & Hoffmann, N. (1983). Discriminant analysis of depressive interactions. *Behavior Modification, 7,* 403–422.

Lindsley, O. R. (1964). Direct measurement and prothesis of retarded behavior. *Journal of Education, 147,* 62–81.

Ling, W., Oftedol, G., & Weinberg, W. (1970). Depressive illness in childhood presenting as a severe headache. *American Journal of Diseases of Children, 120,* 122–124.

Lobovits, D. A., & Handal, P. J. (1985). Childhood depression: Prevalence using DSM-III criteria and validity of parent and child depression scales. *Journal of Pediatric Psychology, 10,* 45–54.

MacFarlane, J. W., Allen, L., & Honzik, M. P. (1954). *A developmental study of the behavior problems of normal children between 21 months and 14 years.* Berkeley: University of California Press.

MacMahon, B., & Pugh, T. F. (1965). Suicide in the widowed. *American Journal of Epidemiology, 81,* 23–31.

Mahler, M. (1961). On sadness and grief in infancy and childhood. *Psychoanalytic Study of the Child, 16,* 332.

Malmquist, C. P. (1977). Childhood depression: A clinical and behavioral perspective. In J. G. Schulterbrandt & A. Raskin (Eds.), *Depression in children: Diagnosis, treatment and conceptual models* (pp. 33–59). New York: Raven Press.

Malouff, J. (1984). Development and validation of a behavioral peer-rating measure of depression. *Journal of Consulting and Clinical Psychology, 52,* 1108–1109.

Masters, J. C., Felleman, E. S., & Barden. R. C. (1981). Experimental studies of affective states in children. In B. B. Lahey & A. E. Kazdin (Eds.), *Advances in clinical child psychology* (Vol. 4, pp. 91–118). New York: Plenum Press.

Matson, J. L., Esveldt-Dawson, K., & Kazdin, A. E. (1983). Validation of methods for assessing social skills in children. *Journal of Clinical Child Psychology, 12,* 174–180.

Matson, J. L., Rotatori, A. F., & Helsel, W. J. (1983). Development of a rating scale to measure social skills in children: The Matson Evaluation of Social Skills with Youngsters (MESSY). *Behaviour Research and Therapy, 21,* 335–340.

McKnew, D. H., Jr., Cytryn, L., Efron, A. M., Gershon, E. S., & Bunney, W. E., Jr. (1979). Offspring of patients with affective disorders. *British Journal of Psychiatry, 134,* 148–152.

Mendelson, M. (1982). Psychodynamics of depression. In E. S. Paykel (Ed.), *Handbook of affective disorders* (pp. 162–174). New York: Guilford Press.

Mezzich, A. C., & Mezzich, J. E. (1979). Symptomatology of depression in adolescence. *Journal of Personality Assessment, 43,* 267–275.

Michelson, L., DiLorenzo, T., & Petti, T. A. (1981). Behavioral assessment of imipramine effects in a depressed child. *Journal of Behavioral Assessment, 3,* 253–262.

Michelson, L., Sugai, D., Wood, R., & Kazdin, A. E. (1983). *Social skills assessment and training with children: An empirically-based handbook.* New York: Plenum Press.

Miller, L. C. (1972). School Behavior Checklist: An inventory of deviant behavior for elementary school children. *Journal of Consulting and Clinical Psychology, 38,* 138–144.

Miller, R. E., Ranelli, C., & Levine, J. M. (1977). Nonverbal communication as an index of depression. In I. Hanin & E. Usdin (Eds.), *Animal models in psychiatry and neurology* (pp. 171–180). New York: Pergamon Press.

Moretti, M. M., Fine, S., Haley, G., & Marriage, K. (1985). Child and adolescent depression: Child-report versus parent-report information. *Journal of the American Academy of Child Psychiatry, 24,* 298–302.

Moyal, B. R. (1977). Locus of control, self-esteem, stimulus appraisal, and depressive symptoms in children. *Journal of Consulting and Clinical Psychology, 45,* 951–952.

Murphy, G. E., Simons, A. D., Wetzel, R. D., & Lustman, P. J. (1984). Cognitive therapy and pharmacotherapy. *Archives of General Psychiatry, 41,* 33–41.

Nezu, A. M., & Ronan, G. F. (1985). Life stress, current problems, problem-solving, and depressive symptoms: An integrative model. *Journal of Consulting and Clinical Psychology, 53,* 693–697.

Nowicki, S., Jr., & Strickland, B. R. (1973). A locus of control scale for children. *Journal of Consulting and Clinical Psychology, 40,* 148–154.

Nurnberger, J. I., & Gershon, E. S. (1982). Genetics. In E. S. Paykel (Ed.), *Handbook of affective disorders* (pp. 109–125). New York: Guilford Press.

Orvaschel, H. (1983). Maternal depression and child dysfunction: Children at risk. In B. B. Lahey & A. E. Kazdin (Eds.), *Advances in clinical child psychology* (Vol. 6, pp. 169–197). New York: Plenum.

Orvaschel, H., Puig-Antich, J., Chambers, W., Tabrizi, M. A., & Johnson, R. (1982). Retrospective assessment of prepubertal major depression with the Kiddie-SADS-E. *Journal of the American Academy of Child Psychiatry, 21,* 392–397.

Paykel, E. S. (Ed.). (1982a). *Handbook of affective disorders.* New York: Guilford Press.

Paykel, E. S. (1982b). Life events and early environment. In E. S. Paykel (Ed.), *Handbook of affective disorders* (pp. 146–161). New York: Guilford Press.

Paykel, E. S., & Tanner, J. (1976). Life events, depressive relapse and maintenance treatment. *Psychological Medicine, 6,* 481–485.

Petti, T. A. (1978). Depression in hospitalized child psychiatry patients: Approaches to measuring depression. *Journal of the American Academy of Child Psychiatry, 17,* 49–59.

Pfeffer, C. R., Conte, H. R., Plutchik, R., & Jerrett, I. (1979). Suicidal behavior in latency age children. *Jour-*

nal of the American Academy of Child Psychiatry, 18, 679–692.

Poznanski, E. O., Cook, S. C., & Carroll, B. J. (1979). A depression rating scale for children. *Pediatrics, 64,* 442–450.

Poznanski, E. O., Cook, S. C., & Carroll, B. J., & Corzo, H. (1983). Use of the Children's Depression Rating Scale in an inpatient psychiatric population. *Journal of Clinical Psychiatry, 44,* 200–203.

Poznanski, E. O., Grossman, J. A., Buchsbaum, Y., Banegas, M., Freeman, L., & Gibbons, R. (1984). Preliminary studies of the reliability and validity of the Children's Depression Rating Scale. *Journal of the American Academy of Child Psychiatry, 23,* 191–197.

Puig-Antich, J. (1983). Neuroendocrine and sleep correlates of prepubertal major depressive disorder: Current status of the evidence. In D. P. Cantwell & G. A. Carlson (Eds.), *Affective disorders in childhood and adolescence: An update* (pp. 211–227). New York: Spectrum.

Puig-Antich, J., Blau, S., Marx, N., Greenhill, L. L., & Chambers, W. (1978). Prepubertal major depressive disorders: A pilot study. *Journal of the American Academy of Child Psychiatry, 17,* 695–707.

Puig-Antich, J., & Gittelman, R. (1982). Depression in childhood and adolescence. In E. S. Paykel (Ed.), *Handbook of affective disorders* (pp. 379–392). New York: Guilford Press.

Puig-Antich, J., Goetz, R., Davies, M., Fein, M., Hanlon, C., Chambers, W. J., Tabrizi, M. A., Sachar, E. J., & Weitzman, E. D. (1984). Growth hormone secretion in prepubertal children with major depression: II. Sleep-related plasma concentrations during a depressive episode. *Archives of General Psychiatry, 41,* 463–466.

Puig-Antich, J., Lukens, E., Davies, M., Goetz, D., Brennan-Quattrock, J., & Todak, G. (1985a). Psychosocial functioning in prepubertal major depressive disorders: I. Interpersonal relationships during the depressive episode. *Archives of General Psychiatry, 42,* 500–507.

Puig-Antich, J., Lukens, E., Davies, M., Goetz, D., Brennan-Quattrock, J., & Todak, G. (1985b). Psychosocial functioning in prepubertal major depressive disorders: II. Interpersonal relationships after sustained recovery from affective episode. *Archives of General Psychiatry, 42,* 511–517.

Rapoport, J. L., & Ismond, D. R. (1984). *DSM-III training guide for diagnosis of childhood disorders.* New York: Brunner/Mazel.

Rehm, L. P. (1977). A self-control model of depression. *Behavior Therapy, 8,* 787–804.

Rehm, L. P., & Kaslow, N. J. (1984). Behavioral approaches to depression: Research results and clinical recommendations. In C. M. Franks (Ed.), *New developments in behavior therapy* (pp. 155–229). New York: Haworth Press.

Reynolds, W. M. (1985). Depression in childhood and adolescence: Diagnosis, assessment, intervention strategies, and research. In T. R. Kratochwill (Ed.), *Advances in school psychology* (Vol. 4; pp. 133–189). Hillsdale, NJ: Erlbaum.

Reynolds, W. M., & Coats, K. I. (1985). A comparison of cognitive–behavioral therapy and relaxation training for the treatment of depression in adolescents. *Journal of Consulting and Clinical Psychology, 54,* 653–660.

Riddle, K. D., & Rapoport, J. L. (1976). A 2-year follow-up of 72 hyperactive boys. *Journal of Nervous and Mental Disease, 162,* 126–134.

Rie, H. E. (1966). Depression in childhood: A survey of some pertinent contributions. *Journal of the American Academy of Child Psychiatry, 5,* 653–685.

Rochlin, G. (1965). *Griefs and discontents.* Boston: Little, Brown.

Sachar, E. J. (1982). Endocrine abnormalities in depression. In E. S. Paykel (Ed.), *Handbook of affective disorders* (pp. 191–201). New York: Guilford Press.

Saylor, C. F., Finch, A. J., Jr., Baskin, C. H., Furey, W., & Kelly, M. M. (1984). Construct validity for measures of childhood depression: Application of multitrait–multimethod methodology. *Journal of Consulting and Clinical Psychology, 52,* 977–985.

Saylor, C. F., Finch, A. J., Jr., Spirito, A., & Bennett, B. (1984). The Children's Depression Inventory: A systematic evaluation of psychometric properties. *Journal of Consulting and Clinical Psychology, 52,* 955–967.

Schwartz, G. E., Fair, P. L., Mandel, M. R., Salt, P., Meske, M., & Klerman, G. L. (1978). Facial electromyography in the assessment of improvement in depression. *Psychosomatic Medicine, 40,* 355–360.

Seligman, M. E. P. (1975). *Helplessness: On depression, development and death.* San Francisco: W. H. Freeman.

Seligman, M. E. P., Peterson, C., Kaslow, N. J., Tanenbaum, R. L., Alloy, L. B., Abramson, L. Y. (1984). Attributional style and depressive symptoms among children. *Journal of Abnormal Psychology, 93,* 235–238.

Simons, A. D., Garfield, S. L., & Murphy, G. E. (1984). The process of change in cognitive therapy and pharmacotherapy for depression. *Archives of General Psychiatry, 41,* 45–51.

Spitz, R. (1946). Anaclitic depression. *Psychoanalytic Study of the Child, 2,* 113–117.

Spitzer, R. L., Endicott, J., & Robins, E. (1978). Research Diagnostic Criteria: Rationale and reliability. *Archives of General Psychiatry, 35,* 773–782.

Sroufe, L. A., & Rutter, M. (1984). The domain of developmental psychopathology. *Child Development, 55,* 17–29.

Strober, M., Green, J., & Carlson, G. (1981). Utility of the Beck Depression Inventory with psychiatrically hospitalized adolescents. *Journal of Consulting and Clinical Psychology, 49,* 482–483.

Strober, M., & Werry, J. S. (in press). The assessment of depression in children and adolescents. In N. Sartorius & T. A. Ban (Eds.), *Assessment of depression.* Geneva: World Health Organization.

Tesiny, E. P., & Lefkowitz, M. M. (1982). Childhood depression: A 6-month follow-up study. *Journal of Consulting and Clinical Psychology, 50,* 778–780.

Tesiny, E. P., Lefkowitz, M. M., & Gordon, N. H. (1980). Childhood depression, locus of control, and school achievement. *Journal of Educational Psychology, 72,* 506–510.

Tisher, M., & Lang, M. (1983). The Children's Depression Scale: Review and further developments. In D. P. Cantwell & G. A. Carlson (Eds.), *Childhood depression* (pp. 181–203). New York: Spectrum.

Toolan, J. M. (1962). Depression in children and adolescents. *American Journal of Orthopsychiatry, 32,* 404–414.

Usdin, E., Asberg, M., Bertilsson, L., & Sjoqvist, F. (Eds.). (1984). *Advances in biochemical psychopharmacology: Vol. 39. Frontiers in biochemical and phar-*

macological research in depression. New York: Raven Press.

Waxer, P. (1976). Nonverbal cues for depth of depression: Set versus no set. *Journal of Consulting and Clinical Psychology, 44,* 493.

Weinberg, W. A., Rutman, J., Sullivan, L., Pencik, E. C., & Dietz, S. G. (1973). Depression in children referred to an education diagnostic center. *Journal of Pediatrics, 83,* 1065–1072.

Weissman, M. M., Orvaschel, H., & Padian, N. (1980). Children's symptom and social functioning self-report scales: Comparison of mothers' and children's reports. *Journal of Nervous and Mental Disease, 168,* 736–740.

Werry, J. S., & Quay, H. C. (1971). The prevalence of behavior symptoms in younger elementary school children. *American Journal of Orthopsychiatry, 41,* 136–143.

Whybrow, P. C., Akiskal, H. S., & McKinney, W. T.

(Eds.). (1984). *Mood disorders: Toward a new psychobiology.* New York: Plenum.

Williams, J. B. W., & Spitzer, R. L. (1982). Research Diagnostic Criteria and DSM III: An annotated comparison. *Archives of General Psychiatry, 39,* 1283–1289.

Williams, J. G., Barlow, D. H., & Agras, W. S. (1972). Behavioral measurement of severe depression. *Archives of General Psychiatry, 27,* 330–333.

Wirt, R. D., Lachar, D., Klinedinst, J. K., & Seat, P. D. (1977). *Multidimensional description of child personality: A manual for the Personality Inventory for Children.* Los Angeles: Western Psychological Services.

Young, W., Knowles, J. B., MacLean, A. W., Boag, L., & McConville, B. J. (1982). The sleep of childhood depressives. *Biological Psychiatry, 17,* 1163–1168.

Zis, A. P., & Goodwin, F. K. (1982). The amine hypothesis. In E. S. Paykel (Ed.), *Handbook of affective disorders* (pp. 175–190). New York: Guilford Press.

5 FEARS AND ANXIETIES

BILLY A. BARRIOS
University of Mississippi

DONALD P. HARTMANN
University of Utah

O ne cannot be a student of behavior therapy and not have some knowledge of children's fears and anxieties. These disorders have had much too conspicuous a hand in shaping the discipline—its theories, treatments, and boundaries—for the disorders to go unnoticed. Consider the three cases of Albert, Peter, and Hans. Watson and Rayner's (1920) attempted conditioning of fear of a white rat in 1-year-old Albert was interpreted as offering early support for behaviorism, and continues to be cited as evidence for a classical conditioning theory of anxiety (B. Harris, 1979). Further early support for this paradigm of behaviorism came from Mary Cover Jones's (1924) desensitization and modeling treatments of 3-year-old Peter's fear of rabbits; to this day, these treatments continue to be used to overcome the fears and anxieties of children. And then there is Freud's (1909/1955) classic case of young Hans—a case whose original formulation by Freud did little to promote behaviorism, but whose reinterpretation by Wolpe and Rachman (1960) did.

While these early examples indicate that children's fear and anxiety disorders served as an important vehicle for the development of behavior therapy's theories and techniques, behavior therapists historically have not viewed these reactions as subjects worthy of study in their own right. This, however, appears to be changing. It is a change that is perhaps best captured by recent work in the adult domain. There, researchers have been actively attempting to delineate the response elements of fears and anxieties (e.g., Barlow *et al.*, 1984), the distinctions between the common types of fears and anxieties (e.g., Turner & Beidel, 1985; Turner, Beidel, & Larkin, 1986), and the possible mechanisms behind their expression (e.g., Cohen, Barlow, & Blanchard, 1985; Lang, 1985). These recent emphases gradually are finding their way into the child domain.

This view of children's fear and anxiety reactions as subjects worthy of study in their own right is obviously one we share. The present chapter is concerned with one aspect of the study of children's fears and anxieties: their behavioral assessment. The chapter is intended to serve not as a cookbook, but as a sourcebook for those researchers and practitioners interested in the measurement of children's fears and anxieties. In the pages that follow, we discuss children's fear and anxiety reactions in terms of definitions that are found in the literature, developmental data, available assessment instruments, parameters of a comprehensive assessment, and unsettled assessment issues.

DEFINITIONAL CONSIDERATIONS

A wide variety of terms have been coined and definitions proposed in an attempt to specify and classify children's fears and anxieties. Among these terms are "fear," "anxiety," "wariness," "phobia," "clinical fear," "anxiety state," and "anxiety reaction." Attempts at classification most commonly have attempted to distinguish among three of these terms: "fears," "anxieties," and "phobias."

Children's fears have been described as reactions to perceived threats that involve avoidance of the threatening stimuli, subjective feelings of discomfort, and physiological changes. Anxieties have been differentiated from fears largely on the basis of the specificity of the threatening stimuli and the accompanying response (Jersild, 1954). Fears are thought to be highly unified reactions to specific stimuli such as natural events (e.g., lightning, darkness) or abstract concepts (e.g., war, rejection), while anxieties are thought to be more diffuse reactions to nonspecific stimuli—what S. B. Johnson and Melamed (1979) refer to as "apprehension without apparent cause" (p. 107). Clinical fears or phobias have been distinguished from nonclinical fears primarily on the basis of their persistence, maladaptiveness, and magnitude; similar bases have been used to distinguish clinical from nonclinical anxieties (e.g., Berecz, 1968; Crider, 1949; Marks, 1969; L. C. Miller, Barrett, & Hampe, 1974; Morris & Kratochwill, 1983b).

Symptoms

Many different responses or symptoms have been ascribed to children's fears, anxieties, and phobic reactions. Consider, for example, Rachman's (1968) description of a 7-year-old child's reaction to a bee and Bankart and Bankart's (1983) description of a 9-year-old child's reaction to a new school. When confronted with a bee, Rachman's 7-year-old became "white, sweaty, cold and trembly, and his legs were like jelly" (p. 4). When confronted with attending a new school, Bankart and Bankart's 9-year-old showed "intense feelings of fear and dread, uncontrollable crying, nausea, bowel disturbance, headache, fever, and insomnia" (p. 81). Other descriptions of fears, anxieties, and phobic reactions have children reporting feelings of terror, panic, impending doom, or imminent death; children exhibiting physiological changes of rapid respiration, dizziness, palpitations, or breathlessness; and children displaying motor acts of urgent pleas for assistance, exaggerated flight, or complete immobility.

Classification Schemes

Numerous schemes have been proposed for the classification of children's fears and anxieties. At one time it was fashionable to provide long lists of exotic-sounding phobias, such as paraliphobia (fear of precipitating disaster by having omitted or forgotten something), pantophobia (fear of practically everything), and phobophobia (fear of phobias). More recent attempts at classification have grouped children's fears and anxiety reactions into broader categories, through either analytical or empirical methods. In Hebb's (1946) system, fears and anxiety reactions are classified according to presumed etiology; those, for example, that are produced by conflicts or sensory deficit form a class of reactions different from those produced by constitutional disturbances or maturation. In several other systems, the results from factor analyses have served as the basis for the groupings. Scherer and Nakamura (1968) classified the fears of children into those of failure and criticism, of social events, of small animals, of medical procedures, of death, of darkness, of home and school, and of miscellaneous events; L. C. Miller, Barrett, Hampe, and Noble (1972) classified the fears of children into those of physical injury, of natural events, and of psychic stress; and Ollendick (1983) classified the fears of children into those of failure and criticism, of the unknown, of injury and small animals, of danger and death, and of medical procedures.

Other groupings of children's fears and anxieties are found in the clinically derived diagnostic system of the American Psychiatric Association (1980) and the empirically derived classes of behavior disorders (Achenbach, 1985; Quay, 1972, 1979). In the third edition of the American Psychiatric Association's *Diagnostic and Statistical Manual of Mental Disorders* (DSM-III), the fears and anxieties of children have been reduced to eight: Separation Anxiety Disorder, Avoidant Disorder, Overanxious Disorder, Agoraphobia, Social Phobia, Simple Phobia, Panic Disorder, and Obsessive Compulsive Disorder. The eight types of disorders are similar in that they all have anxiety as their predominant symptom; they are dissimilar in that the situations to which anxiety is linked are different.

For DSM-III Separation Anxiety Disorder, the reaction is to separation from major attachment figures such as the mother or from familiar surroundings such as the home. This reaction may take some combination of excessive worrying about major attachment figures, school refusal, social withdrawal, sleep disturbances, somatic complaints, crying and pleading, disruptions in work and play, and persistent tracking of major attachment figures. For Avoidant Disorder, the anxiety reaction is to the presence of strangers; it is said to consist of the mixture of persistent and excessive withdrawal from strangers, clear and sufficient disturbances in peer relationships, healthy and satisfying relationships with family members, and clear and sufficient desires for affection and acceptance. For Overanxious Disorder, anxiety is said to be persistent and pervasive, not linked to any apparent situation or object. This persistent and pervasive anxiety is expressed by some combination of preoccupation with past, present, or future events, repeated requests for reassurance, frequent somatic complaints, marked self-consciousness, and marked feelings of tension.

The three types of phobic disorders in DSM-III—Agoraphobia, Social Phobia, and Simple Phobia—are similar to one another in that the child's fear is focused onto a circumscribed stimulus; they are dissimilar to one another in that the child's fear is focused onto different circumscribed stimuli. For Agoraphobia, the child's fear is linked to being alone or in public places from which escape might be difficult or help not forthcoming in the event of sudden incapacitation. Examples of such public places are crowded stores, elevators, tunnels, and buses. This fear of being alone or in public places dominates and constricts the child's life. For Social Phobia, the fear is tied to situations in which the child might be judged foolish by others. Examples of such situations are speaking in the presence of others, eating in the presence of others, and writing in the presence of others. This fear of looking foolish is a significant source of distress for the child and is recognized by the child as excessive and irrational. For Simple Phobia, the fear is connected to any specific stimulus other than the specific stimuli of the aforementioned categories (e.g., separation from significant other,

presence of a stranger, being alone, speaking in the presence of others). Examples of such stimuli are animals, darkness, water, and heights. Like the fear of humiliating oneself in Social Phobia, the fear of a discrete stimulus in Simple Phobia is a major source of distress and an acknowledged overreaction to the objective dangers posed.

Panic Disorder and Obsessive Compulsive Disorder are DSM-III's two remaining categories of children's fears and anxieties. In Panic Disorder, anxiety takes the form of recurrent, unpredictable bouts of panic—a bout of panic being a constellation of four or more somatic symptoms (e.g., chest pain, dizziness, sweating, choking, trembling). The bouts of panic are unpredictable in that they have no discernible precipitant. In Obsessive Compulsive Disorder, anxiety is tied to obsessions or compulsions or both (obsessions being recurrent, repugnant thoughts, and compulsions being repetitive, nonpurposeful behavior). These obsessions or compulsions are either a significant source of distress for the child or a significant obstacle to adaptive living.

Four general classes of behavior disorders have emerged from the numerous factor-analytic studies on children's problems, one of which is the class of anxiety–withdrawal (cf. Quay, 1979). Anxiety–withdrawal is characterized by feelings of tension, depression, inferiority and worthlessness, and by behaviors of timidity, social withdrawal, and hypersensitivity (cf. Quay, 1979).

These traditional definitions of fears, anxieties, clinical fears (i.e., phobias), and clinical anxieties have a number of problems that detract from their utility. First, the distinctions between fears and anxieties, between normal and clinical fears, and between normal and clinical anxieties have been difficult to operationalize. Second, labeling a child as "fearful" or "anxious" is an imprecise description of how the child has reacted in the past and how the child will react in the future. "Fearful" or "anxious" persons have been found to vary from one another in terms of the responses (i.e., subjective, motoric, and physiological) that they emit, the pattern of relationships among the responses, and the stability of that pattern of relationships over time (e.g., Barrios, 1986; Hodgson & Rachman, 1974; Rachman & Hodgson, 1974; Vermilyea, Boice, & Barlow, 1984). The possibility exists, then, that a number of different response combinations will fall under the same label. For example, one child labeled as dog-fearful may think of dogs as dangerous, perspire profusely when in proximity to them, and steadfastly refuse to go near them. Another child, also labeled as dog-fearful, may also think of dogs as dangerous, yet may not perspire when in their presence or refuse to approach them. Third, it is possible to conceive of a number of the classic fear responses being developed and maintained independently of a threatening stimulus. For example, school avoidance can be acquired and maintained by parent-mediated consequences, regardless of the fear-eliciting qualities of the school.

Despite their shortcomings, we employ the traditional definitions of "fear" and "anxiety" in the material that follows. These definitions are compatible with current theorizing on emotions and with behavioral conceptualizations of fears and anxieties. Contemporary theories of emotions (e.g., Izard, Kagan, & Zajonc, 1984; Plutchik & Kellerman, 1980, 1983) all view emotions as having three components—subjective, motor, and physiological—that merge with one another to form a complex, organized state of activity (cf. Izard et al., 1984). Emotions are not seen as verbal reports or overt behavioral acts or somatovisceral responses, but as the unity of all three (e.g., Lang, 1984; Lang, Rice, & Sternbach, 1972). As specific types of emotions, "fear" and "anxiety" are defined in a similar fashion (e.g., Lang, 1984). Current behavioral theories of fear and anxiety also agree on how to define the two (cf. Delprato & McGlynn, 1984): as complex organized states of subjective, motor, and physiological activity (e.g., Borkovec, 1976; Borkovec, Weerts, & Bernstein, 1977; Lang, 1968, 1971; Rachman, 1977).

With the limited data currently available, it is not clear that the aforementioned classification schemes have "carved nature at its joints"; nor is it clear that any of the proposed schemes have been or will be of great use to behavioral assessors (see Morris & Kratochwill, 1983b, for a detailed review of these classification systems). At this time, the most prudent approach—both empirically and theoretically—would be to categorize children's fears and anxieties by the stimulus to which they are linked. Doing so implies that children's fears and anxieties are context-bound and that they are inferred in part from a knowledge of the situation's unique task demands—two assump-

tions shared by most developmental, emotion, and behavioral theorists (e.g., Campos & Barrett, 1984; Delprato & McGlynn, 1984; Izard et al., 1984; Lang, Levin, Miller, & Kozak, 1983; M. Lewis & Michalson, 1983). For these reasons, it is the approach that we employ in the material that follows.

DEVELOPMENTAL CONSIDERATIONS

The incidence and course of children's fears and anxieties have been explored in a number of epidemiological and related investigations (see reviews by Berecz, 1968; Campbell, 1986; Graziano, DeGiovanni, & Garcia, 1979; Jersild, 1954; I. M. Marks, 1969; L. C. Miller et al., 1974; Morris & Kratochwill, 1983b.) Differing procedures and methodological problems make these studies difficult to compare, but a few generalizations can be made with reasonable confidence.

Incidence

Normal children have a surprisingly large number of fears. Jersild and Holmes (1935) noted that mothers reported that their 2- through 6-year-old children averaged between four and five fears and displayed a fearful reaction once every 4.5 days. MacFarlane, Allen, and Honzik (1954), in their classic longitudinal study of normal children aged 2 through 14 years, found that specific fears were reported at least once for 90% of their sample. Investigating a large sample of 6- through 12-year-old children, Lapouse and Monk (1959) indicated that 43% of their mothers reported that their children experienced seven or more fears, and 15% reported that their children displayed three or more anxious behaviors such as nail biting, teeth grinding, and thumb sucking. The results of a smaller ($N = 193$) validation sample further indicated that maternal reports may underestimate the prevalence of these behaviors. In contrast to the children's own reports, mothers reported 41% fewer fears and anxieties. Maurer's (1965) interviews of 112 children aged 5 through 14 found all of them to have at least one specific fear and to average between four and five fears. Ollendick's (1983) sample of 217 children aged 3 through 11 averaged between 9 and 13 extreme fears; Kirkpatrick's (1984) sample of 30 adolescents aged 15 through

17 averaged between two and three intense fears.

Age Trends

Though fears and anxieties in children are numerous, their frequency tends to decline with increasing age (see reviews by Graziano, DeGiovanni, & Garcia, 1979; Morris & Kratochwill, 1983b; L. C. Miller et al., 1974; Rachman, 1968). Holmes (1935), for example, observed common childhood fears such as fear of strangers, of being left alone, and of the dark in 2- through 5-year-olds and found that age was inversely related to the number of fears displayed. MacFarlane et al. (1954) reported similar age trends for 2- through 14-year-olds; Lapouse and Monk (1959) for 6- through 12-year-olds; Maurer (1965) for 5- through 14-year-olds; Bauer (1976) for 4- through 12-year-olds; and Barrios, Replogle, and Anderson-Tisdelle (1983) for 5- through 16-year-olds. Some studies, however, have found no such decline with age (e.g., Croake & Knox, 1973; Dunlop, 1952) or have found an increase in the numbers of fears and anxieties between the ages of 9 and 11 years (e.g., Angelino & Shedd, 1953; MacFarlane et al., 1954; Morgan, 1959).

Accompanying this overall drop in the number of children's fears and anxieties with age is a shift in the nature of those that are predominant. Young infants are frightened by the loss of support, by height, and by sudden, intense, and unexpected stimuli such as loud noises (e.g., Jersild, 1954). As children mature and face new developmental challenges, their fears also change. Children aged 1 and 2 are afraid of strangers, of toileting activities, and of being injured (e.g., L. C. Miller et al., 1974), but are as yet unafraid of snakes (H. E. Jones & Jones, 1928). Imaginary creatures are common sources of fear for preschool children, as are animals and the dark (e.g., Bauer, 1976; Jersild & Holmes, 1935). Young children in elementary school continue to be frightened by small animals and darkness, concerned with their physical safety, and fearful of natural events such as lightning and thunder (e.g., Croake & Knox, 1973; Maurer, 1965). As children enter into the middle school years, academic-, social-, and health-related fears become prominent (e.g., Bauer, 1976; Maurer, 1965; Ollendick, 1983; Scherer & Nakamura, 1968). For example, Kennedy (1965) estimated the incidence of serious phobic reactions to school to be 17 per 1,000; Stricker and Howitt (1965) estimated as many as 16% of all school-aged children as having serious fear and anxiety related to dental treatment; and Scherer and Nakamura (1968) identified terror of principals and teachers as the primary fear of children in middle school. Older schoolchildren increasingly become frightened of physical injury, medical procedures, public speaking, test taking, and economic and political catastrophes such as war (e.g., Allan & Hodgson, 1968; Angelino, Dollins, & Mech, 1956; Herbertt & Innes 1979; Kirkpatrick, 1984).

Seriousness

Although common, most childhood fears and anxieties apparently are not very serious. For example, Rutter, Tizard, and Whitmore (1970) screened the total population of 10- and 11-year-olds on the Isle of Wight and found a prevalence rate for serious fears of only 7 per 1,000, with animal, darkness, school, and disease phobias the most common. Prevalence data of this kind prompted L. C. Miller et al. (1974) to suggest that the intensity of children's fears is best described by a J-shaped distribution curve, with numerous reports of mild fears and infrequent reports of severe fear reactions. The data reported by MacFarlane et al. (1954), for example, provide a good fit with this description. Other investigators have reported data that are not consistent with this description (e.g., Croake & Knox, 1973; Kirkpatrick, 1984; Ollendick, 1983).

Reports based on referrals to treatment agencies suggest that most fears are not sufficiently indisposing to children or irritating to their parents or teachers to require professional care. S. B. Johnson and Melamed's (1979) review indicates that phobic disorders account for only 3–4% of all child cases referred for treatment. Graham (1964), for example, reported only 10 specific phobias in 239 consecutive cases referred to the Maudsley Hospital Children's Department in London. Although behavior therapists spend more of their time treating fearful and anxious clients than any other type (Swan & MacDonald, 1978; Wade, Baker, & Hartmann, 1979), it would appear that these clients are typically not children. Based on a small and perhaps unrepresentative survey of child behavior therapists, Graziano and DeGiovanni (1979) found relatively few children (7–8%) referred for specific fear-related behavior. When children are referred for treatment of fearful behavior, school phobia accounts for the majority of cases (69%, according to L. C. Miller *et al.*, 1974), although it is by no means the most common phobia.

Prognosis

Available research paints a mixed picture regarding the persistence of most childhood fears and anxieties. The majority of evidence from early studies suggests that most of these childhood disorders are short-lived, while the bulk of evidence from later studies suggests that they may be more enduring. Slater (1939), for example, reported that the frequent displays of fearful and anxious behavior (e.g., tics, requests for mothers, and postural tensions) in 2- and 3-year-old nursery school children had almost completely abated after 4 weeks. Cummings (1944, 1946) reported that fears, though not generalized anxiety reactions, were quite transitory in 2- through 7-year-olds. Hagman (1932) similarly reported that most childhood fears were short-lived: 54% had disappeared after 3 months, and the more recalcitrant fears were gone after 3 years.

Other early studies are consistent with this encouraging view of the favorable prognosis for fearful and avoidance behaviors in children. In a 5-year follow-up of an earlier epidemiological study, Agras, Chapin, and Oliveau (1972) found that, of the 10 children initially identified as phobics, all were improved or had recovered. Hampe, Noble, Miller, and Barrett (1973), reporting a 2-year follow-up of treated phobic children, found that only 7% of the children continued to have serious fear reactions, whereas 80% were "symptom-free." Similarly, Robins's (1966) analysis of the adult status of 525 child guidance clinic patients indicated that adults who displayed neurotic behaviors (e.g., nervousness, fears, tics, and shyness) as children had a *lower* rate of neurotic disturbances when they reached adulthood than did members of a control group. Retrospective studies of adult phobics provide results generally consistent with the results of prospective studies. Although adult phobics report having more childhood fears than control group members (Solyom, Beck, Solyom, & Hugel, 1974), the fears of adult phobics typically do not begin during childhood (Agras, Sylvester, & Oliveau, 1969), with the possible exception of specific animal phobias (I. M. Marks & Gelder, 1966).

More recent investigations have found the fears and anxieties of children to be much more stable. For example, Barrios *et al.* (1983) had 74 adolescents aged 14 through 16 rate their fear and anxiety reactions to 50 different stimuli over a 1-month period. The stability coefficients for their subjective, motor, and physiological responses averaged +.82. Approximately 1–2 months after a lightning disaster, Dollinger, O'Donnell, and Staley (1984) questioned the child victims and their parents about fear and anxiety symptoms such as trembling and crying during storms, refusal to sleep alone, and tearfulness upon separation from parents. Of 38 children, 15 continued to show mild upset, 7 to show moderate upset, and 8 to show severe upset, with 4 requiring some form of professional counseling for their fear and anxiety symptoms. The self-reported fears and anxieties of Ollendick's (1983) sample of 60 children aged 8 through 11 remained markedly consistent over a 3-month period (stability coefficients ranged from .55 to .60), as did those of Eme and Schmidt's (1978) sample of 22 fourth-graders over a 1 year period. And in their studies spanning a substantially longer time, Berg and associates (Berg, 1976; Berg, Marks, McGuire, & Lipsedge, 1974) identified a relationship between school phobia in childhood and agoraphobia in adulthood.

The bulk of epidemiological and related evidence suggests that behavior assessors would do well to maintain a developmental perspective when evaluating children's fears and anxieties. According to this perspective, the seriousness of a fear response is partly a function of the extent to which that response is common to children of a similar age. Thus, a fear of ghosts under the bed might be of minor concern if displayed by a 5-year-old, but might be a more serious matter if reported by a 13-year-old. A developmental perspective also might help restrain assessors who are inclined to overinterpret children's fearful reactions. Kanner (1960) provides an amusing example of the salutary effects of developmental norms in evaluation of children's fearful and anxious behavior. In the early years of child psychopathology, the seemingly innocent response of nail biting was variously viewed as "a stigma of degeneration," "an exquisite psychopathic symptom," and "a sign of an unresolved Oedipus complex." A survey disclosing that 66% of school children had been nail biters at one time or another prompted Kanner to remark that it was "hardly realistic to assume that two-thirds of our youth are degenerate, exquisitely psychopathic, or walking around with an unresolved Oedipus complex" (p. 18).

An additional implication for behavior assessors can be drawn from the various sources of data relating to the outcome of children's fears. Treated fears, with the exception of some cases of school phobia, have a favorable outcome. Even many untreated fears can be expected to improve with the passage of time. Although this latter fact may be of little immediate consolation to distressed parents, behavior assessors should consider cost-effectiveness before recommending treatment. Favorable cost-effective outcomes may be limited to inexpensive treatments that produce rapid and significant improvements (Gelfand, 1978) or that also serve preventive functions.

Other Considerations in Deciding Whether to Treat

Although developmental and prognostic factors are important in deciding whether or not to accept a fearful or anxious child for treatment, many other factors will also contribute to that decision. The assessor may want to consider the child's and the adults' views of the problem, the relationship of the fear or anxiety to other problem behaviors, the anticipated costs and benefits associated with available treatments, and other practical and ethical factors. The following questions highlight these issues.

1. *Who is complaining?* Children are rarely self-referred for treatment; instead, they are referred by parents, teachers, or physicians (I. M. Evans & Nelson, 1977). The perceptions of these adults, not the child's fearful or anxious behavior, may be more important in determining whether the child is brought to the attention of a behavior therapist (Lobitz & Johnson, 1975). Thus, even though the child is fearful or anxious, he or she may be unmotivated or otherwise unwilling to participate in treatment. In other cases, the child's behavior may be appropriate, but the adult's demands or expectations for fearless behavior may be unreasonable. When this occurs, the adult rather than the child may be the appropriate recipient of treatment.

2. *How is the behavior a problem?* According to Karoly (1975), a problem exists when a behavior reliably disrupts one's pursuit of personal goals, one's ability to adjust to the environment, or one's sense of comfort, satisfaction, and freedom. With a child client, the behavior assessor would want to examine the impact of the fear or the anxiety on individual, family, and classroom functioning; its interference with normal development and learning experiences; and the resulting curtailment of behavior choices and creation of subjective discomfort.

3. *How are fears related to other areas of the child's behavior?* The fearful or anxious behavior identified by an adult may not be the problem that needs modifying. Enuresis, tantrums, and sleep disturbances may occur in conjunction with anxiety reactions (Kanner, 1957). Anxiety may also be a reaction to other problems, such as learning difficulties, faulty parenting techniques, or physical illnesses, and an acute anxiety attack or phobia may precede or accompany a psychotic reaction (Chess & Hassibi, 1978). The child's fear may be linked to a parent's problems or indicative of maladaptive family functioning (Eisenberg, 1958; Gambrill, 1977; Singer, 1965). The presence of associated difficulties may mean that a problem other than the child's fear or anxiety should be treated, or that both the fear or anxiety and another problem should be treated.

4. *What are the costs of treatment, assuming that there are effective interventions for the problem?* A child might be embarrassed about or resentful of treatment, despite the promise of improved behavior and increased attractiveness to others. For parents and other adults, treatment involves expending time, money, and effort and disrupting regular activities in return for a fearless child.

5. *What would be different for the child and others in his or her natural environment without the problem?* The therapist must examine alternatives to the current situation and determine whether changes would be a positive event for all the persons involved. What are the implications of not treating a child's fear or anxiety? Although epidemiological data suggest that most childhood fears are transient, a therapist's refusal to provide the best available intervention might result in ethical or legal problems. The therapist must also consider the short- and long-term consequences for the child that are associated with a failure to treat. For example, children's fear of dentists, injections, and other medical procedures may be short-lived; the fears'

interference with adequate care, however, may contribute to permanent physical damage, serious disease, and general poor health.

Answers to questions such as these will assist the behavioral assessor in deciding whether treatment is warranted. If the decision is made to treat the child, then the assessor must consider other issues in order to select effective treatment procedures.

INSTRUMENTS FOR ASSESSING FEARS AND ANXIETIES

Classification and Review

In this section, we review the available instruments for assessing children's fears and anxieties. For purposes of presentation and analysis, the instruments have been classified along three dimensions: the nature of the threatening stimulus, the response system assessed, and the method of assessment. As mentioned earlier, the fears and anxieties of children are conceptualized as being context-bound (e.g., Borkovec, 1976; Borkovec et al., 1977; Campos & Barrett, 1984; Lang, 1984; M. Lewis & Michalson, 1983). The stimulus contexts of children's fears and anxieties vary in their specificity, complexity, and generality. Certain threatening stimuli (e.g., small animals, medical procedures, and acts of nature) are fairly distinct, whereas other stimuli (e.g., the future, one's competence, and one's health) are not. The stimuli also vary in the complexity both of their makeup and of the task demands posed. Stimulus conditions such as thunderstorms and darkness are fairly straightforward in their makeup and modest in what they demand from children in the way of appropriate performance. On the other hand, stimulus conditions such as medical procedures and public speaking are more complicated in their makeup and in what they require in the way of adaptive responding. In addition to their specificity and complexity, threatening stimuli differ in terms of their temporal generality. The appearance of some stimuli (e.g., medical procedures and school examinations) are totally predictable, whereas others (e.g., thoughts about the future, one's competence, or one's health) are totally idiosyncratic.

For each stimulus category, the instruments have been separated according to the type of fearful and anxious responding that they assess.

As stated earlier, fear and anxiety reactions are conceptualized as complex, organized patterns of activity from three response systems—subjective, motor, and physiological (e.g., Borkovec et al., 1977; Lang, 1968, 1971; Rachman, 1977). As such, any instrument concerned with the assessment of children's fears and anxieties must focus on activity from one or more of the response systems. Activity from each one of the response systems may take various forms (e.g., Hugdahl, 1981; Kozak & Miller, 1982). Table 1 offers a partial listing of the specific responses (or symptoms) from each system that have heretofore been assessed. Though we have made no attempt to classify the instruments in terms of the specific responses that they assess, we do offer such information in our descriptions of the instruments.

Classified by stimulus category and by response system, the instruments have been further subdivided in terms of their method of assessment. Measurement of most aspects of children's fear and anxiety reactions can be carried out through multiple means (e.g., Cone, 1979; Morris & Kratochwill, 1983b).

For example, information on children's motor responses to separation can be gathered through interviews with the children or the parents, through questionnaires completed by the children or the parents, or through direct behavior observation of the children. Virtually all of the instruments, though, employ one of three basic methods of measurement: self-report, observational, or mechanical (e.g., bioelectronic recording). Thus, our third classification of the instruments employs these three methods of measurement.

Table 2 provides a brief description and appraisal of the available instruments for assessing the fears and anxieties of children. This brief description of each instrument includes information on its administration and scoring. With respect to the administration of each instrument, information is given on the nature and number of assessment stimuli, and on the obtrusiveness and immediacy of data collection. Assessment stimuli or test items may be either naturalistic representations of the threatening conditions (e.g., an actual thunderstorm) or contrived ones (e.g., an audio recording of a thunderstorm). Acting as a representative of the threatening conditions may be either a single test item (e.g., one photograph of a snake)

TABLE 1. A Partial Listing of the Motoric, Physiological, and Subjective Response Components of Children's Fears and Anxieties

Motoric responses	Physiological responses	Cognitive responses
Avoidance	Heart rate	Thoughts of being scared
Gratuitous arm, hand, and leg	Basal skin response	Thoughts of monsters
movements	Palmar sweat index	Thoughts of being hurt
Trembling voice	Galvanic skin response	Images of monsters
Crying	Muscle tension	Images of wild animals
Feet shuffling	Skin temperature	Thoughts of danger
Screaming	Respiration	Self-deprecatory thoughts
Nail biting	Palpitation	Self-critical thoughts
Thumb sucking	Breathlessness	Thoughts of inadequacy
Rigid posture	Nausea	Thoughts of incompetence
Eyes shut	Pulse volume	Thoughts of bodily injury
Avoidance of eye contact	Headache	Images of bodily injury
Clenched jaw	Stomach upset	
Stuttering	Stomachache	
Physical proximity	Urination	
White knuckles	Defecation	
Trembling lip	Vomiting	
Certain verbalizations[a]		

Note. The responses listed have been documented in the following studies: Esveldt-Dawson, Wisner, Unis, Matson, & Kazdin (1982); Glennon & Weisz (1978); Katz, Kellerman, & Siegel (1980); LeBaron & Zeltzer (1984); T. Lewis & Law (1958); Melamed, Hawes, Heiby, & Glick (1975); Melamed & Siegel (1975); Milos & Reiss (1982); Ross, Ross, & Evans (1971); Siegel & Peterson (1980); Simpson, Ruzicka, & Thomas (1974); Sonnenberg & Venham (1977); Van Hasselt, Hersen, Bellack, Rosenblum, & Lamparski (1979); Zatz & Chassin (1983).

[a] In some cases, the distinction between motor and subjective responses may be difficult to draw. For example, the shouted statement "I'm scared!" in response to a large, barking dog is similar to a scream (a motor response) and is, of course, the expression of a feeling (a subjective response).

or multiple test items (e.g., more than one photograph of a snake). Children's reactions to the test items may be monitored in an obtrusive, highly conspicuous fashion, with children fully aware that they are being observed (e.g., role-play assessment of responses to a stranger), or they may be monitored in an unobtrusive, covert fashion, with the children unaware that they are being observed (e.g., a naturalistic assessment of response to a stranger). The interval between the monitoring of children's reactions and the recording of those reactions may be either concurrent or retrospective. And with respect to the scoring of the reactions, each individual response may be examined in isolation, or the responses may be summed to form a weighted or unweighted composite score. (A weighted composite score has certain responses contributing more to the total score than others, whereas an unweighted composite score has all responses contributing equally to the total.)

Table 2 lists over 100 instruments, most of which are concerned with the assessment of

children's fear and anxiety reactions to medical procedures, darkness, school events, separation, and small animals, and with the assessment of generalized anxiety. More instruments are available for the assessment of fears and anxieties concerning medical procedures (33, to be exact) than for the assessment of any other distressing condition. In fact, there are nearly twice as many instruments for medical procedures than for the next-ranking condition—a finding that we suspect reflects behavior therapy's recent interest in behavioral medicine (e.g., Blanchard, 1982; Melamed & Siegel, 1980; Russo, 1984; Varni, 1983). Of the 100-odd instruments, approximately one-half are concerned with the assessment of the motor (or behavioral) aspects of children's fear and anxiety reactions; approximately one-third with the assessment of the subjective aspects; and the remaining one-sixth with the assessment of the physiological aspects. It should come as no surprise that the activity of the motor response system has been examined more extensively than the activity of the other two response

TABLE 2. Description and Appraisal of Instruments for Assessing Children's Fears and Anxieties

Stimulus	Instrument/author(s)	Response system	Method of measurement	Description	Appraisal
Blood	Behavioral avoidance test Van Hasselt, Hersen, Bellack, Rosenblum, & Lamparski (1979)	Motor	Observational	A blood-soaked pillow case 15 feet away is brought 1 foot closer every 15 seconds until the child motions to stop.	Excellent temporal stability across 3 weeks. Scores fluctuate in accord with treatment, but bear no systematic relationship to physiological and subjective measures. Easy to administer and score; suitable for both the laboratory and the clinic for problem identification and treatment evaluation.
	Target Complaint Scale Van Hasselt et al. (1979)	Subjective	Self-report	Subjective fear experienced during the behavioral avoidance test is rated on a 12-point scale, with descriptive anchors (e.g., "none," "pretty much," "couldn't be worse") at every third point.	Excellent temporal stability across 3 weeks. Scores fluctuate in acord with treatment, but bear no systematic relationship to physiological and motor measures. A global rating of ambiguous meaning and suspect soundness and utility. Addition of more response items of distinct content may make the instrument useful to the researcher and clinician in identifying problematic fear and evaluating treatments.
	Heart rate Van Hasselt et al. (1979)	Physiological	Mechanical	Monitored throughout the behavioral avoidance test. Heart rate response score calculated by subtracting the rate for the last 15 seconds of baseline from the rate for the last 15 seconds of final approach item.	Good temporal stability across 3 weeks. No evidence of validity (e.g., fluctuations with treatment, convergence with other measures); thus, no data to support the usefulness of this method of recording and quantifying heart rate activity.
	Finger pulse volume Van Hasselt et al. (1979)	Physiological	Mechanical	Monitored throughout the behavioral avoidance test. Response score calculated by subtracting amplitude for last 15 seconds of baseline from the amplitude for last 15 seconds of final approach item.	Good temporal stability across 3 weeks. No evidence of validity (e.g., fluctuations with treatment, convergence with other measures); thus, no data to support the usefulness of this method of recording and quantifying cardiovascular activity.

(continued)

TABLE 2. (*continued*)

Stimulus	Instrument/author(s)	Response system	Method of measurement	Description	Appraisal
Darkness	Behavioral avoidance test Giebenhain (1985)	Motor	Observational	Room illumination is progressively dimmed in 10 steps, with 30-second interval between steps, until the child tolerates 30 seconds of total darkness or motions to stop.	Excellent temporal stability over 3 weeks. Convergence with other motor and subjective measures of fear. Discriminates between groups known to differ in their fearfulness toward darkness. Easy to administer and score; suitable for use in both the laboratory and clinic for problem identification and treatment evaluation.
	Fear thermometer Giebenhain (1985)	Physiological	Self-report	Level of physiological upset during the behavioral avoidance test is rated on a 5-point scale with animated figures as descriptive anchors at each point.	Poor temporal stability over 3 weeks. Convergence with other subjective measures of fear. A global rating of ambiguous meaning and questionable utility. Addition of more response items of distinct content may make scores more stable and useful in problem identification and treatment evaluation.
	Heart rate Giebenhain (1985)	Physiological	Mechanical	Monitored throughout the behavioral avoidance test. Response score calculated by subtracting mean baseline rate from mean rate for the final approach item.	Poor temporal stability over 3 weeks and no evidence of validity (e.g., convergence with other fear measures, discrimination of known groups); therefore, no support for the usefulness of this method of monitoring and quantifying heart rate activity.
	Modified Timed Behavior Checklist Giebenhain (1985)	Motor	Observational	During the behavioral avoidance test, the occurrence–nonoccurrence of nine responses (e.g., rocking, shuffling feet, clenching fists, nail biting, facial grimacing) is recorded for each gradation. Response score is calculated by dividing the number of gradations tolerated into the total number of occurrences.	Excellent interrater reliability; acceptable temporal stability over 3 weeks. Convergence with other motor and subjective measures of fear. Discriminates between groups known to differ in their fearfulness toward darkness. Need for trained raters probably restricts its use to research for purposes of problem identification and treatment evaluation.

Instrument		Description	Comments
Self-Statement Checklist Giebenhain (1985)	Subjective Self-report	Child rates, on a 4-point scale from "never" to "a lot," the frequency of five fearful thoughts (e.g., "I kept thinking about how scared I was") and five coping or mastery thoughts (e.g., "I kept thinking that I am brave") experienced during the behavioral avoidance test. A response score for each type of thinking is obtained by summing across the five items.	Poor temporal stability over 3 weeks. Convergence with other subjective, motor, and physiological measures of fear. Discriminates groups known to differ in their fearfulness toward darkness. Addition of more response items may render scores more stable. Easy to administer and score; suitable for use in both the laboratory and clinic for purpose of problem identification and treatment evaluation.
Think-aloud statements Giebenhain (1985)	Subjective Self-report	Audiotaped recordings of "thinking aloud" during the behavioral avoidance test are scored for the percentage of fearful, coping, and irrelevant statements. Entire transcript rated for affect on a 7-point scale (e.g., "not at all afraid," "extremely afraid").	Excellent interrater reliability; good temporal stability over 3 weeks. Convergence with other subjective, motor, and physiological measures of fear. Discriminates groups known to differ in their fearfulness toward darkness. Scoring of think-aloud audiotapes is tedious and time-consuming; therefore, the procedure appears to be restricted to use by researchers for the purposes of problem identification and treatment evaluation.
Bedtime Illumination Test Giebenhain & O'Dell (1984)	Motor Observational	Child selects from one of 11 levels (total darkness to total brightness) the nighttime illumination for the bedroom.	Excellent temporal stability over 1 month. Scores fluctuate in accord with treatment. Easy to administer and score. Suitable for both the laboratory and the clinic for purposes of treatment evaluation.
Direct Home Observation Graziano & Mooney (1980)	Motor Observational	Parents record nightly the number of minutes after request the child requires to get to bed, the number of minutes to fall asleep, the occurrence of avoidance and delay behaviors (e.g., requesting a glass of water,	Good interrater reliability; poor temporal stability over 4 weeks. Scores discriminate between groups known to differ in their fearfulness towards darkness and fluctuate in accord with treatment. Temporal stability may be improved through aggregation across response items and sessions. Suitable for both researcher and clinicians for *(continued)*

207

TABLE 2. (continued)

Stimulus	Instrument/author(s)	Response system	Method of measurement	Description	Appraisal
				telling of a story), a rating of willingness to go to bed, and a judgment of whether or not child is afraid.	purposes of problem identification and treatment evaluation.
	Fear Strength Questionnaire Graziano & Mooney (1980)	Motor	Observational	Child's fear reaction is rated along nine dimensions (e.g., frequency, intensity, duration per incident, level of disruption, seriousness, degree of school interference).	Good temporal stability over 4 weeks. Scores fluctuate in accord with treatment. Ease of administration and scoring makes it suitable for both the laboratory and the clinic, but lack of data on interrater reliability and convergence with other fear measures restrict its use to treatment evaluation.
	Darkness Tolerance Test Kanfer, Karoly, & Newman (1975)	Motor	Mechanical	Two variants: one has the child in total darkness for 180 seconds before adjusting the illumination to a comfortable level; the other has the child in total illumination, dimming the light to complete darkness or some intermediate point.	Excellent temporal stability over unspecified time period. Scores on the two forms of the test correlate with each other, converge with subjective measures of fear, fluctuate in accord with treatment, and generalize to other relevant settings. Simple to administer and score; appropriate for both the laboratory and the clinic for purpose of problem identification and treatment evaluation.
	Behavioral avoidance test Kelley (1976)	Motor	Observational	Room illumination is decreased from full brightness in five steps until child tolerates 60 seconds of total darkness or motions to stop. Response score is seconds of the steps tolerated.	No estimates of reliability. Modest relationship to subjective measure of fear. Test performance sensitive to instructional demand for approach behavior. Lack of reliability and validity data argues against its use.
	Fear thermometer Kelley (1976)	Subjective	Self-report	Level of fear experienced during the behavioral avoidance test is rated on a scale of 1–5 by moving a lever up a multicolored board.	No estimates of reliability. Modest relationship to motor measure of fear. A global rating of ambiguous meaning and suspect soundness. Not recommended for use at present.

208

(continued)

Instrument				
Behavioral avoidance test Leitenberg & Callahan (1973)	Motor	Observational	Number of seconds of total darkness tolerated is recorded.	Excellent temporal stability over 4 weeks. Scores fluctuate in accord with treatment. Simple to administer and score; suitable for use in the laboratory and the clinic for purposes of treatment evaluation.
Nighttime Coping Response Inventory Mooney (1985)	Subjective, motor	Self-report	Retrospective 5-point ratings are made of the frequencies of 20 nighttime coping responses from five categories: Self-Control (e.g., "think happy or pleasant thoughts"), Social Support (e.g., "go into bed with Mom or Dad"), Clinging to Inanimate Objects, Control over Inanimate Environment, and Control over Others. A composite score for each response category is obtained by summing across the four appropriate items.	No estimates of reliability. Scores discriminate fear groups known to differ in their fearfulness toward the dark. Easy to administer and score, but difficult to interpret because items addressing the subjective component are lumped with ones addressing the motor component. Separate scales may be developed for the two components. With these modifications and additional reliability and validity data, the inventory may be useful in problem identification, treatment selection, and treatment evaluation.
Nighttime Fear Inventory Mooney (1985)	Subjective	Self-report	Child completes 5-point ratings of the level of worry or fear experienced to 28 images from seven stimulus categories: Personal Security (e.g., "dying or thinking I am going to die"), Separation from Others (e.g., "wonder if Mom or Dad are hurt or not"), Imaginal (e.g., "ghosts or spooks"), Inherent Characteristics, Dreams, Dark, and Neutral. A compositie score for each stimulus category obtained by summing across the four relevant items.	No estimates of reliability. Scores discriminate fear groups known to differ in their fearfulness toward the dark. Ease of administration and scoring makes it appropriate for use in both the laboratory and the clinic. Lack of reliability and validity data argues for cautious use.

TABLE 2. (*continued*)

Stimulus	Instrument/author(s)	Response system	Method of measurement	Description	Appraisal
	Darkness Tolerance Test Sheslow, Bondy, & Nelson (1982)	Motor	Observational	The number of seconds of total darkness tolerated is recorded.	Excellent interrater reliability. Scores fluctuate in accord with treatment. Ease of administration and scoring makes it suitable for use in both the laboratory and the clinic. Lack of temporal stability data calls for cautious use of the instrument to evaluate treatment effectiveness.
Heights	Ladder climb Van Hasselt *et al.* (1979)	Motor	Observational	Number of feet the child goes up a 12-foot ladder is recorded.	Excellent temporal stability over 3 weeks. Convergence with physiological measure of fear and fluctuation in accord with treatment. Suitable for use in laboratory and clinic for purposes of treatment evaluation.
	Target Complaint Scale Van Hasselt *et al.* (1979)	Subjective	Self-report	Subjective fear experienced during the ladder climb is rated on a 12-point scale, with descriptive anchors at every third point (e.g., "none," "pretty much," "couldn't be worse").	Excellent temporal stability over 3 weeks. Fluctuations in accord with treatment. A global rating of ambiguous meaning and suspect utility. Addition of response items of distinct content may yield a reliable instrument of use in problem identification and treatment evaluation.
	Heart rate Van Hasselt *et al.* (1979)	Physiological	Mechanical	Heart rate is recorded upon arrival to the laboratory and immediately prior to the ladder climb. Former is subtracted from the latter to yield a heart rate response score.	Excellent temporal stability over 3 weeks. Convergence with motor measure of fear and fluctuation in accord with treatment. Expensive recording apparatus may restrict this measurement of heart rate to the laboratory, where it might be used for the purposes of problem identification and treatment evaluation.
Illness	Fear-related verbalizations Bornstein & Knapp (1981)	Subjective	Self-report	Parents record on an hourly basis the frequency of fear-related verbal remarks.	Excellent interrater reliability; poor temporal stability. Scores fluctuate in accord with treatment. Ease of data collection makes it suited for both the researcher and clinician for assessing outcome. Stability may be improved through aggregation.

210

Medical procedures					
Maternal Anxiety Rating Bradlyn (1982)	Motor	Observational	Mother rates her child's current level of anxiety according to a 7-point scale.	No estimates of reliability; scores fluctuate with treatment. A global rating of ambiguous meaning and suspect utility. Addition of more items of definite content may render it useful.
Faces—Subjective Units of Disturbance Bradlyn (1982)	Subjective	Self-report	Child indicates present level of anxiety by pointing to one of five faces each depicting a level of fear.	No evidence of reliability or validity. A global rating of uncertain meaning and utility. Addition of response items of distinct content may transform the instrument into a useful one. In its present form, though, it is of little worth.
Hospital Fears Schedule Bradlyn (1982)	Subjective	Self-report	Using the 5-point Faces scale, child rates degree of anxiety to 10 hospital-related situations. Ratings are summed across items to yield a total fear score.	No evidence of reliability or validity. Test score is actually a composite of 10 global ratings; thus, suffers from the same limitations as the global rating (e.g., instability, ambiguous content). Increasing the clarity of the rating scale may improve its reliability and validity.
Observational Behavior Scale Bradlyn (1982); Klorman, Ratner, King, & Sveen (1978)	Motor	Observation	Occurrence–nonoccurrence of 7 motor responses (e.g., kicking, hand to face, crying) is recorded every 15 seconds and summed across responses and intervals to yield a total motor score.	Excellent interrater reliability. Scores are relatively stable across successive exposures to medical procedures. Scores correlate with parental and self-ratings of anxiety. Small number of response categories makes it feasible for both clinical and research use.
Ratings of Anxiety and Cooperation Bradlyn (1982)	Motor	Observational	Physician and nurse or technician rate on a 7-point scale the child's level of anxiety and level of cooperation during the procedure.	No estimates of reliability. Scores fluctuate in accord with treatment. A single-item measure of uncertain meaning and questionable utility. Introduction of more items of specified content may enhance the usefulness of the instrument.
Self-Statements Inventory—Revised Bradlyn (1982)	Subjective	Self-report	Child rates on a 7-point scale the frequency of 18 thoughts of two types (coping, disruptive) experienced during the medical procedure. The 9 coping thoughts (e.g., ''How much were you	No estimates of reliability or validity. May have too few items on each scale for adequate reliability. Addition of more items may enhance reliability, which in turn may enhance the usefulness of the inventory.

(continued)

TABLE 2. (continued)

Stimulus	Instrument/author(s)	Response system	Method of measurement	Description	Appraisal
				thinking that the test didn't hurt and how easy it was to get through it?") and the 9 disruptive thoughts (e.g., "How much were you worrying that the test might kill you?") are summed to yield a composite score for each type.	
	Behavioral avoidance test Freeman, Roy, & Hemmick (1976)	Motor	Observational	Number of steps completed in an 11-step physical examination is recorded.	No estimates of reliability. Scores fluctuate in accord with treatment. Ease of administration and scoring make the procedure well suited for both the laboratory and the clinic. Lack of data on temporal stability calls for caution in using the measure as an index of treatment outcome.
	Behavior Profile Rating Scale—Revised Gilbert, Johnson, Spillar, McCallum, Silverstein, & Rosenbloom (1982)	Motor	Observational	Frequency of several anxiety-related behaviors is recorded during self-injection of insulin. Frequencies are summed to yield a single motor fear score.	Good interrater reliability. No evidence of validity (e.g., convergence with other fear measures, fluctuations with treatment). Employing a weighted as opposed to an unweighted scoring system may enhance the usefulness of the instrument. The need for trained observers restricts its use to research.
	Global Anxiety Rating Gilbert et al. (1982)	Motor	Observational	The child's level of anxiety during insulin self-injection is rated on a scale of 1–10.	Good interrater reliability. No evidence of validity. A single-item measure of unknown meaning and questionable worth. The addition of response items of definite content may improve the instrument's usefulness.
	Observational Scale of Behavioral Distress Jay & Elliott (1984); Jay, Ozolins, Elliott, & Caldwell (1983)	Motor	Observational	Occurrence–nonoccurrence of 11 behaviors (e.g., cry, scream, physical restraint, muscular rigidity) is recorded in 15-second intervals. The behaviors are dif-	Excellent interrater reliability. Convergence with other motor, subjective, and physiological measures of fear. Need for trained observers may restrict its use to research for the purposes of problem identification and treatment evaluation.

212

Measure	Type	Category	Description	Comments
			ferentially weighted according to intensity of distress, and summed to yield a weighted composite score.	
Procedure Behavioral Rating Scale Katz, Kellerman, & Seigel (1980)	Motor	Observational	Occurrence–nonoccurrence of 13 behaviors (e.g., cling, flail, stall, scream) is recorded during entire procedure. Recordings are summed across behaviors to yield a single motor score.	Excellent interrater reliability, good temporal stability over 1½ years. Convergence with other measures of fear. Need for trained observers may restrict its employment to research for the purposes of problem identification and treatment evaluation.
Procedure Behavior Checklist LeBaron & Zeltzer (1984)	Motor	Observational	Occurrence–nonoccurrence and intensity of eight behaviors (e.g., muscle tension, crying, restraint used, physical resistance) are recorded during the entire medical procedure. Intensity is rated on a scale of 1–5. Recordings are summed across behaviors to yield a single occurrence score and a single intensity score.	Acceptable interrater reliability. Convergence with other motor and subjective measures of fear. Need for trained observers may restrict its use to research for purposes of treatment evaluation.
Observer Rating of Anxiety LeBaron & Zeltzer (1984)	Motor	Observational	The child's level of anxiety during a portion of the medical procedure is rated on a 5-point scale.	Acceptable interrater reliability. Convergence with other motor and subjective measures of anxiety. Single-item measure of ambiguous meaning. Addition of items of stated content may enhance the usefulness of the measure.
Faces Test of Anxiety LeBaron & Zeltzer (1984)	Subjective	Self-report	Child rates degree of anxiety experienced during the procedure by pointing to one of five faces, each depicting a level of fear.	No estimate of reliability. Convergence with motor measures of anxiety. Global rating of undetermined content and limited utility. Addition of items of known content may increase the reliability and validity of the test.
Behavior Profile Rating Scale Klingman, Melamed, Cuthbert, & Hermecz	Motor	Observational	The frequencies of 27 behaviors (e.g., crying, refusal to open mouth, rigid posture, kicking) are recorded	Excellent interrater reliability. Convergence with other observational and self-report measures of dental anxiety; scores fluctuate in accord with treatment. Large number of

(continued)

TABLE 2. (continued)

Stimulus	Instrument/author(s)	Response system	Method of measurement	Description	Appraisal
	(1984); Melamed, Hawes, Heiby, & Glick (1975); Melamed, Weinstein, Hawes, & Katin-Borland (1975); Melamed, Yurcheson, Fleece, Hutcherson, & Hawes (1978)			during the dental treatment procedure. Each behavior is weighted according to its degree of disruption, and a total score is obtained by summing across the weighted values.	response categories and need for trained observers confine its use to research. May be of assistance in problem identification and treatment evaluation.
	Children's Fear Survey Schedule—Dental Melamed, Hawes, et al. (1975); Melamed, Weinstein, et al. (1975); Melamed et al. (1978)	Subjective	Self-report	Children rate on a scale of 1–5 their level of fear of 15 dental-related situations. Ratings on the items are summed to yield a single fear score.	Good temporal stability over 7 days. Convergence with other subjective, motor, and physiological measures of dental anxiety; scores fluctuate in accord with treatment. Global nature of the rating scale makes interpretation problematic. Having a more descriptive scale may circumvent this problem.
	Dental Ratings of Anxiety and Cooperation Melamed, Hawes, et al. (1975); Melamed, Weinstein, et al. (1975); Melamed et al. (1978)	Motor	Observational	Dentist rates children on a 10-point scale for their level of anxiety and level of cooperation during dental procedures.	Excellent interrater reliability; acceptable temporal stability over 1 day. Convergence with other observational and self-report measures of dental anxiety. A global rating of unspecified content and dubious utility. Introduction of more response items of an explicit nature would rectify this.
	Fear thermometer Melamed, Hawes, et al. (1975); Melamed, Weinstein, et al. (1975); Melamed et al. (1978)	Subjective	Self-report	Children rate on a 5-point scale their current degree of fear.	Acceptable test–retest reliability. Correspondence with observational measures of dental anxiety and self-report of general anxiety. A single, global rating of undefined content and questionable utility. Addition of more response items of specified content would facilitate interpretation of scores.

Measure			Description	Comments
Heart rate Klingman et al. (1984); Melamed et al. (1978)	Physiological	Mechanical	Heart rate is monitored throughout and sampled at 10- to 30-second intervals. Baseline rate is subtracted from phase rates to yield response scores.	No estimates of reliability. Scores fluctuate in accord with treatment. Expensive recording equipment limits its use to research. May serve as a measure of treatment outcome.
Observer Ratings of Anxiety and Cooperation Melamed, Hawes, et al. (1975); Melamed, Weinstein, et al. (1975); Melamed et al. (1978)	Motor	Observational	Independent observer rates on a 10-point scale the child's level of anxiety and level of cooperation during a dental procedure.	Excellent interrater reliability; acceptable same-day temporal stability. Convergence with other observational and self-report measures of dental anxiety. Global nature of rating makes interpretation of scores problematic. More response items of known content needed to overcome limitations of single-item, global ratings.
Respiration Klingman et al. (1984)	Physiological	Mechanical	Respiration is monitored throughout. Baseline rate is subtracted from phase rates to yield response scores.	No evidence of reliability or validity; thus, no support for its employment. Different system of sampling and quantification may yield more encouraging statistics.
Hospital Fears Rating Scale Faust & Melamed (1984); Melamed & Siegel (1975); Peterson & Shigetomi (1981)	Subjective	Self-report	Children rate on a scale of 1–5 their level of anxiety regarding 16 hospital-related situations and 9 nonhospital-related situations. The ratings for the 16 hospital items are summed to form a single subjective score.	Good internal consistency. No evidence of validity. The measure is a composite of global ratings, and as such suffers from the limitations inherent to all global ratings (e.g., instability, obscure meaning). Adding greater specificity to the rating scale may yield stable and useful measures.
Observer Rating Scale of Anxiety Melamed & Siegel (1975)	Motor	Observational	Occurrence–nonoccurrence of 29 verbal and skeletal–motor behaviors (e.g., crying, trembling hands, stuttering) is recorded for a 3-minute interval. Recordings are summed across behaviors and intervals to form a single motor response score.	Excellent interrater reliability and immediate test–retest reliability. Scores fluctuate in accord with treatment. Large number of response categories and the need for trained observers limit it to research use, where it may serve as a measure of treatment outcome.

(continued)

TABLE 2. (continued)

Stimulus	Instrument/author(s)	Response system	Method of measurement	Description	Appraisal
	Palmar sweat index Faust & Melamed (1984); Gilbert et al. (1982); Melamed & Siegel (1975)	Physiological	Mechanical	A plastic impression on the child's index finger that registers active sweat glands, the number of which serves as the response score.	Excellent interrater reliability. Correspondence with other physiological and motor measures of anxiety; scores fluctuate in accordance with treatment. One of the more practical methods for measuring physiological responses; lends itself to use in both the laboratory and clinic.
	Child Behavior Checklist Peterson, Schultheis, Ridley-Johnson, Miller, & Tracy (1984); Peterson & Shigetomi (1981)	Motor	Observational	Occurrence–nonoccurrence, magnitude, and duration of 16 behaviors (e.g., crying, hair twisting) are recorded per phase of the medical procedure. Magnitude and duration are rated on a scale of 1–3, and behaviors are weighted for degree of disruption. Magnitude rating, duration rating, and weight are combined multiplicatively for each behavior, then summed across behaviors.	Good interrater reliability; poor internal consistency. Scores fluctuate in accord with treatment. Addition of a few more response items may increase internal consistency to acceptable level. Number of response categories and need for trained observers make the instrument practical only for research use as a measure of treatment outcome.
	Child Behavior Observational Rating Peterson et al. (1984); Peterson & Shigetomi (1981)	Motor	Observational	Children are rated on a 5-point scale for their level of anxiety, cooperation, and tolerance during the medical procedure.	Excellent interrater reliability; good internal consistency. Scores fluctuate in accord with treatment. Measure is a composite of three global ratings; therefore, is of indeterminate content and meaning. Increased detail in the three scales may circumvent these problems.
	Child Self-Report Peterson et al. (1984)	Subjective	Self-report	Children use a five-piece thermometer to rate the attractiveness of three hospital-related pictures (e.g., coming to the nurse's desk, getting a blood test) and	No evidence of reliability or validity. Having only three items per category may preclude obtainment of reliable measurement. Additional items may lead to improved reliability, which would allow for investigation of validity.

	Type	Method	Description	Comments
			three nonhospital-related pictures (e.g., playing with favorite toys). A score for each scene category is obtained by summing across the appropriate three pictures.	
Faces Affect Scale Venham, Bengston, & Cipes (1977)	Subjective	Self-report	Children select from eight pairs of calm–upset faces the one that best matches current mood state. A total upset scores is formed by summing across the eight pairs.	Acceptable internal consistency. Low to modest correlations with other subjective, motor, and physiological measures of anxiety. Molar nature of the response items may preclude scores from being sensitive indicators of treatment effects or correlating with other fear measures. Items of greater specificity may prove to be more useful.
Venham Anxiety-Rating Scale Venham, Gaulin-Kremer, Munster, Bengston-Audia, & Cohan (1980)	Motor	Observational	Child's level of anxiety is rated on a descriptive scale of 0 (e.g., relaxed, smiling) to 5 (e.g., loud crying, physical restraint required) for each of three periods. The ratings are averaged to yield a score for the entire procedure.	Excellent interrater reliability. Convergence with other motor, subjective, and physiological measures of anxiety. The multiple descriptive anchors pose interpretive problems. Rating the child on each one of the descriptors would avoid these problems.
Venham Behavior-Rating Scale Venham et al. (1980)	Motor	Observational	Child's disruptive behavior is rated on a descriptive scale of 0 (e.g., no crying or protest) to 5 (e.g., no compliance, physical restraint required) for each of three periods. The ratings are averaged to yield a score for the entire period.	Excellent interrater reliability. Convergence with other motor and subjective measures of anxiety. Multiple descriptive anchors create problems in interpretation of scores. It would be preferable to rate the child on each of these descriptors, thus avoiding confusion as to the scores' meaning.
Global Mood Scale Vernon, Foley, & Schulman (1967)	Motor	Observational	Child's overall mood is rated on a descriptive scale of 1 (e.g., attentive, contented) to 7 (e.g., intense crying,	Excellent interrater reliability. Convergence with motor and physiological measures of anxiety. Scale points have multiple, vague descriptive anchors, which make interpreta- (continued)

TABLE 2. (continued)

Stimulus	Instrument/author(s)	Response system	Method of measurement	Description	Appraisal
				loud screaming) for each of four periods. The ratings are averaged across the periods to yield a score for the entire procedure.	tion of scores problematic. Interpretive problems could be avoided by rating the child on each response descriptor.
	Hospital Scenes Dorkey & Amen (1947); Vernon (1973)	Subjective	Self-report	Child is presented with 14 hospital scenes in which the face of the central child figure is left blank, and is asked to select either a happy or a sad face for the scenes. Total number of sad faces selected serves as measure of subjective response.	Excellent internal consistency; poor test–retest reliability. Convergence with observational measures of anxiety. Global nature of the two scale points produces scores of ambiguous meaning.
	Posthospital Behavior Questionnaire Vernon (1973); Vernon, Schulman, & Foley (1966)	Motor	Observational	Mother rates on a scale of 1 ("much less than before") to 5 ("much more than before") the frequency of 27 child behaviors (e.g., fear of leaving the house, refusal to enter the dark, tailing parents). Ratings are summed across response items to yield a composite motor score.	Good test–retest reliability. Convergence with interview data from mothers. Large number of response categories and retrospective nature of ratings cast doubt on the utility of the instrument. May have some usefulness in the assessment of generalization or social validity.
Separation	Fear-related verbalizations Bornstein & Knapp (1981)	Subjective	Self-report	Parents record hourly the frequency of the child's fear-related verbal remarks.	Excellent interrater reliability; poor temporal stability across 19 days. Scores fluctuate in accord with treatment. Ease with which data are collected makes it attractive for both clinical and research use. Stability of scores may be increased through aggregation.
	Preschool Observational Scale of Anxiety Glennon & Weisz (1978)	Motor	Observational	Occurrence–nonoccurrence of 30 behavioral categories (e.g., trembling voice, lip licking, trunk contortions,	Good interrater reliability; acceptable internal consistency. Convergence with other motor measures of anxiety; scores fluctuate with stimuli differing in threat. The large

Measure	Response class	Description	Comments
		avoidance of eye contact) is recorded for 30-second intervals. Scores are summed across categories and 20 intervals to give a single anxiety score.	number of response categories and need for trained observers may restrict the system's use to research.
Parent Anxiety Rating Scale—Separation Doris, McIntyre, Kelsey, & Lehman (1971); Glennon & Weisz (1978)	Motor / Observational	Parents rate the child on 6 items dealing with separation anxiety and 19 items dealing with general anxiety. Ratings are summed across respective items to form total separation anxiety and general anxiety scores.	No estimates of reliability. Convergence with other observational measures of separation anxiety. May not have sufficient number of items for reliable measurement; reliability could be improved by adding several more items to the scale.
Teachers' Separation Anxiety Scale Doris et al. (1971); Glennon & Weisz (1978)	Motor / Observational	Teacher rates the child at the end of the school day on 11 items related to separation anxiety.	No estimates of reliability. Convergence with other observational measures of separation anxiety. Retrospective nature of the ratings casts doubt on their accuracy and usefulness. May be of some use as a social validation measure.
Global Anxiety Rating Glennon & Weisz (1978)	Motor / Observational	Child is rated on a scale of 1–6 for level of anxiety during testing session.	No evidence of reliability or validity. Suffers from the same limitations of all global, single-item measures (e.g., instability, ambiguous meaning). Additional items of distinct content may improve its worth.
Global Self-Rating Glennon & Weisz (1978)	Subjective / Self-report	Child rates level of anxiety experienced during session by selecting one face from among six faces depicting progressive levels of anxiety.	No evidence of reliability or validity. A single, overall self-rating of ambiguous meaning and worth. Addition of detailed response items may render it useful.
Teacher Rating of Separation Anxiety Hall (1967); Milos & Reiss (1982)	Motor / Observational	Teacher rates on a descriptive scale of 1–5 the child's level of separation anxiety at the onset of the school year, level of separation anxiety for the past 2 weeks, and overall level of separation anxiety. An average of the three ratings is computed.	Acceptable interrater reliability. No evidence of validity. Small number of items spanning different time periods may preclude the measure from being stable and useful.

(continued)

TABLE 2. (continued)

Stimulus	Instrument/author(s)	Response system	Method of measurement	Description	Appraisal
	Observation of Separation-Relevant Play Milos & Reiss (1982)	Motor	Observational	Frequency of anxiety-relevant play (e.g., desire to be with mother, ambivalence in the use of the mother doll) is recorded for 30-second intervals. Frequencies are summed across intervals to produce a total anxiety play score.	Excellent interrater reliability. Scores fluctuate with treatment. Small number of response categories makes it amenable for use by both researchers and clinicians. Limited validity data suggests that its use be confined to treatment evaluation.
	Quality of Play Rating Milos & Reiss (1982)	Motor	Observational	Child's play is rated for degree of expression of separation themes and willingness to master anxiety. A descriptive scale of 1 (e.g., avoidance of separation themes) to 5 (e.g., child doll plays with peers after mother doll leaves) is used.	Acceptable interrater reliability. Correspondence with other observational measure of separation anxiety. Highly global in nature, the rating is of ambiguous meaning, suspect soundness, and suspect worth. The addition of more well-defined response items may increase the utility of the measure.
	Separation Anxiety Neisworth, Madle, & Goeke (1975)	Motor	Observational	Duration of child's crying, screaming, and sobbing for a 3-hour period is recorded.	Excellent interscorer reliability. Congruence with mothers' reports of child behavior; generality across relevant settings. Length of observation period and need for raters may restrict its use to research.
	Speech Disturbance Milos & Reiss (1982)	Motor	Observational	Child responds to six separation-relevant questions (e.g., "What happens when Mommy and/or Daddy leaves?") and four separation-irrelevant questions (e.g., "What do you do on your birthday?"). The number of seven types of speech disturbances (e.g., sentence corrections, word repetitions, sentence incomple-	Acceptable interscorer reliability. Corresponds with other motor measure of separation anxiety; responsive to treatment; discriminates between groups known to differ in their fearfulness toward separation. Tedious and time-consuming nature of the ratings may restrict the instrument's use to research.

220

tions) is recorded. For each category of questions, the total number of speech disturbances is divided by the total number of words spoken. The ratio for the separation-irrelevant questions is subtracted from the separation-relevant questions to yield a single response score.

Category	Type	Instrument	Description	Reliability / Comments
Small animals	Motor	Behavioral avoidance test Bandura, Grusec, & Menlove (1967)	Approach to a live dog is performed in 17 steps. Number of steps performed and degree of fearfulness, vacillation, and reluctance preceding and accompanying each approach response are recorded. The recordings are summed to form a single fear score.	Excellent interrater reliability; acceptable temporal stability over 5 days. Scores fluctuate in accord with treatment and generalize to other relevant settings. Appropriate for use in both the laboratory and clinic for the purposes of problem identification and treatment evaluation.
	Motor	Behavioral avoidance test Davis, Rosenthal, & Kelly (1981)	Approach to a live spider is performed in 27 steps. Number of steps performed and duration of performance are recorded.	Excellent temporal stability over 3 weeks. Measures of approach correlate with self-reports of fear, and fluctuate as a function of treatment. Suitable for use in both the laboratory and clinic for purposes of problem identification and treatment outcome.
	Motor	Behavioral avoidance test P. D. Evans & Harmon (1981)	Latency to approach, number of contacts, and cumulative time of contacts with a live spider are recorded.	Good temporal stability over an unspecified time period. Scores correspond to self-reports of fear and discriminate groups known to differ in their fearfulness toward spiders. Practical for use by both researchers and clinicians for the purpose of problem identification.
	Motor	Behavioral avoidance test Hill, Liebert, & Mott (1968)	Approach to a live dog is performed in three steps.	No estimates of reliability. Scores fluctuate in accord with treatment. Small number of steps allows for only gross discriminations in fear level.

(continued)

TABLE 2. (continued)

Stimulus	Instrument/author(s)	Response system	Method of measurement	Description	Appraisal
	Behavioral avoidance test Kornhaber & Schroeder (1975)	Motor	Observational	Approach to a live snake is performed in 14 steps.	Acceptable temporal stability over 30 minutes. Convergence with subjective measure of snake fear; fluctuations in concert with treatment. Appropriate for use in the laboratory and the clinic for the purposes of problem identification and treatment evaluation.
	Snake Attitude Measure Kornhaber & Schroeder (1975)	Subjective	Self-report	Children select from 10 sets of three animal pictures which one they like and which one they don't like. Nine of the sets contain one picture of a snake; one set contains two pictures of snakes. A response score is computed by subtracting the number of snake pictures disliked from the number of snake pictures liked.	Acceptable temporal stability over 30 minutes. Convergence with motor measure of snake fear and fluctuations in accord with treatment. Administration and scoring of responses relatively simple. Scores, however, yield little information in regard to the subjective component. The addition of more specific rating scales may enhance the usefulness of the instrument.
	Behavioral avoidance test Kuroda (1969)	Motor	Observational	Approach to live frogs, earthworms, and cats performed in three steps.	No estimates of reliability. Scores fluctuate in accordance with treatment. Having only three graduations, it is capable of making only gross discriminations in fear level.
	Active behavioral avoidance test Murphy & Bootzin (1973)	Motor	Observational	Approach to a live snake is performed in 8–18 steps.	Poor temporal stability over 10 days. Correspondence with passive variant of test; fluctuations in accord with treatment. Instability of scores argues against its use.
	Passive behavioral avoidance test Murphy & Bootzin (1973)	Motor	Observational	A live snake is brought progressively closer to the child in 8–18 steps.	Poor temporal stability over 10 days. Correspondence with active variant of test, fluctuations in accord with treatment. Instability of scores argues against its employment.
	Behavioral avoidance test Ritter (1968)	Motor	Observational	Approach to a live dog is performed in 29 steps.	Good temporal stability over 1 week. Scores converge with self-reports of fear

and vary with exposure to treatment. Appropriate for use in both the laboratory and clinic for purposes of problem identification and treatment evaluation.

Social and stranger interaction	Fear and Avoidance Hierarchy Ratings Barlow & Seidner (1983)	Subjective, motor	Self-report	Child rates on a scale of 0–8 the degree of anxiety and avoidance to a 10-item individualized hierarchy of social situations. Ratings are summed across anxiety and avoidance and across items to yield a single fear score.	No estimates of reliability. Converges with mothers' reports of behavior; changes as a function of exposure to treatment. Multidimensional nature of response score makes interpretation problematic. Such difficulties could be circumvented by computing separate subjective and motor response scores.
	Role-Play Test Esveldt-Dawson, Wisner, Unis, Matson, & Kazdin (1982)	Motor	Observational	Child role-plays five situations involving an unfamiliar male (e.g., "asking a man for a donation to a children's hospital"). For each role play, ratings are made of six behaviors (e.g., stiffness, nervous mannerisms) on a scale of either 1–3 or 1–5. Ratings are summed across role plays.	Excellent interrater reliability and temporal stability over 14 days. Some correspondence among the six response measures; scores fluctuate in accord with treatment. Ease with which the role plays can be administered and the performance can be scored makes it suitable for both the laboratory and the clinic. Best used for the evaluation of treatment.
	Behavioral approach test Matson (1981)	Motor	Observational	Approach (in feet) and number of words spoken to a stranger are recorded.	Acceptable interrater reliability; excellent temporal stability over 9 days. Concordance between the two measures and with a self-rating of fear. Changes in scores as a function of treatment. Lends itself to use in both the laboratory and clinic for the purposes of problem identification and treatment evaluation.
	Social Interaction Scale O'Connor (1969)	Motor	Observational	Occurrence–nonoccurrence of five response categories (e.g., physical proximity, verbal interaction with other) is recorded for 15-second intervals. Response occurrences are summed across intervals.	Excellent interrater reliability. Scores fluctuate with exposure to treatment. Schedule of observations may be too demanding for clinical use. Information is needed on how well the individual response categories correlate with one another, and thus can be interpreted as a collective measure. May be best used by researchers as a measure of treatment outcome. *(continued)*

TABLE 2. (*continued*)

Stimulus	Instrument/author(s)	Response system	Method of measurement	Description	Appraisal
	Peer Interaction and Avoidance Ross, Ross, & Evans (1971)	Motor	Observational	Occurrence–nonoccurrence of five social interaction behaviors (e.g., physical proximity, physical contact) is recorded for 15-second intervals. An interval receives a score of 1 if any of the five behaviors occurs. Frequencies of eight avoidance behaviors (e.g., lowering of eyes to avoid visual contact, turning away when a peer initiates contact) during 15-minute periods are recorded and combined.	Excellent interrater reliability. Scores fluctuate in accordance with treatment. Schedule of data collection may be too strenuous for clinical use. Information is needed on the interrelationships among and between the individual behaviors of the two response composites. Scores appear best suited as measures of treatment outcome.
Travel	Fear-related verbalizations Bornstein & Knapp (1981)	Subjective	Self-report	Parents record hourly the frequency of fear-related verbal remarks.	Excellent interrater reliability; poor temporal stability over 29 days. Scores fluctuate with exposure to treatment. Ease with which data can be collected and scored make it appropriate for both research and clinical use. Stability of scores may be improved through aggregation.
Water	Behavior Rating Scale S. Lewis (1974)	Motor	Observational	Child's performance of 16 swimming-related behaviors rated on a scale of 1 (did not try behavior) to 4 (completed behavior quickly and spontaneously). Ratings are summed across behaviors to yield a single approach score.	Excellent interrater reliability and temporal stability over 5 days. Scores correlate significantly with observer ratings of skill, fear, and avoidance, and fluctuate in accordance with treatment. Administered under naturalistic conditions; therefore, probably best suited for research purposes.
School-related events	Revised Timed Behavior Checklist Fox & Houston (1981)	Motor	Observational	Occurrence–nonoccurrence of 12 behavioral signs of public-speaking anxiety (e.g., sways, foot move-	Excellent interrater reliability. Scores correlate with other motor and subjective (State scale of the State–Trait Anxiety Inventory for Children) measures of perfor-

224

Instrument	Response system	Method	Description	Evaluation
			ments, face muscles tense) is recorded. The recordings are summed across behaviors and intervals to yield a composite score.	mance anxiety. Scores do not vary as a function of treatment. Need for trained raters restricts its use to research; insensitivity to presumably active treatments restricts its use to the task of problem identification.
Cognitive Behavior Questionnaire Houston, Fox, & Forbes (1984)	Subjective	Self-report	Children rate on a 5-point scale the frequencies of seven types of thoughts (e.g., "Were you thinking that this is kind of an interesting situation?" "Were you thinking that you have a reason not to worry about the game/test?") for a given time period.	No estimates of reliability. Convergence with the other subjective measure (Think Aloud) of test anxiety; scores vary as a function of stimuli differing in threat. Ease with which it can be administered and scored makes it practical for both research and clinical use. More data are needed on the measure's motor and physiological correlates and on its sensitivity as an index of treatment outcome.
Think Aloud Houston et al. (1984)	Subjective	Self-report	Transcripts of child "thinking aloud" are rated on a 5-point scale for the prominence of seven categories of thoughts (e.g., analytic attitude, performance denigration, preoccupation).	Excellent interrater reliability. Correlates with the other subjective measure (Cognitive Behavior Questionnaire) of test anxiety; scores vary with stimulus conditions differing in threat. Tedious, time-consuming nature of the ratings probably precludes its clinical use. More information is needed on the scores' motor and physiological correlates and responsiveness to treatment.
Teacher Rating Scale Sarason, Davidson, Lighthall, Waite, & Ruebush (1960)	Motor	Observational	Teacher rates on a 5-point scale the level of 17 child behaviors (e.g., voice trembles when asked to speak); the ratings are summed across behaviors.	No evidence of reliability. Scores correlate with the other subjective measure (Test Anxiety Scale for Children) of test anxiety and with measures of academic performance and intelligence. Though practical for both clinical and research use, lack of reliability data calls for caution in its employment.
Test Anxiety Scale for Children Sarason et al. (1960)	Subjective, physiological	Self-report	Children rate on a scale of 0–1 their anxiety to 30 test-related situations. Ratings are summed across items.	Good internal consistency and temporal stability over 4 weeks. Correspondence with observational measures of test anxiety (Teacher Rating Scale, Observation of Classroom Behavior) and with self-report measure of general anxiety (General Anxi-

(continued)

225

TABLE 2. (continued)

Stimulus	Instrument/author(s)	Response system	Method of measurement	Description	Appraisal
					ety Scale for Children). Interpretation is problematic because items addressing subjective responses are combined with those addressing physiological ones. This difficulty could be avoided by having separate subjective and physiological subscales.
	Analogue Test Taking Van Hasselt et al. (1979)	Motor	Observational	Seven letters are presented sequentially on a memory drum. After inital presentation, child is asked to anticipate each letter in the series. The number of trials required for errorless anticipation of the letters is recorded.	Good temporal stability over 1 week. Scores fluctuate in accord with treatment. Practical for both research and clinical use for the purposes of treatment evaluation.
	Finger pulse volume Van Hasselt et al. (1979)	Physiological	Mechanical	Monitored throughout the Analogue Test Taking. Volume for last 15 seconds of baseline is subtracted from volume for 15-second sample of each trial, then summed across trials for sessions.	Good temporal stability over 1 week. No evidence of validity (e.g., convergence with other fear measures, sensitivity to treatments); thus, no support for this method of monitoring and quantifying cardiovascular reactivity.
	Heart rate Van Hasselt et al. (1979)	Physiological	Mechanical	Monitored throughout the Analogue Test Taking. Average baseline heart rate is subtracted from heart rate for last 15 seconds of each trial, then summed across trials.	Good temporal stability over 1 week. No evidence of validity; thus, no support for this specific method of sampling and quantifying heart rate responses to test taking.
	Target Complaint Scale Van Hasselt et al. (1979)	Subjective	Self-report	Child rates level of fear for each session by means of a 12-point scale with descriptive anchors at every third point (e.g., "none," "pretty much," "couldn't be worse").	Excellent temporal stability over 3 weeks. Scores fluctuate in accord with treatment. A global rating of ambiguous meaning and questionable utility. Addition of response items of definite content may enhance the scale's worth.

Observation of Classroom Behavior Wine (1979)	Motor	Observational	Occurrence–nonoccurrence of 22 behaviors (e.g., works quietly, stands, initiates communication with teacher) is recorded in 30-second intervals. The behaviors are grouped into five categories (i.e., attending behaviors, task-related behaviors, activity, communication, and interactional behaviors). Occurrences for each behavior are summed across intervals.	Excellent interrater reliability. Scores correlate with subjective measure of test anxiety (Test Anxiety Scale for Children), discriminate groups known to differ in their anxiety toward test taking, and vary as a function of stimulus conditions varying in threat. Large number of behaviors observed and need for trained observers probably limit the instrument to research use.
Children's Cognitive Assessment Questionnaire Zatz & Chassin (1983, 1985)	Subjective	Self-report	Children rate on a 4-point scale (i.e., "never" to "all the time") the frequency with which they experienced 50 different thoughts during an exam. The thoughts are grouped into five categories: On-Task Thoughts (e.g., "Read each question carefully"), Off-Task Thoughts (e.g., "I wish this were over"), Positive Self-Statements (e.g., "I do well on tests like this"), Negative Self-Statements (e.g., "I am doing poorly"), and Coping Self-Statements (e.g., "Try to calm down"). Ratings are summed across each category's respective items.	Good internal consistency and temporal stability over 6 weeks. Correspondence with motor, subjective, and physiological measures of test anxiety (anagrams, Test Anxiety Scale for Children); discrimination of groups known to differ in their anxiety toward test taking. Easy to administer and score; appropriate for both research and clinical use. At present, best used for the purposes of problem identification.
Personal Report of Confidence as a Speaker Cradock, Cotler, & Jason (1978); T. Johnson, Tyler, Thompson, & Jones (1971); Paul (1966)	Subjective, motor, physiological	Self-report	Child rates "true" or "false" 30 statements describing his or her reactions to speaking before a group (e.g., "My hands tremble when I try to handle objects on the platform"; "I am terrified at the thought of speaking before a	Excellent internal consistency and temporal stability over 6 weeks. Scores converge with motor measure of public-speaking anxiety (i.e., Timed Behavior Checklist) and fluctuate in accord with treatment. Multidimensional nature of the test score makes interpretation problematic. This could be rectified by developing three

(continued)

TABLE 2. (*continued*)

Stimulus	Instrument/author(s)	Response system	Method of measurement	Description	Appraisal
				group of people''; ''I perspire and tremble just before getting up to speak''). Responses are summed across items to produce a single self-report measure of anxiety.	subscales (one for each response component); additional items may, however, be needed in order for subscale scores to be sufficiently reliable. The instrument's sophisticated wording restricts its use to teenagers.
	Role-Play Assessment Esveldt-Dawson *et al.* (1982)	Motor	Observational	Child role-plays five school-related situations (e.g., speaking in front of a class, being accused of cheating by the teacher) and is rated on a 3- or 5-point scale for level of six behaviors (e.g., stiffness, eye contact, nervous mannerisms). Ratings for each behavior are summed across scenes.	Excellent interrater reliability and temporal stability over 15 days. Good correspondence among the behaviors and with a self-rating of fear; scores fluctuate as a function of exposure to treatment. Ease of administration and small number of behaviors to observe make it practical for both clinical and research use.
	Timed Behavior Checklist Cradock *et al.* (1978); Paul (1966)	Motor	Observational	Child is observed every 30 seconds for the occurrence–nonoccurrence of 20 response categories (e.g., pacing, swaying, hand tremors, quivering voice, speech blocking). Occurrences are summed across categories and intervals to produce a composite motor response score.	Excellent interrater reliability. Scores correlate with subjective (Personal Report of Confidence as a Speaker) and physiological measures of public speaking anxiety, and fluctuate in accord with treatment. Schedule of observations and number of behaviors observed appear too demanding for routine clinical use.
General	Children's Fear Survey Schedule—Revised Barrios, Replogle, & Anderson-Tisdelle, (1983)	Subjective, motor, physiological	Self-report	Children rate on a 3-point scale 50 situations for level of subjective, motor, and physiological responses. Ratings are summed across	Good temporal stability over 1 month. Good convergence among the instrument's three scales; moderate correspondence with parental ratings. Ease of administration and scoring makes it practical for both clinical

Instrument	Components	Format	Description	Comments
Children's Manifest Anxiety Scale Castaneda, McCandless, & Palermo (1956)	Subjective, physiological, motor	Self-report	Children indicate which of 53 statements (e.g., "I worry most of the time"; "Often I feel sick to my stomach") apply to them. Those endorsed are summed.	and research use. Aside from the assessment of generalized anxiety, the instrument may serve as a screening device or a measure of treatment generalization effects. Good test-retest reliability and internal consistency. Over 100 pieces of research attesting to its validity. Significant relationships with other subjective (e.g., State–Trait Anxiety Inventory for Children, global self-ratings) and motor measures (e.g., errors on learning tasks) of anxiety, and with behavioral problems. Normative estimates available for a variety of child groups. Interpretation, though, is problematic because of the multidimensional nature of the score. This could be rectified by creating three subscales: one for each of anxiety's three response components.
Cognitive and Somatic Trait Anxiety Inventory Fox & Houston (1983)	Subjective, physiological	Self-report	Children respond to 24 items, 15 of which pertain to Cognitive Trait Anxiety and 9 of which pertain to Somatic trait anxiety. Total scores for the two types of trait anxiety are obtained by summing across their respective items.	Acceptable internal consistency. The two scales correlate highly with one another. Scores on the Cognitive scale are related to scores on subjective (i.e., the Cognitive scale of the Cognitive and Somatic State Anxiety Inventory, the Think Aloud, the Cognitive Behavior Questionnaire), motor (i.g., performance errors), and physiological (i.e., the Somatic scale of the Cognitive and Somatic State Anxiety Inventory) measures of situational anxiety (i.e., test taking). Appropriate for both research and clinical use. May be helpful in problem identification and treatment planning for generalized anxiety and in evaluation of treatments' generalized effects. Information needed on scores' temporal stability.

(continued)

TABLE 2. (continued)

Stimulus	Instrument/author(s)	Response system	Method of measurement	Description	Appraisal
	Cognitive and Somatic State Anxiety Inventory Fox & Houston (1983)	Subjective, physiological	Self-report	Children respond to 27 items, 18 of which pertain to Cognitive state anxiety and 9 of which pertain to Somatic state anxiety. Total scores for both are obtained by summing across their respective items.	Good internal consistency. The two scales correlate well with each other and with subjective measures of test anxiety (i.e., Think Aloud, Cognitive Behavior Questionnaire); the Cognitive subscale also correlates with the Cognitive subscale of the Cognitive and Somatic Trait Anxiety Inventory, and the Somatic subscale with the Somatic subscale of the Trait Inventory. Appropriate for both the clinical and research assessment of any situation-specific fear or anxiety. May be most helpful in treatment planning and selection.
	Parent Anxiety Rating Scale—General Doris et al. (1971); Glennon & Weisz (1978)	Motor	Observational	Parents answer 19 items pertaining to the child's general anxiety; responses are summed across items.	No estimates of reliability. Scores vary in accord with stimulus conditions purported to differ in anxiety-eliciting properties. Lack of reliability and validity data suggests that the instrument be used cautiously.
	Louisville Fear Survey Schedule L. C. Miller, Barrett, Hampe, & Noble (1972)	Subjective, motor	Self-report, observational	Children rate on a 5-point scale their level of fear in 104 situations, or parents rate their children's level of fear in the situations using the same scale. Ratings are summed across items.	Excellent internal consistency. Moderate correspondence with parental ratings. Scores are of ambiguous meaning because of the global nature of the rating scale. Addition of scales of explicit content may improve interpretation and utility. In its current form, the instrument may be of some use as a quick screening device or measure of treatment generalization effects.
	Fear Survey Schedule for Children—Revised Ollendick (1978, 1983)	Subjective	Self-report	Children rate on a 3-point scale their level of fear in 80 situations. Ratings are summed across items to give a general anxiety score.	Excellent internal consistency; good temporal stability over 7 days; acceptable temporal stability over 3 months. Scores converge with other self-report measure of generalized anxiety (i.e., State–Trait Anxiety Inventory for Children) and discriminate anxiety groups known to differ in anxiety.

Instrument	Components	Format	Description	Comments
				Global nature of the rating scale makes interpretation problematic. Addition of scales of specific content may enhance its utility. As is, the instrument may be of use as a screening device or measure of treatment generalization effects.
Children's Manifest Anxiety Scale—Revised Reynolds & Richmond (1978)	Subjective, physiological, motor	Self-report	Children respond to 37 items, 28 of which pertain to anxiety. The responses to these 28 items are summed to form a general anxiety score.	Good internal consistency. Correlations with other subjective and physiological measures of generalized anxiety (i.e., State–Trait Anxiety Inventory for Children). Norms available for preschoolers. Interpretation of scores is problematic because of their multidimensional nature. Establishment of subscales, one for each of anxiety's three components, would facilitate interpretation and use as a measure of generalized anxiety or treatment generalization effects.
Children's Fear Survey Schedule Ryall & Dietiker (1979)	Subjective	Self-report	Children rate on a 3-point scale their level of anxiety in 48 situations. Ratings are summed to form a general anxiety score.	Good test–retest reliability. Scores discriminate groups known to differ in anxiety. Global nature of the rating scale makes interpretation of scores problematic. Introduction of rating scales of specific content would allow for more ready interpretation and use as a measure of generalized anxiety. As is, may be helpful in screening or assessing treatment generalization.
General Anxiety Scale Sarason et al. (1960)	Subjective, physiological	Self-report	Children indicate which of 45 statements (34 pertaining to anxiety) are typical of them. Number of the 34 anxiety-related items endorsed serves as general anxiety score.	No estimates of reliability. Scores correlate with self-report of test anxiety (i.e., Test Anxiety Scale for Children), intelligence, and school achievement. Interpretation of scores is problematic because items addressing the subjective component of anxiety are combined with those addressing the physiological component. Construction of subscales would rectify this problem and enhance the potential usefulness of the instrument. As is, may be helpful in assessing treatment generalization effects. Lack of reliability data calls for cautious use.

(continued)

TABLE 2. (continued)

Stimulus	Instrument/author(s)	Response system	Method of measurement	Description	Appraisal
	Fear Survey Schedule for Children Scherer & Nakamura (1968)	Subjective	Self-report	Children rate on a 5-point scale their level of fear in 80 situations. The ratings are summed across items to form a general anxiety score.	Excellent internal consistency. Scores correlate with other subjective and physiological measures of generalized anxiety (i.e., Children's Manifest Anxiety Scale) and with measures of dental anxiety (i.e., Behavior Profile Rating Scale, Dental and Observer Ratings of Anxiety and Cooperation, fear thermometer, palmar sweat index). Scores are of ambiguous meaning because of the global nature of the rating scale. Addition of rating scales of specific content would allow for more straightforward interpretation. As is, the instrument may be helpful in screening or assessing treatment generalization.
	State–Trait Anxiety Inventory for Children Spielberger (1973)	Subjective, physiological	Self-report	Children respond to two 20-item inventories, one pertaining to situationally linked anxiety and the other pertaining to cross-situational anxiety. Responses are summed across the appropriate items to yield a State anxiety score and a Trait anxiety score.	Good internal consistency; acceptable temporal stability over same day and 3 months. Scores correlate with other subjective and physiological measures of generalized anxiety (i.e., Children's Manifest Anxiety Scale) and with measure of intelligence and school performance. Scores vary with exposure to stimuli varying in threat. Norms are available for different child groups. Interpretation of scores is problematic because subjective component items are combined with physiological component items. Items could be segregated as in the Cognitive and Somatic State and Trait Anxiety Inventories. In its current form, it may be useful as a screening device or measure of treatment generalization effects.

Note. Portions of this table have appeared in "Assessment of Children's Fears: A Critical Review" by B. A. Barrios and C. C. Shigetomi in *Advances in School Psychology* (Vol. 4) edited by T. R. Kratochwill, 1985, Hillside, NJ: Erlbaum. Copyright 1985 by Lawrence Erlbaum Associates. Adapted by permission.

systems involved in fear and anxiety reactions. This emphasis on motor responses is consistent with behavior therapy's theoretical and methodological foundations (cf. Rimm & Masters, 1979) and with the common immediate need to reduce the child's escape or avoidance behavior (Morris & Kratochwill, 1983b). Although the ultimate clinical goal is to modify maladaptive activity from all relevant response systems, behavior therapists have tended to focus initially on the modification of maladaptive motor responses (e.g., escape, avoidance, and disruptive behavior). In part, this is due to the general theoretical agreement that maladaptive motor activity serves to maintain subjective distress and physiological upset (e.g., Bandura, 1978; Foa & Kozak, 1986).

Virtually all of the instruments for assessing the motor aspects of children's fears and anxieties are observational; those for assessing the subjective aspects are self-report; and those for assessing the physiological aspects are mechanical. Though activity from a response system is assessed primarily through one method of measurement, the exact form that this method of measurement takes does vary from instrument to instrument. In what follows, we review the major forms of each of the three methods for measuring children's fears and anxieties: observational, self-report, and mechanical.

Observational Methods

As stated above, nearly all of the instruments for assessing the motor aspects of children's fears and anxieties use direct observations as their method of measurement. That is, they employ an independent person or persons who observe and report on the children's display of certain motor behaviors. The three instruments that assess motor responses through other means—the Children's Fear Survey Schedule—Revised (Barrios *et al.*, 1983), the Fear and Avoidance Hierarchy Ratings (Barlow & Seidner, 1983), and the Nighttime Coping Response Inventory (Mooney, 1985)—have the children themselves observe and report on their motor behavior. As the method of measurement for 58 of the instruments, direct observations take one of four general forms: behavioral avoidance tests, observational rating systems, checklists, or global ratings.

Behavioral Avoidance Tests

Behavioral avoidance tests (BATs) have been used to assess children's motor reactions to blood, darkness, heights, medical procedures, school events, strangers, and water. Although BATs have been in use since the early 1900s (Jersild & Holmes, 1935; M. C. Jones, 1924), those developed in the last 20 years have been patterned after the procedure described by Lang and Lazovik (1963). Generally, this entails placing the child in a setting that contains the feared stimulus, then having the child perform a series of graduated tasks that call for approach to an interaction with the feared stimulus. Some passive variants of the procedure have the child remain stationary and bring the feared stimulus in a graduated fashion closer to the child (e.g., Giebenhain, 1985; Kelley, 1976; Murphy & Bootzin, 1973; Van Hasselt, Hersen, Bellack, Rosenblum, & Lamparski, 1979). Whatever the variant, BATs have as their hallmark tight control over stimulus conditions.

At present, BATs have a number of characteristics that argue for and other characteristics that argue against their utilization. On the negative side is the absence of a standardized BAT, both within and across stimulus categories. Behavioral assessors are inclined to design their own version of the BAT, with its unique set of steps and instructions, rather than to employ an existing BAT. This practice may be consistent with an idiographic bent toward assessment (e.g., Cone, 1981; Nelson & Hayes, 1979, 1981), but it makes comparisons across studies highly problematic. For example, the number of steps in BATs for small animals ranges from 1 (P. D. Evans & Harmon, 1981) to 29 (Ritter, 1968), for darkness from 1 (e.g., Leitenberg & Callahan, 1973; Sheslow, Bondy, & Nelson, 1982) to 10 (Giebenhain, 1985), and for the stimulus categories as a whole from 1 to 85 (Ultee, Griffioen, & Schellekens, 1982). If there is any generality to the adult finding of greater approach with BATs including more gradations (Nawas, 1971), then comparing performances on BATs that differ in number of steps may be very risky.

The BATs also vary widely in the instructions they give to the child—a variability that handicaps attempts to integrate findings from different studies. Some BATs provide factual information about the feared stimulus (e.g., Bandura, Grusec, & Menlove, 1967; Murphy & Bootzin, 1973), while others do not (e.g., Davis, Rosenthal, & Kelley, 1981; P. D. Evans & Harmon, 1981). Having factual information may reduce ignorance of the feared stimulus, which in turn may lead to greater approach (Bernstein & Paul, 1971). The instructions for some BATs try to allay apprehension over possible danger and harm (e.g., Kornhaber & Schroeder, 1975); the instructions for others make no attempt to do so (e.g., Giebenhain, 1985). With adults, reducing uncertainty about threat leads to greater approach and less physiological upset (Lick, Unger, & Condiotte, 1978). It seems safe to speculate that similar reductions in children's uncertainty may also lead to less fearful responding.

Aside from information on the attributes of the feared stimulus, the BATs differ in their instructions for task performance. Some BATs describe all of the steps only at the outset of testing (e.g., Giebenhain, 1985), while others stagger their description of the steps throughout the course of testing (e.g., Kornhaber & Schroeder, 1975). The descriptions of the tasks may be delivered live (e.g., Murphy & Bootzin, 1973; Van Hasselt et al., 1979) or through recordings (e.g., Kornhaber & Schroeder, 1975). And they may ask the child "to perform as many of the steps as you can," "to perform as many of the steps as you can without feeling scared," or "to try as hard as you can to perform all of the steps." With adults, all of these variations have been found to influence BAT performance (cf. Bernstein & Nietzel, 1974). For example, there is greater approach when the instructions for each step are presented live and upon execution of the preceding step than when the instructions for all steps are recorded and presented at the onset of testing (Bernstein & Nietzel, 1973). With children, only the influence of instructional "demand" on BAT performance has been investigated. What this influence is has yet to be determined, for the findings to date have been mixed (Kelley, 1976; Sheslow et al., 1982).

The tight control that is a hallmark of the BATs may also be one of their most serious drawbacks: Performance in the laboratory may not generalize to the naturalistic setting. BATs expose children to a safe form of the feared stimulus in a safe environment. With adults, the approach exhibited within the safety of the laboratory has not always transferred to the possible more dangerous confines of the naturalistic setting (Lick & Unger, 1975, 1977). It is fair to speculate, then, that the BAT performance of children also may not generalize beyond the laboratory.

Despite these shortcomings, the BATs have a number of points that speak in their favor.

First, the BATs are very straightforward procedures; they lend themselves well to reliable administration, and thus to standardization. Second, the BATs allow for the assessment of multiple motor responses. Some of the motor responses that have been measured in conjunction with approach are grimacing, stiffness, eye contact, nervous giggling, hesitation, crying, scanning, and nail biting (Esveldt-Dawson, Wisner, Unis, Matson, & Kazdin, 1982; P. D. Evans & Harmon, 1981; Giebenhain, 1985). And third, the BATs allow for the concurrent monitoring of activity from the subjective and physiological response systems. Thus, they are suitable vehicles for carrying out triple-response-system assessments of children's fears and anxieties (Barrios & Shigetomi, 1985). With their BATs for blood and heights, Van Hasselt et al. (1979) collected measures not only of approach, but also of heart rate, finger pulse volume, and subjective distress. With her BAT for darkness, Giebenhain (1985) collected measures of approach as well as of heart rate, articulated thoughts, subjective distress, and self-statements. The two studies are good examples of the potential of BATs.

Observational Rating Systems

Whereas the BATs have as their hallmark the strict control of stimulus conditions, the observational rating systems have as their hallmark the lack of such control. The rating systems are used to assess children's motor reactions to events in the natural environment—events over which the behavioral assessor typically has little or no control. Children's reactions are observed directly, and the observations are recorded with some immediacy.

Observational rating systems have been developed for the assessment of children's motor reactions to darkness, medical procedures, public speaking, separation, social contact, and test taking. The rating systems vary in the number and type of motor responses they monitor. For example, Milos and Reiss's (1982) Observation of Separation-Relevant Play monitors the frequency of the single molar behavior of anxiety-relevant play, whereas Glennon and Weisz's (1978) Preschool Observational Scale of Anxiety monitors the frequency of 30 molecular behaviors.

Several of the rating systems used to monitor fear and anxiety reactions to medical procedures are sophisticated in their development, design, and scoring. The oldest of these is Melamed and Siegel's (1975) Observer Rating Scale of Anxiety. Developed for use with children undergoing surgery, the Observer Rating Scale of Anxiety consists of 28 response categories such as "crying," "stutters," and "trembling hands," which are monitored for their frequency. The frequencies for all of the categories are combined to form a single (motor response) anxiety score for the entire observation period.

Melamed and her colleagues (Melamed, Hawes, Heiby, & Glick, 1975; Melamed, Weinstein, Hawes, & Katin-Borland, 1975; Melamed, Yurcheson, Fleece, Hutcherson, & Hawes, 1978) have developed a similar instrument for assessing the motor responses of children to dental treatment, the Behavior Profile Rating Scale. The instrument has 27 response categories (e.g., "crying," "kicking," "refusal to open mouth," "rigid posture," "verbal complaints," and "white knuckles"), which are recorded for their frequency of occurrence throughout the observation period, usually a dental session. The frequency score of each category is combined to form a single, weighted composite score for the session; the weights are determined by how disruptive the behavior is to the efficient treatment of the child as determined by the dentist.

Three other impressive observational rating systems for use in medical settings are the Procedure Behavioral Rating Scale (Katz, Kellerman, & Siegel, 1980), the Procedure Behavior Checklist (LeBaron & Zeltzer, 1984), and the Observational Scale of Behavioral Distress (Jay & Elliott, 1984; Jay, Ozolins, Elliott, & Caldwell, 1983). These rating systems were developed for assessment of children's reactions to the same medical procedure, bone marrow aspiration. The three systems are very similar; in fact, the latter two can be viewed as modified versions of the former. In constructing the Procedure Behavioral Rating Scale, Katz *et al.* (1980) first compiled what they believed to be an exhaustive list of anxiety responses to bone marrow aspiration. For response items, they drew upon their own extensive clinical experience with children with cancer and upon the experience of medical personnel who routinely performed bone marrow aspirations. Of the original 25 items generated, 12 were eliminated because of infrequency of occurrence or lack of correlation with other measures of anx-

iety.[1] The remaining 13 items constitute the Procedure Behavioral Rating Scale. Each of the 13 behaviors is monitored for its occurrence–nonoccurrence across an observation session; the total number of behaviors that occur serves as the response score for the session. Examples of the scale's response items and their operational definitions are "cry" (tears in eyes or running down face); "cling" (physically holds on to parent, significant other, or nurse); "scream" (no tears, raises voice, verbal or nonverbal); "flail" (random gross movements of arms or legs, without intention to make aggressive contact); and "muscular rigidity" (any of the following behaviors: clenched fists, white knuckles, gritted teeth, clenched jaw, wrinkled brow, eyes clenched shut, contracted limbs, body stiffness) (Katz *et al.*, 1980, p. 359).

The Procedure Behavior Checklist (LeBaron & Zeltzer, 1984) is identical to the Procedure Behavioral Rating Scale except in its number of items and their scoring. Each of the system's eight behaviors is observed for its occurrence and is rated for its intensity of occurrence on a scale of 1–5. The ratings are summed across behaviors to yield a response score for the observation period.

The Observational Scale of Behavioral Distress (Jay & Elliott, 1984; Jay *et al.*, 1983) differs from the Procedure Behavioral Rating Scale only in its number, recording, and scoring of items. Each of the 11 items on this scale is recorded for occurrence–nonoccurrence every 15 seconds throughout the observation period. Each of the items is weighted for intensity of distress; the weighing is determined by medical personnel experienced in the bone marrow aspiration procedure. Occurrences for individual items are tallied, adjusted for their intensity of distress, then summed.

Among the other noteworthy observation rating systems are the Preschool Observational Scale of Anxiety (Glennon & Weisz, 1978), the Observation of Classroom Behavior (Wine, 1979), and two versions of Paul's (1966) Timed Behavior Checklist—the Revised Timed Be-

---

[1] These item selection procedures may impose an unsubstantiated (and faulty) theory of anxiety and fear—one assuming that all anxiety indicators are common and substantially correlated for all patients—and may impair an idiographically oriented assessment, as items excluded because of their rarity of occurrence or due to low interitem correlations may be highly relevant to some anxious children.

havior Checklist (Fox & Houston, 1981) and the Modified Timed Behavior Checklist (Giebenhain, 1985). Though used to assess children's behavioral responses to separation, the Preschool Observational Scale of Anxiety was designed for use across a broad range of stimulus situations. The scale is comprised of 30 overt behaviors, all of which had appeared in the literature as an observable indicator of children's anxiety, had been screened by clinical child psychologists for their appropriateness, and had been tested for their ability to be reliably and accurately observed. The individual behaviors are observed for their occurrence–nonoccurrence every 30 seconds; the occurrences are summed across 30-second intervals and behaviors to form a motor behavior score for the entire assessment period. Examples of the scale's 30 responses are "gratuitous leg movement," "trunk contortions," "lip-licking," "whisper," and "fingers touching mouth area."

Wine (1979) has developed a detailed scheme for observing children's anticipatory reactions to an academic examination. Though originally used in conjunction with video recordings of the children's classroom behavior, the system appears quite amenable for live use. A 15-minute sample of each child's behavior is divided into 30-second intervals; for each interval, the occurrence–nonoccurrence of 22 discrete observable behaviors is recorded. The behaviors are grouped into five categories: Attending Behaviors (e.g., child orients head and eyes toward the teacher when he or she is addressing the class), Task-Related Behaviors (e.g., child works quietly on assignment), Activity (e.g., child leaves desk), Communication (e.g., child initiates communication with a classmate), and Interactional Behaviors (e.g., child aggresses against another child). Occurrences for each of the 22 behaviors are summed across the 30-second intervals to yield 22 response scores for the observational period.

Paul's (1966) Timed Behavior Checklist has been used in the assessment of older children's reactions to public speaking (Cradock, Cotler, & Jason, 1978) and has been modified for use in the assessment of younger children's reactions to public speaking (Fox & Houston, 1981) and to darkness (Giebenhain, 1985). Based on a factor-analytic study of anxiety signs in speech research (Clevanger & King, 1961), the Timed Behavior Checklist was designed to measure overt anxiety in situations involving public

speaking. The checklist consists of 20 behaviors (e.g., stammering, hand tremors, and foot shuffling) that are monitored every 30 seconds for their occurrence–nonoccurrence. Occurrences are summed across behaviors and intervals to yield a single anxiety response score for the entire period. The Fox and Houston (1981) and Giebenhain (1985) versions of the rating system differ from the original only in terms of the number of response items: The Fox and Houston (1981) adaptation has 12 items, while the Giebenhain (1985) adaptation has 9 items.

Checklists

A third type of observational instrument for the assessment of the motor component of children's fears and anxieties is the checklist. Like the observational rating system, the checklist is composed of multiple responses that are monitored for their occurrence in the naturalistic setting. Unlike the observational rating system, the checklist provides retrospective data, as there may be a considerable delay between the monitoring of the checklist items and the recording of those observations.

Checklists exist for the assessment of children's motor reactions to specific situations (e.g., darkness, separation, test taking) as well as to multiple situations (i.e., generalized anxiety). The checklists vary not only in their stimulus situations, but also in the number and nature of their response items and the timetable for their observations and recordings. This variation is illustrated in the two checklists available for assessment of children's responses to darkness—the Fear Strength Questionnaire and the Direct Home Observation (Graziano & Mooney, 1980)—and the three available for assessment of children's responses to separation: the Parent Anxiety Rating Scale—Separation (Doris, McIntyre, Kelsey, & Lehman, 1971); the Teachers' Separation Anxiety Scale (Doris et al., 1971); and the Teacher Rating of Separation Anxiety (Hall, 1967).

The Fear Strength Questionnaire has nine response items that are observed and reported on for an indeterminate time period. These are the frequency, duration, and intensity of nighttime fear episodes; the episodes' disruption of the child's, the siblings', and the parents' behavior; the seriousness of the fear episodes; the degree of school disruption; and the impairment in the child's social adjustment. The Direct Home Observation has a shorter list of response items, a shorter period of observation, and a short interval between observation and recording than the Fear Strength Questionnaire. Its five items (e.g., number of minutes required to fall asleep, avoidance and delay behaviors displayed) are monitored and marked on a nightly basis.

The three checklists for separation anxiety exemplify similar variations in number and nature of response items, span of observation period, and delay between observation and measurement. The Parent Anxiety Rating Scale—Separation (Doris et al., 1971; Glennon & Weisz, 1978) has six response items that cover an extended, indeterminate period of observation of the child. The Teachers' Separation Anxiety Scale has 11 response items covering a much more circumscribed period of surveillance (i.e., the interval following the parent's placement of the child in school and the parent's departure); the observations, though, are not recorded until the end of the school day. The three-item Teacher Rating of Separation Anxiety asks for reports of both recent and past reactions to separation from the parent. The items ask for a report of the child's reaction to separation from the parent at the onset of the school year, for the last 2 weeks, and for the entire time that school has been in session.

Global Ratings

The fourth type of observational instrument for the assessment of the motor component of children's fears and anxieties is the global rating. The simplest (and surely the most suspect) of all the observational instruments, the global rating calls for a single, overall evaluation of the child's response to the problematic situation. This evaluation takes the form of a single rating on a multipoint scale. Some form of global rating has been used to assess children's reactions to the medical procedures of bone marrow aspiration (LeBaron & Zeltzer, 1984), cardiac catheterization (Bradlyn, 1982), dental treatment (Melamed, Hawes, et al., 1975; Melamed, Weinstein, et al., 1975; Venham, Gaulin-Kremer, Munster, Bengston-Audia, & Cohan, 1980), insulin injection (Gilbert et al., 1982), and surgery (Peterson & Shigetomi, 1981; Vernon, Foley, & Schulman, 1967). The global ratings vary in their number of scale points and their response descriptions of those scale points. The global ratings range from those based upon a 5-point scale (LeBaron & Zeltzer, 1984; Pe-

terson & Shigetomi, 1981; Venham et al., 1980) to those employing a 10-point scale (Gilbert et al., 1982; Melamed, Hawes, et al., 1975; Melamed, Weinstein, et al., 1975). Few of the global ratings provide response definitions for each of the scale points. Three that do provide descriptive anchors are the Global Mood Scale (Vernon et al., 1967), the Venham Anxiety-Rating Scale (Venham et al., 1980), and the Venham Behavior-Rating Scale (Venham et al., 1980). Even these three, though, allow for considerable inference in the assignment of ratings. The descriptive anchors for the two endpoints of the Global Mood Scale are "attentive and active in happy or contented way" and "scream full blast, intense and constant crying." For the midpoint of the Venham Behavior-Rating Scale, the descriptive anchor is "protest presents real problems to dentist, complies reluctantly, body movement"; for the midpoint of the Venham Anxiety-Rating Scale, the descriptive anchor is "shows reluctance to enter situation, difficulty in correctly assessing situational threat, pronounced verbal protest, crying, using hands to stop procedure, protest out of proportion, copes with great reluctance."

Summary

By definition, all four types of observational instruments—BATs, observational ratings, checklists, and global ratings—employ human observers; they must all, therefore, contend with the host of measurement issues that surround (but are not confined to) the collection of observational data. These issues include the accuracy and reactivity of observational assessment and the intrusion of bias, drift, and expectancy into observers' recordings (Foster & Cone, 1980; F. C. Harris & Lahey, 1982a, 1982b; Hartmann & Wood, 1982; Haynes & Horn, 1982; Kazdin, 1981; Kent & Foster, 1977). These issues of construct and external validity (e.g., Cook & Campbell, 1979) have yet to be addressed by the investigators who have developed observational instruments for the assessment of children's fears and anxieties. In the section on the evaluation and selection of assessment instruments, this concern for the validity of the measures is taken up more fully.

Self-Report Methods

Of the 112 instruments listed in Table 2, 39 are self-report in nature. Though the measurement method of self-report lends itself to the assessment of all three components of children's fears and anxieties, most of these 39 self-report instruments have as their sole focus the subjective component. Only 10 of the instruments focus upon another component in addition to the subjective, and only 1 focuses upon a component in the absence of the subjective. From these numbers, it is obvious that behavioral assessors have not ignored the inner child—his or her experiences, thoughts, and perceptions—in their assessment of children's fears and anxieties. Such was not the situation at the time of the first edition of the present volume; few instruments existed then for the measurement of the child's subjective reactions (see Barrios, Hartmann, & Shigetomi, 1981). The many instruments that are now available may be an indication of just how widely accepted the three-systems conceptualization of fear and anxiety is among behavioral assessors (e.g., Morris & Kratochwill, 1983b; Nelson & Hayes, 1981). These self-report instruments for assessing children's fears and anxieties can be divided into three types: global ratings, questionnaires, and think-aloud procedures.

Global Self-Ratings

Global self-ratings differ from global observer ratings only in terms of who serves as the evaluator; in the former the child serves as both the evaluator and the evaluated, whereas in the latter a person other than the child serves as the evaluator. Using the multipoint scale, the child rates his or her overall reaction to a troublesome stimulus setting or condition. The stimulus conditions for which global ratings have been obtained are blood (Van Hasselt et al., 1979), darkness (Giebenhain, 1985; Kelley, 1976), cardiac catheterization (Bradlyn, 1982), bone marrow aspiration (LeBaron & Zeltzer, 1984), dental treatment (Melamed, Hawes, et al., 1975; Melamed, Weinstein, et al., 1975), and test taking (Van Hasselt et al., 1979).

Despite the simplicity of this assessment approach, there is no uniformly accepted format for global rating scales. Instead, there are many global rating scale formats differing in length and in detail. The Target Complaint Scales of Van Hasselt et al., (1979) have the child rate his or her level of fear on a 12-point scale that includes a descriptive term at every third point (e.g., "none," "pretty much," "couldn't be

worse"). Others, such as the fear thermometers of Kelley (1976) and Melamed's group (Melamed, Hawes, et al., 1975; Melamed, Weinstein, et al., 1975; Melamed, et al., 1978) employ a 5-point scale that has a denotative color at every point. Still other global rating scales employ drawings of figures or facial expressions as their descriptive anchors, such as the Faces—Subjective Units of Disturbance (Bradlyn, 1982), the Faces Test of Anxiety (LeBaron & Zeltzer, 1984), the fear thermometer of Giebenhain, (1985), and the Global Self-Rating (Glennon & Weisz, 1978).

Questionnaires

A second type of self-report instrument for assessing the subjective dimension of children's fears and anxieties is the questionnaire. Unlike the global rating, which has a single response item, the questionnaire has multiple response items that are either categorical or continuous in nature. Table 2 lists 25 questionnaires, 14 of which have as their focus the child's reactions to a specific stimulus situation and 11 of which have no such stimulus restrictions. The former are referred to collectively as "specific fear questionnaires," the latter as "general anxiety questionnaires."

Specific fear questionnaires are available for the following situations: darkness (Giebenhain, 1985; Mooney, 1985), medical and dental procedures (Bradlyn, 1982; Melamed, Hawes, et al., 1975; Melamed & Siegel, 1975; Melamed, Weinstein, et al., 1975; Peterson, Schultheis, Ridley-Johnson, Miller, & Tracy, 1984; Venham, Bengston, & Cipes, 1977), small animals (Kornhaber & Schroeder, 1975), social interaction (Barlow & Seidner, 1983), and test taking (Houston, Fox, & Forbes, 1984; Sarason, Davidson, Lighthall, Waite, & Ruebush, 1960; Zatz & Chassin, 1983, 1985). As might perhaps be expected, there is little consistency in the format of these questionnaires, both within and across stimulus situations. The questionnaires vary in their number of response items from 7 (i.e., Cognitive Behavior Questionnaire; Houston et al., 1984) to 50 (Children's Cognitive Assessment Questionnaire; Zatz & Chassin, 1983, 1985). They also vary in the nature and number of subjective responses assessed. Many of the questionnaires ask for repeated ratings of overall fear and anxiety reactions to a number of related aspects of the same troublesome situation. For example, the Hospital Fears Rating Scale (Melamed & Siegel, 1975) has the child estimate how afraid he or she is of 16 hospital events; the Children's Fear Survey Schedule—Dental (Melamed, Hawes, *et al.*, 1975; Melamed, Weinstein, *et al.*, 1975) does the same for 15 dental events; and the Fear and Avoidance Hierarchy Ratings (Barlow & Seidner, 1983) do the same for 10 social events. Other questionnaires ask for ratings of different subjective responses, such as different thoughts and images to a single stimulus condition. For example, the Children's Cognitive Assessment Questionnaire (Zatz & Chassin, 1985) has the child estimate the occurrence of 50 different thoughts related to test taking, and the Self-Statement Checklist (Giebenhain, 1985) has the child estimate the occurrence of 10 different thoughts related to darkness.

Several of the specific fear questionnaires make clever use of visual material in their assessment of children's subjective reactions. One such instrument is the Snake Attitude Measure (Kornhaber & Schroeder, 1975), which consists of 10 target and 6 filler sets of three pictures of animals. For the target sets, one (and for one set, two) of the pictures are of snakes; for the filler sets, none of the pictures are of snakes. The child selects which animal he or she likes most and which animal he or she dislikes most from each picture set. The number of snake pictures liked minus the number of snake pictures disliked serves as a measure of the child's subjective response toward the animal. Another instrument that makes extensive use of visual material is the Child Self Report (Peterson *et al.*, 1984). This device consists of six photographs, three depicting hospital scenes and three depicting positive home scenes. With the assistance of a large photograph of a thermometer segmented into five parts, the child rates the extent to which he or she likes each of the scenes. The ratings for the three hospital scenes serve as a measure of the child's subjective response toward that setting.

The 11 general fear questionnaires can be separated into two groups: those instruments that assess the child's subjective reactions to a wide range of life situations, and those instruments that assess a wide range of the child's subjective reactions to his or her overall life situation. The former group consists of the five fear survey schedules; the latter group consists of the six more trait-oriented instruments (e.g., the Children's Manifest Anxiety Scale and the

State–Trait Anxiety Inventory for Children). Among the five fear survey schedules, the oldest is the 80-item Fear Survey Schedule for Children developed by Scherer and Nakamura (1968). Appropriate for use with children between the ages of 9 and 12, the schedule has the child rate on a 5-point scale the level of fear experienced in regard to each of the 80 stimulus items. In order to render the schedule suitable for use with younger or less intelligent children, Ollendick (1978, 1983) replaced the instrument's 5-point rating scale with a 3-point rating scale. Very similar to these two is the Louisville Fear Survey Schedule (L. C. Miller *et al.*, 1972), which contains 81 items, employs 3-point rating scales, and is appropriate for use with children between the ages of 4 and 18. The other available instruments—the original Children's Fear Survey Schedule (Ryall & Dietiker, 1979) and a recent revision (Barrios *et al.*, 1983)—also employ 3-point rating scales, but with fewer (50) stimulus items.

The group of general fear questionnaires that assess a wide range of children's subjective responses to their overall life situation contains two of the most frequently employed instruments in all of child psychology: the Children's Manifest Anxiety Scale (Castaneda, McCandless, & Palermo, 1956) and the State–Trait Anxiety Inventory for Children (Spielberger, 1973). They are not, however, two of the most frequently employed instruments in child behavior therapy. Nor are any of their variants (e.g., the Children's Manifest Anxiety Scale—Revised and the Cognitive and Somatic Trait Anxiety Inventory) among the most widely employed instruments in child behavior therapy. This pattern of usage may change, though, as the notion of generalized fear and anxiety becomes more widely accepted among child behavior therapists.

The original version of the Children's Manifest Anxiety Scale contains 53 items—42 that assess the child's general anxiety state and 9 that assess the child's tendency to falsify reports. Reynolds and Richmond (1978) revised the scale in order to decrease administration time and required reading level, and to increase item clarity and conformity with test standards. Their revision of the scale contains 37 items— 29 that assess the child's general anxiety state (e.g., "I have trouble making up my mind," "I am afraid of a lot of things") and 9 that assess the child's tendency to falsify reports (e.g., "I am always good," "I never lie").

Patterned after the adult form of the instrument, the State–Trait Anxiety Inventory for Children (Spielberger, 1973) consists of two 20-item scales: a State scale, which measures transitory anxiety reactions to particular situations; and a Trait scale, which measures a stable predisposition to act anxiously, irrespective of the situation. From this inventory, Fox and Houston (1983) have constructed two other instruments: the Cognitive and Somatic State Anxiety Inventory and the Cognitive and Somatic Trait Anxiety Inventory. The two instruments differ from the original in that they further separate the State and Trait scales into subscales for the subjective and for the physiological dimensions of anxiety.

Think-Aloud Procedures

The third type of self-report instrument for assessment of the subjective component is the think-aloud procedure, the mechanics of which ask the child to verbalize his or her thoughts in anticipation of and/or exposure to a distressing stimulus. Recordings of the verbalized thoughts are then scored for certain categories of responses—a not-so-simple task, for it involves the generation and delineation of classes of verbalized thoughts.

To date, we know of only two attempts to assess the subjective aspects of children's fears and anxieties by means of the think-aloud procedure (i.e., Giebenhain, 1985; Houston *et al.*, 1984). The two attempts both have the child say his or her thoughts into a tape recorder; however, they have different systems for scoring the child's spoken thoughts. Houston and his colleagues rate the child's verbalizations for prominence of seven categories of thoughts: analytic attitude (e.g., "I think the game is very colorful"), derogation of other (e.g., "I don't even see why I'm doing this"), justification of positive attitude (e.g., "I just think it's really fun to do things like this because a lot of kids don't get to do this"), performance denigration (e.g., "I'm feeling sort of scared about this"), and situation-irrelevant thoughts (e.g., "Wonder what I'm going to do when school's out"). Giebenhain (1985), on the other hand, scores the child's verbalizations for the percentage of three classes of thoughts: fearful (e.g., "I'm getting scared"), coping (e.g., "I know nothing bad is going to happen to me"), and other (e.g., "I hope Mom makes hamburgers tonight"). In addition to these three re-

sponse scores, the child's entire think-aloud performance is rated for overall level of fear.

Mechanical Methods

Few of the instruments listed in Table 2 employ direct mechanical recording in their assessment of children's fears and anxieties. Of the mere 10 that do, all but 1 have as their focus the physiological component of children's fears and anxieties. Their small numbers attest to the difficulties and complexities involved in directly assessing the activity of the physiological component. Chief among these complicating factors is the absence of a simple response or combination of responses that reliably denotes physiological upset across persons and stimuli (L. C. Johnson & Lubin, 1972). The work of the Laceys (Lacey, 1956; Lacey & Lacey, 1967) clearly demonstrates that there are different patterns of physiological responses to different stressful stimuli, and that for any given stressor there are individual differences in the exact expression of physiological upset. For the assessor of child behavior, these findings imply that adequate measurement of the physiological component of anxieties and fears will entail the measurement of multiple physiological responses.

Adequate measurement of the physiological component also entails the proper selection and operation of equipment across the appropriate parameters of assessment (e.g., Averill & Opton, 1968; Martin & Venables, 1980). What is more, adequate recording and quantification of physiological activity call for sensitivity to such phenomena as adaptation (cf. Barlow, Leitenberg, & Agras, 1969; Montague & Coles, 1966) and initial values (Benjamin, 1963; Lacey, 1956; Ray & Raczynski, 1981; Wilder, 1950), and to such measurement contaminants as room temperature and extraneous movement (e.g., Martin & Venables, 1980; Fehr, 1970; Shapiro, 1975). With children, measurement artifacts are always a concern, for they may find it difficult to remain stationary during physiological recording.

Despite the complexity of physiological assessment, measures of heart rate, finger pulse volume, respiration, and skin conductance have been collected. In some instances elaborate electronic equipment (e.g., a physiograph) has been used to obtain the measures (e.g., Faust & Melamed, 1984; Klingman, Melamed, Cuthbert, & Hermecz, 1984; Melamed *et al.*, 1978;

Van Hasselt *et al.,* 1979); on other instances, less expensive and technical equipment has been employed (e.g., Giebenhain, 1985; Melamed & Siegel, 1975). The latter type of equipment warrants description, for it circumvents the major obstacle to assessment of the physiological component of children's fears and anxieties: its infeasibility.

One of the feasible instruments is the palmar sweat index (R. Johnson & Dabbs, 1967; Thomson & Sutarman, 1953), an instrument that Melamed and her associates (Melamed & Siegal, 1975; Melamed *et al.,* 1978) have used periodically to assess electrodermal responses to medical procedures. The index involves brushing a plastic solution onto either the child's fingertips or palm, two sites that contain a high concentration of sweat glands. When active, a sweat gland leaves a distinct impression on the plastic coating. A measure of the child's electrodermal response is obtained by counting the number of impressions that appear on the coating's surface.

Other practical and relatively inexpensive instruments are the many portable devices for recording physiological activity. One such device—a digital pulse monitor (Lafayette Instruments, Model 77065)— was used by Giebenhain (1985) to assess the heart rates of children to various shades of darkness. The instrument's finger clip, in which the sensing element resides, was decorated to look like a Band-Aid and was referred to as one in order to assuage the children's apprehension about the device. Through use of the digital pulse monitor, Giebenhain (1985) was able to assess the children's physiological responses (i.e., heart rate) as she assessed their motor and subjective responses. Thus, in addition to being economical, the portable recording devices can be employed in concert with instruments assessing other components of children's fears and anxieties.

EVALUATION AND SELECTION

With over 100 instruments to choose from for assessing children's fears and anxieties, behavioral assessors may experience some difficulties in selecting their assessment batteries. The selection, however, will be determined in large part by the decisions that need to be made. In the practice of behavior therapy, decision making is continuous (e.g., I. M. Evans, 1985; Kanfer, 1985). First, one must decide whether or not a problem exists, and, if so, whether or

not to treat the problem. If therapy is seen as appropriate, one must then decide on the nature of the treatment, implement it, and decide on whether or not it is having the desired effect. Assessment data are looked to for help in rendering these decisions, for assessment data determine how tenable the inferences are that underlie these decisions (cf. Barrios & Hartmann, 1986). And the tenability of these inferences is determined by the quality of the assessment data on which the decisions are based.

Once it is decided that a number of instruments provide data appropriate to a particular decision, an instrument is selected that provides "good" data—an instrument with adequate measurement properties.[2] The measurement or psychometric properties that must be considered depend on the inferences to be made. To infer that a child is responding fearfully or anxiously requires the use of a "content-valid" instrument—an instrument that addresses all relevant aspects of fear or anxiety. The extent to which an assessment instrument addresses these aspects depends upon its overlap with the currently accepted conceptualization of fear or anxiety (e.g., Linehan, 1980).

To infer that a child's responding constitutes a problem requires the use not only of a content-valid instrument, but a content-valid instrument for which there are norms. Normative estimates are needed because there is no criterion for problematic fear and anxiety (a predicament that is taken up in the chapter's concluding section). Given the absence of a criterion for problematic fear and anxiety, norms are a convenient and useful background against which to evaluate the problem status of a child's responses (e.g., Hartmann, Roper, & Bradford, 1979).

For a child whose behavior has been judged as problematic, a decision must be made on whether to treat the condition or to allow it to run its natural course. The decision to treat the condition is based in large part upon the inference that the pattern is relatively enduring (and, of course, at least moderately inconvenient); the decision not to treat is based upon the inference that the pattern is fairly transient. The tenability of each of these inferences depends upon the accuracy with which the instrument correctly places individuals into behavioral categories with known prognoses. For it to do so

---

[2]Cost factors must also be considered, but are not discussed in this chapter.

requires that the instrument has well-established empirical validity (e.g., Meehl & Rosen, 1955).

Treatment selection is founded upon the inference that treatment-produced changes in certain variables will lead to desirable changes in the child's performance. The soundness of this inference is reflected in the strength of the relationships between these variables and the child's fear responses. Such relationships are referred to as the measure's "nomological" or "construct" validity (Cronbach & Meehl, 1955). Thus, for the purposes of treatment selection, the need is for instruments with acceptable estimates of nomological validity.

Treatment evaluation requires assessment devices that accurately track changes in the targeted behavior. In order to perform this role, the instrument must be both sensitive and temporally reliable.

Table 2, under the heading of "Appraisal," summarizes the available data on the aforementioned measurement properties (i.e., reliability, validity, and norms) for each of the 112 instruments. The major uses (screening, problem identification, treatment selection, and treatment evaluation) to which each instrument can be put, and the two major settings (the clinic and the laboratory) in which each can be employed, are also summarized. Ideally, instruments would be well suited for use in both settings, for information from both settings contributes to the refinement of behavioral assessment and the understanding of children's fears. Unfortunately, the realities of the clinical situation often prohibit the use of many of the more molecular instruments favored by researchers. The recommendations we offer here are influenced by our recognition of the different needs and demands of the two settings.

Direct Observations

Of the three methods of measurement—direct observation, self-report, and mechanical means—more is known about the psychometric properties of direct observation instruments than is known about the other two. This is not surprising, given that the observational instruments have as their focus the motor component of children's fears and anxieties which historically has been the component of greatest interest to behavioral assessors. Of the 58 observational instruments listed in Table 2, approximately half have estimates attesting to their interscorer reliability, their convergence with other measures of motor activity, and their sensitivity—for example, to treatment. Approximately one-third of the instruments have estimates testifying to their temporal stability[3] and their convergence with measures of the subjective and physiological components of children's fears. Few of the instruments have data on their internal consistency, their ability to discriminate children known to differ in fearfulness, and their generality across relevant settings. None of the instruments have norms.

Of the four types of observational instruments—BATs, observational rating systems, checklists, and global ratings—the rating systems tend to have the best psychometric properties. The superiority of the rating systems may be due to their frequency of use as well as to their format. Observational ratings have been used more frequently than the other observational methods; with more frequent use, psychometric information has become available, which provides feedback for improvement of the instruments. The makeup of the rating systems and the way in which the observations are recorded and scored are especially conducive to reliable assessment. Rating systems are composed of multiple response items, each of which is specifically defined and immediately recorded, and the recordings from these items are summed to yield a composite score. These features help reduce errors in measurement that might be due to the inattentiveness of observers or the instability of single response items; such features promote reliability. And it is only reliable measures that can prove to be valid (e.g., Nunnally, 1978).

Both BATs and checklists have been used irregularly; therefore, a sizable body of information is not yet available on their properties. With more regular use, however, individual BATs may prove to be very valuable instruments for assessing children's fears and anxieties, largely because of their straightforwardness and their suitability for standardization and for the measurement of multiple responses. In their current form, checklists do not appear to have this potential. For many of the checklists, the response items are vague, and the delay between observing and recording may be substantial. The checklists are, however, easy to

[3] Ordinary stability estimates completely confound two sources of inconsistency: actual changes in the targeted behavior that occur over the repeated assessments, and inaccuracy (error of measurement) in the assessment device.

implement—a feature that makes them very attractive to practitioners. In order for the checklists to be both useful and easy to use, they will need to undergo some alternations to remedy their obvious defects.

It is doubtful, though, that any amount of alteration will help make the global ratings sound instruments for assessing children's fears and anxieties. Single-item measures are notoriously unreliable and conceptually barren (e.g., Nunnally, 1978). Be that as it may, some of the global ratings listed in Table 2 have impressive estimates of interobserver agreement, temporal stability, and convergence with other fear measures. What these global ratings lack, though, is clarity of content. They fail to specify what aspects of children's performance are to be observed, and so fail to specify what it is they measure. It is this ambiguity of meaning that is the global ratings' most serious drawback and that argues against their continued use.[4] Despite these misgivings, behavior therapists are unlikely to abandon the global ratings; the ease with which the ratings can be collected all but guarantees their continued use.

Self-Reports

Relative to the observational instruments, little is known about the measurement properties of the self-report instruments, and even less is known about those of the mechanical ones. Of the 39 self-report instruments, information on reliability and validity is available for only a third of them. This lack of information is in large part due to the newness of most of the self-report instruments, which have as their principal focus the subjective component of children's fears and anxieties. Until recently, only a handful of techniques were available for assessing the subjective reactions of children, and those techniques that were available did not appear to be compatible with behavioral conceptualizations of fear and anxiety (Barrios et al., 1981; Barrios & Shigetomi, 1985; Morris & Kratochwill, 1983a). Now several techniques are available—global ratings, questionnaires, and think-aloud procedures—all of which appear to be more or less harmonious with current behavioral accounts of fear and anxiety.

Self-report instruments vary substantially in their utility for the behavioral assessment of children's fears and anxieties. In particular, it is the global self-ratings, such as fear thermometers and faces tests, that appear to have little potential as useful assessment tools.[5] Like the global observer ratings, the global self-ratings are single-item measures, and thus suffer from the same limitations as do all single-item measure: instability, poor discrimination, and ambiguous meaning. And, as with the global observer ratings, it is doubtful that these limitations will override their attractive but less critical features, such as their face validity and ease of administration.

Though the outlook for the questionnaires and the think-aloud procedures is much brighter than for the global self-ratings, these two types of self-report instruments are not without their problems. The fear survey schedules lack the same clarity of content as do the global ratings, which they resemble in design. Both sets of instruments ask for an overall self-evaluation of fear or anxiety that is felt either in single situations (global ratings) or in each of several different situations (fear survey schedules). Both sets leave undefined what it is they measure. One fear survey schedule does not suffer from this shortcoming: the Children's Fear Survey Schedule—Revised (Barrios et al., 1983). This instrument makes use of rating scales for three specific responses—the self-statement "I am afraid," heart rate, and avoidance. Each of the three rating scales is applied to each of the schedules's 50 stimulus situations, yielding three measures of specified content. In order for the other fear survey schedules to be of greater help in understanding children's fears and anxieties, rating scales of similar detail may need to be employed.

Ambiguity of a similar sort pervades the questionnaires that ask for self-ratings of several specific responses to either a discrete situation or situations in general: Which response component of fear and anxiety is being assessed? Many of the traditional questionnaries, such as the Children's Manifest Anxiety Scale and the State–Trait Anxiety Inventory for Children, contain items that address the subjective

---

[4] There is one clear use for global ratings: their use in social validation—the assessment of the social significance and acceptability of treatment (e.g., Kazdin, 1977; Wolf, 1978).

[5] In fact, it could be argued that the major justifiable role for global self-ratings is as therapeutic tools rather than as assessment tools. It is in the facilitation of rapport, motivation, and compliance that the worth of global ratings may lie, and not in their provision of information for clinical decision making.

component of fear and anxiety as well as items that address other components. Problems in meaning (and in interpretation) arise when the items are combined to form a single response score. This ambiguity can be avoided by grouping items by response component, and then summing across items for each grouping. It is this method that was used in developing instruments for assessing cognitive and somatic anxiety from the items of the State–Trait Anxiety Inventory for Children (Fox & Houston, 1983).

By virtue of their instructions—"Say out loud what it is you're thinking"—the think-aloud procedures are clear as to what response component of fear and anxiety they assess. They are less clear as to what might be the best way to score the verbalized thoughts of children. The two applications of the think-aloud procedure differ in the dimensions—such as fearfulness, coping, and mastery—along which the children's verbalizations are examined and the responses subsumed by each of those dimensions. Instead of carrying out a trial-and-error search for the optimum system for scoring children's verbalized thoughts, it may prove useful to draw upon those systems that appear in the adult literature (e.g., Davison, Robins, & Johnson, 1983; Hollon & Bemis, 1981; Merluzzi, Glass, & Genest, 1981).

Mechanical Methods

In general, the direct recordings of physiological responses have not fared well in the measurement of children's fears and anxieties. Little correspondence has been found between the different responses of the physiological component and those of the subjective and motor components. What is more, the physiological measures have not been particularly sensitive to treatment manipulations, to which they presumably should be sensitive. This is not a problem unique to mechanical methods for assessing children's fears and anxieties, as assessors of adults' fears and anxieties have reported similar problems in their efforts to locate reliable and valid physiological measures (e.g., Arena, Blanchard, Andrasik, Cotch, & Myers, 1983; Holden & Barlow, 1986). The situation is one, then, in which many mechanical devices are available for assessing the physiological component of children's fears and anxieties, but none have yet demonstrated the required validity. Some readers may view this situation as grounds for de-emphasizing or even discontinuing the assessment of the physiological responses of children's fears and anxieties. We, however, see it as indicating the need for greater sensitivity to the mechanics of psychophysiological assessment and to the quantification of these data.

ADDITIONAL ASSESSMENT CONSIDERATIONS

Several factors determine the scope as well as the form of an assessment of a child's fears and anxieties. Our previous discussion has emphasized three principal factors: the conceptualization of the disorder, the available instruments for measuring the disorder, and the considerations (such as the child's developmental status) involved in whether or not to treat the disorder. This section focuses on the roles of three other influential factors: treatment prerequisites, familial variables, and ethical guidelines.

Treatment Considerations

Optimum use of available treatments requires certain skills of the child and, in some cases, of the child's parents. To aid, then, in treatment selection, behavioral assessments should include an evaluation of these requisite skills. A description of the procedures and prerequisites for each of the most widely employed behavioral interventions is presented below; a summary of the material is presented in Table 3.

Systematic Desensitization and Its Variants

As a treatment for children's fears and anxieties, systematic desensitization involves the following steps (cf. Hatzenbuehler & Schroeder, 1978; Morris & Kratochwill, 1983a, 1983b): First, the child is trained in deep muscle relaxation; next, the child rank-orders from least distressing to most distressing a series of scenes depicting the feared stimulus; and last, while in a relaxed state, the child imagines each of the scenes in the series. This pairing of the relaxed state with images of the feared stimulus begins with the least distressing scene and ends with the most distressing one, progression through the series being contingent upon imagining a scene without undue discomfort.

For the treatment to be implemented, the child must be able to rank-order the stimulus scenes, generate vivid images of those scenes, and detect subtle changes in his or her bodily state. Thus, the child must be familiar with the concept of ordinality, and have the capacities to image and to distinguish autonomic nervous system changes. Numerous simple and reliable tests for the concept of ordinality are available (e.g., Inhelder & Piaget, 1964). An example of such a test is the Ordinality Check, an instrument used by Giebenhain (1985) in her study of children's reactions to darkness. The instrument consists of drawings of five facial expressions ranging from extreme sadness to extreme joy. The drawings are shuffled and the child arranges them "from the child who is the least happy to the child who is the most happy." The ordering of the faces is highly stable across testing intervals of both a few minutes and a few weeks. Numerous simple and reliable tests for imagery capacity also are available. Among the instruments are the Memory for Objects (Radaker, 1961), the Tri-Model Imagery Scale (Bergan & Macchiavello, 1966), the Visual Imagery Index (Radaker, 1961), and the Image Clarity Scale (Hermecz & Melamed, 1984). In addition, some of the instruments developed for use with adults appear to be amenable for use with children. Among these are the Vividness of Visual Imagery Questionnaire (D. F. Marks, 1973), the Pattern Reconstruction Task (Danaher & Thoresen, 1972), and the Item Location Task (Rimm & Bottrell, 1969). There does not, however, appear to be a ready supply of instruments for assessing children's sensitivity to bodily changes such as fluctuations in heart rate, muscle tension, respiration, and sweating. This could be rectified by adapting the instruments that assess the autonomic awareness of adults, such as the Autonomic Perception Questionnaire (Mandler, Mandler, & Uviller, 1958), the heart-tracking task (Brener, 1977), and the visceral perception test (Pennebaker, Gonder-Frederick, Stewart, Elfman, & Skelton, 1982).

As a treatment for children's fears and anxieties, systematic desensitization does not directly instruct the child in the proper way to interact with the feared stimulus; it is assumed that the child already has this pattern in his or her repertoire. While no instrument is yet available for determining whether or not the child does so—and thus whether or not the child is appropriate for systematic desensitization—such an instrument should be relatively simple to construct. One approach might be to pattern the instrument after LaGreca and Santogrossi's (1980) assessment of children's problem-solving skills. In their procedure children view videotapes of other children in social predicaments, then offer recommendations as to how these problem situations might best be resolved; the responses are audiotaped and then scored for the occurrence of various problem-solving behaviors. In assessing knowledge of adaptive responding, the child would view or listen to taped depictions of other children facing the feared stimulus and then would be asked how best to behave in these situations.

Variations in the basic desensitization procedure involve changes in the number and type of requisite skills. For example, *in vivo* desensitization employs the actual feared stimulus as opposed to an image of it (e.g., P. M. Miller, 1972; Schermann & Grover, 1962); the treatment therefore does not require imagery. Other variants such as group-administered desensitization (e.g., Barabasz, 1973; T. Johnson, Tyler, Thompson, & Jones, 1971) and emotive imagery (e.g., Jackson & King, 1981; Lazarus & Abramovitz, 1962) demand abilities from the child that are similar to those required by the standard procedures.

Prolonged Exposure and Its Variants

In prolonged exposure, the child is asked to confront the feared stimulus immediately and to remain in its presence indefinitely (cf. Morris & Kratochwill, 1983a, 1983b). None of the three variants of the treatment—flooding, implosion, and reinforced practice—offers instruction in how to interact adaptively with the feared stimulus; therefore, each requires the child to be in possession of such knowledge prior to treatment. (Assessment of the child's knowledge of effective responding might be carried out along the lines suggested above.) Flooding entails the intense, extended, realistic presentation of the actual feared stimulus (e.g., Kandel, Ayllon, & Rosenbaum, 1977) or an imaginal representation of it. When the latter is the case, flooding has the additional requisite of an aptitude for imagery (an aptitude that can be assessed using any of the instruments cited above). Implosion also carries the requirement of an aptitude for imagery, for in implosion the child imagines an unrealistic yet nevertheless horrific scenario involving the feared stimulus (e.g., Ollendick & Gruen, 1972; Smith & Sharpe, 1970). The third variant of prolonged exposure, reinforced practice, does not demand

TABLE 3. Considerations in the Selection of a Behavioral Treatment for Children's Fears and Anxieties

Variable	Desensitization			Prolonged exposure			
	Imaginal desensitization	In vivo desensitization	Emotive imagery	Imaginal flooding	In vivo flooding	Implosion	Reinforced practice
Child characteristics							
Repertoire with the disturbing stimulus	+	+	+	+	+	+	+
Concept of ordinality	+	+	+				
Imagery ability	+		+	+		+	
Capacity to discriminate different bodily states	+	+	+	+	+	+	+
Self-management skills							
Attention deficit							
Defensiveness							
Parental characteristics							
Monitoring skills							
Dispenses consequences contingently							
Mood disturbance							
Trait-like attributions to the child's disturbances							

Variable	Contingency management	Modeling	Self-management	Compound intervention		
				Contingency management + self-management	Modeling + self-management (therapist-administered)	Modeling + self-management (therapist and parent-administered)
Child characteristics						
Repertoire with the disturbing stimulus			+			
Concept of ordinality			+	+	+	+
Imagery ability			+	+	+	+
Capacity to discriminate different bodily states						
Self-management skills		+	+	+	+	+
Attention deficit		−			−	−
Defensiveness		−			−	−
Parental characteristics						
Monitoring skills	+		+	+		+
Dispenses consequences contingently	+		+	+		+
Mood disturbance	−		−	−		−
Trait-like attributions to the child's disturbances	−		−	−		−

Note. This table is intended to serve as a framework for treatment selection. It is not meant to be a definitive source, as there are few data on procedures for selecting optimal treatment. A plus (+) indicates that the child or parent characteristic is a requisite of the technique; a minus (−) indicates that the characteristic contraindicates the technique; and an open cell indicates that the characteristic is not clearly relevant.

imagery skill but does require autonomic perception (a skill that can be assessed by the
methods described above). Specifically, the child
must be able to discriminate varying degrees of
autonomic upset, for in reinforced practice the
child is rewarded for remaining in the presence
of the feared object for as long as the emotional
upset can be tolerated (e.g., Leitenberg & Callahan, 1973).

Modeling and Its Variants

Modeling treatments have the child observe
another child interacting adaptively with the
feared stimulus (cf. Melamed & Siegel, 1980;
Morris & Kratochwill, 1983a, 1983b). This
demonstration of effective responding may be
either live (e.g., Bandura *et al.*, 1967) or filmed
(e.g., Melamed *et al.*, 1978) and may be followed by either considerable or little practice
and coaching in the modeled behaviors (e.g.,
Esveldt-Dawson *et al.*, 1982; Faust & Melamed, 1984; S. Lewis, 1974). Because the
modeling therapies provide direct instruction in
adaptive responding, the child is not required
to be proficient in imagery. And since there are
no scenes to rank-order or pair with a relaxed
state, and no emotional upset to tolerate, the
concept of ordinality and the awareness of internal arousal are not necessary.

Other than the capacity to attend to and retain
sensory information, the modeling therapies have
no prerequisites. This capacity to attend to and
retain modeled events is thought to be largely
a function of the sensory equipment of the child
(Bandura, 1969, 1977b). Other important determinants are suggested in the studies of modeling treatments of children's medical fears by
Melamed and her associates (Faust & Melamed, 1984; Klingman *et al.*, 1984; Melamed,
Dearborn, & Hermecz, 1983; Melamed *et al.*,
1978). These additional determinants include
the child's age, prior experience with the feared
stimulus, and dispositional characteristics of
defensiveness and self-control. Younger children, children with previous exposure to the
feared situation, and children high in defensiveness and low in self-control have been found
to retain little of the model-conveyed information and to profit little from modeling treatments. Thus, these child characteristics should
be assessed, and those children who are unlikely to profit from standard modeling treatments should be provided with alternate treatments or with tailored modeling treatments.

Melamed and her colleagues have used the
Defensive Questionnaire (Wallach & Kogan,
1965) to assess children's tendency toward denial. Other instruments that assess the same
tendency are the Children's Version of the
Repression–Sensitization Scale (Peterson &
Toler, 1984) and the Lie scales from the Children's Manifest Anxiety Scale (Castaneda *et
al.*, 1965) and its revision (Reynolds & Richmond, 1978). As a measure of children's tendency toward self-control, Melamed and her
colleagues have employed the Children's Version of the Self-Control Scale (Klingman &
Rosenbaum, 1981; Rimon, 1980; Rosenbaum,
1980).

Contingency Management

Interventions that manipulate the external consequences of children's movement away from
or toward the feared stimulus are referred to
collectively as "contingency management"
procedures (cf. Morris & Kratochwill, 1983a;
Richards & Siegel, 1978). In some instances a
reward is administered for approach (e.g., Vaal,
1973) or taken away for avoidance (e.g., Waye,
1979) or both (e.g., Ayllon, Smith, & Rogers,
1970); Boer & Sipprelle, 1970). In other instances, rewards are delivered for coming progressively closer to the feared stimulus (e.g.,
Luiselli, 1978), or penalties are imposed for
failing to do so (e.g., Tobey & Thoresen,
1976). All that these procedures ask from a
child in the way of prerequisites is that he or
she have the physical makeup to act appropriately.

More often than not, it is a child's parents
who are responsible for implementing the
treatment program; they monitor the child's
performance and dole out the consequences
accordingly. The consistency and thoroughness
with which the parents carry out these duties
appear to be a function of a host of variables,
the most important of which are their mood
state and their causal attributions regarding the
child's maladaptive behavior (cf. O'Dell, 1986).
Parents who are depressed or who see the child's
behavior in trait-like terms typically do not
carry out their treatment duties; consequently,
the treatments tend to be of little benefit. For
fearful and anxious children who have parents
such as these, contingency management is not
the treatment of choice.

Whether or not the parents have appropriate
mood and causal attributions can be determined

with the help of assessment data. Numerous instruments are available for the assessment of adult depression (Lewinsohn & Lee, 1981; Rehm, 1976; 1981); those most frequently employed in this context are the Beck Depression Inventory (Beck, Ward, Mendelson, Mock & Erbaugh, 1961) and the Minnesota Multiphasic Personality Inventory Depression scale (Dahlstrom, Welsh, & Dahlstrom, 1972). Fewer instruments exist for the assessment of parents' causal attribution regarding their child's problematic behaviors, and those that do exist address problems other than fears and anxieties. Simple alterations of these instruments should render them suitable, however. Examples of such instruments are the questionnaires developed by Forehand (Forehand, Wells, McMahon, Griest, & Rogers, 1982; McMahon, Forehand, Griest, & Wells, 1981) and by O'Dell (1982, 1986) for their studies of parent training and child noncompliance.

Self-Management

In self-management, the focus is on changing the child's subjective and physiological reactions to the feared stimulus (cf. Melamed, Klingman, & Siegel, 1984; Morris & Kratochwill, 1983a). The child is instructed in ways to cope with the dangers, whether real or imagined, posed by the feared situation. Typically this instruction takes the form of training in deep muscle relaxation, distracting imagery, and brave and comforting self-talk. And presumably, in order to benefit from this form of training, the child must be sensitive to differing bodily states, adept at imagery, and knowledgeable in adaptive ways of overtly responding to the feared stimulus. Methods of assessing each of these skills have been previously discussed.

The self-management program developed by Peterson (Peterson & Shigetomi, 1981; Peterson & Tobler, 1984) for children with hospital fears illustrates the fourth, and oftentimes overlooked, prerequisite of this form of treatment. Through the use of a puppet, therapist and parent instruct the child in cued muscle relaxation, imaging scenes of quiescence and mirth, and verbal self-reassurance regarding the feared stimulus. Parental instructions and prompts are provided as to when and where the child might best exercise each one of these techniques. The parent, then, is an integral part of the intervention. The ability of parents to carry out their part in self-management programs may be a function of the same variables as the ability of the parents to carry out their part in contingency management programs: mood state and causal attributions regarding their child's appropriateness (in this case) for self-management. Determining a fearful child's appropriateness for self-management should therefore include an assessment of these two parental variables. And such an assessment might be carried out along the lines suggested above.

Compound Interventions

Various treatment combinations have been fashioned from the five interventions previously described. These compound interventions represent not only a combination of the operations of the individual treatments, but also a combination of the prerequisites. Three illustrative programs and their prerequisites are described below.

Graziano and his associates (Graziano & Mooney, 1980; Graziano, Mooney, Huber, & Ignasiak, 1979) have developed a home-based treatment for children's nighttime fears that combines elements of contingency and self-management training; the treatment, therefore, has the requisites associated with both of these treatment components. In their program, the child receives instruction in deep muscle relaxation, pleasant imagery, and courageous self-talk. Each night the child practices the techniques and is rewarded by the parent for his or her behavior during practice and for the remainder of the evening.

In Peterson's (Peterson & Shigetomi, 1981; Siegel & Peterson, 1980) combination of modeling and self-management treatment for children's hospital-related fears, the child and the parent are coached together in the three coping techniques of cue-controlled relaxation, distracting imagery, and comforting self-talk. And, together, they watch a film depicting the hospital facilities, the medical procedure the child is to undergo, and the appropriate reactions to these procedures. The parent is responsible for seeing that the child rehearses the techniques and for prompting the child when to perform the techniques. Requisites for the program are the same as those for self-management and modeling, with the exception of knowledge of adaptive responding, which is provided by the treatment's modeling component.

The list of prerequisites is shorter for Melamed's (Klingman *et al.*, 1984; Melamed *et al.*, 1984) combination of modeling and self-management treatment for children's dental fears. In her program, Melamed has the child watch a videotape of another child using the coping strategies of controlled breathing and distracting imagery as he or she undergoes dental treatment. With each demonstration of each strategy, time is allotted for the child to practice the technique. For a fearful child to be appropriate for this type of treatment, the child must possess the characteristics required for modeling—reasonable self-control and low defensiveness—as well as those imagery skills required for self-management; the treatment does not require the child to know how to respond adaptively to the feared stimulus.

Familial Variables

Because the support for much of children's behavior is provided by their family members, numerous familial variables have been linked to children's fears and anxieties. Among the most frequently cited and heavily researched of these variables are maternal anxiety, child-rearing practices, and sibling anxiety. Despite this research attention, the relationships between each of these three variables and children's fears have not been fully elaborated.

Studies of the relationship between maternal and child anxiety generally have taken one of three forms. One is to correlate measures of mothers' general or trait anxiety with measures of children's anxiety reactions to a particular situation (e.g., Klorman, Michael, Hilpert, & Sveen, 1979; Klorman, Ratner, Arata, King, & Sveen, 1978; Wright, Alpern, & Leake, 1973). Instruments such as the Taylor Manifest Anxiety Scale (J. A. Taylor, 1953) and Trait scale of the State–Trait Anxiety Inventory (Spielberger, Gorsuch, & Lushene, 1970) are used to assess the general anxiety of the mothers. Another approach is to correlate the anxiety reactions of mothers and children to the same situation (e.g., R. Johnson & Baldwin, 1968), 1969; Klorman *et al.*, 1978, 1979; Melamed & Siegel, 1975; Melamed *et al.*, 1978). Either the State scale of the State–Trait Anxiety Inventory (Spielberger *et al.*, 1970) or a specific fear questionnaire such as the Maternal Anxiety Questionnaire (Melamed *et al.*, 1978) is used to assess mothers' responses toward the stimulus. The final strategy is to compare the responsiveness of children to treatment with the reactions of their mothers to that treatment (e.g., Bradlyn, 1982; Peterson & Shigetomi, 1981). Specially developed scales are used to assess maternal reactions to the intervention, such as the Parent Self-Report (Peterson & Shigetomi, 1981).

Findings from all three classes of studies tend to suggest that the younger the child, the stronger the connection between maternal and child anxiety (cf. Winer, 1982). Thus, for younger children it may be necessary to assess and possibly to treat the mother's anxiety. This prescription also is suggested by a major developmental theory of emotions, social referencing theory (Klinnert, Campos, Sorce, Emde, & Svejda, 1983). According to social referencing theory, children seek out emotional information from significant others in their environment whenever they are confronted with an ambiguous situation or a situation that exceeds their ability to appraise its dangerousness. It is upon this information that children predicate their reactions to the situation. Younger children are less likely to have had experience with the stimulus; therefore younger children are more likely to search out a significant other, such as the mother, for cues as to how to interpret and react to the situation. It follows then, that if the mother displays a fearful or anxious reaction to the situation, the young, observing child will as well.

Though sibling anxiety has been investigated considerably less than has maternal anxiety, the findings tend to be more consistent. In general, the fears and anxieties of siblings have been found to parallel one another, the correspondence being stronger for specific fears than for general anxiety (e.g., Bailey, Talbot, & Taylor, 1973; DeFee & Himelstein, 1969; Ghose, Giddon, Shiere, & Fogels, 1969). However, the direction of influence between the specific fears of siblings is unclear. Some data suggest that the line of influence is from older sibling to younger sibling (e.g., Ghose *et al.*, 1969); other data suggest the opposite (e.g., Hawley, McCorkle, Witteman, & Van Ostenberg, 1974). Given this uncertainty over the direction of influence, it would seem prudent to assess the siblings of fearful children for their reactions to the feared stimulus and to treat those reactions if they are judged to be problematic. Assessment of siblings' responses to the feared stimulus could be carried out along the same lines as assessment of the target child's responses.

Child-rearing practices have been the least investigated of the three familial variables that have been linked to children's fears and anxieties (cf. Campbell, 1986; Winer, 1982). With less than a handful of studies conducted, only the most tentative of statements can be made about the relationship between child-rearing practices and children's fears. Permissive child-rearing practices appear to be correlated with the presence of anxiety reactions, but only in young children (e.g., Allan & Hodgson, 1968; Sarnat, Peri, Nitzan, & Perlberg, 1972; Venham, Murray, & Gaulin-Kremer, 1979). Therefore, with young fearful children, it may be useful to assess and possibly to alter their parents' child management behaviors. Instruments for conducting an assessment of child management procedures include the Child Rearing Practice Questionnaire (Venham *et al.*, 1979) and the many inventories available from the area of parent training (cf. O'Dell, 1986).

Ethical Considerations

The ethical consideration most germane to the assessment of children's fears and anxieties involves the notion of the "mature minor." Specifically, a "mature minor" is a child who has sufficient insight into his or her condition and into the relative costs and benefits associated with treatments designed to alter that condition (Melton, 1981). Such a child is accorded full rights of self-determination over mental health services, including the rights of informed consent, confidentiality, and goal setting (e.g., Melton, 1978, 1981). Presumably, most children 15 years of age or older have the cognitive abilities to qualify as a "mature minor."

For the behavioral assessor facing a fearful child aged 15 or over, the immediate task is to determine whether or not the child qualifies as a "mature minor." (This determination is critical, for it establishes who can approve of the instruments used to assess and the techniques used to treat the child's fear reaction.) Assessment of the child's "maturity" or competence will proceed along several different lines. One is an assessment of the child's understanding of his or her problem condition; another is an assessment of the child's understanding of the relative merits of different treatments; and a third is an assessment of the child's understanding of clients' rights—how they can be exercised and when they are being violated (Belter & Grisso, 1984).

Unfortunately, instruments are available only for an assessment of the child's understanding of clients' rights. The procedure developed by Belter and Grisso (1984) for assessing children's understanding of clients' rights employs three videotapes. Before viewing the videotapes, children are instructed to imagine that the person on the screen is their therapist and that they are the person whom their therapist is addressing. The first tape has the therapist presenting information on clients' rights; the second has the therapist describing the nature of therapy; and the third has the therapist violating the rights cited in the first tape. After each tape is shown, the children are questioned on its content.

Similar materials might be developed for measuring children's understanding of common fear reduction methods. In their studies of the therapeutic expectancies generated by common methods of fear reduction, Stanley and Barrios (1984, 1985) describe such materials. Constructed with adults in mind, their instruments should be appropriate for use with children after minor modification.

Development of instruments for measuring children's understanding of their fears and anxieties may prove to be more troublesome because of the difficulties in defining the concept to be measured. One possible solution would be to adopt the definition that is used for insight into one's physical illness: the ability to identify specific agents of the disorder. Such a definition would involve assessing children's ability to identify psychosocial or internal factors that are thought to underlie their fears and anxieties. This assessment may take the form of an interview or a questionnaire, and may have as its list of "acceptable" agents those that are cited in scientific accounts of children's fears and anxieties.

SUMMARY AND RECOMMENDATIONS

A major emphasis in clinical behaviorism is on the intimate relationship between assessment and intervention (e.g., Bandura, 1969; Kanfer & Phillips, 1970; Kanfer & Saslow, 1969; Rimm & Masters, 1979). Assessment data are enlisted in the selection of the target behavior, the selection of treatment, and the evaluation of treatment effectiveness. Information about the child, the problem condition, the circumstances under which the problem occurs, the prognosis of the condition, the reactions of peers, and other variables all presumably help to determine whether or not treatment is warranted. If treatment is judged to be warranted, then presumably all such information helps to identify the specific target, the optimal treatment, and the primary and collateral dependent variables. Unfortunately, reality falls far short of this ideal. At present there is no generally accepted model for selecting target and treatment; consequently, decisions are based primarily on clinical impressions or on the availability of techniques (Ciminero & Drabman, 1977; Mash & Terdal, 1976). Only in developing a technology for measuring dependent variables and evaluating treatment effectiveness have behavior assessors achieved reasonable success (I. M. Evans, 1985; Hartmann et al., 1979).

Need for a Model for Target and Treatment Selection

Several conditions contribute to the general failure of assessment data to assist in identifying problems, treatment foci, and treatment strategies. First and foremost among these conditions is the nonspecific topography of children's fears and anxieties. Assessors have defined children's fears and anxieties as complex patterns of subjective, motor, and physiological responses (cf. S. B. Johnson & Melamed, 1979; Morris & Kratochwill, 1983a; Winer, 1982), but have yet to identify the specific subjective, motor, and physiological responses that constitute the patterns. Most attempts at delineating the response profiles of children's fears and anxieties have assumed invariance across stimuli, across ages, or both. Current data and theorizing on emotional expression suggest that no such invariance exists (e.g., Campos & Barrett, 1984; Campos, Barrett, Lamb, Goldsmith, & Stenberg, 1983; Lang, 1984; Lang et al., 1983). Instead, they suggest that the exact expression of fear and anxiety will vary as a function of the task demands of the stimulus context and the developmental stage of the child. It would appear productive, then, to begin tracing the response profiles of children's fears and anxieties with these two factors in mind.

A second condition is the confusion over the interrelationships among fear and anxiety's three response components. Although subjective, motor, and physiological responses apparently are not independent (e.g., Rachman & Hodgson, 1974; Sartory, Rachman, & Grey, 1977), substantial disagreement exists over the specific form of their organization (e.g., Bandura, 1969, 1977a; Lang, 1971, 1977). Historically, behavior therapists have viewed the three components as being loosely coupled and have offered prescriptions for the assessment of fear and anxiety that are based upon this view (e.g., Borkovec et al., 1977; Lick & Katkin, 1976; Neitzel & Bernstein, 1981; Paul, 1966). Recently, the trend has been to try to pinpoint the conditions under which high concordance or discordance among the response components occur (Bandura, 1978; Barrios, Mitchell, Bosma, & Thacker, 1982; Hodgson & Rachman, 1974; Lang, 1984; Lang et al., 1983). It is this line of investigation that appears more likely to enhance our understanding and assessment of children's fears and anxieties.

Third is the absence of an objective criterion for fear and anxiety. Global parental reports heretofore have served as the criterion for fearful and anxious responding. Such reports are fraught with difficulties. They are suspect from a psychometric standpoint (Nunnally, 1978) and are highly susceptible to bias and distortion (e.g., Christensen, Phillips, Glasgow, & Johnson, 1983; Forehand et al., 1982). What is more, they have been found to relate only tenuously to accepted subjective, motor, and physiological measures of fear and anxiety (e.g., Barrios et al., 1983; Giebenhain, 1985; Jay & Elliott, 1984, Peterson & Shigetomi, 1981). An obvious solution to the criterion problem is the establishment of cutoff scores on accepted, standardized measures of children's fears and anxieties. Such proposals have been put forth for some of the adult anxiety disorders (e.g., Himadi, Boice, & Barlow, 1985). Child behavior assessors may wish to recommend similar guidelines. Of course, such guidelines are predicated on their being standardized measures of children's fears and anxieties. That there are none presently is discussed below.

Fourth is the absence of a widely accepted system for classifying children's fears and anxieties. Of the many systems that have been proposed, the DSM-III (American Psychiatric Association, 1980) categories are the most likely to prevail. They are likely to do so not because of empirical, conceptual, or utilitarian reasons, but because of economic reasons (e.g., Nelson & Barlow, 1981; C. B. Taylor, 1983). Such categories may not, however, be the ones that best advance the understanding, assessment, and treatment of children's fears and anxieties. Epidemiological data clearly show that the objects of children's fears and anxieties vary with age. A classification system that reflects these age-related variations and thus is organized along developmental lines may be one that better serves our needs.

Fifth, according to I. M. Marks (1977) and Graziano, DeGiovanni, and Garcia (1979), none of the theoretical accounts of the acquisition and maintenance of fears and anxieties is sufficiently broad to explain the many cultural, interpersonal, and constitutional factors involved in the disorders. Marks (1977) discusses seven aspects of naturally occurring fears and anxieties that are not well explained by most current models. These are (1) selection of the feared stimulus, (2) individual differences in susceptibility, (3) maturational changes, (4) physiological controlling variables, (5) social influences, (6) the role of trauma, and (7) the association of fears with other psychological disturbances. Although more work clearly is needed in the development of theoretical models, consideration of currently prominent though incomplete models may enhance the assessment process.

For example, the prepotency or preparedness model put forth by I. M. Marks (1969) and Seligman (1971) may provide insights into the selective nature of children's fears and anxieties. According to this theory, some stimuli such as snakes, spiders, dogs, and heights may "act as a magnet for phobias" (I. M. Marks, 1977, p. 194); other stimuli such as wooden ducks, macaroni, and shoelaces may not have this capacity to elicit fear and anxiety. The work of Öhman and his colleagues (Fredrikson & Öhman, 1979; Hugdahl, Fredrikson, & Öhman, 1977; Öhman, 1979; Öhman, Fredrikson, & Hugdahl, 1978) bear out these predictions: they show reliable differences in the rates of conditioning and extinguishing emotional responses to different stimuli. Whether these data support the notion of innate fears is, however, a matter of considerable contention (Delprato, 1980; Delprato & McGlynn, 1984; Jacobs & Nadel, 1985).

The social referencing theory of emotional development (e.g., Campos & Barrett, 1984; Klinnert et al., 1983) may offer clues into the shifting targets of children's fears and anxieties. As a general explanatory framework of emotions, its main tenets apply to all emotions, including fear and anxiety. The theory's cor-

nerstone proposition—that persons seek out information on emotional expression from significant others in their environment whenever they are confronted with a situation that is ambiguous or that exceeds their appraisal capacities (cf. Klinnert et al., 1983)—implies for the developing child that fears arise (and are associated with) the change from a safe, certain environment to an uncertain, unfamiliar environment. For example, fears should develop when the child is removed from the arms of the mother and placed into those of a strange caretaker, when the child is removed from the home and placed into a school setting, and when the child moves from one school setting to another.

Several of the models highlight critical variables that have heretofore been largely overlooked in assessments of children's fears and anxieties. The social referencing model implicates not only novel events, but also the reactions of significant others (e.g., parents, siblings) to those events. Revised respondent conditioning theory (Rachman, 1977) and social learning theory (Bandura, 1969, 1977b) make similar claims. Other models underscore different variables in the acquisition and maintenance of children's fears and anxieties. Critical variables and the theoretical models endorsing them include early infantile conditioning, endorsed by the infantile amnesia model (Jacobs & Nadel, 1985); expectations and images, endorsed by the cognitive–mediational models (e.g., Bandura, 1977a, 1978; Lang, 1977, 1979; Reiss, 1980; Seligman & Johnston, 1973); and basal activity of the autonomic nervous system, endorsed by the physiological model (Lader & Mathews, 1968).

Sixth, for a target and treatment selection model to be useful, it must be founded upon sound, standardized assessment (Mash, 1985)— a situation that does not currently exist for the assessment of children's fears and anxieties. As the present review testifies, there is no shortage of measures of children's fears and anxieties. However, there is a shortage of standardized, content-valid assessments of children's fears and anxieties. Protocols that measure the subjective, motor, and physiological responses of children's fears and anxieties are needed. While such protocols have been developed by Melamed and colleagues and by Peterson and colleagues, many more are needed. Along with more content valid assessment protocols is the need for more data on the psychometric properties of the measures obtained from such protocols, including data on the measures' reliability (i.e., interscorer consistency, internal consistency, and temporal stability across intervals of varying length and for children of different ages), validity (i.e., convergence with measures within and across response components, divergence with measures of presumably distinctive disorders, sensitivity to experimental manipulations, and generality across relevant settings), and norms (i.e., scores of age-appropriate reference groups). It is information of this sort that is likely to be of greatest assistance in selecting targets and treatments for children's fears and anxieties.

At this time, the utility of assessment is not easy to evaluate (Barrios & Hartmann, 1986; I. M. Evans & Nelson, 1977; Kanfer & Nay, 1982). Nevertheless, our working assumption is that the assessment of children's fears and anxieties is valuable—that a thorough and objective formulation of these problems will substantially facilitate their resolution.

REFERENCES

Achenbach, T. M. (1985). *Assessment and taxonomy of child and adolescent psychopathology.* Beverly Hills, CA: Sage.

Agras, W. S., Chapin, H. N., & Oliveau, D. C. (1972). The natural history of phobia. *Archives of General Psychiatry, 26,* 315–317.

Agras, W. S., Sylvester, D., & Oliveau, D. C. (1969). The epidemiology of common fears and phobias. *Comprehensive Psychiatry, 10,* 151–156.

Allan, T. K., & Hodgson, E. W. (1968). The use of personality measurements as a determinant of patient cooperation in an orthodontic practice. *American Journal of Orthodontics, 54,* 433–440.

American Psychiatric Association. (1980). *Diagnostic and statistical manual of mental disorders* (3rd ed.). Washington, DC: Author.

Angelino, H., Dollins, J., & Mech, E. V. (1956). Trends in the "fears and worries" of school children as related to socio-economic status and age. *Journal of Genetic Psychology, 89,* 263–276.

Angelino, H., & Shedd, C. (1953). Shifts in the content of fears and worries relative to chronological age. *Proceedings of the Oklahoma Academy of Sciences, 34,* 180–186.

Arena, J. G., Blanchard, E. B., Andrasik, F., Cotch, P. A., & Myers, P. E. (1983). Reliability of psychophysiological assessment, *Behaviour Research and Therapy, 21,* 447–460.

Averill, J. R., & Opton, E. M. (1968). Psychophysiological assessment: Rationale and problems. In P. R. McReynolds (Ed.), *Advances in psychological assessment* (Vol. 1, pp. 265–288). Palo Alto, CA: Science and Behavior Books.

Ayllon, T., Smith, D., & Rogers, M. (1970). Behavioral management of school phobia. *Journal of Behavior Therapy and Experimental Psychiatry, 1,* 125–138.

Bailey, P. M., Talbot, A., & Taylor, P. P. (1973). A comparison of maternal anxiety levels with anxiety levels manifested in child dental patients. *Journal of Dentistry for Children, 40,* 277–284.

Bandura, A. (1969). *Principles of behavior modification.* New York: Holt, Rinehart & Winston.

Bandura, A. (1977a). Self-efficacy: Toward a unifying theory of behavioral change. *Psychological Review, 84,* 191–215.

Bandura, A. (1977b). *Social learning theory.* Englewood Cliffs, NJ: Prentice-Hall.

Bandura, A. (1978). Reflections on self-efficacy. *Advances in Behaviour Research and Therapy, 1,* 237–269.

Bandura, A., Grusec, E., & Menlove, F. L. (1967). Vicarious extinction of avoidance behavior. *Journal of Personality and Social Psychology, 5,* 16–32.

Bankart, C. P., & Bankart, B. B. (1983). The use of song lyrics to alleviate a child's fears. *Child and Family Behavior Therapy, 5,* 81–83.

Barabasz, A. (1973). Group desensitization of test anxiety in elementary schools. *Journal of Psychology, 83,* 295–301.

Barlow, D. H., Cohen, A. S., Waddell, M., Vermilyea, B. B., Klosko, J. S., Blanchard, E. B., & DiNardo, P. A. (1984). Panic and generalized anxiety disorders: Nature and treatment. *Behavior Therapy, 15,* 431–449.

Barlow, D. H., Leitenberg, H., & Agras, W. S. (1969). Experimental control of sexual deviation through manipulation of the noxious scene in covert sensitization. *Journal of Abnormal Psychology, 74,* 596–601.

Barlow, D. H., & Seidner, A. L. (1983). Treatment of adolescent agoraphobics: Effects on parent–adolescent relations. *Behaviour Research and Therapy, 21,* 519–526.

Barrios, B. A. (1986). *Concordance and discordance among measures of children's fears and anxieties.* Unpublished manuscript, University of Mississippi.

Barrios, B. A., & Hartmann, D. P. (1986). The contributions of traditional assessment: Concepts, issues and methodologies. In S. C. Hayes & R. O. Nelson (Eds.), *Conceptual foundations of behavioral assessment* (pp. 81–110). New York: Guilford Press.

Barrios, B. A., Hartmann, D. P., & Shigetomi, C. (1981). Fears and anxieties in children. In E. J. Mash & L. G. Terdal (Eds.), *Behavioral assessment of childhood disorders* (pp. 259–304). New York: Guilford Press.

Barrios, B., Mitchell, J. E., Bosma, B. M., & Thacker, W. (1982, March). *Perceived self-efficacy and physiological responsivity: The importance of individual difference variables.* Paper presented at the meeting of the Southeastern Psychological Association, New Orleans.

Barrios, B. A., Replogle, W., & Anderson-Tisdelle, D. (1983, December). *Multisystem–unimethod analyses of children's fears.* Paper presented at the meeting of the Association for Advancement of Behaviour Therapy, Washington, DC.

Barrios, B. A., & Shigetomi, C. C. (1985). Assessment of children's fears: A critical review. In T. R. Kratochwill (Ed.), *Advances in school psychology* (Vol. 4, pp. 89–132). Hillsdale, NJ: Erlbaum.

Bauer, D. H. (1976). An exploratory study of developmental changes in children's fears. *Journal of Child Psychology and Psychiatry, 17,* 69–74.

Back, A. T., Ward, C. H., Mendelson, M., Mock, J., & Erbaugh, J. (1961). An inventory for measuring depression. *Archives of General Psychiatry, 4,* 561–571.

Belter, R. W., & Grisso, T. (1984). Children's recognition

of rights violations in counseling. *Professional Psychology: Research and Practice, 15,* 899–910.

Benjamin, L. S. (1963). Statistical treatment of the law of initial values (LIV) in autonomic research: A review and recommendation. *Psychosomatic Medicine, 25,* 556–566.

Berecz, J. M. (1968). Phobias of childhood: Etiology and treatment. *Psychological Bulletin, 70,* 694–720.

Berg, I. (1976). School phobia in the children of agoraphobic women. *British Journal of Psychiatry, 128,* 86–89.

Berg, I., Marks, I., McGuire, R., & Lipsedge, M. (1974). School phobia and agoraphobia. *Psychological Medicine, 4,* 428–434.

Bergan, J. R., & Macchiavello, A. (1966). *Visual imagery and reading achievement.* Paper presented at the meeting of the American Education Research Association, Chicago.

Bernstein, D. A., & Nietzel, M. T. (1973). Procedural variation in behavioral avoidance tests. *Journal of Consulting and Clinical Psychology, 41,* 165–174.

Bernstein, D. A., & Nietzel, M. T. (1974). Behavioural avoidance tests: The effects of demand characteristics and repeated measures on two types of subjects. *Behaviour Therapy, 5,* 183–192.

Bernstein, D. A., & Paul, G. L. (1971). Some comments on therapy analogue research with small animal "phobias." *Journal of Behaviour Therapy and Experimental Psychiatry, 2,* 225–237.

Blanchard, E. B. (Ed.). (1982). Behaviour medicine [Special issue]. *Journal of Consulting and Clinical Psychology, 50*(6).

Boer, A. P., & Sipprelle, C. N. (1970). Elimination of avoidance behavior in the clinic and its transfer to the normal environment. *Journal of Behaviour Therapy and Experimental Psychiatry, 1,* 169–174.

Borkovec, T. D. (1976). Physiological and cognitive processes in the regulation of anxiety. In G. E. Schwartz & D. Shapiro (Eds.), *Consciousness and self-regulation* (Vol. 1, pp. 261–312). New York: Plenum Press.

Borkovec, T. D., Weerts, T. C., & Bernstein, D. A. (1977). Assessment of anxiety. In A. R. Ciminero, K. S. Calhoun, & H. E. Adams (Eds.), *Handbook of behavioral assessment* (pp. 367–428). New York: Wiley.

Bornstein, P. H., & Knapp, M. (1981). Self-control desensitization with a multi-phobic boy: A multiple baseline design. *Journal of Behaviour Therapy and Experimental Psychiatry, 12,* 281–285.

Bradlyn, A. S. (1982). *The effects of a videotape preparation package in reducing children's arousal and increasing cooperation during cardiac catheterization.* Unpublished doctoral dissertation, University of Mississippi.

Brener, J. (1977). Visceral perception. In J. Beatty & H. Legewie (Eds.), *Biofeedback and behavior* (pp. 235–259). New York: Plenum.

Campbell, S. B. (1986). Developmental issues. In R. Gittelman (Ed.), *Anxiety disorders of childhood* (pp. 24–57). New York: Guilford Press.

Campos, J. J., & Barrett, K. C. (1984). Toward a new understanding of emotions and their development. In C. E. Izard, J. Kagan, & R. B. Zajonc (Eds.), *Emotions, cognition, and behavior* (pp. 229–263). New York: Cambridge University Press.

Castaneda, A., McCandless, B. R., & Palermo, D. S. (1956). The children's form of the Manifest Anxiety Scale. *Child Development, 27,* 317–326.

Chess, S., & Hassibi, M. (1978). *Principles and practice of child psychiatry.* New York: Plenum.

Christensen, A., Phillips, S., Glasgow, R. E., & Johnson, S. M., (1983). Parental characteristics and interactional dysfunction in families with child behavior problems: A preliminary investigation. *Journal of Abnormal Child Psychology, 11,* 153–166.

Campos, J. J., Barrett, K., Lamb, M., Goldsmith, H., & Stenberg, C. (1983). Socioemotional development. In M. Haith & J. Campos (Eds.), *Handbook of child psychology* (4th ed.): *Vol. 2. Infancy and developmental psychobiology.* New York: Wiley.

Ciminero, A. R., & Drabman, R. S. (1977). Current developments in the behavioral assessment of children. In B. B. Lahey & A. E. Kazdin (Eds.), *Advances in clinical child psychology* (Vol. 1, pp. 47–82). New York: Plenum.

Clevanger, T., & King, T. R. (1961). A factor analysis of the visible symptoms of stage fright. *Speech Monographs, 28,* 296–298.

Cohen, A. S., Barlow, D. H., & Blanchard, E. B. (1985). The psychophysiology of relaxation-associated panic attacks. *Journal of Abnormal Psychology, 94,* 96–101.

Cone, J. D. (1979). Confounded comparisons in triple response mode assessment research. *Behavior Assessment, 1,* 85–95.

Cone, J. D. (1981). Psychometric considerations, In M. Hersen & A. S. Bellack (Eds.), *Behavioral assessment: A practical handbook* (2nd ed., pp. 38–70). New York: Pergamon Press.

Cook, T. D., & Campbell, D. T. (Eds.), (1979). *Quasi-experimentation: Design and analysis issues for field settings.* Chicago: Rand McNally.

Cradock, C., Cotler, S., & Jason, L. A. (1978). Primary prevention: Immunization of children for speech anxiety. *Cognitive Therapy and Research, 2,* 389–396.

Crider, B. (1949). Phobias: Their nature and treatment. *Journal of Psychology, 27,* 217–229.

Croake, J. W., & Knox, F. H. (1973). The changing nature of children's fears. *Child Study Journal, 3,* 91–105.

Cronbach, L. J., & Meehl, P. E. (1955). Construct validity in psychological tests. *Psychological Bulletin, 52,* 291–302.

Cummings, J. D. (1944). The incidence of emotional symptoms in school children. *British Journal of Educational Psychology, 14,* 151–161.

Cummings, J. D. (1946). A follow-up study of emotional symptoms in school children. *British Journal of Educational Psychology, 16,* 163–177.

Dahlstrom, W. G., Welsh, G. S., & Dahlstrom, L. E. (1972). *An MMPI handbook.* Minneapolis: University of Minnesota Press.

Danaher, B., & Thoresen, C. (1972). Imagery assessment by self-report and behaviour measures. *Behaviour Research and Therapy, 10,* 131–138.

Davis, A. F., Rosenthal, T. L., & Kelley, J. E. (1981). Actual fear cues, prompt therapy, and rationale enhance participant modeling with adolescents. *Behavior Therapy, 12,* 536–542.

Davison, G. C., Robins, C., & Johnson, M. K. (1983). Articulated thoughts during simulated situations: A paradigm for studying cognition in emotion and behavior. *Cognitive Therapy and Research, 7,* 17–40.

DeFee, J. F., Jr., & Himmelstein, P. (1969). Children's fear in a dental situation of birth order. *Journal of Genetic Psychology, 115,* 253–255.

Delprato, D. J. (1980). Hereditary determinants of fears

and phobias: A critical review. *Behavior Therapy, 11,* 79–103.

Delprato, D. J., & McGlynn, F. D. (1984). Behavioral theories of anxiety disorders. In S. M. Turner (Ed.), *Behavioral treatment of anxiety disorders* (pp. 63–122). New York: Plenum.

Dollinger, S. J., O'Donnell, J. P., & Staley, A. A. (1984). Lightning-strike disaster: Effects on children's fears and worries. *Journal of Consulting and Clinical Psychology, 52,* 1028–1038.

Doris, J., McIntyre, A., Kelsey, C., & Lehman, E. (1971). Separation anxiety in nursery school children. *Proceedings of the 79th Annual Convention of the American Psychological Association, 79,* 145–146. (Summary)

Dorkey, M., & Amen, E. W. (1947). A continuation study of anxiety reactions in young children by means of a projective technique. *Genetic Psychology Monographs, 35,* 139–183.

Dunlop, G. (1952). *Certain aspects of children's fears.* Unpublished master's thesis, University of North Carolina–Raleigh.

Eisenberg, L. (1958). School phobia: A study in the communication of anxiety. *American Journal of Psychiatry, 114,* 712–718.

Eme, R., & Schmidt, D. (1978). The stability of children's fears. *Child Development, 49,* 1277–1279.

Esveldt-Dawson, K., Wisner, K. L., Unis, A. S., Matson, J. L., & Kazdin, A. E. (1982). Treatment of phobias in a hospitalized child. *Journal of Behavior Therapy and Experimental Psychiatry, 11,* 77–83.

Evans, I. M. (1985). Building systems models as a strategy for target behavior selection in clinical assessment. *Behavioral Assessment, 7,* 21–32.

Evans, I. M., & Nelson, R. O. (1977). Assessment of child behavior problems. In A. R. Ciminero, K. S. Calhoun, & H. E. Adams (Eds.), *Handbook of behavioral assessment* (pp. 603–682). New York: Wiley.

Evans, P. D., & Harmon, G. (1981). Children's self-initiated approach to spiders. *Behaviour Research and Therapy, 19,* 543–546.

Faust, J., & Melamed, B. G. (1984). Influence of arousal, previous experience, and age on surgery preparation of same day of surgery and in-hospital pediatric patients. *Journal of Consulting and Clinical Psychology, 52,* 359–365.

Fehr, F. S. (1970). A simple method for assessing body movement and potential artifacts in the physiological recording of young children. *Psychophysiology, 7,* 787–789.

Foa, E. B., & Kozak, M. J. (1986). Emotional processing of fear: Exposure to corrective information. *Psychological Bulletin, 99,* 20–35.

Forehand, R., Wells, K. C., McMahon, R. J., Griest, D. L., & Rogers, T. (1982). Maternal perception of maladjustment in clinic-referred children: An extension of earlier research. *Journal of Behavioral Assessment, 4,* 145–151.

Foster, S. L., & Cone, J. D. (1980). Current issues in direct observation. *Behavioral Assessment, 2,* 313–338.

Fox, J. E., & Houston, B. K. (1981). Efficacy of self-instructional training for reducing children's anxiety in evaluation situations. *Behaviour Research and Therapy, 19,* 509–515.

Fox, J. E., & Houston, B. K. (1983). Distinguishing between cognitive and sometic trait and state anxiety in children. *Journal of Personality and Social Psychology, 45,* 862–870.

Fredrikson, M., & Ohman, A. (1979). Cardiovascular and electrodermal responses conditioned to fear-relevant stimuli. *Psychophysiology, 16,* 1–7.

Freeman, B. J., Roy, R. R., & Hemmick, S. (1976). Extinction of a phobia of physical examination in a seven-year old mentally retarded boy—a case study. *Behaviour Research and Therapy, 14,* 63–64.

Freud, S. (1955). Analysis of a phobia in a five-year-old boy. In J. Strachey (Ed. and Trans.), *Standard edition of the complete psychological works of Sigmund Freud* (Vol. 10, pp. 3–149). London: Hogarth Press. (Original work published 1909)

Gambrill, E. D. (1977). *Behavior modification: Handbook of assessment, intervention, and evaluation.* San Francisco: Jossey-Bass.

Gelfand, D. M. (1978). Behavioral treatment of avoidance, social withdrawal and negative emotional states. In B. B. Wolman, J. Egan, & A. O. Ross (Eds.), *Handbook of treatment of mental disorders in childhood and adolescence.* Englewood Cliffs, NJ: Prentice-Hall.

Ghose, L. J., Giddon, D. B., Shiere, F. R., & Fogels, H. R. (1969). Evaluation of sibling support. *Journal of Dentistry for Children, 36,* 35–40.

Giebenhain, J. E. (1985). *Multi-channel assessment of children's fear of the dark.* Unpublished doctoral dissertation, University of Mississippi.

Giebenhain, J. E., & O'Dell, S. L. (1984). Evaluation of a parent-training manual for reducing children's fear of the dark. *Journal of Applied Behavior Analysis, 17,* 121–125.

Gilbert, B. O., Johnson, S. B., Spillar, R., McCallum, M., Silverstein, J. H., & Rosenbloom, A. (1982). The effects of a peer-modeling film on children learning to self-inject insulin. *Behavior Therapy, 13,* 186–193.

Glennon, B., & Wiesz, J. R. (1978). An observational approach to the assessment of anxiety in young children. *Journal of Consulting and Clinical Psychology, 46,* 1246–1257.

Graham, P. (1964). *Controlled trial of behavior therapy versus conventional therapy: A pilot study.* Unpublished doctoral dissertation, University of London.

Graziano, A. M., & DeGiovanni, I. S. (1979). The clinical significance of childhood phobias: A note on the proportion of child-clinical referrals for the treatment of children's fears. *Behaviour Research and Therapy, 17,* 161–162.

Graziano, A. M., DeGiovanni, I. S., & Garcia, K. A. (1979). Behavioral treatment of children's fears: A review. *Psychological Bulletin, 86,* 804–830.

Graziano, A. M., & Mooney, K. C. (1980). Family self-control instruction for children's nighttime fear reduction. *Journal of Consulting and Clinical Psychology, 48,* 206–213.

Graziano, A. M., Mooney, K. C., Huber, C., & Ignasiak, D. (1979). Self-control instructions for children's fear-reduction. *Journal of Behavior Therapy and Experimental Psychiatry, 10,* 221–227.

Hagman, E. R. (1932). A study of fears of children of pre-school age. *Journal of Experimental Education, 1,* 110–130.

Hall, T. W. (1967). *Some effects of anxiety on the fantasy play of school children.* Unpublished doctoral dissertation, Yale University.

Hampe, E., Noble, H., Miller, L. C., & Barrett, C. L. (1973). Phobic children one and two years posttreatment. *Journal of Abnormal Psychology, 82,* 446–453.

Harris, B. (1979). Whatever happened to Little Albert? *American Psychologist, 34,* 151–160.

Harris, F. C., & Lahey, B. B. (1982a). Recording system bias in direct observational methodology: A review and critical analysis of factors causing inaccurate coding behavior. *Clinical Psychology Review, 2,* 539–556.

Harris, F. C., & Lahey, B. B. (1982b). Subject reactivity in direct observational assessment: A review and critical analysis. *Clinical Psychology Review, 2,* 523–538.

Hartmann, D. P., Roper, B. L., & Bradford, D. C. (1979). Some relationships between behavioral and traditional assessment. *Journal of Behavioral Assessment, 1,* 3–21.

Hartmann, D. P., & Wood, D. D. (1982). Observational methods. In A. S. Bellack, M. Hersen, & A. E. Kazdin (Eds.), *International handbook of behavior modification and therapy* (pp. 109–138). New York: Plenum Press.

Hatzenbuehler, L. C., & Schroeder, H. E. (1978). Desensitization procedures in the treatment of childhood disorders. *Psychological Bulletin, 85,* 831–844.

Hawley, B. P., McCorkle, A. D., Witteman, J. K., & Van Ostenberg, P. (1974). The first dental visit for children from low socioeconomic families. *Journal of Dentistry for Children, 41,* 376–381.

Haynes, S. N., & Horn, W. F. (1982). Reactivity in behavior observation: A review. *Behavioral Assessment, 4,* 369–385.

Hebb, D. O. (1946). On the nature of fear. *Psychological Review, 53,* 259–276.

Herbett, R. M., & Innes, J. M. (1979). Familiarization and preparatory information in the reduction of anxiety in child dental patients. *Journal of Dentistry for Children, 46,* 319–323.

Hermecz, D. A., & Melamed, B. G. (1984). The assessment of emotional imagery training in fearful children. *Behavior Therapy, 15,* 156–172.

Hill, J. H., Liebert, R. M., & Mott, D. E. W. (1968). Vicarious extinction of avoidance behavior through films: An initial test. *Psychological Reports, 22,* 192.

Himadi, W. G., Boice, R., & Barlow, D. H. (1985). *Assessment of agoraphobia: Measurement of clinical change.* Unpublished manuscript, Center for Stress and Anxiety Disorders, Albany, NY.

Hodgson, R., & Rachman, S. (1974). Desynchrony in measures of fear: II. *Behaviour Research and Therapy, 12,* 319–326.

Holden, A. E., Jr., & Barlow, D. H. (1986). Heart rate and heart rate variability recorded *in vivo* in agoraphobics and nonphobics. *Behavior Therapy, 17,* 26–42.

Hollon, S. D., & Bemis, K. M. (1981). Self-report and the assessment of cognitive functions. In M. Hersen & A. S. Bellack (Eds.), *Behavioral assessment: A practical handbook* (2nd ed., pp. 125–174). New York: Pergamon Press.

Holmes, F. B. (1935). An experimental study of the fears of young children. In A. T. Jersild & F. B. Holmes (Eds.), *Children's fears* (Child Development Monograph N. 20), pp. 167–296. New York: Columbia University Press.

Houston, B. K., Fox, J. E., & Forbes, L. (1984). Trait anxiety and children's state anxiety, cognitive behaviors, and performance under stresss, *Cognitive Therapy and Research, 8,* 631–641.

Hugdahl, K. (1981). The three-system model of fear and emotion: A critical examination. *Behaviour Research and Therapy, 19,* 75–85.

Hugdahl, K., Fredrikson, M., & Öhman, A. (1977). "Preparedness" and "arousability" as determinants of electrodermal conditioning. *Behaviour Research and Therapy, 15,* 345–353.

Inhelder, B., & Piaget, J. (1964). *The early growth of logic in the child.* New York: Harper & Row.

Izard, C. E., Dagan, J., & Zajonc, R. B. (1984). Introduction. In C. E. Izard, J. Kagan, & R. B. Zajonc (Eds.), *Emotions, cognitions, and behavior* (pp. 1–14). New York: Cambridge University Press.

Jackson, H. J., & King, N. J. (1981). The emotive imagery treatment of a child's trauma-induced phobia. *Journal of Behaviour Therapy and Experimental Psychiatry, 12,* 325–328.

Jacobs, W. J., & Nadel, L. (1985). Stress-induced recovery of fears and phobias. *Psychological Review, 92,* 512–531.

Jay, S. M., & Elliott, C. (1984). Behavioral observation scales for measuring children's distress: The effects of increased methodological rigor. *Journal of Consulting and Clinical Psychology, 52,* 1106–1107.

Jay, S. M., Ozolins, M., Elliott, C., & Caldwell, S. (1983). Assessment of children's distress during painful medical procedures. *Journal of Health Psychology, 2,* 133–147.

Jersild, A. T. (1954). Emotional development. In L. Carmichael (Ed.), *Manual of child psychology* (2nd ed., pp. 833–917). New York: Wiley.

Jersild, A. T., & Holmes, F. (Eds.). (1935). *Children's fears* (Child Development Monograph No. 20). New York: Columbia University Press.

Johnson, L. C., & Lubin, A. (1972). On planning psychophysiological experiments: Design, measurement, and analysis. In N. S. Greenfield & R. A. Sternbach (Eds.), *Handbook of psychophysiology* (pp. 125–158). New York: Holt. Rinehart & Winston.

Johnson, R., & Baldwin, D. C., Jr. (1968). Relationship of maternal anxiety to the behavior of young children undergoing dental extraction. *Journal of Dental Research, 47,* 801–805.

Johnson, R., & Baldwin, D. C., Jr. (1969). Maternal anxiety and child behavior. *Journal of Dentistry for Children, 36,* 87–92.

Johnson, R., & Dabbs, J. M. (1967). Enumeration of active sweat glands: A simple physiological indicator of psychological changes. *Nursing Research, 16,* 273–276.

Johnson, S. B., & Melamed, B. G. (1979). The assessment and treatment of children's fears. In B. B. Lahey & A. E. Kazdin (Eds.), *Advances in clinical child psychology* (Vol. 2, pp. 107–139). New York: Plenum Press.

Johnson, T., Tyler, V., Thompson, R., & Jones, E. (1971). Systematic desensitization and assertive training in the treatment of speech anxiety in middle-school students. *Psychology in the Schools, 8,* 263–267.

Jones, H. E., & Jones, M. C. (1928). Fear. *Childhood Education, 5,* 136–143.

Jones, M. C. (1924). A laboratory study of fear: The case of Peter. *Pedagogical Seminar, 31,* 308–315.

Kandel, H. J., Ayllon, T., & Rosenbaum, M. S. (1977). Flooding or systematic exposure in the treatment of extreme social withdrawal in children. *Journal of Behavior Therapy and Experimental Psychiatry, 8,* 75–81.

Kanfer, F. H. (1985). Target selection for clinical change programs. *Behavioral Assessment, 7,* 7–20.

Kanfer, F. H., Karoly, P., & Newman, A. (1975). Reduction of children's fear of the dark by confidence-related and situational threat-related verbal cues. *Journal of Consulting and Clinical Psychology, 43,* 251–258.

Kanfer, F. H., & Nay, W. R. (1982). Behavioral assessment. In G. T. Wilson & C. M. Franks (Eds.), *Contemporary behavior therapy: Conceptual and empirical foundations* (pp. 367–402). New York: Guilford Press.

Kanfer, F. H., & Phillips, J. S. (1970). *Learning foundations of behavior therapy.* New York: Wiley.

Kanfer, F. H., & Saslow, G. (1969). Behavioral diagnosis. In C. M. Franks (Ed.), *Behavior therapy: appraisal and status* (pp. 417–444). New York: McGraw-Hill.

Kanner, L. (1957). *Child psychiatry.* Springfield, IL: Charles C Thomas.

Kanner, L. (1960). Do behavior symptoms always indicate psychopathology? *Journal of Child Psychology and Psychiatry, 1,* 17–25.

Karoly, P. (1975). Operant methods. In F. H. Kanfer & A. P. Goldstein (Eds.), *Helping people change* (pp. 195–228. New York: Pergamon Press.

Katz, E. R., Kellerman, J., & Siegel, S. E. (1980). Behavioral distress in children with cancer undergoing medical procedures: Developmental considerations. *Journal of Consulting and Clinical Psychology, 48,* 356–365.

Kazdin, A. E. (1977). Assessing the clinical or applied importance of behavior change through social validation. *Behavior Modification, 1,* 427–452.

Kazdin, A. E. (1981). Behavioral observation. In M. Hersen & A. S. Bellack (Eds.), *Behavioral assessment: A practical handbook* (2nd ed., pp. 101–124). New York: Pergamon Press.

Kelley, C. K. (1976). Play desensitization of fear of darkness in preschool children. *Behaviour Research and Therapy, 14,* 79–81.

Kennedy, W. A. (1965). School phobia: Rapid treatment of fifty cases. *Journal of Abnormal Psychology, 70,* 285–289.

Kent, R. N., & Foster, S. L. (1977). Direct observational procedures: Methodological issues in naturalistic settings. In A. R. Ciminero, K. S. Calhoun, & H. E. Adams (Eds.), *Handbook of behavioral assessment* (pp. 279–328). New York: Wiley.

Kirkpatrick, D. R. (1984). Age, gender and patterns of common intense fears among adults. *Behaviour Research and Therapy, 22,* 141–150.

Klingman, A., Melamed, B. G., Cuthbert, M. I., & Hermecz, D. A. (1984). Effects of participant modeling on information acquisition and skill utilization. *Journal of Consulting and Clinical Psychology, 52,* 414–422.

Klingman, A., & Rosenbaum, H. (1981). *Children's Self-Control Scale.* Unpublished manuscript.

Klinnert, M. D., Campos, J. J., Sorce, J. F., Emde, R. N., & Svegda, M. (9183). Emotions as behavior regulators: Social referencing in infancy. In R. Plutchik & H. Kellerman (Eds.), *Emotion: Theory, research, and experience* (Vol. 2, pp. 57–86). New York: Academic Press.

Klorman, R., Michael, R., Hilpert, P. L., & Sveen, O. B. (1979). A further assessment of predictors of child behavior in dental treatment. *Journal of Dental Research, 58,* 2338–2343.

Klorman, R., Ratner, J., Arata, C. L., King, J. B., & Sveen, O. B. (1978). Predicting the child's uncooperativeness in dental treatment from maternal trait, state, and dental anxiety. *Journal of Dentistry for Children, 45,* 62–67.

Klorman, R., Ratner, J., King, J., Jr., & Sveen, O. (1978).

Pedodontic patients' uncooperativeness and maternal anxiety. *Journal of Dental Research, 56,* 432.

Kornhaber, R. C., & Schroeder, H. E. (1975). Importance of model similarity on extinction of avoidance behavior in children. *Journal of Consulting and Clinical Psychology, 43,* 601–607.

Kozak, M. J., & Miller, G. A. (1982). Hypothetical constructs vs. intervening variables: A re-appraisal of the three-systems model of anxiety assessment. *Behavioral Assessment, 4,* 347–358.

Kuroda, J. (1969). Elimination of children's fears of animals by the method of experimental desensitization: An application of learning theory to child psychology. *Psychologia: An International Journal of Psychology in the Orient, 12,* 161–165.

Lacey, J. I. (1956). The evaluation of autonomic responses: Toward a general solution. *Annals of the New York Academy of Sciences, 67,* 123–164.

Lacey, J. I., & Lacey, B. C. (1967). The law of initial value in the longitudinal study of autonomic constitution: Reproducibility of autonomic responses and response patterns over a four year interval. *Annals of the New York Academy of Sciences, 38,* 1257–1290.

Lader, M. H., & Mathews, A. M. (1968). A physiological model of phobic anxiety and desenitization. *Behaviour Research and Therapy, 6,* 411–421.

LaGreca, A. M., & Santogrossi, D. A. (1980). Social skills training with elementary school students: A behavioral group approach. *Journal of Consulting and Clinical Psychology, 48,* 220–227.

Lang, P. J. (1968). Fear reduction and fear behavior: Problems in treating a construct. In J. M. Shlien (Eds.), *Research in psychotherapy* (Vol. 3, pp. 90–103). Washington, DC: American Psychological Association.

Lang, P. J. (1971). The application of psychophysiological methods to the study of psychotherapy and behavior modification. In A. E. Bergin & S. L. Garfield (Eds.), *Handbook of psychotherapy and behavior change* (pp. 75–125). New York: Wiley.

Lang, P. J. (1977). Fear imagery: An information processing analysis. *Behavior Therapy, 8,* 862–886.

Lang, P. J. (1979). A bio-informational theory of emotional imagery. *Psychophysiology, 16,* 495–512.

Lang, P. J. (1984). Cognition in emotion: Concept and action. In C. E. Izard, J. Kagan, & R. B. Zajonc (Eds.), *Emotions, cognition, and behavior* (pp. 192–226). New York: Cambridge University Press.

Lang, P. J. (1985). The cognitive psychophysiology of emotion: Fear and anxiety. In A. H. Tuma & J. D. Maser (Eds.), *Anxiety and the anxiety disorders.* Hillsdale, NJ: Erlbaum.

Lang, P. J., & Lazovik, A. D. (1963). Experimental desensitization of a phobia. *Journal of Abnormal and Social Psychology, 66,* 519–525.

Lang, P. J., Levin, D. N., Miller, G. A., & Kozak, M. J. (1983). Fear behavior, fear imagery, and the psychophysiology of emotion: The problem of affective response integration. *Journal of Abnormal Psychology, 92,* 276–306.

Lang, P. J., Rice, D. G., & Sternbach, R. A. (1972). The psychophysiology of emotion. In N. Greenfield & R. A. Sternbach (Eds.), *Handbook of psychophysiology* (pp. 623–644). New York: Holt, Rinehart & Winston.

Lapouse, R., & Monk, M. A. (1959). Fears and worries in a representative sample of children. *American Journal of Orthopsychiatry, 29,* 223–248.

Lazarus, A. A., & Abramovitz, A. (1962). The use of emotive imagery in the treatment of children's phobias. *Journal of Mental Science, 108,* 191–195.

LeBaron, S., & Zeltzer, L. (1984). Assessment of acute pain and anxiety in children and adolescents by self-reports, observer reports, and a behavior checklist. *Journal of Consulting and Clinical Psychology, 52,* 729–738.

Leitenberg, H., & Callahan, E. J. (1973). Reinforced practice and education of different kinds of fears in adults and children. *Behaviour Research and Therapy, 11,* 19–30.

Lewinsohn, P. M., & Lee, W. M. L. (1981). Assessment of affective disorders. In D. H. Barlow (Ed.), *Behavioral assessment of adult disorders* (pp. 129–179). New York: Guilford Press.

Lewis, M., & Michalson, L. (1983). *Children's emotions and moods: Developmental theory and measurement.* New York: Plenum Press.

Lewis, S. (1974). A comparison of behavior therapy techniques in the reduction of fearful avoidant behavior. *Behavior Therapy, 5,* 648–655.

Lewis, T. M., & Law, D. B. (1958). Investigation of certain autonomic responses of children to a specific dental stress. *Journal of the American Dental Association, 57,* 769–777.

Lick, J. R., & Katkin, E. S. (1976). Assessment of anxiety and fear. In M. Hersen & A. S. Bellack (Eds.), *Behavioral assessment: A practical handbook* (pp. 175–206). New York: Pergamon Press.

Lick, J. R., & Unger, T. E. (1975). External validity of laboratory fear assessment: Implications from two case studies. *Journal of Consulting and Clinical Psychology, 43,* 864–866.

Lick, J. R., & Unger, T. E. (1977). The external validity of behavioral fear assessment. *Behavior Modification, 1,* 283–306.

Lick, J. R., Unger, T. E., & Condiotte, M. (1978). Effects of uncertainty about the behavior of a phobic stimulus on subjects' fear reactions. *Journal of Consulting and Clinical Psychology, 46,* 1559–1560.

Linehan, M. M. (1980). Content validity: Its relevance to behavioral assessment. *Behavioral Assessment, 2,* 147–159.

Lobitz, G. K., & Johnson, S. M. (1975). Normal versus deviant children: A multimethod comparison. *Journal of Abnormal Child Psychology, 3,* 353–374.

Luiselli, J. K. (1978). Treatment of an autistic child's fear of riding a school bus through exposure and reinforcement. *Journal of Behavior Therapy and Experimetnal Psychiatry, 9,* 169–172.

MacFarlane, J., Allen, L., & Honzik, M. (1954). *A developmental study of the behavior problems of normal children between twenty-one months and fourteen years.* Berkeley: University of California Press.

Mandler, G., Mandler, J. M., & Uviller, E. T. (1958). Autonomic feedback: The perception of autonomic activity. *Journal of Abnormal and Social Psychology, 56,* 367–373.

Marks, D. F. (1973). Visual imagery differences in the recall of pictures. *British Journal of Psychology, 64,* 17–24.

Marks, I. M. (1969). *Fears and phobias.* New York: Academic Press.

Marks, I. M. (1977). Phobias and obsessions: Clinical phenomena in search of laboratory models. In J. D. Maser & M. E. P. Seligman (Eds.), *Psychopathology: Experimental methods* (pp. 174–213). San Francisco: W. H. Freeman.

Marks, I. M., & Gelder, M. G. (1966). Different onset ages in varieties of phobia. *American Journal of Psychiatry, 123,* 218–221.

Martin, I., & Venables, P. H. (Eds.). (1980). *Techniques in psychophysiology.* New York: Wiley.

Mash, E. J. (1985). Some comments on target selection in behavior therapy. *Behavioral Assessment, 7,* 63–78.

Mash, E. J., & Terdal, L. G. (1976). Behavior therapy assessment: Diagnosis, design and evaluation. In E. J. Mash & L. G. Terdal (Eds.), *Behavior therapy assessment* (pp. 15–32). New York: Springer.

Matson, J. L. (1981). Assessment and treatment of clinical fears in mentally retarded children. *Journal of Applied Behavior Analysis, 14,* 287–294.

Maurer, A. (1965). What children fear. *Journal of Genetic Psychology, 106,* 265–277.

McMahon, R. J., Forehand, R., Griest, D. L., & Wells, K. C. (1981). Who drops put of treatment during behavioral training? *Behavioral Counseling Quarterly, 1,* 79–85.

Meehl, P. E., & Rosen, A. (1955). Antecedent probability and the efficency of psychometric signs, patterns or cutting scores. *Psychological Bulletin, 52,* 194–216.

Melamed, B. G., Dearborn, M., & Hermecz, D. A. (1983). Necessary considerations for surgery prepartion: Age and previous experience. *Psychosomatic Medicine, 45,* 517–525.

Melamed, B. G., Hawes, R. R., Heiby, E., & Glick, J. (1975). Use of filmed modeling to reduce uncooperative behavior of children during dental treatment. *Journal of Dental Research, 54,* 757–801.

Melamed, B. G., Klingman, A., & Siegel, L. J. (1984). Childhood stress and anxiety: Individualizing cognitive behavioral strategies in the reduction of medical and dental stress. In A. W. Meyers & W. E. Craighead (Eds.), *Cognitive behavior therapy with children* (pp. 289–314). New York: Plenum Press.

Melamed, B. G., & Siegel, L. J. (1975). Reduction of anxiety in children facing hospitalization and surgery by use of filmed modeling. *Journal of Consulting and Clinical Psychology, 43,* 511–521.

Melamed, B. G., & Siegel, L. J. (1980). *Behavioral medicine.* New York: Springer.

Melamed, B. G., Weinstein, D., Hawes, R., & Katin-Borland, M. (1975). Reduction of fear-related dental management using filmed modeling. *Journal of the American Dental Association, 90,* 822–826.

Melamed, B. G., Yurcheson, R., Fleece, E. L., Hutcherson, S., & Hawes, R. (1978). Effects of film modeling on the reduction of anxiety-related behaviors in individuals varying in level or previous experience in the stress situation. *Journal of Consulting and Clinical Psychology, 46,* 1357–1367.

Melton, G. B. (1978). Children's rights to treatment. *Journal of Clinical Child Psychology, 7,* 200–202.

Melton, G. B. (1981). Children's participation in treatment planning: Psychological and legal issues. *Professional Psychology, 12,* 246–252.

Merluzzi, T. V., Glass, C. R., & Genest, M. (Eds.), (1981). *Cognitive assessment.* New York: Guilford Press.

Miller, L. C., Barrett, C. L., & Hampe, E. (1974). Phobias of childhood in a prescientific era. In S. Davids (Ed.), *Child personality and psychopathology* (pp. 89–134), New York: Wiley.

Miller, L. C., Barrett, C. L., Hampe, E., & Noble, H.

(1972). Factor structure of childhood fears. *Journal of Consulting and Clinical Psychology, 39,* 264–268.

Miller, P. M. (1972). The use of visual imagery and muscle relaxation in the counterconditioning of a phobic child: A case study. *Journal of Nervous and Mental Disease, 154,* 457–460.

Milos, M. E., & Reiss, S. (1982). Effects of three play conditions on separation anxiety in young children. *Journal of Consulting and Clinical Psychology, 50,* 389–395.

Montague, J. D., & Coles, E. M. (1966). Mechanism and measurement of the galvanic skin response. *Psychological Bulletin, 65,* 261–279.

Morgan, G. A. V. (1959). Children who refuse to go to school. *Medical Officer, 102,* 221–224.

Mooney, K. C. (1985). Children's nighttime fears: Ratings of content and coping behaviors. *Cognitive Therapy and Research, 9,* 309–319.

Morris, R. J., & Kratochwill, T. R. (1983a). Childhood fears and phobias. In R. J. Morris & T. R. Kratochwill (Eds.), *The practice of child therapy* (pp. 53–85). New York: Pergamon Press.

Morris, R. J., & Kratochwill, T. R. (1983b). *Treating children's fears and phobias: A behavioral approach.* New York: Pergamon Press.

Murphy, C. M., & Bootzin, R. R. (1973). Active and passive participation in the contact desensitization of snake fear in children. *Behavior Therapy, 4,* 203–211.

Nawas, M. M. (1971). Standarized scheduled desensitization: Some unstable results and an improved program. *Behaviour Research and Therapy, 9,* 35–38.

Neisworth, J. T., Madle, R. A., & Goeke, D. E. (1975). "Errorless" elimination of separation anxiety: A case study. *Journal of Behavior Therapy and Experimental Psychiatry, 6,* 79–82.

Nietzel, M. T., & Bernstein, D. A. (1981). Assessment of anxiety and fear, In M. Hersen & A. S. Bellack (Eds.), *Behavioral assessment: A practical handbook* (2nd ed., pp. 215–245). New York: Pergamon Press.

Nelson, R. O., & Barlow, D. H. (1981). Behavioral assessment: Basic strategies and initial procedures, In D. H. Barlow (Ed.), *Behavioral assessment of adult disorders* (pp. 13–43). New York: Guilford Press.

Nelson, R. O., & Hayes, S. C. (1979). The nature of behavioral assessment: A commentary. *Journal of Applied Behavior Analysis, 12,* 491–500.

Nelson, R. O., & Hayes, S. C. (1981). Nature of behavioral assessment. In M. Hersen & A. S. Bellack (Eds.), *Behavioral assessment: A practical handbook* (2nd ed., pp. 3–37). New York: Pergamon Press.

Nunnally, J. (1978). *Psychometric theory* (2nd ed.). New York: McGraw-Hill.

O'Connor, R. D. (1969). Modification of social withdrawal through symbolic modeling. *Journal of Applied Behavior Analysis, 2,* 15–22.

O'Dell, S. L. (1982). Enhancing parent involvement in training: A discussion. *the Behavior Therapist, 5,* 9–13.

O'Dell, S. L. (1986). Progress in parent training. In M. Hersen, R. M. Eisler, & P. M. Miller (Eds.), *Progress in behavior modification* (Vol. 17, pp. 57–108). New York: Academic Press.

Öhman, A. (1979). Fear relevance, autonomic conditioning, and phobias: A laboratory model. In P. O. Sjödén, S. Bates, & W. S. Dockens III (Eds.), *Trends in behavior therapy* (pp. 107–133). New York: Academic Press.

Öhman, A., Fredrikson, M., & Hugdahl, K. (1978). Ori-enting and defensive responding in the electrodermal system: Palmar dorsal differences and recovery rate during conditioning to potentially phobic stimuli. *Psychophysiology, 15,* 93–101.

Ollendick, T. H. (1978). *The Fear Survey for Children—Revised.* Unpublished manuscript, Indiana State University.

Ollendick, T. H., (1983). Reliability and validity of the Revised Fear Survey Schedule for Children. *Behaviour Research and Therapy, 21,* 685–692.

Ollendick, T. H. & Gruen, G. E. (1972). Treatment of a bodily injury phobia with implosive therapy. *Journal of Consulting and Clinical Psychology, 38,* 389–393.

Paul, G. L. (1966). *Insight versus desensitization in psychotherapy.* Stanford, CA: Stanford University Press.

Pennebaker, J. W., Gonder-Frederick, L., Stewart, H., Elfman, L., & Skelton, J. A. (1982). Physical symptoms associated with blood pressure. *Psychophysiology, 19,* 201–210.

Peterson, L., Schultheis, K., Ridley-Johnson, R., Miller, D. J., & Tracy, K. (1984). Comparison of three modeling procedures on the presurgical and postsurgical reactions of children. *Behavior Therapy, 15,* 197–203.

Peterson, L., & Shigetomi, C. (1981). The use of coping techniques in minimizing anxiety in hospitalized children. *Behavior Therapy, 12,* 1–14.

Peterson, L., & Toler, S. M. (1984, August). Self-regulated presurgical preparation for children. In B. Stabler (Chair), *Biobehavioral management of illness in children.* Symposium conducted at the meeting of the American Psychological Association, Toronto.

Plutchik, R., & Kellerman, H. (Eds.). (1980). *Emotion: Theory, research, and experience* (Vol. 1). New York: Academic Press.

Plutchik, R., & Kellerman, H. (Eds.). (1983). *Emotion: Theory, research, and experience* (Vol. 2). New York: Academic Press.

Quay, H. C. (1972). Patterns of aggression, withdrawal, and immaturity. In H. C. Quay & J. S. Werry (Eds.), *Psychopathological disorders of childhood* (pp. 1–29). New York: Wiley.

Quay, H. C. (1979). Classification. In H. C. Quay & J. S. Werry (Eds.), *Psychopathological disorders of childhood* (2nd ed., pp. 1–42). New York: Wiley.

Rachman, S. (1968). *Phobias: Their nature and control.* Springfield, IL: Charles C Thomas.

Rachman, S. (1977). The conditioning theory of fear-acquisition: A critical examination. *Behaviour Research and Therapy, 15,* 375–387.

Rachman, S., & Hodgson, R. (1974). Synchrony and desynchrony in fear and avoidance. *Behaviour Research and Therapy, 12,* 311–318.

Radaker, L. D. (1961). The visual imagery of retarded children and the relationship to memory for word forms. *Exceptional Children, 27,* 524–530.

Ray, W. J., & Raczynski, J. M. (1981). Psychophysiological assessment. In M. Hersen & A. S. Bellack (Eds.), *Behavioral assessment: A practical handbook* (2nd ed., pp. 175–211). New York: Pergamon Press.

Rehm, L. P. (1976). Assessment of depression. In M. Hersen & A. S. Bellack (Eds.), *Behavioral assessment: A practical handbook* (pp. 233–260). New York: Pergamon Press.

Rehm, L. P. (1981). Assessment of depression. In M. Hersen & A. S. Bellack (Eds.), *Behavioral assessment: A practical handbook* (2nd ed., pp. 246–295). New York: Pergamon Press.

Reiss, S. (1980). Pavlovian conditioning and human fear:

An expectancy model. *Behavior Therapy, 11,* 380–396.

Reynolds, C. R., & Richmond, B. O. (1978). What I think and feel: A revised measure of children's manifest anxiety. *Journal of Abnormal Child Psychology, 6,* 271–280.

Richards, C. S., & Siegel, L. J. (1978). Behavioral treatment of anxiety states and avoidance behaviors in children. In D. Marholin II (Ed.), *Child behavior therapy* (pp. 274–338). New York: Gardner Press.

Rimm, D. C., & Bottrell, J. (1969). Four measures of visual imagination. *Behaviour Research and Therapy, 7,* 63–69.

Rimm, D. C., & Masters, J. C. (1979). *Behavior therapy: Techniques and empirical findings* (2nd ed.). New York: Academic Press.

Rimon, D. (1980). *Children's assessment of their self-control: Development of a scale.* Unpublished master's thesis, Tel-Aviv University, Israel.

Ritter, B. (1968). The group treatment of children's snake phobias using vicarious and contact densitization procedures. *Behaviour Research and Therapy, 6,* 1–6.

Robins, L. N. (1966). *Deviant children grown up.* Baltimore: Williams & Wilkins.

Rosenbaum, M. (1980). A schedule for assessing self-control behaviors: Preliminary findings. *Behavior Therapy, 11,* 109–121.

Ross, D. M., Ross, S. A., & Evans, T. A. (1971). The modification of extreme social withdrawal by modeling with guided participation. *Journal of Behavior Therapy and Experimental Psychiatry, 2,* 273–279.

Russo, D. C. (Ed.). (1984). Pediatric health psychology [Special issue]. *Clinical Psychology Review, 4,* (5).

Rutter, M., Tizard, J., & Whitmore, K. (1970). *Education, health and behavior.* New York: Wiley.

Ryall, M. R., & Dietiker, K. E. (1979). Reliability and clinical validity of the Children's Fear Survey Schedule. *Journal of Behavior Therapy and Experimental Psychiatry, 19,* 303–310.

Sarason, S. B., Davidson, K. S., Lighthall, F. F., Waite, R. R., & Ruebush, B. K. (1960). *Anxiety and elementary school children.* New York: Wiley.

Sarnat, H., Peri, J. N., Nitzan, E., & Perlberg, A. (1972). Factors which influence cooperation between dentists and child. *Journal of Dental Education, 36,* 9–15.

Sartory, G., Rachman, S., & Grey, S. (1977). An investigation of the relation between reported fear and heart rate. *Behaviour Research and Therapy, 15,* 435–438.

Scherer, M. W., & Nakamura, C. Y. (1968). A fear survey schedule for children (FSS-FC): A factor analytic comparison with manifest anxiety (CMAS). *Behaviour Research and Therapy, 6,* 173–182.

Schermann, A., & Grover, V. M. (1962). Treatment of children's behavior disorders: A method of re-education. *Medical Proceedings, 8,* 151–154.

Seligman, M. E. P. (1971). Phobias and preparedness. *Behavior Therapy, 2,* 307–320.

Seligman, M. E. P., & Johnston, J. C. (1973). A cognitive theory of avoidance learning. In F. J. McGuigan & D. B. Lumsden (Eds.), *Contemporary approaches to conditioning and learning* (pp. 69–110). Washington, DC: V. H. Winston.

Shapiro, A. H. (1975). Behavior of kibbutz and urban children receiving an injection. *Psychophysiology, 12,* 79–82.

Sheslow, D. V., Bondy, A. S., & Nelson, R. O. (1982). A comparison of graduated exposure, verbal coping skills, and their combination on the treatment of chil-

dren's fear of the dark. *Child and Family Behavior Therapy, 4,* 33–45.

Siegel, L. J., & Peterson, L. (1980). Stress reduction in young dental patients through coping skills and sensory information. *Journal of Consulting and Clinical Psychology, 48,* 785–787.

Simpson, W. J., Ruzicka, R. L., & Thomas, N. R. (1974). Physiologic responses of children to initial dental experience. *Journal of Dentistry for Children, 41,* 465–470.

Singer, E. (1965). *Key concepts in psychotherapy.* New York: Random House.

Slater, E. (1939). Responses to a nursery school situation of 40 children. *Monographs of the Society for Research in Child Development, 11* (No. 4).

Smith, R. E., & Sharpe, T. M. (1970). Treatment of a school phobia with implosive therapy. *Journal of Consulting and Clinical Psychology, 35,* 239–243.

Solyom, I., Beck, P., Solyom, C., & Hugel, R. (1974). Some etiological factors in phobic neurosis. *Canadian Psychiatry Association Journal, 19,* 69–78.

Sonnenberg, E., & Venham, L. (1977). Human figure drawing as a measure of the child's response to dental visits. *Journal of Dentistry for Children, 44,* 438–442.

Spielberger, C. D. (1973). *Manual for the State–Trait Anxiety Inventory for Children.* Palo Alto, CA: Consulting Psychologists Press.

Spielberger, C. D., Gorsuch, R. L., & Lushene, R. E. (1970). *Manual for the State–Trait Anxiety Inventory.* Palo Alto, CA: Consulting Psychologists Press.

Stanley, F., & Barrios, B. A. (1984). *Comparison of therapeutic expectancies generated by three treatment rationales.* Unpublished manuscript, University of Mississippi.

Stanley, F., & Barrios, B. A. (1985, March). *A review of expectancy assessment in behavior therapy outcome research.* Paper presented at the meeting of the Southeastern Psychological Association, Atlanta.

Stricker, G., & Howitt, J. W. (1965). Physiological recording during simulated dental appointments. *New York State Dental Journal, 51,* 204–206.

Swan, G. E., & MacDonald, M. L. (1978). Behavior therapy in practice: A national survey of behavior therapists. *Behavior Therapy, 9,* 799–807.

Taylor, C. B. (1983). DSM-III and behavioral assessment. *Behavioral Assessment, 5,* 5–14.

Taylor, J. A. (1953). A personality scale of manifest anxiety. *Journal of Abnormal and Social Psychology, 48,* 285–290.

Thomson, M. L., & Sutarman, M. (1953). The identification and enumeration of active sweat glands in man from plastic impressions of the skin. *Transactions of the Royal Society of Tropical Medicine and Hygiene, 47,* 412–417.

Tobey, T. S., & Thoresen, C. E. (1976). Helping Bill reduce aggressive behaviors: A nine-year old makes good. In J. D. Krumboltz & C. E. Thoresen (Eds.), *Counseling methods* (pp. 163–173). New York: Holt, Rinehart & Winston.

Turner, S. M., & Beidel, D. C. (1985). Empirically derived subtypes of social anxiety. *Behavior Therapy, 16,* 384–392.

Turner, S. M., Beidel, D. C., & Larkin, K. T. (1986). Situational determinants of social anxiety in clinic and non-clinic samples: Physiological and cognitive correlates. *Journal of Consulting and Clinical Psychology, 54,* 523–527.

Ultee, C. A., Griffioen, D., & Schellekens, J. (1982). The

reduction of anxiety in children: A comparison of the effects of systematic desensitization *in vitro* and systematic desensitization *in vivo*. *Behaviour Research and Therapy, 20*, 61–67.

Vaal, J. J. (1973). Applying contingency contracting to a school phobic: A case study. *Journal of Behavior Therapy and Experimental Psychiatry, 4*, 371–373.

Van Hasselt, V. B., Hersen, M., Bellack, A. S., Rosenblum, N. D., & Lamparski, D. (1979). Tripartite assessment of the effects of systematic desensitization in a multi-phobic child: An experimental analysis. *Journal of Behavior Therapy and Experimental Psychiatry, 10*, 51–55.

Varni, J. W. (1983). *Clinical behavioral pediatrics: An interdisciplinary biobehavioral approach*. New York: Pergamon Press.

Venham, L. L., Bengston, D., & Cipes, M. (1977). Children's response to sequential dental visits. *Journal of Dental Research, 56*, 454–459.

Venham, L. L., Gaulin-Kremer, E., Munster, E., Bengston-Audia, D., & Cohan, J. (1980). Interval rating scales for children's dental anxiety and uncooperative behavior. *Pediatric Dentistry, 2*, 195–202.

Venham, L. L., Murray, P., & Gaulin-Kremer, E. (1979). Child-rearing variables affecting the preschool child's response to dental stress. *Journal of Dental Research, 58*, 2042–2045.

Vermilyea, J., Boice, R., & Barlow, D. H. (1984). Rachman and Hodgson (1974) a decade later: How do desynchronous response systems relate to the treatment of agoraphobia? *Behaviour Research and Therapy, 22*, 615–621.

Vernon, D. T. A. (1973). Use of modeling to modify children's responses to a natural, potentially stressful situation. *Journal of Applied Psychology, 58*, 351–356.

Vernon, D. T. A., Foley, J. M., & Schulman, J. L. (1967). Effect of mother–child separation and birth order on young children's responses to two potentially stressful experiences. *Journal of Personality and Social Psychology, 5*, 162–174.

Vernon, D. T. A., Schulman, J. L., & Foley, J. M. (1966). Changes in children's behavior after hospitalization.

American Journal of the Diseases of Children, 3, 581–593.

Wade, T. C., Baker, T. B., & Hartmann, D. P. (1979). Behavior therapists' self-reported views and practices. *the Behavior Therapist, 2*, 3–6.

Wallach, M. A., & Kogan, N. (1965). *Models of thinking in young children*. New York: Holt, Rinehart & Winston.

Watson, J. B., & Rayner, P. (1920). Conditioned emotional reactions. *Journal of Experimental Psychology, 3*, 1–14.

Waye, M. F. (1979). Behavioral treatment of a child displaying comic-book mediated fear of hand shrinking: A case study. *Journal of Pediatric Psychology, 4*, 43–47.

Wilder, J. (1950). The law of initial values. *Psychosomatic Medicine, 12*, 392–401.

Wine, J. D. (1979). Test anxiety and evaluation threat: Children's behavior in the classroom. *Journal of Abnormal Child Psychology, 7*, 45–59.

Winer, G. A. (1982). A review and analysis of children's fearful behavior in dental settings. *Child Development, 53*, 1111–1133.

Wolf, M. (1978). Social validity: The case for subjective measurement or how applied behavior analysis is finding its heart. *Journal of Applied Behavior Analysis, 11*, 203–214.

Wolpe, J., & Rachman, S. (1960). Psychoanalytic "evidence": A critique based on Freud's case of Little Hans. *Journal of Nervous and Mental Disease, 130*, 135–148.

Wright, G. Z., Alpern, G. D., & Leake, J. L. (1973). The modifiability of maternal anxiety as it relates to children's cooperative behavior. *Journal of Dentistry for Children, 40*, 265–271.

Zatz, S., & Chassin, L. (1983). Cognitions of test-anxious children. *Journal of Consulting and Clinical Psychology, 51*, 526–534.

Zatz, S., & Chassin, L. (1985). Cognitions of test-anxious children under naturalistic test-taking conditions. *Journal of Consulting and Clinical Psychology, 53*, 393–401.

PART IV

DEVELOPMENTAL DISORDERS

6 MENTAL RETARDATION

KEITH A. CRNIC
Pennsylvania State University

O f all childhood disorders, perhaps none has received both the clinical and research attention that has been given to mental retardation. There are various reasons why this has been true, not the least of which include the severity and extent of the problem, the relative ease of identification and classification, and the fact that it is of concern to a variety of allied health professions. The study of mental retardation in childhood has been a focus of concern since the early 1800s (Kanner, 1964), and recent evidence suggests that it was the object of scientific attention as early as 1614 (Woolfson, 1984).

Although research and clinical practice in mental retardation has produced rather stable diagnostic and classification systems, children with mental retardation do not constitute a homogeneous group sharing similar cognitive, behavioral, social, and educational characteristics (Knopf, 1979). There are, in fact, wide variations both between and within mentally retarded children, and such variation occurs both within and across classifications. In fact, variability within the population of mentally retarded children is much the same as that within the normal population. It is precisely this variability that makes an idiographic behavioral assessment approach to these children critical for identifying characteristics that may lead to meaningful diagnoses, treatment planning, and treatment evaluations. An idiographic behavioral assessment approach is one that is unique to a specific child within specifically relevant settings measuring individual target behaviors. Mental retardation during childhood is a condition that requires a holistic approach to behavioral assessment across cognitive, affective, behavioral, social, and ecological domains (e.g., family, school, etc.).

This chapter will present a number of the current issues relevant to the disorder and its conceptualization within the context of behavioral assessment strategies. The major focus is intended to be on the necessity of multimodal approaches to behavioral assessment across skill domains as the only meaningful way of identifying the functional parameters of the disorder. Multimodal approaches imply the need to measure behavior in more than an observational capacity, and include standardized testing, interviewing, and questionnaire or rating scale reports as well. Furthermore, measures must go beyond intellectual ability and account for functioning in associated social, affective, and behavioral areas. The explicit focus on functional parameters implies that most important are the behaviors exhibited by the child as they presently occur in context, rather than in respect to the child's potential capabilities. Frequently, assessments of intellectual disorders attempt to draw distinctions between the functional status of a child's development (current abilities as measured) and the level of which the child may be actually capable (potential ability)—a process that is speculative at best. This chapter includes a basic scheme for behavioral assessment of mental retardation conditions in general by denoting specific areas of functioning that should be assessed and methodologies within a behavioral assessment paradigm to accomplish such assessment. While behavioral assessment strategies are clearly individualistic by nature, they are also specifically directed to measurement of the context in which the disorder occurs or operates. For children, the primary developmental context is the family (Bronfenbrenner, 1979), and families of retarded children both influence and are influenced by their retarded children (Crnic, Friedrich, & Greenberg, 1983). As such, this chapter focuses on the ecological contexts relevant to behavioral assessment of mentally retarded children, with a specific emphasis on the family context. This does not imply that other ecological contexts (e.g., schools, vocational settings) are of lesser importance within behavioral assessment strategies; it only suggests that the family is the primary context and the one that is most frequently critical to the assessment process. Complete assessment strategies include all contexts relevant to the issues to be addressed.

DEFINITION

In defining "mental retardation," behavioral objectivity requires that there be a separation between a general definition of "mental retardation" and the use of that diagnosis as applied to any one individual. This differentiation has, in fact, been one of the reasons why defining the condition has had a difficult history. Nevertheless, providing an adequate definition of the disorder serves the important practical purpose of gaining needed services for retarded children (Hobbs, 1975a, 1975b), and therefore cannot be easily abandoned. For example, classroom placements within special education programs are dependent upon clear definitional criteria for mental retardation, as is eligibility for numerous social services provided by governmental and private agencies.

There have been multiple attempts to define mental retardation on the basis of IQ test scores alone (Zigler, Balla, & Hodapp, 1984), social system perspectives (Mercer, 1973), and operant behavioral theory (Bijou, 1966). The most widely accepted definition of mental retardation is that developed by the American Association on Mental Deficiency (AAMD; Grossman, 1973,

1983). Within the AAMD definition, "mental retardation" refers to significantly subaverage general intellectual functioning existing concurrently with deficits in adaptive behavior, and manifested during the developmental period. This definition establishes three important diagnostic criteria:

1. "Significantly subaverage intellectual functioning" refers to performance on standardized psychological tests of intelligence that is more than two standard deviations below the mean (IQ scores of 70 and below).
2. "Adaptive behavior" represents the effectiveness or degree to which the individual meets the standards of personal independence and social skill or responsibility expected of his or her age or cultural group.
3. Finally, the AAMD definition's inclusion of the developmental period indicates that the conditions of cognitive and adaptive impairment must be present between birth and 18 years of age.

It is notable that the 1983 version from the AAMD places less emphasis on adaptive behavior than the 1973 version, reflecting current trends toward more strictly cognitive influences within the disorder.

This AAMD definition, nevertheless, has a number of characteristics that support its relevance for behavioral assessment. First, the retarded child's performance is evaluated in relation to developmentally appropriate tasks, which requires that contexts and expectations be clearly measured for their age-appropriateness. The definition also makes clear that the measure of cognitive functioning should be a description of present behavior rather than a construct involving potential intelligence—a point again related to the necessity of focusing on present functional abilities rather than capability. Finally, the AAMD definition requires specific behavioral measurement of functional abilities across such skill domains as social, behavioral, adaptive, and affective areas, as well as the more common cognitive measurements. The degree to which the three-part AAMD definition of mental retardation has been accepted within the field is exemplified by the fact that the *Diagnostic and Statistical Manual of Mental Disorders,* third edition (DSM-III; American Psychiatric Association, 1980) incorporates the entire definition into its specific diagnostic criteria for this disorder, specifying an IQ value of 70 or below as the criterion for subaverage intellectual functioning.

Although widely accepted, the AAMD definition and its implications are not without critics. Zigler *et al.* (1984) have recently proposed that mental retardation be defined strictly in terms of an IQ score, arguing that few researchers or clinicians actually use measures of adaptive behavior in their work and that definition by cognitive performance alone will allow for more standard classification schemes. This argument does have merit, and is justified by research findings indicating that few investigators actually use each of the AAMD criteria, and that even when these criteria are used as a basis for subject selection some subjects are mislabeled (Cleland, 1979; Taylor, 1980). This, however, is not necessarily sufficient cause to abandon the adaptive and developmental aspects of the definition. Perhaps it makes just as much sense to attempt to insure that multimodal behavioral assessments are accomplished within both research and clinical settings. Clearly, ignoring the role of adaptive and social functioning in determining mental retardation is to ignore perhaps the more salient and measurable behavioral manifestations of the disorder itself.

A specific limitation of the AAMD definition of mental retardation is that it excludes a sizable group of children whose cognitive and adaptive functioning borders on retardation on the one end and low-average performance on the other. These are children whose performance on IQ tests generally falls between 71 and 84, indicating performance more than one but less than two standard deviations below the mean. No specific diagnostic category is associated with this group of children (although they are sometimes referred to as "borderline" functioners), perhaps again due to the variation so apparent in such populations and the subsequent difficulties that this variation presents in attempting definition. Nevertheless, these children have both intellectual and adaptive impairments. The issues and behavioral assessment strategies presented in this chapter are meant to apply equally to this group of children.

CLASSIFICATION

As noted, children with mental retardation compose a heterogeneous group in terms of (1) their functional behavioral abilities and (2) the etiologies for their retardation. Not surprisingly, then, classification systems have been based on these two major factors, involving either the degree to which functional abilities across skill domains are impaired or an identified organic basis for the deficits. Given the disparity and range of abilities and deficits apparent in children who are mentally retarded, classification systems have proved to be most useful in providing an order by which the nature and severity of the disorder can be conceptualized. Furthermore, the rationale for classification of mental retardation is much like the rationale for definition, in that classification serves the important purpose of distinguishing between subgroups for purposes of deciding on the level and intensity of services to be provided.

The AAMD classification system (Grossman, 1973, 1983) currently enjoys the most widespread acceptance. It is based entirely upon the severity of the disability and includes four categories of mental retardation: "mild," "moderate," "severe," and "profound." The basic criterion for category placement according to this system is a score on an individually administered standardized test of intelligence and some assessment of the commensurate adaptive skill of the individual child. Table 1 provides a description of each of these categories by both IQ score and behavioral competency.

Children classified as mildly retarded compose the largest group, accounting for about 80% of children with retardation. These children generally develop communication and social skills early in their development, can achieve some academic success, and can develop vocational skills adequate for some degree of independence and self-support. Moderately retarded children comprise approximately 12% of all retarded children and generally develop adequate communication skills but have poor social awareness. Vocational training is possible with supervision for most moderately retarded persons. Children with severe retardation include about 7% of the population of retarded children. These children have great difficulty developing adequate communicative speech and social skills, and are generally unable to profit from vocational training. Children with profound retardation make up less than 1% of the total retarded population. These children seldom develop functional language ability, and

TABLE 1. Classifications of Mental Retardation by IQ Scores and Behavioral Competencies

Degree of retardation	IQ scores by test standard deviations[a]		Behavioral competencies	
	15	16	Preschool (0–5)	School age (6–18)
Mild	55–69	52–67	Can develop social and communication skills; minimal retardation in sensory–motor area; often not distinguished until later ages.	Can learn academic skills up to sixth grade; can be guided toward social conformity.
Moderate	40–54	36–51	Can talk or learn to communicate; poor social awareness, fair motor skills; profits from self-help skill training; requires some supervision.	Can profit from training in social and occupational skills; unlikely to progress beyond second-grade level; some independence in familiar places possible.
Severe	25–39	20–35	Poor motor development and minimal language skill; generally cannot profit from training in self-help; little communication.	Can learn to talk or communicate; can be trained in elemental self-help skills; profits from systematic habit training.
Profound	Under 25	Under 20	Gross retardation, with minimal capacity for functioning in sensory–motor areas; requires intense care.	Some motor development present; may respond to very limited range of training in self-help.

Source. U.S. Department of Health, Education and Welfare. Reprinted in *Developmental Psychopathology* (2nd ed.) by T. M. Achenbach, 1982.
[a]The major intelligence tests have standard deviations of either 15 points (e.g., Bayley Scales, Stanford–Binet) or 16 points (e.g., the Wechsler scales). With these differences, the IQ scores by category differ correspondingly.

self-help skill acquisition is minimal and difficult to establish.

A related classification system, based on severity as well, is one that is predominantly educational in nature. This includes two main groupings, roughly equivalent to the AAMD categories of mild and moderate retardation. "Educable mentally retarded" (EMR) children are generally defined as having IQs from 50 to 75, and the assumption is made that these children are capable of academic success somewhere between the third- and sixth-grade levels. "Trainable mentally retarded" (TMR) children are defined as having IQs from approximately 30 to 50, and are generally not expected to develop functionally useful academic skills or to proceed beyond second-grade level (Robinson & Robinson, 1976).

Various schemes for classifying retarded children on the basis of the etiology of the disorder have been proposed over the years (Lewis, 1933; J. A. F. Roberts, 1952; Strauss & Werner, 1941). Most recent among these is a proposal by Zigler *et al.* (1984). In line with their call to use cognitive functioning (IQ) as the sole criterion for mental retardation, they have also proposed a simple two-group classification based on etiology: children with known organic impairments, and those who evidence no organic impairment. This approach is based on the assumption that genetic inheritance plays an important role in the determination of intelligence, with perhaps 50–80% of the variance in IQ due to genetic factors. Various models have attempted to account for the variability in the intelligence phenotype (Cronbach, 1975; Gottesman, 1963; Hunt, 1971); Zigler *et al.* argue that the phenotypic expression of intelligence accounts for IQs in the 50–150 range, and that this range represents the normal variation of the intelligence factor created by natural genetic combinations. The majority of children function within this range where the significant determinant of intelligence (and its subsequent behavioral manifestations) is polygenic inheritance. Left to explain the IQs below

50 are primarily organic causes above and beyond the usual polygenic inheritance factors. Furthermore, Zigler *et al.* make the case that the behavioral manifestations of the two groups differ in such a way as to make this classification scheme meaningful. Table 2 presents the distinctions between what Zigler *et al.* classify as "organic" and "familial" retardation. The differences between these diagnostic groups, which include demographic as well as personality, behavior, and motivational factors, may also be a function of a true difference in the structure of intelligence. Weisz, Yeates, and Zigler (1982) have shown differences between the performance of organically and nonorganically retarded children on a variety of Piagetian cognitive tasks, including conservation, role taking, relative thinking, and moral judgment.

Classification is meaningful in the assessment context only insofar as it is often required for delineation of those services that can be delivered within educational or other institutional settings, or as it is specifically relevant to the treatment approaches being considered. Unfortunately, none of the classification systems available is capable of accounting for the heterogeneity of behavioral response that is apparent across and within groups of mentally retarded children.

PREVALENCE

Given the difficulties in gaining common ground for either a definition or classification system for mental retardation, it is not surprising to find that estimates of the prevalence and incidence of this disorder during childhood vary. Generally, figures range from 1% to 3% of the population (Robinson & Robinson, 1976). Most of the estimates that range around 3% use IQ scores as the sole criterion, and these estimates have also been based on statistical normal-curve models. There are several problems with this approach—notably, that adaptive behavior is

TABLE 2. Classifications by Etiology and Their Correlates

	Organic (IQ 0–70)	Familial (IQ 50–70)
Classification principle	Demonstrable organic etiology	No demonstrable organic etiology and parents having this same type of retardation.
Correlates	Found at all SES level	More prevalent at lower SES levels
	IQs most often below 50	IQs rarely below 50
	Siblings usually of normal intelligence	Siblings often at lower levels of intelligence
	Often accompanied by severe health problems	Health within normal range
	Appearance often marred by physical stigmata	Normal appearance
	Mortality rate higher (more likely to die at a younger age than the general population)	Normal mortality rate
	Often dependent on care of others throughout life	With some support can lead an independent existence as adults
	Unlikely to marry and often infertile	Likely to marry and produce children of low intelligence
	Unlikely to experience neglect in their homes	More likely to experience neglect in their homes
	High prevalence of other physical handicaps (e.g., epilepsy, cerebral palsy)	Less likely to have other physical handicaps

Note. From "On the Definition and Classification of Mental Retardation" by E. Zigler, D. Balla, and R. Hodapp, 1984, *American Journal of Mental Deficiency, 89,* 215–230. Copyright 1984 by The American Association on Mental Deficiency. Reprinted by permission.

generally not considered, and that intelligence is not in fact normally distributed. The distribution is actually skewed, with greater numbers than would be predicted statistically at the extreme low end of the continuum, due to specific organic insults (Dingman & Tarjan, 1960). The 3% figure is also somewhat misleading in that it includes only those individuals with IQ scores below 70. As noted earlier, there is a sizable portion of the population with IQ scores between 70 and 85, suggesting that intellectual disorder is in fact more widespread than the 3% figure would indicate. This was considered by the AAMD during the development of the definition and classification system discussed earlier, but was subsequently excluded from consideration, due to ethical concerns about labeling nearly 16% of the population as retarded.

In spite of the difficulties in determining the precise number of children with mental retardation, the prevalence of the disorder is known to vary in relation to a number of factors. Mercer (1973) found that it is less prevalent in younger children than in older school-age or adolescent children (ages 0–4, 0.7%; ages 5–9, 0.54%; ages 10–14, 1.15%; and ages 15–19, 1.61%). It is twice as prevalent in males as in females (Mumpower, 1970). It is more prevalent in minority groups (although this is an issue perhaps related more to bias in testing and educational programs), as black and Hispanic children with IQs below 80 have been found with rates as high as 15.3% and 12.4% respectively, compared to 1.2% of English-speaking Caucasian children (Mercer, 1970). Retardation is also more prevalent in groups with low socioeconomic status (SES) and varies by geographical region, as the prevalence of mental retardation is somewhat higher in the Southern states (these children generally score 6 points lower on IQ tests than do children from other regions; Robinson & Robinson, 1976) and in regions where services for the retarded are scarce (Knopf, 1979). Regardless of the exact prevalence, mental retardation during childhood is strikingly frequent and is of great concern to families and communities alike.

MENTAL RETARDATION AND BEHAVIOR DISORDERS

An issue of some importance for the behavioral assessment of retarded children is the frequency with which these children exhibit associated behavior problems or psychiatric impairments. There has been a fair amount of recent research exploring the presence of behavior disorders in retarded children, and attempts have been made to identify the parameters of these disorders by age, sex, severity, and context. Research generally indicates that retarded children are more likely to exhibit deviant behavior than are children in the general population (Ingalls, 1978; Jacobson, 1982a, 1982b; Koller, Richardson, Katz, & McLaren, 1982; MacMillan, 1977; Rutter, Tizard, & Whitmore, 1970; Sternlicht & Deutsch, 1972).

As with prevalence estimates of mental retardation, there is a good deal of variation in the estimates of the presence of behavioral disturbance in retarded children across studies. One of the major difficulties in these studies is that many of them use populations of clinic-referred children, excluding from consideration all those children who have not been so identified (e.g., Benson, 1985). In a survey of nearly 7,000 retarded persons ranging in age from infancy through adulthood, Eyman and Call (1977) noted the high prevalence of aggressive behavior (28%) and self-injurious behavior (15%) in this population. Other researchers have found that observational ratings of behavior of retarded children on various behavior scales indicate the presence of at least some problem behaviors in 40–50% of the children; variations are often related to placement in community versus residential settings, with greater frequency of behavior problems in those children in residential settings (Bortwick, Meyers, & Eyman, 1981; Hill & Bruininks, 1981; Landesman-Dwyer, Schuckit, Keller, & Brown, 1977).

Separate from behavior problems, but related, is the issue of significant affective or psychiatric dysfunction in mentally retarded children. Like studies of behavior problems, estimates tend to vary from as low as 1.1% (Hill & Bruininks, 1981) to 100% (Webster, 1970), but most studies show rates closer to 30% (e.g., Menalascino, 1970). The disorders that occur generally include psychoses (delusions and disorientation), inappropriate affect, dysphoric mood, lack of interpersonal relatedness, depression, and extremes of inappropriate social behavior. Again, however, these studies have the difficulty of relying predominantly on clinic-referred samples.

Recent studies by Jacobson (1982a, 1982b) provide a more reliable estimate of the occurrence of behavior problems and psychiatric disturbance of children with mental retardation. Jacobson surveyed over 30,000 retarded persons in New York State, more than 8,000 of whom were children. Within this group of retarded children, 9.8% were found to have some significant psychiatric impairment. He further examined the presence of specific behavior problems between groups of children diagnosed as developmentally disabled (DD) and those diagnosed as having both psychiatric problems and developmental disability (PDD). For this behavior survey, 29 behaviors were grouped into four problem categories: (1) "cognitive," including thought disorders and hallucinations or delusions; (2) "affective," including depression and dysphoric affect; (3) "major behavior problems," such as physical aggression or assault, property destruction, coercive sexual behavior, and self-injurious behavior; and (4) "minor behavior problems," including hyperactivity, tantrums, stereotypies, verbal abusiveness, and substance abuse.

Jacobson's findings showed that PDD children had more frequent problem behaviors than DD children across all categories, with the most frequently occurring problems being lack of interpersonal responsiveness (22.3% vs. 9.1%), physical assault upon others (21.5% vs. 8.5%), hyperactivity (21.0% vs. 9.3%), crying and temper tantrums (20.7% vs. 13.8%), and self-injurious behavior (15.3% vs. 7.7%). Nearly all other behaviors for the PDD group had frequencies below 10%, and only crying and temper tantrums were above 10% for the DD group. The behavior problems that were most frequent for the PDD group were also the most frequent for the DD group, the difference involving only the greater frequency and degree to which these problems were seen in the PDD group. This indicates some equivalence between the groups, at least in the types of behavior problems they presented. It was also notable that the presence of more behavior problems was related to age (with fewer problems in younger children), degree of retardation (with fewer problems in the mild and profound categories than the moderate or severe), and

TABLE 3. Percentage of Behavior Problem Types as a Function of Age and Intellectual Level

Age within level of intellectual functioning	n (cases)	Percent without problem behaviors	Behavior type[a]			
			Cognitive	Affective	Major	Minor
Mild mental retardation						
0–12	708	60	11	14	14	61
13–21	818	45	5	26	19	50
22–59	4,024	50	8	35	14	43
60+	641	57	18	32	11	39
Moderate mental retardation						
0–12	640	53	8	19	14	59
13–21	1,163	40	7	22	24	47
22–59	4,866	45	10	27	20	44
60+	632	56	13	32	13	58
Severe mental retardation						
0–12	652	46	5	15	17	63
13–21	1,208	35	6	14	30	50
22–59	4,754	36	8	20	26	44
60+	841	42	12	29	19	40
Profound mental retardation						
0–12	1,056	62	4	19	22	55
13–21	2,539	43	4	15	33	48
22–59	7,175	25	7	17	33	43
60+	710	33	12	26	22	40

Note. From "Problem Behavior and Psychiatric Impairment within a Developmentally Disabled Population: I. Behavior Frequency" by J. W. Jacobson, 1982, *Applied Research in Mental Retardation, 3,* p. 129. Copyright 1982 Pergamon Press, Ltd. Reprinted by permission.
[a] Among individuals with a problem behavior reported only.

living context (with fewer problems in home or family care, and more in residential care). These findings are similar to those reported in other studies (Eyman, Borthwick, & Miller, 1981; MacMillan, 1977). The findings related to the occurrences of behavior problems in retarded persons in relation to factors of age and degree of retardation are summarized in Table 3.

Clearly, the presence of behavior problems within groups of retarded children is a major concern. A variety of associated behavior problems occur with a frequency and intensity great enough to suggest that routine assessment of these problems should be considered within any behavioral assessment approach to retarded children. That does not imply, however, that one may approach the assessment process with an *a priori* set of expectations. Rather, the need to include measures that address potential behavior problems reinforces the point that adequate behavioral assessment strategies must be multidimensional and multimodal, as opposed to the more traditional "cognitively focused" approaches so often employed (Zigler *et al.*, 1984). Behavioral assessment strategies, especially those that are expressly observational in nature, are particularly well suited to the measurement of problem behavior in retarded children.

ETIOLOGY

Etiological considerations present a specific difficulty in the area of mental retardation during childhood, because so little is currently known about the exact causes of so many of these conditions. There is, however, an exhaustive literature dealing with the etiologies of various conditions associated with mental retardation or retardation itself. Within this section, etiology is discussed with regard to its implications for behavioral assessment. Generally, rough distinctions have been made between those etiological determinants that are primarily genetic, those that are primarily physical and environmental, or those that are primarily psychosocial in nature.

Genetic disorders related to mental retardation are varied, and include chromosomal abnormalities (such as those translocations that result in Down syndrome or other trisomies), sex chromosome abnormalities (such as Turner and Klinefelter syndromes), and dominant and recessive gene disorders (such as tuberous sclerosis and phenylketonuria, respectively). Dominant and recessive genes control the specific characteristics that depend on them and determine single gene traits. Most traits, however, are not simply present or absent. They vary continuously over a range of possible expression. Therefore, polygenic theories of inheritance have developed to account for the continuous distribution of characteristics such as intelligence (Shields, 1973). Within this model, genes occur in discrete pairs, but the combinations of numerous pairs operate in concert to affect a particular characteristic. It is precisely this polygenic model that describes why so few specific etiologies of mental retardation can be identified.

The role played by physical and environmental factors in the etiology of mental retardation has received much attention recently. These factors are operative at prenatal and perinatal stages of development, and to some degree during postnatal development as well. Prenatal factors shown to be related to mental retardation include maternal sociocultural history (e.g., early nutritional status), nutritional status during pregnancy, maternal infections or disease, sensitization to the fetus (Rh factor), parental age, radiation, drugs, environmental toxins, and maternal emotional state (Robinson & Robinson, 1976). Common perinatal events include prematurity, anoxia, postmaturity, head trauma, and maternal infection. Postnatal hazards, generally involving central nervous system (CNS) trauma, include head injury, brain tumors, CNS infections (e.g., meningitis), malnutrition, and exposure to or ingestion of various toxins (Robinson & Robinson, 1976).

An example of a disorder in which the etiology has been clearly established to be prenatal and due to a specific teratogen is the fetal alcohol syndrome (FAS). FAS is a recently described disorder (Jones, Smith, Ullenland, & Streissguth, 1973) resulting from maternal ingestion of ethyl alcohol during pregnancy, and provides a clear example of a known prenatal teratogen that adversely affects the physical, developmental, and behavioral status of the child. Because of the widespread use of alcohol in the general population, the potential magnitude of the birth defects and their associated problems is immense. Incidence has been shown to be between 1 and 2 live births per 1,000, with the frequency of partial expressions of the syndrome at perhaps 3 to 5 live births per 1,000 (Clarren & Smith, 1978). The major features of FAS include CNS dysfunction, mild to moderate mental retardation, motor skill deficits, growth deficiency, and dysmorphic facial characteristics.

Hyperactivity has been found to be among the behaviors associated with this syndrome; in combination with the other deficits apparent in these children, it suggests the importance of multimodal behavior assessment approaches to the accurate identification of all parameters of the disorder. One study of 20 children identified as having FAS (Streissguth, Herman, & Smith, 1978) found that the mean IQ was 65, with a range from 15 to 109, indicating a great deal of variability in cognitive functioning. Only 4 of the 20 children, however, had IQs above 80. The only behavioral problem noted was hyperactivity, which appeared characteristic of most of the children in that sample. No other specific behavior problems were noted, although 2 of the 20 were noted to have personality problems involving inappropriate interpersonal behavior and deficient social skills. Associated school problems were also reported, although these were not assessed in any systematic way. The presence of hyperactivity and school problems was also reported by Shaywitz, Cohen, and Shaywitz (1980) in a study of 15 children with FAS, although again specific measurement or assessment strategies were not clearly reported. Clearly, FAS presents a complicated variety of physiological, cognitive, emotional, and behavioral difficulties associated with a prenatal teratogen; this suggests that an understanding of the child with this syndrome requires a careful systematic behavioral assessment, the results of which are critical to accurate diagnosis.

By far the largest group (75%) of children diagnosed as mentally retarded have undifferentiated mild mental retardation, or mental retardation without an identifiable organic basis. This group of children has been conceptualized in various ways, but commonly has been referred to as having "cultural–familial retardation" or "retardation due to psychosocial disadvantage." It is a matter of some controversy whether this group of children is retarded due to cultural, familial, or psychosocial factors exclusively, or whether these children simply represent the low end of the normal distribution and their functioning is representative of both genetic and environmental factors. The evidence seems more often to suggest the latter (Achenbach, 1982), although there remains a good deal of evidence that environmental factors play an important role (see Skeels, 1966).

Some of the psychological and familial factors that have been shown to be related to intellectual functioning include family structure and size, parental deprivation, early verbal stimulation of children, parent–child relationships, characteristics of the home, abuse or neglect, and poverty, to mention a nonexhaustive few (Robinson & Robinson, 1976).

In all, it should be clear from the foregoing discussion that there is rarely a single cause or clear explanation for any intellectual impairment. In some cases, an organic cause can definitely be identified, but most often the disability is the result of some complex interaction among genetic factors, individual biological conditions, and a wide variety of environmental and psychological conditions. Particularly for those children with undifferentiated mild developmental delays or retardation, genetic mechanisms determine the rank ordering of IQs within particular environmental conditions, and the environmental conditions determine the actual level of intellectual functioning (Achenbach, 1982).

The study of children at high risk for developmental impairment provides an interesting example of the complex interrelationships between biological conditions and psychosocial contexts as etiological factors. Premature infants with very low birth weight (VLBW) became a focus of concern as medical technologies advanced to the point at which infants weighing as little as 600 grams could survive. These infants typically suffer from extreme respiratory problems because of their young gestational ages (e.g., 28–32 weeks), and often have associated complications, such as CNS bleeding. Prematurity, defined by indices of birth weight (less than 2,500 grams) and gestational age (less than 37 weeks), has been found to be associated with a number of maternal demographic factors. The incidence of prematurity has been found to be greater in those mothers from lower-SES groups (Berkowitz, 1981) and to be associated with a number of other relevant risk factors, including maternal age (young teenage mothers and those over 40), less education, smoking, short intervals between pregnancies, and poor previous pregnancy history (Van den Berg & Oechsli, 1984). Early reports of the developmental status of VLBW premature infants indicated that cognitive and behavioral impairments were present, leading to the development of the notion of a "continuum of reproductive casualty" as a primary etiological mechanism (Passaminick & Knobloch, 1961). Implicit in this notion was the primacy of an infant's biological condition, independent of the environmental context, in determining outcome. Furthermore, the biological factor that appeared to be the most powerful in determining outcome was infant birth weight (Bennett, Robinson, & Sells, 1982).

Subsequent longitudinal research with high-risk infants appears to indicate, however, that an infant's biological condition alone is neither a necessary nor a sufficient condition predictive of developmental and/or behavioral outcome (Bakeman & Brown, 1980; Crnic & Greenberg, 1984, 1985; DiVitto & Goldberg, 1979; Field, 1980). In a series of reviews of studies of high-risk children, Sameroff (Sameroff, 1980; Sameroff & Chandler, 1975; Sameroff & Siefer, 1983) has found that psychosocial contexts appear to be better overall predictors of outcome than biological status. Sameroff has proposed a "continuum of caretaking casualty" to describe this process, in which the outcomes of high-risk children are more a function of SES factors and the transactions that occur between these children and the various psychosocial contexts in which they live.

Findings from a number of studies of VLBW prematures appear to support the transactional model proposed by Sameroff. Differences in cognitive functioning are attenuated when children's scores on developmental assessment are corrected for gestational ages (Bakeman & Brown, 1980; Hunt & Rhodes, 1977; Parmelee & Schulte, 1970), and generally few studies note specific major developmental deficits in preterm infants. Numerous studies, however, have described both behavioral and interactional differences between preterm infants and full-term children (Bakeman & Brown, 1980; Brachfield, Goldberg, & Sloman, 1980; Crnic, Ragozin, Greenberg, Robinson, & Basham, 1983; DiVitto & Goldberg, 1979; Field, Dempsey, & Shuman, 1981). The absence of developmental difficulties was noteworthy, and most studies found that SES was more powerfully related to developmental functioning in preterm and full-term children than were factors involving infant biological status. In contrast, there remain studies indicating that biological status is related to preterm outcome. Bennett et al. (1982) followed the development of 161 infants born prematurely and with respiratory illness. They reported that respiratory illness was re-lated to developmental functioning during early infancy (4 months of age), but not at 12 or 24 months. In contrast, birth weight and gestational age (the two major criteria for diagnosis of prematurity) were not related to functioning at 4 months but were related at 12 and 24 months. Furthermore, they reported that birth weight was the best predictor of neurodevelopmental outcomes, although psychosocial variables were not considered in this study. The difficulty in distinguishing between these conflicting reports involves the fact that most of the studies did not adequately measure both biological and social variables, that criteria for subject selection varied, and that the populations differed in terms of their SES.

A recent series of studies (Crnic & Greenberg, 1984, 1985; Crnic, Ragozin, et al., 1983) has begun to indicate that both biological and contextual factors are critical to developmental functioning of high-risk children. In a 5-year longitudinal study, VLBW preterm and normal full-term children did not significantly differ in developmental abilities after age 1; yet numerous family, parent–child interaction, and child behavior factors predicted preterm outcomes to a much greater extent than full-term children's outcomes. These findings suggest an interaction between biological and contextual factors, such that the presence of some biological abnormality or insult creates a condition whereby behavioral factors within the child and family (as well as the child's and family's interactions within other contexts, such as school and the community at large) are more critical to developmental outcome than is the case when no biological risk condition is present. It seems apparent that biological and environmental risk factors operate in concert to dictate outcomes; this again demonstrates a need for multimodal assessments across medical, psychological, developmental, and familial contexts.

The etiology of intellectual impairment and its associated features is complex and not clearly resolved in many cases. Yet etiology and its identification have clear implications for behavioral assessment. The focus of behavioral assessment is on the identification of those variables that control or influence particular behaviors within a particular environmental context. The behavioral expression of the intellectual impairment, whether or not some biological condition is identifiable, is dependent to a large degree on the behavioral and social transactions between the affected child and the various environmental contexts in which he or she interacts. Furthermore, as Zigler *et al.* (1984) note, intellectual deficits resulting from specific organic factors also have behavioral implications that differentiate organic from nonorganic retardation. Identification of those factors that serve to differentiate, promote, or maintain behaviors associated with intellectual impairment not only serves to suggest intervention targets and strategies, but may also identify those specific behavioral and contextual conditions that create the disordered functioning. Behavioral assessment procedures—particularly those that are multidimensional—will identify not only the condition itself and its concomitant features, but also the conditions antecedent to their occurrence. In this way, the data provided by behavioral assessment procedures may offer some understanding of etiological conditions associated with mental retardation.

PREDICTING DEVELOPMENTAL COURSE

Within the assessment context, one of the most difficult and yet frequently asked questions about the diagnosis of mental retardation pertains to its stability over time. Parents are perhaps the most critically concerned with this issue, as perhaps they should be. But those who see these families within clinical settings and identify these children are frequently asked whether change is possible or what the children will be like in 2 years, 10 years, and so on. Often, psychologists are put in the position of providing predictive information—a position that certainly can be an uncomfortable one, given the myriad of factors that can affect cognitive and behavioral stability over time.

To address this question of prediction, it is necessary to assess the stability of IQ over time. A number of large-scale longitudinal studies have attempted to answer the question of IQ stability over time (Bayley, 1949; Bradway & Thompson, 1962; Kangas & Bradway, 1971; Sontag, Baker, & Nelson, 1958), and the general conclusions from these studies are that children's test performance retains generally the same position over time in relation to other children of similar age, especially after age 6. The exact IQ score, however, does not remain constant. Although this suggests good stability from childhood to adulthood, it is notable that

all of these studies found some children whose scores changed dramatically over the years. With respect to children who are mentally retarded, Robinson and Robinson (1976) report that IQ stability is somewhat greater than it is for children who are average or superior, but that, again, there are many children who can and do show rather dramatic changes over time. Sometimes it is possible to account for these changes empirically (as seen in the report by Skeels, 1966) but often those factors responsible for the change are unidentifiable.

One limit on predictability appears to be the age of the child identified as retarded. Scores of infant and preschool-age children on standardized intelligence tests tend to be particularly unstable. This is true for both nondisabled and retarded performers. The exception to this is that group of very young children whose performance on these measures is three or more standard deviations below the mean. Such low scores are suggestive of organicity within the disorder, and stability of the scores is greater under these conditions. It is likewise true for older children as well that the lower the IQ, the greater the stability over time (Ross & Boroskin, 1972).

Although predictability for groups of children is possible, it is difficult to make predictions for any individual child with mental retardation. The exception may be those children who are functioning within the range of very severe to profound retardation, but these children represent only a small proportion of the population overall. It is, therefore, dangerous to attempt prediction for any one individual on the basis of a single assessment. A single assessment measurement at one point in time should serve as a description of the present functional condition and as a baseline for future assessments to be compared with. It is only with multiple measurements over time and within appropriate contexts that developmental course can be predicted with some degree of confidence. Therefore, it is imperative to interpret test and observational data from a single point in time with some restraint. This is often difficult, as prediction is such a general concern of families and other referral sources. Nevertheless, the ability to predict with any degree of certainty is dependent upon multiple assessments over time that involve more than measurement of IQ. Given that behavioral and environmental factors are known to significantly influence IQ, comprehensive, ongoing behavioral assessments add greatly to the potential for accurate prediction, as such assessment allows for analysis of change across skills, behaviors, and contexts.

BEHAVIORAL CONTEXTS

Within any assessment paradigm, the context in which behavior is measured is of critical importance. Within populations of retarded children, the family context is of particular significance (although this significance certainly is not restricted to mentally retarded children). Although families, and the effect that retarded children have on their functioning, have been a focus of clinical concern for some time, it is only recently that research on the family as a system has come to the fore. Inherent in this work has been the notion that the relationships and influences between retarded children and their families are most likely reciprocal and circular (Crnic, Friedrich, & Greenberg, 1983), such that although families are affected by the presence of retarded children, the children are also affected by their families' response and the quality of the home context (Nihira, Meyers, & Mink, 1980). The response that the parents and families have to the children is to some degree dependent upon the stresses engendered and perceived by the family members in response to the presence of the disorder. Families, too, are more than a collection of independent individuals. The family context is a system and an organization that operates on several levels. These levels include the various combinations of family members in specific interactions (mother–child, father–child, mother–father–child, mother–father, and sibling–sibling), as well as the group activities in which families engage (e.g., recreation, chores, community involvements, etc.) The stress frequently associated with the presence of a retarded child affects the family as a system as well as the parents and siblings as individuals (Crnic, Friedrich, & Greenberg, 1983).

Stress

Families vary in their response to a mentally retarded child, and this variation is in part a function of the perceived stress related to the presence of the retarded child (Crnic, Friedrich, & Greenberg, 1983). For some time, adaptational models assumed a pathological outcome for families and their individual members as a function of a stress–reaction hypothesis (Erickson, 1969; W. H. Miller & Keirn, 1978); that is, pathological outcomes were assumed to occur because of the difficulties presented by the presence of the retarded child. "Stress," as conceptualized within this research, generally refers to a perception of chronic burden related to greater and more intense caregiving demands, the social stigma associated with having a retarded child, and the life changes engendered by the retarded child's limitations. The presumed stress associated with having a mentally retarded child was thought to create numerous behavioral, emotional, and social problems for parents and siblings. Among these difficulties were greater emotional distress in mothers, fathers, and siblings; reports of significant marital discord; less social mobility; fewer recreational opportunities; and generally less positive approaches to parenting (Crnic, Friedrich, & Greenberg, 1983). While such a conceptualization made sense at face value, there were two important limitations to this stress–reaction hypothesis. First, none of the studies that discussed these relationships used any objective measures of stress in the parents or families; second, it was clear from clinical and some research reports that not all families showed pathological outcomes in regard to their retarded children (e.g., Mink, Nihira, & Meyers, 1983).

Only recently have measures of stress been included in studies purporting to assess stresses on parents and families in relation to their retarded children. As a rule, these studies indicate that families of retarded children experience more stress than do families of nonretarded children (Friedrich & Friedrich, 1981; Friedrich, Greenberg, & Crnic, 1983; Holroyd & McArthur, 1976), and this stress is further related to the severity of a child's handicap (Beckman, 1983; Holroyd & Guthrie, 1979). Families under stress are not only more likely to be adversely affected without access to adequate coping resources, but are also more likely to have adverse impacts on the children's functioning, such as behavioral responsiveness during interactions and actual school performance (Crnic, Greenberg, Ragozin, Robinson, & Basham, 1983; Nihira et al., 1980).

Familial Response

Few studies of familial response to having a retarded child have been more than unidimensional (measuring only a single factor related to functioning) or unimodal (using only one type of measurement, such as questionnaires). The dominant characteristic of this research has been a focus on a single family member (primarily the mother) or on a single functional domain, such as emotional distress, attitude toward parenting, or marital satisfaction. As such, it is somewhat difficult to judge the extent to which the family system as a whole responds to the stress of a retarded child. Nevertheless, the literature clearly seems to show the risk status of family members of retarded children (Crnic, Friedrich, & Greenberg, 1983). Parents tend to have less positive or developmentally facilitative attitudes toward their retarded children (Ricci, 1970; Waisbren, 1980); to show more personality and emotional difficulties than parents of nonretarded children (Cummings, 1976; Erickson, 1968; W. H. Miller & Keirn, 1978); to have less marital satisfaction (Farber, 1959; Friedrich & Friedrich, 1981); to have greater psychosocial problems, including reduced social mobility and declining SES (Farber, 1970); and to show greater parent–child interaction difficulties, particularly related to lack of reciprocity and responsiveness (Breiner & Forehand, 1982; Cunningham, Rueler, Blackwell, & Deck, 1981; Eheart, 1982; Kogan, Wimberger, & Bobbitt, 1969; Vietze, Abernathy, Ashe, & Faulstich, 1978). There also tend to be more frequent behavior problems among siblings, particularly female siblings (Farber, 1959; Gath, 1973).

A series of recent studies by Nihira and his colleagues indicates the importance of the family context for understanding the retarded child's functioning (Mink, Meyers, & Nihira, 1984; Mink et al., 1983; Nihira et al., 1980; Nihira, Mink, & Meyers, 1982). This research, which focused on the interaction of the home or familial context and the functioning of the retarded child, showed that family adjustment and functioning were related to the severity of a child's handicap and the degree of maladaptive behavior exhibited across settings. In all cases, the more severe the handicap and the more maladaptive the behavior, the worse the family adjustment. Furthermore, this research clearly indicated the complexity of the interactive child–family system: The parents' report of impact was related to the retarded child's lack of adaptive competency, while the child's adaptive competency was related to successful parental coping with the child. Of additional importance

to behavioral assessment considerations was the finding that performance within educational settings was related to the quality of the home and family context for these children. This suggests that behavioral assessments of family functioning will suggest additional contexts (such as school) in which problems may arise. Again, this stresses the need for measurements across contexts.

The studies by Mink et al. (1983, 1984) are of particular importance as well for the identification of family types provided and the behavioral and developmental qualities that the retarded children showed within each family type. Five family types were identified in their research:

1. *Cohesive, harmonious*: Parents provided good physical environments, social maturity, and control.
2. *Control-oriented, somewhat nonharmonious*: Parents provided good physical environment, social maturity, and control, yet relied on physical punishment.
3. *Low disclosure, unharmonious*: Parents indicated low openness and awareness, poorer physical environments, and less social maturity, and made use of physical punishment.
4. *Child-oriented, expressive*: Families were characterized by factors concerned with child well-being (e.g. warmth and affection, lack of physical punishment).
5. *Disadvantaged, low morale*: Families were characterized by low scores on nearly all factors, but especially stimulation through toys and academic stimulation.

Mink and colleagues further described behavior and developmental functioning of children in each of the groups in both home and school contexts, significantly differentiating among the groups of children on these factors.

The research by Nihira, Mink, and colleagues is important not only for the clinical value of the information provided about families of retarded children, but also in terms of the measurement employed. A number of the measures used to study these families may be of use in specific behavioral assessments of families. The Nihira studies employed the Home Observation for Measurement of the Environment (HOME; Caldwell & Bradley, 1979), which is an observational inventory designed to assess seven behavioral factors involving the social, emotional, and cognitive environments available to young children. Research studies have indicated that HOME scores during late infancy and early preschool years are predictive of later cognitive, language, and social development (Elardo, Bradley, & Caldwell, 1975, 1977); these findings substantiate the importance of this measure, at least within research contexts. The social, emotional, and cognitive factors are rated from spontaneous observations of the home environment and naturally occurring behavioral interactions between parent and child. Nihira *et al.* (1980) also developed the Home Quality Rating Scale (HQRS), which consists of 28 items designed to assess various aspects of the home environment on the basis of interviewer or observer impressions. The 28 scales of the HQRS include factors such as quality of parenting; adjustment and harmony in the home; openness of parent and awareness of disability; quality and safety of the residential environment; and parental attitude toward the handicapped child. Both the HOME and the HQRS are potentially useful within behavioral assessment strategies, although their use in other than research capacities has not been empirically established. Nevertheless, the information obtained from these measures can suggest specific areas for more in-depth observational assessment within a stimuli–organism–responses–contingencies–consequences (S-O-R-K-C) model.

From the foregoing discussion of the nature of the family system, it should be clear that no assessment paradigm can avoid measurement of the family context and be considered complete. There are complicated issues to be assessed, and frequently it is difficult from a practical standpoint to conduct behavioral observations or other measurements of entire family units. Nevertheless, a comprehensive assessment is dependent on understanding the complex and often contingent relationships within the family and other relevant ecological systems.

IMPLICATIONS FOR BEHAVIORAL ASSESSMENT

The overview of mental retardation presented in the preceding sections has a number of implications for behavioral assessment. First, it should be clear that the assessment must be multimodal and multidimensional. The findings from various research studies indicate that interviews, rating scales, observations, and standardized testing are all relevant to the identification of the disorder and its associated features. Furthermore, there are numerous areas of potential concern in regard to the child and his or her environmental contexts that must be addressed, including a variety of developmental skill domains, behavioral and affective functioning, social and adaptive skills, and the reciprocal influences between the child and the environmental contexts in which he or she operates. A standardized test with concomitant behavioral observations during performance is not sufficient to address the concerns that are likely to be involved in any referral question. In fact, behavioral assessment strategies are not primarily concerned with actual measurement of developmental skills in cognition, language, or academic areas. Behavioral assessment strategies are perhaps most useful within the context of those deficits related to adaptive functioning and the associated features of the disorder involving deficits in behavioral, social, and affective functioning. Furthermore, behavioral assessment has a particular focus on the contexts in which behavior is measured, both in terms of the conditions that serve to promote and maintain the behaviors of concern and in terms of the impact of the retarded child on the context. The impact that the child has on the context may well serve to maintain the behaviors of concern; this implies the need for careful assessment of behaviors across contexts, such as the home and school.

Although the roles that standardized tests of cognitive and academic functioning play in the assessment process of mental retardation cannot be minimized (cognitive functioning is a critical determinant), the use of behavioral assessment strategies is best conceptualized in regard to the recurring behavioral problems characteristic of the disorder. Both adaptive skills and behavioral problems have been previously discussed as to their significance for this population of children, and the assessment strategies and measures that follow are specifically oriented to addressing these issues. Cognitive and academic assessment are also discussed, but primarily in regard to how they might be conceptualized within a behavioral assessment paradigm, rather than in terms of the more traditional psychometric approach.

REFERRAL ISSUES

The heterogeneity within the population of mentally retarded children is essentially comparable to that within the population of children in general. The range of specific concerns can potentially vary across the spectrum of cognitive, behavioral, emotional, social, or academic difficulties. Given this condition, the process of behavioral assessment truly begins with the parameters of the specific referral question.

The variety in referral questions mirrors that of the potential difficulties within the disorder. Some referral questions are as "simple" as identifying whether or not a given child is mentally retarded. However, most referrals are quite a bit more involved and require not only diagnostic information, but information on education and treatment planning, whether specific learning styles can be modified, whether the problems apparent at any one time will continue indefinitely, whether parents should act as treatment or intervention agents, and whether or not this problem is related to a specific action or occurrence. Furthermore, the referral questions may involve differential diagnosis as a primary issue. It is not uncommon, for example, to see referrals that inquire as to whether a child is autistic or mentally retarded.

Depending upon the source of the referral, a good deal of sensitivity may be required to address the problem being considered. Often parents are the referral source, and although they may suspect that their child is not functioning at the same level as other children of a similar age, they may not have mental retardation in mind as the explanation for this discrepancy. Similarly, when parents are not the referral source, but school personnel or pediatricians are, parents are often anxious and perhaps resentful about an assessment process. In any respect, this can make planning assessment strategies a more delicate process and compliance with procedures difficult at times.

Referral questions can also involve issues regarding behavior problems across various settings (home, school, group home); the identification of developmental rate and change as well as its determinants; and, not infrequently, legal questions as to responsibility for the condition and its long-term consequences. Obviously, referral questions take many forms and can address numerous issues. In most cases, the referral involves a combination of many of the issues addressed above. Regardless, as detailed in the following sections, behavioral assessment approaches are appropriate to address many of the issues for which retarded children and their families are referred.

BEHAVIORAL ASSESSMENT STRATEGIES

General Guidelines

As Eyberg (1985) has noted, behavioral assessment has its historical roots in direct behavioral observation of children, whereby specific behaviors of concern are identified, operationally defined, observed in context for antecedents and consequences, and counted. Over time, this notion has been expanded; behavioral methods have gone beyond the sole reliance on direct behavioral observation, and now encompass an empirically based and developmentally sensitive multimethod approach that utilizes a range of procedures to understand a given child (Mash & Terdal, 1981 and this volume; Ollendick & Hersen, 1984). Such procedures include behavioral and developmental interviews, rating scales, standardized intellectual and academic measures, and direct observations in context.

With the range of potential techniques available, the way in which an examiner structures the behavioral assessment process for any one child will be a function of the specific question at hand. Certainly, it is not always necessary to use each of the techniques described here. Questions that involve behavioral difficulties within a group home setting may not require specific intellectual or academic assessment, just as questions that seek to determine developmental rate over time may not require specific classroom observations of a retarded child. Determining the procedures to be employed will depend on clear formulation of the problems presented; their breadth; and identification of the contexts that serve to promote, facilitate, maintain, or otherwise affect the child and the developmental contexts that contain the child.

With populations of mentally retarded children, standardized IQ tests are employed in the assessment process more often than not, but it is clearly the case that one need not always be given. Many times, recent IQ data may be available from other sources, and readministration of the test is not necessary or represents overassessing a child. This is particularly true once children reach school age and receive periodic assessments as a part of their educational program, and when no outstanding event has occurred that may have been likely to influence a child's cognitive functioning. Likewise, referrals that have primarily to do with behavior issues may not require an IQ assessment. Generally, development of a comprehensive yet meaningful assessment strategy is dependent upon the formulation of clear questions to be addressed from the referral information available, as well as from the data-based interviews that often begin the assessment process.

Developmental Interview

With the need for accurate information to plan the behavioral assessment process, a behavioral–developmental interview is the common starting point. Parents are almost always a major part of the assessment process with retarded children, and they are generally quite good as behavioral reporters if provided with the appropriate structure for responding specifically. Many parents also keep records, in various states of detail, of their child's development and behaviors at various ages. "Baby books" can be invaluable guides for parental recall, and it can be helpful to have parents bring these along to the interview. There is, however, a certain amount of debate over the validity of parental reports; some research indicates that parents are poor reporters (Schnelle, 1974; Yarrow, Campbell, & Burton, 1970), while others have suggested that parent reports have good criterion-related validity (Graham & Rutter, 1968; Herjanic & Campbell, 1977). Behavioral parent interviews have received a fair amount of attention in the literature, and specifics of these interviews have been widely discussed in these presentations (Bersoff & Grieger, 1971; Kanfer & Saslow, 1969; O'Leary & Johnson, 1979; M. C. Roberts & LaGreca, 1981).

The interview process with the parents of a retarded child should not simply be conceptualized as a behavioral interview; it also needs to be considered within a developmental framework. It is important to define the developmental parameters of the child's behavior in the home and other contexts of which the parents are aware, as well as to obtain a sense of the developmental landmarks attained by the child and the age at which these occurred. As with most interview formats, it is most useful to begin with open-ended questions that seek to discover just what the major concerns are from a parental point of view. From the parental response to such open-ended questions as "Tell me why you have brought your son/daughter here," or "Tell me as best you can what you see as the major difficulties present with your son/daughter now," specific areas of concern can be identified and returned to at some later point in the interview, and questions can become more specific to narrow the focus of the concern and its situational determinants and consequences.

In regard to the developmental issues to be addressed, there is specific information that should be obtained to identify the developmental nature of the disorder. First, information should be obtained about when the child reached specific developmental landmarks (e.g., first smile, first sat alone, began crawling, began walking, first words, first simple word combinations, reactions to strangers occurred, toilet-trained, began to acquire dressing skills). Each of these developmental parameters normally occurs during infancy and toddlerhood, and the identification of their appearance or nonappearance will provide information as to when the disorder may have first been discernible. Consistent delay in regard to these milestones is a clear indication of the presence of intellectual disorder early in the developmental period and is common in cases of mental retardation. It is also helpful to ask when parents first suspected there might be something wrong with their child's development, and what specifically brought this suspicion to the fore. There are usually some developmental parameters not met, as well as some comparisons with other children who seem to have done things with more ease or earlier, that act as signals to parents. Furthermore, the developmental information sought should also include specific questions about functioning across developmental skill areas (cognition/learning, language skills, motor skills, self-help skills, and behavior and social skills). This is so because mental retardation during childhood is characterized by relatively consistent developmental deficits across skill areas. Large discrepancies between skill areas are not common and suggest the need for differential diagnosis.

Beyond the specific developmental issues, there are likely to be behavioral concerns as well. Therefore, the interview also needs to include those questions that are more typical of behavioral assessment within the S-O-R-K-C model as proposed by Kanfer and Saslow (1969). Thus, with any given behavior of concern, interview questions must address antecedent events ("What generally occurs prior to the behavior?", "Where does this usually happen?"), a specific description of the behavior ("What exactly does your child do?"), a description of the learning and behavior history ("How often does this occur?", "Is it similar at each occurrence?"), and a description of the consequent events ("What do you usually do or what happens next?"). Left out of these examples is the "O" portion of the model, which addresses the notion of the biological–developmental condition of the child. This information is provided within the context of the developmental aspects of the interview described above. Also, within the scope of the behavioral interview, it is important to obtain information on the child's behavioral assets as well as deficits ("What things does your child do well?"), and to attempt to ascertain potentially powerful consequences ("Tell me what your child really enjoys or is really willing to work to obtain"). Both of these facets can be used in subsequent intervention planning. Finally, it should be noted that the interview format is the best vehicle for establishing rapport with parents. The importance of this facet of the interview should not be overlooked. With retarded children, the information to be given to parents is often difficult to accept; in addition, one may wish to involve parents in intervention programs following the assessment, and good rapport is important to compliance within the sometimes frustrating and demanding context of behavioral interventions.

In most cases, parents are not the only informants with whom behavioral interviews will be important. Frequently, with retarded children, teachers have specific concerns in relation to education programs and behavior management within academic settings. Research tends to indicate that teachers are accurate behavioral reporters (Ollendick, 1981), and they are often most valuable in delineating behaviors related to learning styles and abilities, as well as social skills with peers. The specifics of teacher behavior interviews do not differ appreciably in style from those with parents.

Intellectual and Academic Assessment

Assessment of cognitive or intellectual status is of primary concern in the diagnosis of mental retardation during childhood, although (as noted earlier) it will not always be necessary, depending on the question at hand. It is, nevertheless, necessary to describe the use of standardized tests of cognitive development or intelligence and academic ability that are typically used to identify functioning indicative of retardation.

Valid and reliable tests of intelligence and cognitive functioning are currently available for children of all ages, from infancy through adolescence. Table 4 provides a list of those instruments that are most frequently used with children, along with brief descriptions of the age ranges and major subscales involved. This list is not in any way meant to be exhaustive of those tools that exist, or to imply that tools not listed specifically lack reliability, validity, or utility. Rather, this list is representative of those measures most frequently employed as individual tests of intelligence by psychologists serving populations of mentally retarded children.

Academic achievement tests are frequently part of the assessment process with mentally retarded children as well. The information that can be derived from normed or standardized achievement tests (see Taylor, Chapter 8, this volume) is important in identification of the comparability of actual academic performance with general cognitive ability. For the most part, performance on achievement tests should be in line with performance on measures of intelligence for children with mental retardation.

Academic assessments can take a number of forms. Most common are assessments of general academic skills across such subject areas as reading, spelling, arithmetic, and vocabulary. Achievement tests can also focus on individual skill areas, most frequently oral reading and comprehension. Finally, academic assessment can broadly include tests of specific visual–spatial or auditory abilities, as these are skills that often help to indicate when inabilities in one academic area might be particularly troublesome. Typically, such tests might include indices of visual–motor perception and integration or auditory processing. Individual achievement tests that are frequently employed in assessments of retarded children are presented in Table 5, listed by skill area. Again, this list is not exhaustive, but represents those measures most commonly employed. Anastasi (1976) has noted that numerous difficulties exist

TABLE 4. Most Frequently Used Standardized Cognitive Assessments, with Age Ranges and Descriptions

Test	Age range	Description
Bayley Scales of Infant Development (Bayley, 1969)	0–3 months	Provides indices of early cognitive and motor development and includes a Behavior Rating Index. Most useful above age 4 months. Frequently used with children older than 30 months, with age equivalents rather than standard score reported.
Stanford–Binet Intelligence Scale (Thorndike, Hagen, & Sattler, 1986)	2 years through adulthood	This fourth edition is substantially revised in both format and content from earlier editions. It provides a composite Cognitive Index from 15 subscales involving verbal, visual, and quantitative reasoning and memory.
Kaufman Assessment Battery for Children (K-ABC; Kaufman & Kaufman, 1983)	$2\frac{1}{2}$ to 12 years	Relatively new assessment tool (1983), which provides indices of cognitive functioning divided by major cognitive strategy required (Simultaneous or Sequential). A composite score is computed, which is equivalent to IQ scores. K-ABC also includes an Achievement scale and a Nonverbal Functioning scale.
McCarthy Scales of Children's Abilities (McCarthy, 1974)	$2\frac{1}{2}$ to 8 years	Provides indices of various cognitive abilities and a General Cognitive Index. Materials are enjoyable, and children respond well to tasks. Many clinicians find that scores for retarded children are about 10 points lower than on other tests (no research evidence has been reported).
Wechsler Preschool and Primary Scale of Intelligence (WPPSI; Wechsler, 1967)	4–6 years	Both measures are Wechsler scales oriented to specific age groups. Both tests divide performance into Verbal and Visual–Perceptual Motor Reasoning Scales, and a combined Full Scale IQ index is obtained. These are the most frequently used IQ measures, with a wealth of research to substantiate their use.
Wechsler Intelligence Scale for Children—Revised (WISC-R); Wechsler, 1974)	6–16 years	
Leiter International Performance Scale (Leiter, 1948)	2 years through adulthood	A nonverbal measure of intellectual functioning based on concrete and abstract matching skills. Neither comprehension nor expression of language is required. An IQ is obtained through a ratio formula (MA/CA × 100 = IQ). The norms are quite old (1940s), so current scores are probably overestimates.
System of Multicultural Pluralistic Assessment (SOMPA; Mercer & Lewis, 1978)	5 through 12 years	Standardized measure of cognitive, perceptual–motor, and adaptive ability that incorporates medical, social, and pluralistic information in an attempt to accommodate the effect of cultural bias in assessment. It does provide a standard score. It is questionable whether the SOMPA actually reduces cultural bias.

with the psychometric status of many of the measures of achievement or special abilities, and suggests that they may be more appropriately used as qualitative (as opposed to quantitative) measures. Using such measures as qualitative indications of abilities is compatible with the general model of behavioral assessment strategies.

TABLE 5. Frequently Used Standardized Test of Achievement, Academic Skill, and Related Special Skills

Test	Description
Achievement/academic	
Wide Range Achievement Test—Revised (WRAT-R; Jastak & Wilkinson, 1984)	Standardized instrument for use with preschool ages through adulthood. Provides grade equivalents and standard scores (mean = 100) in three basic academic skill areas: Reading, Arithmetic, and Spelling. The test has separate forms for children younger and older than 12 years.
Peabody Individual Achievement Test (PIAT; Dunn & Markwardt, 1970)	Normed and standardized measure for kindergarten through high school ages. Assesses academic skill in five areas: Math, Reading Recognition, Reading Comprehension, Spelling, and General Information. Standard scores are provided for subtests and total scores.
Woodcock–Johnson Psycho-Educational Battery (Woodcock, 1977)	Standardized measure of cognitive and achievement skills for ages 3 through adulthood. Measure contains 27 subtests, although not all are given at each age. Standard scores are provided with a mean of 100. Can take up to 2 hours to administer entire test. Standard error of measurement is not reported, making profile comparison difficult.
Specific academic abilities	
Gray Oral Reading Test (Gray, 1963)	Standardized assessment of oral reading and comprehension skill for children in first grade through high school. Scoring is based on number of errors and reading time for a particular passage, and grade equivalents are obtained.
Durrell Analysis of Reading Difficulty (Durrell, 1955)	Normed assessment of five specific areas of reading skill, suitable for first through sixth grade. Scores are provided for rate and comprehension of oral and silent reading, and there are related skill assessments for nonreaders.
KeyMath Diagnostic Arithmetic Test (Connolly, Nachtman, & Pritchett, 1976)	Normed and individually administered assessment of math skills. There are 14 subtests organized within three major areas: content, operations, and applications. Norms are for kindergarten through ninth grade, and the scores obtained are grade equivalents. Behavioral objectives are provided for each item.
Specific abilities	
Developmental Test of Visual–Motor Integration (VMI; Beery, 1967)	The VMI has somewhat limited norms, but measures visual–motor abilities in children aged 2 through 15. The test provides an age equivalent based on a child's reproduction of geometric designs.
Bender–Gestalt (Koppitz Scoring System for Children) (Koppitz, 1975)	Test of perceptual–motor ability through the use of paper-and-pencil design or figure reproduction. Norms exist for boys and girls aged 5 through 11.
Frostig Developmental Test of Visual Perception (Frostig, Maslow, Lefever, & Whittlesey, 1964)	Standardized instrument assessing five separate areas of visual–perceptual skill for children aged 3 to 9 years. The test yields perceptual age equivalents for each area, and a perceptual quotient for a total score.
Wepman Auditory Discrimination Test (Wepman, 1973)	Normed test that serves as a screening device in the assessment of discrimination ability in 5- to 8-year-olds. It contains 40 word pairs matched for familiarity, and can be brief to administer.
Illinois Test of Psycholinguistic Abilities (ITPA; Kirk, McCarthy, & Kirk, 1968)	Standardized individual test for children aged 2 through 10, which focuses on the communication base of cognitive abilities and comprises 10 subtests involving either visual or verbal material. Standard scores are provided for each subtest, as are age equivalents, and a total Psycholinguistic Age score is obtained.

Standardized tests of intelligence and achievement or academic skill and their uses with children in general have been described at length in numerous texts (Anastasi, 1976; Sattler, 1982) and are not so described again within the context of this chapter. A number of issues, however, are deserving of attention beyond the significance of standard scores of intelligence for accurate diagnosis, classification, and treatment planning.

Cognitive and academic abilities include more than simply performances on the standardized problem-solving tasks presented in the various measures noted above. The performance on these structured tasks is, in fact, only one component of such evaluation. Just as meaningful in the context of cognitive and academic assessment are the behavioral concomitants of the test performance that are observed during the administration of the tests themselves. There is a good deal of evidence to suggest that test performance varies as a function of a child's behavioral approach to the tasks presented (Anastasi, 1976; Sattler, 1982). Motivation, alertness, affect, attention, distractibility, mood, and learning style, among a myriad of factors, are likely to influence how well a child performs and the choice of factors that might possibly be addressed in interventions within the home and school settings. It is for these reasons that adequate standardized testing requires a careful behavioral observation approach, not only with an eye toward correctness of performance on a particular task, but also with attention to *how* that child performed or failed to perform that task. Behavioral concomitants of performance in structured learning situations such as IQ or developmental tests are of special importance to educational intervention, and are often more needed by educators in the planning of individualized educational programs than the test scores themselves. For this reason, observations during test administration should include clear indications of the child's behavior, both on-task and off-task functioning, within an S-O-R-K-C model. Beyond those variables likely to affect learning and performance, the test situation also provides a context for judging a child's social skills with adults under highly structured conditions, which may also be relevant to both home and school interventions.

Within the conceptualization of behavioral assessment, standardized tests of intelligence and academic ability sample general behavioral skills that have been acquired through learning. Such abilities include children's labeling repertoires, discrimination skills, imitation abilities, ability to attend and follow instructions, and motivation (Nelson, 1975). Items on standardized tests can be considered to reflect samples of behavior, rather than measures of psychological traits or internal qualities. Intellectual and academic skills are viewed more as learned behavioral repertoires. The child's behavior in relation to actual task performance (such as puzzle solving) is conceptualized as under the explicit control of the examiner's verbal instruction, and forms one part of a specific verbal–motor behavioral repertoire.

Standardized tests of intelligence and achievement have a number of important advantages for behavioral assessment strategies with children (Nelson, 1974, 1975), including (1) the provision of developmental norms for children through a standardization sample serving as a control group; (2) elicitation of samples of children's academic behaviors in response to standardized task stimuli; (3) assessment of children's behavioral assests and deficits in comparison to children of similar chronological and developmental age; (4) provision of baseline measures useful in treatment planning; (5) availability for use as screening tools for skills to be assessed in greater depth in different contexts; and (6) appropriateness of use for prescriptive teaching purposes. Likewise, Ciminero and Drabman (1977) note specifically that standardized tests used within behavioral assessment paradigms can assist in the identification of behavioral deficits important to intervention planning.

The observational assessment process described above is entirely possible within the limits of standardization required for the adequate administration of the tests. There are, however, times when for clinical purposes standardization no longer serves to answer the questions that arise during the course of cognitive and academic assessment. Within a behavioral assessment context, it can be desirable to abandon standard procedures when questions arise that can only be answered by manipulating contingencies or antecedents. It should be noted from the start that attempts to complete cognitive and academic assessments with traditional IQ tests should always be made within the limits of standardization. Yet this will not always demonstrate the range or variety of abilities that retarded children show. Once items have been presented in a standard format, it is often of great interest to test the limits of a child's performance by varying parameters of the presentation, by attempting to teach an approach to problem solving (e.g., modeling or demonstration for several trials), or by reinforcing performances that approximate the goal. For example, token reinforcement of correct performance on the Wechsler Intelligence Scale for Children—Revised (WISC-R) has been shown to result in higher scores on this measure with young, mildly retarded children (Johnson, Bradley-Johnson, McCarthy, & Jamie, 1984; Saigh & Payne, 1979; Young, Bradley-Johnson, & Johnson, 1982). Results from such structured observations can serve to further identify cognitive and behavioral strengths and weaknesses, and this information can subsequently be utilized in intervention planning. It is, however, incumbent on the examiner to describe digressions from standard procedures clearly when reporting performance on standard tests under such conditions.

Assessing Adaptive Behavior

As previously discussed, adaptive behavior is of primary concern in the identification of mentally retarded children. For the purposes of this discussion, "adaptive behavior" includes development of self-help or daily living skills, social skills, and behavioral functioning. Each of these areas is at significant risk with mentally retarded children, and behavioral assessment strategies with retarded children can and should measure functioning across the various domains. As adaptive behavior is not a single, discrete skill area, approaches to assessment typically require a variety of approaches. Typical of assessment strategies within this context are behavioral interviews, rating scales, and actual behavioral observations. As the interview format has already been discussed, this section focuses on the use of rating scales and direct behavioral observations.

A number of rating scales have been developed specifically to assess adaptive behavior in populations of retarded children. These are quite different from the general behavior rating scales that are traditionally used to assess behavioral difficulties during childhood. Adaptive skill measures tend to focus more specifically on the development of self-help and daily living skills, as well as on maladaptive social behavior and emotional dysfunction. The number of adaptive scales is rather staggering, as they seem to be proliferating in the wake of the AAMD's requirement that adaptive behavior be included in considering a diagnosis of retardation.

Among the adaptive behavior rating scales recently developed are the AAMD Adaptive Behavior Scale (ABS; Nihira, Foster, Shellhaas, & Leland, 1974); the Adaptive Behavior Inventory for Children, which is part of the System of Multicultural Pluralistic Assessment developed by Mercer and Lewis (1978); the Balthazar Scales of Adaptive Behavior (Balthazar, 1976); the Behavior Rating Inventory for the Retarded (BRIR; Sparrow & Cicchetti, 1978); the Children's Adaptive Behavior Scale (Richmond & Kicklighter, 1980); the Vineland Adaptive Behavior Scales (Sparrow, Balla, & Cicchetti, 1984); and the Wisconsin Behavior Rating Scale (WBRS; Song et al., 1980). Many of these measures have been criticized for various reasons, including applicability to limited or restricted samples, potential response biases, inadequate reliability and validity assessment procedures, and difficulty in administration and scoring (Reschly, 1981; Sparrow & Cicchetti, 1984). Despite their psychometric limitations, however, an increasing amount of research has demonstrated the utility of several of these measures.

The ABS is the most frequently used and best researched of the adaptive behavior rating scales. It is a third-party measure (generally completed by a parent or teacher), yielding reasonably objective ratings of a child's effectiveness in dealing with the natural demands of various environmental contexts. It is divided into two major sections; Part I comprises ratings of developmental and self-help competence, and Part II comprises ratings of maladaptive behavior problems. Part I involves ratings of 10 adaptive domains (Independent Functioning, Physical Development, Economic Skills, Language Development, Numbers and Time, Domestic Activity, Vocational Activity, Self-Direction, Responsibility, and Socialization). Part II assesses 14 categories of possible maladaptive behavior (Violent and Destructive Behavior, Antisocial Behavior, Rebellious, Untrustworthy, Withdrawal, Stereotypies and Odd Mannerisms, Inappropriate Interpersonal Manners, Unacceptable Vocal Habits, Self-Abusive, Hyperactive, Aberrant Sexual Behavior, Psychological Disturbance, unacceptable or eccentric habits, and Use of Medications). Administration of the scale can either be done within an interview format or as a questionnaire completed by the respondent alone. There is also a version that is specifically developed to be used within school contexts by teachers (Lambert & Hartsough, 1981; Lambert, Windmiller, Cole, & Figueroa, 1975). The ABS has generated a wealth of research over the past decade, generally indicating acceptable levels of reliability and validity, although Part I has fared somewhat better than Part II in most studies (Clements, Bost, DuBois, & Turpin, 1980; Clements, DuBois, Bost, & Bryan, 1981; Isett & Spreat, 1979; Meyers, Nihira, & Zetlin, 1979; Stack, 1984; Taylor, Warren, & Slocumb, 1979). The scores obtained on the ABS can be compared with scores from IQ tests to assess equivalence between the cognitive and adaptive domains. This rating scale can also be used as a good starting point for defining behaviors that will subsequently be assessed through direct behavior observations.

Another frequently used rating scale is the Vineland, originally developed by Doll (1964); it has been recently revised by Sparrow *et al.* (1984). There are few data available on which to assess the merits of the new revision, but the old Vineland was useful in determining the social adaptive behavior of mentally retarded children, and in fact was the measure of choice prior to the appearance of the ABS (Song & Jones, 1982). The revised Vineland is generally administered as an interview, and now has three forms: the interview edition and its expanded form, the survey form, and the classroom form. The differences among these forms involve both the number of items administered and the content areas assessed. The survey and the expanded interview form contain a Maladaptive Behavior scale, as well as the general four indices of adaptive behavior (Communication, Daily Living Skills, Socialization, and Motor Skills). This instrument provides standard scores with a mean of 100 and a standard deviation of 15, which makes scores equivalent to most measures of IQ.

Another measure with particularly strong psychometric properties is the BRIR (Sparrow & Cicchetti, 1978). The BRIR was recently expanded to include more items and increase its applicability to a wider age range of retarded persons at more functional levels. The resulting measure was renamed the Behavior Inventory for Rating Development (BIRD; Sparrow & Cicchetti, 1984). The BIRD is comprised of 75 items, each of which is ordinally scaled from lowest to normal levels of adaptive behavior, and covers five domains of adaptive behavior: (1) Communication, (2) Physical Skills, (3) Self-Help Skills, (4) Self-Control, and (5) Social Skills. A factor-analytic study, however, produced only four interpretable factors and no factor specific to Self-Help Skills. Self-Help Skills items tended to load in either Communication or Physical Skills, depending upon the particular self-help skill required. The advantages of the BIRD are that it is relatively short, is constructed such that the higher the score the more adaptive the behavior, can be easily used as either an interview or a questionnaire, and demonstrates good reliability and validity. It is, however, not normed, and Sparrow and Cicchetti (1984) suggest that it be used primarily as a research tool, although it could be used as a screening device within clinical settings. They further suggest that more comprehensive scales be used when programmatic decisions are needed for retarded persons.

One limitation of the measures described above is the lack of many content items for children who function developmentally below 3 years of age. The WBRS (Song *et al.*, 1980) was designed specifically to be used with children from birth to 4 years of age, or with retarded children (particularly the severely or profoundly retarded) who function below 4 years of age in developmental abilities. The WBRS is composed of 11 subscales: Gross Motor Skills, Fine Motor Skills, Receptive Language, Expressive Language, Play, Socialization, Domestic Activity, Eating, Toileting, Dressing, and Grooming. It is criterion-based as well as norm-referenced, and has been found to be more reliable and valid than the ABS for younger children and severely–profoundly retarded populations functioning at this young developmental level. (Song *et al.*, 1984).

The choice of the most appropriate measure of adaptive function depends primarily on the intent of the user (research vs. clinical assessment), the setting in which the measure will be used (clinic, school, home, institution), the availability of informed or knowledgeable reporters, and the age or functional level of the child being assessed. For general clinical and programmatic use, the ABS and the Vineland are perhaps the most comprehensive, although their length and scoring procedures can make them cumbersome. Both these measures include a scale for maladaptive behavior as well, obviating the need for additional measures. For younger and lower-functioning handicapped children, the WBRS is most useful. The BIRD and the WBRS are particularly useful for research, given their ease of administration and lesser time requirements.

The alternative or perhaps additional approach to assessment of adaptive skills is through direct behavioral observations. A number of studies have shown that adaptive skills can be objectively measured through discrete behavioral observations (Landesman-Dwyer, Berkson, & Romar, 1979; Landesman-Dwyer, Stein, & Sackett, 1978; Thompson & Grabowski, 1977). These studies also demonstrate the importance of the contexts in which adaptive behaviors are measured and the conditions that prompt and maintain those behaviors. It is particularly important in planning behavioral observations of adaptive abilities with mentally retarded children that the developmental context be considered. This is often overlooked, but adaptive ability is age-specific, as may be the context of what appears to be maladaptive behavior. Some developmental criterion should be employed. It may be possible to observe behavior in some contexts where other children of a similar age are available to act as controls for observations (school classrooms, institutional settings). It may, however, be necessary to choose behavioral criteria for performance against specific age norms. However this is accomplished, the appropriate application of the S-O-R-K-C model is dependent upon identifying appropriate developmental contexts. As the presence of behavior problems in retarded children is often associated with a problem in adaptive skills, these too must be specifically assessed.

Assessing Behavior Disorders

As noted previously in this chapter, behavior disorders are frequently associated with mental retardation. Curiously, the theory and study of psychopathology in mental retardation have been left largely unexplored, although Matson (1985) has made a recent attempt to define a biosocial model of psychopathology and mental retardation. Within this model, biological, social, and psychological factors are viewed as interactive elements relevant to etiological, assessment, and treatment consideration. Assessment is of particular importance in clarifying psychopathological conditions in mental retardation, and behavioral assessment approaches can be of

particular value. Much like the measurement of adaptive ability, measurements of behavior disorders have typically utilized various rating scales or direct behavioral observation strategies in combination with structured interviews.

Both the ABS and the revised Vineland measures of adaptive abilities have specific scales related to the presence of maladaptive behavior. Although the revised Vineland Maladaptive Behavior scale is too recently developed to have been extensively researched or used, the ABS maladaptive behavior measures (which make up Part II of the instrument) have received a fair amount of attention. As noted in the preceding section, Part II of the ABS has been criticized for its psychometric properties and construction. Recent studies by Clements and his colleagues (Clements *et al.*, 1980, 1981), however, have strengthened the ABS by devising severity ratings for the maladaptive domains, thereby increasing the measure's reliability and validity.

Many of the studies that have reported on the incidence of behavior disorders in mentally retarded populations have relied on broadly defined categories of behaviors in major surveys (e.g., Jacobson, 1982a, 1982b) or on more traditional methods, such as psychiatric interviews and review of case records (e.g., Benson, 1985); as such, they are not particularly useful within individual behavioral assessment approaches. A number of general behavioral rating scales or personality inventories exist that are sensitive to behavior disorders displayed by mentally retarded children—for example, the Child Behavior Checklist (Achenbach & Edelbrock, 1983); the Personality Inventory for Children (Wirt, Lachar, Klinedinst, & Seat, 1977); the Louisville Behavior Checklist (L. C. Miller, 1967); the Eyberg Child Behavior Inventory (Eyberg, 1980); the Conners Parent Rating Scale (Conners, 1970); the Conners Teacher Rating Scale (Conners, 1969); and the Preschool Behavior Questionnaire (Behar & Stringfield, 1974)—but these instruments were not specifically designed for use with retarded populations. An exception is the recently developed Aberrant Behavior Checklist (ABC; Aman, Singh, Stewart, & Field, 1985a). The ABC is a 58-item measure with five subscale factors: Irritability, Lethargy, Stereotypies, Hyperactivity, and Inappropriate Speech. The checklist has adequate reliability and validity, and was in fact validated against actual behavioral observations conducted by independent observers, who used interval recording techniques to assess the frequency of behaviors associated with the five subscale factors (Aman, Singh, Stewart, & Field, 1985b). This measure was developed to be particularly useful for severely and profoundly retarded persons, and also to specifically assess the effects of medication use and behavioral treatment interventions.

Direct behavioral observations are perhaps the most frequently employed behavioral assessment procedure for measuring specific behavior problems, as direct observational approaches provide data not only about the type and frequency of the problem, but also about the antecedent and consequent events that serve to control it. Typically, observational assessment is the initial segment of all behavioral interventions when baseline data are taken. A wealth of research and case study investigations have shown the applicability of this technique with a wide variety of behavior disorders in mentally retarded children (Wetherby & Baumeister, 1981), including attentional deficits (Morrow, Burke, & Buell, 1985), self-injurious behavior (Lockwood & Bourland, 1982), stereotypic behaviors (MacLean & Baumeister, 1981; Thompson & Berkson, 1985), a wide range of conduct disorders (Breiner & Beck, 1984; Thompson & Grabowski, 1977), parent–child interactional deficits (Peterson, Robinson, & Littman, 1983), and severe aggressive and destructive behaviors (Luiselli, Myles, & Liffman-Quinn, 1983). It has also been used in monitoring the effects of drug interventions (Singh & Winton, 1983).

A study of stereotyped behavior of severely retarded children (Thompson & Berkson, 1985) exemplifies an observational approach to assessment of a particularly frequent and difficult behavior exhibited by retarded children. Children received standardized developmental assessments, and were assessed for visual and motor disorders as well. Observations were conducted in classrooms during teaching times, and subsequently in free-play situations. Observations were conducted for 25 minutes, and every 30 seconds an observer recorded the behavior of the child and teacher at that moment (for the classroom episode) or the child only (for the free-play episode). Child behavior was rated in six subgroups: stereotyped behavior without objects, stereotyped behavior with objects, self-injury, simple manipulation of objects, complex manipulation of objects, and

manipulation of self. Teacher attention was recorded in one of four categories: informal play or conversation, formal response concerning curricular activity, formal reaction to the stereotyped behavior, or no interaction. Frequency counts of stereotypic behavior in the two contexts showed that more frequent stereotypic behavior occurred in free play. The results also showed that stereotypical behavior was more frequent in less developmentally functional children and in older retarded children, and that teacher attention was negatively related to stereotypies without objects but unrelated to the occurrence of stereotypies with objects. The complexity of the interaction of age, setting, developmental skill, and type of stereotypies was also found in a similar observational study of a developmentally delayed infant (MacLean & Baumeister, 1981).

Both the use of rating scales and direct observational methodologies are particularly salient to the behavioral assessment of behavioral disorders in retarded children, especially when combined with other developmental assessment information (e.g., Thompson & Berkson, 1985). The particular strength of the observational methodology, however, is the relevance of the data obtained for planning subsequent behavioral interventions.

Social Skills

Although the assessment measures described above in the section on adaptive behavior include some basic notions of social skills, they provide only a global assessment of social behavior and little in the way of identifying specific interpersonal competencies of retarded children that may require attention (Singh & Winton, 1983). Furthermore, measures of adaptive behavior generally focus only on maladaptive social interaction, which differs dramatically in content and meaning from skills that may be only ineffective or nonexistent. An exact definition of what comprises social skills is difficult to detail (see Hops & Greenwood, 1988), as numerous models have been proposed. Several excellent reviews are available (Gresham, 1981; McFall, 1982; Mulick & Schroeder, 1980), but the major salient feature of social skill is consistently identified as verbal and nonverbal interpersonal interaction—an area of deficit characteristic of mentally retarded children (Grossman, 1977).

Social skills are generally situation-specific

(Bates & Harvey, 1978), although there are models based more on trait notions (McFall, 1982). Regardless, the questions relevant within behavioral assessment involve (1) identifying those interpersonal behaviors that are or are not occurring, (2) with whom this is occurring, and (3) in what social context. A specific model for analyzing the interpersonal social skills of retarded persons has been described by Bernstein (1981). It focuses on five measurable behavioral dimensions: (1) content of the interactions (play, eating, work, weather, etc.); (2) intersubjective aspects of the interactions, involving verbal components (questions, statements, directions, demands, requests, etc.); (3) extralinguistic components of the interactions (eye contact, posture, gestures, facial expression, etc.); (4) type of relationship (parent–child, other adult–child, peer–peer, stranger–child, etc.); (5) setting in which the interactions occur (home, school, work, agency, store, theatre, etc.). Bernstein's model presents a specific outline of the salient features of social interactions that can be measured within the specific context of behavioral assessment.

As with the behavioral assessment of adaptive skill and behavior disorders, there are a number of methods available for assessing the social skills or social competency of retarded children. The choice of methods depends upon the specific concerns at hand. Social competency in retarded children has been measured with sociometric strategies typical of social skill assessments in nonretarded populations (Connolly, 1983). The critical features of sociometric procedures are (1) using peers as a source of information and (2) obtaining a restricted number of criterion nominations. One of the most common sociometric procedures is the use of peer nomination, in which children are asked to identify those peers who are their friends or with whom they would like to work or play. The score on such measures is the number of nominations an identified child receives. The social skill correlates of popularity are generally found to be supportiveness, cooperation, leadership, and helpfulness (Coie, Dodge, & Coppotelli, 1982). Peer nomination techniques with retarded children present some difficulties, however, as they are less reliable with developmentally younger children and highlight unpopular children, which can be troublesome in mainstreaming classroom settings (Connolly, 1983). Peer rating procedures, an alternative sociometric measurement, lessen some of the

difficulties, as all children in a setting are asked to rate every other child as to how much they would like to play with the child on a 5-point scale. The score received by any one child is the average of the ratings from the entire class; this provides a more reliable estimate of the child's status.

Peer assessment procedures are also available, in which peers are asked to nominate or rate their peers according to a list of specific descriptors of behavior and characteristics. In one recent study, peer assessments were used to determine perceived behavior correlates of rejection of retarded children by their normal peers (Gottlieb, Semmel, & Veldman, 1978). Items describing behavioral disruptions were found to be most strongly related to rejection. Sociometric assessments by teachers are also frequently used, especially with populations of retarded children, as questions may arise as to the ability of retarded peers to make subtle social distinctions. Several studies have had teachers rank peers on the basis of popularity (Connolly & Doyle, 1981; Greenwood, Walker, Todd, & Hops, 1979) and have found teachers to be more reliable and better predictors of social competence and positive peer interactions. Teachers ratings and peer ratings are, however, generally highly intercorrelated (Connolly, 1983). Several specific teacher assessment measures have also been developed to rate child social skills, including the Kohn Social Competence Scale (Kohn, 1977) and the Pupil Evaluation Inventory (Prinz, Swan, Liebert, Weintraub, & Neale, 1978). The utility of these instruments with populations of retarded children has yet to be specifically established, although teacher rating instruments may be more helpful with retarded children than peer instruments have been.

Observational assessments of the social skills of retarded children have been surprisingly few, but observational methodologies can be particularly useful (Greenwood et al., 1979). Observational studies of the behavior of retarded children have not been sufficient to address clinical issues involving selection of target behaviors (Greenwood, Walker, & Hops, 1977), primarily because behavioral categories observed have been too broad, samples of behavior have been too brief, and observations have focused on frequencies of single behaviors rather than ongoing interactions (Strain, 1983). Recently, Strain (1983) has developed a methodology for assessing social skill target behaviors of retarded children across contexts. Eight positive behavior categories were developed (reward-related activity, complimentary verbal statement, play organizer, sharing, physical assistance, rough-and-tumble play, affection, and conflict resolution). Two broad categories of negative behavior were also included (negative motor–gestural and negative vocal–verbal). Also observed within this system was whether the behavior was a response to some other's behavior or a spontaneous initiation. These behaviors were observed continuously in four settings permitting social interactions: (1) children entering a classroom, (2) classroom free-play period, (3) classroom instructional period, and (4) after school when children were waiting to leave. Strain's results are interesting in a number of respects. They indicated that no setting-specific effects were operative; that high-status handicapped children were more often engaged in sharing, affection, assistance, and play organizing; that low-status handicapped children engaged in significantly more negative initiations; and that nonhandicapped children were not adversely affected by exposure to handicapped peers.

The Strain (1983) study is particularly meaningful, not only for the clarity and potential utility of the specific observational model described, but also because it demonstrates the relationship of sociometric status to social skills in retarded populations. This suggests that greater understanding of the social skills of retarded children can be gained through some combination of sociometric and observational techniques in the behavioral assessment context.

Assessing Stress and Families

So far, this chapter has considered what might seem a fairly exhaustive list of assessment areas. As noted earlier, however, ecological contexts for behavior and development must be considered within the assessment process, because the retarded child does not live or behave in a single noninteractive context. Most important within such considerations is the family, as so much research has indicated that families of handicapped children are at risk for higher stress and greater psychological problems (Crnic, Friedrich, & Greenberg, 1983), and the family provides the primary context in which children develop (Bronfenbrenner, 1979). If we are to reach some understanding of the cognitive, adaptive, and behavioral functioning of the retarded child, we need a clear notion of how the family adapts to the difficulties that such a child tends to present, as well as of how the family interacts with that child.

A sizable literature is developing on family stress and its effects upon individual family members, the target child, and the family as a system (Beckman, 1983; Friedrich et al., 1983; Friedrich, Wilturner, & Cohen, 1985; Holroyd, 1974; Holroyd & McArthur, 1976; Wikler 1981). Basically, this research indicates that families of retarded children experience more life stress generally and much stress specifically related to their retarded children. Furthermore, this stress adversely affects parent–child interactions, child functioning, and parental participation in interventions. With these findings in mind, it is clearly important to assess the amount of stress perceived by family members of retarded children.

There are several ways in which this assessment can be accomplished. First, the interview may be used to assess the degree of impact that parents see a retarded child as having on the family and the functioning of its members. There are also several measures that can be employed to assess the apparent stress. Perhaps the best measure is the Questionnaire on Resources and Stress (QRS; Holroyd, 1974). This is a measure that was specifically designed to be used on populations of families with developmentally disabled children; it identifies specific problems and stresses along 15 dimensions. This measure is, however, quite long (285 items), and the factor structure has not always been found to relate well to the 15 subscales proposed. A recent attempt to revise the QRS resulted in a much shorter measure with four reliable factors (Friedrich et al., 1983). The four subscales are Child Problems, Parent and Family Problems, Pessimism in Relation to the Child's Disorder, and Physical Disabilities in the Child. Although primarily used in research studies to date, this revised version of the QRS could be a valuable clinical tool, if used to suggest the variety of stressors present and the amount of stress perceived. The measure is presented in Figure 1. It should be kept in mind that this tool is not a standardized instrument, as are so many of the other rating scales that have been presented. Other adaptation of the QRS exist as well, with formats much briefer than the original measure and adequate reliabilities and validities (e.g., Salisbury, 1986).

Assessment of the family context also requires measurement of how the family functions as a system across various dimensions important to family integrity. There are two ways in which this can be accomplished. One is to use a rating scale developed to measure family functioning, and the other is to conduct naturalistic and/or structured behavioral observations of family members. There are several rating scales that have proven to be useful within families in general and families with retarded children in particular. The Family Environment Scale (FES; Moos & Moos, 1981) is a 90-item, normed rating scale completed by parents. The FES provides scores in 10 subscales (Cohesion, Expressiveness, Conflict, Independence, Achievement Orientation, Active/Recreational Orientation, Moral/Religious Em-

phasis, Intellectual/Cultural Orientation, Organization, and Control). A number of studies have shown that the FES can be used meaningfully with families of retarded children, and that scores on this measure are positively correlated with perceived stress related to the retarded child (Crnic, in press; Friedrich *et al.*, in press).

Naturalistic or structured observations of the families of retarded children have been few, but those that have been reported suggest that such observations can be important indicators of interactional problems and ability to follow through with intervention regimens. Stoneman, Brody, and Abbott (1983) recently reported an observational study of interactions between mother–child dyads, father–child dyads, and mother–father–child triads in families with a

---

FIGURE 1. A short form of the Questionnaire on Resources and Stress. From "A Short-Form of the Questionnaire on Resources and Stress" by W. N. Friedrich, M. T. Greenberg, and K. Crnic, 1983, *American Journal of Mental Deficiency, 88*, p. 47. Copyright 1983 by the American Association on Mental Deficiency. Adapted by permission.

This questionnaire deals with your feelings about a child in your family. There are many blanks on the questionnaire. Imagine the child's name filled in on each blank. Give your honest feelings and opinions. Please answer all of the questions, even if they do not seem to apply. If it is difficult to decide True (T) or False (F), answer in terms of what you or your family feel or do *most* of the time. Sometimes the questions refer to problems your family does not have. Nevertheless, they can be answered True or False, even then. Please begin. Remember to answer all the questions.

1. _____ doesn't communicate with others of his/her age group.	T	F
2. Other members of the family have to do without things because of _____.	T	F
3. Our family agrees on important matters.	T	F
4. I worry about what will happen to _____ when I can no longer take care of him/her.	T	F
5. The constant demands for care for _____ limit growth and development of someone else in our family.	T	F
6. _____ is limited in the kind of work he/she can do to make a living.	T	F
7. I have accepted the fact that _____ might have to live out his/her life in some special setting (e.g., institution or group home).	T	F
8. _____ can feed himself/herself.	T	F
9. I have given up things I have really wanted to do in order to care for _____.	T	F
10. _____ is able to fit into the family social group.	T	F
11. Sometimes I avoid taking _____ out in public.	T	F
12. In the future, our family's social life will suffer because of increased responsibilities and financial stress.	T	F
13. It bothers me that _____ will always be this way.	T	F
14. I feel tense whenever I take _____ out in public.	T	F
15. I can go visit with friends whenever I want.	T	F
16. Taking _____ on a vacation spoils pleasure for the whole family.	T	F
17. _____ knows his/her own address.	T	F
18. The family does as many things together now as we ever did.	T	F
19. _____ is aware who he/she is.	T	F

(continued)

FIGURE 1. *(continued)*

20. I get upset with the way my life is going.	T	F
21. Sometimes I feel very embarrassed because of _____.	T	F
22. _____ doesn't do as much as he/she should be able to do.	T	F
23. It is difficult to communicate with _____ because he/she has difficulty understanding what is being said to him/her.	T	F
24. There are many places where we can enjoy ourselves as a family when _____ comes along.	T	F
25. _____ is over-protected.	T	F
26. _____ is able to take part in games or sports.	T	F
27. _____ has too much time on his/her hands.	T	F
28. I am disappointed that _____ does not lead a normal life.	T	F
29. Time drags for _____, especially free time.	T	F
30. _____ can't pay attention very long.	T	F
31. It is easy for me to relax.	T	F
32. I worry about what will be done with _____ when he/she gets older.	T	F
33. I get almost too tired to enjoy myself.	T	F
34. One of the things I appreciate about _____ is his/her confidence.	T	F
35. There is a lot of anger and resentment in our family.	T	F
36. _____ is able to go to the bathroom alone.	T	F
37. _____ cannot remember what he/she says from one moment to the next.	T	F
38. _____ can ride a bus.	T	F
39. It is easy to communicate with _____.	T	F
40. The constant demands to care for _____ limit my growth and development.	T	F
41. _____ accepts himself/herself as a person.	T	F
42. I feel sad when I think of _____.	T	F
43. I often worry about what will happen to _____ when I no longer can take care of him/her.	T	F
44. People can't understand what _____ tries to say.	T	F
45. Caring for _____ puts a strain on me.	T	F
46. Members of our family get to do the same kinds of things other families do.	T	F
47. _____ will always be a problem to us.	T	F
48. _____ is able to express his/her feelings to others.	T	F
49. _____ has to use a bedpan or a diaper.	T	F
50. I rarely feel blue.	T	F
51. I am worried much of the time.	T	F
52. _____ can walk without help.	T	F

Down syndrome child. They constructed an observational scheme involving roles that each member could take (e.g., teacher, manager, helper, playmate) and types of behaviors observed in those roles (solitary activity, positive verbalization, negative verbalization, positive affect, negative affect, touch that was either positive or negative in nature, and others). These observations were conducted in each family's home (although this is not necessary for every clinical assessment) during an unstructured play session. Behaviors were coded sequentially to determine the contingent responsiveness between the interactive members, and interval coding was also accomplished, scoring target behaviors that occurred during each 10-second interval (any one behavior was counted only once for each 10-second interval).

Of interest was the fact that measured reliabilities ranged from .81 to .97 for the behavior categories observed. Generally, observations indicated that parents of Down syndrome children were more directive and spent more time managing behavior (which may be intrusive within developmental contexts) than did parents of nonhandicapped children, and that mothers took a superordinate control role when triadic interactions occurred. The Down syndrome children responded less contingently to parental behavior than did nonhandicapped children, indicating that they were more difficult to manage. This less contingent responsiveness found in the Down syndrome children is similar to findings across observational studies of retarded children and their parents (Crnic, Friedrich, & Greenberg, 1983).

Although attempts at observing family units are most desirable, this is difficult at times, given the constraints of parental work schedules and other factors. Frequently, however, problems within a family may involve only one parent and the retarded child. As noted previously, research has indicated that parent–child interactions occurring on a dyadic level are problematic when the child is retarded. This problematic interaction is characterized by greater maternal control, directiveness, and overprotection, and less positive affect, while the retarded child displays unresponsiveness and noncompliance (Breiner & Forehand, 1982; Cunningham et al., 1981; Eheart, 1982; Kogan et al., 1969). In particular, these interactional deficits clearly show the problems that characterize asynchronous and nonreciprocal relationships. (Vietze et al., 1978), and they suggest the need to include assessments of parent–child interactions in behavioral assessments of retarded children. Each of these studies has involved observational techniques and systems that can be individually applied to parent–retarded child dyads, similar to the Stoneman et al. (1983) procedure discussed above.

To illustrate this last point, Breiner and Forehand (1982) observed the behavioral interactions of mother–retarded child pairs within the home context. For comparison purposes, they also observed mother–child interactions with populations of clinic-referred noncompliant children and nonclinic-referred children. Parent–child pairs were observed in their homes under naturalistic conditions for three 40-minute periods on different days. The observational system employed involved the sequential coding of mother and child behavior in 30-second intervals collected in 5-minute blocks. Occurrence or nonoccurrence of deviant child behavior was also recorded in 30-second time intervals. Parental behaviors coded included rewards, total commands made to child (separately coded as being either clear or vague in instruction), and contingent attention (representing verbal or physical praise given within 5 seconds following child compliance). Child behavior coded included deviant behaviors other than noncompliance (e.g., whining, crying, negative behavior, or destructive behavior) and compliance–noncompliance (defined as initiation of a response within 5 seconds of a command being given). This system provided clear reliabilities, due to the behavioral objectivity of the categories being coded. Results from this observational study indicated that mothers or retarded children engaged in significantly more interactive behavior with their children than did mothers in the other two groups studied, giving more rewards, more commands of both types, and more contingent attention. The retarded children, however, were significantly less compliant, again demonstrating the asynchrony typical of these dyads. Such an observational approach to assessing parent–child interaction can be incorporated into behavioral assessment strategies with families of retarded children when these dyads appear particularly problematic.

As families are often involved in interventions for their children, observations of family interactions can be helpful in establishing baseline information on how families perform together; in addition, repeating these observations over time during the course of intervention will provide data on change within the families and/or indicate when problems in the intervention procedures arise. A good example of such a strategy is provided by Kozloff (1979), in a book that describes in great detail a behavioral program for children with various learning and associated behavior problems. Kozloff suggests that baseline observations of each family be done on at least three occasions, and that the family be observed in three different contexts: sessions involving the parents attempting to teach their child a skill, sessions involving short behavioral problems such as temper tantrums or whining, and a free interaction period. He further suggests that videotapes of these interactions be made, although this is not always practical or feasible within clinical assessments. Within these observational contexts, both the parents and the child are observed for behaviors identified in an assessment interview or behaviors relevant to the issue at hand (teaching, behavior problem relationships). This information is then used as a baseline with which to identify areas of needed behavioral intervention and to check later progress throughout the intervention phase. Such a system can also be utilized within educational settings (Kozloff, 1979).

Observations in Extrafamilial Ecologies

Throughout this chapter, I have emphasized the importance of context for assessing the behavior and development of mentally retarded children. Although the focus has primarily been on tools for assessing the child within the context of the family, specific applications have been made to assessments in other contexts. Including other contexts within the behavioral assessment of retarded children is particularly important, because there are other settings in which problem behaviors are a part of the initial concerns brought to the assessment. Most frequently, the other context of concern will be the school setting. A number of rating scales, questionnaires, interview techniques, and observational techniques have been described within specific skill measurement sections of this chapter. In terms of the methods involved in the behavioral observations within the classroom setting, there is little that differs from the methods employed elsewhere, as the techniques previously presented would indicate. There are, however, a number of additional considerations or approaches that may prove helpful within the classroom context.

First, teachers must be enlisted and interviewed as to the problems noted in learning and behavior that are of primary concern to them, and these behaviors should be made the targets of the observations, along with any other identified behaviors. It is important to learn about classroom routine, so that observations can be scheduled at times when the behaviors of concern are most likely to be seen. It is often a useful strategy to randomly choose another child in the classroom to serve as a "control," conducting the same observations on this child as on the target child. This will usually turn up surprising results, especially when the target child is being observed because of concerns involving behavioral disruption. This control child can also serve as a developmental standard within the classroom with which to compare the target child. Finally, recess is a particularly useful observational period, even though teachers frequently like to use this time to discuss the target child with the observer. The playground, however, is perhaps the richest naturalistic source of social skill information available, and the opportunity for observation during this time can be critical.

The other major context in which mentally retarded children are frequently assessed is that of residential or group home placements. Again, the procedures employed in these settings to perform behavioral observations do not vary dramatically from those discussed previously in other sections of this chapter. Ethical concerns do arise within these settings, however, and coercion of residents within specific observational situations has at times offered a problem in this regard, which requires careful attention to the rights of child residents and issues involving invasion of privacy. Nevertheless, the major focus on the family context in this chapter does not imply that alternative ecological contexts are of lesser behavioral significance. The importance of any context for behavioral assessment is defined by the behavior of interest and its salience within the setting being considered.

Issues of Social Validation

The emphasis in this chapter on the behavioral assessment of mentally retarded children has been on a multimodal approach to assessment with these children and their families. Behavioral ratings and observations have become a crucial element of this process, as performance on measures other than intelligence or specific academic skills has gained greater status in the area. Assessment has as its goal not only diagnostic considerations, but also the identification of specific problems or goals for intervention that are relevant to the social context in which they are applied, thereby demonstrating social validity (Wolf, 1978). The concept and process of social validation, then, is a critical concern in assessment of mentally retarded children, as the goals for interventions move toward normalization concepts (Kazdin & Matson, 1981) and functioning within non-handicapped environments.

The basic issue involved in social validation involves selecting a contextually important focus of intervention. Within the assessment process with mentally retarded children, Kazdin and Matson (1981) have indicated that two modes of assessment are appropriate for determining social validity: social comparisons and subjective evaluations. "Social comparison" involves observation of normal individuals to provide information as to the skills necessary to perform at an acceptable level within a specific context (a method that also serves the function of noting the developmental appropriateness of a given behavior). "Subjective evaluation" involves soliciting the opinions of persons who, by virtue of their expertise in retardation or specific knowledge of a particular child, are in a position to judge what skill is necessary to perform at a certain level or what behavior needs to be a focus of concern. Examples of both these methodologies have been described at various points throughout this chapter. Although both of these techniques can have problems that may require attention from both researchers and clinicians, they can provide a greater understanding of the characteristics distinguishing performance between children with and children without intellectual disorders.

Integrating Assessment Results

If one approaches the behavioral assessment of mentally retarded children from a multimodal perspective, then one is left with a large amount of data to be integrated into a coherent whole. This not an easy process, especially given that assessment data from various sources and measures will not always dovetail in a way that is easily explainable. Nevertheless, cognitive, adaptive, behavioral, and social context data can be compared to note equivalence across areas and patterns of specific strengths and weaknesses. Within a behavioral approach to assessment data, a particular caveat involves not going beyond the data collected, or beyond the framework of what is known about the measures employed. For example, a score from a single IQ measure of a 10-year-old with equivalent data from academic and adaptive measures may indicate that mental retardation is present; yet accurately predicting that child's vocational potential is a risky proposition at best. Several questions may be helpful in conceptualizing results from a large data collection:

1. When all standardized test data are collated and compared, are the scores equivalent, or is significant scatter present across skill areas?
2. Are results from previous test data available? If so, how do the present results compare? Do these scores suggest stability or instability of performance over time?
3. In testing limits and alternate strategies during standardized assessment, how did changes in the structure affect performance?
4. What behavioral factors were identified as problematic, and what behaviors were identified as strengths? How did these affect the outcomes of the standardized tests given, if at all?
5. Did performance or behavior vary across settings in which these behaviors were measured? What settings produced what performance or behavior, and what were the critical parameters of these settings that might account for these differences? Was there equivalence across settings?
6. Have historical variables (developmental,

medical, behavioral) been reported during interviews that might be relevant to the performance observed?

This list of questions is certainly not exhaustive, but it can serve as a basic guideline with which to begin integrating one's results. It is worth noting as well that every finding collected may not require integration with every other finding. Individual findings have importance in their own right and can stand on their own merit if found to be reliable.

Providing Feedback

One final consideration in the assessment process, which has received little attention in the literature on assessment of any type, is that of providing the results to parents. This can be an especially critical concern when assessing children suspected of mental retardation, as such a label carries tremendous implications for parents and is generally not well understood. Experience suggests that most parents have the idea that "retardation" implies the inability to learn or progress and eventually requires institutionalization of a child who is capable of doing almost nothing for himself or herself. The "retardation" label also implies a dramatic loss for the parents in terms of the expectations and hopes that they and other family members have for the child. This is a diagnosis that is not easy to hear and not easy to give. This latter point is important: It is not uncommon to find that children have been evaluated in the past on numerous occasions and have functioned each time within a retarded range, but that the term "mental retardation" has never been used with the parents.

Recently, Shea (1984) has presented a model for providing parents feedback about assessments that indicate retardation is present. She notes that a feedback session should have three goals: (1) providing specific information about the child's developmental functioning and answering all of the parents' questions about it; (2) supporting and helping parents as they begin to cope emotionally with the knowledge of their child's handicap; and (3) assisting parents in making plans to carry out recommendations and interventions. Euphemisms are often used to describe children's functioning when it is indicative of retardation. The most frequently used is "developmental delay." While such a term is descriptive and perhaps even appropriate with infants and young preschool-age children, the term "mental retardation" needs to be used honestly and explained fully when it is appropriate to do so.

Shea provides a nine-step procedure to be used as a guideline in providing feedback to parents on a diagnosis of mental retardation. These steps begin with restating the parental concerns presented initially, and move through explaining the assessment procedures, stating the general findings of delayed development, clarifying the specific findings from each data source, comparing chronological and developmental age functioning, explaining the concept of slow development as being synonymous with mental retardation, emphasizing that retarded children do continue to learn and progress, explaining that different degrees of retardation are related to differing rates of development, and making it clear that chronological age catchup is unlikely to occur. One point deserving of attention but not included in this model is the clear notion that behavior is related to development functioning and ability and is an important parameter of the functional description of the disorder. Parents often focus exclusively on the IQ scores, to the detriment of other important factors that can affect intellectual ability.

The basic issues in providing feedback effectively to parents involve notions of honesty in relation to the findings and sensitivity to parental response. It may take more than a single session to adequately cover the material found during the assessment, as well as its implications, and to allow the parents to ask all the questions they have. In fact, parents often do not conceptualize many questions they have until some time after they have had a chance to think about the results presented. Therefore, planning for more than one session is often a good idea. Although the feedback session is often a painful and difficult time for parents, it can also be the beginning of increased awareness or understanding of a child's specific needs and the roles that parents can take to help meet those needs. This is often the first step in enlisting parents as an effective part of successful intervention.

SUMMARY

Behavioral assessment of children with mental retardation is a complex and often time-consuming process, as the heterogeneity within this group of children is so great. A multimodal approach to assessing these children's functioning is necessitated both by the heterogeneity apparent and by the definition of the disorder itself, which requires identification of cognitive, adaptive, social, and behavioral functioning. Beyond standard measures and rating scales, behavioral observations in structured and unstructured situations are critical to clear delineation of the nature of the disorder at hand and to suggestions for specific intervention. Throughout this chapter, the importance of ecological context has been emphasized, both in terms of the effects that families and their responses have on the functioning of retarded children and in relation to the notion that retarded children's behavior is likely to vary across contexts. However, context is important as well in ascertaining the social validity of the behaviors chosen for assessment and subsequent intervention.

REFERENCES

Achenbach, T. M. (1982). *Developmental psychopathology* (2nd ed.). New York: Ronald Press.

Achenbach, T. M., & Edelbrock, C. (1983). *Manual for the Child Behavior Checklist and Revised Child Behavior Profile*. Burlington: University of Vermont, Department of Psychiatry.

Aman, M. G., Singh, N. N., Stewart, A. W., & Field, C. J. (1985a). The Aberrant Behavior Checklist: A behavior rating scale for the assessment of treatment effects. *American Journal of Mental Deficiency, 89*, 485–491.

Aman, M. G., Singh, N. N., Stewart, A. W., & Field, C. J. (1985b). Psychometric characteristics of the Aberrant Behavior Checklist. *American Journal of Mental Deficiency, 89*, 492–502.

American Psychiatric Association. (1980). *Diagnostic and statistical manual of mental disorders* (3rd ed.). Washington, DC: Author.

Anastasi, A. (1976). *Psychological testing* (4th ed.). New York: Macmillan.

Bakeman, R., & Brown, J. V. (1980). Early interaction: Consequences for social and mental development at three years. *Child Development, 51*, 437–447.

Balthazar, E. E. (1976). *The Balthazar Scales of Adaptive Behavior: Section II. The Scale of Functional Independence (BSAB-II)*. Palo Alto, CA: Consulting Psychologists Press.

Bates, P., & Harvey, J. (1978). Social skills training with the mentally retarded. In O. C. Karan (Ed.), *Habilitation practices with the severely developmentally disabled* (Vol. 2). Madison, WI: Waisman Center.

Bayley, N. (1949). Consistency and variability in the growth of intelligence from birth to eighteen years. *Journal of Genetic Psychology, 75*, 165–196.

Bayley, N. (1969). *Bayley Scales of Infant Development: Birth to two years*. New York: Psychological Corporation.

Behar, L. B., & Stringfield, S. (1974). A behavior rating scale for the preschool child. *Developmental Psychology, 10*, 601–610.

Backman, P. J. (1983). The influence of selected child characteristics on stress in families of handicapped infants. *American Journal of Mental Deficiency, 88,* 150–156.

Beery, K. E. (1967). *Developmental Test of Visual–Motor Integration.* Chicago: Follett.

Bennett, F. C., Robinson, N. M., & Sells, C. J. (1982). Hyaline membrane disease, birthweight, and gestational age: Effects on development in the first two years. *American Journal of Diseases of Children, 136,* 888–891.

Benson, B. A. (1985). Behavior disorders and mental retardation: Associations with age, sex, and level of functioning in an outpatient clinic sample. *Applied Research in Mental Retardation, 6,* 79–85.

Berkowitz, G. S. (1981). A epidemiologic study of preterm delivery. *American Journal of Epidemiology, 113,* 81–92.

Bernstein, G. S. (1981). Research issues in training interpersonal skills for the mentally retarded. *Education and Training of the Mentally Retarded, 16,* 70–74.

Bersoff, D. N., & Grieger, R. M. (1971). An interview model for the psychosituational assessment of children's behavior. *American Journal of Orthopsychiatry, 41,* 483–493.

Bijou, S. W. (1966). A functional analysis of retarded development. In N. R. Ellis (Ed.), *International review of research in mental retardation* (Vol. 1, pp. 1–19). New York: Academic Press.

Borthwick, S., Meyers, C. E., & Eyman, R. K. (1981). Comparative adaptive and maladaptive behavior of mentally retarded clients of five residential settings in three western states. In R. H. Bruininks, C. E. Meyers, B. B. Sigford, & K. C. Lakin (Eds.), *Deinstitutionalization and community adjustment of mentally retarded people* (Monograph No. 41, pp. 351–359). Washington, DC: American Association on Mental Deficiency.

Brachfield, S., Goldberg, S., & Sloman, J. (1980). Parent–infant interaction in free play at 8 and 12 months: Effects of prematurity and immaturity. *Infant Behavior and Development, 3,* 289–305.

Bradway, K. P., & Thompson, C. W. (1962). Intelligence at adulthood: A twenty-five year follow-up. *Journal of Educational Psychology, 53,* 1–14.

Breiner, J., & Beck, S. (1984). Parents as change agents in the management of their developmentally delayed children's noncompliant behaviors: A critical review. *Applied Research in Mental Retardation, 5,* 259–278.

Breiner, J., & Forehand, R. (1982). Mother–child interactions: A comparison of a clinic referred developmentally delayed group and two non-delayed groups. *Applied Research in Mental Retardation, 3,* 175–183.

Bronfenbrenner, U. (1979). *The ecology of human development: Experiments by nature and design.* Cambridge, MA: Harvard University Press.

Caldwell, B., & Bradley, R. (1979). *Home Observation for Measurement of the Environment.* Little Rock: University of Arkansas, Center for Child Development and Education.

Ciminero, A. R., & Drabman, R. S. (1977). Current developments in the behavioral assessment of children. In B. B. Lahey & A. E. Kazdin (Eds.), *Advances in child clinical psychology* (Vol. 1, pp. 47–82). New York: Plenum Press.

Clarren, S. T., & Smith, D. W. (1978). The fetal alcohol syndrome. *New England Journal of Medicine, 298,* 1063–1068.

Cleland, C. C. (1979). Mislabeling and replication: Methodological caveats. *American Journal of Mental Deficiency, 83,* 648–649.

Clements, P. R., Bost, L. W., DuBois, Y. G., & Turpin, W. B. (1980). Adaptive Behavior Scale, Part Two: Relative severity and of maladaptive behavior. *American Journal of Mental Deficiency, 84,* 465–469.

Clements, P. R., DuBois, Y., Bost, L., & Bryan, C. (1981). Adaptive Behavior Scale, Part Two: Predictive efficiency of severity and frequency scores. *American Journal of Mental Deficiency, 85,* 433–434.

Coie, J. D., Dodge, K. A., & Coppotelli, H. (1982). Dimensions and types of social status: A cross-age perspective. *Developmental Psychology, 18,* 557–570.

Conners, C. K. (1969). A teacher rating scale for use in drug studies with children. *American Journal of Psychiatry, 126,* 884–888.

Conners, C. K. (1970). Symptom patterns in hyperkinetic, neurotic, and normal children. *Child Development, 41,* 667–682.

Connolly, J. A. (1983). A review of sociometric procedures in the assessment of social competencies in children. *Applied Research in Mental Retardation, 4,* 315–327.

Connolly, J. A., & Doyle, A. B. (1981). Assessment of social competence in preschoolers: Teachers versus peers. *Developmental Psychology, 17,* 415–456.

Connolly, J. A., Nachtman, W., & Pritchett, E. M. (1976). *KeyMath Diagnostic Arithmetic Test.* Circle Pines, MN: American Guidance Service.

Crnic, K. A. (in press). Families of children with Down syndrome: Ecological contexts and characteristics. In D. Cicchetti & M. Beeghly (Eds.), *Down syndrome: The developmental perspective.* Cambridge, MA: Harvard University Press.

Crnic, K. A., Freidrich, W. N., & Greenberg, M. T. (1983). Adaptation of families with mentally retarded children: A model of stress, coping, and family ecology. *American Journal of Mental Deficiency, 88,* 125–138.

Crnic, K. A., & Greenberg, M. (1984, April). *Social interaction and developmental competence of preterm and full term infants from birth to 24 months: Predicting outcomes.* Paper presented at the International Conference on Infant Studies, New York.

Crnic, K. A., & Greenberg, M. T. (1985, April). *Transactional relationships between perceived family style, risk status, and mother–child interaction in two year olds.* Paper presented at the meeting of the Society for Research in Child Development, Toronto.

Crnic, K. A., Greenberg, M. T., Ragozin, A. S., Robinson, N. M., & Basham, R. B. (1983). Effects of stress and social support on mothers and premature and full-term infants. *Child Development, 54,* 209–217.

Crnic, K. A., Ragozin, A. S., Greenberg, M. T., Robinson, N. M., & Basham, R. B. (1983). Social interaction and developmental competence of preterm and full-term infants during the first year of life. *Child Development, 54,* 1199–1210.

Cronbach, L. J. (1975). Five decades of public controversy over mental testing. *American Psychologist, 30,* 1–14.

Cummings, S. T. (1976). The impact of the child's deficiency on the father: A study of fathers of mentally retarded and of chronically ill children. *American Journal of Orthopsychiatry, 46,* 246–255.

Cunningham, C. E., Rueler, E., Blackwell, J., & Deck, J. (1981). Behavioral and linguistic developments in the interactions of normal and retarded children with their mothers. *Child Development, 52,* 62–70.

Dingman, H. F., & Tarjan, G. (1960). Mental retardation and the normal distribution curve. *American Journal of Mental Deficiency, 64,* 991–994.

DiVitto, B., & Goldberg, S. (1979). The effects of newborn medical status on early parent–infant interaction. In T. M. Field, A. M. Sostek, S. Goldberg, & H. H. Shuman (Eds.), *Infants born at risk,* (pp. 311–332). New York: Spectrum.

Doll, E. A. (1964). *Vineland Scale of Social Maturity.* Minneapolis: American Guidance Service.

Dunn, L. M., & Markwardt, F. C., Jr. (1970). *Peabody Individual Achievement Test.* Circle Pines, MN: American Guidance Service.

Durrell, D. D. (1955). *Durrell Analysis of Reading Difficulty.* New York: Harcourt, Brace, & World.

Eheart, B. K. (1982). Mother–child interactions with nonretarded and mentally retarded preschoolers. *American Journal of Mental Deficiency, 87,* 20–25.

Elardo, R., Bradley, R., & Caldwell, B. M. (1975). The relations of infants' home environments to mental test performance from six to thirty-six months: A longitudinal analysis. *Child Development, 46,* 71–76.

Elardo, R., Bradley, R., & Caldwell, B. M. (1977). A longitudinal study of the relation of infants' home environments to language development at age three. *Child Development, 48,* 595–603.

Erickson, M. T. (1968). MMPI comparisons between parents of young emotionally disturbed and organically retarded children. *Journal of Consulting and Clinical Psychology, 32,* 701–706.

Erickson, M. T. (1969). MMPI profiles of parents of young retarded children. *American Journal of Mental Deficiency, 73,* 728–732.

Eyberg, S. M. (1980). Eyberg Child Behavior Inventory. *Journal of Clinical Child Psychology, 9,* 29.

Eyberg, S. M. (1985). Behavioral assessment: Advancing methodology in pediatric psychology. *Journal of Pediatric Psychology, 10,* 123–139.

Eyman, R. K., Borthwick, S. A., & Miller, C. (1981). Trends in maladaptive behavior of mentally retarded persons placed in community and institutional settings. *American Journal of Mental Deficiency, 85,* 473–477.

Eyman, R. K., & Call, T. (1977). Maladaptive behavior and community placement of mentally retarded persons. *American Journal of Mental Deficiency, 82,* 137–144.

Farber, B. (1959). Effects of a severely mentally retarded child on family integration. *Monographs of the Society for Research in Child Development, 24* (Whole No. 71).

Farber, B. (1970). Notes on sociological knowledge about families with mentally retarded children. In M. Schreiber (Ed.), *Social work and mental retardation.* New York: John Day.

Field, T. M. (1980). Interactions of high risk infants: Quantitative and qualitative differences. In D. B. Sawin, R. C. Hawkins, L. P. Walker, & J. H. Penticuff (Eds.), *Exceptional infant: Vol. 4. Psychosocial risks in infant–environmental transactions* (pp. 119–130). New York: Brunner/Mazel.

Field, T. M., Dempsey, J. R., & Shuman, H. H. (1981). Developmental follow-up of preterm and post-term infants. In S. L. Friedman & M. Sigman (Eds.), *Preterm birth and psychological development* (pp. 299–312). New York: Academic Press.

Friedrich, W. N., & Friedrich, W. L. (1981). Comparison of psychosocial assets of parents with a handicapped child and the normal controls. *American Journal of Mental Deficiency, 85,* 551–553.

Friedrich, W. N., Greenberg, M. T., & Crnic, K. (1983). A short-form of the Questionnaire on Resources and Stress. *American Journal of Mental Deficiency, 88,* 41–48.

Friedrich, W. N., Wilturner, L. T., & Cohen, D. S. (1985). Coping resources and parenting mentally retarded children. *American Journal of Mental Deficiency, 90,* 130–139.

Frostig, M., Maslow, P., Lefever, D. W., & Whittlesey, J. R. B. (1964). The Marianne Frostig Developmental Test of Visual Perception, 1963 standardization. *Perceptual and Motor Skills, 19,* 463–499.

Gath, A. (1973). The school-age siblings of mongol children. *British Journal of Psychiatry, 123,* 161–167.

Gottesman, I. (1963). Genetic aspects of intelligent behavior. In N. R. Ellis (Ed.), *Handbook of mental deficiency* (pp. 253–296). New York: McGraw-Hill.

Gottlieb, J., Semmel, M. I., & Veldman, D. J. (1978). Correlates of social status among mainstreamed mentally retarded children. *Journal of Educational Psychology, 70,* 396–405.

Graham, P., & Rutter, M. (1968). The reliability and validity of the psychiatric assessment of the child: II. Interview with the parent. *British Journal of Psychiatry, 114,* 581–592.

Gray, W. S. (1963). *Gray Oral Reading Test.* New York: Bobbs-Merrill.

Greenwood, C. R., Walker, H. M., & Hops, H. (1977). Some issues in social interaction/withdrawal assessment. *Exceptional Children, 43,* 490–499.

Greenwood, C. R., Walker., H. M., Todd, N. M., & Hops, H. (1979). Selecting a cost-effective screening measure for the assessment of preschool social withdrawal. *Journal of Applied Behavior Analysis, 12,* 639–652.

Gresham, F. M. (1981). Social skills training with handicapped children: A review. *Review of Educational Research, 51,* 139–176.

Grossman, H. (1973). *Manual on terminology and classification in mental retardation, 1973 revision.* Washington, DC: American Association on Mental Deficiency.

Grossman, H. J. (1977). *Manual on terminology and classification in mental retardation, 1977 revision.* Washington, DC: American Association on Mental Deficiency.

Grossman, H. (1983). *Manual on terminology and classification in mental retardation, 1983 revision.* Washington, DC: American Association on Mental Deficiency.

Herjanic, B., & Campbell, W. (1977). Differentiating psychiatrically disturbed children on the basis of a structured interview. *Journal of Abnormal Child Psychology, 5,* 127–133.

Hill, B. K., & Bruininks, R. H. (1981). *Physical and behavioral characteristics and maladaptive behavior of mentally retarded people in residential facilities.* Minneapolis: University of Minnesota, Department of Psychoeducational Studies.

Hobbs, N. (1975a). *The futures of children.* San Francisco: Jossey-Bass.

Hobbs. N. (1975b). *Issues in the classification of children* (2 vols.). San Francisco: Jossey-Bass.

Holroyd, J. (1974). The Questionnaire on Resources and

Stress: An instrument to measure family response to a handicapped family member. *Journal of Community Psychology, 2,* 92–94.

Holroyd, J., & Guthrie, D. (1979). Stress in families with neuromuscular disease. *Journal of Clinical Psychology, 35,* 734–739.

Holroyd, J., & McArthur, D. (1976). Mental retardation and stress on the parents: A contrast between Down's syndrome and childhood autism. *American Journal of Mental Deficiency, 80,* 431–436.

Hops, H., & Greenwood, C. R. (1988). Social skill deficits. In E. J. Mash & L. G. Terdal (Eds.), *Behavioral assessment of childhood disorders* (pp. 263–314). New York: Guilford.

Hunt, J. M. (1971). Parent and child centers: Their basis in the behavioral and educational sciences. *American Journal of Orthopsychiatry, 41,* 13–38.

Hunt, J. M., & Rhodes, L. (1977). Mental development of preterm infants during the first year. *Child Development, 48,* 204–210.

Ingalls, R. P. (1978). *Mental retardation: The changing outlook.* New York: Wiley.

Isett, R. D., & Spreat, S. (1979). Test–retest and interrater reliability of the AAMD Adaptive Behavior Scale. *American Journal of Mental Deficiency, 84,* 93–95.

Jacobson, J. W. (1982a). Problem behavior and psychiatric impairment within a developmentally disabled population: I. Behavior frequency. *Applied Research in Mental Retardation, 3,* 121–139.

Jacobson, J. W. (1982b). Problem behavior and psychiatric impairment within a developmentally disabled population: II. Behavior severity. *Applied Research in Mental Retardation, 3,* 369–381.

Jastak, S., & Wilkinson, G. S. (1984). *Wide Range Achievement Test—Revised.* Wilmington, DE: Jastak Associates.

Johnson, C. M., Bradley-Johnson, S., McCarthy, R., & Jamie, M. (1984). Token reinforcement during WISC-R administration: II. Effects on mildly retarded black students. *Applied Research in Mental Retardation, 5,* 43–53.

Jones, K. L., Smith, D. W., Ullenland, C. N., & Streissguth, A. P. (1973). Pattern of malformation in offspring in chronic alcoholic mothers. *Lancet, i,* 1267.

Kanfer, F. H., & Saslow, G. (1969). Behavioral diagnosis. In C. M. Franks (Ed.), *Behavioral therapy: Appraisal and status* (pp. 417–444). New York: McGraw-Hill.

Kangas, J., & Bradway, K. (1971). Intelligence at middle age: A thirty-eight year follow-up. *Developmental Psychology, 5,* 333–337.

Kanner, L. (1964). *A history of the care and study of the mentally retarded.* Springfield, IL: Charles C. Thomas.

Kaufman, A. S., & Kaufman, N. L. (1983). *The Kaufman Assessment Battery for Children.* Circle Pines, MN: American Guidance Service.

Kazdin, A. E., & Matson, J. L. (1981). Social validation in mental retardation. *Applied Research in Mental Retardation, 2,* 39–53.

Kirk, S. A., McCarthy, J. J., & Kirk, W. D. (1968). *The Illinois Test of Psycholinguistic Abilities.* Urbana: University of Illinois Press.

Knopf, I. J. (1979). *Childhood psychopathology: A developmental approach.* Englewood Cliffs, NJ: Prentice-Hall.

Kogan, K. L., Wimberger, H. C., & Bobbitt, R. A. (1969). Analysis of mother–child interaction in young mental retardates. *Child Development, 40,* 799–812.

Kohn, M. (1977). *Social competence, symptoms and underachievement in childhood: A longitudinal perspective.* Washington: Wiley.

Koller, H., Richardson, S. A., Katz, M., & McLaren, J. (1982). Behavior disturbance in childhood and the early adult years in populations who were and were not mentally retarded. *Journal of Preventive Psychiatry, 1,* 453–468.

Koppitz, E. M. (1975). *The Bender–Gestalt Test for young children: Vol. 2. Research and application, 1963–1973.* New York: Grune & Stratton.

Kozloff, M. A. (1979). *A program for families of children with learning and behavior problems.* New York: Wiley.

Lambert, N. M., & Hartsough, C. S. (1981). Development of a simplified diagnostic scoring method for the school version of the Adaptive Behavior Scale. *American Journal of Mental Deficiency, 86,* 138–147.

Lambert, N. M., Windmiller, M., Cole, L. J., & Figueroa, R. A. (1975). *A manual for the Public School Version of the AAMD Adaptive Behavior Scale.* Washington, DC: American Association on Mental Deficiency.

Landesman-Dwyer, S., Berkson, G. B., & Romer, D. (1979). Affiliation and friendship of mentally retarded residents in group homes. *American Journal of Mental Deficiency, 83,* 571–580.

Landesman-Dwyer, S., Schuckit, J. J., Keller, L. S., & Brown, T. R. (1977). A prospective study of client needs relative to community placement. In P. Mittler (Ed.), *Research to practice in mental retardation: Care and intervention* (Vol. 1, pp. 377–388). Baltimore: University of Park Press.

Landesman-Dwyer, S., Stein, J. G., & Sackett, G. P. (1978). A behavioral and ecological study of group homes. In G. P. Sackett (Ed.), *Observing behavior: Vol. 1. Theory and application in mental retardation* (pp. 349–378).

Leiter, R. G. (1948). *Leiter International Performance Scale.* Chicago: Stoelting.

Lewis, E. D. (1933). Types of mental deficiency and their social significance. *Journal of Mental Science, 79,* 298–304.

Lockwood, K., & Bourland, G. (1982). Reduction of self-injurious behaviors by reinforcement and toy use. *Mental Retardation, 20,* 169–173.

Luiselli, J. K., Myles, E., & Littman-Quinn, J. (1983). Analysis of a reinforcement/time-out treatment package to control severe aggressive and destructive behaviors in a multihandicapped, rubella child. *Applied Research in Mental Retardation, 4,* 65–78.

Mash, E. J., & Terdal, L. G. (Eds.). (1981). *Behavioral assessment of childhood disorders.* New York: Guilford Press.

MacLean, W. E., Jr., & Baumeister, A. A. (1981). Observational analysis of the stereotyped mannerisms of a developmentally delayed infant. *Applied Research in Mental Retardation, 2,* 257–262.

MacMillan, D. L. (1977). *Mental retardation in school and society.* Boston: Little, Brown.

Matson, J. L. (1985). Biosocial theory of psychopathology: A three by three factor model. *Applied Research in Mental Retardation, 6,* 199–227.

McCarthy, D. A. (1974). *Manual for the McCarthy Scales of Children's Abilities.* New York: Psychological Corporation.

McFall, R. M. (1982). A review and reformulation of the

concept of social skills. *Behavioral Assessment, 4*, 1–33.

Menalascino, F. J. (1970). *Psychiatric approaches to mental retardation*. New York: Basic Books.

Mercer, J. R. (1970). Sociological perspectives on mild mental retardation. In M. C. Haywood (Ed.), *Sociocultural aspects of mental retardation* (pp. 378–394). New York: Appleton-Century-Crofts.

Mercer, J. R. (1973). *Labelling the mentally retarded*. Berkeley: University of California Press.

Mercer, J. R., & Lewis, J. F. (1978). *System of Multicultural Pluralistic Assessment*. New York: Psychological Corporation.

Meyers, C. E., Nihira, K., & Zetlin, A. (1979). The measurement of adaptive behavior. In N. R. Ellis (Ed.), *Handbook of mental deficiency: Psychological theory and research* (2nd ed., pp. 431–482). Hillsdale, NJ: Erlbaum.

Miller, L. C. (1967). Louisville Behavior Checklist for males, 6–12 years of age. *Psychological Reports, 21*, 885–896.

Miller, W. H., & Keirn, W. C. (1978). Personality measurement in parents of retarded and emotionally disturbed children: A replication. *Journal of Clinical Psychology, 34*, 686–690.

Mink, I. T., Meyers, C. E., & Nihira, K. (1984). A taxonomy of family lifestyles: II. Homes with slow learning children. *American Journal of Mental Deficiency, 89*, 111–123.

Mink, I. T., Nihira, K., & Meyers, C. E. (1983). Taxonomy of family lifestyles: I. Homes with TMR children. *American Journal of Mental Deficiency, 87*, 484–497.

Moos, R. H., & Moos, B. (1981). *Revised Family Environment Scale*. Palo Alto, CA: Consulting Psychologists Press.

Morrow, L. W., Burke, J. G., & Buell, B. J. (1985). Effects of a self-recording procedure on the attending to task behavior and academic productivity of adolescents with multiple handicaps. *Mental Retardation, 23*, 137–141.

Mulick, J. A., & Schroeder, S. R. (1980). Research relating to management of antisocial behavior in mentally retarded persons. *The Psychological Record, 30*, 397–417.

Mumpower, D. L. (1970). Sex ratios found in various types of referred exceptional children. *Exceptional Children, 36*, 621–622.

Nelson, R. O. (1974). An expanded scope for behavior modification in school settings. *Journal of School Psychology, 12*, 276–287.

Nelson, R. O. (Chair). (1975, August). *The use of intelligence tests within behavioral assessment*. Symposium presented at the meeting of the American Psychological Association, Chicago.

Nihira, K., Foster, R., Shellhaas, M., & Leland, H. (1974). *AAMD Adaptive Behavior Scale, 1974 revision*. Washington, DC: American Association on Mental Deficiency.

Nihira, K., Meyers, C. E., & Mink, I. T. (1980). Home environment, family adjustment, and the development of mentally retarded children. *Applied Research in Mental Retardation, 1*, 5–24.

Nihira, K., Mink, I. T., & Meyers, C. E. (1982). Relationship between home environment and school adjustment of TMR children. *American Journal of Mental Deficiency, 86*, 8–15.

O'Leary, K. D., & Johnson, S. B. (1979). Psychological assessment. In H. C. Quay & J. S. Werry (Eds.), *Psychopathological disorders of childhood* (2nd ed.). New York: Wiley.

Ollendick, T. H. (1981). Assessment of social interactive skills in schoolchildren. *Behavioral Counseling Quarterly, 1*, 227–243.

Ollendick, T. H., & Hersen, M. (Eds.). (1984). *Child behavioral assessment: Principles and procedures*. New York: Pergamon Press.

Parmelee, A. H., & Schulte, F. J. (1970). Developmental testing of preterm and small for date infants. *Pediatrics, 45*, 21–28.

Passaminick, B., & Knobloch, H. (1961). Epidemiological studies on the complications of pregnancy and the birth process. In G. Caplan (Ed.), *Prevention of mental disorders in children* (pp. 74–94). New York: Basic Books.

Peterson, S. L., Robinson, E. A., & Littman, I. (1983). Parent–child interaction training for parents with a history of mental retardation. *Applied Research in Mental Retardation, 4*, 329–342.

Prinz, R. J., Swan, G., Liebert, D., Weintraub, S., & Neale, J. M. (1978). ASSESS: Adjustment Scales for Sociometric Evaluation of Secondary-School Students. *Journal of Abnormal Child Psychology, 6*, 493–501.

Reschly, D. (1981). Sociocultural background, adaptive behavior, and concepts of bias in assessment. In C. Reynolds & T. Gutkin (Eds.), *Handbook of school psychology*. New York: Wiley-Interscience.

Ricci, C. S. (1970). Analysis of child-rearing attitudes of mothers of mentally retarded, emotionally disturbed, and normal children. *American Journal of Mental Deficiency, 74*, 756–761.

Richmond, B. O., & Kicklighter, R. H. (1980). *Children's Adaptive Behavior Scale (CABS)*. Atlanta: Humanics.

Roberts, J. A. F. (1952). The genetics of mental deficiency. *Eugenics Review, 44*, 71–83.

Roberts, M. C., & LaGreca, A. M. (1981). Behavioral assessment. In C. E. Walker (Ed.), *Clinical practice of psychology: A practical guide for mental health professionals* (pp. 293–346). New York: Pergamon Press.

Robinson, N. M., & Robinson, H. B. (1976). *The mentally retarded child* (2nd ed.). New York: McGraw-Hill.

Ross, R. T., & Boroskin, A. (1972). Are IQ's below 30 meaningful? *Mental Retardation, 10*, 24.

Rutter, M., Tizard, J., & Whitmore, K. (1970). *Education, health and behavior*. New York: Wiley.

Saigh, P. A., & Payne, D. A. (1979). The effect of type of reinforcer and reinforcement schedule on performance of EMR students on four selected subtests of the WISC-R. *Psychology in the Schools, 16*, 106–110.

Salisbury, C. (1986). Adaptation of the Questionnaire for Resources and Stress—short form. *American Journal of Mental Deficiency. 90*, 456–459.

Sameroff, A. J. (1980). Issues in early reproductive and caretaking risk: Review and current status. In D. B. Sawin, R. C. Hawkins, L. O. Walker, & J. H. Penticuff (Eds.), *Exceptional infant: Vol. 4. Psychosocial risks in infant–environment transactions* (pp. 343–360). New York: Brunner/Mazel.

Sameroff, A. J., & Chandler, M. J. (1975). Reproductive risk and the continuum of caretaking casualty. In F. D. Horowitz, M. Hetherington, S. Scarr-Salapatek, & G. Siegel (Eds.), *Review of child development research*

(Vol. 4, pp. 187–243). Chicago: University of Chicago Press.

Sameroff, A. J., & Seifer, R. (1983). Familial risk and child competence. *Child Development, 54,* 1254–1268.

Sattler, J. (1982). *Assessment of children's intelligence* (2nd ed.). Philadelphia: W. B. Saunders.

Schnelle, J. F. (1974). A brief report on invalidity of parent evaluation of behavior change. *Journal of Applied Behavior Analysis, 7,* 341–343.

Shaywitz, S. E., Cohen, D. J., & Shaywitz, B. A. (1980). Behavior and learning difficulties in children of normal intelligence born to alcoholic mothers. *Journal of Pediatrics, 96,* 978–982.

Shea, V. (1984). Explaining mental retardation and autism to parents. In E. Schopler & G. B. Mesibov (Eds.), *The effects of autism on the family* (pp. 265–288). New York: Plenum.

Shields, J. (1973). Heredity and psychological abnormality. In H. J. Eysenck (Ed.), *Handbook of abnormal psychology* (pp. 298–343). London: Pitman Medical Publishing.

Singh, N. N., & Winton, A. S. (1983). Social skills training with institutionalized severely and profoundly mentally retarded persons. *Applied Research in Mental Retardation, 4,* 383–398.

Skeels, H. M. (1966). Adult status of children with contrasting early life experiences. *Monographs of the Society for Research of Child Development, 31* (Serial No. 105).

Song, A. Y., & Jones, S. E. (1982). Vineland Social Maturity Scale norm examined—the Wisconsin experience with 0- to 3-year-old children. *American Journal of Mental Deficiency, 86,* 428–431.

Song, A. Y., Jones, S. E., Lippert, J., Metzgen, K., Miller, J., & Borreca, C. (1980). *Wisconsin Behavior Rating Scale.* Madison: Central Wisconsin Center for the Developmentally Disabled.

Song, A., Jones, S. E., Lippert, J., Metzgen, K., Miller, J., & Borreca, C. (1984). Wisconsin Behavior Rating Scale: Measure of adaptive behavior for the developmental levels of 0 to 3 years. *American Journal of Mental Deficiency, 88,* 401–410.

Sontag, L. W., Baker, C. T., & Nelson, V. L. (1958). Mental growth and personality development: A longitudinal study. *Monographs of the Society for Research in Child Development, 23* (Serial No. 68).

Sparrow, S. S., Balla, D. A., & Cicchetti, D. V. (1984). *Vineland Adaptive Behavior Scales.* Circle Pines, MN: American Guidance Service.

Sparrow, S. S., & Cicchetti, D. V. (1978). Behavior rating inventory for moderately, severely, and profoundly retarded persons. *American Journal of Mental Deficiency, 82,* 365–374.

Sparrow, S. S., & Cicchetti, D. V., (1984). The Behavior Inventory for Rating Development (BIRD): Assessments of reliability and factorial validity. *Applied Research in Mental Retardation, 5,* 219–231.

Stack, J. G. (1984). Interrater reliabilities of the adaptive behavior scale with environmental effects controlled. *American Journal of Mental Deficiency, 88,* 396–400.

Sternlicht, M., & Deutsch, M. R. (1972). *Personality development and social behavior in the mentally retarded.* Lexington, MA: D. C. Heath.

Stoneman, Z., Brody, G. H., & Abbott, D. (1983). In-home observations of young Down syndrome children with their mothers and fathers. *American Journal of Mental Deficiency, 87,* 591–600.

Strain, P. S. (1983). Identification of social skill curriculum targets for severely handicapped children in mainstream preschools. *Applied Research in Mental Retardation, 4,* 369–382.

Strauss, A. A., & Werner, H. (1941). The mental organization of the brain injured mentally defective child. *American Journal of Psychiatry, 97,* 1194–1203.

Streissguth, A. P., Herman, C. S., & Smith, D. W. (1978). Intelligence, behavior, and dymorphogenesis in the fetal alcohol syndrome: A report on 20 patients. *Journal of Pediatrics, 92,* 363–367.

Taylor, R. L. (1980). Use of the AAMD classification system: A review of recent research. *American Journal of Mental Deficiency, 85,* 116–119.

Taylor, R. L., Warren, S. A., & Slocumb, P. R. (1979). Categorizing behavior in terms of severity: Considerations for Part Two of the Adaptive Behavior Scale. *American Journal of Mental Deficiency, 83,* 411–414.

Thompson, T. J., & Berkson, G. (1985). Stereotyped behavior of severely disabled children in classroom and free play settings. *American Journal of Mental Deficiency, 89,* 580–586.

Thompson, T. J., & Grabowski, J. (1977). *Behavior modification of the mentally retarded* (2nd ed.). New York: Oxford University Press.

Thorndike, R. L., Hagen, E. P., & Sattler, J. M. (1986). *Stanford–Binet Intelligence Scale* (4th ed.). Chicago: Riverside.

van den Berg, B. J., & Oechsli, F. W. (1984). Prematurity. In M. B. Bracken (Ed.), *Perinatal epidemiology* (pp. 69–85). New York: Oxford University Press.

Vietze, P. M., Abernathy, S. R., Ashe, M. L., & Faulstich, G. (1978). Contingency interaction between mothers and their developmentally delayed infants. In G. P. Sackett (Ed.), *Observing behavior: Vol. 1. Theory and application in mental retardation* (pp. 115–124). Baltimore: University Park Press.

Waisbren, S. E. (1980). Parents' reactions after the birth of a developmentally disabled child. *American Journal of Mental Deficiency, 84,* 345–351.

Webster, T. G. (1970). Unique aspects of emotional development in mentally retarded children. In F. J. Menalascino (Ed.), *Psychiatric approaches to mental retardation* (pp. 3–54). New York: Basic Books.

Wechsler, D. (1967). *Manual for the Wechsler Preschool and Primary Scale of Intelligence.* New York: Psychological Corporation.

Wechsler, D. (1974). *Manual for the Wechsler Intelligence Scale for Children—Revised.* New York: Psychological Corporation.

Weisz, J., Yeates, K., & Zigler, E. (1982). Piagetian evidence and the developmental-difference controversy. In E. Zigler & D. Balla (Eds.), *Mental retardation: The developmental-difference controversy* (pp. 213–276). Hillsdale, NJ: Erlbaum.

Wepman, J. M. (1973). *The Auditory Discrimination Test.* Chicago: Language Research.

Wetherby, B., & Baumeister, A. A. (1981). Mental retardation. In S. M. Turner, K. S. Calhoun, & H. E. Adams (Eds.), *Handbook of clinical behavior therapy* (pp. 635–664). New York: Wiley.

Wikler, L. (1981). Chronic stress of families of mentally retarded children. *Family Relations, 30,* 281–288.

Wirt, R. D., Lachar, D., Klinedinst, J. K., & Seat, P. D. (1977). *Multidimensional description of child personality: A manual for the Personality Inventory for Chil-

dren (rev. ed.). Los Angeles: Western Psychological Services.

Wolf, M. M. (1978). Social validity: The case for subjective measurement or how applied behavior analysis is finding its heart. *Journal of Applied Behavior Analysis, 11,* 203–214.

Woodcock, R. W. (1977). *Woodcock–Johnson Psycho-educational Battery.* Boston: Teaching Resources.

Woolfson, R. C. (1984). Historical perspective on mental retardation. *American Journal of Mental Deficiency, 89,* 231–235.

Yarrow, M. R., Campbell, J. D., & Burton, R. V. (1970). Recollections of childhood: A study of the retrospective method. *Monographs of the Society for Research in Child Development, 35* (Serial No. 138).

Young, R. M., Bradley-Johnson, S., & Johnson, C. M. (1982). Immediate and delayed reinforcement on WISC-R performance for mentally retarded students. *Applied Research in Mental Retardation, 3,* 13–20.

Zigler, E., Balla, D., & Hodapp, R. (1984). On the definition and classification of mental retardation. *American Journal of Mental Deficiency, 89,* 215–230.

7 AUTISM

CRIGHTON NEWSOM
Muscatatuck Developmental Center

CHRISTINE HOVANITZ
University of Cincinnati

ARNOLD RINCOVER
Surrey Place Centre

These are very striking children: An intelligent, serious face contrasts sharply with the absence of normal language and social skills and the presence of some highly unusual behaviors. As a result, autistic children, despite their small number, have attracted considerable interest since the disorder was first identified in 1943. Behavioral psychologists were among the first clinicians to approach the problem from an experimental rather than a phenomenological perspective, and they developed the first quantitative assessment methods used with autistic children. By 1962, Ferster had finished a series of experimental studies of reinforcer preference, resistance to extinction, discrimination learning, and drug effects (Ferster & DeMyer, 1961a, 1961b, 1962). Soon afterward, direct observation procedures began to be used routinely by the behavioral clinicians who first implemented treatment programs (e.g., Lovaas, Freitag, Gold, & Kassorla, 1965a, 1965b; M. M. Wolf, Risley, & Mees, 1964).

This chapter selectively reviews contemporary practices in the assessment of autism, emphasizing diagnostic considerations, treatment planning, work with families, and methods for the functional analysis of behavior problems. First, a discussion of clinical diagnosis addresses Kanner syndrome and the Pervasive Developmental Disorders classification of the *Diagnostic and Statistical Manual of Mental Disorders,* third edition (DSM-III; American Psychiatric Association, 1980), with Infantile Autism receiving most of the attention. Next, a critical review of the more prominent diagnostic checklists is undertaken to indicate the current state of the art in efforts to make the diagnosis of autism more objective. Then assessment for treatment planning is considered, addressing intelligence tests, adaptive behavior scales, and ecological assessment methods. Some approaches to the assessment of families are presented next, followed by methods developed specifically for behavior management efforts.

DIAGNOSTIC CRITERIA

Overview

Two important functions served by diagnosis in the field of autism are subject selection in research and client selection for program placement. All investigators in the field of autism agree that progress in research on the characteristics and etiology of the disorder has long been impeded by poor diagnostic practices (Coleman & Gillberg, 1985; Kistner & Robbins, 1986; Rimland, 1974). Current researchers thus have a special obligation to avoid adding to the confusion. Furthermore, even the practitioner who never does research will recognize that the expansion of educational and vocational programs over the past 10 years has created opportunities for autistic children and adolescents that did not previously exist, and that access to an appropriate program may well depend on an accurate and well-substantiated diagnosis.

The description and classification of severely behavior-disordered children have long posed major and still unresolved problems. From the 1930s through the 1950s, many psychiatrists, including Potter (1933), Bender (1947), Kanner (1943), Anthony (1958), and Mahler (1952), described and attempted to classify the severely disordered children they saw. They had only informal observation, basic medical tests, some information on normal development, and psychoanalytic theory to refer to. Consequently, most of the syndromes they identified (usually as subclasses of the ubiquitous "childhood schizophrenia") have not survived in formal nosologies. During the 1960s and 1970s, international committees and task forces with access to a large, expanding empirical literature worked on the problems in this area (e.g., Rutter *et al.*, 1969; Spitzer, 1980). However, little progress has been made, as seen in DSM-III and its proposed revision, DSM-IIIR. The Schizophrenia, Childhood Type diagnosis of DSM-II was replaced by three categories based on age of onset as well as behaviors in DSM-III: Infantile Autism, Childhood Onset Pervasive Developmental Disorder, and Atypical Pervasive Developmental Disorder. The proposed revision of the Pervasive Developmental Disorders classification in DSM-IIIR differs primarily in having only one residual category along with Autistic Disorder and in effectively removing the criterion for age of onset. The provision of only two or three categories to classify the very heterogeneous population of severely disordered children is an indication that the few recent empirical efforts at classification (e.g., Prior, Perry, & Gajzago, 1975; Wing & Gould, 1979) have not yet been replicated and gained the acceptance of the field. The removal of a criterion for age of onset for autism expands its

definition well beyond the infantile syndrome described by Kanner (1943). Some implications of these developments are discussed later. For now it is sufficient to note that DSM-III presents an oversimplified view of severe child disorders, but it is the standard nosology for the field and is therefore used to structure our presentation. In addition to familiarity with the relevant criteria, accurate diagnosis of autism requires an interview with a parent or other informant that elicits a good early history as well as current behaviors, and sensitive observation of the child. Useful adjunctive information can often be obtained from neurological, audiological, linguistic, and psychological testing, which may assist in identifying alternative or additional diagnoses.

In the following sections, the major points to be considered in diagnosing autistic children are addressed. First, there is a brief look at Kanner syndrome. Next, the Pervasive Developmental Disorders of DSM-III are reviewed, with the criteria for Infantile Autism discussed in considerable detail, along with a brief synopsis of current findings regarding etiology. Some guidelines for differential diagnosis follow. Finally, a discussion of some limitations of the DSM-III approach to diagnosis, including possible implications of the currently proposed revisions of the autism criteria, concludes this part of the chapter.

Kanner Syndrome

The "early infantile autism" identified by Kanner in 1943 is a narrower concept than the Infantile Autism of DSM-III or the proposed Autistic Disorder of DSM-IIIR. Over time, the former has become known simply as "Kanner syndrome" or "classical autism" to distinguish it from the more generic syndrome described in DSM-III and most of the literature. The point of mentioning Kanner syndrome, however, is not simply to note its historical significance (valuable as that is in understanding the earlier literature), but to emphasize that this disorder is distinguishable from other autistic syndromes and may differ in etiology (Lotter, 1966; Wing, Yeates, Brierley, & Gould, 1976).

Table 1 lists Kanner's criteria as abstracted from his original paper (1943). The language and cognitive criteria (points 2 and 4) indicate that Kanner initially saw what would now be considered a high-functioning subgroup of autistic children (i.e., those whose intelligence is in the moderately retarded range or higher).

TABLE 1. Diagnostic Criteria for Kanner Syndrome

---

1. Extreme autistic aloneness from birth that ignores or shuts out all exteroceptive stimuli, as indicated by a failure to assume the normal anticipatory posture prior to being picked up in infancy, feeding problems, fear of loud noises and moving objects, unresponsiveness to other people's verbalizations, failure to look at others' faces, failure to play with other children, and failure to notice the comings and goings of the parents.

2. Language abnormalities, including mutism (which appears to be elective) in a minority of children and noncommunicative speech in the majority. The speaking children learn to name objects easily and repeat nursery rhymes, prayers, songs, and lists requiring an excellent rote memory but no comprehension. They also exhibit lack of spontaneous sentence formation and immediate or delayed echolalia, resulting in the reversal of personal pronouns in requests. There is extreme literalness in the use of prepositions and "affirmation by repetition" ("yes" is indicated by simply echoing the question).

3. An anxiously obsessive desire for the maintenance of sameness that nobody but the child may disrupt. Changes of daily routine, of furniture arrangement, of an arrangement of objects, or of the wording of requests, or the sight of anything broken or incomplete produce tantrums or despair. There is a limitation in the variety of spontaneous activity, including rhythmic movements and a preoccupation with objects that do not change their appearance or position except when manipulated by the child.

4. Good cognitive potential, as indicated by intelligent and serious-minded, yet "anxiously tense," facial expressions; excellent memory for previous events, poems, and complex patterns and sequences; and good performance on nonverbal tests such as the Seguin Form Board.

5. Essentially normal physical development, with better fine motor than gross motor skills.

Note. Abstracted from "Autistic Disturbances of Affective Contact" by L. Kanner, 1943, *The Nervous Child, 2*, 217–250.

Later, after seeing many more children, he relegated these two criteria to secondary status and changed the physical development criterion (point 5) to emphasize fascination for objects. "Extreme self-isolation" and "insistence on the preservation of sameness" continued as the primary criteria, the *sine qua non* for the diagnosis (Eisenberg & Kanner, 1956). Unfortunately, the main effect of emphasizing only two essential features was to create the opening wedge for the subsequent broadening of the diagnosis that has bedeviled the field ever since (Newsom & Rincover, 1981; Rutter, 1978). In current clinical practice, Kanner syndrome children are diagnosed as cases of Infantile Autism, but in research the more specific designation of "Kanner syndrome" is preferred when it is warranted (i.e., the child meets all the criteria in Table 1). Kanner syndrome children can be discriminated from other autistic children primarily by the presence of ritualistic routines, distress over changes in the environment, "splinter" skills, and good fine-motor coordination (Prior *et al.*, 1975).

The prevalence of Kanner syndrome can be calculated from the epidemiological studies of Lotter (1966) and Wing *et al.* (1976). They identified "nuclear" autistic children (those showing extreme social aloofness and insistence on sameness, as well as most of Kanner's other criteria) as occurring at a rate of 2.0 per 10,000 children aged 8–10 (Lotter, 1966) and 5–14 years (Wing *et al.*, 1976). Applying this rate to the U.S. population of children aged 5–14 years in 1980 (just under 35 million; U.S. Bureau of the Census, 1983), the number of Kanner syndrome children is only about 7,000. When Rimland's (1971) more stringent criteria are used, including a score of +20 or greater on his Diagnostic Check List for the identification of Kanner syndrome children, the prevalence rate is about 1 in 20,000 (Rimland, 1974), or a total of only 1,750 children. The ratio of males to females is about 4:1 (Kanner, 1971; Prior, Gajzago, & Knox, 1976).

Pervasive Developmental Disorders

"Pervasive Developmental Disorders" is used in DSM-III to distinguish this classification from the "Specific Developmental Disorders" (of language, reading, arithmetic, etc.) listed later in the manual. "Pervasive" also highlights the fact that severe impairments across multiple areas of functioning are present. The use of "Developmental" connotes two important ideas: first, that biological rather than social or psychogenic factors are believed to be paramount in the etiologies of these disorders; and, second, that they are therefore related to other developmental disorders, such as mental retardation and learning disabilities, instead of being childhood versions of adult disorders.

Infantile Autism is the category that applies

to most cases of severe behavior disorders first evident in infancy. After 37 years of informal usage, its inclusion in DSM-III marked its first appearance in the most widely recognized American classification system. The mere availability of a standard set of criteria bearing the imprimatur of a major professional organization has helped to alleviate some of the problems caused by multiple and ever-expanding definitions, discussed at length previously (Newsom & Rincover, 1981).

There are two other categories in the Pervasive Developmental Disorders group in DSM-III. One is Childhood Onset Pervasive Developmental Disorder, a category for children whose abnormalities are of later onset (30 months to 12 years) and who, in addition, do not meet the criteria for Schizophrenic Disorders. (If the Schizophrenic Disorders criteria are met the child is so diagnosed, without the adjective "Childhood.") Atypical Pervasive Developmental Disorder is a residual category for children of any age of onset who show pervasive impairments but do not fully meet one of the other sets of criteria.

Infantile Autism

The DSM-III criteria for Infantile Autism appear in Table 2; their elaboration and empirical support follow.

A. ONSET BEFORE 30 MONTHS OF AGE. The first criterion, more than any other, has done much to reduce diagnostic confusion, simply because it provides a fairly definite cutoff age. The empirical support for this criterion rests primarily with a group of studies on the age distribution of severe childhood disorders. Rutter (1978) observed that studies in England, Japan, and the USSR agree in showing a bimodal distribution in age of onset, with one peak in infancy and another around puberty. Severe disorders of any type with onsets between 3 and 6 years are extremely rare (e.g., 5% of Kolvin's [1971] British sample), and only 6% of the autistic children identified in Wing's epidemiological study had an age of onset later than 3 years (Wing & Gould, 1979). Additional support comes from a classification analysis of severe disorders by Prior et al. (1975). These investigators obtained 142 completed Diagnostic Check Lists (Form E-2; Rimland, 1964) from the parents of children with various child psychosis diagnoses and subjected them to computerized taxonomic analysis. The "best" classification obtained (in terms of the most efficient sorting of the cases) was one that resulted in two classes. The first class contained Kanner syndrome children as well as other children with early onset (before 2 years) and symptoms of self-isolation and impaired communication. The second class contained mostly children with later onset and more varied symptoms. Prior et al. (1975) concluded that the most parsimonious classification of severe disorders is one based on age of onset and relative proportion of autistic behaviors.

Determining age of onset requires profes-

TABLE 2. DSM-III Diagnostic Criteria for Infantile Autism

A. Onset before 30 months of age.

B. Pervasive lack of responsiveness to other people (autism).

C. Gross deficits in language development.

D. If speech is present, peculiar speech patterns such as immediate and delayed echolalia, metaphorical language, pronominal reversal.

E. Bizarre responses to various aspects of the environment, e.g., resistance to change, peculiar interest in or attachments to animate or inanimate objects.

F. Absence of delusions, hallucinations, loosening of associations, and incoherence as in Schizophrenia.

Associated Features

1. Mental retardation (70%).

2. Mood lability.

3. Hypo- or hyper-responsivity to sensory stimuli.

4. Failure to appreciate real dangers in the environment.

5. Repetitive, stereotyped behaviors.

6. Self-injurious behaviors.

Note. From *Diagnostic and Statistical Manual of Mental Disorders* (3rd ed., pp. 88–90) by the American Psychiatric Association, 1980, Washington, DC: Author. Copyright 1980 by the American Psychiatric Association. Used with permission.

sional observation of the child by 30 months of age or, if the child is older, an interview with a parent or other good informant who can at least roughly date the emergence of abnormal behaviors. The child is most likely to be brought for evaluation and diagnosis between $2\frac{1}{2}$ and 5 years of age (Ornitz, Guthrie, & Farley, 1977). The parents will have been worried for 2 to 3 years that the child might be retarded, neurologically impaired, or deaf. Their chief complaint will usually center on the child's failure to develop language, although delayed motor development may also be mentioned (DeMyer, 1979; Ornitz et al., 1977). Specific problems noticed during the first 2 years often include slow or unusual motor development, social unresponsiveness, excessive quietness or irritability, excessive rocking or bouncing, cessation of speech, and hypersensitivity to sounds (DeMyer, 1979). About 20–30% of cases have a period of apparently normal development before a setback or a failure to keep up with developmental milestones (DeMyer, 1979; Lotter, 1966). When interviewing parents of an only child, it may be necessary to question them comprehensively about early social, language, and play behaviors to establish whether or not abnormal signs were present but overlooked. Sometimes parents will simply say that the child seemed "odd" or "strange" as an infant; probes for the specific incidents and behaviors producing this impression may be very informative.

B. PERVASIVE LACK OF RESPONSIVENESS TO OTHER PEOPLE (AUTISM). Identification of the second crucial feature requires that the child's level of social development be significantly below his or her level of intelligence, so that social deficits due solely to mental retardation can be ruled out. In early infancy, there may be no response to a human voice and failure to develop social smiling. The baby may not adopt an anticipatory posture of the arms or shoulders when about to be picked up. Autistic infants tend not to be cuddly when held; instead of adjusting to the parent's body, they remain either very limp or very stiff. The curiosity and visual exploratory behaviors characteristic of normal infants are absent or grossly deficient (Wing, 1976).

Between 1 and 5 years of age, signs of social aloofness become more obvious. Autistic toddlers may not follow their parents around the house or show anxiety when they leave. Unlike normal children, they show no significant preference for interacting with their mothers instead of a stranger in a play setting (Sigman & Ungerer, 1984). Observed among peers in a classroom during unstructured time, they will usually be physically distant from other children, never initiating and only rarely responding to social interactions. They may respond positively to an adult's tickling or rough-and-tumble play, but not to questions or conversations. No cooperative or symbolic play with toys is present. Play consists of repetitive, inappropriate manipulations of objects (e.g., spinning the wheels on a toy truck) or appropriate but limited and stereotyped routines rather than imaginative activities (e.g., repeatedly loading and unloading a toy truck) (Wing, Gould, Yeates, & Brierley, 1977).

Lack of eye contact, or gaze avoidance, is usually considered particularly characteristic of autistic children. Rutter (1978), however, has suggested that their eye contact is not so much lacking as it is deviant. Unlike normal children, they fail to look directly at others' eyes when they want to get their attention or when being spoken to (Mirenda, Donnellan, & Yoder, 1983). Instead, they may look at others only out of the corners of their eyes or use an indirect, off-center gaze that creates the impression of being stared through.

In later childhood, improvements in social behavior usually occur, especially if language and social skills have been directly taught. A certain superficial quality often remains in the child's social interactions, however. Even higher-functioning autistic adolescents and adults tend to show a lack of cooperative group play, failure to make close friendships, and inability to recognize feelings in others or to show deep affection.

C. GROSS DEFICITS IN LANGUAGE DEVELOPMENT. As many as 80% of autistic children are mute when first diagnosed in early childhood (Ornitz et al., 1977), and about 50% remain mute for life in the absence of intensive treatment (Rutter, Greenfeld, & Lockyer, 1967). Most of these individuals are "functionally" mute rather than completely silent. They are able to produce vocal noises, phonemes, and word approximations, but not to articulate words and phrases. As a result, the parent or pediatrician may suspect hearing impairment or elective mutism, but these hypotheses are rarely substantiated in audiological and language evaluations. However, evaluation of auditory perceptual functioning may reveal severe deficits in attending to the multiple acoustic features of speech stimuli (Schreibman, Kohlenberg, & Britten, 1986).

Both retarded and nonretarded autistic children show severe speech delays. Bartak and Rutter (1976) studied autistic children with IQs above and below 70. For the lower group, the mean age of the first use of single words was 4 years, 7 months; for the higher group it was 2 years, 6 months. Comprehension is somewhat less delayed. Parents of autistic children recall the understanding of simple nouns occurring at a median age of 24 months—12 months later than reported by parents of normal children (Ornitz et al., 1977). Frequently, comprehension remains limited to concrete nouns associated with strong reinforcers and punishers, familiar aspects of the daily routine, and commands accompanied by gestures, indicating dependence on visual cues. Even after the initially mute child is taught some communicative speech, problems persist with spontaneity, abstract concepts, feelings, humor, idiomatic expressions, and words varying with speaker and context, such as pronouns and prepositions (Ricks & Wing, 1976). In her comprehensive review of studies on the linguistic functioning of autistic children, Tager-Flusberg (1981) concluded that their language acquisition tends to be highly asynchronous, with phonology and syntax more advanced than semantic and pragmatic development.

Frequently mentioned in association with language deficits are abnormalities or deficits in what are considered "prelinguistic" skills, including babbling (Bartak, Rutter, & Cox, 1975; Ricks, 1975) and imaginative play (Wing et al., 1977). Curcio (1978) found that autistic children fail to engage in behaviors to direct an adult's attention to an object as normal toddlers do unless they want the item. Then they either look and wait or take the adult's hand and guide it to the item.

D. IF SPEECH IS PRESENT, PECULIAR SPEECH PATTERNS SUCH AS IMMEDIATE AND DELAYED ECHOLALIA, METAPHORICAL LANGUAGE, PRONOMINAL REVERSAL. "Immediate echolalia" is the repetition of the utterance of another person within a few seconds. The voicing, intonation, and articulation are usually faithful to the original utterance and better than in the child's own spontaneous speech. Echoes of whole sentences may preserve only the latter part of the sentence, apparently because of auditory memory limitations. Immediate echolalia may be "exact" or "mitigated" (i.e., may include alterations in utterance content or structure).

One major determinant of echolalia is the child's failure to comprehend the utterance just heard (Carr, Schreibman, & Lovaas, 1975; Fay, 1969). Unlike the more common exact echolalia, mitigated echolalia occurs infrequently in autistic children, but when it does, it indicates at least some processing of verbal input and thus a somewhat higher level of language development (Fay, 1980).

The presence of either type of echolalia is significant for language prognosis. Echolalic children invariably progress faster and farther in language acquisition than initially mute children (Lovaas, 1977), particularly if remediation begins when they are young (Howlin, 1981; Lovaas, 1987).

"Delayed echolalia," topographically similar to immediate echolalia but functionally different (Newsom, Carr, & Lovaas, 1979), may occur hours, days, or weeks after the original utterance. The content is often either "melodic" (TV commercials or snatches of songs) or "emotional" (commands, reprimands, fragments of arguments). Delayed echolalia may be intrinsically reinforcing (Lovaas, Varni, Koegel, & Lorsch, 1977), and it can function as an attempt to avoid adult demands (Durand & Crimmins, 1987).

"Metaphorical language" is Kanner's (1946) term for a variety of rare and little-studied idiosyncratic usages in autistic children who have relatively well-developed speech. In some cases, delayed echolalic utterances become functional responses after participating in contingencies of reinforcement or punishment. For example, Furneaux (1966) described an autistic girl who asked, "Do you want to go in the garden?" whenever she wanted to go outside. There is also Kanner's (1946) famous example of the boy whose mother reprimanded him for attempting to throw his toy dog off a hotel room balcony. Thereafter, whenever he was about to engage in any forbidden act, he said to himself, "Don't throw the dog off the balcony!"

In other cases, the child uses words that are only tangentially related to their referents. Kanner (1946) describes cases in which a 55-year-old grandmother was called "Fifty-Five" and the number 6 became "Hexagon." Another child named his five paint bottles after the Dionne quintuplets, then always referred to primary colors by their names in sentences like "Annette and Cecile make purple."

"Pronominal reversal" refers to echoing the second- or third-person pronoun in sentences heard instead of substituting "I," as is required when shifting from listener to speaker. When asked, "Do you want a cookie?" the child might respond, "You want a cookie?" Fay (1980) has noted that the term "pronominal reversal" is possibly misleading, because the child is not deliberately exchanging pronouns but is simply repeating what is heard. Evidence that the phenomenon is due to echolalia and memory deficits rather than deficiencies in self-concept, as once thought, has been provided by Bartak and Rutter (1974) and Fay (1966).

E. BIZARRE RESPONSES TO VARIOUS ASPECTS OF THE ENVIRONMENT, E.G., RESISTANCE TO CHANGE, PECULIAR INTEREST IN OR ATTACHMENTS TO ANIMATE OR INANIMATE OBJECTS. The child may resist changes in the environment, such as the rearrangement of furniture, a new place at the dinner table, or the relocation of toys, any of which may evoke distress or tantrums. The child may also resist changes in his or her own rigidified behavior patterns, including bedtime routines, lining up objects, or repetitive, stereotyped behaviors.

Interest in or attachments to moving objects may be shown by fascination with spinning tops or fans, washing machines, or windshield wipers. Music, flashing lights, or other kinds of sensory stimulation may also be strongly reinforcing (Rincover, 1978; Rincover, Newsom, Lovaas, & Koegel, 1977). "Animate" also means "living," and autistic children tend to be afraid of household pets and other animals, perhaps because they are unpredictable. The child may collect and hoard simple objects like pieces of string or glass, or become strongly attached to a favorite doll or blanket (Marchant, Howlin, Yule, & Rutter, 1974). Higher-functioning children may have obsessions with numbers, letters, timetables, or expressway signs, showing excellent long-term memory for items related to their idiosyncratic interests (Epstein, Taubman, & Lovaas, 1985).

F. ABSENCE OF DELUSIONS, HALLUCINATIONS, LOOSENING OF ASSOCIATIONS, AND INCOHERENCE AS IN SCHIZOPHRENIA. Few autistic children have sufficient language to permit an examiner to determine whether or not schizophrenic phenomena are present, but the sixth criterion can occasionally be helpful when examining higher-functioning older children or adolescents.

ASSOCIATED FEATURES. Even if present to a marked degree, the associated features listed in Table 2 should not weigh heavily in making the diagnosis, because they are frequently seen in other disorders besides autism.

The actual concomitance of mental retardation with autism is difficult to determine precisely, but appears to be higher than the estimate of 70% stated in DSM-III (Table 2, point 1), particularly when intelligence is measured by the Wechsler or Stanford–Binet scales. When the standard procedures of these tests are used, 50–75% of autistic children are found to be untestable (Kolvin, Humphrey, & McNay, 1971; Lovaas, Koegel, Simmons, & Long, 1973; Mack, Webster, & Gokcen, 1980; Rutter, 1966). Of those who are testable, 80–90% obtain Wechsler or Stanford–Binet IQs in the retarded range (Lovaas et al., 1973; Mack et al., 1980; Shah & Holmes, 1985). When the Leiter, Merrill–Palmer, Raven's Progressive Matrices, or other largely nonverbal tests are used, 70–85% of conservatively diagnosed, small samples ($n < 50$) fall in the retarded range (Kolvin, Humphrey, & McNay, 1971; Lotter, 1966; Wing & Gould, 1979). In liberally diagnosed, large samples ($n > 100$), 83–94% are retarded (DeMyer et al., 1974; Lord & Schopler, 1985; Schopler, Reichler, DeVellis, & Daly, 1980). Measures of adaptive behavior indicate a somewhat higher level of overall functioning than is suggested by measures of intelligence (Lord, Schopler, & Revicki, 1982). IQs remain relatively stable in retarded autistic children receiving conventional special education (DeMyer et al., 1973; Freeman, Ritvo, Needleman, & Yokota, 1985) but increase significantly in most children receiving intensive behavior therapy (Browning, 1971; Lovaas, 1987; Lovaas et al., 1973).

"Mood lability" (point 2) refers to observations that the child may suddenly begin to laugh or cry for no apparent reason and just as quickly shift to the opposite emotion. An autistic child may stare into space while giggling, suggesting the possibility of hallucinations, but their occurrence has never been confirmed. It is most likely that some impairment in hormone regulation or neurochemical homeostasis is involved (cf. Coleman & Gillberg, 1985). Another aspect of the lack of emotional control exhibited by autistic children is their tendency toward extreme overreaction to slight frustrations or unexpected changes. Prolonged bouts of crying or screaming occur and may lead to severe tantrums that include self-injurious, aggressive, or destructive behaviors.

Point 3, regarding hypo- or hypersensitivity to sensory stimuli, relates to some investigators' view that sensory or perceptual disturbances are cardinal symptoms of autism (Lovaas, Koegel, & Schreibman, 1979; Ornitz & Ritvo, 1968; Schopler et al., 1980; Wing & Wing, 1971). Both under- and overresponsivity, especially with sounds, may occur at different times in the same child, so that the problem is better characterized as inconsistent responsivity. The child may not cover his or her ears when loud noises occur, or fail to look when called by name, yet orient to the sound of a crinkling candy wrapper. About 60% of autistic children show such behaviors (Kolvin, Ounsted, Humphrey, & McNay, 1971; Prior et al., 1975). Learning and attention deficits have been implicated to a greater degree than any basic sensory impairments (Lovaas et al., 1979; Newsom & Simon, 1977).

The failure to appreciate real dangers in the environment (point 4) results in the child's requiring constant supervision both indoors and out. Like a normal toddler, but at a far older age, an autistic child may walk into the street in front of an oncoming vehicle, climb on bookcases or windows, or ingest household chemicals. Such behaviors remain to be analyzed, but our clinical experience suggests that factors to consider include the positive-reinforcement value of the immediate attention elicited by these behaviors and a failure to learn from previous experience because of a diminished perception or memory of pain (cf. Wing, 1976). Strong punishment may be required to eliminate these behaviors in some children (Risley, 1968), while other children may respond to discrimination training that reinforces the avoidance of dangerous objects (White, Eason, & Newsom, 1981).

Repetitive, stereotyped (self-stimulatory) behaviors (point 5) are seen in most autistic children but are not diagnostic, because they also occur in retarded nonautistic children. However, there is some limited evidence that profiles of specific topographies may differentiate retarded autistic children from other retarded children. Repetitive vocalizations, rubbing surfaces, hand flapping, whirling, and posturing were found to be significantly higher in a sample of young autistic children than in retarded controls (Freeman et al., 1979). Wing et al. (1977) found that retarded autistic children were much more likely than nonautistic retarded children to engage in stereotyped and repetitive routines with toys and objects instead of symbolic play. The stereotypies of autistic children apparently develop out of the normal repetitive behaviors of infancy (Thelen, 1979) and seem to be maintained by the sensory reinforcement they automatically produce for the children (Lovaas, Newsom, & Hickman, 1987; Rincover, 1978).

Self-injurious behavior (point 6) has been reported in the histories of as many as 71% of one sample of retarded autistic children, although it was observed in a brief evaluation in only 6% of the same children (Bartak & Rutter, 1976). Like repetitive, stereotyped behavior, it fails to distinguish autistic children because it is also seen in retarded children. A number of variables have been implicated in the motivation of self-injurious behavior, including organic conditions (e.g., Carr & McDowell, 1980), positive reinforcement in the form of adult attention (e.g., Lovaas & Simmons, 1969), negative reinforcement through escape from demands (e.g., Carr, Newsom, & Binkoff, 1976), and the sensory stimulation provided by the behavior (e.g., Rincover & Devany, 1982).

PREVALENCE. As noted earlier, the best studies of the prevalence of autism were conducted in England by Lotter (1966) and Wing et al. (1976). They used similar methods, including actual observation and testing of the most likely children, and obtained very similar prevalence rates of 4.5 per 10,000 aged 8–10 (Lotter) and 4.8 per 10,000 aged 5–14 (Wing et al.). Using the Wing et al. rate and 1980 U.S. Census data, this means that there are approximately 17,000 autistic children (both Kanner syndrome and other autistic children) in the United States. Similar calculations indicate that in any given year about 1,700 autistic infants will be born. The ratio of males to females is about 3.5:1 (Lord & Schopler, 1985; Tsai, Stewart, & August, 1981).

ETIOLOGY. Most investigators now consider autism to be the result of any of a number of different possible etiologies. Unfortunately, for the majority of cases, the etiology is impossible to establish with any degree of certainty. It seems very likely that a predisposition to autism is inherited, and, in some cases, neurological abnormalities can be identified that seem to have etiological significance. The evidence for the heritability of autism comes from twin and family studies. In twin studies, unusually high rates of concordance for autism are found in identical pairs, and very low rates are found in fraternal pairs (Folstein & Rutter, 1977; Ritvo, Ritvo, & Brothers, 1982). Studies of families have indicated that 2–6% of the siblings of autistic children are also autistic, and 8% of the extended families will include another member who is autistic (Baird & August, 1985; Coleman & Rimland, 1976; Gillberg, 1984). These percentages are low, but when compared with the rare prevalence of autism in the general population, they represent a great increase in risk for developing autism (Coleman & Gillberg, 1985; Rutter & Bartak, 1971). Family studies also reveal an increased prevalence of mental retardation and specific cognitive disabilities in the siblings of autistic children, particularly those who are themselves severely retarded. This suggests that what might be inherited is not an "autism gene," but rather a nonspecific factor that increases the liability for all cognitive impairments, including autism (August, Stewart, & Tsai, 1981; Baird & August, 1985; Folstein & Rutter, 1977). The mode of transmission is unclear, but most cases seem to fit an autosomal recessive model (Coleman & Gillberg, 1985; Coleman & Rimland, 1976), with a minority of males with the "fragile X" syndrome implicating a sex-linked pattern (W. T. Brown et al., 1982; Meryash, Szymanski, & Gerald, 1982).

Evidence that neurological abnormalities can sometimes be identified exists in the occurrence of autistic subgroups among children with genetic, infectious, or metabolic disorders known to affect the central nervous system. These include tuberous sclerosis (Riikonen & Amnell, 1981; Valente, 1971), prenatal rubella (Chess, Fernandez, & Korn, 1978), and phenylketonuria (Knobloch & Pasamanick, 1975; Lowe, Tanaka, Seashore, Young, & Cohen, 1980). Structural, electrophysiological, and biochemical abnormalities that are sometimes associated with autism and may be pathogenic include brain stem dysfunction (Ornitz, 1983; Student & Sohmer, 1978), epilepsy and various other electroencephalographic abnormalities (Deykin & MacMahon, 1979; Riikonen & Amnell, 1981; Tsai, Tsai, & August, 1985), ventricle enlargement (M. Campbell et al., 1982; Damasio,

Maurer, Damasio, & Chui, 1980), hydrocephalus (Damasio et al., 1980), and abnormal levels of serotonin or dopamine (M. Campbell, Friedman, DeVito, Greenspan, & Collins, 1974; Cohen, Caparulo, Shaywitz, & Bowers, 1977; Goldstein, Mahanand, Lee, & Coleman, 1976). A comprehensive review of the biological factors associated with autism appears in the recent book by Coleman and Gillberg (1985), who argue persuasively that autism is not a single entity but a group of related syndromes having multiple etiologies.

The contemporary clinician still occasionally encounters parents who mistakenly believe that they caused their child's condition through faulty child-rearing practices. Such parents should be reassured that there is now considerable evidence that parental personality and rearing practices are not responsible for the development of autism (Cantwell & Baker, 1984; Cantwell Baker, & Rutter, 1978). It is important to be alert to the possibility that interpretations of the development and maintenance of problem behaviors by well-intended but deleterious social contingencies may be misunderstood by parents as blame for the child's autism. The sensitive clinician will make sure that the parents understand that autism is a neurological condition but that the child's behavioral excesses may be explicable in terms of social learning variables, just as they often are in normal children.

Childhood Onset Pervasive Developmental Disorder

Childhood Onset Pervasive Developmental Disorder (COPDD) is basically an "other, later" category, as inspection of Table 3 suggests. COPDD is an even more heterogeneous category than Infantile Autism, and there is very little research behind this new category. The decision to provide specific diagnostic criteria is therefore questionable (Rutter, 1985). However, the inclusion of COPDD does accomplish at least one practical purpose: It provides a category for late-onset (after 30 months) children who are severely behavior-disordered but are neither autistic nor schizophrenic.

The criteria for COPDD (Table 3) describe children with severe social deficits and at least three of the multiple "oddities" of behavior listed in point B. The items listed in points A and B could describe many autistic children; hence the need for the criterion requiring an age of onset over 30 months (point C). The

TABLE 3. DSM-III Diagnostic Criteria for Childhood Onset Pervasive Developmental Disorder

A. Gross and sustained impairment in social relationships, e.g., lack of appropriate affective responsivity, inappropriate clinging, asociality, lack of empathy.

B. At least three of the following:

(1) sudden excessive anxiety manifested by such symptoms as free-floating anxiety, catastrophic reactions to everyday occurrences, inability to be consoled when upset, unexplained panic attacks

(2) constricted or inappropriate affect, including lack of appropriate fear reactions, unexplained rage reactions, and extreme mood lability

(3) resistance to change in the environment (e.g., upset if dinner time is changed) or insistence on doing things in the same manner every time (e.g., putting on clothes always in the same order)

(4) oddities of motor movement, such as peculiar posturing, peculiar hand or finger movements, or walking on tiptoe

(5) abnormalities of speech, such as questionlike melody, monotonous voice.

(6) hyper- or hypo-sensitivity to sensory stimuli, e.g., hyperacusis

(7) self-mutilation, e.g., biting or hitting self, head banging

C. Onset of the full syndrome after 30 months of age and before 12 years of age.

D. Absence of delusions, hallucinations, incoherence, or marked loosening of associations.

Associated Features

1. Bizarre ideas and fantasies.
2. Preoccupation with morbid thoughts or interests.
3. Pathological attachment to objects.
4. Low intelligence.

Note. From *Diagnostic and Statistical Manual of Mental Disorders* (3rd ed., pp. 90–91) by the American Psychiatric Association, 1980, Washington, DC: Author. Copyright 1980 by the American Psychiatric Association. Used with permission.

practical implication is that the history must indicate normal or near-normal development for at least the first 2.5 years.

Information on this category is sparse. Most of the classic work on childhood schizophrenia by Bender (1956), Goldfarb (1974), and others is inapplicable, because their subject populations included undifferentiated mixtures of schizophrenic, autistic, and what would now be termed COPDD children. Some information is, however, available in the epidemiological studies of Lotter (1966), Prior *et al.* (1976), and Wing and Gould (1979). Lotter (1966) contrasted the autistic children he found with a comparison group of severely disordered but nonautistic children. The comparison children differed most in showing far less noncommunicative speech, solitary behavior, ignoring of peers, social aloofness, suspected deafness, elaborate, ritualistic play, and insistence on sameness in daily routines. Prior *et al.* (1976) contrasted "mostly-later-onset" severely disordered children with early-onset children and obtained findings similar to Lotter's. Additionally, the later-onset children were less likely to have organic signs but were similar to early-onset children in terms of pre- and perinatal complications, milestone attainment, intelligence distribution, and family characteristics.

Wing and Gould (1979) subdivided the "severely socially impaired" children they identified into three groups by type of social impairment. Most of the autistic children fell into the "aloof" category. A second category was termed "passive interaction"; it included children who did not make spontaneous social contact but accepted the approaches of others and allowed themselves to be pulled into peers' games. The third category, "active but odd interaction," included children who presumably would fit the definition of COPDD. Such children initiated social interactions, but their interactions were inappropriate because the children used them to indulge some idiosyncratic preoccupation. These children had no real interest in or sympathy for the needs and ideas of others. They tended to annoy others and to be rejected by their peers because of their peculiar behavior.

This category will be called simply "Pervasive Developmental Disorder" in DSM-IIIR and become a frankly residual category for severely disordered children who are not clearly autistic.

Differential Diagnosis

Identifying an autistic child may require a fine discrimination between this and other conditions with similar features. As in other conditions, the difficulties are greatest at the extremes. At the lower-functioning end of the intelligence continuum, autism overlaps with severe and profound retardation, while at the higher end, it overlaps with COPDD, schizophrenic disorders, and learning disabilities (Shea & Mesibov, 1985; Wing, 1981a, 1981b). The following considerations may help in distinguishing autistic from other impaired children.

Mental Retardation

Retardation usually coexists with autism and is diagnosed in addition to autism when warranted by measures of intelligence and adaptive behavior. Retardation is diagnosed *instead* of autism when the deficits in cognitive, motor, social, and language functioning are all at a fairly uniform level, rather than showing peaks and valleys: Autistic children exhibit greater deficits in social and language development, but better motor skills and more unusual responses to environmental stimuli than would be expected on the basis of their overall level of retardation. The fact that autistic children tend to show a higher level of motor development than comparable retarded children is an aspect that is especially useful in distinguishing autistic from profoundly retarded nonautistic children, who may be equally asocial and mute. The most difficult cases involve severely retarded nonautistic children (Wing, 1981b), because they often exhibit immediate echolalia and high levels of stereotypy. Unlike autistic children, however, severely retarded children are usually responsive to simple social interactions. In doubtful cases, it is best to be conservative and defer the autism diagnosis until it is clear whether or not the children meet all the criteria.

Degenerative Neurological Conditions

If there has been a period of normal development before the emergence of autistic symptoms, progressive degenerative disorders should be considered, and the child should receive a thorough neurological evaluation (Coleman & Gillberg, 1985). In these conditions, development appears normal up to 3 or 4 years of age, at which time a profound regression in multiple areas of functioning occurs. Often there is a premorbid period of vague illness with restlessness, irritability, and anxiety. Over the course of a few months, there is a loss of language, social skills, and intelligence. Interest in toys fades, and an extensive repertoire of stereotypies and mannerisms develops (Rutter, 1985). Often the condition may eventually be traced to some type of encephalitis or cortical degeneration, but there are some cases where the etiology is never discovered (Evans-Jones & Rosenbloom, 1978). In girls, Rett syndrome should be considered if the child shows stereotyped handwashing or rubbing movements, jerky ataxia of the trunk, and gross motor deterioration (Hagberg, Aicardi, Dias, & Ramos, 1983).

Developmental Language Disorders

Higher-functioning autistic children differ from children with receptive and expressive dysphasia in the following ways: (1) Autistic children show more echolalia, pronominal reversal, and noncontextual utterances; (2) their comprehension deficits are more severe than those of children with receptive dysphasia; (3) they fail to use gestures and facial expressions as alternative means of communication; and (4) they often fail to use the speech they have for communicative purposes, seldom initiating or sustaining conversations (Bartak *et al.*, 1975).

Schizophrenic Disorders

With higher-functioning children, consideration may need to be given to conditions such as schizophrenia and Asperger syndrome. Schizophrenic children exhibit a progressive narrowing of interests, negativism, interpersonal difficulties, distrust, identification with other persons, animals, or objects, bizarre somatic complaints, irrational and paranoid fears, and delusions (Eggers, 1978). Among the late-onset children studied by Kolvin, 81% had auditory hallucinations and 60% exhibited disorders of thought association, blocking, delusions, and blunted affect. Virtually none showed echolalia, pronominal reversal, or inconsistent responsivity to sounds (Kolvin, Ounsted, Humphrey, & McNay, 1971). Thus, in addition to a later age of onset (usually after 6 years, but sometimes younger; Cantor, Evans, Pearce, &

Pezzot-Pearce, 1982), schizophrenic children show characteristics like those seen in schizophrenic adults, not autistic children.

Asperger syndrome (Wing, 1981a) or "schizoid disorder" (Wolff & Barlow, 1979) more closely resembles autism in normally intelligent children. Speech is stilted, literal, and communicative, but not really conversational. The child is unable to empathize, to learn vicariously, or to follow rules. Unusual, circumscribed topics such as genealogy or astronomy become the focus of interest. Social behavior is naive and inappropriate, due to a lack of understanding the rules and implicit expectations of most social situations. Gross motor movements are clumsy; gait, posture, and gestures show poor coordination. Asperger syndrome children differ from autistic children in lacking their extreme social isolation, severe delays and abnormalities of speech, and gross motor coordination (Wing, 1981a). In test situations, such children are more distractible by internal stimuli and less perseverative than autistic children (Wolff & Barlow, 1979).

Limitations of DSM-III

The current description of the Pervasive Developmental Disorders classification in DSM-III contains certain technical and conceptual problems that are likely to continue into DSM-IIIR. The main limitations are summarized here.

The first problem is that the reliability of the diagnostic criteria is unknown. The DSM-III field trials described in DSM-III, Appendix F, and in Spitzer, Forman, and Nee (1979) included a total of only five children in the Pervasive Developmental Disorders group, with no breakdown of the diagnoses of the children, the reliability of the diagnoses, or the number of clinicians. Similar problems related to finding few or no autistic children in community clinic samples (e.g., Earls, 1982), due to the rarity of the disorder, will leave reliability in limbo until studies are done with larger samples in hospital or school settings.

A second problem is the lack of guidelines in either DSM-III or DSM-IIIR for subclassifying autistic children. The diagnosis provides only one broad term for a very heterogeneous population. Under one label are subsumed children who are profoundly retarded, mute, and totally absorbed in self-stimulation, as well as children whose intelligence is in the normal range, have some communicative language, and

engage in elaborate, highly organized rituals. This situation is likely to continue for some time to come, given the reluctance of the DSM Task Force to subdivide a category when existing subclassification systems have not yet established their clinical utility (Spitzer, 1980). Although a number of schemes, some based on clinical judgment (e.g., DeMyer, Churchill, Pontius, & Gilkey, 1971; Lotter, 1974; Wing, 1981b) and some on quantitative measures (e.g., Deckner & Blanton, 1980; DeMyer, Barton, & Norton, 1972; Fein, Waterhouse, Lucci, & Snyder, 1985; Prior et al., 1975), have been presented over the years, none has yet received replication and widespread adoption. This is due in part to the differing needs of different groups of potential users—for example, medical researchers, psychologists, and educational administrators. The lack of a widely accepted taxonomy may also be due to the continuing existence of controversy in defining autism (cf. Schopler, 1985), suggesting that subclassification may be premature until the boundaries of the condition are better established. In the meantime, communication among professionals is best facilitated by utilizing the multi-axial framework of DSM-III and routinely reporting the child's level of retardation on Axis I along with the Infantile Autism diagnosis, and any neurological or medical conditions on Axis III. Unfortunately, the other axes of DSM-III (with the occasional exception of Axis IV, Psychosocial Stressors) appear to have been designed primarily for persons of normal or near-normal intelligence and are not useful for describing most autistic individuals.

As of this writing, the DSM Task Force on Nomenclature and Statistics is in the process of revising the criteria for Autistic Disorder for DSM-IIIR (American Psychiatric Association, 1985). The proposed criteria are shown in Table 4. Compared to the existing criteria, the proposed criteria are better organized (e.g., all the language characteristics are combined into one category instead of split among two) and have been made much clearer by the provision of five or six alternatives in each category and the inclusion of pertinent, mostly observable, behavioral examples. Such changes should assist in the uniform application of the criteria. However, note that criterion D allows the diagnosis to be made in children over the age of 36 months, in spite of the data discussed earlier indicating that only a very small percentage of autistic children have an age of onset later than

TABLE 4. DSM-IIIR Criteria for Pervasive Developmental Disorders

---

299.00 Autistic Disorder

(Note: Lower-numbered items [and earlier examples within items] are seen in the younger or more handicapped child.)

A. A qualitative impairment in reciprocal social interaction as manifested by at least two of the following:

    (1) marked lack of awareness of the existence or feelings of others (e.g., treats a person as if he or she were a piece of furniture, doesn't notice another person's distress, intrudes on others' privacy without realizing it)

    (2) absent or abnormal seeking of comfort at times of distress (e.g., doesn't come for comfort even when ill, hurt, or tired)

    (3) absent or impaired imitation (e.g., does not wave bye-bye; mechanical imitation of others' actions out of context)

    (4) absent or abnormal social play (e.g., does not actively participate in simple games, preference for solitary play activities, involves other children in play only as "mechanical aids")

    (5) impairment in ability to make peer friendships (e.g., no interest in making peer friendships; despite interest in making friends, lacks understanding of conventions of social interaction)

B. A qualitative impairment in communication as manifested by at least one of the following:

    (1) no developmentally appropriate mode of communication, such as communicative babbling, gesture, mime, or spoken language

    (2) absent or abnormal nonverbal communication, such as use of eye-to-eye gaze, facial expression, body posture, or gestures to initiate or modulate social interaction (e.g., does not anticipate being held, stiffens when held, doesn't look or smile when making a social approach, does not greet parents or visitors, has a fixed stare in social situations)

    (3) abnormalities in the form or content of speech, including stereotyped and repetitive use of speech (e.g., immediate echolalia or mechanical repetition of television commercial); use of "you" when "I" is meant; or idiosyncratic use of words or phrases

    (4) impairment in the ability to initiate or sustain a conversation with others, despite adequate speech

    (5) abnormalities in the production of speech, including volume, pitch stress, rate, rhythm, and intonation

C. A markedly restricted repertoire of activities, interests, and imaginative development as manifested by at least one of the following:

    (1) stereotyped body movements (e.g., hand flicking or twisting, rocking, spinning, head banging)

    (2) persistent preoccupation with parts of objects (e.g., sniffing or smelling objects, repetitive feeling of texture of materials, or spinning wheels of toy cars) or attachment to unusual objects (e.g., insists on carrying around a tin can)

    (3) marked distress over changes made in trivial aspects of environment, e.g., when a vase is moved out of usual position

    (4) unreasonable insistence on following routines in precise detail, e.g., insisting that exactly the same route is always followed when shopping

    (5) absence of developmentally appropriate imaginative activity, such as playacting of adult roles or fantasied characters of animals, or interest in stories

    (6) stereotyped and restricted patterns of interest, e.g., an encompassing preoccupation with lining up objects, pretending to be a fantasied character or animal, or preoccupied with bus timetables

D. Onset during infancy or childhood.

    Specify:

        Infantile onset (before 36 months of age)

        Childhood onset (after 36 months of age)

        Age at onset unknown or not otherwise specified

299.80 Pervasive Developmental Disorder

This is a residual category for disorders involving (. . . a qualitative impairment in the development of reciprocal social interaction and of verbal and nonverbal communication skills . . .) that do not meet the criteria for Autistic Disorder.

Note. From *Diagnostic and Statistical Manual of Mental Disorders* (Draft of the 3rd ed., rev. in Development, subject to change, as proposed by the Work Group to Revise DSM-III, pp. 32–34) by American Psychiatric Association, 1985, October 5, Washington, DC: Author. Used with permission.

3 years (Kolvin, 1971; Prior et al., 1976; Wing & Gould, 1979). This change may be helpful in the very few cases where onset is actually later than 3 years or there is insufficient information to conclude that onset occurred prior to 3 years. The implications of this change for basic research efforts, however, are unclear, because it is not yet known whether children who develop autism after age 3 will turn out to be similar to early-onset children. Extending the diagnosis to children over 3 years of age runs the risk of inappropriate, overinclusive application of the diagnosis that has long compromised the generality of research findings in this field. If the proposed criteria are adopted, it will be important to specify the age of onset as "infantile," "childhood," or, if necessary, "unknown."

DIAGNOSTIC CHECKLISTS

In an effort to put the diagnosis of autism on a more objective, quantitative footing, a number of checklists and one standard observational procedure have been developed (DeMyer et al., 1971; Parks, 1983). At present, none of the available instruments is sufficiently sound to serve as the sole diagnostic tool, but several are still being refined and may eventually gain widespread acceptance. The better-known scales are reviewed below in terms of three crucial dimensions: interrater reliability, concurrent validity, and discriminant validity.

Diagnostic Check List for Behavior-Disturbed Children

The most frequently studied version of Rimland's (1964) Diagnostic Check List, Form E-2, contains 80 items to be completed by the parents regarding the child's development and behavior from birth to age 5. The first 17 questions concern the child's age, sex, birth order, age of onset, possible perinatal complications, sensory–perceptual functioning, self-stimulatory behaviors, motor skills, and intelligence. The next 41 questions address behaviors mentioned by Kanner as part of the classical autism syndrome, such as imitative ability, ritualistic behaviors, visual and auditory responsiveness, social interactions, splinter skills, and physical appearance. Another 17 questions concern language, including its presence or absence, initial and subsequent utterances, echolalia, use of pronouns and "yes" and "no,"

and comprehension. Three questions ask about the parents' educational levels and the occurrence of psychiatric disorders in the extended family. The final question asks the parents to read over all the items and indicate which 10 best describe their child.

The stated purpose of the Diagnostic Check List is to discriminate classically autistic, or Kanner syndrome, children from other autistic and schizophrenic children. A total "classical autism" (Kanner syndrome) score is derived by subtracting "nonautistic" points from "autistic" points, with +20 being the cutoff score for identifying Kanner syndrome. The diagnosis corresponding to scores between +20 and +10 is "uncertain," and children with scores below +10 are definitely excluded from a diagnosis of Kanner syndrome (Rimland, 1971). The scoring key is not in the public domain but may be obtained from the author for research purposes, or the completed forms may be sent to the author for scoring.

Although the Diagnostic Check List is intended to be administered to parents, no assessments of interrater reliability between the mothers and fathers of autistic children have been made. However, Albert and Davis (1971) administered Form E-1 (an early version of the Check List appearing in the first printing of Rimland, 1964) to 62 parents of normal preschoolers and found a significant correlation ($r = .72$) between mothers' and fathers' ratings. Prior and Bence (1975) compared parents' responses on Form E-2 for nine children with those of treatment staff members, who, unfortunately, were not blind to the parental ratings. The parents reported fewer abnormal behaviors than the staff, leading Prior and Bence to suggest that the Check List reflects parents' impressions of behavior in comparison to their children's previous functioning levels rather than in relation to normal children's behaviors. In only one case were the differences in total scores sufficient to change the diagnosis. Davids (1975) and a student completed Form E-1 from the files of 66 children, 41 of whom had been diagnosed with some form of psychosis. The parents of 21 of these children also completed Form E-1 retrospectively. The correlation between the E-1 scores from the case histories and from the parents was a statistically significant but moderate .54.

In a unique but informal approach to concurrent validity, Rimland (1971) analyzed the scores of 22 cases reportedly diagnosed as autistic by Kanner himself. The mean score of the 22 was +13.2, well below Rimland's conservative criterion of +20. Possible reasons for the discrepancy include the unknown reliability of parental reports of Kanner's diagnosis and the intentionally high setting of the criterion to reject false positives at the expense of some true cases (Rimland, 1971).

In the first study of the discriminant validity of Form E-2, Douglas and Sanders (1968) found that it was highly effective in distinguishing autistic from mentally retarded children. Rimland (1971) compared E-2 results for 118 "especially high-scoring" (presumably Kanner

syndrome) children with results for 230 "autistic-like" children who had scored in the −10 to +5 range. The items that best discriminated the Kanner syndrome children from the others are shown in Table 5, along with the percentages of the responses for the answer considered to be most indicative of Kanner syndrome.

DeMyer *et al.* (1971) studied the discriminant validity of both Forms E-1 and E-2 with four small groups (*n* = 8–15) of children independently diagnosed by two psychiatrists as higher-functioning autistic, lower-functioning autistic, early schizophrenic, and nonpsychotic brain-damaged or retarded children. The E-1

TABLE 5. Diagnostic Check List, Form E-2 Sample Items, and Response Percentages

Item	Kanner syndrome		"Autistic-type" (230)
	Speaking (65)	Mute (53)	
21. Did you ever suspect the child was very nearly deaf?			
—Yes	77	94	54
—No			
29. Age 2–5: Is he cuddly?			
—Definitely			
—Above average			
—No	90	88	56
—Don't know			
33. Age 3–5: How skillful is the child in doing fine work with his fingers or playing with small objects?			
—Exceptional skillful	71	75	33
—Average for age			
—A little or very awkward			
—Don't know			
40. Age 3–5: How interested is the child in mechanical objects such as the stove or vacuum cleaner?			
—Little or no interest			
—Average interest			
—Fascinated by certain mechanical things	77	92	56
45. Age 3–5: Does the child get very upset if certain things he is used to are changed?			
—No			
—Yes, definitely	87	86	41
—Slightly true			
71. Age 3–5: Does the child typically say "Yes" by repeating the same question he has been asked?			
—Yes, definitely	94	12	22
—No			
—Not sure			
—Too little speech to say			

Note. From "The Differentiation of Childhood Psychoses: An Analysis of Checklists for 2,218 Psychotic Children" by B. Rimland, 1971, *Journal of Autism and Childhood Schizophrenia, 1,* p. 169. Copyright 1971 by Plenum Press. Adapted by permission. Numbers in parentheses are group *n*'s.

scale, with a criterion of +30 points, discriminated the higher-functioning autistic group from
the others at a significant level. However,
DeMyer *et al.* (1971) noted that group means
were misleading. Only 5 of the 10 higher-
functioning autistic children scored above or
close to +30, and 9 children from other diagnostic groups achieved borderline scores. The
revised scale, Form E-2, failed to discriminate
the four groups or any combinations of groups.
The failure of either version of the Check List
to make better discriminations was probably
due to different definitions of autism. Rimland's Check List defines autism strictly in
terms of the characteristics originally described
by Kanner (1943), whereas the broader DeMyer
et al. criteria were emotional withdrawal before
3 years, noncommunicative speech, nonfunctional, repetitive use of objects, and lack of
role play.

When Prior *et al.* (1975) defined Kanner
syndrome cases as those scoring +17 or higher
on a modified Form E-2, a computer program
was able to distinguish the 37 Kanner syndrome
cases from 105 other cases of pervasive disorder of either early or late onset. Moreover, the
Kanner syndrome cases could be distinguished
from 43 other autistic children by items indicating preservation of sameness, islets of special ability, and fine motor skill.

Leddet *et al.* (1986) compared Form E-2
scores with diagnoses made by experienced
clinicians who used the DSM-III criteria and
had access to each child's developmental history, neurological findings, and psychological
and language assessment data. Form E-2 scores
discriminated autistic children with and without
neurological signs from nonautistic retarded and
nonautistic psychiatrically disordered children.
Furthermore, a group of 16 children clinically
diagnosed as cases of infantile autism without
neurological signs could be discriminated from
a group of 37 diagnosed as autistic with associated neurological conditions, as well as from
the group of 21 cases of nonautistic retarded
and psychiatrically disordered children. However, none of the autistic children achieved an
E-2 score greater than +11, well below Rimland's (1971) recommended cutoff point of +20
for identifying Kanner syndrome cases.

The general conclusion to be drawn from the
studies just reviewed is that both Form E-1 and
E-2 of the Diagnostic Check List identify Kanner syndrome children but reject many individuals who today would be considered to have
infantile autism. Therefore, the Check List is
most useful in situations where there is an
interest specifically in identifying Kanner syndrome children. A continuing difficulty in using
the Check List is knowing where to set the
cutoff score. Most investigators, including
Rimland himself (1971), have noted that +20
for E-2 is extremely conservative, with many
children who seem clinically to fit Kanner's
(1943) criteria failing to achieve it. Only 9.7%
of a sample of 2,218 completed forms yielded
scores at or above +20 in an early study (Rimland, 1971). This small percentage is the basis
for Rimland's (1971) and Kanner's (cited in
Rimland, 1964) conclusion that only about 1 in
10 autistic children is a Kanner syndrome case,
but Rimland (1971) has noted that the optimal
cutoff score may actually lie somewhere in the
range from +13 to +20. Prior and her colleagues have used +17 (Prior *et al.*, 1975) and
+15 (Prior *et al.*, 1976) in classification and
epidemiological studies with satisfactory results, but the implications of using either of
these scores (or some other score) for other
clinical and research purposes are unknown.

Autism Behavior Checklist

The Autism Behavior Checklist (ABC; Krug,
Arick, & Almond, 1978) is part of a package
of five assessment procedures included in the
Autism Screening Instrument for Educational
Planning. Here we discuss only the ABC; the
other four components are described later. The
ABC consists of 57 items divided into five
categories: Sensory, Relating, Body and Object
Use, Language, and Social and Self-Help. Each
item is weighted from 1 to 4, with items weighted
4 considered to be the best predictors of autism.
Thus, the higher the child's total score, the
more autistic he or she is considered to be.
Examples of the items with their weights appear
in the ABC record form shown in Figure 1.
Additionally, profiles of category scores for
autistic and other severely handicapped children
are provided to assist in making the diagnosis.
Individual items for the ABC were initially
selected from previous checklists, then submitted to experts in the field for critical review.
Subsequently, the weights assigned to the items
were determined by analyses of 1,049 checklists completed by special educators in a national survey. Autistic, retarded, severely emotionally disturbed, deaf–blind, and normal
children were represented in the sample of re-

AUTISM BEHAVIOR CHECKLIST

INSTRUCTIONS: Circle the number to indicate the items that most accurately describe the child.

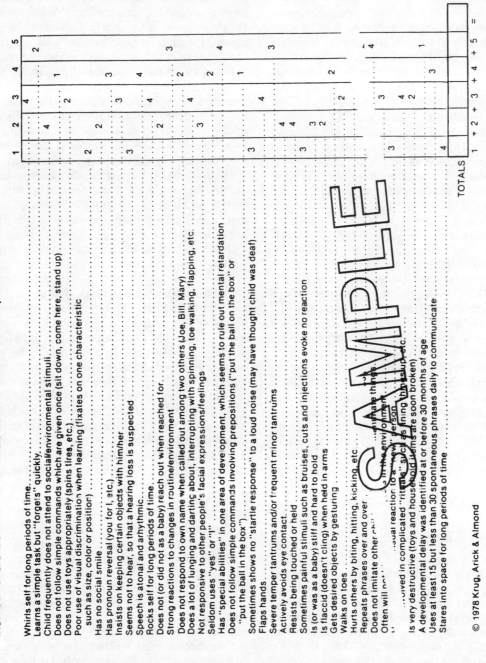

© 1978 Krug, Arick & Almond

FIGURE 1. Autism Behavior Checklist record form (sample items). The numbers in the columns are the weights assigned to the items. The numbers at the top of the columns indicate categories of items, as follows: 1. Sensory; 2. Relating; 3. Body and Object Use; 4. Language; 5. Social and Self-Help. From *Autism Screening Instrument for Educational Planning* by D. A. Krug, J. R. Arick, and P. J. Almond, 1978, 1980, Portland, OR: ASIEP Education. Copyright 1978, 1980 by D. A. Krug, J. R. Arick, and P. J. Almond. Reprinted by permission.

turned checklists. The weight of each item was based on its ability to predict the autism diagnosis according to proportional-reduction-in-error statistics (Krug, Arick, & Almond, 1980).

Interrater reliability for the ABC was examined by having 14 groups of three independent raters complete checklists for each of 14 children (Krug et al., 1980). Agreement averaged 95% across the 42 raters, but descriptions of the children and the raters were not reported. Concurrent validity was examined by administering the ABC to a new sample of 62 children previously diagnosed as autistic. Of this sample, 86% received scores within one standard deviation of the mean of the autistic group in the standardization sample. The other 14% had scores within 1.5 standard deviations (Krug et al., 1980). Details about the sources of the diagnoses and the checklist administration procedure were not given.

Discriminant validity for the ABC was investigated by comparing the mean scores for each of the ABC categories (Sensory, Relating, etc.) and the mean total scores for the autistic group with those for each of the other groups studied (retarded, deaf–blind, emotionally disturbed, normal). The category scores and the total scores were significantly higher for the autistic group than for each of the other four groups. Significant differences between the autistic group and each of the other groups held up when each group was subdivided according to age, sex, residential status, language age, and student–teacher ratio (Krug et al., 1980).

The ABC was developed with the aid of sophisticated analytic techniques at each step. Still needed, however, are stringent reliability checks and better-controlled evaluations of concurrent validity.

Childhood Autism Rating Scale

The Childhood Autism Rating Scale (CARS; Schopler et al., 1980) is used to rate preschool-aged children on 15 subscales: Relationships with People, Imitation, Affect, Use of Body, Relation to Non-Human Objects, Adaptation to Environmental Change, Visual Responsiveness, Auditory Responsiveness, Near Receptor Responsiveness, Anxiety Reaction, Verbal Communication, Non-Verbal Communication, Activity Level, Intellectual Functioning, and General Impressions. The child is observed and the subscales are scored either during or im-

mediately after a testing session with the Psychoeducational Profile (Schopler & Reichler, 1979) or other assessment instruments. For each subscale, there are instructions on how to create opportunities to observe the behaviors of interest. For example, when the Relationships with People category is being rated, an adult should engage the child in activities such as playing with toys and following instructions, varying the amount of direction from "persistent, intensive intrusion" to "complete nonintrusion." The rater is instructed to consider the amount and intensity of intrusion required on the part of the adult to elicit a response, how much interaction the child initiates, and the child's reactions to physical affection (Schopler et al., 1980, Appendix). Each subscale includes definitions for rating the child from 1 ("within normal limits for age") to 4 ("severely abnormal"), and allows ratings at the midpoint between integers (e.g., 1.5, 2.5, etc.) when the child seems to fall between the rating categories.

Total scores on the CARS can range from 15 to 60. Classification rules, based on 537 cases, are as follows: (1) Children receiving scores of less than 30 are considered "nonautistic"; (2) children scoring over 36 and having a rating of 3 (moderately abnormal) or higher on at least five subscales are considered "severely autistic"; (3) all other children are considered "mildly to moderately autistic."

Interrater reliability with the CARS has been assessed by correlating the scores on individual subscales administered by two independent, trained observers, who rated 280 children (Schopler et al., 1980). Correlation coefficients averaged .71 and ranged from .55 (Intellectual Functioning) to .93 (Relationships with People).

Concurrent validity has been addressed by correlating total CARS scores with ratings of "psychosis" by "clinicians" (type, number, and experience unspecified) and with judgments made by a child psychologist and a child psychiatrist (Schopler et al., 1980). The reported coefficients (.84 and .80, respectively) are uninterpretable in the absence of information about the number of cases and the procedures used. Schopler et al. (1980) also analyzed their results in terms of other sets of diagnostic criteria. Diagnostic Check Lists (Form E-2) were obtained for 450 cases and scored by Rimland. Only 8 of the 450 met the criteria for Kanner syndrome. Of these 8, 3 were classified as "nonautistic" on the CARS. When 125 "severely autistic" cases were compared with Rutter's (1978) criteria, which closely approximate the current DSM-III criteria, only 49 (39%) were found to meet them. Apparently, no studies of discriminant validity have been undertaken.

In summary, the CARS allows the user to quantify the severity of a number of behavioral dimensions in pervasively disordered children. It lacks validity for diagnostic purposes, perhaps because several of its subscales (Affect, Near Receptor Responsiveness, Anxiety Reaction, Activity Level) are only tangentially relevant to current conceptions of autism, yet are weighted equally with the other, more relevant subscales.

Behavior Rating Instrument for Autistic and Other Atypical Children

The Behavior Rating Instrument for Autistic and Other Atypical Children (BRIAAC; Ruttenberg, Kalish, Wenar, & Wolf, 1977) has the appearance of a combined developmental–personality scale rather than a diagnostic checklist. In some studies, the total BRIAAC score and some of the individual scales fulfill the stated purpose of measuring changes in autistic children over time and across settings (Wenar & Ruttenberg, 1976; Wenar, Ruttenberg, Dratman, & Wolf, 1967).

The scales are concerned with a wide range of behaviors in the following domains: Relationship to Adult, Communication, Drive for Mastery, Vocalization and Expressive Speech, Sound and Speech Reception, Social Responsiveness, Body Movement, and Psychobiological Development (or "Psychosexual Development" in earlier versions). Each scale contains 10 items or groups of items termed "levels," arranged on a continuum from "severely autistic" to "normal 3- to 4-year-old." Within each scale, the observer distributes 10 points across the levels according to their apparent frequencies of occurrence after observing the child in his or her natural environment. This unique approach to scoring permits observers to weight their scores across different levels within each scale and thus to account for the simultaneous existence of different stages of development. However, the weightings are based on judgments rather than actual counts of observed behaviors. As a result, formidable problems in obtaining reliability are inherent in the procedure, and these are compounded by the highly inferential nature of some of the items.

Interrater reliability, when reported in studies using the BRIAAC, is in the high .80s or .90s (Ruttenberg, Dratman, Fraknoi, & Wenar, 1966; Ruttenberg, Kalish, Fiese, & D'Orazio, 1983; Wenar & Ruttenberg, 1976), but only one early study describes the procedure used to determine reliability. Ruttenberg et al. (1966) found that the total scale scores from four trained observers resulted in rankings of scales that correlated in the middle .80s. No measures of interobserver agreement on the occurrence or weightings of individual levels were made.

In an attempt to establish concurrent validity, Wenar and Ruttenberg (1976) correlated BRIAAC total scores and scores for three scales (Vocalization and Expressive Speech, Sound and Speech Reception, and Relationship to Adult) from 26 "autistic and atypical" children with an experienced clinician's ratings of severity of disturbance. Three of the four correlations were statistically significant, but none of the other scales were evaluated.

As it was not designed primarily for differential diagnosis, it is not surprising to find very little evidence for discriminant validity for the BRIAAC. E. G. Wolf, Wenar, and Ruttenberg (1972) found that scores on the Relationship to Adult, Communication, and Vocalization and Expressive Speech scales were significantly lower in 32 autistic than in 24 retarded children. The scores on Drive for Mastery and Psychosexual Development did not differ. Unfortunately, the samples were not matched on intelligence, so it is not certain that diagnoses rather than mean intelligence levels were being discriminated. In a study reported in Cohen et al. (1978), BRIAAC total scores did not discriminate among autistic, aphasic, psychotic, and retarded children. A study by Ruttenberg et al. (1983) implies that BRIAAC scale scores were significantly different in 3- to 8-year-old autistic children and 2- to 5-year-old normal children. The only data presented showed that there were no significant differences between the autistic children and 1-year-old normal infants, except on the Relationship to Adult scale, on which the autistic children scored lower. These results are theoretically interesting but do not contribute to the validity of the BRIAAC. Finally, it was found that BRIAAC total scores and scores on three scales (Sound and Speech Reception, Social Functioning, and Psychosexual Development) significantly discriminated younger (3–6 years) and older (7–9 years) autistic children (Wenar & Ruttenberg, 1976).

The BRIAAC samples a wide variety of behaviors commonly seen in autistic children. With more objective behavior descriptors and scoring procedures, its reliability might be established, which would then make validity studies meaningful.

Behavior Observation Scale

Unlike the foregoing instruments, the Behavior Observation Scale (BOS; Freeman, Ritvo, Guthrie, Schroth, & Ball, 1978) is not a checklist but a standardized observation procedure. Originally containing a list of 67 behaviors, subsequent analyses of the reliability, stability, and discriminating power of individual items have resulted in apparently only 35 survivors (by our count) in a revised version (Freeman & Schroth, 1984). The procedure is conducted by observing a child through a one-way mirror in a room containing a number of toys, chairs, and a table. Each session is divided into nine 3-minute intervals, with the first and last serving as baselines. During the first 10 seconds of each of the other seven intervals, an adult presents one of several stimuli (e.g., flashing light, spinning top, tuning fork). During one interval the adult attempts to engage the child in ball play. Each BOS item is scored from 0 to 3, depending on its frequency of occurrence. Each child is observed in three sessions on 3 different days.

Factor analyses of BOS results with autistic, retarded, and normal children have been carried out (Freeman, Schroth, Ritvo, Guthrie, & Wake, 1980). The autistic group could best be characterized by behaviors indicating inappropriate interaction with people and objects (i.e., preoccupation with objects, visual scrutiny of details, rubbing surfaces, undifferentiated holding of objects, ignoring the examiner, resisting being held, and deviant ball play). The mentally retarded group was characterized by solitary behaviors, whereas the normal group was characterized by appropriate interactions with people and objects.

Interrater reliability, in terms of percentage of agreement by two trained observers, has been reported for each of the original 67 behaviors in the BOS (Freeman & Schroth, 1984).

Observers were trained to a criterion of 80% agreement with a standard tape and were blind to the diagnoses of the 46 autistic, 32 retarded, and 40 normal children who were scored. Agreement was 75% or better on all but 10 behaviors, 5 of which seldom occurred and have been deleted from the revised BOS. The mean reliability of the remaining 5 was 66%.

Because the BOS is still in development, no concurrent validity studies have been undertaken. The ongoing research strategy appears to be to assume accurate diagnosis of groups of autistic and retarded children and to explore the data base for significant differences, with the ultimate goal of deriving norms for different mental and chronological age groups within diagnostic categories.

The discriminant validity of the BOS was initially found to be poor, due to changes in behaviors across chronological age and mental age in most subjects (Freeman et al., 1978). Subsequently, attention has focused on identifying behaviors that are significantly different between groups when normal-IQ and retarded autistic subjects are matched with normal and mentally retarded controls, respectively (Freeman et al., 1979; Freeman et al., 1981; Freeman & Schroth, 1984). Significant differences in behaviors have been found between groups, but the lists of behaviors vary somewhat across experimental samples. Therefore, analyses of additional measures, such as consistency over time, relative frequency of occurrence, percentage of children engaging in each behavior, and "diagnostic distance" (difference between group means divided by pooled standard deviation), are being used to refine the scale further.

The BOS may not be ready for application for some time, given its developers' stated purpose of establishing norms for autistic, retarded, and normal children at different ages and levels of development. As the most ambitious attempt so far to define autism in terms of standardized observations, it may yet justify the wait. Basic problems requiring solution before that happens include the selection of the behaviors, determination of the best measure of each behavior, and some decisions about the most productive statistical treatment of the data.

As the foregoing review indicates, the attempt to define autism objectively is a relatively active area of research, but much work remains to be done before a generally satisfactory instrument is available. At the present time, the most useful scale for assistance in making the diagnosis of autism appears to be the ABC. When there is a need to identify Kanner syndrome children specifically, Rimland's Form E-2 remains the instrument of choice.

ASSESSMENT FOR TREATMENT PLANNING AND EVALUATION

This section first describes the most frequently used standardized intelligence scales and some "specialized" scales for autistic children that resemble more familiar tests in format and purpose. Adaptive behavior scales are considered next, followed by a discussion of methods representative of "ecological" (L. Brown *et al.,* 1979) or "ecobehavioral" (Rogers-Warren, 1984) approaches to assessment.

Intelligence Scales

Earlier, we have indicated the difficulties involved in trying to answer the "simple" question of what percentage of autistic children are retarded. The problem stems in part from the obvious hazards of trying to use conventional, verbal IQ tests standardized on normal children with children who are severely language-deficient as well as often inattentive and unmotivated. At a practical level, the information on cognitive abilities provided by existing intelligence scales is seldom relevant to treatment planning for autistic children, so that many clinicians would dispense with them entirely but for federal and state regulations. However, there are a few situations in which intelligence testing is important and the effort is worthwhile. First, in diagnosing autistic children, it is important to know the child's general intelligence level in order to judge whether or not the social and language impairments are below what would be expected simply as a function of mental retardation. Second, in studies concerned with treatment outcome and follow-up, pretest–posttest scores are commonly obtained and reported. This practice not only assists in demonstrating changes to the larger professional community in terms they understand, but also indicates changes on what is essentially a standard set of generalization tasks. Third, in research concerned with differences between autistic children and those of other diagnostic groups, or between samples of autistic children at different levels of functioning, intelligence scores can be used as one variable for matching or distinguishing the groups, respectively. Fi-

nally, in the assessment of higher-functioning autistic children for classroom placement purposes, IQ scores, along with the results of other tests, can serve their traditional function of roughly predicting academic achievement. This section provides some suggestions on the use of familiar instruments, then describes some instruments that resemble conventional intelligence tests but have been designed specifically for autistic children.

Standardized Tests

The Stanford–Binet (Terman & Merrill, 1972) and the Wechsler scales (Wechsler, 1967, 1974) can be used with autistic children and adolescents who have at least some receptive language, but the validity of either scale below the mildly retarded level is questionable (Sattler, 1982). An obvious advantage of using one of these established scales whenever possible is their high degree of familiarity to other professionals. In using the Stanford–Binet with functionally mute autistic children, adaptations like those developed for cerebral-palsied children may help. For example, only items that can be answered by pointing may be administered; then an estimated mental age may be computed by prorating (Katz, 1956). When children fail to pass all of the items at the 2-year level, there is an alternative to simply reporting "no basal age established." If the child passes at least one item at the 2-year level, a basal age of 1–6 can be assigned and 1 month's credit given for each item passed at this year level (Sternlicht, 1965).

The Wechsler Intelligence Scale for Children—Revised (WISC-R) may have more construct validity than the Stanford–Binet with autistic children, because its Performance scale contributes to the Full Scale IQ throughout its range, whereas the Stanford–Binet becomes increasingly loaded with Verbal items after the 3-year level. However, it should be remembered that the Performance items on the WISC-R require considerable receptive language ability, with the possible exception of Block Design and Object Assembly, on which autistic children often achieve their highest scores (Rutter, 1966). Unfortunately, the WISC-R does not provide IQs below 40, severely limiting its usefulness with most autistic children. The Wechsler Preschool and Primary Scale of Intelligence creates similar problems with its limited floor and is a more difficult test than the

Stanford–Binet for children in its age range (4 to 6.5 years); consequently, it is used much less often with young autistic children.

For autistic children who are mute, minimally verbal, or deaf, the Leiter International Performance Scale (Leiter, 1969), the Pictorial Test of Intelligence (French, 1964), and Raven's Coloured Progressive Matrices (Raven, Court, & Raven, 1977) are popular alternatives to the Stanford–Binet and Wechsler scales (Clark & Rutter, 1979; Maltz, 1981; Shah & Holmes, 1985). The main advantage of the Leiter is that it can be administered completely without verbal instructions. It does, however, require that the child be able to match to sample in an unusual task format (placing blocks in the slots of a wooden bar), which occasionally makes it unusable with some severely and profoundly retarded autistic children. The Leiter IQ is correlated with but significantly greater than the WISC-R Full Scale IQ in autistic children (Shah & Holmes, 1985).

In testing young and very low-functioning children, a choice can be made between one of the developmental scales (e.g., Bayley Scales of Infant Development, Merrill–Palmer Scale, Cattell Infant Intelligence Scale) or Alpern and Kimberlin's (1970) Cattell–Binet Short Form. The Cattell–Binet is a combination of the Cattell Scale (Cattell, 1960) and the Stanford–Binet in which two items from each age level are used. It has a wide range of applicability with retarded autistic examinees because it extends down to the 2-month age level. Additional advantages include its high correlation (.97) with the full Stanford–Binet, its brief administration time (less than 20 minutes), and its yield of mental ages and IQs that are calculated in a similar way to those obtained from the Stanford–Binet. Disadvantages include the high degree of judgment involved in scoring many of the infant items and the paucity of reliability and validity data beyond those provided in the original article on a small sample of retarded autistic children. In a later study of children with various developmental disabilities, the obtained scores differed by 6 or more points from those obtained with the full Stanford–Binet for about a third of the sample (Bloom, Klee, & Raskin, 1977).

Several neuropsychological researchers have adapted certain standardized tests for use with autistic individuals, including the Halstead–Reitan Neuropsychological Test Battery for adolescents and adults (Dawson, 1983) and the McCarthy and Peabody tests for higher-func-

tioning children (Fein et al., 1985). Adaptations of Piagetian tasks have been used successfully with autistic children by several investigators (Curcio, 1978; Lancy & Goldstein, 1982; Sigman & Ungerer, 1981; Wetherby & Gaines, 1982). Two of these studies cast doubt on the developmental notion that most autistic children are permanently arrested at the sensory–motor stage of development; when properly assessed, some are capable of functioning at a stage appropriate for their chronological age (Lancy & Goldstein, 1982; Wetherby & Gaines, 1982).

In administering a standardized test to retarded autistic children, it is common practice to use food reinforcers, which are delivered noncontingently with praise for cooperation and effort. The scale should be administered as efficiently as possible, with periodic breaks for the child. Still, it may be necessary to spread testing over two or three sessions, especially with disruptive or young children. In addition to providing an IQ and/or a mental age, the administration of an intelligence test allows some informal behavioral observations to be made. The examiner should gain an impression of the child's general language level, fine motor skills, latency of responding ("impulsivity"), and breadth and span of attention. Additionally, the test administration constitutes a situation that is rich in adult demands and therefore provides some information about the child's characteristic responses to this important class of stimuli.

Specialized Tests

Several published instruments have been specifically designed to provide assessments of autistic children, and at least one has been designed for autistic adolescents and adults. They differ from conventional intelligence tests by including many simpler items; some also provide for the recording of maladaptive behaviors. They lack adequate reliability, validity, and normative data and are therefore useful primarily for individual program planning and for within-subject comparisons over time.

The Indiana group was the first to engage in a systematic effort to develop assessment tools to measure general intellectual level in autistic children. In addition to the Cattell–Binet Short Form (Alpern & Kimberlin, 1970) mentioned above, Alpern (1967) also adapted the Cattell Infant Scale for use with autistic children and correlated the results with psychiatrists' ratings and the Vineland Social Maturity Scale. One problem with the "Infant Items Passed" scale, as it was called, was its low ceiling, since items extending only up to the 12-month level were used. This resulted in the subsequent development of the Cattell–Binet to provide more upward range.

A third contribution of the Indiana group was the DeMyer Profile Test (DeMyer *et al.*, 1972). This is a battery composed of items from other published infant and childhood instruments along with some original items. The tasks are divided into five categories: Intellectual, Language, Motor, Perceptual–Motor, and Perceptual. Designed for use primarily with preschool autistic children, the items range in difficulty level from infancy to middle childhood. Items are scored in terms of their mental age equivalents. For comparisons across children, "age-corrected" scores (ratio IQs) can be obtained for each category or major subcategory. No norms are available, but DeMyer *et al.* (1972) do report profiles of the category scores of small groups of high-, middle-, and low-functioning autistic, retarded, and normal children.

The Psychoeducational Profile (PEP; Schopler & Reichler, 1979) is intended for children 1–12 years of age who are functioning at a preschool level. It consists, first, of tasks similar to those found in infant development scales and IQ tests, which are organized into six developmental areas: Imitation, Perception, Motor, Eye–Hand Integration, Cognitive–Performance, and Cognitive–Verbal. In addition, there are a number of specified informal observations to be made in five "pathology" areas: Affect, Relating/Cooperating/Human Interest, Play and Interest in Materials, Sensory Modes, and Language. The developmental scale yields a profile of raw scores, which is keyed to a hierarchy of chronological age norms obtained from a sample of normal children 1 to 7 years of age. A companion scale, the Adolescent and Adult Psychoeducational Profile (AAPEP), consists of three parts. Two checklists cover behaviors in the home and school or work settings, and a series of tests, including vocational tasks, is administered directly. Unfortunately, the tasks tend to be too easy for many autistic individuals and do not closely resemble the tasks found in most sheltered workshops (Sitlington, Marlowe, & Stork, 1985).

The Autism Screening Instrument for Educational Planning (ASIEP; Krug *et al.*, 1978) is a package of five instruments that can be used in combination or separately. Its components include (1) the ABC, discussed previously; (2) a Sample of Vocal Behavior, a procedure for recording 50 representative vocalizations and analyzing them for repetitiveness, communicative function, vocal complexity, syntactic complexity, and language age; (3) an Interaction Assessment, which involves time-sampling several categories of behavior (Interaction, Constructive Independent Play, No Response, and Aggressive/Negative) in a standard play setting; (4) an Educational Assessment, with tasks in the areas of In-Seat Behavior, Receptive Language, Expressive Language, Body Concept, and Speech Imitation; and (5) a Prognosis of Learning Rate, based on performance on a series of shape- and color- sequencing tasks. For each component, profiles of normative data from autistic and nonautistic severely handicapped children are provided. Statistical analyses indicate that the performance of autistic children is significantly different from that of other severely handicapped children on each component (Krug, Arick, & Almond, 1981).

Adaptive Behavior Scales

Although adaptive behavior scales are more useful than intelligence tests in defining important strengths and weaknesses for program planning, there are no scales that have been normed on autistic children. However, Kozloff (1974) has presented a scale for parents and teachers designed primarily for younger autistic children. The Behavior Evaluation Scale organizes 99 behaviors into seven areas: (1) Learning Readiness Skills, (2) Looking, Listening, and Moving Skills, (3) Motor Imitation Skills, (4) Verbal Imitation Skills, (5) Functional Speech, (6) Chores and Self-Help Skills, and (7) Problem Behaviors. An indication of the detailed evaluation the scale permits is indicated by the two items in Table 6 from the Learning Readiness Skills area. The behaviors in each area (except Problem Behaviors) are arranged in an easy-to-difficult sequence, and the most important behaviors are indicated by asterisks and capital letters. The scale also includes questions concerned with the degree and frequency of prompting needed to evoke the behaviors and the child's reactions to attempts to teach the behaviors. The Behavior Evaluation Scale is most useful in parent training programs and in developing classroom programs for young autistic children and severely/profoundly retarded older autistic children.

In most clinical and educational settings,

TABLE 6. Sample Items from the Behavior Evaluation Scale

**A4 THE CHILD *COOPERATES* WITH (FOLLOWS) *SIMPLE* SPOKEN REQUESTS, FOR EXAMPLE, TO CLOSE THE DOOR, HANG UP HIS COAT, SIT DOWN, PUT A PLATE ON THE TABLE. (Circle as many as apply, and underline.)

   a. Child (often; sometimes; rarely; never) cooperates with simple spoken requests.

   b. When child cooperates, it is usually with (a spoken request *all by itself;* a spoken request but only in *certain places;* a spoken request but only if *extra gestures*—body movements—are used to tell him what is wanted).

   c. When child does not cooperate, it is usually because (he seems not to hear or to *notice* the request; he hears but does not seem to *understand* the request; he seems to want to *tease* by not doing it).

   d. When child cooperates it is with (just about anyone; most people; only with certain people).

(Pages 197 to 198 in Chapter 9 tell you how to teach the above behavior.)

**A5 THE CHILD SITS DOWN WITH PARENT OR TEACHER LONG ENOUGH TO EARN REWARDS BY WORKING AT SOME TASK (NO MATTER HOW SIMPLE). (Circle as many as apply, and underline.)

   a. Child (often; sometimes; rarely; never) sits down with someone to work at a task.

   b. If child will sit and work with someone, he *usually* will do it (on his *own;* only when he is *asked;* only when he is *made* to sit down).

   c. If child will sit and work with someone, he will stay sitting without being *forced* (for 30 minutes or more; for 15 to 30 minutes; for 5 to 15 minutes; for less than 5 minutes) before he becomes restless and tries to get up.

   d. Child will sit and work with (almost anyone; most people; only certain people; does not sit and work).

(Pages 199 to 203 in Chapter 9 tell you how to teach the above behavior.)

Note. From *Educating Children with Learning and Behavior Problems* (pp. 406–407) by M. A. Kozloff, 1974, New York: Wiley. Copyright 1974 by John Wiley & Sons. Reprinted by permission of John Wiley & Sons, Inc. The asterisks and capital letters indicate the most important, basic behaviors that should become the initial goals of instruction if not already present.

---

adaptive behavior scales developed for retarded and normal populations are used most often with older autistic children and adolescents. Because these are reviewed elsewhere (e.g., Sattler, 1982; Switzky, 1979; Wallander, Hubert, & Schroeder, 1983) and are already familiar to most clinicians, only a few points will be made here.

The two most widely used instruments are the American Association on Mental Deficiency (AAMD) Adaptive Behavior Scale (Nihira, Foster, Schellhaas, & Leland, 1974) and the recent Vineland Adaptive Behavior Scales (Sparrow, Balla, & Cicchetti, 1984). The AAMD Adaptive Behavior Scale is probably most useful as a criterion-referenced scale in identifying important deficits in a large number of practical domains and in evaluating educational progress (Ando, Yoshimura, & Wakabayashi, 1980; Sloan & Marcus, 1981). The new Vineland, on the other hand, would be the instrument of choice in situations where a norm-referenced assessment of the attainment of developmental milestones is desired in the areas of Communication, Daily Living Skills, Socialization, and Motor Skills. Those working with very young or severely/profoundly retarded older autistic children might also consider the Balthazar Scales

of Adaptive Behavior (Balthazar, 1972, 1973). These scales focus on toileting, feeding, dressing, and some social, communicative, play, and maladaptive behaviors. Instead of relying on an informant's report, the scoring of most areas is done through direct observation. This makes them particularly suitable for objective evaluations of skill training and program changes.

Ecobehavioral Assessment

Conventional evaluations based on interviews, standardized tests and checklists, and observations in one or two contrived settings are increasingly being viewed as insufficient to generate treatment plans that adequately address autistic children's problems in generalizing learning across settings (Rincover & Koegel, 1975) and the need to acquire skills that are functional in everyday environments. Johnson and Koegel (1982), for example, have argued that when educational objectives are based solely on normal developmental sequences, autistic children often receive instruction on tasks or skills that are inappropriate for their chronological age, that are not functional in natural environments, and that are taught and exhibited only in highly artificial settings. Consequently, despite years of special education, autistic adults remain incapable of living independent and productive lives. Others concerned with the education of autistic and other severely handicapped children have made the same argument (e.g., L. Brown *et al.,* 1979; Sailor & Guess, 1983; Snell & Browder, 1986). They advocate that the evaluation process include "ecological" assessments of a child's behaviors in the context of the natural environments and social situations that the child currently experiences, as well as those he or she is likely to experience in the future. Such an approach can be subsumed under the general concept of "ecobehavioral analysis" (Rogers-Warren, 1984), because it is concerned with ecology–behavior interactions—that is, with interactions between settings, activities, and persons and the child's behaviors. Rogers-Warren (1984) has noted that the utility of an ecobehavioral analysis lies in its implications for expanding the range of possible interventions by identifying a larger set of environmental variables that influence behavior than is normally considered.

The ecobehavioral approach is relevant to assessment and treatment development with autistic children in at least three major ways. First, it suggests that the primary assessment question is this: "In what specific ways does this child's behavioral repertoire fail to meet the demands and expectations of his or her environment?" This is a rather different question from the more usual one: "How do this child's cognitions and behaviors differ from those of normal children of the same age?" The latter question is concerned with the mismatch between the child and his or her normal peers, and relates to diagnostic and placement issues; the former is concerned with the mismatch between the child and everyday settings, and focuses attention on individual treatment and educational needs. Although adaptive behavior scales can provide some answers to the former question, it is also useful to conduct supplementary observations in relevant settings to develop valid treatment plans. A possible strategy, based on the suggestions of L. Brown *et al.* (1979), begins with an "ecological inventory" consisting of the following steps:

1. Determine the most important environments in which the child is currently functioning or will function in the near future (e.g., natural home, group home, school, workshop, restaurant, supermarket, etc.).

2. Divide the environments into subenvironments (e.g., kitchen, living room, bathroom, etc.).
3. Delineate the most important activities that occur in each subenvironment (e.g., cooking food, washing dishes, etc.).
4. Delineate the specific skills needed in order for the child to participate fully or partially in the activities.

The delineation of the specific skills needed is based on a "repertoire inventory" for each activity (L. Brown *et al.,* 1979). The steps are as follows:

1. Analyze and record the skill sequences demonstrated by normal persons in performing the activity.
2. Determine which of the steps in the skill sequence the handicapped child can do by observing his or her performance either in the actual environment or in a simulated environment.
3. Compare the child's performance with that of a normal individual to find which skills are missing from the child's repertoire.
4. If necessary, consider possible adaptations of skills, materials, rules, or devices that would allow or enhance participation in the activity. For example, a mute child might be taught to use pictures instead of speech to order food in a fast-food restaurant, or a child who cannot count might be taught to make purchases by handing over the number of dollars indicated on the cash register plus one and waiting for the change.

Many of the steps just described have been employed in recent work with autistic children. Bailey, Prystalski, Kozlowski, Mielke, and Owen (1984) have developed a useful form for evaluating the performance of autistic children in natural environments, as shown in Figure 2, where the performance of an autistic child is compared with that of a normal individual in a fast-food restaurant. Blew, Schwartz, and Luce (1985) assessed the performances of autistic children in reference to task analyses of customary behaviors in several community locations, then employed a normal peer as a tutor to teach them functional skills such as making purchases at a convenience store, crossing a public street, and checking a book out of a library. On a larger scale, Lovaas (1987) focused the treatment of young autistic children on the actual

PERFORMANCE FORM

Student Name __I N__

1. Dom. Voc. R/L (C-at-L) (circle one domain)   Date of N/H person Inventory __7-6-83__

2. Environment __McDonald's (Stratford Square)__   Inventoried by __V. Owen__

3. Sub-environment _____   Date of student inventory __7-7-83__

4. Sub-sub environment _____   Inventoried by __D. Peel__

5. Activity or activities __ordering, finding a table, eating, clean-up__

Natural sD	Performance steps for nonhandicapped person	Criterion for nonhandicapped person	Student Performance + or −	Communication Requirements	Additional Comments
hunger/lunch hour	walk to counter		−	RESPOND TO ANY NEEDED PROMPTS ↓	
	wait in line		−		
Clerk says "May I help you?"	Place order - Coke fries hamburger	respond in 3 seconds	−	look at clerk comprehend "your turn to order"	
Clerk says "Is that "to go" or to stay"	Reply "It's for here"	respond in 3 seconds	−	indicate "for here"	
Clerk says "that will be $2.07"	get money out of wallet – pay clerk	respond with $2.07 or more	−	comprehend "pay for order" will give clerk	if given money will give clerk
Clerk returns change	receive change and return change to wallet		−	comprehend "wait for change"	
Clerk gives food on tray	pick up tray of food		+		
Clerk says "thank you, come again"	carry tray to clean/ empty table	without spilling food	+	possible communicative	
	sit down		+	communication with companions	
	unwrap food		+	interaction with companions	
food consumed no longer hungry	eat food	in an appropriate amount of time depending on conversation	+	companions	needs some assistance–pulls sandwich apart
	Clean-up, putting paper and leftover food on tray		−		
	carry tray to garbage can and empty contents	dispose of disposable contents only	−		drops entire tray into garbage
	walk to door		−		

FIGURE 2. Form for comparing the performance of an autistic child with that of a nonhandicapped person in a natural setting. Item 1 refers to the following curricular domains: Domestic, Vocational, Recreation/Leisure, and Community-at-Large. From "The Curriculum" by S. L. Bailey, P. Prystalski, S. Kozlowski, C. Mielke, and V. Owen, 1984, in S. L. Bailey, V. E. Owen, D. S. Hurd, and C. A. Conley (Eds.), *Instructional Procedures for Educating Students with Autism in the Communication Disorders Program* (p. 44). DeKalb: Northern Illinois University Autism Program. Reprinted by permission.

328

behaviors required successively in home, neighborhood, nursery school, and kindergarten or first-grade environments. At each step, informal observations of normal children in the relevant settings determined each child's "curriculum" of individualized training and treatment objectives (Lovaas, 1987; Lovaas et al., 1981). The success of this model, which resulted in 47% of the children succeeding in regular first-grade classrooms, strongly recommends attention to ecological variables.

A second way in which ecobehavioral methods have been used with autistic children has been in the assessment of relationships between certain settings or activities and a range of typical behaviors. For example, Kozloff (1984) noted that his Behavior Evaluation Scale, described in the preceding section, does not yield a picture of the nature and extent of a child's participation in daily affairs. Therefore, in his parent training program, Kozloff conducts three additional types of assessment activities. First, parents write logs of daily events, which are used to construct a typical day in the life of the family. Second, task analyses of the child's performance of a number of activities are conducted to determine very general strengths and weaknesses across activities. Third, in order to

assess the extent and nature of the child's participation in family life, the child is observed during routine activities to answer the following questions: (1) Was the child present during the activity? (2) If not present, what was the child doing (an alternative, desirable behavior, a maladaptive or disruptive behavior, etc.)? (3) If present, was the child fully integrated, partially participating, not participating but available, or not participating but attending? The information from these additional assessments is used to develop an intervention plan addressing general, functional, and age-appropriate behaviors that will allow the child to participate more fully in everyday family life (Kozloff, 1984).

Working in educational settings, Charlop, Schreibman, Mason, and Vesey (1983) observed five settings in each of three classrooms of autistic children: Group Work, Individual Work with the Teacher, Independent Work, Free Play, and Time Out. The children's behaviors were recorded in eight categories: Out-of-Seat, Self-Stimulation, Echolalia, Tantrum, Appropriate Verbal, Work, Play, and Social. After "mapping" mean levels of the behaviors by settings, the investigators were able to make some data-based recommendations for program redesign. For example, it was found that the

TABLE 7. Definitions of Functional Attributes and Domains

A. Functional Activity Attributes
1. *Functional Materials:* Materials that would be encountered in the student's own community when engaged in similar activities there. Examples include clothing, roller skates, vending machines, and record players. Nonfunctional materials include pegboards, inch cubes, laminated shapes, and buttoning boards.
2. *Functional Tasks:* Tasks that would have to be performed by someone else if the student did not perform the task. Examples include toileting and dressing oneself. Nonfunctional tasks include walking a balance beam and stacking rings.
3. *Age-Appropriateness:* Activities usually performed by nonhandicapped, age-matched peers, without regard for the child's tested mental age. Examples include doing homework and emptying the trash. Non-age-appropriate activities include assembling a wooden inlay puzzle and having an adult tie shoelaces by children over 6 years.
B. Curricular Domains
1. *Recreation/Leisure Activities:* Those that teach the student how to spend leisure time appropriately. Examples include using playground equipment, card games, and roller skating.
2. *Domestic Activities:* Those that teach skills normally required for home living. Examples include washing clothes and setting tables.
3. *Self-Care Activities:* Those that are necessary to exhibit and maintain good grooming, health, and personal safety. Examples include toothbrushing, hair care, and toileting.
4. *Vocational Activities:* Those that contribute directly to the ability of the student to assume a vocation that would enable some degree of economic independence. Examples include tasks performed in sheltered workshops or community jobs.

Note. Abstracted from "A Supervision Program for Increasing Functional Activities for Severely Handicapped Students in a Residential Setting" by K. Dyer, I. S. Schwartz, and S. C. Luce, 1984, *Journal of Applied Behavior Analysis, 17,* pp. 250–251.

highest levels of work-related behaviors and appropriate verbalizations occurred during Individual Work with the Teacher, as expected; however, contrary to the teachers' assumptions, more work and appropriate speech occurred during Independent Work at desks than during Group Work at a table. This finding suggested that the group arrangement be replaced by more time in individual sessions with the teacher alternating with independent tasks at students' desks.

Finally, ecological considerations have begun to influence process measures in evaluations of treatment and educational programs for autistic children. For example, Dyer, Schwartz, and Luce (1984) modified the Planned Activities Check (PLACHECK) procedure (Doke & Risley, 1972) to assess the quality of the activities provided by staff for autistic children in a residential setting. During random daily observation sessions, each child in a residence was observed briefly in turn; the observer scored the activity in which the child was engaged according to three attributes (Functional Task, Functional Materials, and Age-Appropriate Task), and judged whether or not the activity could be categorized into one of four functional curricular domains (Recreation/Leisure, Domestic, Self-Care, Vocational). If a child happened to be receiving a prescribed behavioral treatment for an inappropriate behavior, the "activity" was categorized as Reducing Socially Inappropriate Behavior. The definitions of the attributes and curricular domains are listed in Table 7. A total score for each child was based on the assignment of 1 point for each activity attribute and 1 point for the curricular domain, or a total of only 1 point if Reducing Socially Inappropriate Behavior was scored. For each residence of seven to nine children, an average score was calculated. This measure proved to be sensitive to a supervisory intervention that included posting the definitions of the attributes and domains and providing corrective feedback and praise to staff. A very similar approach was used by Green et al. (1986) to evaluate and establish norms for classroom programs for autistic and other developmentally disabled children.

ASSESSMENT OF FAMILIES

For many years, research on the families of autistic children focused on the possible etiological role of various family factors. This fo-

cus resulted from Kanner's informal observation that most of the parents of the first 11 children he saw seemed to be emotionally cold and perfectionistic (Kanner, 1943). Subsequently, over 150 studies addressed three etiological possibilities: (1) the occurrance of stress or psychological trauma early in the life of the child; (2) the existence of significant psychopathology in the parents; and (3) the presence of deviant parent–child communication or interaction patterns. Cantwell et al. (1978) and Cantwell and Baker (1984) reviewed the literature comprehensively and reached the following conclusions:

1. Early stress cannot explain the development of infantile autism, and, in recent years, this hypothesis has not been considered seriously.
2. The literature does not support the hypothesis that parents of autistic children are excessively cold, introverted, undemonstrative, or mentally disordered.
3. Family communication and interaction patterns are not significantly different from those seen in families with children having other severe disabilities, and are not involved in the etiology of autism, but may play a role in the course of autism after it appears.

As the result of such findings and the increasing involvement of professionals in parent training programs, recent research has focused on identifying specific effects of the autistic child on the family system (Bristol, 1984; DeMyer, 1979; Harris, 1983; Kozloff, 1979; 1984; Schreibman, Koegel, Mills, & Burke, 1984). The scope of the issues involved in working clinically with families can be appreciated by considering Harris's (1983) organization of the kinds of problems they face. First, there are pragmatic problems, including accepting the diagnosis; fatigue; lack of free time; finances; finding professional services, residential services, and schools; burnout; and the child's and the other family members' changing needs as the child grows older. Second, there are emotional problems, such as depression, guilt, and anger. Finally, there are interpersonal problems, including marital relationship issues; sexual problems; siblings; grandparents and other relatives; and the reactions of strangers encountered in the community. Harris has provided a number of examples of each of these kinds of problems and has suggested ways to help parents deal with them over the family life cycle (Harris, 1983; Harris & Powers, 1984).

Most of the data currently available on the stresses experienced by the families of autistic children have come from interviews and questionnaires. DeMyer (1979) used semistructured interviews with the parents of 33 autistic children, who were interviewed for an average of 17 hours. Some of her main findings were that all the mothers reported feelings of physical and psychological tension, and two-thirds reported guilt feelings. In addition, 67% of the mothers felt a partial or complete lack of support from their husbands in caring for their autistic children. When questioned about professional services, 42% of the parents reported that professionals had not been helpful. The three areas most frequently mentioned were insufficient or uninformative communication, questionable diagnostic procedures or results, and a lack of direct help for the children, especially in the area of behavior management. Culbertson (1977) interviewed the families of autistic children and also found that professionals were a significant source of stress. Obtaining a final diagnosis required 6 to 15 professional contacts involving a wide variety of specialists and institutions. In 70% of the cases, the treatment recommendation was for the parents to undergo psychotherapy. Other professional practices identified as troublesome or difficult included inattentive listening, treatment directed at parents instead of children, nondirective therapeutic approaches, recommendations to institutionalize the children, and the withholding of information.

Holroyd and McArthur (1976) used a 285-item questionnaire on resources and stressors developed by Holroyd (1974) to study the parents of autistic and Down syndrome children. Mothers of autistic children reported significantly more embarrassment and disappointment generally than the mothers of Down syndrome children, as well as more stress in areas such as taking their children to public places. The mothers of autistic children also reported that their children had fewer leisure activities, more difficult personality characteristics, more disruptive behaviors, fewer community services, and poorer prospects for employment and independent living.

Increasingly, investigators are supplementing interview data with standardized scales and direct observation measures. Bristol (1984) has reported studies on the families of autistic children in which data were gathered through interviews, the Family Environment Scale (Moos & Moos, 1981), and the Coping Health Inventory for Parents (McCubbin & Patterson, 1981). The Family Environment Scale measures dimensions of Family Relationships (Cohesion, Expressiveness, Conflict), Personal Growth (Independence, Achievement Orientation, Intellectual–Cultural Orientation, Active–Recreational Orientation, Moral–Religious Emphasis), and System Maintenance (Organization and Control). The Coping Health Inventory is a list of coping responses to measure the perceived helpfulness of three major types of coping patterns in handling the stress of a handicapped or chronically ill child: those aimed at maintaining family integration, cooperation, and an optimistic definition of the situation; those aimed at maintaining social support, self-esteem, and psychological stability; and those aimed at seeking information and services and carrying out prescribed activities. In a study comparing 27 families of autistic children with 18 families with dysphasic or conduct-disordered children, Bristol (1984) found that on the Family Environment Scale the families with autistic children scored significantly higher than the control families on Moral–Religious Emphasis and lower on Active–Recreational Orientation. In the total group of 45 families, successful adaptation to the handicapped child, as determined by interviewers' ratings, was closely correlated with high scores on Cohesion (commitment to and support for one another), Expressiveness (open and direct expression of feelings), and Active–Recreational Orientation (participation in social and recreational activities outside the home).

In conjunction with their project comparing clinic and home-based treatment approaches, Koegel, Schreibman, and their colleagues developed a comprehensive set of pre–post measures for assessing multiple effects of 1 year of treatment on both the children and the parents (Koegel, Schreibman, Britten, Burke, & O'Neill, 1982; Schreibman et al., 1984). The procedures that included the parents, and some of the main findings, were as follows:

1. Structured laboratory observations assessed each child's behavior in a standard playroom setting while, in different conditions, the child's mother, a student therapist, and an unfamiliar adult attempted to engage the child in a series of interactions (cf. Lovaas et al., 1973). Each session was videotaped and scored for the

proportion of time spent engaged in three kinds of appropriate behavior (Appropriate Toy Play, Social Nonverbal Behavior, and Appropriate Speech) and four categories of inappropriate behavior (Noncooperation, Self-Stimulatory Behavior, Tantrums, and Psychotic Speech). The results indicated that significant gains in appropriate behavior and reductions in inappropriate behavior occurred only in the condition including the child's regular therapist—that is, only with the mother for the home treatment children and only with the student therapist for the clinic treatment children.

2. Unstructured home observations assessed each child's responses to parents' questions and instructions. Data were recorded from videotapes made during each family's dinner hour, a time when the entire family was together. Children in the home treatment group showed significant improvement in responding appropriately to questions and instructions; children in the clinic group did not.

3. Parent–child interaction measures were obtained during a 15-minute session in which the parent attempted to teach the child a new skill. For each session a particular task (e.g., verbal imitation, color discrimination) was selected from a pool of tasks the child had not yet mastered but were judged to be within his or her ability to learn. The parent's correct use of instructions, prompts, shaping, consequences, and intertrial intervals was scored in 30-second intervals. These teaching techniques have been found to be sufficient to produce learning in autistic children when used by parents (Koegel, Glahn, & Nieminen, 1978) and teachers (Koegel, Russo, & Rincover, 1977). The percentage of intervals scored correct was calculated for each of the five categories of teaching techniques for each session. In addition, an index of whether or not the child was learning in the session was obtained by comparing the number of correct responses in the last 10 trials with the first 10 trials. Posttreatment observations of the mothers' use of the five teaching procedures showed that the mothers trained to work with their children at home used them correctly more often than untrained mothers, and that the home-treated children scored twice as high on the learning index as the clinic-treated children.

4. Standardized instruments were used to assess certain parental personality and relationship factors. The Minnesota Multiphasic Personality Inventory (MMPI; Hathaway & McKinley, 1967) was computer-scored for the 3 validity scales and the 10 clinical scales. The Spanier Dyadic Adjustment Scale (Spanier, 1976) was used to measure each parent's satisfaction with the marriage. Both groups of parents scored within the normal range on all scales of the MMPI and the Dyadic Adjustment Scale both before and after treatment. On the Family Environment Scale (Moos & Moos, 1981), both groups were well below the normative sample prior to treatment, but the parent training group improved significantly on the Expressiveness, Intellectual–Cultural Orientation, and Active–Recreational Orientation scales at posttreatment.

5. Finally, measures of daily activities and satisfaction with treatment were obtained. Daily activity diaries, in which the parents listed each activity they engaged in during one weekday and one weekend day, were used to analyze the amount of time the parents engaged in teaching activities, custodial care activities, and leisure and recreation activities. At posttreatment, parents in the parent training group reported spending twice as much time teaching self-care and academic skills as parents in the clinic group, as well as a sevenfold increase in the amount of time devoted to leisure and recreational activities. Parent satisfaction with the treatment program was measured by a questionnaire addressing seven areas: (a) the staff's ability to provide treatment, (b) the relevance of the treatment to the child's future, (c) the child's improvement, (d) the parents' commitment to provide treatment, (e) the parents' ability to provide treatment, (f) the staff's commitment to provide treatment, and (g) overall satisfaction with the child. The parents in the parent training group reported more overall satisfaction with their children and a greater commitment to provide treatment than the parents in the clinic group.

As this brief overview of family studies has indicated, professionals who work with parents are becoming increasingly concerned with the types of stress parents experience and their ways of coping with them. Another important theme is the impact on the entire family system of interventions focused on the autistic child. In the future, we can expect to see much more research in this area, particularly as ecobehavioral methods are used increasingly in studies of families with autistic children (as they have *what are we going to study* (handwritten annotation)

...t in Natural Environments

...first steps in any behavior manage-
...tation is to obtain some basic in-
...om direct observation and from
...hers, or direct care staff about the
...d events that appear to be related
...s of the problem behavior. At an
...al level, such information can be
...using a recording sheet like that
...Favell (1981) and reproduced in
...e first column in the recording
...escriptions of the type and topog-
...oblem behavior being observed,
...percentage of occurrence across
...intervals, and its intensity (i.e.,
..."mild," "moderate," or "se-
...cond column requires a listing
...which the behavior does not
...those in which it does occur,
...pt consideration of important
...rmer situations that could be
...sequent treatment efforts. The
...provide space for lists of the
...the problem behavior and ap-
...rs. Such lists may point to
...ing the problem behavior and
...nsufficiency of positive rein-
...ropriate behaviors. The use
of such a form during informal observations
helps to direct attention to sequences of behavioral and environmental events that are closely
associated in time. A single behavior episode
may not be revealing, but observation of a
number of episodes should indicate some pattern of antecedents and consequences that is
correlated with episodes and that may be causal.

A useful adjunct to informal observation is a
questionnaire for teachers or parents designed
by Durand and Crimmins (1983, in press). The
Motivation Assessment Scale (MAS) is a list
of 16 questions about a child's most frequent
disruptive behavior. The 16 questions are composed of four questions in four categories, each
category related to one of the following possible
motivational processes: social attention, escape
from demands or other aversive stimuli, sensory consequences, and tangible consequences
such as food or toys. Examples of the questions
related to each process are shown in Table 8.
The sources of motivation shown in Table 8
were selected because they have been found in
experimental studies to be functionally related
to severe behavior disorders in autistic and

...design strategies (Johnston & Pennypacker, 1980; Kazdin, 1982), they permit the
objective analysis of the effect of treatment
interventions. More recently, there has been an
increased emphasis on conducting a thorough
analysis of the problem behavior prior to treatment, because doing so often reveals environmental variables that are functionally related to
the behavior. When a functional relationship is
identified, a treatment derived logically from
the assessment can often be implemented, with
considerable gains in timeliness, effectiveness,
and accountability. Thus, the clinician can go
to the heart of the problem in a way not possible
when assessment is limited to intellectual and
developmental evaluations or to trial-and-error
applications of common treatments.

Some recently developed methods for analyzing the problem behaviors of autistic children are described in this part of the chapter.
They include procedures that are useful in natural environments, as well as procedures for
conducting functional analyses in highly structured analogue situations.

retarded children (see reviews by Carr, 1977, and Carr & Durand, 1985b). The informant answers each question by circling the appropriate rating on a 7-point scale ranging from "Never" (0) to "Always" (6). A mean score is obtained for each of the four categories of maintaining variables. The relative standing of the resulting mean scores indicates the relative contribution of each of the types of motivation to the problem behavior.

In interrater reliability studies, 20 pairs of teachers rated a total of 50 autistic and retarded children. Correlations between the ratings on individual questions ranged from .66 to .92 and were significant at the .001 level (Durand & Crimmins, in press). Rank-order correlation coefficients for the category mean scores were also highly significant. Some initial validity data demonstrated that the primary category of motivation identified by the MAS predicted the subsequent occurrence of problem behaviors in a corresponding classroom analogue situation (described in the next section). For example, children whose disruptive behaviors were rated on the MAS as most likely to occur when

demands were made later demonstrated those behaviors much more frequently in the "Escape" analogue situation, which included difficult tasks, than in the other situations. In fact, ranks of the categories of motivation derived from the MAS ratings correlated .99 with ranked data from the different analogue conditions, indicating almost perfect prediction of the children's performance in the test situations by the teachers' ratings (Durand & Crimmins, in press). The MAS would benefit from further validation, but it can be very helpful in quickly obtaining some initial information about the possible functional significance of problem behaviors.

In many educational and treatment settings, data on problem behaviors are customarily reduced to line graphs of the daily frequency, rate, or percentage of time samples the behavior was observed. Although useful for determining the effectiveness of treatment interventions, such graphs contribute little to the analysis of behaviors because they ordinarily provide no information about the situations that are differentially associated with high, low, and zero

---

BEHAVIOR PROBLEMS: INFORMATION SHEET

Client: _____

Period of Observation: _____

Observer: _____

Type, Frequency, Intensity of Problem	Situations in Which Problem Behavior Does/Doesn't Occur	Consequences of Problem Behavior	Appropriate Behavior and Its Consequences
Type	Does		
Frequency (or %)			
	Doesn't		
Intensity			

COMMENTS:

FIGURE 3. Form for recording initial information about problem behaviors. From *Treating Problem Behavior in Developmentally Disabled Persons* by J. E. Favell, 1981, May, workshop presented at the convention of the Association for Behavior Analysis, Milwaukee, WI. Reprinted by permission.

TABLE 8. Motivation Assessment Scale Categories and Sample Questions

Attention

3. Does this behavior occur when you are talking to other persons in the room?
7. Does this behavior occur whenever you stop attending to him or her?
11. Does your child seem to do this behavior to upset or annoy you when you're not paying attention to him or her?

Escape

2. Does this behavior occur following a command to perform a difficult task?
6. Does this behavior occur when *any* request is made of your child?
10. Does your child seem to do this behavior to upset or annoy you when you are trying to get him or her to do what you ask?

Self-Stimulation

1. Would this behavior occur continuously if the child was left alone for long periods of time?
5. Does this behavior occur repeatedly, over and over, in the same way?
9. Does it appear to you that he or she enjoys performing this behavior, and would continue even if no one was around?

Tangible Reward

4. Does this behavior ever occur to get a toy, food, or game that he or she has been told that he or she can't have?
8. Does this behavior occur when you take away a favorite toy or food?
12. Does this behavior *stop* occurring shortly after you give the child the toy or food he or she has requested?

Note. Adapted from *The Motivation Assessment Scale: A Preliminary Report on an Instrument which Assesses the Functional Significance of Children's Deviant Behavior* by V. M. Durand and D. B. Crimmins. Paper presented at the Berkshire Association for Behavior Analysis and Therapy, Amherst, MA, October 1983. Copyright 1983 by V. Mark Durand. Adapted by permission.

probabilities of the behavior. An alternative method of data presentation that does capture relationships between behaviors and situations is the scatter plot suggested by Touchette, MacDonald, and Langer (1985). One of the investigators' examples, which shows the data of an aggressive autistic adolescent, appears in Figure 4. The ordinate is divided into time periods appropriate to the length of most of the elements of the client's daily schedule; here, they are half hours. The abscissa shows successive days. Within the grid, blank cells indicate nonoccurrence of the problem behavior, and filled cells indicate that the behavior occurred during that interval. Filled circles represent two or more assaults on peers or staff, and open squares represent one assault.

The scatter plot indicates that aggression was most likely to occur during weekdays from 1:00 to 4:00 P.M., when the client was in group prevocational and community living classes. Aggression was least likely to occur during morning one-to-one instruction, Friday afternoon field trips, and evening and weekend activities. Consequently, intervention began with the elimination of afternoon class participation and the scheduling of activities similar to those

available during evenings and weekends (e.g., listening to stories, trying on cosmetics, playing with stickers). The first 2 weeks of treatment are shown in the "Revised Program" panel of Figure 4. Over the following 12 months, the client was exposed to classroom activities for gradually increasing periods of time, eventually spending most of the afternoon in class with minimal aggression, as shown in the third panel of Figure 4.

The usefulness of a scatter plot depends primarily on the use of a code that is easily understood. Touchette *et al.* (1985) caution that using more than two or three symbols (representing "presence"–"absence" of the behavior or "high," "low," and "zero" rates) tends to make the grid difficult to interpret. In applied settings, all that is usually needed for treatment decisions is a code that discriminates "major" or "significant" episodes of a particular problem behavior from "minor" or "negligible" episodes. Inclusion of data on minor episodes, even if the ultimate goal is complete elimination of the behavior, aids in identifying approximations in the desired direction that are especially useful when there are few zero intervals in the baseline. (Although the same information

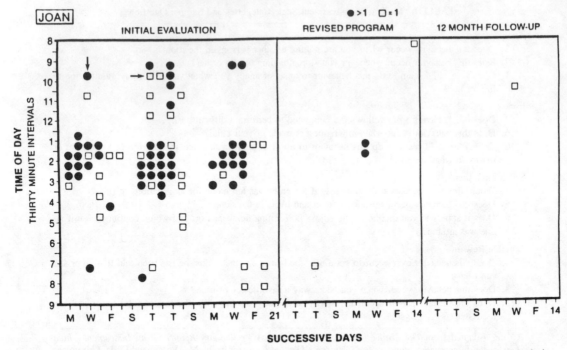

FIGURE 4. Scatter plot of assaultive behaviors by an autistic adolescent. Filled circles indicate 30-minute intervals during which more than one assault occurred; open boxes indicate intervals with only one assault. From "A Scatter Plot for Identifying Stimulus Control of Problem Behavior" by P. E. Touchette, R. F. MacDonald, and S. N. Langer, 1985. *Journal of Applied Behavior Analysis, 18*, p. 347. Copyright 1985 by the Society for the Experimental Analysis of Behavior, Inc. Reprinted by permission.

could in principle be obtained from a multiple-baseline graph, a graph equivalent to the grid in Figure 4 would require at least five or six curves, one for each major portion of the day, and thus would be far more troublesome to plot and to read.) A scatter plot is also useful even if no patterns in the behavior emerge, because it thereby suggests two possibilities with autistic individuals: An unstable, poorly structured environment exists (Touchette *et al,* 1985, Case 3), or the behavior is not under stimulus control but instead is a "pure" operant (Skinner, 1938) maintained by intermittent social or sensory reinforcers.

Functional Analysis in Analogue Settings

Formal functional-analytic procedures include the experimental manipulation of variables that may influence a behavior to determine their actual causal status. Functional-analytic methods have been used in laboratory settings for

over 20 years with autistic children, for the study of behaviors such as self-injury (Carr et al. 1976; Lovaas *et al.,* 1965a; Rincover & Devany, 1982), stereotypy (Rincover, 1978; Rincover, Cook, Peoples, & Packard, 1979), and tantrums (Carr & Newsom, 1985). In these and related studies, only one or two variables (e.g., contingent social attention, adult demands) were compared with a control or baseline condition. What is new is the assessment of the effects of several variables appearing in combinations of conditions scheduled in either reversal (Baer, Wolf, & Risley, 1968) or alternating-treatments designs (Barlow & Hayes, 1979). One condition serves as a control condition, and several additional conditions sample variables that may be related to the behavior under study. Some examples of recently developed analogue assessment procedures are discussed here.

Iwata, Dorsey, Slifer, Bauman, and Richman (1982) created four analogue conditions based on the experimental literature on the motivation of self-injurious behavior (SIB);

1. *Social Disapproval:* The experimenter ignored the subject during toy play but gently reprimanded him or her contingent upon each episode of SIB. The intent was to duplicate the attention that sometimes functions as an inadvertent positive reinforcer for SIB in natural environments (Lovaas & Simmons, 1969).
2. *Alone:* The subject was left alone in the room without toys or other stimulating materials. This condition assessed the maintenance of SIB by its self-stimulatory properties (Favell, McGimsey, & Schell, 1982; Rincover & Devany, 1982).
3. *Academic Demand:* The experimenter instructed, modeled, and prompted performance on classroom tasks and turned away from the subject for 30 seconds contingent on each episode of SIB. This condition assessed whether or not SIB was maintained by the negative reinforcement of temporarily escaping adult demands (Carr *et al.*, 1976).
4. *Unstructured Play:* A variety of toys were made available and the experimenter praised any non-SIB every 30 seconds while ignoring SIB episodes. This condition served as a control procedure in which low levels of SIB were expected (and obtained) due to the absence of demands and the reinforcement of incompatible behavior in an "enriched" environment (Horner, 1980).

Each condition was conducted for two 15-minute sessions (a total of eight randomly ordered sessions a day in a simultaneous treatment design) until responding stabilized or 12 days of sessions were completed. An observer recorded the presence–absence of SIB in continuous 10-second intervals. Overall interobserver reliability, calculated interval by interval, was 97%.

Iwata *et al.* (1982) presented the results of their procedure with nine subjects. Their summary data appear in Figure 5. In order to facilitate comparisons across subjects despite large differences in overall rates of SIB, the experimenters normalized the data in terms of each subject's mean across conditions. Thus, the histograms in Figure 5 present the data for each condition as standard deviations from each subject's mean percent occurrence of SIB. Despite the differences between subjects in overall levels of SIB, most individuals showed higher rates of SIB in one condition than in the others. Four main patterns of responding were identified. First, four subjects (Subjects 4, 6, 7, and 9 in Figure 5) showed their highest levels of SIB during the Alone condition, suggesting that sensory feedback was maintaining their SIB. Second, Subjects 1 and 3 exhibited their highest levels of SIB in the Academic Demand condition, implicating escape as the negative reinforcer of their SIB. Third, Subject 5 engaged in SIB most frequently in the Social Disapproval condition, suggesting the likelihood that attention functioned as a positive reinforcer for this child's SIB. Finally, Subjects 2 and 8 showed an undifferentiated pattern of similar amounts of SIB across two or more conditions. Such a result indicates that the subjects did not discriminate the different conditions, that their SIB was controlled by variables not included in the assessment conditions, or that their SIB served multiple functions.

The Iwata *et al.* (1982) article includes specific treatment recommendations based on their findings about the likely motivation of most of their subjects' SIBs. The procedure is easily adaptable to the assessment of other problem behaviors and has recently been used to evaluate aggression (Mace, Page, Ivancic, & O'Brien, 1986) and stereotypy (Stanley, 1985).

Carr and Durand (1985a) developed and validated an analogue assessment procedure for identifying two common antecedents of various problem behaviors (e.g., aggression, tantrums, object destruction, self-injury) of autistic and other developmentally disabled children in classrooms. Their procedure examined the effects of reducing the level of adult attention and increasing the level of task difficulty in separate conditions. An adult worked with one of two children at a table to approximate a classroom situation for one to three 10-minute sessions per day. In different assessment conditions, the child being evaluated received either an easy or a difficult task (as determined in preliminary testing) and a high or low level of adult attention (instructions, praise, and comments) for task-related behavior. The first condition presented was a baseline condition termed "Easy 100." The child worked on either an easy receptive-labeling task or an easy match-to-sample task and received an instruction, praise, or a neutral comment every 10 seconds (i.e., in 100% of the 10-second intervals into which each session was divided). Because the task was easy and a high level of adult attention was provided, disruptive behaviors could be expected to be low. Following three to six

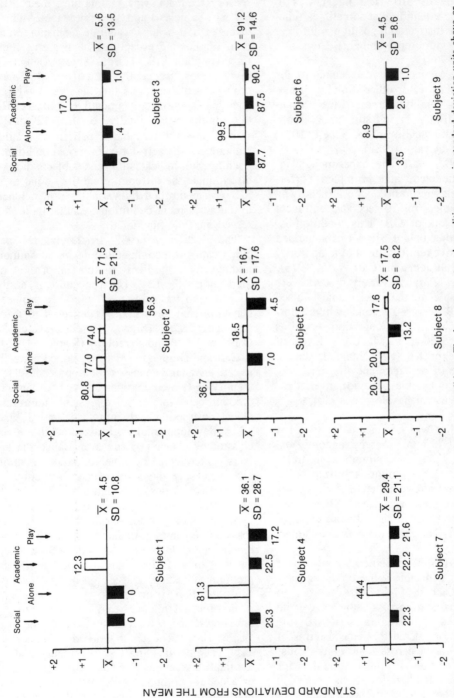

FIGURE 5. Summary data for nine subjects across assessment conditions. The bars represent each condition mean in standard deviation units above or below the subject's overall mean. The numbers to the right of each graph show overall mean percentage of intervals of self-injury and the standard deviation. The numbers above or below each bar indicate the mean percent of intervals of self-injury per condition. From "Toward a Functional Analysis of Self-Injury," by B. A. Iwata, M. F. Dorsey, K. J. Slifer, K. E. Bauman, and G. S. Richman, 1982, *Analysis and Intervention in Developmental Disabilities*, 2, p. 13. Copyright 1982 by Pergamon Press, Ltd. Reprinted by permission.

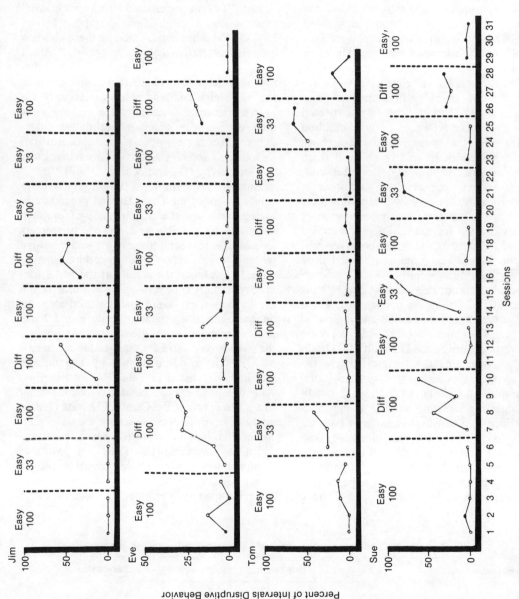

FIGURE 6. Percentage of intervals of disruptive behavior as a function of task difficulty and level of adult attention. Open circles indicate sessions conducted by an informed experimenter; filled circles indicate sessions conducted by naive experimenters. From "Reducing Behavior Problems through Functional Communication Training" by E. G. Carr and V. M. Durand, 1985, *Journal of Applied Behavior Analysis, 18*, p. 117. Copyright 1985 by the Society for the Experimental Analysis of Behavior, Inc. Reprinted by permission.

baseline sessions, two other assessment conditions were alternated with it every three sessions. One condition was "Easy 33," in which the child worked on the easy match-to-sample task but received instructions and praise every 30 seconds (i.e., during 33% of the 10-second intervals). The reduction in adult attention was expected to evoke disruptive behaviors in those children whose disruptive behaviors were normally followed by increased attention. The other condition was "Difficult 100": The child worked on a difficult receptive-labeling task while receiving attention in every time interval. The increase in level of task difficulty was expected to evoke disruptive behaviors in those children for whom such tasks were aversive and whose disruptive behaviors frequently allowed them to escape the task. Data were collected in continuous 10-second time samples by an observer in the room who was cued by a tape recorder. The presence–absence of disruptive responses previously defined for each child was recorded at the end of each interval. Interobserver reliability for disruptive behavior exceeded 80% interval-by-interval agreement.

The results for four children assessed by Carr and Durand (1985a) appear in Figure 6. Three distinctive patterns of motivation are implicated in the data. Two children (Jim and Eve) were disruptive primarily in the Difficult 100 condition only, suggesting that their disruptive behaviors were escape-motivated. One child (Tom) was disruptive primarily in the Easy 33 condition, suggesting attention seeking as the motivation. Finally, Sue was disruptive in both the Easy 33 and Difficult 100 conditions, suggesting that both attention seeking and escape were factors in her disruptive behaviors. Support for the validity of these conclusions appears in a second experiment in the Carr and Durand (1985a) study. They showed that teaching each child a verbal phrase relevant to his or her motivation as an appropriate alternative response reduced disruptive behavior; teaching an irrelevant phrase did not. For example, escape-motivated children were successfully taught to say, "I don't understand," to prompt assistance instead of engaging in disruptive behaviors. On the other hand, teaching these children a verbal attention-seeking response ("Am I doing good work?") did *not* result in less disruptive behavior, because it was irrelevant to the motivation of their behavior. Exactly the reverse occurred with attention-seeking children. Similar assessment and validation procedures have been applied to noncontextual, "psychotic" speech (Durand & Crimmins, 1987) and stereotypy (Durand & Carr, 1987).

Durand and Crimmins (in press) have recently extended the Carr–Durand procedure to include tests for the maintenance of problem behaviors by tangible and sensory reinforcers in addition to social (attention) and negative (escape) reinforcers. Their procedure was designed to validate the results of the MAS (described earlier) with self-injurious children, but the validation procedure can be used alone as an analogue assessment procedure and lends itself to many other problem behaviors because the motivational variables assessed are not unique to SIB. The conditions used by Durand and Crimmins are listed in Table 9. The Baseline, Attention, and Escape conditions were similar to the conditions of the Carr and Durand (1985a) study. The difference was that tangible reinforcers (edibles or preferred toys) were provided on a variable-ratio (VR) 3 schedule of reinforcement for correct responses on picture match-to-sample tasks. The inclusion of tangible reinforcement permitted the assessment of

TABLE 9. Analogue Conditions for Assessment of Motivation of Self-Injurious Behavior

Assessment condition	Task	Performance[a]	Attention[b]	Tangible rewards[c]
Baseline	Easy	100%	100%	VR 3
Attention	Easy	100%	33%	VR 3
Escape	Difficult	33%	100%	VR 3
Tangible	Easy	100%	100%	VR 9
Unstructured	*Ad libitum*	—	*Ad libitum*	*Ad libitum*

Note. Abstracted from "Identifying the Variables Maintaining Self-Injurious Behavior" by V. M. Durand and D. B. Crimmins, in press, *Journal of Autism and Developmental Disorders.*
[a]Percentage of correct responding.
[b]Percentage of 10-second intervals with praise, commands, or comments.
[c]Schedule of reinforcement for correct task responses. VR, variable ratio.

its functional significance in the Tangible condition. There, the schedule of reinforcement was changed from rich to lean (i.e., from reinforcement for every third correct response to every ninth correct response). The logic was that if the child's SIB were being maintained by tangible reinforcement, a sudden reduction in reinforcement density would result in a higher rate of SIB in an effort to reinstate the richer schedule. In the Unstructured condition, task materials and tangible reinforcers were left within reach of the child and were freely available if the child wanted them. Social attention from the adult was also available if the child initiated an interaction. Otherwise, the adult did not interact with the child, who was therefore free to engage in SIB for the intrinsic sensory reinforcement it may have provided. Each condition was presented for three 10-minute sessions in random order. The primary measure was percentage of 10-second intervals during which any predefined SIBs occurred. Interobserver agreement across children and conditions ranged from 80% to 98%.

Durand and Crimmins (in press) presented the results of four pairs of autistic children. The pairs of children were randomly selected from four subgroups previously identified on the MAS as exhibiting SIB that was motivated by attention, escape, tangible reinforcement, and sensory reinforcement. The data from the analogue assessment confirmed the MAS results: Each pair of children showed the highest levels of SIB in the analogue condition corresponding to the source of motivation identified on the MAS.

Multiple-condition analogue procedures like those just described not only help with immediate treatment concerns, but also indicate the value of reconceptualizing problem behaviors in terms of their functional significance for the individual, instead of in ways that simply describe the topographical or emotional aspects of such behaviors. However, it is important to note some difficulties attending the use of these procedures. First, an interpretative problem may arise if the conditions are scheduled according to an alternating-treatments design, as has been characteristic of many of the studies published thus far. In such a design, several different conditions are scheduled in random order each day for several days with counterbalancing across therapists and times of day. The scheduling of multiple conditions per day creates one threat to internal validity (D. T. Campbell & Stanley,

1963) that is especially likely to occur with very young or severely/profoundly retarded autistic children—the possibility that the child will fail to discriminate the different assessment conditions and respond nondifferentially (Iwata et al., 1982). Nondifferential responding across conditions is uninterpretable because it may be due not only to indiscriminable conditions, but also to the possibility that the behavior is multiply determined and therefore responsive to experimental variables in every condition or to the influence of uncontrolled, extraexperimental variables. The problem can be addressed in one or more of the following ways: (1) giving the subject more opportunities to make the necessary discriminations by extending the sessions over several weeks, lengthening the duration of the conditions, or alternating the conditions more frequently within each session; (2) making each condition more discriminable to lower-functioning individuals by pairing a distinctive, arbitrary stimulus with each condition (but not stimuli that must be counterbalanced to control for extraneous factors, such as therapists, settings, and times of day) (Barlow & Hayes, 1979); (3) conducting only two or three conditions at a time (Kazdin, 1982) instead of the four or five found in most of the studies cited; (4) replacing the original conditions with others that more closely model the natural situations in which a particular subject's problem behaviors occur (Mace et al., 1986); or (5) abandoning the alternating-treatments design altogether and using a reversal or multiple-baseline design with no more than two or three conditions, each of which is in effect for several days (Carr & Durand, 1985a; Durand & Carr, in press; Durand & Crimmins, 1987).

A second difficulty with multiple-condition analogue procedures is that the external validity of the procedures published so far is unknown. That is, the extent to which the obtained assessment results reflected actual controlling relationships in the natural environment was not determined in these studies by direct observation methods. Most of the studies did establish strong internal validity for the obtained assessment results by showing that interventions based on them successfully reduced the problem behaviors in controlled environments (Carr & Durand, 1985a; Durand & Carr, 1987; Durand & Crimmins, in press; Mace et al., 1986; Stanley, 1985).

Finally, there are some differences in the conditions used across studies to measure the same behavioral processes. For example, Iwata *et al.* (1982) and Stanley (1985) assessed the functional significance of response-produced sensory feedback in the maintenance of self-injurious and stereotyped behaviors, respectively, by placing the children alone in a barren room to eliminate alternative sources of reinforcement. On the other hand, Durand and Crimmins (in press) provided unlimited access to social and tangible reinforcers in a demand-free setting, reasoning that SIB maintained by social or tangible reinforcement or escape would therefore be unlikely to occur and any remaining SIB must be maintained by its sensory consequences. Currently, it is not known which of these two indirect approaches is preferable. A third, direct alternative frequently exists—that of removing or masking the sensory feedback to see whether doing so reduces the behavior (Rincover & Devany, 1982).

None of the individual procedures or combinations of procedures cited above has yet emerged as a "standard problem behavior assessment" for clinical use. In practice, it seems best to begin with the procedure that seems most applicable to a particular child and the presenting behavior, and then, if necessary, to add or substitute conditions that model problematic situations specific to the individual. For example, Mace *et al.* (1986) used a procedure similar to that of Iwata *et al.* (1982) to analyze aggressive behaviors, but substituted a "Divided Attention" condition for "Alone" for some children as the result of parental reports and informal observations. In "Divided Attention," two adults conversed with each other and attended to the child only when he or she engaged in aggressive or other disruptive behaviors.

CONCLUDING COMMENTS

This review has indicated that the assessment of autistic children is a multifaceted enterprise that frequently crosses traditional boundaries between clinical psychology, psychiatry, applied behavior analysis, and special education. Some familiarity with the relevant contributions of each of these disciplines is necessary to an understanding of the issues bearing on the evaluation of autistic children. Equally important is the need to maintain a pragmatic, functional perspective at the level of the individual child. Of the many available assessment procedures,

only a few are needed at a given point in time. The selection of the specific procedures to be used should depend on the major current needs of the child and the questions raised by parents, teachers, or other referral sources. Selectivity among possible procedures is in any event inevitable with children so pervasively impaired, as their problems are so numerous as to preclude a truly comprehensive assessment in a limited period of time. Because selectivity is inevitable, the selection process should be as well informed as possible, and the overall purpose of this chapter has been to provide some relevant, up-to-date information to assist in the selection process. Additional relevant information can be found in the chapter by Crnic in this volume and in the recent text by Powers and Handleman (1984).

REFERENCES

Albert, R., & Davis, A. (1971). A reliability study of interparental agreement on the Rimland Diagnostic Check List. *Journal of Clinical Psychology, 27,* 499–502.
Alpern, G. D. (1967). Measurement of "untestable" autistic children. *Journal of Abnormal Psychology, 72,* 478–486.
Alpern, G. D., & Kimberlin, C. C. (1970). Short intelligence test ranging from infancy levels through childhood levels for use with the retarded. *American Journal of Mental Deficiency, 75,* 65–71.
American Psychiatric Association. (1980). *Diagnostic and statistical manual of mental disorders* (3rd ed.). Washington, DC: Author.
American Psychiatric Association. (1985, October 5). *Diagnostic and statistical manual of mental disorders* (3rd ed., rev., draft). Washington, DC: Author.
Ando, H., Yoshimura, I., & Wakabayashi, S. (1980). Effects of age on adaptive behavior levels and academic skill levels in autistic and mentally retarded children. *Journal of Autism and Developmental Disorders, 10,* 173–184.
Anthony, E. J. (1958). An experimental approach to the psychopathology of childhood. *British Journal of Medical Psychology, 31,* 211–223.
August, G. J., Stewart, M. A., & Tsai, L. (1981). The incidence of cognitive disabilities in the siblings of autistic children. *British Journal of Psychiatry, 138,* 416–422.
Baer, D. W., Wolf, M. M., & Risley, T. R. (1968). Some current dimensions of applied behavior analysis. *Journal of Applied Behavior Analysis, 1,* 91–97.
Bailey, S. L., Prystalski, P., Kozlowski, S., Mielke, C., & Owen, V. (1984). The curriculum. In S. L. Bailey, V. E. Owen, D. S. Hurd, & C. A. Conley (Eds.), *Instructional procedures for educating students with autism in the Communication Disorders Program* (pp. 13–44). DeKalb: Northern Illinois University Autism Program.
Baird, T. D., & August, G. J. (1985). Familial heterogeneity in infantile autism. *Journal of Autism and Developmental Disorders, 15,* 315–321.

Balthazar, E. E. (1972). *Balthazar Scales of Adaptive Behavior: Vol. 1. Scales of functional independence.* Palo Alto, CA: Consulting Psychologists Press.

Balthazar, E. E. (1973). *Balthazar Scales of Adaptive Behavior: Vol. 2. Scales of social adaptation.* Palo Alto, CA: Consulting Psychologists Press.

Barlow, D. H, & Hayes, S. C. (1979). Alternating treatments design: One strategy for comparing the effects of two treatments in a single subject. *Journal of Applied Behavior Analysis, 12,* 199–210.

Bartak, L., & Rutter, M. (1974). The use of personal pronouns by autistic children. *Journal of Autism and Childhood Schizophrenia, 4,* 217–222.

Bartak, L., & Rutter, M. (1976). Differences between mentally retarded and normally intelligent autistic children. *Journal of Autism and Childhood Schizophrenia, 6,* 109–120.

Bartak, L., Rutter, M., & Cox, A. (1975). A comparative study of infantile autism and specific developmental receptive language disorder: I. The children. *British Journal of Psychiatry, 126,* 127–145.

Bender, L. (1947). Childhood schizophrenia: Clinical study of one hundred schizophrenic children. *American Journal of Orthopsychiatry, 17,* 40–56.

Bender, L. (1956). Schizophrenia in childhood—its recognition, description, and treatment. *American Journal of Orthopsychiatry, 26,* 499–506.

Blew, P. A., Schwatz, I. S., & Luce, S. C. (1985). Teaching functional community skills to autistic children using nonhandicapped peer tutors. *Journal of Applied Behavior Analysis, 18,* 337–342.

Bloom, A. S., Klee, S. H., & Raskin, L. M. (1977). A comparison of the Stanford–Binet abbreviated and complete forms for developmentally disabled children. *Journal of Clinical Psychology, 33,* 477–480.

Bristol, M. M. (1984). Family resources and successful adaptation to autistic children. In E. Schopler & G. Mesibov (Eds.), *The effects of autism on the family* (pp. 289–310). New York: Plenum.

Brown, L., Branston, M., Hamre-Nietupski, S., Pumpian, I., Certo, N., & Gruenewald, L. (1979). A strategy for developing chronological age-appropriate and functional curricular content for severely handicapped adolescents and young adults. *Journal of Special Education, 13,* 81–90.

Brown, W. T., Jenkins, E. C., Friedman, E., Brooks, J., Wisniewski, K., Raguthu, S., & French, J. (1982). Autism is associated with the fragile X syndrome. *Journal of Autism and Developmental Disorders, 12,* 303–308.

Browning, R. M. (1971). Treatment effects of a total behaviour modification program with five autistic children. *Behaviour Research and Therapy, 9,* 319–327.

Campbell, D. T., & Stanley, J. C. (1963). *Experimental and quasi-experimental designs for research.* Chicago: Rand McNally.

Campbell, M., Friedman, E., DeVito, E., Greenspan, L., & Collins, P. (1974). Blood serotonin in psychotic and brain damaged children. *Journal of Autism and Childhood Schizophrenia, 4,* 33–41.

Campbell, M., Rosenbloom, S., Perry, R., George, A. E., Kricheff, I. I., Anderson, L., Small, A. M., & Jennings, S. J. (1982). Computerized axial tomography in young autistic children. *American Journal of Psychiatry, 139,* 510–512.

Cantor, E., Evans, J., Pearce, J., & Pezzot-Pearce, T.

(1982). Childhood schizophrenia: Present but not accounted for. *American Journal of Psychiatry, 139,* 758–762.

Cantwell, D. P., & Baker, L. (1984). Research concerning families of children with autism. In E. Schopler & G. B. Mesibov (Eds.), *The effects of autism on the family* (pp. 41–63). New York: Plenum.

Cantwell, D. P., Baker, L., & Rutter, M. (1978). Family factors. In M. Rutter & E. Schopler (Eds.), *Autism: A reappraisal of concepts and treatment* (pp. 269–296). New York: Plenum.

Carr, E. G. (1977). The motivation of self-injurious behavior: A review of some hypothesis. *Psychological Bulletin, 84,* 800–816.

Carr, E. G., & Durand, V. M. (1985a). Reducing behavior problems through functional communication training. *Journal of Applied Behavior Analysis, 18,* 111–126.

Carr, E. G., & Durand, V. M. (1985b). The social-communicative basis of severe behavior problems in children. In S. Reiss & R. Bootzin (Eds.), *Theoretical issues in behavior therapy* (pp. 219–254). New York: Academic Press.

Carr, E. G., & McDowell, J. J. (1980). Social control of self-injurious behavior of organic etiology. *Behavior Therapy, 11,* 402–409.

Carr, E. G., & Newsom, C. (1985). Demand-related tantrums: Conceptualization and treatment. *Behavior Modification, 9,* 403–426.

Carr, E. G., Newsom, C. D., & Binkoff, J. A. (1976). Stimulus control of self-destructive behavior in a psychotic child. *Journal of Abnormal Child Psychology, 4,* 139–153.

Carr, E. G., Schreibman, L., & Lovaas, O. I. (1975). Control of echolalic speech in psychotic children. *Journal of Abnormal Child Psychology, 3,* 331–351.

Cattell, P. (1960). *Cattell Infant Intelligence Scale.* New York: Psychological Corporation.

Charlop, M. H. Schreibman, L., Mason, J., & Vesey, W. (1983). Behavior-setting interactions of autistic children: A behavioral mapping approach to assessing classroom behaviors. *Analysis and Intervention in Developmental Disabilities, 3,* 359–373.

Chess, S., Fernandez, P., & Korn, S. (1978). Behavioral consequences of congenital rubella. *Journal of Pediatrics, 93,* 699–703.

Clark, P., & Rutter, M. (1979). Task difficulty and task performance in autistic children. *Journal of Child Psychology and Psychiatry, 20,* 271–285.

Cohen, D. J., Caparulo, B. K., Gold, J. R., Waldo, M. C., Shaywitz, B. A., Ruttenberg, B. A., & Rimland, B. (1978). Agreement in diagnosis: Clinical assessment and behavior rating scales for pervasively disturbed children. *Journal of the American Academy of Child Psychiatry, 17,* 589–603.

Cohen, D. J., Caparulo, B. K., Shaywitz, B. A., & Bowers, M. B. (1977). Dopamine and serotonin metabolism in neuropsychiatrically disturbed children: CSF homovanillic acid and 5-hydroxyindoleacetic acid. *Archives of General Psychiatry, 34,* 545–550.

Coleman, M., & Gillberg, C. (1985). *The biology of the autistic syndromes.* New York: Praeger.

Coleman, M., & Rimland, B. (1976). Familial autism. In M. Coleman (Ed.), *The autistic syndromes* (pp. 175–182). Amsterdam: North-Holland.

Culbertson, F. M. (1977). The search for help of parents of autistic children or beware of professional "group think." *Journal of Clinical Child Psychology, 6,* 63–65.

Curcio, F. (1978). Sensorimotor functioning and communication in mute autistic children. *Journal of Autism and Childhood Schizophrenia, 8,* 281–292.

Damasio, H., Maurer, R. G., Damasio, A. R., & Chui, H. C. (1980). Computerized tomographic scan findings in patients with autistic behavior. *Archives of Neurology, 37,* 504–510.

Davids, A. (1975). Childhood psychosis: The problem of differential diagnosis. *Journal of Autism and Childhood Schizophrenia, 5,* 129–138.

Dawson, G. (1983). Lateralized brain dysfunction in autism: Evidence from the Halstead–Reitan Neuropsychological Battery. *Journal of Autism and Developmental Disorders, 13,* 269–288.

Deckner, C. W., & Blanton, R. L. (1980). Classification of abnormal children: Discrimination learning ability. *Journal of Autism and Developmental Disorders, 10,* 405–415.

DeMyer, M. K. (1979). *Parents and children in autism.* Washington, DC: V. H. Winston.

DeMyer, M. K., Barton, S., Alpern, G. D., Kimberlin, C., Allen, J., Yang, E., & Steele, R. (1974). The measured intelligence of autistic children. *Journal of Autism and Childhood Schizophrenia, 4,* 42–60.

DeMyer, M. K., Barton, S., DeMyer, W. E., Norton, J. A., Allen, J., & Steele, R. (1973). Prognosis in autism: A follow-up study. *Journal of Autism and Childhood Schizophrenia, 3,* 199–246.

DeMyer, M. K., Barton, S., & Norton, J. A. (1972). A comparison of adaptive, verbal, and motor profiles of psychotic and non-psychotic subnormal children. *Journal of Autism and Childhood Schizophrenia, 2,* 359–377.

DeMyer, M. K., Churchill, D., Pontius, W., and Gilkey, K. (1971). A comparison of five diagnostic systems for childhood schizophrenia and infantile autism. *Journal of Autism and Childhood Schizophrenia, 1,* 175–189.

Deykin, E. Y., & MacMahon, B. (1979). The incidence of seizures among children with autistic symptoms. *American Journal of Psychiatry. 136,* 1310–1312.

Doke, L. A., & Risley, T. R. (1972). The organization of day-care environments: Required versus optional activities. *Journal of Applied Behavior Analysis, 5,* 405–420.

Douglas, V. I., & Sanders, F. A. (1968). A pilot study of Rimland's Diagnostic Check List with autistic and mentally retarded children. *Journal of Child Psychology and Psychiatry, 9,* 105–109.

Durand, V. M., & Carr, E. G. (1987). Social influences on "self-stimulatory" behavior. *Journal of Applied Behavior Analysis, 20,* 119–132.

Durand, V. M., & Crimmins, D. B. (1983, October). *The Motivation Assessment Scale: A preliminary report on an instrument which assesses the functional significance of children's deviant behavior.* Paper presented at the Conference of the Berkshire Association for Behavior Analysis and Therapy, Amherst, MA.

Durand, V. M., & Crimmins, D. B. (1987). Assessment and treatment of psychotic speech in an autistic child. *Journal of Autism and Developmental Disorders, 17,* 17–28.

Durand, V. M., & Crimmins, D. B. (in press). Indentifying the variables maintaining self-injurious behavior. *Journal of Autism and Developmental Disorders.*

Dyer, K., Schwartz, I. S., & Luce, S. C. (1984). A supervision program for increasing functional activities for severely handicapped students in a residential setting. *Journal of Applied Behavior Analysis, 17,* 249–259.

Earls, F. (1982). Application of DSM-III in an epidemiological study of preschool childhood. *American Journal of Psychiatry, 139,* 242–243.

Eggers, C. (1978). Course and prognosis of childhood schizophrenia. Journal of Autism and Childhood Schizophrenia, 8, 21–36.

Eisenberg, L., & Kanner, L. ()1956). Early infantile autism, 1943–1955. *American Journal of Orthopsychiatry, 26,* 556–566.

Epstein, L. J., Taubman, M. T., & Lovaas, O. I. (1985). Changes in self-stimulatory behaviors with treatment. *Journal of Abnormal Child Psychology, 13,* 281–294.

Evans-Jones, L. G., & Rosenbloom, L. (1978). Disintegrative psychosis in childhood. *Developmental Medicine and Child Neurology, 20,* 462–470.

Favell, J. E. (1981, May). *Treating problem behavior in developmentally disabled persons.* Workshop presented at the convention of the Association for Behavior Analysis, Milwaukee, WI.

Favell, J. E., McGimsey, J. F., & Schell, R. M. (1982). Treatment of self-injury by providing alternate sensory activities. *Analysis and Intervention in Developmental Disabilities, 2,* 83–104.

Fay, W. H. (1966). Childhood echolalia in delayed, psychotic and neuropathologic speech patterns. *Folia Phoniatrica, 18,* 68–71.

Fay, W. H. (1969). On the basis of autistic echolalia. *Journal of Communication Disorders, 2,* 38–47.

Fay, W. H. (1980). Aspects of language. In W. H. Fay & A. L. Schuler (Eds.), *Emerging language in autistic children* (pp. 51–85). Baltimore: University Park Press.

Fein, D., Waterhouse, L., Lucci D., & Snyder, D. (1985). Cognitive subtypes in developmentally disabled children: A pilot study. *Journal of Autism and Developmental Disorders, 15,* 77–95.

Ferster, C. B., & DeMyer, M. K. (1961a). The development of performances in autistic children in an automatically controlled environment. *Journal of Chronic Diseases, 13,* 312–245.

Fester, C. B., & DeMyer, M. K. (1961b). Increased performances of an autistic child with prochlorperazine administration. *Journal of the Experimental Analysis of Behavior, 4,* 84.

Ferster, C. B., & DeMyer, M. K. (1961b). Increased performances of an autistic child with prochlorperazine administration. *Journal of the Experimental Analysis of Behavior, 4,* 84.

Folstein, S., & Rutter, M. (1977). Genetic influences and infantile autism. *Nature, 265,* 726–728.

Freeman, B. J., Guthrie, D., Ritvo, E., Schroth, P., Glass, R., & Frankel, F. (1979). Behavior Observation Scale: Preliminary analysis of the similarities and differences between autistic and mentally retarded children. *Psychological Reports, 44,* 519–524.

Freeman, B. J., Ritvo, E. R., Guthrie, D., Schroth, P., & Ball, J. (1978). The Behavior Observation Scale for Autism. *Journal of the American Academy of Child Psychiatry, 17,* 576–588.

Freeman, B. J., Ritvo, E. R., Needleman, R., & Yokota, A. (1985). The stability of cognitive and liguistic parameters in autism: A 5 year study. *Journal of the American Academy of Child Psychiatry, 24,* 290–311.

Freeman, B. J., Ritvo, E. R., Schroth, P. C., Tonick, I.,

Guthrie, D., & Wake, L. (1981). Behavioral characteristics of high- and low-IQ autistic children. *American Journal of Psychiatry, 138,* 25–29.

Freeman, B. J., & Schroth, P. C. (1984). The development of the Behavioral Observation System (BOS) for autism. *Behavioral Assessment, 6,* 177–187.

Freemen, B. J., Schroth, P., Ritvo, E., Guthrie, D., & Wake, L. (1980). The Behavior Observation Scale for Autism (BOS): Initial results of factor analyses. *Journal of Autism and Developmental Disorders, 10,* 343–346.

French. J. (1964). *Pictorial Test of Intelligence.* Boston: Houghton Mifflin.

Furneaux, B. (1966). The autistic child. *British Journal of Disorders of Communication, 1,* 85–90.

Gillberg, C. (1984). Infantile autism and other childhood psychoses in a Swedish urban region: Epidemiological aspects. *Journal of Child Psychology and Psychiatry, 25,* 35–43.

Goldfarb, W. (1974). *Growth and change of schizophrenic children: A longitudinal study.* New York: Wiley.

Goldstein, M., Mahanand, D., Lee, J., & Coleman, M. 1976). Dopamine-beta-hydroxylase and endogenous total 5-hydroxyindole levels in autistic patients and controls. In M. Coleman (Ed.), *The autistic syndromes* (pp. 57–63). Amsterdam: North-Holland.

Green, C. W, Reid, D. H., McCarn, J. E., Schepis, M. M., Phillips, J. F., & Parsons, M. B. (1986). Naturalistic observations of classrooms serving severely handicapped persons: Establishing evaluative norms. *Applied Research in Mental Retardation, 7,* 37–50.

Hagberg, B., Aicardi, J., Dias, K., & Ramos, O. (1983). A progressive syndrome of autism, dementia, ataxia, and loss of purposeful head use in girls: Rett's syndrome. Report of 35 cases. *Annals of Neurology, 14,* 471–479

Harris, S. L. (1983). *Families of the developmentally disabled: A guide to behavioral intervention.* New York: Pergamon Press.

Harris, S.L., & Powers, M. D. (1984). Behavior therapists look at the impact of an autistic child on the family system. In E. Schopler & G. Mesibov (Eds.), *The effects of autism on the family* (pp. 207–224). New York: Plenum.

Hathaway, S. R., & McKinley, J. C. (1967). *Minnesota Multiphasic Personality Inventory: Manual for administration and scoring.* New York: Psychological Corporation.

Holroyd, J. (1974). The questionnaire on resources and stress: An instrument to measure family response to a handicapped member. *Journal of Community Psychology, 2,* 92–94.

Holroyd, J., & McArthur, D. (1976). Mental retardation and stress on the parents: A contrast between Down's syndrome and childhood autism. *American Journal of Mental Deficiency, 80,* 431–436.

Horner, R. D. (1980). The effects of an environmental "enrichment" program on the behavior of institutionalized profoundly retarded children. *Journal of Applied Behavior Analysis, 13,* 473–491.

Howlin, P. A. (1981). The effectiveness of operant language training with autistic children. *Journal of Autism and Developmental Disorders, 11,* 89–105.

Iwata, B. A., Dorsey, M. F., Slifer, K. J., Bauman, K. E., & Richman, G. S. (1982). Toward a functional analysis of self-injury. *Analysis and Intervention in Developmental Disabilities, 2,* 3–20.

Johnson, J., & Koegel, R. L. (1982). Behavioral assessment and curriculum development. In R. L. Koegel, A. Rincover, & A. L. Egel (Eds), *Educating and understanding autistic children* (pp. 1–32). San Diego: College-Hill Press.

Johnston, J. M., & Pennypacker, H. S. (1980). *Strategies and tactics of human behavioral research.* Hillsdale, NJ: Erlbaum.

Kanner, L. (1943). Autistic disturbances of affective contact. *The Nervous Child, 2,* 217–250.

Kanner, L. (1946). Irrelevant and metalphorical language in early infantile autism. *American Journal of Psychiatry, 103,* 242–246.

Kanner, L. (1971). Follow-up study of eleven autistic children originally reported in 1943. *Journal of Autism and Childhood Schizophrenia, 1,* 119–145.

Katz, E. (1956). The pointing scale method: A modification of the Stanford–Binet procedure for use with cerebral palsied children. *American Journal of Mental Deficiency, 60,* 838–842.

Kazdin, A. E. (1982). *Single-case research designs.* New York: Oxford University Press.

Kistner, J., & Robbins, F. (1986). Characteristics of methods of subject selection and description in research on autism. *Journal of Autism and Developmental Disorders, 16,* 77–82.

Knobloch, H., & Pasamanick, B. (1975). Some etiologic and prognostic factors in early infantile autism and psychosis. *Journal of Pediatrics, 55,* 182–191.

Koegel, R. L., Glahn, T. J., & Nieminen, G. S. (1978). Generalization of parent training results. *Journal of Applied Behavior Analysis, 11,* 95–109.

Koegel, R. L., Rincover, A., & Egel, A. L. (Eds.). (1982). *Educating and understanding autistic children.* San Diego: College-Hill Press.

Koegel, R. L., Russo, D. C., & Rincover, A. (1977). Assessing and training teachers in the generalized use of behavior modification with autistic children. *Journal of Applied Behavior Analysis, 10,* 197–205.

Koegel, R. L., Schreibman, L., Britten, K. R., Burke, J. C., & O'Neill, R. E. (1982). A comparison of parent training to direct child treatment. In R. L. Koegel, A. Rincover, & A. L. Egel (Eds.), *Educating and understanding autistic children* (pp. 260–279). San Diego: College-Hill Press.

Kolvin, I. (1971). Studies in the childhood psychoses: I. Diagnostic criteria and classification. *British Journal of Psychiatry, 118,* 381–384.

Kolvin, I., Humphrey, M., & McNay, A. (1971). Studies in the childhood psychoses: VI. Cognitive factors in childhood psychoses. *British Journal of Psychiatry, 118,* 415–419.

Kolvin, I., Ounsted, C., Humphrey, M., & McNay, A. (1971). Studies in the childhood psychoses: II. The phenomenology of childhood psychoses. *British Journal of Psychiatry, 118,* 385–395.

Kozloff, M.A. (1974). *Educating children with learning and behavior problems.* New York: Wiley.

Kozloff, M. A. (1979). *A program for families of children with learning and behavior problems.* New York: Wiley.

Kozloff, M. A. (1984). A training program for families of children with autism. In E. Schopler & G. Mesibov (Eds.), *The effects of autism on the family* (pp. 163–186). New York: Plenum.

Krug, D. A., Arick, J., & Almond, P. (1978). *Autism Screening Instrument for Educational Planning.* Portland, OR: ASIEP Education.

Krug, D. A., Arick, J., & Almond, P. (1980). Behavior

checklist for identifying severely handicapped individuals with high levels of autistic behavior. *Journal of Child Psychology and Psychiatry, 21,* 221–229.

Krug, D. A., Arick, J. R., & Almond, P. J. (1981). The Autism Screening Instrument for Educational Planning: Background and development. In J. E. Gilliam (Ed.), *Autism: Diagnosis, instruction, management, and research* (pp. 64–78). Springfield, IL: Charles C Thomas.

Lancy, D., & Goldstein, G. (1982). The use of nonverbal Piagetian tasks to assess the cognitive development of autistic children. *Child Development, 53,* 1233–1241.

Leddet, I., Larmande, C., Barthelemy, C., Chalons, F., Sauvage, D., & LeLord, G. (1986). Comparison of clinical diagnoses and Rimland E-2 scores in severely disturbed children. *Journal of Autism and Developmental Disorders, 16,* 215–225.

Leiter, R. G. (1969). *Leiter International Performance Scale.* Los Angeles: Western Psychological Services.

Lord, C., & Schopler, E. (1985). Differences in sex ratios in autism as a function of measured intelligence. *Journal of Autism and Developmental Disorders, 15,* 185–193.

Lord, C., Schopler, E., & Revicki, D. (1982). Sex differences in autism. *Journal of Autism and Developmental Disorders, 12,* 317–330.

Lotter, V. (1966). Epidemiology of autistic conditions in young children: I. Prevalence. *Social Psychiatry, 1,* 124–137.

Lotter, V. (1974). Factors related to outcome in autistic children. *Journal of Autism and Childhood Schizophrenia, 4,* 263–277.

Lovaas, O. I. (1977). *The autistic child: Language development through behavior modification.* New York: Irvington.

Lovaas, O. I. (1987). Behavioral treatment and normal educational and intellectual functioning in young autistic children. *Journal of Consulting and Clinical Psychology, 55,* 3–9.

Lovaas, O. I., Ackerman, A., Alexander, D., Firestone, P., Perkins, M., & Young, D. B. (1981). *Teaching developmentally disabled children.* Baltimore: University Park Press.

Lovaas, O. I., Freitag, G., Gold, V. J., & Kassorla, I. C. (1965a). Experimental studies in childhood schizophrenia: Analysis of self-destructive behavior. *Journal of Experimental Child Psychology, 2,* 67–84.

Lovaas, O. I., Freitag, G., Gold, V. J., & Kassorla, I. C. (1965b). Recording apparatus and procedure for observation of behavior of children in free play settings. *Journal of Experimental Child Psychology, 2,* 108–120.

Lovaas, O. I., Koegel, R. L., & Schreibman, L. (1979). Stimulus overselectivity in autism: A review of research. *Psychological Bulletin, 86,* 1236–1254.

Lovaas, O. I., Koegel, R. L., Simmons, J. Q., & Long, J. S. (1973). Some generalization and follow-up measures on autistic children in behavior therapy. *Journal of Applied Behavior Analysis, 6,* 131–166.

Lovaas, O. I., Newsom, C., & Hickman, C. (1987). Self-stimulatory behavior and perceptual reinforcement. *Journal of Applied Behavior Analysis, 20,* 45–68.

Lovaas, O. I., & Simmons, J. Q. (1969). Manipulation of self-destruction in three retarded children. *Journal of Applied Behavior Analysis, 2,* 143–157.

Lovaas, O. I., Varni, J. W., Koegel, R. L., & Lorsch, N. (1977). Some observations on the non-extinguishability of children's speech. *Child Development, 48,* 1121–1127.

Lowe, T. L., Tanaka, K., Seashore, M. R., Young, J. G., & Cohen, D. J. (1980) Detection of phenylketonuria in autistic and psychotic children. *Journal of the American Medical Association, 243,* 126–128.

Mace, F. C., Page, T. J., Ivancic, M. T., & O'Brien, S. (1986). Analysis of environmental determinants of aggression and disruption in mentally retarded children. *Applied Research in Mental Retardation, 7,* 203–221.

Mack, J. E., Webster, C. D., & Gokcen, I. (1980). Where are they now and how are they faring? Follow-up of 51 severely handicapped speech-deficient children, four years after an operant-based program. In J. Oxman & J. E. Mack (Eds.), *Autism: New directions in research and education* pp. 93–106). New York: Pergamon Press.

Mahler, M. S. (1952). On child psychosis and schizophrenia: Autistic and symbiotic infantile psychoses. *Psychoanalytic Study of the Child, 7,* 286–305.

Maltz, A. (1981). Comparison of cognitive deficits among autistic and retarded children on the Arthur Adaptation of the Leiter International Performance Scales. *Journal of Autism and Developmental Disorders, 11,* 413–426.

Marchant, R., Howlin, P., Yule, W., & Rutter, M. (1974). Graded change in the treatment of the behavior of autistic children. *Journal of Child Psychology and Psychiatry, 15,* 221–227.

Martin, G., & Pear, J. (1983). *Behavior modification: What it is and how to do it* (2nd ed.). Englewood Cliffs, NJ: Prentice-Hall.

McCubbin, H. I., & Patterson, J. M. (1981). *Systematic assessment of family stress, resources, and coping.* St Paul University of Minnesota, Family Stress Project.

Meryash, D. L., Szymanski, L., & Gerald, P. (1982). Infantile autism associated with fragile X syndrome. *Journal of Autism and Developmental Disorders, 12,* 295–301.

Mirenda, P. L., Donnellan, A. M., & Yoder, D. E. (1983). Gaze behavior: A new look at an old problem. *Journal of Autism and Developmental Disorders, 13,* 397–409.

Moos, R. J., & Moos, B. S. (1981). *Family Environment Scale.* Palo Alto, CA: Consulting Psychologists Press.

Newsom, C. D., Carr, E. G., & Lovaas, O. I. (1979). The experimental analysis and modification of autistic behavior. In R. S. Davidson (Ed.), *Modification of behavior pathology* (pp. 109–187). New York: Gardner Press.

Newsom, C., & Rincover, A. (1981). Autism. In E. J. Mash & L. G. Terdal (Eds.), *Behavioral assessment of childhood disorders* (pp. 397–439). New York: Guilford Press.

Newsom, C. D., & Simon, K. M. (1977). A simultaneous discrimination procedure for the measurement of vision in nonverbal children. *Journal of Applied Behavior Analysis, 10,* 633–644.

Nihira, K., Foster, R., Shellhaas, M., & Leland, H. (1974). *AAMD Adaptive Behavior Scale.* Washington, DC: American Association on Mental Deficiency.

Ornitz, E. M. (1983). The functional neuroanatomy of infantile autism. *International Journal of Neuroscience, 19,* 85–124.

Ornitz, E. M., Guthrie, D., & Farley, A. J. (1977). The early development of autistic children. *Journal of Autism and Childhood Schizophrenia, 7,* 207–229.

Ornitz, E. Mn., & Ritvo, E. R. (1968). Perceptual inconstancy in early infantile autism. *Archives of General Psychiatry, 18,* 76–98.

Parks, S. L. (1983). The assessment of autistic children: A selective review of available instruments. *Journal of Autism and Developmental Disorders, 13,* 255–267.

Patterson, G. R. (1982). *Coercive family process.* Eugene, OR: Castalia.

Potter, H. W. (1933. Schizophrenia in children. *American Journal of Psychiatry, 12,* 1253–1270.

Powers, M. D., & Handleman, J. S. (1984). *Behavioral assessment of severe developmental disabilities.* Rockville, MD: Aspen Systems Corporation.

Prior, M., & Bence, R. (1975). A note on the validity of the Rimland Diagnostic Checklist. *Journal of Clinical Psychology, 31,* 510–513.

Prior, M. R., Gajzago, C. C., & Knox, D. T. (1976). An epidemiological study of autistic and psychotic children in the four eastern states of Australia. *Australian and New Zealand Journal of Psychiatry, 10,* 173–184.

Prior, M., Perry, D., & Gajzago, C. (1975). Kanner's syndrome or early-onset psychosis: A taxonomic analysis of 142 cases. *Journal of Autism and Childhood Schizophrenia, 5,* 71–80.

Raven, J. C., Court, J. H., & Raven, J. (1977). *The Coloured Progressive Matrices.* London: H. K. Lewis.

Ricks, D. M. (1975). Vocal communication in preverbal normal and autistic children. In N. O'Conner (Ed.), *Language, cognitive deficits and retardation* (pp. 75–83). London: Butterworths.

Ricks, D. M., & Wing. L. (1976). Language, communication, and the use of symbols. In L. Wing (Ed.), *Early childhood autism* (2nd ed., pp. 93–134). New York: Pergamon Press.

Riikonen, R., & Amnell, G. (1981). Psychiatric disorders in children with earlier infantile spasms. *Developmental Medicine and Child Neurology, 23,* 747–760.

Rimland, B. (1964). *Infantile autism.* New York: Appleton-Century-Crofts.

Rimland, B. (1971). The differentiation of childhood psychoses: An analysis of checklists for 2,218 psychotic children. *Journal of Autism and Childhood Schizophrenia, 1,* 161–174.

Rimland, B. (1974). Infantile autism: Status and research. In A. Davids (Ed.), *Child personality and psychopathology* (Vol. 1, pp. 137–167). New York: Wiley.

Rincover, A. (1978). Sensory extinction: A procedure for eliminating self-stimulatory behavior in psychotic children. *Journal of Abnormal Child Psychology, 6,* 299–310.

Rincover, A., Cook, R., Peoples, A., & Packard, D. (1979). Using sensory extinction and sensory reinforcement principles for programming multiple adaptive behavior change. *Journal of Applied Behavior Analysis, 12,* 221–233.

Rincover, A., & Devany, J. (1982) The application of sensory extinction procedures to self-injury. *Analysis and Intervention in Developmental Disabilities, 2,* 67–81.

Rincover, A., & Koegel, R. L. (1975). Setting generality and stimulus control in autistic children. *Journal of Applied Behavior Analysis, 8,* 235–246.

Rincover, A., Newsom, C. D., Lovaas, O. I., & Koegel, R. L. (1977). Some motivational properties of sensory stimulation in psychotic children. *Journal of Experimental Child Psychology, 24,* 312–323.

Risley, T. R. (1968). The effects and side effects of punishing the autistic behaviors of a deviant child. *Journal of Applied Behavior Analysis, 1,* 21–34.

Ritvo, E. R., Ritvo, E. C., & Brothers, A. M. (1982). Genetic and immunohematologic factors in autism. *Journal of Autism and Developmental Disorders, 12,* 109–114.

Rogers-Warren, A. K. (1984). Ecobehavioral analysis. *Education and Treatment of Children, 7,* 283–303.

Ruttenberg, B. A., Dratman, M. L., Fraknoi, J., & Wenar, C. (1966). An instrument for evaluating autistic children. *Journal of the American Academy of Child Psychiatry, 5,* 453–478.

Ruttenberg, B. A., Kalish, B. I., Fiese, G. H., & D'Orazio, A. (1983). Early infant assessment using the Behavior Rating Instrument for Autistic and Atypical Children (BRIAAC). In J. D. Call, E. Galenson, & R. L. Tyson (Eds.), *Frontiers of infant psychiatry* (pp. 413–424). New York: Basic Books.

Ruttenberg, B. A., Kalish, B. I., Wenar, C., & Wolf, E. G. (1977). *BRIAAC: Behavior Rating Instrument for Autistic and Other Atypical Children:* Chicago: Stoelting.

Rutter, M. (1966). Behavioral and cognitive characteristics of a series of psychotic children. In J. K. Wing (Ed.), *Early childhood autism* (pp. 51–81). New York: Pergamon Press.

Rutter, M. (1978). Diagnosis and definition of childhood autism. *Journal of Autism and Childhood Schizophrenia, 8,* 139–161.

Rutter, M. (1985) Infantile autism and other pervasive developmental disorders. In M. Rutter & L. Hersov (Eds.), *Child and adolescent psychiatry* (2nd ed., pp. 545–566). Oxford: Blackwell.

Rutter, M., & Bartak, L. (1971). Causes of infantile autism: Some considerations from recent research. *Journal of Autism and Childhood Schizophrenia, 1,* 20–32.

Rutter, M., Greenfeld, D., & Lockyer, L. (1967). A five to fifteen year follow-up study of infantile psychosis. *British Journal of Psychiatry, 113,* 1183–1199.

Rutter, M., Lebovici, S., Eisenberg, L., Sneznevskij, A. V., Sadoun, R., Brooke, E., & Lin, T. Y. (1969). A tri-axial classification of mental disorders in childhood. *Journal of Child Psychology and Psychiatry, 10,* 41–61.

Sailor, W., & Guess, D. (1983). *Severely handicapped students: An instructional design.* Boston: Houghton Mifflin

Sattler, J. M. (1982) *Assessment of children's intelligence and special abilities* (2nd ed.). Boston: Allyn & Bacon.

Schopler, E. (1985). convergence of learning disability, higher-level autism, and Asperger's syndrome. *Journal of Autism and Developmental Disorders, 15,* 359–360.

Schopler, E., & Reichler, R. J. (1979). *Individualized assessment and treatment for autistic and developmentally delayed children: Vol. 1. Psychoeducational profile.* Baltimore: University Park Press.

Schopler, E., Reichler, R. J., DeVellis, R. F., & Daly, K. (1980). Toward objective classification of childhood autism: Childhood Autism Rating Scale (CARS). *Journal of Autism and Developmental Disorders, 10,* 91–103.

Schreibman, L., Koegel, R. L., Mills, D. L., & Burke, J. C. (1984). Training parent–child interactions. In E. Schopler & G. Mesibov (Eds.), *The effects of autism on the family* (pp. 187–205). New York: Plenum.

Schreibman, L., Kohlenberg, B. S., & Britten, K. R. (1986). Differential responding to content and intonation components of a complex auditory stimulus by nonverbal and echolalic autistic children. *Analysis and Intervention in Developmental Disabilities, 6,* 109–126.

Shah, A., & Holmes, N. (1985) The use of the Leiter International Performance Scale with autistic children. *Journal of Autism and Developmental Disorders, 15,* 195–203.

Shea, V., & Mesibov, G. B. (1985). The relationship of learning disabilities and higher-level autism. *Journal of Autism and Developmental Disorders, 15,* 425–435.

Sigman, M., & Ungerer, J. (1981). Sensorimotor skills and language comprehension in autistic children. *Journal of Abnormal Child Psychology, 9,* 149–165.

Sigman, M., & Ungerer, J. A. (1984). Attachment behaviors in autistic children. *Journal of Autism and Developmental Disorders, 14,* 231–244.

Sitlington, P. L., Marlow, M., & Stork, B. (1985, October). *Summary of formal vocational assessment instruments and their use with severely autistic youth.* Paper presented at the convention of the Council for Exceptional Children, Las Vegas, NV.

Skinner, B. F. (1938). *The behavior of organisms.* New York: Appleton-Century.

Sloan, J. L., & Marcus, L. (1981). Some findings on the use of the Adaptive Behavior Scale with autistic children. *Journal of Autism and Developmental Disorders, 11,* 191–199.

Snell, M. E. (1983). *Systematic instruction of the moderately and severely handicapped* (2nd ed.). Columbus, OH: Charles E. Merrill.

Snell, M. E., & Browder, D. M. (1986). Community-referenced instruction: Research and issues. *Journal of the Association for Persons with Severe handicaps, 11,* 1–11.

Spanier, G. B. (1976). Measuring dyadic adjustment: New scales for assessing the quality of marriage and similar dyads. *Journal of Marriage and the Family, 38,* 15–30.

Sparrow, S. S., Balla, D. A., & Cicchetti, C. V. (1984). *Vineland Adaptive Behavior Scales.* Circle Pines, MN: American Guidance Service.

Spitzer, R. L. (1980). Introduction. In American Psychiatric Association, *Diagnostic and statistical manual of mental disorders* (3rd ed., pp. 1–12). Washington, DC: American Psychiatric Association.

Spitzer, R. L., Forman, J. B. W., & Nee, J. (1979). DSM-III field trials: I. Initial interrater diagnostic reliability. *American Journal of Psychiatry, 136,* 815-817.

Stanley, A. E. (1985). *Toward a functional analysis of stereotypy.* Unpublished doctoral dissertation, Claremont Graduate School, Claremont, Cal.

Sternlicht, M. (1965). A downward application of the 1960 Revised Stanford–Binet with retardates. *Journal of Clinical Psychology, 21,* 79.

Student, M., & Sohmer, H. (1978). Evidence from auditory nerve and brainstem evoked responses for an organic brain lesion in children with autistic traits. *Journal of Autism and Childhood Schizophrenia, 8,* 13–20.

Sulzer-Azaroff, B. & Mayer, G. R. (1977). *Applying behavior analysis procedures with children and youth.* New York: Holt, Rinehart & Winston.

Switzky, H. N. (1979). Assessment of the severely and profoundly handicapped. In D. A. Sabatino & T. L.

Miller (Eds.), *Describing learner characteristics of handicapped children and youth* (pp. 415–477). New York: Grune & Stratton.

Tager-Flusberg, H. (1981). On the nature of linguistic functioning in early infantile autism. *Journal of Autism and Developmental Disorders, 11,* 45–56.

Terman, L. M., & Merrill, M. A. (1972). *Stanford–Binet Intelligence Scale.* Boston: Houghton Mifflin.

Thelen, E. (1979). Rhythmical stereotypies in normal human infants. *Animal Behavior, 27,* 699–715.

Touchette, P. E., MacDonald, R. F., & Langer, S. N. (1985). A scatter plot for identifying stimulus control of problem behavior. *Journal of Applied Behavior Analysis, 18,* 343–351.

Tsai, L., Stewart, M. A., & August, G. (1981). Implications of sex differences in the familial transmission of infantile autism. *Journal of Autism and Developmental Disorders, 11,* 165– 173.

Tsai, L. Y., Tsai, M. C., & August, G. J. (1985). Implications of EEG diagnoses in the subclassification of infantile autism. *Journal of Autism and Developmental Disorders, 15,* 339–334.

U.S. Bureau of the Census (1983). *1980 census of the population* (Vol. 1, Chap. B, Part 1). Washington, DC: U.S. Government Printing Office.

Valente, M. (1971). Autism: Symptomatic and idiopathic—and mental retardation. *Pediatrics, 48,* 495–496.

Wahler, R. G. (1980). The insular mother: Her problems in parent–child treatment. *Journal of Applied Behavior Analysis, 13,* 207–219.

Wallander, J. L., Hubert, N. C., & Schroeder, C. S. (1983). Self-care skills. In J. L. Matson & S. E. Breuning (Eds.), *Assessing the mentally retarded* (pp. 209–246). New York: Grune & Stratton.

Wechsler, D. (1967). *Wechsler Preschool and Primary Scale of Intelligence.* New York: Psychological Corporation.

Wechsler, D. (1974). *Wechsler Intelligence Scale for Children—Revised.* New York: Psychological Corporation.

Wenar, C., & Ruttenberg, B. A. (1976). The use of BRIAC for evaluating therapeutic effectiveness. *Journal of Autism and Childhood Schizophrenia, 6,* 175–191.

Wenar, C. Ruttenberg, B. A., Dratman, M. L., & Wolf, E. G. (1967). Changing autistic behavior: The effectiveness of three milieus. *Archives of General Psychiatry, 17,* 26–35.

Wetherby, A. M. & Gaines, B. (1982). Cognition and language development in autism. *Journal of Speech and Hearing Disorders, 47,* 63–70.

White, M., Eason, L., & Newsom, C. (1981, May). *Teaching appropriate avoidance behavior to autistic children through discrimination training.* Paper presented at the convention of the Association for Behavior Analysis, Milwaukee, WI.

Wing, L. (1976). Diagnosis, clinical description, and prognosis. In L. Wing (Ed.), *Early childhood autism* (2nd ed., pp. 15–64). New York: Pergamon Press.

Wing. L. (1981a). Asperger's syndrome: A clinical account. *Psychological Medicine, 11,* 115–129.

Wing, L. (1981b). Language, social, and cognitive impairments in autism and severe mental retardation. *Journal of Autism and Developmental Disorders, 11,* 31–44.

Wing, L., & Gould, J. (1979). Severe impairments of social interaction and associated abnormalities in children: Epidemiology and classification. *Journal of Autism and Developmental Disorders, 9,* 11–29.

Wing, L., Gould, J., Yeates, S. R., & Brierley, L. M.

(1977). Symbolic play in severely mentally retarded and in autistic children. *Journal of Child Psychology and Psychiatry, 18,* 167–178.

Wing, L., & Wing, J. K. (1971). Multiple impairments in early childhood autism. *Journal of Autism and Childhood Schizophrenia, 1,* 256–266.

Wing, L., Yeates, S. R., Brierley, L. M., & Gould, J. (1976). The prevalence of early childhood autism: Comparison of administrative and epidemiological studies. *Psychological Medicine, 6,* 89–100.

Wolf, E. G., Wenar, C., & Ruttenberg, B. A. (1972). A comparison of personality variables in autistic and mentally retarded children. *Journal of Autism and Childhood Schizophrenia, 2,* 92–108.

Wolf, M. M., Risley, T., & Mees, H. (1964). Application of operant conditioning procedures to the behaviour problems of an autistic child. *Behaviour Research and Therapy, 1,* 305–312.

Wolff, S., & Barlow, A. (1979). Schizoid personality in childhood: A comparative study of schizoid, autistic and normal children. *Journal of Child Psychology and Psychiatry, 20,* 29–46.

8   LEARNING DISABILITIES

H. GERRY TAYLOR
McGill–Montreal Children's Hospital Learning Centre

Many children encounter difficulties in schoolwork at one time or another (Belmont & Belmont, 1978, 1980; Potter, 1982). These difficulties may involve failure to acquire beginning reading skills as quickly as expected, trouble memorizing spelling lists or math facts, inability to comprehend the thematic structure of prose, or trouble planning and writing a term paper. Common reactions to these difficulties probably include frustration, anxiety, and a sense of isolation. If problems are serious enough, parents and teachers may express disapproval or annoyance, the effects of which may be to lessen even further a child's ability to cope. Fortunately, a majority of such learning difficulties are slight or transitory and do not have any major repercussions for the child. With the passage of time, or with efforts by the child or help from parents or teachers, difficulties are alleviated and the child makes an easy return to the mainstream of education.

These transient periods of difficulty may be similar to what children with learning disabilities experience on an ongoing basis. Like most other behavior disorders of childhood, learning disabilities come in varying degrees, take different forms, and are associated with any number of complications. What distinguishes the learning-disabled child from the "normal" learner are *characteristics* of the learning difficulty, rather than its presence versus absence—characteristics such as pervasiveness, duration, intractability, and atypicality. Whether a child with learning difficulties will be regarded as learning-disabled depends on local expectations, the child's reaction to the problems, and the degree to which the child is able to make compensatory adjustments.

In short, learning disabilities constitute an amorphous and relativistic category of childhood problems. These disabilities are often subtle; their behavioral manifestations are misleading; and their causes are difficult to pin down. Learning problems themselves may be accompanied by lack of motivation, poor social functioning, low self-esteem, and feelings of helplessness on the part of the child (Licht, 1983). Parents may have difficulties adjusting to their child's problems and may place unreasonable blame on themselves, the child, or the school. The school, in turn, may be unable or unwilling to adapt or alter the curriculum in a manner that would allow the child to succeed (Brutten, Richardson, & Mangel, 1973).

The only characteristic shared by all children with learning disabilities is that they do not perform in school in accordance with expectations. Otherwise, presenting symptoms vary tremendously. Complaints range from those that pertain to specific academic skills (reading, spelling, writing, math) to those that involve more general behavioral traits, including speech and language problems, disruptive behavior, poor attention and concentration, low self-confidence, sloppiness and disorganization, over-reactivity, and poor overall academic progress. What parents and teachers typically request from the examiner are judgments regarding reasons for the problems, what to do about them, and what can be expected of the child in the future.

In my experience, parents and teachers of a referred child most often have their own notions as to why the child is not doing well. And they may have responded accordingly by assigning blame, trying to get the child to work harder or behave more appropriately, or arranging for additional assistance with schoolwork. Clinicians may likewise take any one of a number of approaches to presenting complaints. They may focus on the child's academic skills and make recommendations for special class placements. They may analyze the manner in which parents and teachers are managing the child's behavior and initiate a program of behavior modification. Concerned with the child's mental health, they may choose another mode of psychotherapy directed at increasing the child's self-esteem and family harmony. Or they may give the child an extensive test battery to clarify strengths and weaknesses and recommend cognitive rehabilitation.

Any of the above-mentioned strategies may prove worthwhile for a given child. However, the best overall approach to assessment is to consider the child's learning problems from a number of perspectives. The major aims of the present chapter are to portray the many-sided nature of learning disabilities and to propose a model for assessment that takes the complexities of learning failure into account. Due to the need to understand the condition one seeks to evaluate, I begin by discussing the concept of learning disabilities, its historical origins, and definitions. I then review what we know about learning disabilities: incidence, correlates, subtypes, etiology, and prognosis. Following this review, I consider the implications of current knowledge for assessment. I then outline the evaluation model I follow in assessing children with learning problems, and detail specific assessment procedures. I conclude by summarizing current knowledge and needs.

As apparent from this outline, the present chapter is intended more as a guide to the basic elements of assessment than as a clinical manual. By surveying the general literature on learning disabilities, I hope to persuade the reader that the proposed assessment model is defensible in terms of its clinical utility, the adequacy of its conceptualization, and its research support. Proposing such a system may help to discourage simplistic views of learning disabilities, and should underscore the need for more directed research in this area.

REVIEW OF CURRENT KNOWLEDGE

Definition and Historical Background

The term "learning disabilities" is of relatively recent origin. Officially, the term dates back to only 1963. At a keynote address that year to the National Conference on Exploration into the Problems of the Perceptually Handicapped Child, Kirk (1963) proposed that the term be used to denote the difficulties some children have in school-related basic skill areas (e.g., speech and language, reading, spelling, writing, math). In his speech, Kirk emphasized that the time had come to forego speculations regarding causes of learning failure and to begin to focus on identifying and treating the learning problems themselves. The term "learning disabilities," along with behaviors to which it referred, was familiar long before 1963 (see reviews by Hallahan & Kauffman, 1977; Kessler, 1980; Smith, 1983). The importance of Kirk's address is that it signaled the foundation of learning disabilities as a field of its own. Prior to this time learning disabilities were considered one subset of symptoms related to minimal brain dysfunction (MBD). The scientific community was focused more on MBD symptoms—which also included impairment in abstract thinking, perseverative tendencies, impulsivity, inattentiveness, and perceptual disturbances—than it was on accompanying academic disabilities (Taylor, 1984b).

The definition of "learning disabilities" recommended by Kirk and those that followed reflected an increasing awareness of the plight of disabled learners and of the need to identify and treat their problems. The definition put forth by the National Advisory Committee on Handicapped Children, headed by Kirk, was representative of early attempts to operationalize the concept. According to this definition,

Children with special learning disabilities exhibit a disorder in one or more of the basic psychological processes involved in understanding or in using spoken or written language. These may be manifested in disorders of listening, thinking, talking, reading, writing, spelling, or arithmetic. They include conditions which have been referred to as perceptual handicaps, brain injury, minimal brain dysfunction, dyslexia, developmental aphasia, etc. They do not include learning problems which are due primarily to visual, hearing, or motor handicaps, to mental retardation, emotional disturbance, or to environmental disadvantage. (U.S. Office of Education, 1968, p. 34)

Essentially the same definition is cited in U.S. Public Law 94-142 (1977), which serves as a legal guarantee to special education assistance for learning-disabled children in the United States. According to this statute, identification criteria include levels of achievement that are not commensurate with "age and ability levels" in one or more of the following areas of academic achievement: oral expression, listening comprehension, written expression, basic reading skill, reading comprehension, mathematics calculation, or mathematics reasoning. The federal law requires that this discrepancy be "severe"; that it not be due to either limited educational opportunity or the other conditions given above (e.g., emotional disturbance or mental retardation); and that the child's problems be of a sort that cannot be handled adequately within the regular educational stream (U.S. Public Law 94-142, 1977, p. 65083).

The definition's reference to "basic psychological processes" is an attempt to dissociate learning disabilities from problems in learning that reflect environmental disadvantage. But it is not clear what these psychological processes are or how to measure them. Similarly, the definition stresses that learning disabilities are not the consequence of mental retardation, sensory or physical handicaps, or emotional disturbance. Does this mean that children affected by the other conditions cannot have learning disabilities? More specifically, how can we assume, in all cases, that the learning problems accompanying emotional disturbance, mild mental retardation, physical handicaps, or environmental disadvantage would not have existed in the absence of these conditions? A further limitation is that the definition fails to indicate how one might identify disorders of "listening, thinking, talking, reading, writing, spelling, or arithmetic." The definition refers only vaguely to the very abilities on which the learning disabilities movement has place so much emphasis.

Recent reformulations of the definition have come to terms with some of these limitations.

The definition proposed by the National Joint Committee for Learning Disabilities (NJCLD) makes it clear that "learning disabilities" is a generic term as opposed to a specific diagnosis. This revised definition more openly acknowledges the heterogeneity of learning problems, and it admits that learning disabilities may occur "concomitantly with other handicapping conditions," as long as they are not considered to be a consequence of these other conditions (Hammill, Larsen, Leigh, & McNutt, 1981). The NJCLD reformulation thus avoids the illogical pretenses of previous definitions (Hallahan & Kauffman, 1976; Keogh, 1982). Another recent definition that avoids some of the pitfalls of previous definitions is the one proposed in the *Diagnostic and Statistical Manual of Mental Disorders,* third edition (DSM-III; American Psychiatric Association, 1980). Learning disabilities fall under a category referred to as Specific Developmental Disorders (Axis II) in DSM-III. Although learning disabilities are not mentioned specifically, reference is made to very specific disorders of learning, including Specific Reading Retardation (which includes Developmental Dyslexia and Specific Reading Difficulty), Specific Arithmetical Retardation, and Other Specific Learning Difficulties. These disorders are said to be present when academic skills are significantly below expectations, "given the individual's schooling, chronological age, and mental age (as determined by individually administered IQ tests)" (pp. 94–95). Despite some of the advantages that the DSM-III and NJCLD definitions have over previous formulations, these contemporary definitions fail to make the concept of learning disabilities any less "fuzzy" (Stanovich, 1986). Other than suggesting that IQ tests be used, these formulations also fail to provide specifics regarding the methods or criteria that may prove useful in assessing children for learning disabilities.

The several shortcomings of these definitions leave room for a substantial difference of opinion regarding identification procedures. Some experts in the field stress that identification should be based on the existence of deficits in those basic psychological processes that are believed to underlie learning problems (e. g., perceptual–motor abilities), regardless of the child's level of general mental ability (Wepman, Cruickshank, Deutsch, Morency, & Strother, 1975). A small minority holds that measures of psychological processes should be included as diagnostic criteria (Mercer, Forg-none, & Wolking, 1976). But most authori-ties require a discrepancy between academic achievement on the one hand, and expectations for achievement based on age, grade, or IQ on the other. They further demand that intelligence be at least within the broad average range (gen-erally an IQ of 80 or above) (Senf, 1978; Smith, 1983). Practically speaking, the children whom teachers decide to refer for assessment are the ones most likely to be labeled "learning-dis-abled" (Ysseldyke & Algozzine, 1983). For-mal diagnostic procedures are variable and in-consistently applied. In light of the vast dif-ferences in the populations of children served by different schools, and the disparate ways in which special educational needs are met, there is little hope for agreement (Algozzine & Yss-eldyke, 1983; Coles, 1978; Keogh, 1982; Ler-ner, 1981). Hagin, Beecher, and Silver (1982) have even advised that we "abandon the search for a single, all-purpose definition" (p. 56).

As a consequence of the imprecision of ex-isting definitions, they encompass children with a wide array of learning problems. As a group, these children are not readily distinguishable from other underachievers (Stanovich, 1986). Current definitions of learning disabilities also fail to consider the influence of "extrachild" variables, such as the child's educational op-portunities, the standards of achievement ex-pected of the child, and numerous motivational and social influences on learning (Keogh, 1982). According to Smith (1983), learning disabilities are defined in such a way as to place the onus of the problem on the child rather than on the interaction of the child's characteristics with the learning environment.

Despite these limitations, the current concep-tion of learning disabilities has several advan-tages. The most notable of these is the attention this concept has focused on a large number of children and adults who are not suffering from other major handicapping conditions, but who are nonetheless unable to acquire academic-related skills at a normal rate. The concept itself stems in large part from a dissatisfaction with psychosocial accounts of learning failure (Critchley, 1970; Taylor, 1984b). One of the virtues of the concept is that it has forced us to take a careful look at the cognitive skills re-quired for learning (e.g., memory, attention, language, and perception). A further virtue of the concept is its reference to inherent biolog-ical–genetic correlates. Although many other variables influence the nature and severity of learning problems, the concept encourages us to keep the possibility of biological antecedents in mind (Taylor, 1984b). Most importantly, the concept has drawn attention to the existence of a real and potentially devastating clinical prob-lem. Whether or not learning-disabled children are distinct from other low achievers, their problems merit careful evaluation. Early rec-ognition or even prediction of their problems, anticipation of associated or future difficulties, and appropriate recommendations for interven-tion are essential

Prevalence

Estimates of the incidence of learning disabili-ties in children of school age have ranged from 1% to 40% (Hallahan & Kauffman, 1977; Keogh, 1982; Lefebvre & Hawke, 1983). Of those public school children who received spe-cial educational assistance in the United States in the 1981–1982 school year, 38% were con-sidered learning-disabled (Smith, 1983). This number represented 3.4% of the total school population. Such relatively low estimates may reflect governmental and public school policy more than epidemiological fact. More empiri-cally based estimates typically range between 10% and 15% (Gaddes, 1976; Satz, Taylor, Friel, & Fletcher, 1978). Estimates obviously depend on the criteria used to identify learning disabilities. The larger the discrepancy between achievement and IQ that is required, or the greater the number of years below grade ex-pectations, the smaller the figure.

Learning disabilities are more common in boys than in girls, with ratios typically ranging from less than 2:1 to 5:1 (Finucci & Childs, 1981). Although evidence relating incidence rates to age is surprisingly sparse, there is reason to believe that learning disabilities may become both more frequent and more severe as children pass from grade level to grade level, at least during the elementary school years (Satz et al., 1978). This may be due to the cumulative effects of school failure, or to the greater de-mands placed on children at higher grade lev-els. Incidence rates additionally vary in accord-ance with sociodemographic variables, the resources available within the school system, and the tests used to assess the child (Eisenberg, 1978; Luick & Senf, 1979; Rodgers, 1983; Rutter, 1978). Whatever the exact figure, it is clear that a significant proportion of schoolchildren can be regarded as learning-disabled. The sheer number of children affected warrants a careful examination of their problems and needs.

Correlates

The list of child characteristics associated with learning disabilities is almost endless. Although research has failed to confirm any characteristics of learning-disabled children that are distinct from those of other low achievers, a review of the types of problems associated with learning disabilities is worthwhile on several counts. Such a review documents the multiplicity of problems involved. These include cognitive and social–emotional problems as well as academic ones. It leads us to wonder what relationships might exist between these different areas of dysfunction. And it provides clues as to unique sources of learning difficulty.

A clear distinction between learning disabilities and other forms of underachievement is generally not made in the research literature in this area. Research findings reviewed here consequently include those involving comparisons of good and poor learners, as well as those involving children specifically identified as learning-disabled. Good- and poor-learner groups generally comprise children from mainstream education classes. The fact that these children are typically free of other obvious mental, physical, and emotional handicaps helps to legitimize this broader look at correlates.

Academic Abilities

Good and poor learners clearly differ in terms of the magnitude and pervasiveness of their academic problems (Feagans, 1983; Rourke, 1980; Taylor, Fletcher, & Satz, 1982). Poor readers, for example, are less efficient in decoding words, comprehend and remember less of what they read, are less able to guess missing words from context, and are less likely to use strategies in order to improve their comprehension (Carr, 1981; Stanovich, 1986). Problems in one academic area are usually accompanied by problems in other areas (Taylor *et al.*, 1982). Learning-disabled children are less task-oriented than their peers, and they spend a greater percentage of their time off task (T. Bryan, 1974; Forness & Esveldt, 1975). Qualitative differences in the nature of errors made, or in the kinds of difficulties experienced, may also

be present (Batey & Sonnenschein, 1981; Benton, 1975, 1980; Jones, 1980; Reid, 1978).

Cognitive–Neuropsychological Skills

Children with learning problems display a broad range of cognitive and neuropsychological deficiencies. Global speech–language dysfunctions and histories of delayed language development are frequently observed (Ackerman, Peters, & Dykman, 1971; Belmont & Birch, 1966; Ingram, Mason, & Blackburn, 1970; Owen, Adams, Forrest, Stolz, & Fisher, 1971; Warrington, 1967). The speech–language functions involved include the following:

1. Expressive language and listening comprehension, at the level of both single words and connected speech (e.g., Andolina, 1980; Berger, 1979; Fry, Johnson, & Muehl, 1970; Semel & Wiig, 1975; Stanovich, Cunningham, & Feeman, 1984; Wiig & Semel, 1980; Wilkinson, 1980).
2. Accuracy and speed in naming and in articulatory (speech–motor) control (e.g., Bouma & Legein, 1980; Denckla & Rudel, 1976; Ellis, 1981; Rudel, Denckla, & Broman, 1981; Snowling, 1981; Spring & Capps, 1974; Spring & Farmer, 1975; Spring & Perry, 1983; Wiig, Semel, & Nystrom, 1982; Wolf, 1982).
3. Ability to use or access phonological (speech–sound) codes to remember verbal stimuli, to produce rhymes or recognize phonemic similarity, and to segment and blend the phonemes into words (Bradley & Bryant, 1985; Bryne & Shea, 1979; Fox & Routh, 1980; Liberman, Shankweiler, Fisher, & Carter, 1974; Mann, Liberman, & Shankweiler, 1980; Mark, Shankweiler, Liberman, & Fowler, 1977; Rosner & Simon, 1971; Shankweiler, Liberman, Mark, Fowler, & Fisher, 1980).
4. Ability to use verbal coding or verbal rehearsal more generally as an aid to memory (Lindgren & Richman, 1984; Spring & Capps, 1974; Stanovich, 1986; Swanson, 1978; Tarver, Hallahan, Kauffman, & Ball, 1976; Torgesen, 1985; Vellutino, 1978).
5. Awareness of morphological and syntactic structures in language (Menyuk & Flood, 1981; Vogel, 1974).

Children with learning disabilities are also impaired in several cognitive processes that cannot be considered purely linguistic in nature. Deficient nonverbal performance areas include the following:

1. Visual perception and visual–motor skill (Badcock & Lovegrove, 1981; Benton, 1975; Mason & Katz, 1976; Mazer, McIntyre, Murray, Till, & Blackwell, 1983; O'Neill & Stanley, 1976; Stanley & Hall, 1973).
2. Ability to discriminate or remember the temporal order of nonverbal stimuli (Corkin, 1974; Noelker & Schumsky, 1973; Tallal, 1980; Zurif & Carson, 1970).
3. Neurological "soft sign" status, including motor steadiness, motor sequencing and agility, and somatosensory skills (Taylor, 1987).

Dysfunctions in these nonverbal processes are less well established than are verbal impairments. Differences between learning-disabled and normal achievers in nonverbal skills are more dependent on task demands and age. Differences between groups are less consistently present. And there are questions as to the significance of nonverbal deficiencies to the learning problems themselves (Benton, 1975, 1980; Stanovich, 1986). Some investigators have argued that group differences in nonverbal tasks represent differential facility in using verbal coding processes to mediate task performance (Hicks, 1980; Vellutino, 1978).

It is difficult, however, to see how all of the deficits associated with learning disabilities can be ascribed to a common language dysfunction (Carr, 1981; Doehring, 1978; Fletcher & Satz, 1979; Jorm, 1983). The tendency for learning-disabled children to display greater numbers of neurological "soft signs" is a case in point (Taylor, 1987). Factor-analytic studies showing that verbal and nonverbal skills are independently related to academic performance also argue strongly against the notion of a unitary language deficit (Fletcher & Satz, 1979; Satz *et al.*, 1978). Perhaps one of the reasons why learning-disabled children display nonverbal deficits less consistently than they do other cognitive problems is that these children are often matched to normal learners on nonverbal skills to begin with (e.g., matching on Performance IQ). In any case, there is little doubt that many learning-disabled children have impaired nonverbal skills.

In addition to problems that can be described as primarily verbal or nonverbal in nature, dis-

abled learners have a number of more pervasive cognitive deficits. Such "transmodal" or generalized cognitive dysfunctions are apparent in the following areas:

1. Cross-modal and intermodal matching ability (J. W. Beery, 1967; Birch & Belmont, 1965; Muehl & Kremenak, 1966; Vande-Voort & Senf, 1973).
2. Short-term memory for both verbal and nonverbal stimuli (e.g., Morrison, Giordani, & Nagy, 1977).
3. Vigilance and attentional capacity (e.g., Blackman & Goldstein, 1982; Douglas & Peters, 1979; Keogh & Margolis, 1976; Kinsbourne, 1982).
4. Use of strategies that enhance task performance, including accuracy or comprehension monitoring, stimulus encoding, rehearsal, clustering, and elaboration (e.g., Baker, 1982; Bauer, 1982; Bos & Filip, 1982; Douglas, 1980; Hagen, Barclay, & Newman, 1982; Lorsback & Gray, 1985; Torgesen, 1977, 1980; Torgesen & Licht, 1983).
5. Miscellaneous higher-order cognitive abilities, such as the ability to shift mental sets, reason abstractly, solve problems, and conceptualize (McLeskey, 1980; Morrison & Manis, 1982; Swanson, 1980).

No single characteristic applies to all disabled learners. Some of these children have normal language skills, other have normal perceptual–motor abilities, and still others make good use of information-processing strategies (Strang & Rourke, 1983; Symmes & Rappoport, 1972; Torgesen & Licht, 1983). There is no one fundamental deficit. Given a large enough sample of disabled learners, group comparisons will reveal differences along almost any dimension examined.

Groups of disabled learners even tend to score more poorly than groups of normal learners on tests of general mental ability such as the Wechsler Intelligence Scale for Children—Revised (WISC-R). Such group differences are apparent whether or not there has been an attempt to "match" the disabled and normal groups on overall mental ability. As a rough estimate, groups of learning-disabled children have mean IQ scores closer to 90 than to 100 (Feagans, 1983; Stanovich, 1986; Taylor, Fletcher, & Satz, 1984; Torgesen, 1985).

Social–Behavioral Adjustment

Psychosocial correlates of learning failure include work avoidance, difficulties in interpersonal relationships, frustration, anger, lack of motivation, anxiety, and lowered self-esteem (see reviews by Adelman, 1978; Bruck, 1986; T. Bryan & Bryan, 1978; Lict, 1983; Serafica & Harway, 1979). As a group, learning-disabled children are more socially isolated and less popular with their peers than other children (V. L. Bruininks, 1978a, 1978b; T. Bryan, 1976; Garrett & Crump, 1980; Scranton & Ryckman, 1979). They have more difficulty communicating their interests, giving and accepting criticism, and resisting peer pressure (Schumaker & Hazel, 1984). And they make a more negative impression on others than do their peers (J. H. Bryan & Perlmutter, 1979; J. H. Bryan, Sherman, & Fisher, 1980; T. Bryan & Wheeler, 1976; R. B. Chapman, Larsen, & Parker, 1979; Keogh, Tchir, & Winderguth-Behn, 1974). Not surprisingly, parental expectations for achievement are lower for learning-disabled children, and the children themselves have lower expectations for success (Bosworth & Murray, 1983; J. H. Bryan, Sonnefeld, & Grabowski, 1983; Butkowsky & Willows, 1980; J. W. Chapman & Boersma, 1979; Pearl & Bryan, 1982; Pearl, Bryan, & Donahue, 1980). Such downgrading, whether by self or others, diminishes a child's ability to cope with academic difficulties and increases the likelihood of maladaptive behavior patterns (Butkowsky & Willows, 1980; Torgesen & Licht, 1983).

An additional problem area is lack of social perceptiveness. Learning-disabled groups have difficulties interpreting and reacting appropriately to nonverbal social cues. They fail to observe the more subtle rules of social interaction, as is necessary, for example, in knowing when and how to take turns; and they are deficient in responding to and using verbal communication to socialize (Bruno, 1981; J. H. Bryan et al., 1980; T. Bryan, Wheeler, Felcan, & Henek, 1981; Ozols & Rourke, 1985; Spekman, 1981; Wong & Wong, 1980).

Learning-disabled children are also more likely than their peers to experience behavior problems of one sort or another (Bruck, 1986; McConaughy, 1986; McConaughy & Ritter, 1986; McKinney, 1984; McKinney & Feagans, 1983; Peter & Spreen, 1979; Porter & Rourke, 1985). Behavior problems may take any of several diverse forms, ranging from depression and social withdrawal to obsessive–compulsive behaviors, anxiety, impulsivity, and social misconduct. Poor task orientation, lack of initiative and perseverance, and difficulties in independent functioning (i.e., inability to carry out assignments without supplementary help or supervision) are commonly observed. Behavior problems and social incompetence are by no means characteristic of all disabled learners. Nevertheless, these characteristics are common enough to merit careful consideration of behavioral issues in every individual case.

Psychosocial problems may be associated with a child's learning disability in any of three ways (Rourke & Fisk, 1981). The first possibility is that the learning disabilities themselves are secondary to social–emotional disturbance. Although this possibility has been largely rejected as an explanation for the majority of cases (see volumes by Benton & Pearl, 1978; Kinsbourne & Caplan, 1979; Knights & Bakker, 1976), it may hold true for some small proportion of children with learning disabilities. A second possibility is that learning failure may lead to or exacerbate social problems, precipitating a vicious cycle from which the child cannot easily escape (Cunningham & Barkley, 1978; Douglas, 1980). A third possibility is that social problems and learning failure originate from a common source. According to this view, psychosocial deviancy reflects the same cognitive or language problems that underlie the child's academic weaknesses. Evidence that learning-disabled groups suffer from impaired ability to interpret social cues is consistent with the latter view. More research is required to determine which of these alternatives, alone or in combination, is applicable to a given child.

Specificity of Dysfunction

As this brief review makes clear, learning disorders are associated with an almost innumerable list of academic, cognitive, and psychosocial problems. Although we know relatively little regarding the co-occurrence of these problems, it is clear that difficulties in one domain are not necessarily accompanied by difficulties in another domain. The importance of such dissociations is that they uphold the traditional concept of learning disabilities, which demands that disabled learners share some characteristics with those of normal learners. Evidence that dysfunctions can be relatively specific also provides information about unique sources of learning problems.

Several findings indicate that cognitive impairments can in fact occur in relative isolation. To begin with, cognitive deficits are demonstrable in disabled learners who are closely matched to normal learners in Performance IQ, Verbal IQ, or some other general ability measure (Cohen & Netley, 1978; Olson, Kliegl, Davidson, & Foltz, 1975; Sweeney & Rourke, 1978). The association of particular cognitive skills to academic aptitude cannot be readily accounted for by IQ (Richardson, DiBenedetto, Christ, & Press, 1980; Rosner & Simon, 1971; Samuels & Anderson, 1973; Stanovich et al., 1984; Taylor et al., 1982; Taylor, Satz, & Friel, 1979). These cognitive skills range from the ability to manipulate the phonological features of language to other specific language, perceptual–motor, and memory abilities.

A second basis of support for the specificity of some forms of learning disability is evidence for dissociable academic subskills. There are some disabled readers who have difficulties comprehending what they read, despite normal word recognition skills (Cromer, 1970; Isakson & Miller, 1976; Johnson, 1980). Others make good use of context to interpret the meaning of a written passage, despite poor single-word decoding (Boder, 1973; Mitterer, 1982; Olson, in press; Tallal, 1980). Decoding ability itself seems to break down in different ways. Some poor readers show little awareness of phoneme–grapheme correspondences, while others are not able to associate meaning with "whole-word" orthographic spelling patterns. Boder (1973) refers to these as "dysphonetic" and "dyseidetic" patterns of disability, respectively. The dimension of phonetically accurate versus inaccurate spelling errors has also proved useful in describing differences between children with learning disabilities (Boder, 1973; Frith, 1983; Olson, in press).

Even stronger evidence for isolated forms of cognitive impairment is provided by studies that have matched disabled and normal readers in both IQ and academic skill. Bryant and Bradley (1983), for example, found that disabled readers had more difficulty than reading-age-matched controls in recognizing phonemic dissimilarity in groups of orally presented words (e.g., "sun," "sea," "sock," "rag"). Their disabled readers also performed more poorly on a rhyme production task. Using a similar design, Snowling (1980, 1981) demonstrated specific impairments in reading and in pronouncing nonsense words. And Olson (in press) found specific deficits in identifying homophone equivalents of real words, and in the phonetic accuracy of spelling errors. What is most impressive about these several findings is the fact that the groups of disabled readers were on average as much as 4 years older than the younger nondisabled groups.

A final reason for believing that some disabled readers have selective impairments is the fact that groups of these children have been shown to perform as well as normal learners in many areas. Disabled readers frequently do as well as same-age normal readers in tasks involving nonverbal memory (Holmes & McKeever, 1979; Hulme, 1981; Katz, Shankweiler, & Liberman, 1981; Lindgren & Richman, 1984; Swanson, 1978; Vellutino, 1978). Other tasks on which disabled learners have performed at normal levels include ones requiring (1) memory for recency items in immediate recall of serially presented verbal stimuli (Bauer, 1977; Spring & Capps, 1974); (2) discrimination and recognition of nonsense bigrams and trigrams (Cohen & Netley, 1978); and (3) retention or recognition of semantically meaningful materials (Dean & Kundert, 1981; Shankweiler, Smith, & Mann, 1984; Torgesen, 1982; Waller, 1976; Weinstein & Rabinovitch, 1971). Despite the tendency for groups of disabled learners to exhibit mild generalized deficiencies in cognition, there is no doubt that some of these children are more selectively disabled.

Subtypes

Cognitive–Neuropsychological Domain

Contemporary researchers have placed high priority on the identification of distinct subtypes of disabled learners (Rourke, 1985; Satz & Morris, 1981). The discovery of more homogeneous subgroups is essential if we are to predict the types of difficulties that are likely to be associated with a child's learning problems, to specify appropriate treatment, and to anticipate future consequences. To date, most attempts at subtyping have involved analyses of cognitive and neuropsychological skills. Rourke and his colleagues were among the first to examine the implications of different cognitive profiles associated with learning disabilities. In his earlier work in this area, Rourke conducted a series of studies on the significance of Verbal–Performance discrepancies on the WISC (Rourke, Dietrich, & Young, 1973; Rourke & Telegdy, 1971; Rourke, Young, & Flewelling, 1971). Rourke and his associates found, at least for older children, that those with higher Verbal IQs performed better on language and achievement tests. Those children with higher Performance IQs, on the other hand, performed better on visual–perceptual tasks and were more adept in motor and psychomotor activities. A third subgroup, composed of children with comparable Verbal and Performance IQs, displayed a more uniform pattern of abilities than the first two subgroups. The fact that the three subgroups were matched in Full Scale IQ suggests that factors other than overall mental ability accounted for differences between the subgroups.

Mattis, French, and Rapin (1975) employed a method similar to that used by Rourke. These investigators assigned disabled readers to one of three neuropsychological subtypes. Children with language deficits comprised the first subtype. Inclusion in this subgroup was based on difficulties in naming, comprehension, imitative speech, and speech–sound discrimination. Children in the second subtype had what Mattis *et al.* referred to as "articulatory and graphomotor dyscoordination." These children possessed good sound discrimination and receptive language abilities, but had specific difficulties in blending sounds and copying designs. Children in the third subtype had visual–spatial and perceptual disorders. Identifying criteria included lower Performance than Verbal IQs and difficulties in abstract reasoning and visual memory. Although the validity of these subtypes is uncertain, Mattis *et al.* hypothesized that these distinctions have clinical significance.

These and other investigators have subsequently suggested additional subtypes. Mattis (1978), for example, speculates on the presence of a subgroup with sequencing deficits. Special difficulties in immediate memory for digits and in sentence repetition are characteristic of this subgroup of children. Denckla (1977) provides a more detailed description of a similar subtype, which she refers to as the "dysphonemic sequencing" syndrome. According to Denckla, this syndrome is identified on the basis of the child's inability to sequence phonemes correctly, despite normal naming, comprehension, and sound articulation. Still another subtype, also proposed by Denckla, is one associated

with difficulties in verbal memory. Children in this latter subgroup are said to have isolated problems in sentence repetition and in verbal paired-associated learning, but they are otherwise verbally proficient.

Another example of the "clinical–inferential" approach to subtyping is that taken by Richman (1983). Richman proposes three subtypes based on factor analyses of subtests from the Wechsler scales and the Hiskey–Nebraska Test of Learning Aptitude. This first subgroup is composed of children with good abstract reasoning abilities but poor sequencing and memory skills. Children in the second subgroup display the reverse pattern: These children have intact sequencing and memory skills, but do poorly on tasks requiring abstract reasoning. Children with deficits in both sequencing–memory and abstract reasoning skills are included in a third subgroup. Richman and Lindgren (1981) reported that children in the first subgroup tended to have fewer behavioral problems and a greater frequency of familial learning disabilities than did children in the other two subgroups.

Torgesen (1982) has also focused on a subgroup of children with prominent deficits in immediate verbal memory. Torgesen identifies this subgroup on the basis of poor performance on the Digit Span subtest of the WISC-R. His findings indicate that learning-disabled children who score low on Digit Span have deficits unlike those found in other disabled learners. This special subgroup, for example, has particularly poor memory for familiar stimuli such as digits and numbers, but their memory for less familiar stimuli is comparable to that of other disabled learners. He explains these differences by reference to impaired access to phonetic codes. The validity of his subgrouping strategy is supported by the inordinate difficulties this special subgroup shows in following directions, comprehending the surface features of spoken prose, and blending sequentially presented phonemes into words. He further observes that these children benefit less than other disabled learners from structured spelling lessons (Torgesen, 1985; Torgesen & Licht, 1983).

Children with nonverbal disorders of learning are yet another subgroup that has attracted special interest (Johnson & Myklebust, 1967). Difficulty in response organization is a hallmark of this subgroup. Among the more specific features suggestive of organizational problems are the following: (1) inability to efficiently carry out tasks requiring integration of several subskills (e.g., spelling correctly in written expression); (2) slow or clumsy speech and graphomotor skills (e.g., slow or sloppy writing, or many false starts in speaking, reading, or writing); (3) difficulties in following multielement directions, or in maintaining the order of a multistep task (e.g., inability to properly sequence the steps necessary to carry out an arithmetic calculation); (4) special weaknesses with respect to concepts of space and time; (5) attentional problems and distractibility, most noticeable on more complex tasks; and (6) inappropriate social behavior. Strang and Rourke (1983) describe a nonverbal perceptual–organizational–output disability suggestive of this type of disorder. According to these investigators, children with nonverbal learning disorders have special problems in mathematics, in nonverbal reasoning, and in socialization. Variations on the theme of nonverbal disabilities include references to "developmental output failure" (Levine, Oberklaid, & Meltzer, 1981; Siegel & Feldman, 1983), "organizational deficiency" (Jansky, 1980), "the dyscontrol syndrome" (Denckla, 1972), and "sequential–organizational disability" (Denckla, 1983).

A major limitation of clinically based subtypes is that they are defined by the investigator. Criteria for subgrouping depend on what the investigator has deemed sensible, rather than on purely empirical considerations (Satz & Morris, 1981). To avoid this limitation, recent researchers have begun to employ more empirically generated classification techniques. The purpose of Q-factor and cluster-analytic methods is to discover naturally occurring profile subtypes based on multiple test performances. The goal is to place most or even all of the children from a heterogeneous group of disabled learners into these subtypes.

Results of statistical classification studies are promising, and there are some interesting points of commonality (Fletcher, 1985). Collectively, the results of these studies provide tentative support for several subgroups. Disabled learners in one common subgroup are characterized by generalized impairment in language skills. Those in a second subgroup have more specific language deficits (e.g., in auditory–verbal or phonological processing). The children in a third subgroup exhibit perceptual–motor dysfunction. And a fourth subgroup is comprised of children with more global cognitive impairment.

Two additional subtypes also deserve mention. One is characterized by relatively isolated deficits in sequential processing and somatosensory weaknesses (Rourke & Strang, 1983). The other is what has been referred to as an "unexpected" subgroup. Children in this latter subgroup have no obvious impairments in cognitive–neuropsychological skills (Lyon, Stewart, & Freedman, 1982; Satz & Morris, 1981). Whereas motivational rather than cognitive deficiencies may account for the problems of these disabled learners, subtle and undetected cognitive deficits may be present. Alternatively, problems may represent residual effects of past cognitive dysfunctions.

Satz and Morris (1981) found that their subgroups differed significantly from one another on several behavioral and neuropsychological measures. Similarly, Lyon (1985) found that his subgroups responded differently to specific methods of reading instruction. For the most part, current statistical classification systems represent a point of departure for further research. Although these systems provide clues as to unique sources of learning problems, the constructs on which these systems are based need to be clarified, and the validity of the subgrouping better established (Fletcher, 1985).

Academic Domain

A second general strategy in the search for more homogeneous subtypes of disabled learners is to analyze patterns of academic skills. One of the most common distinctions that is made in studies of reading disability is that between audiophonic and visual–perceptual reading disorders (Boder, 1973; Ingram et al., 1970; Johnson & Myklebust, 1967). The best known of these is the distinction referred to earlier between dysphonetic and dyseidetic readers (Boder, 1973; Boder & Jarrico, 1982). Following Boder's procedure, the examiner evaluates the child's ability to sound out familiar and unfamiliar words, and then compares these abilities to the phonetic accuracy with which the child is able to spell. Dysphonetic disabled readers are those whose ability to sound out unfamiliar words is poor, whose spelling accuracy depends little on phonetic regularity, and whose misspellings are phonetically inaccurate. Dyseidetic disabled readers, in contrast, are those who are able to sound out some words despite poor immediate word recognition, whose accuracy in spelling depends on the orthographic regularity of the words, and whose misspellings are more phonetically accurate.

The importance of distinguishing between phonological (i.e., sound–symbol) and orthographic (i.e., whole-word) decoding strategies has been noted by several investigators besides Boder. Nelson and Warrington (1974), for example, found that children whose spelling errors were phonetically inaccurate had lower Verbal than Performance IQs on the WISC. Sweeney and Rourke (1978) divided poor spellers into two subgroups. One of these subgroups displayed a preponderance of phonetically inaccurate errors in their misspellings; the other subgroup made spelling errors that were more phonetically accurate. Consistent with the findings of Nelson and Warrington, these latter investigators observed that phonetically inaccurate misspellers were more linguistically disabled than phonetically accurate misspellers. Obrzut (1979) obtained a similar result, using Boder's classification system.

Still further support for the distinction between phonological and orthographic coding processes comes from a recent study by Olson (in press). In Olson's study, tasks of phonological and orthographic skills were administered to disabled readers. The phonological task required identification of homophones for real words (e.g., "baik," "bape"); the orthographic task involved recognition of the correct spelling of two words that were homophonically equivalent (e.g., "room," "rume"). Olson found that performance on these two tasks varied markedly and to some extent independently. In addition a relationship was discovered between orthographic skills and the pattern of eye movements observed while the children were reading. Children who had poor orthographic skills, and who hence presumably relied more on phonological decoding strategies, read text in a more plodding, word-by-word fashion. Children with relatively good orthographic skills, on the other hand, exhibited more exploratory movements while reading. Qualitative analyses of reading performance by Bakker (1979) are consistent with the findings of Olson and his colleagues.

In another study of reading subskills, my colleagues and I administered tests of word recognition, reading comprehension, and phonics to a heterogeneous group of learning-disabled children (Taylor *et al.*, 1982). Although we found that reading subskills intercorrelated quite highly, we discovered that 18 of 45 children with reading disabilities had a standard score on one of these reading measures that fell 5 or more points below their standard scores on the other two measures. Inspection of the results for individual children revealed substantial variation in subskills in some poor readers. Although our study was essentially descriptive in nature, we also observed that subskill deficits corresponded to some extent with the types of errors children made in reading and spelling and with their neuropsychological performances.

Subdivisions in addition to those mentioned above may be helpful in analyzing the nature of a child's academic disability. It may be possible, for example, to subdivide single-word decoding into knowledge of grapheme–phoneme correspondences, speed of naming, and the ability to sequence and blend phonemes (Marshall & Newcombe, 1973; Whiting & Jarrico, 1980). Analogous suggestions for subdividing reading comprehension skills, oral reading fluency, and spelling have been made by Calfee (1982), Doehring and Hoshko (1977), Harris (1982), Layton (1979), Maria and MacGinnitie (1982), and Royer and Cunningham (1981).

A statistical approach to the classification of reading disorders was undertaken by Doehring and his associates (Doehring, 1985; Doehring, Trites, Patel, & Fiedorowicz, 1981). Doehring analyzed the performance of disabled readers on a battery of reading-related tests involving visual, auditory, and auditory–visual matching of letters, syllables, and words. He also examined disabled readers' abilities to name or read these stimuli. His research provided evidence for three subtypes. Children in Subtype 1 performed well on tests of visual and auditory–visual matching, but did poorly in oral reading of words and syllables. Children in Subtype 2, who also had difficulties in reading words orally, were particularly slow and inaccurate in associating printed and spoken letters, syllables, and words. And the problems of children in Subtype 3 were most impaired in the auditory–visual matching of syllables and words.

According to Doehring's findings, children in Subtype 1 showed least impairment overall in neuropsychological testing, whereas children in Subtype 2 were most impaired. Many children in Subtype 1 had difficulties repeating word strings, whereas children in Subtype 2 were relatively intact in this area. In general, however, Doehring has not been able to document a close correspondence between his three subtypes and performance on neuropsychological and cognitive tests; hence the significance of his subgroup classifications remains uncertain. Doehring (1985) himself advises caution in interpreting the results, which he stresses are merely suggestive of ways in which to distinguish subtypes of reading disability.

Rourke (1980) has taken an alternative approach to subgroup classification. Based on clinical appraisal of performances on the three subtests of the Wide Range Achievement Test (WRAT), Rourke has identified three subgroups. Children with uniform deficiencies on the Reading, Spelling, and Arithmetic subtests are assigned to Subgroup 1. Children with greater deficiencies in Reading and Spelling performance-relative to Arithmetic performance are assigned to Subgroup 2. And children with deficiencies in Arithmetic performance relative to Reading and Spelling performance are assigned to Subgroup 3. Rourke's technique involves matching Subgroups 2 and 3 in absolute level of Arithmetic performance. In this way, any differences between these two subgroups are due to the pattern of deficiencies associated with poor Arithmetic performance, rather than with the absolute level of Arithmetic performance per se. His studies consistently show that the children with specific impairments on the Arithmetic subtest (Subgroup 3) perform more poorly than other disabled learners in visual–perceptual, visual–spatial, and nonverbal reasoning tasks, but that they perform relatively well on measures of verbal and auditory–perceptual abilities (see also Fletcher, 1985). Children in Subgroup 3 also tend to make qualitatively distinct errors in arithmetic. Relative to the children in Subgroup 2, these latter children pay less attention to calculation signs, have difficulties in writing numbers and aligning columns, inadequately monitor the accuracy of their work, and have a poor understanding of mathematical concepts (Rourke & Strang, 1983). Children in Subgroup 3 also tend to be more socially maladaptive and more poorly adjusted than other disabled learners (Porter & Rourke, 1985).

Social–Behavioral Domain

Relatively little attention has been paid to the possibility of subgrouping disabled learners on the basis of patterns of psychosocial adjust-

ment. The promise of this approach to subtyping is illustrated by both McKinney (1984) and Porter and Rourke (1985). McKinney (1984) analyzed teacher ratings of disabled learners' behavior at school (Classroom Behavior Inventory; Schaefer, 1981). His results showed that disabled learners could be placed into one of several subgroups according to differences in ratings of task-oriented behavior, extraversion–introversion, and hostility–considerateness. Porter and Rourke (1985) had parents complete the Personality Inventory for Children (Wirt, Lachar, Klinedinst, & Seat, 1984). They found that children with social–emotional difficulties fell into one of three distinct subtypes. The first subtype was comprised of children who showed symptoms of childhood depression, including low self-esteem, worry, and poor interpersonal relationships. The second subtype consisted of children who had numerous somatic complaints. And the third subtype included children whose behaviors were suggestive of attention deficit disorder. Children in this latter subgroup were characterized as restless, distractible, impulsive, and prone to antisocial behaviors. Although there were a number of learning-disabled children in both of the above-cited studies who failed to display any signs of behavior or psychosocial disturbance, the fact that disabled learners experience more than their fair share of social–emotional problems warrants continued investigation into different types of maladjustment.

Limitations of Subtyping

The major objective of attempts to subtype disabled learners is to identify different sources of learning problems. Despite some progress in this respect, critical appraisal of existing research reveals several shortcomings. Studies frequently fail to establish the reliability of subtype classifications, to distinguish children along dimensions of learning or behavior apart from those used to define the subtypes, or to demonstrate clinical applicability (Fletcher, 1985; McKinney, 1984; Satz & Morris, 1981). Many individual children either do not fit into a given subgroup, or have characteristics in common with several subgroups. No one classification scheme has as yet gained common acceptance.

Some investigators have gone so far as to question the existence of distinct subgroups altogether (Guthrie, 1978; Jorm, 1983; Olson et al., 1985; Rutter, 1978; Stanovich, 1986;

Vellutino, 1979). Harris's (1982) conclusion with respect to reading disability applies to the field in general: "It may be that each case of reading disability involves a unique constellation of handicapping conditions—constitutional, environmental, and motivational—and that the search for relatively small numbers of subtypes into which they can be pigeon-holed is futile" (p. 459). This point of view, echoed by other investigators (Farnham-Diggory, 1986; Keogh, 1982; Taylor *et al.*, 1982; Torgesen, 1982), need not imply that we abandon attempts to create subgroup classifications. It merely underscores the complex environmental influences on learning, and the fact that initially subtle or isolated problems in learning may have a more pervasive impact over time (Benton, 1975; Stanovich, 1986; Torgesen & Licht, 1983). As a result of this complexity, many disabled learners may not fall into one of several clearly separable subgroups.

Etiology

Biological Factors

By definition, the problems of children with learning disabilities cannot be due to extreme forms of social or environmental adversity. Instead, these problems are assumed to reflect intrinsic, brain-related psychological traits. Although the extent to which this assumption is correct is open to debate, review of the evidence suggests that biological factors may be at least partially involved (Taylor & Fletcher, 1983).

Direct evidence for abnormal cerebral status is scant and inconclusive. Studies involving computerized tomography (CT) scans and neurological examinations have generally failed to discriminate disabled from normal learners (Denckla, 1978; Hughes, 1978; J. S. Thompson, Ross, & Horwitz, 1980). Three cases that came to autopsy have yielded suggestive findings (Drake, 1968; Galaburda & Kemper, 1979). However, the individuals studied also had social–emotional and neurological problems. Hence, the relevance of autopsy findings to the individuals' learning disability is uncertain. Abnormalities in the relative size of the two posterior parietal lobes in dyslexics versus normal readers have been observed by Hier, LeMay, Rosenberger, and Pearlo (1978). But the sample size was small; the results need to be replicated; and it is difficult to say whether the abnormalities were specifically related to the dyslexics' problems in reading. The search for direct neuropathological correlates of learning disabilities awaits application to children of noninvasive measures of the brain status (Rapin, 1981).

Nevertheless, a wealth of indirect evidence suggests that learning disabilities do in fact have constitutional–genetic antecedents. One of the most compelling arguments in favor of a biological basis for learning disorders is the fact that these disorders are frequently observed in children for whom any other explanation is untenable. Many learning-disabled children are highly intelligent; they come from intact and supportive families; they have been given every opportunity to learn; and they appear personally well adjusted. Other indirect evidence includes a greater than normal frequency of learning problems in natural parents and other blood relatives; a higher incidence among males than females; an association with prenatal and perinatal complications; and histories of developmental delays, neuropsychological deficits, neurological "soft signs," and electrophysiological abnormalities.

As in so many other areas of research on learning disabilities, investigations of the biological "markers" of learning disabilities are plagued by inconsistent results and numerous methodological problems. In light of the indirect nature of the evidence for biological correlates, this evidence can in no way be construed as proof that constitutional limitations underlie learning disabilities. A biological basis for learning disabilities remains a working hypothesis rather than an established fact. Taken as a whole, however, the indirect evidence noted above supports this hypothesis (Benton, 1975; Taylor & Fletcher, 1983). The significance for an individual child of an indirect biological marker such as a positive family history of learning disabilities is unclear. We may hope that better understanding of the relevance of these indirect markers for individual children will come about as we begin to establish more meaningful subgroup classifications.

There are two subsets of children with learning disabilities for whom medical factors have more direct relevance. The first is that group of children whose learning disabilities are accompanied by histories of definitive neurological disorder. Cases in point are those children with such past or present conditions as cerebral palsy, spina bifida, epilepsy, head injury, central nervous system infections or irradiation, and genetic defects. Research shows that such disorders are often accompanied by specific learning problems that would qualify as instances of learning disability (Fletcher & Levin, in press; Rutter, 1981; Taylor, 1984a). Learning disorders are more frequently associated with some neurological conditions than with others. Consideration of the type of neurological disorder, present neurological status, and a child's developmental history can help in evaluating the extent to which neurological abnormalities may have contributed to learning problems.

A second subset of disabled learners for whom medical considerations have direct relevance are those suffering from chronic medical conditions. Asthma, allergies, diabetes, endocrine disorders, and heart disease are examples of these conditions. Such chronic medical disorders, or medications taken for them, can result in fatigue, physical discomfort, or lowered energy levels.

The relationship of other medically related factors to learning disabilities is less certain. Evidence linking learning disabilities to otitis media, deficient visual functions (e.g., poor fusional amplitudes), or certain dietary substances is inconsistent and methodologically flawed (Barkley, 1981a; Conners, 1980; Keogh & Pelland, 1985; Kinsbourne & Caplan, 1979; Paradise, 1981). This is not to say that such conditions are completely irrelevant. In severe form, poor nutrition or disorders of hearing or vision may be in large part responsible for learning problems. These conditions may also exacerbate pre-existing learning difficulties. What is in question is the relevance of these problems to learning disabilities in general. The clinician needs to be vigilant for evidence of questionable dietary practices, middle ear disease, or outright hearing or visual impairment. Evidence of these conditions may merit follow-up and referral. However, there is little justification for regarding these factors as major causes of learning disabilities.

Social–Behavioral and Environmental Factors

Regardless of the extent to which biological factors are involved, a child's social, environmental, and adaptational characteristics have an important bearing on learning ability. It is possible, for example, that some "constitutionally vulnerable" children learn well by virtue of social and environmental advantages. On the other hand, children who experience social–environmental disadavantages may develop learning problems whether or not they are constitutionally vulnerable. Even in children whom we might consider biologically at risk, the nature and extent of learning problems may be influenced by extraconstitutional factors. Children who receive little encouragement from their parents or who are in classes where their needs are not attended to are more likely to develop learning difficulties than children of similar initial ability who find themselves in more favorable circumstances.

Potential social and environmental influences on learning include the following:

1. Sociodemographic characteristics, such as socioeconomic class and size of family (Eisenberg, 1978; Kavale, 1980; Rutter, 1978; Smith, 1983).
2. Cultural values (Feuerstein, 1979).
3. Family interactions, parental attitudes toward learning, and child management practices (Larsen, 1978; Owen et al., 1971; Rourke & Fisk, 1981; Rutter, 1978).
4. Characteristics of a child that are at least partially independent of academic skills per se, such as the child's interests in school, self-concept, cognitive style or temperament, and ability to compensate for learning difficulties (Kinsbourne & Caplan, 1979; Smith, 1983; Torgesen & Licht, 1983).
5. The degree to which expectations of the child are matched to the child's capacity to perform (Adelman, 1971; Calfee, 1983; Larsen, 1978; Lefebvre & Hawke, 1983; Smith, 1983).

Although there are few formal measures of the above-listed factors, clinical practice shows that they have a strong impact on learning and school performance. This impact may be either positive or negative. Appreciation of social–environmental influences is essential both in understanding how learning disabilities come about and in formulating treatment strategies (Harris, 1982; Keogh, 1982). More systematic research in this area is imperative. To conduct such research will require more objective measures of social–environmental factors, as well as models for analyzing the ways in which these factors actually influence learning.

Prognosis

Given the pervasiveness of problems associated with learning disabilities, one would expect the future of a disabled learner to be in serious jeopardy. In fact, this expectation may prove only partially correct. According to several excellent reviews of the topic, the outlook for children with learning disabilities is highly variable (Bruck, 1985; Horn, O'Donnell, & Vitulano, 1983; Schonhaut & Satz, 1983; Spreen, 1982). Prognosis differs considerably as a function of the particular aspect of future performance examined.

Existing studies leave little doubt that disabled learners are at greatest risk for continued and often lifelong deficiencies in academic skills. Frauenheim's (1978) finding in this regard is especially concerning. Frauenheim tested a group of adults who as children had been diagnosed as dyslexic. His sample consisted of 40 individuals with mean age at diagnosis of 11½ years. The average age of these persons at follow-up was almost 22 years. Initial scores in reading, spelling, and arithmetic were at the third grade level or less. What was most surprising was that only a little over 1 year's gain was made in these skills over the entire 10-year follow-up period.

Other follow-up studies report substantially higher levels of academic achievement for their samples (e.g., Balow & Blomquist, 1965; Bruck, 1985). Grade equivalencies on academic testing obtained by Bruck's (1985) young adults ranged from 6.5 to 10.2. Although the skills of the learning-disabled group were significantly below those of peer controls, Bruck's findings suggest that a large proportion of disabled learners can become functionally literate. Findings by Balow and Blomquist (1965), Kline and Kline (1975), and Preston and Yarrington (1967) also indicate that disabled learners may make significant academic progress.

There is little doubt, however, that academic deficiencies tend to persist if not worsen over time, relative to normal expectations (Ackerman, Dykman, & Peters, 1977; Forell & Hood, 1985; Hall & Tomblin, 1978; Rourke & Orr, 1977; Satz et al., 1978; Trites & Fiedorowicz, 1976). Rourke and Orr (1977), for example, found that only 5 of 19 young children classified as retarded readers made significant gains in reading over a 4-year period. Three-quarters of the group followed by Rourke and Orr made little if any progress. Similarly, Satz et al.

(1978) reported an increase with grade in the proportion of children with severe reading problems. According to Spreen's (1982) review, only a small percentage of children may actually catch up with their peers in academic skills. For most disabled learners, improvements in these skills come with great difficulty, and the gap between their academic skills and those of their peers widens rather than narrows over time. Moreover, even if initially selective, academic difficulties tend to become more pervasive over time. Documentation of this fact is provided by Rudel (1981). Rudel followed several disabled learners who had become functionally literate as adults. Despite adequate overall levels of literacy, these persons continued to experience residual academic problems. They had difficulties in reading comprehension; their reading was slow and belabored; and attempts at written expression indicated errors in "syntax, punctuation, or logical ordering in their writing" (p. 97).

Cognitive deficiencies also persist. In her small sample of adults, Rudel (1981) was impressed by the predominance of deficits in digit and word repetition tasks, and by lack of precision and organization in oral speech. Persistent difficulties in auditory and language skills have been observed by others as well (Blalock, 1982; Johnson, 1980; Satz et al., 1978; Wiig & Semel, 1980). Evidence for an "unexpected" subgroup of disabled learners (e.g., Satz & Morris, 1981) raises the possibility that a subset of these children may have cognitive deficits only initially, even though they continue to have learning problems. The prognostic relevance of distinguishing between persistent and temporary cognitive deficits is unknown. Further investigations of cognitive abilities in learning-disabled adolescents and adults will be required if we are to determine the utility of this distinction in predicting severity of learning disorders during adulthood, or the potential of adults to benefit from remedial academic instruction.

Long-term personal and social adjustment is a further area of concern for children with learning disabilities. Both Spreen (Peter & Spreen, 1979; Spreen, 1982) and Bruck (1985) have found that adults who were learning-disabled as children are prone to maladaptive social adjustment. Compared to his controls, Spreen's young adult disabled learners were rated by their parents as more antisocial. Self-ratings and interviews also indicated more frequent personal dissatisfaction and social isolation in the group of young adults with histories of learning failure. Consistent with these findings, Bruck observed that young adults who had had learning disabilities displayed more signs of social isolation and interpersonal difficulties than nondisabled peers. Difficulties in controlling temper and in dealing with frustration (acting-out behavior) were also more frequent in the learning-disabled group. In both of the above-cited studies, these difficulties occurred more frequently for females than for males. The reasons for this are unclear, but Bruck (1985) speculates that the sex bias may reflect a more negative attitude toward academic failure in girls than in boys, or a bias in referring children for learning disabilities that favors girls with combined learning disabilities and adjustment problems.

These findings do not indicate that all learning-disabled children develop social and interpersonal problems as they grow up. Indications of psychological maladjustment were absent for many of the persons in Bruck's learning-disabled group. Furthermore, over 50% of the persons from this group for whom there were indications of childhood adjustment problems appeared well adjusted at follow-up. The fact that individuals with severe psychopathology as children would tend to be excluded from the learning disabilities category may in part account for these findings. In a small proportion of cases, early learning disabilities may contribute to later emotional disturbances (Rutter, Tizard, & Whitmore, 1970; Saunders & Barker, 1972), but it is difficult to estimate the absolute numbers of children so affected.

Another important prognostic issue is the question of whether learning disabilities lead to serious antisocial acts or to delinquency. For some time, conventional wisdom supposed a direct link between childhood learning disabilities and later delinquency (see reviews by Lefebvre & Hawke, 1983; Smith, 1983; Spreen, 1981; Zinkus, 1979). According to these reviews, a majority of delinquents have histories of school failure, and perhaps as many as a third underachieve relative to their IQs. Retrospective studies that begin with samples of delinquent youths and then look back at their histories to determine the incidence of learning disabilities are necessarily subject to bias. For example, the same social and motivational problems that led to delinquency may have initially predisposed the children to poor performance and underachievement in school. In such instances, persons considered to be delinquent as adolescents may not have been considered learning-disabled when younger. Alternatively, problems in learning may have gradually developed as a consequence of poor motivation.

There is, in fact, some reason to question a direct link between learning disabilities and delinquency. Spreen (1981) studied the incidence of delinquent acts in a sample of adolescents and young adults whom he had followed from an earlier age. Spreen's sample consisted of children referred to a clinic for learning problems. These children were followed into young adulthood and then compared to a sample of nonreferred persons of similar age without histories of learning problems. Although the learning-disabled group received somewhat more severe penalties for delinquent acts committed, the groups did not differ in numbers of such acts. Bruck (1985) also failed to find a higher rate of commission of delinquent acts, encounters with police, or drug or alcohol abuse in learning-disabled versus control group comparisons.

Still, it is premature to completely dismiss the possibility of an association between learning disabilities and antisocial behavior. In a prospective study of a large and unselected school population, Elliot and Voss (1974) reported an association between failure early in school and later delinquency. In a review of two major investigations in this area, Dunivant (1982) has reported a higher rate of adjudicated delinquency in young males with learning problems than in young males without such problems (9/100 vs. 4/100). These rates were based on a study of a large sample of adolescent boys comprised of both nondeliquents and delinquents. According to this review, when the boys who were nondelinquent at the time of the first study were followed up at a later date, those who had learning problems showed a greater prevalence of new delinquent behaviors than was the case for those without learning problems.

The latter findings are hard to reconcile with those of Spreen (1981) and Bruck (1985). Differences in sample composition or the way in which learning problems were defined (e.g., include or exclude children with social–motivational problems) may account for the incongruities. As long as it is understood that learning disabilities do not necessarily lead to delin-

quency—and probably do not in most cases—
it seems fair to conclude that antisocial behavior
sometimes accompanies learning problems.
Failure to make age-appropriate progress in
learning, when not itself due to psychosocial
difficulties, may contribute to eventual delinquency. However, there is no basis for hypoth-
esizing any necessary association between uncomplicated academic problems and eventual
antisocial behavior (Schonhaut & Satz, 1983).

Outcome with respect to educational levels
and occupational status may be reasonably good.
Bruck's (1985) learning-disabled young adults
were no more likely than their siblings to drop
out of school. Those with histories of learning
failure were more likely than their siblings to
go to vocational training schools after high
school. Reduced academic loads were also more
characteristic of the learning-disabled group,
necessitating additional years to complete college or university programs. But the disabled
learners were just as likely as the siblings to
complete high school and to pursue further
schooling. Employment rates and types of jobs
held were also comparable for the two groups.

Not all findings have been as positive as
those reported by Bruck (1985). Follow-up
studies by Cerny (1976), Finucci, Gotfredson,
and Childs (1985), and Hinton and Knights
(1971) revealed lower than expected levels of
educational and vocational attainment. In
Spreen's (1981) study, those young adults with
histories of learning disabilities had higher school
dropout rates and lower occupational status than
nondisabled controls. The fact that socioeconomic status was generally lower for Spreen's
participants than for Bruck's may account in
part for the discrepancies between these two
studies.

But outcome depends on many factors in
addition to the availability of social and economic resources. The available evidence suggests that prognosis is multiply determined
(Bruck, 1985; Horn et al., 1983; Kline & Kline,
1975; Spreen, 1982; Yule, 1973). Relevant
variables include initial severity of the learning
disability, the age at which the disability is
recognized, the specificity of the learning problems, the individual's cognitive abilities and
response to early intervention, and the type of
intervention received. Prognosis may be additionally determined by the degree to which the
child's learning problems are understood and
accepted by parents and teachers, as well as
the child's own motivation and coping skills

(Bruck, 1985; Horn et al., 1983). It is not
possible to make precise predictions regarding
outcome for individual children. However, the
available evidence suggests that much can be
done to enhance a child's potential for normal
development.

IMPLICATIONS FOR ASSESSMENT: AN ASSESSMENT MODEL

Prerequisites for Assessment

The variable manifestations and multiple sources
of learning disabilities make assessment a complicated business. Simplistic approaches to assessment that involve measurement of only a
limited number of skills or that focus on identification of a single presumed cause are necessarily inadequate. Short-cut approaches to assessment may stem from either practical
considerations (e.g., time available for assessment) or theoretical biases. But such approaches are not likely to result in an accurate
portrayal of a child's learning difficulties. An
adequate attempt to understand the sources of
learning problems demands comprehensive assessment of multiple factors, and of the interactions between these factors. The preceding
review shows that a large number of child
factors need to be considered. Among these are
academic skills and school performance, cognitive abilities, and social–behavioral characteristics. Other factors include environmental
and biological influences on the child. Finally,
situational determinants must be taken into account. Among these latter determinants are the
nature of the tasks on which the child has
difficulty, and the standards or expectations
against which the child is judged as having
problems.

The mulitfactorial approach to the assessment of learning disabilities is by no means
new. The importance of assessing a broad perspective on the child with learning disabilities
has been widely acknowledged for some time
(Adelman, 1971; Applebee, 1971; Doehring,
1978; Spreen, 1976). Gaddes (1983) advises
"a combined cognitive, personality, social, and
neuropsychological approach, along with skilled
behavior therapy techniques" (p. 514). Good
clinical judgment is essential and depends on
balanced consideration of a large number of
factors working in concert with one another
(Smith, 1983). An important but often frustrat-

ing task is to disentangle those influences that may represent necessary conditions from those influences that may play more interactive roles. Although it is difficult in practice to distinguish between primary and secondary contributors to the child's problems, an attempt to do so demands that all relevant factors by taken into consideration (Taylor *et al., 1984*).

Prerequisites for adequate assessment of learning problems are as follows:

1. *The actual learning problems must be examined in detail* (Calfee, 1982; Doehring, 1976; Farnham-Diggory, 1986; Guthrie, 1973; Taylor *et al.*, 1982; Torgesen, 1979). Disabilities in reading, spelling, written expression, and math take many forms. Learning problems can also involve difficulties in organizing schoolwork, poor task orientation, and failure to complete work on time. Knowledge regarding the actual academic deficit or school performance problem provides clues that help direct the remainder of the assessment and that allow the examiner to narrow focus on those factors or abilities most relevant to the learning problems themselves (Rapin & Allen, 1983; Torgesen, 1979).

2. *The examiner must entertain the possibility, or even likelihood, that a deficit in one particular academic skill may have more wide-ranging consequence.* Poor single-word decoding skills, for instance, are likely to have implications for subsequent development of reading comprehension and appreciation of written orthography (Carr, 1981; Curtis, 1980; Stanovich, 1986). Deficits in academic achievement have implications for the development of other skills as well, including linguistic competence, memory, and content knowledge (Benton, 1975; Jorm, 1983). Stanovich (1986) refers to these wider-ranging consequences as "reciprocal causation."

3. *The examiner must obtain information regarding those aspects of the child's performance that are of particular concern to parents and teachers, the types of situations in which the problems occur, and the standards or expectations against which the child is compared* (Lefebvre & Hawke, 1983; Smith, 1983). If problems exist at school and at home and involve all aspects of performance, more general deficiencies in attention or intelligence may be involved. If, on the other hand, problems are task- or setting-specific, more circumscribed deficits may be present. Knowing what is expected of the child helps the examiner to establish whether the learning problems are "real," in the sense that they would be regarded as learning problems in most settings, or whether the learning problems are in part "created" by unusually high standards or expectations. Information about knowledge expectations further allows the examiner to gauge the extent to which the child's individual needs are being met. If expectations are unrealistic, accommodation to the child's needs is likely to be insufficient. The latter information may permit the examiner to suggest potential environmental factors that may be contributing to the child's learning problems (e.g., stress and frustration) and to make recommendations.

4. *The examiner must be ready to assess a variety of child characteristics.* These include cognitive abilities and psychosocial–behavioral traits. The fact that children with learning disorders can have any one of a number of deficits justifies wide-based assessment. One of the advantages of wide-based assessment is the opportunity it affords for judging the presence, nature, and specificity of cognitive–behavioral impairments. An additional advantage is the possibility of comparing the child's profile with existing subtype classifications. Many investigators are suspicious of the relevance of cognitive, or "process-oriented," tests to the understanding and treatment of learning disorders (Torgesen, 1979). A general failure to demonstrate clear relationships between learner aptitudes and educational treatments has contributed to this view (Resnick, 1979). The problem with this view is that it ignores the fact that "aptitudes and treatments have rarely been analyzed in terms of similar underlying performance processes that could relate the two" (Pellegrino & Glaser, 1979, p. 85). Neuropsychological research on learning disabilities clearly demonstrates relationships between ability patterns and academic skill deficits (e.g., Rourke & Strang, 1983). Awareness of these ability patterns clarifies the sources of learning failure, and may provide insights regarding the origins of problems in nonacademic settings. The fact that intrinsic child characteristics are fundamental to some children's learning problems is the very essence of the historical concept of learning disabilities.

5. *The examiner must take into account the possibility that cognitive–behavioral characteristics may influence one another.* Certain language deficits, for example, may predispose the child to social isolation or withdrawal. Like-

wise, the child who is temperamentally impulsive may find it difficult to develop appropriate problem-solving skills.

Relationships between various cognitive deficiencies are also of interest. Associations between memory, verbal learning ability, phonological skills, speed of naming, and expressive vocabulary have been noted by several investigators and merit further inquiry (Bradley, Hulme, & Bryant, 1979; Denckla, 1973, 1977; Rudel *et al.*, 1981; Rudel, Denckla, & Spalten, 1976; Spring & Capps, 1974; Torgesen, 1982; Wolf, 1982). One of the purposes of examining associations and dissociations between cognitive–behavioral characteristics is to identify independent sources of learning failure. Another purpose is to distinguish those deficiencies that play a primary role from those that represent secondary effects or from those that have little bearing on the learning problem itself.

6. *Numerous environmental factors must be taken into account as potential influences on the child's cognitive–behavioral characteristics and on school performance and academic achievement.* Environmental factors include longer-term influences such as learning history and social–cultural milieu, or more immediate environmental influences such as incentives to learn, child management practices, and educational methods. The effects of social and cultural factors on learning and development are well documented (Sameroff & Chandler, 1975; Walsh & Greenough, 1976; Werner, 1980). The efficacy of behavior management techniques and strategy training in improving school performance is also well known (Barkley, 1981b; Torgesen & Goldman, 1977). Sociocultural factors may influence academic achievement either by virtue of their effects on the child's attitudes, or via their impact on the develop-

ment of those mental skills required for successful school performance (Feuerstein, 1979; Rutter, 1978; Smith, 1983; Stevenson, Stigler, Lee, & Lucker, 1985). Depending on their social and cultural background, children are more or less conforming, competitive, achievement-oriented, or reflective. These variables are not likely to have a pronounced effect within a given culture or sociodemographic group. But there is no justification for assuming that any performance, even on neuropsychological tests, is completely "culture-free" (Feuerstein, 1979; Taylor *et al.*, 1984).

7. *Finally, biological factors must be considered.* These factors include definitive neurological disorders, as well as medical conditions that are known to have a depressive effect on mental abilities. They additionally include such biological "markers" as family history of learning problems, histories of developmental delays not readily accounted for by environmental influences, prenatal and perinatal complications, and electrophysiological abnormalities. Biological factors are viewed more as restraints on skill acquisition than as direct causes of any deficiencies observed (Ferguson, 1963; Taylor *et al.*, 1984). The influence of biological factors, even if they involve definitive neurological insult, must always be considered in conjunction with environmental variables and with existing premorbid child characteristics (Fletcher & Taylor, 1984; Rutter, 1981).

A Working Model: Nature of Variables to Be Considered

As is apparent from the preceding discussion, a large number of prerequisites must be kept in mind when conducting comprehensive assess-

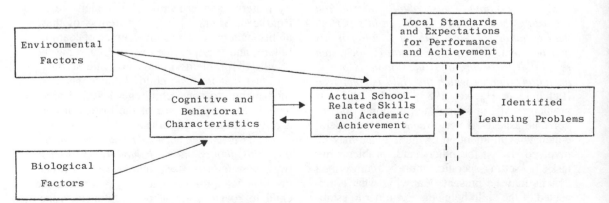

FIGURE 1. Schema for examining the sources of learning problems: An assessment model.

ments of learning-disabled children. I have found the schematic model presented in Figure 1 useful in conceptualizing the several aspects of the assessment process. More than anything else, this model is intended as a vehicle for organizing the components of the assessment process. It illustrates the groups of variables that need to be taken into account (the boxes in Figure 1), as well as the relationships between variables that require consideration (the arrows in Figure 1). The types of factors that comprise each variable set are described below in order to demonstrate the implications of the model for assessment. Only general considerations and informal assessment strategies are mentioned in this section to convey the general content and aims of each component. Details regarding formal assessment techniques follow (see "Formal Assessment Procedures," below).

Identified Learning Problems

The point of departure for any assessment is the set of presenting problems. Information regarding problems is obtained by asking parents and teachers for their views of the problems, the settings and tasks in which the problems are apparent, and the duration, intensity, and frequency of the problems. The objective of such questions is to find out what about the child is disturbing to others. The examiner must make sure to take note of all reported problems, whether they be academic, behavioral, social, or motivational ones. Complaints are rarely unidimensional. Although the primary complaint is usually poor academic productivity, a variety of other reported problems almost invariably accompany this complaint. These problems may include disruptive behavior, lack of initiative, difficulties in paying attention, or specific weaknesses in academic skills. Delineation of problem areas is best accomplished by obtaining written descriptions of problems by parents and teachers, reviewing results of previous testing, examining actual samples of the child's work, and finding out where in the curriculum the child is currently working and how he or she is faring relative to other children in the class. Parent interview is also essential (see "Formal Assessment Procedures").

Local Standards and Expectations for Performance and Academic Achievement

The best way to become familiar with local standards and expectations is to be well ac-

quainted with the child's school and teachers. Average achievement levels (relative to national norms) for students in a given school can sometimes be obtained from principals. It is also helpful to know whether a school is public or private and the kind of curriculum being used. Appreciation of what the child's teacher expects is even more essential. Because expectations vary from teacher to teacher, it may be wise to ask about the child's performance in previous years, or, if the child has several teachers, to obtain impressions from each of them. One way to get a sense of expectations is to ask what the child would need to know in order to improve up to a level that would be considered appropriate for children in a given teacher's class. The examiner may also want to ask the teacher to submit work samples both for the identified child and for children in the class who are considered to be average learners. Another method is to ask teachers to indicate what has been done to deal with the problems. This may provide hints as to a teacher's tolerance and his or her willingness to accommodate to individual differences (Mercer, 1979).

School-Related Performance and Academic Achievement (Direct Assessment)

Clinic assessment of school-related performance and academic achievement is an attempt to confirm and refine what has been gleaned from school observations or parent/teacher ratings. School-related performance skills are just as important as actual achievement levels. Is the child attentive? Can the child remember directions? Does the child complete work efficiently? To evaluate academic achievement, the examiner must explore component abilities as well as overall, or functional, aptitude levels. Evaluating reading skills, for example, requires appraisal of how well the child can cope with the current reading curriculum, as well as a look at specific subskills such as decoding ability, oral reading fluency, and comprehension. In addition to formal tests, watching how a child reads or spells can itself be enlightening. The examiner may note the child's posture, speed, attitudes toward the task or in response to errors, and types of errors (e.g., omissions, substitutions, hesitations, sequencing errors).

Component mathematical skills include awareness of the meanings of numbers, memory for and retrieval of basic math facts, mastery of the mechanical aspects of written coma

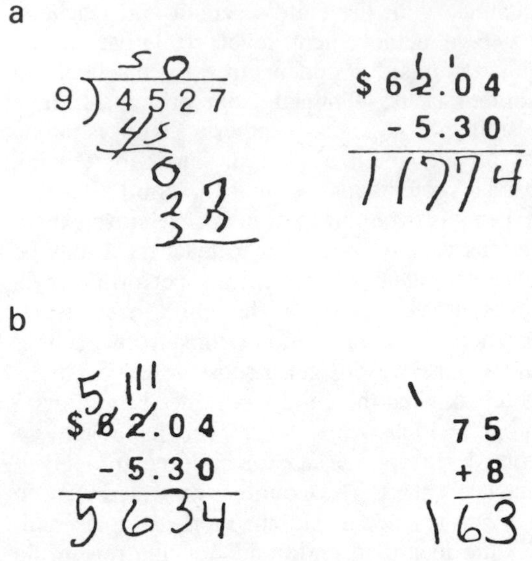

b

FIGURE 2. Samples of problems in math computation: (a) 12-year-old boy; (b) 10-year-old girl.

putation, spatial manipulation of numbers, and mathematical reasoning (Boller & Grafman, 1985; Fleischner & Garnett, 1979–1980; Rourke & Strang, 1983). Calculation errors typical of those made by disabled learners are presented in Figure 2. Figure 2a shows computational mistakes associated with attentional problems. Error analysis suggests that this child's attention drifted prior to the problem on the left-hand side of Figure 2a; in addition, he seems to have switched from subtraction to addition in the middle of the problem on the right-hand side. Figure 2b shows the errors made by a second child. These errors are more suggestive of spatial difficulties and directional confusion.

Assessment of mathematical aptitudes should not be restricted to accuracy measures, but must also entail observations of rate and the child's ability to keep up with classroom work (Fleischner & Garnett, 1979–1980). One child I evaluated displayed math problems reminiscent of the nonverbal learning disorders discussed earlier. According to teacher report, the child was able to complete only 4 addition and subtraction problems in 40 minutes. This compared to the completion of 27 problems in 30 minutes by a low-average child from the same class, and to the completion of 30 problems in 15 minutes by an above-average student from the class. Differences of this magnitude have obvious implications for classroom performance.

Like math, writing and spelling are complex skills. Comprehensive assessment demands attention to functional classroom performance as well as to numerous component abilities. Component spelling skills include the ability to revisualize spelling patterns, to use grapheme–phoneme correspondences, and to spell correctly in the context of writing a sentence or paragraph. Components of written expression include speed and legibility of handwriting, fluency and content of ideas expressed, adherence to writing conventions, an ability to take alternative points of view, literary style, and quality of thought (Bereiter, 1980; Smith, 1983). The writing of learning-disabled children is characterized by inaccuracies and inconsistencies of spelling and syntax, low productivity, limited vocabulary, poor punctuation, and barren thematic content (Myklebust, 1973; Poplin, Gray, Larsen, Banikowski, & Mehring, 1980). Because high school curricula make particularly heavy demands on writing skills, an examination of written expression is essential in evaluating adolescents with learning disabilities (Alley & Deshler, 1979).

The writing of an 11-year-old boy, shown in Figure 3, is illustrative of difficulties in written expression (M. Golick, personal communications, February, 1986). Perusal of the child's writing reveals poorly formed and unevenly sized letters. Frequent retracing of letters attests to the fact that the mechanics of writing are slow and laborious. Analysis of the content of the child's writing is especially enlightening (see Figure 3 caption). The child shows imagination, ingenuity, a rich vocabulary, and a basic grasp of storytelling. But his writing is replete with the types of misspellings and other mistakes so often observed in the written work of disabled learners. Writing problems evident in Figure 3 include the following:

1. Use of single letters to represent syllables ("prsun" for "person').
2. Lack of awareness of how word morphology determines spelling patterns ("tride" for "tried" and "panete" for "panicked").
3. Poor ability to sequence vowel sounds ("wrock" for "work").
4. Idiosyncratic vowel spellings ("anunul" for "animal" and "eleyfint" for "elephant").
5. Erroneous doubling before a suffix ("hopping" for "hoping").

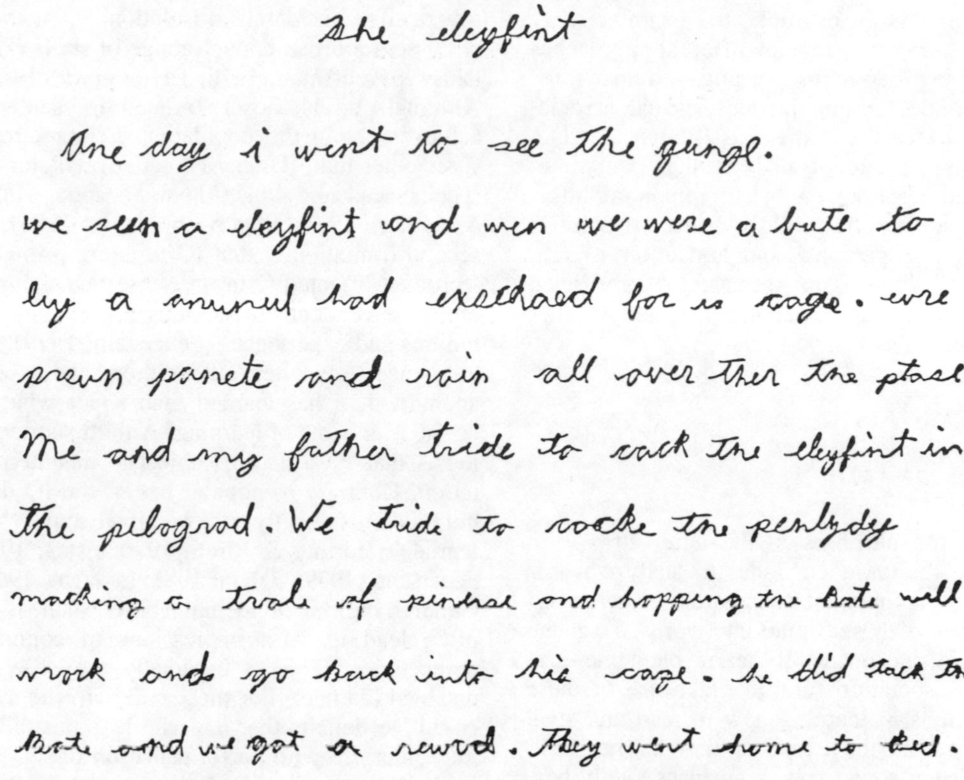

FIGURE 3. Story written by 11-year-old boy. Probable translation: "One day I went to see the jungle. We seen a clephant and when we were about to leave an animal escaped from his cage. Every person panicked and ran all over the place. Me and my father tried to catch the elephant in the playground. We tried to catch the elephant [by] making a trail of peanuts and hoping the bait would work and [he would] go back into his cage. He did take the bait and we got a reward. Then [we] went home to bed." (M. Golick, personal communication, February, 1986. Used by permission.)

6. Poor analysis of sound sequences ("exscdaed" for "escaped").
7. Inconsistent spellings ("catch" spelled as both "cack" and "cacke").
8. Substitution, or writing errors ("liy" for "leave," and "they" for "then we").
9. Difficulties in spelling high-frequency function words ("for" for "from," "a bute" for "about," "evre" for "every," "dy" for "by").
10. Insertion and omission of words at the level of sentence production (". . . and rain all over *ther ptase,*" ". . . and hopping the bate will wrock and (the elephant will) go back into his cage").

Such analyses clarify the nature of writing and spelling difficulties and provide a rich source of information about the child's basic cognitive skills.

Since available standardized tests do not measure all important school-related performance characteristics, it is often necessary to make qualitative observations during testing, or to improvise test procedures. Tasks given to the child might include a set of homework problems assigned by the teacher, or a spelling, writing, or math task similar to what the child has been asked to do in school. To investigate study skills, for example, the examiner may decide to have the child read part of an assigned chapter, and then go through the steps that would be taken to prepare for an upcoming test on that chapter. Such informal task analysis is generally useful in clarifying the elements of a task that pose special difficulty for the child (Smith, 1983).

Trial teaching can also help to isolate stumbling blocks to learning, and to determine the instructional approach that may have best results for the child (e.g., how much structure or cueing to give, best modality and rate of presentation). As an example, the examiner may want to "try out" several different approaches to teaching beginning reading—comparisons, for example, among phonics, visual association, and kinesthetic methods (Lerner, 1981).

The use of letter strips is another example of how trial teaching can yield important information about the child's learning abilities (S. Schwartz, personal communication, March, 1986). A "letter strip" consists of a restricted and specially arranged alphabet. A sample letter strip is as follows:

$$a \; u \; i$$
$$p \; t \; s \; m \; n \; f \; d \; k$$
$$ck$$

One of the purposes of the letter strip is to evaluate the child's abilities to analyze words into their component sounds and, conversely, to synthesize these sounds into words. To gauge the child's capacity to learn phoneme–grapheme associations and to make use of these associations in learning how to read and spell actual words, the examiner first teaches individual letter–sound correspondences. With these few letter–sound correspondences as a foundation, the examiner then points to the letters and asks the child to blend the letters into words (reading); or the examiner says a word and asks the child to point to and then write the corresponding letters (spelling). The speed, agility, and independence with which the child is able to make use of the letter strip to read and spell provides valuable insights into the child's ability to relate sound and letter patterns.

Cognitive and Behavioral Characteristics

Cognitive and behavioral characteristics to be assesssed fall into three categories:

MENTAL ABILITIES AND NEUROPSYCHOLOGICAL SKILLS. Mental abilities and neuropsychological skills compose the first of these categories. IQ tests such as the WISC-R (Wechsler, 1974) or the fourth edition of the Stanford–Binet (Thorndike, Hagen, & Sattler, 1986) measure numerous verbal and nonverbal abilities, and in this way give the examiner a sense of the child's strengths and weaknesses. Summary IQ scores may also help to establish the child's generalized cognitive capacity. Nevertheless, the value of IQ testing is sometimes

overrated. Considered in isolation, IQ tests do not assess a broad enough range of skills (Hallahan & Kauffman, 1976; Taylor et al., 1984). Although IQ is closely related to academic achievement in the population at large, measures other than IQ may be better predictors of specific academic skills (Lloyd, Sabatino, Miller, & Miller, 1977; Stanovich et al., 1984). A second limitation is that IQ tests are primarily "product-oriented," in the sense that they are highly dependent on previous learning opportunities and experiences (Feuerstein, 1979). Intelligence tests often tell us more about what an individual has learned than about what he or she is capable of learning. A third shortcoming is that IQ tests are subject to misinterpretation. Contrary to popular belief, the IQ does not index genetically endowed intellectual "potential" (Bortner & Birch, 1970; Estes, 1981; Feuerstein, 1979; Galvin, 1981; Liverant, 1960). General indices of mental ability such as IQ often lead to false impressions of cognitive competence. This is especially the case for disabled learners. For these children, the same cognitive deficits that underlie learning failure may interfere with performance on the IQ test itself. IQ tests are simply less useful in evaluating some groups of children—such as those with learning disabilities—than they are for the general child population (Brown & French, 1979; Feuerstein, 1979; Smith, 1983).

Due to increasing awareness of the limitations of IQ tests, measures of how the child functions in everyday circumstances, or of adaptive behaviors, are now recognized as useful adjuncts to formal IQ testing (McLoughlin & Netick, 1983; Strawser & Weller, 1985). Neuropsychological and other cognitive tasks are also of value as supplements to more traditional IQ testing. Functions tapped by cognitive–neuropsychological testing include language abilities, memory, visual–spatial and constructional skills, somatosensory and motor proficiency, attention, and problem solving and abstract reasoning. Performances on these tasks clarify strengths and weaknesses.

Broadly speaking, cognitive–neuropsychological testing is designed to assess both the *abilities* and the *processes* required for learning. How the child learns depends not only on basic skills, but also on the child's stock of previous knowledge, the manner in which that knowledge is represented, the efficiency or "automaticity" with which skills are put to use, and the strategies or "control processes" by which the skills are employed in more complex tasks (Brown, Bransford, Ferrara, & Campione, 1983; Hagen *et al.*, 1982; Hunt, 1983; Kail & Bisanz, 1982; Sternberg & Powell, 1983; Torgesen & Licht, 1983). In assessing these several prerequisites for learning, the approach the child takes to a task and probable reasons for failure are just as important as the total score. The extent to which the child plans his or her response or uses learning strategies can be observed by watching what the child does during the task (e.g., covert rehearsal and other self-verbalizations, clustering of items in an attempt to improve memory, checking one problem before going on to the next). Qualitative features of performance can also be inferred by conducting task analysis or by determining under what conditions the child's performance can be improved. Strategic behaviors, or the lack thereof, are most evident on tasks that require response planning and organization. Strategies used to memorize a list of words, tell a story, or draw a complex design are particularly revealing.

BEHAVIORAL CONDUCT, SOCIAL COMPETENCE, AND ATTITUDES. Behavioral conduct, social competence, and attitudes constitute a second subdivision of cognitive–behavioral characteristics. These traits pertain less to the child's raw cognitive capacity than they do to behavioral tendencies that may interface with deployment of those capacities. Any of a wide array of behavior disorders may accompany learning disabilities. In some cases these disorders may exacerbate pre-existing learning difficulties, or may even precipitate learning problems that would otherwise have been managed without special intervention. In other cases, behavior disorders may be manifestations of the same problems that underlie learning failure. Whatever their relationship to learning disabilities, social and behavior problems must be identified by the examiner. These problems are likely to influence the nature and extent of learning disabilities. Moreover, dealing with these problems is a necessary first step in treating the child's learning difficulties.

Although it is important that all behavior and social problems be brought to light, the research findings reviewed earlier suggest that special attention be paid to the following:

1. The child's task orientation (lack of sustained effort; distractibility or impulsivity; poor work completion; disorganized approach to tasks; lack of self-initiative; inability to work independently of the teacher).
2. Incidents of misconduct and rule-breaking behavior (aggression; disruption; speaking out of turn; failure to stay in seat or to return to class on time; need for teacher intervention.
3. Social interactions (general quality of interactions and popularity; resistance to peer pressure; skill at negotiating own interests in joint activities; ability to give and receive both positive and negative feedback; appropriateness of behavior in initiating, sustaining, and terminating interactions with others).

It is also important to survey the child's attitudes toward self, others, and school. Experiences of failure may result in anxiety, low self-esteem, lack of self-confidence, limited mastery orientation, or even "learned helplessness" (Adelman & Chaney, 1982; Douglas, 1980; Harter, 1982; Licht & Dweck, 1984; Torgesen & Lecht, 1983). A vicious cycle is thus set in motion wherein failure leads to expectations of failure, eventuating in further lags relative to the development of peers. Over time and by virtue of the inability of the child to automatize lower-order skills, impairments may accrue in higher-order cognitive strategies (Douglas, 1980). Even if children have the repertoire of skills needed to carry out an academic task, "whether a given strategy is applied may be more related to the children's self-generated learning goals than to their knowledge of appropriate processing strategies" (Torgesen & Licht, 1983, p. 26).

TEMPERAMENT AND PERSONALITY TRAITS. Temperament and personality traits fall into a third class of cognitive–behavioral characteristics. Examples of temperament include bipolar trait continuums such as underfocused versus overfocused, persistent versus nonpersistent, impulsive versus reflective, and convergent-thinking versus divergent-thinking (Chess, 1968; Kinsbourne & Caplan, 1979; Smith, 1983). Where an individual falls on these continuums is not necessarily a measure of degree of behavior disorder. These traits instead represent individual-difference variables that may either facilitate or diminish the child's capacity to compensate for learning problems. For this reason, these traits have special relevance to the evaluation of learning disabilities (Hagin *et al.*, 1982; Jansky, 1978).

Environmental Factors

Environmental factors include social and cultural background, educational history, parent and teacher attitudes toward education, parent and teacher beliefs regarding the sources of the child's problems, opportunities to learn at home and at school, the degree to which the child's special needs are being met, sociodemographic characteristics of the family, stress and conflict within the family, and child management practices. Parents' current understanding of the child's problems are particularly revealing. Some parents attribute their child's problems to lack of motivation, while others place all of the blame on themselves or the teacher. In either case, the parents' attributions serve as a "red flag" for inadequacies in the child's support system. Detailed questioning regarding the manner in which the child's behavior is managed is also critical. Certain management procedures may serve only to worsen the child's school performance or attitudinal problems. It is also revealing to ask parents why they are interested in having the child assessed, how they are presently coping with problems, what they see as the child's future educational or vocational prospects, and whether they agree in these respects.

Information regarding environmental influences is most readily obtained from parent interviews and parent questionnaires (see "Formal Assessment Procedures"). Direct observation of management procedures at home, at school, or in structured laboratory settings may also be useful, especially in problematic cases or where formulation of a behavioral treatment program is a primary concern (Hallahan & Kauffman, 1977; Smith, 1983). Clinical practice suggests that a given environmental stress (e.g., marital conflict) may have clear consequences for some children but no impact whatsoever for others. Determining the significance of environmental factors for an individual child, therefore, rests in large part on clinical judgment.

Biological Factors

I have found it beneficial to ask routinely for information regarding a child's medical history, and to inquire regarding the regularity of the child's medical examinations. These procedures help to assure that any medical concerns that the parents might have are voiced and that the child is receiving proper follow-up. Most of the time, outright disease is not present. In these cases, more indirect evidence for biological contributions for learning problems may come in the form of the biological "markers" referred to earlier (e.g., developmental delays, neuropsychological deficits, neurological "soft signs," prenatal and perinatal complications, electrophysiological abnormalities, and family histories of learning difficulties). Information regarding biological markers is obtained from parents or through review of medical records. These markers do not *prove* that biological factors are responsible for the child's learning problems, but they do raise one's suspicions in this regard (Taylor, 1983).

Assumptions

The proposed model is based on a number of assumptions regarding which variables are relevant to learning failure, and how these variables interact with one another. Each of these assumptions is justified by research findings reviewed earlier in this chapter. Listing of these assumptions is a means of summarizing the essential features of the model.

1. Identified learning problems, or presenting complaints, are a function of (a) the child's actual school performance and academic achievement; (b) what the child is being asked to do and the standards and expectations against which the child's performance is compared; (c) cognitive–behavioral characteristics; and finally (d) environmental and biological factors.
2. The most immediate or proximal sources of identified learning problems are the actual school performance and academic achievement of the child, considered in light of local standards and expectations for performance on a given task.
3. More distal sources of learning failure include the cognitive–behavioral characteristics of the child and environmental and biological factors.
4. Cognitive–behavioral characteristics are a joint function of environmental and biological factors, past and present.
5. The impact of biological factors on learning problems is by virtue of their influence on the basic cognitive–behavioral characteristics of the child.
6. Environmental factors can have either a direct influence on actual school performance

and academic achievement, or an indirect influence via their effect on the child's cognitive–behavioral characteristics.

7. Cognitive–behavioral characteristics and actual school performance and achievement influence one another as the child develops.

8. The factors that comprise each variable set may represent independent influences or characteristics, or they may be associated with one another in some way. (For the sake of simplicity, this assumption is not represented in Figure 1.)

Advantages

Although the proposed assessment model runs the risk of appearing a bit unwieldy and perhaps too general to be useful, a model that is less complex or more focused would not grant adequate coverage to the many factors that influence learning problems. The several advantages of the proposed model offset any disadvantages.

One notable advantage is that assessment commences with a thorough description of the problems as they exist in the actual setting in which the child is expected to learn (e.g., the severity, frequency, duration, and elicitors of the problems). Beginning in this way makes it possible to get to the heart of the child's problems from the outset, thereby establishing directions for further inquiry. By comparing the child's performance in testing with performances observed at home or at school, the examiner can assess situational determinants of learning problems. These include special difficulties in classroom situations or in response to particular management techniques. As an example, some children demonstrate good component reading skills in formal testing, yet are unable to read fluently enough to meet the demands of the classroom. Other children may do well in most classroom circumstances but are found on individual testing to possess component skill deficits. Although some children may be able to compensate for these deficits in earlier grades, they may be vulnerable to future failure in school. The multiple ways in which academic skills can break down make detailed assessments of the child's learning problems essential (Calfee, 1982; Doehring *et al.*, 1981).

A related advantage of the present model is that it sets no restrictions on the type or origins of a child's learning problems. Children referred for assessment will not meet all criteria for learning disabilities. Environmental factors, emotional disturbance, or generalized mental deficiency may be essential antecedents to some children's problems. The examiner must be able to evaluate these several sources of learning problems in any given child. Although the model is useful in determining whether a child meets criteria for learning disabilities as traditionally defined, its orientation to learning problems is essentially noncategorical (Hallahan & Kauffman, 1977). The model also fails to side with one particular explanatory model of learning failure. Neither the medical nor the educational model is judged to have sufficient explanatory power on its own (T. Bryan & Bryan, 1980). The present model eschews such "either–or" thinking and opens up for consideration the possibility of a wide range of potential influences on learning.

Other advantages include the model's denial of simple one-to-one correspondences between biological factors and behavior (Fletcher & Taylor, 1984), and it emphasizes multiple child characteristics. Awareness of child characteristics is essential if the examiner is to see the child from a broader psychological perspective, and to recognize that the same characteristics that lead to learning problems may also be behind difficulties in other areas of functioning (e.g., peer relationships, compliance with parental management, completion of chores). In short, the model encourages the examiner to assess the "whole" child. This requires a thorough understanding of the complexities of child behavior, good clinical judgment, and multidisciplinary involvement.

FORMAL ASSESSMENT PROCEDURES

I have not found any fixed battery of procedures to be sufficient in every case. Nevertheless, I have adopted a set of "core" assessment techniques that I routinely apply. The benefits of using a fixed but limited set of routine procedures is that it insures evaluation of a number of important facets of a child's abilities and development, while leaving time for more thorough assessment of problem areas specific to a particular child. To pinpoint deficits and to find out more about given aspects of behavior or skill development, I draw from a large repertoire of auxiliary assessment procedures. If, for example, the core assessment substantiates parent and teacher complaints of attentional problems, I may ask parents or teachers to complete supplementary ratings of the child's school performance. I may also administer additional psychometric tests to determine what aspects of attentional capacity are most problematic and to investigate implications of attentional difficulties for other performance areas such as memory or problem solving. So long as background information and core assessment findings fail to suggest weaknesses in academic skills, further testing in this area is unnecessary. On the other hand, if initial testing or background information suggests that deficiencies in academic or language skills are present, assessment may entail more careful analysis of these latter problems as well.

The purpose of the present section is to review specific assessment techniques that I have found useful in assessing children with learning problems. The order in which these techniques are described follows the order in which assessment usually takes place. By way of introduction, it should be emphasized that these techniques consist of a constantly evolving collection of less formal clinical strategies and more formal test procedures. The clinical strategies I use follow standard clinical practice (Kinsbourne & Caplan, 1979; Sanders, 1979). The value of these procedures is dependent on the extent to which they yield a broad base of information about the child and his or her family and school. The value of formal tests and measures is determined not only by traditional psychometric criteria, such as reliability and validity (Reynolds, 1982; Rourke, 1976), but also on the basis of sensitivity to developmental differences and to the trait the examiner wishes to measure. If the examiner wishes to assess skills for which no established measures are available, experimental procedures may be necessary, even if these procedures have not as yet been shown to meet accepted psychometric standards. Qualitative features of performance on published or experimental tests are also useful. Qualitative observations may suggest problems not necessarily reflected in the test scores per se, or may offer a means by which to pinpoint skill deficits.

What is most important is that the examiner appreciate variations between children with respect to various academic, cognitive, and behavioral constructs. The examiner's foremost objective is to formulate hypotheses regarding a child's psychological makeup and factors that contribute to current learning problems. This cannot be done by reporting test scores or by doing inventories of strengths and weaknesses. Proper assessment requires the examiner to make inferences based on behavior. To do so, the examiner must have a working knowledge of the concepts reviewed earlier in this chapter and of the many behavioral manifestations of learning problems. Seen from this perspective, a set of specific techniques could never be considered exhaustive of the possibilities for assessment. In fact, I find that I am continually revising my tactics with the emergence of more effective and better-validated assessment techniques.

Obtaining Background Information

The first step in any evaluation is to obtain essential background information. It is usually possible to collect some information over the phone at the time of referral—enough at least to determine the appropriateness of the referral. More complete background information is obtained by means of questionnaires sent to parents and teachers and returned prior to direct evaluation of the child. Information requested in the questionnaires is outlined in Tables 1 and 2.

So that scoring can be completed before the child is seen, I typically send behavior checklists along with the parent and teacher questionnaires. Parents are asked to complete the Child Behavior Checklist (CBCL; Achenbach & Edelbrock, 1983a), and teachers are asked to fill out and return the Teacher's Report Form of the CBCL. (Achenbach & Edelbrock, 1984b). Both checklists are standardized for children from 6 to 16 years of age. The checklists evaluate multiple internalizing and externalizing behavior problems. The narrow-band symptom clusters measured include Schizoid, Depressed, Uncommunicative, Obsessive–Compulsive, Somatic Complaints, Social Withdrawal, Hyperactive, Aggressive, and Delinquent. Social Competence is measured in terms of numbers of activities in which the child participates, number and frequency of social contacts, and parent or teacher ratings of school performance. The Teacher's Report Form also requests teacher judgments of the child's performance in school subjects (rated from far-below-grade to far-above-grade).

Additional materials requested from parents or schools prior to the clinic appointment are as follows: (1) samples of school work; (2)

TABLE 1. Outline of Parent Questionnaire

1. Identifying information
    a. Child's name, birthdate, sex
    b. Parents' names, home address, and phone number
    c. Date, grade, and present school
    d. Special programs, if any
2. Written description of the child: Strengths and weaknesses
3. Parent identification of major problem areas
    a. Problem
    b. Age first noticed
    c. Suspected causes
    d. Steps taken to deal with problem and outcome
4. Educational history
    a. School attended
    b. Special help received or grades repeated
    c. Problems in other grades or schools
5. Current health
    a. Child's physician
    b. Regularity and outcome of medical checkups
    c. Special medical problems or concerns
    d. Medications, if any
6. Medical and developmental history
    a. Pregnancy or birth complications
    b. Illnesses and hospitalizations
    c. Reports of actual neurological disease or head injury, seizure-like behavior, loss of coordination or mental abilities, or unusual physical complaints
    d. Developmental delays relative to siblings or other children
7. Family history
    a. Makeup of child's immediate family
    b. Age, education, and occupation of parents
    c. Problems experienced currently or in past by child's relatives
    d. Other medical or psychiatric problems among relatives

results of any school-administered achievement or cognitive testing; (3) copies of reports written by school psychologists, speech pathologists, or other professionals; and (4) any existing summaries of educational plans. Should the examiner desire more comprehensive informa- tion regarding school functioning, a call to the teacher may be useful (see Sanders, 1979, pp. 263–267, for suggestions regarding topics to be covered in a teacher interview); or the examiner may ask the teacher to complete a standardized rating form, such as the Pupil Rating

TABLE 2. Outline of Teacher Questionnaire

1. Identifying information
    a. Child's name, grade, and school
    b. Teacher's name and date
2. Written description of the child: Strengths and weaknesses
3. Teacher identification of major problem areas
    a. Problem
    b. When first noticed
    c. Suspected causes
    d. Steps taken to deal with problem and outcome
4. Current school program
    a. Type of class and any special characteristics
    b. Type and amount of special help given the child outside the classroom
5. Other educational programs or resources available or recommended

Scale (Myklebust, 1981). The latter scale requests teacher ratings of the child's classroom performance in five different domains: Auditory Comprehension and Memory; Spoken Language; Orientation; Motor Coordination; and Personal–Social behavior.

With this information in hand, the examiner is better prepared for the parent interview. The interview itself constitutes the most important single source of information about the child. Guidelines for conducting parent interviews are given in Table 3.

General considerations to keep in mind during the initial interview with parents are as follows (see also Kinsbourne & Caplan, 1979; Sanders, 1979; Slowman & Webster, 1978):

1. It is usually informative to begin the interview by simply asking the parents why they want the child assessed. This provides information as to what the parents think is most important, and is likely to lead to insight on what motivates their concerns. It is appropriate that the child be in the room with the parents at this time. By having the child present, the interviewer can observe the manner in which parents and child respond to one another, and can convey to the child a desire on the interviewer's part to deal with the problem in an open way.

2. Because parents may have information they would prefer to give without the child present, it may be desirable to have the child leave the room after the first part of the parent interview. This depends, however, on the age of the child and the preference of the parents and child.

3. The purpose of the initial interview is to collect information on the child, assess family functioning, and build rapport with parents. It is important to structure the interview to some extent, making sure to collect needed information and to redirect parents when their com-

---

TABLE 3. Guidelines for Initial Parent Interview: Topics Covered, in Typical Order

1. Reasons for referral
2. Nature of problem(s)
   a. Description(s)
   b. Examples
   c. History
   d. Attempted solutions and how parents are currently helping the child to cope (e.g., homework assistance, tutoring, discussions with teachers or the child)
   e. Parents' perceptions of reasons for problem(s)
   f. Other opinions (e.g., teachers, physicians, psychologists, or other professionals)
   g. Parents' expectations of child in problem areas
   h. Why parents decided to have child assessed at this time
3. Survey of other areas
   a. Review as necessary of educational history (see Table 1): schools attended, problems noted by teachers, special programs, grades retained
   b. Review as necessary of developmental history (see Table 1): perceived lags in earlier development; past and present status relative to siblings or peers in areas not covered above, including attention, memory, comprehension, reasoning, speech and language, coordination, academic abilities, peer relationships, temperament or personality traits
   c. Review as necessary of medical history (see Table 1): current medical or somatic complaints, current medical care, histories of serious illness or injuries, hospitalizations, previous medical diagnoses
   d. Review as necessary of family history and family stresses (see Table 1): history of learning problems in parents, siblings, or other relatives; impact on family of child's problems; supports available to the family; family functioning and stress on family, including conflict within family, pressure from relatives, financial problems, illnesses, and mental health problems
   e. Behavioral adjustment: compliance, self-control, independent functioning and self-initiative, attitude toward self and school, relationships with family members
   f. Disciplinary strategies of parents and other caregivers: general approach to management of child, expectations regarding child's behavior, parental reactions to misbehavior, consistency
   g. Strengths (special characteristics or skills valued by parents, others, or child)
   h. Parents' future aspirations for the child
4. Parents' summarization of questions they would like answered and of their expectations regarding possible outcomes of having the child assessed

ments have gotten off track. At the same time, it is critical to follow the topics brought up by parents themselves to some extent. This strategy makes it more likely that all salient events or beliefs will come to light. Allowing parents to say what is on their minds and encouraging them to express their reactions to events or problems is also an excellent way to build rapport, making it more possible to communicate effectively with parents after the evaluation and to enlist their support in carrying out recommendations.

4. The purpose of the initial interview is to collect information *from* parents, not to give it out. It is usually best to resist temptation to give advice, communicate impressions of the child, or even share general information on child development or developmental problems with parents during the initial interview. If parents question the examiner or ask for advice at this time, a reasonable response is to state that children are complex beings; that we must know a lot about them, their families, and their schools if we are to fully appreciate their problems; and that the examiner will do his or her best after testing to answer all questions. It is also appropriate to briefly review assessment procedures for parents, and to stress that the ultimate aim of the evaluation is to determine how best to help the child.

5. In some cases, it may be instructive to survey the child's performance in nonacademic settings. Nonacademic performances occasionally contrast markedly with school performance or IQ scores. I have found the Vineland Adaptive Behavior Scales (Sparrow, Balla, & Cicetti, 1984) particularly useful in this regard. The Vineland Adaptive Behavior Scales are well standardized and appropriate for children of any age. Parent responses to structured interview questions yield measures of the child's functional level, as manifested in habitual and observable behaviors at home, across four domains: Communication, Socialization, Daily Living Skills, and Motor Skills. The Vineland also yields a composite Adaptive Behavior score.

Evaluating Academic Achievement

Measures I frequently include in core assessment of academic skills are listed in Table 4. When there is good evidence that learning problems do not involve deficiencies in academic skills per se, only the WRAT-R (Jastak & Wilkinson, 1984) may prove necessary to val-

idate that fact. Typically, however, learning problems do entail weaknesses in reading, spelling, math, or other academic skills. Evidence for such weaknesses necessitates administration of several of the measures listed in Table 4. Whatever specific test procedures are chosen, interpretation of test results is facilitated by transforming raw scores to age-related percentiles or standard scores rather than to grade equivalencies (Burns, 1982; Reynolds, 1982).

Procedures complementary to those mentioned in Table 4 for assessing reading and spelling skills include the Brigance Diagnostic Inventory of Essential Skills (1981) and the Interactive Reading Assessment System (IRAS; Calfee & Calfee, 1981). The Brigance tests are useful in assessing oral reading, and in pinpointing problems in the initial acquisition of reading skills. The IRAS measures decoding, vocabulary, understanding of sentences, and text comprehension. Further insights into the manner in which the child reads and spells may be obtained from the Boder Test of Reading–Spelling Patterns (Boder & Jarrico, 1982), and from more experimental measures of phonological and orthographic skill (Olson, in press). Experimental measures may also help to clarify the nature of reading comprehension difficulties (Calfee & Spector, 1981; Dennis, 1983; Torgesen, 1982; Wilkinson, 1980). To further assess component math skills, the examiner may wish to administer the Key Math Diagnostic Arithmetic Test (Connolly, Watchman, & Pritchett, 1971) or the math sections of the Brigance Diagnostic Inventory (Brigance, 1981). The Woodcock–Johnson Psycho-Educational Battery (Woodcock & Johnson, 1977) is useful in evaluating a range of basic academic skills and content knowledge.

Evaluating Cognitive and Behavioral Characteristics (Individual Assessment Techniques)

Core techniques for evaluating cognitive functioning include the WISC-R (Wechsler, 1974), along with some or all of the core neuropsychological tests listed in Table 5. To take maximum advantage of intelligence test results, the examiner may want to explore subtest and recategorization scores. Bannatyne's WISC-R recategorization scores, for example, are purported to assess four different types of abilities: spatial, conceptual, sequential, and acquired

TABLE 4. Core Measures of Academic Achievement

Area	Test	Skill measured	Normed age range (years, except where noted)
Reading	Reading subtest of the Wide Range Achievement Test (WRAT-R), Jastak & Wilkinson, 1984	Word recognition	5–adult
	Gilmore Oral Reading Test (Gilmore & Gilmore, 1968)	Oral reading fluency and comprehension	Grades 1–8
	Word Attack subtest of the Woodcock Reading Mastery Tests (Woodcock, 1973)	Phonological decoding	Grades 1–12
	Reading Comprehension subtest of the Peabody Individual Achievement Tests (PIAT; Dunn & Markwardt, 1970)	Reading comprehension (forced-choice format)	5–18
Spelling	Spelling subtest of the WRAT-R	Spelling to dictation	5–adult
	Spelling subtest of the PIAT	Recognition of correct spelling (forced-choice format)	5–18
	Spelling of Sounds subtest of the G-F-W Tests (Goldman, Fristoe, & Woodcock, 1974)	Spelling of pseudowords	3–adult
Math	Arithmetic subtest of the WRAT-R	Written calculation	5–adult
	Mathematics subtest of the PIAT	Math concepts (forced-choice format)	5–18
Writing	Test of Written Language (Hammill & Larsen, 1983)	Word usage, spelling, written expression, handwriting	7–14
	Story Starter (Deno, Mirkin, & Marston, 1980)	Written expression	Grades 3–6

information (Kaufman, 1981; Vance & Singer, 1979). The Freedom from Distractibility factor—usually composed of the Digit Span, Arithmetic, and Coding subtests—is another derivative of the WISC-R. Low performance on these subtests is common in learning-disabled children and may reflect problems in attention and working memory. The primary value of such factor scores is in exploring a child's strengths and weaknesses. However, it is important to keep the limitations of this technique in mind, and to regard factor scores as suggestive rather than definitive (see Kaufman, 1979, 1981; Sattler, 1982).

Alternative tests of global intelligence include the McCarthy Scales of Children's Abilities (McCarthy, 1970), the British Ability Scales (Elliot, Murray, & Pearson, 1983), the Hiskey–Nebraska Test of Learning Aptitude (Hiskey, 1966), the Kaufman Assessment Battery for Children (K-ABC; Kaufman & Kaufman, 1983), and the fourth edition of the Stanford–Binet (Thorndike et al., 1986). Each of these test batteries measures several distinct cognitive skills. For example, the McCarthy Scales of Children's Abilities (appropriate only for younger children) assesses perceptual skills, language abilities, memory, and motor coordination; the revised Stanford–Binet (ages 2 to adulthood) assesses verbal reasoning, quantitative reasoning, abstract visual reasoning, and short-term memory. Administration of some or all of these

TABLE 5. Core Neuropsychological Measures

Area	Test	Skill measured	Normed age range (years, except where noted)
Language	Expressive One-Word Picture Vocabulary Test (M. F. Gardner, 1979)	Naming vocabulary	2–11
	Expressive One-Word Picture Vocabulary Test, Upper Extension (M. F. Gardner, 1983)	Naming vocabulary	12–15
	Peabody Picture Vocabulary Test (Dunn & Dunn, 1981)	Receptive vocabulary	2–adult
	Token Test for Children (Part V) (DiSimoni, 1978)	Ability to follow spoken directions	3–12
	Auditory Analysis Test (Rosner & Simon, 1971)	Phonological analysis	Grades K–6
	Word Fluency Test (Gaddes & Crockett, 1975)	Word production and retrieval	6–13
	Rapid "Automatized" Naming Test (Denckla & Rudel, 1976)	Naming speed	5–10
Visual–spatial and constructional	Beery Test of Visual–Motor Integration (K. E. Beery, 1982)	Ability to copy designs	4–15
	Recognition Discrimination (Taylor, Fletcher, & Satz, 1982)	Ability to match designs	5–13
Motor	Grooved Pegboard Test (Knights & Norwood, 1980)	Manipulative dexterity	5–14
Memory and learning	Digit Span subtest of the WISC-R (Wechsler, 1974)	Immediate memory for digits	6–16
	Verbal Selective Reminding Test (Fletcher, 1985)	Ability to learn word list	6–18
	Nonverbal Selective Reminding Test (Fletcher, 1985)	Ability to learn dot locations	7–12
Attention and psychomotor efficiency	Underlining Test (Rourke & Gates, 1980)	Speed of visual search	5–14
Abstract reasoning and problem solving	Culture Fair Test Scales 2 or 3 (Institute for Personality and Ability Testing, 1973)	Ability to identify principles of similarity, sequence, and spatial relationships from design patterns	7–adult

alternative test batteries may be useful in fur-
thering understanding of suspected strengths
and weaknesses.

For this same reason, the examiner may wish
to administer neuropsychological tests in addition to those mentioned in Table 5. Examples
of supplementary neuropsychological tests are
listed by skill area below.

1. Language
   • Spreen–Benton Aphasia Tests (Gaddes
     & Crockett, 1975)
   • Illinois Test of Psycholinguistic Abili-
     ties (Kirk, McCarthy, & Kirk, 1968)
   • Clinical Evaluation of Language Func-
     tions (CELF; Semel & Wiig, 1980)
   • Goldman–Fristoe Test of Articulation
     (Goldman & Fristoe, 1969)
   • Sentence Repetition Task (Golick, 1977)
   • Pseudoword Repetition Test (Taylor,
     1986)
2. Visual–spatial and constructional skills
   • Line Orientation Test (Lindgren & Ben-
     ton, 1980)
   • Test of Three-Dimensional Block Con-
     struction (Spreen & Gaddes, 1969)
   • Bender–Gestalt Test for Young Chil-
     dren (Koppitz, 1964)
   • Rey–Osterrieth Complex Figure (Wa-
     ber & Holmes, 1985)
3. Motor and sensory–motor skills
   • Bruininks–Oseretsky Test of Motor
     Proficiency (R. H. Bruininks, 1978)
   • Purdue Pegboard (R. A. Gardner, 1979)
   • Stereognosis Test (Spreen & Gaddes,
     1969)
   • Kløve–Matthews Motor Steadiness Bat-
     tery (Reitan & Davison, 1974)
4. Learning and memory
   • Revised Visual Retention Test (Benton,
     1974)
   • Target Test (Rourke, 1980)
   • Association subtest of the G-F-W Sound–
     Symbol Test Battery (Goldman, Fris-
     toe, & Woodcock, 1974)
   • Learning Potential Assessment Device
     (Feuerstein, 1979)
   • Contingency Naming Test (Taylor, in
     press)
5. Attention and psychomotor efficiency
   • Children's Checking Task (Keogh &
     Margolis, 1976)
   • Matching Familiar Figures Test (Gjerde,
     Block, & Block, 1985)
   • Colorado Perceptual Speed Test (Decker
     & DeFries, 1981)

6. Abstract reasoning and problem solving
   • Category Test (Rourke, 1980)
   • Tactual Performance Test (Rourke, 1980)
   • Word-Finding Test (Pajurkova, Orr,
     Rourke, & Finlayson, 1976)
   • Symbolic Relations and Conceptual
     Matching subtests of the Detroit Tests
     of Learning Aptitude (DTLA-2) (Ham-
     mill, 1985)
   • Matrix Analogy subtest of the K-ABC
     (Kaufman & Kaufman, 1983)

Information regarding social competence and
behavioral adaptation can be obtained from the
previously mentioned CBCL (both the parent
form and the Teacher's Report Form), and
Vineland Adaptive Behavior Scales. Supplementary behavior ratings include the Revised
Conners Parent and Teacher Rating Scales
(Goyette, Conners, & Ulrich, 1978). These
latter measures and the ADD-H Comprehensive
Teacher Rating Scale (Ullman, Sleator, & Sprague, 1984) are particularly valuable in assessing
task orientation and attentional capacity. Other
parent-based behavior ratings are the Personality Inventory for Children (Wirt et al., 1977)
and the Pediatric Behavior Scale (Lindgren,
1985). The former measure is helpful in assessing behavioral deviancy, and the latter in
broadening the range of behavioral observations
made of the child. Various research measures
have been developed to assess social skills (e.g.
behavioral coding techniques, formal observation of children in role-playing situations, sociometric ratings of the target child by other
children in the class). However, many of these
techniques have not as yet been well enough
standardized or validated for general clinical
application (Schumaker & Hazel, 1984). Evaluation, therefore, is largely dependent on the
aforementioned parent–teacher observations and
interviews.

The tactic I use most often to assess attitudes,
temperament, coping style, and self-esteem is
first to observe the child during testing, noting
responses to failure, persistence of efforts, and
general enthusiasm. I then follow up on formal
testing with a semistructured interview of the
child. A way to begin this phase of the evaluation is to ask the child why he or she thinks
the testing is taking place. The examiner may
also wish to ask the child directly about learning
difficulties and about attitudes toward himself
or herself, the school, and the family. In my
experience, however, direct questions often yield
little information. More productive techniques

for exploring the child's attitudes are to ask for likes and dislikes, wishes, things that make the child happy or sad, and things that the child would like to change about himself or herself, the school, or the family. Another useful method is to have the child draw pictures of himself or herself interacting with others at home and at school (D. Tervo, personal communication June, 1984). The child's description of the pictures may provide additional clues as to likes and dislikes. The pictures may also serve as pretexts for further questions regarding the pattern or interactions that take place at home and school, and the child's belief about his or her own abilities. An additional strategy is to make use of projective techniques, such as having the child tell stories to go along with pictures or finish incomplete sentences (e.g., "I wish I could . . ."). The reader is referred to Kinsbourne and Caplan (1979) and Sanders (1979) for further discussion of the use of projective techniques in evaluating children with learning problems.

More formal measures of coping skills and attitudes toward self can be obtained by administering the Intellectual Achievement Responsibility Scale (Licht & Dweck, 1984), the Piers–Harris Children's Self-Concept Scale (Piers, 1984), the Perceived Competence Scale (Harter, 1982), the Middle Childhood Temperament Questionnaire (Hegvik, McDevitt & Carey, 1982), and the Children's Personality Questionnaire (Porter & Cattell, 1975). Information from these measures or from the child interview are frequently valuable in making recommendations as to how parents and teachers might best respond to the child's problems.

Evaluating Environmental Influences

Special circumstances at home or school that serve to either support or stress the child are usually brought out in the initial parent interview (see Table 3). Nevertheless, I frequently ask parents to complete the Life Events Questionnaire (Herzog, Linder, & Samaha, 1981). This questionnaire, which is a modification of Coddington's (1972) Life Events Scale for Children, yields information on both positive and negative life events. Since parental attitudes toward learning and general family characteristics have a bearing on the child's learning problems, these factors deserve close inspection (Harmer & Alexander, 1978; Sameroff & Seifer, 1983; Slowman & Webster, 1978). While

parent interview is revealing with respect to these factors, formal measures include the Home Environment Questionnaire (Sines, 1983) and the Family Environment Scale (Moos & Moos, 1981).

Evaluating Biological Influences

The parent questionnaire and parent interview (Tables 1 and 3) are again helpful in assessing biological contributions to the child's learning problems (see R. G. Thompson & Gottlieb, 1979, for further details on taking a medical history). Reports of actual or suspected medical abnormalities may then be followed by review of medical records or consultation with medical specialists. Although outright neurological problems are rare in learning-disabled children (Taylor *et al.*, 1979), these disturbances may have implications for learning. Children with neurological disorders consequently deserve special consideration (see Fletcher, 1988).

Interpretation and Presentation to Family

Although eligibility for appropriate special services often requires a definitive diagnosis of learning disabilities, the diagnosis itself is otherwise irrelevant. Previous discussion has shown that definitions are arbitrary and inconsistently applied, and that they tend to vary from setting to setting. The real purpose of assessment is to achieve an understanding of a child's problems that will have implications for treatment of that child. To this end, I have found the guidelines given in Table 6 useful in conducting the postassessment interpretive conference with parents or other caregivers.

General considerations in developing a formulation of the child's problems and in conducting postassessment conferences are as follows (see also Kinsbourne & Caplan, 1979; Rockowitz & Davidson, 1979):

1. Before drawing any conclusions, the examiner may wish to conduct further testing to narrow possible explanations and pinpoint deficits. Consultation with professionals may also be appropriate to determine the significance of observations outside of the examiner's area of expertise. For example, the examiner may want to discuss speech and language problems with a speech pathologist, medical problems with a physician, or family dynamics with specialists in the mental health area.

2. Psychological or medical jargon is to be

TABLE 6. Guidelines for Postassessment Parent Conference: Topics Covered, in Typical Order

1. Description of child's strengths and weaknesses as revealed by testing. Includes discussion of how these observations accord with or modify previous observations made by parents and teachers.
2. Discussion of the factors that have most likely contributed to the child's learning problems. Includes known or suspected biological predispositions, deficiencies or delays in basic skill areas, personality–behavioral traits, environmental and family influences, and interactions between and among these various factors.
3. Discussion of the child's needs as implied by assessment findings. Includes objectives for improved academic skills, increased self-esteem, reduced frustration, and more effective behavior management.
4. Specific recommendations for meeting these needs at home and at school, and realistic expectations, given that recommendations are followed.
5. Summary restatement of parents' initial questions, and overall impressions and recommendations.
6. Plans for follow-up. Includes establishing a follow-up appointment date, deciding on purposes of follow-up visit, and setting interim tasks for the examiner and parents (e.g., getting additional information, making contacts with school, writing and sending out reports, setting up appointments as needed with other professionals).

avoided whenever possible. The examiner's primary objective is to translate impressions into descriptions of child characteristics that make sense to parents and teachers. It is best to avoid giving the names of specific tests or reporting exact test scores. The procedure I follow is to give such details only if parents request that I do so. To guard against misinterpretation, mention of any specific scores necessitates some debriefing regarding the limitations of testing and problems associated with over-interpretation of results. Test results are never beyond reproach. The purpose of assessment is merely to develop impressions of the child that are to varying degrees compatible with other information about the child. Single test scores mean far less than consistent patterns of findings, and even these latter patterns are subject to modification, given further observation of the child.

3. Although the evaluation process may reveal a number of needs or issues that should be brought to the parents' attention, it may not be reasonable to deal with all of these issues simultaneously. By virtue of existing belief systems or problems of their own, parents may not be ready to appreciate the finer distinctions of the examiner's impressions of the child, or to respond to certain suggestions. In these cases, or where a child's problems are simply so complex that full-blown discussion would probably overwhelm an already overanxious parent, it is best to limit initial discussion to the most basic impressions and recommendations. More detailed presentation can be taken up in the course of follow-up or in the written report. At times it may prove useful to compare the ex-

aminer's interpretation of the child's problems with the parents' current understanding, or with viewpoints that have been expressed by others. Parents should be given ample opportunity to ask questions, and the examiner may occasionally have to step back into his or her initial role as a reflective listener. Basic impressions and recommendations should also be shared directly with the child. This strategy mitigates against false beliefs that the child might have been harboring about his or her problems or about the purposes of assessment. It also reinforces the need to view the child as an active participant in treatment.

4. Dealing with the child and parents openly and honestly is not only clinically beneficial but ethically imperative. Additional ethical considerations include the following: (a) relating information to parents before passing it along to teachers or others, and obtaining formal parental consent before doing so; (b) assuming that information is otherwise confidential; (c) informing the child of any intentions to disclose information that might be considered personal, and asking for the child's assent prior to disclosure; (d) keeping assessment costs and time to within a reasonable and justifiable limit; (e) seeing that appropriate referrals are made for problems outside of the examiner's area of expertise; (f) doing everything possible to minimize the risk of false interpretation of the child's problems (e.g., proper test administration procedures, lack of reliance on a single test or observation, avoidance of "knee-jerk" case formulations, proper examiner training and experience); and (g) making recommendations that are realistic and constructive, given pro-

gram availability and family values. In carrying out all of these responsibilities, the examiner's most essential duty is to serve as an advocate for the child. This means making sure that the child's difficulties are properly understood and that positive steps are taken on the child's behalf.

Treatment Approaches

Given that assessment substantiates learning problems, the first step in developing treatment plans is to determine how well the child and family are coping, and to identify obstacles to more optimal adjustment. For children whose difficulties are essentially those of many "normal" learners, or whose difficulties in learning are already being managed as optimally as possible, simple reassurance may suffice. More typically, however, the child is caught in a vicious cycle in which learning problems reciprocally interact with behavior difficulties, poor attitude toward self and learning, and negativistic attitudes toward the child on the part of parents and teachers. A primary treatment goal is to break this negative cycle in order that the child's learning problems can be isolated from the child's total pattern of functioning, even if it is not possible to completely eliminate the learning difficulty per se. Gaining proper perspective is especially important for children with learning disabilities. By definition, these children have some abilities comparable to those of normal learners. Isolating the problems is the first step in helping the parents and the child to take some control over them. The best way to isolate the problems is to encourage the child, along with parents and teachers, to recognize strengths and to accommodate in constructive ways to specific weaknesses.

Over and above this primary treatment goal, a variety of intervention strategies can be considered. Some of these involve alternative academic instruction. Other approaches focus on the development of basic cognitive skills, or on improved social or behavioral adjustment (Taylor, in press). Academic remediation of children with learning disabilities usually takes place in one or a combination of three ways. The first way is to alter educational expectations of the child in accordance with the child's weaknesses. The second way is to provide remediation in areas of weakness. The third way is to teach the child how to use strengths in order to compensate for weaknesses. Hartlage and Telzrow (1983) refer to these as the "circumvention," "remediation," and "capitalization on strengths" approaches, respectively. What approaches are best for a given individual will depend on the child's motivation and existing resources.

To be effective, recommendations must be feasible and must deal with all aspects of the child's problems. Recommendations for educational programming need to be accompanied by suggestions regarding behavior management and ways in which circumstances at home and at school could be improved to reduce the child's frustrations. Most of the time, there is no single step one can take to eliminate the learning problems. To quote Sanders (1979), "Most children with learning problems do not present one outstanding symptom, the alleviation of which is sufficient to allow for successful learning" (p. 11). However, there is often much that can be done to curtail the effects of the disability, and to enhance the child's capacity to compensate for it. Proper management of learning problems requires a plan that is sensitive to the developmental needs of the child and that deals effectively with the multidimensional nature of learning problems (Deshler, Schumaker, & Lenz, 1984).

SUMMARY AND NEEDS

The heart of the concept of learning disabilities is affirmation of learning problems not readily accounted for by general mental deficiency, emotional disturbance, sensory deficits, or environmental disadvantage. A significant number of schoolchildren have learning problems that statisfy these criteria. Research supports the prevailing presumption that their learning problems are linked to intrinsic cognitive deficiencies, and that these deficiencies are in part biologically related. More than anything else, however, the evidence reviewed in this chapter underscores the complexities involved in assessing children with learning problems.

Although the learning disabilities movement has encouraged study of the many facets of learning failure, the concept itself has proved less than satisfactory. The generic category of learning disabilities has proved difficult to operationalize. It has yielded a group of children who vary markedly in their individual pattern of abilities and disabilities, and who are similar in many ways to other low-achieving children. Another complication is that the problems of these children do not appear to reflect cognitive and biological limitations alone. Pressure on a child to learn, the appropriateness of expectations, and the support and encouragement given the child all affect academic skills. Child characteristics other than purely cognitive ones also play a moderating role. These latter characteristics include the child's attitude toward learning, compensatory abilities, and behavioral adjustment. The severity of the child's difficulty in coping with the regular educational curriculum and the course and prognosis of learning problems are conjointly determined by these several types of variables.

The complexity of the determinants of learning disabilities most likely accounts for the difficulty the field has had in agreeing on a definition, and for the great diversity of problems encompassed by this category. Criteria for admitting children to learning disabilities programs are ambiguous, inconsistent, and even arbitrary (Algozzine & Ysseldyke, 1983; Shepard & Smith, 1983; Ysseldyke & Algozzine, 1983). In light of this diversity, one must seriously question the use of the term as a diagnostic label, and the sensibility of educational programs designed for "the learning-disabled child."

One major disadvantage of the label "learning disabilities" is that it excludes many children who are in need of special help. Low-achieving children with substandard IQs or with obvious emotional difficulties may not qualify for special instructional assistance. Yet there is no evidence that such children are any less needy than the children who happen to meet a particular set of criteria for learning disabilities (Eisenberg, 1978). Another disadvantage is that the label falsely implies common or distinctive problems. The result is systematic disregard for individual differences, ineffective remedial programs, and unproductive research (Keogh, 1982; Smith, 1983). A final disadvantage is that the label perpetuates the fallacy that learning problems exist only in the child. The fact is that these problems depend greatly on the extent to which variations in learning ability are accommodated within the regular curriculum (Smith, 1983). Bateman (1974) has gone so far as to suggest that we refer to "teaching" rather than "learning" disabilities. This sentiment has been echoed by many others (e.g., Adelman, 1971; Larsen, 1978). Related to this problem is the possibility that the term may serve as an "out" for parents who would prefer to ignore associated family problems or difficulties in emotional adjustment (Sanders, 1979).

From a clinical point of view, it is not important to decide who is learning-disabled and who is not. The goals of assessment are to detail the nature and extent of learning problems, describe possible sources, and recommend treatment. The bases of learning problems are usually diverse and multifaceted. The challenge of assessment is to evaluate all aspects of a child's functioning—academic skills, cognitive abilities, emotional and behavioral adjustment, and medical status—and to do so without losing sight of how each of these aspects might relate to one another (Hagin *et al.*, 1982). Evaluation and treatment are worthwhile only to the extent that the examiner considers the child's total pattern of functioning at home and at school. Effective management may require special educational assistance. But it also demands attention to the child's attitudes, motivation, and coping strategies, and to potential supports provided by parents and teachers. In this sense, much can be done to assist a child with learning problems, whether or not the child meets strict criteria for learning disabilities.

An important legacy of the learning disabilities movement is a widened perspective on the potential determinants of learning failure. The clinical significance of the concept of learning disabilities is the impetus it provides for a closer look at intrinsic child characteristics. However, appropriate assessment and intervention demands that all components of the proposed model be taken into consideration. It is imperative that we rethink the current conceptualization of learning disabilities (Ysseldyke & Algozzine, 1983). Classification of children as learning-disabled or non-learning-disabled is typically based on too limited a set of variables. Simplistic definitions of learning disabilities, such as those based on discrepancies between IQ and achievement, cannot hope to take the complexities of learning problems into account. Employing such definitions is not likely to result in the best possible intervention strategies.

My own bias is that we should begin by identifying children who are not meeting standards for school performance or academic achievement, for whatever reason. We should then explore reasons for this, and design interventions accordingly. The amount of "specialized" education provided would then depend on how well a child's difficulties can be accommodated within the educational mainstream, on the child's coping capacities, and on the likelihood of the child's benefiting from special services. The major virtue of this approach is that it does not presume that children now labeled "learning-disabled" are any different from other low achievers. Rather, it allows us to treat learning problems more globally and to identify characteristics of those children who benefit most from specific types of treatment in a more empirical manner.

While clinical approaches to children with learning problems call for a broader frame of reference, meaningful research in this area requires that we look closely at variations within the larger group of disabled learners. A major goal of research on subtypes is to identify unique sources of learning failure. There are several possible approaches to subtyping. One approach is to subtype heterogeneous samples of disabled learners based on patterns of strengths and weaknesses in the academic, cognitive, and social–behavioral domains. The classifications suggested by recent research provide clues as to how we might proceed (Rourke, 1985). But no particular classification system has as yet gained general acceptance. The reliability and validity of proposed subtype classifications must be better established. Further needs include fine-tuning of the cognitive constructs that distinguish subtypes; new measurement techniques; and study of relationships between and among academic, cognitive, affective, and neurological characteristics of the child (Benton, 1975, 1980, 1984; Carr, 1981; Farnham-Diggory, 1980; Frith, 1981; Rourke & Fisk, 1981; Taylor et al., 1982). Study of relationships between child characteristics and response to intervention is also in order. Despite a general failure of previous attempts to demonstrate treatment × aptitude interactions, response to treatment provides a promising means for validating subtype classifications (Fletcher, 1985; Hartlage & Telzrow, 1983; Lyon, 1985; Torgesen, 1982).

An alternative method for identifying subtypes is to study individual cases in greater depth, or to focus on children whose learning problems are associated with specific types of processing deficits. Torgesen's (1982) work is illustrative of this approach. By isolating a subgroup of disabled learners with short-term memory deficits, Torgesen has been able to test hypotheses regarding the nature of the deficit, examine homogeneity within this subgroup, in-

vestigate the relationship of this deficit to academic skills, and explore implications for instruction. The benefit of such in-depth studies is that they help to establish unique sources of learning problems and to isolate necessary antecedents from moderating influences (Taylor et al., 1982).

Although essential in its own right, the search for subtypes must be tempered by three more general considerations. First, learning problems change as a function of age. As children develop, different aspects of cognitive abilities are critical for learning. Perceptual–motor skills, for example, have more relevance for younger children than for older children (Satz et al., 1978). Similarly, reading ability becomes more dependent on language comprehension skills and less dependent on verbal decoding at more advanced reading levels (Curtis, 1980; Stanovich et al., 1984). The "ripple" effects on subsequent development of poor initial ability to learn may tend to blur distinctions between subtypes over time. Hence it is crucial that we investigate learning problems in young children and follow them longitudinally (Hagin et al., 1982; Jorm, 1983; Stanovich, 1986; Torgesen & Licht, 1983).

A second and more general issue pertains to the goal of research in this area. The aim of research is not merely to classify children into homogeneous subgroups or to construct better definitions. The aim, rather, is to improve our ability to identify etiology, correlates, predictors, course, and preferred treatment. Accomplishing this aim requires theoretical models to help direct research. These models must specify how learning fails to occur, and must take normal acquisition processes into account (Keogh, 1982; Lovett, 1984).

Finally, we must be certain to keep sight of the complexities of learning problems. Between-child variations in coping skills, personality traits, and environmental influences have as much to do with the nature and severity of learning problems as any inherent cognitive deficiencies. Research must attend to the multiple influences on learning (Keogh, 1982). In this respect, the aims of the researcher dovetail with those of the clinician. To return to the point made at the outset of this chapter, many more children may be at risk for problems in learning than those who actually succumb to these problems. An important aim in research and clinical work is to identify all major factors that place children at risk for learning problems, and to indicate how the combined impact of these factors precipitates actual learning failure (Aylward & Kenny, 1979; Garmezy, Masten, & Tellegen, 1984; Rutter & Yule, 1975; Sanders, 1979).

Acknowledgments

I would like to acknowledge the past guidance of Drs. Phillip Zerfas and Fred Theye of the Marshfield Clinic. Their appreciation of the multiple dimensions of childhood problems and of the special difficulties of learning-disabled children helped to shape the clinical approach to assessment detailed in this chapter. Special appreciation is also extended to colleagues at the Child Development Unit of the Children's Hospital of Pittsburgh and the McGill–Montreal Children's Hospital Learning Centre for their many discussions on assessment issues. Finally, I would like to acknowledge the able secretarial assistance of Joan Spence in the preparation and editing of the manuscript.

REFERENCES

Achenbach, T., & Edelbrock, C. (1983a). *Manual for the Child Behavior Checklist and Revised Child Behavior Profile*. Burlington: University of Vermont, Department of Psychiatry.

Ackerman, P., Dykman, R., & Peters, J. (1977). Learning disabled boys as adolescents: Cognitive factors and achievement. *Journal of the American Academy of Child Psychiatry, 16*, 296–313.

Ackerman, P., Peters, J., & Dykman, R. (1971). Children with learning disabilities: WISC profiles. *Journal of Learning Disabilities, 4*, 150–166.

Adelman, H. S. (1971). The not so specific learning disability population. *Exceptional Children, 37*, 528–533.

Adelman, H. S. (1978). The concept of intrinsic motivation: Implications for practice and research with the learning disabled. *Learning Disability Quarterly, 1*, 43–54.

Adelman, H. S., & Chaney, L. A. (1982). Impact of motivation on task performance of children with and without psychoeducational problems. *Journal of Learning Disabilities, 15*, 242–244.

Algozzine, B., & Ysseldyke, J. (1983). Learning disabilities as a subset of school failure: The over-simplification of a concept. *Exceptional Children, 50*, 242–246.

Alley, G., & Deshler, D. (1979). *Teaching the learning disabled adolescent: Strategies and methods*. Denver: London.

American Psychiatric Association. (1980). *Diagnostic and statistical manual of mental disorders* (3rd ed). Washington, DC: Author.

Andolina, C. (1980). Syntactic maturity and vocabulary richness in learning disabled children at four age levels. *Journal of Learning Disabilities, 13*, 372–377.

Applebee, A. N. (1971). Research in reading retardation: Two critical problems. *Journal of Child Psychology and Psychiatry, 12*, 91–113.

Aylward, G. P., & Kenny, T. J. (1979). Developmental follow-up: Inherent problems and a conceptual model. *Journal of Pediatric Psychology, 4*, 331–343.

Badcock, D., & Lovegrove, W. (1981). The effects of contrast, stimulus duration, and spatial frequency on visible persistence in normal and specifically disabled readers. *Journal of Experimental Psychology: Human Perception and Performance, 7*, 495–505.

Baker, L. (1982). An evaluation of the role of metacognitive deficits in learning disabilities. *Topics in Learning and Learning Disabilities, 2*, 27–35.

Bakker, D. J. (1979). Hemispheric differences and reading strategies: Two dyslexias? *Bulletin of the Orton Society, 29*, 84–100.

Balow, B., & Blomquist, M. (1965). Young adults ten to fifteen years after severe reading disability. *Elementary School Journal, 66*, 44–48.

Barkley, R. A. (1981a). *Hyperactive children: A handbook for diagnosis and treatment*. New York: Guilford Press.

Barkley, R. A. (1981b). Learning disabilities. In E. J. Mash & L. G. Terdal (Eds.), *Behavioral assessment of childhood disorders* (pp. 441–482). New York: Guilford Press.

Bateman, B. (1974). Educational implications of minimal brain dysfunction. *Reading Teacher, 27*, 662–668.

Batey, O., & Sonnenschein, S. (1981). Reading deficits in learning disabled children. *Journal of Applied Developmental Psychology, 2*, 237–246.

Bauer, R. (1977). Memory processes in children with learning disabilities: Evidence for deficient rehearsal. *Journal of Experimental Child Psychology, 24*, 414–430.

Bauer, R. (1982). Information processing as a way of understanding and diagnosing learning disabilities. *Topics in Learning and Learning Disabilities, 2*, 33–45.

Beery, J. W. (1967). Matching of auditory and visual stimuli by average and retarded readers. *Child Development 38*, 827–833.

Beery, K. E. (1982). *Revised administration, scoring and teaching manual for the Developmental Test of Visual–Motor Integration*. Cleveland: Modern Curriculum Press.

Belmont, I., & Belmont, L. (1978). Stability or change in reading achievement over time: Developmental and educational implications. *Journal of Learning Disabilities, 11*, 80–88.

Belmont, I., & Belmont, L. (1980). Is the slow learner in the classroom learning disabled? *Journal of Learning Disabilities, 13*, 496–500.

Belmont, L., & Birch, H. G. (1966). The intellectual profile of retarded readers. *Perceptual and Motor Skills, 22*, 787–816.

Benton, A. L. (1974). *Revised Visual Retention Test: Clinical and experimental application* (4th ed.). New York: Psychological Corporation.

Benton, A. L. (1975). Developmental dyslexia: Neurological aspects. In W. J. Friedlander (Ed.), *Advances in neurology* (pp. 1–47). New York: Raven Press.

Benton, A. L. (1980). Dyslexia: Evolution of a concept. *Bulletin of the Orton Society, 30*, 10–27.

Benton, A. L. (1984). Dyslexia and spatial thinking. *Annals of Dyslexia, 34*, 69–86.

Benton, A. L., & Pearl, D. (Eds.). (1978). *Dyslexia: An appraisal of current knowledge*, New York: Oxford University Press.

Bereiter, C. (1980). Development in writing. In L. W. Gregg & E. R. Steinberg (Eds.), *Cognitive processes in writing* (pp. 73–93). Hillsdale, NJ: Erlbaum.

Berger, N. (1979). Why can't John read? Perhaps he's not a good listener. *Journal of Learning Disabilities, 11*, 633–638.

Birch, H. G., & Belmont, L. (1965). Auditory–visual integration, intelligence and reading ability in school children. *Perceptual and Motor Skills, 20*, 295–305.

Blackman, S., & Goldstein, K. M. (1982). Cognitive styles and learning disabilities. *Journal of Learning Disabilities, 15,* 106–115.

Blalock, J. (1982). Persistent auditory language deficits in adults with learning disabilities. *Journal of Learning Disabilities, 15,* 604–609.

Boder, E. (1973). Developmental dyslexia: A diagnostic approach based on three atypical reading–spelling patterns. *Developmental Medicine and Child Neurology, 15,* 663–687.

Boder, E., & Jarrico, S. (1982). *The Boder Test of Reading–Spelling Patterns: A diagnostic screening test for subtypes of reading disability.* New York: Grune & Stratton.

Boller, F., & Grafman, J. (1985). Acalculia. In P. J. Vinken, G. W. Bruyn, & H. L. Klawans (Eds.), *Handbook of clinical neurology* (revised series, pp. 473–481). New York: Elsevier Science.

Bortner, M., & Birch, H. G. (1970). Cognitive capacity and cognitive competence. *American Journal of Mental Deficiency, 74,* 735–744.

Bos, C., & Filip, D. (1982). Comprehension monitoring skills in learning disabled and average students. *Topics in Learning and Learning Disabilities, 2,* 79–85.

Bosworth, H. T., & Murray, M. E. (1983). Locus of control and achievement motivation in dyslexic children. *Developmental and Behavioral Pediatrics, 4,* 253–256.

Bouma, H., & Legein, C. P. (1980). Dyslexia: A specific recoding deficit? An analysis of response latencies for letters and words in dyslexics and in average readers. *Neuropsychologia, 18,* 285–298.

Bradley, L., & Bryant, P. (1985). *Rhyme and reason in reading and spelling (International Academy for Research in Learning Disabilities* Monograph Series, No. 1). Ann Arbor: University of Michigan Press.

Bradley, L., Hulme, C., & Bryant, P. E. (1979). The connexion between different verbal difficulties in a backward reader: A case study. *Developmental Medicine and Child Neurology, 21,* 790–795.

Brigance, A. H. (1981). *Brigance Diagnostic Inventory of Essential Skills.* North Billerica, MA: Curriculum Associates.

Brown, A. L., Bransford, J. D., Ferrara, R. A., & Campione, J. C. (1983). Learning, remembering, and understanding. In J. H. Flavell & E. M. Markman (Eds.), *Handbook of child psychology (4th ed.): Vol. 3. Cognitive development* pp. 77–166). New York: Wiley.

Brown, A. L., & French, L. A. (1979). The zone of potential development—implications for intelligence testing in the year 2000. In R. J. Sternberg & D. K. Detterman (Eds.), *Human intelligence: Perspectives on its theory and measurement* (pp. 217–235). Norwood, NJ: Ablex.

Bruck, M. (1985). The adult functioning of children with specific learning disabilities: A follow-up study. In I. Sigel (Ed.), *Advances in applied developmental psychology* (Vol. 1, pp. 91–129). Norwood, NJ: Ablex.

Bruck, M. (1986). Social and emotional adjustments of learning disabled children: A review of the issues. In C. Ceci (Ed.), *Handbook of cognitive, social and neuropsychological aspects of learning disabilities* (pp. 361–380). Hillsdale, NJ: Erlbaum.

Bruininks, R. H. (1978). *Bruininks–Oseretsky Test of Motor Proficiency, examiner's manual.* Circle Pines, MN: American Guidance Service.

Bruininks, V. L. (1978a). Actual and perceived peer status of learning disabled students in mainstream programs. *Journal of Special Education 12,* 51–58.

Bruininks, V. L. (1978b). Peer status and personality characteristics of learning disabled and nondisabled students. *Journal of Learning Disabilities, 11,* 484–489.

Bruno, R. M. (1981). Interpretation of pictorially presented social situations by learning disabled and normal children. *Journal of Learning Disabilities, 14,* 350–352.

Brutten, M., Richardson, S. O., & Mangel, C. (1973). *Something's wrong with my child: A parent's book about children with learning disabilities.* New York: Harcourt Brace Jovanovich.

Bryan, J. H., & Perlmutter, B. (1979). Immediate impressions of LD children by female adults. *Learning Disability Quarterly, 2,* 80–88.

Bryan, J. H., Sherman, R., & Fisher, A. (1980). Learning disabled boys' nonverbal behaviors within a dyadic interview. *Learning Disability Quarterly, 3,* 65–72.

Bryan, J. H., Sonnefeld, L. J., & Grabowski, B. (1983). The relationship between fear of failure and learning disabilities. *Learning Disability Quarterly, 6,* 217–222.

Bryan, T. (1974). An observational analysis of classroom behaviors of children with learning disabilities. *Journal of Learning Disabilities, 7,* 26–34.

Bryan, T. (1976). Peer popularity of learning disabled children: A replication. *Journal of Learning Disabilities, 9,* 307–311.

Bryan, T., & Bryan, J. (1978). *Understanding learning disabilities* (2nd ed.). Sherman Oaks, CA: Alfred.

Bryan, T., & Bryan, J. (1980). Learning disorders. In H. E. Rie & E. D. Rie (Eds.), *Handbook of minimal brain dysfunctions: A critical view* (pp. 456–482). New York: Wiley.

Bryan, T., & Wheeler, R. (1976). Teachers' behaviors in classes for severely retarded, multiply trainable mentally retarded, learning disabled, and normal children. *Mental Retardation, 14,* 41–45.

Bryan, T., Wheeler, R., Felcan, J., & Henek, T. (1981). "Come on, dummy": Disabled children's conversational skills—the "TV talk show." *Learning Disability Quarterly, 4,* 250–259.

Bryant, P. E., & Bradley, L. (1983). Auditory organization and backwardness in reading. In M. Rutter (Ed.), *Developmental neuropsychiatry* (pp. 489–497). New York: Guilford Press.

Burns, E. (1982). The use of interpretation of standard grade equivalents. *Journal of Learning Disabilities, 15,* 17–18.

Butkowsky, I. S., & Willows, D. (1980). Cognitive–motivational characteristics of children varying in reading ability: Evidence for learned helplessness in poor readers. *Journal of Educational Psychology, 72,* 408–422.

Byrne, B., & Shea, P. (1979). Semantic and memory codes in beginning readers. *Memory and Cognition, 7,* 333–338.

Calfee, R. (1982). Cognitive models of reading: Implications for assessment and treatment of reading disability. In R. N. Malatesha & P. G. Aaron (Eds.), *Reading disorders: Varieties and treatments* (pp. 151–176). New York: Academic Press.

Calfee, R. (1983). Review of *Dyslexia: Theory and research. Applied Psycholinguistics, 4,* 69–79.

Calfee, R., & Calfee, K. (1981). *Interactive Reading Assessment System* (IRAS). Stanford, CA: Stanford University.

Calfee, R., & Spector, J. (1981). Separable processes in reading. In F. J. Pirozzolo & M. C. Wittrock (Eds.), *Neuropsychological and cognitive processes in reading* (pp. 3–29). New York: Academic Press.

Carr, T. H. (1981). Building theories of reading ability: Or the relation between individual differences in cognitive skills and reading comprehension. *Cognition, 9*, 73–114.

Cerny, L. (1976). Experience in the reeducation of children with dyslexia in Czechoslovakia. *International Journal of Mental Health, 4*, 113–122.

Chapman, J. W., & Boersma, F. T. (1979). Learning disabilities, locus of control, and other attitudes. *Journal of Educational Psychology, 71*, 250–258.

Chapman, R. B., Larsen, S. C., & Parker, R. M. (1979). Interactions of first-grade teachers with learning disordered children. *Journal of Learning Disabilities, 12*, 225–230.

Chess, S. (1968). Temperament and learning ability of school children. *American Journal of Public Health, 58*, 2231–2239.

Coddington, R. D. (1972). The significance of life events as etiological factors in the diseases of children: II. A study of a normal population. *Journal of Psychosomatic Research, 16*, 205–213.

Cohen, R. L., & Netley, C. (1978). Cognitive deficits, learning disabilities and the WISC Verbal–Performance consistency. *Developmental Psychology, 14*, 624–634.

Coles, G. (1978). The learning disabilities test battery: Empirical and social issues. *Harvard Educational Review, 48*, 313–340.

Connolly, A. J., Watchman, W., & Pritchett, E. M. (1971). *Key Math Diagnostic Arithmetic Test*. Circle Pines, MN: American Guidance Service.

Conners, C. K. (1980). *Food additives and hyperactive children*. New York: Plenum.

Corkin, S. (1974). Serial-ordering deficits in inferior readers. *Neuropsychologia, 12*, 347–354.

Critchley, M. (1970). *The dyslexic child* (2nd ed.). London: Heinemann.

Cromer, W. (1970). The difference model: A new explanation for some reading difficulties. *Journal of Educational Psychology, 61*, 471–483.

Cunningham, C. E., & Barkley, R. A. (1978). The role of academic failure in hyperactive behavior. *Journal of Learning Disabilities, 11*, 15–21.

Curtis, M. E. (1980). Development of components of reading skill. *Journal of Educational Psychology, 72*, 656–669.

Dean, R. S., & Kundert, D. K. (1981). The effects of abstractness in mediation with learning-problem children. *Journal of Clinical Child Psychology, 10*, 173–176.

Decker, S. N., & DeFries, J. C. (1981). Cognitive ability profiles in families of reading-disabled children. *Developmental Medicine and Child Neurology, 23*, 217–227.

Denckla, M. B. (1972). Clinical syndromes in learning disabilities: The case for "splitting" versus "lumping." *Journal of Learning Disabilities, 5*, 401–406.

Denckla, M. B. (1973). Research needs in learning disabilities: A neurologist's point of view. *Journal of Learning Disabilities, 6*, 441–450.

Denckla, M. B. (1977). Minimal brain dysfunction and dyslexia: Beyond diagnosis by exclusion. In M. E. Blaw, I. Rapin, & M. Kinsbourne (Eds.), *Topics in child neurology* (pp. 243–261). New York: Spectrum.

Denckla, M. B. (1978). Critical review of "Electroencephalographic and neurophysiological studies in dyslexia." In A. L. Benton & D. Pearl (Eds.), *Dyslexia: An appraisal of current knowledge* (pp. 241–249). New York: Oxford University Press.

Denckla, M. B. (1983). Learning for language and language for learning. In U. Kirk (Ed.), *Neuropsychology of language, reading, and spelling* (pp. 33–43). New York: Academic Press.

Denckla, M. B., & Rudel, R. G. (1976). Rapid "automatized" naming (R.A.N.): Dyslexia differentiated from other learning disabilities. *Neuropsychologia, 14*, 471–479.

Dennis, M. (1983). The developmentally dyslexic brain and the written language skills of children with one hemisphere. In U. Kirk (Ed.), *Neuropsychology of language, reading, and spelling* (pp. 185–208). New York: Academic Press.

Deno, S. L., Mirkin, P. K., & Marston, D. (1980). *Relationships among simple measures of written expression and performance on standardized achievement tests (Institute for Research on Learning Disabilities, Research Report No. 22)*. Minneapolis: University of Minnesota.

Deshler, D. D., Schumaker, J. B., & Lenz, B. K. (1984). Academic and cognitive interventions for LD adolescents: Part 1. *Journal of Learning Disabilities, 17*, 108–117.

DiSimoni, F. G. (1978). *The Token Test for Children*. Boston: Teaching Resources.

Doehring, D. G. (1976). Evaluation of two models of reading disability. In R. M. Knights & D. J. Bakker (Eds.), *The neuropsychology of learning disorders: Theoretical approaches* (pp. 405–411). Baltimore: University Park Press.

Doehring, D. G. (1978). The tangled web of behavioral research on developmental dyslexia. In H. L. Benton & D. Pearl (Eds.), *Dyslexia: An appraisal of current knowledge* (pp. 123–140). New York: Oxford University Press.

Doehring, D. G. (1985). Reading disability subtypes: Interactions of reading and nonreading deficits. In B. P. Rourke (Ed.), *Neuropsychology of learning disabilities: Essentials of subtype analysis* (pp. 133–146). New York: Guilford Press.

Doehring, D. G., & Hoshko, I. M. (1977). A developmental study of the speed of comprehension of printed sentences. *Bulletin of the Psychonomic Society, 9*, 311–313.

Doehring, D. G., Trites, R. L., Patel, P. G., & Fiedorowicz, C. A. M. (1981). *Reading disabilities: The interaction of reading, language, and neuropsychological deficits*. New York: Academic Press.

Douglas, V. I. (1980). Higher mental processes in hyperactive children: Implications for training. In R. M. Knights & D. J. Bakker (Eds.), *Treatment of hyperactive and learning disordered children: Current research* (pp. 65–91). Baltimore: University Park Press.

Douglas, V. I., & Peters, K. G. (1979). Toward a clearer definition of the attention deficit of hyperactive children. In G. A. Hale & M. Lewis (Eds.), *Attention and cognitive development* (pp. 173–248). New York: Plenum Press.

Drake, W. E. (1968). Clinical and pathological findings in a child with a developmental learning disability. *Journal of Learning Disabilities, 1*, 488–502.

Dunivant, N. (1982). *The relationship between learning*

disabilities and juvenile delinquency: Executive summary. Williamsburg, VA: National Center for State Courts.

Dunn, L. M., & Dunn, L. M. (1981). *Peabody Picture Vocabulary Test—Revised Manual for Forms L and M*. Circle Pines, MN; American Guidance Service.

Dunn, L. M., & Markwardt, F. C. (1970). *Peabody Individual Achievement Test manual*. Circle Pines, MN: American Guidance Service.

Edelbrock, C., & Achenbach, T. (1984). The Teacher Version of the Child Behavior Profile: I. Boys aged 6–11. *Journal of Consulting and Clinical Psychology, 52,* 207–217.

Eisenberg, L. (1978). Definitions of dyslexia: Their consequences for research and policy. In A. L. Benton & D. Pearl (Eds.), *Dyslexia: An appraisal of current knowledge* (pp. 29–42). New York: Oxford University Press.

Elliot, D. S., & Voss, H. L. (1974). *Delinquency and dropout*. Lexington, MA: D. C. Heath.

Elliott, C., Murray, D. J., & Pearson, L. S. (1983). *The British Ability Scales*. Windsor, England: National Foundation for Educational Research/Nelson.

Ellis, N. (1981). Visual and name coding in dyslexic children. *Psychological Research, 43,* 201–218.

Estes, W. K. (1981). Intelligence and learning. In M. P. Friedman, J. P. Das, & N. O'Connor (eds.), *Intelligence and learning* (pp. 3–23). New York: Plenum.

Farnham-Diggory, S. (1980). Learning disabilities: A view from cognitive science. *Journal of the American Academy of Child Psychiatry, 19,* 570–578.

Farnham-Diggory, S. (1986). Time, now, for a little serious complexity. In S. J. Ceci (Ed.), *Handbook of cognitive, social and neuropsychological aspects of learning disabilities* (pp. 123–158). Hillsdale, NJ: Erlbaum.

Feagans, L. (1983). A current view of learning disabilities. *Journal of Pediatrics, 102,* 487–493.

U. S. Public Law 94–142 (The Education for All Handicapped Children Act). (1977, December 29). *Federal Register,* pp. 65082–65085.

Ferguson, J. D. (1963). On transfer and the abilities of man. In P. F. Grose & R. C. Birney (Eds.), *Transfer of learning* (pp. 181–194). Princeton, NJ; Van Nostrand.

Feuerstein, R. (1979). *The dynamic assessment of retarded performers: The Learning Potential Assessment Device, theory, instruments, and techniques*. Baltimore: University Park Press.

Finucci, J., & Childs, B. (1981). Are there really more dyslexic boys than girls. In A. Ansara, N. Geschwind, A. Galaburda, M. Albert, & N. Gartrell (Eds.), *Sex differences in dyslexia* (pp. 1–9). Towson, MD: Orton Dyslexia Society.

Finucci, J., Gottfredson, L., & Childs, B. (1985). A follow-up study of dyslexic boys. *Annals of Dyslexia, 35,* 117–136.

Fleischner, J., & Garnett, K. (1979–1980). *Arithmetic learning disabilities: A literature review* (Research Institute for the Study of Learning Disabilities, Research Review Series, Vol. 4). New York: Columbia University Teachers College.

Fletcher, J. M. (1985). External validation of learning disability typologies. In B. P. Rourke (Ed.), *Neuropsychology of learning disabilities: Essentials of subtype analysis* (pp. 187–211). New York: Guilford Press.

Fletcher, J. M. (1985). Memory for verbal and nonverbal stimuli in learning disability subgroups. Analysis by

selective reminding. *Journal of Experimental Child Psychology, 40* (2), 244–259.

Fletcher, J. M. (1988). Brain-injured children. In E. J. Mash & L. G. Terdal (Eds.), *Behavioral assessment of childhood disorders* (2nd ed., unabridged, pp. 451–489). New York: Guilford Press.

Fletcher, J. M., & Levin, H. S. (in press). Neurobehavioral effects of brain injury in children. In D. Routh (Ed.), *Handbook of Pediatric Psychology,* Guilford Press.

Fletcher, J. M., & Satz, P. (1979). Unitary deficit hypotheses of reading disability: Has Vellutino led us astray? *Journal of Learning Disabilities, 12,* 168–171.

Fletcher, J. M., & Taylor, H. G. (1984). Neuropsychological approaches to children: Towards a developmental neuropsychology. *Journal of Clinical Neuropsychology, 6,* 39–56.

Forell, E., & Hood, J. (1985). A longitudinal study of two groups of children with early reading problems. *Annals of Dyslexia, 35,* 97–116.

Forness, S. R., & Esveldt, K. D. (1975). Classroom observations of children with learning and behavior problems. *Journal of Learning Disabilities, 8,* 382–385.

Fox, B., & Routh, D. K. (1980). Phonemic analysis and severe reading disability in children. *Journal of Psycholinguistic Research, 9,* 115–119.

Frauenheim, J. G. (1978). Academic achievement characteristics of adult males who were diagnosed as dyslexic in childhood. *Journal of Learning Disabilities, 11,* 480–481.

Frith, U. (1981). Experimental approaches to developmental dyslexia. *Psychological Research, 43,* 97–109.

Frith, U. (1983). The similarities and differences between reading and spelling problems. In M. Rutter (Ed.), *Developmental neuropsychiatry* (pp. 453–472). New York: Guilford Press.

Fry, M. A., Johnson, C. S., & Meuhl, S. (1970). Oral language production in relation to reading achievement among select second graders. In D. J. Bakker & P. Satz (Eds.), *Specific reading disability: Advances in theory and method* (pp. 123–146). Rotterdam, The Netherlands: Rotterdam University Press.

Gaddes, W. H. (1976). Prevalence estimates and the need for definition of learning disabilities. In R. M. Knights & D. T. Bakker (Eds.), *The neuropsychology of learning disorders: Theoretical approaches* (pp. 3–24). Baltimore: University Park Press.

Gaddes, W. H. (1983). Applied educational neuropsychology: Theories and problems. *Journal of Learning Disabilities, 16,* 511–514.

Gaddes, W. H., & Crockett, D. J. (1975). The Spreen–Benton Aphasia Tests—normative data as a measure of normal language development. *Brain and Language, 2,* 257–280.

Galaburda, A. M., & Kemper, T. L. (1979). Cytoarchitectonic abnormalities in developmental dyslexia: A case study. *Annals of Neurology, 6,* 94–100.

Galvin, G. (1981). Uses and abuses of the WISC-R with the learning disabled. *Journal of Learning Disabilities, 14,* 326–329.

Gardner, M. F. (1979). *Expressive One-Word Picture Vocabulary Test*. Novato, CA: Academic Therapy.

Gardner, M. F. (1983). *Expressive One-Word Picture Vocabulary Test, Upper Extension*. San Francisco: Academic Therapy.

Gardner, R. A. (1979). *The objective diagnosis of minimal brain dysfunction*. Cresskill, NJ: Creative Therapies.

Garmezy, N., Masten, A. S., & Tellegen, A. (1984). The study of stress and competence in children: A building block for developmental psychopathology. *Child Development, 55,* 97–111.

Garrett, M. K., & Crump, W. D. (1980). Peer acceptance, teacher preference, and self-appraisal of social status among learning disabled students. *Learning Disability Quarterly, 3,* 42–48.

Gilmore, J. V., & Gilmore, E. C. (1968). *Gilmore Oral Reading Test: Manual of directions.* New York: Harcourt Brace Jovanovich.

Gjerde, P. F., Block, J., & Block, J. H. (1985). Longitudinal consistency of Matching Familiar Figures Test performance from early childhood to late preadolescence. *Developmental Psychology, 21,* 262–271.

Goldman, R., & Fristoe, N. (1969). *Goldman–Fristoe Test of Articulation.* Circle Pines, MN: American Guidance Service.

Goldman, R., Fristoe, M., & Woodcock, R. (1974). *G-F-W Sound–Symbol Tests.* Circle Pines, MN: American Guidance Service.

Golick, M. (1977). *Language disorders in children: A linguistic investigation.* Unpublished doctoral dissertation, McGill University, Montreal.

Goyette, C. H., Conners, C. K., & Ulrich, R. F. (1978). Normative data on Revised Conners Parent and Teacher Rating Scales. *Journal of Abnormal Child Psychology, 6,* 221–236.

Guthrie, J. T. (1973). Models of reading and reading disability. *Journal of Educational Psychology, 65,* 9–18.

Guthrie, J. T. (1978). Principals of instruction: A critique of Johnson's "Remedial approaches to dyslexia." In A. L. Benton & D. Pearl (Eds.), *Dyslexia: An appraisal of current knowledge* (pp. 423–433). New York: Oxford University Press.

Hagen, J., Barclay, C., & Newman, R. (1982). Metacognition, self-knowledge, and learning disabilities. Some thoughts on knowing and doing. *Topics in Learning and Learning Disabilities, 2,* 19–26.

Hagin, R. A., Beecher, R., & Silver, A. A. (1982). Definition of learning disabilities: A clinical approach. In J. P. Das, R. F. Mulcahy, & A. E. Wall (Eds.), *Theory and research in learning disabilities* (pp. 45–57). New York: Plenum.

Hall, P. K., & Tomblin, J. B. (1978). A follow-up study of children with articulation and language disorders. *Journal of Speech and Hearing Disorders, 43,* 227–241.

Hallahan, D. P., & Kauffman, J. M. (1976). *Introduction to learning disabilities: A psycho-behavioral approach.* Englewood Cliffs, NJ: Prentice-Hall.

Hallahan, D. P., & Kauffman, J. M. (1977). Labels, categories, behaviors: ED, LD, and EMR reconsidered. *Special Education, 11,* 139–149.

Hammill, D. D. (1985). *Detroit Tests of Learning Aptitude (DTLA-2).* Austin, TX: Pro-Ed.

Hammill, D. D., & Larsen, S. C. (1983). *The Test of Written Language.* Austin, TX: Pro-Ed.

Hammill, D. D., Larsen, S. C., Leigh, J., & McNutt, G. (1981). A new definition of learning disabilities. *Learning Disability Quarterly, 4,* 336–342.

Harmer, W., & Alexander, J. (1978). Examination of parental attitudes within the diagnostic intervention process. *Journal of Learning Disabilities, 11,* 590–593.

Harris, A. J. (1982). How many kinds of reading disability are there? *Journal of Learning Disabilities, 15,* 456–460.

Harter, S. (1982). The Perceived Competence Scale for Children. *Child Development, 53,* 87–97.

Hartlage, L. C., & Telzrow, C. F. (1983). The neuropsychological basis of education intervention. *Journal of Learning Disabilities, 16,* 521–528.

Hegvik, R. L., McDevitt, S. C., & Carey, W. B. (1982). The Middle Childhood Temperament Questionnaire. *Developmental and Behavioral Pediatrics, 3,* 197–200.

Herzog, J., Linder, H., & Samaha, J. (1981). *The measurement of stress: Life events and the interviewer's ratings* (Project Competence Report No. 1). Minneapolis: University of Minnesota.

Hier, D. B., LeMay, M., Rosenberger, P. B., & Perlo, V. (1978). Developmental dyslexia: Evidence for a subgroup with reversal of cerebral asymmetry. *Archives of Neurology, 35,* 90–92.

Hinton, C. G., & Knights, R. M. (1971). Children with learning problems: Academic history, academic prediction, and adjustment three years after assessment. *Exceptional Children, 37,* 513–519.

Hiskey, M. S. (1966). *Hiskey–Nebraska Test of Learning Aptitude.* Lincoln, NE: Union College Press.

Holmes, D. R., & McKeever, W. F. (1979). Material specific serial memory deficit in adolescent dyslexia. *Cortex, 15,* 51–62.

Horn, W. F., O'Donnell, J. P., & Vitulano, L. A. (1983). Long-term follow-up studies of learning-disabled persons. *Journal of Learning Disabilities, 16,* 542–555.

Hughes, J. R. (1978). Electroencephalographic (EEG) and neurophysiological studies in dyslexia. In A. L. Benton & D. Pearl (Eds.), *Dyslexia: An appraisal of current knowledge* (pp. 205–240). New York: Oxford University Press.

Hulme, C. (1981). The effects of manual training on memory in normal and retarded readers: Some implications for multisensory teaching. *Psychological Research, 43,* 179–191.

Hunt, E. (1983). On the nature of intelligence. *Science, 219,* 141–146.

Ingram, T. T. S., Mason, A. W., & Blackburn, I. (1970). A retrospective study of 82 children with reading disability. *Developmental Medicine and Child Neurology, 12,* 271–281.

Institute for Personality and Ability Testing. (1973). *Measuring intelligence with the Culture Fair Tests: Manual for scales 2 and 3.* Champaign, IL: Author.

Isakson, R. L., & Miller, J. W. (1976). Sensitivity to syntactic and semantic cues in good and poor comprehenders. *Journal of Educational Psychology, 68,* 787–792.

Jansky, J. J. (1978). A critical review of "Some developmental and predictive precursors of reading disabilities." In A. L. Benton & D. Pearl (Eds.), *Dyslexia: An appraisal of current knowledge* (pp. 377–394). New York: Oxford University Press.

Jansky, J. J. (1980). Patterning and organizational deficits in children with language and learning disabilities. *Bulletin of the Orton Society, 30,* 227–239.

Jastak, S., & Wilkinson, G. S. (1984). *Wide Range Achievement Test—Revised.* Wilmington, DE: Jastak Associates.

Johnson, D. J. (1980). Persistent auditory disorders in young dyslexic adults. *Bulletin of the Orton Society, 30,* 268–276.

Johnson, D. J., & Myklebust, H. (1967). *Learning disabilities: Educational principles and practices.* New York: Grune & Stratton.

Jones, D. R. (1980). The dictionary: A look at "look it up." *Journal of reading, 23*, 309–312.

Jorm, A. F. (1983). Specific reading retardation and working memory: A review. *British Journal of Psychology, 74*, 311–342.

Kail, R., & Bisanz, J. (1982). Information processing and cognitive development. In H. W. Reese (Ed.), *Advances in child development and behavior* (Vol. 17, pp. 45–81). New York: Academic Press.

Katz, R. B., Shankweiler, D., & Liberman, I. Y. (1981). Memory for item order and phonetic recoding in the beginning reader. *Journal of Experimental Child Psychology, 32*, 474–484.

Kaufman, A. S. (1979). *Intelligent testing with the WISC-R.* New York: Wiley.

Kaufman, A. S. (1981). The Wechsler scales and learning disabilities. *Journal of Learning Disabilities, 14*, 397–398.

Kaufman, A. S., & Kaufman, N. L. (1983). *The Kaufman Assessment Battery for Children.* Circle Pines, MN: American Guidance Service.

Kavale, K. A. (1980). Learning disability and cultural–economic disadvantage: The case for a relationship. *Learning Disability Quarterly, 3*, 97–112.

Keogh, B. K. (1982). Research in learning disabilities: A view of status and need. In J. P. Das, R. F. Mulcahy, & A. E. Wall (Eds.), *Theory and research in learning disabilities* (pp. 27–44). New York: Plenum Press.

Keogh, B. K., & Margolis, J. S. (1976). A component analysis of attentional problems of educationally handicapped boys. *Journal of Abnormal Child Psychology, 4*, 349–359.

Keogh, B. K., & Pelland, M. (1985). Vision training revisited. *Journal of Learning Disabilities, 18*, 228–236.

Keogh, B. K., Tchir, C., & Winderguth-Behn, A. (1974). Teacher's perceptions of educationally high risk children. *Journal of Learning Disabilities, 7*, 367–374.

Kessler, J. W. (1980). History of minimal brain dysfunctions. In H. E. Rie and E. D. Rie (Eds.), *Handbook of minimal brain dysfunctions: A critical view* (pp. 18–51). New York: Wiley.

Kinsbourne, M. (1982). The role of selective attention in reading disability. In R. N. Malatesha & P. G. Aaron (Eds.), *Reading disorders: Varieties and treatments* (pp. 199–214). New York: Academic Press.

Kinsbourne, M., & Caplan, P. J. (1979). *Children's learning and attention problems.* Boston: Little, Brown.

Kirk, S. A. (1963). Behavioral diagnosis and remediation of learning disabilities. *Proceedings of the Annual Conference on Exploration into the Problems of the Perceptually Handicapped Child.* (pp. 1–7). Evanston, IL: Fund for Perceptually Handicapped Children, Inc.

Kirk, S. A., McCarthy, J. J., & Kirk, W. D. (1968). *The Illinois Test of Psycholinguistic Abilities.* Urbana: University of Illinois Press.

Kline, C. L., & Kline, C. L. (1975). Follow-up study of 216 dyslexic children. *Bulletin of the Orton Society, 25*, 127–144.

Knights, R. M., & Bakker, D. J. (Eds.). (1976). *The neuropsychology of learning disorders: Theoretical approaches.* Baltimore: University Park Press.

Knights, R. M., & Norwood, J. A. (1980). *Revised smoothed normative data on the Neuropsychological Test Battery for Children.* Ottawa, Ontario: Carleton University, Department of Psychology.

Koppitz, E. M. (1964). *The Bender–Gestalt Test for Young Children.* New York: Grune & Stratton.

Larsen, S. C. (1978). Learning disabilities and the professional educator. *Learning Disability Quarterly, 1*, 5–12.

Layton, J. R. (1979). *The psychology of learning to read.* New York: Academic Press.

Lefebvre, A., & Hawke, W. (1983). Learning disorders in children and adolescents. In P. D. Steinhauer & Q. Rae-Grant (Eds.), *Psychological problems of the child in the family* (2nd ed., pp. 350–387). New York: Basic Books.

Lerner, J. W. (1981). *Learning disabilities: Theories, diagnosis, and teaching strategies.* Boston: Houghton Mifflin.

Levine, M. D., Oberklaid, F., & Meltzer, L. (1981). Developmental output failure: A study of low productivity in school-aged children. *Pediatrics, 67*, 18–25.

Liberman, I. Y., Shankweiler, D., Fisher, F. W., & Carter, B. (1974). Reading and the awareness of linguistic segments. *Journal of Experimental Child Psychology, 18*, 201–212.

Licht, B. G. (1983). Cognitive–motivational factors that contribute to the achievement of learning-disabled children. *Journal of Learning Disabilities, 16*, 483–490.

Licht, B. G., & Dweck, C. S. (1984). Determinants of academic achievement: The interaction of children's achievement orientations with skill area. *Developmental Psychology, 20*, 628–636.

Lindgren, S. D. (1985). *Pediatric Behavior Scale.* Iowa City: University of Iowa, Department of Pediatrics.

Lindgren, S. D., & Benton, A. L. (1980). Developmental patterns of visuospatial judgement. *Journal of Pediatric Psychology, 5*, 217-225.

Lindgren, S. D., & Richman, L. C. (1984). Immediate memory functions of verbally deficient reading-disabled children. *Journal of Learning Disabilities, 17*, 222–225.

Liverant, S. (1960). Intelligence: A concept in need of re-examination. *Journal of Consulting Psychology, 24*, 101–110.

Lloyd, J., Sabatino, D., Miller, T., & Miller, S. (1977). Proposed federal guidelines: Some open questions. *Journal of Learning Disabilities, 10*, 69–71.

Lorsback, T. C., & Gray, J. W. (1985). The development of encoding processes in learning disabled children. *Journal of Learning Disabilities, 18*, 222–227.

Lovett, M. W. (1984). The search for subtypes of specific reading disability: Reflections from a cognitive perspective. *Annals of Dyslexia, 34*, 155–178.

Luick, A. H., & Senf, G. M. (1979). Where have all the children gone? *Journal of Learning Disabilities, 12*, 285–287.

Lyon, R. (1985). *Educational validation studies in learning disability subgroups.* Paper presented at the meeting of the Society for Research in Child Development, Toronto.

Lyon, R., Stewart, N., & Freedman, D. (1982). Neuropsychological characteristics of empirically derived subtypes of learning disabled readers. *Journal of Clinical Neuropsychology, 4*, 343–365.

Mann, V. A., Liberman, I. Y., & Shankweiler, D. (1980). Children's memory for sentences and word strings in relation to reading ability. *Memory and Cognition, 8*, 329–335.

Maria, K., & MacGinnitie, W. H. (1982). Reading comprehension disabilities: Knowledge structures and non-accommodating text processing strategies. *Annals of Dyslexia, 32*, 33–60.

Mark, L. S., Shankweiler, D., Liberman, I. Y., & Fowler,

C. A. (1977). Phonetic recoding and reading difficulty in beginning readers. *Memory and cognition, 5,* 623–629.

Marshall, J. C., & Newcombe, F. (1973). Patterns of paralexia: A psycholinguistic approach. *Developmental Medicine and Child Neurology, 2,* 175–199.

Mason, M., & Katz, L. (1976). Visual processing of non-linguistic strings: Redundancy effects and reading ability. *Journal of Experimental Psychology: General, 105,* 338–348.

Mattis, S. (1978). Dyslexia syndromes: A working hypothesis that works. In A. L. Benton & D. Pearl (Eds.), *Dyslexia: An appraisal of current knowledge* (pp. 43–58). New York: Oxford University Press.

Mattis, S., French, J. H., & Rapin, I. (1975). Dyslexia in children and young adults: Three independent neuropsychological syndromes. *Developmental Medicine and Child Neurology, 17,* 150–163.

Mazer, S., McIntyre, C., Murray, M., Till, R., & Blackwell, S. (1983). Visual persistence and information pick-up in learning disabled children. *Journal of Learning Disabilities, 16,* 221–225.

McCarthy, D. (1970). *Manual for the McCarthy Scales of Children's Abilities.* New York: Psychological Corporation.

McConaughy, S. H. (1986). Social competence and behavioral problems of learning disabled boys aged 12–16. *Journal of Learning Disabilities, 19,* 101–106.

McConaughy, S. H., & Ritter, D. R. (1986). Social competence and behavioral problems of learning disabled boys aged 6–11. *Journal of Learning Disabilities, 19,* 39–45.

McKinney, J. D. (1984). The search for subtypes of specific learning disability. *Journal of Learning Disabilities, 17,* 43–50.

McKinney, J. D., & Feagans, L. (1983). Adaptive classroom behavior of learning disabled students. *Journal of Learning Disabilities, 16,* 360–367.

McLeskey, J. (1980). Learning set acquisition: Problem solving strategies employed by reading disabled and normal children. *Journal of Learning Disabilities, 13,* 557–562.

McLoughlin, J. A., & Netick, A. (1983). Defining learning disabilities: A new and cooperative direction. *Journal of Learning Disabilities, 16,* 21–23.

Menyuk, P., & Flood, J. (1981). Linguistic competence, reading, writing problems and remediation. *Bulletin of the Orton Society, 31,* 13–28.

Mercer, C. D. (1979). *Children and adolescents with learning disabilities.* Columbus, OH: Charles E. Merrill.

Mercer, C. D., Forgnone, C., & Wolking, W.D. (1976). Definitions of learning disabilities used in the United States. *Journal of Learning Disabilities, 9,* 47–57.

Mitterer, J. O. (1982). There are at least two kinds of poor readers: Whole-word poor readers and recoding poor readers. *Canadian Journal of Psychology, 36,* 445–461.

Moos, R. H., & Moos, B. S. (1981). *Family Environment Scale manual.* Palo Alto, CA: Consulting Psychologists Press.

Morrison, F., Giordani, B., & Nagy, J. (1977). Reading disability: An information processing analysis. *Science, 196,* 77–79.

Morrison, F., & Manis, F. (1982). Cognitive processes and reading disability: A critique and proposal. In C.

Brainard & M. Pressley (Eds.), *Verbal processes in children: Progress in cognitive development research* (Vol. 2, pp. 59–94). New York: Springer-Verlag.

Muehl, S., & Kremenak, S. (1966). Ability to match information within and between auditory and visual sense modalities and subsequent reading achievement. *Journal of Educational Psychology, 57,* 230–239.

Myklebust, H. R. (1973). *Development and disorders of written language: Studies of normal and exceptional children* (Vol. 2). New York: Grune & Stratton.

Myklebust, H. R. (1981). *The Pupil Rating Scale—Revised.* New York: Grune & Stratton.

Nelson, H. E., & Warrington, E. K. (1974). Developmental spelling retardation and its relation to other cognitive abilities. *British Journal of Psychology, 65,* 265–274.

Noelker, R. W., & Schumsky, D. A. (1973). Memory for sequence, form, and position as related to the identification of reading retardates. *Journal of Educational Psychology, 64,* 22–25.

Obrzut, J. G. (1979). Dichotic listening and bisensory memory skills in qualitative diverse dyslexic readers. *Journal of Learning Disabilities, 12,* 304–314.

Olson, R. K. (in press). Disabled reading processes and cognitive profiles. In D. Gray & J. Kavanagh (Eds.), *Biobehavioral measures of dyslexia.* Parkton, MD: York Press.

Olson, R. K., Kliegl, R., Davidson, B. J., & Foltz, G. (1985). Individual and developmental differences in reading disability. In G. E. MacKinnon & T. G. Waller (Eds.), *Reading research: Theory and practice* (pp. 1–63). New York: Academic Press.

O'Neill, G., & Stanley, G. (1976). Visual processing of straight lines in dyslexic and normal children. *British Journal of Educational Psychology, 46,* 323–327.

Owen, F. W., Adams, P. A., Forrest, T., Stoltz, L. M., & Fisher, S. (1971). Learning disorders in children: Sibling studies. *Monographs of the Society for Research in Child Development, 36* (Serial No. 144).

Ozols, E. J., & Rourke, B. P. (1985). Dimensions of social sensitivity in two types of learning disabled children. In B. P. Rourke (Ed.), *Neuropsychology of learning disabilities: Essentials of subtype analysis* (pp. 281–301). New York: Guilford Press.

Pajurkova, E. M., Orr, R. R., Rourke, B. P., & Finlayson, A. J. (1976). Children's Word-Finding Test: A verbal problem-solving task. *Perceptual and Motor Skills, 42,* 851–858.

Paradise, J. L. (1981). Otitis media during early life: How hazardous to development? A critical review of the evidence. *Pediatrics, 68,* 869–873.

Pearl, R., & Bryan, T. H. (1982). Mothers' attributions for their learning disabled child's successes and failures. *Learning Disability Quarterly, 5,* 53–59.

Pearl, R., Bryan, T. H., & Donahue, M. (1980). Learning disabled children's attributions for success and failure. *Learning Disability Quarterly, 3,* 3–9.

Pellegrino, J. W., & Glaser, R. (1979). Cognitive correlates and components in the analysis of individual differences. In R. J. Sternberg & D. K. Detterman (Eds.), *Human intelligence: Perspectives on its theory and measurement* (pp. 61–88). Norwood, NJ: Ablex.

Peter, B., & Spreen, O. (1979). Behavior rating and personal adjustment scales of neurologically and learning handicapped children during adolescence and early adulthood: Results of a follow-up study. *Journal of Clinical Neuropsychology, 1,* 75–92.

Piers, E. V. (1984). *Piers–Harris Children's Self-Concept*

Scale: Revised manual. Los Angeles: Western Psychological Services.

Poplin, M. S., Gray, R., Larsen, S., Banikowski, A., & Mehring, T. (1980). A comparison of components of written expression abilities in learning disabled and nondisabled students at three grade levels. *Learning Disability Quarterly, 3*, 46–53.

Porter, J. E., & Rourke, B. P. (1985). Socio-emotional functioning in learning disabled children: A subtypal analysis of personality patterns. In B. P. Rourke (Ed.), *Neuropsychology of learning disabilities: Essentials of subtype analysis* (pp. 277–280). New York: Guilford Press.

Porter, R. B., & Cattell, R. B. (1975). *Children's Personality Questionnaire*. Champaign, IL: Institute for Personality and Ability Testing.

Potter, M. L. (1982). *Application of a decision theory model to eligibility and classification decisions in special education* (Institute for Research on Learning Disabilities, Research Report No. 85). Minneapolis: University of Minnesota.

Preston, R. C., & Yarrington, D. J. (1967). Status of 50 retarded readers eight years after reading clinic diagnosis. *Journal of Reading, 11*, 122–129.

Rapin, I. (1981). Disorders of higher cerebral function in children: New investigative techniques. *Bulletin of the Orton Society, 31*, 47–63.

Rapin, I., & Allen, D. A. (1983). Developmental language disorders: Nosological considerations. In U. Kirk (Ed.), *Neuropsychology of language, reading, and spelling* (pp. 155–184). New York: Academic Press.

Reid, D. K. (1978). Genevan theory and the education of exceptional children. In J. M. Gallagher & J. A. Easley (Eds.), *Knowledge and development: Piaget and education* (Vol. 2, pp. 199–241). New York: Plenum.

Reitan, R. M., & Davison, L. A. (Eds.). (1974). *Clinical neuropsychology: Current status and applications*. New York: Wiley.

Resnick, L. B. (1979). The future of IQ testing in education. In R. J. Sternberg & D. K. Detterman (Eds.), *Human intelligence: Perspectives on its theory and measurement* (pp. 203–215). Norwood, NJ: Ablex.

Reynolds, C. R. (1982). The importance of norms and other traditional psychometric concepts to assessment in clinical neuropsychology. In R. N. Malatesha & L. C. Hartlage (Eds.), *Neuropsychology and cognition* (Vol. 2, pp. 55–76). The Hague: Martinus Nijhoff.

Richardson, E., DiBenedetto, B., Christ, A., & Press, M. (1980). Relationship of auditory and visual skills to reading retardation. *Journal of Learning Disabilities, 13*, 77–82.

Richman, L. C. (1983). Language-learning disability: Issues, research and future directions. In M. Walraich & D. K. Routh (Eds.), *Advances in developmental and behavioral pediatrics* (Vol. 4, pp. 87–107). Greenwich, CT: JAI Press.

Richman, L. C., & Lindgren, S. D. (1981). Verbal mediation deficits: Relation to behavior and achievement in children. *Journal of Abnormal Psychology, 90*, 99–104.

Rockowitz, R. J., & Davidson, P. W. (1979). Discussing diagnostic findings with parents. *Journal of Learning Disabilities, 12*, 2–7.

Rodgers, B. (1983). The identification and prevalence of specific reading retardation. *British Journal of Educational Psychology, 53*, 369–373.

Rosner, J., & Simon, D. P. (1971). The Auditory Analysis Test: An initial report. *Journal of Learning Disabilities, 4*, 40–48.

Rourke, B. P. (1976). Issues in the neuropsychological assessment of children with learning disabilities. *Canadian Psychological Review, 17*, 89–102.

Rourke, B. P. (1980). Neuropsychological assessment of children with learning disabilities. In S. B. Filskov & T. J. Boll (Eds.), *Handbook of clinical neuropsychology* (pp. 453–478). New York: Wiley-Interscience.

Rourke, B. P. (Ed.). (1985). *Learning disabilities in children: Advances in subtype analysis*. New York: Guilford Press.

Rourke, B. P., Dietrich, D. M., & Young, G. C. (1973). Significance of WISC Verbal–Performance discrepancies for younger children with learning disabilities. *Perceptual and Motor Skills, 36*, 275–282.

Rourke, B. P., & Fisk, J. L. (1981). Socio-emotional disturbances of learning disabled children: The role of central processing deficits. *Bulletin of the Orton Society, 31*, 77–78.

Rourke, B. P., & Gates, R. D. (1980). *The Underlining Test: Preliminary norms*. Windsor, Ontario: University of Windsor.

Rourke, B. P., & Orr, R. R. (1977). Prediction of the reading and spelling performances of normal and retarded readers: A four-year follow-up. *Journal of Abnormal Child Psychology, 5*, 9–20.

Rourke, B. P., & Strang, J. D. (1983). Subtypes of reading and arithmetic disabilities: A neuropsychological analysis. In M. Rutter (ed.), *Developmental neuropsychology* (pp. 473–488). New York: Guilford Press.

Rourke, B. P., & Telegdy, G. A. (1971). Lateralizing significance of WISC Verbal–Performance discrepancies for older children with learning disabilities. *Perceptual and Motor Skills, 33*, 875–883.

Rourke, B. P., Young, G. C., & Flewelling, R. W. (1971). The relationships between WISC Verbal–Performance discrepancies and selected verbal, auditory–perceptual, visual–perceptual, and problem–solving abilities in children with learning disabilities. *Journal of Clinical Psychology, 27*, 475–479.

Royer, J. M., & Cunningham, D. T. (1981). On the theory and measurement of reading comprehension. *Contemporary Educational Psychology, 6*, 187–216.

Rudel, R. G. (1981). Residual effects of childhood reading disorders. *Bulletin of the Orton Society, 31*, 89–102.

Rudel, R. G., Denckla, M. B., & Broman, M. (1981). The effect of varying stimulus context on word-finding ability: Dyslexia further differentiated from other learning disabilities. *Brain and Language, 13*, 130–144.

Rudel, R. G., Denckla, M. B., & Spalten, E. (1976). Paired associate learning of Morse code and Braille letter names by dyslexic and normal children. *Cortex, 12*, 61–70.

Rutter, M. (1978). Prevalence and types of dyslexia. In A. L. Benton & D. Pearl (Eds.), *Dyslexia: An appraisal of current knowledge* (pp. 3–28). New York: Oxford University Press.

Rutter, M. (1981). Psychological sequelae of brain damage in children. *American Journal of Psychiatry, 138*, 1533–1544.

Rutter, M., Tizard, J., & Whitmore, K. (1970). *Education, health and behaviour*. London: Longmans, Green.

Rutter, M., & Yule, W. (1975). The concept of specific reading retardation. *Journal of Child Psychology and Psychiatry, 16*, 181–197.

Sameroff, A. J., & Chandler, M. J. (1975). Reproductive

risk and the continuum of caretaking casualty. In F. Horowitz (Ed.), *Review of child development research* (Vol. 4, pp. 187–244). Chicago: University of Chicago Press.

Sameroff, A. J., & Seifer, R. (1983). Familial risk and child competence. *Child Development, 54,* 1254–1268.

Samuels, S. J., & Anderson, R. H. (1973). Visual recognition memory, paired-associate learning, and reading achievement. *Journal of Educational Psychology, 65,* 160–167.

Sanders, M. (1979). *Clinical assessment of learning problems: Model, process, and remedial planning.* Boston: Allyn & Bacon.

Sattler, J. M. (1982). *Assessment of children's intelligence and special abilities* (2nd ed.). Boston: Allyn & Bacon.

Satz, P., & Morris, R. (1981). Learning disability subtypes: A review. In F. J. Pirozzolo & M. C. Wittrock (Eds.), *Neuropsychological and cognitive processes in reading* (pp. 109–141). New York: Academic Press.

Satz, P., Taylor, H. G., Friel, J., & Fletcher, J. M. (1978). Some developmental and predictive precursors of reading disabilities: A six year follow-up. In A. L. Benton & D. Pearl (Eds.), *Dyslexia: An appraisal of current knowledge* (pp. 313–347). New York: Oxford University Press.

Saunders, W. A., & Barker, M. G. (1972). Dyslexia as a cause of psychiatric disorder in adults. *British Medical Journal, iv,* 759–761.

Schonhaut, S., & Satz, P. (1983). Prognosis of the learning disabled child: A review of follow-up studies. In M. Rutter (Ed.), *Developmental neuropsychiatry* (pp. 542–563). New York: Guilford Press.

Schumaker, J. B., & Hazel, J. S. (1984). Social skills assessment and training for the learning disabled: Who's on first and what's on second? Part 1. *Journal of Learning Disabilities, 17,* 422–431.

Scranton, T. R., & Ryckman, D. B. (1979). Sociometric status of learning disabled children in an integrated program. *Journal of Learning Disabilities, 12,* 402–407.

Semel, E. M., & Wiig, E. H. (1975). Comprehension of syntactic structures and critical verbal elements by children with learning disabilities. *Journal of Learning Disabilities, 8,* 46–51.

Semel, E. M., & Wiig, E. H. (1980). *CELF: Clinical Evaluation of Language Functions. Diagnostic battery, examiner's manual.* Columbus, OH: Charles E. Merrill.

Senf, G. M. (1978). Implications of the final procedures for evaluating specific learning disabilities. *Journal of Learning Disabilities, 11,* 124–126.

Serafica, F. C., & Harway, N, I. (1979). Social relations and self-esteem of children with learning disabilities. *Journal of Clinical Child Psychology, 8,* 227–233.

Shankweiler, D., Liberman, I. Y., Mark, L. S., Fowler, C. A., & Fisher, F. W. (1980). The speech code and learning to read. *Journal of Experimental Psychology: Human Learning and Memory, 5,* 531–545.

Shankweiler, D., Smith, S. T., & Mann, V. A. (1984). Repetition and comprehension of spoken sentences by reading-disabled children. *Brain and Language, 23,* 241–257.

Shepard, L. A., & Smith, M. L. (1983). An evaluation of identification of learning disabled students in Colorado. *Learning Disability Quarterly, 6,* 115–127.

Sines, J. O. (1983). *Home Environment Questionnaire manual.* Iowa City, IA: Psychological Assessment Services.

Slowman, L., & Webster, C. D. (1978). Assessing the parents of the learning disabled child: A semistructured interview procedure. *Journal of Learning Disabilities, 11,* 73–79.

Smith, C. R. (1983). *Learning disabilities: The interaction of learner, task, and setting.* Boston: Little, Brown.

Snowling, M. (1980). The development of grapheme–phoneme correspondence in normal and dyslexic readers. *Journal of Experimental Child Psychology, 29,* 294–305.

Snowling, M. (1981). Phonemic deficits in developmental dyslexia. *Psychological Research, 43,* 219–234.

Sparrow, S. S., Balla, D. A., & Ciccetti, D. V. (1984). *Vineland Adaptive Behavior Scales.* Circle Pines, MN: American Guidance Service.

Spekman, N. J. (1981). Dyadic verbal communication abilities of learning disabled and normally achieving fourth- and fifth-grade boys. *Learning Disability Quarterly, 4,* 139–151.

Spreen, O. (1976). Neuropsychology of learning disorders: Post-conference review. In R. M. Knights & D. J. Bakker (Eds.), *The neuropsychology of learning disorders: Theoretical approaches* (pp. 445–467). Baltimore: University Park Press.

Spreen, O. (1981). The relationship between learning disability, neurological impairment, and delinquency: Results of a follow-up study. *Journal of Nervous and Mental Disease, 169,* 791–799.

Spreen, O. (1982). Adult outcome of reading disorders: In R. N. Malatesha & P. G. Aaron (Eds.), *Reading disorders: Varieties and treatments* (pp. 473–498). New York: Academic Press.

Spreen, O., & Gaddes, W. H. (1969). Developmental norms for 15 neuropsychological tests, age 6 to 15. *Cortex, 5,* 171–191.

Spring, C., & Capps, C. (1974). Encoding speed, rehearsal, and probed recall of dyslexic boys. *Journal of Educational Psychology, 66,* 780–786.

Spring, C., & Farmer, R. (1975). Perceptual span of poor readers. *Journal of Reading Behavior, 7,* 297–305.

Spring, C., & Perry, L. (1983). Naming speed and serial recall in poor and adequate readers. *Contemporary Educational Psychology, 8,* 141–145.

Stanley, G., & Hall, R. (1973). Short-term visual information processing in dyslexics. *Child Development, 44,* 841–844.

Stanovich, K. (1986). Cognitive processes and the reading problems of learning disabled children: Evaluating the assumption of specificity. In J. Torgesen & B. Wong (Eds.), *Psychological and educational perspectives in reading disabilities* (pp. 87–131). New York: Academic Press.

Stanovich, K., Cunningham, A., & Feeman, D. (1984). Intelligence, cognitive skills, and early reading progress. *Reading Research Quarterly, 19,* 278–303.

Sternberg, R. J., & Powell, J. S. (1983). The development of intelligence. In J. H. Flavell & E. M. Markman (Eds.), *Handbook of child psychology* (4th ed.): Vol. 3. *Cognitive development* (pp. 341–419). New York: Wiley.

Stevenson, H. W., Stigler, J. W., Lee, S., & Lucker, G. W. (1985). Cognitive performance and academic achievement of Japanese, Chinese, and American children. *Child Development, 56,* 718–734.

Strang, J. D., & Rourke, B. P. (1983). Concept formation of non-verbal reasoning abilities of children who exhibit specific academic problems with arithmetic. *Journal of Clinical Child Psychology, 12,* 33–39.

Strawser, S., & Weller, C. (1985). Use of adaptive behavior and discrepancy criteria to determine learning disabilities severity subtypes. *Journal of Learning Disabilities, 18,* 205–211.

Swanson, L. (1978). Verbal encoding effects on the visual short-term memory of learning disabled and normal readers. *Journal of Educational Psychology, 70,* 539–544.

Swanson, L. (1980). Conceptual rule learning in normal and learning disabled children. *Journal of General Psychology, 102,* 255–263.

Sweeney, J. E., & Rourke, B. P. (1978). Neuropsychological significance of phonetically accurate and phonetically inaccurate spelling errors in younger and older retarded spellers. *Brain and Language, 6,* 212–225.

Symmes, J. S., & Rappoport, J. L. (1972). Unexpected reading failure. *American Journal of Orthopsychiatry, 42,* 82–91.

Tallal, P. (1980). Auditory temporal perception, phonics, and reading disabilities in children. *Brain and Language, 9,* 182–191.

Tarver, S. G., Hallahan, D. P., Kauffman, J. M., & Ball, D. W. (1976). Verbal rehearsal and selective attention in children with learning disabilities: A developmental lag. *Journal of Experimental Child Psychology, 22,* 375–385.

Taylor, H. G. (1983). MBD: Meanings and misconceptions. *Journal of Clinical Neuropsychology, 5,* 271–287.

Taylor, H. G. (1984a). Early brain injury and cognitive development. In C. R. Almli & S. Finger (Eds.), *Early brain damage: Research orientations and clinical observations* (Vol. 1, pp. 325–345). New York: Academic Press.

Taylor, H. G. (1984b). Minimal brain dysfunction in perspective. In R. E. Tarter & G. Goldstein (Eds.), *Advances in clinical neuropsychology,* (Vol. 2, pp. 207–229). New York: Plenum Press.

Taylor, H. G. (1987). The meaning and value of soft signs in the behavioral sciences. In D. E. Tupper (Ed.), *Soft neurological signs: Manifestations, measurement, research, and meaning* (pp. 297–335). New York: Grune & Stratton.

Taylor H. G. (in press). Treatment of learning disabilities. In E. J. Mash & R. A. Barkley (Eds.), *Behavioral treatment of childhood disorders.* New York: Guilford Press.

Taylor, H. G., Albo, V. C., Phebus, C. K., Sachs, B. R., & Briel, P. G. (in press). Post-irradiation treatment outcomes for children with acute lymphocytic leukemia: Clarification of risks. *Journal of Pediatric Psychology.*

Taylor, H. G., & Fletcher, J. M. (1983). Biological foundations of "specific developmental disorders": Methods, findings, and future directions. *Journal of Child Clinical Psychology, 12,* 46–65.

Taylor, H. G., Fletcher, J. M., & Satz, P. (1982). Component processes in reading disabilities: Neuropsychological investigation of distinct reading subskill deficits. In R. N. Malatesha & P. G. Aaron (Eds.), *Reading disorders: Varieties and treatment* (pp. 121–147). New York: Academic Press.

Taylor, H. G., Fletcher, J. M., & Satz, P. (1984). Neuropsychological assessment of children. In G. Goldstein & M. Hersen (Eds.), *Handbook of psychological assessment* (pp. 211–234). New York: Pergamon Press.

Taylor, H. G., Lean, D., & Schwartz, S. (1986). *Pseudoword repetition ability in a sample of learning disabled children.* Paper submitted for publication.

Taylor, H. G., Satz, P., & Friel, J. (1979). Developmental dyslexia in relation to other childhood reading disorders: Significance and clinical utility. *Reading Research Quarterly, 15,* 84–101.

Thompson, J. S., Ross, R. J., & Horwitz, S. J. (1980). The role of computed axial tomography in the study of the child with minimal brain dysfunction. *Journal of Learning Disabilities, 13,* 48–51.

Thompson, R. G., Jr., & Gottlieb, M. I. (1979). Medical evaluation and intervention with the learning-disabled child. In M. I. Gottlieb, P. W. Zinkus & L. J. Bradford (Eds.), *Current issues in developmental pediatrics: The learning-disabled child* (pp. 263–295). New York: Grune & Stratton.

Thorndike, R. L., Hagen, E. P., & Sattler, J. M. (1986). *Stanford–Binet Intelligence Scale* (4th ed.). Chicago: Riverside.

Torgesen, J. K. (1977). The role of nonspecific factors in the task performance of learning disabled children: A theoretical assessment. *Journal of Learning Disabilities, 10,* 27–34.

Torgesen, J. K. (1979). What shall we do with psychological processes? *Journal of Learning Disabilities, 12,* 514–521.

Torgesen, J. K. (1980). Conceptual and educational implications of the use of efficient task strategies by learning disabled children. *Journal of Learning Disabilities, 13,* 364–371.

Torgesen, J. K. (1982). The use of rationally defined subgroups in research on learning disabilities. In J. P. Das, R. F. Mulcahy, & A. E. Wall (Eds.), *Theory and research in learning disabilities* (pp. 111–131). New York: Plenum Press.

Torgesen, J. K. (1985). Memory processes in reading disabled children. *Journal of Learning Disabilities, 18,* 350–357.

Torgesen, J. K., & Goldman, T. (1977). Verbal rehearsal and short-term memory in reading-disabled children. *Child Development, 48,* 56–60.

Torgesen, J. K., & Licht, B. (1983). The learning disabled child as an inactive learner: Retrospect and prospects. In J. McKinney & L. Feagans (Eds.), *Topics in learning disabilities* (Vol. 1, pp. 100–130). Norwood, NJ: Ablex Press.

Trites, R. L., & Fiedorowicz, C. (1976). Follow-up study of children with specific or primary reading disability. In R. M. Knights & D. J. Bakker (Eds.), *The neuropsychology of learning disorders: Theoretical approaches* (pp. 41–50). Baltimore: University Press.

Ullman, R. K., Sleator, E. K., & Sprague, R. L. (1984). A new rating scale for diagnosis and monitoring of ADD children. *Psychopharmacology Bulletin, 20,* 160–164.

U.S. Office of Education. (1968). *First Annual Report, National Advisory on Handicapped Children.* Washington, DC: U.S. Department of Health, Education and Welfare.

U.S. Public Law 94-142 (The Education of All Handicapped Children Act). (1977, December 29). *Federal Register,* pp. 65082–65085.

Vance, H. B., & Singer, M. G. (1979). Recategorization of the WISC-R subtest scaled scores for learning disabled children. *Journal of Learning Disabilities, 12,* 487–495.

VandeVoort, L., & Senf, G. M. (1973). Audiovisual integration in retarded readers. *Journal of Learning Disabilities, 6,* 170–179.

Vellutino, F. R. (1978). Toward an understanding of dyslexia. In A. L. Benton & D. Pearl (Eds.), *Dyslexia: An appraisal of current knowledge* (pp. 61–111). New York: Oxford University Press.

Vellutino, F. R. (1979). *Dyslexia: Theory and research.* Cambridge, MA: MIT Press.

Vogel, S. A. (1974). Syntactic abilities in normal and dyslexic children. *Journal of Learning Disabilities, 7,* 103–109.

Waber, D. P., & Holmes, J.M. (1985). Assessing children's copy productions of the Rey–Osterrieth Complex Figure. *Journal of Clinical and Experimental Neuropsychology, 7,* 264–280.

Waller, T. G. (1976). Children's recognition memory for written sentences: A comparison of good and poor readers. *Child Development, 47,* 90–95.

Walsh, R. N., & Greenough, W. T. (Eds.). (1976). *Environments as therapy for brain dysfunctions.* New York: Plenum.

Warrington, E. K. (1967). The incidence of verbal disability associated with reading retardation. *Neuropsychologia, 5,* 175–179.

Wechsler, D. (1974). *Manual for the Wechsler Intelligence Scale for Children—Revised.* New York: Psychological Corporation.

Weinstein, R., & Rabinovitch, M. S. (1971). Sentence structure and retention in good and poor readers. *Journal of Educational Psychology, 62,* 25–30.

Wepman, J. M., Cruickshank, W. M., Deutsch, C. P., Morency, A., & Strother, C. R. (1975). Learning disabilities. In N. Hobbs (Ed.), *Issues in the classification of children* (Vol. 1, pp. 300–317). San Francisco: Jossey-Bass.

Werner, E. E. (1980). Environmental interaction in minimal brain dysfunctions. In H. C. Rie & H. D. Rie (Eds.), *Handbook of minimal brain dysfunctions: A critical review* (pp. 210–231). New York: Wiley.

Whiting, S. A., & Jarrico, S. (1980). Spelling patterns of normal readers. *Journal of Learning Disabilities, 13,* 45–47.

Wiig, E. H., & Semel, E. M. (1980). *Language assessment and intervention for the learning disabled.* Columbus, OH: Charles E. Merrill.

Wiig, E. H., Semel, E., & Nystrom, L. (1982). Comparison of rapid naming in language-learning-disabled and academically achieving eight-year-olds. *Language, Speech, and Hearing Services in Schools, 13,* 11–23.

Wilkinson, A. C. (1980). Children's understanding in reading and listening. *Journal of Educational Psychology, 72,* 561–574.

Wirt, R. D., Lachar, D., Klinedinst, J. K., & Seat, P. D. (1984). *Multidimensional description of child personality: A manual for the Personality Inventory for Children* (rev. ed.). Los Angeles: Western Psychological Services.

Wolf, M. (1982). *"Gulpbirds, screwhorses and chickenleafs": A longitudinal and case study approach to dysnomia and the developmental dyslexias.* Paper presented at the meeting of the International Neuropsychological Society, Deauville, France.

Wong, B. Y. L., & Wong, R. (1980). Role-taking skills in normal achieving and learning disabled children. *Learning Disability Quarterly, 3,* 11–18.

Woodcock, R. W. (1973). *Woodcock Reading Mastery Tests manual.* Circle Pines, MN: American Guidance Service.

Woodcock, R. W., & Johnson, M. B. (1977). *Psycho-Educational Battery.* New York: Teaching Resources.

Ysseldyke, J. E., & Algozzine, B. (1983). LD or not LD: That's the question. *Journal of Learning Disabilities, 16,* 29–31.

Yule, W. (1973). Differential prognosis of reading backwards and specific reading retardation. *British Journal of Educational Psychology, 43,* 244–248.

Zinkus, P. W. (1979). Behavioral and emotional sequelae of learning disorders. In M. I. Gottlieb, P. W. Zinkus, & L. J. Bradford (Eds.), *Current issues in developmental pediatrics: The learning-disabled child* (pp. 183–215). New York: Grune & Stratton.

Zurif, E. B., & Carson, G. (1970). Dyslexic in relation to cerebral dominance and temporal analysis. *Neuropsychologia, 8,* 351–361.

PART V
CHILDREN AT RISK

9 CHILD ABUSE AND NEGLECT

DAVID A. WOLFE
University of Western Ontario

The maltreatment of children has been justified or sanctioned throughout history in relation to cultural norms for disciplining and educating children, pleasing certain gods, or expelling evil spirits (Radbill, 1968). Not only was harsh physical punishment viewed as a suitable cure for unruly child behavior, but until the middle of the 19th century such acts were condoned, supported by law, and often considered salutory (Ross, 1980). Interest in child abuse and neglect slowly increased during the late 19th century, as legal and social precedents for intervention on behalf of maltreated children were established. Despite advances, however, it was not until the early 1960s that social casework joined forces with the medical profession to embrace the view of child maltreatment as a medical and psychiatric problem. During the following decade, child abuse efforts focused on mandatory reporting laws and administrative bureaucracy to protect children from abuse and neglect by parents and other caregivers (Magnuson, 1983). Such rapid cultural changes in awareness and tolerance of abuse and neglect, coupled with medical, social, and psychological interventions, have led to tempered optimism in terms of reducing the incidence of these problems, although a long-standing commitment to the problem is needed to avoid repeating the discouragement associated with such an entrenched social problem (Ross, 1980).

As a result of changing legislative and social policy, the impact of social scientists on the field of child abuse has steadily increased. Sociologists began large-scale probes into the social causes of child abuse in the late 1960s, documenting the relationship between family violence and such conditions as poverty, unemployment, social and physical isolation from community resources, and overcrowded environments (Gil, 1970; Straus, Gelles, & Steinmetz, 1980). Psychologists were initially slow to respond to this problem, most likely because of the difficulty of studying behavior that is illegal, occurs with low frequency in the privacy of the home, and is not viewed as atypical or problematic by most persons who perform it. However, the creation in 1974 in the United States of the National Center on Child Abuse and Neglect under the Federal Child Abuse Prevention and Treatment Act (U.S. Public Law 93-247) resulted in over $50 million being spent on research, demonstration, and evaluation activities between the years 1974 and 1980 (Besharov, 1982). This has stimulated an increasing number of publications and the development of comprehensive social-psychological models of child abuse (e.g., Belsky, 1980; Garbarino & Sherman, 1980), along with assessment (e.g., Friedman, Sandler, Hernandez, & Wolfe, 1981) and intervention strategies (e.g., Gambrill, 1983) for helping abusive families. Despite justifiable criticism that research in this area has been of limited scope and design (e.g., Besharov, 1982; Smith, 1984), we have seen a pronounced expansion of our understanding and treatment of this problem in recent years.

The purpose of the present chapter is to present the reader with a comprehensive review of the major findings on child abuse and neglect in order to develop a multilevel framework for behavioral assessment. The physically abused child receives the primary focus throughout the chapter (which reflects the imbalance in the research literature; see Wolock & Horowitz, 1984), although information relevant to the assessment of child neglect is presented in the context of parent, child, and situational factors that influence behavior among family members. The scope includes definitional issues, a developmental perspective of the abused child, a functional analysis of abusive behavior, and a model for assessing abuse and neglect that involves specific recommendations. Research studies involving members of abusive families are presented in order to facilitate an understanding of the complex interrelationships among social and psychological variables affecting the occurrence of child maltreatment (e.g., parental history, child-rearing skills, stressful events, etc.). The approach to behavioral assessment that is derived from this organization of the research and clinical literature involves a multistage process that profits from recent advances in observational, physiological, and self-report assessment strategies.

CHILD MALTREATMENT AND THE RISK OF IMPAIRED DEVELOPMENT

A composite profile of cases reported to Child Protective Services in the United States from 1976 to 1982, which was analyzed by the American Humane Association, revealed a fairly consistent pattern of child maltreatment. Of these children, 64% experienced "deprivation of necessities" (e.g., inadequate clothing, nutrition, or medical care, exposure to hazards, or being left unattended), while 25% were the victims of physical abuse (e.g., bruised, cut, burned, or internally injured due to nonaccidental behavior of a caregiver). Emotional abuse (e.g., insulting or berating the child) and sexual abuse (e.g., exposing a minor under age 18 to sexual acts or materials) accounted for another 17% and 6% of the reports, respectively (Russell & Trainor, 1984). Compared to all U.S. families with children, maltreated children are twice as likely to live in a single-parent, female-headed household; are four times as likely to be supported by public assistance; and are affected by numerous family stress factors, such as health problems, alcohol abuse, and spouse abuse (Russell & Trainor, 1984).

Children who lack the basic social and psychological necessities of life, such as food, affection, medical care, education, and intellectual and social stimulation, are considered to be at risk for impaired development, relative to children who do not lack such opportunities (Garbarino, 1982). For example, a stressful or disadvantaged environment is associated with pronounced developmental impairments in intellectual, social, and affective functioning of the child (Srole et al., 1978). Epidemiological studies suggest that although a child may be able to tolerate single chronic stressors or risk factors (e.g., poor housing, parental separation, school disruption, etc.) with little or no apparent harm, additional stressors may geometrically increase the risk of such adjustment disorders as delinquency and school failure (Rutter, 1979). Similarly, such traumatic events as abuse, neglect, emotional deprivation, and related forms of maltreatment do not appear to affect children in a predictable, characteristic fashion. Rather, the effects of these events upon children vary as a function of their frequency, intensity, and duration, coupled with the child's own resources and compensating experiences (Garmezy & Rutter, 1983; Lipsett, 1983; Srole et al., 1980). Therefore, to understand the degree of potential risk of impaired development in a case of child maltreatment, we must evaluate the nature and severity of the act in relation to the child's personal and family resources. This calls for a developmental, systems-oriented approach to assessment that focuses on the characteristics of the parent, the child, and the circumstances surrounding the incident(s).

Definitions of Child Abuse and Neglect

The existence of adequate definitions of "abuse" and "neglect" is central to the entire system of service delivery to problem families. This is so because communities must distinguish between families who need help and those who do not, and they also must educate all community members in the currently acceptable and unacceptable forms of child rearing (rightly or wrongly, this is typically accomplished by defining or identifying the "failures" of the system). Although most communities have legal definitions to justify social intervention in cases of child maltreatment, the laws do not clearly specify what is or is not acceptable in operational terms. For example, there is no clear distinction in state statutes between acceptable forms of punishment on the one hand and child abuse on the other (National Institute of Mental Health, 1977). Legal definitions also fall short of practical requirements because, as a function of cultural values, history, and community standards, one person's "abuse" is another person's "discipline" (Wolfe, Kaufman, Aragona, & Sandler, 1981). Furthermore, standards used to determine whether a type of maltreatment has occurred or might occur tend to vary across different agencies within the same community. For example, a hospital staff may define "abuse" very conservatively (e.g., scratches or bruises on the child that are greater in number than those seen on other children attending a clinic), and may become frustrated or angered at the apparent unresponsiveness of the child protection agency in a particular case. *Ipso facto,* the protection agency may feel constrained by the requirements of the juvenile court for physical evidence to justify their involvement in a family's affairs.

The problems of defining abuse are further complicated by what are commonly referred to as "high-risk" suspected abuse cases. An investigation of a report of alleged abuse may fail to conclusively detect that the child has been abused. However, the person conducting the investigation may be aware that many high-risk signs of abuse are present (e.g., an unstable marriage, a problem child, reliance upon physical punishment, etc.). Often such parents reject any offers to help in such circumstances, and agencies are forced to resort to persuasion and threats to compel the parents to accept assistance for their family problems.

The general definition of "physical abuse" that has emerged over the past decade emphasizes the presence of a nonaccidental injury that is the result of acts of commission (physical assault) or omission (failure to protect) by caretakers, and that requires medical attention or legal intervention (National Institute of Mental Health, 1977). Although evidence of physical injury to the child remains a critical factor in defining an act as abusive (especially for legal purposes), more and more emphasis is being placed upon the circumstances and nature of the act (as opposed to the consequences) in differentiating abuse from nonabuse (Smith, 1984). In practice, therefore, the process of deciding whether or not a specific incident constitutes physical abuse involves at least two judgments (Giovannoni & Becerra, 1979):

1. The extent to which the parental act was judged sufficiently deviant to necessitate protection of the child (e.g., the parent did nothing to prevent the child from falling down stairs; the parent used a fist, weapon, or dangerous object to control the child).
2. The "dangerousness" of the current situation *vis-à-vis* salient stress factors affecting the parent and developmental and behavioral characteristics of the child (e.g., parental complaints of "losing control" with the child; complaints of economic or related family problems; an excessively delayed or active child that easily provokes the parent).

The definition of "child neglect," on the other hand, usually takes into strong consideration the chronicity and pervasiveness of parental inadequacy and failure to assume basic responsibilities (National Institute of Mental Health, 1977; Polansky, Chalmers, Buttenwieser, & Williams, 1981). Although these two forms of maltreatment may coexist, most investigators argue the importance of considering abuse and neglect as somewhat distinct forms of parental and family dysfunction (e.g., Bousha & Twentyman, 1984; Herrenkohl, Herrenkohl, & Egolf, 1983). Simply stated, "neglect" can be defined as a chronic pattern of deprivation of necessities that must be remediated in order to prevent sustained and pervasive developmental impairments of the child. Neglect includes, for example, adults' refusing to meet family needs; inadequate supervision; parents' lack of knowledge of child care; inappropriate use of medical facilities; unsafe home environment; and allowing dangerous or unsafe child behavior to occur, such as no evening curfew, no attempts to restrain the child's use of alcohol or drugs, and prostitution (Herrenkohl *et al.,* 1983). As with physical abuse, the determination of neglect is a judgment that must take into consideration such intangible factors as intensity, frequency, and duration of purported incidents, as well as the potential or real harm to the child.

For purposes of assessment and intervention (rather than apprehension and custody), the definitions of "abuse" and "neglect" used herein include cases of high-risk parenting prac-tices. Accordingly, examples of family prob-lems that are addressed by this assessment strat-egy include the reliance upon high-intensity physical punishment; use of excessive criticism and verbal harassment of the child (i.e., "emo-tional abuse"); use of unorthodox disciplinary techniques (e.g., pressure points, shaking, pub-lic ridicule); lack of physical or verbal affection toward the child; failure to provide develop-mentally appropriate stimulation or opportuni-ties to the child; extreme adult inconsistencies and "mood swings" that restrict the child's ability to adapt to his or her family environ-ment; and similar episodes of parental inade-quacy or ineffectiveness that warrant profes-sional involvement. Because the determination of such events involves the judgment of profes-sionals (rather than "evidence" per se), the definitions of "abuse" and "neglect" vary somewhat in accordance with the purpose of the assessment and intervention concerns. This limited ambiguity is considered to be necessary and acceptable, in view of the current state of knowledge and the presumed advantage to the child and family in seeking assistance for wide-ranging problems (as opposed to labeling or punishing family members).

Incidence and Profile

The number of child abuse and neglect reports processed by child protective service agencies across the United States in 1982 was slightly under 1 million, which represents an increase of 123% since 1976. This figure, which is based on substantiated reports, results in a national reporting rate of 2% of all children in the country (20.08 children for every 1,000; Amer-ican Humane Association, 1984). This stands in sharp contrast to a nationwide survey's es-timate that 14% of all children (140/1,000) in the United States are subject to abusive violence each year (Straus, 1979a). These discrepant figures draw into question the representative-ness of reported cases investigated by protective service agencies, as well as the factors that affect child abuse reporting. However, inter-pretation of these incidence figures should take into account the fact that reporting rates are influenced by the allocation of federal money, the strengthening of state laws, education of community members, and similar circum-stances. Furthermore, it is widely recognized that the number of cases handled by child pro-

tective services represents only a fraction of all child maltreatment cases (Russell & Trainor, 1984).

With these considerations in mind, several findings stand out in the analyses of trends in child abuse reporting statistics over the past decade:

1. Earlier concerns about a possible report-ing bias due to race have not been substantiated (i.e., blacks were not more likely to be reported than whites; Russell & Trainor, 1984).

2. The strong relationship that has consis-tently emerged between abuse reports and pov-erty is considered to be a reliable finding, rather than a bias in reporting. In other words, there is a consensus that child maltreatment is related to economic inequality, and occurs dispropor-tionately more often among economically and socially disadvantaged families (National Cen-ter on Child Abuse and Neglect, 1981; Pelton, 1978).

3. The only major reporting bias seems to be related to the child's age: Younger children are much more likely to be reported than ado-lescents (National Center on Child Abuse and Neglect, 1981; Russell & Trainor, 1984).

4. Although child neglect is by far the most commonly reported form of child maltreatment, combined reports of abuse and neglect have been gradually increasing over the years; about 46% of all reports of neglect received each year involve physical abuse as well (Russell & Trai-nor, 1984).

5. A disturbingly large number of abuse–neglect incidents that are known to profession-als are not reported to the proper authorities, even though such reports are mandated by law. The National Study of the Incidence and Se-verity of Child Abuse and Neglect reported that *two-thirds* of the child maltreatment cases that were known to service agencies (e.g., law en-forcement, public and private medical facilities, day care centers, mental health agencies, etc.) were not reported to child protective services (National Center on Child Abuse and Neglect, 1981).

6. Children who were reported as fatalities in 1982 (based on an incomplete sampling of 484 known cases) were much younger (2.04 years) than the average age of all maltreated children (7.14 years). Furthermore, the seri-ousness of child neglect is underscored by the fact that out of this total number of fatalities, 51% died because of neglect (i.e., deprivation of necessities), compared to 40% who died

from major physical injuries and 24% from minor injuries (American Humane Association, 1984).

These cumulative findings provide considerably more detail and understanding of the patterns of maltreatment that have occurred over the past decade than do previous clinical estimates (e.g., Spinetta & Rigler, 1972). Inferences derived from these relationships have considerable importance for the direction and choice of assessment, as presented in the latter part of this chapter.

Background Characteristics of Children and Their Families

Certain child characteristics have been identified through incidence studies that help to identify the overall probability and type of maltreatment (Russell & Trainor, 1984). Regarding age of the victims, since 1976 there has been a consistent pattern of neglect most often affecting the youngest age groups and declining as children grow older. In contrast, reports of sexual and emotional maltreatment occur most frequently among adolescents. Surprisingly, physical abuse affects a sizable proportion of all age groups; however, the highest rate of physical injury is found among the oldest children.

Sex of the victims has not shown a discriminatory pattern over the years, with males and females being reported at approximately the same rate (with the exception of sexual abuse). However, the profile of reports made on black children appears to be distinctly different from the overall group: Black families have been characterized by more neglect and less abuse. One inference drawn from this finding is that reports are now being labeled more correctly; in the past, a concerned individual may have reported "abuse," even though neglect was the primary issue. This explanation may account for the 10% increase in neglect-only reports and concomitant decrease in abuse–neglect reports for blacks between 1976 and 1982 (Russell & Trainor, 1984). White children, in contrast, are underrepresented in the reporting figures (when compared to census data) and are more often the victims of abuse or combined abuse–neglect. Thus, although no age, race, or sex of child is immune to child maltreatment, certain demographic characteristics make children more vulnerable to different forms of maltreatment. Knowledge of these relationships may assist in the determination of services for troubled children.

The perpetrators of child maltreatment are, for the most part, the parents of the children (97%), with a large percentage being natural parents (American Humane Association, 1984). Natural parents show less sexual abuse and more neglect than other perpetrators (who show more sexual abuse and physical injury). Nonrelatives who are caretakers of the child (e.g., foster parents, guardians) commit more physical and sexual abuse and less neglect and emotional maltreatment (Russell & Trainor, 1984). These patterns have been consistent over many studies, and highlight some of the possible dynamics of the perpetrator–child relationship that are linked to maltreatment.

In addition to the finding that perpetrators are most often the parents of the children, incidence data have suggested that they had their children at a younger age than did those in general. As a case in point, the child welfare agency serving my own community discovered that over a 10-year period 95% of the mothers known to the agency for child maltreatment or parental inadequacy had given birth to their first child before the age of 20 years (Young, 1982). The average age of the parent at the time of the report (32 years, nationally) was well beyond adolescence, however. There are also more female than male caretakers of maltreated children (60.8% female vs. 39.2% male), which reflects the predominance of female-headed households. This is significant in terms of type of maltreatment and the implications for assessment and treatment: Males are associated with more major and minor physical injury, much more sexual abuse, and less neglect. This finding is also congruent with the influence of economic factors (discussed above): When only the mother is present in the home, economic difficulties are more prevalent, and neglect is the most common form of maltreatment (Russell & Trainor, 1984).

Information concerning the child welfare system's response to these incidence reports highlights the directions taken to assist abused and neglected children at a national level. First, it should be recognized that in one representative year, 1982 (American Humane Association, 1984), 30% of reported cases of child maltreatment were closed after the initial evaluation (due to lack of evidence or need for services). The majority of cases (58%), however, were opened for protective services. Of these open cases, the vast majority (79%) received "case-work counseling" (a service that is vaguely defined and may range from one or two contacts to extended family intervention); 13% of the children were placed in foster homes; and 18% received mental health services (e.g., individual or group therapy, parent training, etc.). The trend is clearly away from long-term foster placement (a 50% decrease in placements since 1976), and more toward increased provision of mental health services for children and their families (a 50% increase since 1979). Finally, service provision is related to the source of the report and type of maltreatment. Reports made by professional sources and law enforcement are most likely to be served, and cases involving abandonment and sexual abuse receive the most attention from service providers. Neglect and minor physical abuse receive the smallest percentage of services, despite the fact that in 1982, for example, over 50% of reported child fatalities were reportedly related to deprivation of necessities (Russell & Trainor, 1984).

A DEVELOPMENTAL PERSPECTIVE ON CHILD ABUSE AND NEGLECT

What becomes of the maltreated child as he or she grows older is a source of great debate and confusion. Since abuse is typically accompanied by family instability, parental dysfunctioning, and socioeconomic disadvantage, its unique and specific impact on development is difficult to assess. Moreover, concern about child abuse is recent, and while longitudinal studies are increasing in number (e.g., Egeland, Breitenbucher, & Rosenberg, 1980; Elmer, 1977), few well-designed prospective investigations have been conducted. Information about the developmental sequelae of maltreatment that has been accumulated from case histories, clinical interventions, follow-up studies, and comparative investigations of abused and nonabused children over the past decade indicate that abused children, as a group, do not reveal characteristic adjustment patterns or long-term developmental problems that clearly distinguish them from nonabused children (Toro, 1982). On the other hand, the range and extent of problems in this population implicate abuse as a contributory factor involved in a wide range of child (e.g., delinquency, school problems, speech and language delays) and adult (e.g., criminal behav-

ior, marital conflict, child-rearing problems) developmental impairments (Friedrich & Boriskin, 1976; Frodi, 1981).

A developmental perspective on abuse and neglect views the emergence of maladaptive behaviors, such as peer aggression, school failure, and delinquency, within a longitudinal and multidimensional framework (Cicchetti & Rizley, 1981). This perspective does not attempt to relate abuse or neglect in a causal manner to specific developmental outcomes, since the interactive nature of the problems usually limits predictive and linear relationships between maltreatment (the suspected "cause") and particular adjustment disorders (the putative "effect"). Rather, this perspective facilitates an ongoing investigation of the *changes over time* that are observed among samples of maltreated children, and attempts to account for these changes on the basis of both global (e.g., socioeconomic and normative factors affecting all children) and more specific (e.g., type of maltreatment; child and family resources) intervening variables.

The origins of such a framework can be attributed to early clinical and research studies of abused children that reported a high frequency of conduct problems and developmental delays (e.g., Elmer & Gregg, 1967; B. Johnson & Morse, 1968; Kempe & Kempe, 1978). These initial reports led to controlled studies of abused and nonabused infant characteristics, parent–child interactions, and parent and teacher descriptions, in order to determine whether the behavior of abused children (i.e., academic, social, affective, or cognitive aspects of behavior) was distinguishable from their nonabused counterparts. One of the biggest challenges in such research, however, continues to be the difficulty in separating the effects of child maltreatment from the more generic effects on child development arising from abnormal child care (e.g., social isolation, poor prenatal and infant care, and insufficient sensory stimulation) that often accompany abuse and neglect (Green, 1978). Thus, at the present time it is uncertain that child abuse and neglect per se are responsible for developmental impairments; a more cautious statement would be that abuse and neglect are associated with a wide range of developmental deviations (to be discussed below) to such an extent as to warrant assessment and intervention services that curtail both the maltreatment *and* the concomitant environmental/family factors (e.g., insufficient stimulation, economic instability, marital conflict) that are suspected to impair child development.

Infancy

The quality of infant–caregiver attachment is believed to be the product of characteristic styles of mutual interaction over the first year of life (Ainsworth, 1980), involving such parental characteristics as sensitivity and responsiveness to the infant's needs and signals in relation to the infant's temperament and self-regulation (i.e., sleep, feeding, and arousal patterns; Belsky & Isabella, in press; Crittenden & Bonvillian, 1984; Sroufe & Fleeson, 1986). The security or quality of the attachment relationship has been linked to the child's emerging mastery of his or her social and physical environment, and thus secure attachment is seen as promoting a high level of capabilities, goals, and actions throughout development (Schneider-Rosen & Cicchetti, 1984). Because abusive family environments are often characterized by physical and emotional rejection, harsh treatment, insensitivity, and verbal assaults, researchers have been interested in how the developing parent–child interactions may be affected under such adverse circumstances (Aber & Cicchetti, 1984; Ainsworth, 1980; Egeland & Farber, 1984; Egeland & Sroufe, 1981).

Attachment is assessed during an unfamiliar task (i.e., the "strange situation" task, whereby a 12- to 18-month-old infant's exploration of a novel environment in the presence of the mother, reaction to separation from the mother, and reunion with the mother are observed), and two patterns of insecure attachment have been identified. Anxious–avoidant infants explore with little affective interaction in preseparation episodes, treat the mother and stranger similarly, and avoid the mother upon reunion, whereas anxious–resistant infants show little exploration and often struggle, cry, or become rigid when comforted. Evidence suggests that anxiously attached infants may be less easy to care for than other infants, and, in turn, their mothers have been found to be less sensitive and less responsive to their infants' cues (e.g., Egeland & Farber, 1984).

The results of recent comparative and prospective studies indicate that child maltreatment during infancy is associated with insecure attachment relationships with the caregiver (Die-

trich, Starr, & Kaplan, 1980; Egeland & Sroufe, 1981; Egeland & Vaughn, 1981; Schneider-Rosen & Cicchetti, 1984). Infants in these studies who had been abused or neglected by their mothers were significantly more likely than controls to cling to their mothers and/or to display negative affect (e.g., screaming, fear, muscle rigidity). Researchers have speculated that maltreatment during infancy produces an insecure attachment over a period of time that adversely affects the child's later intellectual and socioemotional development (Ainsworth, 1980; Steinhauer, 1983). These conclusions are supported by several well-designed prospective investigations that have begun to link early problems in attachment to patterns of declining developmental abilities over the first 2 years of life (e.g., Egeland & Farber, 1984; Egeland & Sroufe, 1981). Moreover, sex differences may interact with caretaking behavior to produce greater risk to some children, as suggested by the results of a recent study with maltreated infants: Male infants tended to be more vulnerable to caretaking differences (such as maternal sensitivity and responsiveness), whereas female infants appeared to be more vulnerable to stressful life events than males (Egeland & Farber, 1984). These suggestive findings delineate the importance of the early parent–child relationships, and further indicate possible beginnings of parent–child conflict, such as parental avoidance or lack of contingent responding to infant demands (Patterson, 1982; Wahler & Dumas, 1986a), parental failure to provide stimulation and comfort to the infant (Egeland & Sroufe, 1981), and infant characteristics that interact with parental ability (Frodi, 1981).

Early studies of abused infants linked child abuse to handicapping conditions, such as mental retardation, perinatal problems, prematurity, and physical anomalies, which were believed to increase stress upon the parent (see Friedrich & Boriskin, 1976, and Frodi, 1981, for reviews). However, a careful analysis of prospective data indicates that the role of such conditions may have been overemphasized (Egeland et al., 1980; Starr, Dietrich, Fischhoff, Ceresnie, & Zweier, 1984). What has emerged from these studies is a less obvious association between handicapping conditions and abuse: Minor deviations in child behavior (e.g., poor motor coordination, slow language development, being less affectionate), rather than major handicaps, are more often related to the occurrence of abuse (Starr *et al.*, 1984). It is speculated that the parent of a noticeably handicapped child will more often attribute problems to the handicap than will a parent with an infant who appears physically normal. For example, the parent of a child who appears normal but shows subtle deviations in behavior and development may be more likely to attribute problems to things that the child can control, and perhaps may be more likely to blame the child and use punishment to control behavior. This perspective may also relate to the evidence that a significant number of abused infants are treated for a variety of physical illnesses (e.g., coughs, fever, digestive problems) more often than controls (Sherrod, O'Connor, Vietze, & Altemeier, 1984). Such children may be prone to illnesses (a minor handicapping condition) that are not recognized by their parents as minor developmental impairments, and such illnesses become a further source of stress on the parents.

Early Childhood

Early childhood (ages 2–5) includes a period of child development that is commonly considered to be very demanding of caretakers' time, energy, and patience. Preschool children are generally described by their parents as being difficult to control, overly active, and attention-seeking (Achenbach, 1966), all of which can place them in jeopardy of harsh parental treatment or physical abuse (Stevens-Long, 1973). This risk is confirmed by the figures from nationwide incidence studies relating type of maltreatment to children's ages: 60% of major physical injuries were accounted for by children under age 4 (American Humane Association, 1984). Related to risk of physical harm are concerns about the possible long-range impairments that may result from maltreatment during this period of rapid development. The preschooler's cognitive, emotional, and behavioral development requires a nurturant, supportive environment in order to maximize the child's abilities (e.g., verbal and physical responsivity, predictable adult behavior, and limits on the range of permissible child behavior; Carew, 1979), and for this reason child abuse researchers have focused attention upon the abused preschooler's development across a wide range of cognitive and behavioral indicators.

Studies have found that abused preschool children are significantly more likely than peers to show developmental delays, especially in areas related to cognitive development, language acquisition, and the ability to discriminate emotions in others (Appelbaum, 1977; Barahal, Waterman, & Martin, 1981; Friedrich, Einbender, & Luecke, 1983; Frodi & Smetana, 1984; Hoffman-Plotkin & Twentyman, 1984; Main & George, 1984; Sandgrund, Gaines, & Green, 1974). For example, both abused and neglected children had significantly lower scores on all measures of cognitive functioning (i.e., the Stanford–Binet Intelligence Scale, the Peabody Picture Vocabulary Test, and the Merrill–Palmer Scale of Mental Tests) than a matched sample of nonabused children, with an average difference of approximately 20 IQ points (Hoffman-Plotkin & Twentyman, 1984). Lower intellectual functioning may account for the differences in moral and social judgment (e.g., ability to judge the allocation of limited resources, seriousness of punishment, and fairness of rules) shown by some maltreated children, although no firm conclusions can be drawn at this time (Frodi & Smetana, 1984; Smetana, Kelly, & Twentyman, 1984).

Studies of maltreated children's social behavior with peers and adults have found that abused preschool children direct more aggression toward peers (George & Main, 1979; Hoffman-Plotkin & Twentyman, 1984; Sandgrund *et al.*, 1974), and may show a complex array of social behaviors indicative of poor self-control, distractibility, and negative emotion (e.g., low enthusiasm, verbal and physical resistance to directions; Egeland, Sroufe, & Erickson, 1983; Gaensbauer & Sands, 1979). These results are consistent with parent and teacher reports of their children's social immaturity and poor readiness to learn (Hoffman-Plotkin & Twentyman, 1984).

Neglected preschoolers, on the other hand, have been observed as being more socially avoidant (Hoffman-Plotkin & Twentyman, 1984), and seem to have the most difficulty in dealing with challenging tasks or interpersonal situations, in comparison to abused and normal children (Egeland *et al.*, 1983). Although it would be premature to draw firm conclusions, these early findings suggest that neglected preschoolers are relatively inactive and deficient in social skills (i.e., show low rates of verbal and physical interactions with peers and adults) as compared to normal peers, and that abused preschoolers are more overactive and disruptive. As a further example, Herrenkohl, Herrenkohl, Toedter, and Yanushefski (1984) found that children who were victims of neglect ($n = 78$) differed from their normal comparison sample only in their rate of talking to the observer in the home (i.e., no differences were found in rates of task involvement, negative behaviors, visual behaviors, and positive affect). Child victims of abuse ($n = 54$) or combined abuse and neglect ($n = 50$), in contrast, were rated by observers as being less involved in the task, more destructive with objects, and more hostile with other family members (however, actual *rates* of difficult child behavior did not differ among the maltreated and normal samples). Whether these behavioral differences can be attributed to abuse or neglect per se remains an open question. Common factors shared by these children include family instability, marital discord, and socioeconomic disadvantage (to name but a few), which may be the major ingredients affecting the cognitive and behavioral development of children from violent or dysfunctional families (Emery, 1982; Wolfe, Jaffe, Wilson, & Zak, 1985; Wolfe & Mosk, 1983).

Middle Childhood

Significant indicators of developmental delay or deviation among school-age abused children, such as academic failure or peer relationship problems, have been a primary concern. Although few studies have used appropriate comparison groups, the results of a recent investigation document some of the developmental impairments among school-age maltreated children in relation to their peers. Salzinger, Kaplan, Pelcovitz, Samit, and Kreiger (1984) assessed academic and intellectual performance and also obtained parent and teacher behavior ratings for a sample of physically abused ($n = 30$, including mixed forms of maltreatment such as emotional abuse), neglected ($n = 26$), and non-maltreated ($n = 48$) children, matched on age and socioeconomic status. Comparisons on standard achievement tests and current grades found the maltreated group to be poorer in their academic standing than controls. A significantly larger percentage of children in the maltreated sample were 2 years below grade level in verbal abilities (27% vs. 9% for controls) and math abilities (33% vs. 3%), and approximately one-third of the children in the maltreated sample were failing one or more subjects and/or placed in a special class. Although separate analyses were not conducted for the abused and neglected children in the sample,

the results with this heterogeneous group indicate that children raised in maltreating families show disturbances of function in a number of ways during school years. Interestingly, not only the children who had been targets of abuse and neglect performed more poorly in academic work; their siblings (who were an average of 2 years older) were at comparably below-average levels of academic performance. This study reiterates the concern that all of the children in families reported for child maltreatment may be at risk for developmental impairments as a result of endemic social and family factors associated with abuse and neglect (e.g., marital discord, school absenteeism, lack of social supports; Belsky, 1980; Salzinger *et al.*, 1984; Wolfe & Mosk, 1983).

Regarding the behavioral adjustment of school-age abused children, some intriguing yet inconclusive findings have been reported. Several studies using observational coding systems and comparison groups have found that abused children exhibit high rates of aggressive and aversive behaviors, such as yelling, hitting, and destructiveness, when interacting in the home with their parents (Bousha & Twentyman, 1984; Lorber, Felton, & Reid, 1984; Reid, Taplin, & Lorber, 1981). Such findings are in accord with a social learning viewpoint on child abuse (e.g., Friedman *et al.*, 1981; Patterson, 1982; Reid *et al.*, 1981) in suggesting that children who present high rates of discipline problems are more likely to be physically abused than those who do not. However, an exception to this finding was reported by Burgess and Conger (1978), who found that abused children did not behave significantly different from controls (using methodology similar to that of the studies cited above). To account for these conflicting results, studies need to control for the influence of sample characteristics (e.g., clinic-referred problem families who are abusive vs. a random sample of detected abuse cases), child characteristics (e.g., younger children may display more difficult behavior during observations than older children; male children may show higher rates of aggression, etc., than female children), and situational variables (e.g., structured interactional tasks that "pull" for parent–child conflict vs. naturalistic observations without tasks). Moreover, these data on rates of behavior are relevant to abused children only, due to the limited investigation of neglected school-age children.

In contrast with observational data, parent,

teacher, and child report measures of behavior problems (e.g., destructiveness, fighting with siblings) consistently indicate that the abused school-age child is *perceived* as more difficult to manage, less socially mature, and less capable of developing trust with others (Herrenkohl et al., 1984; Kinard, 1980; Salzinger et al., 1984; Wolfe & Mosk, 1983). Interestingly, one study also found that whereas the maltreated children were rated as equally disturbing by parents and teachers, the parents also rated the *nontargeted siblings* as highly disturbing (a finding that was inconsistent with teacher reports). This finding led the researchers to speculate that maltreating parents may have a lower threshold for considering children's behavior to be disturbing, and/or that the target child may show only some very specific behaviors that serve to trigger abuse, which are very difficult to identify through limited clinic and home observations (Salzinger et al., 1984). On the basis of parent and teacher reports, however, vicitimized children do not appear to fit any clinical "pattern" that can be associated with maltreatment; rather, they may exhibit a wide range of both typical problems (e.g., distractibility, overactivity) and unusual behaviors (e.g., hoarding food, self-injury; Green, 1978). This suggests that the intensity, duration, frequency, and type of maltreatment may interact with such child factors as IQ and social development, and such situational variables as removal of the child from the home, to affect different aspects of development.

Adolescence and Adulthood

Most of the controlled studies on the consequences of abuse and neglect have been limited to short-term effects (e.g., the children were assessed within a year of the discovery of maltreatment). More recently, however, several retrospective and longitudinal studies of these child populations have begun to document a moderately strong association between childhood maltreatment and adjustment problems appearing during adolescence. Not surprisingly, this relationship is strongest among samples drawn from delinquent populations, where several authors have noted that the most striking factor distinguishing violent from nonviolent delinquents is the amount of violence in the violent delinquents' past (Lewis, Pincus, & Glaser, 1979; Loeber, Weisman, & Reid, 1983; Tarter, Hegedus, Winsten, & Alterman, 1984).

To illustrate this relationship, Tarter et al. (1984) dichotomized the crimes of delinquents referred by juvenile court according to whether or not they were assaultive, and discovered that 44% of the abused delinquents ($n = 27$) versus 16% of the nonabused delinquents ($n = 74$) committed violent crimes of an assaultive nature.

In addition to these data based upon clinical and/or delinquent populations and retrospective accounts of maltreatment, the New York State Select Committee on Child Abuse (Alfaro, 1981) undertook an empirical study based on the official records of child protective agencies and courts across the state during the period between 1950 and 1972. One large sample ($n = 5,136$) of the children was examined to determine which direction they went after their contact with the child protective services system, while a second sample ($n = 1,963$) was examined to see from which direction they had come before their contact with the juvenile justice system. The findings confirmed an empirical relationship between child abuse and juvenile delinquency or ungovernability (e.g., truancy, runaways), and revealed the striking significance of family violence in the perpetuation of antisocial behavior. That is, approximately 50% of the families reported for abuse or neglect (averaged over eight counties) had at least one child who later appeared in court as delinquent or ungovernable. Furthermore, delinquent children who were reported as abused or neglected tended to be more violent than other delinquents, according to the nature of their court offenses.

Similar findings were reported in a 40-year longitudinal study of 232 males from violent and nonviolent low-income families (McCord, 1979, 1983). After careful tracing of records, the author found that 22% of the abused ($n = 49$), 23% of the neglected ($n = 48$), and 50% of the rejected ($n = 34$) boys (i.e., cases in which the parents demonstrated repeated displeasure with the boys, but they were not abused or neglected) had been later convicted for serious juvenile crimes such as theft, auto theft, burglary, or assault, compared to 11% of the boys from demographically similar normal families ($n = 101$). Whereas each of the three groups differed from the normal group (but not from one another) in terms of juvenile crime, their rates of alcoholism, divorce, and occupational success were all similar. Among the 97 abused or neglected children, however, 44 (45%) either had become criminal, alcoholic, or mentally ill or had died before reaching age 35. Those who showed these signs of juvenile and adult maladjustment also tended to have alcoholic or criminal parents and to have been aggressive during childhood, whereas among the remaining 53 adjusted boys (55%), maternal education and self-confidence were significant correlates of favorable development. In speculating on these findings, it is interesting to consider that this ratio of 45% maladjusted to 55% adjusted adults who were victims of childhood abuse or neglect is a gross indication of the prevalence of negative versus positive adjustment outcomes subsequent to childhood victimization.

While data indicate that childhood abuse is clearly implicated in later antisocial behavior, the mechanisms underlying this relationship have not been clarified empirically. One explanation for the suspected relationship between abuse during early and middle childhood and subsequent adjustment is offered in a study by Herzberger, Potts, and Dillon (1981), who posited that abused children may develop distorted or maladaptive perceptions of parental characteristics, discipline techniques, and emotional acceptance–rejection that affect their subsequent behavior. Interviews were conducted with 14 boys (ages 8–14 years) who had been abused previously and were living in a residential group home. These children had been removed from their parents (and abusive treatment) for an average of 2½ years, and they were compared to 10 males living in the same group home who had not been abused (this sample was matched on IQ, age, months of residence in group home, and months since residence with principal caretakers). The study found that, relative to controls, abused children described their abusive parents in more negative terms and generally believed that their treatment was more emotionally rejecting (i.e., when asked whether or not their parents cared about them, gave them a lot of love, and liked having them around). There was also wide variability in the children's perceptions of their parents and treatment, further indicating that children's interpretations of abusive incidents are important to consider. The authors postulate that seeing abuse as an indicant of *parental rejection* may have more harmful effects on child development than perceiving abuse as being caused by the parents' externally imposed frustrations (e.g., difficult child behavior), because children actively construct a view of their social environment and then respond according to this construction

(Ausubel *et al.*, 1954, cited in Herzberger *et al.*, 1981).

Further causal hypotheses relating child maltreatment to subsequent juvenile crimes and adult maladjustment are suggested by some laboratory (e.g., Bandura, 1973) and field studies (e.g., Loeber *et al.*, 1983) of childhood aggression; these have indicated that perceiving aggression as a legitimate means of resolving conflicts (e.g., parental acceptance and approval of violence in the home) increases the likelihood that the child will model aggression in other social contexts. Combining these theoretical and empirical findings addressing the long-term impact of child maltreatment, therefore, leads one to surmise that abuse and delinquency may be products of a common family environment of which violence is a trademark (Straus *et al.*, 1980); yet the factors that moderate the impact of violence on later outcomes are poorly understood at present (Garmezy & Rutter, 1983; Wolfe *et al.*, 1985).

Summary and Assessment Implications

The perspective on chronically abused and neglected children presented herein has focused upon the wide range of developmental changes and deviations that have been documented among this diverse population. This developmental viewpoint embraces the subtly interacting conditions that work in combination either to attenuate the effects of powerful traumatic events or to turn a minor developmental crisis into a major impairment (Lipsett, 1983). Accordingly, the evidence related to infant–caregiver attachment has revealed that maltreatment during infancy is strongly associated with characteristics of anxious attachment (e.g., clinging, rigidity, withdrawal), which may, over time, adversely affect the child's intellectual and socioemotional development. Similarly, preschool-age abused children have been shown in studies to be more difficult to manage and to have more marked developmental delays in language, self-control, and peer interactions than non-clinic-referred samples of children. Studies of abused school-age children concur with those of younger children, finding that such children often have significant learning and motivational problems at school, as well as a higher rate of aggressive and destructive behavior. Finally, studies of chronically abused children who have reached adolescence have confirmed a correlational relationship between abuse and juvenile crime that exceeds the variance accounted for by family socioeconomic factors alone.

Two issues that have not been adequately addressed in the literature to date concern the differences between abuse and neglect and the differential impact upon girls and boys over the course of development. Although data reveal that child neglect is more prevalent than physical abuse, it has received far less attention from researchers. Wolock and Horowitz (1984) illustrate this state of affairs by documenting the ratio of studies on physical abuse to those on neglect: A computer search of the Social Science Citation Index Data Base in 1983 revealed 662 citations with "child abuse" in the title, compared with only 23 titles containing "child neglect." A similar analysis of titles of papers presented at the Fourth National Conference on Child Abuse and Neglect showed that 43% contained "abuse" alone, 27 "abuse and neglect" and 3% "neglect" alone (Wolock & Horowitz, 1984). These authors cite historical precedents (e.g., media interest, political priorities) and the relation between neglect and poverty as major reasons for the de-emphasis on neglect relative to abuse. As reflected by this state of the literature, very little is known about the developmental impairments subsequent to prolonged neglect. The present review found only a handful of empirical studies of neglected children, who were predominantly of preschool age. The preliminary conclusions drawn from these studies focused on the neglected children's socially avoidant behavior (e.g., isolation from peers) and their delays in cognitive development (e.g., difficulty in dealing with challenging tasks or interpersonal interactions).

Investigations of sex differences in reference to maltreatment are even rarer in the literature. This is perhaps due to the small sample sizes necessitated by most studies, which prohibit subsample analyses. However, such differences have played an important part in understanding children's adjustment in the related areas of family violence (Jaffe, Wolfe, Wilson, & Zak, 1986), divorce (Emery, 1982), and family stress (Rutter, 1971). That is to say, boys appear to be more vulnerable to the effects of stress in the family (Rutter, 1983). On the other hand, children's age has been shown to be less of a factor in explaining differential adjustment to family stressors (cf. Rutter, 1983). Although we do not know from studies of abused children

whether a child's age or developmental level can interact with the onset of abuse to produce a differential pattern of adjustment, a cautious conclusion that can be drawn from the developmental perspective of abuse presented herein is that the *chronicity* (including intensity, severity, and type) and *early onset* of maltreatment are the most important factors affecting developmental outcome.

As noted throughout this section, the effects upon children's development of accompanying family and social factors, such as marital conflict, low income, and spousal violence, as well as lack of knowledge of causal relationships, prohibit drawing any firm conclusions as to the impact of child maltreatment per se on development. This precaution is highlighted by findings from an 8-year follow-up study of 17 abused children, which employed carefully matched comparison groups to control for sociodemographic and medical factors (Elmer, 1977). Clinical assessments of speech problems, school performance, physical and neurological development, and self-concept revealed a high level of dysfunction present across *all* groups of children; yet no significant differences emerged between abused and nonabused children. The author concluded that lower-class status may adversely influence child development as powerfully as abuse does. Disturbances in abused children's social and behavioral development, according to this reasoning, may be partially a function of the "fallout" from family discord and disadvantage, where physical abuse is one frequent concomitant (Gil, 1970; Wolfe & Mosk, 1983). Behavioral assessment of maltreated children, therefore, must take into careful consideration the interacting family, individual, and contextual factors (elaborated on in the following section) that modulate the impact of negative events upon child development.

A BEHAVIORAL ANALYSIS OF CHILD ABUSE AND NEGLECT

While findings from studies of abusive families have originated from discrepant theoretical viewpoints (e.g., psychiatric, sociological, and social-interactional; see Parke & Collmer, 1975), they contribute collectively to a comprehensive data base that brings investigators closer to understanding the major interactive and functional components. From amalgamated clinical and developmental research findings and conceptual models from work with distressed (e.g., Patterson, 1976; Wahler, 1976) and normal (e.g., Belsky, 1984; Garbarino, 1982) families, a social-interactional model of child abuse that stresses the dynamic interplay among individual, family, and social factors has been formulated (Belsky, 1980, 1984; Burgess, 1979; Friedman *et al.*, 1981; Gambrill, 1983; Parke & Collmer, 1975; Reid *et al.*, 1981; Starr, 1979; Vasta, 1982). This interactive-systems model is aimed at understanding abusive behavior in relation to both past (e.g., exposure to parental violence during childhood) and present (e.g., a screaming child) contextual events that affect the parent–child relationship. Within this framework, theories of abuse can be viewed as differing primarily with respect to the emphasis given to particular elements in the system as the principal "cause" of abuse (Wolfe, 1985a). The behavioral assessment of child abuse and neglect, therefore, may actually reflect a combination of (1) methods for analyzing elements within a comprehensive systems model with (2) assumptions about how the elements interact and their relative importance *vis-à-vis* changing the system. Important concerns that underlie the social-interactional model of child abuse include the following (after Burgess, 1979):

1. Abusive parents often lack the skills and resources necessary to cope effectively with child rearing and other stressful life demands (e.g., unemployment, crowded housing, and constant child attention). Ineffective parenting may, in turn, lead to a greater number of child behavior problems, which progressively serve to increase parental stress and poor coping.

2. In recognition of the range and intensity of identified problems among abused children, this model is concerned with the characteristics of the child that may be contributing to and/or maintaining the parent's maladaptive and/or abusive behavior.

3. Child maltreatment is a private and illegal act that occurs at a relatively low frequency, making it difficult to observe and study directly. Therefore, less extreme, routine interactions are studied (e.g., parental commands, criticisms, and types of punishers; child demands, aversive behavior, and prosocial behavior). An important assumption arising from this approach to low-frequency behavior is that there is continuity between everyday interactions and extreme violence or neglect. The validity of observational measures thus rests on a construct (i.e., the expression of annoyance and aggres-

sion), and this construct is very difficult to define. Abusive family members do interact with significantly more negative and hostile behaviors (e.g., criticisms, grabbing, threats) on an everyday basis than do nonabusive families (Wolfe, 1985b); yet the predictive and discriminative validity of such measures has not been fully established. By far the most commonly employed techniques for studying aggression in the laboratory are those based upon a crucial deception in which participants are led to believe that they can somehow harm another person when in fact they cannot (Baron, 1977; Zillman, 1979). Clearly, such methods of direct experimentation and concomitant measures of verbal or physical aggression are unsuitable for assessing abusive families.

4. While abuse would appear to be a specific action between a parent and a single child, it is the case that such episodes are embedded within a network of family events. Therefore, it is necessary to study the entire family.

5. A functional analysis of child abuse and neglect must include conceptually distinct levels of individual, family, and environmental factors. This involves investigation of critical antecedents, significant historical or developmental characteristics of the parent and child, the nature of the aggressive act, the consequences that maintain such behavior, the nature of the family context, and the larger social system in which maltreatment occurs.

6. This paradigm is based upon evidence that child abuse, like other forms of intrafamilial violence, is seldom due to some extremely abnormal or pathological influence. On the contrary, child abuse is viewed as the culmination of interrelated events both within and outside of the family. This argument provides the major basis for studying abusive behavior within the multilevel context of individual, family, and societal events. These events may be extreme forms of things that all families may experience to some degree.

A major implication of this conceptual model is that child abuse and neglect are seldom related to any particular event or to any parent or child attribute. Rather, they are viewed as the product of multiple factors that potentiate one another in the absence of compensatory, protective factors or buffers (Cicchetti & Rizley, 1981). As an illustration of the social-interactional model of abuse, consider such common problems shown by young children as crying, whining, screaming, and noncompliance. When faced with these annoying behaviors, a parent may not be capable of dealing with them other than through the use of physical punishment or verbal threats (the methods most familiar to him or her). Under normal circumstances, the parent may be able to deal with the situation without becoming overly irritated or violent. However, hostile aggression (i.e., abuse) is more likely to occur if the parent is emotionally "aroused" (Baron, 1977; Berkowitz, 1983), such as when he or she has had an encounter with an angry neighbor earlier in the day that has left the parent feeling tense and upset (feelings that he or she may not necessarily recognize or admit). At this point, the risk of overreacting or abusing the child increases, especially if the parent is unaware of the source of extraneous arousal and misattributes it to the provocation—that is, the child's crying or noncompliance (Averill, 1982). As discussed by Patterson and Cobb (1973), physical punishment may "work," or it may lead over time to a standoff between the parent and child, forcing the parent to increase the severity of his or her punishment and the child to escalate his or her aversiveness.

The following discussion reviews the data regarding several key components in the functional analysis of child abuse that are relevant to behavioral assessment, including precursors, parent characteristics, response topography, and major consequences. Distinctions between abuse and neglect are made wherever findings are available, although the bulk of the data addresses physical abuse only. Reference to child characteristics presented previously are included in this analysis.

Precursors to Child Abuse and Neglect

Until recently, most data regarding antecedents to child maltreatment have consisted of broad descriptions of sociodemographic conditions (e.g., Gil, 1970) or clinical reports of the apparent relationship between noxious child behavior and subsequent abuse by the parent (e.g., Kempe & Kempe, 1978). In recent years, the specific circumstances surrounding the occurrence of child abuse and neglect have received greater attention (Herrenkohl et al., 1983; Kadushin & Martin, 1981). These circumstances can be clustered into two conceptually important categories of antecedents: (1) proximal events that may have precipitated the incident, and (2)

distal events that are associated indirectly with maltreatment.

Proximal Events

Child behavior has been implicated as a major factor in triggering abusive episodes. Existing evidence suggests that abusive incidents occur most often during difficult, but not uncommon, episodes of child behavior. In such contexts, aversive child behavior, such as crying, may produce anger and tension in some adults that contributes to aggressive responding (Frodi & Lamb, 1980; Vasta, 1982; Wolfe, Fairbank, Kelly, & Bradlyn, 1983). For example, Kadushin and Martin (1981) identified several immediate precursors to abuse in their large-scale study, such as aggressive behavior, (21%), unspecified child misbehavior (16%), and lying and stealing (9%). A related study of 825 official case records of physical abuse incidents further revealed that abuse was most often associated with oppositional child behaviors, such as refusal, fighting and arguing, accidental occurrences, immoral behavior, dangerous behavior, the child's sexual behavior, and inconveniences due to the child (Herrenkohl et al., 1983). Interestingly, this latter study also revealed that circumstances preceding incidences of *neglect* were characterized more by chronic adult inadequacy (i.e., refusing to meet family needs, inadequate adult supervision, parent's lack of knowledge, inappropriate use of medical facilities, unsafe home environment, and child's dangerous behavior) than by child misbehavior. These findings on the abused child, in particular, are consistent with the interactive model of abuse that stresses the child's contribution to his or her own maltreatment through misbehavior. However, it should be emphasized that the child is not *responsible* for the assault in a legalistic or moralistic sense. Child abuse remains primarily a parental act in which the child is the major victim.

Adult conflict, another suspected powerful antecedent of abuse, has received considerable attention in recent studies. In a major nationwide study, Straus et al. (1980) found that marital disharmony and violence were significantly associated with higher rates of severe violence toward children (the authors estimated that in approximately 40% of the families where the adults were violent toward each other, there was also violence toward a child at some point during a 12-month period). Concurrently, recent findings in the marital and child clinical literature have documented the relationship between adult conflict and increased child behavior problems (Bond & McMahon, 1984; Emery, 1982, Griest & Wells, 1983; Porter & O'Leary, 1980; Wolfe et al., 1985). This is not surprising, in that the escalation of emotional arousal and/or physical aggression that accompanies conflicts between adults (e.g., Levenson & Gottman, 1983) can easily carry over to interactions with children. The child may be caught in the "crossfire" between his or her parents (or other adults in the home), or he or she may precipitate a marital conflict by creating a stress on either or both parents (e.g., disobeying the mother by claiming that the father gave permission). Subsequently, child injuries may occur during attempts to interrupt the fighting, escape from the situation, or continue with routine activities (e.g., finishing dinner, watching television).

Distal Events

Although child- and adult-related conflicts are common antecedents of reported child abuse cases, it is clear that such events account for only a small, albeit significant, percentage of the total variance associated with child abuse (on the order of 6%; Herrenkohl et al., 1983). In addition to proximal events that are directly linked to a particular abusive incident, an understanding of abuse must take into account many contextual factors that are suspected to be indirect precursors to abusive situations. Although such distal variables are numerous, research has pointed to several as particularly important.

Socioeconomic stress—that is, factors associated with poverty and with inadequate physical resources and social support systems—has been documented as the single most influential aggregated variable contributing to child abuse and neglect (Gil, 1970; Pelton, 1978). In one major study (Garbarino, 1976), socioeconomic factors accounted for 36% of the variance in rates of child abuse in Pennsylvania. Unemployment (Light, 1973), restricted educational and occupational opportunities (Gil, 1970), unstable and/or violent family situations (Straus et al., 1980), and similar disadvantages (e.g., housing, privacy, noise levels, and pollution levels) often associated with lower-social-class membership have emerged as major sociocultural factors influencing rates of child abuse in

North America. The suspicion that various aspects of the physical environment can indirectly affect aggressive behavior has been supported by several experimental studies that are relevant to the study of child abuse. For example, heat (Baron, 1978), noise (Donnerstein & Wilson, 1976), and air pollution or ionization (Baron, Russell, & Arms, 1985) have all been found to influence aggressive behavior. Given the general pervasiveness and unremitting nature of socioeconomic stressors, they certainly warrant attention in any assessment of abuse, in that they often exert a major influence upon choice and outcome of family treatment (Blechman et al., 1981; Wahler, 1980).

The perspective that emerges from a consideration of proximal and distal setting events is that child abuse may be understood as a special case of aggression, in which child behavior often represents an immediate aversive stimulus that precipitates adult aggression (Averill, 1982; Knutson, 1978). This perspective also recognizes the significance of contextual factors, such as crowded housing, ambient noise level, and socioeconomic disadvantages, that contribute to the uncontrolled expression of aggression in the family. Although such precursors of abuse are highly relevant to our understanding of the problem, the question remains as to why only a relatively small percentage of adults exhibit such behavior in the presence of these common aversive events. To answer this question, a consideration of parent and situational characteristics that may serve to accent or buffer the impact of such events is required.

Parent Characteristics

Interest in child abusers' psychological functioning has been strong over the past two decades, despite a lack of consistent findings in regard to distinctive personality attributes or serious emotional disturbance among this population (Parke & Collmer, 1975; Spinetta & Rigler, 1972; Starr, 1979). Recent data from studies comparing abusive and nonabusive parents continue to challenge earlier assumptions of major character disorder (cf. Spinetta & Rigler, 1972), such as poor impulse control, inadequate or immature personality, bipolar affective disorders, or antisocial personality. Child abuse is best described as a pattern of behavior rather than as a psychiatric diagnosis (Steele & Pollock, 1968). Behavior patterns that are situation-specific, such as dealing with aversive child behavior, problem solving with other family members, and handling chronic levels of stress, appear to define this population more accurately (Wolfe, 1985a). In the following discussion of abusive parents, a synopsis of research findings is presented that covers the major adult factors associated with child abuse: (1) the parent's prior childhood experiences and history; (2) personality attributes and behaviors; (3) knowledge and perceptions of children; (4) perceived social supports; and (5) other characteristics, such as intelligence and substance abuse.

Childhood Experiences

There has been a great deal of interest in the abuser's early family experiences, since prior abuse and family violence are believed to perpetuate a cycle of violence across generations (Straus et al., 1980). Retrospective studies of abusers and violent delinquents provide the most consistent empirical support for the conclusion that abusive parents have themselves often been exposed to violence as children (Lewis et al., 1979; Monane, Leichter, & Lewis, 1984; Tarter et al., 1984). Violence in one's family background is often cited as a strong predictor of future violent behavior (Standing Senate Committee on Health, Welfare, & Science, 1980).

It must be noted, however, that only a small minority (less than 15%) of adults who were abused as children were themselves found to be abusive toward their own children (as defined by parental methods used to discipline or resolve conflicts) in one nationwide study that involved interviews with hundreds of randomly selected American families (Straus et al., 1980). A number of positive influences, such as supportive adults within and outside of the family, siblings, and successful school achievement, may serve over time to moderate the effect of abuse or other stressors in childhood (Rutter, 1979); therefore, we should exercise caution in weighing the significance of this factor in isolation. Also, the long-term effects of physical abuse and neglect must be considered in relation to concomitant psychological injuries to the child that can be most damaging, such as rejection, lack of affection, and exposure to dangerous situations (e.g., strangers in the home, poor supervision; Herrenkohl et al., 1984), as well as events outside of the family (e.g., aggressive and delinquent peers; Fagan & Wexler, 1984).

Personality Attributes and Behavior

In relation to psychological functioning, abusive parents have been described in various studies as exhibiting a myriad of symptoms and pathological traits, such as unmet dependency needs (Steele & Pollock, 1968), lack of identity (Steele & Pollock, 1968), and impaired impulse control (see Parke & Collmer, 1975, and Spinetta & Rigler, 1972, for reviews). However tempting it has been to view child abuse as a general personality or impulse disorder, evidence has failed to support this conclusion thus far. This is not to imply that abusers are asymptomatic or psychologically well adjusted; they often report elevated physical and emotional symptoms, such as dissatisfaction, irritation, and physical health problems (Conger, Burgess, & Barrett, 1979; Lahey, Conger, Atkeson, & Treiber, 1984; Mash, Johnston, & Kovitz, 1983), which most likely impair their functioning as parents. However, when abusers have been compared to matched controls, most studies have failed to detect symptoms of such severity or magnitude as to be indicative of psychiatric disorder (e.g., Gaines, Sandgrund, Green, & Power, 1978; Spinetta, 1978; Starr, 1982).

An alternative explanation (to psychiatric disturbance) of the relationship between parental adjustment and child abuse focuses upon those parental characteristics that are related, both specifically and globally, to the child-rearing role (Wolfe, 1985a). That is to say, the above-mentioned psychological and physical symptoms noted among abusive parents may reflect the parents' inability to tolerate or cope with the amount of stress impinging upon them from many child-related and non-child-related sources. This is reflected in the finding that abusive parents report *levels* of stress similar to those reported by nonabusive parents; yet they rate the *impact* of these stressors more severely than controls (Wolfe, 1985a). Unfortunately, we are far from understanding the relative importance of individual factors (e.g., IQ, sex, sensitivity to stimulation) that may account for differences in adaptation to stressful environmental demands (Rutter, 1983). Nonetheless, a systems perspective on the interaction among contextual factors, child situations, and parental symptomatology provides guidance for assessing abusive behavior from multiple sources and for avoiding an overreliance upon psychopathology as the "cause" of such aberrant behavior. Moreover, instruments designed to detect psychiatric symptomatology, while important in the clinical assessment of some abusive parents, may be inadequate or inappropriate for assessing more situation-specific disturbances in the parent–child relationship, such as those encountered during disciplinary or instructional situations.

Knowledge and Perceptions of Children

Attention has also been given to the possible role of parental expectations and perceptions concerning child development, child behavior, and the parenting role. Interest in developmental milestones and norms has stemmed from the idea that parental expectations that are inaccurate or incomplete will lead the parent to believe that a young child is performing at a level that is less than expected. This may result in frequent punishment by the parent, because the child will seldom be capable of meeting such age-inappropriate expectations. However, recent evidence suggests that the notion of a preexisting deficit in knowledge of child development among abusive parents has not been strongly supported in the literature (Kravitz & Driscoll, 1983; Wolfe, 1985a). This may be so because studies have chosen to operationalize "unrealistic expectations" by assessing parents' knowledge of developmental milestones; such assessment does not fully take into account the complexity of interactions with the child (e.g., facial expressions, voice tone, context) that contribute to behavioral outcome (Azar, Robinson, Hekimian, & Twentyman, 1984; Egeland & Sroufe, 1981; Frodi & Lamb, 1980).

The suspected link between parental knowledge and perceptions of children and rates of physical abuse may be more fully understood in terms of the parent's expectations and judgments concerning more complex chains of child behavior. To illustrate, Azar et al. (1984) compared 10 abusive, 10 neglectful, and 10 nonmaltreating parents on two dimensions of cognitive deficiency: unrealistic expectations of their children, and problem-solving ability in reference to child-rearing situations. The results underscore the importance in distinguishing between developmental knowledge on the one hand, and the application of that knowledge during realistic situations with the child on the other. Both groups of maltreating mothers showed greater unrealistic expectations and poorer problem-solving skills than did the com-

parison mothers. In addition, the measure that required the parents to rate the appropriateness of expecting various child behaviors (e.g., "There is nothing wrong with punishing a 9-month-old for crying too much") differentiated maltreating mothers from the comparison group, whereas the measure of developmental milestones (e.g., ability to count, climb stairs, etc.) did not.

These kinds of inaccurate perceptions and judgments that relate specifically to the parent's own experience and/or perceptions of the child-rearing role may reflect the developmental immaturity that has been reported among samples of abusive parents (see Kempe & Kempe, 1978; Steele & Pollock, 1968), and the extent to which they accurately recognize the demands and responsibilities that accompany child rearing. From an assessment standpoint, therefore, it is critical that a parent's knowledge of child development be distinguished from the more significant concern of the parent's application of knowledge, experience, and expectations while making judgments and decisions affecting his or her actions toward the child. These cognitive abilities and resultant behavior toward the child can best be revealed in naturalistic observations, discussions of actual situations that have recently occurred with the child, and structured questionnaires that are designed to assess parental opinion in the context of common child-rearing situations (e.g., the Parent Opinion Questionnaire; Azar et al., 1984; Twentyman, Plotkin, & Dodge, 1981).

Social Supports

The mechanisms by which social support appears to enhance parental adjustment include the facilitation of problem solving; access to accurate information about children and culturally normative standards for one's own parenting practices; opportunities for positive-reinforcement practices for investment in the parental role; and affirmation of worth in the parenting role that enhances self-esteem (Cutrona, 1984). Within abusive samples, therefore, it has been long suspected that limited social supports may perpetuate inappropriate child-rearing values and methods (e.g., Spinetta & Rigler, 1972). Studies that have assessed abusive parents' perceived social supports (i.e., the adults' perception that people are available and willing to listen to their problems and/or provide moral support and tangible assistance), as well as studies of the frequency of positive versus negative contacts with nonrelatives in the community (i.e., church attendance, speaking with neighbors, etc.), concur with earlier clinical impressions that abusers tend to avoid social contacts and fail to develop positive support networks (e.g., Garbarino, 1976; Salzinger, Kaplan, & Artemyeff, 1983; Wahler, 1980). For example, maltreating mothers were found to be more isolated from supports (especially peer networks) and to spend less time with the persons whom they identified as being a part of their peer support network (Salzinger *et al.*, 1983).

The question of what produces such isolation remains unanswered, prompting speculation that general deficiencies in social skills, combined with unmanageable stress, may be responsible (Salzinger *et al.*, 1983). That is, the large number of socioeconomic factors (e.g., limited economic resources, large family size, poor education, and limited job skills), singly and in combination, increase the likelihood that a person will have frequent aversive exchanges with others in the community (Burgess & Youngblade, 1987; Wahler, 1980). The concept of social supports (and social skills) may have particular merit in future research investigating patterns of family interaction within the broader framework of "social competence" (Wolfe, 1985b). As detailed by Anderson (1984; cited in Burgess & Youngblade, 1987), three conditions must be met in order for a person to use interpersonal skills effectively to meet the demands of a situation in a positive manner: (1) The person must have a capacity for displaying interpersonal positiveness, such as praising and showing affection; (2) displays of social skill must be rewarding for both interactants; and (3) the person must be able to observe the demands of specific situations accurately in order to select the most appropriate response. Social incompetence, therefore, may be the theoretical concept linking the various indicators of child maltreatment. That is, maltreaters are more likely to be poor observers of child behavior; to be noncontingent responders; to exhibit less positive and more negative behavior toward family members; and to have a pattern of social isolation, poor work history, and so on (Burgess & Youngblade, 1987). The degree of pervasiveness of this pattern of socially incompetent behavior may reflect the extent and severity of the parent–child problems that warrant assessment.

Other Characteristics

Several other stable characteristics of the abuser have received attention, but unambiguous conclusions about them are difficult to reach at present. Deficits in the parent's intellectual functioning were identified in a review of early studies (Spinetta & Rigler, 1972), but IQ deficiencies per se (as opposed to the more general notion of social incompetence) have received only limited documentation. In their review of factors associated with maternal risk of child maltreatment, Crittenden and Bonvillian (1984) noted that from 30% to 77% of parents in the maltreating samples they examined were reported to be of borderline or subnormal intelligence. However, studies often have not distinguished between abusive and neglectful parents, and therefore the relative importance of this factor is not presently clear. Similarly, there is little convincing evidence linking drug and alcohol abuse to a significant number of child-abusive incidents (Herrenkohl *et al.*, 1983; Monane *et al.*, 1984). In Gil's (1970) nationwide study of factors associated with child abuse, 12.9% of the perpetrators were described as being intoxicated at the time of the incident. Despite the inconclusiveness of current data, intellectual functioning, substance abuse, and psychiatric status may be major etiological factors in a minority of abuse cases and therefore deserve careful screening.

In sum, abusive parents can be characterized as coming from multiproblem families of origin, where they were exposed to traumatic or negative childhood experiences, such as family violence and instability. As adults, they often are incapable of managing the levels of stress found in their environment, and tend to avoid social contacts that could be perceived as additional sources of stress. Inadequate or inappropriate exposure to positive parental models and supports (in both the present and the past), coupled with limited intellectual and problem-solving skills (i.e., the ability to make appropriate judgments during child-rearing situations), may serve to make child rearing a difficult and aversive event. Consequently (or concomitantly), abusive parents may report symptoms indicative of health and coping problems, which further impair their ability to function effectively as parents. While it is clear that the abusive parent is often a multiply handicapped individual, differences in situationally defined parental competence (i.e., interpersonal positiveness, social skill, and accurate observation and judgment in the parental role) may be a useful framework for investigating failures and successes among diverse child-rearing populations.

Response Topography

Child abuse reports indicate a wide variability in the types and severity of abusive acts; yet there has not been much recognition of the continuum of abusive behavior (Friedman *et al.*, 1981). The vast majority of incidents investigated by child protective service agencies involve inappropriate actions by the parent to gain control of the child, such as striking the child with an object, burning, beatings, and severe spankings that result in injury to the child (Herrenkohl *et al.*, 1983; Kadushin & Martin, 1981). When viewed from a social-interactional perspective, the parent's child management techniques can be investigated by observing other (low-intensity) behaviors that occur more frequently, such as criticisms of the child, threats, and harsh methods of controlling the child (e.g., grabbing, slapping) that are presumed to be related to the more extreme abusive actions (Burgess, 1979; Friedman *et al.*, 1981).

The long-held suspicion that abusive parents are significantly more harsh and punitive toward their children has received a great deal of attention from researchers. The results support the overall conclusion that abusers are significantly *less positive* than nonabusers (primarily measured in terms of praise, physical contact, voice tone, and frequency of neutral and positive statements), and that this produces an imbalance in the proportion of negative to positive behavior shown during interactions with the child (Wolfe, 1985a). Accordingly, abusers are proportionately more likely than nonabusers to rely upon aversive control, such as threats and physical methods of punishment and control (Lorber *et al.*, 1984; Reid *et al.*, 1981).

Neglecting parents are similar to abusers on this dimension of infrequent positive interactions with their children. Two observational studies found that neglecters interact less frequently in the family than do normals (Bousha & Twentyman, 1984; Burgess & Conger, 1978) and tend to ignore child behavior (Disbrow, Doerr, & Caulfield, 1977). Thus, during parent–child situations in the home, abusers and neglecters show similarly disproportionate patterns of low-frequency, negatively imbalanced interactions; however, circumstantial evidence (i.e., from case records and reconstructions of incidents) indicates that the neglecter more often *avoids* interacting with the child (e.g., ignores the child's appropriate bids for assistance and/ or contact, escapes from noxious situations), whereas the abuser tends to administer excessive forms of verbal and physical control that are incongruent with the demands of the situation (e.g., strikes the child; Herrenkohl *et al.*, 1983).

In conjunction with naturalistic studies of parent–child interaction, laboratory investigations of abusers' emotional reactivity have supported the theoretical contention that they show more conditioned arousal to noxious child behavior than do nonabusers, as indicated by changes in heart rate, skin conductance, skin temperature, respiration, and/or facial expressions during experimental analogues of child-rearing situations (Disbrow *et al.*, 1977; Frodi & Lamb, 1980; Wolfe *et al.*, 1983). The conditioning, or learning, process may occur over an unknown time period (e.g., gradually, such as during early parent–infant contact or struggles with a difficult toddler; or more suddenly, such as during high-stress periods in which the parent is less tolerant of child behavior or experiences a very aversive encounter with the child). These conditioning experiences, in turn, affect later parent–child interactions in terms of expected outcome (e.g., frustration, anger) and behavior (e.g., threats, punishment). The preliminary findings from studies investigating the issue of emotional reactivity suggest that the abusive parent may show an idiosyncratic arousal pattern that serves to mediate aggressive reactions, in accordance with theoretical studies on anger and emotional arousal (cf. Baron, 1977; Berkowitz, 1983; Zillman, 1979). However, the range of noxious events that may elicit such arousal and aggression, as well as predispositions to respond in such a manner, have not been investigated by child abuse researchers; therefore, the relationship between conditioned arousal and physical abuse remains tentative at present.

In order to account for the high-intensity nature of abusive acts, two components of the abusive response deserve careful attention: (1) the everyday family interactions and observable expressions of interest and concern for the child; and (2) the parent's reactivity (i.e., emotional and cognitive arousal/awareness) to aversive events, which is believed to mediate anger and aggression (Vasta, 1982). The first component of the response may be under operant control and governed by its consequences (see below), and the other component may be under respondent control and elicited by certain classes of stimulus events in individuals with such a disposition. Therefore, it is necessary to observe parental behavior (e.g., rates of praise, criticism, and physical negatives), as well as to assess the parent's level of arousal and distress during age-representative types of family situations, such as infant care, feeding, and stimulation (with very young children) and compliance tasks, teaching, and disciplinary situations (with older children).

Consequences of Aggressive Behavior

Drawing upon related research with problem families (Patterson, 1982), parental aggression toward a child is believed to be shaped and maintained by its reinforcing consequences and by the reciprocation of aversive behavior between the parent and child, which escalates in intensity and frequency over time (Reid *et al.*, 1981). Whether the initial stimulus is child behavior or not, a parent's use of coercive methods (e.g., verbally and physically threatening gestures) to control aversive events (e.g., loud children, bothersome neighbors) may be negatively reinforced by the termination of the event or a reduction in his or her unpleasant mood state, or positively reinforced by approval from significant others (Friedman *et al.*, 1981). A pattern of negative reinforcement, however, may occur at a less intense level for many families; therefore, in order to explain the high intensity of abusive behavior, the behavioral model stresses the importance of the bidirectional shaping process. That is, the child (and perhaps other family members as well), who is the common target of such coercion, may also be learning to be more coercive and aggressive in his or her manner of dealing with the parent, since this shaping process involves the reciprocation of behavior between interactants.

To illustrate this process, consider the example of a parent who lacks the ability to teach directly, or to model, prosocial skills to the child and to manage stressful events. When this situation is coupled with a child who becomes progressively more difficult to manage, the stage is set for increased use of more intensive punishment. The child, moreover, may begin to

habituate to the level of punishment and/or may learn to counteraggress in a blatant or subtle manner. According to aggression theories, the adult may begin to respond to cues that have previously been associated with frustration and/or anger (e.g., child's voice tone, facial expressions), and his or her behavior toward the child may be intensified by these experiences (Berkowitz, 1983; Vasta, 1982). The role of anger, in particular, has been recently emphasized as the possible mechanism that escalates bickering into battering (cf. Averill, 1982). Empirical support for this "dual-component" conceptualization of abuse (i.e., the involvement of both operant and respondent conditioning principles; Vasta, 1982) has begun to emerge. For example, laboratory studies of the effects on maternal behavior of varying the consequences of punishment (e.g., undesirable child behavior decreases or increases, under the experimenter's control), or of varying the child stimuli (e.g., a very inattentive child vs. a very compliant child), demonstrate the significance of salient cues and feedback to the parent in moderating his or her type of punishment (Mulhern & Passman, 1979; Vasta & Copitch, 1981).

Finally, it should be stressed that a cycle of aggressive and abusive behavior may exist to some extent because of the *absence* or lack of awareness of clearly defined and enforceable negative consequences. The legal statutes that exist in all states and provinces in North America are often not known to the public, and many parents are not aware that the methods used during their own childhood may result in a charge of child abuse today. Similarly, consequences for abuse are nonspecifically defined and are inconsistently and arbitrarily enforced in many cases, leading to further confusion that may negate the intended effects of the sanctions. For assessment purposes, therefore, one must consider the parent's *perceptions* of the consequences (positive and negative) of his or her aggressive behaviors, as well as more objective data, in attempting to understand how such behaviors are maintained.

Implications for Assessment

The preceding overview of theoretical and empirical explanations of child abuse has emphasized the interplay of a constellation of factors involving the entire family. This constellation is known to include the parent's childhood and early adult history, child-rearing skills, recent stressful events, and social relationships, and features of the child, among others. We have also seen that the causes and outcomes of abuse are entwined with general background factors that may impair child development, such as low income level, birth status, health status, and family instability.

In view of the complexity of this problem, several implications for the behavioral assessment of abusive families emerge. While home and clinic observations of behavior have demonstrated their value for pinpointing specific problem areas, such observations may be insufficient by themselves to reveal the range and significance of contextual events that may be dramatically influencing parent and child behavior (Wolfe, 1985a). Therefore, indirect methods (e.g., self-report and collateral report instruments, interviews, and standardized psychological tests) that assess such things as parental attitudes, perceived social supports, and physical and emotional health are important methods for examining low-frequency behaviors and qualitative factors that relate to parental competence and possible marital, social, or financial problems (Griest & Wells, 1983).

Another assessment issue that deserves emphasis is that of the extremely wide range of behaviors that may be shown by abused and neglected children. Typically, functional components of the abuse process, such as marital conflict, family instability, and elevated expressions of anger, are associated with an unusual pattern of child behavior. However, it is not uncommon to find maltreated children who either lack any signs of overt problems or distress or exhibit very self-defeating behavior with no obvious function. Rather than assuming that an apparent absence of distress is indicative of the benign effects of abuse, the clinician must carefully consider other alternatives.

One consideration in understanding the diversity of child reactions to abuse and neglect is that some children appear to be able to handle unusually high levels of family and environmental stress (e.g., spouse abuse, divorce, and parental psychopathology) without apparent long- or short-term harmful effects (cf. Emery, 1982; Rutter, 1979, 1983; Wolfe et al., 1985). These children may possess certain coping abilities and predispositions that help them to adapt in a positive manner (i.e., the "invulnerable" child), or they may have the advantage of positive life experiences (e.g., supportive adults, successful educational and peer experiences,

etc.) that serve as "buffers" against traumatic or stressful circumstances. On the other hand, some children may disguise their distress very effectively when around nonrelatives, possibly out of fear that they will be removed from their parents, forced to live in a foster home, or harmed. Similarly, a small number of maltreated children may seem to "prefer" to be hit or mistreated by adults, despite attempts at positive child management. For example, in our treatment project several abused children residing in foster care continued to perplex social workers and foster care staff with their bizarre and self-destructive behavior, which would occur at very unpredictable times. At the foster homes these children would hoard food in their rooms, urinate on their personal belongings, or aggress toward a peer in the presence of an adult, resulting in considerable upset and punishment. Similar reports have prompted speculation that abused children may suffer from a form of posttraumatic stress disorder (Green, 1983), or may have adapted to the punitive atmosphere of their families of origin in such a way that their behavior is more likely to produce a consistent, predictable (i.e., reinforcing) outcome—anger and punishment (Wahler & Dumas, 1986b). These observations indicate that ongoing assessment of abused children's development and behavior over an extended time period may be necessary to understand the relationship of the behavior to previous and current experiences, as well as to determine the (possible) adaptive nature of their coping and adjustment patterns at different developmental periods.

BEHAVIORAL ASSESSMENT OF ABUSIVE AND NEGLECTFUL FAMILIES

The assessment of abusive and neglectful families is a multistage process, often beginning with impressionistic data from reporting and referral sources and narrowing toward the evaluation of more specific intervention needs. The psychologist's role should be coordinated with the role of the child protective service agency to promote an interdisciplinary approach toward working with multiproblem families. Consultation with the family social worker can serve to review the allegations, evidence, proceedings, and decisions that affect the evaluation, and can help in the formulation of appropriate assessment questions. The social worker's per-

FIGURE 1. Referral Questionnaire. From *The Child Management Program for Abusive Parents* by D. A. Wolfe, K. Kaufman, J. Aragona, and J. Sandler, 1981, Winter Park, FL: Anna. Copyright 1981 by Anna Publishing. Reprinted by permission.

REFERRAL QUESTIONNAIRE
(Confidential)

Family Being Referred: _____

Referral Person: _____

Position Title: _____

Instructions: Please rank the following in terms of importance to the above family for receiving treatment/instruction in that area. Circle the appropriate number above each category.

No importance Need no treatment in this area			Somewhat important			Highly important
1	2	3	4	5	6	7

1. CHILD MANAGEMENT SKILLS
The skills covered would include positive reinforcement of appropriate child behaviors, methods of reducing undesirable child behavior and fostering healthy parent/child relations. The emphasis is upon the parents learning to problem-solve for themselves and to acquire viable alternatives to punishment.

1	2	3	4	5	6	7

2. CHILD DEVELOPMENT
Instruction that highlights areas of normal and abnormal child development, with an emphasis upon understanding "norms" of development and reasonable expectations from their child(ren) at certain ages. Description of typical child-rearing responsibilities: feeding, bathing, toilet training, etc.

1	2	3	4	5	6	7

3. CRISIS INTERVENTION
Assistance in managing a runaway, separation, acute depression, financial, health, or any other circumstance that immediately bears upon the family's current situation. The need for this form of service should be differentiated from chronic disturbance.

1	2	3	4	5	6	7

4. ANGER/IMPULSE CONTROL
This includes relaxation training, preparing for and dealing with stressful child behaviors and related problems, and developing coping skills that reduce the frequency and intensity of verbal and physical outbursts.

(continued)

---

spective on the family should be carefully outlined, as well as preliminary goals that the worker has prepared with the family. The Referral Questionnaire (shown in Figure 1) may assist in obtaining the social worker's assessment of the family's needs and priorities in several major areas.

While the task of assessing abusive families overlaps considerably with the assessment of families with conduct problem children (Forehand & McMahon, 1981 and Chapter 3, this volume), family conflict (Foster & Robin, Chapter 17, this volume), and other dysfunctional family systems (Conger, 1981), several unique aspects deserve attention:

1. The abusive family often has been referred for psychological services involuntarily or under duress. This makes it more difficult both to elicit the necessary, accurate information from the parents and to establish the credibility and rapport that will increase their motivation to change their parenting style. In

FIGURE 1. (*continued*)

1   2   3   4   5   6   7

5. FINANCIAL ASSISTANCE OR MANAGEMENT
Learning to apportion one's income more carefully and responsibly, shopping wisely, and reducing or avoiding financial stress. This includes but is not limited to AFDC and other forms of family support.

1   2   3   4   5   6   7

6. MARITAL COUNSELING
Partners need to agree or compromise on decisions, and learn to settle disputes without reliance upon threat or force. Development of communication skills.

1   2   3   4   5   6   7

7. PSYCHOLOGICAL DISTURBANCE
One or more members of the family displays deviant behavior to such extent that individual psychotherapy, medications, and/or hospitalization is warranted.

1   2   3   4   5   6   7

8. SOCIAL ISOLATION
Family members need the help of "support systems" to provide feedback to parents on their behavior, the behavior of their children, and to provide resources for coping with stress.

1   2   3   4   5   6   7

9. SUBSTANCE ABUSE
One or more family members need to participate in a program to reduce reliance/dependence upon drugs or alcohol. This includes modifying other behaviors (e.g., disciplining children) that appear to be mediated by drugs or alcohol.

1   2   3   4   5   6   7

10. EMOTIONAL NEGLECT
Caregiver(s) need assistance in developing affectional patterns, becoming responsive to the child's psychological needs, accepting affection from the child.

1   2   3   4   5   6   7

11. OTHER (Please Describe)

_____

_____

_____

Additional Instructions: Please go back over the list of treatment areas and indicate the three (3) most important areas by placing a check mark next to the title of that area.

general, such clients are more reserved and defensive than self-referred clients in regard to their need for mental health services and their willingness to establish and meet therapeutic goals.

2. Abuse represents an extreme form of parent–child conflict in which the target behavior cannot be readily observed. However, once a parent has "lost control" of his or her response to a child, the possibility of recurrence becomes an ongoing concern. This may necessitate more careful monitoring and detailed assessment than would typically be the case with nonabusive parent–child problems.

3. The task of learning unfamiliar child management procedures may appear overwhelming to the parents, strengthening their desire to adhere to more familiar, aversive control methods. This "resistance to change" is also embedded in sociodemographic factors (e.g., proclivity toward physical punishment and rigid control) that may conflict with the therapist's

style of assistance and intended goals for the family.

4. Abusive and neglectful families are a very heterogeneous group of multiproblem families that possess unique combinations of assets and liabilities. Thus, each family often requires a uniquely tailored, ongoing assessment strategy that is sensitive to the family's particular needs.

These added concerns require a management strategy that establishes priorities among assessment and treatment needs for each family, in order to maximize the probability of benefit.

Common Assessment Purposes

The behavioral assessment of abuse and neglect must meet several intermediate goals prior to case management decisions or initiating recommendations for intervention. An overview of a child abuse assessment strategy is presented in Table 1, which includes several decisions and precautionary statements that may

be associated with each assessment purpose. The first two assessment purposes are directed at general concerns requiring initial screening and attention; these are then followed by more specific detail where indicated (i.e., identifying parental and child needs).

A very common and salient issue that arises in the assessment of abuse and neglect is the detection of possible maltreatment among clinical child populations, and the overriding concern of potential risk to these children of further maltreatment. The examiner may be asked to assist in the pending decision to place a child in foster care, and he or she must carefully weigh the risks and benefits of this shared decision. Situations in which abuse might be suspected include those in which (1) the history of the child's injury given by the parent is incompatible with the present injury; (2) the parent's account of the "accident" changes during the course of questioning; (3) repeated episodes of trauma or accidents are known to

TABLE 1. Child Abuse and Neglect Assessment Strategy: An Overview

Purpose	Pending decisions	Precautions
A. Determining dangerousness and risk to the child in cases of detected or undetected maltreatment	Apprehension of child Alternative placement of child	Removing and returning child to family is highly stressful Initial impression of family may be distorted

B. Identifying general strengths and problem areas of the family system
  Family background
  Marital relationship
  Perceived areas of stress and supports
  Symptomatology
	Identification of major factors (antecedents, consequences, and individual characteristics) suspected to be operative within the family
	Directions for protective services, supports, additional community services
		Involvement of too many professionals may overwhelm family
		"Crises" that family members report may change dramatically
		Parent–child problems may be embedded in chronic family problems (e.g., financial; marital) that resist change

C. Identification of parental needs *vis-à-vis* child-rearing demands
  Child-rearing methods and skills
  Anger and arousal toward child
  Perceptions and expectations of children
	Behavioral intervention planning and establishing priority of needs	Parental behavior toward child may be a function of both proximal (e.g., child behavior) and distal (e.g., job stress) events
		Numerous treatment interferences must be identified (e.g., resistance, socioeconomic status, marital problems)

D. Identification of child needs
  Child behavior problems with family members
  Child adaptive abilities and cognitive and emotional development
	Referral to school-based intervention
	Behavioral interventions (e.g., parent training)
	Returning child to family
		Unclear or delayed expression of symptom/impairments
		Child's behavior may be partially a function of recent family separation and change

the agency, setting, or interagency records; and (4) there is an inexplicable delay in seeking treatment for the child's injury or illness. Typically, such assessment or screening is done by emergency care staff in hospitals and child protection agencies, although any professional who comes into contact with families may be called upon to offer his or her opinion about the nature and probable cause of an atypical pattern of child injuries, delays, or behavior. While the decision to take a child into protective custody ultimately rests with child welfare department officials, mental health professionals may have significant input at this stage in terms of treatment directions.

After the initial detection of maltreatment, the examiner must begin to identify the major strengths and problem areas of the family system (see Table 1) in preparation for involvement of additional community resources, directions for protective services, and specific treatment needs. An interview with the parent(s) may facilitate a preliminary screening for possible major psychopathology (e.g., thought disorder, homicidal–suicidal ideation, etc.) and identifying the most probable and significant etiological factors. The interviewer should pay particular attention to defining the family's current situation in terms of specific problems currently existing that may be correlates of maltreatment (e.g., financial, housing, legal), and the course and nature of these problems (i.e., historical origins, attempts to modify the problems, attenuating and accentuating circumstances that have been identified). Precautionary considerations during this stage of assessment include recognizing that involvement of too many professionals or resources may be counterproductive, and avoiding premature decisions based upon a parent's report of transient crises.

The second major focus in assessing abusive families is the identification of parental and child needs (see Table 1). At this point the examiner is concerned with the identification or development of possible treatment alternatives for the family, and this requires more specialized assessment instruments and skills. A detailed functional analysis of the parent's response patterns and the child's behavior can be completed (as detailed below), allowing for the establishment of priorities for the family and a timetable for meeting the agency's, court's, or practitioner's objectives. The following sections delineate specific assessment methods that have been developed for the assessment of abusive family systems, with an emphasis on parent and child focal areas. These methods are also applicable in the assessment of neglecting families, as indicated.

Assessment of Parent(s)

The assessment of abusive parents is a multistage process that must be tailored to the needs of the referral source and each particular family. Due to the complex array of factors that contribute toward abuse and neglect, this necessitates an assessment approach organized in a manner that attends to the major problem areas in a progressive fashion without becoming overburdened by the number of potential concerns. Guidelines for parental assessment are presented below in two major sections that correspond with the recommended progression:

1. Identifying general problem areas. This section includes interview and psychometric methods that facilitate inquiry into the family background, marital relationship, perceived areas of stress and supports, and symptomatology.

2. Assessing parental response to child-rearing demands. This section addresses response mechanisms such as anger and arousal, perceptions and expectations of children, and child-rearing methods that may require continuous baseline assessment and treatment planning.

Because the possible consequences associated with the family's participation during assessment and issues of confidentiality are often unclear, parents may initially behave in a cautious or defensive manner. It is important that the interviewer explains his or her professional role (i.e., to assess areas in need of change) and standards concerning client confidentiality; however, it is equally important to clarify for the parents the legal obligation to report any suspicions of child maltreatment to protective services. Usually this can be done in a matter-of-fact manner during the beginning of the session, by stating, "I'll be asking you to tell me a lot of details concerning your child's behavior and your feelings and actions related to your child. My role is to find out whether the problems you have can be lessened in any way. Please understand that I'm not here to make any judgments about your parenting ability without your agreement and understanding. I am under no obligation to report to anyone outside of this room about what we discuss unless it may lead to the harm of your child.

This means that if you tell me that you have hurt your child or may hurt him (her), I must notify your caseworker (or protective services). Beyond the immediate safety of your child, I will not discuss anything with your caseworker unless we have both agreed to this beforehand (such as your efforts to work on your problems). If you have any other concerns about your situation and my role, let's discuss them now before proceeding with the interview.'' (Mental health professionals who have been asked by the court to prepare a written report

on parental competence and risk will have to modify this statement to clarify for the parents exactly what the court is asking and what the professionals do and do not have to report.)

Identifying General Problem Areas

Much of the initial information concerning parent and child functioning is obtained during a semistructured interview with the parent. To assist in organizing the material in a comprehensive fashion, a Parent Interview and As-

---

TABLE 2. Parent Interview and Assessment Guide: Abuse and Neglect

The following is a selected summary of the major factors associated with child abuse and neglect, requiring further interviewing and assessment of the parent, as indicated. The framing and emphasis of each question are left up to the discretion of the interviewer.

I. Identifying general problem areas
  A. Family background
    1. Early rejection or abuse during own childhood; relationship with biological and/or psychological parents
    2. Methods of punishment and reward received during own childhood
    3. Family planning and effect of children on the marital relationship
    4. Preparedness for and sense of competence in child rearing
    5. Early physical, emotional, behavioral problems of child (i.e., illnesses, trauma, temperament)
  B. Marital relationship
    1. Length, stability, and quality of present relationship
    2. Examples of conflict or physical violence
    3. Support from partner in family responsibilities
    4. Substance abuse
  C. Areas of perceived stress and supports
    1. Employment history and satisfaction
    2. Family income and expenses, chronic economic problems
    3. Stability of occupation, income, and living arrangements
    4. Perceived support from within or outside of the family
    5. Daily/weekly contacts with others (e.g., neighbors, social workers)
    6. Quality of social contacts and major life events (i.e., positive vs. negative influence on the parent)
  D. Symptomatology
    1. Recent or chronic health problems; treatment; drug and alcohol use
    2. Identifiable mood and affect changes; anxiety; social dysfunction
    3. Previous psychiatric evaluations or treatment

II. Assessing parental responses to child-rearing demands
  A. Emotional reactivity
    1. Perception of how particular child differs from siblings or other children known to the parent
    2. Feelings of anger and "loss of control" when interacting with child (describe circumstances, how the parent felt, how the parent reacted)
    3. Typical ways of coping with arousal during/following stressful episodes
  B. Child-rearing methods
    1. Parental expectations of child (i.e., accuracy of expectations for child behavior and development, in reference to child's actual developmental status)
    2. Examples of recent efforts to teach new or desirable behavior to child
    3. "Preferred" and "typical" manner of controlling/disciplining child
    4. Attitudes toward learning "different" or unfamiliar child-rearing methods
    5. Perceived effectiveness of parent's teaching and discipline approach
    6. Pattern of child behavior in response to typical discipline methods (i.e., accelerating, decelerating, manipulative, responsive)

sessment Guide is presented in Table 2; this provides an overview of the major issues that are referred to in each of the subsections below: (1) family background; (2) marital relationship; (3) areas of perceived stress and support; and (4) symptomatology.

In conjunction with interview procedures and topics, several relevant psychometric instruments for assessing problems encountered in the family context are also presented throughout each subsection. These methods provide a comprehensive and normative comparison of a parent's functioning in those areas associated with abuse (i.e., marital, family experiences, symptomatology, and coping with stress and children), and they are becoming essential components of a child abuse assessment battery.

FAMILY BACKGROUND. The importance of careful investigation of previous childhood experiences that may affect current behavior cannot be overstated. Abusive parents can often relate to the examiner several significant events, such as early rejection or abuse during childhood, or strong cultural values (e.g., adherence to corporal punishment and disavowal of "bribery methods") that have influenced or guided their behavior within the family. While these events and perceptions may have little to do with changing current behaviors per se, they may suggest to the examiner the type of treatment approach that might be most effective (i.e., emphasis on cognitive and attitudinal change, modeling, problem solving, etc.). Most importantly, knowledge of a parent's history will enable the therapist to develop an intervention plan that is most likely to succeed in relation to the parent's expectations, abilities, and needs.

The interview should trace the origins and development of significant areas of stress within the family system, beginning with family planning and the effects of children on the marital relationship. This discussion includes, for example, whether the abused child was planned, the effect of the pregnancy on parental attitudes and life style, support of the biological father, the mother's preparedness and sense of competence in child rearing (i.e., emotional maturity, family support, peer influences), and early childhood problems (e.g., illnesses, trauma, temperament). It is often useful to allow for general discussion of the child throughout the interview, because the parent may have justified or rationalized his or her actions on the basis of the child's "difficult behavior." The parent

can be encouraged to describe the child's desirable and undesirable behaviors, and to discuss how he or she would like to see these changed.

The Child Abuse Potential Inventory (CAPI; Milner, 1986) is a self-report instrument that has been specifically designed to measure problem areas related to parental and family background (such as those described above) that are associated with an increased probability of abuse. Since its development in the late 1970s, this instrument has undergone psychometric investigations by the author and his colleagues (e.g., Milner & Ayoub, 1980; Milner, Gold, Ayoub, & Jacewitz, 1984) that have produced norms for general and abusive populations, and reliability and validity information. For example, in a study of predictive validity, high scale scores were significantly correlated ($r = .34$, $p < .01$) with subsequent reports of abuse. The major scale on the instrument contains seven factor-analyzed subscales (i.e., Distress, Rigidity, Child with Problems, Problem with Family and Others, Unhappiness, Loneliness, and Negative Concept of Child and of Self) that permit a more detailed understanding of the parent's problem areas. In addition, there is a Lie scale that indicates the degree of deceptive responding (e.g., "I love all children"). The 160 items on the scale are written at the third-grade reading level and require only an "agree" or "disagree" response (e.g., "I am often mixed up," "A child should never talk back," "My parents did not understand me"). The CAPI appears to be measuring parents' general psychological functioning and child-rearing attitudes, and as such may be an alternative to standardized psychological tests (e.g., the Minnesota Multiphasic Personality Inventory, the Beck Depression Inventory).

MARITAL RELATIONSHIP. Because a parent's child-rearing effectiveness and appropriateness are often related to his or her interactions and experiences with other significant adults (cf. Griest & Wells, 1983; Wahler, Leske, & Rogers, 1979), the interviewer should be careful to assess areas of non-child-related stress within the family. In many instances of child maltreatment, the marital (or common-law) relationship is a primary source of added conflict and stress that interferes with child rearing. A discussion of the length, stability, and quality of the present relationship may provide insight into the manner in which adult conflict may influence parent–child interactions, such as tolerance for child misbehavior, noise, and interruptions. In addition, the interviewer should be sensitive to other signs of major distress or conflict in the family system that may be the primary source of child maltreatment, especially physical violence between partners, extramarital relationships, substance abuse, interference from relatives, and lack of spousal assistance in handling family affairs. These topics may need to be addressed during private, individual sessions with each partner as circumstances require. Instruments that offer assistance in assessing problems associated with adult relationships are discussed below.

Marital conflict and satisfaction can be assessed through several methods, including interviews, standardized instruments, and observation of interactions during conflict resolution tasks (see Weiss, 1984, for a full description). For child-abusive families (where the spouses have not requested marital counseling and are often hesitant to discuss other issues), it is often useful to follow the interview procedure (above) with a brief measure of satisfaction, such as the Dyadic Adjustment Scale (DAS; Spanier, 1976). The DAS is a self-report measure of marital satisfaction that is similar in form and content to the earlier Locke and Wallace (1959) measure of marital satisfaction. The DAS contains 15 items reflecting areas of common disagreement in marriages (e.g., family finances, friends, sex relations), and each partner is asked to indicate his or her degree of agreement or disagreement with the partner on a 6-point scale ("always agree" to "always disagree"). This is followed by 11 items concerned with the frequency of positive and negative interactions (e.g., "How often do you discuss or have you considered divorce, separation, or termination of your relationship?"). Finally, each partner rates his or her degree of happiness in the relationship, and chooses a statement that best describes how he or she feels about the future of the relationship. The DAS produces a standardized score that enables the clinician to interpret the degree of dissatisfaction in the relationship in relation to distressed and nondistressed norms.

Because of the strong association between child abuse and marital conflict, the interviewer should also address the possibility of physical violence between partners. The Conflict Tactics Scales (CTS; Straus, 1979b) have been specifically designed to elicit information concerning conflict resolution tactics between adults and/ or between parents and child in a sensitive and revealing fashion that makes their use with abusive families especially pertinent. The instrument is administered in an interview fashion, whereby each partner is separately asked to rate the frequency of occurrence (on a 7-point scale, ranging from "never" to "more than 20 times") of tactics that he or she has used toward the partner during disputes over the past 12 months. These tactics include, for example, "discussed the issue calmly," "insulted or swore at the other one," "threatened to hit or throw something at the other one," "kicked, bit, or hit with a fist." Ratings of 18 items form three subscales (Reasoning, Verbal Hostility, and Physical Aggression) that measure the degree of positive and negative methods of conflict resolution. The CTS have been widely used in clinical and research studies to assess verbal and physical aggression in the family (e.g., Straus et al., 1980; Wolfe et al., 1985). However, Jouriles and O'Leary (1985) found that agreement between partners on the occurrence of violence was low to moderate on the CTS; that is, husbands tended to underreport their own violent behavior, and wives tended to overreport the violence performed by husbands. Thus, information obtained from this approach should be combined with data from other sources (e.g., interview, direct observation) to provide the best estimate of marital conflict resolution tactics.

Observation of marital interactions during discussion of common problems and events provides a very rich source of information on affect and behavior expressed over time (Gottman, 1979). One common procedure, described by Levenson and Gottman (1983) and Weiss (1984), requires the partners to discuss the events of the day as if they were home alone at the end of the day, and then to discuss a conflictive problem area in their marriage. These interactions are videotaped and shown at a later date to each partner *separately* to provide their subjective ratings of affect (i.e., each partner is asked, "Rate how you felt when you were actually in the interaction," on the dimension of "very positive" to "very negative"). Investigations of this "video recall" procedure (Levenson & Gottman, 1983) have shown that ongoing self-reports of affect discriminated high-conflict from low-conflict interaction, correlated significantly with marital satisfaction, and were significantly correlated with observers' coding of couples' affect (Gottman & Levenson, 1985). Variations of this interactional approach to assessing marital conflict exist, such as ratings of efficacy, progress, and satisfaction based on repeated 10-minute interactional sequences; detailed observational systems for sequential or conditional analyses are also available (Weiss, 1984).

AREAS OF PERCEIVED STRESS AND SUPPORTS. The major purpose of assessing the family's degree of stress and supports is to locate areas that are perceived as highly stressful (either to a parent individually or to the family as a unit), and to determine what resources family members use to manage these areas of stress, either effectively or ineffectively. Assessment of socioeconomic factors that may be highly stressful can be accomplished during the interview by discussing employment history and satisfaction, family income and expenses, housing and living arrangements, and similar circumstances that may be contributing to family problems. An instrument such as the Life Experiences Survey (LES; Sarason, Johnson, & Siegel, 1979) is a useful tool during the initial stages of assessment to engage the parents in a discussion of major events affecting the family. The LES requires an adult to rate the positive or negative impact over the past 12 months of 47 events, such as changes in income, divorce, or death of a family member, on a scale from "very negative" (-3) to "very positive" ($+3$). A total negative score derived from this instrument has been shown in previous research to be a reliable measure and the best predictor of subjects' anxiety, academic achievement, and malajustment (J. H. Johnson & Sarason, 1979).

The indirect manner in which such socioeconomic factors and life events influence child development and child-rearing practices can also be determined from the following instruments that have been designed to assess aspects of the child's environment, parental stress, and social supports.

Polansky et al. (1981) developed the Childhood Level of Living Scale (CLLS) to assess the extent of positive and negative influences present in a child's home environment. This instrument is particularly well suited for assessing neglectful families, in that it lists the major areas of concern to children's minimal health, safety, and stimulation requirements. The CLLS has two main scales: Physical Care, comprising five subscales (General Positive Care, State of Repair of House, Negligence, Quality of Household Maintenance, and Quality of Health Care and Grooming), and Emotional/Cognitive Care, with four subscales (Encouraging Competence, Inconsistency of Discipline and Coldness, Encouraging Superego Development, and Material Giving). The 99 items are rated by home visitors as "yes" or "no." The authors provide preliminary normative data for this instrument, with cutoff scores indicating neglectful care, adequate care, and good child care, although reliability and validity data are limited (with the exception of one report indicating discriminative validity between neglectful and control families; Polansky et al., 1981).

The Home Observation for Measurement of the Environment (HOME; Bradley & Caldwell, 1979) is a well-researched criterion checklist that reflects the quality of the child's environment more precisely than designations of social class or socioeconomic status alone. This inventory was designed to sample certain aspects of the quantity and quality of social, emotional, and cognitive support available to a young child (different forms are available for children from birth to 3 years and from 3 to 5 years of age). The HOME is completed following visits to the family's residence, and items not obtained via direct observation (e.g., "takes child out of home more than twice per week") are based on parental report. The rater's "yes–no" responses to the 45-item checklist result in six subscales: Emotional and Verbal Responsivity of the Mother, Avoidance of Restriction and Punishment, Organization of the Physical and Temporal Environment, Provision of Appropriate Play Materials, Maternal Involvement with the Child, and Opportunities for Variety in Daily Stimulation. Bradley and Caldwell (1979) report significant correlations between subscale scores and later child IQ scores, along with numerous studies in support of the scale's reliability and validity.

Assessment of stress in the parenting role is a promising new approach to measuring global and specific aspects of the family system. The Parenting Stress Index (PSI; Abidin, 1983) is a well-validated instrument that incorporates a wide range of items linked to dysfunctional parent–child relationships. The PSI (Form 6) contains 101 items to which the parent responds on a 5-point scale ("strongly agree" to "strongly disagree"). The instrument is especially useful with abusive parents, since the items are understandable at the fifth-grade reading level and can be completed in 20–30 minutes. In addition, the items appear to be personally relevant for parents having problems in their role (e.g., "My child wakes up in a bad mood," "I feel trapped by my responsibilities as a parent"). An attractive feature of the PSI is that it defines "stress" in the parenting system in a multidimensional fashion, emanating from three major sources: (1) Child Domain, comprised of six subscales (Adaptability, Acceptability, Demandingness, Mood, Distractibility/Hyperactivity, and Reinforces Parent); (2) Parent Domain, comprised of seven subscales (Depression, Attachment, Restriction of Role, Sense of Competence, Social Isolation, Relationship with Spouse, and Parent Health); and (3) Life Stress, comprised of 19 items dealing with stress related to events such as divorce, death, finances, and so on. Responses to the items may provide very useful clinical information, and the percentile rankings allow for an analysis of the sources of stress in the family system (e.g., child demandingness, social isolation). In addition, Abidin (1983) provides clinical cutoff scores in the manual, and offers a sample profile of abusive families based on 30 cases (which, interestingly, reveals high elevations on all subscales in both the Child and the Parent Domains). This instrument may signal a trend toward recognizing the parenting role within the unique context of the family system.

The identification of sources of perceived social support has also received considerable interest in recent years, resulting in several new measurement devices, although it is important to recognize that this construct may be confounded with pronounced family deprivation, psychiatric symptoms, and life events (Dohrenwend, Dohrenwend, Dodgson, & Shrout, 1984). A discussion of frequency, nature, range, and quality of daily or weekly contacts between family members and sources of perceived stress or support can begin during the initial interview process and follow-up with the use of a brief questionnaire. A very useful instrument for this purpose is the Perceived Social Support Questionnaire (PSSQ; Procidano & Heller, 1983), which addresses the parent's *perceptions* of support, rather than the mere presence of a potential support network. The instrument contains two scales, each containing 20 items to which the respondent is to select one of three answers: "yes," "no," or "don't know." The two scales indicate perceived social supports *within* the family and *outside* of the family, respectively. The scale is worded very simply (e.g., "I rely on my friends for emotional support," "My family enjoys hearing about

what I think") and enables the clinician to identify areas of perceived social support (or lack thereof) that are useful in guiding the direction of intervention. The Community Interaction Checklist (Wahler *et al.*, 1979) can also be used for the purpose of assessing the family's social environment. This instrument differs from the PSSQ, however, in that it prompts recall of all *social contacts* (rather than perceived supports) that occurred during the preceding day, and asks the respondent to rate the quality of each social contact on a negative–positive dimension. This procedure enables the clinician or researcher to determine the frequency and quality of the family's social contacts (i.e., contacts with police, unfriendly neighbors, store clerks, etc.) and provides a further delineation of socioeconomic correlates of child maltreatment that occur at the macro level of analysis (cf. Belsky, 1980; Garbarino, 1976).

SYMPTOMATOLOGY. During the interview, a history of the parent's clinical symptomatology may be addressed by discussing mood and affect changes, anxiety, recent or chronic health problems, and medical treatments. This interview procedure may be assisted by the administration of a standardized psychiatric symptom checklist or inventory to rule out particular forms of psychopathology and/or to determine the extent of psychopathology. The General Health Questionnaire (Goldberg & Hillier, 1979), for example, is an effective method for assessing symptoms of emotional and physical health. This instrument measures somatic problems, anxiety and insomnia, social dysfunction, and depression in adults as rated over the past few weeks. The 28 items require the respondent to indicate the frequency of various symptoms on a 4-point scale, ranging from "not at all" (0) to "much more than usual" (3). The items are phrased in simple-to-understand language (e.g., "Have you recently been feeling perfectly well and in good health? . . . felt that you are ill? . . . felt capable of making decisions about things?") and help to identify potential problem areas that may affect parent–child interactions.

Assessing Parental Responses to Child-Rearing Demands

Despite the formidable influence of parental background, psychological functioning, and situational life stressors upon abusive behavior, child maltreatment is strongly linked to events that involve the child in some manner (Wolfe,

1985a). Therefore, a comprehensive assessment of the parent's typical daily behavior with his or her child includes self-report and observational data in reference to situations that lead to anger and that may be precursors to abusive episodes. This requires an analysis of idosyncratic arousal patterns, fluctuations in mood and affect, and characteristic response styles during commonly occurring child-rearing situations. During the interview, the parent should be encouraged to discuss his or her expectations of the child, such as at dinnertime, while getting dressed, going to bed, and so forth, and to discuss his or her preferred or typical manner of controlling the child. These interview topics can then be followed up by an assessment of emotional reactivity and child-rearing methods, as presented below.

EMOTIONAL REACTIVITY. The parent's reactivity to unpleasant or aversive environmental events is an important factor believed to mediate anger and aggression (Berkowitz, 1983). Because emotional reactivity involves involuntary somatic responses (e.g., changes in cardiovascular function, temperature of peripheral organs, muscle tension) that are very difficult to observe or measure under realistic conditions, self-report ratings of annoyance, anger, or unpleasant changes in affect have been the most commonly used assessment methods. Abusive parents are often willing to describe their feelings of anger and "loss of control" when provided with distinctive cues or examples, such as interacting with their child in a high-conflict situation or discussing a recent conflict (e.g., Koverola, Elliot-Faust, & Wolfe, 1984). That is, feelings of anger, tension, and frustration can be identified by asking parents to provide recent examples of irritating child behaviors, the circumstances in which they occurred, how they felt, and how they reacted. At the same time, the clinician can ask the parents to identify fluctuations in mood (especially depression, anxiety, and agitation) that precede or follow incidences of parent–child conflict.

Physiological recordings—specifically, heart rate, electromyographic (EMG) activity, galvanic skin response (GSR), blood pressure, and peripheral temperature—during live or videotaped examples of aversive child behavior have proven useful for research purposes in assessing emotional reactivity among abusive parents. Compared to nonabusive parents, abusers have shown rapid elevations or changes in somatic functions in response to infant cries (Frodi &

Lamb, 1980) and child misbehavior (Wolfe et al., 1983), and these covary with their self-reports of annoyance or displeasure. However, such recordings have limited applicability in clinical practice, due to concerns of intrusiveness, excessive expense, and potential measurement artifact. Alternatively, self-monitoring of annoyance, anger, or similar feelings that precede aggressive responding toward the child in actual situations can be obtained using an Anger Diary (Wolfe et al., 1981), which the parent completes in the home or clinic. The parent is instructed to record a description of each incident in which the child did something that led to his or her feelings of anger, frustration, or tension. The parent also indicates how he or she dealt with the problem, how it finally was resolved or ended, and how he or she felt afterward about the entire incident (also see Trickett & Kuczynski, 1986). Parental compliance with this self-monitoring task is often forthcoming if the procedure is described as one in which the parent can inform the therapist more precisely of "the problems you have to face every day with your child's behavior" rather than the manner in which they react to their child. Although the connection between the child's problem behavior and the parent's inappropriate actions is a two-way street, it is often more fruitful to focus the parent's efforts initially on his or her "problems with the child," followed by increasing recognition of responsibility during subsequent treatment sessions.

Another useful clinical method for monitoring the client's distress and arousal level vis-à-vis child behaviors is the Subjective Units of Distress Scale (SUDS). The SUDS is a 10-point Likert-type scale (0 = "no distress," 10 = "high distress") that reflects parental distress during imaginal or in vivo situations involving the child. The parent is instructed to raise his or her finger whenever distress is felt (e.g., irritation, tension, anger). The therapist can then initiate relaxation and coping instructions (either overtly or covertly through a transmitter device) that have been previously rehearsed with the parent. Self-monitoring procedures, such as the Anger Diary, or the SUDS, establish the assessment basis for proceeding with an important goal in treatment: controlling anger and arousal during actual problem situations with the child (Koverola et al., 1984).

A "video recall" procedure, similar to the method used to assess marital conflict (Gottman & Levenson, 1985), may also be used to determine the parent's anger and arousal by providing a continuous record of affect during parent–child interactions. This method has the advantage of being highly salient to the parent (i.e., he or she is involved in typical interactions with the child), and facilitates multimodal assessment of affective responding (i.e., physiological, cognitive, and behavioral measures optionally may be used during the procedure). Parents with young children (under age 4) are asked to engage in "low-conflict" and "high-conflict" tasks during 10-minute laboratory observations that are videotaped behind a one-way mirror. These tasks are open-ended, but they can be chosen to elicit the most typical interaction patterns described by the parent during the interview. For example, for a low-conflict task, a parent may be asked to talk to his or her child about things they like to do together, and for a high-conflict task, the parent should be instructed to have the child comply with directions (e.g., pick up toys). For parents with older children, these tasks can be extended to more general discussion of conflicts that occur frequently in the home (e.g., getting ready for school on time). The videotaped interactions are then viewed by the parent on a separate day (without the child present) for the purpose of assessing affective responding. The parent's self-monitored "affect ratings" are recorded throughout this recall presentation, using a mechanical sliding lever (e.g., Bauer & Twentyman, 1985) labeled from 1 ("not annoyed") to 7 ("very annoyed"), or a rating dial (Gottman & Levenson, 1984) that traverses a 180-degree arc over a 9-point scale labeled from "very positive" to "very negative." These data can then be analyzed to determine mean affect ratings, latency to peak annoyance, peak annoyance, and so forth, over low- and high-conflict situations.

Although the reliability and validity of the video recall procedure have not been investigated specifically with abusive parents, it has been shown to be a valid procedure for obtaining self-report of affect in marital interaction (Gottman & Levenson, 1985). It appears that, regardless of whether emotions are aroused during an interaction or while viewing a videotape of previous interactions, there is isomorphism between responses that occur in the original setting and those that occur while re-experiencing the situation. This procedure shows promise for assessing each parent's distinctive pattern of emotional arousal in reference to typical situations involving his or her own child. However, it is important to provide the parent and child with time for enjoyable activities prior to leaving the clinic, in order to protect against possible carryover effects of arousal.

CHILD-REARING METHODS. Interest in patterns of parenting has gradually shifted over the past two decades away from specific child care issues, general approaches to discipline (e.g., permissive vs. authoritarian), or general child-rearing attitudes (Dowdney, Mrazek, Quinton, & Rutter, 1984) to the molecular analysis of reciprocal patterns of parent–child interaction, with particular emphasis on developmental abilities (Harris & Ferrari, 1983). This emphasis has led to a corresponding shift toward increasing use and availability of observational measures, questionnaires, and other forms of self-report in order to assess family interactions.

Research aimed at distinguishing interaction patterns between abusive and nonabusive families has highlighted the importance of identifying the ratio of positive to negative behaviors exhibited, as well as the frequency and quality of prosocial behavior (Wolfe, 1985a). Likewise, researchers investigating parent–child interactions with other clinical and nonclinical populations have converged upon similar dimensions of parenting that discriminate desirable from nondesirable methods (e.g., Conger, McCarty, Yang, Lahey, & Kropp, 1984; Maccoby & Martin, 1983). The main dimensions of parenting emerging from these studies include parental responsivity, affect, social communication, and patterns of control (Dowdney, et al., 1984). Representative methods for assessing these dimensions are reviewed here in light of practical setting and sampling restrictions.

The consensus among child abuse researchers appears to support the validity and feasibility of direct observations with this population (Wolfe, 1985a). There are several ways to approach this task, each with advantages and disadvantages. For example, observing families in the home may provide the most naturalistic setting; however, the family's typical pattern of interaction may be so disrupted that little information may be gained (this is especially problematic with abusive families who have not requested service). In terms of setting criteria, structured clinic observations have gained wide acceptability and support as a valid assessment method for parent–child interactions (Hughes

& Haynes, 1978). One potential advantage of clinic observations is the feasibility of video-taping interactions. In addition to coding behavior from the tape, the scenes may be played back in order to have the parent retrospectively indicate his or her emotional reactions, level of arousal, and thoughts during the interaction. Another consideration for using structured clinic observations is that observations of low-frequency behaviors (such as yelling, grabbing, etc.) yield more relevant data in a more efficient manner when structured tasks are presented (e.g., Burgess & Conger, 1978; Friedman *et al.*, 1981; Herrenkohl *et al.*, 1984; Mash *et al.*, 1983; Wolfe et al., 1981).

Quantitative assessment of family interactions is best approached by using an existing or modified structured procedure for coding family interactions. Since there are no particular behavior categories that are unique to abusive families, the investigator can choose from among an expanding variety of family observation systems, and can base his or her choice upon considerations such as diversity of definitional codes, ability to conduct sequential interactions, and field experience. Systems that seem especially suited for aggressive families and have considerable field research and development include the Behavioral Observation Scoring System (Burgess & Conger, 1978; Conger *et al.*, 1984), the Family Process Code (Patterson, 1982), the Dyadic Parent–Child Interaction Coding System (Robinson & Eyberg, 1981), the Response-Class Matrix (Mash *et al.*, 1983), the Standardized Observation Codes (Wahler, House, & Stambaugh, 1976), and the Behavioral Coding System (Forehand & McMahon, 1981). These observational systems all contain definitional codes for the major dimensions of parenting discussed previously (e.g., verbal and physical positive behaviors, criticism, commands, verbal and physical negative behavior, etc.), which allow for a comprehensive appraisal of the parent's and child's aversive and prosocial behaviors. The increasing availability of computer entry and scoring systems accompanying these methods will markedly enhance data collection and analysis.

A final issue that currently poses a challenge to observational systems involves methods of assessing the "quality" of parental competence in child rearing (see discussion by Wolfe & Bourdeau, 1987). One approach is to use a criterion-based performance measure or index based upon observations. For example, my colleagues and I (Wolfe *et al.*, 1981) have presented a checklist for assessing the skill dimensions of positive reinforcement, commands, and punishment, which is completed following observations of parent–child interactions. Items on the checklist correspond to common training objectives with problem families (e.g., "parent uses clear, firm voice," "enthusiastic," "avoids unnecessary criticism," etc.). Crittenden and Bonvillian (1984) and Conger *et al.* (1984) approach the task of assessing parenting quality by combining behavioral codes into an index of parent "sensitivity" or "affect," resulting in a summative measure that may be more meaningful than any single behavior codes for evaluating treatment directions (although this is a supposition that remains to be determined). Other promising directions for assessing the qualitative dimensions of parenting (e.g., social communication, affect) emerge from related literature on measuring emotions in humans. Research on parent–child interaction could profit from informative approaches to coding hostility, anger, and similar emotional expressions from facial movements, such as the Facial Affect Scoring Technique (Ekman, 1982). Gottman and Levenson (1985) have also developed 11 specific affect codes (e.g., anger, disgust, fear) that are based on subjects' verbal content, voice tone, facial expression, gestures, and body movements, and they have shown these measures to be highly related to the subjects' self-report and physiological changes during assessment of marital interaction. Although these coding procedures are time-consuming, they hold promise for improving the measurement of the qualitative dimensions of parent–child interactions that are often not defined in behavioral coding systems.

Assessment of Child

The developmental perspective presented earlier has highlighted many of the documented and suspected problems exhibited by abused and neglected children. However, no distinctive or circumscribed pattern of behavior has been discovered among this population. Therefore, a thorough investigation of a maltreated child's development and social behavior across settings is often necessary to determine his or her current needs. As with the abusing parent, the task of assessing all potentially relevant areas can become unmanageable unless a systematic, problem-solving approach is used. Since maltreated children have generally been shown to display a variety of behavior problems and developmental delays, a useful strategy is to formulate major assessment questions around these two concerns:

1. Child behavior problems with family members. What is it about this child that places him or her at risk of maltreatment? This concern directs the clinician's attention toward noticeable and/or reported features of the child that stand out as being problematic within the context of his or her family, such as behavior excesses or deficits.

2. Child adaptive abilities and cognitive development. How is the child's overall physical, emotional, cognitive, and behavioral development affected by the current circumstances? This concern focuses the clinician's attention toward aspects of the child's development and adaptive behavior that may require remedial assistance.

Child Behavior Problems with Family Members

The abused child is often described as being "difficult," which could be either a cause or an effect of physically coercive child-rearing methods. Such descriptions may, in part, represent biased parental perceptions reflecting only the worst side of the child's behavior. On the other hand, several observational studies have found abused children to behave in a more obnoxious fashion than comparison children (Wolfe, 1985a), which supports the parents' contentions. Since both objective and subjective sources of information are essential to understanding the abused child, parental self-report and direct observational measures of child behavior are considered in this section.

PARENTAL REPORT. The child's primary caregiver, usually the parent, is a critical source of information concerning the child's development and behavior. Parental report of child behavior is a useful starting point for assessment and intervention planning, because it permits the clinician to obtain a broad spectrum of information as to the parent's perception of problem areas in the parent–child relationship. Most parents who have been accused of abuse or who had admitted to their fear of harming their children share a willingness to discuss the children's misdeeds and to complete a checklist of behavioral strengths and weaknesses that best describe their children. Although the degree of parental distortion or exaggeration of problems is not known, at least one study has demonstrated interparent agreement (Pearson correlation for Internalizing problems = .61; correlation for Externalizing problems = .84) in a sample of abusing parents who completed the Achenbach Child Behavior Checklist (Wolfe & Mosk, 1983).

The Achenbach Child Behavior Checklist (CBCL; Achenbach & Edelbrock, 1983) is a 118-item parent rating scale of a child's behavior. The child's social competence (e.g., completion of chores, involvement with friends) and behavior problems (e.g., "won't talk," "can't concentrate") as judged over the past 6 months are measured by this instrument on a 3-point scale (0 = "not true," 1 = "sometimes or somewhat true," 2 = "very true or often true"). Computer or hand scoring produces a Child Behavior Profile that can be compared to age- and sex-based normative data (for ages 2–16 years), and T scores and percentile rankings are produced. The three Social Competence factor scales (Activities, Social Involvement, School Performance) permit an understanding of the child's strengths and/or needs for participation and involvement with others. Conversely, the Behavior Problem factor scales (Somatic Complaints, Anxious/Obsessive, Depressed/Withdrawn, Hyperactive, Delinquent, Aggressive, and others that are unique to age and sex groups) provide assistance in determining the range and severity of child problems as expressed by the parent. These Behavior Problem scales have been further factor-analyzed into broad-band scales labeled Internalizing (i.e., affective and/or self-deprecatory behaviors such as crying, withdrawal, and anxiety) and Externalizing (i.e., behaviors that often interfere with task completion or annoy others, such as hitting, yelling, and being overly active). The CBCL requires a sixth-grade reading level and takes about 20 minutes to complete. Following scoring, it is useful to review the items marked by each parent to clarify further the nature of and specific circumstances surrounding child behavior problems.

The Eyberg Child Behavior Inventory (ECBI; Eyberg & Ross, 1978) is a briefer (36-item) parent-completed checklist of child conduct problems, suitable for use with children aged 2–12. The inventory contains common examples of child behaviors that may be a problem for the parent (e.g., "dawdles in getting dressed," "physically fights with siblings"), and requires that the respondent rate the "intensity" or frequency of each potential problem on a 7-point scale (1 = "never," 7 = "always"). The ECBI yields both an intensity and a problem score, based on the ratings and on the parent's indication that the behavior is a problem for him or her; these scores enable the examiner to pinpoint problem areas for further discussion and elaboration. Interpretation of the scores is aided by referring to clinical cutoff scores provided through normative studies.

Ancillary reports from significant adults who know the child can provide useful reliability checks (as to parent's accurate description of the child's behavior), as well as additional clinical information regarding the child's adjustment at school or in the community. The CBCL or the ECBI may be completed by a foster parent or social worker who has known the child for several months. Although the test norms would no longer be applicable, the perspective of these individuals may serve to confirm or clarify the problems that have been noted by the abusing parent, or to suggest the degree of situational specificity of such problems. (For example, do the problems occur more or less often in the foster home? Does the foster parent view this child's behavior as significantly different from others he or she has known?) The child's classroom teacher can also complete a questionnaire similar to the parent report (e.g., the Teacher Report Form of the CBCL; Achenbach & Edelbrock, 1983) to provide normative comparisons of this child to other children in a school setting.

OBSERVATIONAL PROCEDURES. Observations of child behavior conducted in the home or clinic serve two assessment functions: They provide a measure of the child's "typical" behavior with his or her parent, and they also allow the examiner to view the child's range of behavior under controlled conditions. By observing the parent and child from behind an observational mirror, the examiner may record selected target behaviors during contrived situations and free interaction. For very young children and infants, these situations are limited primarily to basic caregiving, such as feeding, holding, verbal and physical forms of communication, and simple compliance or instructional tasks (e.g., attending to parent's voice commands). Preschool and older children may be given more specific instructions by the parent to engage in activities that resemble common areas of conflict at home (e.g., to complete one activity and then switch to another). During parent–child interactions, the observer should watch for child "avoidant" behaviors, such as dodging, flinching, staring at the parent, or similar hypervigilance suggesting that the child is fearful of the parent. Similarly, the observer should determine the manner in which the child approaches both parents. Often the preschool-age abused child will seek to gain a parent's attention by highly aversive means, such as grabbing, pinching, tugging, or whining, despite the parent's attempts to punish such behavior. The child's use of eye contact, appropriate speech, attention span, compliance, and positive and negative physical contact with the parent are additional examples of behavior categories that may be recorded during structured observations by using standardized coding systems (such as those discussed previously).

To gain an understanding of the child's range of developmentally appropriate behavior, the examiner may wish to interact with the child while the parent observes from behind the mirror or another part of the room. This enables the examiner to elicit the child's response to adult praise and attention, unfamiliar learning tasks (such as a puzzle or matching-figures game), compliance tasks (e.g., cleaning up and putting the toys away), and if necessary, time out or similar punishment procedures, which the parent may not be capable of eliciting during the assessment period. The examiner may also instruct the child to play alone with a desirable and/or a less desirable toy, in order to address the child's attention span and distractibility. Following this procedure, the parent can share his or her impressions of the child's recent behavior, which serves as a method for eliciting more objective descriptions from the parent of recent child behavior (without the bias or influence of being part of the same interaction).

Adaptive Abilities and Cognitive and Emotional Development

The developmental consequences of child abuse can become major handicaps if left unattended, placing the child in jeopardy of school failure, peer problems, and long-term adjustment disorders. Abused children may be at risk due to their birth status (e.g., retardation, physical impairments, prematurity), or they may begin to show early signs of developmental retardation as a consequence of abuse or neglect.

Specific areas of functioning that require assessment involve the child's adaptive abilities in such areas as language and self-care, as well as the child's cognitive and emotional development in the areas of interpersonal problem solving, coping methods, and family perceptions. These areas can be assessed through parent report methods and structured tests administered directly to the child.

PARENT REPORT. The parent, foster parent, or other adult who is familiar with the child's development can be a source of useful information concerning adaptive abilities and handicaps. A number of adaptive behavior scales for children are widely available that enable the interviewer to assess the range of the child's adaptive abilities. The Pyramid Scales (Cone, 1984) and the revised Vineland Adaptive Behavior Scales (Sparrow, Balla, & Cicchetti, 1984) survey the child's developmental progress and adaptive functioning through interviews with the caregiver. The Pyramid Scales are particularly useful for lower-functioning parents and children, because they contain several scales of adaptive behavior that are organized according to basic self-help skills (e.g., eating, dressing, toileting, etc.) as well as social interaction skills (e.g., receptive and expressive language). These are criterion-referenced instruments; that is, the interviewer determines the level of performance that the child has mastered in important developmental areas by asking the parent to indicate, for example, whether the child presently can walk up stairs unassisted, eat with a fork, speak in two-word sentences, and so on. The child's adaptive ability is assessed in reference to the criteria contained in the instrument, ranging from simple sensory–motor skills to more complex social interaction. For age-norm comparisons (which are especially relevant if significant delay is suspected with infants or toddlers), a developmental test can be administered (e.g., the Denver Developmental Screening Test; Frankenburg & Dodds, 1968). This procedure involves the presentation of stimuli to the infant or child, such as sounds, shapes, and verbal commands. The child's responses to the stimuli are compared to developmental norms that provide an estimate of the child's developmental progress or delay.

CHILD INTERVIEW AND SELF-REPORT. An individual assessment with the infant, preschooler, or school-age child can assist the examiner in understanding the child's overall functioning and can provide insight as to current fears or anxiety that might be quite debilitating. The possibility that the older child (age 6 or older) has developed a distorted perspective of family life in which violence is commonplace or acceptable should be investigated by discussing attitudes about interpersonal aggression, sex roles, and responsibility for aggressive behavior. The child may also respond to the examiner in a very guarded manner that is not a valid reflection of his or her typical behavior, out of possible fear of reprisal or confusion over the events that have occurred. For this reason, the examiner should enable the child to establish a sense of trust and comfort prior to discussing the family's problems.

A good beginning point is the discussion of the child's comprehension and reaction to family problems using a semistructured interview format. Our research team at the University of Western Ontario has developed a number of interview questions that address what has happened to the child in the family; his or her feelings about these events; and his or her perception of blame, responsibility, and the family's future. The interview begins with a general discussion of activities and events that the child enjoys, which leads into a more specific discussion of recent crisis events. The child's "crisis adjustment" is assessed in reference to (1) his or her feelings about changes in the family (e.g., foster care, parental separation); and (2) the completion of the Life Events Checklist for Children (J. H. Johnson & McCutcheon, 1980). This latter checklist asks the child to indicate what events have happened to him or her; whether each was a good or bad event; and whether each had no effect, a little effect, or a lot on his or her own routine. The checklist contains 31 major life events (e.g., moved to a new house; Mom or Dad lost job; special recognition for good grades) and enables the clinician to elicit essential information about the child's view of the specific circumstances surrounding violence in the home.

Safety skills (e.g., "What do you do if Mom and Dad are arguing?", "How can you tell when Mom or Dad is angry?", "Who do you call in an emergency?") are also important areas to consider during the child interview. The child's comprehension of personal safety and knowledge of appropriate actions to take provides useful information for planning for the immediate needs of the child (e.g., out-of-home placement; alternative actions to avoid high-conflict situations). This discussion can then turn to the child's attitudes and responses to interpersonal conflict and expression of anger, by encouraging the child to discuss events and circumstances that "make you really mad," followed by identification of his or her actions, feelings, and attitudes about such "anger situations." We find it useful to describe attitudes toward and reactions to anger provocation in reference to favorite television characters, in order to determine the child's ability to recognize the artificiality and inappropriateness of aggressive behavior. For example, some abused children reveal the influence of aggressive modeling in the family or on television through their inability to recognize nonviolent means for resolving interpersonal conflicts. Although this is by no means unique to abused children, the presence of such rigid adherence to coercive problem solving signals a need for exposure to alternative strategies.

The Parent Perception Inventory (PPI; Hazzard, Christensen, & Margolin, 1981) is a recently developed interview method for eliciting sensitive information from children over age 5, and is a useful procedure for encouraging discussion of family topics. The PPI includes nine positive and nine negative parental behaviors, to which the child responds according to the frequency of their occurrence at home. The rationale provided to the child is very important and must be stated clearly to avoid misunderstanding: "I would like to know how much you think your mom and dad do certain things at home. I only want to know about your ideas, so there aren't any right or wrong answers. I won't talk to your parents about what you tell me, so please tell me what you really think. If you don't want to answer a question, that's okay." The child is then provided with a chart containing five vials, one empty and the others colored to increasing amounts of fullness, and labeled "never" (empty vial) to "always" (full vial). For example, the child is asked by the interviewer, "How often does your mom and dad say nice things to you, praise you, compliment you?" and "How often does your mom or dad take away things when you misbehave, like not letting you watch TV, ride your bike, or stay up late?" The scale is completed separately in reference to the mother and father, which results in a total score of positive and negative perceptions for each parent (comparative norms for boys and girls are available).

Studies using this instrument with populations of abused children have not yet been reported, and therefore the validity and reliability of this method remain to be established. Its clinical and research utility for revealing a child's perspective on parental treatment appears to be warranted, but the examiner must be careful to avoid communicating value judgments to the child concerning his or her family.

Assessment of the child's current anxieties and fears may also be conducted through observation (during the interview) and self-report instruments. The interviewer should be sensitive to the child's verbal and somatic indices of anxiety or negative affect (e.g., poor eye contact, twitching movements, long silences, sadness) and should make every attempt to determine the origins or reference for such emotion (which is often linked to foster care placement, uncertainty over family reunion, and/or fear of further maltreatment). The State–Trait Anxiety Inventory for Children (STAIC; Spielberger, 1973) and the Children's Manifest Anxiety Scale—Revised (Reynolds & Richmond, 1978) are two self-report instruments that have been specifically developed to assess children's anxiety. The instruments are easy for children to understand (sample item from the STAIC: "I worry about making mistakes [hardly ever, sometimes, often]") and provide complete norms for comparison with age and sex groups. The Fear Survey Schedule for Children—Revised (Ollendick, 1983) is an 80-item fear inventory with a 3-point response format ("none," "some," "a lot") suitable for assessing fears in children aged 6 and above. It is an attractive instrument for assessing maltreated children, because of its extensive listing of common and less common fears that can potentially interfere with children's family and social adjustment.

Integrating Child Assessment Information

What should emerge from an assessment of the child's current adaptive abilities and cognitive and emotional development is an understanding of his or her resources for coping with the level of family problems that may exist, as well as current attitudes, beliefs, and emotional and behavioral expression vis-à-vis his or her role in the family. Children who have been removed from the home (or who have had their parents separate or leave the home), as well as older children who have experienced prolonged family conflict and abuse, often display the more extreme signs of adjustment difficulties (e.g., aggression, withdrawal, peer problems, anger at family members). This finding presumably reflects the relationship between child behavior and critical situational variables that must be considered throughout the interpretation of the child's needs. Information provided by the parent, child, and caseworker, and gathered through interview procedures, should be integrated in a fashion that permits a comparison of how the parent views the child with how the child views his or her own situation, behavior, and affect; this should follow from the assessment procedures described herein. Furthermore, objective information on the child's cognitive development and behavioral adjustment, obtained through observational or normative assessment devices, can provide a framework for establishing treatment priorities that are consistent with the child's abilities and needs.

SUMMARY

This chapter has described the multifaceted issues surrounding the assessment of child abuse and family dysfunction. Research over the past 10 years has improved our understanding of the functional relationships among diverse etiological variables, and these advances are reflected in the availability of a variety of assessment strategies and methods for abused and neglected children and their families. The emphasis throughout this chapter has been on examining maltreatment within the context of family and other situational variables, rather than on limiting the focus primarily to faults of the parent and/or child. Consideration of the developmental consequences of child maltreatment indicates increasing support for the position that family violence and discord interferes with the child's development of adaptive and prosocial behavior. Characteristics of the parent and child have been discussed here in terms of how they interact with significant environmental events to affect the likelihood of aggressive and abusive behavior. Major antecedents of abuse (e.g., difficult child behavior and marital conflict) have been identified, as have several variables that mediate the expression of aggressive behavior (e.g., the parent's emotional responsivity, perceived social supports, and child management skills).

Due to the nature of child abuse and neglect, the scope of behavioral assessment procedures is often limited by restrictions on observing low-frequency, private behaviors occurring between family members. This challenge has been met by behavioral investigators who have attempted to define higher-profile behaviors that can be observed during parent–child interactions. In addition, this chapter has argued that in order to assess crucial aspects of parent and child behavior, behavioral assessment procedures can be expanded and integrated with other approaches to yield complementary information. Accordingly, a wide variety of assessment procedures have been presented, including direct observation in structured and naturalistic settings, parent self-report of problem situations and emotional reactivity, standardized tests, interviews, and self-monitoring techniques. This approach to the assessment of the abusive family is intended as a comprehensive set of procedures that will enable practitioners to select those methods that are most suitable for different assessment purposes.

It is worth restating that the heterogeneity and complexity of physically abusive families make agreement on definitional, assessment, and intervention criteria very difficult. Consequently, no single approach to this problem can handle the entire range of contributing factors in a manner that is practical and defensible. Behavioral researchers and practitioners are relative newcomers to the field of family violence, which has been the major responsibility of direct service providers and government programs. Cooperative efforts among mental health professionals have grown immensely, but they continue to lag behind expectations. The past decade has seen a vast increase in public awareness and concern for this problem, growing from 10% of the American population in 1974 who considered child abuse to be a serious national problem to 90% in 1983 (Magnuson, 1983). Early views of the abusive parent as being a seriously disturbed individual are slowly fading in favor of more comprehensive, ecological explanations (e.g., Belsky, 1980), and research is documenting more of the major factors that may be important in preventing this tragic social problem. This has resulted in a number of promising treatment approaches to enhance parental competence and reduce situational stress among high-risk families (e.g., Kelly, 1983; Lutzker, 1983; Wolfe et al., 1981). Community-based intervention strategies (e.g., Cohn, 1982) and innovative research programs that strive to understand the causal relationships among these discrepant factors (e.g., Egeland *et al.*, 1980) have also appeared. Although this optimistic view of progress in the field must be countered by the lack of clear evidence that these efforts have as yet been effective in reducing the problem, the contribution of behavioral assessment methods to this burgeoning field will probably continue to be paramount in the years to come.

REFERENCES

Aber, J. L., & Cicchetti, D. (1984). The socio-emotional development of maltreated children: An empirical and theoretical analysis. In H. Fitzgerald, B. Lester, & M. Yogman (Eds.), *Theory and research in behavioral pediatrics* (Vol. 2, pp. 147–199). New York: Plenum.

Abidin, R. (1983). *Parenting Stress Index—manual*. Charlottesville, VA: Pediatric Psychology Press.

Achenbach, T. M. (1966). The classification of children's psychiatric symptoms: A factor-analytic study. *Psychological Monographs, 80* (Whole No. 615).

Achenbach, T. M., & Edelbrock, C. S. (1983). *Manual for the Child Behavior Checklist and Revised Child Behavior Profile*. Burlington: University of Vermont, Department of Psychiatry.

Ainsworth, M. D. S. (1980). Attachment and child abuse. In G. Gerbner, C. J. Ross, & E. Zigler (Eds.), *Child abuse: An agenda for action* (pp. 35–47). New York: Oxford University Press.

Alfaro, J. D. (1981). Report on the relationship between child abuse and neglect and later socially deviant behavior. In R. J. Hunner & Y. E. Walker (Eds.), *Exploring the relationship between child abuse and delinquency* (pp. 175–219). Montclair, NJ: Allanheld, Osmun.

American Humane Association. (1984). *Highlights of official child neglect and abuse reporting—1982*. Denver, CO: Author.

Appelbaum, A. S. (1977). Developmental retardation in infants as a concomitant of physical child abuse. *Journal of Abnormal Child Psychology, 5*, 417–423.

Averill, J. R. (1982). *Anger and aggression: An essay on emotion*. New York: Springer-Verlag.

Azar, S. T., Robinson, D. R., Hekimian, E., & Twentyman, C. T. (1984). Unrealistic expectations and problem-solving ability in maltreating and comparison mothers. *Journal of Consulting and Clinical Psychology, 52*, 687–691.

Bandura, A. (1973). *Aggression: A social learning analysis*. Englewood Cliffs, NJ: Prentice-Hall.

Barahal, R. M., Waterman, J., & Martin, H. P. (1981). The social cognitive development of abused children. *Journal of Consulting and Clinical Psychology, 49*, 508–516.

Baron, R. A. (1977). *Human aggression*. New York: Plenum.

Baron, R. A. (1978). Aggression and heat: The "long, hot summer" revisited. In A. Baum, S. Valins, & J. E. Singer (Eds.), *Advances in environmental research* (Vol. 1, pp. 186–207). Hillsdale, NJ: Erlbaum.

Baron, R. A., Russell, G. W., & Arms, R. L. (1985). Negative ions and behavior: Impact on mood, memory, and aggression among Type A and Type B persons. *Journal of Personality and Social Psychology, 48*, 746–754.

Bauer, W. D., & Twentyman, C. T. (1985). Abusing, neglectful, and comparison mothers' responses to child-related and non-child-related stressors. *Journal of Consulting and Clinical Psychology, 53*, 335–343.

Belsky, J. (1980). Child maltreatment: An ecological integration. *American Psychologist, 35*, 320–335.

Belsky, J. (1984). The determinants of parenting: A process model. *Child Development, 55*, 83–96.

Belsky, J., & Isabella, R. (in press). Maternal, infant, and social–contextual determinants of attachment security. In J. Belsky & T. Nezworski (Eds.), *Clinical implications of attachment*. Hillsdale, NJ: Erlbaum.

Berkowitz, L. (1983). Aversively stimulated aggression: Some parallels and differences in research with animals and humans. *American Psychologist, 38*, 1135–1144.

Besharov, D. J. (1982). Toward better research on child abuse and neglect: Making definitional issues an explicit methodological concern. *Child Abuse and Neglect, 5*, 383–390.

Blechman, E. A., Budd, K. S., Christophersen, E. R., Szykula, S., Wahler, R., Embry, L. H., Kogan, K., O'Leary, K. D., & Riner, L. S. (1981). Engagement in behavioral family therapy: A multisite investigation. *Behavior Therapy, 12*, 461–472.

Bond, C. R., & McMahon, R. J. (1984). Relationships between marital distress and child behavior problems, maternal personal adjustment, maternal personality, and maternal parenting behavior. *Journal of Abnormal Psychology, 93*, 348–351.

Bousha, D. M., & Twentyman, C. T. (1984). Mother–child interactional style in abuse, neglect, and control groups: Naturalistic observations in the home. *Journal of Abnormal Psychology, 93*, 106–114.

Bradley, R. H., & Caldwell, B. M. (1979). Home Observation for Measurement of the Environment: A revision of the preschool scale. *American Journal of Mental Deficiency, 84*, 235–244.

Burgess, R. L. (1979). Child abuse: A social interactional analysis. In B. B. Lahey & A. E. Kazdin (Eds.), *Advances in clinical child psychology* (Vol. 2, pp. 142–172). New York: Plenum.

Burgess, R. L., & Conger, R. (1978). Family interactions in abusive, neglectful, and normal families. *Child Development, 49*, 1163–1173.

Burgess, R. L., & Youngblade, L. (1987). Social incompetence and the intergenerational transmission of abusive parental practices. In R. J. Gelles, G. T. Hotaling, D. Finkelhor, & M. A. Straus (Eds.), *New directions in family violence research*. Newbury Park, CA: Sage.

Carew, J. (1979). Commentary: The Ypsilanti–Carnegie Infant Education Project. *Monographs of the High/ Scope Educational Research Foundation, 6*, 75–80.

Cicchetti, D., & Rizley, R. (1981). Developmental perspectives on the etiology, intergenerational transmission, and sequelae of child maltreatment. In D. Cicchetti & R. Rizley (Eds.), *New directions for child development: Developmental perspectives on child maltreatment* (pp. 31–55). San Francisco: Jossey-Bass.

Cohn, A. H. (1982). Stopping abuse before it occurs: Different solutions for different population groups. *Child Abuse and Neglect, 6*, 473–483.

Cone, J. D. (1984). *The Pyramid Scales: Criterion-referenced measures of adaptive behavior in handicapped persons*. Austin, Tx: PRO-ED.

Conger, R. (1981). The assessment of dysfunctional family systems. In B. B. Lahey & A. E. Kazdin (Eds.), *Advances in clinical child psychology* (Vol. 4, pp. 199–242). New York: Plenum Press.

Conger, R., Burgess, R., & Barrett, C. (1979). Child abuse related to life change and perceptions of illness: Some preliminary findings. *Family Coordinator, 28,* 73–78.

Conger, R., McCarty, J.A., Yang, R. K., Lahey, B. B., & Kropp, J. P. (1984). Perception of child, childrearing values, and emotional distress as mediating links between environmental stressors and observed maternal behavior. *Child Development, 55,* 2234–2247.

Crittenden, P. M., & Bonvillian, J. D. (1984). The relationship between maternal risk status and maternal sensitivity. *American Journal of Orthopsychiatry, 54,* 250–262.

Cutrona, C. E. (1984). Social support and stress in the transition to parenthood. *Journal of Abnormal Psychology, 93,* 378–390.

Dietrich, K. N., Starr, R. H., & Kaplan, M. G. (1980). Maternal stimulation and care of abused infants. In T. M. Field, S. Goldberg, D. Stern, & A. M. Sostek (Eds.), *High-risk infants and children: Adult and peer interactions* (pp. 25–41). New York: Academic Press.

Disbrow, M. A., Doerr, H., & Caulfield, C. (1977). Measuring the components of parents' potential for child abuse and neglect. *Child Abuse and Neglect, 1,* 279–296.

Dohrenwend, B. S., Dohrenwend, B. P. Dodgson, M., & Shrout, P. E. (1984). Symptoms, hassles, social supports, and life events: Problem of confounded measures. *Journal of Abnormal Psychology, 93,* 222–230.

Donnerstein, E., & Wilson, D. W. (1976). Effects of noise and perceived control on ongoing and subsequent aggression behavior. *Journal of Personality and Social Psychology, 34,* 774–781.

Dowdney, L., Mrazek, D., Quinton, D., & Rutter, M. (1984). Observation of parent–child interaction with two- to three-year-olds. *Journal of Child Psychology and Psychiatry, 25,* 379–407.

Egeland, B., Breitenbucher, M., & Rosenberg, D. (1980). Prospective study of the significance of life stress in the etiology of child abuse. *Journal of Consulting and Clinical Psychology, 48,* 195–205.

Egeland, B., & Farber, E. A. (1984). Infant–mother attachment: Factors related to its development and changes over time. *Child Development, 55,* 753–771.

Egeland, B., & Sroufe, L. A. (1981). Attachment and early maltreatment. *Child Development, 52,* 44–52.

Egeland, B., Sroufe, A., & Erickson, M. (1983). The developmental consequence of different patterns of maltreatment. *Child Abuse and Neglect, 7,* 459–469.

Egeland, B., & Vaughn, B. (1981). Failure of "bond formation" as a cause of abuse, neglect, and maltreatment. *American Journal of Orthopsychiatry, 51,* 78–84.

Ekman, P. (1982). Methods for measuring facial action. In K. R. Scherer & P. Ekman (Eds.), *Handbook of methods in nonverbal behavior research* (pp. 45–90). Cambridge, England: Cambridge University Press.

Elmer, E. (1977). A follow-up study of traumatized children. *Pediatrics, 59,* 273–279.

Elmer, E., & Gregg, G. S. (1967). Developmental characteristics of abused children. *Pediatrics, 40,* 596–602.

Emery, R. (1982). Interparental conflict and the children of discord and divorce. *Psychological Bulletin, 92,* 310–330.

Eyberg, S., & Ross, A. (1978). Assessment of child behavior problems: The validation of a new inventory. *Journal of Clinical Child Psychology, 7,* 113–116.

Fagan, J. A., & Wexler, S. (1984, August). *Family origins of violent delinquents.* Paper presented at the Second National Conference for Family Violence Researchers, University of New Hampshire, Durham.

Forehand, R., & McMahon, R. (1981). *Helping the non-compliant child: A clinician's guide to parent training.* New York: Guilford Press.

Frankenburg, W. K., & Dodds, J. B. (1968). *The Denver Developmental Screening Test—manual.* Boulder: University of Colorado Press.

Friedman, R., Sandler, J., Hernandez, M., & Wolfe, D. (1981). Child abuse. In E. J. Mash & L. G. Terdal (Eds.), *Behavioral assessment of childhood disorders* (pp. 221–255). New York: Guilford.

Friedrich, W. N., & Boriskin, J. A. (1976). The role of the child in abuse: A review of the literature. *American Journal of Orthopsychiatry, 46,* 580–590.

Friedrich, W. N., Einbender, A. J., & Luecke, W . J. (1983). Cognitive and behavioral characteristics of physically abused children. *Journal of Consulting and Clinical Psychology, 51,* 313–314.

Frodi, A. M. (1981). Contribution of infant characteristics to child abuse. *American Journal of Mental Deficiency, 85,* 341–349.

Frodi, A. M., & Lamb, M. E. (1980). Child abusers' responses to infant smiles and cries. *Child Development, 51,* 238–241.

Frodi, A. M., & Smetana, J. (1984). Abused, neglected, and nonmaltreated preschoolers' ability to discriminate emotions in others: The effects of IQ. *Child Abuse and Neglect, 8,* 459–465.

Gaensbauer, T. J., & Sands, K. (1979). Distorted affective communication in abused/neglected infants and their potential impact on caretakers. *Journal of the American Academy of Child Psychiatry, 18,* 236–250.

Gaines, R., Sandgrund, A., Green, A. H., & Power, E. (1978). Etiological factors in child maltreatment: A multivariate study of abusing, neglecting, and normal mothers. *Journal of Abnormal Psychology, 87,* 531–540.

Gambrill, E. (1983). Behavioral interventions with child abuse and neglect. *Progress in Behavior Modification, 15,* 1–56.

Garbarino, J. (1976). A preliminary study of some ecological correlates of child abuse: The impact of socioeconomic stress on mothers. *Child Development, 47,* 178–185.

Garbarino, J. (1982). *Children and families in the social environment.* Chicago: Aldine.

Garbarino, J., & Sherman, D. (1980). High-risk neighborhoods and high-risk families: The human ecology of child maltreatment. *Child Development, 51,* 188–198.

Garmezy, N., & Rutter, M. (Eds.). (1983). *Stress, coping and development in children.* New York: McGraw-Hill.

George, C., & Main, M. (1979). Social interactions of young abused children: Approach, avoidance, and aggression. *Child Development, 50,* 306–318.

Gil, D. G. (1970). *Violence against children: Physical child abuse in the United States.* Cambridge, MA: Harvard University Press.

Giovannoni, J. M., & Becerra, R. M. (1979). *Defining child abuse.* New York: Free Press.

Goldberg, D. P., & Hillier, V. F. (1979). A scaled version of the General Health Questionnaire. *Psychological Medicine, 9,* 139–145.

Gottman, J. M. (1979). *Marital interaction: Experimental investigations.* New York: Academic Press.

Gottman, J. M., & Levenson, R. W. (1985). A valid procedure for obtaining self-report of affect in marital interaction. *Journal of Consulting and Clinical Psychology, 53,* 151–160.

Green, A. H. (1978). Self-destructive behavior in battered children. *American Journal of Psychiatry, 135,* 579–582.

Green, A. H. (1983). Dimension of psychological trauma in abused children. *Journal of the American Academy of Child Psychiatry, 22,* 231–237.

Griest, D. L., & Wells, K. C. (1983). Behavioral family therapy with conduct disorders in children. *Behavior Therapy, 13,* 37–53.

Harris, S. L., & Ferrari, M. (1983). Developmental factors in child behavior therapy. *Behavior Therapy, 14,* 54–72.

Hazzard, A., Christensen, A., & Margolin, G. (1981). Children's perceptions of parental behaviors. *Journal of Abnormal Child Psychology, 11,* 49–60.

Herrenkohl, R. C., Herrenkohl, E. C., & Egolf, B. P. (1983). Circumstances surrounding the occurrence of child maltreatment. *Journal of Consulting and Clinical Psychology, 51,* 424–431.

Herrenkohl, E. C., Herrenkohl, R. C., Toedter, L., & Yanushefski, A. M. (1984). Parent–child interactions in abusive and nonabusive families. *Journal of the American Academy of Child Psychiatry, 23,* 641–648.

Herzberger, S. D., Potts, D. A., & Dillon, M. (1981). Abusive and nonabusive parental treatment from the child's perspective. *Journal of Consulting and Clinical Psychology, 49,* 81–90.

Hoffman-Plotkin, D., & Twentyman, C. T. (1984). A multimodal assessment of behavioral and cognitive deficits in abused and neglected preschoolers. *Child Development, 55,* 794–802.

Hughes, H. M., & Haynes, S. N. (1978). Structured laboratory observation in the behavioral assessment of parent–child interactions: A methodological critique. *Behavior Therapy, 9,* 428–447.

Jaffe, P., Wolfe, D. A., Wilson, S., & Zak, L. (1986). Family violence and child adjustment: A comparative analysis of girls' and boys' behavioral symptoms. *American Journal of Psychiatry, 143,* 74–77.

Johnson, B., & Morse, H. A. (1968). Injured children and their parents. *Children, 15,* 147–152.

Johnson, J. H., & McCutcheon, S. M. (1980). Assessing life stress in older children and adolescents: Preliminary findings with the Life Events Checklist. In I. G. Sarason & C. D. Spielberger (Eds.), *Stress and anxiety* (Vol. 7, pp. 111–125). Washington, DC: Hemisphere.

Johnson, J. H., & Sarason, I. G. (1979). Recent developments in research in life stress. In V. Hamilton & D. Warburton (Eds.), *Human stress and cognition: An information processing approach* (pp. 205–233). London: Wiley.

Jouriles, E. N., & O'Leary, K. D. (1985). Interspousal reliability of reports of marital violence. *Journal of Consulting and Clinical Psychology, 53,* 419–421.

Kadushin, A., & Martin, J. A. (1981). *Child abuse: An interactional event.* New York: Columbia University Press.

Kelly, J. A. (1983). *Treating abusive families: Intervention based on skills training principles.* New York: Plenum.

Kempe, R. S., & Kempe, C. H. (1978). *Child abuse.* Cambridge, MA: Harvard University Press.

Kinard, E. M. (1980). Emotional development in physically abused children. *American Journal of Orthopsychiatry, 50,* 686–696.

Knutson, J. F. (1978). Child abuse as an area of aggression research. *Journal of Pediatric Psychology, 3,* 20–27.

Koverola, C., Elliot-Faust, D., & Wolfe, D. A. (1984). Clinical issues in the behavioral treatment of a child abusive mother experiencing multiple life stresses. *Journal of Clinical Child Psychology, 13,* 187–191.

Kravitz, R. I., & Driscoll, J. M. (1983). Expectations for childhood development among child-abusing and nonabusing parents. *American Journal of Orthopsychiatry, 53,* 336–344.

Lahey, B. B., Conger, R. D., Atkeson, B. M., & Treiber, F. A. (1984). Parenting behavior and emotional status of physically abusive mothers. *Journal of Consulting and Clinical Psychology, 52,* 1062–1071.

Lewis, D. O., Pincus, J. H., & Glaser, G. H. (1979). Violent juvenile delinquents: Psychiatric, neurological, psychological, and abuse factors. *Journal of the American Academy of Child Psychiatry, 18,* 307–319.

Levenson, R. W., & Gottman, J. M. (1983). Marital interaction: Physiological linkage and affective exchange. *Journal of Personality and Social Psychology, 45,* 587–597.

Light, R. (1973). Abused and neglected children in America: A study of alternative policies. *Harvard Educational Review, 43,* 556–598.

Lipsett, L. (1983). Stress in infancy: Toward understanding the origins of coping behavior. In N. Garmezy & M. Rutter (Eds.), *Stress, coping, and development in children* (pp. 161–190). New York: McGraw-Hill.

Locke, H., & Wallace, K. (1959). Short marital adjustment and prediction tests: Their reliability and validity. *Marriage and Family Living, 21,* 251–255.

Loeber, R., Weissman, W., & Reid, J. (1983). Family interactions of assaultive adolescents, stealers, and nondelinquents. *Journal of Abnormal Child Psychology, 11,* 1–14.

Lorber, R., Felton, D. K., & Reid, J. (1984). A social learning approach to the reduction of coercive processes in child abusive families: A molecular analysis. *Advances in Behavior Research and Therapy, 6,* 29–45.

Lutzker, J. R. (1983). Project 12-Ways: Treating child abuse and neglect from an ecobehavioral perspective. In R. F. Dangel & R. A. Polster (Eds.), *Parent training: Foundations of research and practice* (pp. 260–297). New York: Guilford Press.

Maccoby, E. E., & Martin, J. A. (1983). Socialization in the context of the family: Parent–child interaction. In E. M. Hetherington (Ed.), *Handbook of child psychology* (4th ed.): Vol. 4. *Socialization, personality, and social development* (pp. 1–101). New York: Wiley.

Main, M., & George, C. (1984). Responses of abused and disadvantaged toddlers to distress in agemates: A study in the day care setting. *Developmental Psychology, 21,* 407–412.

Magnuson, E. (1983, Sept. 5). Child abuse: The ultimate betrayal. *Time,* pp. 16–18.

Mash, E. J., Johnston, C., & Kovitz, K. (1983). A comparison of the mother–child interactions of physically abused and nonabused children during play and task situations. *Journal of Clinical Child Psychology, 12,* 337–346.

McCord, J. (1979). Some childrearing antecedents of criminal behavior in adult men. *Journal of Personality and Social Psychology, 9,* 1477–1486.

McCord, J. (1983). A forty year perspective on effects of

child abuse and neglect. *Child Abuse and Neglect, 7,* 265–270.

Milner, J. S. (1986). *The Child Abuse Potential Inventory: Manual (Revised).* Webster, NC: Psytec Corporation.

Milner, S., & Ayoub, C. (1980). Evaluation of "at-risk" parents using the Child Abuse Potential Inventory. *Journal of Clinical Psychology, 36,* 945–948.

Milner, J. S., Gold, R. G., Ayoub, C., & Jacewitz, M. M. (1984). Predictive validity of the Child Abuse Potential Inventory. *Journal of Consulting and Clinical Psychology, 52,* 879–884.

Monane, M., Leichter, D., & Lewis, D. O. (1984). Physical abuse in psychiatrically hospitalized children and adolescents. *Journal of the American Academy of Child Psychiatry, 23,* 653–658.

Mulhern, R. K., & Passman, R. H. (1979). The child's behavioral pattern as a determinant of maternal punitiveness. *Child Development, 50,* 815–820.

National Center on Child Abuse and Neglect. (1981). *Study findings: National Study of the Incidence and Severity of Child Abuse and Neglect* (DHHS Publication No. OHDS 81-30325). Washington, DC: U. S. Government Printing Office.

National Institute of Mental Health. (1977). *Child abuse and neglect programs: Practice and theory.* Washington, DC: U. S. Government Printing office.

Ollendick. T. H. (1983). Reliability and validity of the Revised Fear Survey Schedule for Children (FSSC-R). *Behaviour Research and Therapy, 21,* 685–692.

Parke, R. D., & Collmer, C. W. (1975). Child abuse: An interdisciplinary analysis. In E. M. Hetherington (Ed.), *Review of child development research* (Vol. 5, pp. 509–590). Chicago: University of Chicago Press.

Patterson, G. R. (1976). Aggressive child: Victim and architect of a coercive system. In E. J. Mash, L. A. Hamerlynck, & L. C. Handy (Eds.), *Behavior modification and families* (pp. 267–316). New York: Brunner/Mazel.

Patterson, G. R. (1982). *Coercive family process.* Eugene, OR: Castalia.

Patterson, G. R., & Cobb, J. A. (1973). Stimulus control for classes of noxious behaviors. In J. Knutson (Ed.), *The control of aggression: Implication from basic research* (pp. 145–199). Chicago: Aldine.

Pelton, L. H. (1978). Child abuse and neglect: The myth of classlessness. *American Journal of Orthopsychiatry, 48,* 608–617.

Polansky, N., Chalmers, M., Buttenwieser, E., & Williams, D. (1981). *Damaged parents: An anatomy of child neglect.* Chicago: University of Chicago Press.

Porter, B., & O'Leary, K. D. (1980). Marital discord and child behavior problems. *Journal of Abnormal Child Psychology, 80,* 287–295.

Procidano, M., & Heller, K. (1983). Measures of perceived social support from friends and from family: Three validation studies. *American Journal of Community Psychology, 11,* 1–24.

Radbill, S. X. (1968). A history of child abuse and infanticide. In R. E. Helfer & C. H. Kempe (Eds.), *The battered child* (pp. 3–17). Chicago: University of Chicago Press.

Reid, J. R., Taplin, P., & Lorber, R. (1981). A social interactional approach to the treatment of abusive families. In R. B. Stuart (Ed.), *Violent behavior: Social learning approaches to prediction, management, and treatment* (pp. 83–101). New York: Brunner/Mazel.

Reynolds, C. R., & Richmond, B. O. (1978). What I think and feel: A revised measure of children's manifest anxiety. *Journal of Abnormal Child Psychology, 6,* 271–280.

Robinson, E., & Eyberg, S. (1981). The dyadic parent–child interaction coding system: Standardization and validation. *Journal of Consulting and Clinical Psychology, 49,* 245–250.

Ross, C. J. (1980). The lessons of the past: Defining and controlling child abuse in the United States. In G. Gerbner, C. J. Ross, & E. Zigler (Eds.), *Child abuse: An agenda for action* (pp. 63–81). New York: Oxford University Press.

Russell, A. B., & Trainor, C. M. (1984). *Trends in child abuse and neglect: A national perspective.* Denver, CO: American Humane Association.

Rutter, M. (1971). Parent–child separation: Psychological effects on the children. *Journal of Child Psychology and Psychiatry, 12,* 233–260.

Rutter, M. (1979). Protective factors in children's responses to stress and disadvantage. In M. W. Kent & J. E. Rolf (Eds.), *Primary prevention of psychopathology: Social competence in children* (pp. 49–74). Hanover, NH: University Press of New England.

Rutter, M. (1983). Stress, coping, and development: Some issues and some questions. In N. Garmezy & M. Rutter (Eds.), *Stress, coping, and development in children* (pp. 1–41). New York: McGraw-Hill.

Salzinger, S., Kaplan, S., & Artemyeff, C. (1983). Mothers' personal social networks and child maltreatment. *Journal of Abnormal Psychology, 92,* 68–76.

Salzinger, S., Kaplan, S., Pelcovitz, D., Samit, C., & Kreiger, R. (1984). Parent and teacher assessment of children's behavior in child maltreating families. *Journal of the American Academy of Child Psychiatry, 23,* 458–464.

Sandgrund, A., Gaines, R. W., & Green, A. H. (1974). Child abuse and mental retardation: A problem of cause and effect. *Journal of Mental Deficiency, 79,* 327–330.

Sarason, I. G., Johnson, J. H., & Siegel, J. M. (1979). Assessing the impact of life changes: Development of the Life Experiences Survey. *Series in Clinical and Community Psychiatry, 6,* 131–149.

Schneider-Rosen, K., & Cicchetti, D. (1984). The relationship between affect and cognition in maltreated infants: Quality of attachment and the development of visual self-recognition. *Child Development, 55,* 648–658.

Sherrod, K. B., O'Connor, S., Vietze, P. M., & Altemeier, W. A. (1984). Child health and maltreatment. *Child Development, 55,* 1174–1183.

Smetana, J., Kelly, M., & Twentyman, C. (1984). Abused, neglected, and nonmaltreated children's judgments of moral and social transgressions. *Child Development, 55,* 277–287.

Smith, J. E. (1984). Nonaccidental injury to children: I. A review of behavioral interventions. *Behaviour Research and Therapy, 22,* 331–347.

Spanier, G. B. (1976). Measuring dyadic adjustment: New scales for measuring the quality of marriage and similar dyads. *Journal of Marriage and the Family, 38,* 15–28.

Sparrow, S. S., Balla, D. A., & Cicchetti, D. V. (1984). *Vineland Adaptive Behavior Scales* (rev. ed.). Circle Pines, MN: American Guidance Services.

Spielberger, D. C. (1973). *Manual for the State–Trait Anxiety Inventory for Children.* Palo Alto, CA: Consulting Psychologists Press.

Spinetta, J. J. (1978). Parental personality factors in child abuse. *Journal of Consulting and Clinical Psychology, 46,* 1409–1414.

Spinetta, J. J., & Rigler, D. (1972). The child abusing parent: A psychological review. *Psychological Bulletin, 77,* 296–304.

Srole, L., Langner, T., Michael, S., Kirkpatrick, P., Opler, M., & Rennie, T. (1978). *Mental health in the metropolis.* New York: Academic Press.

Sroufe, L. A., & Fleeson, J. (1986). Attachment and the construction of relationships. In W. W. Hartup & Z. Rubin (Eds.), *Relationships and development* (pp. 51–72). Hillsdale, NJ: Erlbaum.

Standing Senate Committee on Health, Welfare, and Science. (1980). *Child at risk.* Hull, Quebec: Ministry of Supply and Services Canada.

Starr, R. H., Jr. (1979). Child abuse. *American Psychologist, 34,* 872–878.

Starr, R. H., Jr. (1982). A research-based approach to the prediction of child abuse. In R. H. Starr, Jr. (Ed.), *Child abuse prediction: Policy implications* (pp. 105–134). Cambridge, MA: Ballinger.

Starr, R. H., Jr., Dietrich, K. N., Fischhoff, J., Ceresnie, S., & Zweier, D. (1984). The contribution of handicapping conditions to child abuse. *Topics in Early Childhood Special Education, 4,* 55–69.

Steele, B. F., & Pollock, C. B. (1968). A psychiatric study of parents who abuse infants and small children. In R. E. Helfer & C. H. Kempe (Eds.), *The battered child* (pp. 89–133). Chicago: University of Chicago Press.

Steinhauer, P. D. (1983). Assessing for parenting capacity. *American Journal of Orthopsychiatry, 53,* 468–481.

Stevens-Long, J. E. (1973). The effect of behavioral context on some aspects of adult disciplinary practice and effort. *Child Development, 44,* 476–484.

Straus, M. A. (1979a). Family patterns and child abuse in a nationally representative American sample. *Child Abuse and Neglect, 3,* 213–225.

Straus, M. A. (1979b). Measuring intrafamily conflict and violence: The Conflict Tactics (CT) Scales. *Journal of Marriage and the Family, 41,* 75–88.

Straus, M. A., Gelles, R. J., & Steinmetz, S. (1980). *Behind closed doors: Violence in the American family.* Garden City, NY: Doubleday/Anchor.

Tarter, R. E., Hegedus, A. E., Winsten, N. E., & Alterman, A. I. (1984). Neuropsychological, personality, and familial characteristics of physically abused delinquents. *Journal of the American Academy of Child Psychiatry, 23,* 668–674.

Toro, P. A. (1982). Developmental effects of child abuse: A review. *Child Abuse and Neglect, 6,* 423–431.

Trickett, P. K., & Kuczynski, L. (1986). Children's misbehaviors and parental discipline strategies in abusive and nonabusive families. *Developmental Psychology, 22,* 115–123.

Twentyman, C. T., Plotkin, R., & Dodge, D. (1981, November). *Inappropriate evaluations of parents who maltreat their children: Initial descriptive survey and cross-validation.* Paper presented at the 15th Annual Convention of the Association for Advancement of Behavior Therapy, Toronto.

Vasta, R. (1982). Physical child abuse: A dual component analysis. *Developmental Review, 2,* 164–170.

Vasta, R., & Copitch, P. (1981). Simulating conditions of child abuse in the laboratory. *Child Development, 52,* 164–170.

Wahler, R. G. (1976). Deviant child behavior within the family: Developmental speculations and behavior change strategies. In H. Leitenberg (Ed.), *Handbook of behavior modification and behavior therapy* (pp. 516–543). Englewood Cliffs, NJ: Prentice-Hall.

Wahler, R. G. (1980). The insular mother: Her problems in parent–child treatment. *Journal of Applied Behavior Analysis, 13,* 207–219.

Wahler, R. G., & Dumas, J. (1986a). "A chip off the old block": Some interpersonal characteristics of coercive children across generations. In P. Strain, M. Guralnick, & H. Walker (Eds.), *Children's social behavior: Development, assessment, and modification* (pp. 49–91). New York: Academic Press.

Wahler, R. G., & Dumas, J. (1986b). Maintenance factors in abusive mother–child interactions: The compliance and predictability hypotheses. Journal of Applied Behavior Analysis, 19, 13–22.

Wahler, R. G., House, A. E., & Stambaugh, E. E. (1976). *Ecological assessment of child problem behavior.* New York: Pergamon Press.

Wahler, R. G., Leske, G., & Rogers, E. S. (1979). The insular family: A deviance support system for oppositional children. In L. A. Hamerlynck (Ed.), *Behavioral systems for the developmentally disabled: Vol. 1. School and family environments* (pp. 102–127). New York: Brunner/Mazel.

Weiss, R. L. (1984). Cognitive and behavioral measures of marital interaction. In K. Hahlweg & N. S. Jacobson (Eds.), *Marital interaction: Analysis and modification* (pp. 232–252). New York: Guilford Press.

Wolfe, D. A. (1985a). Child abusive parents: An empirical review and analysis. *Psychological Bulletin, 97,* 462–482.

Wolfe, D. A. (1985b). Prevention of child abuse through the development of parent and child competencies. In R. J. McMahon & R. DeV. Peters (Eds.), *Childhood disorders: Behavioral–developmental approaches* (pp. 195–217). New York: Brunner/Mazel.

Wolfe, D. A., & Bourdeau, P. A. (1987). Current issues in the assessment of abusive and neglectful parent–child relationships. *Behavioral Assessment, 9,* 271–290.

Wolfe, D. A., Fairbank, J., Kelly, J. A., & Bradlyn, A. S. (1983). Child abusive parents' physiological responses to stressful and nonstressful behavior in children. *Behavioral Assessment, 5,* 363–371.

Wolfe, D. A., Jaffe, P. J., Wilson, S. K., & Zak, L. (1985). Children of battered women: The relation of child behavior to family violence and maternal stress. *Journal of Consulting and Clinical Psychology, 53,* 657–665.

Wolfe, D. A., Kaufman, K., Aragona, J., & Sandler, J. (1981). *The child management program for abusive parents: Procedures for developing a child abuse intervention program.* Winter Park, FL: Anna.

Wolfe, D. A., & Mosk, M. D. (1983). Behavioral comparisons of children from abusive and distressed families. *Journal of Consulting and Clinical Psychology, 51,* 702–708.

Wolock, I., & Horowitz, B. (1984). Child maltreatment as a social problem: The neglect of neglect. *American Journal of Orthopsychiatry, 54,* 530–543.

Young, R. (1982). *Characteristics of families receiving services at Family and Children's Services of London/ Middlesex: 1970–1980.* Unpublished manuscript.

Zillman, D. (1979). *Hostility and aggression.* Hillsdale, NJ: Erlbaum.

INDEX